Market
Regulation

The Addison-Wesley Series in Economics

Abel/Bernanke/Croushore
*Macroeconomics**

Bade/Parkin
*Foundations of Economics**

Bierman/Fernandez
Game Theory with Economic Applications

Binger/Hoffman
Microeconomics with Calculus

Boyer
Principles of Transportation Economics

Branson
Macroeconomic Theory and Policy

Bruce
Public Finance and the American Economy

Byrns/Stone
Economics

Carlton/Perloff
Modern Industrial Organization

Caves/Frankel/Jones
World Trade and Payments: An Introduction

Chapman
Environmental Economics: Theory, Application, and Policy

Cooter/Ulen
Law and Economics

Downs
An Economic Theory of Democracy

Ehrenberg/Smith
Modern Labor Economics

Ekelund/Ressler/Tollison
*Economics**

Fusfeld
The Age of the Economist

Gerber
International Economics

Ghiara
Learning Economics

Gordon
Macroeconomics

Gregory
Essentials of Economics

Gregory/Stuart
Russian and Soviet Economic Performance and Structure

Hartwick/Olewiler
The Economics of Natural Resource Use

Hoffman/Averett
Women and the Economy: Family, Work, and Pay

Holt
Markets, Games, and Strategic Behavior

Hubbard
Money, the Financial System, and the Economy

Hughes/Cain
American Economic History

Husted/Melvin
International Economics

Jehle/Reny
Advanced Microeconomic Theory

Johnson-Lans
A Health Economics Primer

Klein
Mathematical Methods for Economics

Krugman/Obstfeld
*International Economics**

Laidler
The Demand for Money

Leeds/von Allmen
The Economics of Sports

Leeds/von Allmen/Schiming
*Economics**

Lipsey/Courant/Ragan
*Economics**

Melvin
International Money and Finance

Miller
*Economics Today**

Miller
Understanding Modern Economics

Miller/Benjamin
The Economics of Macro Issues

Miller/Benjamin/North
The Economics of Public Issues

Mills/Hamilton
Urban Economics

Mishkin
*The Economics of Money, Banking, and Financial Markets**

Mishkin
*The Economics of Money, Banking, and Financial Markets, Alternate Edition**

Murray
Econometrics: A Modern Introduction

Parkin
*Economics**

Perloff
*Microeconomics**

Perman/Common/McGilvray/Ma
Natural Resources and Environmental Economics

Phelps
Health Economics

Riddell/Shackelford/Stamos/ Schneider
Economics: A Tool for Critically Understanding Society

Ritter/Silber/Udell
Principles of Money, Banking, and Financial Markets

Rohlf
Introduction to Economic Reasoning

Ruffin/Gregory
Principles of Economics

Sargent
Rational Expectations and Inflation

Scherer
Industry Structure, Strategy, and Public Policy

Sherman
Market Regulation

Stock/Watson
Introduction to Econometrics

Stock/Watson
Introduction to Econometrics, Brief Edition

Studenmund
Using Econometrics

Tietenberg
Environmental and Natural Resource Economics

Tietenberg
Environmental Economics and Policy

Todaro/Smith
Economic Development

Waldman
Microeconomics

Waldman/Jensen
Industrial Organization: Theory and Practice

Weil
Economic Growth

Williamson
Macroeconomics

*denotes myeconlab titles. Log onto www.myeconlab.com to learn more.

Market Regulation

Roger Sherman

University of Houston

Boston San Francisco New York
London Toronto Sydney Tokyo Singapore Madrid
Mexico City Munich Paris Cape Town Hong Kong Montreal

Publisher: *Greg Tobin*
Editor in Chief: *Denise Clinton*
Sponsoring Editor: *Noel Kamm*
Editorial Assistant: *Courtney E. Schinke*
Managing Editor: *Nancy H. Fenton*
Senior Production Supervisor: *Kathryn Dinovo*
Supplements Coordinator: *Heather McNally*
Senior Media Producer: *Bethany Tidd*
Senior Marketing Manager: *Roxanne Hoch*
Marketing Assistant: *Ashlee Clevenger*
Senior Author Support/Technology Specialist: *Joe Vetere*
Senior Prepress Supervisor: *Caroline Fell*
Rights and Permissions Advisor: *Shannon Barbe*
Senior Manufacturing Buyer: *Carol Melville*
Cover Designer: *Gina Hagen Kolenda*
Production Coordination, Text Design, Composition, and Illustrations: *Nesbitt Graphics, Inc.*
Cover image: *Sonia Delaunay-Terk (1885–1979). Rythme couleur, 1939. Oil on canvas. Photo: R. G. Ojeda.*
Photo credit: *Réunion des Musées Nationaux / Art Resource, NY*
Image credit: © L & M SERVICES B.V. The Hague 20070505

Many of the designations used by manufacturers and sellers to distinguish their products are claimed as trademarks. Where those designations appear in this book, and Addison Wesley was aware of a trademark claim, the designations have been printed in initial caps or all caps.

Library of Congress Cataloging-in-Publication Data

Sherman, Roger, 1930-
    Market regulation / Roger Sherman.
        p. cm. — (Addison-Wesley series in economics)
Includes bibliographical references and index.
ISBN 978-0-321-32232-6
1. Economic policy. 2. Competition. 3. Monopolies—Government policy. I. Title.
HD87.S543 2008
338.8—dc22

2007024459

IBSN-13: 978-0-321-32232-6

ISBN-10: 0-321-32232-0

1 2 3 4 5 6 7 8 9 10–CRW–11 10 09 08 07

BRIEF CONTENTS

CONTENTS

PREFACE

Markets can be pretty, not visually pretty like the Grand Canyon or the Eiffel Tower, but intellectually pretty like an elegant mathematical proof or a good joke. Pretty markets work wonders by blending decentralized decisions so those who make them get the most satisfaction from their resources. Such wondrous results cannot be assured, however, even when markets are competitive. Individuals may not have the information they need to make good decisions in competitive markets, and technology may interfere with competition. If decentralized decisions in a market do not account for all of the resulting costs or benefits, even a competitive market will be inefficient. When such conditions intrude, markets are not so pretty, but some form of external regulation may make them prettier. How markets can go wrong and how best to regulate them when they do are the subjects of this book.

All over the world, countries increasingly use markets to organize economic activity, and at the same time side effects of economic activity, such as air pollution that can cause global warming, grow more serious. Fortunately, a host of remedies can alleviate many market problems once they are successfully diagnosed, and the goal of this book is to help with both diagnosis and remedy. The reader should gain a thorough understanding of markets in order to recognize flaws and develop ways to fix them. Markets can achieve remarkable results and do much good in the world, so market regulation is an important aim.

CONTENT AND ORGANIZATION

Although it is not visible to the typical consumer, governmental market regulation has a long history, not only in preventing monopoly through antitrust policy but also in accepting and then controlling monopoly through some form of industry regulation. External effects—for example, the pollution that occurs when producers emit toxins into the air—are now the subject of a large regulatory effort. The problems of maintaining competition, regulating industries, and treating problems like pollution make up the three main parts of this book.

These three problem areas—regulating competition, industry regulation, and social regulation—are often treated as if they were independent subjects. I treat them coherently as failures of markets to regulate themselves through competition, because they all result from particular failures in self-regulating markets. Chapter 1, which describes this approach and provides background information, begins a three-chapter "Introduction." Chapter 2 presents the ideal self-regulation that perfect competition can produce and explains its assumptions. Chapter 3 then relaxes each of these assumptions and traces the consequences, thereby identifying the market problems that are examined in the three main parts of the book. This approach prepares the reader to diagnose problems in the functioning of markets.

Factors that limit the number of firms in a market, complicate entry, or invite differentiated products illustrate the challenges to competition that are the subject of Part 1, "The Regulation of Competition." The Sherman Act was an effort to constrain monopoly and support competition, and over the past century antitrust law has developed into an effective set of rules that guide a host of business firm actions. Understanding this process requires knowledge of industrial organization because the way that industrial markets are organized affects the strategies business firms can use and may tempt them into inefficient strategies that antitrust laws are designed to prevent. In Part 1, Chapter 4 examines modern business firms and Chapter 5 addresses market organization, or market structure. Chapter 6 considers resulting strategic possibilities and Chapter 7 emphasizes one strategy, innovation. Then Chapter 8 explores the origin and present content of antitrust law and Chapter 9 describes applications that show the form of its guidance today. Part 1 also shows how economic knowledge improves the development of new antitrust law when markets change.

The technologies used in some industries can derail competition and thus invite government regulation. In the last 30 years or so, government regulation of industries has changed dramatically, as some of the tasks once assigned to regulatory agencies have been turned over to competitive forces. In many instances this has required the redesign of markets, like wholesale markets for electricity, and the process is continuing. In Part 2, "The Regulation of Industries," Chapter 10 introduces this process of industry regulation, describing why competition fails and when government might intervene, with attention to a range of new and more modest roles for government regulation. This chapter also considers how to judge success. Chapter 11 presents pricing principles for these situations, and Chapter 12 reviews institutions of industry regulation. Considering industry regulation and especially the changes of recent decades requires knowledge of the industries themselves, so most of Part 2 is devoted to careful studies of six regulated industries: postal service, communications services, communication for news and entertainment, transportation, energy, and electricity. Although Part 2 begins with principles that apply generally to industry regulation, it is devoted mainly to the different forms that industry regulation takes.

Even in competitive markets outcomes may not be ideal. If decentralized decisions do not account for all costs and benefits, for example, competitive outcomes will not be efficient. Or if those making decisions are ill informed, the outcomes may not be pretty. Part 3, "Social Regulation," examines these problems of competitive markets and shows that many problems thought to be broad social problems originate in failures of markets. Chapter 19 introduces social regulation and explains the main sources of such market failures: externalities and imperfect information. Chapter 20 explains a range of remedies that may be pursued. The remainder of Part 3 discusses government policies that try to protect the environment, workers, consumers, and investors from harm. Chapter 21 presents a broad description of the environment and describes methods of protecting it, including the important program of trading rights to emit sodium dioxide. Chapter 22 examines protection of workers, considering first the protections that markets offer and then the statutory protections, not only for health and safety but also for employment discrimination and for retirement pensions. Chapter 23 considers first the protections that courts offer consumers and then considers state and federal statutes in areas of food and drugs, traffic safety, and consumer products. One side effect of relying on competitive markets is that some firms fail, sometimes spectacularly as in the case of Enron. Firm failure imposes costs not only on investors, but on employees, retirees, and even consumers. Chapter 24 addresses protections that moderate the negative effects of firm failures and also treats corporate governance regulation and regulatory efforts to avoid firm failures.

Market Regulation is intended for advanced undergraduate economics and business students and for graduate business students. The use of mathematics is confined mainly to appendices and occasionally to boxes in the text, and it is not crucial to student understanding. The book contains more material than can be covered in a three-hour, one-semester course, and this allows instructors to combine chapters in many different ways depending on their purposes. Industrial organization can be emphasized with Chapters 1 through 7 and the early chapters of Part 2. When students are more advanced, Chapters 1 through 3 are less important, but noting them is still desirable because they express the book's organizing concept. Antitrust policy is presented in Chapters 8 and 9, although treatment of it will benefit from covering Chapters 4 through 7 as background. In Part 2, after covering general material about industry regulation with Chapters 10 to 12, instructors can choose which of the six industries in Chapters 13 through 18 they wish to cover. Part 3 begins with Chapters 19 and 20 on general social regulation material and then in Chapters 21 through 24 instructors can choose to treat protection of the environment, workers, or consumers, or protection from the effects of firm failure. Important terms are bold-faced in text and are defined in an end-of-book Glossary, and references to supporting works are indicated by author name and date of publication in the text and are listed in a References section at the end of the book.

ADDITIONAL RESOURCES AVAILABLE ONLINE

I have prepared an Online Instructor's Manual that includes student learning goals, suggested assignments, teaching tips, and answers to end-of-chapter questions. It also contains true/false questions for use in class or on tests and, when applicable, additional discussion points and references. This Online Instructor's Manual is available for download as Microsoft Word files or as Adobe PDF files from the Instructor Resource Center (www.aw-bc.com/irc).

Another resource, the Companion Website, provides learning objectives, discussion questions, quizzes, Web links to online resources referenced in the text, and glossary flashcards to further students' comprehension outside the classroom. The Web links come complete with descriptions of the content available at each site, providing easy access to relevant data sources. Visit the Companion Website at www.aw-bc.com /sherman for more information.

ACKNOWLEDGMENTS

A book such as this draws on a large literature and we all must be grateful for the skillful analysis that contributors to this literature provide. I am also grateful personally for helpful contributions to my own thinking from teachers and colleagues over many years, including Simon Anderson, James Buchanan, Darren Bush, Steve Craig,

Michael Crew, Keith Crocker, Dick Cyert, Otto Davis, Trenery Dolbear, Cathy Eckel, Ken Elzinga, Bob Feinberg, Nick Feltovitch, Gary Fournier, Don Fullerton, Paul Gregory, Gurcan Gulen, John James, Bill Johnson, Janet Kohlhase, Lester Lave, Han Lee, Ben McCallum, Tom Mayor, Allen Meltzer, David Mills, Len Mirman, John Mullahy, Ed Prescott, Roy Ruffin, Joel Sailors, Gordon Tullock, Michael Visscher, Jacqueline Weaver, Nat Wilcox, and especially Emin Dinlersoz, Charlie Holt, Richard Schramm, and John Whitaker. For research help I want to thank Recai Aydin, Faruk Balli, Eugenia Belova, Cahit Guven, Monica Hartmann, Han Lee, and Sevil Yaman.

Reviewers who have contributed importantly to the substance of the book include the following:

Donald L. Alexander, *Western Michigan University*
Carson Bays, *East Carolina University*
Anthony Becker, *St. Olaf College*
Gilbert Becker, *Saint Anselm College*
Klaus Becker, *Texas Tech University*
Subir Bose, *University of Illinois at Urbana–Champaign*
Morris Coats, *Nicholls State University*
Michael Crew, *Rutgers University*
Robert Feinberg, *American University*
Gary Fournier, *Florida State University*
Devra Golbe, *Hunter College, CUNY*
Daniel Hollas, *University of Texas, San Antonio*
David Huffman, *Bridgewater College*
Marilyn Kaplan, *University of Texas, Dallas*
Brian Kench, *University of Tampa*
William Koch, *Western Illinois University*
Nicholas Kreisle, *Federal Trade Commission*
Tom Larson, *California State University, Los Angeles*
Li Way Lee, *Wayne State University*
Matt Lewis, *The Ohio State University*
Dave Loomis, *Illinois State University*
Ellen Magenheim, *Swarthmore College*
Eric Mitchell, *Randolph College*
Diana Moss, *University of Colorado, Boulder*
Bernardo Mueller, *University of Brasilia*
Jon Nelson, *Penn State University*
Michael Noel, *University of California, San Diego*
Michael Pollitt, *University of Cambridge*
Nicholas Powers, *University of Illinois at Urbana–Champaign*
Eric Rasmusen, *Indiana University*
Barak Richman, *Duke University*
Michael Rothkopf, *Rutgers University*
F. Paroma Sanyal, *Brandeis University*
Raymond Sauer, *Clemson University*
Bruce Seaman, *Georgia State University*

William Shughart, *University of Mississippi*
H. Scott Wallace, *University of Wisconsin, Stevens Point*
Dennis Weisman, *Kansas State University*
Larry Wohl, *Gustavus Adolphus College*
James Zinser, *Oberlin College*

The publisher of the book, Addison Wesley, provided most congenial aid throughout, and for their help I want to thank sponsoring editor Noel Kamm, assistant editors Julia Boyles and Sara Holliday, and editorial assistant Courtney Schinke. Freelance development editor Jennifer Jefferson and copy editor Lou Bruno made the text clearer. For the nuts and bolts of actually producing the book I thank the senior production supervisor, Kathryn Dinovo, and I appreciate the smooth management of the project by Mary Sanger.

I want to give special thanks to Zhenhui Xu, who got me started on this book more than 10 years ago. In its earliest form, the book was a series of class notes, used over the past 10 years by students at the University of Virginia and the University of Houston. I am grateful to those students for forcing me to be clear, and for their innumerable suggestions for improvement as the class notes developed into this book.

My wife Gerry Moohr not only improved the book substantially but also eased the task of writing it. The book is most gratefully dedicated to her.

Roger Sherman
Houston, Texas
June 1, 2007

INTRODUCTION

Life in a market economy leaves the regulation of economic activity largely to the forces of competition. Democratic capitalism uses democratic institutions to control capitalism, in which owners of capital hire inputs, such as labor and capital, directly through decentralized markets or oversee managers who do. The economy's performance then depends, first, on how well the markets bring benefits to citizens. When competition regulates markets poorly, or when it fails, democratic controls are imposed in the form of governmental market regulation.

This book covers three areas of governmental market regulation: (1) *antitrust regulation,* which keeps competition functioning (mainly by preventing monopoly), (2) *industry regulation* where conditions do not support competition (such as electricity), and (3) *social regulation,* which cuts across industries where externalities (such as air pollution) or imperfect information may hamper decentralized markets. These three areas of regulation are described in the Introduction, Chapters 1–3, and are then examined in detail in the three main parts of the book.

Chapter 1 discusses property rights, the law, politics, and institutions such as the corporation and markets. Because competition plays such an important role in a market economy, Chapter 2 reviews how competition ideally functions and conveys desirable results. Emphasis is placed on the assumptions that must be met for competition to function well. Problems can arise in competition, however, and Chapter 3 reveals them by examining consequences when each assumption of perfect competition is not satisfied. Chapters 2 and 3 thus set the stage for diagnosing problems with competition that elicit the three main forms of governmental market regulation.

1

Introduction to Market Regulation

Buy a ticket at your favorite movie theater, search online for a book, or make any of your other daily economic choices, and you will probably be influenced by some form of governmental market regulation, even if you can't see it. You may not know that the firm from which you buy complies with antitrust laws or, if you buy from a firm in a regulated industry like electricity, is subject to more detailed regulation. Government regulation also protects against environmental hazards, bans harmful consumer products, opposes dangerous working conditions, and even limits losses when business firms fail (e.g., by protecting retirement pensions). Yet, in keeping with the way markets generally function, government regulation is only partly visible to the consumer.

Many forms of government regulation exist in a capitalistic market economy, where economic activity is organized around the decisions of those who own capital and who act through decentralized markets. The owners of capital either employ inputs like labor directly or oversee managers who do, with inputs as well as product outputs being bought and sold in markets. How markets function then determines how the economy performs. Market regulation therefore influences the effectiveness of a market economy in bringing benefits to its citizens.

One must realize that market regulation can occur naturally from market competition, which limits the prices sellers can charge and sets the qualities they must deliver. This competitive process can regulate markets without intervention from any outside party, and it offers one standard against which to judge the effectiveness of government intervention. Regulation also comes from social norms. For instance, a social norm calls on you to pay voluntarily for goods you have chosen in a store. Social norms have even served historically to enforce contracts. Competition, however, even when supported by social norms, does not always regulate effectively.

Outside authorities may impose market regulation, and this kind of regulation is what the phrase "market regulation" usually brings to mind. Laws may establish new practices or norms, either in product design features for business firms, such as motor vehicle seat belts, or in behavioral mandates for consumers, such as a requirement that passengers must wear seat belts. Laws also create regulatory agencies.

Courts interpret and enforce legislation and regulatory agency rules. Such government market regulation can affect the price you pay, the form, effectiveness, and safety of the goods you purchase, the marketing practices that attract you, the workplace of those who serve you, and the environmental effects of their production.

Because economic affairs are regulated primarily by the forces of competition, knowledge of competition helps to reveal when it is not working well and, thus, when to seek other forms of market regulation. These other forms include regulation of competition through *antitrust law,* which supports competition, and *industry regulation,* which may modify or even replace competition. A third form, called *social regulation,* cuts across many industries to affect what a firm can release from its smokestacks, how it is governed, how it organizes its workplace, and even how it designs its products. Section 1.1 describes the three realms of market regulation. Then Section 1.2 sketches the context for market regulation, including the private property basis for transactions, economic incentives, and important players like the corporation, in markets that make up a democratic capitalism. Section 1.3 treats the roles of law and politics, because government regulation is created and imposed through legal and political institutions.

1.1 | GOVERNMENTAL MARKET REGULATION

We begin with descriptions of the three main areas of governmental market regulation—regulation of competition, regulation of industries, and social regulation—and the purposes behind them.

Regulation of Competition

Out of the great expansion in economic activity that followed the U.S. Civil War there emerged large combinations of firms within many industries, combinations that were called "trusts," after the voting trusts that appeared in the 1880s. Trusts allowed effective boardroom voting control of groups of firms in the same industry. Reports about ruthless abuse of the growing market power of trusts were legend. Yet the trusts could not be controlled by common law, because their actions were not unambiguous offenses. Under such circumstances, with little economic knowledge on which to draw and with conflicting interests to be reconciled, Congress passed the *Sherman Act* in 1890 to initiate antitrust economic policy in America. The Sherman Act made monopolizing, or attempting to monopolize, illegal, and it was the first government effort to preserve competition in the United States.

Nevertheless, firms continued to form business combinations and trusts. The Sherman Act expressed sentiment for an objective but gave no clear instruction for reaching it, and it was slow to have effect. After the Sherman Act began to take hold, the *Clayton* and *Federal Trade Commission Acts* were passed in 1914 because the Sherman Act alone was thought inadequate to achieve its purpose. The Clayton Act specified offenses in more detail than the Sherman Act. The Federal Trade Commission Act targeted unfair practices and created the Federal Trade Commission to prevent

BOX 1.1 Gasoline Pricing

Price discrimination occurs when different buyers are charged different prices for the same good. In 1914, the practice, which was thought to require monopoly power, was outlawed by the Clayton Act because of the unfairness and inefficiency caused by different prices for the same good. In a careful study in the 1990s Professor Andrea Shepard attempted to see whether price discrimination occurred in the generally competitive gasoline retailing market by separating Boston, MA, gasoline stations into three categories: (1) only self service, (2) only full service (where an attendant pumps the gas), and (3) both self service and full service. There were reasons to believe that costs were comparable at all the stations. Stations in the third category, offering both self service and full service, were found to set higher prices than self-service or full-service stations alone, by about 13 cents per gallon in 2006 dollars. Stations offering only one level of service simply set prices to maximize profit for that service level. Stations offering two levels of service could experiment with both prices, and even if the full service price was set too high for some customers they would probably not be lost because the customers could shift to self service at the same station. So the stations offering two services were accomplishing a modest bit of price discrimination, even in fairly competitive conditions.

See A. Shepard, "Price Discrimination and Retail Configuration," *Journal of Political Economy*, February, 1991, Vol. 99, pp. 30–53.

them. These modifications to the Sherman Act contained no startling new initiative or sharp change of direction, but they supplied details. Two further changes were made in 1976 through the *Hart-Scott-Rodino Antitrust Improvements Act*, which required preapproval by the federal government of large mergers and allowed state attorneys general to bring antitrust suits on behalf of their citizens. Although U.S. antitrust law remains the product of late nineteenth-century America, it has been substantially modified by later legislation and by a century of court decisions.

The large business firm, usually in the form of a corporation, is the subject of antitrust law. Proprietorships and partnerships are numerous, but they tend to be smaller, in part because owners under this form of organization are liable to meet financial obligations even beyond the assets of the firm. The many owners of a corporation, on the other hand, can lose only the amount of their investments (which they also can sell on well-organized stock exchanges). This limited liability helps the corporation to raise large amounts of capital. The corporation can also be overseen by a board of directors, so the individual shareholder need not devote time to its management. Yet the shareholders are strongly motivated because they have a claim on what is left over after costs are subtracted from revenue; they claim the residual, so they want revenue high and cost low. They seek directors who will represent their interests by getting managers to pursue profit.

The structure of a product market—competition or monopoly or something in between—can influence how firms in the market behave and consequently how the market performs. Firms face a wide range of decisions, from selecting their product lines to choices of manufacture and means of distribution to the final consumer, or of merger partners. As residual claimants, owners of firms have strong profit-seeking incentives. So if they have monopoly power they will want to use it to their advantage, which may harm consumers if the power is unchecked. Beside their product markets, firms are constantly involved in other markets—capital markets or labor markets, for instance—where they can be affected by competitive forces and make strategic decisions. And they are subject to technological imperatives that restrain firms' sizes and methods of operation. Through research and development efforts firms may attack even these limitations.

Antitrust law is an added constraint on firm behavior. It does not pursue firms that run the trucks of competitors off the road, as ordinary criminal law serves that purpose, but antitrust law guides and restrains firms in their competition. When it is effective, it limits practices that firms may be tempted to use, such as fixing prices among themselves, restraining trading opportunities, or obtaining and exercising monopoly advantage. Offending actions usually involve either some form of collusion among otherwise separate parties, some form of exclusion that prevents intrusion from other parties, or some form of monopoly advantage and using it in an objectionable way. Antitrust policy generally regulates competition and preserves its role in guiding economic decisions so they serve the general welfare.

In the United States, the main institutions that pursue antitrust policy are the Antitrust Division of the Department of Justice and the Federal Trade Commission. Many private suits to collect damages for illegal actions are also motivated under the law, and state attorneys general can bring such suits on behalf of their citizens. Courts must interpret legislative statutes, and in the case of antitrust law the interpretation has changed considerably over time. Many other countries now have institutions that regulate competition similar to U.S. antitrust agencies, and because competition is increasingly global these agencies attempt to coordinate their regulation. The Competition Commission of the European Union prevented General Electric and Honeywell from merging in 2001, for example, and has been more vigorous than the United States Department of Justice in limiting actions by Microsoft. The Organization for Economic Cooperation and Development (OECD), a group of 30 countries including the United States that support reliance on markets, provides data and analysis valuable to the countries in shaping their competition policies.

Part 1 describes the problems that arise in competition by considering the structure of markets and how it affects the strategies available to firms in the markets. Part 1 also shows the current state of antitrust law and policy that is intended to support competition. Understanding antitrust policy affords insight into how competition functions and into the rules that can help it function better.

Regulation of Industries

Market economies throughout the world face the same problem: how to deal with technologies that complicate the smooth functioning of competition. Television, telephone, water, natural gas, electricity, airlines, and railroads illustrate large and complex technologies, often organized into networks, which can complicate the functioning of competition. Use of such technologies is guided in many countries by administrative

---

BOX 1.2 The Rise and Rivals of Southwest Airlines

Although economic regulation of prices and entry in the airline industry ended in the late 1970s, other political restrictions have been applied that are even less defensible. Southwest Airlines began operations in 1971 at Love Field in Dallas, Texas, rather than at the big, new Dallas/Fort Worth International Airport. In the years that followed, American Airlines and the Dallas/Fort Worth airport tried unsuccessfully to block Southwest's access to Love Field through the courts. Then Texas Congressman Jim Wright, when he was House majority leader, attached to an unrelated piece of legislation a rider that limited Southwest flights from Love Field to be within Texas or to just four neighboring states. After suffering under this restriction for years, Southwest mounted a campaign in 2004 to end the so-called Wright amendment, using the dramatic claim "Wright is wrong!" A Missouri Congressman added an amendment to a bill that allowed Southwest flights from Dallas to St. Louis, and after the bill became law, prices on that route fell and traffic soared. Then American and the cities of Dallas and Fort Worth opened negotiations with Southwest and reached an agreement that restricts the use of Love Field by cutting the number of gates in half while allocating 80 percent of them to Southwest and allowing it to fly one-stop flights anywhere. Also, the number of gates in the Dallas region is not to be increased. The Dallas/Fort Worth airport is pleased to contain the threat from Love Field, especially because it recently lost a large amount of Delta Airlines traffic, and American and Southwest avoid new competition from airlines such as Jet Blue. The agreement is not good for consumers, however, as you might suspect, when legislation introduced in Congress to codify it proposes a blanket antitrust exemption to the airlines that participate in it.

See S. Pearlstein, "Southwest Undercuts Competitors, and Competition," *Washington Post*, July 28, 2006, p. D1.

---

institutions in monopoly circumstances rather than by competitive markets. New arrangements are now transforming many of these industries and allowing more room for competitive forces to operate.

In the United States many of these services are provided exclusively by privately owned firms that public agencies regulate. The firms are often called public utilities, another name (like antitrust) that goes back to the nineteenth century, and they are seen as providing goods or services in which the general public has a great interest. The public regulatory agencies that oversee them are commonly operated at the state level, as a Public Service Commission, State Corporation Commission, or similarly titled agency, although federal agencies also play important roles. The vast majority of electricity, natural gas, television, and local telephone service, and large amounts of water, public transportation, and other services have at some time been provided by such privately owned and governmentally regulated public utilities. Services may also be provided by public enterprises, which are publicly owned and operated. Public enterprises are especially common in water and public transportation services, and they are more widely used as an organizational form in many countries. The largest public enterprise in the United States is the U.S. Postal Service.

Some industries that were closely regulated 30 years ago, such as the airlines, or long-distance telephone service, are no longer regulated in the same way today. Others, including natural gas, local telephone service, and even electricity generation, are exposed increasingly to new forms of competition. One may reasonably expect that the degree of regulation will vary with time as technologies and institutions change, and the current trend is to rely less on regulation of entire industries and to deregulate where possible. Competition may be introduced at one level of an industry's activities, for example long-distance telephone service in the telecommunications industry, or it may be introduced by requiring a monopoly owner of an essential resource to allow competitors to use the resource, as when a local telephone network must complete calls for rival long-distance companies. These modifications of institutions, and of property rights, are part of the move toward the deregulation and restructuring of industries, placing greater reliance on competition and less on administrative regulatory guidance.

Traditional forms of industry regulation offered only weak incentives for efficiency. If a monopoly firm is allowed to earn only a specified level of profit, for example, the firm is not motivated to make more sales or to lower costs because it cannot keep resulting gains. The traditional regulatory arrangement for industries in the United States was *rate-of-return regulation,* which resulted from court decisions aimed mainly at limiting prices set by monopoly providers of public services by limiting the returns they could earn on their assets. This compromise between contending parties, the consumers on one hand and the shareholders on the other, limited allowed profit and failed to generate incentives for the efficient operation of regulated firms. Deregulation has attempted to return such industries to competitive status. Even where deregulation has not been complete, a restructuring of the industry has brought new forms of regulation that rely more on competitive forces and improve efficiency incentives.

Rate-of-return regulation set prices for regulated industries that would cover costs, including profit at a reasonable rate of return on the firm's assets. That set a limit on profit, which almost eliminated the role of the residual claimant and left little incentive for the firm to keep its costs low or to innovate. As it functioned, rate-of-return regulation also produced a bias in the firm's input decisions, tempting the firm to use more capital than was efficient, relative to other inputs, because profit was allowed only on capital assets. New regulatory arrangements are being devised that offer better incentives—more cost control, better input choices, better pricing, more innovation—than rate-of-return regulation. Many countries are participating in the search for better regulatory institutions, and when arrangements adopted in one country prove effective they are often used by other countries.

Public rather than private ownership of important enterprises is common in many countries, although the United States tends to rely more heavily than others on private ownership. Government ownership may be accomplished through a substantial government stake in an otherwise private firm, through independent wholly state-owned, or public, enterprises, or otherwise through government departments or bureaus. There has been a tendency in recent years for quite a few countries to "privatize," or to sell stock ownership in, formerly public enterprises. The aim is to improve incentives by creating a group that has a claim on benefits from good performance by the enterprise, and who will, therefore, press for its achievement. Private owners, or shareholders, provide this motivation because when costs are subtracted from sales, the residual as profit falls to them. They are "residual claimants," and they seek high sales and low costs to make their residual large. Of course governments can raise substantial sums of money from privatizing (that is, selling) public enterprises, too. Still organized as public enterprises in the United States are the U.S. Postal Service, the Tennessee Valley Authority that operates a huge system of dams, and the Corporation for Public Broadcasting, among many others.

Greater awareness of the importance of incentives has stimulated the movement toward less regulation that began in the 1970s. Although normative guidelines could be developed as goals for alternative regulatory institutions, incentives to pursue such goals were often weak or nonexistent. Indeed, designing ideal institutions to pursue social goals is not a simple matter, and creating real institutions with that aim is even more difficult. Moreover, regulators had no strong incentive to bend firms to the efficient service of their consumers. There was no regulation of the regulators. Private ownership, through corporate organization, is not adequate, as we have noted, if the profit the firm can earn is limited—as it was under rate-of-return regulation—because then even a badly managed, inefficient monopoly may be able to meet its profit limit and satisfy its shareholders. As weaknesses in these regulated monopolies grew more apparent, ways to use competitive forces, with their strong incentives, were developed in the 1980s and 1990s, when a deregulation and restructuring movement began to alter regulated industries.

Today, in the United States, many institutions guide industry regulation, including state Public Utility Commissions, the Federal Communications Commission, the Federal Energy Regulatory Commission, and the Surface Transportation Board. Other agencies that once regulated important industries, such as the Civil Aeronautics Board (airlines) no longer exist today. In Europe many institutions regulate specific industries, but the European Commission has implemented some ways to introduce competitive forces in those industries.

Part 2 concerns principles that can be used to guide the design and operation of either government providers, such as public enterprises, or privately owned public utilities or other firms, to regulate—through competition or other means—the markets in which they operate. The chapters in this part focus on new forms of competition with stronger incentives and greater efficiency than traditional regulatory institutions. Chapters in Part 2 cover not only principles used in the design of new regulatory institutions but also applications in a range of important industries whose efficiency affects the strength of the economy.

Social Regulation

Even when competition seems to function, the results may not always satisfy citizens or their democratically elected representatives. As a result, political institutions may move to restrain or modify competitive forces in some way, perhaps through government regulation or new market institutions that harness poorly aimed incentives. Impure food, air pollution, unsafe products, dangerous workplaces, the possibility of bank or insurance company failure, or the failure of a corporation that causes the collapse of its pension fund are all examples of problems that might be eased by some form of social regulation. Finding good solutions to any of these problems calls for careful diagnosis, which again depends on understanding how markets function.

The main areas of social regulation all involve some problem in how markets function. Environmental pollution, for example, is a classic example of an externality. An **externality** is an effect that spills over from a decision and affects a party who did not participate in the decision, as when you play your stereo set too loudly and bother your neighbor. Or if you drive your automobile recklessly, you can endanger others (as well as yourself). Externality has been the subject of great attention in economics, because it can interfere with the effectiveness of the decentralized decisions that are central to a competitive market economy. *Information* is another source of concern. Safety of consumer products, or of workplaces, may be improved if information about dangers, good practices, or good product and equipment design can be widely disseminated. Much is known about imperfect information and the problems it creates in markets, and this knowledge can be helpful in dealing with workplace health and safety regulation and with consumer product regulation. Another aim of social regulation is to avoid harmful effects from the failure of firms, especially of banks or insurance companies.

Social problems can arise in markets precisely because high-powered incentives motivate private corporations so well. If no restriction limits their release of pollutants into the air, for example, polluting is the low-cost way of operating that improves profit. Profit-seeking competitors may be forced to pollute, because the firm that incurs greater cost to reduce its pollution will be handicapped by those greater costs when it tries to sell its product. If workers and consumers are poorly informed, they may suffer in unsafe workplaces or consume unsafe products. When information is poor, a firm that is able to skimp on safety for its workers or its consumers may be more likely to survive. Social regulation attempts to limit these potentially perverse effects of strong incentives.

The first national effort to control the quality of products in the competitive U.S. economy came in 1906 with passage of the Pure Food and Drug Act. Unsanitary practices in the handling of meat in Chicago's stockyards prompted this action, which was aimed at setting standards for food purity and quality, and then inspection to ensure that producers met the standards. More than half a century later, primarily in the 1960s, concern about environmental effects of modern farming practices led to limitations on them. The first target was the insecticide DDT, which improved crop yields but was banned because it entered rivers and lakes with unintended (and unforseen) poisonous effects on animals and people. Soon afterwards, more general environmental concerns led to the Clean Air Act and the Clean Water Act to protect air and water from pollution and to the formation of the Environmental Protection Agency. States also undertook actions with similar aims. Regulation of this sort can be analyzed effectively by viewing it as an effort to deal with an economic problem, such as the spillover or externality effects that using DDT to kill insects may have on innocent bystanders.

BOX 1.3 Cross-Border Air Pollution

Not only is air pollution an externality, an effect that strikes those who did not cause it, but it may even strike those in another country, thereby raising jurisdictional issues that complicate legal remedies. Although the United States is one of the world's biggest air polluters, it also suffers air pollution that drifts from other countries while other countries suffer from U.S. air pollution. Air- and ground-based sensors reveal that as much as 30 percent of the ozone in the United States may come from Mexico and Asia, and dust from the Sahara desert adds to unwanted particles in the air in Miami and other southern cities. Even mercury from power plants in China reaches lakes and streams in the United States. On the other hand, Canadian cities have complained formally and persuasively about health problems caused by U.S. air pollution. Many other disputes arise between nations that are close to each other, and such disputes are likely to become more common as pollution increases.

See T. Watson, "Air Pollution from Other Countries Drifts into USA," *USA Today,* March 14, 2005 p. 1A.

In the 1960s and 1970s other dangers became apparent. An increasingly dangerous workplace led Congress to create the Occupational Safety and Health Administration, aimed at improving workplace health and safety. The number of highway deaths had also grown alarmingly, and Congress formed the National Highway Traffic Safety Administration to try to reduce them. Consumer products did not escape this movement to make the nation safer, and Congress created the Consumer Product Safety Commission in an effort to contain the dangers from consumer products.

Problems that cause social regulation can be difficult to solve. Consider the problem of the National Highway Traffic Safety Administration in reducing the danger to passengers of motor vehicle travel by requiring that seat belts be installed in new vehicles by their manufacturers. Notice how the chance of an accident is an important consideration in the economic evaluation of making seat belts mandatory in *every* vehicle. If every vehicle is involved in one accident over its useful life then every vehicle's seat belts will be used on average. Relative to the value of the protection that seat belts can then afford, the cost of mandating them will be quite low. On the other hand, if only one vehicle in a million can be expected to have an accident, the protective value in one accident must be weighed against the cost of installing seat belts in one million vehicles, a substantially higher cost per effective use.

Another example is building a new highway in place of one that is proved to be dangerous, so lives may be saved. The new highway is expensive, and resources are limited. Some means of valuing lives relative to other goals can be useful in facing such decisions about how to use society's limited resources. Some understanding of how we handle risk and how we differ in our tolerance of risk can be useful as well. Therefore, in addition to environmental protection, worker protection, and consumer protection, topics that foster clearer thinking about problems of social regulation are considered in Part 3.

Part 3 also treats aspects of the regulation of banking, insurance, and pensions. These activities are subjects of social regulation for two main reasons. First, both the banking and insurance industries are important to the rest of the economy because they interact with so many firms and industries beyond their own boundaries. Second, as with all of the issues treated under social regulation, a problem may be caused by the way markets function, in this case the problem of firm failure. In most competitive industries, firms fail all the time and are replaced by others—all without great inconvenience to consumers. The failure of a bank or an insurance company, however, can bring disaster for affected customers, who often are not able to assess the risk of such failures. The same applies to employees of any company that fails without having its pension plan properly funded, which means employees may not receive the retirement benefits that were promised. In part to avoid harmful consequences of this routine side effect of competition—firm failure—these industries and funds are subject to special forms of regulation. Regulation of accounting, for instance, can prevent concealment of high-risk actions that would make failure more likely.

Many separate institutions guide social regulation in the United States. At the federal level, the Environmental Protection Agency pursues environmental protection, while the Occupational Safety and Health Administration is concerned about safety and health in the workplace. The Food and Drug Administration, The National Highway Traffic Safety Administration, and the Consumer Product Safety Commission seek to protect consumers from unsafe products. The Federal Deposit Insurance Corporation and other agencies provide protection against bank failure. Most states have corresponding agencies for many of the same purposes and they provide the main protection against insurance company failure. The Public Company Oversight Board serves to avoid deceptive corporate accounting reports that could conceal risks and hasten failure. The federal Employee Retirement Income Security Act is a main instrument of pension regulation. In addition to laws and agency efforts, resort to the courts provides remedies for some harms, and knowing that such recourse is available motivates firms to avoid harms, especially to workers and consumers.

1.2 | THE CONTEXT OF MARKET REGULATION

Markets and market regulation depend on institutions, including legal arrangements like property rights that facilitate transactions between private parties. In the next section, we examine property rights, consider how incentives develop and drive economic activity, and discuss the corporation, the most important private actor in the economy. In the following section, we examine markets, first noting how property was exchanged in early markets and then considering the modern market economy that combines political with economic institutions.

Transactions, Incentives, and Corporations

Markets foster transactions, which convey private property from one party to another. Rights to private property make these transactions possible. How property rights are collected in an organization determines the organization's economic incentives, which can play an important role in its success. Corporations are especially important collections of property rights organized to pursue profit through economic activity.

Property Rights

What does it mean to own something? How can you prove ownership? These questions are important if you want to acquire property or if you want to sell property you already own. The advantage of specialization is often given as a reason to motivate transactions. Instead of all of us running our own farms and kilns and other operations to produce whatever it is we need, we specialize in something we can do well and exchange the results of our effort for items we want. In a market economy, such specialization requires—and allows—the exchange of goods and services for some forms of payment in transactions. Such transactions require well-defined **property rights**, which specify the rights that accompany ownership of property and, thus, inform traders about what they are exchanging.

A wide range of property rights exists today. One ticket gives you the right to sit in a particular theater seat on one evening, for example, while another lets you reclaim your coat after the performance. For certain valuable items, such as automobiles or real estate, government agencies provide evidence of title to property, and they thereby facilitate the transfer of such property. To some extent the title that is granted explains the rights and responsibilities of ownership, but these are seldom defined in perfect detail.[1] So there can be uncertainty, or lack of full information, about property rights.[2]

Private property gives an owner legal claims, even when ownership is separated from possession. Indeed, duties and liabilities accompany ownership, and the law upholds them.[3] A property owner ordinarily is free to use the property in a way that does not interfere with others' rights, which means, for instance, that the owner of property may be restrained from causing air pollution. The right to sell property may also be proscribed, for instance, to prevent a home seller from refusing to sell to a potential buyer because of the buyer's race. Excluding others from the use of property is also a right an owner may have to forgo when regulators require that access to a limited resource—such as a railroad bridge—be granted to others.

Rights are not always defined in a way that invites socially desirable action. Take the case of an oil well. Owners of several parcels of land may be able to drill into the same underground reservoir of oil, and all who can do so will lay claim to the oil. In such situations the **rule of capture** defines property rights, which means that rights to the property (oil) are granted according to the amount each claimant can extract. A problem called the **common-pool problem** results, because the reservoir is like a common pool and each party wishes to extract the oil as rapidly as possible (before others take it). For technical reasons, rapid extraction allows less oil to be extracted from the reservoir.

---

[1] For example, consider constraints on the use of a motor vehicle: driving only after proving competence and being licensed, on only part of the road, at restricted speeds, according to many other detailed traffic rules, often with a motor vehicle that is inspected, insured, and licensed.

[2] For legal analysis of property, see Joseph W. Singer (2001, 2002).

[3] Nobel laureate Ronald Coase (1960) provides a classic analysis of the role of property rights in the functioning of markets.

Property rights can sometimes be difficult to define. No one owns the air, for instance, so it may be used to discard wastes, perhaps through a factory smokestack, which not only cause discomfort to neighbors but also can pollute rivers and forests hundreds of miles away. That is how poorly defined property rights give rise to externality, where one party is affected by another's decision, which applies to the common-pool problem. Once property rights in such a situation are defined, however, parties might conceivably negotiate a solution.[4] An example of this process is land itself, which was once so plentiful in England that it was not owned by any private party and was used by all. When population grew and land became scarce, assigning property rights led to more efficient use, because the owner of each parcel of land sought its most valuable use. Air or water cannot be divided as easily to create the kinds of transferable ownership rights that are feasible for land. Constraining rights to discharge unwanted wastes into air and water is still possible to avoid the pollution that can result when decentralized decisions are unregulated.

An economy based on private property has to have property widely dispersed among the population to induce market transactions. Obviously, if all property is concentrated in the hands of a few, as it was in feudal societies, those property owners are bound to be well served. The general public, however, would not be served so well, and the advantages of market competition for serving general welfare could be lost. In the United States, there is substantial inequality of income. The top 20 percent receive more than 45 percent of national income, while the bottom 20 percent receive only about 5 percent.[5] Indeed, the United States has less equality of income than almost any of the leading private industrial economies today. Yet property is held widely enough through the population that a market economy can flourish, aided by redistribution policies that moderate the concentration of income and wealth.

Property has to be reasonably well defined and reasonably dispersed among us, therefore, to be traded or exchanged effectively in markets. Traders must have something to exchange, and they have to know what they are trading. Clear property rights can make exchange simple and easy, so markets with many buyers and sellers can function smoothly. Creating property rights is not costless, and law can help clarify, define, and, as necessary, change property rights. Once they are defined, property rights bring incentives into play as property owners seek value from the rights they own.

Incentives

Most of us want to own property, which wealth permits, so in a world with private property the promise of income or wealth serves to motivate us. Such incentives make markets work. You might be willing to work harder to keep a job that pays $25 per hour than a job that pays $10 per hour, for example, or take more time to learn

---

[4] See Coase (1960).

[5] Brazil has a less equal distribution of income than the United States, with the top 20 percent accounting for almost 65 percent of income and the lowest 20 percent receiving only 2.5 percent. That might be one reason that security—in forms such as armored cars—is of great concern there. See Simon Romero, "Cashing In on Security Worries," *New York Times*, July 24, 1999, p. B1. Indeed, international terrorism might be motivated in part by unequal distribution of world income.

how to perform the higher paying job. Proper incentives can move us in socially desirable directions, but incentives can also lead us in socially undesirable directions. For example, the incentive to withdraw oil from a common pool—before others withdraw it—is flawed when it induces an excessively high rate of extraction of oil from the ground.

To see different types of incentives, suppose you are responsible for a department in a business firm. You may hire employees and pay them either by **salary**, as a fixed amount per hour or other time period worked, or according to work performed, the so called **piece rate** that pays a certain amount per unit of output. Which payment plan you choose may affect how your employees function, because different compensation plans reward different kinds of behavior. We should expect workers to behave in a way that improves their incomes. Under the piece rate, they have the incentive to produce output, because that is what adds to their incomes, but they may not give as much care to the quality of their work. Incentive to meet a quality standard can be created within the piece rate, by giving the per-unit payment only for units that meet the quality standard, where a test of quality is feasible. If a salary is paid instead, the employees may attend to quality but they may not move quickly, or give an all-out effort, because income is not directly affected (and less work is usually preferred to more work).

Anytime one party—the **principal**—seeks to obtain effort for a certain purpose from another—the **agent**—we have what is called a principal-agent problem. If the principal offers a fixed salary, the agent's reward does not depend directly on effort, so the agent may not work as hard, and more supervision is needed. If the principal offers a piece rate, supervision may be easier, but monitoring of quantity and quality is needed to insure that rewarded work is actually accomplished. As another way to create incentive, the principal may share profit with the agent, but then the agent has to bear risks and may not be in a position to do that. So the principal-agent problem may have no perfect solution.

The incentive problem is even more complicated than these payment-plan examples suggest. Workers may be motivated in other ways, such as possibilities for promotion, pride, self-respect, concern for community, and even spite. Still, in a crude way, incentives can be categorized by how strong they are and then examined separately for their effects on efficiency. For instance, it is easy to see that a piece rate, or a per-unit payment, gives a stronger incentive to produce units than does a fixed payment for working a unit of time, such as a rate of pay per hour.

An even more "high-powered" incentive can be created. For example, as the owner of a private firm, you would receive the revenue from units sold less the cost of units produced. You can influence both sales and production costs, and what is left over from sales minus costs is yours to keep. We call the amount left over as profit the residual, and as the owner you are the **residual claimant** because you get to keep it. We know that owners—the shareholders of a corporation who formally own its capital—have a strong incentive to keep sales high and costs low, because the difference between sales and costs goes to them. The resulting **high-powered incentive** is stronger than a per-unit incentive. With this high-powered incentive, there is no guarantee of a per-unit profit, and effort to make sales and to control costs might

---

BOX 1.4 Incentives for Innovation

A patent creates an ownership interest in an innovation and, thus, motivates its discovery. A prize offers an even more direct incentive, focused on specific performance. For example, in the 1920s hotel owner Raymond Orteig offered a cash prize of $25,000 for a successful flight from New York to Paris. Nine attempts were motivated, and aviators spent well over $100,000 in the effort. The prize was won in 1927 when Charles Lindbergh landed in Paris. In 1996, a New Spirit of St. Louis organization was formed to offer $10,000,000 as an "X Prize" for accomplishing two private flights within two weeks into space (100 kilometers or 62 miles above the earth) carrying the equivalent of three human adults. The X Prize was won on October 4, 2004, when the space vehicle SpaceShipOne, designed by aviation legend Elbert L. Rutan and financed by philanthropist Paul G. Allen, made its second successful space flight (the first had been on September 29).

Netflix, the DVD movie rental service has offered a prize of $1,000,000 to anyone who—within five years—can improve its Cinematch program (by a well-defined 10 percent), which predicts movies you would like based on movies you have chosen in the past. Deep down, Netflix executives thought they had the greatest possible program in Cinematch, but many leaders in a field called machine learning have downloaded Netflix's 100 million movie ratings and considerable improvement has already been achieved. Progress can be tracked at a leader board at Netflix's website, www.Netflix.com.

See D. Leonhardt, "You Want Innovation? Offer a Prize," *New York Times,* January 31, 2007, p. B1.

even fail. If sales do not exceed costs, money is lost. If sales exceed costs by a large amount, shareholders can be handsomely rewarded. Thus, a corporation, offers high-powered incentives to its owners, as shareholders, who face a principal-agent problem because collectively they are the principal and they must induce managers to pursue goals they set.

Corporations

The present-day **corporation** allows shareholders a very sophisticated property interest in a business enterprise. This *ownership interest* can be separate from actual *operation* of the business, as any holder of a few shares of stock in a large corporation well knows, because shareholders of a corporation may elect a board of directors to oversee the salaried top managers of the business. At the same time, shareholder liability is limited to the amount of money invested, so a corporation shareholder need not worry about being dragged into court to settle further obligations of the enterprise. As noted, shareholders retain a residual claim to net income and to the net assets of the corporation. Like a person, the corporation may sue or be sued and it pays taxes. As long as it is solvent so it can pay its bills, however, it does not die; it has perpetual life.

In contrast to the corporation, the proprietorship and partnership forms of business enterprise end abruptly when the owner or a partner dies. Portions of a partnership cannot be purchased or sold without agreement among all partners. A proprietor or partner may also be held liable for obligations beyond investments made in the business. So it is not surprising that proprietors and partners often take a careful and active interest in managing the businesses they own.

Corporations are the most significant actors in the U.S. economy. According to recent findings of the Census of Manufacturers,[6] about 80 percent of manufacturing firms were organized as corporations and they accounted for 98 percent of the value added in manufacturing. The **value added** by a firm is essentially the difference between its sales and the inputs it purchases. A maker of steel purchases iron ore, for example, works it into steel, and sells the steel. The difference between the value of purchased ore and sold steel is the *value* the firm *added* to the inputs. Corporations play a vital role in the market economy, and they have evolved into newer, ever more economical forms as times have changed.[7]

Complicated **functional organizations**, with divisions for functional activities like sales, production, and finance, developed late in the nineteenth century. Primarily in the twentieth century, manufacturers began to extend their organizations by integrating into retailing to distribute products to consumers. **Multidivisional organizations** also developed in which each division handled all activities for a particular product line. And **conglomerates**, which combine many apparently unrelated products, appeared, followed by **multinational enterprises**, which operate in more than one country. These new organizational forms could deal more effectively in changed circumstances, and they flourished, showing how the search for more profitable operations can alter the shape of the business firm.

At the end of the seventeenth century, when it was first used in Europe as a so-called joint stock company, the shareholder or corporate form of business organization was seriously misused. A number of early joint stock companies formed in England and France collapsed when their organizers either ran off with funds or proved incompetent. One of the most famous cases is that of the South Sea Company, which assumed England's national debt in 1711 in return for an annual payment of interest, plus a monopoly over British trade with the South Sea Islands and South America. Speculation drove the price of shares in the company far out of proportion to their value and the collapse that followed exposed fraud. The event became known as the "South Sea Bubble," and it led in 1720 to what was called the Bubble Act in England, a law that prevented widespread use of this organizational form for 100 years. Because of this history, any organization resembling a corporation was regarded with suspicion in the United States during the early colonial period.[8]

In eighteenth-century America, the archetypal corporation actually was a municipality, and only in the nineteenth century did the corporate form come into use in private business.[9] New York State first allowed a business firm to incorporate itself in 1811. Under that law, the corporation could have capital up to $100,000 and a life of only

---

[6] See U.S. Census Bureau at www.census.gov.

[7] See Chandler (1962, 1977, 2001).

[8] Costly corporate bankruptcies such as those of Enron and Worldcom, in the early years of the twenty-first century show that this problem with the shareholder form of organization still exists.

[9] See Horowitz (1977).

20 years.[10] The real significance of the New York law was that it allowed voluntary incorporation as a routine procedure under specific terms, rather than by special act of a state legislature. Special acts were open only to businessmen with political influence, sometimes through corruption,[11] so having standard terms for incorporation improved fairness. By midcentury, railroads predominated among corporations. They developed the line-and-staff form of organization, which separated decision makers who had line responsibilities from specialized supporting staff. Manufacturing corporations became numerous after the Civil War, and by 1900 corporations conducted much of U.S. commerce.

The individual state governments retained power to create corporations after they came into use in the early 1800s, and they imposed strict requirements through most of the nineteenth century. A corporation typically had to serve a well-defined purpose, for example, such as providing railroad transportation between two specific points. As in New York, corporations had a limited life and could accumulate only a specified amount of capital. One corporation also was forbidden from owning stock in another. By the 1890s, however, following improvements in transportation and communications, more commerce was moving across state lines, and a firm with interstate business could choose where to incorporate. States began to compete with one another to raise revenue by granting corporate charters, and their competition took the form of easing restrictions on corporations.[12]

In 1890, New Jersey allowed one corporation to own another, thereby giving corporation status to holding companies and **trusts**. The word *trust* refers to the "voting trust" that first came into use in 1882 when shareholders of 50 oil refineries surrendered their stock for certificates in the Standard Oil Trust.[13] The Standard Oil Trust coordinated actions among firms in the industry. Restraining such organizations was the aim of a movement that gave us the laws we still call *antitrust laws.*

Business firms exist because there are costs to using markets, and organizing some activities within a business firm can be more efficient than relying on transactions in markets.[14] The firm offers a governance structure to ensure pursuit of chosen ends, and it avoids some problems that arise from contractual relationships in markets.[15] We are unable to anticipate every possible eventuality when we write a contract so we may be surprised by an opportunist who takes advantage of us through a loop hole in our contract. Units that share the same goal within a firm may avoid these contractual problems of markets. This does not mean, however, that firms are always more efficient, for the market can motivate and discipline agents sometimes better than the organization. The point is that firms draw lines separating them from markets largely to minimize costs. Beyond giving the firm this choice of whether to keep activities within the firm or to use markets, markets can offer many other advantages.

---

[10] See Mason (1968).

[11] See Seager and Gulick (1929).

[12] Today more than half of all publicly traded companies are incorporated in Delaware, which took over leadership from New Jersey early in the twentieth century after rules adopted by New Jersey put firms incorporated there at a disadvantage. See Bebchuk and Hamdani (2002).

[13] See Clark (1928, pp. 518–519).

[14] See Coase (1937) for the classic statement of this trade-off between organizing an activity within the firm or using the market.

[15] For rich descriptions of these influences on the corporation see Williamson (2000, 2002).

Markets

Markets developed historically as changes in property rights created incentives that markets could serve, and new institutions were also created. Western Europe provides an example. There, for more than a thousand years from about 500 AD to 1500 AD, feudal manorial organization instead of markets guided economic activity. Typically, land was not divided into plots that were individually owned, in the modern sense of being readily salable. Economic activities were sustained mainly by tradition. Goods were made largely for local consumption instead of being purchased, transported, and resold at another location as they commonly are today.

During this early period, transportation was not easy and military weapons such as gunpowder or even the crossbow had not been developed. Not surprisingly, the important political entities were small kingdoms, which at that time could be defended easily, rather than the great nations of today.[16] Workers who tilled soil and tended animals in these predominantly agrarian societies became early settlers in the Americas, and they brought ideas for an industrial revolution and a new kind of democratic capitalism.

The Industrial Revolution in England

If we could watch the sort of trading that occurred in English market towns late in this medieval period we might think it chaotic. Imagine parties haggling amid piles of produce without any currency, let alone credit cards. Behind the scenes, however, trade was closely controlled. As early as the eleventh century, for example, guild organizations were given royal charters to regulate trade in English towns. Great trading companies like the famous East India Company (and the infamous South Sea Company) held royal charters to oversee foreign trade. By the fifteenth century they exercised power in foreign countries much as an arm of government would. At that time, the granting by kings of exclusive royal charters to particular groups seemed a sensible way to control trade. By the end of the sixteenth century, however, Queen Elizabeth began the practice of making grants of trading rights to individuals, and they took on more obvious monopolistic elements. Some grants went to foreigners in an effort to attract their technology to England, but some grants were sold, virtually to raise revenue for the Crown, and others went as rewards to loyal friends.

After abuse of monopoly grants by the Crown became apparent, Parliament, the political body that had grown from small advisory councils of local leaders in the medieval period, sought to restrain monopoly. Parliament found an avenue for this in the arguments of Sir Edward Coke, chief justice under King James I, who insisted that the common law (and not the king) was the supreme law of the land. While some decisions at common law courts were already helping competitive trade, the merchants and traders—who were well represented in Parliament—passed laws that changed property rights to foster even more commercial activity.

An example of the changes that occurred by legislative act in England is the enclosure acts, which changed property rights to allow the fencing of fields for individual or

---

[16] There were economic as well as military advantages in small kingdoms. See Howard (1976).

BOX 1.5 The Enclosure Acts

The enclosure acts Parliament passed in England in the seventeenth century reduced the common uses of land and permitted the formation of enclosed, or private, estates and small lots. Enclosures allowed efficient use of land for crops that had become relatively more valuable in the seventeenth century. When new livestock feed crops, such as clover, were introduced from America and the turnip was brought from Holland, changes in the sizes and shapes of plots were warranted. Enclosure and exclusive property rights fostered the formation of farms that could take advantage of these developments. The Enclosure Acts alone did not *cause* the Industrial Revolution; they affected only a fraction of all land, and the Industrial Revolution occurred in some countries that adopted no such enclosure scheme. The enclosures, however, typify the move toward more exact property rights that facilitated trade.

See P. Deane, *The First Industrial Revolution,* Cambridge: Cambridge University Press, 1965; D. C. North and R. P. Thomas, *The Rise of the Western World,* Cambridge: Cambridge University Press, 1973; and J. G. Sidak and D. F. Spulber, *Deregulatory Takings and the Regulatory Contract,* New York: Cambridge University Press, 1997.

---

private use rather than common use by all. Common use of land had developed when land had been plentiful (almost like common use of air and water today). When a resource is scarce, however, common rights to use it causes a common-pool problem. Because the resource is free, too many claims are made on it. In the sixteenth century, land grew scarce and the price of wool went up, so private, exclusive, rights to use land became valuable. Exclusive rights could be desirable because, with such a right, one would not overgraze the land as many sheep herders would when all were trying to use the same land. Indeed, by avoiding overgrazing, exclusive rights to land raised wool production.[17]

The trade and commerce that developed in England, especially after the Revolutionary War and independence for America, was spectacular. Paved roads were built, canals were dug, and in the 1800s railroads stretched from city to city. A system of banks developed and facilitated the raising of capital. Between 1780 and 1860 more political restraints on trade were removed. For instance, laws from the 1400s had regulated the supplies of small grains to keep their prices high. After much debate, these laws, called the Corn Laws, were repealed in 1846. New technological discoveries were made, and modern science found profitable application. Where life had stood almost in the same place for many centuries, in the eighteenth and nineteenth centuries the modern world began to emerge.

Of this burst of economic activity historian Arnold Toynbee observed ". . . [t]he essence of the Industrial Revolution is the substitution of competition for the medieval regulations which had previously controlled the production and distribution of wealth."[18] The working of this competitive market process was described masterfully

---

[17] Enclosure of pastoral land arose in common law as early as 1236 in the Statute of Merton. See North and Thomas (1973, p.150).

[18] See Toynbee (1969, 1984). I am grateful to Professor Max Hartwell for pointing out this Toynbee passage.

by Adam Smith (1776), who saw how actions by individual agents, all seeking their own best interests, could serve society well if all agents were subject to competitive pressures. Any one seller might seek to profit handsomely on a transaction; but, if customers could go elsewhere, each seller would be constrained by competitors' prices. As a result, market prices would tend to approximate the full costs of goods that were efficiently produced, without excessive profit.

Democratic Capitalism

The Industrial Revolution in England marked the emergence of capitalism, which organizes economic activity around markets and places central decision power in the hands of those representing capital. The corporation shows the capitalist form, with shareholders as residual claimants running the show. In the modern age, that central power is tempered by governmental political power through **democratic capitalism**. Here, democratic political power—operating from a "one person, one vote" principle—restrains the economic power of businesses. Through legislative and executive political institutions, governmental regulatory functions are defined and put into effect to produce a regulated species of capitalism.

Democratic capitalism is not the only way to organize economic activity. Indeed, history shows repeated conflict within and between nations that organized their political and economic affairs differently. Some citizens have even been forced to leave their countries in such disputes, but otherwise citizens tend to favor arrangements followed by their own country and may even fight to protect them. In pointing out the remarkable economic performance of capitalist countries over centuries, Dennis Mueller (2001) noted that despite the loyalty one usually has for one's own country, the last two centuries have seen a steady immigration to the United States, suggesting that citizens of other countries are not immune to its appeal. Democratic capitalism is not necessarily ideal, and it takes many forms in many countries, but it is so successful in raising living standards and is so widely adopted that understanding how it works and how it is regulated are obviously worthy goals.

Market Regulation

In the right circumstances effective competition can bring prices roughly into line with costs of production. Competition challenges producers to lower costs to raise profits. In addition, competitive market prices that reflect costs let consumers guide production, because in comparing prices consumers are actually comparing costs and deciding which goods should be produced. When monopoly is present and unregulated, this market process is not as effective. Monopoly blocks new entry, so the price of a good or service may lie above long-run cost without expanded production. A monopoly usually wants to limit the supply of the good or service to keep its price high, and its market power enables it to do that. More production of the good would benefit consumers because they value it so highly. When consumers buy from a monopoly that sets its price high, the value that consumers place on those units exceeds their cost. Monopoly prices do not reflect the costs of goods the way competitive prices do, so consumers cannot guide production as they do in competition.

Now the true advantage of competitive prices can be seen. A consumer who is deciding which of two goods to purchase looks at their prices. When those prices reflect marginal costs of production, the consumer can make a decision based on the *relative marginal costs* of the two goods. Having consumers choose what to purchase based on the costs of goods leads to efficient results, because goods that offer more value for consumers per unit of cost are the goods that are chosen. To the extent relative prices do not reflect relative marginal costs when there is monopoly, consumers' decisions are not based on the true relative costs of goods, and overall economic efficiency cannot be achieved. If effective competition could be introduced into the monopoly market, expansion and entry would force a reduction in price to the level of costs, and more of that good would be chosen by consumers.

The production of new knowledge raises special problems. Without property rights in new ideas, incentive for their discovery would be limited. To help motivate discovery, a patent monopoly is granted for new ideas. Of course, patent monopolies complicate antitrust policy because they are legal and legitimate monopolies, yet monopolies are generally attacked under the law. Modern antitrust policy attempts to support well-functioning competitive markets where competition is thought to be

---

BOX 1.6 The Pay of a Blocking Lineman in Professional Football

Professional sports leagues are granted some exemptions from antitrust law on grounds that cooperation can foster more appealing competition in the sport. One example is the common draft, or selection, of players into professional football, which the league designed to have weaker teams choose players earlier to strengthen those teams. Once selected in this draft, a player was tied to the team selecting him, and his bargaining power came only from his threat to withhold services; he could not negotiate with another team. All that changed in 1993 when, to settle labor strife in pro-football, a new labor agreement was reached. A cap was placed on a team's total salaries for all players. The cap would rise in proportion to team revenue. After a time, drafted players could negotiate with other teams, which made players free agents and created a market for them.

Before these changes, linemen were the poorest paid members of a team, partly because their work was out of the public's view and they could rarely become stars. This was true even as linemen who could rush the quarterback to disrupt his passes became valuable, and linemen who could block them became *very* valuable. In the market that free agency produced, in just a few years, salaries of those blocking linemen rose to five times as much as they had been before, and a talented lineman often became the second highest paid player on a team, after the quarterback and ahead of players who ran with the football. Thus, in contrast to earlier times when teams owned players and could pay low salaries to unheralded linemen, the introduction of a free-agent market for players was able to induce monetary payments based on players' individual contributions to a team's success, no matter what their position.

See M. Lewis, *The Blind Side: Evolution of a Game*, New York: W. W. Norton, 2006.

feasible, and patent monopolies complicate that task. This form of market regulation is examined in Part 1 of the book.

When *economies of scale* are very great, monopoly organization of a market may offer advantages. Economies of scale can arise in *networks,* such as those for telephone or mail delivery, because one more telephone call or one more letter may be handled at very low cost. If the technology can achieve lowest cost at such a large scale of operation that one firm serves the entire market, a monopoly organization may be preferred. An example is the traditional public utility, which is regulated in an effort to avoid monopolistic behavior. Perhaps one stage in the production of a service may be open to competition, however, such as the generation of electricity, while other stages, such as the distribution of electricity, are regulated by government. Competitive forces may also be created by allowing other providers of a service to use the resources of a monopoly, even in the distribution of electricity. These kinds of regulatory issues are examined in Part 2.

In other circumstances, competition can function but may not produce ideal outcomes, as when production of a good causes excessive air pollution, a cost that is not borne by the polluter and thus not perceived as a cost of production. Decentralized decisions that ignore such costs when they are borne by others are inherently inefficient. Other problems follow when information is imperfect, especially for consumers in the marketplace, for workers in the workplace, or for employees in the

---

BOX 1.7 A Business Model for Satellite Radio

When the Federal Communications Commission (FCC) allowed radio spectrum to be auctioned for satellite radio service in the 1990s it was not sure the new technology would compete with ordinary broadcast radio. So the FCC required that there be at least two satellite radio stations, which are now XM and Sirius, to force them to compete with each other. XM and Sirius collect monthly fees from subscribers and offer different, advertising-free, programming content. The services are incompatible in that you can receive the programming of a service only if you subscribe to it, and the services offer different programming. Sirius famously pays Howard Stern $100,000,000 a year and delivers professional football and Nascar races, while XM has Oprah Winfrey and professional baseball. To catch both Howard and Oprah (or both football and baseball), you would have to pay fees to both XM and Sirius. Competition from ordinary (free) broadcast radio, as well as from each other, limits the fees XM and Sirius can charge subscribers, yet at the same time they compete with each other for program content and drive up its price. Partly as a result, they are losing money. They have scale economies and may not develop sufficient subscribers to allow profit. But they are attempting to merge into one service, which could give compatibility to subscribers and more monopsonistic, or single buyer, advantages in buying program content at lower prices. This case contains many issues, and illustrates the difficulty that new technologies bring to the docket of the Federal Communications Commission.

See J. Nocera, "I Want My Howard Stern and Oprah," *New York Times,* January 20, 2007, p. B1.

labor market. One side effect of competition is that firms fail, sometimes causing enormous losses for investors, employees, and even retirees. Remedies are sought for such problems to preserve the effectiveness of decentralized markets in meeting social goals. Problems in the functioning of decentralized markets and their remedies are examined in Part 3.

1.3 | LAW AND POLITICS

One instrument that is much relied on to improve market outcomes is the process of the law. Courts settle many commercial disputes and rule on regulatory matters. The political realm is also important in market regulation, for legislatures provide laws and institutions to guide competition, to regulate an industry, or to limit effects of market imperfections such as pollution. Political institutions, operating largely under majority rule, are able to reach decisions over often controversial issues but are not focused on economic efficiency. Indeed, the institutions are not always charged with the best possible purposes, may not be well designed for the purposes they are given, and, like some business firms, may not be effectively managed.

Having emphasized incentives in markets, we must also acknowledge their important role in political institutions. A legislator serves constituents, whose votes are needed for political survival. Votes can also be influenced through advertising and other election campaign expenses that financial contributions from voters and special interests can support. So many forces affect the rules for governmental market regulation in democratic capitalism, including the interests of those who are to be regulated.

The Legal System

All civilizations have had to form some system of law to organize governments and to settle disputes.[19] Indeed, among Western nations that rely heavily on private property rights and markets to guide their economic activities there is no exception. Just as laws themselves change, what law *is* changes with time. Sir Henry Maine (1920) claimed, for example, that for settling disputes the gradual shift from hierarchy, with authority or status, to contract under law was a good development for social relations. Contrasting views by Karl Marx (1867) challenged the indispensability of law, arguing that defects and inequalities in society were due not to the nature of humans but to the way their economic affairs were organized. Law was seen by Marx as an instrument of domination that could decline in influence just as the state itself eventually could decline.

A great many sociological theories of law have been advanced in the last two hundred years. These theories were often normative, in that they sought scientific principles that could guide the improvement of society. They were intended to explain

---

[19] For a history of American law, see Friedman (1985).

how law works. Jeremy Bentham (1879, 1945) saw laws as balancing the collectivist interests of society against the private interests. More purposefully, Roscoe Pound (1959) viewed law as a way to engineer an efficient social structure, thereby to balance individual interests, public interests, and social interests. A modern realism school uses social science to examine the legal process. In this view, law is generally accepted as "what the judges decide" and can be improved by using knowledge from the social sciences to predict more fully the ultimate effects of legal decisions. More recently, critical legal scholars have incorporated ideas from deconstruction and other post-modern philosophical theories into the realist's framework to provide insights into the purpose and operation of the legal system.

Systems and Sources of Law

The two main systems of law used by Western nations are *Roman law* and *common (or English) law*. **Roman law** is the earliest form of law. It relies on deliberate lawmaking by legislative and judicial bodies to produce clear rules for regulating human affairs. Most western European countries use it. To decide cases under Roman law, courts look to the text of numerous statutes or legal codes.

In contrast, **common law** courts look more to past judicial decisions. In England, where common law originated, the criteria for judicial decisions are acts of Parliament, the principles followed in previous judicial decisions (judicial precedent), or immemorial custom. England has no constitution to serve as a source of law, but if no primary law or principle is available to help in deciding a case, a court may turn to foreign law, textbooks, or even social values as sources of law. While common law gives greater scope to judges in interpreting the law on a case-by-case basis, the hallmark of the common law system is that judicial precedent set in previous decisions is binding on judges (Clark, 1928, p. 28), through the doctrine of *stare decisis*. **Stare decisis** requires that courts hearing similar cases must adhere to the rules of law developed in preceding cases.[20] A settled hierarchy of courts determines which rules are binding, for *stare decisis* is brought into operation by reference to the decisions of higher courts. This common law process allows social norms to be accommodated into the law, because the law can be used to enforce the social norms.

The United States, with slight exceptions, follows common law rather than Roman law. (Under French influence, the state of Louisiana adopted much Roman law, and California and Texas retain traces of Spanish law, which is of the Roman type.) Accordingly, judges use statutes, judicial precedent, and custom as major sources of American law. In addition, the U.S. Constitution is the touchstone by which laws are evaluated.

Civil, Criminal, and Administrative Law

In describing the process of law in more detail it is useful to distinguish criminal law from civil law. First, **criminal law** is a set of rules we all must obey or face punishment

---

[20] After time for appealing a court decision has passed, that decision is binding on the parties involved and cannot be disputed in any subsequent proceeding between them, according to the legal principle called *res judicta*.

by the state. State and federal governments force adherence to criminal law, which may vary from place to place but includes violent crimes against the person (assault, rape, murder), infringements of property rights (arson, copyright infringement, forgery), and regulatory crimes (antitrust violations, environmental harms, workplace injuries) because the rules are judged to be needed for society's benefit.

In contrast to criminal law, **civil law** encompasses rules to settle private disputes, such as those involving business affairs, the transfer of property, or the recovery of money for injuries through the fault of others. **Torts** are particular civil wrongs for which an injured party may recover damages because the injury was deliberate or due to negligence. Slander, trespassing, or personal injury are torts.

Civil and criminal law are not mutually exclusive, for many offenses may be both civil and criminal. The standards of proof required to find guilt under these two types of law differ, however. For example, the former football star, O. J. Simpson, was found not guilty of the crime of murdering his wife or Ronald Goldman in 1995, but liable for civil damages in a wrongful death civil suit in 1997, perhaps because the standards of proof for finding guilt are more demanding in a criminal case than for finding liability in a civil case.

Administrative law governs the actions of government agencies and is relevant in many regulatory agency proceedings. Indeed, these agencies specialize in the areas being regulated and are thereby able to develop expert knowledge for resolving the complex issues that arise. The Federal Trade Commission enforces antitrust law, for example, while the Federal Communications Commission guides regulatory policy in the telecommunications industry, and the Environmental Protection Agency regulates air, water, and land pollution. Regulatory agencies make rules that can have the force of statutes. Agencies also rely on their own previous decisions that, like common law decisions of courts, shape expectations about future regulatory policies and actions for those who are subject to them.

Dispute Resolution in the Civil Context

The lawsuit may be the best known legal procedure for resolving private disputes. One party, the **plaintiff**, files a complaint in court against another party, the **defendant**. Before the actual trial begins the parties make extensive preparations, with court rulings governing such matters as the information each party is entitled to obtain from the other under what are called **discovery procedures**. During this process some negotiation can occur, and as a result the dispute may be settled by a **plea bargain** in which the defendant might agree not to continue a certain practice or even to pay compensation and, in exchange, not have to participate in a trial. Over 90 percent of federal criminal cases end in plea bargains, as do about 90 percent of antitrust cases and the great majority of white-collar-crime cases. Agreement in a plea bargain saves parties the cost of a trial, and it avoids uncertainty about the outcome, but it leaves no detailed public record so it does not develop the law the way a decision in a public trial does. In antitrust there is a special leniency provision that rewards the first firm to confess, say in a collusion case, by forgoing fines or prison terms. A firm must apply for leniency, however, and uncertainty about whether it will be granted limits the use of the provision.

A case that goes to trial takes place in either a state court or one of 90 Federal District Courts and involves arguments about both fact and law. Criminal defendants always can insist on a jury trial. Parties in civil actions may request trial by jury. For example, an antitrust-case defendant in a criminal monopoly action may insist on a trial by jury while a defendant in a civil treble-damage action (under the Sherman Act three times the damage caused by illegal action may be collected by a plaintiff) may only *request* trial by jury.

Once the trial ends either party may appeal the decision. From a federal district court, an appeal would go to the next higher level of federal court, the Appeals Court for its region (there are eleven),[21] and states have similar court structures. An appeal can only concern points of law, not findings of fact. Eventually the case may even be appealed to the third and final federal level, the U.S. Supreme Court and heard there if four of the nine members of the Court find the point of law in the appeal sufficiently important to warrant attention.[22] With time for appeals, an antitrust or regulation case may take five years or longer to complete. The way a point of law is finally settled is binding in future cases under the *stare decisis* principle.

Law in Economic Affairs

Many legal concepts are relevant to economic affairs. The notion of a contract, for example, is important in law and is basic to economic transactions. Similarly, the law of property can be critical in fostering beneficial exchanges, just as the right of exclusive ownership allowed more efficient allocation of land in the example of the Enclosure Acts in England. Property rights encouraged efficient land use because they allowed land to be exchanged and adapted to new uses, rather than merely being held by tradition in common ownership and consequently overused. Most market regulation is effected through administrative agencies and courts, which inevitably involve the law.

Legislation of some kind is widely regarded as ". . . indispensable to the efficient regulation of the modern state" (Dias, 1964, p. 77). And as long as they do not conflict with the Constitution, legislative statutes take priority over judicial opinion. Of course in the United States, the judicial branch also has responsibility for interpreting the Constitution. Indeed, federal courts may find an act of legislation to be in conflict with the Constitution and overturn it. Or an act of legislation may be worded vaguely and judges must interpret its statutes, trying to plumb the purpose of the legislation so they can render a judgment accordingly. Legislation itself results from a political process that obviously has an important role in shaping policies for market regulation.

The Political System

Where, if anywhere, should power to control economic affairs be lodged? We have seen that the right to own, use, or exchange property has developed over many hundreds of years to the point where all sorts of goods and services are exchanged reliably

---

[21] There is also a federal circuit court that hears patent cases, claims against the U.S. government, and federal employee matters.

[22] When referring to the U.S. Supreme Court, the first letter in the word *Court* is capitalized, whereas in references to other courts no capital letter is used.

in markets by means of subtle forms of the property right, from theater tickets to shares in the ownership of corporations. If distributed somewhat evenly among us, these rights to property can disperse economic power into many hands and thereby support democratic government, with little need for centralized power. But, if unevenly distributed, economic power can cause political power to be unevenly distributed also, making the rich—even when their riches are owed to monopoly advantage—hard to control.

Limitations on Government Action

Well-defined property rights actually have prevented governments from interfering with the affairs of its citizens, whether for antitrust or for a different goal. On several occasions in the nineteenth century the Supreme Court found laws of individual states unconstitutional because they violated the right to contract.[23] That limitation seriously constrained state action against monopoly power. The right of a state to regulate the price of a public service was finally established in the famous *Munn v. Illinois*[24] decision in 1877, which paved the way for establishing state regulatory commissions to oversee public utilities.

We must remember that the Fourteenth Amendment was added to the Constitution after the Civil War and it requires that". . . no person shall be deprived of life, liberty, or property without due process of law." When the Supreme Court accepted the private corporation essentially as a person in 1886, it thereby extended to corporations the protection of the Fourteenth Amendment, which meant that corporations were entitled to due process as persons. As a result, states could not penalize corporations arbitrarily under state antitrust laws (Miller, 1976, pp. 41–49). Much debate about the Sherman Act focused on whether it would conflict with the Fifth Amendment, which requires the federal government to follow due process procedures.[25]

Government action, such as that involved in antitrust policy, may therefore encounter principles of equity that can stand in the way of improving the functioning of our market process. The question those nineteenth-century cases faced might go something like this. If a business firm has behaved according to the rules of the game implicit in current laws and previous court decisions, making sizeable investments on the presumption those rules will continue in force, is it reasonable to change them, say by passing a radically new law, or reaching a new and unexpected court decision? Actions that change property rights and rules of the game may benefit some and harm others. Not only may they be unfair, but arbitrary changes may lead parties to worry about possible future changes and not plan as efficiently as a result. Some changes are necessary, of course, but stability and continuity are also desirable. Government action must be taken carefully so policy can develop consistently and not upset and frustrate sound planning by business firms and other actors in the

---

[23] See *Fletcher v. Peck*, 10 U.S. 87 (1810), and *Trustees of Dartmouth College v. Woodward*, 17 U.S. 518 (1819). Both opinions were written by John Marshall.

[24] *Munn v. Illinois*, 94 U.S. 113 (1877).

[25] Ways for government to influence economic processes are quite different among Western countries. For discussion see Lasok and Bridge (1973).

economy. Yet if we follow that line of reasoning too far, powerful economic interests may persist indefinitely in unfair and inefficient performance.

What we are noting here is that perfect remedies may not be available for many of the situations that governmental market regulators face. Advantages currently enjoyed by some producers may be so long established that changing them now will be difficult. Those who are benefitting financially from their current positions have resources. They can hire excellent counsel, present their case persuasively to legislators and government administrators, and perhaps as a result keep the rules working in their favor.[26] Not only does government lack unlimited power to alter contract, property, and other legal relations in our society, it also is influenced by those very persons it is called upon to control. This is how democracy works. As an example, throughout American history many have believed small business units to be the backbone of an ideal Jeffersonian democracy and have sought to foster rugged individualism of the sort possessed by frontier farmers. Those same aims might be claimed by increasingly powerful businessmen, who could associate individualism with laissez-faire policy that would prevent government interference with established economic power.

Sources and Uses of Political Power

The making of laws lies in the hands of those who control the legislative machinery, and to a lesser extent the judicial machinery, of government. They are not just a small group so it is not surprising that laws usually reflect the status quo, tending to continue the existing order but accommodating peacefully and orderly to change. Although behavior in keeping with our laws has long been cloaked in respectability and legitimacy, from time to time laws have been challenged. They have been labeled "wrong," and significant numbers of citizens have refused to obey them. Close observation of the political process and of recent cases of civil disobedience shows that laws can indeed be wrong; they are authored by politically dominant groups who can insinuate their own preferences into law. Moreover, those in positions of power are also the target of a host of special interests that are trying to reshape the world to their liking.[27] We point out this potential fallibility in law and in law making, not so much to criticize the process as to remind readers that the process is imperfect and that any study of it should take this possibility into account.

Congress is influenced by corporations and other interest groups, who employ lobbyists and contribute mightily to election campaigns. These interest groups can influence actions that are taken, sometimes—as illustrated in Box 1.8, Voting on Clean Air—when a majority favors a less efficient outcome. Interest groups may also block action, with the result that Congress may fail to deal with certain problems. Two examples are gun control and the health effects of tobacco use, where delay was probably due to the great influence of affected industries in Congress. In these two examples, recent lawsuits focused on changing the ways gun manufacturers and tobacco companies design and sell their

---

[26] Or other political actions may be taken. For example, in response to a 1998 effort to increase competition by deregulating taxi cabs in Rome, taxis gathered in large numbers and deliberately clogged the Piazza Venezia.

[27] For a description of the effects of special interests in politics see Grossman and Helpman (2001).

BOX 1.8   Voting on Clean Air

Coal-burning power plants are a substantial source of air pollution, especially sulphur dioxide that causes acid rain. In the 1970s Congress and the Environmental Protection Agency considered two alternative remedies for this pollution problem: (1) require power plants to use low sulphur coal, perhaps by imposing a tax on the sulphur content of coal or on smokestack effluent, or (2) require power plants to install devices called "scrubbers," that clean the effluent as it passes through smokestacks. The scrubber solution was far more costly than switching to a different type of coal. Yet, under pressure from Congress, scrubbers were mandated by the Environmental Protection Agency. The pressure for this decision was traced to the many Midwestern and Eastern states that produce high sulphur coal. They preferred mandatory adoption of the scrubber technology—despite its great cost—because demand for their states' coal would be maintained if its high-sulphur content could be removed by the scrubbers. And because of their political, or voting, power in Congress, they prevailed over the fewer, mainly Western, states that produce low-sulphur coal. This example illustrates an inherent problem with lawmaking about economic issues in which the constituents of political representatives have divergent interests and their votes, rather than analysis of all benefits, determine outcomes.

See B. Ackerman and W. T. Hassler, *Clean Coal, Dirty Air.* New Haven, Conn.: Yale University Press, 1981.

products, and the suits have had very important effects on those industries.[28] Here a perceived problem, which ordinarily would be handled through legislation, is instead pursued through the legal system to a remedy. This shows how the legal system can be an element in the political process and is a reminder that many different forces can influence the degree and forms of market regulation.

Regulatory Agencies and Their Jurisdictions

Regulation involves more than legislation. Laws often create regulatory agencies. These agencies are intended to serve regulatory purposes, but their functioning may reflect other influences as well. Indeed, a **capture theory** holds that a regulatory agency will be captured by the very interests it is supposed to regulate. Such an outcome is possible in part because regulators, who presumably are chosen for their knowledge and experience, may come from the industry being regulated and may, therefore, share the values and aims of the industry. They may also expect to return to the industry (through what is dramatically labeled as the **revolving door**) and will prefer to find friends rather than enemies there. To benefit their industries, these regulators would need to have considerable discretion, which they often possess. Congressional committees also exercise power over federal agency budgets, and through that power they can continue to influence agency policies and decisions. Congressmen, lobbyists, and others may also influence the selection of leaders for regulatory agencies.

---

[28] See Barry Meier, "Bringing Law Suits to Do What Congress Won't," *The New York Times,* March 24, 2000, Sec. 4, p.3.

Federal government agencies play important roles in (1) regulating competition, through the Department of Justice and the Federal Trade Commission, (2) regulating industries, through such agencies as the Federal Communications Commission, the Federal Energy Regulatory Commission, or the Nuclear Regulatory Commission, and (3) regulating social issues, through agencies like the Environmental Protection Agency, the Consumer Product Safety Commission, or the Occupational Safety and Health Administration. These agencies pursue broad but defined goals across the country and enlist state agencies in support of those goals.

State versus Federal Scope

The federalist governmental structure of the United States creates citizens with dual sovereignty, to both national and state governments. State and local governments also engage in economic regulation. Monopoly franchises for electricity have been awarded and regulated by state or local governments for years, for example, with federal coordination of interfirm, or wholesale, transactions and special regulation of nuclear power. Under the Constitution, states are independent of the federal government but delegate to it certain of their powers. In principle, this federalist system allows regulation to occur at the level of government where it is most appropriate.

State Differences. Many differences among the states can be useful or appropriate, such as differences in minimum drinking ages, tax systems, speed limits, gambling proscriptions, or insurance rate distinctions. Citizens in a region suffering from industrial pollution may have concerns quite different from those in a wilderness area, and decentralized jurisdictions are able to serve the needs of each group. Of course, if pollution from the industrial area causes harm in the wilderness area a broader governmental jurisdiction may be appropriate, perhaps even an international one. When similar problems are faced, separate jurisdictions can be valuable because their different governmental approaches can foster innovation. Separate states, struggling with their own problems, might innovate in ways that would not be attempted under centralized control. A useful competition among decentralized states can then develop, because citizens are free to locate in the states they find most appealing.

Centralization. Centralized federal regulation also offers advantages. First, some regulations derive from guarantees awarded to all citizens nationwide, such as equal employment opportunity, which may require federal enforcement. There may also be economies in federal action, as in some central testing of food or pharmaceuticals by the Food and Drug Administration. Testing costs are then borne only once. National producers also have only one set of regulatory standards to meet, rather than, say, 50 different sets of rules for 50 different state requirements. Even where federal concerns are broad, as in environmental protection, the Environmental Protection Agency has granted authority to states, both for setting limited levels of pollution for firms to meet, and for enforcement, largely because circumstances differ across states and local knowledge is valuable.

National regulation can preempt state regulation when Congress explicitly calls for it in a statute.[29] Although there may be some cost savings, because firms do not have to comply with 50 different state regulatory standards when there is federal preemption, advantages of local state action may also be lost. Whether the federal government can regulate better is especially pertinent in those cases in which federal regulation is weaker, or less ambitious, than regulation in some states. In such cases, compliance only with federal law may afford consumers less protection. The recent trend is in the direction of greater preemption of authority by the federal government. This trend burdens the federal court system and alters the balance between state and federal jurisdictions by reducing local influence and control.[30]

SUMMARY

The Industrial Revolution is behind us. As a society we can no more reject large organizations to pursue only family and parochial production concerns or do without capital and scientific method and return to a hunter/gatherer life than we as individuals can forget all we have learned since the first grade in school. Neither can we claim that the spectacular transition of the last 200 years, from agrarian communities to modern industrial nations, has gone perfectly. Modern life seems to require ever more elaborate political and economic organizations. We find again and again that our organizations are imperfect and must be modified. So we approach this examination of regulatory policy in a critical way, with the hope that readers can find improvements that may very well be needed in the near future.

This chapter describes the three areas of regulation that are examined in the book; competition, industry, and social. It provides background information about institutions of the market economy, such as the corporation, and the idea of a property right that makes possible the efficient exchange of goods. We briefly examine markets because it is valuable to understand how markets can function to see why regulation from outside the market might improve outcomes. (Indeed, the remainder of the Introduction deals with competition, as Chapter 2 reviews the ideal competitive market system and Chapter 3 sketches the major problems from which it may suffer.) Chapter 1 also considers the legal and political systems that support the functioning of markets. Understanding how these institutions can influence market regulation is important because their effects are not always ideal. Designing remedies for market problems therefore calls for understanding political and legal institutions as well as markets themselves, which are the subject of the next two chapters.

---

[29] This is not the only source of preemption. See Moohr (1997).
[30] See Moohr (1998).

QUESTIONS

1. Choose an item of property that you own. Can you prove ownership of the item you have selected? Would you be able to sell it to someone else?
2. As noted in Section 1.1., land was once so plentiful it was commonly owned. But as use of it grew, its common ownership caused land to be overused. Is this essentially the "common pool" problem? Whatever the problem was, did the Enclosure Acts in England solve it?
3. Air still can be regarded as commonly owned, and, like land before it, it is being overused, in that it is being polluted. If property rights could be extended to air, would that solve this problem of overuse? Property rights to air cannot be defined as easily as they are for land. Why does this complicate the creation of policies to control air pollution?
4. Identify five important ways by which a corporation differs from a proprietorship.
5. What is the main difference between civil law and criminal law?
6. Give several reasons why a legislative body may be handicapped in making economic policy.
7. Does the principle of majority rule protect minorities?
8. Consider the case of XM and Sirius radio, as sketched in Box 1.7. List separately the advantages and disadvantages of a merger between XM and Sirius radio. For each advantage or disadvantage, try to describe data that would help you decide its lasting importance.

2

Competition as Market Regulator

I deally, competitive markets regulate themselves. For example, suppose chewing gum is sold at a price that exceeds its long-run cost of production. Gum producers earn high profit, which spurs their expansion and invites entry by new producers. The lure of profit in competitive markets motivates the shift of resources—capital, workers, managers, materials—to increase the production of chewing gum. As chewing gum grows more plentiful, that forces down the market price until it is again close to the cost of production, when further expansion is no longer motivated. Competition has regulated the market.

Just how the competitive market process can regulate markets, and what good effects it can achieve, are reviewed in this chapter. First, we review cost ideas, because costs drive the actions of business firms in competitive markets. We then look at how perfect competition functions. Setting out a standard that can be used to judge the performance of a competitive market system is our final goal here, and it requires a measure of economic welfare. The potential effectiveness of competition in delivering economic welfare to citizens is a major reason for organizing an economy through markets, and that is one reason many countries rely on a market economy to provide most of their goods and services.[1] Although competitive markets can be very effective in serving citizens, knowledge of how they function and malfunction is still needed to help diagnose and remedy problems that can arise. The perfect competition that we describe does not exist in pure form, and Chapter 3 shows problems that can arise to motivate government regulation.

This opening description and review of the theory of competitive markets provides background that is important throughout the book. Even where material is familiar or straightforward, do not pass over it quickly. Try to focus on market adjustments, the short-run reactions to changes, and then the longer-run responses. The goal is to understand very well the principles behind an ideal competitive market system.

---

[1] There are other reasons. In particular, a market economy fosters decentralized action, consistent with dispersion of economic power, which supports democratic political institutions that can be important beyond economic well-being. See Acemoglu, Johnson, and Robinson (2001).

Just as a good understanding of a mechanical clock is needed before trying to repair one, a good understanding of market competition is needed to recognize and remedy its shortcomings, and to improve its regulation. Chapter 3 describes the main problems that can arise in competitive markets, setting the stage for the rest of the book.

Production costs of the firm are examined in Section 2.1., to provide a basis for business firm decisions. Competition among such firms is the subject of Section 2.2. Section 2.3 introduces a measure of economic welfare to serve as a standard for market performance.

2.1 | THE FIRM'S PRODUCTION COSTS

Should Intel produce its own advertising or hire an advertising agency? Each firm strikes a balance between conducting activities within its organizational boundaries (where monitoring costs must be incurred) and relying on transactions in markets (which are accompanied by other kinds of costs, like negotiating contract details). Here we ignore such influences on firm size and shape, except for the important effect of entry. We simply present cost information and assume that in its drive to maximize profit and survive in competition the firm uses the best available technology and minimizes cost.

To focus on the central role of costs, we assume first that a firm exists to produce a single good. Again, this very simple representation of costs assumes away the transaction costs of markets and does not explicitly consider the many incentive issues that can arise within the firm other than maximizing profit. A simple representation of the efficient firm is provided by its *total cost function,* which is something of a skeleton of the firm, reflecting cost consequences that are crucial influences in many of the firm's market choices. In the first subsection we examine costs for this classic single-product firm, which can determine market supply for a single product. The second subsection makes distinctions between short-run and long-run costs and shows how entry can be affected. The third subsection examines cost representations of the more common multi-product firm.

The Single-Product Firm

If a firm makes only one product, say chewing gum, it must know how its output affects its total cost of operating. Once this relation between output and total cost is clear we can easily trace the effect that an increase in output has on total cost. The small increase in total cost caused by producing one more unit of output is called *marginal cost,* and it is important in profit-maximizing choices. At any point, dividing the total cost by output yields *average cost* per unit. These values of marginal cost and average cost guide short-run and long-run decisions of the firm.

The Total Cost Function

The competitive firm minimizes cost to maximize profit, which it must do to survive in a competitive market. That minimized cost is represented by the **total cost function**, which identifies the total cost of producing any chosen output. The cost function includes all costs, even a normal return to capital that accountants would call profit, because a normal rate of profit is needed to attract investment resources. As with all inputs, the normal rate of profit is determined by market forces that reflect the benefit given up, or the opportunity cost, of devoting resources here rather than elsewhere. If profit *above* the normal level is earned, we call that amount the **economic profit**. Economic profit motivates expansion or new entry.

Technology dictates the resources—and hence the cost—needed to produce any chosen level of output. Subject to this constraint from technology, which limits how the firm can convert inputs into outputs, the firm attempts to minimize its cost for producing its output. When cost is minimized, a unique total cost function can be obtained that identifies the minimum cost for every possible level of output (we can list all the possible output levels and list next to them all the associated levels of minimized total costs). The result is a functional relationship between total cost and output: $C = C(q)$, where $C(q)$ is the function that identifies total cost for any quantity of output, q.

A firm trying to minimize its costs is concerned with the increase that each input can make to output. The increase in output that can be obtained by adding one more unit of an input, a marginal unit, is called that input's **marginal product**, and the marginal product typically decreases for each input as that input alone is increased. When total cost is minimized, the marginal product of every input,[2] divided by that input's price, is the same for every input. Think about this mark of production efficiency: All inputs are used so the marginal product (the increase in output caused by the marginal unit of input) per unit of cost (that is, per dollar of input cost) is equal. If this was not true, an input with greater marginal product per dollar should be used more and an input with lower marginal product per dollar should be used less. Then more marginal output or product could be obtained for the same expenditure on inputs. A general solution to the cost minimizing problem thus yields useful guidelines for achieving the solution, and those guidelines also help to predict how cost-minimizing firms behave.

Marginal Cost and Average Cost

From the total cost function one can derive measures of *marginal cost* and of *average cost,* which are important because of their role in decisions by the firm. The firm decides under short-run or long-run time horizons, and the time horizon affects the meaning of the cost definitions. The definitions themselves are quite simple, however. **Marginal cost (*MC*)** at any output level is the increase in total cost that results from a one-unit increase in output. Mathematically, marginal cost can be represented as the derivative of the total cost function, or $dC/dq = MC(q)$, where MC is a function of q. **Average cost (*AC*)** at any output level is total cost divided by total quantity at that output level, so it is the cost per unit of output. Mathematically, average cost can be represented as total cost divided by quantity $= C(q)/q = AC(q)$, where AC is a function of q.

---

[2] Suppose we number inputs from 1 to n, with n the total number of inputs. Then an index, i, can represent one input when i is set at any number from 1 to n. Then the marginal product of input i is the marginal increase in output that can be obtained from an increase in one unit of input i. That statement applies to every input.

The Short Run and the Long Run

Firms treat these cost ideas differently, depending on the time scale of the decision they face. Often the firm must choose an output to produce right *now,* in a short time period that is called the **short run**, using the technology it already has in place. *Short-run marginal cost* and *short-run average cost* are defined for such a short period of time. Some inputs cannot be changed quickly in response to short-run changes. These inputs that are unchangeable in the short run are called **fixed inputs**, and they might include the building the firm operates in. In making short-run output choices the firm is guided by the effect on total cost of small, or marginal, adjustments in its output, which have to be made by adjusting those inputs that can be changed in the short run. These are **variable inputs** and might include labor or materials. The marginal effect on total cost of an output change, therefore, is **short-run marginal cost (SRMC). Short-run average cost (SRAC)** is just total cost divided by output, or cost per unit, at any level of output in the short run.

Long-run marginal cost (LRMC) and **long-run average cost (LRAC)** are cost measures that permit changes in *all* inputs. By definition, the long run is a period long enough to allow all inputs to be changed. No input, not even the building the firm owns, is fixed in the long run, because there is enough time to modify it. If the firm is considering a long-run decision, for example whether to enter an industry, it focuses on its long-run average cost, which cannot exceed price if profit is to be earned.

Certain patterns are common for these cost functions. For instance, short-run marginal cost usually rises as short-run output increases, as shown in Figure 2.1.

Figure 2.1 *Short-Run Marginal Cost Rises with Output*

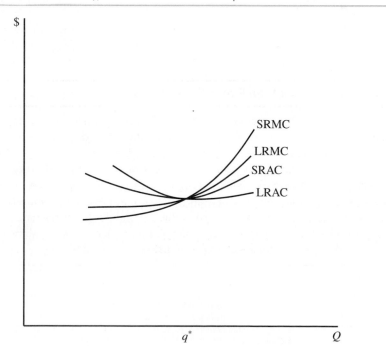

At low output levels the firm can combine inputs in a low cost way, especially if it has abundant fixed inputs, so short-run marginal cost is low. As short-run output grows larger, however, while fixed inputs cannot be changed, the input mixture changes and marginal cost increases. At some point the output will be perfectly suited to the fixed inputs, as at q^* in Figure 2.1. There at q^*, short-run and long-run average cost will be at a minimum.[3] Maneuvering is easy in a warehouse that is not very full but may be difficult as output rises in the short run and the warehouse becomes congested with more parts being stored for the increased production (that is, parts have to be stacked higher and are harder to reach). At some point the fixed warehouse, which cannot be altered in the short run, may impose a severe limit on output and make short-run marginal cost rise to a very high level.

Short-run average cost is the cost per unit to produce any output when some inputs cannot be adjusted. If long-run choices have been made for output q^* in Figure 2.1, an ideal input mixture for that output is possible in the short run. At all other output levels, however, limits to the adjustment of inputs in the short run make the short-run average cost higher than the long-run average cost.

The long-run average cost will conceivably continue to decline as output increases, even up to where one firm is producing all that is demanded in the market. Marginal cost must be lower than average cost if average cost declines with increased output. This falling average cost allows greater economies as the firm increases its scale of operations, and it is given the name, *economies of scale.*

Economies of Scale

Economies of scale exist if long-run average cost declines while output increases, indicating that there are economies (that is, average cost is lower) as the scale of output increases.[4] As quantity increases, the marginal change in average cost is marginal cost minus average cost, all divided by q, or $dAC/dq = (MC - AC)/q$.[5]

BOX 2.1 The Logic of the Firm's Cost Curves

Think through the firm's cost curves shown in Figure 2.1. Short-run average cost is higher than long-run average cost at any output other than q^* (where inputs are optimally adjusted), because when output is not at q^* the short-run input mixture is not ideal. Short-run marginal cost follows a different pattern. Why is short-run marginal cost lower than long-run marginal cost at outputs below q^*? Short-run marginal cost excludes fixed cost, which does not change in the short run and so is not marginal. On the other hand, short-run marginal cost is higher than long-run marginal cost when output exceeds q^*, because resources that are part of fixed costs now constrain output and working around their limitations increases marginal cost.

---

[3] At the point, q^*, where average cost is minimized, SRMC = LRMC = SRAC ≑ LRAC.
[4] Mathematically, if average cost declines as output increases, $dAC/dq < 0$.
[5] The relationship can be derived by taking the derivative of AC with respect to q: $dAC/dq = d(C/q)/dq = (qdC/dq - C)/q^2 = (dC/dq)/q - C/q = (MC - AC)/q$.

Figure 2.2 *Economies of Scale*

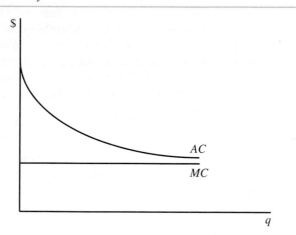

Thus, when marginal cost is above average cost, increases in output raise average cost ($MC - AC$ is positive). But with economies of scale, when increases in output lower average cost, marginal cost is below average cost ($MC - AC$ is negative). Figure 2.2 shows this latter case of economies of scale, which exist where all market demand can be met by one firm, as when a firm operating to the left of q^* in Figure 2.1 could meet all the demand in the market. When one firm can serve the entire market at lowest cost, having many firms for competition could be inefficient.

We say there are economies of scale if marginal cost is below average cost in the long run. That is, long-run marginal cost is below long-run average cost, and long-run average cost is decreasing—or $dAC/dq < 0$. Average cost is lower as the scale of operations is greater. The degree of scale economies can be represented by a measure of cost elasticity, C_E:

$$C_E = (dC/dq)q/C = MC(q)/AC(q),$$

which equals the ratio of marginal cost to average cost. This elasticity is less than one when economies of scale exist, so its reciprocal is usually used as a measure of scale economies, S_C:

$$S_C = AC(q)/MC(q) = 1/C_E.$$

This S_C measure exceeds one when scale economies exist and is larger as scale economies are greater.

The Short Run, the Long Run, and Entry

We now delve a little deeper into the way time affects the firm's decisions, to see that the time horizon for a decision affects the way costs are viewed. Costs are viewed differently when a firm is choosing an output than when it is deciding whether to enter an industry.

Fixed Cost and Variable Cost

Because firms make some decisions under a short-run time horizon, an important distinction arises between *fixed cost* and *variable cost*. **Variable cost** is cost that varies with output in the short run, while **fixed cost** does not vary with output in the short run. Remember that the long run is a time period long enough to allow adjustment of all inputs, so in the long run all costs are variable. When firms must make output decisions over shorter time periods, however, some costs can be fixed and unrelated to output. Rent for warehouse space, for instance, is a fixed cost in the short run, and a small change in output will not affect fixed costs. Marginal costs derive from variable costs, not from fixed costs.

Average cost, sometimes called average total cost, is based on *all* costs, fixed as well as variable. In the short run, AC can effectively be separated into average fixed cost and average variable cost:

$$AC(q) = C/q = [F + V(q)]/q = F/q + V(q)/q = AFC(q) + AVC(q),$$

where F is fixed cost and V is variable cost, and AFC and AVC each depend on q. If only the costs that vary with output are divided by total quantity we obtain **average variable cost**, or $AVC(q)$. If only fixed cost is divided by total quantity we obtain **average fixed cost**, $AFC(q)$. Average cost, $AC(q)$, is the sum of $AVC(q)$ and $AFC(q)$.

Average variable cost imposes a limit on short-run firm behavior. If market price falls below average variable cost in the short run, the firm will stop producing. With price below average variable cost, the firm is losing money on every unit it produces. With *any* positive output, the losses will be greater than if the firm simply does not produce at all. On the other hand, if price is above average variable cost in the short run, the firm is better off producing, because revenue will cover variable cost and contribute toward fixed cost. The firm will then lose more money if it shuts down.

Sunk Costs and Avoidable Costs

Costs that are fixed in the short run can be sorted into two categories. Fixed costs that cannot be terminated for a very long time are called **sunk costs**. Those that can be terminated, or avoided, are called **avoidable costs**. This distinction between sunk costs and avoidable costs is not always perfectly sharp, in that sunk costs might be retrievable but at substantial cost, and avoidable costs might be avoidable but not entirely without cost. Still, a distinction can be made, and it has great importance because if costs must be sunk, that can discourage entry and reduce its role in forcing competitive outcomes in markets. Avoidable costs may be fixed, in that they are not related to output, but they are less of a commitment because they can be terminated. They can be avoided, in other words, when stopping them is appropriate.

Avoiding costs is easiest when contract terms allow it, such as lease terms for an apartment that allow termination on 30 days notice. Such terms are more likely when the asset has alternative uses, and its owner will not suffer greatly when the contract is terminated. A grocery store rental lease might be canceled with small penalty, as another example, in part because a grocery store may be used by another grocer or converted into a clothing store. On the other hand, a nuclear power plant will be much more difficult to sell. It is specialized to a very specific purpose. (It is hard to

---

BOX 2.2 Example: Are the Costs of Airplanes Sunk?

An airline may have fixed costs in its airplanes, but it can move them easily from one market to another, or it can even sell them. Often there has been a good international market in airplanes. Then airlines in any one market may have avoidable costs rather than sunk costs, and avoidable costs can be terminated when they are no longer needed. On the other hand, if the total market for air travel is declining, the airplanes may be sunk costs because then they cannot be sold. A railroad locomotive, as another example, is a cost commitment that is more difficult to terminate because it is less mobile and, therefore, not as easy to sell as an airplane. The cost of a nuclear power plant is even more of a sunk cost because it cannot be moved or converted to any other use.

---

turn a nuclear power plant into a clothing store, let alone much else!) Costs are more sunk when they go for specialized assets that have limited alternative uses. The extent to which costs are sunk depends on **asset specificity**—the degree of specialization that is required of the assets.

Entry

Costs that cannot be terminated—costs that are sunk and are not avoidable—can prevent easy entry, and easy entry will be seen in section 2.2, Competition as Regulator, to underlie perfect competition. Investments that are committed to one specialized purpose and cannot be retrieved (because they involve sunk costs) are undertaken very carefully. Firms can be expected to hesitate about entering an industry with high sunk costs because if prospects turn sour, the firms in the industry have no escape.[6] That is why sunk costs cause problems for entry.

Scale economies can also make entry difficult when they reduce the number of firms that can produce efficiently in a market. Suppose, for example, that when four firms divide the total demand in a market equally, they can all be at a point of minimum average cost. Although no further scale economies remain, it would be very hard for a fifth firm to enter. As a potential entrant to this market, the fifth firm knows that to achieve a competitive level of costs its output will have to increase industry output substantially. That is bound to bring a drop in price, which the entrant must anticipate. Because the price after entry will be lower than the existing market price, the four firms already in the market might raise the price above their minimum average cost and still not induce entry. The reason is that the entrant cannot make a profit after the drop in price its entry will cause.

When a very large investment is needed for entry, that itself can also be a barrier to entry, because a potential entrant may have difficulty raising the necessary funds. After all, a potential entrant is unknown, and investors' information about it is imperfect. In-

---

[6] For analysis of sunk costs and their effects on market structure see Sutton (1991) and Schmalensee (1992).

forming potential investors about itself is an added cost for such an entrant, in part because it is hard to be convincing without a track record. Gathering information to make investment decisions is a cost for investors, and that cost can have more effect on a small fledgling firm than on an established one.

The Multi-Product Firm

Most firms sell more than one product. Representing production by a firm producing more than one product, called a **multi-product firm**, requires some new ideas. First, the cost function that connects outputs with costs must be stated for a multi-product firm. We also need a way to represent the effects on cost of changing the output of one product when there are several products, or some scope in the product line. One reason firms produce more than one product is that there are economies of doing so, and they are represented as *economies of scope*. We also introduce a condition of very easy entry, which leads to markets called *contestable markets* where entrants can have so much importance they make the number of firms less important. These ideas allow us to see when a multi-product firm is cross subsidizing some of its products by raising extra revenues from products.

The Multi-Product Total Cost Function

The multi-product firm is like the single-product firm except for the number of products, and a total cost function can be derived for the multi-product firm by the same process that was used for the single-product firm. Technology again influences the size and shape of a firm to the extent it determines the costs of producing different amounts of different products.[7] The production function of the multi-product firm must relate its outputs—however many there are—to the inputs needed to produce them. With prices of the inputs known, a total cost can still be minimized for any combination of outputs, so a total cost function can be obtained that relates cost minimizing levels of inputs to all possible combinations of outputs. Instead of $C(q)$, the cost function for the single-product firm, the cost function for, say, two goods, is denoted $C(q_1, q_2)$, and it represents the total cost of producing any given combination of the two outputs, q_1 and q_2. The multi-product cost function captures the possibility that a single firm can produce two (or more) outputs at lower cost than two (or more) separate firms can. That is important because it affects how profit seeking firms organize.

A multi-product firm's cost function possesses the same marginal cost properties of the single-product firm's cost function. Marginal cost is still the increase in total cost that results from a one-unit increase in any one output, given all the firm's other outputs. For a two-product firm, marginal costs for the two outputs can be represented as

$$\partial C(q_1, q_2)/\partial q_1 = MC_1 \text{ and } \partial C(q_1, q_2)/\partial q_2 = MC_2.$$

---

[7] See Langlois and Foss (1999) on the importance of production costs in the theory of economic organization.

Notice, however, that each marginal cost may depend on the levels of *both* outputs (e.g., $MC_1 = MC_1(q_1, q_2)$).

In the multi-product firm's cost function, the idea of an average cost for each product can be lost. In the single product firm, total cost can always be obtained by multiplying average cost times output. If there are fixed costs in the multi-product firm, however, including, for example, the cost of the corporate headquarters, allocating such costs soundly among the individual products may not be possible. Then there may be no set of average costs for individual products that, when multiplied by their quantities, account for all costs. In the multi-product firm an alternative measure for each product is called *incremental cost,* and it yields an average incremental cost for each product that can be used somewhat like an average cost in the single-product firm.

Incremental Cost and Average Incremental Cost in the Multi-Product Firm

For the multi-product firm, the best representation of the effect on cost of adding or subtracting any single product is **incremental cost**, which is the cost of producing a product in a firm compared with *not* producing it. Incremental cost for the ith product is, thus, the difference between total cost for all products and total cost for all *except* the ith product. For example, in a two-product firm, incremental cost for q_1, denoted IC_1, is $C(q_1, q_2) - C(0, q_2)$. Incremental cost reflects the effect on total cost of producing not the marginal unit of q_1, but rather the whole output of q_1, whatever that is, compared with producing none of it.

This measure of incremental cost has an important role when we consider regulated industries in Part 2, in defining **sustainable prices**, prices that allow an efficient multi-product firm to set prices that prevent entry by a less efficient firm. It also allows a definition of **cross-subsidy**, which occurs when some consumers contribute to the well-being of others because of the prices that are charged. Yet another advantage of the incremental cost measure is that it yields an average cost representation, **average incremental cost**, which can indicate the degree of scale economies by product in a multi-product firm.

Average incremental cost for the ith good, AIC_i, is incremental cost for the ith good divided by the quantity of the ith good. For good 1 in the two-product case, average incremental cost is

$$AIC_1 = [C(q_1, q_2) - C(0, q_2)]/q_1.$$

The scale economy index for one good that can be constructed from average incremental cost imitates the index in the single-product case but substitutes AIC for AC:

$$S_i = AIC_i/MC_i.$$

If S_i exceeds 1 we can say there are scale economies in production of the ith good, whereas there are scale *dis*economies in the production of good i if S_i is less than 1.

Although S_i offers a measure of economies of scale in producing each good, it does not offer a measure of overall economies of scale for the multi-product firm. To do that, the outputs of the firm can be collapsed into one product and analyzed like a one-product firm. For instance, if the firm produces two goods, q_1 and q_2, define some combination of the two goods as $q = wq_1 + (1 - w)q_2$, where $0 < w < 1$, and check for economies of scale in q. Ideally, all combinations of q_1 and q_2 would be evaluated (all possible values of w), but even one combination can give an indication whether overall economies of scale exist. In addition to complicating scale economies into measures by each product separately and for the overall firm, the multi-product firm offers an effect on cost from having multiple products. If multiple products can be produced in one firm at lower cost than in separate firms, we have *economies of scope*.

Economies of Scope

The multi-product firm raises a new issue: **economies of scope**, the idea that producing more than one good in a single firm is more economical than producing the goods in separate firms.[8] Economies of scope can explain why multi-product firms exist.

To illustrate, consider the cost function of the two-product firm, $C(q_1, q_2)$. Suppose that two separate firms with the same cost function could also produce the two goods, with each firm producing one of the goods. These two firms, producing good 1 alone and good 2 alone, would then have cost functions $C(q_1, 0)$ and $C(0, q_2)$. Economies of scope exist if

$$C(q_1, q_2) < C(q_1, 0) + C(0, q_2),$$

that is, if the cost of producing q_1 and q_2 in a single firm is lower than the combined cost of producing q_1 and q_2 in two separate firms.

We can construct an index of economies of scope, S_o, on the basis of this simple definition:

$$S_o = [C(q_1, 0) + C(0, q_2) - C(q_1, q_2)]/C(q_1, q_2).$$

If $S_o > 0$, producing goods in separate firms is more costly than producing them in a single firm, so we say that scope economies exist.

Scope economies usually arise from some resource that can be shared in production by two or more different products. A truck maker might add capacity to make car bodies, for example, and build car engines in an already existing engine factory, with economies not available to the maker of either vehicle alone. As a result, cars and trucks could be produced more economically in a single firm.[9] In distributing products, a store selling salad ingredients and salad dressings might also have economies of scope. These producing or marketing economies may sometimes require that firms be larger and operate in more than one product market to succeed. Thus scope economies may also make new entry difficult by requiring simultaneous entry into more than one market. In turning now to consider competition as regulator of markets, we focus on single-product firms for simplicity. Multi-product firms come in for more attention later.

---

[8] Economies of scope are described in Baumol, Panzar, and Willig (1982). For empirical estimates of their importance see Friedlaender, Winston, and Wang (1983), Pulley and Braunstein (1992), and Cohn, Rhine, and Santos (1989). The latter find economies of scope in universities across graduate and undergraduate students. For further consideration of effects of costs on market structure, see Eaton and Schmitt (1994).

[9] Friedlaender, Winston, and Wang (1983) show support for this possibility.

BOX 2.3 Economies of Scope in a University

The university has been examined as a multi-product firm to see whether undergraduate and graduate education, and research, are produced under economies of scale or scope. Despite grave difficulties in estimating the cost function for a university, in which teaching quality is not easy to standardize and research output can be difficult to measure, results of studies find economies of scope for both public and private universities. Economies at the level of increases in all outputs are stronger in private universities, which tend to be smaller in size than public universities. At the same time, product-specific scale economies for research and graduate enrollments are found in public universities and not found in private universities. The main lesson is that carrying out research while teaching both graduate and undergraduate students is economical for an institution of higher education.

See E. Cohn, S. L. Rhine, and M. C. Santos, "Institutions of Higher Education as Multi-Product Firms: Economies of Scale and Scope," *Review of Economics and Statistics,* May 1989, Vol. 71, pp. 284–290.

Contestable Markets and Cross Subsidy

Suppose no cost must be "sunk" in an industry, investment needs are not great, and no other barrier exists; so entry can be very easy. These conditions describe a **contestable market**.[10] Entry is so easy in a contestable market that even a small rise in price induces entry, and output expansion from entry returns the price to its competitive level. The significance of market contestability is that it reduces the importance of the number of firms that are already in a market. Because new entrants can quickly affect the market, the number of firms already in the market is less crucial.

The pure contestable market has three requirements:

1. **Entry is very free.** Incumbent firms have no advantage that potential entrants cannot duplicate.
2. **Low price wins.** Any firm that can survive in a market with a lower price than others wins the entire market. The incumbent is presumed to win a tie, so an entrant must have a *lower* price to win.
3. **No cost is sunk.** A firm can enter and—because no cost is sunk—can immediately leave if it chooses, allowing what is called "hit-and-run" entry.

These assumptions are strong, but they also have strong implications. In particular, even one firm in a single-product contestable market must set price at average cost. If it attempts to set a monopoly price it will lose the market to an entrant. Indeed, a price even slightly above average cost can lose the market to an entrant. The price that can preserve the incumbent's position, the sustainable price, equals minimized

---

[10] For treatment of contestable markets see Baumol, Panzar, and Willig (1982).

average cost. The incumbent firm must strive to minimize cost, because otherwise a more efficient entrant that can set a lower price will displace it.

In the multi-product firm, if the price of one product is below cost while the resulting loss is covered by prices of other products that are above their costs, the first product is benefitting from a cross subsidy. Historically, determining whether a subsidy is present has been complicated because it is not easy to see whether the price of a product is "above cost," but sustainable prices help to solve this problem. A crucial requirement for sustainable prices in the multi-product firm is that prices be **subsidy free**.[11] To see what subsidy free means, suppose that an incumbent firm in a market breaks even: total revenue equals total cost. Then, to be subsidy free, the revenues from any subset of products must not exceed the costs of serving that subset by itself.

If one subset of a firm's customers are contributing more to cover costs than other customers are (remember, the firm breaks even, so if some customers pay more than costs, others must pay less), they will not like it. Indeed, the subset of customers paying more will want to serve themselves and go their own way, so the incumbent will fail to retain them. They will *stand alone,* and the incumbent will fail what is called the **stand-alone test**. As an example, suppose that General Motors were to sell Chevrolet models at three times their average incremental costs and charge low prices (below variable costs) on all its other automobile product lines. Chevrolet customers would not be willing to pay these high prices when they could turn to available alternatives, and General Motors would be losing money on its other customers, so such a cross subsidy could ruin General Motors.

Another way to think about cross subsidy is to ask whether revenues for any subset of goods are at least great enough to cover the incremental costs of that subset. If they are not, the remaining consumers would be better off if that subset was simply not served. If any subset of goods is not covering its incremental cost, the incumbent firm fails the **incremental cost test** for cross subsidy. In the General Motors illustration, all product lines other than Chevrolet would not be covering their incremental costs, and it would be better for Chevrolet customers if General Motors sold off all of those other product lines so it could lower Chevrolet prices. Having the incumbent break even insures that these two requirements, the stand-alone requirement and the incremental cost requirement, are consistent. One of them implies the other.

If one good is subsidizing another, it should come as no surprise that entry may be motivated. The good that is providing the subsidy must be priced too high, so entry should be possible. The incumbent multi-product firm or firms must choose prices carefully to avoid cross subsidy, to prevent entry to its market by a firm that might not even be as efficient. Indeed, when an incumbent firm can choose prices that prevent entry by a less efficient firm, those prices are sustainable. To be sustainable, prices must be subsidy free.

Potential competition is extremely important in the contestable market model, so important that it upstages the main threat to firms in ordinary competitive markets, the

---

[11] This analysis of subsidy and price sustainability is from Faulhaber (1975).

BOX 2.4 Is the Airline Industry a Contestable Market?

The airline industry was thought to come close to meeting requirements for contestability when it was deregulated at the end of the 1970s. Entry into particular airline routes can be quite easy, though it does require landing time slots, airplane gates, counter space at airports, and some advertising to inform consumers of the availability of service. There are variations in consumer preferences, however, by time of travel and other characteristics so there can be product differentiation, which moderates the vigor of price competition. Although sunk costs are few in the airline industry, they are not totally absent. Airplanes are very mobile, so an existing airline can deploy them easily to a new market, and their great mobility supports a broad market in used aircraft so in normal times aircraft can be bought and sold quite easily. Setting up a new service involves commitment, however, if only to advertising, and that results in some sunk costs.

    Empirical evidence suggests that the airline industry is not perfectly contestable. Several studies have found that the number of carriers on a route or the amount of entry affects fares for the route. Contestable market theory calls for no effect of the number of firms and little need for entry, so these findings are not consistent with it. Still, contestable market theory is useful for its emphasis on the role of very easy entry and for its careful treatment of the assumptions needed to make entry a powerful enforcer of the competitive process. The airline industry can also offer many features of a contestable market.

See S. H. Baker and J. B. Pratt, "Experience as a Barrier to Contestability in Airline Markets," *Review of Economics and Statistics,* May, 1989, Vol. 71, pp. 352–360; G. D. Call and T. E. Keeler, "Airline Deregulation Fares and Market Behavior: Some Empirical Evidence," in A. Daugherty, ed., *Analytical Studies in Transport Economics,* New York: Cambridge University Press, 1985, pp. 222–247; T. G. Moore, "U.S. Airline Deregulation: Its effects on Passengers, Capital, and Labor," *Journal of Law and Economics,* April, 1986, Vol. 29, pp. 1–28; and A. Peteraf, "Sunk Costs, Contestability and Airline Monopoly Power," *Review of Industrial Organization,* 1995, Vol. 10, pp. 289–306.

competition in price from other firms already there. Critics point out, however, that there are asymmetries of information between existing firms and entrants that reduce the precision of the entry response.[12] As in the case of perfect competition, evidence suggests that perfect contestability may not exist. Laboratory experiments indicate, however, that even in the presence of modest sunk costs, competitive forces are quite strong.[13]

2.2   COMPETITION AS REGULATOR

Armed now with these ideas about cost, we can examine how competition can regulate markets. This section considers an ideal form of competition, which regulates markets very well. A desire to maximize profit motivates firms' decisions in this

---

[12] See Cairns (1994).
[13] See Coursey, Isaac, Luke, and Smith (1984).

competitive world. Firms' costs influence such decisions. Consumer demand also affects decisions, but costs determine the supply of goods that come from firms and industries in response to consumer demand.

Perfect Competition

In looking at perfect competition, let's begin by constructing an economic model for a market economy. Models can represent in simplified form the workings of an entire economy, or the process taking place in part of the economy, to show important consequences. Simplifications require assumptions, and we begin with strong ones. Chapter 3 discusses the effects on outcomes that relaxing these assumptions can have. The question of interest here is: Under ideal conditions, how effective is competition in promoting economic welfare?

The model of **perfect competition** assumes ideal conditions. In this model, strong assumptions allow precise representation of suppliers and demanders so that we can examine equilibrium outcomes. The assumptions for a perfectly competitive market model are:

1. **Free Entry and Exit.** No barrier stands in the way of entry to, or exit from, a market.
2. **Many Sellers and Many Buyers.** Many sellers ensure that no one has control over price, and all must accept the price determined in the market. Extremely free entry and exit can make this assumption unnecessary because the threat of easy and immediate entry by outsiders constrains the price that can be charged, even by a single existing firm; but having many sellers brings that force inside the market. Many buyers prevent any buyer from influencing market price.
3. **Perfectly Divisible, Homogeneous Good.** Only a single good is offered for sale in a market, so consumers cannot distinguish one firm's product from another's. Units of the good can be extremely small, so indivisibility of output never complicates responding, say, to a small change in price.
4. **No Externality.** When a cost or benefit is borne by someone not part of, or external to, a market decision, the result is called an externality. We assume those who make decentralized decisions in a market economy bear all of the consequences of those decisions, so there is no externality. No producer pollutes the air, for example, for that would impose costs on others who were not party to the production decision.
5. **Perfect Information.** All parties are informed about prices and qualities, and about technologies, which are known and unchanging.
6. **No Monitoring or Transaction Costs.** No cost must be incurred either to supervise and motivate workers within the firm or to transact in the market.

The demand for a good represents the willingness to pay of all consumers who would gain satisfaction—or utility—from consuming the good. These demanders are independent of one another, so we can aggregate their behavior into a market **demand curve**. At any market price, which is known to all, those willing to pay that price—or a higher price—will purchase the good. Any consumer who is just willing to buy at the market price may be called the marginal consumer, because others who buy ordinarily are willing to pay more. Thus, the consumers can be ordered, so those willing to pay the most are in position to purchase at the highest prices. That is how we can construct a demand curve for all potential buyers, to represent the aggregate behavior of all consumers. As long as some consumers are willing to pay more than others, we can expect demand curves to slope down. That is, as total quantity consumed increases, the marginal consumer's willingness to pay decreases.

The suppliers are independent of each other in a perfectly competitive market, so we can combine their behavior into a **supply curve** for the market. In a perfectly competitive market, the market supply curve and the market demand curve are also independent of each other. Then the supply and demand can balance when a market price brings forth a supply quantity that matches exactly the quantity consumers wish to purchase at that price.

Profit Maximization

Each firm in a competitive market attempts to earn as much profit as possible and must perform efficiently to survive. If other firms surpass its earnings, it may not be able to attract resources. The need to survive in competition therefore implies the goal of profit maximization.

The owner's claim on residual profit creates a strong incentive to maximize it. And the maximization of profit motivates the minimization of cost, because profit can be high only if cost is low. Minimizing cost serves to define the exact relationship between output and cost that is the total cost function of a firm. Without cost minimization, inputs might be combined in different ways to produce any given output level, so we would not have a unique value for the cost of any output.

Many competitive firms make short-run, profit-maximizing output decisions based on their marginal cost functions, as a simple description demonstrates. Suppose the competitive market price is *above marginal cost* at output q_1 in Figure 2.3. The firm wants to increase its short-run output, because any sale at a price above marginal cost adds to profit. With marginal cost rising as output increases, marginal cost comes to equal price at output q^*, and then the firm stops increasing output. If market price is *below marginal cost,* as at output q_2, the firm wants to *reduce* its output, because all the units produced beyond q^* will lose money.

A major qualification to this prescription for short-run profit maximization follows from the distinction between fixed cost and variable cost. If the firm is maximizing profit by choosing output so that short-run marginal cost and price are equal, and it finds that price and marginal cost are lower than average variable cost, the firm is better off if it shuts down. The firm can terminate variable cost by stopping sales, which also stops the loss on operations. As long as price is above average variable cost, however, the firm can either maximize profit or minimize loss by producing an optimal output in which marginal cost equals price, even if price is *below* average total

Figure 2.3 *Short-Run Profit Maximizing by the Firm*

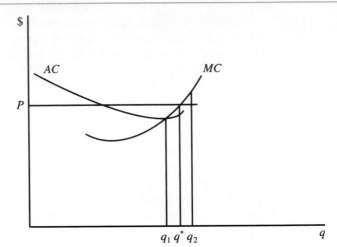

cost! As long as price is above average variable cost, every unit produced contributes something toward covering fixed cost. If the firm stopped producing, the full amount of fixed cost would be lost, whereas producing some positive output can lower that loss.

Thus, firms maximize profit in the short run by choosing an output that sets marginal cost equal to price, as long as price exceeds average variable cost. If the firm is losing money, setting marginal cost equal to price is minimizing the loss, but that is also profit maximizing in that profit—while negative—is still as high as possible. Only later does the firm evaluate the level of its maximized profit. Profit may be positive or negative, depending on whether price is above or below average cost. If price is greater than average cost, expansion may be motivated. We can also have entry by others who observe price above average cost. On the other hand, if price is below average cost, and is expected to stay there, renewal of long-run investments is not warranted. Rather than invest further, firms leave the industry. That is how average cost is crucial to the long-run decisions about expansion, entry, or exit.

Supply and the Perfectly Competitive Equilibrium

Because the competitive firm solves its short-run problem of maximizing profit by setting its marginal cost equal to market price, that marginal cost curve above the *AVC* curve predicts its behavior as a **short-run firm supply curve**. For any market price, that curve tells what output the firm will offer to the market. Aggregating the supply curves for all firms in an industry yields a **short-run market supply curve**. How the firm considers longer-run prospects, given the information it has about its short-run position, yields the **long-run firm supply curve**, and adding the possibilities of entry and exit yields the **long-run market supply curve** for the industry. When combined with demand, a supply function produces a market *equilibrium*.

Short-Run Equilibrium

Let us now put demand and supply together to obtain a market equilibrium. We can aggregate individual consumer demands into a **market demand curve**. That is, at any market price for a particular good, the quantities all consumers want to consume of the good can be added together to determine total market demand. The market supply function and the market demand function capture the behavior of suppliers and demanders. Only where the functions intersect can both suppliers and demanders be content, or in equilibrium.

Figure 2.4 shows market supply and market demand functions. Remember that both functions describe behavior. The supply function tells how much all existing suppliers supply at any price. The demand function tells how much all consumers together demand at any price. If price is above the intersection of the two functions, more units are supplied than are demanded and suppliers have difficulty finding buyers for all their units. We can then expect suppliers to lower price to attract buyers. If price is below the intersection of the two functions, more units are demanded than are supplied, and buyers want to bid the price up, which encourages more production. When supply and demand intersect, neither suppliers nor demanders are motivated to raise or lower price or change output or consumption. This is an **equilibrium** in the short-run competitive market.

Long-Run Equilibrium

Unlike the short run, the long run involves *entry* and *exit* decisions. These long-run decisions depend on economic profit, the excess above a normal level of profit, which turns on the level of price relative to *average* cost rather than *marginal* cost. When a market yields economic profit, firms not in the market want to enter for that above-normal level of profit, and existing firms in the market may want to expand. On the other hand, firms in a market that yields economic losses may decide to exit, especially

Figure 2.4 *Short-Run Equilibrium*

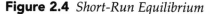

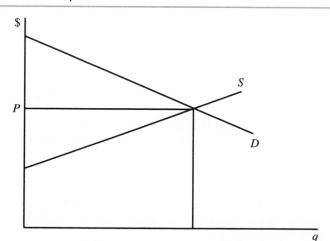

BOX 2.5 Price Formation by Auction

A classic way to price objects is through an auction. In one type of auction, known as the English auction, the price rises until only one bidder remains. The "last bidder left standing" essentially wins at the maximum price that the *second* highest bidder was willing to pay for the object, because when the second highest bidder no longer responds to the auctioneer's call to exceed the then highest bid, the bidding stops. That is why the English auction is also called a "second-price" auction. The main alternative is the Dutch, or "first-price," auction, in which the winning bidder pays what is bid without ever knowing what it takes to top the second highest bidder. Sealed-bid auctions, as for construction contracts, are usually first-price auctions, because the bidder does not know the second price, the price at which other bidders would stop bidding.

Each bidder in the English auction can bid what he or she thinks the object is worth and not be disappointed. Bidding your value in the English auction is wise. If you bid less than the value you place on the object you may lose it at a price you gladly would have paid. And if you bid more than the value you place on the object you may win it at a price above what it is worth to you. The Dutch auction invites more strategic bidding because to enjoy any surplus in such a first-price auction you have to bid below the value you place on the object. You try to bid only high enough to beat what you think others will bid. A seller chooses the type of auction that will raise the most money, and that can depend on the number of bidders, the range of private valuations that bidders have for the object, and other factors.

---

if staying in the market requires them to renew their commitment to the market by replacing worn out assets.

The long-run market supply function is fundamentally different from the short-run market supply function. The short run belongs to firms already in the market. The long-run supply function, however, reflects the possibility of entry by firms not already in the industry or exit by existing firms. This wider scope of possible actions brings a different shape to the long-run supply function in an industry. Entry replicates existing firms, at the minimum of the average cost curves that prevail. If input prices do not change with expansion of the market, average costs may remain at the same level, and we can represent industry supply as a flat line at the level of minimum average cost, as the supply curve S_1 in Figure 2.5 shows. Where the long-run supply function intersects market demand, no further action is motivated in any firm, and the market is in **long-run equilibrium** at Q^*.

As the industry grows larger or smaller, the prices of inputs—and, hence, the level of the firms' costs—might be affected. Changes in one firm's output does not ordinarily affect input prices, but a *market* expansion may be so great that the price of a specialized input is affected. For instance, expansion of aluminum production may raise the price of the ore, bauxite, which is raw material that all firms use for the production of aluminum. In a case like that, the long-run supply curve rises with market output, as curve S_2 does in Figure 2.5.

BOX 2.6 Expand Your Firm or Exit the Market?

You manage a firm that has adjusted its output until marginal cost equals price, where short-run profit is being maximized. Suppose market price is *above* average cost at that point, and average cost includes a normal profit level. Then the profit your firm earns will be above normal, and you may want to expand, or grow larger. You have to expect new entrants to the market, and you may want to move before they do. On a gloomier note, what if market price is *below* average cost when you are maximizing short-run profit? If market price is below average variable cost, you will want to shut down because not even variable costs can be covered. If market price is below average cost and above average variable cost, you can reduce your losses by operating, but you may shrink from a commitment to renew assets that will become fixed costs. At renewal time, those costs become variable. If it is unprofitable to renew them, you will not want to make the commitment that is needed to remain in the market, so you may decide to exit.

Figure 2.5 *Long-Run Equilibrium*

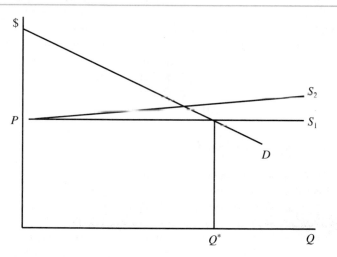

<table>
<tr><td>**2.3**</td><td>**THE ECONOMIC WELFARE GOAL OF MARKET REGULATION**</td></tr>
</table>

One clear goal of market regulation is to achieve economic efficiency, which is usually expected of well-functioning competitive markets and is sought when government regulation modifies competitive markets.[14] One aim of this chapter is to give meaning to

---

[14] Markets may be regulated for reasons other than efficiency, however. Because legislators can be expected to respond to political influences, some regulation may favor those who have political power. Then regulation may be unfair or inefficient, producing poor economic outcomes, in which case it should be replaced with better policies.

the word, *efficiency*. Out of the discussion will come a more exact language for discussing equity, or fairness, and a measure of benefit to consumers. The welfare measure that indicates what is good about the performance of an economy gives a dominant role to consumers, and it falls under a general topic that is known as **welfare economics**. Welfare economics studies the welfare of those who participate in the economy.

When we say that competition could regulate economic activity "well," we have in mind some notion of what is desirable, something that goes beyond the process of competition itself. For in asking a monopoly supplier to choose socially desirable prices, we clearly must be able to describe what "desirable" prices are. A set of precise concepts for thinking about such questions has been developed over many years, and these concepts have been related in various ways to observable measures so they can have useful application. Because market regulation presumably is undertaken to advance economic well-being, it cannot be fully understood without some knowledge of welfare economics.

In addition to efficiency, another virtue of fairness, or equity, is also a desirable goal of market regulation. But a policy that helps one group usually disadvantages another, so fairness is not easy to define. That is why the announced goal of fairness can be used to support many purposes. One aim of fairness may be income redistribution, usually to aid poorer members of the community, and market regulation may be used to further that aim. Often, however, there are more efficient ways, such as tax policy, to serve that goal than through market regulatory means.

Even when goals are agreed upon, finding practical means for achieving them is not easy and must usually be worked out in each specific setting. Wise, detailed analysis is needed to choose and apply policies even after sound goals have been found through the aid of a broad welfare framework. The welfare framework is, however, an essential starting point, and that is why we give it careful attention.

Representing Economic Welfare

Some representation of welfare is needed if policy is to serve it, so we now define a representation of welfare for individuals and relate it to observable demand behavior for a single good or service. We then present a representation of producer surplus. Economic welfare is represented by the sum of consumer surplus and producer surplus. To obtain measures of welfare for a group of consumers we aggregate individual welfare measures. In aggregating representations of individual well-being, however, we must face the issue of income distribution, so we discuss the assumptions typically made about income distribution in measures of welfare. Finally, we briefly discuss risk and welfare.

Consumer Surplus

We begin with a representation of consumer benefit from a market transaction based on demand curves. A **consumer's surplus** is the net benefit that the consumer enjoys from being able to purchase a good or service.[15] Consumer surplus thus represents the amount a consumer would be willing to pay for the opportunity to purchase at a

---

[15] The first description of consumer's surplus was by the French engineer and economist Jules Dupuit (1844), although that label for the idea is due to Alfred Marshall.

Figure 2.6 *Consumer Surplus*

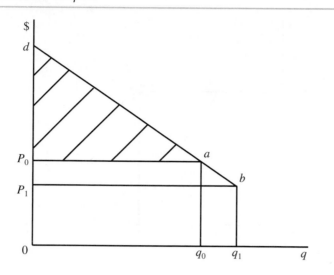

certain price.[16] In Figure 2.6 the demand function, $q(P)$, identifies the price (P) that a consumer would be willing to pay for various quantities (q) of a particular service. We assume that the consumer's money income and the prices of all other goods are known and constant. The triangular area, P_0ad, represents the consumer's benefit, that is, the consumer's surplus, from purchasing at price P_0. That area captures the difference between what the consumer is willing to pay for each unit, indicated by the demand curve, and the payment actually required for each unit, the price P_0. Thus, the area $P_0\,ad$ represents the maximum amount the consumer would be willing to pay for the opportunity to purchase q_0 units at price P_0 per unit. At the lower price, P_1, consumer surplus would be larger, at $P_1\,bd$.

The idea of consumer surplus comes up often because it captures the benefit of economic activity. Notice that the consumer in Figure 2.6 would have been willing to pay roughly an amount d for the first unit, a slightly lower amount for the second unit, and so on until paying P_0 for the q_0th unit. The sum of the evaluations that a consumer is willing to pay for the separate units (area daq_00), less the amount actually paid for the units (P_0 *times* q_0), is the consumer surplus (CS) from consuming q_0 units of the good at price P_0.

Producer Surplus

A **producer's surplus** may be identified in a manner that is similar to consumer's surplus. The producer surplus (PS) of a firm is the area above its marginal cost curve and below price. Any positive difference between price and marginal cost is a surplus because it is a benefit to the producer. For example, the firm operating at marginal

---

[16] This definition is due to Marshall (1920, p. 124).

Figure 2.7 *Producer Surplus*

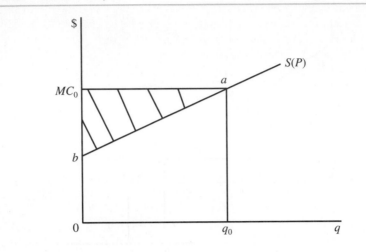

cost (MC_0) along supply function $S(P)$ in Figure 2.7 with no fixed cost has producer surplus represented by the area MC_0ab. The supply function in Figure 2.7 assumes that price equals marginal cost, or $P = MC_0 = MC(S(P))$. If price equaled MC_0, total revenue (TR) would be represented by the area MC_0aq_00. Total cost (TC) is the accumulation of all the separate marginal costs for the units produced up to any particular output level. Total cost, thus, would be represented by the area baq_00. The difference between these two areas, MC_0ab, is the producer surplus, or PS = TR − TC.

Economic Welfare

Consumer surplus and producer surplus represent benefits to the consumer and the producer. So it makes sense to take as a measure of welfare (W) the sum of consumer surplus (CS) and producer surplus (PS), or W = CS + PS. No measure of that sum (CS + PS) needs to be calculated for operational purposes under ideal competition, because no issue depends on the value of the surpluses when well-functioning markets adjust and change through individual transactions. Surplus measures become useful, however, when a question must be decided collectively, as in a public decision whether to build a bridge or in setting the price for a public service, because the surplus measures can define a welfare goal.

The following are important qualifications about using consumer plus producer surplus (CS + PS) as a welfare measure.

Income Effects. Consumer surplus does not always yield a precise measure of welfare for an individual in the simple way Figure 2.6 suggests, because income as well as price affect demand. As the price of a good falls, for example, while the consumer's money income remains constant, the real income of the consumer increases, because the lower price allows more goods to be purchased. The change in real income, by itself, may affect consumption of the good.[17] An increase in real income could shift the demand curve out to the right, for example, when there is a substantial price reduction for a good that takes a large portion of the budget. The price reduction could enable a person to buy more of everything, including the good that had its price reduced. Figure 2.6 does not include such an effect of income, and so it is not adequate to represent that possibility. Income effects tend to be small, however, so that in most analyses they may be ignored.[18]

Income Distribution. When welfare is represented by *aggregate* consumer and producer surplus, it is predicated on the *existing* income and wealth distribution. After all, consumer surplus estimates depend on observable demands, which rest on the current distribution of income. Accepting the existing distribution of income, which aggregating demands into consumer surplus measures does, essentially ignores the issue of income distribution. It sees each dollar gain in consumer and producer surplus as equally good, no matter who receives it. If the existing income distribution is regarded as unsatisfactory, the issue normally should be attacked directly on its own merit, rather than through regulatory policies. Even if a preferred income distribution were known, using regulatory policy to effect it would be undesirable if more efficient ways to redistribute income exist, and they usually do.

Individuals Gain on Average. Using consumer plus producer surplus as a guide to decisions leads to adoption of policies that increase total welfare. While total welfare increases, and many individuals are made better off by the policies, some individuals may actually be made worse off. For example, a regulatory price reduction might benefit consumers of the good while harming shareholders of the firm producing the good. Following consumer plus producer surplus as a welfare guide rests on a crucial presumption. It presumes that, over many actions, the gain in welfare (consumer plus producer surplus) will reach us all. Even though some of us may be harmed by some actions, over time, and in the aggregate, all of us will share in the benefits indicated by the greater welfare obtainable from welfare maximizing policies.

The Benefits of Competition

Although it may seem strange to describe a system of competitive markets as a communication and information system, that is really a useful way to view it. A competitive market system enables consumers to tell suppliers what to produce. Furthermore, their instructions to suppliers can be based on knowledge of the true costs of alternative goods and services, knowledge provided to them through market prices. As an institution for informing consumers and relaying their instructions to producers, the market

---

[17] In Figure 2.6, the income elasticity of demand for the good is zero, meaning that income does not affect demand.
[18] Generally income effects are smaller for a good that accounts for a smaller fraction of consumers' budgets and that has a low income elasticity of demand. For an analysis of these factors affecting the significance of income effects see Willig (1976).

system is really quite remarkable. When its prices provide the right signals it manifests a high level of efficiency.

Competition Brings Efficiency

Production is efficient when no transfer of existing resources among producers can increase output. A competitive price system for inputs can deliver production efficiency because all producers face the same competitive input prices. In minimizing costs, the producers then choose inputs so the value of the marginal product of each input equals its price. Because in a perfect competitive market input prices are the same for every producer, each one faces the same ratio of prices, and, therefore, each producer's cost minimizing ratio of marginal products is the same. If marginal products differed, it would be efficient to switch inputs from a low marginal product use to a high one. When no such switch is possible, we have production efficiency.

All consumers also adjust to the same prices in competitive product markets. When consumers maximize their well-being, or their utility, each consumer's marginal utility per dollar spent should be the same for every good; otherwise the consumer could be better off consuming differently. The ratio of marginal utilities available from any pair of goods is then the same for every consumer, because they all face the same prices. This means that no consumer would wish to trade, so consumption is efficient.

BOX 2.7 A Dutch Auction for Flowers

An efficient market is on display in the Dutch town of Aalsmeer. Every day about 20 million cut flowers and plants are sold there. The Bloemenveiling Aalsmeer, a cooperative with 3,300 members, operates the world's largest flower auction in a sprawling, climate-controlled auction building that covers 250 acres (about the size of 165 football fields). It is cited in the *Guinness Book of World Records* as the largest commercial building in the world. There are five separate auction theaters where flowers are displayed on stage in moving trolley carts and buyers in the audience push buttons at their desks to make bids.

Each round of bidding begins from a high price indicated by a large electronic display above the theater stage (the display also identifies the item on offer, the supplier, the quantity offered, and other details). The bidders have already inspected batches of flowers and listened to details about them through headphones. As the price declines on the display board, the bidders decide when to bid, which they do by pushing a button. The first to push his button wins the batch on offer and pays the price displayed at that moment. Because prices start high, the first price is the highest price, and it wins this Dutch, or first-price, auction. The transaction is completed in an instant, the display board returns to the high price that starts the next batch and it begins its descent. Flowers and plants from all over the world pass through this auction and move on to beautify life from flower stands everywhere.

See E. Pope, "Let a Billion Flowers Bloom," *New York Times,* March 28, 2004, Sec. 5, p. 6.

Not only does an ideal market economy deliver efficiency for consumers and producers, it also coordinates their decisions about how much of which goods and services are produced. There can be little benefit from producing, even at minimum cost, goods that consumers do not want. A competitive market system drives product prices equal to marginal costs. When consumers can choose goods at prices equal to marginal costs, their choices direct resources where their strongest demands are. Consumers' relative valuations for every pair of goods is the same, because they equal the price ratios for the pairs of goods, and the price ratio equals the ratio of marginal costs for that same pair of goods. At an equilibrium for the ideal market economy, no reduction in output of one good—to increase output of another—can improve consumer satisfaction, so the right goods are being produced.

The real key to achieving economic efficiency is having the price of a product equal its marginal cost, the value of all the resources—such as labor, material, land, capital equipment, fuel, or other inputs—that are absolutely needed to make the marginal units of that product. When the prices of products are equal to their marginal unit costs, all consumers—in making their purchase decisions—face prices that reflect precisely the current technical opportunities open to them. After comparing competitive prices, a person's choice of a Polo shirt rather than a sweater is based not only on the person's taste but also on how easy it is for society to turn out a Polo shirt or a sweater, which is reflected in the prices of Polo shirts and sweaters.

Freedom of entry is crucial for delivering this ideal competitive equilibrium. A price above average cost indicates a profit opportunity. Remember that average cost includes a normal profit as part of cost, so a price higher than average cost signals a profit opportunity that is above normal. That excess, above normal profit, is what is called economic profit. Under competition, economic profit attracts more resources to the production of the profitable product. Each firm that newly enters the market may have a small effect on price, but as more and more firms enter, more units are produced than can be sold at the old price, so market price tends to fall. The last unit produced is valued less and less by consumers as price falls until finally the price equals average cost. No extra high profit, no economic profit, remains as incentive then to enter the industry. Average cost is as low as possible, because inefficient high-cost producers lose money and are unable to survive.

Competitive Prices Allocate Resources Efficiently

These efficiency ideas and the essence of the market process itself are simple, but they are sufficiently abstract and subtle that they are often misunderstood. It may be easier to see the advantages of having prices equal marginal costs if we look at prices that persistently do not reflect marginal costs. If one consumer pays less than cost, the final outcome is both unfair and inefficient. It is unfair because others must somehow bear the remaining cost of what this one consumer buys. It is inefficient because the cost of producing marginal units of the product are higher than the value attached to them by the consumer. Even if production costs at that output level are minimized, we must still label the result as inefficient. The resources used to serve this consumer (who does not pay the resources' full cost) would be worth more to consumers in other markets where prices equal marginal costs and where consumers are willing to pay them. Consumption goes beyond an optimal level when it is based on a price that understates true cost and, thus, misleads consumers.

Price can also remain above marginal cost, where marginal cost reflects true costs through competitive prices elsewhere in the economy. The resulting inefficiency in that case is precisely the sort of inefficiency we associate with monopoly. At the marginal value consumers place on the last unit of the good (marginal value being represented by the price of the good), they do not consume as much of it as the society's resources and technology would allow them to consume. In this case, the consumers pay more than the value of resources needed to produce those marginal units, while someone pockets the difference, thus making it unfair as well as inefficient. The outcome is inefficient because consumers are discouraged from consuming, even though they would value any additional units more than it would cost society to produce them.

Figures 2.8 and 2.9 illustrate these effects of prices that do not equal marginal costs. Suppose the measures of quantities in the figures are defined for a specific time period such as a week, a day, or an hour. Assume marginal cost (MC) is constant regardless of market output quantity, Q. The amount consumers are willing to pay to clear the market of any quantity is represented by the downward sloping linear demand curve, dd. In Figure 2.8 the price is below MC; consumers pay the amount represented by the area P_0AQ_20, whereas total cost is the larger amount CBQ_20. The difference, represented by P_0ABC, is a transfer that must come from somewhere else to these consumers. If the firm is a multi-product firm, profit from other products might be subsidizing the product represented in Figure 2.8. When a subsidy benefits one product using revenues from another, we say there is a cross subsidy.

In Figure 2.8, notice that every unit of output beyond quantity Q_1 is valued by consumers along demand curve dd at *less than* its marginal cost of MC. In going beyond point D, the triangle DBA captures the difference between marginal cost and the lower valuation by consumers. This area represents a welfare loss to society, because it represents the negative difference between what units cost and how much consumers value them. Another way to see DBA as a welfare loss is to realize that

Figure 2.8 *A Price Too Low (Subsidy)*

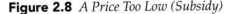

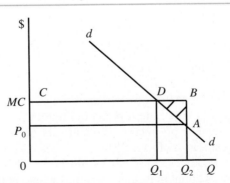

Figure 2.9 *A Price Too High (Monopoly)*

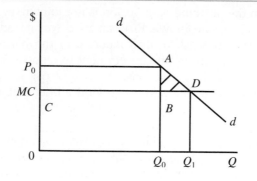

consumers gain consumer surplus in the area $CDAP_0$ when price is reduced from MC to P_0, but the producer loses the area $CBAP_0$ at the price, P_0. The loss area is larger, and the difference between these two areas is the net social loss, DBA.

In Figure 2.9 the price is above marginal cost, perhaps because of a seller's market power. Consumers pay the amount represented by the area P_0AQ_00, whereas total cost is the smaller amount CBQ_00. As part of their payment, the consumers give to the seller $P_0AQ_00 - CBQ_00 = P_0ABC$ as profit. Notice that up to the output at D, every unit that was not produced was valued more by consumers, as revealed by the demand curve, than it would have cost. For example, at output Q_0, marginal cost is B and willingness to pay of consumers is higher at A. An amount of potential social benefit, represented by the triangle, ABD, is being lost as long as the price is held above marginal cost. This loss that continues as long as price is above marginal cost is called the **dead-weight loss**. In moving from price P_0 to a price equal to marginal cost MC, the consumer would gain in consumer surplus P_0ADC and the producer would give up only P_0ABC in profit. The possible gain to society is again ABD, an amount that is lost as long as price remains at P_0.

Perfect competition would eliminate the situations shown in Figures 2.8 and 2.9. In the situation depicted in Figure 2.8, firms lose money. With free entry and exit, firms would not want to replace equipment to remain in the industry, and so they would not remain for the long run. They would reduce output, and some might exit from the industry. Gradually, lower output together with unchanged demand would cause price to rise, until it reached marginal cost, MC, which in this case is also average cost, AC, where further exit would not be motivated. In the situation depicted in Figure 2.9, firms make above normal profit (normal profit plus economic profit). Competition in this situation brings expansion and new entry in pursuit of the extra profit available, which in turn forces price lower as sellers compete for buyers. We can expect price to fall to marginal cost and average cost but not lower. No seller wants to price below marginal cost, and no firm wants to enter if price is below average cost. That is how competition, marked by free entry, tends to force price equal to average and marginal cost.

Risk and Welfare

Risk is present when the outcome of an action is not known, even if the chances of different possible outcomes are known. Risk can affect welfare, and so it can motivate regulation. For example, the risk of firm failure and the harm it would bring to innocent people helps to motivate the government to regulate banks, the insurance industry, and employer-provided pensions. The role of risk in consumer protection regulation is also pronounced. This section presents a brief sketch of expected utility as a way of representing welfare in the presence of risk, and it discusses expected consumer surplus as a welfare measure.[19]

First, we consider measuring individuals' own evaluations of their situations, through representations of their levels of satisfaction, or their utility. Utility reflects satisfaction of an individual's preferences, so it represents their well-being. Usually evaluations can be made that depend only on ordinal measures of utility, which do not offer an absolute measure of utility but can merely indicate which of two situations is better. To deal with risk, however, we need a real, cardinal measure of utility, because the amounts of utility gained and lost have to be calculated.

To see how risk can affect an individual's utility, consider a lottery that offers two outcomes: income y or larger income Y. The lottery offers income y with probability w and income Y with probability $1-w$. Thus, the expected value, or average outcome, of the lottery is

$$E(value) = wy + (1 - w)Y. \qquad \textbf{2.1}$$

A measure of utility can guide individuals who face decisions under risk. Utility of income y is $u(y)$ and utility of income Y is $u(Y)$. Then the utility of the expected value of the lottery is

$$u(E(value)) = u(wy + (1 - w)Y). \qquad \textbf{2.2}$$

As values of y and Y change, the expected utility of the lottery differs from the expected value of the lottery as long as utility is not directly proportional to the level of income. This relationship between utility and income is crucial to the effect of risk on decisions. An individual deciding whether to accept the lottery focuses on the *expected utility* from the lottery, which reflects the individual's well-being. Expected utility from the lottery is

$$E(utility) = wu(y) + (1 - w)u(Y). \qquad \textbf{2.3}$$

Now we are in position to consider the effect of risk on utility. The expected utility of the lottery weights the utility levels of the two possible outcomes according to their probabilities. By considering utilities for the possible (risky) outcomes, the expected utility can represent an effect due to risk. On the other hand, the utility of the expected value simply evaluates utility at the average value, or expected value, of the

---

lottery. Because it does not consider the utility of either possible outcome, it essentially ignores the risk involved in the lottery. This means that a difference between the expected utility of the lottery, expressed in equation 2.3, and the utility of the expected value of the lottery, in equation 2.2, can indicate the effect of risk on utility that the lottery possesses.

A risk-neutral person sees no difference between the expected utility of a lottery, equation 2.3, and the utility of the expected value of the lottery, equation 2.2. To a **risk-neutral** person, risk is irrelevant. A **risk-loving** person finds equation 2.3 yields a greater value than equation 2.2. Risk is attractive to the risk lover. A **risk-averse** person finds equation 2.2 yields a greater value than equation 2.3. Risk is unattractive to the risk averse. A tendency toward risk aversion is widespread in the population. Perhaps we learn from experience to avoid risk, because it brings pain when we lose our gambles. As a trait, aversion to risk possibly raises the chance of survival. Those of us who have it tend to remain in the population—we survive (risk aversion may add to fitness for a "survival of the fittest" world). Risk aversion is also consistent with diminishing marginal utility, because the gain in utility from winning a fair, fifty-fifty bet is not as great as the loss in utility from losing.

The curve in Figure 2.10 shows a functional relationship between income and utility that indicates risk aversion. Notice that utility rises with income for the risk-averse person, but at a decreasing rate. The income axis shows lottery outcomes y and Y. We assume, for simplicity, the probabilities of winning to be $w = 1/2 = (1-w)$. Notice that the utility of the expected value (from equation 2.3 above, $u(y/2+Y/2)$) is higher than the expected utility of the lottery (from equation 2.2, $u(y)/2 + u(Y)/2$). The individual with the utility-of-income function shown in Figure 2.10 would rather have the expected value of the lottery with certainty than accept the lottery. The gain

Figure 2.10 *Diminishing marginal utility of income and risk aversion.*

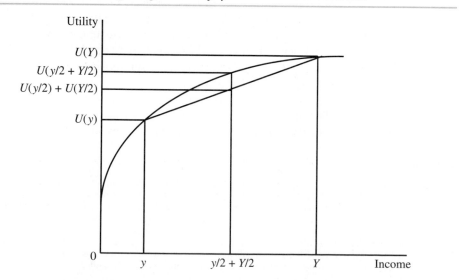

in utility from winning Y is not valued as much in utility terms as the loss of y. Because the risk of the lottery involves gambling on receiving a value that is not valued as much more when it is higher (Y) compared with a loss at the lower (y), the risk-averse person prefers having $y/2 + Y/2$ for sure to that uncertain lottery. Thus, the person whose utility is shown in Figure 2.10 prefers not to bear the risk of a bet, even when it is fair.

The shape of the utility-of-income function for the risk-averse person in Figure 2.10 is consistent with diminishing marginal utility of income. The marginal utility of income at any income level is the slope of the curve that represents levels of utility for all levels of income, or the slope of the curving utility-of-income line in Figure 2.10. In moving to the right in Figure 2.10, to higher incomes, the slope of the utility curve becomes flatter, or lower, indicating for this individual that marginal utility of income is diminishing as income is increasing. Before ordinal utility[20] came into use, economists routinely assumed diminishing marginal utility of income to describe individual behavior. Ordinal utility focused on comparisons among goods rather than on measurable levels of utility. Consider that when marginal utility of income diminishes with increasing income, the gain in winning an even-money bet—a fifty-fifty bet with the same amount to be gained or lost—gives a smaller increment in utility than the loss in losing takes away. So an even-money bet is unattractive to a person with diminishing marginal utility of income. The person with diminishing marginal utility is therefore, averse to risk.

Other relationships between utility and wealth are conceivable. The opposite curvature to that in Figure 2.10 would have utility rise by greater amounts as income increased. Such curvature in the utility-of-wealth function would represent increasing marginal utility of wealth, which is consistent with risk-loving, or gambling, behavior. Because marginal utility increases for the person described by such a utility-of-wealth function, the gain from winning $10 in a fifty-fifty bet is worth more than the loss of $10 from losing it. So this "risk lover" accepts an even-money bet. A person with a linear relationship between utility and wealth, on the other hand, would be regarded as risk-neutral. Such a person cares about average outcomes, not the risks of outcomes. Indeed, if he or she faces many of the same types of decisions repeatedly, an individual might be able to expect risk influences on outcomes to be much reduced, because they cancel each other out,[21] and risk-neutral behavior might then be optimal.

In circumstances where maximizing profit across a large number of relatively independent decisions is possible, risk-neutral behavior may actually be preferable for a firm, because the law of averages tend to deliver an average outcome and essentially reduce or eliminate risk. The opportunity to face many similar decisions may

---

[20] Ordinal utility makes no assumption about how utility changes as income increases, except that more income is preferred to less. It focuses on preferences between goods in comparisons and on willingness to substitute one good for another, through those preferences between goods, without any metric or quantitative measurement or utility.

[21] If the risk influences are independent of one another, more decisions are like a larger sample, and the law of large numbers will reduce the variance of the mean outcome in a large sample. Facing the same decision many times may thus enable the decision maker to ignore risk and assume that average values will quite reliably be achieved.

arise in a large organization, which would prefer that decision makers act in a risk-neutral way. Individuals might be risk averse in single, isolated choices, however. A manager who is responsible for a small part of the firm—and who faces few decisions—may behave in a risk-averse way to avoid personal failure, because that could harm a career in the firm. So the firm may find it difficult to persuade employees to use the law of averages when they see only part of the many decisions that would make its use appropriate.

We use expected utility to represent welfare on occasion, and expected consumer surplus is also noted. The latter measure essentially assumes risk neutrality, because shifts in demand are the source of uncertainty and the measure is average consumer surplus. The results of using expected consumer surplus can easily be compared to analysis under certainty.

SUMMARY

Production costs influence firms' actions in competitive markets. Cost minimization, which is motivated by profit maximization under the pressure of competition, is able to reveal a total cost function for the firm that associates a unique level of cost with any level of output. Once we know this cost function, we can derive measures of marginal cost and average cost. They influence short-run and long-run decisions of the competitive firm, marginal cost forming the short-run supply function of the firm and average cost signaling whether entry or exit should occur over the longer run. Some technologies offer great economies of scale, which allow firms operating at large scale to achieve low average cost.

We can separate average cost into average variable cost and average fixed cost. Whenever average variable cost is above price, the firm should shut down to avoid short-run losses. Fixed costs might be (1) avoidable, when it is possible to terminate them, or (2) sunk, which means they cannot be escaped for a long period of time. Sunk costs would continue to be incurred, even if prospects for sales in the industry turned sour. Costs can also explain the multi-product firm, when scope economies allow goods to be produced at lower cost in a single organization rather than in separate firms.

This chapter also introduces a model of perfect competition. Consumers, who pursue their own welfare, make purchases that are beneficial to them. Their willingness to purchase results in demands for individual goods. Analyzing competition also requires analysis of production costs in simple, one-product, firms. When such firms seek to maximize profit, their cost functions imply supply behavior that can describe short-run industry responses to changes in either costs or demands, and that can identify the short-run market equilibrium. From the short-run equilibrium, we can infer longer-run actions, such as entry or exit, and we can describe a long-run market equilibrium. The importance of this process—reaching short-run equilibrium and then examining longer-run responses to find a long-run equilibrium—cannot be overemphasized. This market process is essential to understanding a market economy, and without that understanding flaws in the system cannot be properly diagnosed. An important conclusion of the analysis is that in ideal conditions competitive markets can deliver the desirable outcome that economic welfare ideas define.

A major goal of this chapter is to express precisely the individual benefit from an economic decision and to translate it into a measure of economic welfare. When carefully aggregated, such individual benefits form a welfare measure, and that measure can guide regulatory policy in those industries that require such guidance. A welfare measure helps to answer questions such as: How does a change in the price of a government-regulated good or service affect social well-being? We cannot claim a perfect and unique measure of social benefit, but a practical measure that is based on observable demand curves—consumer surplus—is reasonably accurate for many uses. We can similarly represent a measure of benefit to suppliers in the form of producer surplus. If a social decision affects more than one price, we must take care in considering effects in substitute or complement markets.

We consider the aggregation of individual measures into social welfare measures, which for consumer surplus can be described as going from a consumer's surplus to aggregate consumers' surplus. To make this transition in the simple cases considered here, individuals must be weighted somehow to make up a combined representation of social welfare. One solution is to weight individuals in society as their current incomes indicate, through observable demands, in a measure of consumer surplus. This weighting essentially accepts the present income distribution, and it regards any benefit as equally desirable for society, no matter who receives it. This chapter also discusses individuals' attitudes toward risk, because risk plays an important role in many regulatory situations.

The perfectly competitive market process discussed in Section 2.2 can deliver the economic efficiency conditions that were set out in Section 2.3. Prices serve to coordinate the actions of consumers and producers. As long as all buyers respond to existing common prices, then all will reach the same ratio of marginal utility to price for every good. The ratios of all consumers' marginal utilities for any particular pair of goods will then be equal, as required for consumption efficiency. The reason for this result is that marginal-utility ratios equal price ratios when consumers maximize their utilities, or when they are doing the best they can for themselves in their consumption choices. Because price ratios are the same for all consumers— consumers all face the same prices—utility ratios also have to be the same, and that marks consumption efficiency. Production efficiency results in a similar way. All producers face the same prices for inputs, so in maximizing profit they use inputs until they all have the same marginal product per dollar, and this brings production efficiency.

Overall economic efficiency, as measured by total surplus, also follows from perfect competition, and the process of entry largely drives it. First, notice that marginal cost equals average cost at a long-run competitive equilibrium, because that occurs at the minimum cost point of the average cost curve. If relative prices for any pair of goods do not match relative marginal costs (or relative average costs), a profit opportunity exists. Production of the good with the higher price, relative to marginal cost, should be expanded while production of the other good should be reduced. Expansion and contraction according to profit signals ultimately brings overall economic efficiency, where relative prices equal relative marginal cost for every pair of goods.

The profit-maximizing firm is thus forced to operate efficiently to survive the competition from other firms. The prices in markets that are regulated by perfect competition can inform consumers about production costs and at the same time can inform producers about consumer preferences, leading to an informed equilibrium. Economic activities are efficiently performed at this equilibrium, and consumer welfare is as large as possible. Problems may arise, however, to prevent achievement of this ideal outcome. The major potential problems for market regulation by perfect competition is the subject of Chapter 3.

QUESTIONS

1. Consider the single-product total cost function, $C = 10 + Q$, where C is cost and Q is quantity.
   a. Express average cost for this case.
   b. Express marginal cost for this case.
   c. Present an effective index of scale economies. Do scale economies exist? (Use the index to show why or why not.)

2. Consider the single-product total cost function, $C = 10 + q + q^2$.
   a. Express average cost for this case.
   b. Express marginal cost for this case.
   c. Present an effective index of scale economies. Do scale economies exist? (Use the index, or use the average cost curve, to show whether the total cost function has scale economies in any output range.)
   d. If all firms have this same cost function, would you expect a competitive market for their product to exist and to function properly?
   e. Suppose market demand is represented by $P = 10.4868 - 0.01Q$. Any number of firms can produce according to the cost function described. Find a competitive equilibrium.

3. Consider the single-product total cost function, $C = 100 + 10q + q^2$. Construct a table with output in one column, total cost in one column, and average cost in the third. (Hint: Begin in the output column with $q = 7$ and increase q one unit at a time until $q = 12$.)
   a. What is the minimum average cost for this cost function? At what output does the minimum average cost occur?
   b. How can the table you have constructed be used to obtain a column containing approximate values for marginal cost?
   c. When the average cost is at its minimum, what is the marginal cost?

4. Suppose a firm produces two goods, Q_1 and Q_2, and has the cost function, $TC = 15Q_1 + 15Q_2$.
   a. Does the cost function possess economies of scale?
   b. Does the cost function possess economies of scope?
   c. What is the average incremental cost for good Q_1 when $Q_1 = 10$ and $Q_2 = 10$?

5. Consider the two-product total cost function, $C = 15 + 0.5q_1 + 0.3q_2$.
   a. Does this cost function possess economies of scale? Explain.
   b. Does this cost function possess economies of scope? Explain.
   c. Now suppose alternative methods exist to produce q_1 and q_2 in independent firms, according to the two cost functions $C_1 = 10 + 0.5q_1$ and $C_2 = 10 + 0.3q_2$.

   Do these new cost functions each possess economies of scale? Does either cost function possess economies of scope?
   d. Given that these different, separate methods exist to produce q_1 and q_2, would you expect q_1 and q_2 to be produced by a single-product firm or by a multi-product firm?

6. Suppose four neighboring farmers want irrigation and flood control systems for their farms. Each farmer can install a system for $15,000 and is willing to do so. If two farmers go together they can build a joint system for $25,000, and three farmers can build one system for three farms at a cost of $30,000. If a single system provides for all four farms, its cost is $44,000. What is the most efficient arrangement for irrigating the four farms? Does the technology of irrigation and flood control possess economies of scale?

7. Imagine two identical twins who—we assume—have exactly the same utility function. One twin is rich while the other is poor. Suppose that one day when they were walking together the twins found an envelope containing $100. After trying unsuccessfully to find the owner of the envelope, they decide to split its contents. If they wish to give each twin the *same gain in utility*, which twin, the rich twin or the poor twin, should receive the bigger share of the $100? If they wish to obtain the greatest gain in their aggregate, or combined, utility, which twin should receive the bigger share? Explain reasons for your conclusions.

8. Consider the consumer's and producer's surpluses presented in Figures 2.8 and 2.9. If the goal was to maximize consumer plus producer surplus from a transaction by simply setting a price in the market, what price would serve best? Describe that price in the clearest way you can, and indicate why it is the best price. If there is a single consumer and a single producer and they bargain, do you think they will reach the price you just described as best? Why or why not?

9. Consider a market for good Q where short-run demand is $P = 10 - 0.01Q$ and short-run supply is $P = 2 + 0.01Q$.
   a. What is the short-run competitive equilibrium price and quantity in this market?
   b. At this equilibrium, what is the value of consumer surplus? What is the value of producer surplus? And what is the total welfare from this market at equilibrium?
   c. Is there enough information for you to analyze the long-run equilibrium?

3

Problems for Competition as Regulator

The competitive process does not regulate every market well. Understanding its failings not only gives an appreciation for how and when competition works, it also suggests remedies for when it does not work. For example, when a monopoly takes over a market and raises price above a competitive level, knowing the source of the monopoly may lead to a remedy. As another example, the producer of a product may use a process that fouls the air for nearby residents. A pollution tax could make the producer take those costs into account to restore efficiency to the market. Competition can be a superb regulator, but when its assumptions are not satisfied we need to examine the resulting conditions. Some departures from the assumptions may cause minor problems, while other departures may cause serious inefficiencies. In this chapter we relax the six assumptions that underlie perfect competition and examine the consequences.

The model of perfect competition was not intended to fit the world perfectly. It describes broad patterns, and, most importantly, it indicates movements and adjustments that ripple through the economy, motivated by consumers seeking their own satisfaction and by firms seeking profit. These movements and adjustments can reveal how an entire complex economy functions to benefit consumers. To see these movements and adjustments, however, we need the simplicity of an economy operating under idealized conditions; we need the model of perfect competition.

In a market economy, the existence of one seller who is protected from entry in a market, a monopoly, provides the sharpest contrast to competitive market organization. There might also be just a few firms in a market, called *oligopoly*, and that market may not function as a competitive market would. We refer to the way a market is organized, say under monopoly, oligopoly, or competition, as its *market structure*.

A great influence on market structure is the condition for entry. Entry into markets must be easy if competition is to function properly (the first assumption). Yet technological conditions, such as great economies of scale that make entry at a small size infeasible, can complicate entry. Entry barriers and scale economies together can lead to monopoly, which violates the second assumption that there are many firms in the market, and can lead to higher prices and a host of other problems for consumers.

Having a single buyer, called a monopsony, can have comparable effects. Because monopoly or monopsony can have so many effects and is such a serious challenge to competitive markets, it receives the most attention in this chapter.

The third assumption of perfect competition is that products are homogeneous. When firms compete with *differentiated* rather than homogeneous products, dimensions other than price are involved in the competition, and evaluating market outcomes is more difficult. Each seller can have some advantages like a monopoly, and the tools we develop to examine monopoly let us examine the consequences in less-than-monopoly circumstances. Fourth, perfect competition assumes no externality, and this lack of externality allows decentralized market decisions to consider all social benefits or costs. Decentralized decisions may not serve society so well if some consequences are not considered in a decision—as when I play my radio too loudly without earphones and interfere with your peace and quiet. A fifth problem that handicaps competition as regulator is imperfect information. When consumers are ill informed, say about product quality, high-quality products may not be offered for sale. Finally, market transactions are costly. So are monitoring and other costs of conducting activities within firms instead of in the market. Decisions based on transaction costs can affect the sizes and shapes of business firms, which in turn can affect how well markets perform.

Actual industries can therefore differ from ideal, perfectly competitive industries and violate their assumptions, and the industries may function less effectively as a result. For review, the six assumptions for perfect competition in markets are

1. Free entry and exit
2. Many sellers and buyers
3. Perfectly divisible, homogeneous good
4. No externality
5. Perfect information
6. No monitoring or transaction costs

In this chapter we trace the consequences that follow when each of these assumptions underlying perfect competition is not satisfied. Recognizing any of these consequences enables us to diagnose their cause by tracing them back to failed assumptions. We begin with free entry and then consider each of the remaining assumptions of perfect competition.

3.1 | ENTRY AND EXIT BARRIERS

New entrants can expand and improve an industry's performance, and perfect competition assumes both free entry and free exit (assumption 1). Free does not literally mean that entry or exit is costless. Rather, it means a new entrant can enter an industry by making the same investment that was required of an already established, or incumbent, firm. Yet entry may be difficult for a new firm if one or a few firms already in the industry possess a cost advantage, perhaps because of economies of scale. Or large sunk costs may be needed for entry, which adds risk for a new entrant who cannot exit if things should go badly. Such barriers to entry may favor existing firms and allow higher prices or less appealing products to persist without entry by new firms to eliminate them. Major reasons for entry difficulty are economies of scale, an absolute cost advantage for existing firms, a need for sunk costs, imperfect information that complicates raising investment funds, and governmental restrictions, like patents, that may serve other purposes.

Economies of Scale

Adam Smith traced scale economies to the division of labor into specialized tasks. Economies of scale can also arise from basic physical relationships, such as the surface area needed in a pipe to allow a certain volume of liquid to flow through the pipe per minute.[1] Some technological devices, such as hydroelectric dams, must be built at very large scale if they are to be effective. Network organization, such as the techniques for telephone service or postal delivery, require a network that is initially very costly but once in place can provide service at low marginal cost.

When a larger scale of operations allows lower unit costs, we say there are economies of scale. Technology contributes directly to the creation of a monopoly or to a market with a few firms in an oligopoly market structure, when economies of scale are significant relative to the demand for the product. Consider, for example, the case in which one firm has average cost declining with output even when output reaches a level that satisfies *all demand* for the product. When average cost is declining, marginal cost must be lower than average cost, so two firms competing in such a market could be tempted to price below average cost and, thus, lose money. Whichever firm could outlast the other could be a monopoly.

In Figure 3.1, suppose each of two firms has the average cost function *AC* and the market demand is *DD*. In this case both firms may be able to operate at a scale that is efficient, in that their output is large enough to achieve a low level of average cost before all demand is satisfied. The two firms don't face competitive circumstances, where an impersonally determined market price leaves them only a choice of output, because here the two firms may be able to see how their actions affect each other and the market outcomes. So the firms can make strategic choices.[2] When a firm has average cost function *AC* in Figure 3.1 but demand is *D'D'*, only one firm can serve the market at lowest cost. Having just one firm could lead to some form of government regulation in the industry, a topic examined in Part 2.

Economies of scale complicate entry when they require a large output of a new entrant. Even if it is possible to enter with a large output, that large output lowers market price and may make entry unprofitable. At first glance, one might think that

---

[1] See Chenery (1949) and Coockenboo (1949).
[2] Larger markets might help offset such effects by accommodating more firms. For example, reduced transportation costs might allow firms to reach larger scale by selling in many domestic markets where they face strengthened competition.

Figure 3.1 *An Example of Economies of Scale*

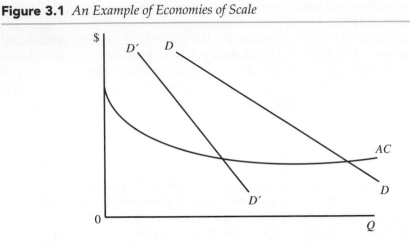

antitrust laws simply should insist on competition in markets and deny any monopoly. However, the production technology best suited for some lines of business may not support competition. Economies of scale may be so great that a single firm can serve a market at lower cost than, say, two firms. Then a monopoly could be the lowest cost way to organize the industry.

Absolute Cost Advantage

An incumbent firm may have an **absolute cost advantage** over potential entrants because of experience in learning a production technique, which can occur when one firm begins production ahead of others and so accumulates more experience. The existing firm with an absolute cost advantage can earn profit while an entrant only breaks even, and the existing firm can cause an entrant more serious harm by lowering price further. Such exposure to harm discourages entry. Economies of scale can also benefit an incumbent firm relative to a new entrant who may have to operate first at smaller scale. Or to achieve competitive cost a new entrant may have to enter at such a large scale that its addition to industry output lowers market price. Existing firms may consequently earn above-normal profit without inviting entry, because entrants expect a fall in price after they enter.

Sunk Costs

Exit barriers may exist when sunk costs are needed, and exit barriers discourage entry. When costs must be sunk, an entrant will want more assurance that prospects will not turn sour after entry, because the firm will not be able to exit. Sunk costs follow when an investment is long lasting and has very limited alternative uses. Limited alternative uses may result from specialization, as when a supplier creates dies to form a specific customer's product shape and, thus, irretrievably commits to serving that customer. For any other customer, the dies are worthless, so the costs are sunk in that they can be used only for an existing customer. At the other extreme, with no sunk cost, we can have what is called a *contestable market*, where entry is so free that even a single firm in a market must behave competitively to avoid losing out to a new entrant.

Imperfect Information

We will return to consider imperfect information later in this chapter, because it is a departure from the perfect information condition that is assumed in perfect competition (assumption 5). For now we note that a lack of perfect information for investors can be an entry barrier. If a very large expenditure is necessary for entry, such as a large investment in capacity to build, distribute, and service automobiles, for example, it can be hard for an unknown potential entrant to raise so much money. In such a case, *imperfect information* may prevent a promising idea from entering a market because it keeps investors from knowing about the idea. Their evaluation of the idea would require a larger investigative effort than they wish to make. Already existing firms may be well known, while a new entrant has to spend large sums of money on advertising and sales promotion to attract attention to its product. The good news is that advertising helps the entrant to deliver this message, but to do so the entrant has to be able to finance the needed expenditure on advertising.

Patents

A patent, which creates a property right granting exclusive use of the new idea for its inventor, can also block entry. A patent creates a monopoly position through its holder's right to exclusive use of an idea as reward for its discovery. New ideas lower the costs of old products or bring more effective products into existence, so an incentive for developing them is desirable. While the patent award thereby motivates discovery of the idea, it does so by creating a monopoly over its use for a limited period of time, with the attendant drawbacks that a monopoly brings. Striking an ideal balance with patents is difficult, deciding how much protection they should allow and for how long a time period. Surveys show patents to be important incentives now for firms in some industries, such as drugs and electronics, but unimportant in others. Patents seem to be less important as an incentive to larger firms than smaller ones, perhaps because some large firms have large market shares in their industries and can thereby appropriate many of the benefits of an innovation even without a patent. We can say that patents help to encourage inventive activity, but to be set against that benefit there is a social cost, in the excess of price over cost that marks monopoly pricing of a product.

Chapter 5 specifically examines entry barriers as an element of market structure. Another key element of market structure is the number of sellers in a market. At the opposite end of the spectrum from the many firms of perfect competition with its easy entry, we have the one-firm structure of monopoly, which we now consider.

3.2 **MONOPOLY**

Perfect competition assumes a market with many firms (assumption 2), all vying to sell to consumers. What if there is only one seller, a monopoly? Here we examine pricing and other effects of monopoly, which will be a persistent threat to desirable competitive outcomes through Parts 1 and 2.

Entry barriers foster monopoly by keeping out possible competitors. Other main causes of monopoly are scale economies and network organization, which give advantages to a single large firm. This section examines the consequences of monopoly, beginning with the range of noncompetitive pricing practices it invites. Other effects are also considered, such as inefficiency in operations or in choice of products to offer and whether to lease them or sell them. The possibility that a monopoly might be available can invite efforts to obtain it. Such efforts are called *rent seeking* because the extra profit available to a monopoly is called a "rent." Rent seeking to obtain monopoly positions can bring wasteful side effects.

Pricing by Monopoly

When a monopoly sets the same price for every unit it sells, we can expect that price, which is called a *uniform price*, to be higher than the competitive price. We begin by examining just how the profit maximizing monopoly chooses its uniform price. Alternatively, the monopoly may be able to vary the price of its product, perhaps with the quantity purchased, in which case it has a *nonuniform price*. We show the monopoly's advantage in pricing this way. The monopoly may also separate its customers and charge them different prices, which is *discriminatory pricing*, and its consequences are described. Finally the monopolist's attempt to harm others by its *predatory pricing* is considered.

Uniform Pricing

Suppose the monopoly sets a **uniform price**, the same price for every unit sold. Unlike a firm with many competitors, a monopoly firm can see how its uniform price affects its sales: to sell more output it must lower its price. Essentially, the monopoly can observe the downward sloping demand curve for the entire market, which enables it to calculate its **marginal revenue**, which is the revenue it will obtain from selling one more unit of output. Marginal revenue for a firm in competition is simply the market price, because that is the revenue the firm obtains by selling another unit. For a monopolist, however, marginal revenue reflects not only the added revenue obtained by selling another unit but also the revenue *lost* when price is lowered to make that additional sale.

Figure 3.2 illustrates marginal revenue for a monopolist for a few discrete units of a good. At a price of $6, the monopolist sells one unit. To sell two units, the monopolist must lower the price to $5. Although the monopolist obtains revenue of $5 from selling the second unit, $5 is not the marginal revenue because the first unit, which originally sold for $6, is now selling for only $5. That loss of $1 ($6 − $5) on that unit should be subtracted from the $5 received on the second unit to determine the actual *marginal* revenue from selling the second unit; that is, marginal revenue is $5 − $1 = $4. By the same reasoning, to sell a third unit the price must be lowered to $4. Be-

Figure 3.2 *Marginal Revenue for a Monopoly*

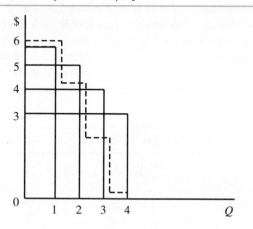

cause two units that were selling for $5 are now sold for only $4, that is a $2 loss from the previous situation. So marginal revenue is the $4 gain in selling a third unit minus that $2 loss, or $4 − $2 = $2. The dashed line in Figure 3.2 traces marginal revenue and shows that in selling four units, the monopolist's marginal revenue is zero.

Figure 3.3 shows that for a linear, or straight line, demand curve, the marginal revenue curve is a dashed line that falls exactly halfway between the linear demand curve and the vertical axis.[3] To maximize profit, the monopoly chooses output to set marginal revenue equal to marginal cost. Assume marginal cost is zero. Then profit is maximized at the output where marginal revenue is zero. Up to that output level, every unit adds to

Figure 3.3 *Uniform Pricing by a Monopoly*

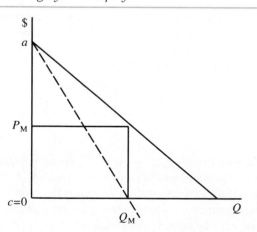

---

[3] By reconsidering the case in Figure 3.2, note that the marginal revenue curve goes down two steps when the demand curve goes down one. The marginal revenue curve has twice the slope of the demand curve or is twice as steep as the demand curve. That is why it lies halfway between the demand curve and the vertical axis in Figure 3.3.

profit because marginal revenue exceeds marginal cost. Beyond that output level, marginal revenue is less than marginal cost (less than zero), so every unit produced beyond Q_M will lose money. Because it reflects revenue lost from lowering the price, the monopolist's marginal revenue is always *lower* than price. So in setting marginal revenue equal to marginal cost, a monopoly sets its price *above* its marginal cost.

Box 3.1 shows that the monopoly price involves a markup over marginal cost, $(P - c)/P$, that is inversely proportional to the elasticity of demand. That is, if the

---

BOX 3.1 A Mathematical Solution for the Uniform Monopoly Price

Suppose a monopoly faces the linear inverse demand curve, $P = a - bQ$, and with constant marginal cost, c, has total costs equal to cQ. In this case, total revenue will be $PQ = (a - bQ)Q$, and profit for the monopoly will be $\pi = (P - c)Q = (a - bQ)Q - cQ$. To maximize profit we should take the derivative of profit with respect to Q and set it equal to zero (and check to be sure we have a maximum and not a minimum). Because profit is total revenue minus total cost, maximizing profit sets marginal revenue minus marginal cost equal to zero, or marginal revenue equal to marginal cost. To demonstrate,

$$\partial\pi/\partial Q = a - 2bQ - c = 0,$$

which we can solve for the monopoly value of Q_M,

$$Q_M = (a - c)/2b.$$

Substituting this value for Q_M into $P = a - bQ$ yields the monopoly price, P_M,

$$P_M = (a + c)/2.$$

Figure 3.3 shows that the monopoly price, P_M, is halfway between a and c, as this price of $(a + c)/2$ implies.

A more general representation of the monopoly's profit maximizing solution follows from using a more general demand function such as $P(Q)$, not necessarily a linear demand. Then the monopoly seeks to maximize profit, $\pi = P(Q)Q - cQ$. Taking the derivative of this expression and setting it equal to zero for a maximum yields

$$d\pi/dQ = P + QP' - c = 0,$$

where $P' = dP/dQ$. We can solve this condition for

$$(P - c)/P = -QP'/P = -1/E,$$

where $E = (P') P/Q = (dQ/dP)(P/Q)$ is the *own-price elasticity of demand*. The expression, $(P - c)/P$, is an expression for the monopolist's markup. At the profit maximum, that markup is set equal to the inverse of the market demand elasticity. This simple rule is known as the monopolist's *inverse elasticity pricing rule*. The monopolist's profit maximizing price can also be solved for P directly, as

$$P = c/(1 + 1/E).$$

elasticity of demand in response to the product's price, the own-price elasticity of demand, is $E = (dP/dQ)(P/Q)$, then

$$\frac{P - c}{P} = \frac{1}{-E}$$

This is called the inverse elasticity pricing rule because the ratio of price minus marginal cost over price on the left-hand side of the equation equals the inverse (the reciprocal) of the demand elasticity. We can solve the inverse elasticity pricing rule for P as

$$P = c/(1 - (1/-E)).$$

In the monopoly case where $-E$ is greater than one but is not infinitely large, $1 - 1/(-E)$ is less than one (remember that E is negative in sign so $-E$ is positive). If $1 - 1/(-E)$ is less than one, then P has to be greater than marginal cost, c. Notice that the price makes sense only if $-E > 1$, or demand is elastic, for if instead demand is inelastic and $-E < 1$, then $1 - (1/-E)$ will be negative. It is not reasonable for $1 - (1/-E)$ to be negative because then either c or P must be negative, and we cannot expect that. Box 3.1 also shows that with a linear demand like $P = a - bQ$, and with constant marginal cost of c, the monopoly price is halfway between a and c: $P = (a + c)/2$. We will see this pattern in future exercises that involve linear demand and constant marginal cost.

Box 3.2 explains why the monopoly prefers to operate where demand is elastic. We can see this by looking at the inelastic region of demand in Figure 3.3. Demand is inelastic in the range of demand where outputs are greater than Q_M and prices are below P_M. Elasticity, which can be represented also as $E = (\Delta Q/Q)/(\Delta P/P)$, will have to be less than one in that range because the percentage change in quantity ($\Delta Q/Q$) will be smaller than the percentage change in price ($\Delta P/P$). Also in that range, where outputs are above Q_M and prices are below P_M, Figure 3.3 shows that marginal revenue is negative. We know profit is maximized by setting marginal revenue equal to marginal cost, but that cannot be done in the inelastic region of the demand curve unless marginal cost is negative (which is not likely), because marginal revenue is negative. The monopolist wants to operate where demand is elastic because marginal revenue is not negative there, so with a positive marginal cost profit can be maximized.

The monopoly's uniform price reduces social welfare from the ideal. The value consumers place on marginal units—reflected in the price they pay the monopoly—exceeds the monopoly's marginal cost. So in comparing monopoly goods with competitive goods, consumers consume too much of the competitive goods relative to the monopolized goods. If the output of a monopolized good increases, social welfare increases. The marginal social benefit from another unit of this good is the price paid, while the marginal social cost is the monopolist's marginal cost, which is lower. So social gains are possible until the monopoly price equals marginal cost. In Figure 3.3, therefore, the potential consumer surplus to the right of Q_M is lost when price is P_M, and that loss is often called the dead-weight loss caused by monopoly pricing.

Nonuniform Pricing and Price Discrimination

What if the monopolist's price is not uniform? Rather than charge all consumers the same uniform price, a monopoly may charge one consumer one price and another

---

BOX 3.2 Why a Monopoly Wants Demand to Be Elastic

The monopoly always wants to operate where demand is elastic. This may seem coun-terintuitive. You may be tempted to say the monopoly should operate where demand is inelastic, because from there you could raise price and make more profit. But that is the point. If demand is inelastic, the monopoly *should* raise price, and keep raising price, until demand is no longer inelastic. When demand is inelastic, raising price raises revenue without increasing cost (quantity sold cannot increase), so it must in-crease profit. The monopoly is not in equilibrium when demand is inelastic precisely because raising price can increase profit.

Remember that when demand is inelastic, $|-E| < 1$. Consider the pricing rule, $(p - c)/p = -1/E$, with $|-E| < 1$. After all, $|-E| < 1$ would imply $-1/E > 1$, which would require that $(P - c)/P > 1$. We could expect $(P - c)/P > 1$ only if $P < 0$ or $c < 0$, but we do not expect negative prices or negative marginal costs.

Another way to see why the monopoly avoids inelastic demand is to consider marginal revenue in the inelastic region of demand. When demand is inelastic, an in-crease in price increases total revenue and a decrease in price decreases total rev-enue. (This follows because with inelastic demand the percentage decrease in quan-tity is less than the percentage increase in price.) This means that when demand is inelastic the effect of an increase in quantity on revenue is *negative*, so in the inelastic region of demand, *marginal revenue is negative!* As long as marginal cost is positive, which we should ordinarily expect, it is impossible to maximize profit when marginal revenue is negative. Thus, a monopolist does not want to operate in an inelastic re-gion of demand.

---

consumer another price. This practice of charging different prices to different customers is called **price discrimination**. We just noted that when charging only a single price the monopolist must lower that price to sell more units, giving up some revenue on sales that were being made before the price was reduced. That is how marginal revenue was defined. If the monopolist can lower price to some customers while not lowering it to others, it can avoid its loss on already existing sales and thereby increase its marginal revenue.

Suppose the monopoly seller can distinguish between consumers, for example between a truck and a car using a toll bridge. As a commercial vehicle with a valuable load, a truck may be willing to pay more than a car to cross the bridge. Rather than starting with a high uniform price that attracts only trucks, and then considering a lower price to attract cars, the monopolist might set two different prices, a higher price for trucks and a lower one for cars. Compared with a uniform price, the monop-olist can make more profit by keeping the high price for trucks and setting a lower price for cars, thus winning the business of both customer groups at different prices. Such discrimination in price can only work when customers willing to pay different prices can be recognized and the product or service cannot easily be resold (bridge trips, or medical care as another example, cannot be resold). Resale, or trading of units among consumers, would lead to a single uniform market price. This kind of price discrimination, based on separating roughly recognizable demands, is called **third-degree price discrimination**.

Another possible form of price discrimination is the **two-part tariff**. This pricing arrangement requires that to consume a good the consumer must pay (1) a fixed fee and (2) a price per unit. The resulting price has two parts and is not uniform across units because the first unit—which requires payment of the fixed fee—effectively has a higher price than subsequent units. We can see the advantage to the firm of this pricing arrangement in Figure 3.4, which illustrates the two-part tariff for one consumer. Suppose the price per unit is set at marginal cost. What fixed fee can the monopolist set that the consumer will pay in exchange for the right to consume at that marginal-cost price? Remember that we can interpret the consumer surplus—the area below demand and above price per unit—as the amount the consumer is willing to pay to consume the good at that given price. The fixed fee, therefore, can be almost as large as all the surplus the consumer would enjoy from consuming the good, which the triangular area in Figure 3.4 indicates. In this case, the consumer is willing to pay such a fee to consume at a price per unit equal to marginal cost.

With many consumers, some will have more consumer surplus than others, and the monopolist will try to set fixed and marginal prices to obtain the most revenue from consumers. A range of rate structures might be offered, for example, with higher fixed fees entitling consumers who pay them to a lower marginal price per unit. Such a rate structure would allow the consumers to choose which category to consume in, so there is price discrimination through differing rate structures, but each consumer can select a best category. Consumers then self-select into categories rather than be placed by the seller into categories. Such discrimination is called **second-degree price discrimination**.

Figure 3.4 *Nonuniform Pricing by a Monopoly*

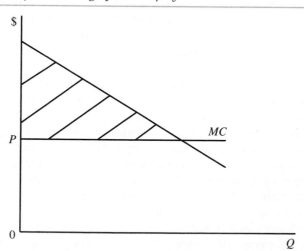

Conceivably, a monopolist could set a separate two-part price such as the one in Figure 3.4 for every consumer and obtain virtually all consumer surplus. This perfect price discrimination is called **first-degree price discrimination**, but it is seldom seen. The extreme form of first-degree price discrimination is clear and so is the idea of recognizing different groups of consumers for third-degree price discrimination. Second-degree price discrimination focuses on pricing by the monopolist who lacks information about consumers' preferences but can offer them choices that let them sort themselves into categories that involve some discrimination.

Although price discrimination transfers income from consumers to the monopolist, it need not interfere terribly with economic efficiency. Indeed, when compared with uniform pricing by the monopoly, price discrimination can often increase quantities consumed and raise social welfare. When two consumers adjust to different prices for the same good their consumption is not efficient; therefore, trades could improve their welfare. When those consumers who are charged high prices are very willing to pay them, however, while those willing to pay only low prices are charged low prices, perhaps even close to the level of marginal cost, the efficiency of consumption choices may actually be improved, at least relative to a monopoly's uniform prices. With price discrimination in the form of two-part prices, for example, the last units purchased by many consumers may be valued at close to their marginal cost, and that is good for efficiency. On the other hand, the fixed fee part of the two-part price may prevent some consumers from consuming the good at all, and that will be inefficient.

The public's objection to price discrimination is based not so much on its efficiency effects as on its consequences for income distribution. The discriminating monopoly takes more income from consumers than an ordinary, uniform-pricing monopolist does. Such transfers are opposed in part because they seem to go from poor individuals to rich corporations and society ordinarily favors transfers that benefit the poor.

Predatory Pricing

A monopoly intends to harm a potential competitor when it uses **predatory pricing**. A monopoly uses a predatory price as a strategic weapon, perhaps in an effort to create or preserve its monopoly position. For example, one seller might set price low in an effort to drive others out of the market and obtain a monopoly. The strategy might be so drastic that all parties lose money and the one who can hold out the longest wins, meaning it will then be in position to raise price. Such a contest is essentially a "war of attrition," in that it lasts until only one firm is left standing. Whether it can be useful to a firm depends on how easy entry and exit are. For if entry and exit are easy, other firms can exit to avoid transactions at money-losing prices. As soon as price is returned to a profitable level, these other firms can reenter. With easy entry and exit, predatory pricing is not very effective in driving competitors from the field for a long time.

If entry is difficult, however, predatory pricing can cause some firms to exit, find other activities that are profitable, and not wish to return. Proven cases of genuine predatory pricing remain few, and what might appear as predatory pricing often involves other considerations. For example, present sales may lead to future sales. That can motivate low, seemingly predatory, prices that may be justified by the business rationale of winning future sales. A seller may expect to learn how to lower cost with experience, and then price low to gain sales and production experience that will result in lower unit costs later. Still, when entry is difficult it is possible that a firm with some monopoly advantage may price low, perhaps in one geographic region or in one product line, with the aim of driving possible competitors from the field.

Other Effects of Monopoly

In addition to its pricing, a monopoly may reduce economic efficiency in other ways. Having no pressure from competitors, it may grow lazy and operate inefficiently or it may not offer some varieties of product to the market. A monopoly may want to lease rather than sell a durable product for reasons that do not arise for competitors. The reward of being a monopoly is so attractive that some resources may be wasted in an effort to obtain the monopoly. Here we consider these other effects of monopoly.

Cost Inefficiency

Lacking pressure from competing producers, a monopoly may not keep its costs low. There are many stories of once-monopoly organizations, swollen with incompetent workers (maybe relatives of the boss) and saddled with poor investments or other management mistakes, that ultimately failed. The very protection monopolists enjoy from the intrusion of new methods and ideas can leave them unchallenged, and as a result they may not work hard. Indeed, the cost function is not even well defined when the firm does not have to be efficient to survive.

From medieval times, the best of all monopoly positions has been that enforced by the power of government.[4] Questions about the efficiency of postal service, the army, or the county highway department arise too often to be entirely without merit. In the private sector, telephone companies, television networks, railroads, airlines, trucking companies, and electric and gas companies, to name a few, have sometimes been regulated with debatable effectiveness while being protected from new competition through exclusive certification or franchising procedures. National defense industries, those involved in foreign trade, and others, have benefitted from large outright subsidies. Congress has heavily subsidized American merchant vessels, for instance. It has paid almost half the cost of building some ships and more than half the cost of operating them, while the shipping companies nevertheless fail to compete effectively for international shipping. The monopoly power of government can be used to protect and sustain a failure as well as an excessively profitable situation.

Product Choices

A business firm chooses what products to sell and how well to make them. Does a monopoly choose products or product quality any differently from competitive firms? Suppose quality is well defined, say in the form of how long a product will last, its durability, and there is an optimal degree of durability that brings lowest cost to consumers over the life of a product. Then as long as it attempts to maximize profit,

---

[4] See, for example, Green (1973).

BOX 3.3 Discipline from the Capital Market

Even when a product market is under monopoly control, some pressure for efficient operation of an unregulated private monopoly firm can arise through the capital market, where ownership shares in the firm are traded. This force operates through what is called the market for corporate control. On recognizing inefficient operation, an investor can buy enough shares to gain a controlling position in the firm in what is called a raid, or a take over. This raider then sacks the poorly performing management and returns the firm to efficient operation, thereby making a gain on the value of the purchased shares. Corporate control of the firm has been transferred to more efficient hands. Operations have to reach a sorry state to motivate such action, because it is always risky. In addition, a successful raid to gain control of a sizeable corporation may require a vast sum of money, and, even if control is achieved, it is not a simple matter to find and cure the sources of inefficiency. Lack of good information may also keep an investor from knowing of the opportunity to improve earnings in the first place. So without competition in the product market, there is no guarantee that a product will be produced by the most efficient means available.

---

a monopoly produces the same quality as a competitive industry.[5] As long as the monopoly can be motivated to maximize profit, it will be motivated to minimize costs and produce attractive products, just as competitive firms are.

Different consumers may prefer different degrees of durability, however, and, if so, the monopoly may provide different choices than a competitive industry would provide. Replacing the durable good may require time, for example, and some consumers may value their time more than others. Those who are least willing to spend time replacing the good would be most willing to pay for greater durability. Of course goods of different durabilities can still substitute for one another, and some durabilities may be more profitable to a seller. Then the monopoly may find it is more profitable not to offer some of the choices if they draw sales away from more profitable varieties. In such a case, variety may not be as great under monopoly as it would be under competition.

To Sell or Lease a Durable Product

By itself, a durable product may actually handicap a monopoly in its pursuit of monopoly profit. Consider the extreme case of a good that lasts forever, perhaps an indestructible aluminum car that is the only kind of car that can be produced. The monopoly would like to discriminate in price over time, selling at a higher price to early buyers and a lower price to later ones. Consumers may realize that the monopoly seller will try to exploit the demand for such a car over time in this way. Being so durable, used cars will substitute well for new cars. Consumers will then be reluctant to pay a high

---

[5] See Swan (1970, 1977).

BOX 3.4 Quality Degradation Can Improve Profit

Light bulbs can be made to last a short time or a long time. Instead of refusing to offer the consumer light bulbs of a certain durability, or lasting power, the monopoly may simply *distort* levels of durability away from some consumers' preferred levels to reduce substitutability. For example, suppose those consumers whose time is most valuable, and who consequently do not want to change light bulbs often, will pay a great premium for light bulbs that last a long time. To profit most from those customers, the monopoly might not offer short-lived light bulbs that could serve as substitutes. Instead, to make short-lived light bulbs less attractive as a substitute, the monopoly might make the short-lived light bulbs *very* short-lived. Those consumers who prefer low-cost light bulbs want more durability than the very short-lived bulbs offer, but they will accept very short-lived light bulbs if that is the only low-price kind that is offered. Against a substitute that is so unattractive because of its very short life, the consumers who place high value on time will pay a higher price for longer-lived bulbs. This degraded durability of short-lived light bulbs, together with high-priced, long-lasting light bulbs, may therefore be the most profitable set of products for the monopoly to offer.

---

price for the initial new car, out of fear that the value of their investments in the cars will decline when the monopoly later lowers the price in an effort to sell more cars. The monopolist might later sell at prices all the way down to marginal cost. Anticipating this possibility can keep consumers from paying the monopoly price.[6]

The monopoly can escape this result by retaining ownership of the car and leasing or renting it. Renting rather than selling changes the monopolist's incentives. No longer can the monopoly imagine initial sales at high prices, because it still owns the cars and has only a rental rate as means of income. As it produces more and more cars, the monopoly cannot escape the loss in value of vehicles produced earlier, because it continues to own them and receives only the rental rate for their use. Consumers should recognize this inability of the monopolist to escape ownership consequences. So they may be willing to rent where they were reluctant to buy. As a result, renting can be more profitable for the monopoly than selling.[7]

Rent Seeking

There is no doubt that having a monopoly position is attractive. Anticipating its existence can even invite a potentially self-defeating form of competition, called **rent seeking**, in the effort to achieve it.[8] The extra profit a monopoly can earn is called a

---

[6] See Coase (1972).

[7] Examples with discrete demands can upset this conclusion that renting is more profitable. Consumers with discrete demands either want a unit at a particular price or not. See Bagnoli, Salant, and Swierzbinski (1989).

[8] See Tullock (1967) and Posner (1975, pp. 8–15).

rent because the monopoly is in position to collect it, rather like a landlord collects a rent from a tenant. If a monopoly position is to be awarded, several parties may seek the opportunity to earn rent from it, and that is rent seeking. The potential monopoly position tempts candidates to devote real resources in an effort to obtain the position, yet those resources serve little social purpose.

The objection to rent seeking is that it can draw real resources into obtaining a monopoly, resources that otherwise would have been productive elsewhere. When that happens, the ultimate monopoly profit is not available as an increase in social welfare, for it must go to pay for resources used to obtain the monopoly position in the first place. For example, suppose two contenders for a monopoly television station hire lobbyists to argue their cases before the Federal Communications Commission. Each calculates it has a fifty-fifty chance to win the monopoly profit stream. Each may therefore devote resources to the effort equal to half the value of the expected monopoly profit, so the resources devoted to the effort by the two firms equal all the potential monopoly profit. The welfare loss due to monopoly then includes not only the dead-weight loss from monopoly pricing but also the real resources—perhaps equal to the entire expected monopoly profit—that were devoted to obtaining the monopoly position. Little true monopoly profit may remain.

3.3 | DIFFERENTIATED PRODUCTS

Perfectly competitive markets deal in **homogeneous products** (assumption 3). Sellers, however, do not always offer homogeneous products. When sellers offer different products that serve the same purpose and can substitute for each other (e.g., Ford and Chevrolet automobiles), we say the market has **differentiated products**. This section begins by describing product differentiation. Whether genuine differences exist among products or not, if consumers *think* there are differences then the products are differentiated. When consumers think the products are different, the goods in the market are no longer perfect substitutes. Each seller may then have a degree of market power, allowing it to raise its price above marginal cost and not lose all of its customers. So one way of analyzing sellers of differentiated products is to treat them as competing monopolies in a model of monopolistic competition.

Product Differentiation

There are two main types of product differentiation. Products that are similar in quality and offer different characteristics are **horizontally differentiated**. A Ford Taurus and a Chevrolet Lumina are horizontally differentiated. When products differ in quality they are **vertically differentiated**. A Chevrolet and a Cadillac are vertically differentiated. In the vertical dimension, all consumers prefer higher quality but may differ in how much they are willing to pay for quality. In the horizontal dimension, choice depends on the consumer's preference for specific combinations of features or characteristics.

The market power of a seller in a differentiated product market may not be strong, especially if there are many sellers of competing differentiated products. Also, entry may be easy, in which case sellers can earn no persistent economic profit. Economist Harold Hotelling (1929) considered a localized differentiation, as in the locations of stores, where the consumers would be more attracted to those sellers that were nearby, as a form of horizontal product differentiation. This representation can also have locations in one direction preferred by all consumers because they offer higher quality as a form of vertical product differentiation.

Not only can different firms in the same general market produce different products, but one firm may also produce more than one product and sell in more than one market. Chapter 2 described a multi-product firm as having advantages in production costs when economies of scope exist, because one firm could then produce two products, say, more cheaply than two firms could produce them. A manufacturer of automobiles for example, such as Ford or General Motors, may try to differentiate its products so consumers will like the whole group. Then they may start by purchasing an inexpensive model and move up to more expensive ones as their incomes increase. In addition to production economies a motive to sell more than one product may arise because of interrelations in the products' demands, often because products complement each other. In these situations a seller may try to differentiate two or more products yet also make them fit together, as makers of video games match them with game consoles to achieve differentiated outcomes.

Monopolistic Competition

Differentiated products depart from perfect competition and can raise questions about the effectiveness of competition as regulator. Each differentiated product has something like monopoly power in that some consumers prefer it, but makers of other products are free to enter into a form of monopolistic competition.[9] The main question is whether this monopolistic competition provides the "right" variety of products or services in the market. That is, are all varieties that can be economically produced available in the market for consumers to buy?

In the **monopolistic competition** model, products are differentiated in that one consumer prefers one variety of a product more than other varieties. The typical consumer shifts to a competing variety if the price of that consumer's preferred brand increases sufficiently. As a result of such loss in sales from raising price, one firm's residual demand is downward sloping, and it can be affected by prices of *all* other varieties of the product. This brings an important change. The Bertrand objection to Cournot's model—namely that firms vary price rather than quantity and undercut each other until price equals marginal cost—does not apply when products are differentiated. Price competition is not so violent when products are differentiated, and it may not drive price down to marginal cost.

---

[9] Economist Edward Chamberlin (1933) first represented monopolistic competition. See also the similar representation of imperfect competition by Joan Robinson (1933).

The major difference between monopolistic competition and monopoly is that in monopolistic competition there is entry when profit opportunity warrants it. Entry in monopolistic competition can force economic profit to zero. Economist Edwin Chamberlin allowed for the possibility that a few firms would recognize their mutual dependence and, as a consequence, would choose cooperative actions. Entry, however, could upset that short-term cooperation, and a larger group of firms would cause the zero profit outcome. Each firm seeks to win business from competitors in what is called the **business-stealing effect**. The situation is illustrated in Figure 3.5, where one firm is shown with its downward sloping demand, *dd*. The firm's share of the total market demand, assuming all firms kept their prices the same, is indicated by demand curve *DD*.

Whether equilibrium in the monopolistic competition model has desirable welfare properties is a long standing question. Consider the equilibrium position of the firm shown in Figure 3.5 whose own independent demand is *dd*. If other firms in the market all raised their prices along with this firm, the firm would move up curve *DD*, which is this firm's "share" of the market demand. Instead this firm and others adjust independently to a zero-profit equilibrium. There price equals average cost, at *C* in Figure 3.5, and with downward sloping demand there, the firm's average cost curve also slopes down. When price is equal to average cost and average cost slopes down, price must be above marginal cost, which is not ideal. The average cost now includes costs for product design and advertising and, while average *production* costs might be constant, economies of scale in advertising might explain the apparent economies of scale. In any case, the equilibrium for this and other firms affords a variety of products. Having different preferences, consumers like variety. The question is whether the equilibrium affords the socially optimal amount of variety.

Too little or too much variety is possible at equilibrium in the monopolistic competition model. Too much variety can result because of the business-stealing ef-

Figure 3.5 *The Firm in Monopolistic Competition*

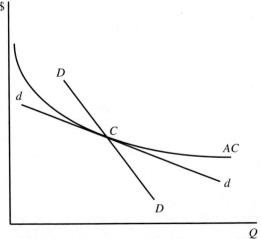

fect. One firm may gain from offering a new product, but the gain to that firm may come because consumers switch—for little consumer surplus gain—from other sellers. The firm offering the new variety gains, while other sellers lose. Moreover, if each variety involves its own fixed costs, prices might rise as a result of the additional product variety. In this case, the new entrant gains more than consumers do, and the result is too much variety. Too little variety can result also in the monopolistic competition model, if the firm can appropriate for itself only a portion of the social benefit of producing a new product. It is possible for the consumer surplus from a new variety of product or service to be substantial, even when a private firm cannot make a profit producing it. In that case there will be too little variety.

Differentiated products therefore introduce into markets product design and advertising, along with greater cost-function complexity. They affect market structure and raise new questions as they open a trade-off between product variety and product cost.

3.4   EXTERNALITY

A market economy achieves efficiency in part because decentralized decisions serve that end. That is why perfect competition assumes that decentralized decision makers consider all costs and benefits from their decisions. There is no externality (assumption 4), meaning that no cost or benefit from one decision spills over and affects someone not involved in the decision. Action by one person, however, often affects others. You add to highway congestion and air pollution when you drive downtown, you disturb others' quiet when you play your television set loudly, and you mar a community's beauty if you discard a candy wrapper on the street. On the other hand, keeping a tidy lawn, wearing attractive clothes, and even going to school are activities that can benefit others.

When a decision maker does not take them into account, such consequences for others are called externalities. They can be either costs or benefits felt by persons who are external to a decision. These external costs or benefits are real, but they do not influence the decision-maker's choice. Production examples are even clearer than those in consumption: a factory that pollutes the air imposes costs on citizens. The externality costs of air pollution are genuine costs, including higher laundry bills and medical care for respiratory diseases such as emphysema. They do not appear as costs for the polluting firms, however, and so are not considered by them. Because they do not take all cost consequences into account, the firms' decentralized market decisions are inefficient.

An External Effect

To see an external effect, examine Figure 3.6. Allen's demand for maintenance that affects the appearance of his home is represented by D_A. At a price of P, which equals the marginal cost of this maintenance service, the demand curve indicates that Allen will choose the maintenance quantity q_1. Suppose Bob lives across the street from

Figure 3.6 *The Maintenance of Allen's Home*

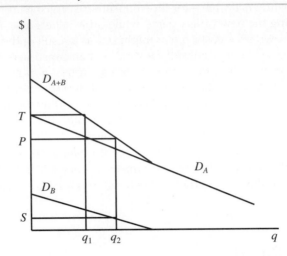

Allen and prefers to see Allen's house in good repair. That is, Bob has an interest in Allen's house maintenance. The demand curve D_B represents Bob's willingness to pay for a higher rate of maintenance by Allen. Currently, however, Bob has no influence on Allen's decision.

Only one level of maintenance is possible for Allen's house; we cannot have one quantity for Allen and a different quantity for Bob. Because only one quantity of maintenance may be chosen for Allen's house, we must construct a total market demand curve differently. We usually obtain market demand by adding together the *quantities* that different persons would choose at a single price. Here, because the quantity of Allen's maintenance must be the same for both parties, to combine individual demands we should add the benefits, or the willingness to pay, at every level of maintenance. That yields how much both persons are willing to pay for any particular quantity of Allen's maintenance.

If we add together the marginal benefit, or willingness to pay, of Allen and Bob for every level of Allen's maintenance quantity, we obtain the marginal combined or social benefit (to both Allen and Bob) for every level of maintenance quantity. Demand curve D_{A+B} represents that combined benefit. For every quantity of maintenance, D_{A+B} represents the amount Allen would pay for the quantity, as indicated by D_A, *plus* the amount Bob would be willing to pay for that same quantity, indicated by D_B. At the level chosen by Allen, which is q_1, the total benefit to both Allen and Bob is T, which exceeds marginal cost, represented by P. So Allen's private maintenance decision is not great enough to be socially optimal. There is a benefit to Bob from Allen's maintenance decision that Allen is not taking into account. That benefit, which is external to Allen's own decision, is an externality.

Total welfare is maximized when marginal social benefit equals marginal *social* cost. That occurs at the level of maintenance q_2 where marginal social benefit (D_{A+B})

equals marginal cost (p). Reaching the q_2 solution in Figure 3.6 is possible if Allen can take into account the benefit to Bob of his maintenance decision. There are several ways that might happen. Home owner Allen's pride alone might do it, or, if Bob's maintenance decision at his house affects Allen in a similar way, the two neighbors might be "neighborly" and consider the satisfaction of the other in deciding on their maintenance levels. Because only two parties are involved, they might also bargain explicitly to reach optimal maintenance levels. Government restrictions might be imposed that require property owners to maintain their homes at the level of q_2, but such restrictions could be hard to define or agree on and they could be costly to enforce. We might even consider a subsidy to be paid by Bob to Allen, of an amount S per unit of Allen's maintenance in Figure 3.6. That subsidy would lead Allen to internalize Bob's benefit and choose the ideal quantity, q_2. Without some remedy, however, decentralized decisions in markets do not reflect all costs or benefits when externalities are present.

Network Externalities

A **network** connects separate units so they are more effective than they are separately. The familiar telephone is connected to others in a telephone network, for example, with or without wires, and the network idea is applicable to a wider range of circumstances. Television sets can be connected by cable into a wired network or through a broadcast system for transmitting signals, and either system creates a network of television sets. Another example of a network is the U.S. Postal Service, which can operate one mail delivery system without the duplication of many mail services. Also think of software programs, which form a network because users of the same

---

BOX 3.5 The Externality of Global Warming

Light from the sun warms the earth and then heads back to space as heat radiation. The heat, however, is held in the earth's atmosphere by greenhouse gases, so named because like greenhouse windows they let heat in, and keep it from escaping. The main greenhouse gas is carbon dioxide (CO_2). It is produced largely from burning fossil fuels such as coal, oil, or gas, and their growing use contributes to global warming. Indeed, if no change is made in our growing production of greenhouse gases in the next 50 years or so, scientists who study the problem predict an increase this century in the average global temperature of as much as 5 °F. Based on historical records, this worst case would melt enough of the polar ice cap to raise the sea level by up to 80 feet, enough to cover parts of Boston, New York, London, and many other major world cities and most of Florida. Yet we burn coal and oil in our home furnaces and we drive our motor vehicles without thinking of future global warming. In part because the predicted global warming effects are so remote from us, global warming is a good example of an externality, and a serious one at that.

See J. Hansen, "The Threat to the Planet," *The New York Review of Books*, July 13, 2006, pp. 12–16.

Figure 3.7 *A Simple Star Network*

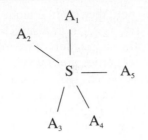

program can more easily exchange materials—and advice—with other users. The issues that arise in networks apply in some degree to any situation in which many parties rely on some form of a single central framework.

Figure 3.7 illustrates a network that resembles a telephone network. Each location, such as A_1, has access to a central switch indicated by S on a path such as A_1S. Parties at A_1 and A_2 can be connected for a telephone call along the path A_1SA_2. A network can offer production scale economies, allowing greater output (phone calls) at lower average cost, and such economies are even called **network economies**. More connections can be provided at lower cost by one network than by two networks because two networks would have to duplicate each other's paths for connections, thus, incurring greater total cost.

Networks not only lower cost as they grow larger, they also may offer greater value to users. A telephone is more valuable to you as you can reach more people. If Figure 3.7 is taken to be a telephone network, and paths from the switch to every phone is regarded as a separate service, the paths in Figure 3.7 are **complements**. That is, they are needed together. Paths A_1S and A_2S are both needed to connect A_1 with A_2.

So highways, railroads, electricity lines, mailboxes, natural gas pipelines, cable TV receptors, and even ATMs all serve as examples of networks. Networks such as those for telephone, highway, or railroad allow two-directional, or two-way, use of the network. Others, such as ATMs, over-the-air or cable television, and oil or natural gas pipelines, normally operate as one-way networks. In all cases there is a **compatibility** requirement. Where railroad tracks join, for instance, the tracks must be the same size for them to be compatible with the same railroad trains. Tracks of the same size meet the same **standard**, and standards help to provide the coordination required to build an effective network.

Externalities are common in networks, where they arise in both production and consumption activities. On the production side, once a network is constructed the marginal cost of serving another user is very small, which results in declining average cost or in economies of scale. Once the U.S. Postal Service has committed itself to a particular delivery plan, for example, adding one more letter adds little to total cost, just as one more telephone call may add little to total cost once an extensive telephone network is in place.

Externalities also arise in consumption. You would not want to have a telephone if no one else had one, and if you have one its value increases with the number of other users you can call. Because your benefit increases with the number of users on the network, those users affect you in a way that is external to their decision to have a phone. Similarly, competing software companies try to win over consumers to make their product more attractive to other consumers because a software program's users can then exchange files easily with more users. Having a large number of customers also makes it more attractive for programmers to write application programs for their software, because the applications will then reach more users, and having more applications can attract more users to the software. Part III, which considers environmental protection, examines externalities in detail, but external effects also arise in many other forms in Parts I and II.

3.5 IMPERFECT INFORMATION

Marrakech, Morocco, offers the classic Middle Eastern bazaar, where information is described by the late cultural anthropologist Clifford Geertz (1978, p. 29) as "poor, scarce, maldistributed, inefficiently communicated, and intensely valued." By contrast, information is also valued at the New York Stock Exchange, the Aalsmeer flower auction in Holland, or the Internet auctions on eBay, but it is efficiently communicated and widely available in a centralized market where well-defined items can be exchanged through a public array of bids and offers. Needless to say, the latter markets allow more mutually beneficial trades, and they show that information is important to effective market performance.

Perfect competition assumes consumers are extremely well informed about price and quality; they have perfect information (assumption 5). Suppose they are not well informed.[10] Suppose, for instance, that consumers know the quality of the product they wish to buy but are uninformed about the prices charged for it by different stores, of which there are quite a few. This **imperfect information** about prices is a relatively simple problem if the quality and reliability of the product are known. A second information problem arises when one party, say the seller, is better informed about product quality than the buyer. We call this a problem of **asymmetric information**. We begin by considering imperfect information about prices.

Imperfect Price Information

A simple model illustrates the possible consequences of imperfect price information. Suppose consumers incur a cost, c, to visit a store to buy bread, and they randomly choose which store to visit first. The perfectly competitive price for a loaf of bread, the marginal-cost price we would expect to prevail under full information, is p_c. Suppose

---

[10] See Salop (1976) and Stiglitz (1989, 2000) for reviews of this imperfect information literature. An early analysis is from Scitovsky (1950).

that the local newspaper collects prices and reports the average bread price regularly. The interesting question in this special situation is, Will the stores that sell bread adopt price p_c as an equilibrium price? To answer that question, start with all firms charging that price, p_c, and ask whether one firm would want to *change* its price. We are essentially asking whether the price p_c is an *equilibrium* price when consumers lack price information and must incur costs to acquire it.

If you were operating a bread store in this situation, would you raise your price above the competitive price, p_c? Think of the calculation to be made by a consumer who has already visited your store. Even assuming that the price is p_c at another store, the consumer cannot obtain bread for that price because the consumer knows it will cost c to go to another store. To switch stores, the consumer must incur the cost, c, which can be called a **switching cost**. To go to another store and purchase the bread, the consumer can expect to pay $p_c + c$. So if you raise your price by an amount less than c you should make a sale to the consumer who is already in your store. This is a reason for you to raise your price.

All stores make exactly the same analysis, and all stores are tempted to raise their prices. Once the average price rises and the local newspaper reports it for all to see, the expected price at another store will be higher for a consumer who is already at your store. So you may find it profitable to raise your price again. And so will other stores. By this process, the stores may even keep raising the price until they reach the monopoly level! In this illustration it doesn't matter what the costs of going to another store are as long as they are not entirely insignificant. If c is lower, stores will attempt smaller price increases, but it will just take more rounds of price increases to reach the monopoly price level. If there are only a few stores then the information problem is easier for consumers because they can *infer* more from information about the average price. With two stores, for example, knowing one store's price plus the average price would enable a consumer to infer the other store's price. The consumer, however, would still have to incur the cost c to go to the other store.

Asymmetric Quality Information

Markets, then, may not perform well when consumers are uninformed about prices. Consumers may also lack information about such important matters as product quality. For instance, one party to a transaction may know more about the quality of an item than the other party. This is a case of asymmetric information. Consider the sale of a used car about which the seller probably knows more than the buyer. Despite a lack of information, the buyer is not totally defenseless in approaching the transaction, for the buyer may expect the worst and assume that the quality of the used car is low. This means the seller may also suffer from the information problem because buyers who lack information may offer less (they assume the worst). Improved information could benefit both parties, which may explain why there are laws seeking to improve information or its reliability in markets (such as state laws that prevent tampering with recorded mileage on the odometer of a car).

The market with asymmetric information is often called the market for "lemons," after an influential analysis by Nobel laureate George Akerlof (1970). The analysis applies to complex products, like automobiles, tailored suits, or upholstered furniture, where quality is hard to judge without taking the product apart. Although some general information about the relative proportions of, for instance, good cars and bad cars for each brand and year may be available, the quality of any given used car is uncertain, and buyers of used cars expect the sellers to know more than they do about the car's quality. Without convincing evidence to the contrary, the buyers may assume the cars are low in quality and be willing to pay only the price of a low-quality car. The reason is that if they cannot be assured of high quality, buyers will assume the worst, and be willing to pay only for the low quality. When consumers are unable to distinguish good products from bad products, good and bad sells at the same (low) price. Experimental markets have repeatedly demonstrated that market price can fall to the level of a low-quality item when there is asymmetric information.[11] This outcome is reasonable, and its implications are important.

This result, where there is a single, low price for all cars and only the owners of poorer quality cars want to sell, is called **adverse selection**. The selection is adverse because only poorer quality products are selected for sale in the market. The result applies beyond markets for used cars. Producers of new products will choose to offer lower quality if consumers are unable to recognize higher quality—and more costly—products. This effect is something like an externality, where social and private benefits differ, so private decisions do not yield ideal outcomes. The added quality the producer can provide would have social benefit, but because the high-quality product is not distinguishable from average products, the producer cannot collect added revenue for providing the greater social value.[12]

When quality is hard to determine, the seller of a high-quality product may guarantee customer satisfaction, or may provide Internet or telephone-hot-line assistance to customers, in an effort to earn a reputation for quality that wins sales. To enforce its support of quality, the seller may offer an explicit **warranty**, which assures the buyer that the product will meet certain standards or be replaced. Warranties can be convincing to consumers when the seller of a poor-quality product who offered the warranty would be flooded by warranty claims and lose money unless its product had good quality. Another way for a seller to sell a high-quality product in these circumstances is to describe its quality through advertising.

The Role of Advertising

Advertising can inform consumers about prices and can signal product quality, so it is not surprising that more than 2 percent of our gross domestic product (GDP) is spent on it. Economists criticized spending on advertising when it was first examined in the mid-1900s because they saw it as creating loyal customers and thereby conveying some degree of monopoly advantage. They also saw high advertising-to-sales ratios in

---

[11] See, for example, Holt and Sherman (1990, 1999).

[12] For an experimental market treatment of this situation see Holt and Sherman (1990). Where deception is not an issue, market processes may elicit information; see Jovanovic (1982b).

BOX 3.6 Can You Lose Weight with a Pill?

Often, information is imperfect about what a product is able to accomplish, and in such a situation the federal government tries to prevent deception. In early 2007, for example, four sellers of diet pills were forbidden by the Federal Trade Commission from making unsubstantiated claims for their diet pills, and were fined a total of $25,000,000 for having done it. Continued sale of the pills was allowed, because the pills were not found to cause any harm, but neither were they found to cause any loss in weight, and that is why claims to that effect were forbidden. Among the Federal Trade Commission's responsibilities is to prevent unfair or deceptive practices, and that includes making unsubstantiated claims for a product.

See E. Iwata, "Diet Pill Sellers Fined $25M," *USA Today,* January 5, 2007, p. B1.

some industries as barriers to entry to the extent they would require larger advertising expenditures by new entrants.

Recent views of advertising have been more accepting. Firms' strategic choices may still lead to nonoptimal outcomes, in part because the advertisers' motives differ from those of the consumers,' but much of the information provided to consumers is valuable. Indeed, advertising of local price information, as by grocery supermarkets, can moderate the problem of imperfect price information and enhance competition. In support of this possibility, an influential study across states found the prices of eyeglasses to be lower in states that allowed advertising.[13] Advertising may be more useful for goods that consumers can judge, such as basic foods, many clothes and everyday staples that are called **search goods**. The idea is that consumers can judge the qualities of search goods, and advertising helps them in their search to find the most attractive terms.[14]

The quality of other goods cannot be determined so readily by inspection and must be experienced to be evaluated. These goods are called **experience goods**, and they create greater problems for both consumers and producers. Much upholstered furniture would fall in this category, along with tailored suits and golf or Ping-Pong balls. Consumers would want to try these goods to know their quality, but that is not always sensible or even possible.[15] Producers always want consumers to try their products, especially when the products are of higher quality because they can expect consumers will be satisfied and will continue to consume. This logic suggests that producers at the high end of the quality range may advertise more, and consumers might infer that a producer who advertises extensively has a higher-quality product. The fact of the extensive advertising itself may then carry more information than the substantive content of the advertising (which may present fuzzy images rather than hard facts) and could even lead to more than an optimal amount of advertising. Evidence for this positive relationship between advertising and quality is not strong,[16] but the idea of

---

[13] See Benham (1972).
[14] The idea is from Nelson (1970).
[15] One can experiment easier with a golf ball than with a tailored suit.
[16] See Caves and Green (1996).

a difference between experience goods and search goods is still important. Consumers take different approaches to evaluating search and experience goods, and producers follow different strategies in attempting to sell the two categories of goods.

There are other reasons why firms may choose nonoptimal amounts of advertising. In some markets, where advertising is used to differentiate products, firms can see the benefit to themselves from advertising, but they do not see the lost sales felt by competitors. (So this effect on the sales of others is an externality.) Because firms are motivated to steal business from one another by advertising, they may carry advertising to excessive levels. When products are similar and not easily differentiated by advertising, however, the advertising of one firm actually might aid competitors by making the generic product more prominent in buyers' minds. As firms cut their advertising to avoid benefitting each other, the result can be less than the ideal level of advertising.

Technological Change

In addition to perfect information, perfect competition assumes a known and unchanging technology (also part of assumption 2), whereas the real world changes everyday. The possibility of technological change raises two questions: (1) How does technological change affect the functioning of markets? and (2) How can technological progress be motivated? The second question arises because the rest of us can free ride on anyone who devotes time and effort to discovering something new (especially if we are all informed about technology, even the new discoveries). Without incentive, the time and effort needed to discover may not be forthcoming. What if the discoverer is granted a monopoly over use of a discovery? That is precisely what a patent offers. A patent motivates research effort by granting the discoverer exclusive use of the discovery for 20 years.

Other devices also reward discovery to motivate its creation. Copyright protects artistic works, for example, which includes some software as well as books and music. A property right can also be extended to trademarks, which identify the producer of a

---

BOX 3.7 Record Companies versus the Internet

Having resisted transmission of music over the Internet in an effort to preserve their control over recorded music, major record companies are finally facing the music: at least one label may release music on the Internet with no copyright restriction, and all major labels are considering it. Most of the independent labels already sell digitally compressed tracks in the MP3 format, mainly to promote future sales. The industry had hoped that sales through Apple iTunes would preserve its control over recorded music, but iTunes sales have not offset the loss of record sales in physical form. The new hope lies in selling copies as singles or through subscription services, or through free distribution on Internet sites that can offer advertising income. Such a change would illustrate how technology effectively alters property rights and forces new means of transacting.

See V. Shannon, "Record Labels Contemplate Unrestricted Digital Music," *New York Times*, January 23, 2007, p. C5.

particular product. Like the patent, these are forms of intellectual property, granting property rights to their discoverers in part to motivate the discoveries. The granting of such rights limits use of the discoveries, which is not good for society, but the limits usually last for only a limited period of time. And granting such rights can motivate the discoveries, which eventually pass into the public domain for use by anyone. The cost and benefit trade-off may not be perfect in every case, but in addition to motivating some discoveries, patents can bring about disclosure of the information the discoveries contain.

3.6 | TRANSACTION COSTS

Transactions in markets take time and are costly. Perfect competition assumes that dealing in markets involves no costs beyond the item purchased; there are no **transaction costs** (assumption 6). In reality, the costs of supervising workers or using markets determine where the firm stops and the market begins. A firm might either produce its own inputs or buy inputs from others in markets, but the former route involves supervising and monitoring costs and the latter requires market transaction costs. Resolving this trade-off between transacting within the firm or through the market determines the shapes of firms. Nobel laureate Ronald Coase (1937) showed that such organizational decisions by firms seek the lowest overall transaction costs.

Costs of Transacting

Engaging in transactions is costly. There are direct costs of transacting—learning about product features, prices, and qualities, for example, and picking up a purchase at the store or paying for shipping costs. There are also costs resulting from uncertainties in transactions that are not easily overcome even by writing contracts. For example, a storm or the discovery of a new technology can bring changes we did not anticipate when writing a contract. We have **bounded rationality**; that is, we are unable to think of all possibilities. Circumstances may change in a way that allows one party to exploit the other through what is called **opportunistic behavior**. Such exploitation is more likely as there is more specialization, which requires commitment to a narrow line of activity. If a firm invests in assets that are specific to the needs of one customer and that have no other use, that firm can be exploited. With great asset specificity, when a buyer cancels its contract, the supplier may be saddled with assets it cannot use. By threatening to switch suppliers, the customer essentially can "hold up" the committed and specialized supplier and bargain for a lower price.

Motivating and Monitoring Workers

These transaction costs may discourage the firm from using markets. Sometimes the firm can merge, joining perhaps with suppliers of inputs or with distributors of outputs to keep more transactions within the firm. Activities within the firm, however, are not costless either. A firm has to motivate its own employees, who otherwise may not seek the best interest of the firm, and there is a fundamental problem in doing so. When one party (the firm, or the principal) engages another (the employee, or the agent) to perform a task that is subject to some risk, and only the *result* of the agent's work, rather than the agent's effort, is observed by the principal, we have a principal-agent problem. The principal can motivate the agent by letting the agent share in results. Notice, however, that the only way the principal can establish a strong incentive program for the agent also forces the agent to bear risk, because risk partly determines good and bad results. The agent may not be willing or able to bear risk. The firm can ease this problem by monitoring the agent to observe effort, but that is costly. Motivating and monitoring are management activities within the firm, and these activities are not free.

Once the costs of transacting in markets and the costs of managing employees are acknowledged, the firm can be expected to compare them. If the transaction costs of using the market are lower than the management costs of carrying out activities within its boundaries, the firm will use the market. If management costs are lower, it will conduct activities within the firm. Choosing the organization that offers the lowest cost serves the firm and can be most efficient.

Some Firms Fail

The usual assumptions of perfect competition do not treat its dynamic operation, which includes technological change and other surprises, or perhaps even managerial mistakes, that cause some firms to fail. This problem is implicitly assumed away. Yet a competitive market economy almost invites a degree of firm failure, by welcoming entry to markets in which some firms may perform better than others, and the poorly performing firms may not survive. The sudden departure of a supplier on which you have relied can be seen as an added, and usually unexpected, cost of relying on markets. Government policies are pursued to moderate the effects of firm failure when it can be very harmful to innocent bystanders, such as those who rely on a bank or insurance company that fails or even those who rely on an employer that has promised pension benefits it can no longer deliver.

SUMMARY

This chapter describes market imperfections that violate the six assumptions of perfect competition and thus move us closer to the public policy problems of real-world industries. Entry and exit were first considered because they are so important to competitive outcomes yet may not exist because of production scale economies, an incumbent's cost advantage, sunk costs, imperfect information, or government barriers such as patents. Scale economies can require an entrant to be large in size, which means the entrant probably must raise a large sum of money. This may be difficult when investors have little information about the entrant. In addition, the entrant may add so much to market output that price falls. Then to survive, the entrant must be able to profit even at the lower price. Incumbent firms, having been operating for a while, may have a cost advantage over an entrant. Technologies that require large and long-lasting investments, called sunk costs, also make entry risky because they make exit difficult. Government restrictions, such as public utility monopolies or patents, also can virtually prevent entry.

Entry barriers can result in monopoly, that sharp departure from the many firms assumed to operate in perfect competition. A monopoly has many ways to increase profit that are not open to firms in competition, and the monopoly ways usually make the economy less efficient. These include setting higher prices, discriminating in prices, and even engaging in predatory pricing to ruin possible competitors. Monopolies may also survive even when they are inefficient, and they can choose the products they offer in a way that is not socially optimal. Sometimes monopolies or oligopolies arise because scale economies call for large firms relative to the size of the market. Networks bring scale economies in consumption as well as in production, and such economies can complicate the functioning of a competitive market.

Another complication for competitive markets is that products in a market may not be homogeneous, as perfect competition assumes. Goods that serve the same purpose may instead be differentiated in their features or designs. As sellers advertise the advantages of their own versions of the product, a new issue is raised: How many varieties of the product are optimal? Competition also assumes no externalities, so each decentralized decision in a market can take into account all its consequences for social costs. Decentralized decisions are not efficient if they do not consider all the costs and benefits they cause, and omitted costs or benefits are called externalities. Because externalities can prevent private decisions from reflecting social costs, they can keep decentralized market decisions from producing desirable social outcomes. Imperfect information can also handicap parties in the market, for example, by making price information costly to obtain or by making quality uncertain to buyers. If a seller knows more about the quality of the product being sold than the buyer, the buyer may make a pessimistic assessment of quality. As a consequence, high-quality products may be driven from the market, and the market may even collapse and cease to exist.

Finally, transactions in markets are costly. They require time and effort, and all possibilities cannot be anticipated in contracts so they involve risks as well. Forgoing use of the market by bringing activities inside the firm does not always solve this problem, because activities within the firm are also costly. Employees must be motivated and monitored. So in its effort to achieve lowest cost, a firm must choose what activities to bring inside the firm and what activities to leave to the market. The boundaries of firms are then influenced by their attempts to organize in the lowest cost way. In the extreme, firms may err and fail, and even though they agreed to transactions they may not carry out their end of them. If the firm that fails is a bank or an insurance company, very serious harm can result. Ordinary firms that fail without paying promised pensions also can cause great harm to their employees and retirees.

The rest of this book explores government regulation to overcome problems that follow when assumptions of perfect competition are not met. Part 1 treats policies in the antitrust area, intended to improve the effectiveness of competition as regulator and to avoid monopoly. How market structure affects firm behavior is examined, along with technological change and modern antitrust law. Technological conditions in an industry, such as economies of scale or network economies, may complicate the functioning of competition and lead to some form of governmental regulation of the industry. Part 2 considers cases where government regulation may improve the performance of an industry. We examine problems of pricing in pursuit of welfare and of finding incentives for efficiency in the very different circumstances that arise in a range of regulated industries. General problems of imperfect information and externalities can call for social regulation, which Part 3 explores. Here we examine broad problems of environmental protection and consumer and worker protection, along with other problems of a market economy such as the consequences of a side effect of market competition: firm failure.

QUESTIONS

1. Consider the case of asymmetric information discussed in Section 3.5, in which a seller may know that her product is high in quality but a buyer may not know it. Describe two different steps the seller might take to avoid the adverse selection problem, which otherwise could put her out of business.

2. Explain how a barrier to exit can be a barrier to entry.

3. Suppose demand for the good in a market is given by the equation $P = 1 - 0.01 Q$, where P is price and Q is quantity of the good. Suppose a monopoly serves the market for the good, and there is no possibility for entry. The firm has total cost, C, of $C = 9 + 0.1 Q$.

   a. Does the cost function indicate that economies of scale exist?

   b. Find the monopoly price and quantity and the monopoly profit.

   c. If entry were possible, a competitive outcome might be expected; however, do you see a problem for the functioning of competition?

4. A monopoly firm sells the same energy bar in two markets that have the demands, $P_1 = 800 - 2Q_1$ and $P_2 = 200 - Q_2$. Suppose the firm is efficient, has no fixed cost, and is able to sell at different prices in the two markets if it wishes.

   a. If the marginal cost for energy bars is constant at $0, what are the profit-maximizing prices and quantities for the two markets? Are these prices discriminatory?

   b. If the marginal cost for energy bars is constant at $100, what are the profit-maximizing prices and quantities for the two markets?

   c. If the marginal cost for energy bars is constant at $200, what are the profit-maximizing prices and quantities for the two markets?

5. Now suppose the firm in question 4 cannot sell at different prices in the two markets because consumers are able to buy in either market, wherever the price is lower. This forces one price for the energy bars. So the two markets are now

combined into one. (*Hint*: The two demand curves can be rearranged so each is solved for quantity rather than price. For example, $P_1 = 800 - 2Q_1$ is rearranged as $Q_1 = 400 - P_1/2$. It is then possible to solve for $Q_1 + Q_2 = Q$ with only price, because $P_1 = P_2 = P$, and the result is a single equation.)

a. If there can be only one price and marginal cost is $0, what will that one price be if the monopoly firm maximizes profit?

b. If there can be only one price and marginal cost is $100, what will the profit maximizing price be?

c. In the situation of question 4b, what is the socially optimal price for energy bars? Would the same price be socially optimal for both markets in the conditions of question 4b, where two prices could be charged in the two markets?

d. Would you expect free entry to produce the socially optimal price or the price you found in question 4b?

6. Suppose a firm faces demand for its product of $P = 100 - Q$ and has total cost $TC = 10 + Q/2$. Its production process, however, generates a pollution side effect that imposes a total cost on all others of $Q/2$ per unit.

a. What is the profit maximizing quantity and price for the firm?

b. What is the socially optimal quantity of this product? Compare your solutions in 6a and 6b to show that an externality is present.

c. Determine a tax that, if imposed per unit of output on the firm, would "internalize" the externality.

7. Suppose a firm produces two goods that have demands $P_1 = 20 - 0.02Q_1$ and $P_2 = 40 - 0.04Q_2$. The cost function of the firm is $TC = 15Q_1 + 15Q_2$.

a. Determine welfare maximizing prices and quantities for these two services.

b. Determine profit maximizing monopoly prices for these two services. Would a firm be willing to pay to be able to charge these prices (that is, might there be rent seeking)?

c. Calculate the ratio of Q_1/Q_2 for your answer in 7a and for your answer in 7b. Can you give a reason for any similarity in these ratios?

8. Let the demands for products q_1 and q_2 be $q_1 = 10 - 2p_1 + p_2$ and $q_2 = 10 - 2p_2 + p_1$, where q_i's are quantities and p_i's are prices for good i. Assume production costs are zero, so costs can be ignored.

a. Suppose that there are two separate monopolies, one for good q_1 and one for good q_2. Calculate the prices, p_1 and p_2, that the two separate monopolies would charge if each treated the other's price as constant. (*Hint*: Because situations are symmetrical, the solutions of the two monopolists should be the same, and you can substitute one into the other to simplify the problem.)

b. Now suppose the two monopolies merge, so a single monopoly now controls both goods and, thus, can set both prices, P_1 and P_2. Calculate the prices that the single monopoly would set for the two goods. If you do not find an exact numerical solution, explain in words how the single monopoly will modify the prices (up or down?) set by separate monopolies. Are the goods substitutes or complements? Explain why the price changes would benefit the single monopoly compared with two separate monopolies.

c. Now suppose that, instead of the demands at the start of question 8, the demands were $q_1 = 10 - 2p_1 - p_2$ and $q_2 = 10 - 2p_2 - p_1$. Find the prices, p_1 and p_2, that two separate monopolies would charge for the two goods in this case.

d. Now for the demands in question 8c, find the prices, P_1 and P_2, that a single monopoly over both goods would charge.

e. How would the prices of one monopoly versus two monopolies differ with the demands in 8c and 8d compared with demands in 8a and 8b? That is, in each of the two demand cases, which set of prices will be higher, those of the two monopolies (p_1 and p_2) or those of the single monopoly (P_1 and P_2)? Explain any difference you find in the pattern of prices for the two cases.

$$P_1 = 800 - 2Q_1$$
$$2Q_1 = 800$$
$$Q_1 = 400 - P_1/2$$

$$P_2 = 200 - Q_2$$
$$\therefore Q_2 = 200 - P_2$$

$$Q_1 + Q_2 = Q$$

$$400 - \frac{P_1}{2} + 200 - P_2 = Q$$

$$600 - \frac{1}{2}P_1 - P_2$$

PART 1
THE REGULATION OF COMPETITION

Competition regulates markets well, but it may not always flourish. Some firms may gain market power, for example, or use unfair practices that handicap competitors or mislead consumers. Antitrust policy originated with the Sherman Act in 1890 to combat market power and to prevent practices that interfere with the beneficial effects of competition. Original legislation was imprecise, and early applications were problematic, but progress in economic knowledge over more than a century has brought an increasing role for economics to guide antitrust policy.

Understanding antitrust regulation first requires knowledge of modern business firms and major influences on their sizes and shapes and the incentives that lie behind their behavior. Ways to represent real industries through measures of market structure are also necessary, and they make possible the study of business strategy, which depends on the options that market structure affords. One element of business strategy, research and development, is so important it deserves special attention. Present-day antitrust policy, the main instrument for the regulation of competition, can be appreciated by knowing these economic foundations and antitrust's history. An examination of legal cases reveals its present form.

Part 1 begins by treating the main player in the market economy, the modern business firm, and considering influences on its size and shape, in Chapter 4. The structure of a market is then characterized in Chapter 5, which shows why some observable features, such as entry difficulty, can indicate how a market functions. Although Chapter 5 sets out incentives and possibilities given by market structure, the full range of considerations and the resulting strategic actions available to firms are taken up in Chapter 6, which considers the business strategies that arise when a few firms compete. Chapter 7 treats one very important category of strategic decision for a business firm, research and development and market innovation.

Under these imperfect market circumstances, when market power can arise, it is usually necessary to forgo absolutes and to pursue reasonable social goals such as efficiency and innovation. Policies that allow progress toward one of these goals may complicate reaching another. Chapters 8 and 9 deal with antitrust policy in the face of such difficulties, first by tracing the origin and development of antitrust law in Chapter 8 and then describing the current state of antitrust law, based on recent cases, in Chapter 9.

4

Focus of the Law: The Modern Business Firm

We cannot discuss markets without treating business firms anymore than we can discuss the theater without treating actors and actresses. The business firm is the big player in any major market, and antitrust policy focuses on business firms. Antitrust policy also takes into account the structure of the market in which a firm operates, but it is the firm that is the target of antitrust action. Regulators do not sue markets; they bring charges against business firms.

Why do business firms have the sizes and shapes they have? Why are they organized the way they are? Some influences are more obvious than others. Economies of scale allow larger firms to achieve lower production costs, and economies of scope can give multi-product firms efficiency advantages. Beyond these technological influences on firms' shapes, however, lie other questions about where the boundaries of firms stop and the market begins. When there are no economies of scope, for example, what affects a firm's choice of which products to produce and which to buy from others? Does Apple Computer, Inc. make its own processor or buy from Intel Corporation or Advanced Micro Devices, Inc.? Will it sell its products to final consumers directly or distribute them through independent retailers?

The business firm plays an obvious and important role in the economy. Section 4.1 considers forces that help to determine the boundaries of the firm. The hierarchy and the control or governance mechanisms of the firm need attention, because they affect achievement of the firm's profit goal, which is discussed in Section 4.2. A mixture of stocks and bonds usually provide capital to the firm, so Section 4.3 considers capital structure, and Section 4.4 treats the question of who controls the corporation. The chapter then turns in Section 4.5 to mergers, which show the clearest form of organizational change. Horizontal mergers are among firms that are in the same line of business, while conglomerate mergers involve firms in unrelated businesses. In Section 4.6 we look at vertical relationships along the path from raw material to final product, whether they involve merger through vertical integration or not. Study of these relationships shows why the firm might operate its own sales agencies or rely instead on independent sales representatives.

4.1 | THE BUSINESS FIRM AND THE MARKET

Have you ever wondered why firms have the boundaries they have? Why does an automobile manufacturer buy steel instead of making it, or sell its automobiles through independent dealers rather than through sales agencies that it owns? The question really is, Where does the firm stop and the market begin? If the firm does not produce its own inputs or does not sell its outputs directly to final consumers, it buys inputs from other suppliers or sells outputs to intermediaries that exist in markets. Seventy years ago, Nobel laureate Ronald Coase (1937) showed that such organizational decisions by firms depend on which arrangement yields the lowest transaction costs.

Transaction Costs

When you deal in a market you incur transaction costs. **Transaction costs** are incurred to learn about buyers or sellers, their prices, and their qualities, and include the risks borne when signing contracts. Anyone who has purchased a used car, a wireless phone, or even a banana, knows that merely engaging in a transaction is costly. Yet estimating these transaction costs is not a simple matter. The easiest costs to estimate are the direct costs of transacting—searching among possible sources to learn prices and qualities, for example, and even traveling to pick up a purchase or incurring shipping costs and delays. The hardest costs to estimate follow from the uncertainties that surround transactions.

Transactions often involve contracts. Results may differ from those envisaged by the contracting parties because of surprises as simple as changes in the weather. Our limited intellectual capacity, or our bounded rationality, prevents us from considering in advance all the possibilities that might arise, so our contracts are incomplete. We simply can't see all that might happen, and the possibility of unwanted consequences are added costs of transacting. This problem of incompleteness in our contracts is greater as uncertainties are greater.

One of the main problems with contracts in changing conditions is opportunistic behavior, which occurs when one party takes advantage of the other,[1] and the problem is more serious when specialization is necessary. For example, suppose one firm must invest in specific assets to supply a product to another firm. To serve their purpose, the assets may be so specialized that they have no other use. This asset specificity makes the potential supplier think twice about undertaking a commitment to supply, for if the customer has another supply opportunity, and takes it, the supplier is saddled with assets it cannot use. The number of firms in a market can affect the degree of asset specificity, because when there are many potential buyers, the possibility of finding another use for assets tends to be greater. When potential buyers are limited, however, the customer literally can "hold up" the supplier who is committed to specific assets by threatening to switch suppliers and can, thus, bargain for a lower price.

---

[1] See Williamson (1985).

Early in the history of the auto industry, the Fisher Body Company built auto bodies for General Motors Corporation. Of course, Fisher Body would be uneasy about committing to serve General Motors, because its commitment to specific assets could be lost if General Motors stopped buying its auto bodies. On the other hand, General Motors also would make a large commitment to purchase bodies from Fisher and could be harmed if Fisher Body backed out. Each party could suffer from the other behaving opportunistically. To minimize the discomfort of this situation, the parties signed a long-term (10-year) contract, with prices to be adjusted by formula. But the formula was not perfect. It included a cost-plus pricing adjustment that could weaken Fisher Body's incentive to minimize costs and might not motivate plant locations that would be ideal for General Motors. The formula also may not have brought adequate responses when demand changed markedly.[2] The shapes of car bodies and the means of making the bodies changed, too, in the direction of closed rather than open bodies, requiring the use of more metal fabrication and less wood. General Motors decided to purchase the Fisher Body Company and to integrate vertically by producing its own auto bodies.[3]

General Motors' acquisition of Fisher Body occurred in a complicated setting, and many forces may have contributed to it. Nobel economist Ronald Coase (2000), who first drew attention to transaction costs and their effect on the organization of the firm, argues that contracts could have solved the problems between General Motors and Fisher Body. He sees the desire of General Motors to engage directly the services of the six, talented Fisher brothers as crucially important to the acquisition. Economist Robert Freeland (2000) supports this view and even argues that the Fisher brothers actually held up General Motors after the integration occurred through bargains over their human capital. Economists Ramon Casadesus Masanell and Daniel Spulber (2000) add further support by showing that General Motors sought greater coordination of production and inventories and an adequate supply of auto bodies, as well as the talents of the Fisher brothers. All of these considerations involve transaction costs as influences on the shape of the business firm.

To the extent that all eventualities cannot be covered in contracts, firms might prefer not to use the market and to rely instead on organizational units that are owned and controlled through internal procedures. That is, firms might bring activities inside rather than use the market to avoid being exploited when the opportunity arises for the other party in a contract to do so. The firm has to compare the costs of using the market with the cost of carrying out activities itself, to find which arrangement has the lowest cost. For activities cannot be managed costlessly within the firm, because workers must be motivated and monitored.

Motivating and Monitoring Workers

Transaction costs do not arise solely from contracting in the market. If they did, we might have one large firm in the economy and little reliance on markets. It is also costly for a firm to motivate and monitor its own employees, who do not always want

---

[2] See Klein (2000).

[3] See Klein, Crawford, and Alchian (1978).

BOX 4.1 An Electric Utility's Contract for the Supply of Coal

Transaction costs can affect the contracts electric utilities negotiate with coal suppliers when asset specificity is involved. Electricity generating plants that burn coal sometimes locate near coal mines to save on the considerable cost of transporting coal. We call such a plant a "mine mouth," because it depends on a single mine for coal. If alternative sources of coal for the generating plant are some distance away, the transportation cost makes those sources more costly. Then the utility's location becomes a specific asset, so bargaining power with the nearby mine is not strong and the mine may behave opportunistically. Professor Paul Joskow studied the contracts for coal that were agreed upon by utilities in a range of situations. He expected that mine-mouth utilities would enter into longer-term contracts with the mines near them to reduce their exposure to opportunistic behavior, especially when alternative sources of coal were far away. He found the duration of contracts in such mine-mouth situations averaged 16 years longer than when alternative mine sources were available, indicating that the mine-mouth utilities were attempting to reduce transaction costs by negotiating longer contracts.

See Paul L. Joskow "Contract Duration and Relation-Specific Investments: Empirical Evidence from Coal Markets," *American Economic Review*, 1987, Vol. 77, pp. 168–185.

to do exactly what is in the best interest of the firm. A firm employing a lawyer, for example, may have difficulty evaluating her performance. As an alternative, the firm might obtain the services for each specific lawyering task as needed through the market. The market provides motivation for law firms to develop favorable reputations to attract clients, so using the market might reduce the motivational task. The firm can also arrange payments in the market for services just as they are needed, according to the specialties required and at the times they are needed, so the management problem can be easier. In these respects, using the market might be less costly than organizing the lawyering task within the firm.

A basic incentive problem, called the **principal-agent problem**, arises when one party (the principal) engages another (the agent) to perform a continuing task, and the principal cannot observe the agent's performance. For example, suppose you engage a farmer to manage a farm you own in another community some distance away. As one option, you may pay the farmer a fixed fee for working the farm. Alternatively, you may reward the farmer by grant of some fraction of the harvest (like a piece rate). A third arrangement would have the farmer pay you a fixed fee, or rental, for use of the farm, and you then allow the farmer to keep any profit from operating the farm. In this third case, the farmer would be the residual claimant to profit from the farm. As we move from the first to the third arrangement, note how the incentive for the farmer grows stronger and stronger.

Strength of incentive, however, is not the only consideration. In addition to the farmer's effort, the harvest depends on factors beyond the farmer's control—such as the weather—which you cannot evaluate well because you are so far away from the farm. Offering a fraction of the harvest, or making the farmer the residual claimant, forces the farmer to bear *risk*, due to uncertainties of the weather, and that can be unappealing to the farmer. You, the property owner, may actually be in a better position to bear such risk. Your desire to motivate the farmer, thus, conflicts with the ideal sharing of risk between you and the farmer.[4] An age-old solution to this incentive problem is the **share-cropping** formula, which is a compromise that compensates partly by granting the farmer a fixed payment and partly by granting the farmer a share in the harvest.[5]

These costs of motivating and monitoring employees within the firm are called **agency costs**, because they are costs that arise when a principal tries to control the actions of an agent. They may be higher or lower in cost than relying on contracts through the market. Striking just the right balance to obtain the best effect requires management effort, which involves agency cost that may extend to employee promotion decisions, health and retirement plans, and other aspects of organizational life. Whatever arrangement allows the firm to operate at lowest expected cost, where expected cost may take into account a wide range of possible outcomes, is best for the firm. At least it is best if the firm seeks to maximize its profit by operating efficiently.

4.2 THE GOAL OF THE FIRM

With few exceptions, profit is the presumed goal of a business firm. Profit is not perfectly precise, however, because time plays a role. When is profit actually reported? A firm may pursue short-run profit at the expense of greater profit later or it may sacrifice short-run profit to obtain greater profit later. Merely by observing a firm's policies one may have difficulty telling whether the firm is maximizing profit. We begin by discussing the profit incentive, then the time element, and, finally, we show how thumb rules may actually maximize profit.

Profit Incentives

Private firms ordinarily seek profit. Admittedly, a range of nonprofit organizations exists, where profit seeking is not a primary goal. Some of these organizations—such as the National Science Foundation, which pursues research—are clearly not profit-seeking. Others are concerned with profit but, as nonprofit corporations, are limited in the amount they can retain. An example of a nonprofit corporation is the RAND Corporation, which performs research for hire. We may also question whether some regulated firms seek maximum profit, insofar as they are limited in the amount of profit they can earn. Regulatory profit limitation can sap their motivation because it disallows added profit from added effort.

---

[4] Because high risk may make incentive payments less appealing to agents, one might expect to find a negative correlation between risk and incentive payments. As Prendergast (1999, 2000, 2002) has shown, the evidence is ambiguous. She points to other influences that complicate the trade-off, such as complexity in situations that require the agent to respond with discretion to developments as they occur.

[5] Garrett and Xu (2003) provide evidence supporting the efficiency of share cropping relative to owner-operated farms and rented farms.

If a private firm does not maximize profit, it may not survive against competitors in its product market who do. Other firms will be able to offer better services or lower prices. To succeed, the firm must satisfy not only customers but also shareholders. Capital markets are competitive, so pressure from shareholders is ever present. Even if a firm has no competitor in its product market, its owners may turn out its management if the management does not generate as much profit as its monopoly market situation allows. Or an investor, called a *raider*, may take a sufficient financial interest in the company to throw out the existing management and install new, profit maximizing management, so shares will increase in value and the raider can sell them for considerable profit.

Because managers can keep their jobs by successfully maximizing profit, we can expect firms to maximize profit. Profit maximization requires cost minimization, which includes the minimization of transaction costs as well as operating costs, and thus influences the shape of the firm. Now there are practical reasons for questioning whether profit is really the firm's goal. Remember that the principal has to motivate an agent to do its bidding and that motivational problem exists in any business firm. The hierarchy of the firm, and who actually controls it, can influence its incentive structure and determine how effectively it pursues profit.

Owners of corporations are concerned about motivating their top managers, who in turn want to motivate those below them. That is one reason why the compensation of top executives often includes profit-sharing elements. Moreover, executives are often granted shares in ownership directly, on favorable terms, or granted stock options that allow them to purchase shares profitably when they rise in value. Such incentive arrangements are intended to bring executives' objectives more into line with those of the shareholders. Remember that, throughout the organization, this problem of motivation is part of the general trade-off between carrying out operations within the firm and relying on the market through outside contracts. Investors are interested in profit, and shareholders—through boards of directors—try to motivate management to deliver it.

The Long Run

Even if corporations are motivated to maximize profit, a time element can rob that goal of some of its clarity. To repeat, Does the firm maximize profit in this immediate, or short-run, accounting period? Or does it pursue maximum profit over a longer time period? Although firms need short-run profit maximizing in many narrow circumstances, it is the long run that determines the firm's survival and success. Indeed, the broad or long-run aim is generally to maximize the present value of all the firm's future earnings.

Two streams of payments that extend into the future can be hard to compare, to decide which is greater. The **present value** of a stream of payments is the amount that stream is worth right now. One advantage of the present value is that, as a single number, it allows comparison of two (or more) streams. To calculate present value, however, requires a discount rate at which to trade-off present and future payments.

To illustrate, suppose you are promised $110 to be received one year from today. The present value of that promise depends on the **discount rate**, the rate you could earn in alternative uses of your funds. If that rate is 10 percent, the present value (PV) of that promise of $110 a year from today is $100:

$$PV = \$110/(1 + 0.10) = \$100,$$

or generally, with X, the payment next year, and d, the discount rate, $PV = X/(1 + d)$. It may seem more straightforward to determine the future value (FV) one year from now of $100 today, which is obtained by reversing the calculation:

$$FV = \$100(1 + 0.10) = \$110.$$

Analysis of present value can help the firm choose its investment projects. For example, if $100 invested in a project today returns $120 in one year, *and if the appropriate discount rate is 10 percent* (suppose the best alternative investment earns 10 percent), one does better investing in the project. With a discount rate of 10 percent, $120 one year from now has a present value of $120/1.1 = $109.1, which exceeds $100.

Essentially, the value of a corporation in the stock market is the present value of all its future dividends. Some estimate of earnings—and some discount rate—is thus implicit in the valuation of stock shares. Uncertainty about outcomes makes evaluation of long-term management decisions difficult. It is another reason why the share values of the firm are used as a measure of the success of the firm, because investors are always judging the present value of the firm's future earnings.

Rules of Thumb and Satisficing

Even if any of us could know all details of how a large organization functions, writing them down would be hard. That complexity is one reason large organizations may employ a host of simple rules in their decision making. Such thumb rules can allow more senior managers to retain responsibility for more important decisions. Repetitive decisions can be made efficiently by well-chosen rules of thumb, which permit decentralized decisions according to rules that are chosen at higher levels in the organization. The rules can be quite general, in which case they would be called policies.

By observing a firm, one cannot easily tell whether it is maximizing profit. Firms may appear to set prices for groups of products to meet profit goals, for example, rather than to maximize profit. There is evidence from observations of firms and interviews with managers that firms often set markups over cost as a basis for prices.[6] Many other studies have fashioned rules of thumb from observation of actual decisions, involving such actions as department store pricing and even portfolio management, with quite remarkable predictive success.[7] That is, computer programs built around rules of

---

[6] See Hall and Hitch (1939), Kaplan, Dirlam, and Lanzillotti (1958), Lanzillotti (1958), and Kahn (1959).
[7] See Cyert and March (1963).

thumb reproduced with great accuracy the behavior of the observed deciders. Such procedures can be consistent with profit maximization, however, because they still allow the policies that are implicit in the decision mechanisms—such as a price markup—to be altered with circumstances in profit maximizing ways. The important point is that the policies can be decided at higher levels in an organization.

The late Nobel laureate Herbert Simon described a process he called **satisficing**, in which a decision maker in a large organization worked in turn on different goals. The goals might be effected through rules of thumb, such as pricing markups, as well as through a variety of related actions. When one prescribed goal was met, rather than pursue it further the decider turned to focus on another goal. Simon described accepting a goal, rather than continuing to maximize, as *satisficing*. The decider would continue by satisficing in that fashion from goal to goal, returning in time to the first goal, only to repeat the cycle of attending to the entire set of goals. Not only was performance improved in pursuit of the goals, but goals would also be adjusted, in consultation with higher management and based on success achieved previously. All of these activities may be performed better as a firm matures, and that can improve its life expectancy.[8]

4.3 | CORPORATE FINANCE

Incentive problems extend even to the financing of a corporation because the method of financing influences its governance. **Corporate governance** is the means by which corporations and their managers are governed. As Chapter 1 reported, some seventeenth century business organizations that were based on shareholder ownership—the joint stock companies—were badly governed, and as a consequence their shareholder owners suffered financial losses. The managers of these companies did not serve the owners faithfully.

Despite its inauspicious beginning, the corporate form of organization is now in widespread use, owing to a combination of factors, and taking slightly different forms in different countries. Information is more widely available now and it can be certified for reliability, security dealers are well informed, and exchanges where shares are traded are well organized. The process is not perfect. In 2001, the seventh largest company in the United States, Enron, declared bankruptcy and saw its once $85 shares fall below $1 in value. Complicated accounting practices, which were not discovered by certifying accountants, were implicated in the firm's demise.[9] Today, regulations also circumscribe the behavior of securities dealers and exchanges, and of corporations as well, although not perfectly. The suppliers of capital to modern day corporations—mainly shareholders, bondholders, and other creditors—also have differing interests. Because managers may have their own aims, conflict is always possible.

---

[8] For evidence on firm prospects and changes with age, see Carroll and Hannan (2000).

[9] See, for example, Floyd Norris, "Companies Are Warned About Rosy Numbers," *New York Times*, December 5, 2001, p. C1.

Shareholders and Bondholders

Corporations are owned by **shareholders**. Their ownership right, or what they own after accounting for the corporation's debt obligations, is called their **equity** in the firm. Shareholders, also called stockholders, hold shares of *stock* issued by the corporation. In addition to capital supplied by shareholders, corporations raise additional capital by selling *bonds*. Those who hold bonds, the **bondholders**, are owed the value of the bond and are usually paid a fixed interest rate for this capital they have provided to the corporation. The mixture of shareholder equity and bond debt make up the **capital structure** of the corporation. Others besides bondholders and shareholders, including employees and managers, suppliers and customers, and retirees (who may depend on company profits for pension income), have a stake in a corporation. Substantial change has occurred in relations among some of these parties in the last few decades.[10]

Bonds exist because the less daring among potential investors are willing to invest only if they have to bear little risk. The bond is a low-risk investment vehicle that tempts these more timid souls to join the ranks of investors. Bonds offer lower risk because they promise first priority to interest payments out of earnings, before any dividends can be paid to shareholders. The interest payments are fixed, however, and they do not increase further when times are very good. Bondholders have first claim to assets, too, in the event of corporate bankruptcy. A side effect of making such a lower risk offer to bondholders is that the offer increases the risk in common stock shares. If the capital structure includes bonds, a fixed payment must always be made first to bondholders, and, as earnings fluctuate, the residual earnings left over for shareholders fluctuates even more. Shareholders can thus expect to receive higher returns after debt is issued, but only as long as the average return on assets is greater than the interest rate paid to bondholders.

Through their boards of directors, the shareholder-owners try to reconcile the differing views of major players in a corporation. For instance, bondholders are naturally concerned that a change in policy would greatly increase the firm's debt, because that would increase the chance of bankruptcy. In addition to protecting bondholders by assigning them priority claim to assets, boards of directors often agree to **bond covenants**, such as a limit on the fraction of debt to be allowed in the capital structure of the firm, to help protect the position of the already existing bondholders. These assurances to bondholders can also benefit the owners, by helping to keep low the interest rate to be paid on the bonds. Such covenants can even lower the cost of borrowing from banks, which have similar concerns. Boards of directors also want to motivate managers so they will serve the shareholders' interests. To do so they design management incentive contracts that often include stock options, which give managers the right to an equity interest in the firm and tie their fate to that of the corporation's equity shareholders.[11]

---

[10] Important differences in the corporate form and its constraints exist across countries. For description and analysis of differences between U.S. and European corporations, see Lynch-Fannon (2003).

[11] The financial ownership interest of management grew more substantial as the twentieth century drew to a close and was presumably intended to align management incentives with the goals of other shareholders.

The ratio of debt in the capital structure (debt divided by the total of debt plus equity) is called **leverage**. This name reflects the fact that shareholders can earn greater average returns by *leveraging* their investments through the use of debt. There is leverage in that the same equity investment of shareholders can support greater investment when bonds are added to the capital structure, because bonds can lower the capital needed from shareholders. On the smaller capital investment by shareholders, the average return is higher, because the return earned on the capital supplied by bond sales usually exceeds the payment made to the bondholders, which allows added profit to shareholders. If the return earned on capital is lower than the interest payment to bondholders, however, the shareholders are worse off than if there was no debt. When the leverage is very great, and bonds provide much of the firm's capital, that leaves little margin for error. The shareholders can make a higher return, on average, than is required to cover the low-risk interest payments they make to bondholders. Yet they also bear greater risk of low (and even negative) returns as leverage is higher, because the fixed burden of bond interest payments becomes so large.

The corporation's capital structure can also affect management incentives within the firm.[12] Consider a manager who owns 100 percent of a firm that has absolutely no debt.[13] The manager is the residual claimant for profit and so has every incentive to put forth effort. Suppose the firm needs more capital and the manager sells shares until he owns only 50 percent of the firm. This restructuring weakens his incentive. One half of whatever benefit his effort produces must be shared now with other owners. If the firm issues bonds instead of shares, on the other hand, and their quantity is not great, the manager remains the 100 percent residual claimant on profit. So the manager continues to render full effort. If debt is increased further, however, a point may be reached where the manager will consider very risky investments. If the investments succeed, with great leverage, he will make a fortune. If the investments fail, the bondholders will be big losers.

The Valuation of Shares in the Capital Market

Determinants of corporations' share values have been explained only in the past 40 or 50 years.[14] The central idea is that the value of one firm's shares is affected by how those shares move relative to all other shares in the stock market, because investors consider each share based on how well it fits into a portfolio with other shares.[15] Investors are averse to risk, so they like shares that, when combined with others, tend to lower the overall risk of their portfolios.

To take advantage of the valuation principles, separate single-product firms need not be merged together into conglomerate firms. The effect that a particular

---

[12] See Hart (2001).

[13] For early treatments of this incentive problem in the firm, see McEachern (1975) and Jensen and Mechling (1976).

[14] For one of the classic statements of the valuation process, see Nobel laureate William F. Sharpe (1965). See also Richard A. Brealey (1969) for a very clear exposition.

[15] Shleifer (2000) describes other influences on share valuations in real markets based on behavioral patterns.

BOX 4.2 Valuation in the Stock Market

Economist Jan Mossin described the principles of stock valuation this way: "Loosely speaking, a rain-wear manufacturer is worth relatively more if everybody else produces ice cream and suntan lotion." When ice cream makers and suntan lotion makers have bad times—that is, when it rains—the rain-wear manufacturer does well. By the same token, when the sun shines the rain-wear manufacturer does not do so well, but shares in ice cream and suntan lotion companies carry the portfolio. So the overall portfolio containing all three producers has a more stable earnings stream.

See J. Mossin, "Security Pricing and Investment Criteria in Competitive Markets," *American Economic Review*, 1969, Vol. 59, pp. 753–763.

firm's shares may have on a portfolio's value is already an influence on that firm's value because of the way shares are valued in stock markets. On the other hand, to the extent it lowers their bankruptcy risk, bondholders may welcome the formation of multi-product firms with diversified earnings to protect the bonds. Managers may also prefer to manage a portfolio of firms—as in a single conglomerate firm—because the profit stream fluctuates less. With a smooth profit stream, the manager is less likely to suffer a bad year.[16] This potential conflict in organizational incentives raises the question, Who is in control of the firm?

4.4 | HIERARCHIES AND CONTROL

Business firms are organized into units that can be arrayed in *hierarchies*, or in a defined chain of command. The Board of Directors is above the President, for example, who in turn is above Vice Presidents, perhaps of functional areas such as Sales, Manufacturing, and Finance. This ordering gives those higher in the organization nominal control over those who are lower. One advantage of such an organization is that important information can be passed up through successively higher (and, with subsidiary units included, larger) units of the organization, thereby allowing coordinated decisions that can reflect effects across the subsidiary units. The Vice Presidents of Sales, Manufacturing, and Finance pass information to the President to allow a coordinated decision that affects the entire firm. Organizing around functions such as sales, manufacturing, and finance leads to what is called a functional organization, but that is not the only way to organize a business firm.

An alternative organizational form is the multidivisional organization, called the **M-form**, in which each broad division is responsible for a different product or service. The functional form of organization was common among large firms early in the twentieth century, but it gradually gave way to the M-form of organization as firms grew

---

[16] There is evidence that managers of firms operating in more than one industry were paid 12 to 14 percent more compared with firms in single industries, but because the job required better managers, not because managers were entrenched. See Rose and Shepard (1997).

larger and engaged in a wider range of activities.[17] The M-form has the advantage that top management can delegate responsibility for profit to divisions, thereby opening opportunities for incentives and for performance evaluation, whereas in the functional form the contributions of the separate functional divisions to profit are difficult to infer.

Ownership and Control

From the joint stock company experience of almost three centuries ago, the question arises whether owners and those higher in an organization can actually control those that are lower.[18] In 1932, Adolph Berle and Gardiner Means alleged that ownership of increasingly large corporations was being separated from control.[19] They argued that owners were no longer running corporations, at least not the way the owners ran partnerships and sole proprietorships, largely because there was no small block of owners of large corporations who could get together easily to control the managers. Ownership was dispersed through many small shareholdings, inviting **free-rider** behavior as each shareholder counted on others to watch over management.

Partnerships and proprietorships lack the limited liability feature of corporations. Owners of partnerships and proprietorships are consequently responsible for losses even beyond their investment in the firm, and that responsibility helps to keep owners attending to business. They are motivated by the possibility they may lose all they own, which could go well beyond their investments in their firms to include their homes and other property. In corporations, on the other hand, without owners in control, hired managers might serve their own interests, which are not entirely consistent with the shareholders' interests. As a consequence, corporations might be less efficient. This concern is greater in cases where firms possess market power, which can give managers more discretion in how they operate the firms.

A wide range of organizational possibilities exists at the top management level of corporations, and some may be more effective than others in preserving shareholder control. The least shareholder control might follow when (1) there is no large shareholder and (2) top managers of the firm also fill a majority of the seats on the board of directors. These so-called inside boards pass considerable control to managers and have been discouraged by stock exchanges and regulators. Such boards might agree too readily to excessive management compensation packages, for example, that do not tie executive pay to firm performance effectively.

Takeovers

There are limits to what managers of a corporation can do without the owners' support. The board of directors, whose members often have substantial investments in the corporation, formally represent the shareholders. These directors can be expected

---

[17] See Chandler (1962).

[18] For description of modern high-stakes, capital-market thievery and its pursuit, see Stewart (1991).

[19] See Berle and Means (1932).

to act—perhaps by replacing the chief executive officer (CEO), for example—if the corporation's performance is poor. When the directors include officers of the firm, they may resist such action. Remember, however, that the shares in a corporation are transferable—they can be bought and sold. This means that any observer with resources—not necessarily a current director—who thinks the firm can be made more profitable can organize a raid. The raider buys a large stake in the firm, organizes a takeover by winning board representation, and installs new management. If the judgment is correct, profitability improves, the value of shares in the corporation rise, and the purchased shares may be sold by the raider at a profit. Such transactions constitute the **market for corporate control**.

Attempting to gain control of a corporation can be very costly. Hence, a takeover is motivated only when the performance of the firm is substantially below what might be achieved, so a considerable profit improvement can be anticipated that more than covers the costs of the effort. The Williams Act, which guides takeovers at the federal level, together with state legislation, tends to add to that cost by delaying takeovers. Managements also have acted to make takeovers more difficult. A management will understandably try to convince shareholders that they are already well served and, indeed, that they will suffer if the corporation is taken over. Going further, the management may try to have voting rules adopted that will make a takeover more difficult. Management can require more than a simple majority to gain control, for example, a **super-majority** requirement, making a takeover effort to win shareholder approval more difficult.

Managements have used more colorful devices to resist takeovers. They have sometimes persuaded boards or shareholders to grant them high severance payments in the event of a takeover— payments called **golden parachutes**—which serve to discourage takeovers and at least reward managements in the event that takeovers succeed. Managements may also make shares of stock available at low prices only to original shareholders—not to the new, takeover, shareholders. Because it dilutes the value of the latter's shares, this is called the **poison-pill** defense against takeovers. Another strategy is to buy shares from the would be raider at a premium—a payment called **greenmail**—to deflect the takeover effort. Or the incumbent management may try to attract a more congenial partner, called a **white knight**, to take over the firm instead of the advancing raider. With so many strategies available to the incumbent management, taking over a poorly performing corporation is not an easy task.

These efforts by managements to resist takeovers all tend to lower the probability that a takeover will succeed. On the other hand, if the takeover does succeed in the presence of these defensive efforts, the returns to shareholders tend to be greater. If adopted by a firm, the major defensive maneuvers, such as super-majority requirements, greenmail, or poison-pill arrangements, tend to lower the price of the firm's shares. After they have been adopted, however, if a takeover nevertheless is successful, the average gain to shareholders appears to be greater. Such a consequence might be expected to follow because only the more attractive mergers can be pursued in the presence of such serious obstacles.

There appears to be growing dissatisfaction among shareholders with managements' resistance to takeovers. Many poison pills that were adopted 10 or 15 years ago are now expiring, and shareholders in some large companies are opposing their renewal. Shareholders have expressed opposition to poison pills for some time, noting their negative effects on share values, but managements have ignored them. Managements stress that the poison pill enables them to negotiate more effectively with a potential buyer, and they point to evidence that shareholder gains are greater in successful takeovers with poison pills in place. But, again, the barrier they represent may allow only the especially profitable mergers to occur.[20]

The mergers that do occur in these contested circumstances generally seem to improve efficiency in the economy. Returns to shareholders from mergers are positive. The returns are generally higher in the acquired firms than in the acquiring firms, which is to be expected because the firm that is acquired is the target that is sought after, sometimes by competing potential acquirers who essentially must bid against each other. Acquired firm shareholders gain from an increase in stock price, running roughly 15 to 35 percent and tending to be higher for firms acquired through takeovers.[21] Again, returns to acquiring firms are much smaller. Indeed, from small positive returns of about 4 percent in the 1960s, returns tended to fall over time and became small or slightly negative in the 1980s and 1990s.[22]

Firms may be refinanced so that managers formally become owners of the firm, and then they can legitimately exercise control. In these so called **"going-private"** transactions, the management of the firm buys a controlling interest, which is why we call such transactions **management buyouts**, or **MBOs**. When the funds for such transactions are raised by issuing debt, we call such deals **leveraged buyouts**, or **LBOs**. LBO transactions may involve others besides the managers. These MBO and LBO transactions were especially common in the 1980s. The bonds used to finance them, which carried unusually high risk and paid unusually high interest rates, especially for LBOs, were called **junk bonds**. Such buyouts obviously can align the manager and owner interests, because managers become owners, and the increased incentive for management in such arrangements often seems to have improved performance.[23] In "going private" reorganizations, the returns to shareholders tend to be even higher than in takeovers. But this is not always true, and shareholders sometimes resist the change in ownership.[24]

A corporation organized in the M-form may offer advantages in disciplining management. The divisions, being devoted to separate outputs and having independent profit responsibility, are like corporations except they do not issue their own shares. Instead of the capital market, they have top management overseeing them and, if necessary, disciplining them. This evaluation and correction activity may possi-

---

[20] The Chubb Corporation defied a shareholder vote to remove their poison pill arrangement. See Joseph B. Treaster, "Seeking the Death of the Poison Pill," *New York Times*, May 9, 1999.

[21] See Romano (1992).

[22] See Ravenscraft and Scherer (1987c) and Andrade, Mitchell, and Stafford (2001).

[23] See Marais, Schipper, and Smith (1989).

[24] See Dennis K. Berman and Sarah McBride, "Clear Channel Showdown Signals Investor Wariness of Private Buyouts," *Wall Street Journal*, January 27, 2007, p. A1.

bly be performed better within the firm, through the M-form of organization, than in the market, through takeovers.[25]

Corporate Governance

High-level decisions in a business firm require sound information. Business decisions often depend on marginal or average cost, for example, which must be estimated properly if the decisions are to be sound. As for the organization's behavior, how employees perform has to be measured so the employees can be accorded proper compensation to motivate them. Performance has to be monitored even at the highest reaches of the organization, to insure that the organization meets its goals. Top managers have an advantage over their monitors, however, because they control the information that is available about their performance. *Corporate governance* is the broad subject of how owners control levels of organization in a firm to achieve firm goals.

Aligning incentives so they motivate achievement of goals is part of corporate governance. **Stock options** may be used to compensate top executives of a firm, for example. A stock option allows its holder to buy shares of stock at a price that is usually set below market value, called the strike price. A fall in share value keeps the option from having any value at all, while an increase in share value gives the stock option the value of a share less the strike price. Top executives who have options may want short-term gains in stock value, so they can cash the stock options, even when such gains may not serve the long-run interests of the shareholders.

Compensating executives through the award of stock options grew handsomely in the 1990s, in part because—under accounting rules—the options were not regarded as an expense at the time they were issued, so they seemed like a low-cost way to compensate executives. Stock options were treated as an expense only when they are exercised, or cashed in, which might come some time after they are issued. Apparently, however, top executives may have promoted extensive use of stock options for their own benefit. Indeed, firms that allocated a greater fraction of stock options to their top executives performed worse through the 1990s than firms that distributed them more widely through the firm.[26]

The typical ownership structure of firms has changed in the past 30 years. Before the 1980s, managers served their corporations loyally, but not their shareholders in particular, and the market for corporate control was not well developed.[27] Managers were often directors of their companies, and they sat in on board meetings. International competition was not as strong and markets were not as global as they are today. Excess capacity existed in many industries by the 1980s and managers had

---

[25] See Williamson (1985).

[26] See Blasi, Kruse, and Bernstein (2003). Among other things, they show that of all options that were awarded in firms, the fraction to the top five executives was inversely related to shareholder returns.

[27] See Ravenscraft and Scherer (1987b, 1987c) and Jensen (1988, 1993).

BOX 4.3 The Stock Options Scandal

In 2006, some results of a broad investigation into the timing of stock option grants came to light. The Securities and Exchange Commission and many state regulators questioned more than 120 companies about whether they had "backdated" their grants of stock options to executives, actually granting them today, for instance, but claiming they were granted, say, two weeks earlier when the stock value was 10 percent lower. When recipients exercise their option grants they usually purchase them at the price as of the day the options were granted and sell them at the later market price, so backdating to a low-price date means greater gain. It is an entirely risk-free gain, because the rise in price since the backdated time has already occurred. Backdating makes options less a motivational device and more a way to pass extra money to executives that observers may not notice.

To be legal, backdating must not involve any forged document and must be disclosed to shareholders, because they pay the added compensation that backdating gives executives. Extra money received by recipients of the options is a company expense, and the company's accounting must reflect that fact. The Sarbanes-Oxley Act of 2002 required that stock options be reported to the SEC within two days after they are granted, and this has reduced the problem. Good news, however, can be issued by the firm after options are awarded to achieve a similar effect.

See R. A. Heron and E. Lie, "Does Backdating Explain the Stock Price Pattern Around Executive Stock Option Grants?" *Journal of Financial Economics,* 2007, Vol. 83, pp. 271–295, and S. Saul, "Study Finds Backdating of Options Widespread," *New York Times,* July 17, 2006, p. C1.

not acted to correct resulting problems, sometimes subsidizing losing activities with profitable ones, and corporate governance was "soft" on managers.[28] For example, proxy fights, in which some shareholders try to win the support of enough others to force change, were rare, and raiders seldom attempted takeovers. Incentives for management were not closely tied to shareholder interests, either.[29] Equity-based compensation still accounted for less than 20 percent of executive income going into the 1980s, but it grew to exceed 50 percent by 1994. Stock options were granted to 30 percent of CEOs in 1980, and grew to 70 percent in 1994.

The shape of the shareholder population also changed by the end of the twentieth century. The fraction of shares held by institutional investors—such as pension funds and mutual funds that manage investment portfolios—increased from under 30 percent in 1980 to over 50 percent in 1996,[30] while ownership of shares by individuals dropped from 60 percent to 48 percent.[31] After many years of passive behavior, these fund managers withdrew their loyalty to incumbent managers and became

---

[28] Conglomerates seemed especially guilty of management slackness, and part of the restructuring that occurred in the 1980s returned firms to narrower and more specialized goals.

[29] See Hall and Liebman (1998).

[30] See Gompers and Metrick (2001).

[31] See Poterba and Samwick (1996).

aggressive in seeking returns. They controlled the large blocks of shares needed for takeovers, which they could facilitate, either by helping directly through share commitments to raiders or by selling blocks of shares.[32] These conditions in the 1990s may have prompted restructurings and consequent changes in incentives, and their effects appear to be lasting.

The 1990s did not see as many hostile takeovers as the 1980s did. Large institutional investors began to require returns that exceeded the costs of capital, though, and they monitored its achievement. Management incentives were based much more on how well they benefitted shareholders than had been true in earlier decades. Stock options had this effect because they allowed managers to buy stock on favorable terms when it rose in value,[33] although they did not punish poor performance as much as real stock ownership would. The incentives of directors were also aligned more directly with goals of shareholder owners.[34] Corporations became more decentralized and more willing to use markets rather than internal operations when warranted by profit opportunities. New sources of venture capital sprang up to support new companies with new ideas.[35] External capital markets were playing a more important role in investment allocation, leaving less discretion to managers and a greater role for investors.

As residual claimants, shareholders have created strong incentives for boards of directors and managers, through such devices as compensation in the form of stock options. Despite efforts of the organization that sets U.S. accounting standards, the Financial Accounting Standards Board (F.A.S.B.), to count stock options as an expense when they are awarded, they had seldom been regarded as an expense until 2004.[36] This nonexpense status encouraged their abundant use. Stock options may in some cases have given managers short-sighted financial goals, because they reward an *increase* in the stock price. Managers may also have awarded themselves stock options just before announcing good news for their company, thus insuring themselves handsome gains.[37] In the 1990s, Congress eased reporting requirements by corporations and weakened their accountability by making officers less liable for overly optimistic earnings forecasts and by making it harder for shareholders to bring lawsuits.

As the twenty-first century opened, there was growing concern that pressure to produce increasing earnings may have tempted top managers and accountants to skirt the rules of sound reporting, and to report misleading results. The year 2001 saw an increase in large-firm bankruptcies, and in 2002 the record was worse. Auditors check the correctness of publicly disseminated facts about firms, and the **Securities**

---

[32] See Donaldson (1994) and Holmstrom and Kaplan (2001).

[33] See Hall and Liebman (1998, 2000).

[34] See Perry (2000).

[35] See Gompers and Lerner (2001).

[36] In March 2004, the Financial Accounting Standards Board proposed that companies report the value of stock options as an expense when they are awarded, which may significantly reduce reported profit at many companies. See Floyd Norris, "Accounting Board Wants Options to be Reported as an Expense," *New York Times*, April 1, 2004, p. C1.

[37] See Gretchen Morgenson, "In the Timing of Options, Many, Um, Coincidences," *New York Times*, December 5, 2004, Sec. 3, p. 1.

and Exchange Commission (SEC), the federal agency that oversees corporation financing, requires audits of publicly owned corporations. The accountant is to tell whether the firm complies with *generally accepted accounting practices* and thus to insure that its reports reveal its true financial condition. The reliability of this auditing process has been questioned after recent failures, such as the collapse of Enron in 2001 and WorldCom in 2002. Such failures happened in part because of misleading asset valuations and earnings reports.

What guidelines do the independent accountants follow? Two important panels set standards for accounting practices. There is an **International Accounting Standards Board (IASB)**, which many countries follow to make their accounting practices sound and consistent. The United States has its own **Financial Accounting Standards Board (FASB)**, which maintains a body of **generally accepted accounting principles (GAAP)** that accountants are to follow throughout the country. The Securities and Exchange Commission requires corporations to submit to independent audits that follow FASB practices if they issue shares to the public. This means that to be listed on the New York Stock Exchange, an international company has to reconcile accounts for the two different systems.

In 2002 Congress passed the Sarbanes-Oxley Act[38] in response to large bankruptcies at the start of the twenty-first century, such as those of Enron and Worldcom. The Act increased many penalties for executive criminal behavior and fraud. One of the Act's provisions also created a new **Public Company Oversight Board**, to oversee the accounting profession. This Board would be able to evaluate the effect of generally accepted accounting practices and FASB accounting standards. It could also insure that the incentives faced by accounting firms would not lead to deceptive information about corporations' financial health.

Suppose a stockholding senior executive, who knows the facts about the firm, buys or sells stock based on that information. Current law makes it a felony for the executive to trade on such **insider information**, that is, on information not available to the general public. This law is enforced by requiring the reporting of trades by insiders of the firm. Until the Sarbanes-Oxley Act, such reports did not arrive until about a month after the trade, which was often too late to evaluate the action.[39] The Sarbanes-Oxley Act calls for faster reporting of trades by insiders to make such information available within a few days.

Although some steps have been taken to improve the reliability of the information corporations report, problems still exist. Obtaining transparency at the top, so facts about the financial performance of the corporation are visible, is difficult when managements may see strategic advantage in controlling such information. There is evidence, however, that firms with better governance structures, which preserve more rights for shareholders, perform better. From rules of governance across about 1,500 firms in the 1990s, economists Gompers, Ishii, and Metrick (2003) formed an index of governance soundness, and they found that firms with better governance rules were

---

[38] See Sarbanes-Oxley Act of 2002, PL 107–204. 116 Stat. 745 (HR 3763, July 30, 2002).

[39] See Floyd Norris, "S.E.C. Seeks Tighter Curbs On Insiders," *New York Times*, April 12, 2002, p. C1.

more profitable, more valuable, had higher sales growth, and made fewer acquisitions. Acquisitions can complicate governance because, as the organization of the firm grows more complicated, reports are harder to decipher. The next two sections, on mergers and vertical relationships, consider further influences on the shape of the firm, influences that usually complicate the organization.[40]

4.5   CORPORATE MERGERS

This chapter began by noting how the boundaries of a firm are set by a trade-off, a choice between minimizing the transaction costs of either using outside markets or motivating and monitoring employees within the firm. We then looked at incentives, financial instruments, organizational hierarchies, and control, including the market for corporate control and takeovers. We now turn to consider in more detail the most dramatic way the shape of the firm can be changed—bringing formerly separate firms together in a merger.

The technology that influences firms' sizes and shapes may change, and when that happens firms can adapt most quickly through merger. Firms usually grow as their market opportunities grow, and those opportunities may be influenced by the firm's technical, sales, or other skills. But circumstances change, tastes change, and technologies change. Firms may feel the need to alter their shapes as a consequence, usually by merging with another firm to become larger. And the market for corporate control can also play a role, in that stock values matter. Acquiring another firm by merger is more attractive to a corporation when its own stock value is high, because more assets can then be acquired for each share in the acquiring firm's stock. A firm may also spin off a unit and become smaller.

Merger joins two firms into one, typically for the purpose of enhancing their effectiveness. Firms may join together to improve efficiency and lower cost, or for market power to raise price and improve profit, or possibly for other purposes. Mergers are usually placed in one of the three categories: horizontal mergers, vertical mergers, and conglomerate mergers.[41] This section examines horizontal and conglomerate mergers. Special features of vertical relationships include not only merger, called *vertical integration*, but also *vertical restraints*, which are contractual, and other arrangements to deal with special problems that can arise on the way from raw materials to final products. These special features of vertical relationships are taken up in the following section.

Some of the main motives for merging are explored first. Because antitrust authorities review large mergers before they are carried out to assess whether the

---

[40] For analysis of firm size and shape over the life cycle of a competitive industry, see Jovanovic and McDonald (1994a, 1994b).

[41] An additional category, called *diagonal* merger, has been analyzed by Higgins (1997). Diagonal mergers blend horizontal and vertical elements. For example, suppose two markets have interrelated, say substitute, demands, and one uses an input from an upstream industry. If a firm in this upstream industry merges with a firm in the industry that does *not* use its input, that would seem harmless. The merged firm may, however, through influence on the price of the input, harm the substitute industry and benefit itself.

merger will raise or lower welfare, we also examine horizontal and conglomerate mergers to emphasize the forms of market power they may achieve.

General Motives for Mergers and Acquisitions

Here we explore five of the most important reasons for corporate mergers: (1) improved efficiency, (2) enhanced market power, (3) advantageous financial or tax effects, (4) management self interest, and (5) shareholder self interest. While all of these motives may play some role in mergers, the search for improved efficiency seems to be the strongest.

1. **Efficiency.** Combining resources of two firms in a merger may lower costs, improve quality, or lead to new products or new ways to distribute products to consumers. Possible economies of scale can motivate the merger of firms with similar activities to lower costs. Economies of producing more than one product in a single organization can also invite mergers that can improve efficiency. Selling complementary products together can save consumer effort and yield an *economy of scope in consumption* when it saves consumers' time or adds to their pleasure. Vertical relationships, as between a manufacturer and the retailer of its product, may result in greater profit opportunities when the firms are combined than when they are separate.

   Many studies have focused on how merger announcements change the values of stock shares in the merging firms, and they reveal the expectations that investors have about the mergers. The studies tend to show returns almost as handsome as in takeover cases: shareholders of *acquired* firms enjoy over 20 percent premiums, and shareholders of *acquiring* firms receive small or negative returns.[42] There is also some evidence that such stock market evaluations of mergers serve to predict the ultimate effects of the mergers reasonably well.[43] On the whole, these results suggest that mergers improve efficiency.

2. **Market Power.** Market power can be based legitimately on patented ideas, prime retail locations, or otherwise superior products or services, which can all be reasonable influences on firms' decisions. A desire for increased market power can also inspire mergers. In the most obvious example, two firms in the same market merge to gain more control of the market through a larger combined market share. Or two firms may integrate vertically so one can gain a more reliable source of supply while withholding that supply from competitors. Antitrust authorities search for these and other possible anticompetitive effects before allowing large mergers to occur.

---

[42] See Andrade, Mitchell, and Stafford (2001).
[43] See Sirower and O'Byrne (1998).

To explore possible market-power effects, studies of how firm share values change upon merger announcements have included firms not involved in the merger. In its simplest form, the idea is that if values of nonmerging firms in the industry go down, the merger brings efficiencies that challenge rivals. On the other hand, if the values of nonmerging firms go up, the merger may increase market power, because the merged firm can raise price and that helps rivals. Effects of the announcement of antitrust opposition to a merger were studied in the same way. Economist Laurence Schumann has argued that effects on values of merging firms relative to nonmerging firms can implicate both efficiency and market power and so cannot resolve which cause is more important.[44]

3. **Financial or Tax Effects.** We might expect a financial benefit from joining unrelated firms into a conglomerate, because doing so adds diversification to reduce risk. Profit outcomes from several firms should contain less risk than the profit outcome from a single firm, because of the pooling, or diversification, that occurs with the sample of several firms, especially when their activities are somewhat independent of one another. The result is a lower risk of bankruptcy, so a conglomerate merger might save costs related to bankruptcy or allow greater use of debt in the firm's capital structure. Except for this possible reduction in the cost of bankruptcy, however, investors in the capital market do not generally gain

---

BOX 4.4 Some Mergers Increase Market Power

Two horizontal mergers that were opposed by the Federal Trade Commission after they were completed show increased market power through postmerger price increases. The mergers involved the Xidex Corporation, which produced two special forms of microfilm—diazo and vesicular. The microfilm products were sufficiently homogeneous to imply constant price ratios across the products. These price ratios allowed detection of price changes after Xidex merged, first with diazo producer Scott Graphics in 1976, and then with vesicular producer Kalvar Corporation in 1979. Both mergers increased the Xidex market share by 10 percent or more, and prices increased significantly after both mergers. Indeed, prices increased by enough to pay the merger costs in a period of only two years. Another study of mergers isolated price effects of mergers in cement, titanium oxide, and corrugated paperboard markets. Prices fell after the cement merger, probably from efficiencies achieved together with competitive forces, but prices rose after mergers in the other two industries. So when we can observe price effects, we can see that horizontal mergers that substantially increase market share seem to bring higher prices.

See D. M. Barton and R. Sherman, "The Price and Profit Effect of Horizontal Merger: A Case Study," *Journal of Industrial Economics,* December 1984, Vol. 33, pp. 165–187, and L. Schumann, R. P. Rogers, and J. D. Reitzes, *Case Studies of the Price Effects of Horizontal Mergers,* Washington, D.C.: Federal Trade Commission Bureau of Economics, 1992.

---

[44] See Schumann (1993).

when a conglomerate forms. They already have the opportunity to combine stock shares into investment portfolios to reduce risk and even to cushion the consequence to them of a rare bankruptcy.

Firm growth can offer a tax benefit to shareholders if the growth leads to increased share values rather than increased dividends when the tax on capital gains is lower than the tax on ordinary income, which has often been the case. **Capital gains** are gains on assets sold at a profit. The gain on the capital asset is the difference between the sale price and the purchase price. So by purchasing stock that then rises in value, holding it long enough to qualify for capital-gains tax treatment and selling it, you may pay a lower tax than you would if you only collected dividends. Most investors, then, regard more highly a firm that can arrange income in the form of capital gain.[45] Firms seeking to merge, however, do not often make great improvements in capital values, so this tax reason is seldom relevant.[46]

4. **Management Self Interest.** Managers' interests may differ from stockholders' interests. Rather than lose their jobs, managers might resist takeovers, for instance, even when a takeover might serve shareholder interests. Managers may also prefer conglomerate organization, even when it has little benefit for shareholders, because diversification by a conglomerate allows managers to preside over a less risky enterprise, so they are less likely to have to explain poor overall earnings at a stockholders meeting. It is conceivable, however, that control of divisions within a conglomerate through an M-form organization can be more strict and more effective for shareholders than the discipline exercised by the capital market, in which case conglomerate organization can serve the interests of shareholders.

Firm growth can be a managerial goal that mergers may enhance. Managers seek the better reputations that go to those who can generate growth and are rewarded accordingly. Managers may pursue some mergers to better their own careers rather than to serve long-run shareholder interests,[47] but that is probably not a reason for very many mergers.

5. **Shareholder Self Interest.** Stakeholders of a firm include all parties that have an interest in its success—shareholders, bondholders and other creditors, employees and managers, suppliers and customers, retired former employees, and neighbors of the firm. By exercising initiative through their controlling position, the shareholders may pursue mergers to shift power in their favor. For instance, they may pursue a merger

---

[45] See Sherman (1972) and Stiglitz (1972), who show how conglomerates can redirect investments to growth areas and more readily offer capital-gain income.

[46] Forty years ago, if a firm lost money it could "carry over" the loss into later tax years, and this made some firms that accumulated very large tax losses valuable merger partners for profitable firms because their tax losses could be used to shield profits from tax. This motive is no longer important, however, because tax law has changed.

[47] See Morck, Shleifer, and Vishney (1990).

through financial means that allows higher returns to shareholders but increases the risk borne by those who hold the firm's debt or overturns what shareholders see as unfavorable labor contracts.[48] Evidence has shown that some harm to bondholders[49] and unionized workers[50] can come from mergers. The evidence from many other studies indicates, however, that expropriating power from stakeholders has not been an important motive for mergers.[51] This is not to say that shareholders are not self-interested. Indeed, beginning in the 1980s they became more aggressive in pursuing those interests, and the consequence was another kind of *merger wave*.

Mergers have tended to occur in clusters, or **merger waves**, stimulated when new technologies arrive, high stock values exist, government regulation changes, or new ways of organizing are found. The late Nobel laureate George Stigler (1950) saw the early wave of mergers around 1900 as mergers for monopoly, a refuge chosen by trusts that were the target of the Sherman Act.[52] He found that the cluster of mergers in the 1920s pursued not monopoly but oligopoly, that is, an industry containing a few large firms. These were waves of horizontal mergers. The 1960s witnessed a conglomerate merger wave, involving unrelated firms that were not in the same industries. Conglomerate mergers may have come in response to effective limitations on horizontal mergers from the Celler-Kefauver Act of 1950. The takeover was the noticeable merger form of the 1980s, and it flourished again in less hostile form in the late 1990s. The late 1990s saw another spurt of mergers, many with an international element. These mergers of the 1980s and 1990s were of a new kind that had strong financial incentives.[53]

Mergers in the 1980s involved takeovers and corporate restructuring more radical than in earlier decades.[54] Nearly half of all major U.S. corporations received takeover offers in the 1980s.[55] Use of debt greatly increased in the decade, as corporations borrowed to pay for takeovers or for financial restructuring to increase leverage. They even repurchased their own shares, often as part of leveraged buyouts. Total corporate equity actually declined in the 1980s, while corporate debt increased, some of it in the form of risky, lowly rated bonds, called "junk bonds," that financed some buyouts. The value of mergers averaged $200 billion per year at the end of the wave in the late 1980s, but it mushroomed to over a trillion dollars a year from 1998 to 2000.[56] Many of these late 1990s mergers involved international firms, and this brief wave has been characterized as an international merger wave.[57]

---

[48] For an example, see Shleifer and Summers (1988).

[49] See Warga and Welch (1993).

[50] See Peoples, Hekmat, and Moini (1993).

[51] See Holmstrom and Kaplan (2001).

[52] See also Bittlingmayer (1985).

[53] For review of merger waves and their causes, see Mueller (1997).

[54] See Holmstrom and Kaplan (2001).

[55] See Mitchell and Mulherin (1996).

[56] See White (2002).

[57] See Black (2000) and Pryor (2002).

Horizontal Mergers: Welfare Trade-Offs and Demand Interrelationships

Horizontal mergers offer a threat to competition, because they reduce the number of firms in a particular market and create one firm with a larger market share, but two merging firms may also achieve lower costs by joining their operations. A cost reduction, extending as it would across all units produced, can often make a greater contribution to welfare than the dead-weight welfare loss from a slightly elevated price.[58]

Figure 4.1 shows the trade-off between effects of efficiency and effects of market power. The two firms have premerger constant marginal cost of MC_1, which equals market price, P_1. After the merger, efficiencies lower the cost to the level of MC_2, while the new merged firm's market power allows a higher price, P_2. Horizontal stripes in Figure 4.1 show the efficiency gain from lowered cost, which greatly outweighs the dead weight loss from raising price that the vertical stripes show. Despite this increase in market power, the overall effect of the merger on welfare is positive because the cost saving is so large. If the merged firm's gain in market power can lead to further increases in market power in the future, however, this static analysis of effects is inadequate.

Demand interrelationships that involve substitutes and complements can also motivate mergers. The added profit that a multi-product firm can obtain when it controls the pricing of complements or substitutes might motivate horizontal or even conglomerate mergers. Indeed, consider the example of PepsiCo, Inc., a company selling both substitutes (one soft drink or another; or one snack food or another) and complements (soft drinks and snack foods). PepsiCo was a broad food and restaurant

Figure 4.1 *Efficiency Gains versus Market Power Increase in Merger*

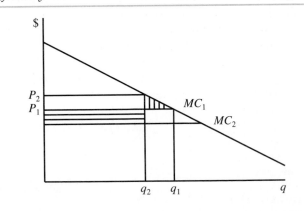

---

[58] For this argument see Williamson (1968), who is the source of the analysis in Figure 4.1.

conglomerate until 1996. In that year its restaurant division was spun off, as the company chose to focus more narrowly on soft drinks and snack foods, where substitute and complementary relations are especially strong.[59]

Antitrust authorities are now able to block horizontal mergers that lower welfare, with the result that few are available for us to observe. Around the turn of the twentieth century, before antitrust law was effective against trusts, some evidence indicates that stock values of firms formed into trusts increased, while values of nonmerging competitors decreased.[60] This reduction in the values of competitors suggests that economies might have been involved, making the merged firm a more challenging competitor. The larger merged firms possibly saw nonmerging firms as targets of predatory actions, but information from the time suggests that is unlikely. Studies of the few recent horizontal mergers that we can observe suggest they can have both efficiency and market power consequences.[61]

Conglomerate Mergers: Economies of Scope and Multi-Market Contact

Unlike horizontal mergers between firms in the same industry, conglomerate mergers are mergers between unrelated firms. The best motivation for conglomerate mergers is the presence of economies of scope, which can allow reduced cost and thus increased social benefit. Demand interrelationships can also invite mergers that appear to be conglomerate but involve, say, complementary goods, where a single supplier can economize on effort of the consumer to obtain goods that are used together (for example, computer and monitor). Such mergers offer an economy of scope in consumption, which can save consumers effort and, thus, improve efficiency.

Strategic possibilities also can arise from conglomerate organization of firms, which allows them to meet each other in more than one market, something called **multi-market contact**. Their competition—or cooperation—can then extend across markets. Some empirical evidence from effects of airline mergers on fares suggest that increased contact across markets among airlines can lead to higher fares, perhaps because airlines then have more means of disciplining each other.[62] The question has also been examined experimentally, by having subjects participate repeatedly in two market games at the same time and with the same other person.[63] Results indicate that greater cooperation is possible in such a situation, perhaps because subjects can test each other in one market and then apply any lessons learned in the other. Subjects can also have more ways to discipline one another when they have this equivalent of multi-market contact.

---

[59] See Constance L. Hays, "An Aisle Unto Itself?," *New York Times*, July 31, 1999, p. B1.

[60] See Banerjee and Eckard (1998).

[61] See Schumann (1993) and Paulter (2001).

[62] See Kim and Singal (1993) and Evans and Kessides (1994). See also Feinberg (1985) on effects of multi-market contact.

[63] For experimental analysis of this issue, see Feinberg and Sherman (1988).

BOX 4.5 The Power, and the Problems, at Time Warner

Although its different activities all lie in information and entertainment fields, the merger of America Online (AOL) and Time Warner illustrates the kind of complementarities among services that the modern conglomerate can offer consumers, even though this merger was not an entirely successful one. When Warner Brothers studio opened the movie *Harry Potter and the Sorcerer's Stone* in 2001, AOL, which served half the homes on the Internet, advertised the movie and provided links to related merchandise that it had either licensed or produced itself. Warner Music Group sold CDs and tapes from the soundtrack. Moviefone, also owned by AOL Time Warner, promoted the movie and sold tickets to it. AOL Time Warner publishes over 160 magazines, including *Time* and *Sports Illustrated*, which offered feature stories as well as advertisements for the movie. The company also provided 20 percent of the cable connections into American homes and supplied broadcasting service through 4 of the top 10 cable networks, so it advertised and promoted the movie that way as well. Coordinated actions through these many avenues bolstered the success of the movie and thus added to profit for the company. Gathering all of these activities within one firm instead of relying on the market is not without serious management problems of motivation and monitoring, however. Despite the advantage of complementarity among its services, Time Warner has had difficulty managing its empire, lost money in 2003, and became the target of takeover and break-up proposals in 2006.

See K. Auletta, "Leviathan: How Much Bigger Can AOL Time Warner Get?," *The New Yorker,* October 29, 2001, pp. 50–61; D. D. Kirkpatrick and J. Rutenberg, "AOL Reporting Further Losses: Turner Resigns," *New York Times,* January 30, 2003, P. A1; and M. Karnitschnig, "Time Warner's Malaise Persists," *Wall Street Journal,* June 23, 2006.

4.6   VERTICAL INTEGRATION AND VERTICAL RESTRAINTS

Horizontal or conglomerate relationships between firms differ from vertical relationships. Firms in vertical relationships are positioned in the path a product takes from raw materials to finished product, from primary origins to final consumption, and they are inherently complementary. Mergers among such vertically related firms bring about vertical integration, which can foreclose competitors from markets or can facilitate price discrimination. We examine these two possibilities first. More generally a seller at one level, say a manufacturer, may have vertical relations with many retailers and may allow them to compete with one another in selling its product. Or the manufacturer may instead restrict competition by granting retail sellers *exclusive territories* so in its own territory each retailer can capture all benefits from its sales efforts. If each of the sellers has some monopolistic advantage, and each sets its own markup over costs, the resulting price to consumers can be above the profit maximizing price that a single firm would charge. Not only does welfare fall as a result, but the firms earn lower profit than coordinated pricing would allow. This *double-marginalization* problem, and vertical integration or vertical restraints to overcome it, occupies the remainder of the section.

Vertical Integration for Price Discrimination or Market Foreclosure

One must note first two unwholesome possible incentives for vertical mergers.[64] First, firms may merge vertically to price discriminate. Suppose a manufacturer with market power sells its product in two markets that have differing market demand elasticities. The manufacturer would like to discriminate in price between the two markets. But if it sells in the lower-price, higher-demand-elasticity market, buyers can purchase there and resell in the higher-price market, thereby under-cutting the discrimination. If the manufacturer can merge with firms in the market that has more elastic demand, it can prevent them from reselling at a low price in the other market, allowing the firm to maintain a higher price there. Although antitrust authorities would probably oppose such an ambitious merger program, it could allow the firm to obtain the effect of profitable price discrimination between the two markets.

A second unwholesome incentive for vertical mergers is to **foreclose**, or prevent entry to, markets. Before 1944, the Alcoa Aluminum Company had a very large fraction of the market for newly produced aluminum. Through its integrated operations it could set the price of raw aluminum ingots high and the price of rolled sheet aluminum low. This combination of prices made it impossible for an independent producer, or fabricator, to buy ingots and operate as a maker of rolled sheet aluminum, because the "spread" between ingot price and rolled sheet price was too small to allow any profit. By influencing prices at the two levels Alcoa could "squeeze" producers operating in between them and essentially foreclose to entrants the market for rolled sheet aluminum alone. To enter the industry successfully, then, an entrant would have to undertake more levels of production than rolled sheet aluminum, which could make entry much more difficult.

The integrated firm may also gain less dramatic advantage over a downstream competitor than squeezing it out of business. Suppose there are two channels of distribution to the final consumer that a manufacturer may use, the first through its own, vertically integrated, retailers, and the second through independent retailers. The integrated firm might find the independent retailer useful as a way to reach some potential consumers. Yet the integrated firm's influence over prices, at both manufacturing and retailing levels, could still give it bargaining advantages in pricing to the independent retailer.[65]

Vertical Relationships More Generally: Retail Competition and Free Riding

In comparing firms along the vertical path from raw material to final consumer, the firm closer to the final consumer, say a retailer for example, is called the **downstream firm**, while the firm closer to the raw materials, say a manufacturer, is called the **upstream firm**. Double marginalization can arise if both firms, acting independently,

---

[64] For more general evaluation of vertical mergers, see Riordan and Salop (1995).

[65] For experimental results showing this bargaining advantage from integration, see Martin, Normann, and Snyder (2001).

mark up their costs in setting prices. Because the downstream firm is adding a markup to a product that already includes the upstream firm's markup, the final price can actually be higher than an integrated firm would charge.

A manufacturer wanting to distribute a product can simply allow competition at the retail level. Competition eliminates a large retail markup over marginal cost and, thus, allows the manufacturer to affect the retail price. The manufacturer could set a monopolistic price for its product to retailers, for example, and count on the forces of competition among them to make the final product price only higher enough to cover the added retailing cost.

The competitive solution may fail to bring about the optimal level of sales services from the retailer, however, because revenue to pay for such services may be insufficient under competition. With competition, presale effort by one high-service retailer can benefit another retailer who offers a lower price. A customer could visit the high-service retailer to become informed and even educated about the product, and then purchase from a discounting retailer. The discounting retailer is free-riding on other retailers' sales efforts. Skimping on information offered to customers saves on costs, which allows the discounter to win customers through lower prices. The problem for the manufacturer is that, where such spill-over effects of services across retailers can occur, competition may drive high-service retailers from the market. And without effective service at the retail level, the manufacturer's overall sales could ultimately suffer.

Exclusive Geographic Territories

This example of free-riding illustrates how granting retailers exclusive territories can have advantages for the manufacturer. A retailer with an exclusive geographic territory has no competing retailer of the same brand of product in the territory, although customers in the territory may still purchase the product from a store in another territory. Being free from immediate competition in the **exclusive territory** can overcome the discount-retailer problem. So in cases where sales effort by retailers is important to a manufacturer's success, the manufacturer may grant exclusive territories. It is possible that when several different upstream brands compete, as when several manufacturers sell similar products such as automobiles, their use of exclusive territories at the retail level might serve to soften their competition.[66] Because exclusive territories give each retailer some freedom from competition within its own brand, that could help to moderate competition between brands. When competition between upstream manufacturing firms is vigorous, however, their use of exclusive territories can make their competition more effective.

Having an exclusive territory motivates the retailer to promote the manufacturer's brand, by means such as local advertising, product explanations and demonstrations, and reliable repair or other services, in part because no competitor can free-ride on such effort. If the retailer agrees not to carry competing brands, through **exclusive dealing** contracts, the motive to provide such services is even stronger.

---

[66] Rey and Stiglitz demonstrate this possibility (1995).

Competition between brands may be more vigorous as a result. In exchange for receiving an exclusive territory, a retailer also may accept a quota or minimum quantity it will agree to accept per time period. This **"quantity-forcing"** practice not only helps the manufacturer to overcome the double-marginalization problem, it also gives the manufacturer a predictable volume of sales.

Internet retailing has no respect for geographic territories. Manufacturers, then, who need product demonstrations, or immediate product availability for consumers, may not retail via the Internet. When Internet retailers compete with brick-and-mortar retailers they may free-ride, like a discounter, and take sales from brick-and-mortar dealers who explain and demonstrate the product. Internet retailers may offer low prices, but they have limited means for providing product demonstrations, and they need time for shipment to customers. The high-service, brick-and-mortar retailers may decide not to sell the product any longer if they lose sales to low-price, low-service Internet retailers. And with the product no longer properly demonstrated, the manufacturer may face a decline in sales, as the distribution system no longer presents effectively the characteristics of its product.[67]

The manufacturer therefore must consider possible effects of competition among retailers in deciding whether to adopt competition for its retailers or instead grant them exclusive territories. Granting exclusive territories can avoid the loss of desirable retail services that may result from free-riding among competing retailers, but it raises a problem of two successive markups that is called *double marginalization*.

The Double-Marginalization Problem in Vertical Relationships

A major problem, called double marginalization, can arise for two firms when they both possess a degree of monopoly power and one sells to the other, who in turn resells to others. **Double marginalization** occurs when the separate firms independently set markups. The problem is that when the manufacturer marks up its costs the retailer takes the resulting price as its cost and marks it up to a level for final consumers that is above what a monopolist would charge. A single seller operating at both manufacturing and retail levels would simply markup its marginal cost once, and then the ultimate price to consumers would be lower and the seller could also earn more profit.

The manufacturer's monopoly power could derive from a patented product while the retailer might be the only seller in an exclusive territory. The manufacturer might assign exclusive territories if explanation of its product is needed to sell it. By creating for its brand a degree of monopoly power at the retail level, the manufacturer is inducing the retailer to demonstrate its product to customers and win sales, because it alone—and no competing retailer in the territory—benefits from such efforts. Similarly, a retailer may have a strong market position based on its location, and it could agree to have all of a certain product supplied by one manufacturer to assure it a reliable supply. Either example would result in successive sellers having some degree of monopoly power.

---

[67] For analysis of this situation see Carlton and Chevalier (2001).

BOX 4.6 The Mathematics of Double Marginalization

Consider a manufacturer and a retailer using monopoly pricing in a simple case with linear demand and constant cost. The manufacturer's cost per unit of the product produced is c, and she sells it to a retailer at a price of r. The final-product demand at the retail level is $p = a - bq$, and the retailer's cost is simply rq. From Chapter 3 we know that with demand $p = a - bq$, and total cost $C = rq$, the monopoly retailer chooses profit maximizing quantity $(a - r)/2b$, and the monopoly retail price is $p = (a + r)/2$. This is the downstream, or final-product, price.

We can obtain the retailer's quantity solution by substituting this monopoly retail price, $p = (a + r)/2$, into the demand function, $p = a - bq$, which yields $q = (a - r)/2b$. This equation reveals the demand that the manufacturer sees, and we can rearrange it in the form $r = a - 2bq$. Choosing r (and thus q) to maximize profit when cost is $C = cq$, the manufacturer's profit-maximizing quantity is $q = (a - c)/4b$. Substituting this value for q into the demand curve faced by the manufacturer, $r = a - 2bq$, yields the manufacturer's price, $r = (a + c)/2$. At this solution, the retailer's profit is

$$\pi_R = pq - rq = [(a + r)/2][(a - r)/2b] - rq = (a^2 - r^2 - 2ar + 2r^2)/4b = (a - r)^2/4b,$$

while the manufacturer's profit is

$$\pi_M = rq - cq = [(a + c)/2][(a - c)/4b] - cq = (a^2 - c^2 - 2ac + 2c^2)/8b = (a - c)^2/8b.$$

Total profit is, thus,

$$\pi_R + \pi_M = (a - c)^2/8b + (a - r)^2/4b = (a - c)^2/8b + (a - [a + c]/2)^2/4b = 3(a - c)^2/16b.$$

Now suppose the retailer and the manufacturer join together by integrating vertically. They would then face the combined profit maximizing problem with demand $p = a - bq$ and cost $C = cq$. The solution for this problem is a quantity of $q = (a - c)/2b$ and a price of $(a + c)/2$, which yields the combined profit of

$$\Pi = [(a + c)/2][(a - c)/2b] - cq = [(a + c)/2][(a - c)/2b] - c[(a - c)/2b] = (a - c)^2/4b.$$

That profit is *greater* than the sum of the two separate profits, $\pi_R + \pi_M$, because

$$(a - c)^2/4b > 3(a - c)^2/16b.$$

Combining into an integrated firm thus allows more profit.

In addition, the final-product price at the combined solution, $P = (a + c)/2$, is *lower* than the final-product price when separate decisions are made, which was $p = (a + r)/2 = (a + [a + c]/2)/2 = (3a + c)/4$. The inequality of these prices,

$$(a + c)/2 < (3a + c)/4,$$

holds because it reduces to $c < a$, which must be true. The vertical demand intercept, a, must be greater than marginal cost, c, for demand to exceed cost. If $c > a$, there can be no market transaction.

These successive sellers on the path a product takes to the consumer are selling complementary goods. The sales are complementary because both are needed if the good is to reach the consumer. If the two sellers merged into one, the single firm would make more profit with just one profit-maximizing markup over costs. Welfare would be greater also, because the resulting price to the final consumer would be lower. Yet firms cannot always merge to solve the double-markup problem. For instance, a grocery store sells many items and may not want to merge with, say, a cereal manufacturer. Double marginalization illustrates the subtleties that can arise in the transaction costs of vertical relationships. It is a problem for the firms because it yields less-than-maximum profits. It is also a problem for society—it brings a final product price that is higher than even a monopolist would want. Solving the double-marginalization problem, therefore, can be socially valuable. Box 4.6 describes mathematically the double-marginalization problem. We now turn to solving it.[68]

Vertical Integration and Vertical Restraints: Solutions for Double Marginalization

This section discusses five important solutions to the double-marginalization problem—(1) vertical integration, (2) a two-part price, (3) franchising, (4) profit sharing, and (5) resale price maintenance. Among these solutions, arrangements (2) through (5) are called vertical restraints. **Vertical restraints** do not involve common ownership, as vertical integration does, but they restrain the behavior of the parties through contractual terms.

1. **Vertical Integration.** To this problem of double marginalization, or double monopoly and its faulty final-product prices, one solution is vertical integration: The manufacturer and the retailer merge. The resulting single firm takes into account all costs and can choose optimal pricing policies, as shown in The Double-Marginalization Problem in Vertical Relationships section. The integrated firm may also respond faster to some changes in distribution channels because it has more power to move decisively.[69] This solution may not be available, however, if, say, a specialist manufacturer sells through retailers who carry many different products.

   Manufacturers do not always have the expertise to succeed at the retail level. Automobile manufacturers do not have local information about customers and other factors important to the retailing of cars, for example, so they rely on franchised retailers instead of integrating into retailing. Success at the retail level may also involve selling many products besides that of the manufacturer, so integration may not be feasible. Integrating into the retail level may also require enormous capital resources,

---

[68] An advanced treatment of these topics is available in Tirole (1988).

[69] See Gertner and Stillman (2001) for description of responses by apparel firms to opportunities opened by the Internet.

and raising them can be difficult, even for a large and established firm. A new manufacturer may simply be unable to finance vertical integration.

2. **Two-Part Price.** Now suppose the manufacturer limits competition among retailers through exclusive territories. Resulting market power at the retailer enables it to provide product demonstrations and other consumer services that may be important for sales success. However, creating market power for the retailer brings back the double-marginalization problem.

   We can trace the double-marginalization problem to the simple contract we have assumed between retailer and manufacturer that involves a uniform per-unit price. Rather than this simple per-unit price, suppose the manufacturer sells its product using a two-part price, one part being a fixed fee and the other part a marginal charge per unit. In addition to the fixed fee, a two-part price allows the manufacturer to offer a marginal price equal to the good's marginal production cost. Then there would be only one markup above marginal cost (by the retailer), which would eliminate double marginalization. The retailer would obtain the maximum monopoly profits, which the manufacturer could share through the fixed fee it collects.

   Exclusive territories reduce competition among retailers selling the same brand of product, which we call **intrabrand competition** or competition *within* the brand. The resulting market power for the retailer of the brand allows the two-part price to work, because market power allows the retailer to set price high enough to pay the fixed fee, F, and still earn profit. Although for years antitrust policy prevented such limitations to intrabrand competition, the courts now evaluate them on a case-by-case basis, and if their competitive effects are positive the courts allow them.[70] What is usually crucial to their positive effects is the presence of sufficient competition *between* brands, called **interbrand competition**.

BOX 4.7 The Two-Part Price to Solve Double Marginalization

Let a manufacturer set a two-part price, $T = F + cq$ for $q > 0$. The retailer pays F to the manufacturer for the right to purchase units at the unit price c. Repeating our analysis of double marginalization for the retailer, the optimal quantity is now $q = (a - c)/2b$, the optimal price is $p = (a + c)/2$, and profit is

$$\pi_R = (a - c)^2/4b - F.$$

The manufacturer can set the fixed fee, F, equal to $(a - c)^2/4b$, to obtain all profit, or to a level that permits a greater share for the retailer, depending on their bargaining. An efficient (for a monopoly) pricing arrangement between manufacturer and retailer is possible without vertical integration however, if a two-part price is used.

---

[70] See *Continental T. V., Inc. v. GTE Sylvania Inc.*, 433 U.S. 36, 97 S.Ct. 2549, 53 L.Ed.2d 568 (1977).

When interbrand competition is strong, reduced intrabrand competition from the vertical restraint is not so troublesome.

3. **Franchising.** The two-part tariff as a pricing arrangement between manufacturer and retailer is very similar to a franchising contract, because the franchisee (retailer) usually pays a franchise fee that is much like the fixed fee part of a two-part tariff. Franchising involves many other features, perhaps requiring the franchisee to purchase inputs from the franchiser (for example, the manufacturer), and adherence by the franchisee to many operating policies established by the franchiser. The franchiser may also control the location of the franchisee in part to avoid the kind of intrabrand competition that would prevent franchisees from being able to pay a fixed fee.

   Franchising offers a manufacturer, or other central supplier, an opportunity to expand rapidly by drawing resources of others to be franchisees.[71] There may even be a tendency for franchisers to expand too much, in plans conceived separately and then carried out despite similar efforts by competing providers of the same goods or services.[72] Aiming to replace small pharmacies, which may have greater difficulty dealing with the world of managed care, drugstore chains have expanded in this way. In the late 1990s several drug chains carried out two-year and three-year expansion plans in New York City, which, for a time, created a surplus of drugstores there.[73]

4. **Profit Sharing.** While still limiting intrabrand competition through exclusive territories, it is also possible to accomplish a result similar to the two-part tariff by having both manufacturer and retailer agree to *share* the profit of the retailer in a specific way, rather than through a prearranged fixed fee. For example, the manufacturer might sell the product to the retailer at its cost of c per unit and then receive, say, one-half of the retailer's profit. Because it faces a cost per unit of c, the retailer would then choose the monopoly price and output, thus, maximizing profit for the manufacturer and retailer combined.

   Compared with a two-part price, however, the profit-sharing arrangement offers weaker incentives to the retailer. Retailer incentives are important because the manufacturer may deal with many retailers and be unable to observe each one carefully. Profit sharing has two incentive problems for retailers, one from having only a share of profit to motivate the retailer and the other from the retailer's ability to influence that share. The first problem under profit sharing is that the retailer receives only some fraction of the profit it can develop. If the profit is shared equally, for example, the retailer receives only half of the marginal contribution its effort makes to profit, rather than all of the marginal

---

[71] Lafontaine (1993) shows the growth of franchising.

[72] For analysis of this possibility, see Baye, Crocker, and Ju (1996).

[73] See Terry Pristin, "Drug Chains at War in New York," *New York Times*, August 1, 1999, p. 21.

contribution as would be the case after paying a fixed fee. Because it benefits less from marginal effort, the retailer's motivation can be less strong in the profit-sharing case than in the two-part pricing case.

Secondly, there is a moral hazard problem, because the retailer can benefit by finding a self-serving way to report lower profit. A **moral hazard** is a temptation that keeps an agent from acting as might be expected under a contract. In this case, after agreeing to a profit-sharing contract, the retailer might add to its store some items that afford personal pleasure and entertainment (such as a television set, exercise equipment, meals, sleeping accommodation, swimming pool, etc.). Even though the cost of such items reduces reported profit, the retailer receives only some fraction, such as half, of that profit, and enjoys *all* the pleasure of the features added to the store. This change the profit-sharing contract causes in retailers' motives is the moral hazard problem. To help overcome it, the sharing payment might be based at least in part on a measure of output, which usually cannot be manipulated as easily as profit can be. One reason a franchiser might require the franchisee to purchase inputs from it is that the franchiser can verify the franchisee's output, which can then be used as the basis for a profit-sharing contract.

Despite its incentive problems, profit sharing may be more attractive when uncertainty is great. Profit sharing allows the retailer and the manufacturer to share risks of demand fluctuations, rather than have the risks fall on one party as they do on the retailer in the two-part price example. Profit sharing is similar in this respect to the share-cropping arrangement discussed in Section 4.1, with the profit-sharing retailer in the position of a share cropper, rather than paying a fixed fee to the landlord and consequently bearing all risk of profit fluctuations. Some franchising contracts contain profit-sharing features, probably in part to

---

BOX 4.8 The Moral Hazard of Profit Reporting

Contracts between a movie studio and a screenwriter or between the studio and an actor or actress have revealed a moral hazard problem. Here the writers, actors, and actresses are the upstream agents, in place of the manufacturer, and the studio is the downstream party, like the retailer. Contracts between them have included profit-sharing arrangements that ended in law suits after writers, actors, and actresses were told there was no profit for them to share. They then sued over whether the particular film they worked on had actually earned a profit. Another example is the 1997 agreement between Disney and Blockbuster that allowed Blockbuster to obtain videos from Disney at $7 each, rather than the former price of about $65 each, in return for promoting the videos and sharing profits from their rental. The relationship turned acrimonious as Disney sued Blockbuster for $120 million, claiming that poor accounting and record keeping had denied Disney that much revenue.

See "Disney Sues Blockbuster Over Contract," *New York Times,* January 4, 2003, p. B2.

capture this risk-sharing advantage. Neither party may want the full exposure to risk, although in some cases the manufacturer—who may be able to diversify across regions—is in better position to bear it.

5. **Resale Price Maintenance.** A manufacturer may be able to overcome double marginalization by controlling the final price at which retailers can sell its product through a **resale price maintenance (RPM)** contract. The practice of RPM has been barred as illegal over much of our history, but it was allowed in 1997 when a gasoline retailer was effectively prevented from raising its price above what the State Oil Company, its source for gasoline, allowed it to charge.[74] RPM can also impose a minimum price, but the courts have not yet endorsed a minimum resale price, in part because it might support seller collusion against consumers.[75] A minimum price could avoid the free-rider (or discounter) problem among retailers, though, for by cutting price the discounter would violate its RPM contract. Instead of ever granting exclusive territories a manufacturer could then avoid double marginalization by using competition among retailers who are bound not to cut price by RPM contracts. Without discount stores, the RPM contracts could allow retailers enough revenue to support the provision of needed retail services.

An RPM agreement for a minimum price may also offer a stability advantage for the manufacturer when demand fluctuations are expected. If demand falls, individual retailers might be tempted to cut prices and sell the supplies they have. The manufacturer realizes that the added sales come only at such a low price as to be harmful for long-run sales and, in taking a long-term view, may try to avoid retail price fluctuations. RPM can prevent retailers from cutting prices in low demand periods and thereby help to keep the market more stable for the manufacturer.[76]

BOX 4.9 Resale Price Maintenance (RPM) to Solve Double Marginalization

A maximum price set by a manufacturer through RPM can keep a retailer from raising price and, thereby, can overcome the double-marginalization problem. For example, in the double-marginalization problem in Box 4.6, suppose the manufacturer sets a final-product price of $p = (a + c)/2$ and maintains it by RPM agreement. The manufacturer can also set the price to the retailer below $r = (a + c)/2$ thus leaving the retailer with some profit. Problems would arise if retailers lost money, but the point is that control of both prices opens another way for the manufacturer to deal with double marginalization.

---

[74] See *State Oil Co. v. Kahn*, 871 U.S. 96 (1997).

[75] The Supreme Court may allow a minimum retail price, as Chapter 9 shows.

[76] Deneckere, Marvel, and Peck (1997) describe this possibility. For a classic description of the advantage of a stable price in markets with low elasticity of demand, see King (1939).

SUMMARY

The modern business firm chooses its size and shape to keep the costs of transacting low. When it is less costly to transact in the market, firms use the market, and transactions are carried out within the firm when that is less costly. That fixes the boundaries of the firm. Costs of using the market can involve possibly opportunistic behavior by others, especially when uncertainty is great. Within the firm, costs arise from the need to motivate and monitor employees to achieve desired aims.

These problems of motivating and monitoring extend to the highest reaches of the business firm's hierarchy. Different sources of capital for the firm—mainly shareholders and bondholders—can have conflicting financial interests, as consideration of factors affecting their assets' values show. Shareholders prefer to control these differences, in order to maximize the value of the firm, but even shareholders may have difficulty eliciting ideal performance from top managers of the firm. Competitive product markets help to discipline managers, because they allow less scope for managerial discretion. The capital market can help in enforcing the will of shareholders, also, in part because the transferability of corporate ownership allows takeovers by outsiders who judge improvement to be possible. Such takeover transactions are difficult and risky, but they foster a market for corporate control that can improve the efficiency of corporations.

The most dramatic way a firm can influence its size and shape is through merger, which brings already existing firms together in a single enterprise. Mergers are vertical, horizontal, or conglomerate, depending on whether the merging firms are in a buying and selling relationship to each other (vertical), are in the same industry (horizontal), or are essentially unrelated (conglomerate). Although mergers can often produce economies that can improve welfare, they can also enhance market power. Demand interrelationships may also motivate mergers to allow control of prices or marketing of complementary or substitute goods when some monopoly advantage exists.

Corporations are usually hierarchical organizations, overseen by a board of directors elected by the shareholder owners. These shareholder interests were pursued more vigorously in the 1980s and 1990s than in earlier decades. One reason is that institutions now hold more shares than individuals, and the institutions have favored strong incentives for managers. Venture capital is also more available to help fledgling firms challenge established ones. The compensation of managers and directors depends more than it used to on the success enjoyed by shareholders, and capital markets play a greater role than before in allocating investment resources.

Firms in vertical relationships sometimes adopt vertical restraints to create the best incentives for serving customers and for setting final retail prices. Two parties in a vertical relationship—such as a manufacturer and a retailer—stand in a complementary relationship to each other. If either raises its price independently, the price to the final consumer is higher and the quantity demanded is lower than coordinated profit maximizing actions could attain. Thus, one firm may want to influence both prices, just as a seller of two complementary goods wants to control those two prices. One firm, say a manufacturer, can control retail prices in such a situation by integrating into retailing, but such integration may not always be advisable or even feasible.

The manufacturer may rely instead on competition among retailers to control the final product price. Discount retailers, however, may compete by lowering price and free riding on other retailers who provide sales effort, and if that sales effort is important the manufacturer's marketing plan may suffer. Retailers who demonstrate and explain the product may lose sales to discounters and may no longer be willing to sell the product. Alternatively, the manufacturer can assure retailers that there is to be no other seller in their exclusive territories. This avoids free riding and gives retailers both the market power and the incentive to provide needed sales effort. By failing to consider the complementarity in their sales, however, independent pricing by manufacturer and retailer is then inefficient, because of what is called double marginalization. Where feasible, vertical integration can solve this problem by bringing central control over final product price. Alternatively, a variety of vertical restraints, in the form of contracts, overcome this failure through control over price. These vertical restraints include two-part pricing, franchising, profit sharing, and resale price maintenance. They can achieve efficient pricing and distribution of goods on a decentralized basis.

The market in which a business firm operates determines its environment, and how the market is organized, that is, its market structure, is especially important to the firm. We now turn to Chapter 5 to represent those aspects of market structure that most affect how firms behave.

QUESTIONS

1. Suppose the management of a corporation asks the shareholders to permit the sale of bonds, the proceeds of which are to be used to buy shares of the firm in the capital market. The management owns some shares now, and after this transaction—involving the sale of bonds and the purchase of stock shares—the management will control the firm (there will be fewer other shares outstanding). Under what conditions, and why, might shareholders accept the proposal? Sketch possible advantages and possible disadvantages.

2. Suppose you are to start from scratch to devise a means of ensuring that corporations reveal their financial conditions honestly. Propose institutional arrangements for accounting oversight that are feasible and that offer motivation for issuing true reports and for discovering faulty ones.

3. Consider the stock option scandal described in Box 4.3. Propose a remedy that will prevent backdating or other tricks having to do with the issuing of stock options.

4. Suppose you own 100 percent of a business that has assets of $50,000,000. You manufacture a patented product and sell it through your own retail stores in the eastern half of the country. You have an opportunity to expand to the western half of the country, which requires the investment of an additional $50,000,000. Although there is always the risk of a new discovery or of a change in consumers' tastes, you should enjoy the same or greater success in the West as you

have had in the East, where the annual rate of return on your assets has averaged 12%. A reporter for *Business Week*, who has an excellent record for such predictions, has estimated that in the West you will earn 10% half the time and 18% half the time, for an average of 14%. There are two main ways to finance the needed $50,000,000 (you do not have it yourself). (1) Issue $50,000,000 in bonds. Two investment bankers have assured you this can be done by paying interest to bond holders at a rate of 10% a year. (2) Issue $50,000,000 in new common stock, which will expand the number of owners and cut your ownership interest from 100% to 50%. This means that you will be entitled to half rather than all the company's profit, but of course on average the company's profit should be at least twice as large as before. Consider three issues:

a. Assuming the *Business Week* reporter is correct in her prediction, how will these two means of financing your expansion (bonds or common stock) affect your expected profit (or rate of return) and your risk (represented perhaps as the fluctuations in your profit)? That is, can you expect to have higher average profit, or greater risk, if you use bonds or if you use common stock to finance the expansion?

b. Will the decision about these two means of financing affect your own incentive to work hard and to make entirely efficient decisions?

c. Suppose that, just as you receive the proceeds from your financing, a new approach to the expansion comes to light. The new approach would require the same investment but would allow a higher average rate of return and bring more risk. The return would be 0 percent half the time and 60 percent half the time, for an average of 30 percent. Will the choice of which method to use to secure the $50,000,000 financing (either bonds or common stock) affect the attractiveness of pursuing this new approach to expansion?

5. In the 1990s, Congress eased the reporting that corporations were required to make and weakened their accountability by making officers less liable for overly optimistic earnings forecasts and by making it harder for shareholders to bring lawsuits against managements. Congress also opposed Financial Accounting Standards Board rules to treat stock options as an expense. Give a plausible explanation for why Congress might weaken regulation in these ways.

6. Suppose you are expanding your business, which now covers the eastern half of the country, into the western half of the country. One way to reduce the investment you need to make the expansion is to use independent retailers, who invest themselves, instead of owning all the retailers. This raises the question whether transactions between independent units can be as efficient as transactions within your single organization when you own all the retail units.

To simplify analysis we consider all the retailers together as if they were one firm. According to your plan, each retailer is located far enough from others that each has market power because of location, so they are not in competition and aggregating them is not entirely foolish. We also assume this retailer's costs are zero, except for what they pay you for the product. Final-product demand is represented graphically by Figure 4.2 or, in tabular form, (at selected intervals), by:

Price (Dollars)	Final Market Quantity (Millions)
5	0
4	100
3	200
2	300
1	400

Please answer these questions:

a. Suppose you raise money to finance the creation of your own retailer in your expansion (considered as one retailer for simplicity), so you control all retail activities. If your marginal cost to manufacture the product is $1 per unit, what final-product price will maximize your profit, and what will that profit be?

b. Suppose instead that you use an independent retailer who owns the retail store that distributes your product. From the information given, estimate the demand from the retailer for your product. That is, at any price you set for your product, how many units will the retailer purchase? (Imagining and solving the retailer's decision is a crucial step, so consider it carefully.) Draw the demand curve in the diagram or amend the table to include it.

c. If your marginal cost of manufacturing is $1 per unit, and given the demand you see from retailers, what price allows you to maximize your profit?

d. From the price you determined in part c, what price does the retailer choose? How many units will be sold? What profit will you earn, and what profit will the retailer earn?

Figure 4.2

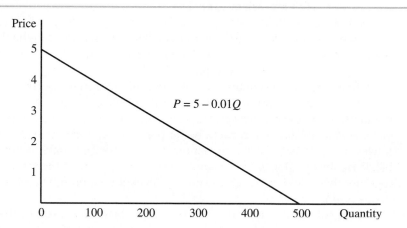

  e. What is the combined manufacturer-plus-retailer profit in part d, and how does it compare with the profit when the manufacturer in part a owns the retailers? In which case, that of owned retailers or independent retailers, is the final product price to consumers higher?

  f. Describe two alternative steps you could take to improve the profit that you and the retailer earn and to lower the final product price to consumers when you work through independent retailers.

7. Suppose a manufacturer comes to you seeking advice about the distribution of its product. The manufacturer wants to know whether there is an inefficiency in its product distribution system and, if there is, how to remedy it.

   The manufacturer sells its product through a retailer, and it sells to the retailer at a price of m per unit of its product. The manufacturer knows the final demand for its product is $q = a - p$, but it does not control the final price p, the retailer does. The manufacturer presumes the retailer maximizes its profit,

$$\pi_r = q\,(p - m) = (a - p)(p - m),$$

and so sets $p = (a + m)/2$. By substituting this value for p into demand $q = a - p$, the manufacturer obtains the demand that *it* experiences, $m = a - 2q$, or $q = (a - m)/2$. Because it's cost per unit is c, the manufacturer can express its own profit as

$$\pi_m = q\,(m - c) = ((a - m)/2)\,(m - c).$$

  a. The manufacturer wants to know whether, if it chooses m to maximize its profit, it can use that profit maximizing price, m^*, to obtain the final product price in terms of parameters (a and c). Express in terms of a and c the final price, p, that results from this independent retailer and manufacturer profit maximizing.

  b. The manufacturer wants to know whether this final-product price obtained in part a is higher or lower than the price would be if the manufacturer sold into the final market directly without the retailer. Express the manufacturer's profit maximizing final product price, p^*, if it sold directly in the final-product market without the middleman retailer.

  c. Compare the price obtained by direct sale in part b with the price obtained in part a when sales take place through a retailer. Which price is higher? Which price affords the greatest total profit, retailer plus manufacturer profit in part a, or manufacturer profit only in part b?

  d. If you find that the present arrangement of selling through the retailer (part a) offers greater total profit than the manufacturer selling directly in the final market (part b), explain why that is true. If you find that direct sale (part b) yields greater profit, that means a better outcome is conceivable. Assume, however, that direct sale by the manufacturer without a retailer is not feasible. Describe two policies the manufacturer could use with the retailer so that together they could approach the greater level of total profit you obtained in your solution in part b.

8. Double marginalization is an important pricing problem for a product that passes through successive stages on its way from raw materials to the consumer.

   a. Consider a manufacturer who effectively grants retailers exclusive territories through its policy of retailer location. In this situation compare and contrast a profit-sharing contract with a two-part price for overcoming double marginalization.

   b. To the extent that resale price maintenance contracts have been allowed by the Supreme Court, can a manufacturer use such contracts to avoid double marginalization?

   c. If the manufacturer could design resale price maintenance contracts, would they encourage effective competition among retailers so the manufacturer would not have to protect them by granting exclusive territories?

9. If the appropriate discount rate is 10 percent, what is the present value of $110 to be received *two* years from today?

5

Market Structure

The biggest influence on a business firm is the structure of the market in which it operates. Structure ranges from competition to monopoly. Coke and Pepsi are neither monopolists nor firms in perfect competition, and they pursue strategies that firms in perfect competition or pure monopoly would not pursue. Even if they sell the same product, a few firms may not behave like many firms in a competitive market because when they are few the firms can see how their actions affect one another and the market price. Market structure represents the way a market is organized, which influences firm behavior and, thus, determines how competitive the market is.

When entry by new firms is difficult, existing firms may not have to compete vigorously, especially when they are few in number. Entry conditions, along with the number and the relative sizes of firms, are the most basic elements of market structure. A pure monopoly has no competitor and faces no potential entrant, so it can choose price to maximize its profit; a firm in perfect competition has to accept a price dictated by the market. A few firms in a market face some combination of these conditions, depending on how many they are and on how easy is entry. These elements of market structure are the main subject of this chapter.

After a brief discussion of market structure in Section 5.1, we begin our study in Section 5.2 by examining the effects on market outcomes of having a small number of firms in the market. We consider homogeneous-product markets on the strong assumption that entry is effectively barred and firms are equal in size. These markets reveal how market structure affects incentives that in turn determine firms' behavior. Next, we consider in Section 5.3 how the possibility of new entry can alter the outcomes and, when combined with observed properties of firms' costs, lead to a range of firm sizes. With firms of different sizes, we need practical ways to characterize the number of firms and their sizes, and for that we have *concentration measures* described in Section 5.4. Finally, in Section 5.5, we examine some empirical evidence about the effects of market structure on firm behavior and market performance.

5.1 | MARKET STRUCTURE

Classical models of duopoly and oligopoly proposed by the early French scholar Augustin Cournot is our starting point. A market with only two firms is called a **duopoly,** and a market with just a few firms is called an **oligopoly**. The Cournot model reveals nicely the motives of firms when they are few in number by making them equal in size, thereby linking the number of firms directly to market share for its effect on motives. Actual markets take a wider variety of forms than these duopoly and oligopoly markets allow, however. Firms in actual markets face the possibility of entry by new firms, and they differ in size and shape from the stylized, equal-size, firms of the usual Cournot model, so a richer descriptive vocabulary is necessary to portray real industries. The range of strategies available to firms goes far beyond those considered by Cournot, and they are the subject of Chapter 6.

When entry by new firms is easy, firms already in the market are threatened by potential entrants and by already existing competitors. Barriers to entry prevent new firms from joining a market and thus close off that source of competition. Sometimes incumbent firms have a cost advantage over new entrants, and that makes entry difficult. Some technologies also require very large investments, and financing them can be difficult when information is imperfectly available to investors. When capital investments are lasting and have few alternative uses, they represent sunk costs, because they cannot readily be converted to another use. Sunk costs make exit from the market difficult if things turn sour, so sunk costs discourage entry. Scale economies can be an entry barrier when they are so great that there is room for only a few firms large enough to achieve low costs in a market. The rate of entry into an industry can influence the sizes of its firms.

Real-world firms in many industries have constant average costs over wide ranges of output, so the firms can be quite different in their sizes. When firms in a market have different sizes and shapes, characterizing the structure of the market becomes a more difficult problem, because the number of firms by itself is no longer adequate. It would be useful to have a simple measure to capture the competitiveness of a market, if only crudely, by representing both the number of firms and their market shares. Concentration measures serve that purpose. Entry is also important to market outcomes, so the difficulty of entry also needs to be represented if we are to describe market structure.

In many markets, products are not homogeneous. The strategy of offering *differentiated products* and, thus, trying to create a preference among consumers for a particular product affects market structure. Brands of automobile, computer, or even toothpaste present significant differences to consumers and invite forms of *nonprice* competition, such as advertising and sales promotion efforts. We explore product differentiation in Chapter 6, in connection with market strategy.

With barriers to entry and few firms in a market, there is a possibility that one or more of the firms has *market power*, the power to raise price above a competitive level and keep it there. How long can a firm sustain such market power? Some economists argue that although monopoly control may be observed at any one time it seldom persists, because the high profit of a monopolist attracts entrepreneurs ingenious enough to share in it.[1] Others argue that such a process of new entry takes time, and those attempting entry can face obstacles in their paths, perhaps placed there unfairly by the firm with market power.[2] How long the market process should be left on its own to erode monopoly advantage is one question that we face repeatedly, for it is at the heart of the question whether government should intervene in some forceful way to support competition.

5.2 | DUOPOLY AND OLIGOPOLY

When firms are few, each can have a noticeable effect on the others, especially when new entry is difficult. Then the market ceases to be an impersonal mechanism, and its equilibrium may reflect whatever relationships the few firms establish with each other. There may be no unique price that the firms reliably reach. The same is true of other dimensions of firm competition, such as levels of advertising or research. Nevertheless, we can analyze the specific ways that actions by the firms affect one another. How their profits are interdependent can influence, in turn, the way the firms behave, and knowing the way each firm's actions affect others helps to identify the possible solutions.

The element of market structure to be examined first is the number of firms, or the related measure of market share, and to do that we assume there is no possibility of entry. Decision makers in duopoly or oligopoly markets may not always be able to choose an action and know its consequences, even with some probability, because the unknown actions of other firms influence the outcome. The payoffs for alternative actions can still influence behavior in much the same way that payoffs influence economic behavior in countless other settings. We can make a good beginning to the study of oligopoly, then, by examining how the actions of interdependent firms affect their profits. The earliest analysis of a few firms in a market made their behavior deterministic to predict exactly what the firms would do. We trace such models in this section to see the incentives they identify, and we consider broader and less deterministic strategies in Chapter 6.

Cournot's Early Solution

Market price is determined easily by a monopoly or routinely by many firms in competition. When firms are few in number, however, they are dependent on one another, and this creates a problem in determining market price. In 1838 a French scholar, Augustin Cournot (1963), solved this problem with a remarkable mathematical analysis of a market.[3] He assumed identical products—specifically, water from mineral springs at zero marginal cost—and he had firms decide how much mineral water to offer for sale in the market; that is, he made quantity the decision variable of

---

[1] See, for example, Israel Kirzner (1973) and Richard Posner (1975).
[2] See, for example, Joe S. Bain (1956) and Mark J. Green (1973).
[3] See Cournot (1963, orig. 1838, trans., N. T. Bacon, 1927).

each firm. In this framework he studied effects of changing the number of firms in the market, from one to many.

With one firm, Cournot reached the monopoly solution, but with, say, two firms in a market, how could they proceed to a solution? So that each firm could attempt independently to maximize its profit, Cournot introduced a notion known now as a **conjecture**, an assumption that one firm would make about the amount that others would offer for sale. The conjecture Cournot ascribed to each firm was simple: each firm assumes that every other firm produces the same quantity in the current period as it did in the previous period. Without such a conjecture, the profit-maximizing problem for a few firms would be indeterminate because no firm knows what others will do. Cournot's conjecture, however, allows dynamic quantity-adjustment paths to converge to an equilibrium price and quantity; and, once there, no firm is motivated to change its output.

We can apply this Cournot solution quite generally. It explains the final solution of a monopolist if there is only one firm (other firms produce nothing) or of a competitive market if there are infinitely many firms. Cournot showed how independent, profit-maximizing behavior would produce a unique market quantity for given costs and demand, depending entirely on n, the number of firms. He also showed how firms' motives to limit output would change as the number of firms, n, and thus market shares, changed. Cournot's solution requires no information regarding a competitor's profit. Only information about the competitor's current output is required, in addition to the firm's own cost and demand information, as a basis for each firm's next-period output decision. Cournot provided not only a solution but also a process for reaching it.

Forty-five years after Cournot's mathematical analysis appeared another French scholar, Jacques Bertrand (1883), criticized the assumption that firms adjust quantities.[4] Bertrand argued that sellers would set price instead of quantity, and, because products were homogeneous, the price would be forced down to marginal cost as soon as more than one firm operated in a market. After another 40 years, in England, Professor Francis Y. Edgeworth showed how capacity limits could moderate such severe price competition.[5] When firms reach capacity limits, they have no capacity to serve customers who might be won through lower prices, so price competition stops. Indeed, if other firms have no capacity remaining, each can raise its price until enough excess capacity returns to again motivate price competition. This process could bring a troublesome pricing instability, but it mainly shifts attention to the firms' choice of capacity. Because capacity is related to quantity, a capacity choice can be seen to be following Cournot's quantity-choice theory.

Cournot therefore sees firms as committing to quantities first and accepting whatever market price results, whereas Bertrand's firms commit to price first and later produce whatever outputs those prices imply for them. Economists Kreps and Scheinkman (1983) showed that if firms would commit to quantities first, in the form of their capacity decisions, and then compete in price given those capacities, the result would be a Cournot equilibrium.[6]

---

[4] See Bertrand (1883).

[5] See Edgeworth (1925, pp. 111–142).

[6] Sherman (1969) carried out experimental investigation of this two-stage, capacity-and-then-price decision. He found effects of capacity cost and risk attitudes on capacity choices, which in turn influenced price decisions.

Oligopoly and duopoly theories of great ingenuity have resulted from this line of research.[7] Despite their abundance, the theories probably cannot do justice to the range of behavior from real-world oligopolists. Still the Cournot model itself reveals important motives, as does the leader-follower model of Stackelberg (1952) to be examined later. To help us consider these motives and to see an equilibrium, we first note basic ideas from game theory.

Game Theory

We learn about strategic interaction early in our lives, from childhood games such as checkers, hop-scotch, or computer games, or even tennis or soccer or softball or baseball. Out of World War II, with its emphasis on applying strategic methods, came the development of **game theory**, which was intended to capture the essence of strategic interactions and to reveal the most effective strategies. Indeed, in their very influential book on game theory that appeared in 1944, *The Theory of Games and Economic Behavior*, John von Neumann and Oskar Morgenstern intended to provide a new foundation for economics.[8] Although it is not quite a new foundation, game theory is a valuable framework for considering strategic choices.[9]

Game theory offers a framework for considering interdependent actors who are trying to reach some goal but are affected by others who have different aims. It focuses on the rules of a game, which indicate

1. Who the *players* are,
2. The *alternative actions* available to each player,
3. The timing . . . *when* each player chooses, and
4. The *payoffs* from all combinations of actions.

Typically, we assume the rules of a game are common knowledge. **Common knowledge** means not only that all players know the rules of the game but also that all know that they all know the rules.

If players choose in sequence, first one and then the other, we would have a **sequential-choice game**. If player one chose first and announced the choice, then player two would have an overwhelming advantage from knowing what player one had already chosen, and this is the pattern in Stackelberg's leader-follower market model. Alternatively, if players choose at the same time, we have a **simultaneous-choice game**, which is how two firms in a Cournot market move. Even if, say, player one moves earlier, we would call it a simultaneous-choice game if, when deciding on an action, player two cannot know the action that was taken by player one.

We now contrast results for two or three firms in the Cournot and Stackelberg models with equilibrium results for the monopoly model and the competitive model. The Cournot duopoly is considered first, where two firms have separate outputs, q_1

---

[7] For reviews of the classic theories, see Fellner (1960).
[8] See von Neumann and Morgenstern (1944).
[9] For experiments in game situations, see Holt (2007).

and q_2, which add to total market quantity, Q ($Q = q_1 + q_2$). We draw on a simple case where the market demand is linear, $p = a - bQ$, and a firm's total cost is cq_i.

Cournot Duopoly

Let us first consider graphically in Figure 5.1 how duopoly firms choose their outputs in Cournot's model. Although there are two firms rather than one, each firm can still sense that increasing output will lower market price and thereby lower profit. That is, Cournot's duopolists can also sense the awareness a monopoly has of declining marginal revenue from seeing the entire market demand, DD. Essentially, each duopolist subtracts the other firm's (constant) output from the total market demand, to obtain its own, *residual*, demand, $d_R d_R$. The duopolist effectively calculates marginal revenue for this **residual demand**, the demand it sees after subtracting the other firm's output. The duopolist can calculate marginal revenue because, along this residual demand, the duopolist can see the effect that changes in its own output have on market price. Figure 5.1 illustrates the result at an equilibrium, where the other firm's output is $q_D - q_d$. Firm 1 chooses $q_1 = q_D - q_d$, a quantity that sets marginal revenue from its residual demand equal to its marginal cost, c. With the other firm doing the same thing, they reach the same quantity.

A Market Model

With market demand $P = a - b(q_1 + q_2)$, firm 1 faces the profit function:

$$\pi_1 = Pq_1 - cq_1 = [a - b(q_1 + q_2)]\, q_1 - cq_1.$$

The profit maximizing problem for firm 1 has the market price depend on total output, $q_1 + q_2$, while revenue and cost for firm one depend only on firm 1's output. Taking q_2, the other firm's output, as fixed, say at the same level as before, firm 1 can maximize π_1 with respect to q_1 and obtain

$$\partial \pi_1 / \partial q_1 = a - 2bq_1 - bq_2 - c = 0.$$

Figure 5.1 *Cournot Duopolist's Solution*

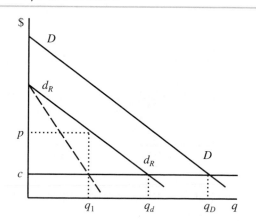

This condition does not yield a profit maximizing level of q_1 that is independent of q_2. But it does yield a profit maximizing level of q_1 for any *given* level of q_2:

$$q_1 = (a - bq_2 - c)/2b.$$

This profit maximizing level of q_1 for any given level of q_2 is firm 1's best response for that level of q_2. This best response gives a way to see the Cournot solution, because the **best-response function** gives a firm's best output choice as a function of the other firm's output. Figure 5.2 plots the best-response functions for the two firms. The best-response function of firm 1 is $q_1 = (a - bq_2 - c)/2b$, while that of firm 2 is $q_2 = (a - bq_1 - c)/2b$. Consider firm 1's reaction function $(q_1 = (a - bq_2 - c)/2b)$. If firm 2 chooses $q_2 = (a - c)/b$, the competitive market output, firm 1 produces zero. If firm 2 chooses to produce an output of zero, firm 1 produces the monopoly output, $q_1 = (a - c)/2b$. And if firm 2 chooses to produce the Cournot output, $(a - c)/3b$, firm 1 also chooses that same output.

The Nash Equilibrium

The only point where behavior can be consistent is where both firms are on their best response functions, which of course is where the two functions intersect. Firm 2's best-response function substituted into firm 1's yields the quantity $q_1 = (a - c)/3b = q_2$. Cournot showed that when firms were away from this intersection point they would be drawn to it, so it would have equilibrium properties. There was inconsistency in Cournot's equilibrating process, however, for while each firm assumes the others will maintain last period's quantity, as they moved toward the equilibrium point they change those quantities. Yet, at each step they move toward the equilibrium. Nobel laureate John Nash (1950) defined the equilibrium rigorously and more generally.[10]

Figure 5.2 *Duopolists' Best-Response Functions*

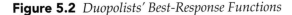

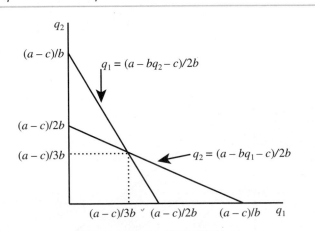

---

[10] See the biography of John Nash by Sylvia Nasar (1998), which was also made into the popular movie *A Beautiful Mind*.

The equilibrium for a situation like that in the Cournot duopoly is called a **Nash equilibrium**.[11] One must remember that an equilibrium strategy works reliably only when others are using their best strategies. When that happens a powerful definition of equilibrium is available in the Nash equilibrium idea. The essence of a Nash equilibrium is that *each player takes the action that is best for that player against the actions taken by others, which in turn are best for them.* The intersection of best-response functions provides a Nash equilibrium to the simultaneous-choice Cournot game.

Duopoly firms facing linear market demand, $p = a - bQ$, and firms' cost of cq_i, therefore choose the quantity $q_1 = q_2 = (a - c)/3b$. Because $Q = q_1 + q_2$, this value for q_1 and q_2 means that $Q = 2(a - c)/3b$ is the Cournot solution for market output. Recalling from Chapter 3 that the monopoly output is $Q = (a - c)/2b$, we see that this duopoly output, $(a - c)2/3b$, is larger. Indeed, substituting the duopoly output into demand, $p = a - bQ$, yields the duopoly price,

$$p = a - 2b(a - c)/3b = (a + 2c)/3,$$

which is lower than the monopoly price of $(a + c)/2$.[12] Cournot demonstrated that as the number of firms in the market increased, the quantity-setting solution—along the lines we have just explored—would approach the competitive solution; with very many firms, price would be driven to equal c.

BOX 5.1 A Numerical Example for the Cournot Equilibrium

Let us consider a numerical example. Assume that a market has linear inverse demand, $p = 1 - 0.01 (q_1 + q_2)$. If average cost is constant at $c = 0.20$, substituting these numbers into the duopoly quantity equations in the text will yield outputs $q_1 = q_2 = (1 - 0.2)/3(.01) = 26.7$, and $Q = q_1 + q_2 = 53.3$. This output is greater than the monopoly output, $(a-c)/2b$, or $(1-0.2)/2(.01) = 40$. The duopoly price is $(a + 2c)/3 = (1 + 0.4)/3 = 0.47$, which is lower than the monopoly price of $(a + c)/2 = (1 + 0.2)/2 = 0.60$. Although lower than the monopoly price, the duopoly price is still higher than the competitive price, which would equal marginal cost of $c = 0.20$. Thus, duopoly improves welfare compared to monopoly by lowering price and increasing output, but it still is not as good as competition for serving welfare, because the duopoly p exceeds marginal cost of c. So in this numerical example, we have three market structures:

	Price	Quantity
Monopoly	0.60	40
Duopoly	0.47	53.3
Competition	0.20	80

---

[11] See Nash (1950). For a portrait of Nash's development of the idea, see Nasar (1998).

[12] To see that $(a + c)/2$ is greater than $(a + 2c)/3$, consider the following. First, note that $a > c$, because the inverse demand function intercept, a, must exceed cost, c, if a market is to exist. At $a/2 + c/2$, the monopoly price weights a more heavily and c less heavily than the duopoly price weighting of $a/3 + 2c/3$, which is why the monopoly price is higher. Or assume $a/2 + c/2 > a/3 + 2c/3$, and simplify $(a/2 - a/3 > 2c/3 - c/2)$ until you reach $a > c$, which is known to be true.

Cournot and the Number of Firms

Now consider how market price declines as the number of firms in the Cournot market increases. As the number of firms, n, increases, Cournot showed that the markup over marginal cost c, decreases according to the following rule:

$$(p - c)/p = 1/n(-E),$$

where E is market demand elasticity, $E = (dQ/dp)(p/Q)$. Recalling again from Chapter 3 that the monopoly pricing markup is

$$(p - c)/p = 1/(-E),$$

we see that the Cournot model reduces the monopoly markup as n increases because it multiplies it by the fraction, $1/n$. Notice how general the Cournot markup rule is. When $n = 1$, the monopoly case, $(p - c)/p = 1/n(-E)$ reduces to $(p - c)/p = 1/(-E)$, the correct monopoly markup rule. When $n = 2$, the price is lower, and this reduction in price continues as n increases. Indeed, when n is very large, $1/n(-E)$ is essentially zero, implying that the markup is zero, and price essentially equals marginal cost. This is how Cournot showed that market outcomes vary depending on n, the number of firms, from monopoly to competition.

An important lesson of this analysis is that the firm's willingness to markup its marginal cost varies with the fraction of the market it can expect to win. We see that the fraction, $1/n$, is the market share of one firm. As long as that share is significant (as Figure 5.1 demonstrates for 2 firms, where each has a 50 percent market share), the firm appreciates how its output affects market quantity and, hence, price, and so it restrains its output. This appreciation is most complete for the monopoly, who controls the entire market, but it extends to smaller but still substantial market shares. When the firm has only a small share of the market, it can see its own gain from an increase in its quantity, but because that quantity is a small fraction of the market it anticipates only a small effect—if any—on market price. Thus, the opportunity a monopoly has to see the effect of its actions on the whole market is available also to each of a few firms that have large market shares. It withers away, however, as the number of firms increases until each firm has only a very small market share and can see no effect on market price from its actions.

The effect of changing the number of firms, n, is shown in Table 5.A2.1 of Appendix 5.2, which is reproduced here as Table 5.1. Profit per firm, π_i, falls as n increases. Industry profit, Π, falls with n also, but not as fast because π_i is multiplied by the growing n to obtain industry profit, Π. Table 5.1 also shows how output per firm, q_i, market output, Q, and market price, p, vary with the number of firms at market equilibria. As the number of firms increases, output per firm declines, market output increases, market price declines, and, as already noted, profit per firm and profit for the entire industry decline.

The Stackelberg Leader-Follower Model

Cournot assumed that all firms chose simultaneously. Suppose one, the **leader**, decides its output before the other, or **follower**, firm does, and suppose the leader also anticipates the behavior of the follower. Heinrich von Stackelberg (1934) con-

TABLE 5.1 Illustrative Cournot Outcomes with Linear Demand and Constant Cost

n	q_i	Q	p	π_i	Π
1	40	40	0.60	16.00	16.00
2	26.7	53.3	0.47	7.13	14.26
3	20	60	0.40	4.00	12.00
4	16	64	0.36	2.56	10.24
5	13.3	66.7	0.33	1.73	8.64
6	11.4	68.6	0.31	1.30	7.80
7	10	70	0.30	1.00	7.00
80	1	80	0.20	about 0	about 0

ceived this possibility, which allows the leader to take advantage of information it has about the follower.

In the Cournot model, each of two firms assumes the others' output is constant. The firms then adjust their outputs until they reach an equilibrium, which is really the intersection of their best-response functions or the simultaneous solution of those functions. Instead, by having one firm move first as leader with knowledge of the follower's behavior, Stackelberg showed how that leader could improve its profit relative to the amount it would earn at the Cournot solution.

Figure 5.3 demonstrates the Stackelberg solution. As in the Cournot case in Figure 5.1, we begin with the market demand curve. Instead of subtracting a *constant* quantity from market demand to obtain the individual firm's residual demand curve, we now subtract the other firm's best-response function output from market demand. That is, we subtract the output the follower chooses for any output set by the leader. Subtracting the follower's output from the market demand yields the residual demand curve faced by the leader, $d_R d_R$ in Figure 5.3. The leader then maximizes profit by setting marginal revenue for this residual demand curve, MR_R, equal to marginal cost, c.

The Stackelberg problem is different from the Cournot problem, first because the Stackelberg firms make sequential rather than simultaneous decisions. Not only that, but the leader knows how the follower will react, so the best-response function of the follower firm becomes part of the leader's profit function *before* that function is maximized. Then when the leader maximizes profit with respect to q_1, the leader's output is found to be $q_1 = (a - c)/2b$. This is the monopoly quantity. We can substitute the leader's quantity into the follower's reaction function, $q_2 = (a - bq_1 - c)/2b$, to yield the follower's best-response output: $q_2 = (a - c)/4b$. The leader and follower together thus have total output of

$$Q = q_1 + q_2 = (a - c)/2b + (a - c)/4b = 3(a - c)/4b,$$

Figure 5.3 *The Stackelberg Leader Solution*

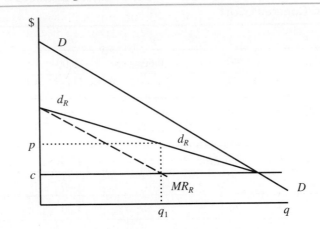

which means the market price is $p = (a + 3c)/4$. The output for two Stackelberg firms is actually the same as the output of a Cournot market that contains *three* firms.

Relative to Cournot's solution for the same number of firms, the Stackelberg solution therefore features larger market quantity, lower price, and lower total profit. Despite lower total profit for both firms, the leader makes more profit than a Cournot duopolist and so prefers the leader's role. But Stackelberg acknowledged that as the firms grow in number, many may seek the leader's roll and predictions are more diffi-cult, so an equilibrium might not even emerge.

The classic Cournot, Bertrand, Edgeworth, and Stackelberg models all assume that entry is barred. We now want to move from these models toward the real world, and we begin by considering possible effects of entry.

5.3 | ENTRY CONDITIONS

A few Cournot or Stackelberg firms may have market power because entry to their industries is not possible, so the few firms can raise price and not have their market invaded by entrants. We know, however, that free entry can prevent monopoly, and it can also destroy the independent tendency of oligopolists to restrict their outputs. Even if oligopolists can agree to raise price, that may attract new entrants to the mar-ket whose added output can bring price back to the competitive level. Because of its great importance, the process of business firm entry that has been ignored thus far is worth studying in some detail. Here we briefly review major entry barriers, beginning with the complete absence of barriers in a contestable market and proceeding to government entry barriers, absolute cost advantage, exit barriers, and imperfect information. Then we examine in more detail economies of scale and cost function properties as entry barriers and the effect of entry conditions on the size distribution of firms in an industry.

A Review of Entry Barriers

As a reminder of how markets can work without entry barriers, consider contestable markets. Contestable market theory emphasizes the role of entry, and its assumptions make entry drive the competitive process. The theory assumes away sunk costs and other entry barriers, and without them entrants can discipline a contestable market even when its firms are few in number. One firm may seem to control a contestable market, yet if it tries to raise price above average cost it can lose the market to an entrant. Essentially, entrants replace exiting firms as the source of competition so they make the number of firms already in the market less important. Now consider entry barriers that can upset this force of entry.

Governments create legal entry barriers, as when Queen Elizabeth I decreed that no one but her groom could import playing cards into England. Governmental entry barriers can be extreme, as when only one public utility is allowed to supply electricity in a given area. In some countries, government authorities put serious barriers in the way of entrants to all industries, such as lengthy application procedures and substantial fees. Such barriers can reduce efficiency and can even invite corruption.[13] In many American cities, taxicabs are separately certified and entry to provide service in the city is limited. The rational of such regulation is to ensure standards of fairness in the treatment of consumers, but the influence of existing operators to block entry almost certainly plays a role. In New York, the value of certification for one taxicab often exceeds $200,000 and represents the added profit that certification allows because entry is limited.[14] Another example of a governmentally created entry barrier is a patent, which, in many countries including the United States, gives exclusive use of an idea to an inventor for 20 years. A comparable invention may have to be made in order for another firm to be able to enter and compete, and that task can be a serious barrier.

Some entry barriers may develop naturally with time. An absolute cost advantage can develop for an incumbent firm—due perhaps to experience in learning a technique—which puts any entrant at a disadvantage. The existing firm with an absolute cost advantage can earn profit while an entrant only breaks even, and because the incumbent firm can cause an entrant more serious harm, entry is discouraged. These cost advantages for incumbents are not easily remedied because they arise without any misbehavior, and they take many forms. For instance, simply by beginning production ahead of other firms, the recipient of a government-awarded patent may achieve cost advantages that last beyond the intended patent period.

Even an exit barrier, which makes exit difficult, can be an entry barrier. Exit barriers can exist when costs must be sunk, because sunk costs cannot easily be recovered, and a firm hesitates to enter whenever costs are hard to retrieve.[15] The investment in a nuclear power plant is sunk, because it lasts a long time and has no other use. This is the important difference between sunk costs, which a firm cannot

---

[13] See Djankov, La Porta, Lopez-de-Silanes, and Shleifer (2002).

[14] See Frankena and Pautler (1984).

[15] For review of the effects of sunk costs, see Schmalensee (1992) and Sutton (1991).

retrieve for a long time, and avoidable costs, which a firm can easily terminate. When costs must be sunk, an entrant wants more assurance that prospects will not turn sour after entry, because the firm will not be able to exit. Sunk costs follow also from asset specificity, or specialization, such as stamping dies that involves essentially irretrievable commitment to a specific product shape.

Imperfect information may also be a barrier to entry. No matter how promising, a small, striving firm may be unable to persuade investors to finance its entry into a market. Some technologies require very large investments, often because they require large-scale operations to achieve efficiency. Such a need for large investments can be an entry barrier with imperfect information among investors because an unknown firm will find it hard to raise large sums of money. Vertical integration can increase the necessary capital requirements for entry, because it means that firms must be larger— they must operate in more of the activities needed to produce a final good—to succeed. Large capital requirements can thus give already existing firms an advantage over potential entrants that is not really unfair, in that existing firms made the investments, but the advantage can be a barrier to a new firm, nonetheless. When large capital requirements are related to economies of scale, that creates a more specific entry barrier.

Economies of Scale and Limit Pricing

Scale economies can inhibit competition by making entry difficult in a way that goes beyond the problem of needing a large investment. In the perfectly competitive case, a new firm can enter with scarcely any effect on market price. With significant economies of scale, however, a newly entering firm must produce enough output to achieve a competitive level of average cost, which may require a significant fraction of industry output. If its output is a significant fraction of industry output, the entrant must consider the effect its entry will have on market price.

Suppose, for example, that a new entrant must increase industry output by 10 percent to reach efficient size. It then has to anticipate that its entry will lower market price. The potential entrant might think that to win a 10 percent share of the market it must force price down by, say, 5 percent. Then the firm will not even attempt entry unless the current market price is at least 5 percent above the level at which it can make a reasonable profit. The highest price that does not stimulate entry—because entry would force price below average cost—is called a **limit price**. It is an upper limit on the price the existing firms can charge without attracting new entry. This is an example where existing firms have market power because they can raise price above a competitive level without inducing entry.

In these circumstances, a reduction in transportation costs may enlarge the sizes of markets and improve their effectiveness. Because the minimum efficient size for a firm is a smaller fraction of a larger market, that means entry has a smaller effect on price, which in turn lowers the limit price. That is how international trade can enforce competition. Many countries have a domestic market too small to support a single automobile producer, but producers from other countries compete for their business as long as no one has a commanding advantage in transportation cost. When the techniques of production, then, offer significant economies of large scale, and only a small number of efficient-sized suppliers exist in one country, tariff policies and transportation costs can become crucial in determining whether competition functions effectively.

When a market is small enough, and if firms that have significant economies of scale would be satisfied with only modestly elevated profits, they might tacitly employ limit pricing to discourage entry. To benefit from preventing entry, however, the existing firms themselves must resist the temptation to expand. For limit pricing to succeed in maintaining elevated profit levels, a few firms would have to have large enough market shares to forgo expansion, as the Cournot model might imply, or they would need real, or tacit, agreement to constrain their outputs.

Thus, even if new entry is prevented, internal expansion may upset a cooperative agreement on price. It is true that if every firm has a rising long-run average cost curve, price can remain above the level of minimum average cost and yet firms within the industry may not want to expand. They are operating in the rising-average-cost portion of their long-run average cost functions, so the firms' marginal costs can be higher than their average costs, and marginal cost can equal a price that remains above average cost without motivating expansion.

If every firm experiences falling or constant average cost in the relevant output range, however, barring entry alone cannot maintain a high price, because capacity expansion can appear profitable to a firm within the industry whenever price is above average cost. This desire to expand can be stronger in a firm that has a small market share, as the Cournot model shows. Firms with small market shares do not resist this urge to expand, so even if larger firms appreciate the Cournot benefit from restraining capacity, smaller ones may force price reductions by expanding.[16]

Entry and the Size Distribution of Firms

Real-world industries may not contain firms that are all the same size, and this helps to foster different goods and services from different companies based in part on firm-size differences. Chapter 2 began with a representation of costs for firms in competition, on grounds that firms' costs determine their decisions about output and investment, and those costs led firms to all be about the same size. The firms' average cost curves were shaped like the bottom of the letter U, so firms had economies of scale at small outputs and diseconomies of scale at large outputs. When industries with these U-shaped cost curves are in equilibrium, and many firms are operating at the low points of their average cost curves, they are all about the same size. In most real-world industries, however, average cost does not reach a minimum at a unique output, but instead remains constant over a wide range of outputs. Over that range, technology allows firms to operate under constant returns to scale, with the same average cost.[17] Not surprisingly, then, firms in those industries may come in a wide variety of sizes, as constant average cost over a range of different outputs would suggest.

---

[16] For evidence of such an effect, see Sherman (1971b, 1972). Experimental evidence indicates that the cost of capacity affects the tendency to constrain capacity expansion (Sherman, 1971a).

[17] For classic studies finding widespread constant average cost, see Johnston (1960) and Walters (1961).

Figure 5.4 *The Size Distribution of Firms in the U.S. Automobile Industry*

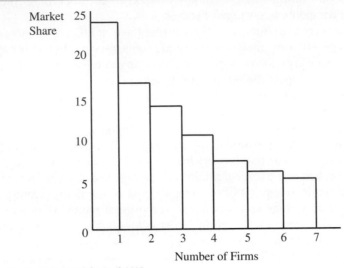

Source: *Ward's AutoInfoBank for April, 2005.*

Figure 5.4 shows the number of firms and their market shares in the U.S. automobile industry, with firms ordered so the first firm is the largest. A few firms have quite large market shares and as there are more firms we move to successively smaller market shares. This pattern of sizes and numbers of firms is called the **size distribution of firms** for the industry. A perfectly competitive industry would tend to show a series of equally tall columns, representing little difference in the sizes of firms. In contrast, the automobile industry shows a variety of firm sizes, and that can affect the terms of competition

When stimulated by product innovations, new industries pass through stages of growth, beginning with the innovator introducing the product.[18] More new entrants usually follow. At some point a "shake-out" ensues, as the number of firms declines because exiting firms exceed entering firms. The industry finally settles down to a mature stage with the possibility of modest entry, and it eventually declines, perhaps even being replaced by a newer innovation. In the mature stage, which usually lasts longer than other stages, the rate of new firm entry into the industry typically influences the distribution of firms by size. Until significant entry into the U.S. automobile market by foreign firms in the 1980s and 1990s, there had been almost no entry for nearly 60 years, and that had produced a size distribution with few firms of unequal sizes. Industry size distributions range from concentrated, where a few large firms have a large fraction of sales, to unconcentrated, where firms tend to be more equal in size, no firm has a large share of the market, and even the largest firms are not very much larger than others.

---

[18] For description of this process, see Gort and Klepper (1982). See also Jovanovic (1982b), and Jovanovic and McDonald (1994a, 1994b), where imitation and innovation are examined.

In most stable or mature industries, some firms fail while others succeed. Without new firms coming into existence through the process of entry, the dynamic evolution of the industry by itself tends to produce larger firms. Without entry, as some firms fail the successful ones take over more of the industry. The late Nobel laureate Herbert Simon, working with another economist, Charles Bonini, provided a dynamic model of firm and industry development that considered such factors.[19] They found empirically that, when industries are more difficult to enter, they tend to become more concentrated.

To see the Simon and Bonini argument, consider the evolution of a growing industry over time, where some firms succeed better than others in serving consumers. If there is no new entry, the more successful firms grow more than the average, while the less successful grow less or decline or fail. Over time, from such a process of firm growth without new entry, we might expect a concentrated industry, led by a few repeatedly successful firms. On the other hand, if many firms are entering all the time, there can be new challengers at every turn, and more firms can attract consumers. A steady infusion of new firms works against the concentration of the industry, simply by offering more sources of successful enterprise and more survival strategies.

The regularity in market structure that tends to follow from patterns of entry and firm growth probably helps to make simple measures of concentration crudely effective as indicators of competitiveness. The main purpose of measures of concentration is to indicate the degree of competitiveness in an industry in a simple way, even when firms differ in size. To the extent that rate of entry and firm growth opportunity regularly influence the size distribution of firms, any simple representation of that size distribution—either the top-four-firm concentration ratio or the Herfindahl-Hirschman Index—is able to reflect competitiveness. The pervasive underlying forces help to make simple representations of market structure effective in predicting consequences.

Competition may work differently when there is a mixture of large and small firms. Large firms may commit to larger and more specialized production facilities, for instance, that require steady production to be economical, while small firms are more adaptable and can adjust output more readily as industry demand changes over time.[20] Large and small firms may have different financing opportunities, different labor relations, and different selling methods. The large firms may constitute the more efficient and more successful of the many firms that are constantly entering the industry at small sizes. Large firms may even grow to a point where they can make entry difficult for others and thus interfere with the process of competition.

Ways to characterize the firms and their different sizes are called **concentration measures**. We have seen that because firms in many industries have constant average costs over wide ranges of output, and may enter the industry at different times, there may not be equal-size firms, as in the Cournot or even the perfectly competitive models. Instead, the firms may differ in size, so the number of firms alone does not indicate competitiveness, and some other way is needed to represent it. That is the purpose of concentration measures.

---

[19] See Simon and Bonini (1958).

[20] For evidence of this pattern in the lumber industry, see Mills and Schumann (1985).

5.4 | CONCENTRATION MEASURES

Classical duopoly or oligopoly models are simple. They ignore entry by assuming it away. While they capture incentives that arise among a small number of firms in a market, they usually assume all firms are the same size, so the number of firms alone tells how concentrated decision making is in the industry. The real world is more complex, not only because entry is important but also because firms differ in size, and we need simple ways to characterize such complexity.

Industry concentration focuses on an industry and can be measured as the percentage of sales, employment, or other activity that occurs in the largest 3, 4, 8, or 20 firms. Industry concentration indicates the concentration of decision-making power within one industry. Industry concentration reflects both the number of firms in the industry and their market shares, to place the industry between competition (almost no concentration) and monopoly (100 percent concentration in one firm). A very crude measure of economic power in a whole economy is **aggregate concentration**, the percentage of an economy's total sales, employment, value added, or other measure of activity that originates in the largest 50, or perhaps the largest 200, firms. This idea of concentration at an aggregate level, across an entire economy, reflects the potential political influence that comes with economic power. We consider industry concentration and aggregate concentration in turn.

Industry Concentration

When firms in a single market are few in number, each can have a noticeable effect on the others, especially if new entry is difficult, and a few firms might establish cooperative relations with each other. As a consequence, for markets with few firms any of several prices (or levels of advertising, or of research, and so forth) might be maintained for some time. Nevertheless, we can analyze the specific ways that actions by the firms affect one another. How their profits are interdependent can influence, in turn, the way the firms behave, and knowing the way each firm's actions affect others helps to identify the possibilities and sort harmful ones from constructive ones. Measures of industry concentration provide a crude indicator of the nature of this interaction.

Any measure of industry concentration requires an industry definition to identify the firms to be included in the calculation of concentration, and defining industries can be a difficult problem. The Bureau of the Census in the United States provides an extensive system of industry definitions and dates back to 1810. The resulting industry boundaries do not always match the boundaries of economic activity well, but despite the many problems, the system and the data collected according to it are extremely valuable. The units of observation in this census are **establishments**, which are physical production locations such as factories.

The new **North American Industry Classification System (NAICS)** provides definitions that are consistent with those used by Canada and Mexico, thus, improving opportunities for trade analysis. The NAICS places an establishment in an industry based on the establishment's activity rather than, say, the main activity of the firm that owns the establishment. A Standard Industrial Classification (SIC) system for defining industries was adopted in the 1930s. That SIC system is currently being replaced by the new NAICS industry definitions. The census of manufacturers has broadened since the 1930s, and it was thoroughly revised for 1997 by adoption of the NAICS to be more consistent with Canada and Mexico and to identify more industries, especially in the service sector. The census of manufacturers is now carried out every five years, in years ending in 2 (such as 2002) or 7.

The new NAICS system is related to the older SIC system, with 460 industry categories either unchanged or reproducible from older categories. The NAICS contains 710 industries, however, that are either new or revised so they have no counterpart in the SIC, which means that long-run trends are difficult to follow for these industries. Like the SIC, the NAICS is hierarchical, with 20 broad sectors at the top (the SIC had 10 sectors as its broadest groups). The NAICS includes many new sectors, such as Information; Professional, Scientific, and Technical Services; Educational Services; Health Care and Social Assistance; Arts, Entertainment, and Recreation, for examples, all covering activities that used to be included in the SIC's single Information Division. Within each sector are successively more detailed breakdowns into more narrowly defined industries. Table 5.2 illustrates how the NAICS breaks the hierarchy of industries within the Manufacturing Sector into parts. One of many subcategories within Manufacturing is Food Manufacturing, and among categories under Food Manufacturing is Cookie, Cracker, and Pasta Manufacturing, which in turn break into three more narrow industries.

Section 5.2 showed that in the Cournot model the number of firms in an industry affects the firms' motivations. This motivation was also an effect of market share because the firms were equal in size and the number of firms determined their market shares. When sizes of firms differ, we can expect their relative sizes to influence the forms of their interdependence and their strategies. Using industry data, several simple ways of representing both number of firms and relative sizes in a market can crudely indicate the scope for anticompetitive behavior. The leading measures of industry concentration are the *concentration ratio* and the *Herfindahl-Hirschman Index*. After each measure is discussed, their values for a few sample industries will be given to illustrate them.

TABLE 5.2 Illustration of North American Industry Classification System Hierarchy

NAICS Code	Industry Group
311	Food Manufacturing
31182	Cookie, Cracker, and Pasta Manufacturing
311821	Cookie and Cracker Manufacturing
311822	Flour Mixes and Dough Manufacturing
311823	Dry Pasta Manufacturing

The Concentration Ratio

The **concentration ratio** measures the percent of an industry's sales, assets, employment, or value added[21] that is in the hands of a small number of the largest of all the firms in the industry. The value of shipments, representing sales, is the measure most frequently used.[22] Aggregate concentration measures, to be considered in the next subsection, examine the largest firms in the economy, while industry concentration focuses on one industry at a time. The industry measure is most relevant for assessing the competitiveness of an industry.

The simplest measure of industry concentration used in the United States is called the **top-4-firm concentration ratio,** or **C4**. It is the percentage of activity (usually value added or value of shipments or employment) in an industry represented by its *largest* four firms. Some European countries use a top-3-firm concentration measure. As an example of the C4 measure, suppose an industry contains five equal-sized firms, so each firm has 20 percent of the market. Then the top-4-firm concentration ratio is 80 (20 + 20 + 20 + 20 = 80). Table 5.3 shows the number of firms and industry profit from Table 5.1 and relates them to the concentration measures that the number of equal-sized firms produce. If instead the largest firm has 60 percent and four other firms each has 10 percent, the top-4-firm concentration ratio is 90 (60 + 10 + 10 + 10 = 90). The C4 or similar concentration ratio measure is used in part because it is so easy to calculate. Sometimes a top-8-firm concentration ratio, C8, or even a top-20-firm measure of concentration, C20, is used.

TABLE 5.3 **The Relation between Concentration and Profit**

n	Π	C4	HHI
1	16.00	100	10,000
2	14.26	100	5,000
3	12.00	100	3,267
4	10.24	100	2,500
5	8.64	80	2,000
6	7.80	67	1,667
7	7.00	57	1,436
80	about 0	5	125

[21] Value added is the difference between an enterprise's value of shipments and the value of its purchases, which is essentially the value that is added to those purchases by the enterprise. This value added is the net contribution of an enterprise to the nation's gross domestic product.

[22] Value of shipments approximates sales but can include sales from a previous period, while sales can include items to be shipped in a future period. Value of shipments is used because it tends to be a reliable and verifiable measure.

BOX 5.2 Herfindahl-Hirschman Index (HHI) Calculations

Squaring the percentage market shares of firms and summing them for the HHI:

One firm: $100 \times 100 = 10,000$,
Two firms: $50 \times 50 + 50 \times 50 = 5,000$,
Three firms: $33 \times 33 + 33 \times 33 + 33 \times 33 = 3,333$,
Four firms: $25 \times 25 + 25 \times 25 + 25 \times 25 + 25 \times 25 = 2,500$,
Five firms: $20 \times 20 + 20 \times 20 + 20 \times 20 + 20 \times 20 + 20 \times 20 = 2,000$, and
One hundred firms: $(1 \times 1) 100 = 100$.

The Herfindahl-Hirschman Index

A slightly more sophisticated measure of concentration is called the **Herfindahl-Hirschman Index (HHI)**, and it involves calculating the market share of each firm, squaring it, and summing those squares. To calculate the HHI, all firms' market shares of a particular measure of activity for an industry—again, the activity is usually value added or value of shipments or employment—are expressed in percentage form and then squared. The sum of those squares is the HHI. Box 5.2 illustrates the HHI using market shares (measured, let us say, by value of shipments) for firms of equal size, when there are 1, 2, 3, 4, 5, or 100 firms in the market. Notice that the HHI declines, from 10,000 to 2,000, as the number of equal-sized firms in the market increases from one to five, and that it falls to 100 with 100 equal-sized firms.

Like the concentration ratio, the HHI is most useful as a way to compare roughly the structures of industries that have different numbers and different *sizes* of firms. For example, consider sales measures when five firms have equal market shares of 20 percent. Box 5.2 shows that with five equal-sized firms the HHI is obtained by

---

BOX 5.3 The Effect of Squaring Market Shares in the HHI

We can observe a general pattern in sets of numbers in which the number of numbers is the same and each set yields the same total. An example is one set of five numbers—20, 20, 20, 20, 20—and another set of five numbers—60, 10, 10, 10, 10—where the total is 100 in each set. Squaring and summing the first set of equal numbers yields 2,000, while the second set of unequal numbers yields 4,000. When the numbers in a set are equal and those numbers are squared and summed, that sum of squares is *smaller* than the corresponding sum of squares for any set that reaches the same total but contains unequal numbers. Squaring the market shares in the HHI thus tends to produce a larger concentration measure when firms are unequal in size, because the larger numbers produce still larger squares. Because market power is potentially greater among firms that are unequal in size, where a large firm can have more influence, this property in a measure of industry concentration is desirable.

calculating $20^2 = 400$ for each firm and then adding the results for five firms to obtain 2,000. Now instead, suppose the five firms in the market have shares of 60, 10, 10, 10, and 10 percent. We then have the HHI $= 60^2 + 10^2 + 10^2 + 10^2 + 10^2 = 3,600 + 100 + 100 + 100 + 100 = 4,000$. Activity is more concentrated in the latter case, because one firm has 60 percent of the sales, and the HHI reflects that concentration in an index of 4,000 instead 2,000 when all firms have equal shares of 20 percent.

Even the market with an HHI of 2,000 is quite concentrated, because there are only five firms in it. The extreme of concentration, however, is the case of one firm having 100 percent of the market, which yields the highest possible HHI of $100^2 = 10,000$. At the other extreme, if there are many firms and all have tiny shares, the HHI is virtually zero.

Interpreting Industry Concentration

Although concentration measures can characterize the size distribution of firms in a variety of circumstances, they also apply where firms are equal in size, as in the Cournot model. There they also reveal a clear positive connection between concentration measure and industry profit.

As concentration falls in Table 5.3, whether measured by the top-4 concentration ratio or the HHI, profit also falls. As Cournot incentives change with an increase in the number of firms, industry output increases, and industry profit declines. The Cournot model also assumes no entry, so this connection between concentration and profit presumes that entry is very difficult.

Table 5.4 presents the number of firms, the value of shipments, concentration ratios based on the top 4, 8, and 20 firms, and HHIs for a variety of U.S. manufacturing industries for the year 2002. The largest value of the HHI for these industries is 2,662, in the Electronic Computers manufacturing industry, and the largest value for the top-4-firm concentration ratio is 87, found in the Primary Batteries industry. Not surprisingly, the top-4-firm concentration ratio and the HHI are correlated. Other highly concentrated industries include Breakfast Cereals and Motor Vehicle manufacturing.

Table 5.4 can be used to show weaknesses that follow from relying on national data. National data can *understate* the degree of concentration for a market, such as Ready-Mix Concrete, which has an HHI of 63 and a top-4-firm concentration ratio of 11. Remember, these are numbers for the entire United States. Ready-mix concrete makers serve local markets because ready-mixed concrete is very costly to transport. National measures here can overstate the competitiveness of local markets, which may sometimes have only one firm. National data do not reflect the market power that may exist locally.[23]

Another problem results because concentration data come from only domestic manufacturers. The Motor Vehicles and Car Bodies industry in the United States has an HHI of 2,324 and a top-4-firm concentration ratio of 81, both numbers indicative of high concentration. These measures *overstate* the concentration, however, because they omit shipments from foreign countries, which amount to more than one-fourth of industry sales to U.S. customers. In industries such as motor vehicles, where

---

[23] Ways to consider local markets and multiproduct markets do exist. See Hayes and Ross (1996).

TABLE 5.4 Concentration Measures by U.S. Manufacturing Industry for the Year 2002

Industry	Number of Companies	Value of Shipments ($ millions)	Top 4 in Value of Shipments	Top 8 in Value of Shipments	Top 20 in Value of Shipments	Herfindahl-Hirschman Index
Breakfast cereal manufacturing	45	9,103	78	91	98	2,521
Soft drink manufacturing	294	32,082	52	63	78	896
Snack food manufacturing	411	17,047	56	65	78	1,980
Men's slacks	92	5,154	80	87	94	2,515
Women's dresses	525	3,627	22	32	48	186
Soaps detergents	699	16,596	61	72	81	2,006
Ready-mix concrete	2,614	21,620	11	17	28	63
Electronic computers	465	47,730	76	89	96	2,662
Primary batteries	33	2,890	87	97	99+	2,573
Motor vehicles	308	240,767	81	91	98	2,324

Source: Concentration Ratios: 2002, Report ECO2-31SR-1, U.S. Department of Commerce, U.S. Bureau of the Census, available at http://www.census.gov/prod/ec02/ec0231sr1.pdf. For general information on the NAICS, see http://www.census.gov/epcd/www/pdf/naicsdat.pdf.

imports are important, omitting them results in understatement of competitiveness and overstatement of possible market power. One reason for developing the NAICS is that imports—at least from North American countries—can properly be accounted for in concentration calculations.

Aggregate Concentration

Overall concentration across an entire economy reflects economic power. Aggregate concentration measures are intended to answer questions such as, What portion of the whole economy do the largest 50 firms control? The question raised by aggregate concentration is not about monopoly, which can arise only within one industry, but rather about economic power more generally, perhaps as influence in Congress, for example.

Concern about the economic power of large firms goes back to early populist sentiments in the United States. It influenced the formation of the Interstate Commerce Commission in 1887 to restrain railroad power, for instance, and the passage of the Sherman Act in 1890 to harness monopoly power. This concern about economic power goes beyond monopoly power, which affects one market, to economic power generally that may create legislation, influence bureaucrats, and even persuade the public. Aggregate concentration is a crude measure of how much economic power some number of large firms in the economy control.

To give a sense of the degree of aggregate concentration in the manufacturing part of the U.S. economy, Table 5.5 presents measures of aggregate concentration in value added, employment, value of shipments, and new capital expenditures for manufacturing in the year 2002. The value of shipments is essentially the sales of the 50, 100, 150, or 200 largest companies, but sales may not indicate market power. A company that purchases a large portion of what it sells, as a grocery store does, for example, may have larger sales than a company that makes its product from scratch, perhaps an aluminum producer, but the latter company may have many more employees, more assets, and more economic significance. Employment might serve better than sales as the measure of economic significance that we seek when calculating aggregate concentration.

Value added is a good measure to use in evaluating aggregate concentration because it captures the magnitude of firms' contributions to economic activity. The difference between value of shipments, or sales, and value of purchases, or inputs, is the increase in the value of output that a firm produces, which is why we call it value added. Measuring aggregate concentration in value added thus indicates the economic significance of the largest 50, 100, or other number of firms. Among other measures shown in Table 5.5, employment comes closest to capturing these value-added effects, because value is added to inputs primarily by labor. Assets also

TABLE 5.5 Percentage of Manufacturing Sector Accounted for by the Largest Enterprises in 2002

Largest Enterprises*	Value Added	Employment	Value of Shipments	New Capital Expenditures
Top 50	25.3	12.1	24.5	19.9
Top 100	33.7	17.4	33.3	28.5
Top 150	38.7	21.3	38.4	33.8
Top 200	42.4	24.4	43.2	42.6

*Ranked according to value added in manufacturing.
Source: Bureau of the Census; http://www.census.gov/prod/ec02/ec0231sr1.pdf.

contribute importantly to value added. But assets are difficult to measure reliably. They are long lasting, which means they may become obsolete, and their value at any one time depends on accounting rules for depreciation that may not capture their true value. Value added is a better measure of economic significance.

In 2002 the 50 largest enterprises accounted for 25.3 percent of value added, 24.5 percent of the value of shipments, and slightly more than 12 percent of employment, which is a substantial portion of the nation's manufacturing activity. The largest 200 firms accounted for more than 42 percent of value added, over 43 percent of the value of shipments, more than 24 percent of all employment, and over 42 percent of new capital expenditures. Whether these percentages mean that large firms have political power and influence is not clear, but these measures do raise that question. The 200 largest firms are decidedly an important part of the economy. Data for the aggregate concentration measures in Table 5.5 are from NAICS. Rank according to value added in manufacturing was used to identify the largest enterprises in Table 5.5.

Because it may be difficult to conclude whether levels of aggregate concentration in Table 5.5 indicate troublesome economic power, an indication of growth or decline might be of interest. Professor Lawrence White gathered aggregate concentration data for manufacturing from 1947 to 1997 using the value-added measure.[24] These concentration data show some increase in aggregate concentration from 1947 to 1962, and since then aggregate concentration in manufacturing has been remarkably stable.

Manufacturing is only part of the U.S. economy, and a declining part of it at that. In 1947, manufacturing accounted for about 30 percent of private sector Gross Domestic Product in the United States, but at the end of the century it accounted for only about 20 percent.[25] A broader compilation of aggregate concentration would go beyond manufacturing to the entire private sector. At the request of Professor White (2002), the Bureau of the Census prepared such a measure for the 1988 to 1999 period, but it could only be done using employment and payroll data. There was a slight decline in these three categories from 1988 through the mid-1990s, followed by a modest rise at the end of the period, a decline that continues in 2002, but the aggregate concentration has remained quite stable.

Aggregate concentration shows that a modest number of firms, such as the largest 100 or the largest 200, control substantial resources and can have a significant effect on the economy. The concentration in manufacturing is greater than in other parts of the economy and has remained quite stable over four decades despite a decline in the importance of manufacturing in the economy. From the late 1980s into the late 1990s aggregate concentration in the entire private sector was also fairly stable. Merger activity was intense at the end of the 1990s, but it does not seem to explain changes in aggregate concentration, largely because mergers occur more commonly among firms that are not extremely large. Moderately large firms are growing in importance relative to the very largest and very smallest size classes.[26]

---

[24] See White (2002, p. 144).
[25] See White (2002, p. 143).
[26] See White (2002, pp. 158–159).

5.5 | EMPIRICAL EVIDENCE

The hypothesis that motivated early empirical studies in *industrial organization* was that some measures of market structure would affect the conduct of firms, which in turn would influence the industry's performance. Stimulated by calls for empirical investigations from Harvard Professor Edward Mason (1939), researchers examined, first, industries as individual case studies and, second, data from many industries in cross-sectional form, seeking general connections between measures of industry structure and measures of industry performance. After all, Cournot's model showed that having barriers to entry and fewer firms in a market would lead to higher industry profit. The development of industrial organization as a special field of economics grew in part from this effort to make concrete empirical measurements that could reflect the organization of an industry, to gauge the effect of industry organization on how the industry performed.

Many cross-sectional studies were carried out, and they came to be called Structure-Conduct-Performance studies. Early measures of industry structure included the concentration measures described above, especially the top-4-firm or top-8-firm concentration ratio, and crude means of judging entry difficulty. These structural factors were expected to affect how the firms behaved, which in turn was expected to determine the industry's performance. Performance was first taken to be reflected in profitability. High profitability was interpreted as a mark of poor performance on the assumption that cooperative behavior among few firms in an industry would result in higher prices and greater profits. More recent studies analyze possible behavior in more sophisticated ways and use better empirical techniques. Some focus on different measures of performance. While it is not possible to examine in detail the many studies of this sort, some illustrations convey the types of conclusions they allow.

Structure-Conduct-Performance (SPC) Studies

At the beginning of this SPC research, empirical measures had to be invented, and by today's standard they were crude. For example, economist Joe S. Bain (1956) used top-8-firm concentration ratios, C8, and subjectively classified industries into three categories by difficulty of entry, which he labeled "low to moderate," "substantial," and "very high." He used rate of return as a performance measure, but he drew rates of return only from the leading firms in the industries studied. Classifying the industries into categories showed that when industries were both difficult to enter and were highly concentrated, they tended to earn higher rates of return. Many later studies, over different time periods, supported this general finding.[27]

Now it is possible to say that these early studies were flawed. First, the measures used were imperfect, and considerable discretion was involved in determining factors such as entry difficulty. There is also the inherent difficulty that some performance measure, such as price or industry rate of return, may actually influence structure, such

---

[27] See, for example, Mann (1966).

as industry concentration, as when a very profitable firm grows larger. If that can happen, the entire idea behind structure-conduct-performance studies is wrong. Structure is not *causing* performance, in part it may be *caused* by it. We cannot know that, however, because the assumption that structure causes performance is built into the framework of tests. Nevertheless, one must understand the tests that have been performed and see what recent efforts have produced. We thus turn to measures of the three elements of structure-conduct-performance studies.

1. **Structure.** To reflect the number and relative sizes of firms, cross-section studies used concentration ratios, and a variety of measures for entry barriers. First, researchers categorized industries into two groups by whether the top-8-firm concentration ratio was above or below 70 percent. They also crudely categorized industries on a judgmental basis into the three categories noted, "low to moderate," "substantial," and "very high." Researchers gradually developed less subjective entry barrier measures. Cost function estimates yielded information about **minimum efficient size (MES)** by industry, for example, which indicated how large a firm had to be to succeed. Those estimates formed entry barrier measures, either as MES directly or by estimating the funds needed to create a firm of minimum efficient size, which would reflect the difficulty of raising capital to enter the industry.

2. **Conduct.** A range of firm conduct can affect industry performance. A small number of firms might compete less aggressively in price than many firms would, for example, because a few firms might see the effects of such competition on themselves and resist it. To the extent entry is difficult and firms emphasize choice of capacity, or quantity, an effect from the Cournot model could make firms with larger market shares prefer to restrain output. The firms might also decide differently a host of strategic variables, such as advertising or research, based on market structure.

3. **Performance.** Performance measures are even more problematic. Because a market structure that allows firms to exercise market power can yield higher than average profit, attention focused on profit measures to indicate market performance, with high profit indicating low performance. Price itself is a measure that should signal market power when it is high, but judging when a price is high can be difficult without some other reference point, such as cost. Chapter 3 showed the price-cost margin to be related (inversely) to elasticity of demand in monopoly pricing ($(P - MC)/P = 1/(-E)$), and some studies used that measure. The price-cost margin might be high in an industry for another reason, however. If the industry required large investment, it would need high profit margins just to generate funds to compensate investors. To take this effect of investment into account, researchers used the **rate of return on investment**. The rate of return is the revenue of the firm, minus its costs, all divided by the value of the firms's assets. Rate of return thus captures the concerns of investors for profit in relation to the investment required of them. Recall that a "normal" profit rate defined economic profit, which is profit

Figure 5.5 *Relationship of Concentration and Entry Barriers to Rates of Return in Early Studies*

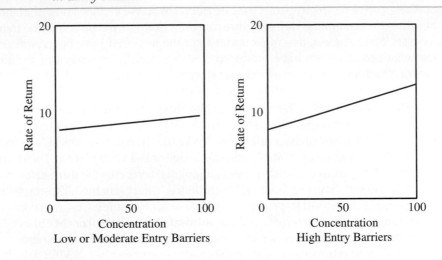

above that normal rate. A high rate of return can indicate that profit is high, meaning that economic profit is being earned, because it takes into account the investment that industry requires.

Figure 5.5, which is from a summary Leonard Weiss (1971) made of early studies by Bain (1956) and Mann (1966), illustrates how the effect of concentration on rate of return can depend on entry barriers. Results of such SPC studies are not robust, however. Economist Yale Brozen (1971) criticized Bain's use of rates of return that were taken from leading firms only, rather than from all firms in an industry, and Brozen duplicated the studies for other time periods and obtained much weaker findings. The measures themselves have also been subject to strong criticism, especially the use of accounting data to calculate rates of return.[28]

The rate of return relies on accounting data for profit in the numerator and for the value of assets in the denominator. The value of assets is especially hard to estimate in part because the life of an asset is not known, and yet the rate-of-return estimate depends on it. The accounting value of assets that is used in rate-of-return estimates does not reliably reflect the market values of the assets. Accounting value is based instead on the historical cost of each asset minus some estimate of loss in value due to depreciation. The resulting accounting value is called **book value**. The depreciation rate in book-value estimates is inherently arbitrary, because it must be decided before the useful life of the asset is actually known.[29]

---

[28] See Fisher and McGowan (1983). Large samples may moderate this weakness, according to Long and Ravenscraft (1984).

[29] Estimates of depreciation are often based on general formulas, such as *straight-line* depreciation, that at best are crude. This depreciation rule divides the original cost of an asset by the number of years it is expected to be useful, and then that fractional value is subtracted each year from original cost to represent loss in the asset's value due to depreciation.

Inflation is another serious problem that arises from using accounting data to value assets.[30] A period of rapid inflation can make historical costs poor indicators of current values, which are now higher, and this problem becomes more serious the longer the asset lives. Suppose you are comparing two industries, one with assets that are replaced every five years and another with assets that are replaced every 25 years. If inflation seriously changes the value of the currency every year, inflation will have less effect on the industry with shorter-lived assets than on the industry with longer-lived assets.

Growth rates also can affect the distortion in asset values caused by inflation. Two industries may have the *same* asset lives, for example, but suppose their growth rates differ. On average, the faster growing industry will have newer assets, because it is adding new assets more rapidly. Inflation will distort accounting values in the faster growing industry less than those of the slower growing industry, where a smaller fraction of assets will be new. Thus, because inflation tends to understate the current value of assets, a slow-growing industry with long-lived assets will appear to have a lower value of assets and thus a higher rate of return than other industries.

There are other accounting problems. Some expenses of the firm actually are genuine investments, and they should be counted as assets in rate-of-return calculations. Examples are advertising and research and development, which can take a long time before they generate revenue and profit. Taxes complicate comparisons also. Industries differ in the taxes they pay, so after-tax data are needed. We can also expect rates of return to differ according to risks in industries, with those possessing more risk requiring higher returns to satisfy their investors. A higher rate of return, then, may be the result of greater risk rather than market power. The measurement of rate of return through accounting data is thus open to serious imperfections.

Using price as a performance measure has the advantage that price is always current. It avoids many of the problems that plague the rate-of-return measure of industry performance. Economist Leonard Weiss (1989) reviewed some of these studies and found that if concentration increased by 10 percent, price tended to increase by 1 to 5 percent. More recent studies have confirmed such an effect of concentration on price in specific industries such as banking[31] or airlines.[32] Other studies have reached comparable conclusions in most cases and have involved natural gas transportation, ocean shipping, local cement markets, hospital prices, and retail food products.[33]

Other Studies

A variety of studies has found effects of market structure, but it is difficult to review and summarize them all. Here, we briefly explore two approaches that reveal important connections between structure and performance. One tries to identify separate

---

[30] An excellent study by Steven Cross (1982) examined problems that are caused by inflation in monetary measures, like asset values, that are the basis for decisions in firms.

[31] See Neumark and Sharpe (1992) and Hannan and Liang (1993).

[32] See Borenstein (1990); Brueckner, Dyer, and Spiller (1992); Morrison and Winston (1990); and Kim and Singal (1993). Airport market share, the importance of an airline in a specific airport's landing capacity, may be a more important influence than passenger share alone. See Evans and Kessides (1993) and Brueckner (2002).

[33] See the review of such studies by Pautler (2001).

effects of market share and concentration to see which is a larger influence on market performance. The other examines the effect of entry condition in a range of markets.

Industry Concentration or Firm Market Share?

If we associate concentration with high prices or other signs of market power, the question arises whether it is really collusive actions of a small number of firms with concentrated decision power. It could simply be the large market shares of firms, which can motivate restrained outputs and higher prices because of incentives that Cournot showed larger firms to have. Firm market shares also tend to be high when concentration is high, so it is difficult to separate their effects. Considerable evidence suggests, however, that large market shares are more important determinants of market performance.[34]

Economist David Ravenscraft (1983), followed by John Kwoka and Ravenscraft (1986), examined this question using the Federal Trade Commission's Line-of-Business (LOB) survey, which considers narrower lines of business than any category in the NAICS (or in the SIC system that preceded it). The LOB survey identifies 261 manufacturing lines of business and 14 others in fields outside manufacturing. One company may operate in as many as 47 of these lines of business, while the average firm operates in 8 of them. This narrow focus on lines of business allows better estimates of effective market shares, which gives better opportunity to compare their effect on market performance with that of concentration. When explaining profitability by both market share and concentration across this LOB sample, market share had a significant positive effect on profitability, while concentration did not.

Effects of Entry

Early studies found that concentration had more effect on performance when entry barriers were high. Using a clever application of limit pricing, economists Timothy Bresnahan and Peter Reiss (1991) consider the effect of entry on competition by examining how larger markets can elicit entry by more firms. They examined five product lines and professions, namely doctors, dentists, druggists, plumbers, and tire dealers, in a variety of 202 local markets in the western United States. They estimated entry thresholds, which are roughly limit prices, the amounts incumbent firms can charge above costs without inducing entry for each product line or profession.

Bresnahan and Reiss expected the entry threshold to be higher for the first firm to operate in a market, a little lower for two firms, and successively lower as more firms were able to operate in larger markets. They found entry thresholds to vary in this way with market size and with the number of firms. The thresholds tended to drop markedly from one to two firms and considerably from two to three firms, but not very much further after that. With respect to tire dealers, the authors examined price data and found prices also fell most with changes from one to two firms, fell less with changes from two to three firms, and did not fall by much after that. Such results are consistent with either concentration or market share affecting price, but it is not possible to tell which cause is crucial. These results, however, are crudely consistent with implications of the Cournot model.

---

[34] Shepherd (1972) and Sherman (1971a, 1971b) provided early evidence for the importance of market share.

BOX 5.4 Who Has the Capacity, and What Does It Cost?

Experimental research has found that capacity levels affect pricing actions when individual subjects operate as firms in laboratory markets. Economists Charles Holt, L. Langan, and Ann Villamill showed, for example, that the number of firms can be less important in influencing market power than the distribution of capacity among the firms, if one firm has control over sufficient capacity that it can affect the market price. More specifically, it can elevate that price when industry demand is so high that the firm's capacity can determine industry capacity. Even if the number of firms is larger, sufficient capacity in the hands of one firm can still lead to higher prices than a market with equal-sized firms. Other experimental markets have shown that high capacity costs can discourage expansion, and resisting expansion helps to sustain higher prices.

See C. A. Holt, L. Langan, and A. Villamill, "Market Power in Double Oral Auctions," *Economic Inquiry,* January 1986, Vol. 28, pp. 107–123; R. Sherman, "Risk Attitude and Cost Variability in a Capacity Choice Experiment, *Review of Economic Studies,* October 1969, Vol. 36, pp 453–466; and R. Sherman, "An Experiment on the Persistence of Price Collusion," *Southern Economic Journal,* April, 1971, Vol. 37, pp. 489–495.

SUMMARY

We can characterize market structure by aspects of the organization of a market—the number of firms and their relative sizes, the conditions of entry and exit, and other factors. A few firms in a market might behave differently from the way a very large number of firms would behave, because the few firms realize how their actions affect each other and how their outputs affect the market price. This conclusion should be modified if there is no entry barrier and no sunk cost in a contestable market. Then easy entry and exit can serve the same purpose as many competitors in a market. Entrants expand industry capacity whenever price rises above the competitive level. In a contestable market, even a single firm, being subject to easy entry from all sides, must operate like a firm in competition.

Product market competition is more complex when there are few firms and entry is difficult. When firms are so few that their profits depend visibly on one another's behavior, we cannot reliably predict any unique market price or quantity. The French economist Augustin Cournot first suggested an independent behavior pattern that would produce a unique equilibrium, a monopoly solution when there is one firm and a competitive solution when there is a very large number of firms. When a market has two firms and entry is not possible, each of the firms can appreciate how its output decisions affect market price, and each may possess some of the monopolist's motive to limit its output and thereby raise price. Each firm can see a residual demand for itself, after the other firm's output is subtracted away from the market, and marginal revenue from that residual demand curve can be set equal to marginal cost at an output lower than the competitive one. The same pattern can arise with three firms, leading to lower price but still above marginal cost. As the number of firms becomes very large, price approaches the competitive level at average cost.

To perpetuate the higher price that a few firms might reach, the firms must be able to limit industry capacity to supply the good. That is, there must be barriers to the entry of new firms. Already existing firms must also resist expansion. Limits on entry that interfere with the ordinary competitive process may allow above normal profits to persist for some time. Entry may be difficult when producers must make large, specialized, and durable investments. Because of economies of scale, producers may need a substantial fraction of the sales in their markets to keep their costs low, and at the resulting equilibrium there may be too few firms to support competition.

Besides their direct influence on the number of firms, entry barriers affect the rate at which firms can enter an industry over time, and that affects the size distribution of firms in the industry. Because average cost tends to be constant in many industries after a minimum efficient size is reached, so firms can have the same costs even when they differ in size, industries may contain firms that differ in size. That makes it difficult to represent competitiveness by the number of firms alone, and that gives rise to other ways to represent it: concentration measures. The industry share of activity controlled by the top 4 firms, called the top-4-firm concentration ratio, or C4, is one measure, and the sum of squares of market shares, the Herfindahl-Hirschman Index, or HHI, is another. Such measures are related to profit in an industry, and they serve to characterize competitiveness.

After a description of the modern business firm in Chapter 4, this chapter has emphasized the environment of the firm in its market structure and has described some measures and effects of market structure. Cournot's analysis shows incentives of the firm but traces essentially deterministic predictions without the range of considerations that open up strategies for the firms. Strategies that market structure may allow have not all been treated yet, and they include cooperatively raising prices above the Cournot level, cutting price below, or designing products that differ from competitors' to win a following of consumers. We consider such market strategies in Chapter 6.

QUESTIONS

1. Consider a market with 1,000 equal-sized firms, where each firm has exactly 0.1 percent of the market.
   a. What is the top-4-firm concentration ratio for this industry? What is the Herfindahl-Hirschman Index for the industry?
   b. Suppose 50 firms in the industry merge into 1 firm. What is the top-4-firm concentration ratio for the industry now? What is the Herfindahl-Hirschman Index for the industry now?
2. Consider a market where demand for the good is given by the equation

$$P = 1 - 0.01Q,$$

where P is price and Q is quantity of the good. Suppose a monopoly serves the market for the good, and there is no possibility for entry. The firm has total cost, TC, of

$$TC = 9 + 0.1Q.$$

a. Does the cost function indicate that economies of scale exist?
b. Find the monopoly price and quantity and the monopoly profit.
c. If entry were possible, can you see any problem for the functioning of competition? Explain in words what the important effect of entry will be and identify when—or essentially why—equilibrium will occur in the market with free entry.

3. Consider a market where demand for the good is given by the equation

$$P = 1 - 0.01Q,$$

where P is price and Q is quantity of the good.

a. Suppose there is only one monopoly firm to serve the market for the good; that is, no entry is possible. The firm has total cost, TC, of

$$TC = 5 + 0.1Q.$$

Find the monopoly price and quantity and the monopoly profit.
b. Now suppose there are two, equal-sized firms whose outputs are q_1 and q_2, and there is no further entry. Total market output is now $q_1 + q_2 = Q$. Each firm has the same cost function as the monopoly in part a, that is, $TC_i = 5 + 0.1q_i$. Find the Cournot outputs and the market price, assuming the firms will be equal in size. Will each firm cover its fixed cost?
c. Now suppose there are three, equal-sized firms whose outputs are q_1, q_2, and q_3, and there is no further entry. Total market output is now $q_1 + q_2 + q_3 = Q$. Each firm has the same cost function as the monopoly in part a, $TC = 5 + 0.1q_i$. Approximate the Cournot outputs and the market price.
d. Finally, suppose there is free entry into the market for the good. What price and quantity outcome would you predict then? If you do not find an exact numerical solution, explain in words what the important effect of entry will be, and describe the conditions that you should expect to find satisfied at a free-entry equilibrium.

4. Consider the market for a good for which demand is

$$P = 2 - 0.01Q,$$

where P is price and Q is quantity.

a. Suppose there is only one monopoly firm to serve the market. It has total cost, TC, of

$$TC = 15 + 0.2Q.$$

Find the monopoly price and quantity.

b. Now suppose there are two equal-sized firms whose outputs are q_1 and q_2. Total market output is now $q_1 + q_2 = Q$. Each firm has the same cost function as the monopoly in part a, $TC = 15 + 0.2Q$. Approximate the Cournot outputs and the market price.

c. Now suppose there are three equal-sized firms whose outputs are q_1, q_2, and q_3. Total market output is now $q_1 + q_2 + q_3 = Q$. Each firm has the same cost function as the monopoly in part a, $TC = 15 + 0.2q_i$. Approximate the Cournot outputs and the market price.

d. Consider the equilibrium price and quantity you obtain in part c. If entry was possible, would it be motivated at the Cournot equilibrium you obtained?

5. In New York City, 12,147 taxicabs are authorized to operate, a number only slightly changed since 1937. Taxi rates are controlled by the New York City Hack Bureau. Each cab must bear a medallion granted by the Hack Bureau, indicating that it has the right to operate. These medallions can be bought and sold. The price of a medallion has grown quite steadily since 1980 and now ranges above $200,000.

a. Can you explain why medallions are so valuable? Does this price of a medallion help to control entry? Where are the monopoly profits that the entry limitation creates? Can you find any rationale for limiting the number of taxicabs in New York?

b. New York City Mayor Michael R. Bloomberg proposed selling 900 more medallions over three years.[35] How would you expect such a sale to affect the value of medallions?

6. Suppose entry to an industry is easy. Any firm's production technology is given by the cost function, $TC = 500 + 100q$.

a. If demand is given by $p = 500 - 25q$, how many firms would you expect in the industry and roughly what price and output would you expect for the market?

b. If demand is given by $p = 500 - 10q$, how many firms would you expect in the industry and roughly what price and output would you expect for the market?

---

[35] See Tim Gray, "A Lender Hopes to Profit from the New Taxi Math," *New York Times*, January 25, 2004, p. BU 8.

APPENDIX 5.1 Cournot's Solution to Duopoly

When there are two firms in a market, neither knows what the other will do. Recall that Cournot had each firm assume the other would hold output at the same level as before, but each firm will make small changes in its output each period, and the firms will move to an equilibrium. Knowing that each firm is responding to the other, it is possible to capture the end result of their actions directly. To see how, begin with firm 1 facing the profit function,

$$\pi_1 = [a - b\,(q_1 + q_2)]\,q_1 - cq_1.$$

The profit maximizing problem for firm 1 has the market price—the quantity in brackets above—depend on total output, $q_1 + q_2$, while revenue and cost for firm one depend only on firm 1's output. Taking q_2, the other firm's output, as fixed, say at the same level as before, firm 1 can maximize π_1 with respect to q_1 and obtain

$$\partial\pi_1/\partial q_1 = a - 2bq_1 - bq_2 - c = 0.$$

This condition does not yield a profit maximizing level of q_1 that is independent of q_2. It does yield, however, a profit maximizing level of q_1 for any *given* level of q_2,

$$q_1 = (a - bq_2 - c)/2b.$$

Because it prescribes the best possible response for firm 1, given any output of firm 2, we call this equation a best-response function, or a **reaction function.**

Cournot imagined that firm 2 would make the same analysis, and would develop the symmetrical profit maximizing condition,

$$\partial\pi_2/\partial q_2 = a - 2bq_2 - bq_1 - c = 0,$$

which yields the reaction function of firm 2,

$$q_2 = (a - bq_1 - c)/2b.$$

Now suppose firm 1 recognized that firm 2 could develop this reaction function. Firm 1 could then substitute this value of q_2 into its own reaction function and obtain an equation in q_1 alone,

$$q_1 = [a - b(a - bq_1 - c)/2b - c]/2b,$$

which we can solve for

$$q_1 = (a - c)/3b.$$

Because the same solution emerges from the same calculation by firm 2, $(a - c)/3b$ is the Cournot solution for the outputs of both duopoly firms.

In a Cournot duopoly with simple linear demand and with two firms that have the same constant costs, total output is $Q = q_1 + q_2 = (a - c)/3b + (a - c)/3b = 2(a - c)/3b$. Recalling that the monopoly output is $Q = (a - c)/2b$, we see that the duopoly output is larger. Indeed, substituting the duopoly output into the inverse demand yields the duopoly price,

$$p = a - 2b(a - c)/3b = (a + 2c)/3,$$

which is lower than the monopoly price of $(a + c)/2$. To see that $(a + c)/2$ is greater than $(a - c)/3b$, consider the following. Because $a > c$ (the inverse demand function intercept, a, must exceed cost, c, if a market is to exist), the monopoly price that weights a more heavily and c less heavily, $a/2 + c/2$, is higher than the duopoly weighting, $a/3 + 2c/3$. Or assume $a/2 + c/2 > a/3 + 2c/3$, and simplify $(a/2 - a/3 > 2c/3 - c/2)$ until you reach $a > c$, which is known to be true.

APPENDIX 5.2 Cournot from Monopoly to Many Firms

An oligopoly is a market with few firms, which we can see by expanding to three firms the example of a duopoly market. The steps are the same as in the duopoly case. Again suppose the inverse market demand is linear, $p = a - b(q_1 + q_2 + q_3)$, but with three producers. Each firm still has simple constant average cost, c, so total cost for the ith firm will be cq_i. Firm 1's profit is now

$$\pi_1 = [a - b(q_1 + q_2 + q_3) - c]\, q_1,$$

and we can maximize it by taking the derivative with respect to q_1 and setting it equal to zero,

$$\partial \pi_1/\partial q_1 = a - 2bq_1 - bq_2 - bq_3 - c = 0.$$

Solving for q_1 yields the best-response or reaction function, $q_1 = (a - b(q_2 + q_3) - c)/2b$. By realizing that firms 2 and 3 derive symmetric reaction functions, and, further, that all q_is will be the same in equilibrium, we can solve this condition for

$$q_1 = q_2 = q_3 = (a - c)/4b.$$

This output per firm with three firms is smaller than at the duopoly solution, which was

$$q_1 = q_2 = (a - c)/3b,$$

because $(a - c)/4b < (a - c)/3b$. By adding the three firms' outputs, however, we find that $q_1 + q_2 + q_3 = Q = 3(a - c)/4b$, which is larger than the duopoly market output of $q_1 + q_2 = Q = 2(a - c)/3b$. Thus, each firm's output is smaller when there are three firms rather than two, but total market output is larger when we add together the outputs of the three firms. Substituting the three-firm quantity $(Q = 3(a - c)/4b)$ into the demand function yields price $p = (a+3c)/4$ in the three-firm case, which is lower than the duopoly price of $p = (a+2c)/3$. One can show that $(a+3c)/4 < (a+2c)/3$ by reducing it to $a > c$, which is known to be true (remember, there can be no market if $c > a$).

For a numerical example, consider the linear inverse demand,

$$p = 1 - 0.01(q_1 + q_2 + q_3),$$

and assume average cost $c = 0.2$, as before. In this three-firm case we have $q_1 = q_2 = q_3 = (1 - 0.2)/4(.01) = 20$, and $q_1 + q_2 + q_3 = 60$. This is a smaller output per firm than in the case of duopoly, at 20 versus 26.7, but a larger output for the whole market, at 60 versus 53.3. Substituting into the demand function, we find price is now 0.40, compared with 0.47 for duopoly and 0.60 for monopoly (and price equals 0.20, or marginal cost, for competition).

We can also construct a horizontal-merger paradox in a Cournot model in which the merged firm does less well after the merger.[36] Suppose there are three firms, and two of them decide to merge. The reason for this result, however, is the assumption in the Cournot model that all firms are always equal in size, so the two firms that had enjoyed two-thirds of the premerger market have only one-half of the postmerger market. That is why mergers are not motivated in the simple Cournot model. Because of this equal-firm-size assumption, the firm that does not participate in the merger is the one that gains from it, going from one-third of the market to one-half. More general analysis, combining Cournot behavior with that of the Stackelberg leader-follower model, yields a possible incentive for merger. That incentive to merge, however, may exist even for mergers that do not improve welfare.[37]

We can obtain Cournot solutions for any number of firms. Table 5.A2.1 shows cases up to $n = 80$, based on the linear inverse demand $p = 1 - 0.01Q$, where $Q = q_1 + q_2 + \ldots + q_n$ and firms' costs are constant at 0.20 per unit. Table 5.A2.1 also shows for its various numbers of firms output per firm, q_i, market output, Q, market price, p, firm profit, π_i, and industry profit, Π, at equilibria. As the number of firms increases,

TABLE 5.A2.1 Illustrative Cournot Outcomes with Linear Demand and Constant Cost

n	q_i	Q	p	π_i	Π
1	40	40	0.60	16.00	16.00
2	26.7	53.3	0.47	7.13	14.26
3	20	60	0.40	4.00	12.00
4	16	64	0.36	2.56	10.24
5	13.3	66.7	0.33	1.73	8.64
6	11.4	68.6	0.31	1.30	7.80
7	10	70	0.30	1.00	7.00
80	1	80	0.20	0	0

[36] Salant, Switzer, and Reynolds (1983) showed this paradoxical result.
[37] See Feltovich (2000) and Ruffin (2007).

output per firm declines, market output increases, market price declines, and profit per firm and profit for the entire industry decline.

We can analyze the Cournot model generally for any number of firms, n. In a market with n firms, identify any particular firm by giving it a number from 1 to n. Then refer to any firm as the ith firm, where i can vary from 1 to n. Total market quantity is $Q = q_1 + q_2 +, \ldots, + q_n$. Maximizing profit with any number of firms, rather than just two or three, can then be represented for firm 1 as

$$\max_{q_1} \pi \; (q_1, q_2, \ldots, q_n) = q_1 \, p(q_1 + q_2 +, \ldots, + q_n) - c \, q_1.$$

Let $\partial p / \partial q = p'$. Differentiating with respect to q_1 and setting the result equal to zero yields

$$\partial \pi / \partial q_1 = p(q_1 + q_2 +, \ldots, + q_n) + q_1 \, p'(q_1 + q_2 +, \ldots, + q_n) - c = 0,$$

which we can solve for

$$(p - c)/p = - (\partial p / \partial q)(q_1 / p).$$

In equilibrium we expect all firms to be the same size, so $Q = nq_1$. Multiplying numerator and denominator of the right-hand side yields

$$(p - c)/p = - (\partial p / \partial q)(n q_1 / p)(1/n) = 1/n(-E),$$

where E is market demand elasticity: $E = (\partial q / \partial p)(p/Q)$.

This result shows how changes in n affect the equilibrium markup. Recall that the monopoly pricing markup is

$$(p - c)/p = 1/(-E),$$

which means that the Cournot model reduces the monopoly markup as n increases, because it multiplies it by $1/n$. Notice how general the Cournot markup rule is. When $n = 1$, the monopoly case, $(p - c)/p = 1/n(-E)$ reduces to $(p - c)/p = 1/(-E)$, the correct monopoly markup rule. When $n = 2$, the price is lower, and this reduction in price continues as n increases. Indeed, when n is very large, $1/n(-E)$ is essentially zero, implying that the markup is zero, and price equals marginal cost. This is how Cournot showed that market outcomes vary depending on n, the number of firms, from monopoly to competition.

APPENDIX 5.3 Entry in the Cournot Model

As is common in the analysis of markets with few firms, the duopoly and oligopoly models assume that entry is not possible. Often when there are few firms, entry is very difficult, so the behavior of the few existing firms is the issue, and Cournot analysis can be helpful. Entry may be possible, however, and examining its consequences is useful. If marginal and average costs are equal and constant, meaning there are no sunk costs, the market is contestable. If price rises above the level of average cost there is entry, and price is driven to the level of average cost. But what if each firm experiences fixed capacity costs? Average cost then declines with output, so marginal cost lies below average cost. What kind of equilibrium might emerge?

Remember that entry turns on average cost, rather than on marginal cost, which is crucial to a short-run output decision. Entry is a longer-run decision, and the potential entrant takes it only if it can see average cost being covered by the market price. If entry is possible, the number of firms can be **endogenous**, meaning it is determined in the model instead of being given by conditions outside the model, or **exogenous**. If potential entrants can anticipate economic profit, that gives them incentive to enter. Entry continues until it is no longer motivated, which is when profit from entry no longer exceeds zero. With a finite number of firms, a small profit may exist when there are n firms, and losses may be incurred when there are $n+1$ firms. We assume the $n+1$st firm can anticipate the effect of its entry and resist entering if it will lose money. The result will be an equilibrium where profit is virtually zero and entry is not motivated.

Consider the Cournot oligopoly model with any number of firms, n. Any particular firm is called the ith firm. The last, or nth, firm to enter determines the number of firms in the market. For any value of n, we have $Q = q_1 + q_2 +, \ldots, + q_n$. In the simple case considered earlier in the chapter, cost for the ith firm equaled cq_i, where c was a constant that was the same for every firm. With such simple constant costs and with free entry, any price above c would attract new entry, so we could expect the market price to be driven to c.

When there are fixed costs, the number of firms, and the market price, depends on the level of those fixed costs. Assume that each firm must incur a fixed cost of F to produce any output at all. F does not vary as output varies, but there is a constant cost, c, per unit of output. The ith firm attempts to maximize its profit, given the number of firms, n,

$$\pi\,(q_1, q_2, \ldots, q_n) = q_i p(q_1 + q_2 +, \ldots, + q_n) - F - c\,q_i.$$

The ith firm seeks maximum profit all the time, even as the number of firms that are producing output changes. At any equilibrium, we continue to assume that all firms are the same size, so $Q = nq_i$. For profit to be earned at any point, we must have $(p - c)q_i > F$. And we know that profit is no longer earned, and further entry is no longer motivated, when $(p - c)q_i = F$, or, equivalently, when price equals average cost: $p = c + F/q_i$. Once profit equals zero, entry is no longer motivated.

Consider the linear demand function just examined, $p = 1 - 0.01Q$. With fixed cost, F, instead of total cost equaling $0.2q_i$, total cost will equal $0.2q_i + F$. What if $F = 4.00$? Or what if $F = 1.00$? How many firms will operate in either of these two cases? We can obtain an answer to this question by knowing how much contribution can be made to profit when there are different numbers of firms. Subtract fixed cost from this profit contribution for the typical firm in all the cases of different numbers of firms. Table 5.A2.1 from Appendix 5.2 contains profit per firm for the demand of interest, but when the cost function has no fixed cost. That is, it is appropriate for $F = 0$. Using Table 5.A2.1, can you predict the number of firms in the market if $F = 4.00$, or if $F = 1.00$?

Focus on the column containing π_i. Table 5.A2.1 represents a case in which there is no fixed cost, so the firm-profit column, or π_i, indicates how much is available to cover fixed costs if they exist. Suppose fixed cost is 4.00. With three firms in the market, Table 5.A2.1 shows that profit per firm will be 4.00 if there is no fixed cost. This means that if fixed cost is 4.00, with three firms in the market profit is zero. Thus, if fixed cost is 4.00 we can expect three firms at the free-entry market equilibrium. On the other hand, if fixed costs are 1.00, each of the three firms realize a profit of 3.00 (4.00 − 1.00 = 3.00), so we should expect further entry. If fixed costs are 1.00, entry continues until the profit per firm, π_i shown in Table 5.A2.1 (which assumes no fixed cost), is 1.00, just enough to cover the fixed cost of that amount. This occurs with seven firms in the market, and so if fixed cost is 1.00, we should expect seven firms in the market.

Introducing entry into a Cournot model shows the entry process at work, but the obtained equilibrium is not socially ideal. Notice, first, that price exceeds marginal cost. This was true in the Cournot oligopoly equilibrium, where we found $(p - c)/p = 1/n(-E)$, which we can expect to exceed zero unless there are many firms. When we add fixed costs to the example of Table 5.A2.1 and consider entry, we find the same outcome. With $F = 1.00$, for example, we expect an equilibrium with seven firms where price equals 0.30, which exceeds marginal cost of 0.20. Fixed costs can essentially determine the number of firms when entry is free, but price is still above marginal cost. Even though the number of firms is exogenous, the equilibrium is still a Cournot equilibrium, where existing firms effectively appreciate the effects of their actions on market price and moderate their competitiveness as a consequence.

There is another problem with the equilibrium that results in this Cournot model with entry. Any firm that produces in this entry model incurs fixed cost, F, which means that if n firms produce, they cause costs for society of nF. To minimize industry costs for the socially optimal outcome, there should be only one firm, which would cause a cost to society of only F. More than one firm in the market increases the fixed cost that must be incurred. Such a structure is not socially ideal unless the resulting competition brings sufficient productive efficiency to overcome the cost advantage of a monopoly market structure that incurs F only once.

Having more than one firm might be preferable to having a monopoly, however, perhaps to spur cost minimization in the industry. Such incentive considerations should not be needed in this model, where all costs are given. The free-entry Cournot market does not produce an ideal outcome because there may be more than one firm at the equilibrium, and one firm could produce any output at lower cost than more firms because of the saving in fixed costs. On the other hand, if we consider incentives, the competition in the Cournot outcome forces efficient operation, whereas the single firm might have to be regulated by less effective, nonmarket means to avoid monopolistic outcomes.

Although illustrative, the Cournot model with entry is admittedly contrived. In the presence of entry, would you expect a Cournot oligopolist to behave exactly as it would without entry? That is what each firm does in this market model. If entry was expected, these firms could no longer presume that they would share the market demand, so they probably would depart from their Cournot behavior. This means that confining attention solely to the responses of other already-existing firms in this situation is potentially foolish. Knowing that one firm would be the ideal way to organize the industry, firms might even behave aggressively in an effort to win that position. Thus, our assumption of Cournot behavior, including its implied equal quantities for all firms, may not be appropriate when entry can upset the equilibrium it would produce.

The Cournot model with entry does serve a useful purpose, however. It stresses the independent incentive that arises in each of a small number of firms to constrain output, because each firm can see a portion of the marginal revenue idea that the monopoly sees. As long as that independent incentive persists, even in the face of entry, as it might, a Cournot equilibrium is possible after entry determines the number of firms. The model demonstrates the zero-profit condition that drives entry, and it shows how entry can be endogenous in an oligopoly model.

APPENDIX 5.4 Stackelberg's Leader-Follower Solution

Two Cournot firms follow the same behavior pattern and reach a solution where their reaction functions intersect. In the Stackelberg model one of the firms is a leader who anticipates the reaction function behavior of the follower and takes advantage of it. We briefly review the Cournot solution and then introduce the Stackelberg leader-follower behavior.

Recall that with two firms in Cournot's duopoly market, firm 1 faced the profit function,

$$\pi_1 = [a - b(q_1 + q_2)] q_1 - c q_1.$$

To review, the Cournot firm 1 takes q_2 as fixed at the same level as before, which allows firm 1 to maximize π_1 with respect to q_1 and obtain

$$\partial \pi_1 / \partial q_1 = a - 2bq_1 - bq_2 - c = 0,$$

which yields firm 1's reaction function,

$$q_1 = (a - bq_2 - c)/2b.$$

Following the same reasoning, firm 2 obtains its reaction function,

$$q_2 = (a - bq_1 - c)/2b.$$

Solving these two reaction functions for their equilibrium values yields the Cournot solution,

$$q_1 = q_2 = (a - c)/3b.$$

The Stackelberg firm 1 does not simply solve two reaction functions for an equilibrium. When the Stackelberg leader recognizes what firm 2's reaction function is, it uses the value of q_2 implied by that reaction function in its own profit maximizing problem. Firm 1 no longer merely substitutes firm 2's reaction function into its own reaction function, as in the Cournot case. As the leader, or **first mover**, firm 1 now substitutes the reaction function of firm 2, the follower, into *its original profit maximizing problem*, and *then* maximizes profit. So the leader considers the follower's behavior when maximizing its profit. Its profit can be stated as

$$\pi_1 = [a - b(q_1 + [(a - bq_1 - c)/2b)])]q_1 - c\,q_1.$$

To repeat, this problem is different from the Cournot firm's problem, because here the reaction function of the other firm, the follower firm, is incorporated into the profit function of the leader *before* that function is maximized. On maximizing the leader's profit function with respect to q_1, we find the leader's output to be

$$q_1 = (a - c)/2b.$$

Do you recognize this quantity solution? The leader's Stackelberg quantity is the same as the monopoly quantity. Now substitute this value for the leader's quantity into the follower's reaction function, $q_2 = (a - bq_1 - c)/2b$, and find the follower's output to be

$$q_2 = (a - c)/4b.$$

Thus, the Stackelberg market with two firms, one leader and one follower, has as total output

$$Q = q_1 + q_2 = (a - c)/2b + (a - c)/4b = 3(a - c)/4b,$$

which is the same as the output of a Cournot market that contains *three* firms.

6

Market Strategy

Market structure determines the scope a business firm has for strategic behavior. A firm in a perfectly competitive market is not very strategic, nor is a single monopoly firm except for steps it might take to extend its monopoly. A few firms in a market have room for strategic behavior as each tries to make the environment more favorable for itself—that is, more profitable. Some strategic actions can benefit consumers and, thus, be desirable. Other strategic actions may be aimed at harming competitors and weakening competition, which is undesirable. Distinguishing the desirable from the undesirable strategies can be difficult, and this potential ambiguity is a problem for antitrust policy. Here we examine strategic behavior, both to understand it and—insofar as it is possible—to be able to recognize the undesirable forms.

Within the constraints it faces, a business firm chooses its own shape. Its boundaries depend on the costs of transactions in markets versus the costs of operating within the firm, but the firm also selects products or services to offer and it may attempt to differentiate its product to gain an element of monopoly advantage. The firm pursues financial arrangements best suited to its circumstances. It engages employees in continuing relationships. It decides on production techniques, marketing, and distribution methods in an effort to achieve the most profit and success. It also plans for the future, perhaps with research and development efforts, building and equipment investments, and employee training. As a result, the firm is drawn into a great range of decisions that affect its shape and its future, and these decisions are often strategic.

Decisions are strategic when at least one other firm may be competing, and the decisions influence the form of that competition. Perfectly competitive markets call for firms to make output decisions independently based on market price and their own costs. Few firms, however, make business decisions in such an independent way, without any influence from other, often competitive, firms, or even from consumers and investors. If one firm cuts price or introduces a new variety of product, that affects its competitors, and each firm attempts to choose actions that improve its own well-being.

One strategic action a firm may take is to create a product that is different from others, with the aim of attracting enthusiastic consumers to the new product. Product differentiation involves differences among products sold to similar consumers, such as Apple and Dell in the computer market. Even physical location near one group of consumers is a form of product differentiation, in that one location can be more attractive to some consumers than to others. With product differentiation, each seller may have a degree of monopolistic advantage to the extent some consumers prefer its form of the product (or its location, or its channel for distributing its product), but at the same time, competition from other varieties of the product limits the degree of market power. More dimensions for competition are now possible, and they can take a variety of *non-price* forms. Firms may compete in research and development, for instance, perhaps to gain a product improvement ahead of rivals and deny them its use. They may also invent different service arrangements or different ways of advertising and distributing their products.

Opening up broad strategies goes beyond Cournot-style representations, which lead to equilibria but require narrow assumptions about firm behavior. Cournot results are valuable, and they offer lessons about incentives and how incentives vary with costs and sizes of firms, but they depend on strong assumptions. Our focus now is on the wide range of choices available to firms, and on the multidimensional strategic considerations that arise in these choices.

Section 6.1 elaborates on game theory to show its advantages as a framework for representing strategic action. Section 6.2 discusses strategic price competition, and Section 6.3 discusses strategic non-price competition. Section 6.4 examines the use of advertising.

6.1 | THE TOOLS OF STRATEGY

Our examination of market structure showed its main influences on firms, but it did not explore the range of strategic possibilities that markets can open up. Here we consider those broader possibilities, beginning with some that may be rewarding but are not ordinary equilibrium outcomes.

Some Game Examples

We can represent a variety of situations in game-theory terms.[1] The **prisoner's dilemma** is a game situation that offers a mixture of cooperative and competitive motives. Using it to represent a small part of the output or pricing choices available to two firms in a Cournot duopoly market can reveal possibilities we did not consider in Chapter 5. Consider the payoff table of Table 6.1, and suppose both firms set high outputs (H,H), so each earns a profit of 5 (in the lower right hand corner of the payoff

---

[1] Classical treatments by McDonald (1950) and Williams (1954) present many more situations. For examples from law, see Baird, Gertner, and Picker (1994).

TABLE 6.1 Prisoner's Dilemma (H = high, L = low)

Player 1/Player 2	L	H
L	15, 15	−5, 25
H	25, −5	5, 5

table). Now if both firms lower their outputs (to L,L) they move—essentially up the market demand curve—to a more profitable point where each makes 15. If one sets a high output while the other's output remains low (H,L), although the price falls the firm with the high output serves more customers and receives a payoff of 25, while the other firm with the low output loses 5. The low-output firm has to increase its output. Once both set the high output again, each receives the modest payoff of 5. Thus, the dilemma. Cooperating at L,L yields the most joint profit, that is, profit for both firms together. Each firm is also tempted to double-cross the other so it can do even better for itself.

In Table 6.1, there is a best strategy from each player's *private* point of view. Consider player 1. If player 2 chooses L, player 1 is better off choosing H (25 > 15). If player 2 chooses H, player 1 is still better off choosing H (5 > −5). Setting a high output dominates. The same result follows when we consider player 2. Both players have a dominant strategy, which is to set a high output. Thus, at a Nash equilibrium, where no player wants to make any change, we should expect both players to have high outputs. This is also the Cournot equilibrium, but notice the possibility that players may do better by cooperating at the low output. That is not an equilibrium outcome, because with both firms at the low output, each firm has private incentive to increase its output. That is why there is a dilemma; both choices offer advantages.

Table 6.2 elaborates on Table 6.1, allowing two firms to choose among three outputs, high (H), medium (M), and low (L), where the high output wins customers but causes financial losses. High outputs in a Cournot market can have this property. Strategy M dominates strategy H because one player's payoffs are always greater for M than for H no matter what strategy the other player chooses. If strategy H is ruled out, the remainder of the game is a prisoner's dilemma like Table 6.1, with strategies M and L, that has M as a dominant strategy. There is, however, the nonequilibrium choice, L, that allows cooperating players more profit.

TABLE 6.2 The Market Situation with Three Choices

Player 1/Player 2	L	M	H
L	15, 15	−5, 25	10, 5
M	25, −5	5, 5	0, 0
H	5, 10	0, 0	−5, −5

TABLE 6.3 Chicken Game (T = tough, Y = yield)

Player 1/Player 2	T	Y
T	−10, −10	20, 0
Y	0, 20	1, 1

To see another game framework, consider the **chicken game**, which involves a form of conflict in which one's payoff depends on the other's action in a dangerous way. Imagine two cars driving on a highway toward each other, each with one wheel over the yellow line down the middle of the road in such a way that they will crash if neither departs from their vehicle course. If they both remain tough (T,T) they crash, represented by a −10 for each player in Table 6.3. If both yield (Y,Y), each receives a small payoff of 1. When one is tough and the other yields (Y,T or T,Y), the tough player receives a big award of 20 and the yielding player receives nothing. This game characterizes the situation that exists when two entrepreneurs each promote a conference center in a town that is large enough to support only one. Then each can be successful only if the other one gives up the effort.

In a **coordination game**, players have to coordinate their actions. The payoff table in Table 6.4 is an example in which two friends are to meet at a coffee shop at 2:00 PM on a Sunday afternoon, so each can obtain a satisfaction level, or utility level, represented by 10. If one of them should come at another time, say 5:00 PM, they both receive a payoff of nothing, unless they both arrive at 5:00 PM, which yields a positive payoff but not as good as at 2:00 PM. They must coordinate their actions to reach a preferred outcome.

Rivalry

We have imagined that players in a game want to maximize their payoffs, but they might be concerned with *relative* payoffs, rather than absolute payoffs. The player who persists in the tough strategy in the chicken game, for example, may be trying to obtain the largest margin of payoff advantage over the opponent. Indeed, instead of actual payoffs, for a rivalrous player we might focus on *differences* between payoffs in each cell. Table 6.5 presents player 1's payoffs from the chicken game as differences in the players' payoffs—player 1 minus player 2 payoffs. These might represent payoffs to the rivalrous player who seeks to maximize payoff difference in the

TABLE 6.4 Coordination Game

Player 1/Player 2	2:00	5:00
2:00	10, 10	0, 0
5:00	0, 0	5, 5

TABLE 6.5 The Difference of Player 1 Minus Player 2 Payoffs

Player 1	T	Y
T	0	20
Y	−20	0

---

chicken game. The rivalrous player who saw payoffs this way might suffer a loss when matched with another rivalrous player, because they would both choose the tough strategy. Such **rivalrous behavior** can lead to solutions that differ from the payoff maximizing solutions.

Suppose two firms in the same industry are competing for the same source of financing. The firm with the better relative performance can expect to win the financing. By causing each firm to consider its own gains *relative* to those of other firms, this situation may induce rivalrous behavior, because it leads to new effective payoffs in which the parties directly oppose each other. If the influence of relative payoffs is strong, it can alter each firm's behavior to make the firm more aggressive and vigorous in its competition.

An example of induced rivalry might arise when two firms have different cost functions, and the firms may not agree readily on a single common price to adopt. If the two firms turn to threatening or attacking each other, differences in their cost functions can make unequal the amount of damage that one can inflict upon the other. If firms have the same constant marginal cost but different fixed costs, even though the relation between their profits lacks symmetry, the firms have a unique cooperative point that affords maximum joint profits. The different fixed costs might make agreement less likely because the firm with greater fixed cost may want a larger output. Investors compare firms in the same industry for profitability, and larger output may allow the high-fixed-cost firm to improve its profits *relative* to its competitor. When each firm seeks a better profit than the other, their behavior is rivalrous.

Bargaining

Profit interdependence among firms continues through time. Over time, further considerations can enter the firms' strategies. First, a firm may use **threats**. If one firm can convince another or others that, unless cooperation is maintained, it will increase output (or cut price) for many future periods, that firm may persuade others to cooperate at a lower output (or a higher price). To be effective, however, any such threat must be **credible**. If carrying out its threat goes against a firm's own interest, its threat may not be credible. If the threat is not credible, it is not an effective threat, so it may be ignored.

A threat can be more effective when firms choose capacities as well as outputs, because capacity decisions require a **commitment** that fosters credibility.[2] Suppose

---

[2] Sherman (1972) examined capacity choices in an experimental market.

BOX 6.1   Commitment in the Lysine Cartel

A famous example of commitment in a case of international collusion involved an amino acid, lysine, which promotes growth in chickens and cattle. The firm, Archer Daniels Midland Company, entered the lysine market in 1991 by building enough capacity to upset the market, or at least to break up the price-fixing agreements that currently existed. The intended effect of this capacity was to give Archer Daniels Midland bargaining power with firms already cooperating in a price-fixing conspiracy. Building capacity was a commitment that made credible the threat of increasing production, which would have forced a lower price in the market. Archer Daniels Midland and coconspirators later pleaded guilty to price fixing.

See Eichenwald (2000) and Lieber (2000) for descriptions of the antitrust case. The duration and effect of collusion by the firms is still disputed. See the symposium on "The Lysine Cartel" in the *Review of Industrial Organization*, February 2001, 18: 1–52.

---

an existing firm wishes to threaten a potential entrant with increased output if the firm should enter. It can attempt to give hints about the response to be expected of it, but such threats probably are not credible. It can add to its credibility, however, by making a commitment. Suppose, for example, the existing firm expands its capacity beyond what seems to be needed to meet present demand. Such a commitment suggests that the firm will expand output in response to entry, both because it has unused capacity at the ready and because—with that idle capacity—its marginal cost will probably be low. Or it might use capacity as a bargaining tool in cartel negotiations, as in the lysine cartel described in Box 6.1. A firm might also expand capacity and lower price in a predatory effort to drive others from the market. Such behavior could foster a *reputation* that might discourage future entry, but the commitment to large capacity would help to sustain it. That is how commitment can make a threat credible.[3]

Commitment of a different kind arises in the "chain store paradox," a strategic situation in which a decision depends on credibility for its effectiveness. Nobel laureate Reinhard Selten (1978) proposed that a powerful chain with 20 stores might face entry in one of its markets. In one market, the chain's best response is to accept entry, and with it a small reduction in profit, rather than to incur costs fighting the entrant. If entry then occurs in other markets, however, the ultimate result is not so modest, and profit consequences would be serious. So the chain may respond vigorously to punish the first entrant, perhaps by steep price cuts, to show its commitment to fighting entry. It might even expand its stores so they are positioned to serve added customers after lowering prices in response to entry. The chain seeks a reputation for responding vigorously to entry in order to ward off further entry into its other markets. The paradox is whether the chain should accept the first entrant or incur the costs of destroying the first entrant to discourage others.

---

[3] Chapter 8 shows that the Alcoa corporation was accused of "spotting plants," that is, building plants before they were needed, to discourage entry into the aluminum industry.

6.2 | PRICE COMPETITION AMONG FEW FIRMS

Of all the strategic variables available for a few firms to choose, price may be the most treacherous. If two of us are competing and our consumers are well informed, our products are similar, and my price is lower than yours, you may have a serious immediate problem, more immediate than if our capacities differ, or if I spend more on advertising or research and development than you do. Powerful incentives can arise in this prisoner's-dilemma-game form, where two firms can profit more if they set *the same* high price, yet each firm can then be motivated to cut price. If firms are not widely separated, if they sell virtually the same product, and if buyers are very well informed, then, as Bertrand (1883) and Edgeworth (1925) indicated long ago, price competition among a few firms can be violent.

The Problem of Price Competition

Jacques Bertrand (1883) attacked Cournot's remarkable market theory on the ground that firms would choose prices rather than quantities as Cournot assumed. Where Cournot had derived a gradual tendency for price to fall from the monopoly to the competitive level as there were more firms in a market, Bertrand saw a sudden drop in price as soon as the number of firms in the market exceeded one. Economist F. Y. Edgeworth (1925) tempered Bertrand's implication when he drew attention to the capacities of firms and developed another classical theory of behavior with firms few in number. With two firms in a market, for instance, he emphasized how, upon cutting price, one firm might fill all of its capacity. Its competitor could then raise its price without losing sales, because the first firm would have no free capacity left to supply consumers.[4] Kreps and Scheinkman (1983) showed that choice of capacity in such situations can lead to Cournot outcomes. Capacity limits can thus soften the effect of price competition that Bertrand emphasized and return attention to Cournot, because his argument for quantity choice can be interpreted as choice of capacity. Nevertheless, a pricing strategy can be more volatile than the quantity strategy, and the difference deserves attention.

Buyers may be well informed about prices, especially when the prices of only a small number of sellers need to be checked. Moreover, some buyers make enormous expenditures—think of an auto manufacturer's purchases of steel—and because a slight savings per unit is then so valuable, it is worthwhile for them to become very well informed about sellers' prices. Each seller may be forced to meet the lowest price set by other firms if it is to sell any of its output. Establishing the same price can then be the ultimate *coordination* problem for sellers. Agreement on price could move competition to non-price areas, such as advertising or location, where differences are not as volatile.

To avoid prisoner's dilemma consequences, firms can jointly control both market price and quantity explicitly, and an arrangement to do so is a **cartel**. Although illegal within the United States since passage of the Sherman Act in 1890, cartels

---

[4] Holt, Langan, and Villamil (1986) showed this possible effect of capacity in experimental markets.

operate in parts of the world where they are not illegal, and they have operated in international commerce, such as ocean freight and international air travel, which escape regulation by any one nation.[5]

Price Coordination

When agreement on some price is so important to firms, a form of coordination game arises. A large number of factors might influence what price finally is chosen, but firms may seek means of fostering coordination. By common practice, for instance, firms may recognize only a few very prominent alternative prices. As an example, if only the three prices, $4.95, $5.95, or $6.95, are considered as possibilities rather than all prices in that range, agreement from among this reduced set of options is easier. Nobel laureate Thomas Schelling (1963) elaborated a variety of influences on choice in uncertain situations, where some agreement is advantageous, and has shown that people search with both logic and imagination to find some **focal point** on which to converge. Precedent, notions of fairness, common experience, and even aesthetic charm can play a role in helping each party find a common basis with another (or others) for forming expectations about what the other will do. Identical products, production costs, and ways of selling to customers also may facilitate tacit agreement by a few firms on what price to charge, by making firms face more similar circumstances.

Even if firms can agree on a collusively high price, it will not persist all by itself. Each party to the tacit—and perhaps explicit—agreement has an incentive to violate it, provided that the others do not immediately violate it also, as is evident at the cooperative solution in the prisoner's dilemma. Instead of cutting its price across the board in an effort to get all of the business in a market, a firm might give rebates or favored treatment to only a few customers. Cheating by making an occasional price concession in this way is not as easily detected by other sellers. If widespread, however, such a practice can undermine price collusion.

The late Nobel laureate George Stigler brought out how a small number of buyers could upset seller collusion by revealing price cuts.[6] When there are only a few buyers and one shifts purchases in response to a price cut, the event is evident in the switch of a substantial purchase from one firm to another. With a small number of buyers it is difficult to have "secret" price cuts because the responses to price changes are more dramatic and noticeable, and that may help sellers enforce their collusive agreements. At the same time, when there are a few large buyers a seller who makes a concession may win a very profitable sale, and that could encourage warlike competition among sellers.

---

[5] For an example, see Bennathan and Walters (1969). For analyses of OPEC as a cartel, see Adelman (1982), Griffin and Teece (1982), and Griffin and Xiong (1997), and for more general reviews see Eckbo (1983) and Griffin (1985). For a recent extensive review of conspiracy studies see Levenstein and Suslow (2006). Cartels are discussed further in Chapter 9.

[6] This argument applies when products are homogeneous. See Stigler (1964). When products are not homogeneous, inferences by collusive firms about secret price cuts based on shifts in patronage are less reliable. But when there are fewer buyers they may exercise more bargaining power to limit sellers' gains. For this argument, see Galbraith (1952).

Price Leadership

The threat of losses as a consequence of price warfare gives firms a common interest in agreeing on *some* price. When there are few firms, they might follow one leader, thereby managing to keep their prices the same. Independent action is destructive, so coordination of all firms may be accorded a higher priority than complete freedom and independence in price choices. Then one very large firm in a market, sometimes called a dominant firm, may act as price leader and other firms will accept the price it sets. A smaller firm may occasionally assume the role of leader, too. It might have a lower marginal cost and therefore prefer a lower price that others would have to follow. As circumstances change, a different firm might take the initiative and act as leader. If that happens often, however, the role of the leader becomes less clear, because if several firms can initiate price actions, the orchestration possibilities of a single leader are lost.

Price leadership can take several forms.[7] **Dominant-firm price leadership** is a form in which all price-setting power resides in the dominant firm. That firm sometimes is presumed to be so large, relative to the total market, that it can anticipate the combined reactions of all other firms to any price it sets and reckon then what it will have available in the market. On the basis of such anticipated adjustments by others, it sets a price that maximizes its own profit, a price that is apt to be below the level a monopolist would charge but above the level of a competitive industry. The dominant firm behaves like the Stackelberg leader in Chapter 5, who constructs a residual demand by anticipating reactions of others to its action.

Another form of price leadership, which is called **barometric price leadership**, presumes no such mastery of the market. One firm initiates changes in price and others follow, but they are forced to do so, for reasons such as we have discussed. The leader may merely be reacting to cost or other changes that also could bring price reactions from a competitive industry. Because it fails to elevate price substantially, this form of price leadership is not thought to be as anticompetitive as dominant-firm leadership is presumed to be.

Adherence to pricing policies that would preserve some **status quo market shares** offers another way to prevent drastic price cutting among firms that come to respect a "normal" situation, or a status quo. Any aggressiveness in a firm's pricing might vanish when the firm reached its historic market share. Such an understanding about market shares would soften price wars. As with price leadership, adopting such a convention means some sacrifice by each firm of its independence, in favor of market stability in support of a status quo. Of course if one or more firms should seek an increase above its status quo market share through aggressive competition, the convention would be violated and price warfare could result. New entry might also upset the status quo.

If firms cooperate jointly in raising price they move up the industry demand curve, and if they independently raise price they move up their own, more elastic, demand curve. Suppose the firm is pessimistic. It expects all firms will join it if it

---

[7] For classic treatments, see Markham (1951) and Stigler (1947).

lowers price, so it will move down the industry demand curve, but it expects no one to join it if it raises price, so it moves up its own more elastic demand curve. The result is a kink in the effective demand curve, the effective curve being flatter for price increases than for price decreases. This is called a **kinked demand** situation, and it discourages each firm from changing its price. Any tendency of firms to maintain the same price, for this or other reasons, is apt to inhibit the adjustment of price to changes in demand. As a consequence, where agreement on one price is important to prevent disruption of the relations among firms, fluctuations in demand are most likely to be met with an unchanged price. The goal of maximizing profit may be sacrificed somewhat then, because a refined price adjustment could be difficult for the firms to agree on and carry out. The unchanging price that results may aggravate employment instability, because the quantity adjustment—and, thus, employment adjustment—is apt to be larger if price does not adjust at all when demand rises or falls.

The incentive to maintain a constant price is strongest among a few firms in an industry when they know that shifts in their total market demand coincide with general economic activity and their quantity demanded is less responsive to changes in market price. Profit risk is important to such firms, because their profit moves with the economy so profit risk cannot easily be diversified away. Firms in that situation can reduce profit fluctuations by not cutting price during periods of low demand. The automobile industry falls into this category. The demand for automobiles is more responsive to changes in national income than to changes in the price of automobiles, and so a few producers have much to lose and little to gain by price competition when demand falls.[8]

Markup Pricing

Some firms set their prices by adding a certain percentage, or **markup**, to their unit costs. Individual firms may set prices in relation to average cost when demand risk is present if they are concerned about profit fluctuations or the risk of losses, because constant prices can lower profit risk. As long as price is below the monopolistic level, cutting price when demand is low and raising price when demand is strong makes profit fluctuate more. In the eyes of investors, such added profit fluctuation is undesirable, and it may actually lower the value of the firm in the stock market.[9]

Large firms produce and sell many products, particularly if we consider different sizes and optional features. Even a talented and valuable (scarce) top executive cannot set the price of each variety of product. The firm might, however, set a markup formula as a **pricing policy** for subordinates to administer as an across-the-board price policy. Such a policy would allow higher-ranking, higher-skilled, higher-paid executives to make those important pricing decisions. When costs are similar among firms, such markup pricing can also tend to make prices (which are some markup of those costs) similar across the different firms, too, and thus help to coordinate the setting of equal prices.

---

[8] See, for example, Chow (1957) and the classic analysis by King (1939).
[9] See Schramm and Sherman (1977).

When the demand curve of each firm slopes down, it is less important for firms to have the same price. Among products that have been assigned prices based on the same markup, the firm tends to sell more of the products that it can produce at a lower cost. Multi-product firms want to price their different products so that their lowest-cost, highest-return-on-investment products and divisions will grow, and markets can help them judge what these lower-cost and higher-return products are. If firms follow markup pricing, markets can automatically signal expansion of their relatively low-cost and most profitable lines of products. Firms following such a passive policy can also avoid deliberate price cutting to take business away from other firms and this will reduce the volatility of profit swings.

Avoiding volatile profit swings may even be part of a firms' goal, because investors value smooth profit streams more than less consistent, seemingly riskier, streams. In response to demand fluctuations, a firm may try to improve its market value by smoothing its profit. Because advertising is in some degree an investment that has later benefits, the firm might advertise more in otherwise high-profit periods and less in otherwise low-profit periods, a strategy that can be more attractive as the demand faced by the firm is less elastic (in absolute value).[10] Such a possibility arises because, when individual firms face downward sloping demands, perhaps because their products are differentiated, other forms of competitive strategy arise, forms generally called non-price competition.

Multi-Product Pricing

Two goods—*substitutes* like two brands of printer—may replace each other. Two other goods—*complements* like printer and cartridge—may support each other. If a *rise* in the price of one printer causes the quantity consumed of another printer to *rise*, we say the goods are **substitutes**. As the price of good 2 rises, some consumers shift from consuming the printer with the increased price to consuming the other printer. On the other hand, if a rise in the price of a cartridge causes the sale of printers to *fall*, the goods are **complements**. In this case, some consumers must have decided not to consume a particular printer when the cartridge price for that printer increased. Because printers and cartridges are used together, the buyer considers the cost of both in its decision. When two products are either complements or substitutes a firm that has some market power can be tempted to sell both products because it can make more profit by controlling both products' prices. We explore motives for pricing complements and substitutes by comparing (1) how independent firms would price them with (2) how a single firm controlling both products would price them. First, we turn to the case of complements.

Complements

To show the effects of demand interrelationships, in Box 6.2 two independent profit-maximizing firms price two complementary goods. Then in Box 6.3 a combined or multi-product firm that sells both of the goods prices them in a coordinated way.

---

[10] See Schramm and Sherman (1976).

BOX 6.2 The Mathematics of Independently Pricing Complements

Consider a single firm, firm 1, selling good q_1 with demand $q_1 = a - 2p_1 - p_2$. The appearance of $- p_2$ in this demand function means that the quantity sold of good q_1 depends on the price of p_2 and the price of p_1. The negative sign on p_2 means that raising p_2 lowers q_1, just as raising p_1 does. If a price increase has the same effect on both goods, that means the two goods are complements. Suppose that a similar demand relation holds for firm 2, which produces good q_2 with demand $q_2 = a - 2p_2 - p_1$. Just to make comparisons easy, the two demands have the same intercept term, a, and are symmetrical. Suppose costs for the two firms are $C_1 = c_1 q_1$ and $C_2 = c_2 q_2$. Later we will assume $c_1 = c_2 = c$, again to make comparisons simple.

The first goal is to find prices that maximize profit for the independent firms. We can then compare such prices with prices that maximize profit for the combined firm selling both goods. Later we can make the same sort of comparison about pricing to maximize profit on substitute goods. Firm 1's profit for this complementary good case is

$$\pi_1 = (p_1 - c_1)(a - 2p_1 - p_2).$$

Maximizing this profit with respect to p_1 yields

$$\partial \pi_1 / \partial p_1 = a - 4p_1 - p_2 + 2c_1 = 0,$$

which we can solve for

$$p_1 = (a + 2c_1 - p_2)/4.$$

Maximizing firm 2's profit in the same way yields

$$p_2 = (a + 2c_2 - p_1)/4.$$

We can solve these two equations for p_1 and p_2 in terms of the parameters, a, c_1, and c_2. By substituting p_2 into the expression for p_1 and then solving for p_1, we obtain

$$p_1 = (3a + 8c_1 - 2c_2)/15.$$

Following the same procedure for p_2, we obtain

$$p_2 = (3a + 8c_2 - 2c_1)/15.$$

So that comparisons are very easy to make, suppose the firms' costs are equal, $c_1 = c_2 = c$, which makes the two prices the same,

$$p_1 = p_2 = a/5 + 2c/5 = p.$$

Similar to the way a monopolist notices the entire demand curve in its market, the single seller of both goods notices that by lowering the price of one of the two complimentary goods it increases the demand for the other. It is consequently more profitable for the single firm to set the prices of both complementary goods. Not only that, but prices of complements will be lower than two firms would set if pricing them

---

BOX 6.3 The Mathematics of Pricing Complements Jointly

The prices of the two goods sold by the combined firm are P_1 and P_2, and the total combined profit from selling both goods in one firm are

$$\pi_1 + \pi_2 = \Pi = (P_1 - c_1)(a - 2P_1 - P_2) + (P_2 - c_2)(a - 2P_2 - P_1).$$

Maximizing this combined profit with respect to P_1 yields

$$\partial\Pi/\partial P_1 = a - 4P_1 - P_2 + 2c_1 - (P_2 - c_2) = 0.$$

This condition differs from $\partial\pi_1/\partial p_1$ for the independent firm 1 above by the addition here of the $-(P_2 - c_2)$ term that comes from having π_2 and π_1 in the objective function (Π) of the combined firm. The term, $-(P_2 - c_2)$, is the effect that a marginal change in P_1 would have on the profit of product 2, and it would be ignored if firms were separate. Taking such terms into account by joining the two firms allows greater possible profit.

Setting $\partial\Pi/\partial P_1 = 0$ and solving yields

$$P_1 = (a + 2c_1 + c_2 - 2P_2)/4,$$

and following the same maximization procedure with respect to P_2 yields the symmetrical equation,

$$P_2 = (a + 2c_2 + c_1 - 2P_1)/4.$$

Now substituting P_2 into P_1 yields

$$P_1 = a/6 + c_1/2,$$

and substituting P_1 into P_2 yields

$$P_2 = a/6 + c_2/2.$$

If we again assume $c_1 = c_2 = c$, to simplify comparisons, we find that the two prices are again the same:

$$P_1 = P_2 = a/6 + c/2 = P.$$

---

independently, so consumers are also better off when one firm sets both prices for complements.

In the profit-maximization process considered in Box 6.2, neither firm is able to control the other's price. Each maximizes profit independently. Suppose the two firms joined into one. They could then maximize the combined profit on both goods by setting both prices with that purpose. With similar demands and similar costs for goods, the two firms reached the same price, p, for both goods in Box 6.2. The same assumptions are used in Box 6.3 to examine pricing by the combined firm, so the prices of both goods will again be equal, but in the combined firm that common price is represented by P.

A comparison of $p = a/5 + 2c/5$ from Box 6.2 (for independently priced complements) with $P = a/6 + c/2$ from Box 6.3 (for jointly priced complements) shows

$p > P.$[11] That is, the combined firm sets *lower* prices (P) than independent firms (p) for both of the complementary goods. The combined firm benefits itself with higher profit and its consumers with lower prices.

We find an example of this combination of complementary goods at PepsiCo. In addition to soft drinks, such as Pepsi-Cola, the company sells complementary Frito-Lay snack foods. It attempts to take advantage of this combination of goods by locating them together in supermarket aisles and by creating joint promotions in which one product enhances the sale of the other.[12] It is possible that through strong market positions in both lines of goods, and with attempts at product differentiation, there is an element of monopoly pricing of these complementary products. Compared with separate pricing by independent firms, pricing Pepsi-Cola and Frito-Lay jointly by PepsiCo could benefit consumers as well as PepsiCo.

Substitutes

The same comparison between one-firm profit maximizing and two-firm, or independent, maximizing can be applied to substitute goods but with a different result. When the pricing of substitutes is combined in a single firm, prices may be higher than separate firms would set. Now, raising each price *increases* sales of the other product. Prices for substitutes are determined independently and jointly in Appendix 6.1 by the same method used in Box 6.2 and Box 6.3, with the independently determined price p and the jointly determined price P. Comparing from Appendix 6.1 p for separate firms with P for the combined firm yields $p = a/3 + 2c/3 < a/2 + c/2 = P,$[13] which means that, when the goods are substitutes, prices set by a combined firm are *higher* than prices set by separate firms. The combined seller earns more profit than two separate firms taken together, but in this case of substitutes the combined seller offers less welfare for consumers than separate firms would.[14]

Table 6.6 provides a summary of profit-maximizing prices, either independently determined or jointly determined, for both complements and substitutes. The special case we consider has symmetric, or equal, linear demands in Box 6.2 and Box 6.3 and in Appendix 6.1, with equal costs also assumed to make comparisons easy. Comparing prices for separate versus combined firms in Table 6.6 shows the combined-firm prices to be lower than prices of separate firms for complements, but the prices of the combined firm are higher than those of separate firms for substitutes. This conclusion can be shown analytically for any $a > 3c$ and is illustrated in parentheses in Table 6.6 for values of $a = 600$ and $c = 30$. The prices of substitutes are always higher than the prices of complements, whether firms are separate or combined. Complement or substitute relations between products can therefore affect the privately optimal prices

---

[11] Proving $p > P$ actually takes two steps. First, the demand curve, $q_1 = a - 2p_1 - p_2$, requires that $a > 2p_1 - p_2$ to have the reasonable case where $q_1 > 0$. Substituting solution values for p_1 and p_2 into this inequality, we obtain $a > 3c$. Second, returning to $p = a/5 + 2c/5 > a/6 + c/2 = P$, we find that it reduces to $a > 3c$, which we know to be true. So $p > P$ is true.

[12] See Constance L. Hays, "An Aisle Unto Itself?" *New York Times*, July 31, 1999, p. B1.

[13] The inequality can be reduced to $c < a$, which must be true for q to be positive.

[14] For an analysis of gasoline sales that demonstrates this point, see Shepherd (1991).

TABLE 6.6 Comparison of Complement and Substitute Prices Set Independently and Jointly (Numerical values in parentheses are based on $a = 600$ and $c = 30$.)

Product Interrelationship	Separate Firms	Combined Firm
Complements	$a/5 + 2c/5$ (132)	$a/6 + c/2$ (115)
Substitutes	$a/3 + 2c/3$ (220)	$a/2 + c/2$ (315)

of firms selling them. The desire to take advantage of such demand interrelationships can also influence the way that firms are organized.

Compatibility

Razors and razor blades are complements that are used together. They can be compatible, so the blades of one manufacturer fit into the razor of another manufacturer, or they can be incompatible, so one manufacturer's blades fit only that manufacturer's razor. Compatibility would seem to open more choice for consumers and, thus, benefit them. With computer processing units and monitors compatible, for example, consumers could pair them as they wished. Compatibility, however, is not always better for consumers than incompatibility. If they are compatible, the two goods can be sold separately and used flexibly, so the goods will be priced independently. Separate and independent pricing of two complementary goods can lead to higher prices than pricing of the two goods by one firm. On the other hand, incompatibility forces coordinated pricing on each seller of razors and razor blades. Because coordinated pricing of complements by a single firm may be preferable, incompatibility may be more beneficial to consumers than compatibility.

Think of two other complementary differentiated goods, video games and game consoles. If they are compatible, the products of different sellers can be mixed and each seller prices them separately. If they are incompatible across different sellers, however, consumers must purchase a matching video game and console from one seller, and because they are complements that seller can be expected to set lower prices for them. The prices can therefore be lower when the video games and consoles from different sellers are incompatible. Incompatibility forces sellers to offer complementary goods, which in turn motivates them to set lower prices. When both the games and the consoles offer scope for innovation, however, a seller may want to pair them technologically, and as a result they may be incompatible.

Despite the advantage of pricing incentives of complementary goods, there may also be disadvantages. Suppose complementary goods are hardware and supplies that together provide a service. If the seller of both hardware and supplies refuses to sell the supplies to other providers, that may prevent competition in supplies and consumers may suffer. Such a case involving Kodak products and supplies will be examined in Chapter 9 under the subject of "refusals to deal."

Technology opens a range of network compatibility issues. When color television was first developed, for instance, there were several ways of transmitting signals, and yet having a single method offered clear network advantages. Compatibility would allow every receiver to receive every signal. Serving as arbiter, the Federal Communications Commission chose one system. When the recording of television video signals later became feasible, two main formats were developed, Beta and VHS. Unlike broadcasting, the recording was done on a decentralized basis, so both methods were allowed to exist. Consumers were free to choose between them, and over time the VHS format came to dominate.

Tying and Bundling

A seller may force consumers to accept an interrelationship between products. For instance, a multi-product firm that has a monopoly over one product might force the consumer to buy a related product (or products), by *tying* it to the monopolized one. Under a **tying** arrangement, to buy one product you must agree to buy a second one also. Tying arrangements were used by IBM for punched cards, cards in which holes were punched to represent data so the data could be entered from the cards into early computers. The tied product, punched cards, was a supply item to be used with the computer, which was based on monopoly patents.

Tying can be used to discriminate in price, and the example of punched cards tied to computers shows how. The user of more punched cards would probably have a more intense demand for the computer and be willing to pay more for it. So an extra high price for the tied supply—the punched card—would bring a greater total payment from those with the most intense demand. If those who value the service more use it more, as we should expect, they will pay a higher effective price—a discriminatory price.

The monopolist over a tying product also can gain advantage over other sellers in markets for the tied products. In the punched card example, IBM would be able to win the punched card business of those who valued its computer, so the tying practice could be unfair to competing makers of punched cards. Indeed, tying can be used to create a barrier to entry into the market for the tied supply item, punched cards in this example when they are tied to the monopoly computer. If tying was permitted, any producer of punched cards would also have to succeed in the computer industry to be in position to sell punched cards. Thus, IBM could **foreclose** the punched card market in that no other producer of punched cards could enter. By tying punched cards to its computer, IBM could control the punched card market.

When two goods are offered together they are **bundled**. The two goods may be sold separately at a higher combined price, or they may not even be offered separately. For instance, Microsoft bundled its Internet Explorer web browser with its Windows operating system.[15] Because Microsoft had a dominant position in operating systems, this bundling practice made Microsoft Internet Explorer browser more easily available to users than any competing Internet browser, such as Netscape's

---

[15] Bundling or tying can be difficult to evaluate in the software market, because the software maker has great discretion in designing products. See Mariotti (2000).

Navigator browser. Bundling the Internet browser would not appear to generate revenue directly, because Microsoft provided Internet Explorer in the bundle at no apparent added cost. The future use of the Internet, however, would depend on browsers, and bundling a browser with its dominant operating system helped Microsoft to a strong browser market position. Courts found this specific bundling practice violated antitrust law, although Microsoft was subject to mild penalties.

6.3 | NONPRICE COMPETITION

One way firms may moderate the problems of price competition is by developing differentiated products and winning a portion of consumers to one version of a product. In the market for soft drinks, for example, sellers offer different products from Coke to Pepsi to 7 Up and beyond, all appealing to our different tastes. This adds a new element to the market structure, differentiated products, and creates a new realm for business strategy. Whether genuine differences exist among products or not, if consumers *think* there are differences in branded products we can regard the products as differentiated. When they think products are different, some consumers may prefer one while others prefer another. That is, they do not see the goods as perfect substitutes, so a firm can raise its price and not lose all of its customers. As a result, each seller has a degree of market power, and that helps to overcome the disadvantages to the seller of price competition.

The monopoly power of a seller in a differentiated product market can be quite limited. First, there may be many purveyors of differentiated products, producing abundant competition. Second, entry may be so easy that firms can earn no economic profit. Indeed, economist Edward Chamberlin (1933) called his classic representation of this market with differentiated products monopolistic competition to capture the mixture of competitive and monopolistic elements involved. He imagined a representative consumer choosing among many varieties of product—many types of toothpaste, for example—and he illustrated the effects by analyzing a representative firm. An alternative representation, formulated earlier by Harold Hotelling (1929) is more concrete because it considers physical location as a source of differentiation. Then consumers are concerned primarily about those sellers located near them, either physically by distance or by location in some other dimension like the sweetness of a soft drink.

Let's distinguish two kinds of product differentiation. Horizontally differentiated products are similar in quality but offer different characteristics, while vertically differentiated products actually differ in quality, some being higher in quality and some lower. A General Electric or an Amana refrigerator may be horizontally differentiated while a General Electric and a custom-made Sub-Zero refrigerator are vertically differentiated. In the horizontal dimension, the consumer may choose from any of the offerings, depending on the specific combination of features or characteristics she most prefers. In the vertical dimension, the trade-off is not between characteristics as much as it is between money and quality. A particular consumer may be willing to pay for a certain level of quality and not stray very far from that quality in either direction.

Location Models

The monopolistic competition model is vague and abstract in its claim of product differentiation because the differentiation is not measured. A genuine downward sloping demand can result, however, when firms' products are differentiated by the firms' locations, a possibility that was examined by the great early twentieth-century economist, Harold Hotelling (1929). Measurable influences, like distance, or sweetness, or time, lie behind Hotelling's representation of differentiation, and they open the way to more concrete analysis.

The location representation can apply to situations where physical or geographical distance is not the measure of location. There may be a spectrum of chocolate flavors that vary with the adjustment of one crucial ingredient, for example. Individual consumers may have preferences about the chocolate flavor that fall from one end of the flavor spectrum to the other. If a consumer who prefers a particular flavor cannot have it, the flavor closest to that flavor on the spectrum will be next preferred. As another example, consider airplane departure times, which can be represented in the time dimension, and different individuals may prefer different departure times. Departure-time choices that are nearer a consumer's most preferred time are better for that consumer than choices far from that time.

Distance in the location model, even if it is in time, or flavor, or some other dimension other than actual geographic distance, can serve to differentiate products for any given consumer. A consumer may prefer one variety over another and be willing to pay more to obtain her preferred offering. By offering lower prices, sellers may persuade consumers to accept less-than-ideal choices. So the demand curves seen by individual sellers can slope down. Consumers are able to trade off having their most preferred variety against money by accepting a less-preferred variety for a lower price. Again, remember Bertrand's criticism of Cournot for having firms choose quantity instead of price. Bertrand thought price competition would immediately drive price equal to marginal cost. When consumers have preferences for locations (distance, flavor, time, or some other measure), however, sellers at certain locations face downward-sloping demands, and price competition need not force prices equal to marginal costs.

Price variation with differentiated products yields a form of profit interdependence similar to quantity variation with homogeneous products. Imagine a market with sellers spread over a wide geographical area and consumers living at different locations. Consumers incur travel costs to reach any particular seller location so the effective price for any consumer includes travel cost as well as the price for the good or service purchased. Then even if all firms sell the same product each seller faces a downward-sloping demand curve, because some consumers are closer to that seller's location and some are farther away. Firms usually prefer situations in which price changes bring small and gradual changes in the number of consumers they can attract, rather than the sharp disruptions that can follow from price changes when they cause large numbers of consumers to change sellers.

Figure 6.1 *Hotelling's Main Street*

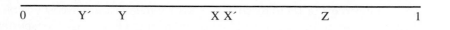

| 0 | Y´ | Y | X X´ | Z | 1 |

Location in the Hotelling Model

Hotelling appreciated the Cournot-Bertrand-Edgeworth development that explained how a few firms might behave in a market. But Hotelling saw another reason why price competition need not force price to marginal cost: the existence of *separate markets*.[16] Hotelling accepted a homogeneous physical product, but he imagined sellers at different locations, so each seller had an advantage in winning the business of customers who were close to it. To create a model that focused on the locations of stores selling a homogeneous good, Hotelling imagined a long and narrow city, with one main street in the long direction, as Figure 6.1 loosely illustrates. Suppose consumers are located uniformly along that street—that is, they are equally spread out along the street, which is, let us say, one mile long. We focus attention on only one good, and we assume consumers purchase one unit of it every day.

Consider, first, the problem of a single firm locating along this main street. In addition to whatever price they pay for the good, consumers have to incur transportation cost to reach the seller. The only firm entering this market can be expected to choose the center of Main Street, at X in Figure 6.1, a location apt to be within reach of all customers. Indeed, this location for a single firm is also socially ideal, because it minimizes the total transportation cost of customers while also maximizing the firm's profit.

For simplicity, think of the cost of transportation to travel the full length of the street, from 0 to 1, as being equal to 1. Then some simple calculations can answer questions about both profit maximizing and welfare-maximizing outcomes. The consumers's **effective price**, or the **full price**, includes not only the price of the good at the store but also the transportation cost to reach the store. To reach the monopoly store at X in the center of the street, what cost would the average consumer incur? The cost of traveling from 0 to X is 1/2 (and the cost of traveling from 1 to X is also 1/2), and the cost of traveling from X to X is zero. Because consumers are uniformly located along the street, the average consumer in that part of the street from 0 to X incurs a transportation cost equal to the average of 1/2 and 0, or an average cost of 1/4. The same is true for consumers between X and 1. Even as a monopoly, the firm realizes that keeping total transportation costs low for consumers keeps the effective price to consumers, including transportation cost they must incur, low. No other location can offer average transportation cost as low as 1/4. If located at either end of the street, for example at 0 or at 1, the average consumer would incur a transportation cost of 1/2.

Now consider a second firm entering the market. If you were able to start over and make socially ideal locations for both firms, where is it best to locate the two

---

[16] Hotelling (1929) was inspired by Piero Sraffa (1926), who imagined firms operating with some monopoly advantage in separate markets. Sraffa was trying to explain why an equilibrium could exist with price above marginal cost when firms had economies of scale, and he saw separate markets as an explanation.

firms? You should be able to show that Y and Z, at 1/4 and 3/4 in Figure 6.1, are the socially ideal locations for the two firms. The most distant consumers from Y and Z incur transportation cost of 1/4 to reach a store, which means average cost will be 1/8. Remember, one store in the middle of Main Street resulted in average transportation cost of 1/4. Locating two stores at Y and Z puts the stores closer to consumers and reduces their total transportation costs.

Let us return to the goal of profit maximization. Suppose, again, that the first firm locates at X. If you are the second firm and you seek maximum profit, where should you locate? First, assume the price of the good is fixed. Then wherever you locate you can expect to split the consumers that are located between you and the firm located at X. You will win all consumers on your side of the firm at X. What should you do to maximize your profit? To keep down the number of consumers you must share with the firm at X, you should locate as close to X as possible, say at X' in Figure 6.1.

The location can be on either side of X, but should be close to X, because then you can win virtually half the consumers. All the consumers on your side of X will find it less expensive to travel to you at X' than to X. Notice also that if the first profit maximizing firm anticipates that you will enter second, it still can do no better than to locate at the center of the street at X. If the first firm chooses any other location, you could again choose to be close, and you could also locate on the side of the first firm that contains the most consumers.

Does profit-maximizing entry by your second firm improve welfare? In locating at X', the second firm adds virtually no benefit for consumers, because travel time will not change much at all. The second firm gains by attracting customers away from the firm at X, however, and this is called the business stealing effect. We have ignored any costs of the seller, but if each seller must incur some fixed cost then new entry, while not benefiting consumers, would lower the combined profit of all firms together by the amount of the second firm's fixed cost. That means that after a second firm enters, even if it is closer to some consumers' preferences, welfare can decline. More fixed costs must be incurred for the added firm. More than two firms might also fall into an unstable location game. As each tries to capture a large portion of the market, a third firm may be trapped with few customers between the other two firms and would seek to relocate. Further entrants will reduce welfare unless their locations reduce travel cost enough to overcome the increase in fixed costs.

Thus far, we have assumed prices are fixed. But two firms next to each other at the center of the Hotelling street would face direct price competition, much as Bertrand assumed. The resulting price competition could be severe and would seriously erode profit. Location in a product dimension, however, allows product differentiation that can moderate price competition. The firms can move away from each other and, thus, from price competition, and choose instead to compete in product locations.

Avoiding Price Competition in the Hotelling Model

If transportation costs for consumers are very great, or if the costs increase more than proportionately with distance, say with the square of distance, then firms can be motivated to avoid price competition. If firms can relocate easily (the hot dog vendor

Figure 6.2 *The Full Price for Consumers to Reach Firm 0 or Firm 1*

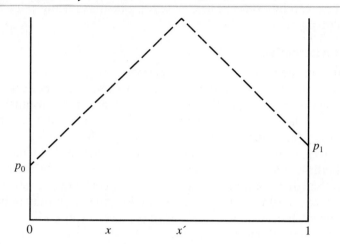

with a rolling cart on a New Orleans street can do this readily) they might realize that price competition is less strong if they are far apart. This reality can motivate them to locate at the ends of the Hotelling street, and that can be an equilibrium.[17]

Figure 6.2 shows two competing stores, called firm 0 and firm 1, at opposite ends of the Hotelling street, which again has consumers located uniformly along it. The sloping lines, which include the price at each store plus transportation costs that vary with the consumers' locations, show the full price to consumers of reaching each store. As shown, firm 0 has a slightly lower base price, or price at the store, than firm 1. Assuming that consumers go where the full price is lower for them, slightly more than half of all consumers would prefer to buy from firm 0.

The full price for a consumer located at x who buys from firm 0 is p_0 plus transportation cost, t, times x, so full price is $P_0 = p_0 + tx$. For consumers who buy from firm 1, full price is p_1 plus transportation cost, which for distance from 1 is t times $1 - x$. Thus, the full price for a consumer at x who purchases from firm 1 will be $P_1 = p_1 + t(1 - x)$. We can find the location of the marginal consumer at x', who is indifferent between purchasing at firm 0 or firm 1, by setting the full prices equal at $P_0 = p_0 + tx = P_1 = p_1 + t(1 - x)$ and solving for x,

$$x' = 1/2 + (p_1 - p_0)/2t.$$

The value of x' in Figure 6.2 is slightly greater than 1/2 because p_0 is slightly below p_1.

When firms locate far apart, as at the two ends of the street in Figure 6.2, notice that despite having a higher price, firm 1 does not lose all its sales to firm 0. The stores are differentiated by distance, so their price competition is muted. A firm that lowers price also loses revenue on all sales it had been making at its higher price so, like a

---

[17] d'Aspremont, Gabszewicz, and Thisse (1979) presented the stability problem in Hotelling's model and showed how increasing transportation cost can yield a solution with locations that have maximal product differentiation at opposite ends of the street.

monopolist or a monopolistic competitor, it has a marginal revenue calculation to make. Each firm can be expected to choose a profit-maximizing price based on the downward-sloping demand it faces.

The Internet Alternative

To examine the pricing problem more fully, suppose consumers have an alternative to purchasing from the two stores at the end of Hotelling's street. They can also purchase from an e-retailer on the Internet. Suppose at the e-retailer the consumer can purchase and have the good delivered at the full price, I. Figure 6.3 shows this situation and indicates that for the prices indicated, x_0 consumers will purchase from firm 0, $x_1 - x_0$ consumers will purchase on the Internet, and $1 - x_1$ consumers will purchase from firm 1.

Now the firms have a new location motive. If firm 0 and firm 1 move toward each other, rather than locate at the ends of the street, they can attract more consumers away from the Internet. They do so by locating to minimize transportation cost for consumers, thus making travel to their physical locations more attractive relative to transacting over the Internet. Figure 6.4 illustrates locations for firm 0 at x_0 and firm 1 at x_1 that will win consumers away from the Internet. Notice that although these locations are close to 1/4 and 3/4, the socially optimal locations, that result is not assured. Firms may locate to preserve product differentiation and avoid vigorous (Bertrand) price competition, but the locations may also be better for society.

Many factors can alter a solution such as that in Figure 6.4, and the trade-off between price competition and product differentiation is complicated. Location decisions may not be ideal, but an alternative such as the Internet can spur firms to pay more attention to consumers' transportation costs in an effort to serve them better, rather than trying to outfox competing firms.[18]

Figure 6.3 *The Full Price for Consumers to Reach Firm 0, or Firm 1, or the Internet*

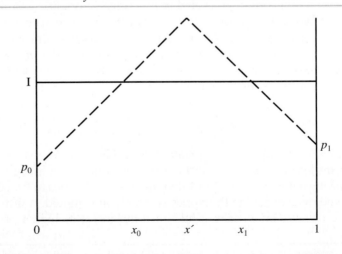

---

[18] Professor Steven Salop (1979) represented locations on a circle, like a circular street that has no end point.

Figure 6.4 *Locations for Firm 0 and Firm 1 That Compete with the Internet*

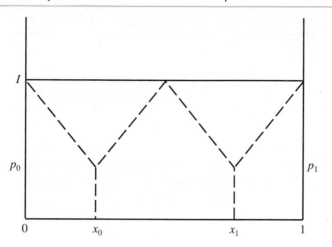

Quality as "Vertical" Product Differentiation

Along the Hotelling Main Street, any store location is preferred by the consumer who occupies that location, and locations differentiate stores. Moving some distance to another location is undesirable, whether the distance is geographic, as in the Hotelling model, or is measured in some other dimension, perhaps the intensities of chocolate flavors or the departure times of airplanes. Such product differentiation is generally regarded as horizontal differentiation. Horizontal product differentiation has the property that if one seller moves in a positive direction, toward 1 along Hotelling's "street" for example, some consumers gain and other consumers lose.[19] Consider a product differentiation such that when a seller moves in a positive direction, and there is no price increase, *all* consumers gain. This is vertical differentiation. With vertical product differentiation, the location dimension reflects quality, and products higher in the dimension have higher quality.

Figure 6.5 contrasts vertical product differentiation with horizontal product differentiation. The upper part of Figure 6.5 shows an example of horizontal differentiation, similar to Figure 6.1, while the bottom part of the figure shows vertical differentiation. In the upper part of Figure 6.5, a consumer at X prefers location X to location Y. In the lower part of Figure 6.5, all consumers would prefer location Y to location X. With vertical differentiation, moving from 0 to 1 along the street raises quality. The main point is that with vertical product differentiation, *all* consumers prefer locations closer to 1, because products at those locations are higher in quality. The question for any consumer is whether a quality gain is worth the added price.

When products are vertically differentiated, all firms do not produce products of the highest, and thus most preferred, quality, because quality is costly. Some

---

[19] See Phlips and Thisse (1982) for description of horizontal and vertical product differentiation.

Figure 6.5 *Horizontal and Vertical Product Differentiation*

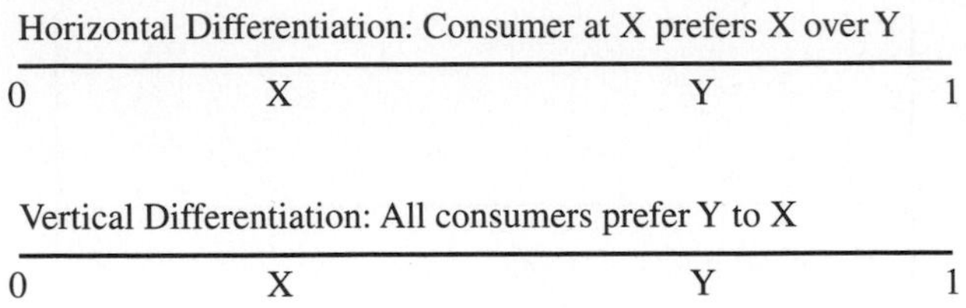

Horizontal Differentiation: Consumer at X prefers X over Y

| 0 | X | Y | 1 |

Vertical Differentiation: All consumers prefer Y to X

| 0 | X | Y | 1 |

consumers do not value added quality enough to pay for its added cost. In considering vertically differentiated products, consumers trade-off quality and price, so sellers locate themselves along the quality dimension where they think their quality per unit of price can appeal most profitably to consumers.

6.4 | ADVERTISING

Many other forms of competition exist beyond price choices, especially when products are differentiated. Automobiles, magazines, cell phones, or toothpastes are not all the same within their markets. Sellers of even similar products may each try to convince us theirs is different and preferable, because if we develop loyalty to a product we may be willing to pay more and not be tempted away by competing products. Even as price competition is moderated when products are differentiated, competition can continue in other areas that contribute to the differentiation. Examples of such non-price areas of competition include advertising, sales promotion, product design, and product development, to name only a few.

Advertising today is both admired and ridiculed, but it is an inescapable part of modern life. Each development in communications, such as newspapers, radio, television, and the Internet, has allowed sellers to present messages directly to potential buyers in ways that were impossible before. For example, manufacturers advertised to buyers by radio and television to sell products through intermediaries, such as retail stores, that they did not own or control. This possibility changed retailing. Now sellers can advertise to buyers and sell to buyers directly over the Internet.

Advertising and Monopoly

We can expect a monopoly to use any means that increases its profit, including providing information to consumers through advertising. Lacking interference from competitors makes the monopoly's problem well defined and therefore easier to tackle. So we begin with the monopoly's optimal advertising decision. Box 6.4 derives conditions for optimal advertising by a profit maximizing monopoly, and they take the following form:

$$E_a/E_p = sa/pq = \text{(advertising expenditure)/(total revenue)}.$$

BOX 6.4 Predicting the Advertising-to-Sales Ratio: The Dorfman-Steiner Condition

Suppose the amount of advertising by a monopoly is a, and the marginal cost of advertising is s. Assume that the quantity of a good sold, q, depends on both its price, p, and its advertising, a, as $q = q(p, a)$. Then the monopolist's profit function is

$$\Pi = (p - c) \, q \, (p, a) - sa.$$

When we introduce advertising into the monopoly model in this way, we assume the firm chooses advertising and price to maximize profit. Maximizing Π with respect to q yields the monopoly price, $(p - c)/p = 1/E_p$, where E_p is the absolute value of the own-price elasticity of demand.

Maximizing Π with respect to a requires that the marginal effect of advertising on profit equals the marginal cost of advertising. The marginal effect of advertising on profit is the increase in quantity from a marginal unit of advertising, or $\delta q/\delta a$, times the marginal profit earned on each added unit, $(p - c)$. Thus, the profit maximizing condition for optimal advertising, that marginal profit equal marginal cost, is

$$(\partial q/\partial a) \, (p - c) = s.$$

From the profit maximizing condition, $(p - c)/p = 1/E_p$, we can obtain $(p - c) = p/E_p$. So p/E_p can be substituted for $(p - c)$ in the optimal advertising condition, yielding

$$(\partial q/\partial a)p/E_p = s \text{ or } (\partial q/\partial a)/E_p = s/p.$$

Now multiply both sides by a/q, to obtain

$$((\partial q/\partial a)a/q)/E_p = sa/pq.$$

The right-hand side, sa/pq, is the ratio of advertising expenditure to sales, or to total revenue, a ratio called the advertising-to-sales ratio. The numerator of the left-hand side, $(\partial q/\partial a)a/q$, is the percentage change in quantity for a percentage change in advertising, or the advertising elasticity of demand, $(\partial q/\partial a)a/q = E_a$. Thus, the left hand side reduces to E_a/E_p, so we have

$$E_a/E_p = sa/pq = \text{(advertising expenditure)/(total revenue)}.$$

This equation is known as the Dorfman-Steiner condition for optimal advertising by a monopoly.

See R. Dorfman and P. O. Steiner, "Optimal Advertising and Optimal Quality," *American Economic Review*, December 1954, Vol. 44, pp. 826–836.

E_a in this equation is the **elasticity of advertising**, $(\partial q/\partial a)a/q$, equivalent to the percentage change in quantity divided by the percentage change in advertising. The left-hand side of this equation is the ratio of the elasticity of advertising to the price elasticity of demand (in absolute value), and the right-hand side is the ratio of advertising expenditure to sales, also known as the **advertising-to-sales ratio**. This relationship between the ratio of advertising elasticity to price elasticity on the left side and the advertising-to-sales ratio on the right side was derived by economists Robert Dorfman and Peter Steiner (1954) and is known as the **Dorfman-Steiner condition**.

When the monopoly sets both price and advertising optimally by the Dorfman-Steiner condition, the advertising-to-sales ratio is greater as quantity responds more to advertising at the margin (E_a is large), and the advertising-to-sales ratio is smaller as price elasticity of demand is greater (the absolute value of E_p is large). When advertising is marginally more effective, it should be used more per dollar of sales. On the other hand, as price elasticity of demand is higher the optimal markup over price is lower and a marginal unit produces less revenue, so advertising is then marginally less effective per dollar of sales.

By focusing on the marginal consumer, the monopolist may not choose a socially optimal level of advertising. Profitability does not depend on consumer surplus, which would determine socially optimal advertising, so the monopolist's choice of advertising may not be optimal. It may be too high or too low, relative to the socially ideal level.[20]

Advertising and Competition

With competition, it matters whether products are inherently similar or can be differentiated by advertising or other means. When products are inherently very similar, firms are reluctant to advertise, because one firm's advertising can benefit its competitors. No single dairy farmer wants to advertise milk, for example, because all farmers would benefit, so industry-wide dairy associations advertise milk. When firms can differentiate their products, say through advertising, they pursue their visible private benefits without taking into account any harm to other firms—harm caused by business-stealing effects—and they may advertise beyond a socially optimal level.

The advertising choices of firms can also draw them into another prisoner's dilemma game. In the prisoner's dilemma game, increasing advertising is analogous to cutting price—each firm privately wants to do it, but if all do it the firms are worse off than if they advertised less. The welfare effects differ though. Whereas lower prices that the prisoner's dilemma invites are socially better, the advertising it motivates can be too high, or socially excessive. If all firms together can restrain their advertising, and settle on lower advertising expenditures, they might enjoy higher profits, just as firms colluding at high prices can. Liquor companies have voluntarily avoided television advertising. Perhaps they believe that public policy would restrict them if they advertised on television. They might also refrain from television advertising in part because it is more profitable for them to limit advertising in some degree. Indeed, cigarette advertising on television was banned in 1970, and initially the ban led to improved profit for cigarette companies.

Advertising may also be a sunk cost because, like an investment, it lasts for some time, and it cannot be used for any other purpose. An industry with large sunk

---

[20] See Becker and Murphy (1993). For a similar argument concerning optimal product quality, see Spence (1975).

costs, which discourages entry, may have fewer firms and be more concentrated. Large advertising expenditures are like a sunk cost because they are not useful to any-one else and so cannot be sold. John Sutton (1991) has noted that, where advertising can foster product differentiation, firms will advertise heavily. One result, he argues, is that advertising sunk costs may be high, which in turn affects market structure by making entry difficult. Firms may make strategic commitments to advertising in an effort to develop their market opportunities while also imposing greater entry costs on potential competitors. To the extent that entry is more difficult in such situations, we can expect more concentration.

Multi-Product Advertising

A complementary relationship between the demands for two products may draw firms into offering both of them. If each of the two complementary products itself is differentiated, so some monopolistic element is present, we know that a single firm can improve profit by controlling the prices of both. It is also possible that advertising both products can be more productive than advertising each alone. For example, one advertisement might mention two complementary products, resulting in more prod-uct exposures per dollar of advertising. To the extent that the productivity of advertis-ing can be improved as a result, the advertising elasticity of demand, $(\partial q/\partial a)a/q = E_a$, increases. From the Dorfman-Steiner condition,

$$E_a/E_p = sa/pq = \text{(advertising expenditure)/(total revenue)},$$

we might expect an increase in E_a to lead to more advertising per dollar of sales for both goods. On the other hand, the prices of the goods might be reduced because of their complementarity, and reducing marginal profit per ad could lower the amount of advertising.

The main point is that complementarity of products can alter advertising and sales promotion strategy as well as pricing strategy. PepsiCo offers an example of how complementarity can be exploited. It can use its positions in complementary soft drinks and snack foods to promote those products together in supermarkets. Bundling and tying are other means of advertising and selling complementary goods in combinations.

SUMMARY

Game theory provides a framework for considering strategic actions by business firms. It focuses on players, available actions and their timing, and payoffs, in ways that allow illustration of choices, analysis of likely behavior by others, and equilibrium outcomes. Product market competition becomes more complex in oligopoly markets, where there are few firms, because the resulting wide range of actions makes strategic behavior more important. When firms are so few that their profits depend significantly on one another's behavior, we cannot reliably predict unique market price or quantity. Knowledge of the way each firm's actions affect another firm can suggest the types of solution that emerge, and attention to the firms' payoffs for alternative actions can help to organize our thinking.

With only two or three or a few firms, a cooperative solution might emerge, or rivalrous competition might develop. When products are homogeneous there is a strong pressure for one price, because price differences can bring strong shifts in sales and serious difficulties for firms. Several means are available to help firms coordinate their prices, including several possible forms of price leadership. Pricing in real industries can be very complicated. Single firms sometimes set prices for thousands of items, and each price may include complex but related terms of sale, such as who pays the freight and when payment is actually due. Still, illustrations of profit interdependence reveal the opportunities that exist, and the motives for cooperation and competition that they create.

Product differentiation opens broader forms of competition. It brings out the role of entry in introducing new product varieties, and yet such a market may not offer the optimal amount of product variety. Location models can represent products that are differentiated in geographic location or in other dimensions, such as departure times for airplanes or flavors for ice cream. One horizontally differentiated product usually has competitors that are "close" to it, such as airplane departure times at 5:00 PM and 6:00 PM. Or products may be vertically differentiated, where one is better but costs more than another, such as a Cadillac relative to a Chevrolet automobile.

When products are differentiated, firms may be able to compete less in price and more in non-price ways, and in part because non-price competition tends to be less volatile, they may seek out ways to differentiate their products. Product differentiation raises the number of dimensions at issue beyond price and quantity to firm or store location, product design and features, product and process research and development, advertising and sales promotion, and other factors. These can be aspects of market structure that influence how firms behave and how markets perform. Advertising offers a good example of non-price competition, and it can be related to a variety of market conditions. Goods can even be categorized in different ways according to how effective advertising might be as an influence on purchasing decisions.

Private business firm decisions may not maximize welfare when products are differentiated. In location models there can be too many firms, or too much variety, relative to the ideal. In the monopolistic competition model of product differentiation, there can be too little as well as too much variety. One cause of this result is a "business-stealing" effect, where a new firm gains by stealing business from other sellers while not adding much to welfare generally. Too little variety results when a new firm cannot capture much of the benefit that a genuinely new variety of product might add to consumer satisfaction. No easy remedy can correct these non-optimal outcomes, even if they were easy to discover, which they are not. We have a hard time telling whether too many different types of automobiles are offered for sale, and even if we knew, there is no readily acceptable way to correct the situation. Moving to non-price competition makes the market a less reliable test of what is socially optimal. Although markets still function quite efficiently and are accepted, non-price competition brings complaints. Advertising is one area of non-price competition that elicits especially vigorous objections.

Cost conditions, demand elasticity, and advertising elasticity may influence optimal advertising by a firm. Relationships among products, such as complementarity, may also influence advertising. When competition can occur in forms or dimensions other than price, equilibria that are not socially optimal are more likely. Many non-price forms of competition can be important to firms trying to position themselves for a profitable future. One of the most important ways to do this is through new product and new process research for innovation, which is the subject of Chapter 7.

QUESTIONS

1. A large retail store is considering its advertising expenditure. The store feels sure that it can obtain a 10 percent return (regardless of any competitor responses) in an alternative project.

   a. The store is confident that, barring a response by a large competitor, an increase in advertising of $10,000 per month would raise sales $100,000 per month. Gross profit would amount to 20 percent of any such sales increase, not counting the advertising cost. (The advertising cost would have to be subtracted from that gross profit to determine net profit.) In addition, capital investment would have to increase by 50 percent of the monthly sales increase to provide working capital (inventories and so on) that is necessary to support the expanded sales. This amounts to $50,000. What would be the rate of return on that increase in working capital (there are no income or other taxes)?

   b. If the store's large competitor were to match the advertising increase, the sales increase would be only $60,000 per month. Profit would still be 20 percent of the sales increase, not counting the advertising cost; and capital investment would still be 50 percent of the monthly sales increase, so it would amount to $30,000. What would be the rate of return on that increase in working capital (there are no income or other taxes)?

   c. Show how to analyze this investment choice problem between advertising and the other project (the alternative project that can yield a 10% return) as a game, to present rates of return under the different possibilities (advertising increase or alternative project, and competitor matches or does not match the advertising increase). Assuming you are risk neutral and simply want to maximize your expected profit, what probability that the competitor would match the advertising expenditure would cause you to abandon the advertising program?

2. Describe a situation from your life that can be represented as a game. Indicate who the players are, how they interact, what strategies are available to them, what goals the players pursue, and what their payoffs are.

3. The following table represents profits as payoffs in a normal form game for two Cournot duopolists in a market with zero costs (as Cournot assumed) and demand of $P = 10 - 0.01Q$:

		FIRM TWO		
	Output Quantities	250	333	500
FIRM ONE	250	1,250	1,388	1,250
		1,250	1,042	625
	333	1,042	1,110	835
		1,388	1,110	556
	500	625	556	0
		1,250	835	0

a. Would the two firms be privately motivated to stay at the output of 500 each?
b. Would the two firms be privately motivated to stay at the output of 250 each?
c. Is there a prisoners' dilemma within the payoff table? If not, explain what is lacking in each possible case (there are four). If there is a prisoners' dilemma, say where it is and explain why it is a prisoner's dilemma.
d. Is there a Nash equilibrium in this game? If there is none, explain why. If there is one, or more, indicate it (them).

4. Consider a market for a homogeneous product where two sellers compete in price and have cost of zero. Market demand is given by $q = 4 - p$. The price, p, is the lower of the two prices the firms set, and if one firm has a lower price it serves the entire market. If the two firms have the same price they divide the market equally ($q_i = (4 - p)/2$ for the ith firm).

a. Assume that each firm cares only about its own profit. Using only whole integers as possible prices for each firm, create a table that contains the firms' outputs for all combinations of prices that the two firms might choose in the game. Using those outputs, and the prices, create a table of profits for all combinations of prices that the two firms might choose.
b. Does a price of 3 dominate a price of 4?
c. Is there a dominant strategy for firm 1? If there is a dominant strategy, explain what it is and why it is a dominant strategy. If there is none, explain why.
d. What is the best response to a price by the other firm of 4? What is the best response to a price of 3? What is the best response to a price of 2?
e. What is the Nash equilibrium price in this game? Would your answer be the same if there were three firms in the market?

5. The Multi-Product Pricing section of this chapter solves profit maximizing conditions for firms selling complementary goods to obtain solution prices in terms of known parameters. Provide the same sort of solution for prices of substitute goods, which are discussed but not fully derived in the text.

6. Consider a location problem for two stores along Hotelling's Main Street. Show that locating stores at Y and Z in Figure 6.1 minimizes transportation cost for customers. Will two stores choose these ideal locations?

7. Consider a small number of firms producing a single, uniform product. How would the following conditions affect the likelihood that the firms would reach agreement at a price above the competitive level: (a) demand for their product is less elastic, (b) their total costs vary relatively less with short-run output, and (c) their capacities are larger relative to quantities now demanded. Be clear what effects each of these conditions would have on the attractiveness of cooperation (perhaps by illustrating effects on payoffs in a two-firm prisoner's dilemma case).

8. Two firms independently sell two substitute goods, q_1 and q_2. Each firm seeks maximum profit through the best choice of prices, p_1 and p_2. Demands faced by the two firms are

$$q_1 = 100 - 2\,p_1 + p_2 \text{ and } q_2 = 100 - 2\,p_2 + p_1.$$

Assume production costs are zero and can be ignored.

a. Find equations that yield the profit-maximizing prices, p_1 and p_2, chosen by the independent firms. (Hint: Because situations are symmetrical, the solutions of the two firms should be the same, and you can substitute one into the other.)

b. By solving these two pricing equations simultaneously, find values for the market prices, p_1 and p_2.

c. Now suppose the two firms join into one through merger. Express profit for the combined enterprise, using as prices in this case, P_1 and P_2.

d. Find equations for profit-maximizing prices, P_1 and P_2, for the combined firm.

e. By solving these two pricing equations simultaneously, find values for the prices, P_1 and P_2.

f. Determine whether p_1 and p_2 from independent profit maximizing or P_1 and P_2 from joint maximizing are larger. Explain the reason for your result.

9. Table 6.6 gives numerical values for prices of complements and substitutes when they are priced independently or together by a combined firm. Show that the same results hold for $a = 300$ and $c = 60$. Table 6.6 is repeated here without numerical values.

Product Interrelationship	Separate Firms (Independent Pricing)	Combined Firm (Joint Pricing)
Complements	$a/5 + 2c/5$	$a/6 + c/2$
Substitutes	$a/3 + 2c/3$	$a/2 + c/2$

10. Here are the payoffs for two firms based on the outputs they choose, high (H) or low (L), in a market as shown in Table 6.1.

Player 1/Player 2	L	H
L	15, 15	−5, 25
H	25, −5	5, 5

Suppose the two firms are rivalrous in their motives, perhaps because the best performing firm wins access to financing and the other firm does not. Show how the fact of their rivalry alters the payoffs for player 1 by making a new payoff table that contains player 1's rivalrous payoffs. Based on these payoffs, what output is best for rivalrous player 1 and why? What outcome would you expect the two firms to reach in this case if they are both rivalrous?

APPENDIX 6.1 Independently Pricing Substitutes

Consider a single firm, firm 1, selling good q_1 with demand $q_1 = a - 2p_1 + p_2$. The appearance of $+ p_2$ in this demand function means that the quantity sold of good q_1 depends on the price of p_2 as well as the price of p_1. The positive sign on p_2 means that raising p_2 will raise q_1. If a price increase in p_2 raises q_1, that means the two goods are substitutes. Suppose that a similar demand relation holds for firm 2, which produces good q_2 with demand $q_2 = a - 2p_2 + p_1$. Just to make comparisons easy, the two demands have the same intercept term, a, and are symmetrical. Suppose costs for the two firms are $C_1 = c_1 q_1$ and $C_2 = c_2 q_2$. Later we assume $c_1 = c_2 = c$, again to make comparisons simple.

The first goal is to find prices that maximize profit for the independent firms. We can then compare such prices with prices that maximize profit for the combined firm selling both goods. Firm 1's profit for this substitute-good case is

$$\pi_1 = (p_1 - c_1)(a - 2p_1 + p_2).$$

Maximizing this profit with respect to p_1 yields

$$\partial \pi_1 / \partial p_1 = a - 4p_1 + p_2 + 2c_1 = 0,$$

which we can solve for

$$p_1 = (a + 2c_1 + p_2)/4.$$

Maximizing firm 2's profit in the same way yields

$$p_2 = (a + 2c_2 + p_1)/4.$$

We can solve these two equations for p_1 and p_2 in terms of the parameters, a, c_1, and c_2. By substituting p_2 into the expression for p_1 and then solving for p_1, we obtain

$$p_1 = (5a + 8c_1 + 2c_2)/15.$$

Following the same procedure for p_2, we obtain

$$p_2 = (5a + 8c_2 + 2c_1)/15.$$

So that comparisons are very easy to make, suppose the firms' costs are equal, $c_1 = c_2 = c$, which makes the two prices the same,

$$p_1 = p_2 = a/3 + 2c/3 = p.$$

7

Market Innovation

Technological change has been with us since people first began making tools about 500,000 years ago. Even against the geological time scale of prehistorians, such early technological change came very slowly. The potter's wheel and the wheeled vehicle came into use only 6,000 years ago, and the simple spindle no more than 2,000 years ago.[1] Today we take for granted vast bodies of technical knowledge, and we have come routinely to expect prodigious annual additions to that knowledge. Because much of our technical knowledge resides in industry, it is natural to ask how market structure or size of firm might affect technology and the rate of technological change.

Simple models of markets are static in nature and thus well defined, so firm actions are channeled narrowly into price or output forms or even to non-price dimensions such as advertising. Yet digital phones, Skype, DVD movies, Google, YouTube, Yahoo!, and Amazon.com show that markets are not static, and change is the order of the day. Naturally, competing firms want to influence change in strategic ways, and they can affect the shape of the future by developing new organizational forms, conducting research to find new products, developing new materials, or finding improvements in their products and processes. New organizational forms are especially important when new technologies—such as development of the Internet— bring new possibilities for communicating and transacting. New products, materials, and processes shape a new world, and the first firms to occupy positions there can have great advantages. This is the dynamic world of technological change and market innovation.

Market innovation rides on new ideas, and property rights to these ideas, called intellectual property, can help to motivate them. We begin by discussing in Section 7.1 four kinds of intellectual property: copyrights, trademarks, patents, and trade secrets. When the public is not readily informed about new ideas, or when there is imperfect

---

[1] These estimates are taken from Singer, Holmyard, and Hall (1954, ch. 9). This five-volume work, published by Oxford University Press, is fascinating to sample and is a thorough account of the development of technology into the early part of the twentieth century. See also Usher (1954).

information, that can help an innovator to appropriate some of the benefits of her innovation. Section 7.2 examines this appropriability question by tying it to the incentive for innovation, and it considers alternative forms of compensation for discovery. Patents, market structure, and dynamics are treated in the next three sections: Section 7.3 focuses on patents and their role in motivating research, Section 7.4 treats the effect of market structure on innovation, and Section 7.5 considers dynamic effects such as competitive races to win patent awards. Finally, Section 7.6 considers the Internet as an example of dramatic and far-reaching technological change.

7.1 INTELLECTUAL PROPERTY AND TECHNOLOGICAL CHANGE

Technological change comes through new ideas, which firms pursue more aggressively when they can own the ideas and exploit them for financial gain. Ideas can be owned as property in the form of copyright, trademark, or patent, and they can be protected as trade secrets. Research efforts can discover new ideas, which firms can develop into saleable and profitable products. Market structure not only influences the incentive to discover, it also can be influenced by discoveries, so it is related to technological change. We examine intellectual property before turning to technological change and market structure.

Intellectual Property

Intellectual property is property related to ideas, and it can be protected by copyright, trademark, or patent, and, in a different way, as a trade secret. Copyright, trademark, and patent grant a property interest, which allows ownership, whereas a trade secret can be protected against theft. A **copyright** protects the expression of an idea, not the idea itself, and grants the owner the exclusive right of first publication and of commercial copying. The expression of an idea is a concrete form of the idea, such as a book manuscript.[2] Writings, works of art, certain compositions, recordings and performances, and some computer programs, can be the subject of copyright protection.[3] We are more concerned with patents, because of their close relation to technological change, and with trademarks and trade secrets because they can be related to technological change, but copyright is an important subject on its own.[4]

Trademarks, patents, and *trade secrets* are especially important in markets.[5] Use of a **trademark** is centuries old. It began as a sign of ownership (like branding cattle), and later—by monopoly guilds in England for example—it was used as a sign of authenticity in production, to insure quality in the presence of imitators. As trademarks

---

[2] See *Harper and Row Publishers, Inc. v. Nation Enterprises.*, 471 U.S. 539 (1985).
[3] See 17 U.S.C. § 102, 117 (1998).
[4] See Landes and Posner (1989).
[5] See Landes and Posner (1987).

of this kind became valuable, they were misappropriated by others in an effort to make products more attractive to buyers. Initially, such unauthorized use of a trademark was regarded as a deception, the offering of an imitation product as if it were an original. As time passed, however, courts accorded trademarks value as property—intellectual property—and regarded misappropriation of such property as theft whether it was deceptive or not.[6]

Firms can register trademarks with the federal government,[7] under terms of the **Lanham Trade-Mark Act** of 1946,[8] or with states that have adopted similar statutes. What for years were called trade names, which would represent a company and its products or services and took the form of words, can now be registered federally as **service marks** rather than as trade names. Firms acquire some rights merely by using a name or service mark, or trademark, but before firms may bring federal infringement claims they must register the service mark. Anyone who might be damaged by its use can also oppose registration of a trademark. For example, while claiming no connection to Babe Ruth, the baseball star, the Curtiss Candy Company that made the Baby Ruth candy bar certainly benefitted from the similarity in names, and it successfully opposed Ruth's use of the name "Babe Ruth Home Run Bar."[9] Decisions in such cases can be appealed to the courts of the judicial system. After being registered five years without objection, the right to a trademark is virtually incontestable, at least in the geographical area where it has been used.

A **patent** is a device intended explicitly to give an inventor a property right to a discovery.[10] It did not arise in the ordinary course of business, as trademarks did. The right was created either as a proper and rightful action to reward social contribution or to follow the design of some purposeful social calculus to elicit social contribution. The natural law idea, which has justified the use of patents in some countries, regarded the discoverer as *deserving* the right to benefit from a discovery. The patent is a convenient way to effect that right, and by compensating the individual who makes a socially valuable discovery it also serves the public. A related view sees the patent as a reward that is morally due an inventor and as having a value presumably comparable to—or in proportion to—the value of the work.

We might also think of a patent as payment to the inventor in exchange for publication of the new idea, because working plans for a patented invention must be publicly available. Under this rationale, society benefits from the *knowledge* of the discovery, while its profit possibilities are reserved for the inventor. Finally, we can view the patent purely as an incentive that invites research, and that may even finance further research. Such a rationale for granting patents presumes that patents actually provide a good incentive for research and that without them an inadequate amount of research would be conducted. The United States sets this incentive advantage against the loss of efficient use that the monopoly property right causes, through

---

[6] See McManis (1992).

[7] Specifically, they are registered with the Patent and Trademark Office of the U.S. Department of Commerce.

[8] See 15 U.S.C. §§ 1051–1127 (1946).

[9] In 1921, when the Baby Ruth candy bar was introduced, the patent office considered trademarks. For more on this case, see Ira Berkow, "A Babe Ruth Myth Is Stirred Up Again," *New York Times*, April 7, 2002, p. 2 YNE SP.

[10] For an economist's description of the patent institution, see Machlup (1968).

BOX 7.1 Who Owns the Smile?

The yellow smiling face that is familiar to Wal-Mart shoppers was registered as a trademark in France in 1971, and since then in 98 other countries, by a company called Smiley World. The Smiley World image began as part of a French newspaper campaign to highlight cheerful news, and after the face was registered it was licensed to other newspapers and then to other firms in Europe, including Levi Strauss for jeans, Mars for M&M candies, and Agfa for film packaging. When Smiley World applied to use the symbol in the United States, the Patent and Trademark Office refused to register it on the ground that the design was already in widespread use. Then in 1997, Smiley World sought to register the word *smiley* in conjunction with the smiley face. Wal-Mart opposed this Smiley World application and then sought to register the trademark for its own use solely in the field of retailing. Smiley World opposed the Wal-Mart application, saying Small World had already been denied a similar request. The right to use the smiley face in the United States will be decided by the U.S. Patent and Trademark Office, but that decision will apply mainly in the United States, where prior usage is important. Each country tends to decide these matters independently, which can cause conflict in a global economy.

See T. Crampton, "Smiley Face Is Serious to Company," *New York Times*, July 5, 2006, p. B3.

---

monopoly pricing over the life of the patent. The monopoly right is limited in duration, however, and when it expires the work moves into the public domain for all of us to use and enjoy. For the purpose of promoting the progress of science and the useful arts, the U.S. Constitution explicitly states this trade-off between offering incentive for creators and allowing efficient use by the public.[11]

The protection of a copyright or a patent is not perfect, and to protect its rights a holder must object when others use its property. Firms often can learn about research efforts of others and are even able to duplicate their discoveries by the time they are patented,[12] although patents make the task of using results more difficult. Rights are not always perfectly clear. For instance, technology now permits the copying, downloading, uploading, and transmitting of music over the Internet. In 2000, however, a federal court barred a young company, Napster, Inc., from helping consumers to do these things. In its appeal, Napster argued that its scheme was in harmony with the Audio Home Recording Act of 1992, which granted consumers the right to use audio tape players and similar recording devices to make copies of digital music for their personal, noncommercial use.[13] But Napster lost its case when the appellate court ruled that the Audio Home Recording Act of 1992 did not apply to digital recording.

---

[11] See U.S. Constitution, Article 1, §8, para. 8. Among powers granted Congress is the power "[t]o promote the Progress of Science and useful Arts, by securing for limited Times to Authors and Inventors the exclusive Right to their respective Writings and Discoveries."

[12] See Levin, Klevorick, Nelson, and Winter (1987).

[13] See Carl S. Kaplan, "A Question of Music Piracy," *New York Times*, Sept. 22, 2000, p. D1.

Trade secrets also receive legal protection, even though they are not publicly disclosed. A firm's list of clients might be a trade secret, for example. If the holder of a valuable trade secret takes measures to protect it, such as telling employees of its status as a secret, then the employee who reveals it to others can be prosecuted for doing so.[14] A trade secret is not property like a patent is, for as long as no theft or misappropriation is involved, any independent discoverer of the contents of the secret may use it.[15]

For a discovery that qualifies, the inventor may either seek a patent, which requires disclosure of the idea and conveys a right to its use for a limited period of time, or may instead attempt to keep the idea a trade secret. In that secret form, it can last indefinitely, so it allows monopoly control of the idea and keeps it from the public. On keeping the idea a secret, the inventor can be legally protected from disclosure or use by others through impropriety or breach of confidence. The holder of a trade secret, however, must take steps to keep it secret to be in a position to object and to pursue damages if someone steals the secret.

Although a patent requires disclosure of the protected idea, and that protection is limited in the United States to a 20-year life, a patent's property value gives it an important advantage over a trade secret. Remember that a trade secret is not really property like a patent. If someone else discovers the content of the trade secret independently, the original possessor has no right to prevent its use. The original possessor of a trade secret can keep those entrusted with it from using it or giving it to others, but that person has no general property right in the secret itself. A famous example is the formula for Coca-Cola, which has remained a trade secret for decades.

The Process of Technological Change

Technological change takes many forms and arises for many reasons, but modern forms usually result from systematic research and development effort, which falls in three broad categories. First is **basic research**, which may not lead to specific applications but will support later discoveries that will do so. Developing the theory behind laser technology is an example of basic research. Second is **applied research**, which is focused to achieve a specific outcome. Laser printing or laser eye surgery are examples. The third category is **development**, which is the effort that goes into moving a new application into a profitable product, such as a laser printer, and arranging ways to present it to the public.

The prospect of an ownership right in the ideas developed, which can be secured, for example, by a patent, can motivate all of these steps. These forms of intellectual property can motivate efforts to create them, and that is their desirable instrumental effect. It is possible to grant too great a property award, which may close off further development and leave a smaller store of public intellectual property from which to draw new ideas. Initially we ignore this problem of the optimal award.

[14] See Moohr (2002) for description of criminal penalties for such misappropriation of trade secrets under the Economic Espionage Act of 1996, which greatly increased the protection of trade secrets.
[15] For analysis of the economics of trade-secrets information, see Kitch (1980).

Rather, we focus on discovery that is stimulated by the prospect of winning the right to intellectual property, which gives its owner appropriate benefits of the discovery.

Results of technological change can affect production processes, and be called **process innovations**, or can lead to new products, in which case they are called **product innovations**. Process innovations usually lower costs, but they may also make feasible the large-scale production of a product that was formerly too expensive to produce. Product innovations create new products that can serve new uses.[16]

Broader effects follow from truly giant innovations, such as the steam engine, oceanic navigation, the railroad, the telegraph, the telephone, the airplane, radio, television, computers, and the Internet. By altering how transportation and communications occurred, these innovations affected firms' activities, sizes, and locations. Changes came in how products and services were designed and in how they were sold.[17] Such dramatic innovations create uncertainty in the midst of the changes they induce, until the world settles down to operate in the new ways they engender. The enterprises that come to thrive in the new regime even help to draw the rules for that new regime.[18]

Market Structure and Other Influences on Technological Change

In his book, *Capitalism, Socialism and Democracy*, the great economic historian Joseph Schumpeter argued that competition "from the new commodity, the new technology, the new source of supply, the new type of organization" was more important than price competition because it "strikes not at the margins of the profits and outputs of existing firms but at their foundations and very lives."[19] Monopoly power played a positive role in Schumpeter's process of "creative destruction," in which large firms are more likely to carry out research, and monopoly or oligopoly power help to drive innovation.

Telling whether degree of monopoly or size of firm has any effect on the rate of technological change has been difficult, and the task remains unfinished. Economists have carefully studied technological change itself only in the past 50 years or so, and just part of their efforts focused on such topics as the effects of monopoly or large firm size on innovation. Innovation can affect market structure, because a new idea can make one firm dominant in a new market arena. We can, then, raise many questions about technological change and market structure.

Some of the findings about technological change have been surprising. In the United States, for instance, increasing use of machines accounted for only a small part of the increase in output per working hour in the twentieth century. Instead, education and health improvements in the work force have been credited with about 40 percent of the increase; and general advances in science and technology

---

[16] As an example, see Petrin (2002) for estimation of effects of the introduction of the minivan.

[17] For description of such changes, see Chandler (1962).

[18] See Spar (2001) for description of this giant-innovation process. Dinlersoz and Hernandez-Murillo (2005) describe how the Internet compares with earlier innovations.

[19] See Schumpeter (1942, p. 84).

with over a third of it.[20] These less tangible aggregate sources of growth are hard to trace to specific industries and harder still to impute to differences in degree of monopoly or firm size. Nevertheless, degree of monopoly and size of firm can both affect the resources that an industry devotes to research and development, and they can affect the chance that any potential innovation, once discovered, is promptly implemented.

To see how markets can encourage new discoveries, we treat new information as a commodity and consider the incentives that markets offer to produce it. Not only can information have value, but who has it *first* can affect how that value is distributed among us. Imperfect information conditions provide an incentive for research by helping to keep a discovery in the hands of its discoverer.

7.2 APPROPRIATING GAINS FROM INNOVATION

Innovation can benefit the person who perpetrates it only if that person is in a position to appropriate some of its rewards. The innovation can benefit others by bringing new pleasures, or old pleasures at less cost, and can harm those who were doing well under old methods. Even for the would-be innovator, rewards are not assured. Time and resources devoted in an attempt to discover and implement a new method may fail. Or before one completes the attempt, another inventor may already have discovered it. Even if the effort succeeds, its value may turn out to be less than was hoped for, or the discoverer may not appropriate a significant portion of the possible gains, perhaps because information about the idea spread to others too quickly. All of these factors, the resources required, the potential value of the discovery, and the opportunity a discoverer has to appropriate that value, influences the net gains expected from research and, hence, the pecuniary incentive to undertake it.

Information and Change

The sale of information, and indeed its commercial exploitation generally, is handicapped by the fact that information may suddenly become less valuable because newer information comes into existence and alters its relevance. Similarly, one who attempts to solve a particular problem by investing in research may not be the first to solve it and consequently may not enjoy a very handsome return (or indeed any return!). Yet it is also possible that discovery may be valuable even without patenting, because the temporary but profitable advantage it allows can lead to further improvements and continued leadership. Discovery alone may be gratifying enough to satisfy some innovators, especially when they can be identified with the discovery and respected for it. An example is the development of open-source software, whose

---

[20] See initial work by Nobel laureate Robert M. Solow (1957) and further analyses by Denison (1962a and 1985). Denison (1967) compared the sources of growth in nine western countries.

developers forgo proprietary claims. The main contributions come typically from a small number of leaders who are identified personally with their achievements.[21]

There may sometimes be conflicting information and clashing views about the future, and yet each holder of one view is confident *that* view is correct. As a result we can expect markets for **speculation**, and that too can be useful. Such markets allow some persons either to avoid bearing risks or to gamble on future price expectations by entering contracts that apply to the future. A variety of contractual arrangements is available in many markets to suit the desires and expectations of differently placed individuals and to accommodate and somehow reconcile different expectations about the future.

Thus we see how imperfect information can help to make new information valuable to its holder. The holder of the new information may have to exploit its promise directly, because successful sale of information is difficult. Discoverers can make gains in other ways as well, however, and those gains afford incentive for private parties to carry out many types of research.

Optimal Reward for Innovation

In principle, a fixed sum of money could be paid as a **reward** to inventors, perhaps by the government. Then their inventions could be freely used by all, because eliminating the monopoly property right eliminates monopoly pricing. The main problem with the reward system lies in estimating the value of reward for a new discovery ahead of time. Not only is it hard to find a basis for the optimal reward, it is also difficult to finance it. As Box 7.2 indicates, the reward system can also be difficult to administer. When government grants an intellectual property right in the use of an idea, such as patent or copyright, the owner of the property right can appropriate the value of the idea through market sales and profits, which reflects, at least approximately, the value of the discovery. While the award of property right may ultimately provide reasonable compensation, it also brings monopoly pricing, but only for a limited period of time.[22] This pricing also helps to allocate the cost of the research to those who benefit from it.

In adopting a property-right plan to motivate and compensate inventors, an important decision is the length of the period the inventor has exclusive use of the idea, the length of the monopoly patent period. Making that period longer potentially raises the incentive to innovate by giving the inventor more time to collect profit as compensation. It can also make further innovation more difficult because patent protected methods can stand in the way longer. The inefficiency of monopoly pricing also persists longer. During the patent period there is another question of how fully the patent-monopoly power can be exploited. For example, should monopoly practices such as tying and price discrimination be allowed? Antitrust law limits the allowed

---

[21] For analysis of open-source software development, see Lerner and Tirole (2002).

[22] For an evaluation of intellectual property as an incentive system, see Gallini and Scotchmer (2001). See Shavell and Ypersele (2001) for analysis of rewards versus intellectual property rights as means of compensating the creators of new information.

BOX 7.2 Paying a Reward for Innovation

Governments have used rewards to motivate socially important discoveries in the past. In the 1700s, for example, safe navigation by ships at sea was widely recognized to be a problem, and devastating shipwrecks punctuated its discussion. People did not sufficiently understand the movement of stars in the heavens to fix the positions of ships by astronomy, and they could not measure time accurately enough, especially in sea-going conditions, to locate longitudinal meridians by timing the motion of the Earth through observations of the sun. As a result, sea-faring nations supported observatories, hoping to master the movements of the stars, and they longed for accurate timepieces, because a breakthrough in either field might solve what was called the longitude problem.

In 1714, after advice from such leaders as Sir Isaac Newton and Edmond Halley (for whom the comet was named), the British Parliament passed the Longitude Act to award a prize for the discovery of a way to determine longitude at sea. The Act formed a Board of Longitude to administer a competition for three prizes, worth £20,000, £15,000, and £10,000, depending on the accuracy of the method discovered. A self-taught clock maker named John Harrison developed a remarkable clock that was able to meet the most demanding prize standard. Yet in a saga that displays all of the infighting that might arise over such a large prize (which would be worth millions of dollars today), Harrison had to battle doggedly for the prize. He finally received the value of the largest prize in 1773, more than 40 years after he began producing remarkably accurate clocks that were able to solve the longitude problem.

See D. Sobel, *Longitude: The True Story of a Lone Genius Who Solved the Greatest Scientific Problem of His Time*, Harmondsworth, England: Penguin Books, Ltd., 1996.

---

practices and, thereby, limits the value of a patent. When the cost of imitating a patented idea is low, then imitators may offer substitutes for the idea and, thereby, reduce its value.[23]

7.3 | PATENTS AND THE APPROPRIABILITY OF GAINS

The patent is not a modern arrangement. In 1474 the Republic of Venice adopted the first formal patent law. Misuse of patent rights in England, for fund raising and granting of favors, is one reason that Parliament passed the Statute of Monopolies in 1623. This statute outlawed earlier monopoly grants and laid down rules governing patent awards, which were to run for a period of 14 years. The 14-year period was chosen because the apprentice training period then lasted 7 years, and 14 years was long enough for two generations of apprentices to be trained. In special cases, the statute

---

[23] See Gallini (1992).

granted protection for three apprentice training periods, or 21 years. Some of the American colonies adopted patent laws based on the Statute of Monopolies. The first U.S. patent law, adopted in 1790, extended the patent for a life of 17 years from the date the patent was awarded, a compromise between England's 14-year and 21-year possibilities. Amid tariff negotiations to make patent lives more similar across countries in 1994,[24] Congress raised the patent life in the United States to 20 years, beginning with the date of the patent *application*. The **American Inventors Protection Act**, passed in 1999, requires public access to patents 18 months after the application date, even if the patent office has made no decision about the application. This law also protects inventors who have reduced the same idea to practice and used it commercially ahead of the patent application.

Just what a patent is, and how it can enable its holder to appropriate gains from a discovery, still varies to some extent from country to country. A patent typically offers an exclusive right to using a clearly described new and useful technical invention, and its holder can use the enforcement power of government to exclude others from such use over a specified time period. Countries have differed in the time period over which they grant patent protection,[25] in details about how they define the patent right, and in procedures for awarding patents.

An international convention in 1883 first enabled participating countries to coordinate patent protection. They adopted rules that protect foreigners in any country on the same basis as nationals of that country, and they specify other terms that are intended to avoid abuse of patent systems. For instance, the rules make it difficult for a nonpatent holder to exploit in one country some manufacture that exists under patent protection in another country. Despite the existence today of a well-developed international patent institution, there is still concern that patents are abused, and reform of the patent systems is continually debated.[26] The benefits achieved by the patent system depend on the value of the new discoveries it has elicited, discoveries that would not have occurred without it. This effect is hard to judge,[27] but survey results indicate that the effect of patents varies considerably among industries and technologies.[28]

Patents in the United States

In the United States, a patent lasts 20 years from the date of application.[29] To be granted a patent, an applicant must satisfy the patent office that a process, machine, manufacture, or composition of matter is new and useful. To be new, neither can practitioners

---

[24] Consistency in patent lives among countries was part of the General Agreement on Tariffs and Trade in 1994. See Berndt (2002, p. 62).

[25] Argentina, Chile, and Germany have offered two or three different periods of protection (in Germany one as short as three years), depending on the type of invention involved. Such discretion in determining patent life is difficult to exercise in practice. But it does permit greater precision in the grant of protection and may help to prevent abuses that tend to develop whenever a patent holder can extend protection over a very long time period.

[26] See, for example, Polanyi (1944), Neal (1968), and Gallini (2002).

[27] See Taylor and Silberston (1973).

[28] See Levin, Klevorick, Nelson, and Winter (1987) and Schankerman (1998).

[29] Current law starts its 20-year patent life at the date of *application*; but, before that law was passed in 1994, a U.S. patent had a life of 17 years from the date it was *issued*.

regard it as totally obvious nor can someone else already have accomplished it. To be useful it must simply promise some practical application. It usually has to be reducible to plans and drawings, too. For example, a process that is designed to produce a chemical may be patentable while the formula for the chemical is not. Examination by the patent office establishes tentative priority for the invention. The U.S. patent system goes beyond the patent systems in some countries, which merely register all patent requests and determine later whether they meet requirements to be patents. It is less demanding, however, than still other patent systems, which require a period of notification and delay during which opposition to the patent award may be registered.

Patent awards have surged in recent years, increasing 60 percent in the United States from 1996 to 2001, and the number of patent applications has grown even faster. An easing of standards is one possible reason for this increase, as software and business methods have sometimes been granted patents, but a great variety of new products include a vast number of patents.[30] One of the most active accumulators of patents is the International Business Machines Corporation (IBM), which obtained a record 3,411 patents in the year 2001.[31] The company manages its portfolio of patents as a genuine resource. With 150,000 engineers and scientists, IBM carries out research in many fields, and it seeks innovations across a wide range of possibilities. Not only do the patents provide legal protection of ideas that are used, they can also protect the control of ideas that otherwise might be used by competitors, or they can be used for bargaining over cross-licensing arrangements, which enable firms to use each others' patents.

The United States issues patents only to individuals who make inventions not to organizations. As a practical matter, employees normally assign to their employers the rights to any inventions they make in connection with their work. Indeed, if the employee leaves the firm, these rights assignments often cover discoveries made for a year or two after the employee departs. Employers usually carry out the administrative work of applying for the patent, too. At the beginning of the twentieth century, individuals retained over three-fourths of the patent rights; at the beginning of the twenty-first century, individuals retained only about one-fourth, with the balance being assigned to organizations.

Although the patent is justified in part as an incentive for invention, the inventors themselves do not always profit greatly from their inventions. Indeed, Robert Dean (1999), an inventor, has argued that truly watershed inventions are made overwhelmingly by individuals, take a long time to reach a market, and reward their inventors—if at all—only after many years of sacrifice.[32] Entrepreneurs, even if not inventors, pursue the profit opportunities that patents protect, so patents can still offer incentive effects. Yet the patent system does not always treat the lonely inventor well. Charles Townes and Arthur Schawlow, who developed the laser for Bell Laboratories in 1960, did not make extra money directly from the patent, although rewards to inventors are more common in the United States than in many other countries.[33]

---

[30] For instance, the parts of an IBM Thinkpad notebook computer contained about 5,000 patents.

[31] See Steve Lohr, "I.B.M. is First Company to Collect Over 3,000 Patents," *New York Times*, January 11, 2002, p. C11.

[32] Dean (1999) examined major, or watershed, inventions over the period from 1745 to 1972.

[33] See John Markoff, "A Rebel in Japan Is Hailed as an Innovator in U.S.," *New York Times*, September 18, 2002, p. C1, and Ken Belson, "Japan Court Says Company, Not Inventor, Controls Patent," *New York Times*, September 20, 2002, p. C4.

BOX 7.3 The Tragic Inventor

Edwin Howard Armstrong, who invented FM radio in 1933, did not enjoy its benefits. The FM technology was not popular with broadcasters, who had already invested in AM radio broadcasting equipment, and Armstrong had to set up his own FM transmitting station. FM radio became popular after World War II, but broadcasting companies stopped paying royalties to Mr. Armstrong. After five years of court battles over royalties, Mr. Armstrong ran out of money in 1954 and committed suicide by jumping from an apartment building in New York City. His widow, Marion Armstrong, persisted and received more than $10 million in royalties by 1967, when the last patent infringement suit against a broadcaster was settled.

See L. Lessig *Man of High Fidelity: Edwin Howard Armstrong*, Philadelphia: Lippincott, 1956, and T. P. Hughes *American Genius: A Century of Invention and Technological Enthusiasm, 1870–1970*, New York: Viking, 1989.

Patent Breadth and Cumulative Effects

The length of a patent, now 20 years from the date of application, is quite well defined, but its breadth, or scope, is not. When it is the subject of a patent, the scope of an idea involves the number of areas, or patent subclasses, that the idea is related to or may affect. Examiners of a patent application assign it to patent subclasses where searches are conducted to evaluate whether knowledge of each relevant subclass already contains the idea. The broader the idea, the more subclasses it involves. A broad patent can thus protect its inventor's rights against a greater range of alternative ideas.[34]

The scope of a patent award is especially important where discoveries come through cumulative efforts, one discovery paving the way for the next. This is the pattern of modern inventions, where we can expect a continuum of improvements to follow a pioneering invention (Gallini, 2002; Merges and Nelson, 1990; Scotchmer, 1991). A broader patent can prevent more of these improvements from being implemented, however, because earlier patents can prevent them. Broader patents may infringe upon earlier patents, so when innovation is a cumulative process, stronger and broader patents may actually bring less innovation.[35] Thus, although stronger and broader patents may at first glance seem to raise the benefits for inventors, they also stand in the way of future inventors; therefore, they can interfere with rapid change in technology.

The Role of Courts in the United States Patent System

By itself, the granting of a patent does not assure exclusive rights to its holder. Courts ultimately settle such rights, and courts tend to be more demanding than the patent office. If the holder of a patent finds the patent being used by an unauthorized

---

[34] For estimates of patent breadth and evidence that it affects patent value, see Lerner (1994).
[35] See O'Donoghue, Scotchmer, and Thisse (1998).

person, she must take action through the courts to deny such use of the idea. If the other person also has a claim—perhaps with an application for a slightly different patent pending—the courts determine who has the patent right. A body of law and precedent exists for such cases, and it goes well beyond the question of which party first received a patent from the patent office. Evidence bearing on the date of discovery is important. The courts also consider the diligence with which each party pursued its development. If one does not show reasonably diligent and persistent effort, that may indicate a failure to realize the effect and value of the idea, which can be reason to lose the patent. In any case, courts ultimately decide disputed property rights to inventions, and the holder of a patent must be prepared to go to court to enforce the right.

A special federal circuit court, the U.S. Court of Appeals of the Federal Circuit, hears appeals of patent cases. This specialist court brings greater consistency and thus predictability to decisions about the validity of patents and their possible infringement. In the period 1953 to 1978, before the federal circuit heard appeals, the various courts that heard cases upheld 62 percent of patents that had been found to be valid and infringed. In the period 1982 to 1990, when the federal circuit heard appeals, a much higher 90 percent were upheld.[36] Also, the federal circuit more often issued preliminary injunctions, which help the patent holder by blocking use of patented materials while infringement is being litigated.[37]

BOX 7.4 What Does It Take to Infringe a Patent?

The Supreme Court recently strengthened the position of patent holders by ruling that a product that is essentially equivalent, even though not identical to the patented product, can infringe a patent. The Court's decision allowed a producer of synthetic food dyes, Hilton Davis Chemical Company of Philadelphia, to protect its technique for purifying dyes against a similar process advanced by a Milwaukee company, Warner-Jenkinson. A jury had concluded that the differences in the processes used were so insignificant that the patent had been infringed. Warner-Jenkinson argued that the process had to be identical to warrant an infringement claim, and that in offering its new technique it should have the benefit of the doubt because it did not intentionally copy the patent. The Court ruled that intentions did not matter, and it upheld the lower-court jury's judgment of patent infringement.

See *Warner-Jenkinson Co., Inc. v. Hilton Davis Chemical Co.*, 520 U.S. 17, 117 S.Ct. 1040 (1997). This doctrine of equivalence is carefully constructed as a rule for determining infringement. See, for example, S. Chartrand, "The Supreme Court and Patents," *New York Times*, June 3, 2002, p. C2.

---

[36] See Jaffe (2000).
[37] See Lanjouw and Lerner (2001), who also point out that preliminary injunctions are awarded more often to larger firms.

Special Problems of the Pharmaceutical Industry

The 20-year U.S. patent life, dating from the time of application, may not work well for pharmaceuticals. Between applying for a patent and actually marketing a drug, there are lengthy delays for approvals, and such delays reduce the effective life of the patent. A firm may need years to gain approval for safety and efficacy from the Food and Drug Administration (FDA), and that approval is required before a firm can market a drug. Approval for *safety* has been required under the Food, Drug, and Cosmetic Act of 1938, which was passed after the death of more than 100 children from a drug failure. Amendments to that Act in 1962 required approval for *efficacy* as well, meaning that the drug must *work*; it must perform as claimed. In support of such approval, the drug company must provide evidence drawn from clinical trials, and that takes time.

After applying for a patent, a drug company could devote as much as a dozen years to obtaining these approvals for safety and efficacy. Because the effort to gain approval begins with the patent application, when the 20-year patent life also begins, the time spent in the approvals process shortens the *effective* life of the patent. In this extreme example that requires 12 years for approval, the effective patent life would be reduced to 8 years. The approval process would usually begin with tests on animals, and—with success there—move to clinical tests on humans, first for safety and then for effectiveness. Completion of all phases of these tests can consume as many as 10 years, and the FDA review of results might take two more years. To offset this decline in effective patent life, Congress passed the **Drug Price Competition and Patent Term Restoration Act** in 1984.[38]

The Drug Price Competition and Patent Term Restoration Act has two aims. First, the Act extends patent protection for the branded drug by the amount of time required for the FDA review plus one-half of the time devoted to required clinical trials, subject to some other limiting constraints. This provision returns some of the patent protection time that the requirement of FDA approvals for safety and efficacy consumes. Second, when this extended period of patent protection expires, the Act makes approval easier for generic producers of the drug, thus increasing competition at the end of the patent period.

Before the 1984 Act, generic drug producers had to go through almost the same process as that undertaken by the discoverer of the branded drug to win FDA approval. Repeating that process delayed competitive entry after the original patent on the branded drug expired. The 1984 Act allowed a generic producer to submit an Abbreviated New Drug Application, which requires showing only that key ingredients in the generic drug are effectively equivalent to the originally patented drug. The first generic producer also can remain the sole generic producer for six months, giving it a status as the *only* generic producer of the drug for that period. So although patent protection was extended under the Act to protect longer the original patent holder of the branded drug, once that patent protection came to an end the Act could facilitate production of the drug by generic producers, thus ending the patent protection more

---

[38] Monopoly advantage for a drug may extend beyond the patent period. See Caves, Whinston, and Hurwitz (1991).

abruptly. Generic drugs account for about half of the prescriptions filled at retail pharmacies today, thanks in part to money-saving policies at corporations' health plans that urge their use, so the issue of speeding their availability is a significant one.[39]

In practice, the Drug Price Competition and Patent Term Restoration Act was not totally successful in bringing generic drugs to market rapidly. By going to court, sometimes armed with patents awarded for minor variations on the original discovery, holders of the soon-to-expire, branded-drug patents were able to delay the introduction of generic drugs.[40] The Act was badly constructed, and it almost invited such suits, because it allowed the branded-drug patent holder to bring a patent infringement suit as soon as a generic producer applied to the FDA for permission to produce. In such a case, the law also prevented the FDA from deciding on the generic application for 30 months while the patent suit was underway.

If you were making, say, $1 million a day from a patented branded drug, and could delay loss of the patent for two and a half years by bringing a law suit, you would probably sue. Some cases have even involved additional suits, brought by the branded-drug company against the generic to extend protection beyond the 30-month period.[41] A policy change by the FDA in 2002 intended to stop frivolous patent suits and allow only one 30-month delay.[42] In 2002, the Senate passed legislation to reform the faulty 1984 legislation, but the House of Representatives did not act on it.[43] In a 2003 settlement with the Federal Trade Commission, Bristol-Myers-Squibb agreed not to bring lawsuits aimed at postponing the arrival of generic competitors, and this settlement might affect the practices of other pharmaceutical companies.[44]

Sometimes patent holders of branded drugs have reached accommodation with the one firm that is approved to produce a generic version for six months. By agreement, the one approved generic producer is paid *not* to produce a generic version of the drug. Thus, for six months at least, only two parties are able to produce the drug, the original patent holder and the generic producer. A monopoly can make more money than two firms in the same market, so it is easy to imagine that the firms could do better if only one of them produced the drug and they shared the resulting profits. A class-action antitrust lawsuit was brought against Abbott Laboratories for restraining trade in this way for the branded drug Hytrin.[45] The company was accused of paying Zenith Goldline Pharmaceuticals, Inc., up to $2 million a month to refrain from producing Hytrin as a generic drug. Such cases have been so numerous that they help

---

[39] See Milt Freudenheim, "Generic Drug Sales Flourish Thanks to Big Companies," *New York Times*, November 2, 2002, p. B16.

[40] For a brief description of this process, see Berndt (2002, pp. 63–64).

[41] States, consumers, and competitors sued Bristol-Myers-Squibb, claiming it illegally kept generic substitutes for their branded Taxol and BuSpar out of the market. See Melody Petersen, "Bristol-Myers-Squibb to Pay $670 Million to Settle Lawsuits," *New York Times*, January 8, 2003, p. C1.

[42] See Robert Pear, "Bush Seeks Faster Generic Drug Approval," *New York Times*, October 22, 2002, p. A24.

[43] See "A Good Week for Copycats," *The Economist*, Aug. 3–9, 2002, p. 55.

[44] See "Bristol-Myers Will Settle Antitrust Charges by U.S.," *New York Times*, March 8, 2003, p. B2.

[45] See Sheryl Gay Stolberg and Jeff Gerth, "How Companies Stall Generics and Keep Themselves Healthy," *New York Times*, July 23, 2000, p. A1. For an example of how delay can be extended because of wording in the law, see Milt Freudenheim, "Generic Drug Maker Challenges AstraZenaca Patent for Prilosec," *New York Times*, May 4, 2002, p. B1, and "AstraZenaca has Won a Battle, But Its War with Generic Drug Makers Is Continuing," *New York Times*, October 14, 2002, p. C2.

BOX 7.5 Monopoly Profit Exceeds Duopoly Profit

In July of 2006, the U.S. Justice Department announced a criminal investigation of payments by two drug makers to a Canadian company, Apotex, that the latter company not produce a generic version of Plavix, a blood thinner that is the world's second largest selling drug with world wide sales of about $6 billion a year. The two drug makers, Sanofi-Aventis in France and Bristol-Myers-Squibb in the United States, jointly market Plavix. They had sued to block Apotex from producing the generic version, claiming that it violated their patent. But the Food and Drug Administration approved Apotex's version of the drug in January 2006. The companies then negotiated a settlement in which Bristol and Sanofi would (1) pay Apotex not to produce its generic version until November, 2011 when the patent was due to expire, and (2) grant Apotex a 6-month period after it began production before they would introduce a generic version of the drug. Although the amount of the payment to Apotex is not known, it is estimated at $60 million. After the government objected to that agreement on grounds that it would limit competition, a secret deal is alleged to have been made that took some of the features, such as the payment to Apotex, away from public eyes. State attorneys general and the Federal Trade Commission rejected this agreement also, and Apotex then began shipping its version of the drug for sales to customers. Bristol and Sanofi won an injunction to stop Apotex sales until their patent case against Apotex is settled. But Bristol has been faulted for opening negotiations with Apotex, and in September of 2006 the company fired its CEO. Stopping sales of the generic is valuable to Bristol and Sanofi because it allows their monopoly profit to continue, and monopoly profit is greater than duopoly profit.

See S. Saul, "Patent Deal on a Drug Scrutinized," *New York Times*, July 28, 2006, p. B1; J. Carreyrou, "States Reject Deal on Plavix, in Blow to Bristol-Myers," *Wall Street Journal*, July 29, 2006, p. A2; S. Saul, "New Details in Reported Secret Deal Over Generic Drug," *New York Times*, August 18, 2006, p. C6; S. Saul, "Generic of Plavix is Blocked," *New York Times*, September 1, 2006, p. C1; and S. Saul, "Drug Maker Fires Chief of 5 Years," *New York Times*, September 13, 2006.

---

to motivate those seeking revision of the 1984 Act.[46] Change may be needed also because the Bush administration did not pursue these cases as aggressively as called for by the economic arguments against monopoly outcomes.[47]

7.4 MARKET STRUCTURE AND INCENTIVE FOR INNOVATION

Does the monopolist or the competitor have the greater potential gain from carrying out research? From theoretical considerations, the potential gain can seem to be greater for the competitor, who starts with no economic profit and can move to a

---

[46] Delays in marketing generics and noncompetitive pricing also seem to reduce the effectiveness of the Act in lowering drug prices. See Milt Freudenheim, "As Drug Patents End, Costs for Generics Surge," *New York Times*, December 27, 2002, p. C1.

[47] See Stephen Labaton, "New View of Antitrust Law: See No Evil, Hear No Evil," *New York Times*, May 5, 2006, p. C5.

handsome protected position. The monopolist's gain is smaller, because the monopolist already enjoys a large profit, and its *increase* in profit is not as great. The competitor, however, may have less abundant *means* with which to carry out the research. Also, patent or other protection is more important to a competitor, because it does not control the industry as the monopolist does. The monopoly, however, does not want to lose the comfortable position it already enjoys. The empirical record is not absolutely clear, but it suggests that neither extreme—the more nearly monopolized industry nor the most perfectly competitive one—offers the best market structure for encouraging research and development.

We still do not reliably know the effects of firm size and market organization on research and innovation. There is agreement, and some evidence, that in industries most like the perfectly competitive model, firms have only limited opportunity to engage in research.[48] Little commercial research is carried on, for instance, in industries having top-four-firm concentration ratios below 10 percent.[49] Beyond that point, however, there is some question whether a structure closer to the competitive or to the monopoly extreme is more conducive to research and innovation. Neither extreme can be defended as ideal.

Gains from Discovering a Process (Cost-Reducing) Innovation

Let us use an example to contrast the gains from research under competition with those under monopoly.[50] Assume in each case that the innovator can appropriate the gains from innovation by means of a well-functioning patent system. Consider first a cost-reducing innovation, where the production process has constant average cost and the innovation can reduce that average cost. In a monopoly regime, the monopolist is able to increase output and earn greater profit by making the innovation, and the gain is the difference between this greater level of profit and the level being earned before making the innovation. On the other hand, in a competitive regime a single innovating firm can win the entire market at a price slightly below the average cost of the old technology.

An innovation could lower average cost so dramatically that, based on the level of cost after the innovation, the new monopoly price would lie below the old competitive price. In cases of such **major innovations**, an innovating former competitor could enjoy exactly the same profit level as a monopolist who had discovered the same innovation. The competitor could set the monopoly price and no former competitor could match it, because that price is below the former competitive price. Moreover, having come from a low profit level, the competitor would enjoy a greater *net* gain than a monopolist would. For the monopolist would have enjoyed a monopoly profit before the innovation, and in moving to the greater monopoly profit after innovation its *net profit* gain would be smaller than the competitive firm's. Comparing

---

48 See Scherer (1967).

49 See Scherer (1967, pp. 529–530). Top-four-firm concentration ratios represent the portion of industry activity (usually sales, but perhaps assets or employment) accounted for by the largest four firms.

50 The following discussion relies on Arrow (1962).

new situations with old, the former competitor enjoys all the new-found profit, whereas the continuing monopolist gains only the difference between the new profit level and the old monopoly profit level. So the *net* gain in profit for the former competitor is greater than it is for the monopolist.

Other, **minor innovations**, do not lower average cost so dramatically. In these cases, the monopoly price after innovation lie above the original level of average cost. Then a single firm in a competitive industry is not able to earn a monopoly level of profit after it discovers and implements the cost-reducing innovation. Although it owns a monopoly right to the innovation, it cannot set price above the old average cost without losing sales to former competitors, who can still produce profitably at that price. Whether a monopoly or a competitive firm would gain more in this case is not obvious, so we examine it in more detail.

Consider a minor innovation, where the monopoly price after innovation is higher than the old level of average cost. As noted, under a competitive regime the new price after the innovation can be no higher than the old price before the discovery, because we can expect other suppliers to enter at that price. Even though under competition the full monopoly price cannot be realized after the innovation, the profit gain, and hence the research incentive, tends to be greater for a competitor in this minor innovation case.

The reduction in average cost from c to c' in Figure 7.1 represents the minor innovation. Profit for the monopolist before the innovation is the area $(p_M - c)q_M$, while monopoly profit after the innovation is the area $(p'_M - c')q'_M$ and the gain is the increase in profit the innovation allows. Suppose an outsider, whom we call the competitor, makes the innovation. The competitor cannot exploit its discovery fully, by setting the monopoly price, because the monopoly is still there and can charge less than that. We assume, however, that it can win all the sales at a price slightly below, yet practically equal to c, or to p_c, a price the monopoly cannot match, which means

Figure 7.1 *Gains from Innovation for Competitor and Monopolist*

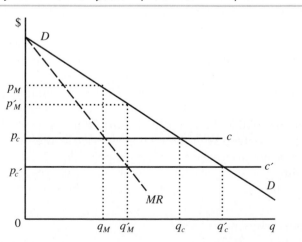

essentially that its quantity is q_c. Alternatively, others could be licensed for a royalty, which would accomplish the same result. Because its average cost after innovation is c', the competitor can enjoy the profit area $(p_c - c')q_c$. Now if we hold to the assumption of linear demand and constant average cost, we can show that the competitor has the greater gain and, thus, the greater incentive to innovate.

Because the innovation is a minor one, the new monopoly price, p'_M, is above the old cost of c, so q_c at price p_c exceeds the monopoly output, q'_M at price p'_M, or $q'_M < q_c$. The gain to the monopoly is the difference in profit before and after the innovation,

$$(p'_M - c') \, q'_M - (p_M - c) \, q_M.$$

The question is whether this exceeds the gain to the competitor, which is its postinnovation profit less its preinnovation profit of zero, which is $(p_c - c')q_c - 0$, or $(c - c')q_c$. Substituting q'_M for q_M can only enlarge the monopoly gain, and this substitution makes the monopoly gain

$$[(p'_M - c') - (p_M - c)] \, q'_M, \text{ or } (p'_M - p_M + c - c') \, q'_M.$$

Notice that $(p'_M - p_M) \, q'_M$ is negative, so if the monopoly gain is to exceed the competitor gain, then $(c - c') \, q'_M$ must exceed $(c - c')q_c$, or $q'_M > q_c$. We already concluded that $q'_M < q_c$, so that is impossible. Thus, the competitor's gain exceeds the monopolist's gain.

This proves our original claim that the competitor has a greater incentive than the monopolist to innovate when the innovation is minor as well as when the innovation is major. Professor Jean Tirole (1988) calls this lesser gain of the monopoly the **replacement effect**, because the monopoly in part *replaces* some of its already existing profit with profit from the discovery.

Bidding for a Discovery Once It Is Made

A firm in a competitive market may realize a greater *gain* from making a major or a minor cost-reducing discovery than a monopoly would. That does not mean, however, that the competitor would outbid the monopoly if they vied with each other to obtain the new method once it had been discovered elsewhere. After all, the monopoly has more to *lose* than the competitive firm.

Suppose both an established monopoly and a potential competitor learn at the same time of a lower-cost process discovered by a separate research laboratory. If it is a major discovery, they see the same possible gain in the future, but the monopoly is alone and the competitor may have the monopoly still hanging around. The survival of the monopoly—as a monopoly—is at stake, so the committed monopoly, needing less further investment, may outbid the competitive firm.[51] If it is a minor discovery, the competitive firm has to contend with the monopoly because the monopoly's technology prevents the competitor from achieving the monopoly price. The monopoly, on the other hand, has no existing producer to deal with, so it can preserve its monopoly position and expect greater profit than can a competing outsider. The new firm essentially has the

---

[51] See Gilbert and Newberry (1982).

prospect of operating in a duopoly market, and even though it has a cost advantage it is constrained by the former monopoly in the price it can set. So the new competitive firm earns less profit from the innovation than the monopoly, who has the market for the innovation entirely to itself. That is why we can expect the monopoly to bid more for rights to a minor innovation made by a third party outside the industry. This is consistent with the willingness of brand name pharmaceuticals to make payments to potential producers of generic drugs, to persuade them not to produce the drugs.[52]

The Number of Firms and Research Incentive

We can elaborate the Cournot model to include research expenditure as a decision variable, where greater research expenditure can lower the marginal process cost. This elaboration was performed by Dasgupta and Stiglitz (1980), who added research expenditure, x_i, to the ith firm's profit function and made marginal cost depend on x_i, as $c(x_i)$. Research expenditures can lower marginal cost. They first found the familiar Cournot conclusion that at equilibrium the price-cost margin would equal $1/n(-E)$ (n is the number of firms and $-E$ is demand elasticity), which would be lower as n is larger:

$$(p - c(x_i))/p = - (\partial p/\partial q)(nq_i/p)(1/n) = 1/n(-E).$$

They also found that the profit maximizing level of x_i sets marginal benefit equal to marginal cost:

$$(-dc(x_i)/dx_i)\, q_i = 1.$$

The left-hand side of this equation is the marginal benefit of a dollar spent on research, the marginal effect of x_i on marginal cost, $c(x_i)$ (which is negative), times output, q_i. The right-hand side is the cost of that marginal dollar spent on research, or 1.

As there are more firms in a Cournot market, the equilibrium output of each firm is smaller. In the profit maximizing condition, q_i is smaller and $(- dc(x_i)/dx_i)$ is larger. On the plausible assumption of diminishing returns to research expenditure, having $(- dc(x_i)/dx_i)$ larger means that the research expenditure of each firm is lower. As there are more firms, however, it is not possible to tell which of these two effects is greater, the larger number of firms or the smaller research expenditure per firm, so we cannot tell from this model whether more firms will raise total industry research spending.

The model suggests that demand elasticity is an important influence on research spending, however. For total research spending to increase when the number of firms increases, price elasticity of demand must be *large* (in absolute value). This allows a larger output increase with a smaller price reduction, so the research spending per firm need not fall very much, and of course there are more firms. On the other hand, if demand is not so elastic, more firms force smaller outputs per firm and a greater price decline, which discourages more research.

---

[52] See Sheryl Gay Stolberg and Jeff Gerth, "How Companies Stall Generics and Keep Themselves Healthy," *New York Times*, July 23, 2000, p. A1.

Dasgupta and Stiglitz (1980) explore free entry in this Cournot model with research spending by imposing a zero-profit condition to determine an equilibrium number of firms. They find that at this equilibrium, research spending for the industry, divided by industry sales, equals $1/n^*E$ (where E is the absolute value of demand elasticity, and n^* is the equilibrium number of firms). Thus, if E is reasonably constant, research expenditure per industry sales dollar falls as the free-entry equilibrium number of firms is greater, because $1/n^*E$ is smaller as n^* is larger. This result is consistent with the Schumpeterian argument that monopoly, or a few firms, will carry out more research than many firms will.

New-Product Innovation

The case of a new product innovation differs from a new process, or cost reduction, innovation. A totally new product offers the same rewards to competitor and monopolist alike, because neither one has to give up anything to enjoy profit from the new product. To the extent that a new product discovery is related to existing products, there may be differences between competitor and monopolist incentives, but they require case-by-case analysis. If the monopolist produced more products, for example, we might expect that interaction of new and existing products could have an influence. The substitution of a new product for an existing product could reduce the monopolist's incentive to offer the new one, for example, because it could reduce sales of the existing product, but the monopolist might profit more from introducing a complementary new product than would the smaller and less diversified competitor.

As in the case of product differentiation, research activity may be more or less than is socially ideal. With more than one firm in a market, there may be an excessive incentive to discover. Each firm sees the gain it can enjoy by stealing business from a competitor through the development of a new product. This "business-stealing" effect is essentially an externality, in the form of a loss to the competitor that is not taken into account by the developer of the new product. So with competition it is possible

---

BOX 7.6 The Changing Role of New Products

The introduction of new products is now more common, and more rapid, than it was years ago. Technologies for inventing new products are more developed, and information and communications channels for marketing them are faster and cheaper. Developers of new products can promote their sales more effectively, and imitators can also copy more quickly. There is still a first-mover advantage, but it is not as great as it was 100 years ago. A study of 46 product introductions over the century from 1887 to 1986 shows that the product life cycle has fallen from about 33 years to nearly one-tenth as long, an average of 3.4 years. Because change is so rapid, the development of new products is a much more important form of competition today than it was a century ago.

See A. Agarwal and M. Gort "First-Mover Advantage and the Speed of Competitive Entry, 1887–1986," *Journal of Law and Economics*, April, 2001, Vol. 44, pp. 161–177.

that there can be too much innovative effort. We also must consider consumers' surplus from an invention. If consumers' surplus from an innovation is large, it may offset the business-stealing externality effect, and then the competitive incentive is not excessive. Indeed, it may even be inadequate relative to the ideal level, meaning the effort to develop new products can be too small.[53]

Other Effects of Market Structure on Innovation

The competitive industry can thus offer a greater incentive than the monopolistic industry for cost-reducing innovations. Once a discovery is made, however, a competitive firm may not be willing to bid as much for it as a monopoly will. So there still is some question whether greater innovation actually results from more competitive structure in our industries. First, imperfections in the patent system might serve to inhibit a competitor who has many potential interlopers, but they might not reduce so much the incentive of a monopolist, because *the monopolist controls the entire market*. More reliable appropriation of gains is possible, even without patent protection, if you are the only game in town. Second, firms in competitive industries simply may not have enough money to finance research and innovation, whereas a monopolist might willingly apply some of its excess profit to research. Moreover, relatively more effort appears to be devoted to new product rather than new process research, and in new product research firms in competitive markets may have no greater incentive.[54]

That large and dominant firms can finance more and larger projects is an argument many economists accept. Joseph Schumpeter (1942) persuasively articulated this argument, which others have elaborated. Richard R. Nelson (1959) pointed out long ago, for instance, (1) that the large firm's diversity makes its research more apt to be usable within its own range of activities, (2) that the large firm can take a longer view and thus can wait longer for its payoff, and (3) that with a larger share of a market the large firm can more reliably share in the social gains from its discoveries. But persuasive arguments have also been made going the other way, that small enterprises, with fewer vested interests, may be driven to bolder innovation.[55]

Firms in monopolistic or oligopolistic industries may be under less pressure to carry out research. There is evidence, from industries where it can be studied, that the largest firms either spend a smaller proportion of their sales on research and development (R&D), or there is no relation between size and R&D expenditures at all; the largest firms have not apparently spent relatively more on R&D. Economies of large-scale research might make large firms able to carry out more research even though they spend proportionately less money. Other evidence suggests, however, that for the same level of R&D expenditure, the productivity of R&D may decline as size of firm increases.[56]

---

[53] Petrin (2002) found the minivan, as a new product, produced consumer benefits far in excess of development costs, and Hausman and Leonard (2002) found new bath tissue brought consumers both lower prices and increased variety.

[54] See Comanor (1967) and Denison (1962).

[55] See, for examples, Jewkes, Sawers, and Stillerman (1958), Mansfield (1964), and Dean (1999).

[56] See Mansfield (1968).

If a firm needs large size and much capital to enter an industry, that may also affect R&D activity. Professor William Comanor (1967) measured R&D activity by the number of R&D-related employees in a firm, and he found that industries with moderate size and capital requirements—not requiring investment of $100 million or production at a scale accounting for 10 per cent of the market, but also not so modest as to call for less than $20 million in investment or 4 per cent of the market to achieve an efficient plant size—had proportionately more R&D-related employees.

All other things equal, it is the medium-range, top-four-firm concentration ratio that seems to invite maximum scientific and engineering employment, too. Concentration in the 50 to 55 percent range produced the most intense scientific employment according to F. Michael Scherer's (1967) study, with greater concentration beyond that range offering no noticeable advantage. Oliver Williamson (1965) found that concentration had a negative influence on the relative innovativeness of the largest four firms in an industry.

Even if evidence showed that monopolistic industries carried out relatively more research (all other things equal), a conclusion that monopoly should be encouraged in some industries to stimulate research does not follow. It is possible that a more competitive market organization might raise output and sales in an industry, so even if research per unit of sales was lower, *total* research activity could still be higher under competition. Moreover, there is no reason why the allocation of resources to inventive activity by industry is efficient if it is undertaken according to the degree of monopoly power that exists by industry. Allocation of effort among industries might better be decided on some other basis, such as expected gain by equally situated industries. On such a basis, we can expect natural differences in the returns from research effort by industry. Firms could also better make decisions about allocating effort to research without relying on market power.[57]

Licensing and Research Joint Ventures

Patent holders license a substantial fraction of patents to other, often competing, firms. **Licensing** allows the licensee to use the patent for a fee. Why would a firm that has had R&D success license the benefit to other, competing, firms?[58] To answer that question, consider a cost-reducing discovery. Through a contract with the licensee, the patent holder can extract a royalty payment almost equal to the cost savings per unit that the innovation makes possible. Such a contract arrangement lowers only slightly the effective cost of the competitor, after royalties are paid. The market price also is little affected, because the competitor's net cost saving is small. The patent holder, then, receives practically the same profit as before the license arrangement, plus added profit from license payments, so the patent holder gains by licensing. Society also gains from the licensing, because what was cost for the competitor is now profit for the patent holder, and profit adds to welfare.

---

[57] See, for example, the extremely high social rate of return estimated by Griliches (1958) from largely government investment in agricultural research, where private firms probably would not have undertaken the research. For a review of research joint venture arrangements, see Brodley (1990).

[58] For a review of licensing arrangements, see Kamien (1992).

Research joint ventures—efforts bringing together, say, two firms in the same industry—may enhance research productivity.[59] By joining together for a research project, firms can moderate the wasteful aspects of patent races. Although no relaxation is encouraged toward other antitrust violations, such as cooperative pricing, 1984 legislation endorses some relaxation of antitrust concerns about cooperative research. The **National Cooperative Research Act** of 1984 invited firms conducting joint venture research to register with the government and thus to be free from responsibility for treble damages or punitive damages from antitrust suits about the research. Joint ventures are growing in the United States, and they increasingly involve firms from other countries, which may help to foster the spread of discoveries across national boundaries.

Joint ventures are especially appealing to firms when all share the benefits of discovery, or when there are scale economies in conducting research. Discoveries might be shared, for example, when they involve an input that all firms are able to use at lower cost. Firms in vertical relationships can easily share in discoveries, so joint ventures are easy to arrange in such circumstances.[60] Scale economies might arise when expensive equipment is crucial to the research, and one laboratory can use it more intensively than can two or more. Research joint ventures also can help to overcome the potential waste in races to acquire patents, to which we now turn.

7.5 PATENT RACES AND OTHER DYNAMIC EFFECTS OF COMPETITION

An important property of a patent is that it goes to only one winner. There is no second prize in the winner-take-all form of patent competition.[61] So when two or more parties seek the same discovery, if they do not form a joint venture, they can fall into a patent race. All trying to be first brings duplication of effort and maybe too-hasty innovation. Still, the earlier timing of the innovation should be better for society than the timing of innovation chosen by a monopoly. A firm may also gain advantage by experience, called *learning by doing*. Learning by doing accentuates the advantage of being first. If production experience can lead to lower cost, being first and winning sales can lower costs and thus be an advantage in competition.

By being in control of a market, a monopoly can choose its own optimal time to introduce an innovation. For example, it might wait until equipment it is using in its old process wears out. Optimal timing allows the greatest present value to be realized by one firm—if no one else intervenes. A competitor upsets that calculation. A competitor simply wants to be first and is not otherwise concerned about optimal timing. For the competitor cannot protect its commitment to older methods; it must forge ahead to avoid defeat by others.

---

[59] See, for example, Shapiro and Willig (1990).

[60] See Oerlemans and Meeus (2001), who relate joint venture arrangements to transaction costs in vertical relationships.

[61] For a review of work on patent races and the timing of innovation, see Reinganum (1989).

TABLE 7.1 Profit Streams from Alternative Investments of $300

Year	Invest at Once in Innovation	Invest in Alternative	Invest in Alternative, Innovate at Year 3
1	$50	$100	$100
2	$100	$100	$100
3	$150	$100	$150
4	$200	$100	$200
5	$400	$100	$400
Net Present Value	$600	$500	$650

Privately Optimal Timing

By calculating the present value of the streams of payments from different innovation strategies, one can find the optimal timing for a single innovator.[62] Table 7.1 presents profit streams from three investment plans. Introducing an innovation requires an initial outlay of $300 to produce a new product that will have a life of five years. Under the first plan, the money goes immediately into an innovation brought to a growing market. Market quantities are implicit in the profit streams, because a profit of $1 per unit is earned, so units are the same as profits. The investment of $300 will last five years in this case and then be worthless because the product will be obsolete. Profit is only $50 in year 1, but with market growth it grows to $400 in year 5, after which sales end. Assume the discount rate is 0 percent, so the net present value of the profit stream is the sum of yearly profits. Then the profit stream for the first plan has a present value of $600 ($900 in profit minus $300 investment that becomes obsolete).

An alternative investment pays $100 per year every year. Investing in the alternative has the advantage that the invested money can be withdrawn and then invested in another project, such as the innovation. This leads to a third option of investing in the alternative and then switching in year 3 to the innovation. The result is a greater present value because earnings in the first year can be better. By avoiding the low earnings of the earlier years with the innovation, this plan produces a larger present value of $650 ($950 in profit minus $300 investment that becomes obsolete), even though it uses the investment only three years. Thus, in this example, it is better for a single monopoly firm to delay the innovation until year 3, the optimal timing for innovation, because that is most profitable. This assumes the same cost for the innovation in year 3 as in year 1, whereas the cost could be lower after delay, and that would add to the benefit of waiting.

---

[62] See Barzel (1968) for an early version of this analysis.

Socially Optimal Timing

Table 7.1 focuses only on profit streams. It does not consider consumer surplus. Innovation can be expected to raise consumer surplus while existing activities, including the alternative investment, does not. Table 7.2 shows how a small consumer surplus advantage can make immediate innovation socially preferable to the optimal timing that a monopolist might choose. Consumer surplus is assumed in Table 7.2 to be one-half as great as the monopoly profit from innovation.[63] Because we obtain some consumer surplus in the first two years under the first plan of immediate implementation, this plan offers the greatest present value of consumer surplus. In this case the gain in consumer surplus is great enough to make total welfare—consumer surplus from Table 7.2 plus profit from Table 7.1—greater with immediate innovation. Now the first plan, which involves immediate innovation, yields consumer surplus plus profit of $450 + $600 = $1050, greater than the third plan of innovating in year three, which yields $375 + $650 = $1025. Again, we assume no reduction in the cost of innovating as time passes.

With competition in the market, the timing that was optimal for a single monopoly firm is no longer relevant. Because the first plan has a positive present value, it is attractive to a competitor, more attractive than waiting until year 3. Table 7.1 is constructed on the assumption that only one firm has the innovation. If there is competition in pursuing the innovation, the firm that waits until year 3 loses its chance to pursue it.

Welfare effects are not reliably predictable here. Even though Table 7.1 contains firms' profit streams, and Table 7.2 adds consumer surplus streams, they represent a single example that is not general. Consumer surplus from immediate innovation usually offsets reductions in the present value of profit, to make welfare greater, but delay can be socially optimal, especially if the cost of innovating falls with time.

TABLE 7.2 Consumer Surplus Streams from Alternative Investments of $300

Year	Invest at Once in Innovation	Invest in Alternative, Innovate in Year 3	Advantage of Investing at Once
1	$25	$0	$25
2	$50	$0	$50
3	$75	$75	$0
4	$100	$100	$0
5	$200	$200	$0
Present Value	$450	$375	$75

---

[63] The full monopoly solution with a linear demand yields consumer surplus that is one-half the monopoly profit. For illustration of this result, see Question 6, part (a).

Competition usually motivates immediate innovation, even when consumer surplus benefit is not large and delay could be better for society. Usually, however, the social benefits are greatest with the earliest innovation.

Effects of Learning by Doing

Now suppose the process underlying the example in Tables 7.1 and 7.2 allowed the producer to gain further economies as its cumulative production increased, as a result of the producer's **learning by doing**. As cumulative output grows, the firm learns more about its production process and about how it can lower costs. As experience accumulates, profit then grows more than Table 7.1 indicates. Might this make any of the three plans more attractive than numbers in Table 7.1 presently indicate?

Table 7.3 assumes that the profits come at the rate of $1 per unit, as in Table 7.1. Profits grow additionally in Table 7.3, however, according to *accumulated* output, because accumulated output creates learning that can lower costs. Thus, Table 7.3 adds 10 percent of accumulated output from the innovation as profit each period. For example, the firm that innovates immediately has outputs of 50, 100, and 150 in the first three years. With learning it gains an extra profit of $5 in period 1 (10 percent of accumulated output of 50), $15 in period 2 (10 percent of accumulated output of 150), and $30 in period 3 (10 percent of accumulated output of 300). Adding these amounts to the profits for this first option in Table 7.1, including amounts to later periods on the same basis, yields profits for those options shown in Table 7.3. Because the third option of delaying the innovation until period 3 reduces the effect of accumulated output in promoting learning, and thereby in raising profit, it is less attractive when learning is important.

Learning by doing makes the first plan of investing in the innovation immediately even more attractive. If learning was more rapid in the early production stages, this advantage would be stronger. Economies gained through learning in the first couple of years are great enough in this example to make the present value of profit

---

TABLE 7.3 Effect of Learning by Doing on Profit Streams from Alternative Investments of $300

Year	Invest at Once in Innovation	Invest in Alternative	Invest in Alternative, Innovate at Year 3
1	$55	$100	$100
2	$115	$100	$100
3	$180	$100	$165
4	$250	$100	$235
5	$490	$100	$475
Present Value	$790	$500	$775

under the first plan, $790, exceed the present value under the third plan, $775, which involves waiting until year 3 to innovate. Thus, option 1 now yields greater profit and is preferable even without considering its advantage in consumer surplus gain.

Effects of learning by doing can be more important when there is competition than when there is a monopoly producer. Learning by doing encourages rivalrous behavior to gain sales in an effort to win lower cost. Any advantage a firm gains in lowering cost persists. As a result, each competitor seeks greater sales to gain greater experience, all with the goal of achieving a cost advantage over its rivals later. This incentive can prompt firms to set very low prices—even prices that produce current losses—in an effort to win more sales, with the hope of gaining cost advantages that will pay off later. Such competition can speed the introduction of an innovation.

Winner-Take-All Patent Races

We have seen that the optimal timing for an innovation can be earlier for a competitive firm than for a monopoly. This extends with great force to the competition *for* patents. Remember that in a patent race, only winning matters. So it is possible for competitors to incur seemingly wasteful expenditures as both attempt to be the first to discover and to patent. A monopoly may attempt to intimidate potential competitors by conducting extensive research efforts, and by doing so early. With a big head start, the monopoly may discourage others from even attempting the same innovation. Breakthroughs come in surprising ways, however, and if it is possible for a smaller firm to leap-frog ahead of the monopolist, it may remain in the race.

Patents are not always crucial in these forms of competition. A survey of research and development executives in the United States indicated that winning market success through sales and service efforts is more important than patents for appropriating rewards from a research effort.[64] So is moving down the learning curve

---

BOX 7.7 Technological Change with Learning

The earlier the innovation, the earlier employees can begin to learn how to lower costs, and, thus, the greater the cost reduction they can achieve. A study across a number of processes in the chemical industry found on average that a doubling of cumulative output would lead to a price reduction of 23 percent. An increase in cumulative output by a firm also led to an increase in the number of patents the firm received. At the same time, the firm that has mastered one technology through learning may hesitate to switch to new and better technology, and it may even be overtaken by a less experienced firm that opts for new technology.

See M. B. Lieberman "Patents, Learning by Doing, and Market Structure in the Chemical Processing Industries, *International Journal of Industrial Organization*, 1987, Vol. 5, pp. 257–276, and B. Jovanovic and Y. Nyarko, "Learning by Doing and the Choice of Technology, *Econometrica*, November, 1996, Vol. 64, pp. 1299–1310.

---

[64] See Levin, Klevorick, Nelson, and Winter (1987) and testimony of Professor F. M. Scherer at www.ftc.gov/opp/global/scherer.htm.

to obtain lower production costs. The executives also rated having some lead time over others and preserving secrecy as more crucial to success than gaining patent protection. These may reflect the views of larger firms, however, and smaller firms might rely more on patents. It is no wonder that Thomas Edison, first among great modern inventors, approached the government of New York City about rights for distributing electricity before he had perfected the invention of the electric light bulb. He anticipated the importance of sales success to any benefit from his research success.

Market organization also affects the speed with which new discoveries are implemented. The monopolist may tend to delay an innovation, in part because it has a vested interest in present methods, including perhaps a desire to let some equipment wear out before replacing it. In contrast, the competitor may press any advantage in an effort to move faster, hoping to take business away from other sellers. Still, larger firms usually are better able to finance innovation than small firms. A monopoly has more money rolling in than firms in competition, which might enable the monopoly to move faster in supporting innovation. There is some evidence, too, that when the cost of an innovation is very great, a larger firm may be more likely to exploit it promptly, although the same is not true for lower-cost innovations.[65] Diffusion of the results of R&D throughout the rest of an industry also appears to be slightly faster in less concentrated industries.[66]

Assessing the Patent System

Besides the expenses of administering the patent system, and the resources that firms devote to the development of patentable innovations, costs of the patent system also include the restrictiveness introduced by monopoly patent awards. By limiting allowed technologies, patents may prevent later innovations. The price of a product also will be higher when produced and sold by a patent-holding monopolist than when produced by many competitors in an environment where no such property right as a patent exists. In exploiting a monopoly over the use of a patented invention, the monopolist simply chooses a price higher than the marginal cost of production, a price that stands in the way of economic efficiency. That is why a reward system that would make a one-time payment to the inventor, rather than granting a patent property right, is attractive. We still rely on the patent to motivate discovery, however, largely because estimating the amount of any reward is so difficult.

The patent is a winner-take-all arrangement that involves high risk, not only about whether the discovery will be made but also whether it will be made *first,* so that a patent can actually be claimed. Waste from duplicate efforts is a possible result. Two or more efforts may be undertaken, and only one can succeed.[67] The importance of being first brings haste to a patent race, as well as waste from duplication. Yet we have accepted the patent monopoly idea nevertheless, largely to serve as incentive to publish

---

[65] See Mansfield (1963).
[66] See Mansfield (1961).
[67] Oerlemans and Meeus (2001) show that research cooperation, especially between firms in vertical relationships, may economize research effort.

new ideas and to try to discover them in the first place. The monopoly grant provides a reward that is roughly comparable with the value society places on the invention. Besides inviting haste and waste, however, the scheme also violates our static efficiency norm (at least for the life of the patent) by allowing price to exceed marginal cost.

The reward the patent offers inventors, the spur it gives to innovation, and the access that patents afford to information about inventions, thus come at the cost of some inefficiency in the economy, much of which depends on the length of the patent protection. Monopoly pricing is inefficient, while long and broad patents can stand in the way of further innovation. Whether a shorter patent period is in order in some cases is a difficult question to answer objectively. We need to guard against possible abuses also. Individual firms may obtain patents simply to prevent the use of alternative and equivalent techniques by others or to extend the effective life of their monopoly beyond 20 years. Firms also may collude in preserving monopoly advantages that they can share. The patent is a time-tested means of granting a property right to an idea, however, and as such it stands as a significant private-property social invention itself.

7.6 THE INTERNET AS AN EXAMPLE OF MAJOR INNOVATION

Starting in 1969 as a research aid, and opening commercial applications in 1990, the Internet has fostered a far-reaching communications revolution. Giant innovations, such as the telegraph, railroad, radio, television, or the Internet cause upheaval, even chaos, and they force parties to grapple with a changing environment.[68] At first the Internet was used for tasks that were already being done, to do them in different ways. Soon, however, tasks were undertaken—such as searching quickly for an author's work—that were not possible without the Internet.[69] Online e-commerce does not involve every good or service in the economy, but it changes the form of some (for example, newspapers and magazines) and changes the way others are bought and sold (for example, books, CDs, and DVDs). It raises new issues of intellectual property protection, and it has inspired stronger laws for that purpose. And its long-run changes in market forms may be so substantial that they are impossible to predict.

Revenues on the Internet are over $500 billion annually[70] and are climbing rapidly, involving more than five million web sites.[71] Productivity has also increased.[72] At the moment we are essentially following an infant industry policy,

---

[68] For analysis of giant innovations and their effects, see Spar (2001). For development of electronic commerce on the Internet, see Dinlersoz and Hernandez-Murillo (2005).

[69] See Borenstein and Saloner (2001).

[70] This sum represents a total value of all transactions; the total value of transactions could easily exceed the nation's Gross Domestic Product, which only includes newly produced goods and services. For other reasons, estimates of total e-commerce activity are problematic. See Fraumeni (2001).

[71] See, for example, Wiseman (2000).

[72] See Baily and Lawrence (2001) and Litan and Rivlin (2001) for estimates of productivity effects.

a policy that exempts a new technology from regulation and taxation while the institution—if that is the right word—grows. When the Internet reaches sufficient size, the tax advantages that Internet retailers now enjoy over physical, brick-and-mortar, retail stores, or over sellers in taxing countries, will not continue.[73] Already the cross elasticity of demand between Internet and physical stores can be reasonably high, indicating that active competition between them is ahead, at least for some goods.[74] Internet e-commerce does face some handicaps. Not surprisingly, the handicaps come partly from other regulated interests, such as the brick-and-mortar liquor stores in many states that were able to win passage of laws preventing out-of-state (that is, California) wine ordered over the Internet from being delivered into the state. The Supreme Court did stop states that were allowing shipments from in-state wineries, but not from out-of-state wineries, yet broader barriers are still in place in many states.[75]

Consumer Opportunities

On the consumer side of Internet transactions, the Internet greatly enhances search possibilities, channeling useful information to consumers at lower cost than before.[76] The effect of such improved information, especially about seller prices, can be more vigorous competition. There is evidence that this reduction in the cost of collecting information results in lower prices.[77] Information obtained from the Internet can actually influence some purchases made through traditional brick-and-mortar stores, especially for durable goods of high value such as electronic products or automobiles.[78]

Examples of sites that help consumers learn about sellers and their products are search engines Alta Vista, Google, or Yahoo!, with Yahoo! also being one of the providers of a business directory. Examples of specialized sites are Expedia, Orbitz, and Travelocity for airline tickets and other travel needs, Dealtime for books and music, Pricewatch and Computer ESP for computers and components, Shopper.com and Yahoo! Shopping for electronics, or Bizrate, which rates retailers for their products and their service quality. Many other shopping robots, or bots, check hundreds of on-line merchants to report price information.

Along with this enhanced information, the Internet changes the structure of costs that shoppers face.[79] The costs of ordinary shopping at retail stores recalls the location model of product differentiation. To reach a store, the shopper incurs a transportation cost that varies by distance from the store and then pays a price for the

---

[73] Goolsbee (2000) shows how variations in retail prices due to taxes affect decisions to purchase on line. See also Goolsbee (2001a).

[74] See Goolsbee (2001b).

[75] See Linda Greenhouse, "Supreme Court Lifts Ban on Wine Shipping," *New York Times*, May 17, 2005, p. A1.

[76] See the 16-page Special Survey, "Crowned at Last: A Survey of Consumer Power," *The Economist*, April 2, 2005, after p. 48.

[77] See, for examples, Brown and Goolsbee (2002), Smith and Brynjolfsson (2001), and Morton, Zettelmeyer, and Silva-Risso (2001).

[78] For examples of Internet influence on sales methods at the retail level, see Bakos (2001).

[79] For description of this change in shopping costs and its effects, see Dinlersoz and Pereira (2005) and Mazon and Pereira (2002).

good purchased. To shop on the Internet, on the other hand, in addition to the cost of the good purchased, the shopper incurs a cost for access to the Internet, product search, and delivery, all of which are quite independent of distance from the Internet source. Some consumers may find the Internet more attractive than other consumers, because they all face different forms of cost and benefit depending on such factors as distance from the physical store and urgency of need. Brick-and-mortar stores may still want to serve both physical and Internet customers, either because the two channels reach separate groups of shoppers or because Internet and brick-and-mortar retailing can support each other in serving the same consumers.[80]

Seller Opportunities

While consumers have new search possibilities that improve their information about sellers, sellers on the Internet are able to obtain information about the consumers. The Internet also allows sellers to communicate product information to potential buyers at low cost. Interactive web pages can give effective sales presentations. Information about consumer choices, even at other retailers, is also available in new forms for Internet retailers, and it allows them to understand their shoppers' wishes better. Sellers can then focus efforts more productively by tailoring products and messages to more promising buyers.

Compared with a brick-and-mortar store, with its limited shelf space, the Internet retailer can carry a wider range of items. Although an Internet shopper cannot hold the product in her hands, a well-designed web site can provide abundant information about the product at low cost. Perhaps more revolutionary, on the Internet it is easier to customize the product to suit a shopper's preferences, as Dell Computer does in selling computers online. The Internet seller can differentiate its product also by designing a web page that consumers like. Better product information can lead to a more satisfying and less price sensitive choice for the consumer.[81] It can add to profit.

Another transaction that the Internet alters is that between one business and another.[82] These so-called business-to-business, or **B2B transactions**, include wholesale trade and company purchases of parts, components, and capital equipment. Almost as soon as it started, the dollar volume of commercial B2B e-commerce exceeded Internet retail sales to consumers. Savings from B2B e-commerce start by their elimination of most of the paper work in transactions, going straight to computer files instead, and saving errors as well as costs in the process. The Internet lowers the search costs of firms, as of consumers, but in the case of B2B transactions, there are instances where whole sets of intermediaries who once made markets are no longer necessary. A range of ownership forms exist for B2B market making, from

---

[80] Current tax policy calls for a seller (online, by mail-order catalog, or by telephone) to collect state sales tax if it has a physical presence (including a warehouse or a call center) in the state. This gives Amazon, with a presence in only Washington State and North Dakota, a tax advantage over stores like Barnes and Noble that have physical locations in many states. See Bob Tedeschi, "The Battle Over Online Sales Tax Turns Acrimonious," *New York Times*, February 17, 2003, p. C1.

[81] See Lynch and Ariely (1998) and Smith and Brynjolfsson (2001).

[82] For description of business-to-business e-commerce, see Lucking-Reiley and Spulber (2001).

industry sponsorship to private offering, and only a small number of markets survives for any industry. Thus, we expect e-commerce among businesses to lower the costs of using markets. Given the trade-off firms face, between keeping activities inside the firm or using the market, a lower cost of using markets could lead to smaller and more nimble firms and a wider range of B2B transactions.

Sellers are also able to learn about their competitors' products and their competitors' prices on the Internet. The sellers can then follow pricing policies automatically, and the pricing protocols they choose can definitely affect market outcomes.[83] Thus, we have new pricing and searching possibilities on the Internet that can reduce transaction costs and influence firm and industry organization.[84]

Property Rights

The Internet raises truly new property rights issues. Intellectual property has often been bound up in physical form, as books, records, videos, or DVDs for examples, which meant that control over production of these physical forms could largely control use. When digitalized music and videos can be delivered over the Internet, however, copyright holders can have greater difficulty controlling the use of their property. A prominent example is the MP3 and Napster controversy, in which Napster supported the sharing of music among listeners cheaply and on a large scale. As a result, fewer records or CDs might be sold, and then recording companies and original artists would receive less compensation for their work. In time, new institutional arrangements may solve these problems, as they did in the business of renting movie videos, where movie studios sued early firms until terms were settled for compensation.[85] The issues are many and complex, because Internet content takes many forms, such as movies, so the issues may not be resolved for some time.[86]

Legal scholars now debate whether private contracts, plus Internet markets, can guide transactions involving intellectual property better than legislation can.[87] The market may not lead to the best outcome. We face a different, and possibly more ambitious, task in Internet markets because the circumstances of transactions differ from what we are used to, and the rules can take new forms.

Market Forms

Markets take many forms, as when buyers set prices, or sellers set prices, or buyers and sellers bid and offer in double auctions. The Internet offers more scope for the use of auctions as a means of price discovery. Auctions normally have large numbers

---

[83] See, for example, Deck and Wilson (2000).

[84] See Merges (1997).

[85] Legal online music service is now available from about a dozen providers, including America Online. They call for monthly fees (about $10) and fees per song of about $1 to download, copy to a CD, or convert to a computer file format like MP3. Other services involve "tethered downloads," which are unlimited in number but prevent copying or sending music on to others. See Saul Hansell, "E-Music Sites Settle on Prices. It's a Start," *New York Times*, March 3, 2003, p. C1.

[86] See Matt Richtel, "Plaintiffs Sought Timeout After Turn in Napster Case," *New York Times*, January 31, 2002, pp. C5.

[87] See, for examples, Cohen (1998), O'Rourke (1995), and Merges (1997).

BOX 7.8 From Russia, Without Permission

In December 2006, several U.S. music recording companies sued the operator of AllofMP3. com, a Russian online music service, to prevent it from selling copyrighted music online without permission. The suit also asks that AllofMP3. com surrender its domain name, which essentially would close it down. The site offers some music that is not authorized for sale online, such as that of Led Zeppelin, yet at the same time it claims to comply with Russian copyright law. The lawsuit follows diplomatic efforts by U.S. trade representatives and some general promises by the Russian government, all thus far to no avail. The German and Danish governments have taken some steps to prevent AllofMP3. com from having access to their citizens, and the record companies seek a similar outcome in the United States.

See J. Leeds, "Music Labels' Lawsuit Seeks Shutdown of Russian Online Service," *New York Times,* December 22, 2006, p. C3.

---

of interested parties on each side of a market, as in many stock exchanges.[88] A prime example on the Internet is eBay, an auction house where people can buy and sell nearly all things, including fine art.[89] Onsale.com operates a market for consumer goods patterned after stock-exchange procedures. These possibilities require information of reasonably good quality, or guarantees, to avoid the "lemons" problem that can arise in any market when parties have different amounts of information, or there is asymmetric information.

The Internet even changes market forms. Special features of information products that can take digital form, including newspapers and magazines, allow them to change their form which in turn alters how they collect revenue.[90] This is another example of change in the structure of costs faced by consumers. New forms for collecting revenue are site licenses, common for software; per-use fees, which apply to music CDs; bundling, which can combine different items into one service (as a newspaper now combines stories together); and new forms of subscription to on-line versions of printed materials. Firms often can easily tailor these products to match consumers' preferences, with a consumer choosing her most preferred collection from a package of options.[91]

The Internet also presents brand new problems of market design. Law Professor Lawrence Lessig has argued that the powerful and innovative uses we see in the Internet may be greatly influenced by the rules chosen, and he emphasizes that software code contains those rules.[92] He finds that social norms from regular space, not cyberspace, have guided early Internet relations. These social norms developed in part

---

[88] Stock exchanges themselves will change with the Internet. See Barber and Odean (2001). New challengers to Nasdaq, the over-the-counter stock market, allow electronic trading and have eroded Nasdaq's volume. Nasdaq has responded with a new electronic trading system (called "SuperMontage"). See Stephen Labaton, "Nasdaq Wins Battle at S.E.C. on New System of Trading," *New York Times,* August 29, 2002, p. C1.

[89] See Alexandra Peers and Nick Wingfield, "Sotheby's, eBay Form Alliance to Sell Fine Art on the Internet," *Wall Street Journal,* January 31, 2002.

[90] See Bakos and Brynjolfsson (2000).

[91] For examples, see Bakos (2001).

[92] See Lessig (1999a, 1999b, 2001).

with the aid of law that sanctioned certain kinds of behavior and encouraged others. In cyberspace, to quote Lessig, "If a regulator wants to induce a certain behavior, she need not threaten, or cajole, to inspire the change. She need only change the code— the software that defines the terms upon which the individual gains access to the system, or uses assets on the system." These systems have a design, or architecture, built around the software code that can control operations and access. Lessig sees closed, or proprietary, architecture as easier to regulate from outside, largely because of the power that resides in code. Open, or nonproprietary, architecture has advantages of freedom but is harder to regulate. He suggests that neither extreme is ideal, and that we should give careful thought to these choices for shaping the Internet.

Law from regular space has been applied to Internet issues in the Microsoft antitrust case, discussed in Chapter 9. The case involves proprietary software in a network world.[93] In 1998, after many private complaints and earlier litigation, 19 states joined the Department of Justice in a suit that accused Microsoft of engaging in a pattern or practice of illegal behavior.[94] The government plaintiffs saw Microsoft as aiming to prevent widespread use of a competitor for its own Internet Explorer browser, the Netscape Navigator Internet browser. Microsoft wanted to advance the use of its own Internet Explorer browser because browser access to the Internet is so important for controlling other applications. The court found Microsoft guilty of antitrust law violations, but the penalties imposed on it were mild.

SUMMARY

The force of competition goes beyond setting price and output in static markets. Firms compete in the ways they organize, and in their research efforts to develop new products and processes that can change the world they (and we) inhabit. These forms of competition are growing, in market environments that are constantly changing, where adaptation is required to survive the innovations of others. New ideas play a key role in this form of competitive life, and some of the ideas can be protected in different ways as patents, trademarks, and trade secrets. Such protections, and the workings of markets and their structure, influence the rate and direction of technological change.

Information is valuable, especially when the information is new. In a world in which information is *not* costlessly available to everyone, the person who discovers new information *first* can gain. The discoverer may alter consumption plans, or he may speculate based on price changes anticipated as a result of the new information. He may sell the information directly, although that may be difficult when the buyer

---

[93] For treatment of antitrust applications in an Internet world, see Eisenach and Lenard (1999).

[94] Based on a 1962 Supreme Court decision, the pattern or practice of illegal behavior can be supported by internal documents that reveal such a pattern or practice within the firm, whether every one of its challenged acts was a violation or not. See *Continental Ore Co. v. Union Carbide and Carbon Corp.*, 370 U.S. 690 (1962).

cannot learn its value without seeing it. By any of these means, the discoverer may be able to share in gains available from the discovery, and that prospect may serve as incentive to spur individuals and organizations alike to make more new discoveries.

Property rights in new ideas may help to motivate their discovery by allowing owners of the ideas to appropriate part of the benefit they bring. Copyright, trademark, patent, and trade secret protection help to define intellectual property. Copyright protection applies to the forms that many ideas can take. Trademarks help sellers of branded products to have buyers identify their wares. And while they do not involve property, trade secrets can be protected from theft, and that protection can encourage their development.

The patent is a specific means of assuring that a discoverer receives a right to gains from the use of the discovery. For a limited period of time, the discoverer receives a monopoly patent right over the use of the invention, although the discover must divulge information about the invention to receive the patent. A monopolist who already enjoys exclusive control of a market has little need for a patent, because it can reliably appropriate the gain from a discovery through its market control. Without a patent, on the other hand, others might immediately copy a single competitor's invention. The patent helps the competitor to appropriate gains from the invention, and, thus, it adds incentive for a single competitive firm to undertake research.

Assuming that the potential gain from a cost-reducing invention can be appropriated by its inventor, perhaps through a patent system, the gain from discovering a new (cost-reducing) process tends to be greater for a single competitor than for a monopoly. Monopoly profits at the start make the monopolist's *incremental* gain from discovery less great. On the other hand, the monopoly wants to protect its already existing high profit. So if a third party makes a threatening discovery, the monopoly is willing to bid more than a competitive firm to purchase it. Once such a new discovery is made, a monopoly can value it more highly than a competitor because the monopoly controls the market for the discovery. The competitor, in contrast, has to contend with the former monopoly in a market with at least two firms. The profit of each of two firms is less than the profit of a monopoly in the same market.

Competitors may wish to move faster than monopolies to innovate, though we cannot be sure, in part because monopolies may be able to earn greater profits through their control of markets and thus have more resources available for research and development effort. The monopoly that waits for an optimal time to innovate, perhaps until its existing plant is worn out or until a competing product it also sells is in decline, may lose out to a competitor. A competitor simply seeks marginal gain, and with no existing plant to preserve and no product replacement effect to worry about, it may beat the monopoly to the innovation.

Without the benefit of excess profits, competitive firms have less *means* for undertaking inventive activity. Evidence indicates that very little research is carried out under conditions in which the firm size and amount of capital required are very small and top-four-firm concentration is below 10 percent. Evidence also suggests, however, that the largest firms do not carry out proportionately more research. The industry with medium-size capital requirements for entry and 50 to 55 percent top-four-firm concentration ratio seems to employ the most R&D personnel.

The Internet brings a revolutionary change in communications speed and cost, as well as disorder and even chaos from rapid change. Previous major innovations engendered the same atmosphere of change and uncertainty. A large innovation brings a time of bold entrepreneurial efforts, many smaller innovations, and a repainting of the market landscape. Effects on market form and on firm size and shape can be substantial, and we cannot yet predict what they will be. The development of the Internet illustrates well the process of dramatic technological change.

Social policy with respect to research still is difficult to settle. Social gains from invention are greater than private gains, suggesting that the resources devoted to research are less than ideal. At the same time, however, some of the devices used to serve as incentives, such as patents, bring high prices and are abused. Even if monopolies *did* carry out more research, it would not be possible on that account alone to favor more monopolistic organization of industry generally. Technological change and invention, including effects such as better health and education, have accounted for more growth in our output than any other factor. Yet we are not sure exactly how best to induce more of it in the future. Antitrust policy has been concerned with innovation as well as market structure and strategy, as we shall see in Chapter 9. We first turn to consider antitrust law and its origins in Chapter 8.

QUESTIONS

1. Explain why, in contrast to the "ideal" perfectly competitive model with full and perfect information, imperfect information actually can induce *more* research.
2. "An individual may want to carry out research either because the risk involved is attractive or because the risk in the situation is unattractive." Comment on this statement, noting conditions that might tend to make research activity add to or subtract from the risk of a firm.
3. Construct a figure like Figure 7.1, but in which the cost reduction is so great that the monopoly price after the technological change is lower than the average cost before the change. Show for this situation whether the gain to a competitive firm from the innovation still exceeds the gain to a monopolist.
4. Suppose monopolistic industries actually carried out more research per dollar of sales than competitive ones. Make a convincing argument for or against relaxation of antitrust law enforcement in that case to foster monopolies and, thus, more research.
5. In June, 2006, Merck & Co., Inc.'s patent on Zocor, a cholesterol-lowering drug, expired. Zocor has been an alternative to another cholesterol-lowering drug, Lipitor, which is the largest selling drug worldwide with sales of $12 billion a year. Lipitor is made by Pfizer, Inc., the world's largest drug company, whose patent does not expire until 2011. Generic producers of Zocor will reduce the price of their equivalent medicine by at least 30 percent and possibly by considerably more. This will hurt the profit of the Merck company, which has been

selling $4.4 billion worth of Zocor a year worldwide. Explain whether the expiration of the Zocor patent will also affect the Pfizer company.

6. Consider an unregulated monopoly producing and selling a product with demand

$$P = 100 - Q,$$

where P is price, and Q is quantity sold. Total cost is $TC = 500 + 40Q$, where 500 is fixed cost, which is also *sunk*, and 40 is marginal cost.

a. Find the monopoly price and output, monopoly profit, and consumer surplus.
b. Suppose a new process can make the product with $TC = 1000 + 20Q$ (1000 is fixed and sunk, and 20 is marginal cost). Would the monopolist have strong profit incentive to introduce the new process? Why or why not?
c. Would a competitive firm that discovered the new process have stronger profit incentive to introduce it? Would consumer surplus be greater if the new process were introduced? Why or why not?

7. Can classifying a new product innovation as a trade secret serve to protect it as well as a patent could?

8. As generic drugs were introduced under the Drug Price Competition and Patent Term Restoration Act, the price of the related branded drug fell. On average, the price reduction, from the level of the branded drug when it was the only drug being sold, depends on how many generic drugs have been introduced. The following table shows the pattern (from *FDA Analysis of Retail Sales Data from IMS Health*, IMS National Sales Perspective, 2005, based on data from 1999 to 2004):

Number of Generic Producers	Fall in Price from Branded Drug Price Level
1	6 percent
2	48 percent
3	56 percent
4	61 percent
5	67 percent

When five generic drugs were being sold on average the price level had fallen 67 percent, or two-thirds, from the price level of the branded drug, but when only one generic drug is being sold the price falls only 6 percent. Explain this pattern of price reductions based on your knowledge of the Drug Price Competition and Patent Term Restoration Act and how it functions.

9. Evaluate how the possibility of taking out an insurance policy against innovation or new discoveries might harm your current position. The insurance would be intended to protect the value of your current business holdings and positions. Would such insurance be socially desirable?

8

The Origin and Development of Antitrust Law

After the American Civil War, firms in many industries in the United States combined into units called "trusts," named after their voting trusts that collected together the shares of many firms in the same industries. A trust allowed the firms in a single industry to coordinate their actions for their mutual benefit. Great concern developed over their growing power, which could not be controlled through common law because their actions were not unambiguous offenses. In 1890, with little economic knowledge to draw on, Congress passed the Sherman Act to restrain the power of trusts, and this Act introduced *antitrust law* in the United States.

The Sherman Act did not immediately stop businesses from forming trusts. The law stated an objective but did not say how to reach it, and it was slow to have any effect. Indeed, Congress passed the Clayton and Federal Trade Commission Acts in 1914 because the Sherman Act alone was thought inadequate to achieve its purpose. The new statutes did not change the direction of antitrust law, however, and antitrust law today has its origins in late nineteenth-century America. We can better understand current antitrust laws if we view them in light of the attitudes and circumstances of the time that prompted their enactment. The logic of the law today, however, depends on how cases have been decided under it. Antitrust policy is also affected by two recent trends: rapid technological change and growing globalization. Both strengthen the role of competition in regulating markets.

Antitrust law is complex. We can see it as restraining monopoly and monopolistic practices, controlling mergers to influence market structures, and preventing restraints of trade and unfair and deceptive practices, all to support a competitive market economy. Defining monopoly took years, and a precise definition is still unavailable. Merger control also developed slowly over the twentieth century and now follows guidelines that inform firms about allowable mergers. Unfair and deceptive practices go back to early efforts by sellers to substitute low-quality products for better ones, and antitrust authorities try to curtail their use to keep trade relations as fair and transparent as possible.

We know the undesirable effects of monopoly and restraints of trade, and we also know how they can appeal to profit-seeking firms. Here we see the steps taken to combat them. This chapter first sketches in Section 8.1 early vestiges of antitrust policy in England, which helped to inspire U.S. law although it did not provide very exact guidance. A brief portrait of America a century ago, when antitrust policy began, helps to explain the form that antitrust policy took. Separate sections describe antitrust legislation—Section 8.2 on the Sherman Act, and Section 8.3 on the Clayton Act and the Federal Trade Commission Act—and then Section 8.4 discusses antitrust enforcement agencies, specifically federal and state enforcement agencies, plus available remedies for violations of the law. Section 8.5 traces early decisions of courts that helped to identify monopoly. Section 8.6 then examines merger policy, which has developed as a way to influence market structure, and Section 8.7 discusses unfair and deceptive practices.

8.1   THE BEGINNINGS OF ANTITRUST POLICY

Framers of the Sherman Act claimed they were merely codifying common law, largely from England, upon which early antitrust cases had drawn. But the common law of late medieval England that United States courts considered covered so many offenses in commerce, changed so often, and was so inconsistent that it did not provide a very clear basis for modern antitrust policy.[1] *Monopoly* was not a word in the vocabulary until the sixteenth century, and guilds, which were professional trade and even social organizations dating back to Roman times, had rights to hold markets that were granted as royal franchises. Conduct was banned more often for being a threat against established economic power than an abuse of it. So the circumstances of early common law offenses were very different from those of the antitrust era in the United States. A brief description of that time shows how antitrust legislation came to be passed.

British Origins

Antimonopoly actions closer to modern antitrust efforts began at the end of the sixteenth century in England, when the great power of guilds—and also of the Crown—was slipping, while Parliament and the common law were becoming more important. A famous example is the Case of Monopolies[2] in 1603 in which an importer of playing cards was sued because Queen Elizabeth had granted her groom the sole right to import playing cards into England. The Court of Queen's Bench voided this grant of a playing-card monopoly, saying it was counter to common law. Grants of monopoly were increasingly viewed as harming potential competitors and harming the public through higher prices and poorer quality. The idea of monopoly was not being

---

[1] A description of common law background is available in Thorelli (1955). See also the historical development in Bork (1966), Heilbroner (1962), Letwin (1965), and Moore (1966). The usefully brief treatment by Gelhorn and Kovacic (1994) also sketches historical origins.

[2] *Darcy v. Allein*, 11 Coke 84, 77 Eng. Rep. 1260 (K.B. 1603). Darcy was Queen Elizabeth's groom, and Allein was a haberdasher who imported playing cards.

rejected, however. Indeed, some years after the playing card monopoly was taken from Darcy the groom, Parliament awarded a monopoly over playing cards to another party. It was the acts of some monopolists, rather than their holding monopoly positions, that common law rejected.

In 1623 Parliament went further and, to void monopolies, passed the **Statute of Monopolies**, which framers of the Sherman Act studied carefully. The Statute of Monopolies cannot be seen as a sharp turning point in antimonopoly history, however, for its effective use against monopolies came many years later. For one thing, it preserved as exceptions Parliamentary grants of monopoly, patents, and the monopolies held by towns or guilds to control trading. So monopoly organization still governed a very large share of economic activity. Furthermore, England was moving toward a political revolution in which the members of Parliament would oppose the king. The Statute of Monopolies (along with other statutes) could not be uniformly effective while the legitimacy of Parliament was in doubt.[3]

The eighteenth and nineteenth centuries brought economic change on a scale never before experienced, a transition to modern life appropriately called the **industrial revolution**. In England during this period legislative statutes came to supersede much of the common law precedent. There was the Statute of Monopolies to use against monopolies, where the common law had grown particularly weak, the Trade Union Acts to supersede common law against combinations of workers, and an abolition of common law against forestalling, an offense essentially against new middlemen that favored existing firms. Common law was relevant only for restraint of trade, and there it was not applied consistently. Although English common law was relied upon to some extent in America in the late 1800s, it did not provide a firm foundation for the Sherman Act.

America in 1890

We can hardly imagine life at the time Congress passed the Sherman Act. There were some electric lights in 1890 but no neon signs or television. Indeed, the first radio signal was not sent by Marconi until 1895. That was also the year celluloid film was first employed as a vehicle for moving pictures, but successful combination with recorded voice into "talking pictures" was decades away. None of today's miracle medicines existed, despite the zany claims made for patent medicines, produced largely from alcohol, that were peddled at the time. Although railroads were sweeping westward, most transportation was by water or by horse. The horse imparted an odor to urban life that would be unacceptable today. Cities were growing but did not yet have skyscrapers, for architecture was only beginning to follow the forms that steel and glass later would allow. The nation was agrarian, individualistic, even entrepreneurial, without the European feudal tradition and without the entrenched and symbolically reinforced economic and political power of European nation states. It is not surprising, then, that we were drawn into something of an economic free-for-all.

---

[3] For a description of this period see Hill (1961).

The end of the Civil War in America had ushered in a period of truly dramatic economic growth.[4] From the Civil War to 1900, 14 million immigrants swelled the American work force and more land was settled than in the roughly four centuries since the continent had been discovered. Railroads laced western settlements together in economic activity with the East. A national banking system was established that helped firms raise capital and grow to serve emerging national markets. It was in this period that the corporation, as a form of business organization, began to spread from canals and railroads, where innovation in large-scale business organization began, to industry and commerce generally.

Along with its benefits, the rapid economic development of the late 1800s brought oppression to the underprivileged and scandal among the privileged. City dwellers, including many children, worked long hours in dirty, poorly lit, and unsafe places, and that working life was combined with slum conditions at home. Labor and local businesses both fell under the power of corporations in trusts and business firm combinations that grew steadily more powerful, often by forcing competitors to sell out under the threat of ruin. City officials who gave out valuable lighting, water, street railway, and other contracts were bribed routinely. Western farmers felt they were suffering from the steadily falling general price level and the growing power of railroads as well as combinations of firms in other industries. Stock prices were manipulated in merger schemes as trusts and combinations proliferated. Trust stood for monopoly, and this is the period that gave monopoly its bad name.

How to remedy this trust problem was not at all obvious, particularly to Congressmen who sympathized with private business and to a public that believed in private enterprise. Many states had adopted antimonopoly constitutional provisions or statutes, but, with few exceptions, they did not enforce them. State attorneys general lacked resources, and even where they had them they were naturally reluctant to drive large employers from their states. Courts also limited the actions that could be taken against corporations by treating corporations as if they were persons, thereby extending to them due-process legal protections. So the formation of trusts and business combinations continued.

After the Civil War, a remarkable battle for control of railroads illustrated excesses of the trust movement.[5] These early railroad leaders played a sophisticated version of the present day Monopoly board game, and although they were charged frequently with illegal acts, they seldom went to jail. In 1887 Congress created the **Interstate Commerce Commission (ICC)** to regulate railroads. The ICC was the first of our **federal administrative agencies**. These administrative agencies are part legislative, part executive, and part judicial. They are able to develop specialized expertise in the areas they regulate, and they play important roles in many areas of market regulation. Whether the railroads actually favored the creation of the ICC—so competition could be better controlled—is still debated, because all of them did not resist.[6] Meanwhile, not far behind the railroads in ruthlessness were efforts of small groups

---

[4] See Davis (1917), Heilbroner (1977), Morison, Commager, and Leuchtenburg (1969), or Robertson (1955).

[5] For detailed description of this and other exploits of the period, see Josephson (1934).

[6] For pro and con arguments about the railroad's embrace of regulation, see Kolko (1965) and Martin (1974).

of individuals to control meat, oil, tobacco, steel, sugar, lead, whiskey, gun powder, and other industries. Despite public unrest, no clamor for antitrust legislation arose because it was not obvious that legislation could solve the problem.

8.2 | THE SHERMAN ACT

The initiative for a new federal law to deal with trusts came from President Harrison, who won election in 1888 by claiming the Republicans would find ways to compel competition while at the same time raising protective tariffs. Although Congress introduced a number of antimonopoly bills at Harrison's urging, the President's intent for this legislation seems to have been partly cosmetic, to make his tariff increases more acceptable to the public. At the time, there was no federal income tax, and tariff proceeds were the nation's most important source of revenue. The McKinley Tariff of 1890, which President Harrison favored, expanded coverage and raised tariff rates so they averaged 50 percent of the value of goods traded.

Why Congress passed the Sherman Act is not easy to summarize, especially given the conflicting intentions of those supporting it.[7] A problem of monopoly power was evident, but the knowledge to understand and deal with it was not at hand. The law's namesake, John Sherman, was an aging and respected senator from Ohio who had almost become the Republican Party's candidate instead of Harrison for the 1888 election. Whether an antitrust law would be constitutional and whether it could be enforced were much debated questions, along with details such as what words to use to express violations of the law and how to penalize them. In the end a bill that had been entirely rewritten by the Judiciary Committee was readily adopted and named for Senator Sherman.

Many of the Congressmen most active in writing the Sherman Act[8] claimed it to be an affirmation of an old common law doctrine, and they made an attempt to express the Act in language from common law. The drafters even sketched the interpretation they placed on the common law,[9] but no very exact meaning was then in use for the words adopted, such as "conspiracy," "restraint of trade," or "monopolize." Moreover, Congress neither provided potent remedies for violations of the Act—except for allowing treble damage claims[10]—nor voted any new funds for the already overworked Department of Justice to see to its enforcement. We might suspect that the large firms that were to be subject to this new act had influenced it, at least in adding to its vagueness and lack of remedies. Legislators appear to have passed a difficult problem along to the courts while hoping at the same time to satisfy the voters'

---

[7] For analysis of the passage of the Act, see Bork (1966), Elzinga and Breit (1976), Letwin (1965), and Thorelli (1955). A time line for major antitrust legislation is provided in Appendix 8.2.

[8] In addition to Senator Sherman were Senators Edmunds of Vermont, Hoar of Massachusetts, and George of Mississippi, who were by no means alike in their proposals.

[9] See Bork (1966).

[10] A successful plaintiff could win compensation equal to three times the damage suffered from a defendant's illegal acts.

desire for action, because the Sherman Act was worded in very broad terms, almost like constitutional provisions, prohibiting restraint of trade and monopolization.

Section 1 of the Act, as amended,[11] makes **restraint of trade** a crime by providing that

> [e]very contract, combination in the form of trust or otherwise, or conspiracy, in restraint of trade or commerce among the several States, or with foreign nations, is declared to be illegal.

To prove a contract, combination, or conspiracy, courts must find some definite agreement among at least two parties that affects interstate commerce, and that agreement must restrain trade unreasonably.

Section 2 of the Act, as amended,[12] made **monopolizing** or **attempting to monopolize** illegal by declaring that

> [e]very person who shall monopolize, or attempt to monopolize, or combine or conspire with any other person or persons, to monopolize any part of the trade or commerce among the several States, or with foreign nations, shall be deemed guilty of a felony.

No precise definition of monopoly exists in the Act. Section 2 can be seen as prohibiting any private party from having power to control price in a particular market, or to prevent entry into it, as long as that power was sought or obtained by methods that show an intent to exercise it. In these two sections, the Sherman Act declared a national policy, but it left to the courts the task of determining the meaning of its prohibitions in specific applications.

These Sherman Act provisions went beyond simple codification of existing common law. For one thing, the Act provided for private parties to bring civil suits against one another by granting to a successful plaintiff three times the extent of damages suffered. The Hart-Scott-Rodino Antitrust Improvements Act of 1976[13] expanded this incentive to prosecute because it allowed state attorneys general to sue on behalf of residents and, if successful, to collect treble damages for the state. The Sherman Act also made some violations crimes, thereby enlisting the government's obligation to enforce the Act for society. This and subsequent legislation led to the creation of federal government agencies to pursue antitrust policy.

Early Enforcement

President Harrison instituted only seven suits under the Sherman Act, President Cleveland (in his second administration) instituted eight, and President McKinley three. These suits seemed utterly ineffective in slowing the trend to corporate consolidation and monopoly. In 1895, in the first Sherman Act case to reach the Supreme

---

[11] Sherman Act, 15 U.S.C. Sec. 1 (Supp. V 1975).

[12] Sherman Act, 15 U.S.C. Sec. 2 (Supp. V 1975).

[13] See the Hart-Scott-Rodino Antitrust Improvements Act of 1976, 15 U.S.C.A. Sec. 15c (1977).

Court, the Court failed to prevent the formation of the E. C. Knight sugar trust.[14] Most of the successful cases prosecuted during President Cleveland's administration were against labor unions. More business combinations were formed in the McKinley administration than ever before. Yet Congress did not amend the Sherman Act.

There are many reasons for the Act's initial ineffectiveness against trusts. It is not easy to absorb a new statute and see exactly what cases should be brought under it. Moreover, the Department of Justice could not have moved at once on all potential Sherman Act fronts even if funds had been available or if the influential first attorney general under President Cleveland, Richard Olney, had been sympathetic to the Act (which he was not). Other important problems distracted politicians in these last years of the nineteenth century, including war with Spain. Many urged that a new navy be inaugurated. Pensions for war veterans were needed. Tariff policy was continually debated, for while high tariffs brought government revenue (remember, there was no income tax) and benefitted big business by reducing foreign competition, the public objected to them because they raised the prices of goods. There was no sound system of taxation. The western states demanded the coinage of silver, while issuing currency without backing in any rare metal was also debated. In addition to outrageous business scandals, an enormous spoils system corrupted the national government. With all of these serious problems, the economy faltered, and the last years of the nineteenth century were economically depressed.

Just as Congress passed the Sherman Act to stop combinations and trusts, a separate development at the state level supported them. Responding partly to a financial crisis, the state of New Jersey enacted an incorporation law that abandoned most of the restraints on corporate behavior. New Jersey also repealed its antitrust law. In effect, the state set out to make money by granting lenient corporate charters, and it was so successful in attracting corporation filing fees and franchise taxes that in 10 years it paid off its debt.[15] New Jersey first allowed one corporation to own another, making the holding company legal, and it later granted unlimited life and size to corporations and the use of financial instruments and devices that facilitated mergers. Because a firm incorporated in one state could operate in others, combinations essentially like trusts that operated anywhere could become legal by incorporating in New Jersey. Many of the goals of a trust were now illegal because of the Sherman Act, but a trust's mere existence in corporate form no longer violated state incorporation statutes. Rather than suffer charges of conspiracy under the Sherman Act, it was safer for firms to merge.[16]

Antitrust action under the Sherman Act was to come, but its foundation remained dormant while federal prosecutors around the nation began to initiate investigations that would lead to prosecutions. Soon the Act would radically alter the administration of law in matters concerning competition. Divergent state rules were

---

[14] The E. C. Knight trust was allowed to continue to exist on the grounds that it was a manufacturer not in interstate commerce, even though it controlled more than 95 percent of the nation's sugar market. See *United States v. E. C. Knight Co.*, 156 U.S. 1 (1895).

[15] Other states followed New Jersey. Today, the state where the most corporations are chartered is Delaware.

[16] For the argument that antitrust law actually spurred mergers, see Bittlingmayer (1985).

now supported by a uniform federal law. More importantly, restraining trade and monopolizing were branded as crimes under the act, punishable as violations of the rules needed to maintain society and, thus, warranting government enforcement. Private parties, either as individuals or as corporations, and—in 1976—state governments as well, were given incentive to enforce the law because they could sue to recover three times the damages they suffered.

Before the end of the nineteenth century, as cases made their way on appeal to the Supreme Court, the Sherman Act began to take effect. In 1892 the federal government sued the Trans-Missouri Freight Association, made up of 15 railroads that controlled rail traffic west of the Mississippi, seeking its dissolution. The government sued on the ground that, as a combination fixing rates and setting uniform rules, the Association restrained trade and thus violated Section 1 of the Sherman Act.[17] The association agreed that it had formed for mutual protection by maintaining reasonable rates, rules, and regulations. It also claimed these activities were acceptable under common law and that Section 1 prohibited only those restraints that had been held unlawful under common law. In 1897 the Supreme Court found the association unlawful because Section 1 condemned *every* restraint of trade.

The ways in which restraints of trade had been handled under common law were considered carefully in the *Addyston Pipe and Steel* case, a price-fixing case decided in favor of the government by the Circuit Court of Appeals in 1898.[18] Defendants in the case were manufacturers and sellers of cast iron pipe who accounted for 65 percent of production capacity over roughly three-fourths of the United States. Conceding that a committee of them fixed their price, they argued that, because they did not control the whole market, their final price was reasonable. In an immensely important decision for shifting attention to market power (rather than market conduct, or behavior, alone), the court held that the agreement would be invalid under common law because it gave the parties *power* to charge unreasonable prices. Whether they charged unreasonable prices or not, the combination was condemned for its power. Not long after the decision in this case, the defendant firms merged, thus showing that merging was safer than price fixing.[19]

These two decisions at the close of the nineteenth century fell like bombshells on the business community. The Sherman Act had teeth after all, at least in the area of price-fixing. Businessmen were dismayed; they resented this intrusion into their affairs and feared an even more general breach of the private enterprise faith. Businessmen did not resist all change, for at the time one new innovation after another appeared, with chemicals leading the way and industrial research laboratories already making their appearance.[20] Businessmen, however, resisted the idea that the government could restrain their accumulation of economic power.

In 1901, in his first message to Congress, President Theodore Roosevelt urged 25 reforms, including regulation of trusts, railroads, and banks. He was responding to

---

[17] *United States v. Trans-Missouri Freight Assn.*, 166 U.S. 290 (1897).

[18] *United States v. Addyston Pipe and Steel Co.*, 175 U.S. 211 (1899).

[19] See Bittlingmayer (1982).

[20] See Jewkes, et al. (1969).

a growing public concern. Under increasingly lenient state incorporation laws, trusts continued to be formed at a rapid rate, largely through the efforts of certain large insurance companies and great banking houses, such as J. P. Morgan and Company, in New York City. They worked to form trusts and combinations because the manipulation of share values allowed their promoters to gain handsomely.

President Roosevelt turned his great energy to the antitrust problem. He quickly formed the Department of Commerce and recommended that it study corporations. The resulting examination of the conduct of interstate corporations furnished material for important antitrust cases in oil, steel, tobacco, and other industries. For the first time, government deliberately set aside resources for antitrust enforcement. In 1902, Attorney General Philander C. Knox proceeded against a giant railway consolidation that would have brought many of the great railroads together in what is known as the *Northern Securities* case.[21] In 1904, by a five to four vote, the Supreme Court enjoined the holding company in the Northern Securities Company case from exercising control over competing railroads and did not allow the railroads to pay dividends to the holding company. That decision came as another big shock to Wall Street.[22]

Essential Facilities

If one firm owns a facility that all competitors need to provide a service, then without forming a trust the owner might control the industry by controlling its essential facility. An **essential facility** is a resource owned by one company that is essential to the provision of a service. In 1912 the Supreme Court required the Terminal Railroad Association, an organization of railroads that jointly owned a railroad bridge and other facilities in St. Louis, to allow other railroads to use its facilities.[23] On the same principle, local telephone companies today must allow long distance companies to complete their calls through their local exchange telephone networks, and owners of high-voltage transmission lines must also grant access to generators of electricity to transmit power.

A court that requires a monopoly owner to allow others access to its essential facility has probably presumed that the monopoly would otherwise behave in an anticompetitive way.[24] It has been argued that existing antitrust law could effectively counter such anticompetitive behavior, so there is no need for special "essential facilities" consideration.[25] Yet whenever monopoly control exists over a facility needed by all suppliers of a good or service, it is readily claimed that other suppliers should have access to the facility, so that they can compete. The *Terminal Railroad Association* case,

---

[21] *Northern Securities Co. v. United States*, 193 U.S. 197 (1904).

[22] Banker J. P. Morgan and businessman Mark Hanna attempted personally to intercede with the president, but the decision stood.

[23] See *United States v. Terminal Railroad Association of St. Louis*, 224 U.S. 383 (1912) and 236 U.S. 194 (1915).

[24] See Gerber (1988).

[25] See Ratner (1988).

then, opened up a broad range of possible arguments for granting competitors access to essential facilities.[26]

There is little question that the Terminal Railroad Association sought, and successfully achieved, monopoly control over all facilities needed to handle freight or passenger railroad traffic in the transcontinental rail center of St. Louis. A possible remedy would have been divestiture of facilities, so that no one party could control them; however, the Court found efficiency advantages under a single owner, the Terminal Railroad Association, so it ordered the Association to allow other railroads to join the Association. If they did not join, they were to be offered terms for using the facilities that would "place every such company upon as nearly an equal plane as may be with respect to expenses and charges as that occupied by the proprietary companies."[27] Thus, if a railroad did not join the Association, it was still to have access to its facilities at charges as close as possible to those of Association members. So in addition to opening an essential facility for use by others, this decision articulated a basis for the terms to be required for access. Access forces some degree of competition in the final good or service when competitors can use the essential facility.

The Rule of Reason

The antitrust movement really began to bloom in 1911 when the Supreme Court held that the Standard Oil Company was an illegal monopoly under Section 2 of the Sherman Act.[28] The firm had come to dominate domestic oil production and distribution, and it left behind a trail of mergers and consolidations often coerced by its economic power. Indeed, its vicious and oppressive tactics against numerous competitors revealed unmistakably that its goal was monopoly. For example, it would cut price in the area of a small oil company and then offer to buy it out to end its misery. It ran afoul of the Sherman Act at almost every turn, and the record of its actions remains today an excellent example of ruthlessly monopolistic behavior.[29] Chief Justice White, in stating the Court's opinion, clearly expressed the illegality of the actions, and he went further. Instead of resting on the clear basis of "every" restraint being illegal, the Court set out a "reasonableness" test called the **rule of reason**.

This rule of reason came to mean that being a monopoly, or even attempting to be a monopoly, need not violate the Sherman Act. To act illegally, a firm also had to behave unreasonably. The rule of reason called for evaluation of the consequences of a firm's behavior in the circumstances of each case. Reasonable action was all right; unreasonable action was illegal. The rule of reason suggested that courts would analyze behavior and its implications for market performance rather than rely on clear and simple rules. Clear, or "bright-line," rules would brand certain actions as illegal, and evidence of participating in them would make a firm guilty "per se."[30] Standard

---

[26] For a broad review of the essential facilities principle, see Lipsky and Sidak (1999).

[27] 224 U.S. at 411.

[28] *Standard Oil Co. of New Jersey v. United States*, 221 U.S. 1 (1911).

[29] For an accounts of the behavior, see Seager and Gulick (1929) and Destler (1967).

[30] For analysis of advantages and disadvantages of per se rules, see Wood (1993).

Oil had behaved unreasonably, and in the Court's opinion it was this unreasonable behavior that led to its conviction. The decision thus indicated not only that a firm needed monopoly power to violate the Sherman Act but it also had to wield the power in an unreasonable way. This focus on reasonableness departed from earlier decisions and from the letter of the law, and it complicated application of the Sherman Act for decades. But there was a long-term benefit from the principle. Examining the consequences of actions in each case under the rule of reason, rather than adhering to per se rules, allowed courts to introduce new economic knowledge to improve the effectiveness of antitrust law.

Chief Justice White had earlier favored this reasonableness requirement (he had dissented in the 1897 *Trans-Missouri Freight Association* case and in similar cases). A basis for his position could be found in the common law, where precedents actually had made illegal only the restraints of trade that were deemed unreasonable, and only the monopolies that were contrary to the public interest. Of course the Sherman Act had no such qualification. Indeed, it explicitly opposed *every* restraint of trade and *every* monopoly. By introducing the rule of reason and looking to market conduct rather than to the possession of market power alone, the Court seemed to be in conflict with the intentions of Congress.

8.3 THE CLAYTON AND FEDERAL TRADE COMMISSION ACTS

Many congressmen disliked the rule of reason because it swerved away from the stated Sherman Act goal of opposing every monopoly and restraint of trade, whether reasonable or not. This view, together with the reforming efforts of President Woodrow Wilson, led in 1914 to the enactment of the *Clayton Act* and the *Federal Trade Commission Act*.[31] We can regard the Clayton Act as an effort to define unreasonable behavior more specifically to make it easier to prove, thereby harnessing the rule of reason to good effect. Even as it was passed, however, many regarded the Clayton Act to be a weak law, because it was a compromise between those who sought detailed specification of offenses and those who preferred generality.

The Clayton Act

The **Clayton Act** is more specific than the Sherman Act in making particular business practices unlawful. Business practices can be opposed not for causing monopoly with certainty, but rather where the effect of these business practices could "substantially lessen competition or tend to create a monopoly in any line of commerce." Section 2 of the Clayton Act, which was amended by the Robinson-Patman Act in 1936 and

[31] For description of the reform period, see Hofstadter (1955).

is now identical with that Act's first section, prohibits discrimination in price,[32] which occurs whenever different prices are charged to different customers for the same good (or, conceivably, where the same price is charged for different goods). Under Section 2 of the Clayton Act, it is unlawful to discriminate in price among those who purchase goods of like grade and quality in interstate or foreign commerce where the effect

> may be substantially to lessen competition or tend to create a monopoly in any line of commerce, or to injure, destroy, or prevent competition with any person who knowingly receives the benefit of such discrimination, or with customers of either of them.

Other provisions of Section 2 allow some scope for different prices to different customers if they can be justified by cost differences, or if the lower price is undertaken in good faith to meet the equally low price of a competitor. Further subsections of the Act control brokerage payments that may be part of the price and the use of promotional services or facilities. Such activities constitute alternative effective prices or costs that allow buyers and sellers to achieve the main aims of price discrimination without appearing to use it. Although Section 2 can prevent some very unfair pricing practices, it has been most troublesome in application. Largely because of its great concern for injury to competitors, which can follow from genuine competition without really harming the process of competition itself, its sanctions have sometimes inhibited genuine competitive behavior.

Section 3 of the Clayton Act prohibits anticompetitive exclusive-dealing arrangements, total-requirement obligations, and tying, whether in sale or lease arrangements.[33] Exclusive dealing commits a purchaser to buy from a single supplier and no others; a **total-requirements contract** has the same effect of obliging a buyer to use the same source of supply over the period of a contract, whatever the buyer's needs may be. With **tying** contracts, one or more goods are made available for sale only on the condition that another good or goods also be purchased. As noted in Chapter 6, tying can deny competitors access to potential customers so it can make entry difficult. It can also enable a firm to discriminate by the way it prices its tied supply item. As with other parts of the Act, these practices are unlawful only where their probable effect "may be substantially to lessen competition or to tend to create a monopoly."

Another important part of the Clayton Act is Section 7, which deals with **corporate acquisitions and mergers**, the joining of two or more firms into one. It was amended importantly in 1950 by the Celler-Kefauver Act to define mergers more fully and to include mergers effected through the sale of assets and not just through the sale of stock shares alone. Under this law, one corporation cannot acquire another "where in any line of commerce in any section of the country, the effect of such acquisition may be substantially to lessen competition, or to tend to create a monopoly."[34]

---

[32] Robinson-Patman Act, 15 U.S.C. Sec. 13 (1970).

[33] Clayton Act Sec. 3, 15 U.S.C. Sec. 14 (1970).

[34] Clayton Act Sec. 7, 15 U.S.C. Sec. 18 (1970).

Since the tightening of this proscription in 1950, many mergers among competing firms of significant size in the same industry—called horizontal mergers—have been prevented.

The Clayton Act contained other provisions as well. It outlawed **interlocking directorates**, which are the same directors controlling several firms in the same industry, when the firms are beyond certain sizes. It contained provisions that made officers of corporations personally responsible for violations of the law, but courts rejected this view and the government could not win early cases under these provisions. The Act also clarified a matter that had confused early Sherman Act cases: it exempted labor unions from the antitrust laws.

The Federal Trade Commission Act

Also intended to improve competition in markets and Sherman Act effectiveness, the **Federal Trade Commission Act** was passed in 1914 and amended in 1938, 1973, and 1975. It set up a nonpartisan **Federal Trade Commission (FTC)** of five members appointed for seven-year terms by the President to interpret and enforce its provisions, subject to review by courts. The Act made unlawful unfair methods of competition and unfair acts and practices. Further, it authorized their investigation by the Commission, which can issue "cease and desist" orders against a corporation or, if that fails, can take the corporation to court. The amended Act now makes a sweeping declaration that "[U]nfair methods of competition in or affecting commerce, and unfair and deceptive acts or practices in or affecting commerce, are declared unlawful."[35]

Because it does not deal so directly with problems of monopoly, this Act may not appear to be an antitrust law. It is concerned with the functioning of competitive markets, however, and it is clearly aimed at regulating competition. Since it was amended in 1938 by the **Wheeler-Lea Act**[36] to stress "deceptive acts or practices," the FTC Act generally has been concerned with problems of imperfect information such as deceptive advertising rather than of monopoly. Nevertheless, any violation of the Sherman Act also violates the FTC Act and can lead to FTC action. Efforts by the FTC in enforcing fair competition have been related to the Clayton and Sherman Acts.

The FTC is an administrative agency like the Interstate Commerce Commission, intended to bring technical expertise to bear on social problems. But in its early days it seemed to be formulating codes and trade practices as if it were in league with businessmen. The FTC Act brought no quick revision in business practices, and America entered the depression decade of the 1930s with most of the sales in many industries concentrated in a few powerful corporations—almost as if only slight effort had been made to control them.

---

[35] Federal Trade Commission Act, 15 U.S.C. Sec. 45 (Supp. V 1975).
[36] Wheeler-Lea Act, 15 U.S.C. Sec. 45 (1970).

BOX 8.1 Advertising and the Federal Trade Commission

The FTC has vigorously pursued misleading advertising, especially since the 1970s. This may be partly because of new additions to its resources that came in the 1970s; from 1970 to 1977 the FTC budget tripled. Early actions by the FTC in that period focused on small points and grappled with the difficult question of when advertising can mislead. For example, the FTC successfully opposed a television ad that depicted a razor shaving sandpaper, when the sandpaper was not real. In time, rules have developed that guide advertisers in what they can do without seriously misleading. Through its ad substantiation program, the FTC requires that advertisers have evidence to support their claims. It has also developed a materiality standard to judge whether information would have a material effect on a consumer's decision.

See *F.T.C. v. Colgate-Palmolive Co.*, 380 U.S. 374, 85 S.Ct. 1035, 13 L.Ed.2nd 904 (1965).

A Quiet Period for Antitrust

Little new antitrust action took place from the passage of the Clayton and FTC Acts until the middle of the twentieth century. Soon after passage of new antitrust legislation in 1914, the nation was engulfed in World War I, and financial and industrial segments of the private economy were engaged to support it. The War Industries Board, which Congress gave sweeping powers to mobilize the nation's resources for war, fostered centralization. All trust-busting efforts ceased.

At war's end the main concern of government and business alike was to return the economy to private ownership and operation, an aim pushed consistently by Republicans Warren Harding, Calvin Coolidge, and Herbert Hoover, who held the presidency from 1920 to 1933. The main legislation in that period was the **Esch-Cummins Transportation Act** of 1920, which sought consolidations of railroads. The law charged the Interstate Commerce Commission with controlling rates so a fair return would go to stockholders and fair rates would govern freight and passenger traffic. The Transportation Act was not entirely successful, in part because the railroads were falling on hard times. Buses, private cars, and trucks traveling on roads built at public expense had become common. Then, in 1929, after a spectacular spurt of economic growth, came the *Great Crash*. Banks collapsed, about one-third of the work force was unemployed, and stock values fell unbelievably in the 1930s in a period known as the Great Depression.

The precarious nature of the economy in the 1930s led to a further postponement of antitrust efforts. Government attention instead focused on legislation and reform that would promote economic recovery and prevent a repetition of the financial collapse of 1929. One may fairly say that the curative and preventive measures adopted during this period showed no great faith in market competition. Some efforts actually promoted monopoly. For example, the **National Industrial Recovery Act** was used in 1933 to support business consolidations in the hope of reviving the economy. After these steps were deemed unsuccessful, the National Industrial Recovery Act was ruled unconstitutional by the Supreme Court.[37]

In the 1930s small shopkeepers had political power in their numbers and were able to use it for their own benefit, in part because politicians were grasping for ways to stimulate the flagging economy. The **Robinson-Patman Act** of 1936 rewrote the Clayton Act provisions against price discrimination to help small retailers combat a dawning supermarket revolution. The law made it more difficult for vendors to give supermarket chains favored price treatment on their larger purchases. As time passed and supermarket chains grew, the law became less effective in protecting small retailers.

The **Miller-Tydings Act** of 1937[38] exempted manufacturers and retailers from prosecution under Section 1 of the Sherman Act when the retailers adhered to minimum prices, wherever state laws allowed them to do so. The **resale price maintenance (RPM)** scheme allowed under Miller-Tydings helped retailers to avoid price competition. However, in the right circumstances RPM could also enable manufacturers and retailers to achieve more efficient outcomes without integrating vertically. They could avoid double marginalization, so RPM can sometimes be justified on efficiency grounds. These latter two acts, Robinson-Patman and Miller-Tydings, opened issues that would not be settled for some years to come.

The 1930s also raised questions about the control exercised by owners (the many shareholders) of the very corporations they owned. Dominant ownership by one person or family, which was common in the 1800s, had gradually given way to more widely dispersed ownership as corporations came to have thousands of shareholders. Concern now shifted from robber barons to a phenomenon called **managerial control**, in which owners no longer controlled their hired managers, who could play one of many owners against another. Critics complained about the pricing behavior of large enterprises because in many industries price did not seem to fall with demand, as competitive theory said it should.[39] This contrary pattern of pricing, called **administered pricing**, was never convincingly proved to be harmful or to be in widespread use, but its use was suspected and it was widely debated.

Aside from the Cellar-Kefauver Act of 1950, which closed a loophole to make the Clayton Act's merger requirements effective, there was little antitrust legislation until the 1970s. The **Magnuson-Moss FTC Improvements Act** of 1975[40] expanded the powers of the FTC by broadening its concern from anything "in" interstate commerce to anything "in or affecting" interstate commerce. It also allowed the FTC to seek more remedies than just the cease-and-desist order and to promulgate rules for regulating trade. The Hart-Scott-Rodino Antitrust Improvements Act of 1976 required firms planning a large merger to notify the FTC and the Department of Justice in advance of the merger so they could evaluate it. The Act also allowed state attorneys general to bring suits on behalf of state citizens. Other seemingly small but potentially important

---

[37] See Hawley (1966).

[38] Miller-Tydings Act, 15 U.S.C. Sec. 1 (1970).

[39] See Berle and Means (1932, 1968).

[40] Magnuson-Moss FTC Improvements Act of 1975, 15 U.S.C.A. Sec. 45 (1977).

changes made in the laws in the 1970s involved penalties.[41] In 1974, the maximum fine for antitrust violations was raised to $1 million for corporations and $100,000 for individuals, and the maximum prison sentence was raised from one year to three.[42] Although focused on corporate governance rather than antitrust, in 2002 the Sarbanes-Oxley Act created new offenses and increased sentences for many corporate misdeeds up to 20 years.[43]

Congress has granted formal exemptions from antitrust law. Most notably, the Clayton Act specifically excluded labor unions. In 1922 professional baseball was also exempted on the grounds that it was a part of sport and not commerce. Congress never extended this exemption to football or other games, and it recently limited the exemption for baseball.[44] Congress has exempted public utilities where they follow instructions from their states or other regulatory authorities, but they are held accountable to antitrust law when they act in competitive industries. Roughly the same boundary line holds for banking and insurance industries. Quite a wide range of private agricultural and fish marketing agreements would violate antitrust law if several acts of Congress did not specifically allow them. Congress also has exempted transportation and allowed agreements among exporters that otherwise would violate antitrust law.

8.4   ENFORCEMENT AGENCIES AND REMEDIES

The court case is generally the best way to enforce antitrust law, because it articulates a legal standard and provides concrete examples of conduct that violates that standard. Federal district courts usually hear federal antitrust cases. Recall that a defendant in a criminal case can always request a trial by jury. Even though a treble-damage action under the Sherman Act is a civil case, the right to a trial by jury is extended to such cases as well. Judges, however, try many cases because parties accept the expert knowledge that a judge possesses. Such specialized knowledge is so important in antitrust cases that when there is a jury it typically receives extensive instructions from the judge about what issues it is to treat and what the law requires in deciding them. After the jury or the judge renders a decision, appeals may be made to the regional appeals court and, finally, to the Supreme Court. Consequently, a complicated antitrust case may take five years or longer to settle.

Antitrust laws encourage private suits, and the treble-damage provision of the Sherman Act motivates them. Extending the treble-damage incentive through the Hart-Scott-Rodino Antitrust Improvements Act in 1976 to civil suits brought by states greatly expanded the possibilities for antitrust suits. For instance, states played important roles

---

[41] For a concise presentation of antitrust law as perceived in this period, see Gellhorn and Kovacic (1994).

[42] Antitrust Procedures and Penalties Act, 15 U.S.C. Sec. 16 (Supp. V 1975).

[43] See 116 Stat 745.

[44] For excellent descriptions of the antitrust exemption and other laws affecting baseball, see Abrams (1998) and Weiler (2000).

in cases brought against tobacco companies and Microsoft. Two federal agencies initiate federal antitrust activity, the Antitrust Division of the Department of Justice and the Federal Trade Commission, and we shall briefly examine each.

The Department of Justice

The Sherman Act authorizes the **Department of Justice (DOJ)** to initiate both civil and criminal actions. The DOJ can also take a defendant to court under the Clayton Act, but, because its violations are not regarded as criminal acts, the Clayton Act itself prompts only civil suits. Criminal and civil actions differ in that criminal actions are to punish wrongdoing, whereas civil actions have the object of compensating for damages suffered. Requiring damage payments in civil suits can also discourage harmful actions in the future, and this effect is specifically intended in the treble-damage provision of the Sherman Act.

In bringing a criminal proceeding under the Sherman Act, the DOJ must first seek a grand jury indictment. Grand juries can only be used for criminal cases; they investigate and decide whether to charge a defendant with a crime. Under the guidance of prosecutors, grand juries have sweeping powers. Both criminal and civil actions can be undertaken against the same violation, so one remedy may be imposed even though the other fails. Indeed, a civil action may be undertaken even where a criminal action already has been lost. The DOJ might still win the civil case because the standard of proof for a civil wrong is not as high as for a criminal offense.

The outcome of a civil action is not limited to an award of damages or to an order that some objectionable conduct be stopped. To prevent future violations, the DOJ may obtain an injunction. The **injunction** can limit the behavior of the offending firm in many ways, or it can require reports to the DOJ and subject the firm to special government oversight for a specified amount of time. A court decision in a civil case may even call for the dissolution, or splitting up, of a firm. **Consent decrees** sometimes result from civil proceedings. They are judicial orders that only a court can alter or interpret and from which it can punish violations. Consent decrees arise out of agreement by government and defendant before a case is decided at trial and often before any evidence is introduced. They do not have the force of precedent. They often are practical compromises, sometimes saving a firm the bother of a case and the embarrassment of confessing error and liability or saving the government from prosecuting what it has come to see as a weak case.

The Federal Trade Commission

The other main enforcement agency for federal antitrust law is the Federal Trade Commission (FTC).[45] It is not a court, it is an administrative agency, and its procedures are less formal than those of a court. A complaint that is brought to the FTC is adjudicated through an FTC hearing, overseen by an administrative law judge, who recommends a decision to the Commission at the close of the hearing. The Commission then issues

---

[45] Winerman (2003) provides a history of the FTC.

a decision that can be quite broad in scope, often going beyond the particular complaint to forbid the firm to accomplish its aim by other means as well. FTC decisions are subject to review in federal courts of appeal. If appeal is not pursued, the FTC order is final. Each violation of such an order—a separate violation can occur every day that the order is disobeyed—can incur a fine of up to $10,000.

In appointing the FTC's five members to their seven-year terms, the President must choose persons from more than one political party. The Senate confirms the appointments. These steps are to make the Commission more expertly specialized and less political than the executive branch's attorney general. Usually a complaint from industry or from someone in government starts an investigation, but the FTC also initiates studies on its own through its staff in Washington or using the resources of its regional offices.

The FTC was created to compel compliance through administrative procedures. Its main weapon has been an order to firms to cease and desist from using objectionable practices. Since 1975, it has been able to go to court and seek other remedies and it has more power to issue regulations. In certain circumstances, consumer redress actions may be instituted in the courts if the Commission finds that a refund or payment of damages is in order.

The Department of Justice and the FTC share enforcement responsibility for the Clayton Act, and their jurisdictions can overlap in other areas as well. Such overlapping jurisdictions could lead to difficulties. Each agency is careful to inform the other of its proposed investigations before it proceeds with them, however, so that they can effectively coordinate efforts where needed. Although a clearer division of duties has been urged,[46] and it might simplify governmental enforcement efforts, problems of conflict and lack of coordination do not appear to have been debilitating.[47] It is even possible that, as in the private economy, the competition of two government agencies can usefully stimulate their efforts.

Remedies for Violations of Antitrust Law

Both before and after passage of the Sherman Act, Congress debated many possible remedies for violations.[48] There were proposals to withhold federal services from antitrust violators, such as access to federal courts or even mail service, or to limit the transportation of their goods in interstate commerce, or even to make them forfeit their property. Some legislators urged a reduction in tariff protection for industries guilty of antitrust violations, while others suggested taxes, particularly for industries unaffected by tariffs. Some recommended simple publicity, based mainly on systematic government inspection of a company's records, although rewards to informers were also suggested. Congress, however, adopted none of these remedies. Look at the five main remedies it did adopt.

---

[46] See Stigler (1969).
[47] See Areeda (1967, p. 33).
[48] See Elzinga and Breit (1976).

1. **Treble Damages**. After debating whether to allow compensation for single, double, or treble the amount of damages suffered due to antitrust violations, Congress finally adopted threefold damages, from the English Statute of Monopolies. These treble-damage payments have no upper limit, as long as the damage injury can be proved. The damage payments are tax deductible by the defendant, however. In addition to the treble-damage payment, the winning plaintiff can collect court costs, including a reasonable attorney's fee. The treble-damage provision gives incentive for private enforcement of the law, which is its main aim. It has not been entirely successful as a remedy, mainly because it motivates too many suits that are unwarranted and, thus, burdens both firms and courts.

   To recover damages, a private party has to show *harm* because of some action that is forbidden under the antitrust laws, and proof of damages can be difficult. When an excessively high price damages a buyer, a case for harm can be made from available data. For example, the buyer can multiply the difference between that high price and an estimated competitive price times the actual quantity bought, to obtain a reasonable estimate of damages suffered. But if an illegal practice prevents someone from entering a line of business, that person has no exact record to show what he or she might have earned. It is then difficult to show evidence of the loss.

2. **Fines**. By 1974 amendments to the Sherman Act, a guilty individual in a criminal case may be fined up to $100,000 and a guilty corporation up to $1,000,000 for each violation of a section of the Sherman Act.[49] The effect of the fines can be magnified, too, because unlike treble-damage awards, corporate fines are *not deductible* from corporate income for tax purposes. Furthermore, in cases where individuals are fined, their reimbursement by the corporation they work for often is not allowed. A record of fines levied under antitrust laws beginning in 1890 shows that in those criminal cases where fines were imposed the average fine per case did not reach $100,000 until the 1960s.[50] For the large corporations involved, that was only a tiny fraction of sales or profit. More recent fines have involved millions of dollars, but fines of that magnitude are not common.

3. **Jail Terms**. An individual can be sent to prison for three years for violating the Sherman Act, which has been considered a felony since 1974.[51] A compilation at about that time showed that jail sentences grew more common after they were used for those found guilty in a conspiracy to fix prices for electrical equipment in the early 1960s.[52] Nevertheless, of 90 defendants subject to criminal sanction from 1966 through 1973, when the crime was a misdemeanor with a maximum sentence of one year,

---

[49] Sherman Act, 15 U.S.C., Secs. 1, 2 (Supp. V 1975).

[50] See the analysis by law professor (now Judge) Richard Posner (1970).

[51] Antitrust Procedures and Penalties Act, 15 U.S.C. Sec. 16 (Supp. V 1975).

[52] See Elzinga and Breit (1976).

only 25 served time in jail, the longest stretch being nine months. The Sarbanes-Oxley Act of 2002 raised possible jail time for many violations to 20 years.

4. **Injunctions**. An injunction may forbid a certain action without imposing any penalty for its having been carried on in the past. Indeed, the injunction may involve no real penalty, although most injunctions do prohibit an antitrust defendant from some specified future business conduct. When the injunction constrains a firm from actions, essentially forever, it can impose a cost or limitation amounting to a significant penalty. For example, Swift & Company was not allowed certain merger actions under terms of a 1903 injunction;[53] that limitation has almost certainly constrained the company from operating as it would have wished. But usually the conduct that is forbidden is undesirable and should be prevented. Sanctioned firms do not always comply faithfully with terms of the injunction, and further lawsuits sometimes follow to seek effective compliance.

5. **Structural Changes**. Structural relief is the most dramatic weapon in the antitrust arsenal because it involves changes in the size and shape of the business unit itself. Appropriate structural relief is seldom easy to devise, however, and is usually hard to accomplish. Deciding what part of the firm to put into a separate unit, or to divest, is especially difficult when the firm involved is very large. A district court judge cannot be expected to know all the consequences of such an action. Accomplishing divestiture is also difficult because inevitable delays can thwart the intended purpose. By the time a divestiture decree is carried out, for example, that portion of a firm to be divested may have been stripped of its strategic value. Economist Kenneth G. Elzinga (1969) studied 39 cases involving such decrees and found three-fourths of them seriously deficient or unsuccessful.

The Role of the States

States also have antitrust laws. Indeed, most states had antitrust laws before the federal antitrust effort began in 1890. And even though states did not want to drive businesses away, state enforcement efforts under the Sherman Act rivaled those of the federal government into the twentieth century.[54] Perhaps state authorities could identify Sherman Act violations more readily because they had already been pursuing some antitrust cases at the state level. As the federal enforcement effort grew more ambitious, however, the states allocated fewer resources to the antitrust purpose.

Many states enacted new antitrust laws in the 1970s.[55] States tend to focus on narrower cases than the federal government, such as local horizontal output restraints or bid-rigging violations. After the Reagan administration relaxed antitrust enforcement in the 1980s, states began to examine more complex cases, which the

---

[53] See *Swift and Company v. United States*, 196 U.S. 375 (1905).
[54] See May (1990).
[55] See Folsom (1990).

federal government was not pursuing, cases involving mergers, for instance, and vertical restraints such as resale price maintenance. States, however, emphasize practices to which federal authorities give little attention, such as "below cost" pricing, which about 30 states prohibit by statute.

States also bring suits under federal antitrust law. The Hart-Scott-Rodino Antitrust Improvements Act of 1976[56] included the *parens patriae* (parent of the state) provision, under which a state attorney general can bring a civil action on behalf of the residents of that state. If an antitrust violation can be shown to have damaged residents, the state can collect treble damages. State attorneys general have undertaken numerous antitrust cases since the Act, including, for instance, participation by 19 of them in the late 1990s case against Microsoft. This *parens patriae* provision of the Act was intended to enlist the efforts of states in the enforcement of federal antitrust laws, and it was a reaction to a decision by the Supreme Court that had limited the right of states to collect treble damages. State laws have also broadened the reach of such damage claims by states to motivate antitrust effort.

States seem to be less accepting than federal authorities of the benefits of mergers. States show evident concern for the effect of mergers on employment in the state involved. States also resist some product distribution practices more than federal authorities do. It is desirable to avoid inconsistency between state and federal antitrust effort, however, and the National Association of Attorneys General works with federal authorities to minimize effects of such inconsistencies.

8.5 | SHOULD COURTS OPPOSE MONOPOLY CONDUCT OR MONOPOLY POWER?

The Sherman Act did not define the crucial antitrust word, *monopoly*, and early court decisions were not consistent in deciding what was objectionable, the monopoly power itself or the way it was used. Despite the passage of the Clayton and the Federal Trade Commission Acts in 1914, the courts continued to struggle to define monopoly and to determine whether the laws referred to monopoly conduct or monopoly power.

The Sherman Act did not squarely oppose the existence of monopoly; it opposed monopolizing (Section 2, remember, makes it unlawful to monopolize, attempt to monopolize, or combine or conspire with others to monopolize trade). Early cases attacked "every" restraint, as the Sherman Act seemed to require, but then the courts began examining conduct and judging whether its effect was undesirable, through the rule of reason. The rule of reason allowed courts to evaluate consequences of a firm's conduct and to apply discretion in rendering judgments. In Section 8.3, we noted that Congress did not welcome the rule of reason, and it responded with the Clayton Act, to spell out offenses in more detail, and the Federal Trade Commission Act, to create a separate agency to enforce antitrust law. Yet courts continued to judge the reasonableness of firms' conduct.

---

[56] Hart-Scott-Rodino Antitrust Improvements Act of 1976, 15 U.S.C.A. Sec. 25c (1977).

Monopoly Conduct and the Rule of Reason

We have seen that when the Supreme Court decided that the Standard Oil Company was an illegal monopoly in 1911, it emphasized the unreasonableness of the company's conduct rather than the fact that the firm possessed monopoly power.[57] Giving such attention to the reasonableness of a monopoly's conduct in deciding Section 2 Sherman Act cases follows the rule of reason. In the same year as the Standard Oil decision, the Supreme Court held that the American Tobacco Company acted illegally, largely because of unreasonable conduct, and dissolved it into 14 separate companies.[58] These 1911 decisions rejected the narrow scope for antitrust that had controlled the E. C. Knight case,[59] and they broadened the Court's view of the scope of the Act to include manufacturing more generally. But in establishing the rule of reason the Court also altered the ground for judging monopoly, shifting attention to the firm's conduct rather than to its power alone.

The rule of reason did not have to affect crucially the outcome of either the Standard Oil case or the American Tobacco case, because monopolization in those cases was easy to see. The reasonableness judgment served simply to clinch the Court's findings of guilt. Starting in 1916, however, that rule would undercut antitrust efforts became clear. In that year the American Can Company, which had controlled 90 percent of the production of tin cans, was not convicted of violating the Sherman Act because it "had done nothing of which any competitor or consumer of cans complains, or anything which strikes a disinterested outsider as unfair or unethical."[60] In the court's view it had not been unreasonable in its conduct.

There followed in 1920 an even more remarkable four-to-three Supreme Court decision, finding the United States Steel Corporation had not violated antitrust law. The corporation had been formed from about 180 companies. It controlled two-thirds of the steel industry in 1901, when it was also fixing prices with other firms, as evidence clearly showed. But the Court deemed the company's monopoly attempt unsuccessful and judged its price-fixing ineffective, because by 1920 it had stopped meeting with rival steel producers. The corporation still controlled half the industry in 1920, but the Court said "[T]he law does not make mere size an offense, or the existence of unexerted power an offense."[61] This U.S. Steel decision forced the Justice Department into a more modest view of monopoly antitrust violations.

Alcoa and the Importance of Monopoly Power

The passage of the Clayton and Federal Trade Commission Acts in 1914 did not stop courts from using the rule of reason, because courts could view these laws as legitimizing their attention to business firm conduct rather than to monopoly power itself. The nation then became engaged in war, which—together with the range of problems that

---

[57] *Standard Oil Co. of New Jersey v. United States*, 221 U.S. 1 (1911).

[58] *United States v. American Tobacco Co.*, 221 U.S. 106 (1911).

[59] *United States v. E. C. Knight Co.*, 156 U.S. 1 (1895).

[60] *United States v. American Can Co.*, 230 F. 859, 861 (1916).

[61] *United States v. United States Steel Corp.*, 251 U.S. 417, 451 (1920).

followed it—claimed the attention of Congress. The war period showed the value of centralized control through large organizations, and awareness of these advantages helped to ease the suspicion against large firms. Antitrust effort began to revive, though, when Thurman Arnold became the aggressive head of the Antitrust Division of the Justice Department in 1938. Even the thorough cases he developed might have accomplished little, however, without a profound decision in 1945 that tempered the rule of reason, a decision written by a respected judge in the Second Circuit in New York, Judge Learned Hand.

The *Aluminum Company (Alcoa)* case came to Learned Hand's court under unusual circumstances. From 1903, Alcoa essentially had controlled aluminum production, at first because it held crucial patents. In 1937 the government charged that Alcoa had monopolized the manufacture of virgin aluminum and the sale of aluminum products and that it had maintained its monopoly through unfair practices. Among these practices were "spotting plants"—discouraging new entrants by building plants before demand was great enough to sustain them—or ruining fabricators who bought aluminum to make final products. Fabricators could be ruined if the price spread between finished goods and raw aluminum was "squeezed." Alcoa was dominant at both final good and raw aluminum levels, and it could set the final product price low and the raw aluminum price high. The resulting price squeeze would make life difficult for a fabricator buying at the high raw price and selling at the low finished price. As remedy, the government asked for the dissolution of Alcoa into at least two firms that would have to compete with one another.

When a trial court found that Alcoa had not violated the Sherman Act, the government immediately appealed. Because they had participated in earlier Alcoa litigation, four justices of the Supreme Court disqualified themselves from hearing the appeal, leaving the Supreme Court without a quorum of six. Congress then amended the judicial code so an appeals court could serve as court of last resort in this peculiar circumstance, and that is how the case came before a judicial panel headed by Judge Hand.

The approach taken by Judge Hand was to see first whether monopoly power existed. To answer this question he focused on defining the market. At the time, Alcoa manufactured more than 90 percent of virgin aluminum production, in ingot form, that was consumed in the United States (the rest was imported). If scrap was included as part of the market, the company still accounted for more than 60 percent. If scrap was included and Alcoa's consumption of its own ingots was excluded, as the company argued it should be, its share would fall to a third of the market, or 33 percent. Judge Hand thought 90 percent of a market would constitute monopoly, but 60 percent was doubtful and 33 percent was not monopoly. He concluded that because aluminum scrap was the result of earlier Alcoa virgin ingot production, the virgin ingot market was the crucial one, and, in view of its 90 percent control there, he accepted the government's position that Alcoa had a monopoly in aluminum.

Judge Hand then went on to consider whether Alcoa had simply competed so successfully that it emerged as a monopoly. To use his words, "The successful competitor, having been urged to compete, must not be turned on when he wins." But Judge Hand did not find that Alcoa had "monopoly thrust upon it" merely by its competitive skills. The company began with patent monopoly protection and substantial economies of scale. After patent protection expired, he found that Alcoa extended its control by building capacity in advance of need. The commitment of extra capacity provided a credible threat to potential entrants that Alcoa could flood the market with aluminum in response to entry. It also used a "price squeeze" by setting the aluminum ingot price high and the price of rolled sheet aluminum low, so no competitor could buy ingots to turn out rolled sheet aluminum at a profit. These he determined to be exclusionary practices aimed at maintaining Alcoa's monopoly.

Alcoa claimed that even if monopoly power existed it had not been unreasonably exercised, that is, its conduct had been reasonable. On this question of reasonableness, Learned Hand boldly took a compelling position against the rule of reason in the monopoly setting. He regarded the distinction between monopoly power and its exercise as "purely formal; it would be valid only so long as the monopoly remained wholly inert; it would disappear as soon as the monopoly began to operate; for, when it did—that is, as soon as it began to sell at all—it must sell at some price and the only price at which it could sell is a price which it itself fixed"[62] He argued it was absurd to hold per se unlawful a collusive agreement among several firms in a market (as the Sherman Act did) when, if the same firms all merged into one and behaved "reasonably" there would be no violation of law. As he saw it, Congress "did not condone 'good trusts' and condemn 'bad' ones; it forbade all."

The decision about a remedy in this case was postponed until 1950, when aluminum plants built during World War II and owned by the federal government were disposed of, and the remedy was modest.[63] Alcoa had to license patents and sever its connection with Aluminum Limited of Canada, while wartime aluminum plants that had been built by the government went to the Kaiser and Reynolds companies which, with Alcoa, came to share the market for aluminum. Judge Hand had achieved a redefinition of monopoly, however, and antitrust effort was invigorated. For example, in a 1946 case of conspiracy against the three leading cigarette producers, collusion was inferred for the first time from evidence of identical buying and selling prices.[64] No special intent was said to be needed as long as the effect of monopoly resulted, although this view was not a lasting one.

The Special Burden of Market Dominance

An interesting elaboration of this revived Section 2 of the Sherman Act came from Judge Charles Wyzanski in his *United Shoe Machinery Corporation* decision in 1953.[65] He argued that when monopoly power was due substantially to barriers caused by its own practices, even though the practices were not predatory or otherwise counter to Section 1 of

---

[62] *United States v. Aluminum Co. of America*, 148 F. 2nd 416, 428 (1945).

[63] *United States v. Aluminum Co. of America*, 91 F. Supp. 333 (D.C.N.Y. 1950).

[64] *American Tobacco Co. v. United States*, 328 U.S. 781 (1946).

[65] *United States v. United Shoe Machinery Corp.*, 110 F. Supp. 295 (1953).

the Sherman Act, the resulting monopoly was unlawful under Section 2. He effectively imposed a higher standard of behavior on dominant firms as monopolies. The United Shoe Machinery Corporation produced 90 percent of U.S. shoe manufacturing equipment. Judge Wyzanski found its practices of leasing machines and not selling them, of using certain exclusive long-term contracts, and of possible price discrimination, while not necessarily illegal for a firm in a less secure market position, were enough to allow United Shoe Machinery to exclude competitors and so were illegal.[66] Judge Wyzanski ordered that these practices be abandoned and that patents be licensed to competitors.

The behavior of the IBM Corporation was limited in similar ways in 1956, when its domination of the computer industry led to a consent decree, an agreement in which a firm promises to change its behavior in the future but admits no guilt.[67] In this era that preceded the personal computer, IBM leased many of its large mainframe computers to customers. In part, this practice reduced the risk that customers might bear in owning costly computers, about which they knew little, but it also fostered a form of price discrimination. Through effective tying, IBM required its computers to use IBM punched cards, which were then the means of entering information into computers. On the manufacture and sale of these punched cards, IBM earned high profits. With the prices of punched cards high, customers who saw the computer as more valuable, and therefore used it more intensively and consumed more cards, would effectively pay more for it through the high prices they were charged for the cards. The court saw this as a monopoly price discrimination tactic.

To avoid prosecution, IBM was required under terms of the consent decree to sell as well as to lease computers. In addition, it had to license to others the printing press equipment that it used in the production of punched cards, equipment on which it held patents, and it had to reduce its share of the punched card market from about 90 percent to 50 percent or less. Thus, the consent agreement broke the connection between computers and punched cards that might have allowed IBM to price discriminate among its customers.

The Supreme Court moderated any special burden that comes with market dominance in its review of the *Grinnell* case, which contributed to the quiet period for antitrust—except for merger cases—from the 1950s to the 1980s.[68] As in his *United Shoe Machinery Corporation* decision, Judge Wyzanski, who also decided *Grinnell*, held that Grinnell's 87 percent share of the market for fire protection that linked business premises to a central alarm station gave it a special burden to show that its practices were not anticompetitive. But in reviewing the decision on appeal, the Supreme Court found that the company had consciously acquired and exerted monopoly power, and the Court saw no need for imposing a special burden to find Grinnell guilty of violating Section 2. The Court distinguished between the use of market power to maintain or extend market control from "growth or development as a consequence of superior product, business acumen, or historical accident," which could have been forgiven.

---

[66] For a defense of the U.S.M.C. practice of leasing, based on modern analysis of transaction costs, see Masten and Snyder (1993), and for a less sympathetic view of the leasing see Brodley and Ma (1993).

[67] The issues were actually settled in *International Business Machines Corp. v. United States*, 298 U.S. 131, 56 S.Ct. 701, 80 L.Ed. 1085 (1936), and the consent decree in 1956 enforced that finding.

[68] See *United States v. Grinnell Corp.*, 236 F. Supp. 244 (D.R.I. 1964).

Judging between these two explanations of behavior by a firm with market power, market power or business skill, has been difficult for courts ever since.

8.6 | GOVERNMENT CONTROL OF MERGERS

Before the *Alcoa* decision, if all firms in an industry merged and did not seem to behave unreasonably, they might have had the effect of a trust and yet escaped prosecution. Even after *Alcoa*, mergers could threaten competition, and as time passed, control over mergers came to be seen as a way to influence market structure. But, first, government needed effective antimerger law to have genuine control over mergers. Next, antitrust authorities needed a basis for deciding when a merger would be anticompetitive. Once past those two hurdles, the authorities still needed an operational way to prevent problematic mergers, a way that would block such a merger before it occurred. Proceeding through these steps brought government control of mergers.

Effective Antimerger Law

As an antimerger law, the Clayton Act was ineffective. Through an oversight, it did not cover mergers carried out through a direct sale of assets, so a merger effected by sale of assets could escape its reach. In 1950, the Celler-Kefauver Act extended government oversight to include such mergers. Moving against mergers with the aid of the Celler-Kefauver Act was seen as a way to slow further concentration in industries, which antitrust laws and administrative court decisions had not yet been able to control. Vigorous enforcement, with the revised Section 7 of the Clayton Act due to Celler-Kefauver, greatly reduced horizontal mergers, and seriously reduced vertical mergers (that is, mergers between the buyers of a particular input and suppliers of that input). This policy was difficult to carry out, however, because grounds for blocking a merger were not clearly understood, and remedies were not easy to fashion after a merger had already taken place.

Another kind of merger, called a **conglomerate merger**, grew in the 1960s, among firms that had no very obvious business relationship. The pure conglomerate merger might involve, say, a hotel chain and an oil company, so their merger would not change the concentration in either industry. We can think of two other categories of mergers, geographical extension mergers and product extension mergers, as conglomerate because they do not affect one market's concentration. **Geographical extension mergers** might bring together two firms in the same product line, such as two grocery store chains, but in different sections of the country, so no relevant market concentration measure would be affected. **Product extension mergers** could be between producers of different products that share the same manufacturing process, or similar marketing methods, so the merger again would not change concentration in any one product market.

The conglomerate merger brought consternation to those responsible for enforcing antimerger sanctions. Although these mergers did not raise the level of control by one firm over any single line of commerce, they still seemed to harbor anti-competitive possibilities, especially for firms that met one another in several different industries. Antitrust authorities were concerned that such "multi-market contacts" might lead to understandings among firms, and possibly to reciprocal buying arrangements between them that could work to the disadvantage of other firms. Sometimes such mergers might eliminate potential entrants to a market, and with fewer potential entrants there would be less chance of entry into the market at a later date.

The Antitrust Division of the Justice Department attempted to prevent different kinds of mergers on various grounds, and there is no doubt the effort prevented a number of them. But enforcement was not consistent, so business leaders found it hard to judge when a particular merger would be considered illegal. In 1968, to help warn businesses in advance, the Department of Justice published guidelines indicating the types of mergers it would oppose. The DOJ revised the guidelines in 1982, 1984, 1992, and 1997, focusing more and more on horizontal mergers and less on other kinds. Today the guidelines inform firms about the kinds of mergers the Justice Department will examine, and these are primarily horizontal mergers.[69]

Market Definition

As already noted, mergers are classified as horizontal, vertical, or conglomerate, based on the markets affected. Defining the relevant market is important in the consideration of any merger, because it is the basis for tracing effects of the merger. For example, in the 1950s, when the DOJ was opposing vertical and other mergers, it prevented E. I. du Pont de Nemours and Company (DuPont) from owning 23 percent of General Motors Corporation (GM) stock.[70] There was no actual merger, but DuPont's holdings of GM stock were thought able to give it advantages over other suppliers in winning the automaker's purchases of paints and fabrics. Such a problem of market foreclosure becomes an issue in many vertical mergers, and solving it depends on a careful definition of the market.

Early definitions of markets were crude, however. Their use focused too heavily on concentration effects alone, and they were sometimes faulty. In *Dupont*, for example, the Supreme Court focused on the markets for "automobile finishes and fabrics," and found that if GM purchases went to DuPont they would represent about 20 to 25 percent of those markets. Concluding that such fractions were substantial, the Court did not allow the DuPont holding of GM stock to continue. It could be argued, however, that no clear separate market for automotive finishes and fabrics really existed, because the same products were sold for many other uses.[71] Indeed, taking into account all uses for these DuPont paints and fabrics, GM's share of total purchases would be only 3.5 percent for paint and 1.9 percent for fabrics. The actual degree of

[69] The complete guidelines may be found at www.usdoj.gov/atr/public/premerger.htm.
[70] *United States v. Dupont*, 353 U.S. 586 (1957).
[71] See Markham (1957).

foreclosure would be much smaller under this definition of the market, and so its use might have led to a different conclusion in the case.

In early cases under the expanded Celler-Kefauver law against mergers, federal authorities were aggressive and successful in blocking mergers by emphasizing effects on market shares in defined markets. In 1962 the Supreme Court decided against one such attempted merger between the Brown Shoe Company, Inc., and the G. R. Kinney Company, Inc.[72] Both firms manufactured shoes and sold them at retail, so the case had both horizontal and vertical aspects. The Supreme Court noted from the record in the case that the industry showed a tendency toward concentration. Because the Court interpreted the law as intending to prevent a lessening of competition in its incipiency, only a probability of damage to competition was needed as proof, not a certainty that it would result. After a careful sorting into submarkets of men's, women's, and children's shoes and studying local competitive effects through market shares, the Court found that even though the merger might have achieved some economies it was sufficiently threatening to competition that it should be denied.[73]

Larger market shares were involved in the *Philadelphia National Bank* case[74] a year later. The Philadelphia National Bank and Girard Trust Corn Exchange Bank were the second and third largest in what the Court judged to be the market for banking services in the Philadelphia area. The Court concluded that bringing together firms with 22 percent and 15 percent shares of that market would, in the absence of evidence to the contrary, substantially lessen competition. Then, in *U.S. v. Von's Grocery*[75] the Court prevented a merger of two grocery store chains that would have had just 7.5 percent of the Los Angeles market.

Thus, mainly with concentration arguments after passage of the Celler-Kefauver Act, the government succeeded in virtually all of its Section 7 cases against horizontal mergers. Courts also treated genuine vertical mergers with suspicion, and few significant ones occurred in the years immediately after 1950. Conglomerate mergers seem unlikely to create monopoly, because they involve completely unrelated firms, but if one of the firms is a prominent potential new entrant to the other's industry, courts have disallowed their merger.[76] Or if the merger would lead to a situation where one part of the new firm could extract from any former supplier some obligation to purchase its other products in turn, courts could also turn aside the merger.[77] Courts might also prevent a conglomerate merger if one of the firms involved was among the largest two hundred in the nation, or if they discern any other anticompetitive effect.

This strong policy of preventing mergers began to wane by the 1970s. Observers criticized court decisions based narrowly on market shares and concentration rather

---

[72] *Brown Shoe Co. v. United States*, 370 U.S. 294 (1962).

[73] For analysis showing the possible foreclosure in this case was not great, see Peterman (1975).

[74] See *United States. v. Philadelphia National Bank*, 374 U.S. 321 (1963).

[75] See *United States v. Von's Grocery Co. et al.*, 384 U.S. 270 (1966).

[76] See, for example, *FTC v. Proctor and Gamble*, 386 U.S. 568 (1967).

[77] See, for example, *FTC v. Consolidated Foods Corp.*, 380 U.S. 592 (1965).

BOX 8.2 Merger Policy in the Bush Administration

> The George W. Bush administration was lenient in allowing mergers. For example, in 2006 the appliance maker Whirlpool was allowed to acquire Maytag for $1.7 billion, even though the resulting firm would control roughly three-fourths of the market for some home appliances where entry was not particularly easy. The Justice Department relied in its decision on what it said was confidential commercial information that it would not release to the public. It defined the market very broadly to include some foreign companies that were not aggressive exporters, and it placed great weight on an economic efficiency defense for the merger. The administration also allowed many telecommunications mergers, such as AT&T's merger with Bell South.

See S. Labaton, "New View of Antitrust Law: See No Evil, Hear No Evil," *New York Times*, May 5, 2006, p. C5.

than broader economic consequences, including possible efficiency benefits of the merger. An example of more moderate decisions is the *General Dynamics* case, where a district court allowed two leading coal producers to merge even though the number of coal producers was declining and the two firms would have half the market.[78] The reason the court allowed the merger was that one of the firms in the merger possessed coal reserves that were virtually exhausted, so that firm would no longer be a force in the market in any case. Attention to other economic factors besides market share, especially entry conditions that could influence the consequences of concentration, were to guide mergers after that.

Premerger Notification

After the Celler-Kefauver merger law made the Clayton Act limitations on mergers effective, and the government learned how to define markets and identify anticompetitive mergers, there was still a problem. The government could oppose any merger that would "tend to create a monopoly or lessen competition," but the merger might already have taken place. As a result, the target of the government's attention could now be a large, complex organization that had just successfully merged separate activities. Breaking up such a merged firm would never be easy.

The Hart-Scott-Rodino Antitrust Improvements Act of 1976 helped to prevent anticompetitive mergers by requiring that large corporations notify the federal government *before* merging. Although there are qualifications, such notification is necessary if one firm in the proposed merger has annual sales or total assets exceeding $100,000,000, while the other firm has sales or assets exceeding $10,000,000, and the acquisition price for the transaction is $15,000,000 or more. The Act requires that both the Antitrust Division of the Justice Department and the Federal Trade Commission have advance notice of these large mergers, and the firms must wait 30 days before implementing the merger. Within that time either of the two government agencies

---

[78] See *United States v. General Dynamics*, 415 U.S. 486 (1975), 94 S.Ct. 1186, 39 L.Ed.2d 530.

may declare that it will oppose the merger, or it may request further information and extend its time to consider the merger.

Being informed before possible mergers gives the government agencies an opportunity to oppose them. The agencies can then prevent objectionable mergers from happening, rather than attempt to pry apart a combined enterprise after a merger has occurred. In response to this legislation, the Justice Department's Antitrust Division elaborated its merger guidelines to provide useful information to firms about the nature of the government's concerns and to describe aspects of a merger seen as problematic. Now merger policy is almost a regulatory process, with administrative agencies following more predictable guidelines so that courts have a less dominant role.[79] Premerger notification allows a more informed, more routine, more regulatory, process for considering mergers of large firms, and it has become an important element in antitrust policy. There has been a tendency for the agencies to use consent decrees increasingly, for example, rather than follow law suits to their trial conclusions.

Takeovers

Mergers may come against the will of some parties, when the merger takes the form of a takeover. A **takeover** is a dramatic form of merger, in which one firm attempts to gain control of another firm without the other's approval, perhaps by purchasing shares of the target firm in the capital market. Takeovers can discipline firms and their managements. By removing inefficiencies, they serve a desirable and productive social purpose.

Takeover oversight occurs at both state and federal levels. Federal regulation arises mainly out of the Williams Act,[80] passed in 1968 and administered by the Securities and Exchange Commission. This legislation imposes disclosure and other requirements on the bidders in a takeover process. Of course such requirements tend to delay an acquisition. Spreading information about attempts to acquire a firm, and delaying the acquisition, effectively fosters an auction for the target firm. Information alerts other firms that a target is "in play," and delay gives them time to act.[81] Premerger notification and waiting period requirements of the Hart-Scott-Rodino Act, which apply to mergers when larger firms are involved, can have reinforcing effects. The Williams Act helps takeover targets to receive more favorable terms, but it also makes takeovers more costly and more difficult and, thereby, makes them less frequent and so reduces their potential economic benefit.

State regulation of takeovers is also important. A state can apply its own takeover laws to firms that are incorporated in it, and for some purposes state law can be applied to firms with physical operations in the state even though they are incorporated elsewhere. In reviewing early state laws that called for disclosure of bid

---

[79] See Panel Discussion, 1998. "The Regulatory Character of Modern Antitrust Policy," Association of Law Scholars Annual Conference, San Francisco, January 9.

[80] Public Law No. 90-439, 82 Stat. 454 (1968) (codified as amended at U.S.C. §§ 78g, 78l-78n, 78s (1988)).

[81] See Romano (1992) and the discussion in Chapter 4.

attempts, the Supreme Court ruled they were unconstitutional for interfering in inter-state commerce. Later state laws were less restrictive and have been upheld. The main role of states lies with courts, which oversee the bidding process and can allow a range of added defensive tactics to resist takeovers. State legislation and court actions together are often more restrictive than the Williams Act, which is why state regulation has important effects.

Although it is difficult to know what would happen without the Williams Act or other takeover regulations, the net effect on welfare may not be positive. Returns to acquiring bidders in takeovers tended to go negative after states enacted takeover legislation.[82] Moreover, states that enacted takeover laws had smaller increases in the number of takeovers than states without such laws. The bid premiums—the increases in values for the targets—were not greater in those states that enacted laws either.[83] Such evidence suggests that regulation reduced the number of takeovers, which seems undesirable itself, and there were no gains to shareholders to be counted as offsetting benefit.

Takeover policy is a complicated subject involving a range of possible consider-ations. Employment effects are given much attention at the state level, for example, to forestall the short-run loss of employment that can accompany takeovers. Yet resist-ing takeovers may prevent efficiency gains that lead to lower prices with longer-run benefits in the state and elsewhere. The federal Williams Act and state laws, thus, handicap the market for corporate control. Yet that market places resources in the hands of those who are able to use them most efficiently.

8.7 UNFAIR AND DECEPTIVE PRACTICES

Competition cannot be expected to function well when some parties are deceived by unfair practices. So it is not surprising that a significant body of law, with origins traceable to British common law, regulates unfair and deceptive trade practices.[84] What in England was called "unfair competition" was the deception of pretending that goods were made by a more reputable seller than the actual one. This "palming off" of one good as another could be accomplished by copying the reputable maker's mark onto the inferior product. As time passed, courts came to see these trademarks as intangible property, and such property could be protected through tort law even without any deceptive intention. The cases involving deceptive intention were deemed to be matters of unfair competition.

Early cases of deception often occurred in vertical relationships. Suppose a manufacturer sells its product through a retailer and the retailer substitutes—or palms off—a lower quality product in its place. That would be illegal. There is nothing wrong if the retailer tries to persuade the buyer to buy the other product, as long as

---

[82] See Bradley, Desai, and Kim (1988).

[83] See Hackl and Testani (1988).

[84] For a summary of this law, see McManis (1992).

the retailer tells the buyer what the alternative product is. If you ask for a "Coke" in a restaurant you may be offered other possibilities instead, but it is wrong for you to be given some substitute without being told about it.

Common law generally affords legal protection to trade and contractual relations. Actions that interfere with such relations can be illegal, based on long-established common law principles. For example, persuading a person to break what is known to be a contractual responsibility to enter another contract can be attacked. When it involves deception or is undertaken for an anticompetitive or predatory purpose, it is an illegal interference with contractual relations.

The FTC Act contains public remedies for a great range of false or misleading advertising and labeling practices. In 1938, the Wheeler-Lea Act amended the FTC Act to protect consumers rather than just competitors from unfair practices. Under the Act the FTC shares with the Food and Drug Administration the responsibility to prevent false advertising of foods, drugs, therapeutic devices, or cosmetics. Further legislation gives the FTC authority over a host of specific practices, such as the labeling of wool, fur and textile products, the packaging of many products, and the regulation of other practices such as credit and debt collection, credit reporting, and the issuing of warranties. In 1975 the Magnuson-Moss FTC Improvements Act, which covered unfair methods of competition and unfair or deceptive acts or practices when they were "in *or affecting* commerce," expanded the FTC's jurisdiction and broadened its authority. If a practice merely had to *affect* commerce, the FTC could oppose a purely local practice.

The Magnuson-Moss Act also made meetings with industry representatives about impending FTC rules open to the public. Federal enforcement of unfair trade law is pursued mainly by the FTC, under terms in the amended FTC Act. Many federal and state laws provide sanctions against unfair practices, such as bribery to win contract advantage or engaging objectionably in a variety of games, giveaways, lotteries, and other devices to attract consumers. For instance, many states have adopted a Uniform Deceptive Trade Practices Act, which gives companies a right to sue other companies for using misleading practices aimed at consumers.

BOX 8.3 Regulating Funeral Homes

The FTC first brandished its 1975 Magnuson-Moss Antitrust Improvements Act authority in the funeral industry, where it made rules in decisive ways. So that bereaved next of kin are less apt to be exploited by funeral directors, the FTC issued a rule requiring that funeral directors give prices over the telephone, display inexpensive caskets along with expensive ones, get permission before embalming, and itemize funeral costs. Funeral directors bitterly opposed this ruling. Industry representatives had previously been able to influence FTC rule-making by quietly cultivating the rule-makers, but as interpreted by the FTC, the Magnuson-Moss Act makes all meetings with industry representatives public. This robs industries of what was once substantial behind-the-scenes influence. The FTC rules clearly caused substantial change in the funeral industry.

The FTC has also tried to curtail the opportunity that conglomerate firms have to conceal information about their separate product lines. Although strictly speaking it may not be a deceptive practice, combining information about separate activities across a conglomerate firm can reduce the amount of information that is disclosed about individual products. Separate corporations whose shares are traded on major stock exchanges must publish annual reports to satisfy requirements set by the Securities and Exchange Commission (SEC) to insure that investors can be informed. However, if the firms merged as a conglomerate their one report could conceal information by product line, so they are required to issue reports by major product line.[85] Even when separate reports are still required the conglomerate's managers might be able to lump together successful and unsuccessful activities, perhaps to hide their own mistakes or to keep potential competitors from knowledge of their successes.

A firm that keeps needed information from consumers or investors can be using an unfair or deceptive practice. By not reporting information by its lines of business a conglomerate firm might keep information secret and at the same time save the expense of reporting. The FTC has proposed line-of-business reporting by all firms to make information by each product line publicly available. Slightly more than half the firms that received line-of-business questionnaires from the FTC filed suit to stop the reporting program, however, objecting to the cost of preparing the reports. The FTC can point out that merely enumerating the cost of reporting does not support nondisclosure, because the lack of information may be more costly in faulty resource allocation than the cost of the reports. But the dispute continued and the reporting program ultimately was scaled back.

SUMMARY

As the nineteenth century drew to a close, corporations seemed beyond control in the United States. Consolidation of businesses and exploitation of resources both moved at a rapid pace. When state efforts at control proved unsuccessful, Congress passed the Sherman Act, not as a clear instruction that civil servants could execute but as a broad aim for courts to take in settling disputes. The Act made monopolizing and restraining trade crimes, and it created treble-damage awards to motivate private damage suits against violators of the law. Time passed before the courts could absorb and enforce the Sherman Act, however, and it was not until the turn of the twentieth-century that the Act began to block trusts and combinations. Amid swelling public concern, Theodore Roosevelt added vigor to enforcement of the Sherman Act and put in place new institutions like the Department of Commerce to study industry

---

[85] The resulting firm would be required by the SEC to provide sales and income data for any line of business that accounts for 10 percent of sales or more. In a large corporation many activities do represent 10 percent of sales. To some extent the sales categories are left to the firms to define, so they still have considerable control over what is reported.

problems. After some progress, however, the Supreme Court interpreted the Sherman Act so not every monopoly or restraint of trade was illegal, only the "unreasonable" ones, and this limited interpretation came to be called the "rule of reason."

Largely in response to the Courts' rule-of-reason evaluation of monopoly conduct, which the Sherman Act did not call for, Congress passed the Clayton Act and the Federal Trade Commission Act. These laws specified unreasonable behavior and created new means of enforcement. They were modified later, mainly to remedy flaws. The main legislation since then is the Hart-Scott-Rodino Antitrust Improvements Act of 1976, which required advance notice of mergers and allowed state attorneys general to bring treble-damage suits on behalf of their states' residents. Antitrust policy today remains essentially a late-nineteenth-century institution, based on the 1890 Sherman Act, which was refined by more legislation but not altered in a fundamental way since then.

Two large government agencies, the Antitrust Division of the Justice Department and the Federal Trade Commission, enforce antitrust laws. Enforcement effort also comes from private parties and state attorneys general seeking treble damages from federal violations and from cases under state laws. Court decisions guided by legislation have resulted in specific rules of law, such as the illegality of price-fixing, that are almost unambiguous, although Chapter 9 explores possible exceptions. Still, many decisions have been difficult to predict, so the very large record of cases is not always a clear one.

The five main remedies for violation of antitrust laws have not seemed perfectly effective. They are treble-damage payments, fines up to statutory limits, incarceration of officers and employees responsible for violations, injunctions or consent decrees to prevent objectionable behavior, and structural changes such as business firm dissolution or divestiture. These remedies leave much scope for discretion in working out solutions. With lawsuits taking place primarily in different district courts, the remedies were not always applied uniformly, and they were sometimes applied timidly.

Policy toward mergers and acquisitions has grown into an important means of controlling market structure, especially since the Hart-Scott-Rodino Antitrust Improvement Act was passed in 1976. Under this law large firms planning a merger must notify the Federal Trade Commission and the Department of Justice before the merger is carried out, and it gives these agencies time to decide whether they should oppose the merger. To guide firms, government agencies provide detailed descriptions of the possibly anticompetitive conditions that concern them. The agencies consult with the firms and can often specify changes in the merger proposals—such as selling portions of the merging firms that would cause reduced competition in certain markets—to make the mergers acceptable.

Takeovers are mergers that the acquired firm does not initially welcome, and they are part of a market for corporate control. The Williams Act of 1968, which requires disclosure about any takeover and delays the process, provides the federal legislation for regulating takeovers. The Securities and Exchange Commission and federal courts administer the Act. State laws and courts also guide the takeover process, in part because states control incorporation and thereby establish the rules that may apply. Limits on this takeover process exist in many states. Both federal and state efforts serve primarily to make takeovers more difficult, and since takeovers often have efficiency benefits, we can question the usefulness of such regulation.

Antitrust policy also extends to controlling unfair and deceptive practices, primarily to preserve faith in market processes. Originally, in British common law, business firms were to be protected from having sellers claim falsely that one product was really another. As time passed, protection of consumers became more important, and the Federal Trade Commission, aided by the Wheeler-Lea Act in 1938, pursued deceptive advertising and other ways of misleading consumers. The Food and Drug Administration protects against similarly misleading actions involving food, drugs, cosmetics, and medical devices.

A century of increasingly subtle antitrust decisions gradually came to represent sound economic knowledge and to focus on economic effects of business practices. As a result, antitrust policy supports competitive outcomes quite effectively today. We now turn to applications of antitrust law and policy in Chapter 9 to see how it achieves that effect.

QUESTIONS

1. How did the Robinson-Patman Act alter the Clayton Act? What reason can you give for its passage? Is it an important piece of antitrust legislation?
2. The Sherman Act set out a new economic policy in the United States. In your own words, try to describe the essence of that policy.
3. Four firms in an industry have market shares of 40 percent, 30 percent, 20 percent, and 10 percent.
   a. What is the Herfindahl-Hirschman Index (HHI) for this industry (Appendix 8.1 gives the formula for HHI)?
   b. Suppose the two smallest firms in the industry merge. After the merger, what is the Herfindahl-Hirschman Index? Would the government want to review this merger, according to the Horizontal Merger Guidelines summarized in Appendix 8.1?
   c. How might entry conditions in the industry influence a government decision about the merger?
4. Consider a market with 10 equal-sized firms, where each firm has exactly 10 percent of the market.
   a. What is the top-four-firm concentration ratio for this industry? What is the Herfindahl-Hirschman Index for the industry?
   b. Suppose five firms in the industry merge into one firm. What is the top-four-firm concentration ratio for the industry now? What is the Herfindahl-Hirschman Index for the industry now? Would the government want to review this merger, according to the Horizontal Merger Guidelines summarized in Appendix 8.1?
   c. How might entry conditions in the industry influence a government decision about the merger?

5. Resale price maintenance is a practice by which manufacturers control the minimum price at which retailers can sell the manufacturer's product. Because manufacturers make their profit based on their price to the retailers, why would they wish to control the retail price at which the retailers, in turn, sell their product? Explain fully.

6. Explain how the 1945 Alcoa decision altered the importance of market structure, as opposed to firm behavior, as the crucial matter in deciding antitrust questions.

APPENDIX 8.1 Horizontal Merger Guidelines

The Horizontal Merger Guidelines from the Department of Justice and the Federal Trade Commission provide a lengthy statement, explaining in detail the purposes and assumptions of horizontal merger guidelines. The guidelines identify five possible problems that a merger among large firms may create. First, if the merger increases concentration in a product market it may raise questions about effects on competition. Second, there may be other adverse effects on competition, and a search for them will be made. Third, if entry is easy a merger may be allowed because any increase in market share from the merger need not persist. Fourth, efficiency gains from the merger that could not otherwise be achieved will be examined. Fifth, merger might be permitted if one firm in the merger would otherwise fail and its resources would leave the industry.

This appendix reproduces the crude concentration standards that are imposed for screening mergers, but the guidelines themselves are much fuller and richer in their descriptions.[86] The Herfindahl-Hirschman Index (HHI) of concentration in industry decision making is calculated by squaring all firms' percentage market shares and adding up the results. With s_i representing the ith firm's market share, and with n firms in the industry, the industry's HHI is given by

$$\sum_{i=1}^{n} s_i^2.$$

A monopoly industry, with 100 percent of the market, would have an HHI of $(100)^2 = 10,000$, which is the greatest possible value for the HHI. The government divides HHI measures into three regions:

Unconcentrated	below 1,000
Moderately Concentrated	1,000 to 1,800
Highly Concentrated	above 1,800

The post-merger HHI for a proposed horizontal merger is calculated after first combining premerger shares of the merging firms into one firm. This provides an estimate of what the concentration will be after the proposed merger takes place. The government's concern about the effect of a merger on the level of concentration is represented in the following guidelines:

a. *Postmerger HHI Below 1,000.* Unlikely to have adverse competitive effects and ordinarily requires no further analysis.

b. *Postmerger HHI Between 1,000 and 1,800.* Mergers that increase the HHI by less than 100 points and have a postmerger HHI in this moderately concentrated range are seen as unlikely to have competitive consequences, and they ordinarily require no further analysis. If the merger raises HHI by more than 100 points, it may raise potential adverse competitive effects, which are discussed elsewhere in the guidelines.

---

[86] The guidelines are available in many places. See, e.g., Goetz and McChesney (1998). Or go to the Department of Justice web site: www.usdoj.gov/atr/public/premerger.htm.

c. *Postmerger HHI Above 1,800*. Mergers that increase the HHI by less than 50 points are seen as not likely to have adverse competitive consequences, even in these highly concentrated markets, and they are unlikely to require further analysis. Mergers that increase the HHI by more than 50 points in this highly concentrated range will potentially raise serious competitive concerns. Mergers that increase HHI by more than 100 points and yield a postmerger HHI in this highly concentrated range are seen as likely to create or enhance market power or facilitate its exercise, though the parties involved may attempt counter arguments.

In addition to these rough categories, which serve as a screening device for mergers, an extensive discussion in the guidelines is intended to assist firms in judging whether the government agencies will move to block a particular merger.

APPENDIX 8.2 Time Line for Major Antitrust Legislation

1890 Sherman Act made monopolization and restraint of trade illegal.

1914 Clayton Act specified antitrust offenses such as price discrimination and merger that tend to lessen competition or create a monopoly, and Federal Trade Commission Act created the Federal Trade Commission (FTC) to prevent unfair competition and enforce antitrust laws.

1920 Esch-Cummins Transportation Act authorized Interstate Commerce Commission to regulate railroad rates.

1937 Miller-Tydings Act exempted manufacturers and retailers from prosecution under Section 1 of the Sherman Act when they engage in resale price maintenance.

1938 Wheeler-Lea Act protected consumers, not just competition, from unfair practices.

1950 Celler-Kefaufer Act defined mergers to make Clayton Act sanctions against mergers effective.

1968 Williams Act required disclosure of takeovers and tended to delay their completion.

1975 Consumer Goods Pricing Act repealed the Miller-Tydings Act to remove antitrust exemption for resale price maintenance.

1975 Magnuson-Moss Antitrust Improvements Act expanded FTC powers.

1976 Hart-Scott-Rodino Antitrust Improvements Act required advance notice to the government before large mergers and allowed state attorneys general to bring antitrust law suits on behalf of the state's residents.

2002 Sarbanes-Oxley Act imposed new corporate governance requirements and raised penalties for violations.

9

Applications of Antitrust Law

The effect of legislation, particularly legislation such as the Sherman Act that leaves wide scope for court interpretation, depends on how it is enforced. For more than a century, the Antitrust Division of the U.S. Department of Justice and the Federal Trade Commission have played crucial enforcement roles. In addition, many private suits have sought treble damages for antitrust violations, and state attorneys general have sued to recover damages suffered by their states' residents. The ways courts decided the resulting large number of concrete legal disputes shaped and elaborated antitrust law, so its form today is far richer than a reading of the original legislation would suggest.[1]

Antitrust law guides the functioning of competition in the United States, and it developed from early legislation through court interpretations into the workable form it has today. Early departures from strict interpretation of the Sherman Act, fostered by the rule of reason, were inconsistent. In time, however, the rule of reason became a more constructive force, as it allowed careful consideration of the economic effects of various practices and invited more thorough economic arguments in antitrust cases. As economic knowledge grew, the economic arguments improved, and more subtle distinctions came into the law. This chapter traces improvement in antitrust law and shows the form it takes in current applications.

Consistency in enforcement of the Sherman Act has been difficult to achieve, in part because the Act was imprecise. There were some literal interpretations of the Sherman Act against price fixing in the late 1890s, but some of the early Court decisions also seemed to stray from the letter of the law.[2] Congress responded by adding the Clayton Act, to spell out specific undesirable practices, and by creating a new federal agency, the Federal Trade Commission, through the Federal Trade Commission Act. Additional legislation since these beginnings has pursued no bold new direction and has aimed largely at improving enforcement of the principles contained in the early

---

[1] Federal antitrust cases may be reviewed at www.stolaf.edu/people/becker/antitrust/.

[2] The Court expressed its duty to ban *every* conspiracy in *Trans-Missouri Freight Association* and in *Addyston Pipe and Steel* cases, but it ruled that the *E. C. Knight Co.* case was not a matter of interstate commerce (so federal law was not controlling) and found Standard Oil in violation not on a strict reading of the law but because of its *unreasonable* behavior.

legislation. Courts have continued to modify and sharpen the meaning of antitrust law, however. This chapter examines some of the main effects of this long process through court decisions in the broad areas of monopolization and restraint of trade.[3]

Briefly, for review, recall that the antitrust laws make illegal the practice to

1. *Monopolize,* to attempt to monopolize, or to combine or conspire to monopolize trade (Sherman Act, Section 2),

2. Enter a contract, combination, or conspiracy in *restraint of trade* (Sherman Act, Section 1) like *collusion* among existing sellers, *exclusion* of other sellers (also Clayton Act, Section 3), or *price discrimination* (Clayton Act, Section 2 as amended by Robinson-Patman Act), that reduces competition,

3. Condition sale through *tying* or *exclusive dealing* (Clayton Act Section 3 and other antitrust laws) when it reduces competition,

4. *Merge* if the effect may substantially lessen competition or tend to create a monopoly (Clayton Act, Section 7 as amended by Celler-Kefauver Act and Hart-Scott-Rodino Antitrust Improvements Act), and

5. Use *unfair or deceptive practices* (Federal Trade Commission Act, Section 5 as amended).

While the statutes just sketched provide a skeleton for antitrust law, actual court decisions provide the muscles and flesh that make the skeleton work. We examine this enforcement activity as it affects (1) the firm and market structure, (2) the firm and market strategy, and (3) the firm and innovation. Attempts by firms to change market structure to increase market power or make the market more monopolistic are considered first, through the topics of merger, price discrimination, predatory pricing, and matters involving essential facilities and refusals to deal. Section 9.2 examines strategic steps taken by firms to improve their positions through restraints of trade rather than by altering market structure. Restraints of trade are some of the most clearly defined offenses, such as collusion, exclusion, or tying, yet new ones are being invented every day. Understanding their possible effects requires careful analysis and that is where economic knowledge has made especially important contributions. Finally, in Section 9.3 we treat the firm and market innovation. Antitrust enforcement is complex in dynamic industries, and authorities have been lenient with innovative firms where change is occurring that benefits consumers.

9.1 │ THE FIRM AND MARKET STRUCTURE

Recall from the *Alcoa* and *United Shoe Machinery* cases that simply being a monopoly was not illegal. Anticompetitive behavior was also necessary, although being more of a monopoly made it harder to avoid being anticompetitive. Courts have still retreated

---

[3] The history of antitrust case decisions is described in many books on antitrust or public policy toward business. See, for example, Gellhorn and Kovacic (1994), Goetz and McChesney (1998), and Neale (1970). For a recent summary of main trends, see Kovacic and Shapiro (2000).

from strict interpretation of Section 2 of the Sherman Act, however, especially where technology is changing. First, courts have not readily found that firms were in violation of the law for being dominant in their markets as long as they served consumers effectively. Second, courts have allowed dominant firms to behave aggressively, again as long as consumers can be shown to benefit.

The U.S. government began to pursue market power in the early 1900s, retreating somewhat by applying the rule of reason to evaluate firm behavior, then returning attention to market structure with the Alcoa case in 1944, but carrying out little effective antitrust activity against monopoly or dominant firms after that. It brought monopolization or attempted monopolization cases against a number of dominant firms from the 1960s to the 1980s, including AT&T, DuPont, Exxon, Firestone, Goodyear, General Foods, Kellogg, IBM, Sunkist, and Xerox. Yet it achieved success of any kind only against AT&T, Sunkist, and Xerox. The other cases were very costly failures. The Exxon case lasted 8 years, the Kellogg case 9 years, the IBM case 13 years, and the government failed in all of them. Economic arguments that were gaining wider acceptance at that time offered less reason for government interference in markets, while growing international competition also served to reduce market power in many industries. The most significant of the cases was an unusual one against AT&T, a regulated monopoly accused of practices that handicapped potential competitors. A negotiated settlement broke up AT&T into seven regional companies and one long-distance company, which was allowed to compete with other long-distance companies in a market that was created for long-distance telephone service.

Outright attacks on monopoly have seldom succeeded since the *United Shoe Machinery* case. Nevertheless, specific monopolistic practices have been successfully attacked by the Department of Justice (DOJ) and the Federal Trade Commission (FTC). We shall consider four kinds of possibly objectionable conduct that may alter market structure: (1) mergers, (2) price discrimination, (3) predatory pricing, which can also be a restraint of trade, and (4) control of essential facilities and refusals to deal.

Regulating Mergers

Although it came 50 years after widespread concern about mergers, the Celler-Kefauver Act in 1950 finally gave antitrust authorities the power to prevent mergers that would lessen competition or tend to create a monopoly. Authorities used this power in an effort to prevent anticompetitive market structures from arising in the first place. Passage in 1976 of the Hart-Scott-Rodino Act, which requires merging firms to notify the DOJ and the FTC in advance of a large merger, further strengthened this ability to preempt the development of market power by assessing the effects of a merger before it occurs.

What sort of merger will the DOJ or the FTC oppose? The agencies publish guidelines in the form of an analytical framework to highlight for firms the matters that concern the agencies.[4] The present guidelines explain market definitions and

---

[4] Appendix 8.1 gives a sketch of part of the merger guidelines. Most recently issued in 1997, the guidelines are available at www.usdoj.gov/atr/public/guidelines/horiz_book/hmg1.html.

concentration measurements, discuss adverse competitive effects of mergers, provide analysis of entry conditions and their importance, and cover treatment of efficiencies from a merger and special consideration for possibly failing firms. Before examining these guidelines, we review market definitions in previous antimerger cases.[5]

Shares of the Relevant Market and Other Factors

Defining the relevant market is important to the consideration of any merger, because that is where effects of the merger can be traced out. An example already noted came in the 1950s, when vertical and other mergers were being opposed, and the DuPont Corporation was prevented from owning 23 percent of General Motors (GM) stock. DuPont was thought to gain advantage over other suppliers in winning GM's purchases of auto industry paints and fabrics, a definition that was too narrow because the paints and fabrics had many other uses.[6] Then the Brown Shoe Company was not allowed to merge with the G. R. Kinney Company[7] in 1962, even though the merger promised economies and the automobile was expanding retail competition by allowing consumers to shop over wider areas.[8] In *United States v. Von's Grocery*,[9] the Supreme Court prevented the merger of two grocery store chains that would have had about 7.5 percent of the Los Angeles market, which was growing more competitive, again as the automobile expanded competition among retail stores. After Celler-Kefauver, in addition to supporting virtually all cases against horizontal mergers, courts also treated genuine vertical mergers with suspicion.

Withering criticism followed these decisions, largely because they were based narrowly on market shares rather than on broader economic consequences, including prospects for entry and possible efficiency benefits of mergers. After considering other factors, two leading coal producers were allowed to merge in the 1975 *General Dynamics* case despite its leading to a combined firm with a 50 percent market share, because one of the firms in the merger possessed coal reserves that were virtually exhausted.[10] Attention to other economic factors besides market share, such as easy entry that would undo efforts to exploit market share, was to guide mergers after that.

Even after the Celler-Kefauver merger law made the Clayton Act limitations on mergers effective, there was still a problem putting merger policy into effect. The government could oppose any merger that would "tend to create a monopoly or lessen competition," but the merger might already have taken place. As a result, the target of the government's attention could now be a large, complex organization that had successfully merged separate activities, and the surgery necessary to break it up would never be easy. To avoid this problem, the Hart-Scott-Rodino Act of 1976 required that large firms considering merger notify the DOJ and the FTC *before* a merger took place, so the authorities could oppose it in advance if they had reason to do so.

---

[5] Merger actions under the guidelines are discussed at www.usdoj.gov/atr/public/guidelines/215247.htm.

[6] *United States v. Dupont*, 353 U.S. 586 (1957).

[7] *Brown Shoe Co. v. United States*, 370 U.S. 294 (1962).

[8] For analysis showing the possible foreclosure in this case was not great, see Peterman (1975).

[9] See *United States v. Von's Grocery Co. et al.*, 384 U.S. 270 (1966).

[10] See *United States v. General Dynamics*, 415 U.S. 486 (1975), 94 S.Ct. 1186, 39L. Ed. 2d 530.

To analyze the effects of a merger before it occurs, the government now focuses systematically on a relevant market for a product, or group of products, and a geographic area. The substitution opportunity of consumers is crucial to defining the relevant market, which is identified by considering consumer responses to a hypothetical monopoly. The question is asked: What could consumers do in response to a price increase by a profit-seeking monopoly in the product group or the area, either by switching to other product offerings in the same area or by switching to other geographic areas? Under such a procedure Dupont paints and fabrics products would be examined with no focus on automotive uses alone. The smallest product group, and the smallest geographic area, that would invite the monopolist to raise its price defines the relevant market. This procedure for defining a relevant market is described in the federal merger guidelines.

Federal Merger Guidelines

Even before premerger notification was required, the DOJ began in 1968 to publish merger guidelines that would inform firms of its concerns and reasoning, originally emphasizing four-firm concentration (C4) ratios.[11] The guidelines were revised in 1982, when the Herfindahl-Hirschman Index (HHI) replaced the C4 concentration measure, and in 1984, when substantial efficiencies from a merger were added as reason to support a merger. Potential harms from merger were more fully portrayed in 1992 guidelines, together with much fuller treatment of how entry conditions would be considered. Revision in 1997 added discussion of costs savings and described how they could be documented to support a merger. The guidelines now contain quite a detailed statement of merger policy. Besides defining the relevant market and its participants, the guidelines explain the calculation of market shares and the HHI values that raise problems, describe in some detail the problems that mergers can cause, explain the influence entry conditions can have, and discuss efficiency or "failing firm" arguments in support of merger.

BOX 9.1 One Reason Behind the Urge to Merge

Providers of telecommunications services have been reorganizing and changing the services they offer in response to technological changes, such as those that have brought new cell phone services that allow purchase of drinks at vending machines, video sequences, or Internet telephone service. Behind that evident turmoil, suppliers of gear to those industries are busy merging, largely to be in position to supply the range of equipment needed by the expanding service providers. Vigorous change in products and services invites changes in the ways firms are organized, and merger is a major way to accomplish rapid change in an organization.

See Ken Belson and Ian Austen, "A Mania in Telecom to Merge," *New York Times*, June 20, 2006, p. C1.

---

[11] See the 1997 guidelines at www.usdoj.gov/atr/public/guidelines/horiz_book/hmg1.html.

TABLE 9.1 Allowed Gains in HHI Due to Merger

Postmerger Concentration	Postmerger HHI	Permitted Gain in HHI
Highly concentrated	Above 1,800	50
Moderately concentrated	1,000 to 1,800	100
Unconcentrated	Below 1,000	Up to 1,000

To evaluate a merger, the market shares of merging firms are ordinarily combined into one firm, and a postmerger HHI is calculated on that basis. Allowed postmerger concentrations for a relevant market are presented in Table 9.1. Almost any merger is allowed if it does not cause the relevant market HHI to exceed 1,000 after the merger. If the postmerger HHI lies in the range from 1,000 to 1,800, which is deemed moderately concentrated, then the increase in HHI as a result of the merger should not be greater than 100 or the merger will be questioned. If the postmerger HHI exceeds 1,800, making the industry highly concentrated, then a merger that increases the HHI by 50 points or more may be questioned.

After expressing these rough benchmarks, the guidelines describe what authorities look for, such as a heightened opportunity for firms to coordinate their actions and even to punish firms that do not join in coordinating their actions. Differentiated products are given special attention, and firms' production capacities are also discussed. A separate section of the guidelines discusses entry, and points out that when entry is easy enough to prevent increased prices from being sustained a merger will not raise antitrust concern. In evaluating ease of entry the authorities examine how quickly it can occur, to see how effective it would be in preventing anticompetitive effects. The authorities also examine how well motivated entry would be to assess how likely it is to occur. Finally, authorities judge whether entry is likely to return prices to premerger levels. If entry can prevent price increases in the market that might arise because of a merger, the merger may be allowed even when it exceeds the concentration guidelines.

A count of the number of cases in which antitrust authorities did or did not oppose merger categorized by final levels of HHI concentration (row) and change in HHI concentration due to the merger (column) are shown in Table 9.2 for years 1996 to 2003. Each row in the table gives the industry HHI after the merger, while each column indicates the increase in HHI that the merger caused. Each cell gives two numbers. The first is the number of proposed mergers of that type that the government challenged, and the second gives the number of proposed mergers that were not challenged. By looking at any postmerger HHI (row) and increase in HHI caused by the merger (column), it is possible to see how many mergers with that combination were challenged and how many were not challenged. Although many mergers arose at levels beyond the guidelines, many such proposals were opposed.

The percentage of mergers that were challenged is shown for each HHI condition in Table 9.3, where the number of challenged mergers in each cell is divided by the total mergers in that cell. Overall, 78 percent of mergers were challenged. But this

TABLE 9.2 Number of Challenged Mergers/Not Challenged Mergers by HHI Condition, 1996–2003

Postmerger HHI	Change in HHI Due to Merger								
	0–99	100–199	200–299	300–499	500–799	800–1,199	1,200–2,499	2,500+	Total
0–1,799	0/14	17/20	18/8	17/4	3/2	0/1	0/0	0/0	55/49
1,800–1,999	0/4	5/4	5/3	12/1	12/2	0/0	0/0	0/0	34/14
2,000–2,399	1/1	1/5	7/4	22/11	31/8	1/1	0/0	0/0	63/30
2,400–2,,999	1/1	4/1	4/3	13/4	41/11	25/3	0/0	0/0	88/23
3,000–3,999	0/2	2/2	3/1	6/1	15/6	49/11	28/7	0/0	103/30
4,000–4,999	0/0	0/2	1/1	3/0	8/1	6/0	42/2	0/0	60/6
5,000–6,999	0/0	0/2	3/2	3/1	6/0	7/1	63/12	20/2	104/18
7,000+	0/0	0/0	0/0	1/0	2/0	5/0	41/1	81/2	100/3
Total	2/22	31/34	41/22	77/22	118/30	93/17	144/22	101/4	607/173

Source: Malcolm B. Coate and Shawn W. Ulrick, *Transparency at the Federal Trade Commission: The Horizontal Merger Review Process, 1996–2003*, Working Paper, Bureau of Economics, Federal Trade Commission, Washington, D. C., February, 2005.

TABLE 9.3 Percentage of Challenged Mergers by HHI Condition, 1996–2003

Postmerger HHI	Change in HHI Due to Merger								
	0–99	100–199	200–299	300–499	500–799	800–1,199	1,200–2,499	2,500+	Total
0–1,799	0	46	69	81	60	0	—	—	53
1,800–1,999	0	55	62	92	92	0/0	—	—	71
2,000–2,399	100	20	64	67	79	100	—	—	68
2,400–2,999	100	80	57	76	75	89	—	—	79
3,000–3,999	0	100	75	86	71	82	80	—	77
4,000–4,999	—	0	100	100	89	100	95	—	91
5,000–6,999	—	0	60	75	100	88	84	91	85
7,000+	—	0/0	0/0	100	100	100	98	98	97
Total	8	48	76	78	80	85	87	96	78

Source: Based on data in Table 9.2

percentage of challenged mergers tends to be lower when the postmerger HHI is low or the increase in HHI is low. Fifty-three percent of mergers were challenged when postmerger HHI was below 1,800 for example, while 97 percent were challenged when postmerger HHI was above 7,000. And only 8 percent of mergers were challenged when they would increase HHI by less than 100, while 98 percent of those that would increase HHI by 2,500 or more were challenged. Although the concentration guidelines alone were not controlling these decisions of whether to challenge a merger, many decisions seem to have taken into account the industry HHI and the increase in HHI the merger would cause.

Antitrust policy in the United States has come increasingly to depend on control of market structures through merger policy and to depend less on limiting firm conduct. The merger guidelines now articulate policy clearly, and the Hart-Scott-Rodino Antitrust Improvements Act allows intervention before a merger occurs. Still, conduct involving price discrimination or predatory pricing can harm competitors and thus affect market structure, and refusing to deal or denying access to an essential facility also can have market structure effects.

Price Discrimination

Price discrimination was explicitly made unlawful by Section 2 of the Clayton Act in 1914. In opposing price discrimination, Congress initially was not overly concerned with consequences for consumers. Rather, it was concerned about the market structure effects of having competitors destroyed, as when a large corporation kept product prices low in a particular geographic area for that purpose. The Robinson-Patman Act revised Section 2 in 1936 to make offenses clearer in the vertical transactions of wholesaling and retailing, largely to prevent chain stores from driving small retailers out of business. Concern over the use of price discrimination by powerful sellers to force competitors to exit, or to prevent their entry, and thereby to affect market structure, has a long history in antitrust. So does its use by powerful buyers to gain advantage over smaller rivals by obtaining lower prices for their purchases. The Robinson-Patman Act essentially protected smaller firms from larger ones.

Although it revised and elaborated the Clayton Act sanctions against price discrimination, the Robinson-Patman Act was passed in 1936 mainly to ward off the growth of chain stores and to protect neighborhood stores from their competition. With many retail outlets, chain stores were able to purchase larger quantities of goods for resale, and they used their greater buying power to obtain lower prices. The chain stores also performed some wholesaling and other intermediary functions themselves, and they argued for lower prices on this basis. Resulting price differences could give chain stores advantages in competition against traditional neighborhood stores. Because the affected neighborhood stores were numerous, they were able to wield substantial political power by organizing, which they managed to do to win passage of the Robinson-Patman Act. Efficiencies in the new alternative distribution schemes of chain stores proved valuable, however, and in part because they brought benefits to consumers the Robinson-Patman Act was unable to prevent their ultimate success.

BOX 9.2 Price Discrimination in the Ming Dynasty in China

Price discrimination has a long history. Charges for commercial shipping on the Grand Canal in China were based on a boat's cargo-carrying capacity and on the value of its cargo, plus other fees. The value of cargo is a basis for discriminating in price, in that prices are not related to costs but instead depend on the richness of the shipments. In the United States, the Interstate Commerce Commission set railroad rates for years using a "value of service" principle, under which a more valuable cargo would pay a higher rate. Transportation was seen as a smaller fraction of the final cost of a more valuable cargo, and with transportation claiming a smaller fraction of delivered cost of the item, demand for that transportation was expected to be less elastic. Thus, shippers of more valuable cargo could be willing to pay more. Discriminatory prices could even help to cover fixed costs and thus allow more efficient prices per unit that were closer to marginal cost.

See R. Hung, *The Grand Canal During the Ming Dynasty, 1368–1644*, Ph.D. dissertation, University of Michigan, 1964; and Andrew Odlyzko, "The Evolution of Price Discrimination in Transportation and Its Implications for the Internet," *Review of Network Economics*, September 2004, pp. 323–346.

The Robinson-Patman Act seeks to avoid "injury to competition," but it is widely criticized for its complexity and its vagueness. It distinguishes three levels of injury to competition from price discrimination. **Primary line** injury involves direct competitors of the discriminating firm. Injury to such a direct competitor is considered an injury to competition only if its purpose or effect is to drive a rival out of business. Such a purpose can be profitable only when the dispatched competitor cannot return, or be replaced, because entry is difficult. It may, as a result, be rare. In addition, bringing such cases too readily might discourage genuinely competitive actions.

Secondary line injury to competition arises among possible buyers from the discriminating firm, and it is the main target of the Robinson-Patman Act. It occurs when a seller gives a discriminatory lower price to one buyer, such as a chain store, and as a consequence that buyer has an advantage over its competitor, perhaps a small neighborhood store that pays a higher price for the same good. To prove injury to competition a plaintiff must show price differentials that are lasting and substantial.[12] **Tertiary line** injury is defined in the Act and involves harm to competitors of the buyers' customers. Such harm is rarely found, however, and so the injury is not important.

Antitrust attacks on price discrimination have been notoriously unsuccessful. Price discrimination exists under the Robinson-Patman Act when two customers pay different prices for goods of like grade and quality that are sold in interstate commerce.[13] When physical goods look the same, they may not be identical when they go to different customer locations, have different associated services provided, or are delivered at different times of day, week, or year. That is, marginal costs for providing

---

[12] See *Federal Trade Commission v. Morton Salt Co.*, 334 U.S. 37, 68 S.Ct. 822, 92 L.Ed. 1196 (1948).

[13] The law applies only to commodities, or goods, and not to services such as advertising or telephone service. Electric power has been considered a commodity and subject to the Act. See *Metro Communications Co. v. Ameritech Mobile Communications, Inc.*, 984 F. 2d 739 (6th Cir. 1993).

the good or service can differ by location, related services provided, or time of production or delivery, and differences in marginal costs can justify different prices. Thus, confirming that price discrimination actually has occurred is difficult, and that makes price discrimination difficult to prove.

Price discrimination can also be part of competition. When a business firm ferrets out a situation where a slightly lower price might beat a competitor and win business, the competitive effect can be desirable. Aggressive antitrust pursuit of all differences in prices could chill this competitive action, which actually bolsters competition and thereby improves welfare. For this reason, courts may judge price discrimination by a small firm to be suitably aggressive competitive behavior, whereas they oppose the same action by a dominant firm, and that is why minor forms of price discrimination are quite common.

There are three defenses to the charge of injury to competition through price discrimination: (1) showing of cost differences, which can justify price differences, (2) showing that the reduced price was to meet the equally low price of a competitor, or (3) showing that the party claiming injury had access to the same low price to which it objected. Showing cost differences as a basis for price differences is difficult, in part because the defendant has the burden of proving not only that cost differences exist, but that they can justify the price differences.

A seller can mount a good defense against the charge of price discrimination if it acted in good faith to meet an equally low price of a competitor. This is called the "meeting competition" defense, and is it is justified by the idea that competitive behavior is to be preserved. The seller does not have to prove that the price it thought it met actually had been offered by another seller, but merely that it had reason to believe it had been offered. For example, a reliable customer may have told the firm about the price and the firm may then have met that price in good faith. Even though the customer might have misled the seller and quoted a lower price than had been offered, as long as the seller believed the offer had been made, it was reasonable to match it. Showing that a complaining party had access to the same price also can be an effective defense against price discrimination. Such evidence means the discrimination could not harm the complainant.

Thus, the main problem with strict enforcement is that price discrimination can actually improve welfare. For example, when different buyers pay different prices, and those prices contribute different amounts to cover the seller's fixed costs, possibly welfare will be greater. The reason is that some consumers may be willing to pay more for the seller's good and, because fixed costs must be covered, collecting more from those willing to pay more can help. Total output with discriminatory prices can be greater then, and total consumer surplus can also be greater. If price discrimination can possibly be so "good," it is hard to oppose it at every turn.

Predatory Pricing

Through predatory pricing strategies, a firm might alter market structure by annihilating other firms through deliberate, although temporary, low prices. Price discrimination may serve this purpose when a firm uses profit obtained from high prices in one market to harm competitors in another market by undercutting their prices. Or it may set predatory prices generally and suffer losses with the aim of harming and then out-lasting its competitors. Yet it is very difficult to determine whether a firm with market power uses that power in a predatory way. After all, the firm could be acting competitively, trying to serve customers and win their lasting business. A competitive rationale is more persuasive when learning allows a firm to lower its production costs as it increases its sales. Then as the firm accumulates further production experience, employees learn to improve methods so the firm can have lower costs later. The firm might also set a low price to win consumers to a continuing relationship (for example, through a form of membership or as a subscriber) that will have a future payoff. Is a particular pricing action a sign of vigorous competition or is it destroying competition? That question has been hard to answer.

A major effort to answer the question was stimulated by Professors Phillip Areeda and Donald Turner (1975, 1978), who proposed a cost test for predatory pricing: *If the monopolist's price is below marginal cost it is predatory.* Because marginal cost can be difficult to observe they offered, as a practical alternative benchmark, average variable cost. Long-run benefits—such as lower cost from learning by doing, or a gain in new customers—conceivably could motivate short-run pricing below marginal cost or average variable cost, but a monopolistic firm would have to prove such benefits to overcome this proposed cost test. Many courts have accepted that pricing below average variable cost is unlawful, unless the firm provides a persuasive, non-predatory justification. Prices that are between average variable cost and average total cost are presumed legal unless entry is difficult, which raises another issue.

The cost test, which focuses totally on the relation between price and cost, is relevant only when entry barriers exist to help sustain a monopoly. Would a firm price below cost and lose money to drive others from the market if it could not later raise price and recoup its loses? The answer is no. To succeed in predatory pricing, the firm must be able to earn high profit later, to offset its losses from below-cost pricing. If entry is so easy that it occurs whenever a firm raises price above the competitive level, predatory pricing cannot succeed. Before the cost test would be relevant, Professors Joskow and Klevorick proposed a second test to determine whether entry is so difficult that later recoupment of losses would be possible.[14] Many courts impose this entry test where price is between average variable cost and average total cost. Moreover, the Supreme Court endorsed this two-pronged test for predatory pricing in a 1993 case. The Court found that Liggett and Myers, Inc., had failed to show that entry barriers would allow the Brown and Williamson Tobacco Corporation, whom it had accused of predatory pricing in the generic cigarette market, to recoup the losses it had incurred from setting low prices.[15]

Some courts are reluctant to find a party guilty of predatory pricing at all. On the one hand, courts do not want to chill the competitive urges of firms by attacking

---

[14] This test was called a "structural filter," because it would focus on a question of market structure. See Joskow and Klevorick (1979) and Elzinga and Mills (1989, 1994).

[15] See *Brooke Group Ltd. v. Brown and Williamson Tobacco Corp.*, 113 S. Ct. 2578, L. Ed. 2d 168 (1993). The case is complicated by the fact that Brown and Williamson might have benefitted in the branded cigarette market by reducing the threat in the generic market. For further analysis see Burnett (1994) and Elzinga and Mills (1994).

those who set low prices. Courts also suspect that a firm objecting to low prices may simply be less efficient than others, and the Supreme Court has indicated that a high standard is appropriate to prove predatory pricing. An example of what could convince the Court came when 21 Japanese sellers of television sets were charged by U.S. competitors with conspiring for 20 years to cross-subsidize sales at predatory prices in America from monopoly profits earned in Japan. The Court found the charge that Japanese sellers were losing money unconvincing because almost no amount of future profit could offset losses over a period of 20 years.[16]

Essential Facilities and Refusals to Deal

An essential facility, such as a railroad bridge, is one that competitors need if they are to compete in a market yet cannot reasonably reproduce on their own. When a monopolist controls an essential facility and refuses to let competitors use it, even when that could easily be done, the monopoly can run afoul of the essential facilities doctrine.[17] Courts may require a monopolist in these circumstances to grant competitors access to the essential facility and to suffer their competition. Whenever refusal to deal involves a monopolized essential facility, it may be seen as an essential facilities case.[18]

The essential facilities doctrine goes back almost 100 years to the early *Terminal Railroad Association* case,[19] where railroads that jointly owned a bridge and other facilities could have refused to deal with other railroads wanting access to St. Louis. Although it had prevented no railroad from using its facilities, a court required the Terminal Railroad Association of St. Louis to allow other railroads to use them. Illustrative later cases have involved access to a centralized fruit and produce market in Providence, R.I.[20] and access for a second football team to play at RFK Stadium in Washington, D.C.[21] The principle has also been applied in many regulated industries, such as a local telephone company that must allow use of its lines by a long-distance telephone company to complete calls, and an electric power company that must carry power over its lines for another company. The monopoly owner of the essential facility cannot refuse to deal with competitors who need only that facility to provide service.

When does a monopoly violate Section 2 of the Sherman Act simply for refusing to deal? The Supreme Court said in *United States v. Colgate and Co.* "[i]n the absence of any purpose to create or maintain a monopoly, the act does not restrict the long-recognized right of trader or manufacturer engaged in an entirely private business, freely to exercise his own independent discretion as to parties with whom he will deal."[22] But the Court saw refusing to deal as serving the "purpose to create or maintain a monopoly" in *Eastman Kodak v. Southern Photo Materials Co.* in 1927.

---

[16] See *Matsushita Electric Industrial Co., Ltd. v. Zenith Radio Corp.*, 475 U.S. 574, 106 S.Ct. 1348, 89 L.Ed.2d 538 (1986).

[17] See *MCI Communications Corp. v. American Tel. And Tel. Co.*, 708 F. 2d 1081 (7th Cir. 1983).

[18] For a broad review of essential facilities cases, see Lipsky and Sidak (1999).

[19] See *United States v. Terminal Railroad Association of St. Louis*, 224 U.S. 383 (1912) and 236 U.S. 194 (1915).

[20] See *Gamco, Inc. v. Providence Food and Produce Building, Inc.*, 194 F.2d 484 (1st Cir. 1952), *cert. denied*, 344 U.S. 817 (1952).

[21] See *Hecht v. Pro-Football, Inc.*, 570 F.2d 982 (D.C. Cir. 1977), *cert. denied*, 436 U.S. 956 (1978).

[22] See *United States v. Colgate and Co.*, 250 U.S. 300, 39 S.Ct. 465, 63 L. Ed. 992 (1919).

In that case, Kodak refused to provide supplies at wholesale to a retailer that would not agree to be purchased by Kodak.[23] The Court saw Kodak's strong-armed attempt to integrate forward into the distribution of photographic supplies as the reason for its refusal to deal. For some time, this was the main form of refusal-to-deal cases: a seller with a dominant position in one market attempts to extend that position into a related upstream or downstream market.

A significant refusal-to-deal monopoly case, which added another consideration to the essential facilities doctrine, came as a private suit in 1985. It involved the Aspen Skiing Company, which the court determined to have a monopoly of downhill skiing services in Aspen, Colorado.[24] Aspen Skiing Company owned three of four ski slopes. It had participated with its smaller competitor on the fourth slope in marketing a common ticket, which allowed skiers to ski on any of the four mountain ski slopes. When the Aspen Skiing Company refused to continue to participate in offering the common ticket, its sole competitor sued, and the Court found Aspen Skiing Company guilty of monopolization. In its appeal, the Aspen Skiing Company argued that it should not be obliged to cooperate with smaller rivals in a marketing arrangement to avoid prosecution under Section 2 of the Sherman Act. But the Court saw its refusal to participate as a use of its market power to handicap a smaller competitor, and it sustained the monopoly conviction. Thus, the owner of dominating resources in a market must have a persuasive business justification for refusing to deal, or courts can find it to have violated the Sherman Act as it would in an essential facilities case.

The Aspen decision raises a troublesome precedent in suggesting that a monopolist can violate Section 2 of the Sherman Act merely by changing the way it markets its service, and that it can avoid a violation only by participating in a joint marketing scheme. The case may discourage a firm from joining cooperative agreements, even, say, for research, because withdrawal from such an agreement later can be difficult. Courts have narrowed the effect of the case, for instance by indicating that it applies only where some cooperation is indispensable to effective competition.[25] Nevertheless, we can expect courts to look carefully to see whether a monopoly justification lurks behind competitive efficiency claims.

Another important refusal-to-deal case arose from a charge that Kodak had monopolized the vertically related parts and services markets for its photocopiers.[26] Kodak manufactures and sells photocopiers, and at the time of this case it had about 20 percent of the photocopier market. Kodak provided service for the photocopiers and sold parts that were unique to its photocopiers. From the early 1980s it had sold parts to competing independent service organizations (ISOs) that serviced its machines. When Kodak refused to continue selling parts to ISOs in the late 1980s, 18 of them sued. The district court dismissed the case on the ground that the conduct at issue was not illegal. The court agreed with Kodak that having only 20 percent of the photocopier market would prevent it from imposing undesirable restraints in the

---

[23] See *Eastman Kodak Co. v. Southern Photo Materials Co.*, 273 U.S. 359, 47 S.Ct. 400, 71 L.Ed. 684 (1927).

[24] See *Aspen Skiing Co. v. Aspen Highlands Skiing Corp.*, 472 U.S. 585 (1985).

[25] See *Olympia Equipment Leasing Company v. Western Union Tel. Co.*, 797 F.2d 370 (7th Cir. 1986).

[26] Micrographic equipment and photocopiers were involved, but the issues were the same for both products so we only examine photocopiers.

parts and service market for its installed base of photocopiers.[27] An appeals court, however, overturned the trial court's dismissal, the Supreme Court agreed and sent the case back to the appeals court,[28] which found that Kodak had monopolized the market for its photocopier's parts and service.[29]

This *Kodak* case raises complex and subtle issues, involving not only original photocopying equipment but also its complementary parts and service. Some evidence indicated that the ISOs' prices were lower and that their service in some cases was better. Kodak argued that customers would look at the total cost of buying and using the equipment over its lifetime, and because Kodak did not have a dominant position in the original photocopying equipment market, it could not raise the price of parts and service without seeing the sales of new equipment decline. But evidence indicated no decline in sales after parts and service prices rose, suggesting that new equipment customers might be poorly informed about lifetime equipment costs. The parts and service also could be effectively tied, because service was impossible without parts. By withdrawing from selling parts to its repair-service competitors, Kodak could ensure service as well as parts business for itself on its own brand of photocopiers. On this evidence, the court decided that Kodak had a monopoly of the parts and services market for already installed Kodak photocopying equipment and that such power could harm consumers.[30]

Kodak raises the same troublesome question as the *Aspen Skiing Company* case, about whether a firm is obliged to deal with its competitors. Indeed, the *Aspen* point—that only competitive reasons can support refusal to deal—is reinforced. *Kodak* strengthens the case against a single brand monopolizing the aftermarket products for its original equipment. Clearly, as in the *Aspen* case, Kodak's change in policy stimulated the lawsuit, which it might have avoided if it had provided its own parts and service from the start. The decision thus invites firms to consider carefully the future implications of their initial product and parts distribution choices. In essence, Kodak's willingness to sell parts initially established the scope and value of its patented property, and courts might have seen future changes from that status quo as an attempt to expand its established rights. Had Kodak initially controlled the provision of all its aftermarket parts and services by itself, it probably would have escaped Sherman Act scrutiny. There would be no need to change policy and no independent dealers to complain of any change.

9.2 | THE FIRM AND MARKET STRATEGY

A firm may undertake a host of strategies in its effort to gain advantage over other firms. Some of these strategies are aided by market power, while others may enhance market power, but they do not focus on altering market structure. These strategies

---

[27] For this argument, see Elzinga and Mills (2001).

[28] See *Eastman Kodak Co. v. Image Technical Services, Inc.*, 504 U.S. 451 (1992).

[29] See *Image Technical Services, Inc. v. Eastman Kodak Co.*, 125 F.3d 1195 (1997).

[30] For defense of the efficiency effects of this decision, see Salop (2000).

restrain trade and thus interfere with the operation of competition. They usually favor one seller and disadvantage another, or they may benefit all sellers as they harm consumers. We first consider restraints of trade among competitors, called horizontal restraints, and then examine vertical restraints, which occur along the path from raw material to the final consumer.

Horizontal Restraints of Trade

Horizontal restraints of trade—that is, trade restraints among firms in the same industry—can produce some of the same effects as monopoly. Indeed, such possibilities were the main concern of those who framed the Sherman Act. Firms in a market may collude to fix prices, they may form a hidden conspiracy, or, when few in number, they may engage in tacit oligopolistic coordination. Firms may also participate in joint ventures or information exchanges where it is possible to restrain trade. Firms might even merge to accomplish the effects of horizontal restraints of trade. If merger might accomplish the same effect as a restraint, that raises the question whether the courts would permit such a merger. If antitrust policy would allow merger, then courts may permit the restraint.

Early price-fixing and dividing-markets cases involved explicit horizontal agreements, which parties freely admitted, but the Sherman Act made them illegal. After courts found the firms in these cases guilty of conspiracy to fix prices, attempts to collude to fix prices were more guarded, or concealed, and the question of whether there was an agreement at all became an important issue. Understandably, some conspiracies attempt to keep their actions secret to escape detection, because joint rather than unilateral action is generally needed to prove that an agreement exists.[31] We may sometimes infer a tacit agreement, however, from the behavior of participants, so finding compelling evidence of conspiracy—a "smoking gun"—is not absolutely necessary. Competing firms do establish explicit agreements in joint ventures or in information exchanges. Policy may allow such agreements, but it places restrictions on how they may function.

We examine six horizontal restraints: price fixing, market allocation, hidden conspiracy, tacit collusion, joint ventures, and information exchanges.

Price Fixing

When firms in a market fix all their prices they restrain trade. The railroads in the *Trans-Missouri* case explicitly agreed to fix prices for freight haulage, and the producers of cast iron pipe in the *Addyston Pipe* case divided markets and participated in a combination to fix prices, all admitting they had fixed prices but claiming the prices were not unreasonable. Under the Sherman Act the Court found such price fixing to be **per se illegal**, which means simply participating in the practice is illegal; there is no need to show unreasonable consequences. Under the rule of reason, courts trace the consequences of a practice to see whether it actually causes harm. When economic arguments can determine effects of a practice well enough to justify a change in the law, the rule of reason can bring about that change.

---

[31] See Kovacic (1993).

Per se illegality has advantages over the rule of reason. It gives those subject to the law a better idea of what is legal, so they can be guided accordingly. A per se rule also fosters a quicker and easier court decision than rule-of-reason analysis. If the precise line of legality is too strict, however, it might prevent the use of some practices that would actually be efficient. Indeed, the rule of reason calls for an evaluation of the effects of an arrangement to ensure that efficient practices are not forbidden. Although the rule-of-reason evaluation takes more time and may produce standards of legality that are less clear, its advantage is that it may allow practices that will raise economic efficiency.

The possibility for reasonableness considerations for pricing arrangements was expressed clearly as early as 1918 by Justice Brandeis in the *Chicago Board of Trade* case.[32] The government had charged that a practice of setting prices for grain that arrived after the Chicago Board of Trade closed amounted to illegal price fixing, even though Board of Trade members who participated in the sales set prices independently for the purpose. Justice Brandeis argued that whether a practice restrains trade illegally is not easy to determine, because all agreements could restrain trade in some way. According to Justice Brandeis, the important question is whether the restraint merely regulates, and perhaps thereby promotes competition, or whether it suppresses or even destroys competition. The Court ruled that the Chicago Board of Trade arrangement for setting hours of operation, and then determining prices outside those hours, was legal based on an evaluation of the practice and its overall effects, not just on an assessment of whether any resulting price was "high."

Rule-of-reason analysis of price fixing is not easy, however. Except for a contradictory judgment supporting the legality of a price-setting sales agent for 137 bituminous coal producers in Appalachia during the depression conditions of 1933,[33] the Supreme Court maintained for a long time that Section 1 of the Sherman Act is to protect consumers by forbidding price-fixing or the rigging of markets in *any* way.[34] Virtual per se illegality for price fixing was reestablished in 1940 in the *Socony* case, which articulated a per se rule that clearly condemned all price fixing arrangements.[35] In this case, market conditions for oil were almost as bad as those for coal in Appalachia in 1933, and large oil companies agreed to buy the oil of independent producers who lacked storage facilities and to resell it in "an orderly way." The Court found claims about the reasonableness of resulting prices to be no defense and declared the arrangement to be illegal because it was "directly interfering with the free play of market forces." So it is almost true that the court would condemn any agreement to fix prices, however reasonable the result might appear. This helps to explain why government enforcement against price fixing was so successful.

Courts have granted exceptions to the harsh per se rule against price fixing, however, when an exception allows production to be more efficient. Consider, for example, the high transaction costs a composer faces in seeking revenue from the

[32] See *Chicago Board of Trade v. United States*, 246 U.S. 231 (1918).
[33] See *Appalachian Coals, Inc. v. U.S.*, 288 U.S. 344 (1933).
[34] For thoughtful criticism of the per se illegality position against price fixing and of some applications of the rule of reason in such cases, see Phillips (1959).
[35] See *United States v. Socony-Vacuum Oil Co.*, 310 U.S. 150, 60 S.Ct. 811, 84 L.Ed. 1129 (1940).

performances of musical compositions and in detecting unauthorized performances. In 1914, a few composers formed the American Society of Composers, Authors, and Publishers (ASCAP) as a clearing house to allow copyright owners and users to negotiate license arrangements. Today, members grant ASCAP nonexclusive rights to license, collect, and distribute royalties to copyright owners, based on the nature and amount of usage of the works and other factors. In 1939, ASCAP doubled its fees for radio stations and raised its charges to networks. Members of the broadcast industry then created a similar agency, Broadcast Music, Inc. (BMI), in response.[36] BMI also represents authors, composers, and publishing companies. Typical arrangements involve blanket licenses over stated periods, which allow unlimited use of the affiliated members' works for a fixed fee or a percentage of revenues.

Columbia Broadcasting System (CBS), which had supported the formation of BMI, later attempted to pay only for materials it used, but BMI required it to follow the blanket license terms.[37] CBS saw ASCAP and BMI as monopolies and sued, claiming that the blanket license amounted to illegal price fixing and involved misuse of copyright, tying, and concerted refusal to deal. A district court found that the arrangement did not fall in the class of per se illegal price fixing, in part because direct negotiation with the copyright owner was still available (ASCAP and BMI rights to grant licenses are nonexclusive). An appeals court overturned this decision, however, finding illegal price fixing, and the case went to the Supreme Court.[38] The Supreme Court observed that "the line of commerce allegedly being restrained, the performing rights to copyrighted music, exists at all only because of the copyright laws." Such laws give copyright owners clear rights to collect payments for performance of their works. The Court saw desirable efficiency results in the operation of ASCAP and BMI arrangements, which grew out of practical marketplace realities. The blanket license lowers transaction cost, because it requires few transactions rather than thousands and it avoids close monitoring of networks to ensure that they pay for what they use. The Court supported use of the blanket license employed by ASCAP and BMI.

The Court also applied the rule of reason in a case involving National Collegiate Athletic Association (NCAA) control over appearances of college football teams on television, and ruled against the NCAA practice.[39] An agreement among member colleges in the NCAA restricted how often their teams could appear on television. The agreement involved horizontal output limitation and price fixing, with the NCAA representing the colleges. The Court did not find the arrangement necessary to the production of television broadcasts (ASCAP and BMI had been deemed necessary), important to the preservation of attendance at college games, or valuable for maintaining competitive balance, so the arrangement was not allowed.

Thus, exceptions to the per se rule against price fixing are possible. As a general rule, however, defendants must have a persuasive rationale for an arrangement that includes price fixing, and there is little scope for the rule of reason to be applied.

---

[36] For description of this development, see Kleit (2001).

[37] For accounts of CBS's earlier conflict with ASCAP, see Cirace (1978) and Sterling and Kittross (2002, pp. 212–214).

[38] See *Broadcast Music, Inc. v. Columbia Broadcasting System, Inc.*, 441 U.S. 1, 99 S.Ct. 1551, 60 L.Ed.2d 1 (1979).

[39] See *National Collegiate Athletic Association v. University of Oklahoma*, 468 U.S. 85, 104 S.Ct. 2948, 82 L.Ed.2d 70 (1984).

BOX 9.3 Price Fixing in Grants of College Student Financial Aid

The case of *United States v. Brown University* grew out of an agreement among a group of private northeastern universities about the financial aid packages they would offer to admitted students. Although this practice involved the fixing of a form of price, that is, the level of scholarship to be awarded, the court noted that the goal of the scholarship agreement was to allow study by more students who lacked the means to attend the institutions. That is, a fixed amount of scholarship funds could be dispersed across a larger number of students if the scholarships were fixed at a lower amount than would result from competition among the universities. The court saw the agreement as advancing that goal of supporting more students and so allowed it, although the participating institutions later ended the practice.

See *United States v. Brown University*, 5 F.3d 658 (3rd Cir. 1993).

Market Allocation

Another way to reduce competition is to divide markets up and allocate parts to different sellers. If one of two sellers sells west of the Mississippi River and the other east of it, for example, that would be called a **geographic division**. Or sellers might allocate markets by **class of customer**. For example, one seller may sell wireless phones to consumers who use them for pleasure, while another sells to professional or business users. Attempts to justify such divisions of markets are based on grounds that they permit more efficient marketing, in part because they alter the selling representatives' incentives, and sometimes for production savings. But like price fixing, courts tend to regard such divisions or allocations of markets as per se illegal.

Although the *Addyston Pipe* case is known for price fixing, the agreement among firms contained market divisions that were also condemned. In a number of later cases courts denied market divisions, but whether they were per se illegal was not established. Then, in 1972, the Court specifically ruled market allocations per se illegal, quite separate from whether price fixing or other horizontal restraints were involved.[40] But in the same way that the rule of reason came back into price fixing cases, attention went to the specific effects of some market divisions. In *Rothery Storage and Van Co. v. Atlas Van Lines, Inc.*, a lower court reviewed an Atlas Van Lines policy of requiring Atlas agents to form a separate affiliate if they wished to carry goods on their own account. Using the rule of reason, the court found that affiliates could carry goods on their own without harming competition, and it cited *BMI* and *NCAA* as cases suggesting that rule of reason analysis could be appropriate.[41]

When a producer considers arrangements for bringing its product to customers, it may wish to assign to separate selling agents **exclusive territories**, which are almost like geographic divisions with one seller in each territory. The advantage to the

---

[40] See *United States v. Topco Associates, Inc.*, 414 U.S. 801, 94 S.Ct. 116, 38L.Ed. 39 (1973).
[41] See *Rothery Storage and Van Co. v. Atlas Van Lines, Inc.*, 792 F.2d 210, 253 U.S.App.D.C. 142 (D.C.Cir. 1986).

producer is that dealers are more willing to advertise and provide product information and product demonstrations to consumers, because other dealers will not free ride on their selling effort. Exclusive territories can be made solely through control of locations, however, and are not permitted to go further and prevent sales in one territory to customers from other territories. Once located, a dealer must be allowed to sell to customers from anywhere, so markets are not explicitly divided. With no dealer selling the same good in the same area, however, competition within the same brand of product—intrabrand competition—is weaker. As long as the producer faces substantial competition between its brand and others—as long as there is substantial interbrand competition—such distributional arrangements may be allowed. We examine these arrangements as vertical restraints, because they usually arise in the relations between successive sellers in the vertical path from raw materials to the ultimate consumer.

Hidden Conspiracy

If sellers cannot openly fix prices or divide markets they may form secret agreements, which allow them to act in concert rather than independently. Conspirators might escape punishment if they can keep their agreement about price-fixing or market allocations secret. A much celebrated antitrust case that involved **hidden conspiracy** is called "the great electrical equipment price conspiracy."[42] The conspirators were representatives of 29 electrical equipment companies who communicated secretly, sometimes in coded messages, and even arranged clandestine meetings at hotels under assumed names. As bidders on large contracts for heavy electrical generators, transformers, and switchgear, they agreed among themselves who would offer the lowest price.

Choosing who would be low bidder followed simple mechanisms, from alphabetical rotation among themselves to random selection, like picking the name out of a hat, and even to a complicated system based on phases of the moon. The agreed upon low bidder would inform others of that bid, and they would then submit higher bids. Some of those higher bids were identical, however, which caused suspicion. And some winning bids were the same, so contracts were awarded by drawing lots among

---

BOX 9.4 Territorial Allocation in Europe

The issue of territorial allocation is an important issue for competition policy in many countries. In the summer of 2000, the European Competition Commission imposed large fines on Volkswagen—about $85 million—for attempting to prevent dealers in Italy from selling to customers from other countries. General Motor's Opel unit was also fined about $35 million for preventing sales in Holland to customers from other countries.

See "EU Fines Opel's Dutch Unit for Violating Antitrust Law," *Wall Street Journal*, Sept. 20, 2000, p. 1.

---

[42] See *City of Philadelphia v. Westinghouse Electric Corp.*, 210 F. Supp. 483 (E.D. Penn, 1962). For further accounts of this remarkable conspiracy, see Smith (1961), Fuller (1962), and Walton and Cleveland (1964).

BOX 9.5 The Lysine Conspiracy

A well-known price-fixing conspiracy involved the Archer Daniels Midland Company (ADM) and international conspirators in the world market for lysine, an amino acid that is an important ingredient in animal feed and in other markets. In 1989, ADM decided to enter the lysine market with an ambitious modern production facility that, when completed, could represent about 40 percent of the industry's capacity. This extensive capacity was introduced with a price war that brought ADM a large share of the American market. ADM apparently then used its capacity commitment to bargain for a large market share in a price-fixing conspiracy among five international companies. A colorful informant who had a Ph.D. degree in biochemistry and was president of ADM's BioProducts Division revealed the conspiracy. A detailed trial record, augmented by the informant's tape recordings from secret meetings, tells the story. Although there is some dispute about the length and effect of the conspiracy, it certainly existed, and it led to record fines of $70 million and treble damage claims of nearly $200 million.

For two books that describe the conspiracy, see K. Eichenwald, *The Informant: A True Story,* New York: Random House, 2000, and J. B. Lieber, *Rats in the Grain: The Dirty Tricks and Trials of Archer Daniels Midland,* New York: Four Walls Eight Windows, 2000. For more analysis see L. J. White, "Lysine and Price Fixing: How Long? How Severe?" *Review of Industrial Organization,* February, 2001, Vol. 18, pp. 23–31.

the bidding conspirators. Submitting identical bids led to the conspiracy's undoing. For when bids on Tennessee Valley Authority projects were repeatedly identical—to many decimal places—it attracted attention that led to discovery of the conspiracy.

Forming conspiracies that would be illegal under antitrust law can be allowable internationally, where no antitrust authority holds sway, although one country that is affected by such a conspiracy may attack it. Economist Helga Nussbaum (1986) estimates that in the depression years between 1929 and 1937, international cartels controlled 40 percent of world trade. International cartels are much less effective today, but they still influence trade in important ways, as newspaper accounts of actions by the Organization of Petroleum Exporting Countries (OPEC) illustrate. There is some recent evidence of increased international cartel activity.[43] The study of international cartels can provide insight into the formation and operation of hidden conspiracies in the United States, where they would be illegal.

Reviewing a large number of studies of price-fixing conspiracies in the United States, Professors Margaret Levenstein and Valerie Suslow (2006) found three general conditions that abetted price fixing: (1) few firms or high concentration in the market, (2) a homogeneous product, and (3) when the number of firms was large, the existence of a trade association helped.[44] These patterns suggest that small numbers, or the assistance of an organization such as a trade association, ease the problem of organizing and communicating among conspirators. A homogeneous product makes negotiations simpler and therefore easier. The economists show similar findings from a host of international cartels. For example, shocks in the form of changed market

---

[43] See Connor (2001).

[44] The study by Levenstein and Suslow (2006) contains a wealth of information about legal and illegal cartels.

conditions can cause a cartel agreement to breakdown, probably because it disrupts the well-defined conditions that made agreement simple and easy.

Although it may be difficult to detect a hidden conspiracy, it is not impossible. Once detected, such a conspiracy may stand little chance in court because evidence of its agreement and its illegal purpose are probably both at hand. In such cases there is a "smoking gun" that makes guilt easy to prove.

Tacit Cooperation in Oligopoly

An even more difficult problem of detecting collusion arises when the few firms in a market tacitly accept it. Tacit acceptance comes without formal agreement or even negotiation. But it can arise because a few (oligopolist) firms can see the effects that their actions have on one another and they can recognize their dependence on each other, especially when entry is difficult and their relationships are lasting. Then **tacit collusion** is possible without sending any message except the message implicit in their own pricing and other actions. Because business behavior of this sort manifests no coded messages or meetings in hotel rooms, no party need confess to a self-evident misdeed. Separate firms can simply act in a cooperative way as they pursue their own best interests. Although their behavior may not appear very competitive, it is hard for a court to rule that it is illegally anticompetitive.

The Supreme Court was willing to find *implied* conspiracy among tacitly cooperating firms as early as 1914. In that year the Court prevented a lumber dealers' trade association from circulating among its members the names of wholesalers who were selling directly to consumers. There was evidence in the case that dealers would refuse to do business with these offending wholesalers when their names were circulated, and this evidence was taken to reveal a conspiracy.[45] The Court again inferred a conspiracy in an important 1939 case from the signing by eight film distributors of similar contracts with a theater chain operator.[46] Among other things, the contracts fixed admission prices. Each signer knew the others were signing the contracts, and the Court accepted that as evidence of conspiracy under the Sherman Act.

The Court took the inferential conspiracy case farthest against the Big Three cigarette manufacturers, American Tobacco Company, Liggett and Myers, Inc., and R. J. Reynolds Tobacco Company, along with associated companies and individuals, in a suit settled in 1946.[47] There was no evidence of meetings or illegal communications, yet defendants' concerted action was alleged to have prevented effective competition through their "parallel action" of keeping their prices the same, The Court accepted that argument. Although the evidence of market power was circumstantial, by drawing on *Northern Securities* and Judge Hand's *Alcoa* decision, the government successfully argued that possession of power was all that had to be shown, not that it was exercised or that any specific harm to a competitor or other party was needed.

The Court also found agreement by competitors to be illegal for tacit collusion when they used identical contract provisions, identical patent licensing provisions,

---

[45] *Eastern States Retail Lumber Dealers Association v. United States*, 234 U.S. 600 (1914).
[46] *Interstate Circuit, Inc. v. United States*, 306 U.S. 208 (1939).
[47] *American Tobacco Co. v. United States*, 328 U.S. 781 (1946).

and other identical policies. Then, however, this line of argument faltered. The Court rejected parallel action alone as proof of conspiracy in several 1953 and 1954 decisions,[48] and the Antitrust Division and the FTC turned their attention to mergers and other matters. Even during the period when the Court had more easily found tacit collusion, the remedies—usually denial of certain practices—had not been painful to the firms involved. The problem of sympathetic action by oligopolistic firms remains almost untouched by antitrust policy even today. It is opposed indirectly, by fostering structural competition wherever possible and by opposing arrangements that might facilitate cooperation.

Joint Ventures

Joint ventures allow cooperation among competing firms and appear to be horizontal restraints of trade. But firms that are otherwise competing are allowed to undertake a variety of cooperative arrangements as **joint ventures**. Joint ventures are usually contractual arrangements for specific purposes, sometimes involving creation of a new corporation whose stock is held by participating firms. Such ventures are not mergers or consolidations of the firms, however, for they have narrower purposes and often shorter lives. They can serve many socially useful purposes, such as pursuing research or other goals that cannot be achieved by one firm for lack of skills and resources, including an inability to face attendant risks. Two or more firms might undertake a research and development project that neither could undertake alone. They might gain scale economies in pursuing the project, or avoid duplication of effort and risk, and research joint ventures can foster more effective research efforts. Joint ventures might even make possible new entry into an industry.

Because they involve otherwise competing firms, however, joint ventures also raise potential anticompetitive problems. Independent efforts by several firms might bring a wider range of competitive product designs or marketing plans than would a joint venture, so social benefits of a joint venture are not always assured. While working together on a joint venture, personnel from separate firms might also develop sympathies for each other that would reduce the aggressiveness of their competition. For these reasons, joint ventures are subject to a careful rule-of-reason analysis, setting potential benefits against the risk of anticompetitive results.

Two main considerations guide antitrust policy toward joint ventures. First, courts consider the venture for its effects as if it were a merger, under merger laws. Second, courts evaluate the joint venture for its purposes and effects, which may cause them to allow it even though they would prevent a merger. These evaluations must rely on predictions about institutions that may not yet be functioning, so it is hard for courts to make perfectly sound analyses of effects. The practice of investment bankers to form underwriting syndicates to market new security issues illustrates the problem and the benefit. In such a case the court realized that many sellers *briefly* agreeing on an offering price plus a distribution plan could place a new security issue in the hands of many buyers smoothly and quickly, and so it permitted the practice.[49]

---

[48] See, for example, *Theater Enterprises, Inc. v. Paramount Distributing Corp.*, 346 U.S. 537 (1954).
[49] See *United States v. Morgan*, 118 F. Supp. 621 (D.C.N.Y. 1953).

Joint ventures can include a variety of restrictions that limit the actions of parties. For example, a joint buying association of regional grocery chains, called Topco Associates LLC, was created as a joint venture to allow the regional chains to buy goods in large volume at lower prices and market them under a private brand. Because the association included territorial restrictions, however, to prevent parties in the joint venture from competing over the private brand, the Court found the association violated the antitrust laws.[50] The Court forbade the restrictions in a per se ruling that did not consider the effect of the restrictions. This is surprising, because the restrictions could have been implemented had the grocery chains merged, and the Court probably would have permitted such a merger.

Analysis of transactions costs has improved evaluation of the effects of many ancillary restrictions in joint ventures, by showing the advantages in efficiency that they can offer. Now the ancillary restrictions that are attached to joint ventures are subject to three tests. First, do the participants in a joint venture have market power? If they do, a restriction may not be allowed. Second, does a restriction increase or decrease the total output of the joint venture? If output is increased, as it was with the ASCAP and BMI blanket licenses for works of composers and authors, the restriction may be allowed. Third, could less restrictive means reach the same justifiable end? The joint venture must show that its restriction is reasonable for achieving its aim because other means are less effective.

Information Exchanges

If competitors pass information among themselves, is that a restraint of trade? **Information exchanges** are arrangements that allow competitors to share information, such as the prices they charge, in a convenient way. Sometimes industry **trade associations** serve as information exchanges, and they perform other functions as well. Businesses selling the same products often form trade associations, which gather information that firms in the industry may use. Much of this information gathering may involve forecasts of input availability and prices, or inventory levels, which can help firms plan and thereby improve market efficiency. Trade associations may also foster efficiency by setting uniform standards where that is useful, or by advertising at the industry level when that avoids a free-rider problem. A single dairy may not want to advertise milk, for example, because doing so would benefit its competitors as well as itself, while a trade association can (and does) advertise collectively for all dairies. But trade associations or information exchanges might also foster collusion, by helping firms to agree on prices and sales territories or by barring some potential members from joining.

Trade associations and information exchanges usually involve contracts, suggesting agreement, so the question arises whether their actions unreasonably restrain trade. Over a series of court cases, standards of conduct have emerged that allow the exchange of information but constrain its form. Specifically, price information should only involve *past* prices. Exchange of future prices, and especially promises to abide by announced future prices, violates Section 1 of the Sherman Act. Prices also should not

---

[50] See *United States v. Topco Associates, Inc.*, 405 U.S. 596, 92 S.Ct.1126, (1972).

identify parties in particular transactions, and they should be available to the public in general, including customers, as well as to members of the information exchange.[51] Direct rivals are not allowed to verify each others' prices, either. Although that practice could stabilize prices and not necessarily raise them, it could easily enable all competitors to offer the same price to buyers.[52]

Business-to-business (B2B) exchanges over the Internet are raising new antitrust issues that go beyond guidelines about the exchange of price information.[53] The so-called B2B web sites give companies in the same industry a place to buy or sell goods, and the sales at such sites already exceed those of better-known consumer sites, such as Amazon.com. The broader capabilities of these sites can raise antitrust issues. The FTC and the Department of Justice carried out investigations of a site planned by the big three automobile manufacturers, for instance, and another site organized by six large meat packing companies, while the Senate Commerce Committee has held hearings on the airline industry's joint web sites.

Both buyers, as in the case of auto companies behind a site called Covisint, and sellers, as in the case of steel manufacturers behind MetalSite, Inc., have organized web sites, often as joint ventures. The web sites instantly bring together enormous amounts of information and can deal with more information, more quickly, than the older information exchanges could achieve. There are concerns about possible price collusion through these web sites as a result, perhaps even tacit collusion, based on a wealth of information firms may obtain about one another's costs. In addition, it might be possible for some competitors to be excluded from the sites, which could put them at a competitive disadvantage. That is why the FTC promises continuing review of Covisint's operation in the auto industry.[54] A close forerunner of these web sites, the computer reservations systems created by major airlines generated similar concern for years.

Computer airline reservation systems came into use in the late 1970s to tame the complex problem of presenting alternative flight information to passengers or their travel agents. Information exchanges effectively existed under economic regulation by the Civil Aeronautics Board until the 1980s, because airline prices were listed that the airlines promised to follow—they were regulated prices. First, the major airlines developed their own internal reservation systems. Then, as travel agents became important in the booking of flights, the airlines broadened these systems to include other airlines' flights and sold reservation-system services to travel agents. Two airlines owned the two major systems, however, and they gave priority to their own flights by having them come up first on the screen. The Civil Aeronautics Board, as one of its last acts before closing down as a regulatory body, held hearings that led to extensive rules for the computer reservations systems to ensure fairness among participants.

---

[51] Two important price-exchange cases are *Wilcox v. First Interstate Bank of Oregon, N.A.*, 815 F.2d 522 (9th Cir. 1987) and *Tag Manufacturers Institute v. Federal Trade Commission*, 174 F.2d 452 (1st Cir. 1949).

[52] See *United States v. Container Corp. of America*, 393 U.S. 333, 89 S.Ct. 510, 21 L.Ed.2d 953 (1969) and *United States v. United States Gypsum Co.*, 438 U.S. 422, 98 S.Ct. 2864, 57 L.Ed.2d 854 (1978).

[53] See David Leonhardt, "Business Links on Web Raise Antitrust Issues," *New York Times*, July 7, 2000, p. C1.

[54] See Federal Trade Commission, *Covisint*, File No. 001 0127, September 11, 2000, and for review of such developments in the auto industry see Kwoka (2001) and Garicano and Kaplan (2001).

The speed with which airlines could exchange price information, and the possibilities that rapid exchange offers for collusive agreement on price, caused the Department of Justice to investigate the Airline Tariff Publishing Company (ATPCO). This company provides price-change information to airline and travel agent computer systems, and it is owned by the airlines. The case was settled privately when the airlines agreed to forgo certain practices, such as presenting information about *future* price changes.[55] Although the lack of a court decision keeps it from being a binding precedent, the outcome is consistent with earlier price-exchange decisions.

Vertical Restraints of Trade

Restraints of trade arise not only from seemingly competitive firms. They also arise in the vertical chain of firms that produce and move products from raw material to final consumer. Vertical restraints are of two main types, those that restrict the distribution of products and those that exclude some firms from participating in a market. Restrictions on product distribution include territorial and customer restrictions and resale price maintenance. Exclusionary practices include tying, exclusionary conduct, and the Robinson-Patman Act. Each of the two types will be examined in turn.

Restrictions on Product Distribution

Until about 30 years ago, courts judged virtually all vertical restrictions to be illegal per se. They were seen as inappropriate extensions of control by sellers after transactions had been completed and property rights had been exchanged. Courts did not consider possible beneficial effects. This position changed as more knowledge of potential advantages for these restraints came to be recognized. Since 1977, courts have considered vertical restrictions other than resale price maintenance on a rule-of-reason basis, and where beneficial results can be shown vertical restrictions may be allowed. In 1997, the Supreme Court supported the use of resale price maintenance, so that practice also can now be subject to a rule of reason evaluation.

Territorial Allocations and Customer Restrictions A manufacturer might assign to retailers an exclusive right to sell from a defined location without other dealers nearby or to a particular type of customer. Some products can be so complex as to require explanation for effective sale or the provision of good maintenance service for effective use. With many retailers competing, some might free ride on the sales and maintenance efforts of others by dropping such efforts and cutting price, which might upset the product distribution plan of the manufacturer. To avoid such competition among the retailers on price alone, manufacturers might grant their retailers exclusive territories. Producers use this argument to justify the assignment of exclusive selling rights for automobiles, bicycles, mens' suits, and other products through separate dealer locations.

The territorial restriction is probably the most important form of vertical restraint, because to some extent it gives a single agent rights to sales in a defined

---

[55] For description of this case, see Borenstein (1999).

geographic area. For years such arrangements were essentially illegal per se, like resale price maintenance, although occasional cases examined specific practices to consider them more fully.[56] A per se limit on territorial restrictions came, for example, in an analysis of complicated distribution practices for Schwinn bicycles in 1967.[57] That is why the *Continental T.V., Inc. v. GTE Sylvania Inc.* case of 1977 [58] is so important. It called for rule-of-reason evaluation of such restrictions, with emphasis on economic effects rather than formalistic analysis of property rights.

GTE Sylvania, Inc., was a small manufacturer of TV sets in the United States with only 1 to 2 percent of the national market. In the early 1960s it changed its distribution arrangements, selling directly to franchised dealers rather than through the independent or owned wholesalers it had been using. The franchised dealers could sell to anyone, anywhere, but only from locations approved and controlled by Sylvania. When Sylvania opened a new franchise in San Francisco, another dealer first objected and then moved its franchise to Sacramento. This violated the terms of the franchise and, when Sylvania terminated it, the former franchisee sued.

The Court held that a reasonableness standard had to be applied. It noted a variety of reasons why the control of franchise locations might reduce intrabrand competition or competition among sellers of the same, Sylvania, brand of TV sets. But control of locations could also strengthen interbrand competition, the competition among different brands. With no other Sylvania dealers in the vicinity, an exclusive dealer would be motivated to advertise and seek consumers more aggressively, because consumers could turn to no other (price-cutting) dealer of the same brand. Interbrand competition was vigorous for Sylvania, and the Court could see that such competition would help to keep prices from rising far. So the Court allowed Sylvania's assignment of store locations.

Sylvania breathed fresh air into the analysis of distributional relationships. Since *Sylvania*, courts have rarely overturned non-price vertical restraints.[59] The *Sylvania* case has led to the use of two main considerations. First, does the firm employing vertical restraints face strong competition in the ultimate, interbrand, market? As long as market power is lacking there, the use of vertical restraints can often be justified.[60] Second, if the firm does have power in the interbrand market, the court considers whether its use of a restraint can be given a plausible business rationale, to show it serves proper competitive aims rather than anticompetitive ones.[61]

Resale Price Maintenance In addition to controlling competition among the sellers of its product, a producer may also want to control the prices they set. For instance,

---

[56] See *White Motor Co. v. United States*, 372 U.S. 253, 83 S.Ct. 696, 9 L.Ed.2d 738 (1963).

[57] See *United States v. Arnold, Schwinn and Co.*, 388 U.S. 365, 87 S.Ct. 1856, 18 L.Ed.2d 1249 (1967).

[58] See *Continental TV v. GTE Sylvania*, 433 U.S. 36 (1977).

[59] See Ginsburg (1991).

[60] In addition, the Supreme Court has required that dealers in territorial arrangements be free to seek and accept customers from each others' territories. This condition is especially important if the dealers take legal title to the product they retail and if the manufacturer is a leading one. See, for example, *United States v. General Motors Corp.*, 384 U.S. 127 (1966).

[61] In one case in which exclusive territories were not allowed, the firm had 70 to 75 percent of the market and could not give a persuasive competitive business justification for the restraint. See *Graphic Products Distributors, Inc. v. Itek Corp.*, 717 F.2d 1560 (11th Cir. 1983).

suppose business firms at two levels of product distribution, such as a manufacturer and a retailer, each possess some market power. Then each is tempted to mark up prices over costs independently, which results in the double marginalization problem that was treated in Chapter 4. Manufacturing and retailing are complementary to each other, and their independent decisions may not reflect the benefits—including lower price and higher profit—that a centralized policy could achieve. Resale price maintenance allows a manufacturer to set a price at which a retailer can sell the product, and, thus, enables separate manufacturing and retailing firms to overcome the double marginalization problem without actually integrating into a single firm.

As noted in the Price Discrimination section, many states adopted resale price maintenance (RPM) in the Great Depression, largely on political grounds, to protect small local retailers from chain stores. The laws permitted stores to set minimal prices, which no store was to undercut. Enthusiasm for such laws was so strong that Huey Long, governor of Louisiana, said he wanted to protect the state from "thieves and chain stores." The laws were euphemistically called "fair trade" laws, and Congress supported them with enabling legislation that prevented RPM from violating any federal law in a state that adopted it.[62] The rise of discount stores after World War II, however, made enforcement of these fair trade laws impossible. Too many stores violated the laws, some even advertising that they faced law suits because their prices were "too low!" States repealed the fair trade laws, and in 1975 the federal government repealed its supporting legislation.

Except for RPM laws from the Great Depression years, courts have seen resale price maintenance as a form of vertical price fixing and did not allow it.[63] An early effort by a manufacturer to control the retail price of its product involved a secret proprietary medicine of Dr. Miles Medical Company. The company accused a wholesaler of obtaining the medicine from other wholesalers at reduced prices, by persuading them to breach agreements they had made with Dr. Miles concerning their selling prices. Relying on what it claimed was the common law doctrine of that time, the Court ruled that, having sold goods to a wholesaler, the manufacturer could not control the terms at which the wholesaler resold the goods.[64]

There can be reasons for resisting control by the manufacturer of a retail price. Such control could lead to a horizontal conspiracy, for instance, either among sellers of the single good or even involving sellers of seemingly competing goods. Fear of such outcomes might drive decisions such as *Dr. Miles*. Indeed, the Court has even rejected imposition by a manufacturer of a *maximum* price that retailers might charge.[65] Yet we know that vertical pricing restraints can achieve useful results. For instance, a minimum price can keep some competing retailers from free riding on others, and it can induce them instead to provide customers with advertising and other information without fear of having the customers then go to a cut-rate seller of the product to make their purchases.

---

[62] This legislation was the Millar-Tydings Act of 1937.

[63] Consistent with the property-law basis of the *Dr. Miles* decision, manufacturers can accomplish resale price maintenance by retaining title to the goods and bearing risks of their sale. See *United States v. General Electric Co.*, 272 U.S. 476, 47 S. Ct. 192, 71 L.Ed. 362 (1926).

[64] See *Dr. Miles Medical Co. v. John D. Park and Sons Co.*, 220 U.S. 373, 31 S. Ct. 376, 55 L.Ed. 502 (1911).

[65] See *Albrecht v. Herald Co.*, 390 U.S. 145, 88 S. Ct. 869, 19 L.Ed.2d 998 (1968).

In a path-breaking 1997 decision, the Supreme Court overturned the *Albrecht v. Herald Co.* decision,[66] which had banned vertical maximum price fixing per se. In *State Oil Co. v. Kahn*, the Supreme Court effectively allowed the imposition of a maximum price on a gasoline dealer.[67] The Court held that the rule of reason can be applied to cases of resale price maintenance. As in the *Sylvania* case, valuation of economic effects under the rule of reason led the Court to stress effects of the pricing on interbrand competition, or competition against other brands of gasoline. The Court found that interbrand competition was vigorous and was well served by the resale price maintenance policy. Thus, rather than adhering to property rights principles alone, with pricing authority tied only to ownership, we can now evaluate the economic effects of resale price maintenance under the rule of reason.

Whether the Supreme Court will extend the logic of the *State Oil v. Kahn* decision, which allowed a seller to set a maximum resale price, to the maintenance of a minimum resale price remains to be seen. At the end of 2006, the Court accepted for review a case involving Leegin Creative Leather Products, Inc., who makes the Brighton line of leather products and who set minimum prices for retailers.[68] On learning that a retailer, Kay's Kloset in Lewisville, TX, was discounting Brighton products, Leegin suspended shipments to it and in response Kay's Kloset sued, claiming that Leegin was violating antitrust law. Kay's Kloset won $1 million in damages, to be tripled under the Sherman Act treble-damages provision. A decision by the Supreme Court in favor of Leegin would extend rule-of-reason analysis to all resale price maintenance cases, whether involving minimum or maximum resale prices.

Exclusionary Practices

Practices that may have the effect of excluding competitors from a market can be anticompetitive in their effect and, therefore, illegal. Tying can have this effect, for example. Suppose a seller requires that to obtain one product (the tying product over which it may have a monopoly) customers must purchase from it a second product (the tied product). Competitors offering the second product are handicapped in this case, not because their product is inferior, but because they are not producers of the tying product. By requiring use of its film, for example, a monopoly camera manufacturer could keep other film manufacturers from the film market. An exclusive contract, under which a retail dealer carries only one manufacturer's product and no other's can also exclude those others if the retailer is significant in the retail market. Price discrimination that favors some dealers can also handicap others and effectively exclude them from a market. Here we examine such possibilities.

Tying and Bundling A tying contract typically requires that a consumer buy a second product to obtain the one wanted; the second product is "tied" to the first, or the "tying," product. Because it gives the seller of one product an advantage in selling the second one, tying can exclude others, and that is deemed to be unfair. Section 3 of

---

[66] *Albrecht v. Herald*, 390 U. S. 145, 88 S. Ct. 869 19 L. Ed. 2d 998.

[67] See *State Oil Co. v. Kahn*, 871 U.S. 96 (1997).

[68] See Linda Greenhouse, "Antitrust Ambiguity to Be on Justices" Docket, *New York Times*, December 8, 2006, p. C1.

the Clayton Act specifically outlawed tying contracts.[69] Tying usually requires a monopoly of the first product, so if the monopoly is not legal—if it is not due to a patent, for example—the use of tying might be attacked as evidence of monopoly under Section 2 of the Sherman Act. It is also a restrictive practice under Section 1. By raising the price of the tied good, thereby obtaining more revenue from more intense users of the tying good, it is also possible through tying to achieve the effect of price discrimination.

Tie-ins often arise from monopoly power that exists legally, as through a patent. When such tie-ins are opposed, that limits the extent, and thus the value, of the patent monopoly. For example, the Motion Picture Patents Company, allowed its patented motion picture projector to be used only to show the company's films. After a purchaser of the projector who used it to show other films was sued, the Court found illegal the practice of tying films to the projector.[70] The Court saw the seller as attempting to use its legal monopoly in the projector market to obtain a monopoly in the film market.

A classic example of tying occurred in the *International Salt* case. There the International Salt Company leased two patented machines, one that dissolved rock salt into brine and another that injected salt into canned goods. International Salt leased both machines to customers, and it required its lessees to buy from it all the salt they used with the machines.[71] The Court saw this tying practice as foreclosing competitors from selling salt to users of these machines, which amounted to a substantial market. Again, they saw it as extending the monopoly power over a patented product into monopoly control of other markets.

Tying can be found illegal per se. To do so a court must find that the seller of two separate products has a dominant position in one—the tying product—and requires the buyer to purchase the other—the tied product—as a requirement to obtain the tying product. Also, a substantial amount of commerce in the tied product must be affected. In examining whether a defendant firm meets these conditions, a court often considers the effects of the practice. Using the rule of reason, the court may analyze whether the practice harms consumers. Bundling is similar to tying, and a major example is examined in this chapter's section titled The Microsoft Case.

Exclusionary Conduct More specific than a tying contract, an exclusive dealing contract may specify that one party must deal only with the other. A manufacturer may arrange an exclusive dealing contract with a retailer, for example, that prevents the retailer from carrying any other manufacturer's brand. Exclusive dealing thus limits the brands that a retailer can carry. Exclusive dealing may therefore reduce the access that other potential sellers have to that retailer and, perhaps, to the market. It often reduces intrabrand competition, because the retailer wants limited competitors retailing the same brand if it is to accept the arrangement. Exclusive dealing does not

---

[69] The Clayton Act applies only to goods and not to services; however, tying services can be attacked under Section 1 of the Sherman Act as a restraint of trade.

[70] See *Motion Picture Patents Co. v. Universal Film Manufacturing Co.*, 243 U.S. 502, 37 S.Ct. 416, 61 L.Ed. 871 (1917).

[71] See *International Salt Co. v. United States*, 332 U.S. 392, 68 S.Ct. 12, 92 L.Ed. 20 (1947).

prevent interbrand competition, because it bars other brands only from one retailer. But if retailers are few it can handicap the distribution of competing products (other brands) because they are blocked from one retailer. After existing retailers have exclusive dealing contracts, further competitors can be foreclosed from selling in the market, somewhat like the tying contract foreclosed other salt suppliers from the market in the *International Salt* case.

When a producer restricts a dealer to carrying that producer's line of products exclusively, it approaches what is called a **total requirements contract**, an agreement by a buyer to accept all that might be needed of a certain line of product from a single seller. Section 3 of the Clayton Act forbids such a contract if it will "substantially lessen competition or tend to create a monopoly in any line of commerce." When they were dominant in their industries, producers were repeatedly prevented by courts from using such contracts in the early part of the twentieth century.[72]

Since the 1950s, the FTC has required that actual injury be likely from exclusive dealing contracts, and the Supreme Court also has required a showing of significant effect. A rule-of-reason approach to cases predominates now. Where exclusive dealing contracts are attractive, the parties tend to be committed to narrow product lines (such as gasoline), rather than broad product lines (such as groceries).[73] Where narrow lines are involved, it would be feasible to achieve the same ends through vertical integration. Realization of this possibility invites the light-handed approach that now prevails.

BOX 9.6 Exclusive Contracts with Gasoline Stations

An important analysis of exclusive dealing came in 1949 in the *Standard Stations* case. The Standard Oil Company of California sold gasoline under exclusive dealing contracts to many independent service stations. These stations represented 16 percent of the gasoline outlets in seven western states, and they accounted for 7 percent of retail gasoline sales in the same seven-state area. The Court attempted an examination of economic effects of the contracts, and it focused on the foreclosed line of commerce, retail gasoline sales in the seven western states. It deemed 7 percent a significant fraction of that market to be foreclosed or unavailable to other suppliers, especially when Standard Oil Company of California was the largest of seven sellers in the area. All sellers used exclusive dealing contracts and entry seemed to be restricted as a consequence. The Supreme Court did not allow the practice. The contracts could be ended on short notice by either party, however, which limits their power of foreclosure, and such a feature might make the contracts allowable today.

See *Standard Oil Co. of California v. United States*, 337 U.S. 293, 69 S.Ct. 1051, 93 L.Ed. 1371 (1949).

---

[72] See, for example, *FTC v. Eastman Kodak Co.*, 274 U.S. 619 (1927).

[73] Despite a decision assuring that Los Angeles discount houses could not be prevented from obtaining automobiles in *United States v. General Motors Corp.*, 384 U.S. 127 (1966), franchised dealers continue as the main means of selling automobiles. Dealers must be willing to sell to consumers from each others' areas, however, or they may be found guilty of agreeing to divide markets.

9.3 **THE FIRM AND MARKET INNOVATION**

A patent is effectively a legal exclusive contract, in that it allows the patent holder to exclude others. When fully exercised, that power to exclude can be converted into market power, yet an innovating firm may be treated leniently under antitrust law. Indeed, over the last 30 years, courts have frequently absolved dominant firms from behaving illegally as long as they have been introducing new products or more competitive ways of operating that benefit consumers. Market definitions are more flexible where markets are changing rapidly and new entrants are expected. Where every day brings change, practices that would otherwise restrain trade may also be allowed if they improve a product or a service for consumers. There is a resistance to chilling competitive urges, especially in dynamic settings where progress is advancing rapidly so even a substantial market advantage may not be long lived. Some examples show this altered interpretation, and the *Microsoft* case is considered in detail.

Broader Interpretation in Dynamic Industries

In the 1970s, International Business Machines Corporation (IBM) redesigned its mainframe computers so rival peripheral products were incompatible with them, but a court allowed the redesign because it found it qualitatively superior to the old design.[74] The FTC also allowed aggressive expansion of production capacity in the titanium dioxide industry by powerful Du Pont.[75] In its decision, the FTC made clear that it did not want to block aggressive competition, even when monopoly might be a possible result.

In another example of the considerations that arise in dynamic industries, a maker of cameras, Berkey Photo, Inc., argued that Eastman Kodak Company had used exclusionary tactics to protect its strong market position in photographic film. Kodak had introduced a new film to go with its newly designed Instamatic camera, and Berkey sought early disclosure of the new camera design so it could make a competing camera that also would use the new film. The court held that such early disclosure would allow competitors to free ride on Kodak's research and development efforts, thereby reducing its incentive to innovate. The court also thought that a requirement for disclosure would be extremely difficult to administer.[76]

Today, the government is usually successful whenever it opposes a merger, but mergers in new and fast-changing markets may be more difficult for the government to prevent. For example, in 2004 the DOJ attempted to block the merger of two U.S. providers of software for maintaining financial and employee records in large businesses, Oracle Corporation and PeopleSoft, Inc. Oracle had tried a hostile takeover of PeopleSoft, and their battle had lasted 15 months and spawned other lawsuits before this decision. But the federal district court judge in San Francisco found the DOJ

---

[74] See *California Computer Products, Inc. v. International Business Machines Corp.*, 613 F.2d 727 (9th Cir. 1979).

[75] See *E.I. du Pont de Nemours & Co.*, 96 F.T.C. 650 (1980).

[76] See *Berkey Photo, Inc. v. Eastman Kodak Co.*, 603 F.2d 263 (2nd Cir. 1979).

definition of the relevant market, which focused on large-firm applications, too narrow, especially in the particularly dynamic software business where many potential entrants exist, including Microsoft.

In many of these cases, owners of intellectual property acted aggressively to win consumers in changing situations. Courts are very reluctant to chill such efforts because doing so would discourage competitive action. So they look to see whether benefits of innovation go to consumers, and where they find benefits they tend to go easy on the active firm.

The *Microsoft* Case

A new antitrust activism arose in the 1990s. It was stimulated by new technologies—Internet commerce and its network characteristics on the one hand, and developments in economics such as game theory and transaction costs on the other. In the 1990s Microsoft Corporation came to dominate the operating systems of personal computers with its Windows operating system, which ran more than 90 percent of the world's Intel-compatible personal computers. Private firms complained about Microsoft, and the federal government considered whether to take action.

The *Microsoft* case is important because it involves new and complex technology, with network relationships, that is changing rapidly. An operating system is like a network in the way it ties together users and defines their needs. Those who write application programs, such as word-processing programs, want to write them for the most widely used operating system because its network offers the largest market for the application. So more applications are written for the most widely used operating system, thereby reinforcing its position. A firm with the dominant operating system has network advantages it may try to preserve by blocking alternative operating systems. That was the charge against Microsoft.

Background

In 1993, the Department of Justice took over an investigation begun by the Federal Trade Commission in 1989, and concluded that several Microsoft practices were objectionable. First, Microsoft granted discounts to computer manufacturers—called original equipment manufacturers (OEMs),—when they agreed to pay for installing the Windows operating systems in all the computers they sold. That is, payment was based on the total number of computers shipped rather than the number that actually contained the Windows operating system. Once entered into, this contract motivated the OEM to install Microsoft's product in all units shipped because the OEM would have to pay for the product in all the units it sold anyway, so the producer of a competing operating system would have difficulty selling it to that OEM. Competitors also accused Microsoft of tying, by requiring customers to purchase Microsoft applications to obtain the Windows operating system. To prevent such contracts, the Antitrust Division of the Justice Department negotiated a settlement with Microsoft in 1994.

A federal judge must approve any antitrust settlement that the Justice Department proposes, and the judge of the U.S. Court for the District of Columbia rejected it on grounds that it was inadequate to contain the anticompetitive designs of Microsoft. But in 1995, the appellate court reversed the judge and approved the settlement, in which Microsoft agreed to stop using its offending contracts.[77] The appellate court required that the case be assigned to another judge to oversee compliance, and it was assigned to Judge Thomas Penfield Jackson. Many observers wondered at the time whether questions concerning Microsoft's royalty contracts with OEMs and tying arrangements with customers were really settled.

Almost immediately after the agreement was approved, competitors complained that Microsoft was violating it. An especially vigorous complaint came from the Internet browser, Netscape Navigator (later purchased by America Online, Inc.), charging that Microsoft required consumers to buy its own Internet browser, Microsoft Internet Explorer, to obtain its Windows 95 operating system. Because Microsoft Windows was the dominant operating system, what Netscape saw as a tying or bundling arrangement—Microsoft's Internet Explorer browser bundled with its Windows operating system—could seriously affect its ability to attract users to its Netscape Navigator browser. The Justice Department agreed with Netscape and in 1997 asked Judge Jackson to hold Microsoft in contempt for violating the 1995 agreement. Ordinarily a contempt order would impose a fine for the violation, but Judge Jackson proposed injunctive relief, which would simply prevent the practice. In 1998, an appeals court disallowed the injunction and permitted Microsoft's combination of an Internet browser with its operating system on grounds that it was convenient for consumers and could be accomplished at lower cost.

The Main Illegal-Behavior Case

In 1998, 19 states joined the Department of Justice in a suit that accused Microsoft of engaging in a "pattern or practice of illegal behavior." Under such a charge the defendant can be guilty whether or not every one of its challenged acts was a violation. Based on a 1962 Supreme Court decision,[78] the pattern or practice of illegal behavior can be supported by internal documents that reveal such a pattern or practice within the firm. One of the objectionable practices of Microsoft was tying its Internet Explorer browser free with its Windows operating system. Netscape Navigator, which at the time had been charging a fee for the use of its browser, claimed it was handicapped by this tying, or bundling, practice, and the government agreed. In addition, the government plaintiffs accused Microsoft of making questionable arrangements with Internet service providers and OEMs to carry Microsoft's Internet Explorer browser instead of Netscape Navigator's browser and of following other unlawful strategies in an effort to thwart competition. And they accused Microsoft of undermining Java software, which could adapt applications to any operating system and thus make Microsoft Windows less important as a network.

The government plaintiffs described Microsoft as intending to prevent two developments that could weaken its dominance. First, Microsoft wanted to prevent widespread use of Netscape Navigator Internet browser when it burst on the scene in

---

[77] See *U.S. v. Microsoft Corp.*, 1995–2 Trade Cas. CCH Para. 71,096 (D.D.C. 1995).

[78] See *Continental Ore Co. v. Union Carbide and Carbon Corp.*, 370 U.S. 690 (1962).

the mid-1990s. Browsers potentially could make possible many computer applications through Internet access, with simple operating systems other than Microsoft's. So control of browser access to the Internet would help Microsoft maintain its grip on the operating systems market. Second, Microsoft wanted to prevent the ascendancy of Sun Microsystem, Inc.'s Java software, because it would allow many applications to be adapted smoothly to alternative operating systems. With the operating system as a platform, Java designed cross-platform applications, applications that could function on any operating system. If applications did not have to be written for the Windows operating system, that would eliminate the network advantage of operating system dominance that was benefitting Microsoft.

Judge Jackson handled the trial expeditiously without a jury; it ended in July of 1999. Judge Jackson issued findings of fact in November, 1999, essentially accepting the position of the government plaintiffs that Microsoft had violated antitrust law. In April, 2000, Judge Jackson issued his Conclusions of Law. He found Microsoft in violation of the Sherman Act by using exclusionary practices in an effort to control operating systems for Intel-compatible, or IBM-style, personal computers through a pattern or practice of illegal behavior. The company had unlawfully tied its Internet Explorer browser to its dominant Windows operating system in an effort to monopolize the market for Internet browsers. By distributing its browser free of charge, it was also guilty of predatory pricing. And by several practices, Microsoft illegally discouraged use of cross-platform Java software.

In June of 2000, Judge Jackson ordered that Microsoft be divided into two companies. One company would produce and sell Microsoft's operating systems products, and the other would sell its software applications and products related to the Internet. Structural remedies such as this are desirable in principle, to the extent they can address problems directly and avoid the need for continuing oversight and enforcement. But structural remedies in cases of monopolization such as Microsoft's, which was not achieved by merger or by collusion, are rare and have not been particularly successful.[79] Structural remedies were often imposed in times of change, and other events overwhelmed their effects. Separation into two companies was to avoid tying or bundling opportunities between Microsoft's applications and its operating system. But there is also a vertical, or complementary, relationship between the two new organizations that would be created, the operating system company and the applications company. Separate firms selling complements may have private incentives to set higher prices than a single firm would set.

In addition to this structural remedy, Judge Jackson ordered conduct remedies. These remedies would require that Microsoft give non-Microsoft software developers the same application program interface information that goes to Microsoft software developers, and that it charge uniform license fees to all original equipment manufacturers, unless cost differences could justify variations. Microsoft also could not discriminate among OEMs or Internet service companies in providing technical or promotional assistance, unless justified by a business reason, and it had to give greater freedom to computer manufacturers in designing the opening screen of the

---

[79] For a thorough review of such cases since the Sherman Act was passed, see Crandall (2001).

Windows operating system. Microsoft would have to offer unbundled versions of integrated new product capabilities and forego exclusive dealing arrangements with original equipment manufacturers and Internet service providers. These remedies were not to be put into effect until all appeals were completed.

Microsoft's Appeal and the Settlement

Microsoft appealed the decision, and in June 2001, the Court of Appeals for the District of Columbia affirmed part, reversed part, and remanded part of the decision to a new district court for determining whether tying had occurred and to decide remedies. Microsoft would not be broken into two firms. The Court of Appeals agreed that Microsoft had a monopoly in the market for operating systems, but being a monopoly is not enough to violate Section 2 of the Sherman Act. A firm must also be found to have engaged in anticompetitive behavior. In its licenses with OEMs, Microsoft did not allow removal of icons from the start page, with the result that its Internet Explorer browser had to be shown. OEMs were reluctant to show two browser icons because that would raise their customer support costs. Consequently, the license that required the Internet Explorer icon effectively excluded the Netscape Navigator browser, and the court found the licenses to be exclusive contracts that violated Section 2 of the Sherman Act. Microsoft also made exclusive dealing agreements with Internet access providers, independent software vendors, and even Apple Computer, to make Internet Explorer the default browser or the only browser available to their customers. Because they blocked usage of Netscape Navigator, these exclusive agreements violated Section 2 of the Sherman Act.

Microsoft also behaved illegally in its actions to discourage the use of the cross-platform Java language. First, Microsoft signed exclusive agreements with independent software vendors to promote a Microsoft version of Java, which lacked the cross-platform capability because it actually worked only with the Windows operating system. Microsoft also offered a set of software development tools to independent software developers to help them in designing Java applications. Microsoft deceived the developers of Java applications, however, who never expected that the resulting applications would run only in the Windows environment. Microsoft also threatened harm to Intel to prevent it from supporting Java in ways that could have reduced reliance on Windows. The court found these actions against Java to be illegal, in violation of Section 2 of the Sherman Act.

The Justice Department settled with Microsoft in November 2001 on a proposed consent decree containing a mild set of penalties. Importantly, the agreement allows Microsoft to add anything it wishes to the Windows operating system, but the company accepted certain restrictions on its actions for a period of five years, to be extended if willfully violated. The review period has been extended two years to November 2009, mainly to ensure that the new Microsoft Internet Explorer browser will not favor a Microsoft search engine over competing search services such as Google.[80] Microsoft also is not allowed to retaliate against a software or hardware

---

[80] See Steve Lohr, U.S. Says "Microsoft Browser Is No Threat to Competition," *New York Times*, May 13, 2006, P. B3.

company for its competitive action. And Microsoft can no longer prevent an OEM from installing non-Microsoft software. Moreover, it is to sell to all OEMs under the same terms. Nine of the states participating in the litigation found the proposal too lenient and refused to support it.[81]

In November 2002, Judge Colleen Kollar-Kotelly of the Federal District Court in Washington ruled that the proposed consent agreement, with some additional features, would settle the case. The most important new feature Judge Kollar-Kotelly added to the agreement would have Microsoft disclose information to rival software companies so they can write applications software that will work smoothly on the Windows operating system. In addition, she required Microsoft to take compliance actions within the firm, by appointing a compliance officer and a compliance committee of its board of directors.

The antitrust effort against Microsoft is an exception to the tendency during the latter part of the twentieth century to prevent monopoly and oligopoly through merger policy. Since passage of the Hart-Scott-Rodino Antitrust Improvements Act in 1976, which requires prior approval for mergers involving large firms, the DOJ and FTC have tried to prevent monopoly and oligopoly from arising in the first place, by moving to stop mergers that would create them. Merger policy may not reach a rapidly growing firm in a new technological field, however, where a firm can grow to a dominant position without merger. Microsoft merged with many smaller firms, but it was a firm that grew rapidly to a dominant position in its market. As long as consumers appear to benefit from the products of such a dominant firm it may receive sympathetic treatment in U.S. courts.

BOX 9.7 Microsoft in Europe

The European Union has dealt more sternly with Microsoft than have U.S. authorities. In March 2004, after a five-year investigation, the European Competition Commission found that Microsoft had illegally tied the Windows Media Player to the Windows operating system. The Commission required that Microsoft offer a separate version of Windows, without Windows Media Player, and that any version that contained Windows Media Player was not to have a lower price than the version that lacked it. The Commission also fined Microsoft more than $500 million. Rivals approached the European Commission in early 2007, after Microsoft introduced its Vista operating system, to complain that the XAML web language it contains, which is intended to replace the current HTML, is entirely dependent on Windows and, therefore, represents an effort to extend Microsoft's operating system dominance.

See Ian Ayres and Barry Nalebuff, "Going Soft on Microsoft? The EU's Antitrust Case and Remedy," *The Economist's Voice*, 2005, 2: 1–10; and for an overview of European competition policy see http://ec.europa.eu/comm/competition/antitrust/overview/.

---

[81] These states were California, Connecticut, Florida, Iowa, Kansas, Massachusetts, Minnesota, West Virginia, and Utah. The District of Columbia also refused to support it

SUMMARY

Several major antitrust enforcement efforts that can affect market structure may be distinguished since the Sherman Act was passed, starting with one from 1904 to 1920 against turn-of-the-century monopolists, and then another from 1938 to 1953 aimed largely at oligopoly firms. An effort against mergers was undertaken in the 1950s and 1960s. With added 1976 legislation, which requires advance notification to the government of mergers and virtual approval before large mergers can take place, merger policy has become almost a routine administrative process. Also, important antitrust cases undertaken in the past 30 years have tended to bring antitrust policy closer to modern economic thinking.

A first category of antitrust effort to alter market structure involves the dominant, or monopoly, firm, which was treated inconsistently over the last century. Although monopoly trusts were broken up early in the twentieth century, use of the rule of reason in 1920 permitted the survival of dominant firms as long as they did not behave unreasonably. This policy changed in the middle of the twentieth century, after Alcoa was deemed to dominate the United States aluminum industry and to engage in anticompetitive behavior. Today a dominant firm is not illegal for reaching its position through superior performance. It can escape antitrust penalty if it can show it is not anticompetitive and it is serving consumers effectively.

A dominant firm that controls a facility needed by other competing firms may be required to allow competitors to use it under the "essential facilities" doctrine. It may be difficult for a dominant firm to stop participating in an arrangement with competitors if such nonparticipation handicaps a competitor. A firm in a dominant position that resorts to predatory pricing or harmful price discrimination should also expect to run afoul of antitrust law.

Strategic actions that restrain trade bring antitrust attention. Restraints of trade can usually be sorted into two kinds: horizontal restraints that affect competition directly, and vertical restraints that affect competitiveness along the product distribution chain. A major horizontal restraint is price fixing, which is almost illegal per se. Allocations of markets through arrangements such as exclusive dealerships may reduce competition between dealers in the same brand, but may be allowed if they enforce competition between brands. Horizontal conspiracies challenge directly the force of competition and generally are opposed. Joint ventures or information exchanges among firms may be allowed but must meet conditions to ensure that they do not restrain trade.

Vertical restraints have been treated more carefully in recent years under rule-of-reason procedures. Restrictions on product distribution arrangements, such as territorial allocations or assignment of different customer types to different dealers are now evaluated for their effect on market outcomes. Per se objection to vertical restraints other than resale price maintenance ended with the *Continental T.V., Inc. v. GTE Sylvania* case in 1977,[82] which opened the way for rule-of-reason evaluation of economic effects of vertical restraints. A restraint that offers economic benefits may be accepted. Similarly, resale price maintenance was virtually illegal per se for many years, but setting maximum retail

---

[82] See *Continental T.V., Inc. v. GTE Sylvania Inc.*, 433 U.S. 36, 97 S.Ct. 2549, 53 L.Ed.2d 568 (1977).

price was allowed after a rule-of-reason analysis in 1997 (*State Oil Co. v. Kahn*), and a pending case may extend the analysis to minimum price setting. If they support competition and efficiency, these practices are allowed; if they are thought not to do so they are denied. Exclusionary practices such as tying and exclusive dealing are usually opposed, but if they can foster competition and efficiency the courts may allow them.

A number of court decisions show that the benefit of the doubt is given to innovative firms competing in fast-changing, high-tech circumstances. Courts have allowed innovative dominant firms great discretion in choosing distribution schemes to bring new products or services to market. As long as the dominant firm can show that its products are better, courts have allowed it to follow innovative policies even when they are also exclusionary.[83]

Antitrust authorities resist the use of monopoly advantage in one market to gain advantage in another, even by an innovative firm. For example, the court found Microsoft guilty of using its monopoly power in operating systems for Intel-compatible personal computers to gain advantage in other markets. Specifically, it was able to reduce Netscape Navigator's share of the Internet browser market and to foil the cross-platform effectiveness of Java software. The court saw these and other steps as anticompetitive ways of preserving and strengthening Microsoft's monopoly in personal computer operating systems, but it imposed mild punishments.

Each legal decision involves great effort to settle the matter at issue in a sensible way while complying with proper legal procedures and compelling legal precedent. The Supreme Court chooses cases to consider on appeal and can choose them to treat important issues or to reconcile differing judgments across lower courts. In part because the outcome of an important case is deemed equitable in the circumstances and focused mainly to that end, it may not be the simplest to administer in the future. Indeed, the process seems almost oblivious to how cases arise, because rules are numerous and complicated, and tactics, such as delaying, can have an economic effect on outcomes. Yet the antitrust laws have surely affected the structure of American industries, and they have tended quite generally to broaden the scope for competition.

Antitrust policy seeks to preserve competition, but in some industries technology prevents competition from functioning well on its own. Then some extra-market regulation may be introduced to bring about socially desirable results. The regulation of such industries is the subject of Part II.

QUESTIONS

1. Suppose six firms in an industry have 15 percent shares of the market and a seventh firm has a 10 percent share.
   a. What is the Herfindahl-Hirschman Index (HHI) for this industry?
   b. Suppose two of the firms with 15 percent shares of the market merge. After the merger, what is the Herfindahl-Hirschman Index? Would this merger be

---

[83] For differing views on the wisdom of this policy, see Ordover and Willig (1981) and Sidak (1983).

allowed, according to the Horizontal Merger Guidelines that are contained in Appendix 8.1?

2. Suppose you manufacture a floor sweeping product, called a "Swisher," that sweeps wood and tile floors (not carpeted floors) and requires disposable paper inserts, which you also manufacture. Explain how you might price these products so you can price discriminate among your customers. Is your pricing practice legal?

3. The Miller-Tydings Act allowed states to pass retail-price-maintenance (RPM) laws without violating federal law. How would the existence of RPM affect contracts between manufacturers and retailers? Could the existence of RPM possibly be socially beneficial?

4. The Microsoft antitrust case attracted much attention. Its resolution may affect the monopolization standard that will be used in high-tech antitrust cases for some time to come. On one hand, through its more than 90 percent control of operating systems, Microsoft exerted control in applications (such as word processing) markets. Microsoft has handicapped competitors, such as the Netscape Navigator browser, by requiring its own Internet Explorer browser in licenses to original equipment manufacturers and by limiting convenient access to Netscape in other ways. On the other hand, the operating system and the applications are related in a vertical way, effectively making them complementary goods from the standpoint of consumers. So Microsoft is motivated to keep the combined price—the price across both operating system and applications levels—lower than separate monopolies in the two levels would charge.

   Using these two issues, tying and complementarity, discuss the proposal to split Microsoft into two firms, an operating system company and an applications company. Explain any problem that follows from creating two vertically related companies in this way. And discuss advantages that might follow from breaking the relationship between the applications and the operating system by creating two separate companies.

5. Consider the case of parts and service for Kodak photocopiers that was considered in the section Broader Interpretation in Dynamic Industries. If applied generally, and if firms were to consider its future effects, what might the decision in this case do to entry conditions in affected markets?

6. In March 2004, after a five-year investigation, the European Competition Commission found that Microsoft had illegally tied the Windows Media Player to the Windows operating system, and it required that Microsoft offer a version of Windows both with and without Windows Media Player. And the version that contained Windows Media Player was not to have a lower price than the version that did not have it. The Commission also fined Microsoft more than $500 million.

   a. Discuss the advantages and disadvantages for both Microsoft and consumers of the bundling of Windows Media Player with the Windows operating system.

   b. Would you expect the remedy chosen by the Commission to be an effective one?

PART 2
THE REGULATION
OF INDUSTRIES

For many years, when problems were found with competition, government regulation often replaced it. Whether a governmental solution would be better than market competition was not fully evaluated, nor was a governmental solution carefully designed. Problems were eventually seen with the resulting regulatory institutions, and some industries, starting with transportation, were deregulated and returned to regulation by competition. Other regulated industries were restructured to allow a greater role for competition.

To examine regulated industries, we must first consider the problems these industries caused for the functioning of competition and then study the institutions that governments created to regulate them. To serve social aims, industry regulation has to give practical form to those aims, from pricing principles to organizational forms. Knowledge about designing institutions has improved in recent years and is described in the early chapters of Part 2. Because problems can differ by industry and depend on the characteristics of each industry, a range of industries is then examined to show how these principles can be applied.

Postal service, examined first, is provided by a government owned monopoly public enterprise, and although liberalization has opened some services to competition, the monopoly remains. So a major postal service issue is pricing. Two industries, telecommunications and electricity, were regulated as monopolies and have recently had their structures radically changed to introduce elements of competition. In each case, technology opened the possibility of competition in part of the industry, and legal ways were found to allow competition. Transportation industries, on the other hand, most notably airlines, were deregulated so competition could replace regulators. Energy regulation treats coal, nuclear power, oil and natural gas, and a host of renewable resources like solar energy. Broadcasting is in large part a public good, and that complicates its competition with cable services, which are extending more broadly into telecommunications to offer telephone and Internet services. Thus, once-separate industries are now providing competition for each other.

10

Industry Regulation

When new airlines were allowed to enter the deregulated airline industry roughly 30 years ago, they brought new services, new methods, and lower prices to air travel, and the airline industry is still adjusting to the changes they caused. For over four decades after its creation in 1938, the Civil Aeronautics Board controlled prices and allowed no new entry on major routes, thus inhibiting changes in procedures and even in route structures. Setting aside the terrorist attacks in 2001, which seriously harmed the industry, the deregulation of airlines demonstrates vividly the effectiveness of competition in forcing changes that benefit consumers.

Although competition can bring self-adjusting market regulation, it can also be hampered in performing that regulatory role. For instance, entry may be difficult when large and inflexible investments are necessary, because then exit from the industry becomes so difficult. On the other hand, the *extremely easy* entry of a contestable market may make government regulation unnecessary, because the threat of competitive entry can then discipline even one firm in a market. Without such unusually easy entry, however, when scale economies are great the government may install a monopoly producer and guide the market by some form of government regulation. It may still be possible for competition to function in part of the industry while a government agency regulates the remainder.

In the choice between competition and government regulation, when should government intervene? And once government intervenes, because technology often influences the form of that intervention, a change in technology raises the question, How should government regulation be changed? What goals should be pursued when extramarket guidance is deemed necessary? Welfare economics offers a way to represent individuals in society, to assess their well-being, and thereby to evaluate the effects of alternative regulatory policies. Thus, conditions that interfere with competition may invite regulation by other means, but the aim is still to maximize economic welfare, as consumer plus producer surplus.

Technologies that complicate the smooth functioning of competition are those underlying television, telephone, water, natural gas, electricity, and railroad transportation to name a few examples. These are large, complex, usually network technologies, the use of which is guided in many countries by administrative or regulatory agencies rather than competitive markets. What is it about these technologies that prevents competition from serving the public well? Or what special features in the design of institutions or rules allow such technologies to be effective in serving the public welfare?

The legislatures that decide whether and, if so, how to intervene in markets do not function as precise mechanisms. In particular, they cannot make the small marginal adjustments that are possible in markets, and they afford only crude means of distilling and pursuing public goals. Legislators have their own goals, and corporate constituents who lobby expensively may win them to their views. As a result of this and other causes, governmental market regulation may not improve on competition and may even yield inferior results.

This chapter first considers reasons why competition fails, followed by a look at some problems inherent in government regulation. These factors are at the heart of optimal choices for market regulation. The chapter next explores how regulation by government has been transformed in recent years to allow competition to play a greater regulatory role. Finally, the chapter looks at criteria from welfare economics that can guide regulatory policies toward efficient outcomes.

10.1   WHEN COMPETITION FAILS TO REGULATE

Although competition can be a superb regulator, some technological conditions interfere with its functioning. One must understand these conditions to diagnose problems and fashion remedies. We begin by reviewing and elaborating conditions that handicap competition, such as economies of scale, high sunk costs, and network arrangements.

Economies of Scale and Economies of Scope

The functioning of competition is complicated when a technology offers great economies of scale. Economies of scale characterize the production of an output if operating at a larger scale lowers average cost. Even if it is not an entry barrier, economies of scale can complicate competition. Remember that if average cost is falling with output, marginal cost must lie below average cost. If a few competing firms all have scale economies, and force market price to the level of marginal cost as we expect, then that price lies below average cost, and all the firms lose money! Indeed, when economies of scale are very great relative to the size of the market, profit may be earned only after all but one of the firms have left the industry, and that one firm may operate as a monopoly. Generation, transmission, and distribution of electricity to customers approximated economies of scale in the past. In response, in the early twentieth century, one by one, states gradually eliminated competition. They created legal monopolies for their electricity industries and imposed governmental regulation.

Another technological property that can complicate the functioning of competition is the presence of economies of product scope. When one firm produces more than one product at lower cost than any combination of several more specialized firms could, it has economies of scope. The firm that is extensive enough to offer more products may then enjoy a cost advantage over other firms. A large telephone service provider may economically offer a range of products that a new entrant is unable to match. Monopoly is not a necessary outcome when economies of scope exist. If they are serious, however, and are combined with scale economies, the scope economies can make entry of new firms difficult. The entrant might have to offer many products from the beginning to achieve low costs, and raising large sums for that purpose can be difficult for a new and unknown firm. With scale economies as well, competing firms may be few in number and may struggle to find the optimal mix of products. Thus, especially when combined with economies of scale, economies of scope can handicap the competitive process.

Sunk Costs

Whether assets that are needed in a production process are specialized and long lasting also matters, because such properties affect the ease of entry to the industry. Entry is easier if the assets needed to enter an industry are few and inexpensive, or if they have many alternative uses and can be resold easily upon exit from the industry. Entry is easy then in part because *exit* is easy. Sunk costs are costs that cannot be withdrawn easily; they require commitment because they have to be in place a long time and that prevents easy exit. A nuclear power plant is a good example of sunk cost because it is costly, long lasting, and has no alternative use. When costs must be sunk, the entry decision is more formidable. With no sunk costs, entry is easy, and easy entry makes markets contestable. An entrant can challenge even a single incumbent firm in a contestable market if, given the quality of its products, the incumbent firm sets its prices too high.

Sunk costs thus tend to be greater when the lowest cost technology calls for very durable, specialized, and very costly capacity. Firms can often have capacity engineered so its durability is consistent with the time period over which it will be reliably used, or it may be designed to be flexible and to have other uses.[1] As a result, however, production is apt to be more costly per unit. Separate competing firms might maintain less durable and more flexible capacity, despite potentially higher costs. The uncertainty that invites this action could be due in part to lack of knowledge by each firm about others' actions. If that strategic source of risk could be removed through monopoly organization, durable and more efficient equipment might be used. By reducing uncertainty and fostering more coherent long-run planning, monopoly organization might thus permit more efficient production with more durable capacity.

This problem of nonoptimal technological choice might arise in competition when sunk costs are large. If each of several competing firms had in their cost structure a great proportion of sunk, fixed cost and a low proportion of variable cost, then a

---

[1] This argument is set out in Baumol and Willig (1981). See also von Weizsacker (1980).

drop in sales could lead to large losses because costs would barely decline at all. To avoid being caught in such an unprofitable condition, each competitor might prefer a less efficient but more flexible,[2] or less long-lived form of capacity. This could even be a desirable development if it brought forth investment capital more readily, but over the long run the result also could be less efficient than using the more durable, and more costly, technique.

Regulated monopoly, then, might be considered in place of competition to reduce investor risk and allow choice of more efficient technology. Building a dam for electricity generation and for water supply (and even for recreation) serves as an extreme example. Undertaking large, durable investments collectively through a public institution does not avoid the risks inherent in them, but it does spread those risks over so many individuals that each bears only a small amount.[3]

It is possible to overemphasize the need for coordination of large, durable investments as a reason for accepting monopoly rather than competitive markets. Coordination was once claimed necessary for the connection of telephone callers, for example, which could be complicated if each caller had to determine which (of many) firms served the party being called and then try to arrange the connection. But deregulation of long-distance telephone service was possible because contracts for service, aided by computer software to make connections, fostered sufficient coordination among competing suppliers. Similarly, digging up streets to lay electricity or communication lines may be claimed to interfere less with street use if one organization plans it rather than many separate ones. Perhaps if firms were charged for digging up city streets, incentives might be created to coordinate the needed construction and thus limit the interference it caused, although duplication might still be inefficient. Anytime competition can induce sufficient coordination, its well-known incentives for efficiency may bring benefits.

Network Economies and Compatibility

Industries that are subject to government regulation are often network industries. Highways, railroad tracks, electricity wires, mailboxes, natural gas pipelines, cable TV receptors, and even automated teller machines (ATMs) are connected through networks. Telephone, highway, or railroad networks allow two-directional use, while ATMs, over-the-air or cable television, and pipelines usually operate as one-way networks.

Networks offer both scale economies and externalities. Network externalities arise because separate network paths are actually complements. Adding one new path can make many new connections possible. If service is defined in terms of total connections, this positive externality can cause an *economy of scale*. Scope economies

---

[2] Stigler (1939) examined such possible effects of production flexibility. For examples in practice, see Mills (1984,1986) and Mills and Schumann (1985).

[3] See Arrow and Lind (1970) and McKean and Moore (1972).

Figure 10.1 *Two Star-Shaped Networks Connected by a Gateway*

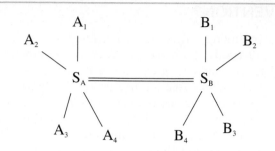

also arise in network industries because one firm with a central switch and network can offer more goods—calls to more parties, for example—at lower cost than can many different providers.

Figure 10.1 shows two star-shaped networks that are connected through a gateway between the two central switches. Externalities can exist within and across the two networks, and for connections to be possible between them, the systems must be *compatible*; they must be able to work easily with each other. If two railroad networks are to join at some point, for example, to be compatible their rails must be the same distance apart so trains can operate across both networks easily.

Quite different ownership configurations are possible for a network. Both A and B networks in Figure 10.1 may have the same owner, or there may be one owner of A and a different owner of B. Ownership of the entire network by a single party favors compatibility, because a single owner would want interconnection between networks to realize a greater network externality benefit. On the other hand, that single owner would like to limit competition. Separate ownership may offer more competition, but it can complicate the functioning of the network, including agreement on compatible technology. Separate network owners might even differ over the advantages of compatibility, perhaps depending on whether it would bring more opportunity by invading others' networks or more intense competition on one's own network. Compatibility may be favored when one technology offers much lower cost than any other, because then excluding others by choosing a different technology may be costly. Even with compatible technology, the networks would have to agree on prices for each others' services when both networks are involved in serving a customer.

Thus, there are technological conditions—such as economies of scale or scope, sunk costs, or network relationships—that may call for modification, in some form, of the customary practices underlying competition. Regulatory policy in such conditions requires an understanding of the technology and the social goals to be pursued, and the idea of economic welfare can help to show what outcomes are desirable. Although government regulation may function where competition does not, it may also weaken incentives for efficiency and not respond adequately to change.

10.2 COMPETITIVE MARKETS OR GOVERNMENT INTERVENTION?

When can competition among sellers work to ensure their efficient production and cause sound pricing of goods and services? When can competition fail to do so?[4] Competition would seem to fail with great scale economies, particularly when costly and durable investments (sunk costs) are necessary. Competitors would then drive prices to marginal cost, below average cost, and lose money. In such circumstances the government has often installed a single producer, as a **natural monopoly**, meaning that the industry is best organized as a monopoly. The government also protected that single producer from new entry through a statutory grant of monopoly franchise. Public utilities provided electricity through this form of organization for most of the twentieth century. Such government control raises questions about which economic goals might emerge from the political process that sanctions it.

In the last quarter of the nineteenth century, the public's faith in markets was not high, whereas regulation by governmental institutions—which was rare—was thought to be reliable and costless. So when problems arose in markets, governments chose to regulate. The late Nobel laureate, George Stigler, humorously likened this embrace of governmental regulation of markets to a judge of two singers in a contest; on hearing the first singer, the judge immediately awards the prize to the second. Today we are less likely to turn markets over to government regulators at the first sign of problems, because a century has made us more aware of the difficulties of government regulation, and we are now more willing to accept alternative market arrangements when they appear workable.

Whether competition or the government regulates a market, its technology may change, and the change can improve or worsen the effectiveness of competition to regulate. That means that after a problem is diagnosed and a regulatory solution is found and implemented, the basis for the solution may change. Then a new diagnosis of the regulatory institution is needed so it can adapt to the new technology.

Theories of Regulation

Many institutions influence economic activity in Western countries. Political institutions create regulatory institutions, for instance, and courts become involved when regulatory agencies and firms disagree.[5] Political institutions seldom function as well as markets in generating economic welfare, and some awareness of their different structure is valuable in considering their role in the process of regulation.

Social choice and **public choice** are fields of study concerned specifically with how collective choices might be well made, even between possible Pareto optima.[6]

---

[4] Conditions that can keep markets from serving welfare goals are treated in Part III. There competition can operate but does not have ideal effects. The problem here in Part II is that competition might not even be able to function effectively.

[5] For a review of political influences, see Wilson (2003).

[6] See Section 2.3 in Chapter 2. For classic social choice analyses, see Arrow (1963), Buchanan and Tullock (1965), Feldman (1980), and Mueller (1989). Applications of social choice methods to regulation may be found in Buchanan (1968) and in Maloney, McCormick, and Tollison (1984).

The prevalent institution of social choice in Western democracies is that of voting by individuals, even in legislatures, and problems of reaching socially desirable outcomes gives rise to other theories of regulation. A public interest theory was developed early. It presumed that well-intentioned public representatives would pursue normative goals, but outcomes did not comply with this prediction. Lobbying and rent seeking explained outcomes more often, and sometimes a regulated industry seemed to be captured by those from the industry when they ran it as regulators. An economic theory of regulation takes several of these influences into account, but it is still too broad in its implications to allow good empirical tests of which theory is best. All may be useful in trying to explain a particular governmental regulatory outcome.

Social Choice and Public Choice

For reaching collective decisions, one common voting rule we are all familiar with is majority rule. As a social choice rule, majority voting is surprisingly different from individual choice. For instance, majority voting easily can lead to intransitive, or inconsistent, choices that we assume a rational individual would never make. Problems in finding agreement in legislatures lie behind most of the political influences on regulation.

Consider three possible expenditures a community might make: to construct an airport (A), a bridge (B), or a coliseum (C). A majority of the community's citizens may favor an airport over a bridge, another majority may favor the bridge over a coliseum, and still another majority may favor the coliseum over an airport, whereas one individual would never be expected to fall into such irrationality.[7] Table 10.1 shows the preference or rankings of airport, bridge, and coliseum by three thoroughly rational individuals, A, B, and C. A majority (A and C) prefers airport to bridge, a majority (A and B) prefers bridge to coliseum, and a majority (B and C) prefers coliseum to airport.

One way to avoid such inconsistency is to offer only two options to the public for a vote. Then an odd number of voters assures a social choice by majority rule. Even then, whoever controls the voting agenda and chooses the two options can greatly

TABLE 10.1 An Example of Inconsistency in Majority Voting

	Individual Preference Rankings		
Project	**A**	**B**	**C**
Airport	1	3	2
Bridge	2	1	3
Coliseum	3	2	1

---

[7] This voting problem has been known as Condorcet's problem for over 200 years. For the original treatment, see Condorcet (1785). It was given fuller, modern, form by Nobel laureate Kenneth Arrow (1963). For a voting analysis in the context of nuclear power plant location, see Wood (1981).

influence the outcome.[8] Our tendency to array political issues on a greatly simplified scale, from "right" to "left," may actually help to make majority rule more effective, although it also cedes power to those who set the agenda.

Political institutions such as majority rule are also capable of generating unwanted outcomes, as Nobel laureate James Buchanan (1962)—a leading public choice theorist— demonstrated. Professor Buchanan argued against replacing market institutions with governmental or political institutions because of imperfections or market failure, such as an externality, without noting possible imperfections in the alternative institution being embraced. For instance, he pointed out how, in the absence of carefully considered restrictions, a majority could bring repeated harm to a minority under seemingly democratic political procedures.

Realizing the limitations of political mechanisms for social choice can be useful in tracing possible consequences when economic issues reach political institutions. Their inherent imperfections owe much to the fact that voting is less precise than market transactions as a means for expressing or for serving citizen preferences. Voting and political institutions in general often are called upon to deal with difficult economic choices that markets cannot easily handle, so it is not surprising that problems arise in making the choices. Those problems may invite parties who can exploit the imprecision of public choice to bring forward issues that they can use to their advantage in a political decision process.

BOX 10.1 Politics and Prices: Some Examples

Political influences in public utility and public enterprise pricing are present to a considerable degree, as a few examples show. Professor Sam Peltzman (1971) found evidence that customers benefitted in regulated liquor pricing. The customers were more numerous and, therefore, more important politically. He did not find this result for public utility pricing, however, perhaps because the managers of regulated firms had more influence through regulatory hearings. Economists Stephen Littlechild and J. J. Rousseau (1975) found that the rulings of a state regulatory commission favored residents of the state, relative to customers who were not residents. That pattern was found also in the setting of rates for Union Pacific Railroad, an issue deliberated in the *Smyth vs. Ames* (1898) decision (Huneke 1983). Political influence was seen by economists Leonard Waverman (1977), who found public enterprise telephone pricing in Great Britain favored richer customers, and Leroy Jones (1985), who observed lower prices for urban rather than rural customers of public enterprises in developing countries. Judge Richard Posner (1971) regarded regulatory agencies generally as taxation authorities, able to confer benefits on politically effective customer groups at the expense of unorganized consumers.

---

[8] See Plott and Levine (1978).

Public Interest Theory

An early **public interest** theory of regulation urged regulatory intervention when ideal outcomes would not be achieved, as when economies of scale were great relative to demand, which was the case in electricity years ago, or when externalities prevented competitive markets from reaching efficient outcomes. The basis for this view is normative in that, compared with an ideal outcome, analysis shows flaws in the market. There could be a failure to reach minimum cost with economies of scale or a failure to avoid serious negative externalities.

Under the public interest theory, political representatives act to pursue ideal outcomes. They faithfully follow normative guidelines and seek efficiency or other wholesome aims. Empirical evaluations, however, have not supported the public interest theory. Politicians have their own concerns, such as reelection to public office. Each business firm has intense interest in certain political outcomes and not only support politicians who favor them but also hire lobbyists who understand the political process and can advance firm or industry interests.

Lobbying and Rent Seeking

Interested parties **lobby**, or try to persuade, government leaders to support their positions. Indeed, history suggests that regulation frequently benefits the regulated parties.[9] Social choice theory shows how political forums, such as legislatures, face a high cost of reaching agreement, and this is especially true when agreement is necessary for regulatory purposes.[10] To persuade legislators to incur such costs requires strong, or costly, lobbying efforts. Many possibilities exist for government authority to improve the position of a particular business, from tax advantages, such as not counting stock options for managers as a company expense, to rules that make declaring bankruptcy more difficult for consumers.

The mere possibility that governmental authority will grant a desired outcome can change the political situation fundamentally, for it leads parties to expend effort to obtain that outcome.[11] Consider the effort to obtain monopoly rents, which are the benefits from a monopoly position. That effort is called rent seeking, and it can alter our assessment of the welfare loss from monopoly. Suppose the award of a statutory monopoly position yields profit. Then those who want to attain the monopoly position might devote effort to do so, and that effort could use up resources. Indeed, contending parties might even use resources equal to all the expected profit. If that happens, the monopoly profit that ultimately results will not be the social benefit of producers' surplus, because real resources will have been used up—perhaps in lawyers' and lobbyists' time—trying to obtain the monopoly profit. Also, if government attempts later to deregulate and eliminate monopoly profit, it will encounter difficulty, because affected parties will lose the real resources they devoted to obtaining the monopoly

---

[9] See Posner (1969, 1975).

[10] See Ehrlich and Posner (1974).

[11] See Posner (1975) and Tullock (1967).

BOX 10.2 Lobbying Congress

A well-known Washington, D.C. lobbyist, Jack Abramoff, organized campaign contributions to federal legislators, job opportunities for their staffers or spouses, lavish trips for them to exotic locations, tickets to sporting events, and meals at upscale restaurants. In return, according to his January, 2006, guilty plea agreement, Abramoff won help from politicians in appropriating funds and advancing legislation that benefitted him and his clients. Abramoff's plea agreement, and that of his former business associate, Michael Scanlon, implicated one member of Congress specifically. Investigation of other legislators continues in this case, but in the past members of Congress have claimed wide scope for their actions in "the sphere of legitimate legislative activity." And they have rarely been convicted without very specific evidence that they used their offices to award benefits in return for the favors they received.

See Anne Marie Squeo, "Round 2 in Abramoff Scandal," *Wall Street Journal*, February 4, 2006, p. A4.

and will fight hard to recover them.[12] This rent seeking incentive, to devote resources in an effort to acquire monopoly or other benefit, was not foreseen when economic regulation was first undertaken.

Capture Theory

Over time, the firms in an industry may **capture** the government regulators who regulate them. Capturing regulators means that the individuals who serve as regulators sympathize with the industry and favor the firms they are supposed to regulate. Regulators may be captured when they are drawn from executive positions in the regulated industry because of their knowledge of the industry. That knowledge of the industry, however, can also encompass loyalty to the firms in the industry.

Another means of capture arises from the frequent movement of individuals not only to regulatory positions but also from government back into the industry. Such movement is so common that it has been characterized suspiciously as the **revolving door**. It first produces regulators who are sympathetic to the industry because of their experience in the industry. Then it invites them further to be supportive with the promise of even more important positions within the industry after they leave their regulatory posts. That is, the prospect of continued employment in the industry helps to keep them from acting against firms in the industry who might later provide their main employment opportunities.

Economic Theory

The economic theory of regulation first envisaged a demand from the public at large for correction of inefficient or inequitable market practices, a demand to which politicians responded.[13] But the economic theory has proceeded with many careful analyses

---

[12] See McCormick, Shughart, and Tollison (1984).
[13] See Johnson (1984).

of the regulatory process, usually finding parties acting in their own self interest. Instead of a vague demand from the public, Nobel laureate George Stigler (1971) conceived that potential supplier benefit (benefit for businessmen) provided a *demand for regulation,* while politicians, in response, control the *supply of regulation.* The demand may come when businessmen hire lobbyists who try to persuade politicians to support their private aims. Stigler's explanation is consistent with the view of Nobel laureate James Buchanan, who with Gordon Tullock (1965), conceived and represented self-interested parties in the political decision process rather than the altruistic actors postulated in the public interest theory. Unlike the public interest theory, this self-interest approach can explain the regulation of industries such as trucking, in which competition functioned quite well but trucking firms that wanted protection from competition influenced legislators to win helpful regulation.

Many examples support the economic theory. Historian Gabriel Kolko's (1963) interpretation of early railroad leaders trying to obtain regulation that would limit destructive competition is consistent with this self-interest pattern but is not explained by the public interest theory.[14] Economist Sam Peltzman (1971) found public utility prices influenced for political reasons. These are also the effects that Judge Richard Posner (1971) reflected when he portrayed regulatory agencies as taxation authorities conferring benefits on politically effective groups.

Thus, a range of theories helps to explain government regulation. There is a measure of wishful thinking in the public interest theory, because public officials may serve their own interests. Social choice theory shows how difficult it is to reach decisions through political institutions, and lobbying, rent seeking, and capture theory reveal how the institutions of government may be exploited for private benefit. The economic theory of regulation encompasses incentives more broadly than other theories and expects the analysis of private motives to explain regulatory outcomes.

The Scope of Regulation

One influence on whether industries are regulated by competition or by government is how effectively entry can discipline firms in an industry. Here we review contestable market theory and show how it can influence the form of government regulation.

Contestable Markets and Sustainable Prices

A contestable market offers competitive incentives for efficiency. When sunk costs are not present, entry to (and exit from) an industry can be free and easy because funds need not be sunk in irretrievable form. A new firm need not raise enormous sums of money, and whatever must be applied to the entry effort can be recovered if prospects in the market should collapse. Properties of production and cost that support free entry can make regulation unnecessary. The resulting market is contestable, because entrants can challenge an incumbent firm even when it is the only firm in the market.[15]

---

[14] Stigler and Friedland (1962) had given empirical support to this view by finding that prices were not very much lower in states that introduced regulation. For examples in specific industries, see Anderson (1981) or Brock (1981).

[15] For a description of contestable market theory, see Baumol, Panzer, and Willig (1982).

In a contestable market, an efficient monopoly that enjoys scale or scope economies can set prices that sustain its position. Such prices are called **sustainable** prices. When prices are sustainable, a less efficient supplier cannot enter to upset the efficient outcome. Because entry is otherwise easy, however, the monopoly cannot set high prices to earn extra profits without losing markets to equally efficient entrants. Thus, if sustainable prices can exist, entry can serve to discipline even a single supplier because efficient performance can protect it from entry. Then extra regulatory institutions are unnecessary.[16]

To better understand how the most efficient arrangement may not protect a firm when prices are not sustainable, imagine four neighboring farmers who want irrigation and flood control systems for their farms and face costs shown in Table 10.2. Each farmer can install a one-farm system for $100,000. If two farmers get together they can build a joint system for $150,000. Three farms can build a three-farm system for $180,000. If a single system serves all four farms, the cost will be $260,000. What is the most efficient solution to the problem for the four farms, and can a single price per farm sustain that solution in the sense that all of the farms will be happy to pay that price?

If you considered all possible combinations of solutions (4 single-farm systems, 1 single-farm system with 1 three-farm system, 2 two-farm systems, and 1 four-farm system), you should find that one four-farm system, at $260,000, is the least costly way to irrigate all four farms. That suggests that a price of $65,000 per farm ($260,000/4) leads to the best arrangement. If that price of $65,000 per farm is set, however, three of the farmers may band together and install the three-farm system for $180,000, or $60,000 each. Then the fourth farm would be left having to go it alone for $100,000. And the four farms would have to spend $180,000 + $100,000 = $280,000, which is inefficient compared with the four-farm system costing $260,000. Thus, the most efficient four-farm system is not sustained by a uniform price per farm that will cover all costs. In this example, free contracting, which is like free entry, does not guarantee an efficient outcome.

Notice that if a supplier was required to supply the entire market at any offered price, the price of $65,000 per farm in this example *would be sustainable*.

TABLE 10.2 Costs of Irrigation Systems

Number of Farms	Total Cost	Cost per Farmer
1	$100,000	$100,000
2	$150,000	$75,000
3	$180,000	$60,000
4	$260,000	$65,000

---

[16] These ideas also allow a precise definition of cross subsidy. See Faulhaber (1975).

Only the four-farm system can serve all farms at its $65,000 price. The problem arises when a supplier can serve only part of the market (three farms). There is, thus, a difference between allowing **partial entry**, such as entry to serve only three farms in this case, and requiring **full entry**, which makes an entrant promise to serve all who wish to consume at whatever price the entrant announces. One should distinguish *sustainability* against *partial* entry from *sustainability* against *full* entry, because sustainability against *partial* entry is more difficult to achieve.

One property of the firm's cost function that is necessary for prices to be sustainable, although it is not sufficient, is *subadditivity*. Consider a single-product firm's cost function $C(q)$, where q is the sum of outputs that might be produced in the firm or in separate firms, each firm indicated by i. In the latter case, we have

$$\Sigma_{i=1}^{n} q_i = q; \; q_i \geq 0$$

The cost function is subadditive if

$$\Sigma_{i=1}^{n} C(q_i) > C(\Sigma_{i=1}^{n} q_i).$$

Essentially, subadditivity exists when the sum of costs of producing a product in separate organizations ($\Sigma_{i=1}^{n} C(q_i)$) exceeds the cost of producing that amount of the product in one organization ($C(q)$), and it thus characterizes economies of scale. The various quantities, or q_i's, in the inequality above are the different amounts of the *same* good that different organizations produce. Because it means that a monopoly could produce at lower cost than competing firms, it is also called a *natural monopoly* condition.

With slight modification the inequality for subadditivity can define economies of scope for a multi-product firm. Let the different values of i represent quantities of different *products*. Then the condition is:

$$\Sigma_{i=1}^{n} C(q_i) > C(q_1, q_2, \ldots q_n).$$

This inequality states that the cost of producing n different products in n different firms ($\Sigma_{i=1}^{n} C(q_i)$) is greater than the cost of producing the n products in one firm ($C(q_1, q_2, \ldots q_n)$). This is the requirement for economies of scope to exist.

The average cost function $AC(q)$ in Figure 10.2 illustrates these ideas for the special case of only one output. First, observe that the firm could satisfy demand D_1 by setting price equal to average cost of P_M^*. No other firm using the same technology and efficiency could enter at a lower price and survive. So the price P_M^* is sustainable when demand is at D_1. It is sustainable against partial entry and full entry.

The average cost function $AC(q)$ satisfies the subadditivity condition up to an output of $\bar{q}$. Beyond output $\bar{q}$, market quantities could be divided between two firms and each could achieve lower average cost than the single firm, which at $\bar{q}$ is experiencing decreasing returns and increasing average cost. At output q_M, which is less than $\bar{q}$, the cost function is still subadditive, because breaking the output of q_M into two parts and producing them separately costs more. For example, $C(q_e) + C(q_{M-e}) > C(q_M)$.

Figure 10.2 *Subadditivity and Sustainability*

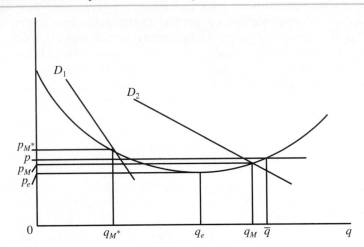

Despite this subadditivity, if demand is at D_2, a price of P_M is not sustainable against partial entry, where partial entry is entry to serve only a part of the market. In Figure 10.2, for instance, a new entrant using the same technology could enter at the lower price of P_e, supply only part of the industry—the quantity q_e—and break even. In that case, the incumbent firm would be left with the task of producing $q_M - q_e$ at higher cost. Clearly the result would be less efficient than having a single supplier. This example demonstrates that, while a subadditive cost function is necessary for sustainable prices, it does not guarantee them. Subadditivity is not sufficient; it does not ensure sustainability.

Now consider a policy of requiring full entry. Under full entry, at whatever price the entrant announces, all consumers who wish to be served must be served. In regulating the household goods moving industry, for instance, the Interstate Commerce Commission implemented this policy by requiring carriers designated as **common carriers** to serve anyone who wants service at announced rates. In Figure 10.2, if such full entry is required of all entrants, even with demand at D_2, the price P_M is sustainable. The reason is that an entrant who must serve the full market cannot provide only q_e units; consumers prefer a larger quantity at the price, p_e. At the point where p_e meets the demand curve, the entrant's average cost exceeds price, so the entrant loses money and the price p_e does not succeed against a policy that requires full entry, where all can buy at that announced price. Thus, with demand at D_2, the price P_M is sustainable against full entry even though it is not sustainable against partial entry.

The airline industry was deregulated at the end of the 1970s in part because it was judged to be close to a contestable market. Entry into particular airline routes is quite easy, although product differentiation can moderate price competition and evidence since deregulation indicates that the airline industry is not perfectly contestable. Nevertheless, prices appear to be sustainable and deregulation brought to the industry innovative new entrants with lower costs.

Subsidy-Free Prices

Another requirement that must be met for prices to be sustainable is that the prices be subsidy-free, meaning that no product is contributing to the cost of another product. To examine the subsidy possibility, we first require that total revenues equal total costs. Two conditions, which are consistent with each other as long as total revenues equal total costs, describe subsidy-free prices: (1) the stand-alone test—the revenues (prices times quantities) paid by any subset of products must not exceed the full costs of serving that group of consumers alone, and (2) the incremental-cost test—revenues (prices times quantities) for any subset of goods must be at least great enough to cover the incremental costs of adding that subset of goods. When these conditions are not satisfied, a subsidy must be present in the prices. If such a subsidy is present, the prices are not sustainable. One or more products that provide revenue to cover the subsidy are priced too high, so entry is possible. When an entrant serves the consumers who had been paying too much, that is the equivalent of those consumers standing alone.

Subsidy-free prices thus yield sufficient revenue to cover the cost of meeting market demands at announced prices. In addition, the revenue from *any* subset of the goods produced—or from *any* subset of customers—cannot exceed the cost of producing that subset by itself; this is the stand-alone test. If this test is not satisfied, the consumers who pay more than the cost of serving them can do better. They can go into business for themselves, or an entrepreneur may recognize the situation and enter the market to serve them. As a result, they can stand alone. If prices do not at least cover incremental costs for any subset of goods, the other consumers would find it in their interest to have the firm stop selling those goods. That is why prices that are not subsidy-free are not sustainable: if prices are not subsidy free, some of the parties involved can do better. In such a case, a regulator might have to bar entry to protect against inefficient entry.

In the example involving the irrigation of four farms, we found that the price of $65,000 per farm would not be sustainable against partial entry. We can now see that the price of $65,000 in that case was not subsidy free. It would not pass the stand-alone test, because three farms could make a more favorable arrangement on their own at $60,000 each. If technology changed, say to make a four-farm system cost $220,000 instead of $260,000, then the resulting price of $55,000 per farm ($220,000/4) *would* be sustainable, and it would be subsidy free. That shows how technological change might alter the means of, and the need for, regulation.

Technological Change and Regulation

Technological change may alter the features of an industry or part of an industry. Microwave technology reduced the scale economies in long-distance telephone service, for example, and combined-cycle turbines reduced the scale economies in electricity generation. When technological changes affect how competition can function in a market, regulatory institutions may take different roles than before. Indeed, where competition had been unworkable it might become feasible because of changes in technology. However, legislative institutions, being deliberative, may be slow to mandate change in regulatory institutions after such technological changes, in which case the institutions can get in the way of efficiency.

Technological changes might affect only one level, or stage, in the series of tasks needed to provide a service. Microwave technology affected the long-distance stage in the production of telephone calls, for example, and only that stage was initially opened to competition. Local service continued to be organized in monopoly form. Competition is now guiding electricity generation in some markets, fostered by access to networks that transmit electricity from one area to another. New electricity generating technology is helping also by making lower costs possible at smaller scales than before. The distribution of electricity to final customers still tends to be organized in regulated-monopoly form, but that also might change. So when changes in technology occur, regulatory changes may also be appropriate; yet the changes may be complex, and recognizing the need to change and then designing appropriate changes in institutions may be difficult.

In telecommunications in the 1980s and electricity in the 1990s, legislators and courts considered allowing competition at some level in the vertical chain of otherwise regulated industry activities. A court allowed competition in long-distance, but not local, telephone service early in the 1980s, for example, and in the 1990s state legislatures allowed competition in the generation of electricity but not in its transmission. Competition was created in each case when budding competitors could access resources that enabled them to compete. In the telecommunications industry, suppliers of long-distance service needed access to local networks to complete customers' calls, and they were granted it. Electricity generators were given the right of access to transmission lines, which allowed them to compete in the vertical chain of services on the way to the final consumer. These changes in view opened the possibility of intervening not simply to regulate, but to design competitive markets into portions of regulated industries, a possibility that has transformed market regulation.

10.3 | THE TRANSFORMATION OF REGULATED INDUSTRIES

When technological problems make regulation by competition problematic, government may impose regulatory institutions in its place. Industries that are primarily local, such as electricity, have been regulated at the state level, with an important federal role in overseeing interstate transactions. In industries with extensive interstate activity, such as the telephone industry, federal authorities play a larger role. Some important interstate industries, such as airlines that fly all over the country or television stations that broadcast over large geographic areas, have been regulated primarily by a federal agency. Airlines were regulated by the Civil Aeronautics Board (CAB), although local authorities operate individual airports, and radio and television stations and broadcasting networks are subject to regulation by the Federal Communications Commission.

Government Regulation of Industries

Institutions that provide regulation in place of competition initially regulated whole firms and whole industries. The U.S. Postal Service is a single enterprise, for example, that has a monopoly on the delivery of letters and is regulated by the U.S. Postal Rate Commission. AT&T was a monopoly long-distance provider for years, regulated by the Federal Communications Commission, and it also controlled much of the nation's local telephone service, where it was subject to regulation by state public utility commissions. Electric utilities were integrated enterprises that generated, transmitted, and distributed electricity to consumers. Each electric utility would be subject to regulation by a state public utility commission that oversaw its pricing and other aspects of its behavior. These regulatory arrangements have changed greatly in recent years.[17] Evidence showed that airlines, regulated as to the routes they could fly and the prices they could charge, were less efficient than unregulated airlines, and after they were successfully deregulated, deregulation swept through other transportation industries. Other weaknesses in regulation were seen, and a movement to restrain the scope of government regulation was born.

Deregulation, Liberalization, and Restructuring

Over the course of the twentieth century a variety of regulatory institutions regulated many industries, and studies showed that some of these regulatory institutions were less than ideal as substitutes for the competitive markets they replaced. This is not surprising in the case of the CAB, because when it began regulating airlines in 1938 it was specifically charged with *promoting* the fledgling airline industry rather than regulating it for antimonopoly purposes. After four decades with virtually no new entry into the industry, the promotional purpose was no longer appropriate, and flaws in the regulation could be seen. Because entry to a specific route was easy, contestable market theory suggested the industry could operate without regulation. There followed a move to deregulate airlines—that is, to stop regulating economic aspects of the industry. Evidence supported the success of this movement, and deregulation was extended to other transportation industries such as railroads and trucking.

Congress deregulated airlines in part because of superior performance by airlines that operated entirely within single states (Texas and California), and so were not subject to CAB regulation. These intrastate airlines had much lower fares per mile and more seats filled in their planes than did CAB regulated airlines.[18] One can see from this example the value of having an alternative regulatory regime to make possible comparisons and thus more objective evaluations. The CAB itself sought to introduce limited price competition and to expand the possibility for new entry into airline markets, and it also urged deregulation of the airline industry. Congress's passage of the Airline Deregulation Act of 1978 resulted in free entry by early 1980 and freely set fares shortly afterwards.

---

[17] A brief description of current regulatory institutions in several industries is available at http://www.globalregulatorynetwork.org/PDFs/NRRIPrimer.pdf.

[18] See Keeler (1972).

An easing of entry in a limited way that opens more scope for competition has come to be called **liberalization**. For example, allowing more parties beyond the U.S. Postal Service to deliver advertising mail to our mail boxes would be liberalization of postal service. Liberalization does not deregulate, but it allows competition into a part of the industry. Such liberalization of postal service has occurred in various forms in many countries. Liberalization allows a partial deregulation, perhaps by allowing entry to a market but restricting the price that may be charged. More radical steps are needed to make competition feasible in some industries, and such steps transform the way those industries are regulated.

Competition is introduced into some regulated industries by **restructuring** the industry. A restructured industry is not deregulated, because government regulation continues to play a role, but the structure of the industry is changed. The electricity industry is restructured, for example, when competition is allowed in the generation of electricity, yet transmission and distribution of electricity are still regulated. Considerable regulation continues in the telephone industry, while competition also flourishes, not only in the long-distance part of the industry but also from new technologies that make digital phones and Internet telephony possible.

The Transformation of Industry Regulation

In addition to the deregulation of formerly regulated industries such as airlines, regulation by competition has been extended into areas where special rules are required to support its functioning. Even where technological conditions can undermine competition, and bring regulatory means in its place, regulators have found clever ways to extend the effectiveness of competition and to preserve its usefulness when a few decades ago it would have been abandoned.

In both telecommunications and electricity, competition plays a new role today, in part because the owner of a crucial facility must allow others to use it rather than exploit its monopoly advantage. Sharing the use of an essential facility goes back to a 1912 Supreme Court decision about a railroad bridge and other facilities that established the essential facilities doctrine.[19] That Court decision said the terms to be offered to nonowners should "place every such company upon as nearly an equal plane as may be with respect to expenses and charges as that occupied by the proprietary companies."[20] On this principle telephone companies have to open their networks so other companies can complete their calls, and electric utilities have to offer electricity transmission services to generators of electricity. Once their calls can be completed on local networks in a nondiscriminatory way, the providers of long-distance telephone service are able to compete, and so can small electricity generators once they can use others' transmission lines.

---

[19] The case that opened this right of access to essential facilities was decided in 1912, when the Supreme Court required railroads jointly owning a railroad bridge to allow other railroads to use it. See *United States v. Terminal Railroad Association of St. Louis*, 224 U.S. 383 (1912) and 236 U.S. 194 (1915). For descriptive evaluations of the essential facilities doctrine, see Kovacic (1992) and Lipsky and Sidak (1999).

[20] 224 U.S. at 411.

BOX 10.3 Competition in Long-Distance Telephone Service

After a contentious history in which AT&T repeatedly blocked access to its network, the Department of Justice (DOJ) filed an antitrust complaint against it in 1974. The Department of Justice (DOJ) charged AT&T with monopolization, or attempting to monopolize, telecommunications markets. AT&T had excluded potential competitors from completing calls on its network, and it also bought equipment only from its own subsidiary, Western Electric. As remedy in the case, the DOJ first proposed that AT&T divest, or sell off, Western Electric. Second, AT&T would separate its long-distance service operations from the local networks of the Bell Operating companies. In retaining its long-distance operations, AT&T would compete for customers with new long-distance service providers that were trying to enter those markets, such as MCI. Behind this case lurked the development of microwave technology, which moderated the economies of scale in long-distance technology that had long supported AT&T's monopoly.

A solution to this case was finally negotiated by AT&T and the Department of Justice, and called the *Modification of Final Judgment*, where Final Judgment stood for a 1956 Consent Decree that had limited AT&T to regulated activities. AT&T divested seven Regional Bell Operating Companies and their ownership passed to AT&T shareholders. These operating companies, with AT&T's assistance, gave all long-distance service providers equal access to their local exchange networks. The decision vastly changed the telecommunications industry. It allowed all long-distance operators to complete calls on local networks, and they could compete for long-distance customers. It also opened the way for more thorough reorganization of the industry, which came with passage of the Telecommunications Act of 1996.

Competition is the main result of granting others access to a crucial resource; but broader changes are underway. In principle, a long-distance telephone company has the right to lease resources from a local network to offer local telephone service, and an electricity marketer can buy electricity from a generator and hire local distribution service to deliver electricity to residential or commercial consumers. Thus, industry regulation is a much richer and more multifaceted institution than it used to be, with attention to the structure of the industry that includes a search for ways to make competition possible.

Access as a Source of Competition

One of the most revolutionary changes in the regulation of industries is that of granting competitors access to essential facilities, or "bottleneck" facilities. A monopoly owner typically operates such facilities. Access to them enables others to supply the good that otherwise could come only from the monopolist. Actions to open such bottleneck facilities have arisen in the past two decades in a variety of industries where regulators have sought to foster competition. Often—but not always—access becomes an issue after a change in technology makes competition feasible at one stage among the separate stages needed to produce a final service. Competitors at that one stage need access to another stage to compete in the final service.

Access and Property Rights

Consider the example in Figure 10.1 that shows two local networks connected by a long-distance gateway. Suppose an integrated firm operates network A and owns the gateway. Should such ownership be allowed, or should operators be confined to one level of service? This is a question about property rights. For example, local telephone networks could operate only at that level in 1982, and they retained their monopoly positions, while competitors could enter long-distance markets (these arrangements were modified by the Telecommunications Act of 1996). If the integrated firm that owns network A and the gateway is allowed to operate, should it be granted access so it can complete calls to telephones located in network B? Is it right to allow network B to use the gateway (along with network A) to reach locations in A?

These are all questions about access. Perhaps scale economies in operating long distance gateways are modest, so the operator of network B may be able to provide its own gateway to network A. There is still the question whether to allow the network B operator to use network A to complete calls, just like the question whether to allow the network A operator to use network B. When a facility is not easy to duplicate, and yet is essential to providing a service, its owner may be required to grant others access to it so they can compete in providing the service.

Forcing the owner of an essential facility to grant access alters property rights, as an example will show. A railroad train route is represented in Figure 10.3 as ABC. The single length of railroad track from B to C is essential for service from A to C, but it has one (monopoly) owner. Two railroads have tracks from A to B, but there is only one track from B to C. Perhaps movement from B to C requires a bridge over a river. Or perhaps mountains prevent construction of alternative lines from B to C or make them prohibitively expensive. The B-to-C facility is a bottleneck facility, or an essential facility.

The holder of a monopoly position for the B-to-C passage who owns one of the A-to-B tracks might *want* to grant access to competitors. Granting access could help it profit from its monopoly position by bringing in more travelers and more trains. The monopoly would charge high prices for its own service from A to C, and it would also charge a high price to competitors for using its B-to-C connection, so their prices for A-to-C service would also be high.

Regulation at two levels, or stages, might resist monopoly effects. First, the owner of the bottleneck asset may be denied exclusive control over its use and forced to grant others access to it in exchange for an access fee. This would probably require some regulatory oversight of the access fee, because it could easily be set so high that monopoly profit levels would persist. And requiring access clearly changes the right

Figure 10.3 *Railroad Train Route*

A ══════ B ─────── C

the monopoly would ordinarily have over its property. With rights to the BC track, competitors could serve customers by using their own AB facilities. This competition could bring pressure on the monopoly to be as cost efficient as the competitor on AB, which is a desirable effect.

The second stage of regulation could attempt to deny monopoly profit. One way is to regulate the price of train travel, to regulate for instance the price of travel from A to C. Another way is to regulate the price the monopoly can charge others for access to the B-to-C passage. That regulated access fee, plus other operating costs of the competitors, would then set a cost standard that the monopoly would have to meet in competing for travelers going from A to C.

Double Marginalization and Asymmetry in a Telephone Network

Forcing access to another network, say for a long-distance carrier to complete a call through a local network, can be justified by viewing the local network as an essential facility, to be made available to other—perhaps competing—networks so competition can function. A local network may similarly use a long-distance network, and another local network, to complete a call it originates. Bringing competition inside the large network requires compatibility, so callers on different networks can be interconnected, and it raises new issues that are still being worked out.[21] For instance, complex pricing issues can arise as calls are exchanged across networks. The issues arise in part from having the senders, or the originators, pay for the costs of calls instead of the recipients, a traditional practice in telephone and postal service that places the cost on the party initiating the communication. This means that the initiating network, which collects whatever fee is charged for the call, is expected to pay the cost of access to the terminating network.

Let us examine the complications that can arise from independent pricing decisions across networks. When a call travels over two networks, the networks stand in relation to each other much as a manufacturer and a retailer in producing and moving a product to a consumer. We considered in Chapter 4 how a manufacturer and a retailer, both facing downward sloping demands and making separate pricing decisions, can reach a price for the consumer that is higher than would be charged by a single owner of both manufacturing and retailing functions. The separate manufacturer sets a price above its own cost to the retailer, who views this price as its cost and, in turn, marks it up to set a price for the consumer. A single monopoly over both manufacturing and retailing would set a single price by marking up its true cost once. Having two separate markups over cost is called double marginalization, as noted in Chapter 4, and it leads to higher prices and less profit than that obtained by a single marginal analysis. By the same independent pricing process, two separate telephone networks, each with some monopoly power, may thus end up with higher prices for consumers than a single monopoly operator would choose. To the extent competition can reduce this monopoly power, it might also help to solve the double marginalization problem.

---

[21] For analysis of network pricing problems, see Shy (2001), and for applications to telecommunications, see Laffont and Tirole (2000).

The volume of call traffic between networks is also an important influence on outcomes. Suppose calls go from network A to network B and from network B to network A. This means there is the possibility of double marginalization in both directions, or **double double marginalization**. If volumes in the two directions are about equal, however, a reciprocity exists that may help the networks agree on a solution to double marginalization. They can simply grant each other access to their networks at marginal cost. Like a manufacturer selling to a retailer at its marginal cost, access at marginal cost avoids two successive markups and defeats double marginalization. Because of their reciprocal relationship, each party can choose one optimal markup. Their equal call volumes bring the two parties equal compensation for access, so neither party needs an additional payment.

Now consider two monopoly telephone networks that complete each others' calls but have unequal call volumes in the two directions. Suppose, for example, the networks are in two different countries, and one receives more calls than it originates. Then that country can profit from high charges for call termination, so we can expect it to bargain for high charges. Calls between countries, which are often handled as if each country were a monopoly, tend to have high charges for access, that is, for terminating calls, even though the best terminating, or access, charge equals marginal cost because that allows each network to set a monopoly price to maximize profit without double marginalization.[22] However, asymmetry in call volumes between two countries can prevent their agreement on access fees that equal marginal cost.

The situation changes if the two networks are in the same country and compete with each other for the same consumers. Suppose, because of product differentiation and long-term contracts, their competition is imperfect. Assume that the portion of the first network's calls that are completed on the second network match the second network's overall market share, a reasonable assumption because a network's market share represents the fraction of all phones that subscribe to it. If one network is larger than the other, more of its customers' calls can be connected on its own network, and so it pays less to the other network in total access charges. This advantage of having a larger market share might motivate each network to seek it and then to set lower prices to consumers to achieve it. On the other hand, each network also wants to set a higher access price for completing its competitor's calls, because that is profitable and handicaps the competitor while also making prices to consumers higher. So ideal pricing may not result.

These examples illustrate the incentives that can arise within networks when there is no external regulation. Some rules, perhaps constraints on access pricing for example, may be appropriate in such circumstances. Allowing price discrimination may even improve outcomes. If government regulation can overcome these coordination problems within networks, a constrained form of competition fosters stronger incentives, both to keep costs low and to develop services that consumers want.

Rules for Access Pricing

The pricing of access to an essential facility is important because it can foster competition, and the desirable incentives for efficiency that competition offers. Because

---

[22] See, for example, Wright (1999).

alternative providers of service compete with the owner of the bottleneck facility, the terms under which they are granted access determines their prospects and the prospects for the bottleneck owner, too. Many considerations can come into play, but pricing to preserve two incentives is especially important. First, it is desirable that the access price be high enough to motivate the resource owner to *offer* access. Second, it is desirable to set the access price so that only *efficient providers* are motivated to avail themselves of access.

Access fees that accomplish these two goals, to have access offered but only to efficient service providers, are said to satisfy the *efficient component pricing rule (ECPR)* for access pricing.[23] Setting the access price too high could prevent access, and setting it too low could discourage access from being offered or, if it is offered, it could induce inefficient producers to enter and offer the service. A more general principle of optimal pricing, called **Ramsey pricing** after its originator, mathematician Frank Ramsey,[24] can also be applied to access pricing. Ramsey prices use only enough monopoly power to cover fixed cost to break even, and they do so with the least possible loss in welfare.

To better understand the ECPR, let's return to the ABC railroad example. Suppose the monopoly owner of the B-to-C section of railroad track charged a fee to other railroads equal to its monopoly profit on a trip all the way from A to C. This access fee would equal its *opportunity cost* of granting access, because that profit is the amount it might lose on a customer who switches to another railroad. Because it replaces the monopoly's lost profit, this access fee makes the monopoly willing to grant access. After paying this access fee, the competitor can only match the monopoly's price for the entire ABC trip *if it is equally efficient* on the A-to-B portion of the trip. Thus, this access fee meets the ECPR requirements of (1) motivating the monopoly to offer service and (2) inducing only efficient providers to enter as competitors.

The ECPR neither solves the problem of monopoly pricing on the A-to-C route nor is it intended to. Granting access under the ECPR only introduces competitive pressure to make the monopoly operate efficiently. If the price of railroad service from A to C is regulated, to moderate the monopoly pricing and profit on that service, the ECPR can still induce competitive pressure. Whatever profit results at the regulated A-to-C service price can serve as opportunity cost in the ECPR to set the price of access to the B-to-C section of track. Thus, the ECPR remains an effective rule for access pricing regardless of whether the final service price is regulated.

Court actions in industries where disputes have arisen are currently considering these issues of access and its pricing. How these disputes are settled may affect the pricing of access in the future, even in other industries. A number of examples of successful access show that it can be very effective in enlarging the role that competitive forces play in otherwise regulated industries. It is not the only means of introducing competitive forces in government regulated industries, but it is an important one.

Whether the question is about allowing access or about pricing access, we need some framework when governmental administrative action modifies the competitive

---

[23] For exposition of the ECPR, see Baumol and Sidak (1994a, 1994b).
[24] See Ramsey (1927).

market process. Over many years, the field of welfare economics has developed the most useful and effective framework for evaluating the effects of such alternative actions.

10.4 | ECONOMIC WELFARE REVISITED

When we say that competition can regulate economic activity "well," we have in mind some notion of what is desirable, something that goes beyond the process of competition itself. For in asking a monopoly supplier to choose socially desirable prices, we must be able to describe what "desirable" prices are. Chapter 2 introduced a set of precise concepts for thinking about such questions. We have related these concepts in various ways to observable measures that we can usefully apply in industry regulation. Even ideas that we cannot apply directly can inform our thinking about regulatory issues. Because regulation presumably is undertaken to advance economic well-being, we can better understand it by better understanding welfare economics.

An appealing and simple notion of economic welfare is called **Pareto optimality**. Pareto optimality is achieved when no action remains that could improve one person's situation, as that person sees it, without harming any one else. An attractive feature of this criterion is its dependence on individuals' own evaluations of their situations, rather than on the value judgments of outside observers. The disadvantage is that there are many Pareto optimal positions, one for every possible distribution of income, and regulation usually calls for one choice from among the many possibilities.

An ideal competitive market economy achieves Pareto optimality by meeting three conditions. The first is consumption efficiency, which is met when every consumer has the same ratio of marginal valuations between every pair of goods and, therefore, the same willingness to exchange them. In a market, all consumers can have the same willingness to exchange when they all face the same price ratio, and uniform prices can bring that about. The second condition is production efficiency, which requires that every producer have the same ratio of marginal productivities for every pair of inputs. If this condition was not satisfied between two producers, an exchange of inputs from the low-valued use to the high-valued use could increase output. The first condition gives rise to a price ratio for every pair of goods, while the second condition yields a ratio of marginal costs for producing every pair of goods. The third condition is overall economic efficiency, which requires that the relative marginal costs of any two goods in production match the price ratio implicit in the common ratio of marginal valuations of consumers in exchange. This third condition requires that the goods so efficiently produced are also the goods that satisfy consumers' strongest needs.

The Pareto criterion offers no basis for choosing among many possible Pareto positions, so it often does not resolve regulatory issues. A stronger representation of social welfare can be created that allows choices among Pareto positions, but it requires a weighting of individual consumers. In this situation, some consumers are given greater weight, or importance, than others. This approach requires strong assumptions about income distribution and other conditions, but it is very useful for analyzing regulatory problems.

We can weigh individuals in a welfare representation by specifying an income distribution. Under reasonable assumptions, we can then show the Pareto features described—consumption efficiency, production efficiency, and overall economic efficiency—yield a unique Pareto optimum, a maximum of such economic welfare for the given distribution of income. Practical measures of welfare, such as consumer surplus (which we can usually infer from demand information) and producer surplus (which is related to profit), essentially accept the *existing* distribution of income. This condition seems a reasonable point of departure because it represents the current status quo, the base from which any change is to be made. These welfare ideas are valuable for evaluating prices and other policies in the absence of competition and in interpreting a host of regulatory issues.

The Pursuit of Economic Welfare

Competition forces firms to pursue economic welfare, because while they pursue profit, their competition limits the profit they can earn to a reasonable level. No such mechanism exists under monopoly. Even if we can define ideal prices for a regulated monopoly to follow, it is hard to motivate a regulated monopoly firm to pursue them. Inducing the pursuit of welfare under monopoly regulation or alternative arrangements is an important goal, so the choice of regulatory institution is influenced by the extent to which it can entice the monopoly to pursue welfare. Such motivation is not easily induced.

Suppose one producer, and no other, is authorized to produce a basic service. The monopoly franchise may be awarded to a single firm because of economies of scale or economies of scope, which make the single producer able to achieve the lowest possible cost. The chosen producer may be the first to make the product, or it may be technologically superior to other producers. The question remains, How will this one enterprise be organized, and, in particular, how will it be owned?

The sharpest distinction in ownership arrangements is between public and private. Whether it is privately owned or publicly owned, simply asking an enterprise to pursue the general welfare may not bring about that result. A privately owned firm may pursue its own benefit instead, for example, and those in charge of a publicly owned firm may pursue their own interests—including an easy life—rather than the general welfare. To begin with, welfare is not well defined like profit is, and no clear incentive induces its pursuit like profit does in a private firm. Philosophical differences over this question of public or private ownership have divided nations. One way to approach the question is to ask which arrangement functions best, where best essentially means most efficiently.

Considering the institution of private ownership coldly for its instrumental effectiveness in promoting efficiency, rather than accepting or rejecting it because of its ideological foundation, is quite a new approach. Many nations are seeing debates today about how to organize public services and other parts of their economies, and there is a general trend toward greater reliance on markets. Planned economies are making growing use of markets, and market economies are taking some steps toward privatization of firms that formerly were publicly owned. Wherever these trends may ultimately settle, the idea of evaluating economic institutions on the basis of their probable effectiveness for specific purposes, rather than their conformity with ideological beliefs, is bound to be a constructive force.

What if the technology that is used to produce a good or service offers economies of scale or economies of scope so great that an enterprise still experiences them, even when all market demand is satisfied? The lowest total cost to society can then be obtained if production is concentrated in a single firm, rather than being shared by many competing firms. It is conceivable that continuing competition for the position of being sole supplier can force efficient production of desirable output, if capacity costs have alternative uses and so are not sunk when committed to this industry. If we can then find prices that sustain the monopoly by preventing inefficient entry, we can call the market contestable.[25] Such a market may pursue welfare aims even when it contains only one active firm, as long as entry is not prevented. If a regulated market is contestable regulators might liberalize it by removing regulatory entry barriers to bolster incentives for efficiency.

Market Entry and Incentives

In a contestable market, a new firm can enter easily to challenge an existing supplier. At any given output, efficient use of technology allows a minimum level of average cost. If prices rise above that level in a contestable market, we might expect entry, so price is forced to equal average cost. Free entry thus pressures the incumbent to control costs. Free entry also tends to prevent cross-subsidization, avoiding the inefficiency, and the redistribution of income across consumer groups that go with it. Indeed, free entry can even make an incumbent supplier act to pursue economic welfare in the forms of low cost and good service.

What if capacity cost is sunk once it is undertaken in the industry and cannot be retrieved, say by resale for other uses? A new entrant probably is reluctant to challenge an established firm then because an entrant could commit excessive resources to the industry, leading to low prices for a sustained period. Indeed, when costs are sunk in this way, the market is not considered contestable, and competition through potential entry cannot insure an efficient result. A monopoly may be created by legislative statute instead, in the form of an exclusive right to provide a specific service in a defined area. Such an exclusive franchise position is awarded particularly if one firm is thought able to achieve the lowest cost. Then the statutory monopoly is regulated, so it serves the public and does not take unfair advantage of its monopoly position.

When a statutory monopoly is created without free entry, is welfare pursued? Professional engineering standards may contribute positively to technical decisions, and devoted bureaucrats may attempt faithfully to serve the public, but the incentives in such a monopoly organization do not impel it to maximize economic welfare. Indeed, a welfare goal is difficult to describe in concrete terms, and it certainly is hard

---

[25] Baumol, Panzar, and Willig (1982) describe this possibility of a contestable market.

to measure. Eliciting the pursuit of welfare through some sort of incentive scheme is thus an ambitious aim.

Governments often grant a monopoly franchise to the provider of a public service, with the provider being given statutory protection from entry. Without competition in the form of free entry, a single supplier must be expected to follow many understandable tendencies of monopolies. Pricing above marginal cost may be desirable as a way to make revenues cover costs when marginal cost is lower than average cost. To raise revenues, markets with less elastic demands have prices proportionately farther above marginal costs. Some reliance on differences in demand elasticities, Ramsey pricing, is desirable when fixed costs must be covered.[26] A monopoly may not choose optimal service offerings, however, and it may rely excessively on demands with low elasticities, when doing so allows it to raise more revenue.

Unless service quality is clearly defined and easily monitored, it may be lowered by a monopoly whose price is regulated. Reliability of service may suffer, too. For example, when there is no threat from alternative suppliers, consumers may be forced to wait longer for service while the monopoly earns greater profit. Or costs may rise because managers shirk or avoid difficult decisions. Innovation may not occur either, for the enterprise has no great incentive to make its present ways of doing things obsolete. These tendencies are natural in any organization, and they are most prevalent when there is little competition.

Where it seems to be workable, industry regulators have relied on contestability to create competitive pressures. This reliance is present, for example, in the airline industry. In addition, government regulators have opened monopoly resources to others by requiring access. As noted, regulators have required local telephone networks to give long-distance carriers access for origination and completion of long-distance calls, and this has spurred competition among long-distance carriers. Regulators have similarly required electric power transmission grids to transmit power for small power generators, which allows competition in electricity generation. The pricing of access rights continues to raise difficult issues, especially when the firm that is granted access is a competitor for the supplier of access. Then the access price can give advantage to one party or the other. But allowing competition to function through such institutions is opening the way for efficiency gains.

The Ownership Interest

Whether an enterprise is privately or publicly owned has a large effect on the enterprise's incentives. Private ownership of the means of production raises many kinds of issues, but most observers agree on one consequence: strong, or "high powered," incentives that arise from profit seeking. When disciplined by competition in well-functioning markets, this profit incentive can induce socially desirable outcomes. Without competition, it can cause monopoly behavior that is harmful to consumers. Government regulation, on the other hand, may destroy the profit incentive and, thus, lead to an inefficient bureaucracy with high costs.

---

[26] See Ramsey (1927) and Boiteux (1956).

Admittedly, less strong, or less narrow, incentives than those in privately owned firms may sometimes be preferable in an institution of public service, although any exacting discussion requires detailed information about the institution at issue and its incentive arrangements. When goals or purposes are many and diffuse, a bureaucracy of professional staff may serve better, in part because their self-interest is less apt to interfere with institutional purposes. If short-run profit is pursued under an incentive system it might lead to perverse outcomes, as when production at a fixed price per unit of a good or service invites lower quality as a way to achieve lower cost. Service quality might even be better maintained when there is no profit incentive. Also, a publicly owned enterprise that is devoted to a well-defined purpose may accomplish desired goals, such as pricing at marginal cost or redistributing income through pricing policies, which a privately owned firm might find financially impossible. When aims are clear enough for a public enterprise to be formed, however, ways can often be designed to accomplish these aims through private firms. Indeed, mixed public and private ownership may even be an effective arrangement if it can combine the incentives of private ownership with responsibility to the public.

The profit incentive of private ownership originates with the shareholder. It is the shareholders who hire and fire management to enforce pursuit of profit, and pursuit of profit extends from there through the organization. One must realize that making the shareholders' interests salable enhances this profit incentive, by making it operate even in a protected monopoly. For if the salable private ownership interest in a monopoly is not yielding as much profit as is possible, then it can be worthwhile for someone to purchase the monopoly and make it do so, as long as the cost of carrying out such a transaction is not too great.[27] But will these incentives be preserved if the privately owned and salable monopoly is regulated by a government authority? That question, along with the question of whether antisocial monopoly behavior can be tamed, determines whether a sound institution of regulation can be designed for a monopoly firm. If we forgo competition, can a government regulated monopoly do better for society?

SUMMARY

Technological conditions, such as economies of scale or economies of scope, can interfere with the smooth functioning of competition, along with entry barriers owing to such conditions as sunk costs. Properties of network industries also raise problems for competition. They often lie behind economies of scope and economies of scale, but they raise a host of other problems such as compatibility and coordination. The advantages of networks may be preserved while allowing some competition, if competitors can be afforded access to crucial parts of the network. Access to such bottleneck facilities, or essential facilities, ordinarily allow competitors to put together all of the stages needed to produce a service for consumers. Then competition is possible at

---

[27] See Williamson (1975).

the final consumer service level, even though only one party may own an essential stage in the process.

When competition does not function well, it raises the question whether government intervention can do better. Political institutions are less subtle than markets, because they deal with difficult either-or choices and they reach decisions by devices such as majority rule that are not always effective. Many influences, including special interest lobbying, may affect political outcomes, and economic welfare is not always well served. Many regulatory problems need careful diagnosis, and political institutions may not be situated well to provide that. Still, ideal benchmarks that represent economic welfare are useful for regulatory guidance.

One consideration that can influence the need for government regulation is the contestability of a market. Certain technological features lead to subadditivity of the cost function, which is necessary for sustainable prices that can support a contestable market. Such prices must also be subsidy-free. When these technological conditions are combined with low sunk costs, a contestable market can exist and it can eliminate the need for government regulation, because it allows the pressure of potential entrants to discipline incumbent firms.

Recent developments in economics have broadened the conditions in which competition can function and have brought to once-regulated industries the possibility of entry, called liberalization, restructuring that allows competition in part of an industry, and outright deregulation. These developments have transformed government regulation by expanding the types and means of regulation and how they are applied to industries. Allowing competitive access to essential or "bottleneck" resources is usually an important element in these new forms of regulation.

This chapter reviews measures of social benefit that are useful in guiding regulatory policy. It is not easy to persuade a monopoly to pursue welfare, however. As an organizational goal, welfare is not as well defined as profit and is difficult to pursue, even if an organization can be motivated to pursue it. That is why the force of market entry can be so valuable, when it can exist, to force cost minimizing and welfare maximizing actions. Private ownership creates strong profit incentives, and with the right market conditions it can bring effective pursuit of welfare. Replacing those market forces, which regulation often must do, can dampen pursuit of welfare. Early regulatory institutions were not designed soundly, and even today it is difficult to find institutions that can achieve desirable welfare goals whenever competition does not function.

QUESTIONS

1. Consider the following cost function for producing two services:

$$TC = 1000 + 10q_1 + 10q_2.$$

   a. Does the cost function exhibit economies of scale?
   b. Does the cost function exhibit economies of scope?

Suppose demands for the services are $P_1 = 100 - q_1$ and $P_2 = 100 - q_2$.

   c. If the markets for these services are contestable, are prices sustainable? If no, explain why. If yes, indicate the level of a sustainable price.

   d. If the markets for these services are contestable, is regulation needed? Why or why not?

2. Consider the following network arrangement:

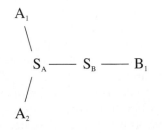

Explain the network externality effect on possible connections if the B location is connected to the A network through the long-distance gateway, S_AS_B.

3. Possible agricultural irrigation systems for up to four farms were described in Question 6 of Chapter 2. One farm could be served for $15,000 (assume that each of the four farms is willing to pay at least that much), two farms for $25,000, three farms for $30,000, and four farms for $44,000.

   a. Find the price per farm for the lowest cost system, overall, that would serve all four farms.

   b. Would your price per farm in part a be sustainable? (If, at a given price, entry could occur that would result in a less efficient irrigation system, the price is not sustainable.) Why or why not?

4. Consider the brief description of long-distance telephone service contained in Box 10.3.

   a. Is this a case of deregulation, liberalization, or restructuring, and why?

   b. Competition in long-distance service requires access to local networks for completion of calls. How might such access be priced?

   c. Explain major problems that price setting in this situation might present.

5. Consider irrigation technology for farms that can serve one farm for $30,000, two farms for $48,000, and three farms for $75,000.

   a. If three farms are to be irrigated, which combination of irrigation systems offers the lowest total cost for all three farms?

   b. Suppose the lowest cost arrangement is constructed by a third party who charges all participating farms the same price (each farm pays an equal share of total cost). Is that price sustainable?

   c. No account is taken of consumer benefit in parts a and b. All consumers are simply assumed willing to participate. But suppose farmer 1 values the irrigation service at $23,000, farmer 2 values it at $30,000, and farmer 3 values it at $40,000. If you may charge different fees to different farms, what

fees would you propose to provide irrigation for
situation?

d. Are the fees that you proposed in part c sustain
the fees that you proposed in part c subsidy-fre

e. For the situation described in part c, what is th

6. The section Theories of Regulation in this chapter
are quite different in purpose and form. Try to brin
mary theory of regulation by writing a short pape
for your summary theory.

11

Pricing Principles

The U.S. Postal Service (USPS) has long been the sole provider of letter mail service in the United States. Given that it operates under economies of scale, how should it choose prices for its stamps? Setting prices equal to the marginal costs of services maximizes welfare, but with economies of scale the revenue that results from marginal cost prices does not cover total costs. General tax revenues are needed for that, which means that a taxpayer who does not use the service may help to pay for it, and that seems unfair. Postal prices can be raised so they cover costs, but because such prices are above marginal costs they are ineffi- cient. Thus, finding ideal prices is not easy when competition does not determine them.

Welfare economics can help to resolve this pricing question by offering meas- ures of benefit, such as consumer surplus and producer surplus, to evaluate alterna- tive prices. Here we use welfare measures along with simple representations of cost to illustrate such pricing principles. Among the principles examined are *marginal-cost pricing* and *peak-load pricing*, plus Ramsey pricing. *Ramsey pricing* departs from marginal-cost pricing to avoid a deficit. Departing from marginal-cost pricing intro- duces a welfare loss, but Ramsey pricing minimizes that welfare loss. *Nonuniform pricing*, or setting different prices for different units, can involve price discrimination, but it can be useful for raising revenue to cover fixed cost. We also explore the pricing of *access* to resources when one agency's resources are to be made available for use by others—say, for example, when one railroad's bridge over a river is to be used by other railroads.

When competition functions imperfectly, whatever institution replaces it can find guidance in the pricing solutions of this chapter. We begin with an application of marginal-cost pricing called peak-load pricing, and then we consider Ramsey pricing for cases where such pricing is not appropriate. We next consider nonuniform pricing, which includes two part pricing that involves a fixed fee and a per-unit fee, and which can sometimes raise revenue more efficiently than uniform pricing. We end by describing access prices, for cases where access to a crucial resource can stimulate a degree of competition.

11.1 PEAK-LOAD PRICING

The soundness of marginal cost pricing for resource allocation in an economy often can repay the effort to use it many times over. We consider here an especially important opportunity to have prices reflect marginal costs, that of **peak-load pricing**. Price schedules can vary by time of day, day of week, month of year, and so forth, as needed to reflect higher costs. That is, when demand follows a periodic cycle, demand predictably being high so cost is high at some times, prices can vary with those times. Such prices are common for many goods and services, such as seasonal resort accommodation, airplane fares, time-of-day electricity rates, movie theater admissions, and restaurant meals.

Peak loads are the highest demand levels, so high they burden available capacity. That makes the cost of capacity expansion part of marginal cost because more capacity is needed to increase output. Until capacity can be expanded, higher prices are motivated to ration the limited capacity. Having prices vary with time periods allows the enterprise to reflect its higher cost when demand is high. Prices that vary with time can also moderate the extremes of the demand cycle and therefore allow more effective use of capacity.

Electricity use follows a daily cycle as needs for factories, cooking, lighting, and so forth pass through a daily routine, and it also follows a yearly cycle due largely to seasonal temperature changes. Higher prices during periods of higher demand can discourage use and thus save costly capacity, and, at off-peak times when demands are low, lower prices can encourage the use of otherwise idle capacity. We are concerned here with the form of this pricing problem and the nature of the optimal solution. We first analyze a situation that involves only one method of production, or one technology. After that we consider a case that offers a choice between diverse

---

BOX 11.1 Marginal-Cost Pricing at a Lemonade Stand

Suppose the leaders of a small community grant an 18-year-old member a monopoly right to sell lemonade to cars that stop at a little byway off the main highway into town. The deal is that the monopolist can include 50 cents per cup of lemonade as normal profit and otherwise set the price per cup at marginal cost. The town provides a table and a mixing bowl. The cost of lemons needed per cup plus sugar, ice, and the cup itself are part of marginal cost, and that marginal cost does not vary as the number of cups changes. Estimated costs for these items add up to $1.50 per cup and, after adding the 50 cent profit allowance, the (regulated) monopolist charges $2 per cup.

The service begins operating between 4 and 5 PM weekday afternoons, and quantity settles down to about 40 cups per day, or 200 cups per five-day week. This is an example of marginal-cost pricing that includes a profit allowance and has a service provided by a regulated monopoly at reasonable cost. More lemonade pricing problems will follow.

BOX 11.2 Peak-Load Pricing at the Lemonade Stand

The monopoly operator of the lemonade stand described in Box 11.1 notices that traffic is greater between 5 and 6 PM than it is during the current operating hours of 4 to 5 PM. As an experiment, the operator extends the hours of operation to 6 PM. Sales turn out to be twice as great in the 5 to 6 PM hour, at 80 cups per day or 400 cups per week, just in that hour alone (200 cups a week are still sold from 4 to 5 PM). This increase in volume causes delays in service so cars back up in the little byway where the lemonade stand operates, and they can even block highway traffic. To avoid this traffic problem by serving cars faster in the 5 to 6 PM hour, the operator proposes changes. She hires another clerk. In addition, she hires a person to make fresh lemonade on the spot in that second hour to meet the higher demand level. Because the operator no longer makes every cup of lemonade, she agrees to a reduction in profit per cup in the second hour to 25 cents. After these changes, the 5 to 6 PM period turns out to be a peak period with higher costs than the 4 to 5 PM period. Including the smaller 25 cent profit allowance, the peak marginal cost is estimated to be $2.50 per cup. To price at marginal costs, the operator charges $2.00 from 4 to 5 PM and $2.50 from 5 to 6 PM.

Under the new regime, these estimates turn out to be sound, except that quite a few cars show up just before the price increases at 5 PM. To moderate this effort by drivers to avoid the 50 cent price increase at 5 PM, the operator decides to change the price more gradually, to $2.25 at 4:50 PM and to $2.50 at 5:10 PM. Such a transition period is called a "shoulder" period in peak-load pricing. Using an intermediate price from 4:50 to 5:10 PM reduces the strategic behavior of drivers enough so it is no longer a problem, and the quantities are very close to 200 per week in the first hour and 400 per week in the second. The local authorities welcome the longer operating hours and approve the new pricing and payment arrangement.

---

technologies that differ in their fixed and variable cost elements (nuclear-or coal-powered electricity generation, as examples).

Single Technology

The pricing problem is especially clear when we assume a simple technology so we postpone consideration of the situation in which several different technologies are available. Let capacity cost per unit of output be B, and suppose capacity is divisible so we may choose any number of units of capacity at that cost.[1] One difficulty of using marginal-cost pricing can be traced to problems in uncovering the value of marginal cost, but we assume marginal cost per unit of output is known and equal to b. No unit

---

[1] The classic treatment of this problem is from Boiteux (1960). Williamson (1966) examined indivisible capacity, and Crew (1968) treated that issue and differences in cost. Steiner (1957) provided another early solution to the peak-load pricing problem.

can be produced unless capacity exists for it. Thus $\overline{Q}$ units of capacity at cost $B\overline{Q}$ would allow production of any output $Q \leq \overline{Q}$ at operating cost bQ. This technology implies a cost function with fixed costs at $B\overline{Q}$ and operating cost per unit that is constant at the level of b up to $Q = \overline{Q}$. At that maximum output, $\overline{Q}$, short-run marginal cost essentially rises vertically to infinity, because the firm cannot produce any output beyond $\overline{Q}$.

The situation is illustrated for linear demands in Figure 11.1. For 12 peak hours of the day, demand D_1 is given by $P_1(Q_1)$, and for 12 off-peak hours demand D_2 is given by $P_2(Q_2)$. (If peak and off-peak services had the same price, we would have $Q_2 \leq Q_1$.) Consumer plus producer surplus represents welfare to be maximized. With the simple constant-cost technology that is assumed, producer's surplus turns out to be zero at a welfare-maximizing solution, so consumer surplus is effectively maximized. Suppose there is zero income elasticity of demand, and zero cross elasticity of demand between peak and off-peak services, so demand curves do not move as prices change. We accept the current income distribution, so to focus on efficiency we need give no concern to income distribution. Now the operating cost, b, is defined for a 12-hour period; that is, this cost of b must be incurred to produce one unit of service in each 12 hour period. The capacity cost, B, on the other hand, is defined for an entire day (24 hours). This means that once the cost, B, has been incurred, it is possible to produce a unit of service in each of the two 12-hour periods.

Two possible situations exist in which peak and off-peak pricing can be useful, and the one in Figure 11.1 is the simpler of the two. It has prices that are clearly equal to marginal costs at the peak and off-peak periods. Peak users pay capacity and operating cost per unit, $P_1 = b + B$, while off-peak users pay only operating cost, $P_2 = b$. Notice that the peak users *cause* capacity to be built for them. To increase output by one unit at the peak requires one additional unit of capacity, which costs B, as well as added operating cost of b. That total of $b + B$ is, thus, the marginal cost of providing

Figure 11.1 *Peak and Off-Peak Demands*

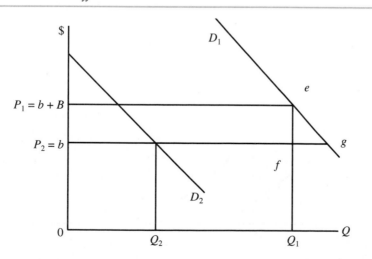

another unit at peak demand. This is true whether off-peak users exist or not, and it gives a basis for determining how large the optimal capacity should be. Optimal capacity, $\overline{Q}$, is equal to Q_1, the quantity demanded by peak demanders when they pay $b + B = P_1$, the long-run marginal cost. At off-peak times, output quantity can be increased one unit by the mere expenditure of b, because capacity is already plentiful at such times, and a price of b covers marginal (operating) cost. Thus, the solution that has $P_1 = b + B$ and $P_2 = b$ has prices that equal peak and off-peak marginal costs. Such a solution maximizes welfare.

You may have noticed that, for this solution in Figure 11.1 to work, the peak and off-peak demands cannot be close together, or capacity cost B cannot be very high. If the peak and off-peak demands are close together or capacity cost B is very high, the lower price, $P_2 = b$, might attract a larger quantity at the off-peak time than P_1 was expected to attract at the peak. If that happens—despite demand D_1 being generally greater than D_2—period 1 no longer experiences the peak demand! This is the second form of the peak and off-peak pricing situation, which Figure 11.2 illustrates. There, we assume $b = 0$, and "off-peak" quantity demanded at $P_2 = b$ actually is *greater* than "peak" quantity demanded at $P_1 = b + B$.

Applications of peak-load pricing have sometimes followed the method of Figure 11.1, in which peak users were expected to pay peak operating plus capacity costs while off-peak users only paid operating costs, only to find the quantity demanded at what was expected to be the off-peak period actually exceeded the quantity demanded at what was to be the peak. Natural gas from the North Sea was introduced on this basis into England and led to greater usage at what were supposed to be off-peak times. From such experiences, this phenomenon was named the **shifting peak** case. To deal with the shifting peak case shown in Figure 11.2, peak and off-peak users must share capacity cost, because not just the peak users, but users in both periods need capacity if quantity is to increase at the margin. From the

Figure 11.2 *Sharing Capacity Costs at Peak and Off-Peak Times*

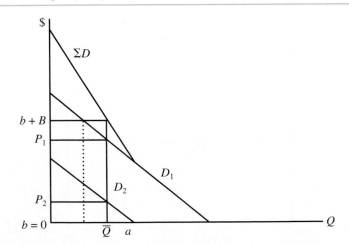

shifting-peak case that is illustrated, the off-peak price should rise and the peak price should fall so the same quantity is demanded in both periods. Such ideal pricing allows consumers to fully use capacity in both peak and off-peak periods.

To illustrate the capacity situation, and to play down operating cost to focus on the sharing of capacity cost, Professor Peter Steiner (1957) set operating cost (b) at zero, as we have done in Figure 11.2 with $b = 0$. Again, the peak and off-peak demands are equal in length (two periods per day of 12 hours each). For any level of capacity, let us ask the question; How much are all users willing to pay for an additional unit of capacity? For any quantity, the combined willingness to pay is the sum of the demand *prices* for the two demands at every level of capacity. Because the time periods are equal they can be weighted equally, so we can add the demands vertically and obtain for every capacity level the sum of what peak and off-peak demanders are willing to pay. That total willingness to pay for an added unit of capacity is the key to solving this pricing problem.

At each possible level of capacity in Figure 11.2, we can form a total value-of-capacity curve, labeled ΣD. We do so by adding together the willingness of both peak and off-peak users to pay for a marginal unit of capacity. To the right of the point where D_2 meets the horizontal axis at point a, the off-peak willingness to pay is zero, and D_1 alone represents the combined value-of-capacity curve (ΣD). Where that value-of-capacity curve equals marginal capacity cost, B (really $b + B$, but $b = 0$), capacity is optimal. For at that level of capacity, labeled $\overline{Q}$ in Figure 11.2, the consumers together value a marginal unit of capacity at exactly what it costs society to provide. Now observe that charging prices P_1 and P_2 at peak and off-peak times supports that capacity level perfectly, because P_1 plus $P_2 = B$. This results because ΣD was formed by adding the willingness to pay for capacity of both D_1 and D_2 demanders, so P_1 plus P_2 add to B at the quantity $\overline{Q}$ where B equals ΣD.

We can carry out the same analysis as that in Figure 11.2 if the operating cost, b, is greater than zero, as long as it is constant. Then b could be subtracted from each price so an analysis like that in Figure 11.2 could be carried out using $P_1 - b$ and $P_2 - b$ instead of P_1 and P_2. The reason we want $P_1 - b$ and $P_2 - b$ is that, as price minus operating cost, they represent the *contribution* each payment makes toward capacity. We should find that $(P_1 - b) + (P_2 - b) = B$ at the optimum. The same method could also be applied to the problem in Figure 11.1. The simple solution like that in Figure 11.1, in which peak users pay all capacity cost, would occur if there was a much smaller value of B in Figure 11.2. Indeed, peak users would pay all capacity cost if the level of capacity cost, B, intersected D_1 to the right of point a (where off-peak demanders in D_2 place no value on marginal capacity). This procedure for deriving ΣD should always be followed in solving peak-load pricing problems because it avoids the surprise of the shifting peak case, when quantity demanded in the peak period turns out to be smaller than the quantity that was expected in the off-peak period.

Simple addition of willingness to pay from demand curves is only possible when the time periods are of equal lengths. As Professor Oliver Williamson (1966) showed, we can weigh demands in the time periods in other ways, such as two to one for 16-hour and 8-hour time periods in the day, to solve a peak and off-peak pricing problem. It is also possible to accommodate any number of time periods. Having a choice among technologies can help to deal efficiently with this peak and off-peak problem. We call that diverse technology.

Diverse Technology

Now suppose that two techniques are available and they have different operating and capacity costs; this is a case of **diverse technology.** Electricity is generated by several techniques, using coal or nuclear power for examples, and because one has more fixed cost than the other these techniques can be efficiently used together to meet peak and off-peak demands. Figure 11.3 shows how peak and off-peak demands might look in a simple example of what is called an electricity **load duration curve,** which shows how demand for generated electricity, or the electrical load, is distributed over the hours of the day or any other periodic cycle. In Figure 11.3 the cycle is T hours long (if the time shown horizontally is a day, $T = 24$). The load on the electric power system is shown at two levels, Q_1 and Q_2 (on the vertical axis) for peak and off-peak levels. These loads in Figure 11.3 assume that prices have already been set that are consistent with this pattern of demand. The load demanded is Q_1 for t hours of the day and Q_2 for $T - t$ hours.

To meet the demand shown in Figure 11.3, one level of load, or quantity of service, Q_2, can be provided over the entire cycle of T hours, including the off-peak time. Then an additional quantity of service, $Q_1 - Q_2$, can be provided for just t hours, or the fraction, t/T of the total cycle, to generate a total of Q_1 units at the peak. Let us represent capacity and operating costs by B and b, as before, except we now define both costs for the entire cycle. Let one technique have capacity cost of B_1 and operating cost of b_1 and the other have capacity cost of B_2 and operating cost of b_2. Assume that $B_2 > B_1$ and $b_2 < b_1$, and that $B_2 + b_2 < B_1 + b_1$. These assumptions roughly fit coal-generated power as technique 1 and nuclear power as technique 2, because

Figure 11.3 *Simplified Load Duration Curve*

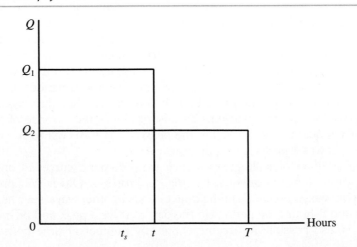

nuclear power has higher fixed costs but lower operating cost than coal power, and nuclear power can be produced at lower cost if plant utilization is very high.

These assumptions about cost magnitudes make technique 2, with costs B_2 and b_2, the lower cost technique if it can be fully utilized, or operated all of the time. But high-capacity costs can make technique 2 uneconomical at low utilization. As Figure 11.3 illustrates, it is possible to operate the technique that has low cost when fully utilized, technique 2, for the entire cycle of T hours, and the other technique for t hours. That use of the techniques is economical because technique 1 has lower fixed costs and can cost less than technique 2 at low levels of utilization.

When we adjust the techniques optimally, their average costs should be equal if operated t hours per day, or at utilization rate t/T.[2] The logic behind this claim is that at 100 percent utilization, technique 2 has the lowest cost, $B_2 + b_2 < B_1 + b_1$. But at a lower utilization rate, say only t_s hours which is less than t hours per day or at a utilization rate of t_s/T, the high fixed cost of technique 2 (B_2) could make the average cost of that technique higher than the average cost of technique 1. Higher cost results because if B_2 is utilized only t_s/T of the time. The amount, $B_2 T/t_s$, has to be recovered per unit to cover the capacity cost, B_2. So when t_s is low we can expect $b_1 + B_1 T/t_s < b_2 + B_2 T/t_s$.

As we decrease the utilization for both techniques from 100 percent of the cycle, at some level of utilization the average cost of technique 2 equals the average cost of technique 1. Then at lower rates of utilization, technique 1 has the lower average cost. By dividing the full demand cycle into parts (by setting the period of length t) at that utilization point where average costs are equal, one technique is better for moving in one direction, toward greater utilization, and the other technique is better for moving in the other direction. The firm is in the best possible position when the peak period covers t/T of the demand cycle, and at that level of utilization average costs are equal for the two techniques. From there, expanding the peak period (increasing t/T) makes technique 2 less costly, and reducing the peak period (reducing t/T), makes technique 1 less costly.

Now let us express the equality of unit costs for the two techniques as

$$b_1 + B_1 (T/t) = b_2 + B_2 (T/t).$$

By solving for t/T, we find that equal unit cost implies

$$t/T = (B_2 - B_1)/(b_1 - b_2)$$

If this condition can be satisfied, the optimal prices for peak and off-peak periods are particularly straightforward:

$$P_1 = b_1 + B_1 (T/t) \text{ and}$$
$$P_2 = b_2$$

The peak price P_1 is the price we should have expected if the capacity of technique 1 was needed only to serve peak users, which is indeed the case. Those who use the service at the peak time are required to pay for having technique 1 capacity stand idle in the rest of the demand cycle, as they should because such capacity was installed to

---

[2] Economist Ralph Turvey showed this result (1968, pp. 28–31).

serve them. But peak users also are paying the capacity cost of technique 2, which is covered by their payment P_1 (remember that $b_1 + B_1 (T/t) = b_2 + B_2 (T/t)$), leaving off-peak users to pay only $P_2 = b_2$, which is the operating cost of technique 2.

Pricing rules for this diverse technology problem can become more complicated. For example, problems arise when the demand periods cannot be made to match techniques ideally, as when peak demand is much longer or much shorter than the ideal of t/T for the demand cycle.[3] But peak and off-peak pricing can be used when demands follow regular time patterns, so prices can be set according to those time periods. Finding optimal prices at peak and off-peak periods still requires that costs be known, for costs remain the basis for setting prices.

Limitations of Marginal-Cost Pricing

When technology interferes with the functioning of a competitive market, government may replace it with another institution, perhaps a regulated statutory monopoly. Competitive pricing would then be a desirable standard to follow, but when competition cannot function, competitive pricing cannot be imitated. Marginal-cost pricing is better defined. When competition is replaced, the question of what prices should be set for the monopolist's outputs arises. Because pricing at marginal cost is such a prominent and attractive possibility, it is useful also to realize its limitations.

Recall that in Chapter 2 we found welfare-maximizing pricing was marginal-cost pricing, unless some limitation or constraint interfered. Marginal-cost pricing was ideal, regardless of how the market was organized. Indeed, the decision whether to rely on competition, or to oversee an economic activity by some other means, such as public utility regulation, might depend in part on whether competition could achieve and sustain the marginal-cost-pricing standard.

Although the principle of pricing at marginal cost may serve desirable efficiency goals, in pure form it is not always workable, even when it yields enough profit that firms can survive.[4] Marginal costs of some goods and services change markedly at different locations and times of day and, even if it were feasible, having prices respond to those changes can be disruptive. Taxi service from an airport to a city, for example, has different short-run marginal costs at different times and places. When many people want rides from the airport into town, marginal cost may be high, because additional passengers can be served only by quickly gathering together drivers, vehicles, fuel, and other scarce resources to serve them. On the other hand, when almost no one wants a ride from the airport, marginal cost may be low because there are idle taxis and drivers.

In reality, taxi fares tend to be the same at all times, often because they are set at publicly regulated levels that can only be changed through a regulatory hearing process. There is an advantage in such price stability; it enables consumers to control their financial outlays by knowing what the taxi charges are. The drawback of the constant price is that taxis may be scarce at peak times because the price does not rise to attract

---

[3] For analysis of this problem, see Wenders (1976) and Crew and Kleindorfer (1986).

[4] See Nobel laureate William Vickrey (1948, 1955) for classic descriptions of difficulties with marginal cost pricing.

more resources into service. Consumers have to wait longer for rides and as a consequence they have less control over their time. Indeed, delays caused by road congestion at peak travel times might even make taxi operation less profitable then, and unless a premium is granted at peak times some taxis may be discouraged from operating.

If there is a regular periodic pattern over the day or the week, as there often is for electricity demand or for telephone usage, preset prices that depend on time of day such as the peak and off-peak prices just considered may reflect changing costs reasonably well.[5] Even when demands follow such conveniently predictable patterns, they may be difficult to translate into a rate schedule that is simple enough to be readily understood by consumers. Moreover, some unpredictable departures from the patterns almost certainly occur. So it may be difficult to achieve the goal of marginal cost pricing, which is to inform consumers all the time of true alternative costs of their available choices while also giving producers information about consumers' preferences.

Determining marginal cost, especially at precise times and places, can also be a difficult accounting problem, because data are seldom collected over time intervals short enough to pinpoint the marginal costs for different levels of output at different times. Consequently, true marginal cost may not even be known. Should this problem of estimating a changing marginal cost be solved, there are still difficulties in using such estimates as a basis for pricing. First, it is not easy to inform consumers about continuously changing marginal-cost prices. Even if they can be informed, consumers may not be able to change their plans quickly enough to avoid high prices when marginal costs are high or take advantage of low prices when marginal costs are low. For all of these reasons, we seldom use momentary marginal costs as an influence on price. Regulators have instead tried to create more stable pricing arrangements that can easily be known and understood by consumers. Modern communication technologies make it easier to inform consumers, however, and in the future may allow greater use of prices based on real-time marginal costs.

Regulated industries often have prices set through quasijudicial procedures, which are so time-consuming they are seldom undertaken unless their results last for some time. As a result, regulated prices tend to be more rigid than competitive prices. Some responses to input price changes can lead automatically by prearranged formula to regulated output price changes. For example, fuel-adjustment clauses tie the price of electricity partly to the prices of fuels used to produce it. And as noted, whenever demand patterns are sufficiently predictable, prices can be set in advance at different levels according to the time of day, week, or year as peak and off-peak prices.[6]

Finally, a major problem arises with economies of scale. In the presence of economies of scale, pricing at marginal cost causes a loss, which threatens survival of an enterprise unless general tax revenues cover the enterprise's deficit. To avoid unfairness when some taxpayers pay for but do not use the service, regulators may require the enterprise to break even. That makes users pay all the costs they cause.

---

[5] See Hausman and Neufeld (1984) and Houthakker (1951).

[6] The optimality of a price equal to the marginal cost presumes that prices elsewhere in the economy equal marginal costs. Even if that is not the case, Davis and Whinston (1965) show that pricing at marginal cost is still useful for improving welfare.

But prices that do not equal marginal costs cause a loss in welfare. Ramsey pricing can minimize that loss.

11.2 | RAMSEY PRICING

When competition fails, representations of economic welfare enable us to identify efficient and socially desirable outcomes. We cannot claim that regulation should always replace the market, for identifying an efficient price is not enough if there is no workable way to put it into effect. It may be possible to set out a price that is ideal, yet no institution may be motivated to adopt it. Moreover, an ideal price may be difficult to agree on, because of conflict over what is ideal. All of these problems must be solved if the regulation of price is to be effective, and we cannot solve them all here. The aim in this section is to sketch briefly some of the main issues that arise when average costs decrease with output and to indicate the types of optimal pricing results that welfare analysis can provide. Box 11.3 begins by showing the solution to a pricing problem that allows a firm with fixed costs to breakeven.

We define *Ramsey prices* carefully in a moment, but for now let us say they are like discriminatory monopoly prices, but instead of allowing monopoly profit Ramsey prices are just high enough for the firm to breakeven or meet some other budgetary requirement. When the average cost of a public-service is declining with output, as when fixed costs exist, it can be socially desirable to raise money to cover fixed costs. That is what Ramsey prices do, they discriminate efficiently—as monopolies do—to raise money for fixed costs, but they do it just enough to cover those fixed costs.

One must see how technology may prevent the ideal ($P = MC$) solutions from serving satisfactorily under market competition. First, uniform prices equal to marginal costs at all outputs may not be feasible, in part because marginal costs may change with output levels that are unpredictable. More importantly, economies of scale cause marginal or incremental costs to lie *below* average costs. This means, then, that whether competition among firms or regulation drives prices to equal marginal costs, all firms lose money. To avoid that result one firm may be franchised as a regulated monopoly, and price may be set so that firm can breakeven.

Ramsey pricing by a monopoly firm may be appropriate when marginal costs lie below average costs. Marginal-cost pricing would still be more efficient then, but public revenue would have to make up the firm's deficit and that could be unfair to citizens who contribute tax funds for that purpose but do not use the service. To avoid such unfairness, regulators may require the enterprise to break even by setting prices above marginal costs. Ramsey prices consider demand elasticities in attempting to raise enough revenue through departures from marginal-cost prices to cover the deficit. In doing so, Ramsey prices cause the smallest possible welfare-loss inefficiency. Ramsey prices allow the firm to breakeven but, unlike marginal-cost prices, they are not ideal. While Ramsey prices are not ideal because they exceed marginal costs, they are the best prices in this specially constrained situation, so we call them **second-best prices**.

BOX 11.3 Fixed Cost at the Lemonade Stand

Suppose the operator of the lemonade stand in Box 11.2 discovers that when operating two hours a weekday and delivering 600 cups of lemonade a week (120 a day) a new technology can be less expensive than the current method. The new technology is contained in a machine that allows one operator to produce cups of lemonade very rapidly, so it can overcome the peak-load problem. By obtaining more juice from the lemons, it also lowers marginal cost to $1.00 per cup, not counting any profit allowance or any fixed cost. The operator is willing to be paid $150 per week (a little less than under the old arrangement but no hiring and firing is now required and the weekly $150 income is assured). The new technology has a fixed cost, however, of $500 per week.

The operator devotes two weeks to price experiments from which she estimates demand over the two hours from 4 to 6 PM to be

$$P = 3.3 - 0.002Q.$$

The operator agrees to charge a price of $2.00 per cup, which yields a quantity of 650 per week. This price is $1.00 higher than marginal cost, and that difference yields $650 to cover the $500 needed for fixed costs plus $150 for the operator. The demand estimate turns out to be correct and the new regime, shown in the figure, works very well.

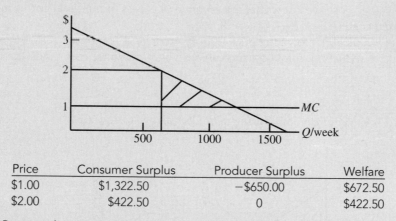

Price	Consumer Surplus	Producer Surplus	Welfare
$1.00	$1,322.50	−$650.00	$672.50
$2.00	$422.50	0	$422.50

Because the price now exceeds marginal cost, there is a welfare loss compared with pricing at marginal cost. The table shows consumer plus producer surplus at each price, $1.00 (marginal cost) and $2.00. The loss in welfare is the difference between welfare under a $1.00 price ($672.50) and under the $2.00 price ($422.50). That difference of $250 ($672.50 − $422.50) is the dead-weight loss that is striped in the figure. (That dead-weight loss area is one-half the base times the height of the triangle (1/2 bh). The height of the striped triangle is $2.00 − $1.00, or $1.00, and the base is the quantity at a price of $1.00 (1150) minus the quantity at a price of $2.00 (650), or 500. The base of 500 times the height of $1.00 times one-half equals $250, the striped dead-weight-loss area.)

Suppose that a service can be produced at constant marginal cost per unit, b, up to a capacity limit. There is also a total fixed cost of B. With constant marginal cost, average cost is decreasing with output. Because average cost is lower at a greater scale of operations, we say there are economies of scale, which cause a problem because a price equal to marginal cost is below average cost and does not yield enough revenue to cover total cost.

The Marginal-Cost Pricing "Solution"

Let's see how marginal-cost pricing can cause a loss. Suppose quantity demanded is given by $Q = Q(P)$, where P is market price, and total cost is given by $TC = B + bQ$ if $Q > 0$. This cost function possesses economies of scale, for as Q gets larger, average cost $AC = b + B/Q$ falls. Because marginal cost $MC = b$, $MC < AC$ ($b < b + B/Q$). Thus, pricing at marginal cost causes a loss. Figure 11.4 illustrates this case. Average cost, $AC = b + B/Q$, falls as Q is larger, and $MC = b$ is always below AC.

Consider welfare to be represented by consumer surplus plus producer surplus, or $W = CS + PS$, where producer surplus $PS = TR - TC$. Thus, welfare $W = CS + TR - TC$. Suppose, first, that price equals P_{AC}, a price that equals average cost where the demand curve and the average cost curve intersect. In that case, consumer surplus is the area above P_{AC}, up to the demand curve, and—because price equals average cost—producer surplus is zero. Moreover, because the firm breaks even when price equals average cost, we know that the revenue in excess of marginal cost is just equal to the fixed cost: $(P_{AC} - P_{MC}) Q_{AC} = B$.

Now think about lowering price from P_{AC} to P_{MC}. As output increases in response to this price reduction, total cost increases by only marginal cost times the quantity

Figure 11.4 *Marginal-Cost Pricing with Decreasing Average Cost*

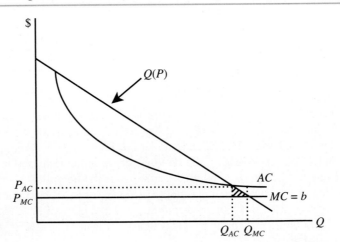

increase, or b $(Q_{MC} - Q_{AC})$. Consumers pay this cost increase because $P_{MC} = b$. The fixed cost, B, is no longer covered when price equals marginal cost, however, because no revenue is left to go toward fixed cost B. Thus, B is now the amount of the firm's loss, which means the gain in producer surplus from lowering price is $\Delta PS = -B$. Consumer surplus increases by $B = (P_{AC} - P_{MC})Q_{AC}$ plus the area of the striped triangular area in Figure 11.4. By the one-half-the-base-times-the-height rule for the area of a triangle, the area of the striped triangle is $\frac{1}{2}$ $(P_{AC} - P_{MC})$ $(Q_{MC} - Q_{AC})$. Thus, the gain in consumer surplus from lowering price from P_{AC} to P_{MC} is

$$\Delta CS = (P_{AC} - P_{MC}) Q_{AC} + \frac{1}{2} (P_{AC} - P_{MC}) (Q_{MC} - Q_{AC})$$
$$= \frac{1}{2} (P_{AC} - P_{MC}) Q_{AC} + \frac{1}{2} (P_{AC} - P_{MC}) Q_{MC}.$$

We know the gain in producer surplus is negative, at $\Delta PS = -B$. Whether welfare improves depends on whether $\Delta CS - \Delta PS > 0$. Because $\Delta PS = -B = -(P_{AC} - P_{MC})Q_{AC}$, we can see that ΔCS is larger because it is half of ΔPS, or $\frac{1}{2} (P_{AC} - P_{MC}) Q_{AC}$, plus half of a greater number, or $\frac{1}{2} (P_{AC} - P_{MC}) Q_{MC}$ (the latter number is greater because $Q_{MC} > Q_{AC}$).

Thus, lowering price to marginal cost improves welfare. Again, however, lowering price to marginal cost may be unfair, because there is a deficit (equal to B) and some who do not consume the good or service may be asked to pay taxes to cover that deficit. Pursuing efficiency by pricing at $P_{MC} = b$ could, thus, make some citizens worse off. In specific cases, losers might object so vociferously that no project could win approval through political institutions, even when—if the gains and losses from many projects were distributed evenly over the population—there would be net gains in efficiency.

Notice that if political institutions become involved in a decision about the pricing of a service, the number of persons who gain and the number who lose could be crucial in any voting outcome. If majority rule is used in the decision, for example, and those benefitting from a price below average cost outnumber those who do not use the service but are forced through taxes to contribute to its support, the community might adopt a price below average cost. This result illustrates how an efficient outcome might be chosen through political institutions, but the efficient marginal-cost price can be unfair and can harm minority interests. The vote might also go the other way and require the service to break even. Even though we cannot count on political institutions to balance subtly the equity and efficiency interests in economic problems, the public often regards such institutions as the legitimate arbiters, so their role inevitably is important.

In the example in Figure 11.4, even though welfare is greater when pricing at marginal cost, it causes a loss, and taxes do not exist that cover the loss without distorting our consumption choices. For instance, using excise, or per-unit, taxes to cover a deficit in one market makes effective prices higher than marginal costs in other markets. If all means of raising money to meet the deficit in one market cause price distortions in other markets, then the marginal cost price is not efficient either. The price should be raised at least enough to share with other available means the task of covering the general deficit. Modifying the problem, to require that revenues cover cost, takes

---

BOX 11.4 A Mathematical Solution to the Second-Best Problem

For the mathematically inclined, we can explore the second-best problem by appending to the welfare maximizing problem a constraint requiring that revenues equal total costs, or $PQ = B + bQ$. The constrained welfare maximization problem is:

$$L(Q,\lambda) = \int_0^Q P(Q)dQ - (B + bQ) + \lambda[P(Q)Q-(B+bQ)].$$

Maximizing L with respect to Q and λ, we obtain

$$(P - b)/P = (\lambda/(1 + \lambda))(1/E),$$

where $E = -(\partial Q/\partial P)(P/Q)$ is the price elasticity of demand. For total revenue to equal total cost when there is only one service, we know that price must equal average cost. (As output increases, average cost must intersect the demand curve from below to yield an equilibrium.) This is the breakeven solution at price P_{AC} in Figure 11.4. Because b equals marginal cost, the price is like a monopoly price except for the $\lambda/(1 + \lambda)$ term on the right-hand side. To simplify, let $\lambda/(1 + \lambda) = K$. This term, $\lambda/(1 + \lambda) = K$, is less than one, and it lowers the markup over long-run marginal cost to the level that allows the firm merely to break even. The second-best price also is some fraction of a monopoly price in the multiple-product (or multiple-service) case, where "average cost" may not be well defined.

---

us to the general problem of *second-best* pricing. The next section treats optimal pricing by a firm that is required to breakeven, and the resulting prices are Ramsey prices.

Ramsey Prices

One way to deal with cases in which pricing a service at marginal cost results in a deficit is to charge a higher price, so those who do not use the service need not pay taxes to support its deficit. Thus, the community might require that all costs of the service be met by payments from users of the service. The community can still pursue a socially optimal price, but subject to the requirement that sufficient revenues be raised to cover all costs. The resulting problem belongs to a general class of problems that are called *second best* because a constraint (that the firm break even) prevents the achievement of a first-best, or ideal, solution. Solving a second-best problem here yields Ramsey prices, which come as close as possible to ideal or welfare maximizing prices but subject to the constraint that the enterprise break even. Such prices are called Ramsey prices after the discoverer of their properties in the form of optimal taxes.[7] A simple one-product form of the more complex multi-product problem that mathematician Frank Ramsey solved is in Box 11.4.

For years, Interstate Commerce Commission (ICC) regulators in the United States used an approximation to Ramsey pricing called "value-of-service" pricing in

---

[7] See Ramsey (1927).

setting regulated railroad rates. The aim was to have these rates cover not only marginal transportation cost but also the substantial fixed costs of railroad operations. Commodities for which railroad service was very valuable were priced farther above their transportation costs than were commodities for which the value of the transportation service was low. When the value of service is high, demand is less elastic, and transportation prices are high. Another example arises in the pricing of postal services, where Ramsey principles receive attention. In the United States, First Class Mail, which has a low elasticity of demand, has a greater markup than, say, parcels, for which demand is more elastic. Fixed costs are large in both railroad and postal cases, and marginal-cost pricing was ruled out by the fairness argument. Raising additional revenue from the services to cover fixed cost was accepted as a desirable goal.

Let us state the Ramsey pricing rule. If $I = 1, \ldots, n$ services are to be provided, and they are independent of one another (all cross elasticities are zero), the pricing rule for the ith service is

$$(P_i - MC_i)/P_i = K/-E_{ii}, i = 1, \ldots, n.$$

On the right-hand side, K is a constant that is less than one. With multiple services, average cost per service may not be easy to define, because fixed cost may be a sum that cannot be allocated to individual services. Costs such as the corporate headquarters, for example, which supports every service, are hard to allocate to any one service so that its average cost can be estimated. But the solution value of K plus values of marginal costs (MC_i's) and demand elasticities (E_{ii}'s) yields Ramsey prices (P_i's) that allow total revenue to cover total cost.

The similarity of Ramsey pricing to multi-product monopoly pricing is striking. Every ratio of price minus marginal cost over price is modified from the monopoly level by the constant, $K < 1$, to yield revenue merely sufficient to cover total cost. It is as if all elasticities are multiplied by the same constant to make them larger, and then the problem is solved as a monopoly would solve it. The result is the Ramsey prices that eliminate the deficit while minimizing the loss in welfare from setting prices above marginal costs.

With zero cross-elasticities of demand among the firm's multiple products, we can also call the Ramsey pricing rule the **inverse-elasticity pricing rule**. The pricing rule makes all the departures from marginal costs over price (as $(P_i - MC)/P_i$) inversely proportional to demand elasticities. The inverse relationship means that when demand elasticity is *low* in absolute value, the ratio of price minus marginal cost over price is *high*.

Using some approximations, we can see another form of the Ramsey pricing rule. First, let the departure from marginal cost be $P_i - MC_i = \Delta P$, and, in the elasticity formula, let $\partial Q_i/\partial P_i = \Delta Q_i/\Delta P_i$. Then we can express the inverse-elasticity rule as

$$\Delta P_i/P_i = K/(\Delta Q_i/\Delta P_i)(P_i/Q_i).$$

On canceling out the $\Delta P/P$ terms, this equation reduces to

$$K = \Delta Q_i/Q_i.$$

Because K is a constant, this means that as prices move away from marginal costs to Ramsey prices, *all* quantity adjustments are in the *same* proportion. Thus, in moving away from marginal-cost prices to Ramsey prices for two goods, i and j, the quantity adjustments should satisfy

$$\Delta Q_i / Q_i = \Delta Q_j / Q_j.$$

This equation means that whatever ratio existed between outputs Q_i and Q_j when prices equaled marginal costs still holds at Ramsey prices. That is, Q_i / Q_j is the *same* at Ramsey prices as at marginal-cost prices.

This alternative quantity-ratio form of the Ramsey pricing rule is more general than the inverse-elasticity pricing rule. The equal proportionate reduction in all quantities applies even when cross elasticities are not zero, whereas we need to modify the inverse elasticity pricing rule for that case. In practice, the proportional quantities relation is sometimes helpful in working out solutions to Ramsey pricing problems.

Here is an intuitive rationale for Ramsey pricing. If all goods, services, and pleasures could be taxed, raising revenue for public services would cause no problem. An equal percentage tax could be imposed on everything, so it would not affect price ratios or relative prices, and it would therefore introduce no inefficiency. But it is not possible to tax everything because leisure cannot be taxed (we don't really purchase leisure)! So any tax makes leisure more attractive, relative to either work (income tax) or to purchasing goods (sales tax), and that distorts relative prices. You may be thinking that you can tax leisure effectively by subsidizing work. This is correct, but subsidizing work will not raise revenue, so it does not provide a solution to the problem. Given that leisure cannot be taxed, a second-best approach asks what the next best policy is. That second-best policy is Ramsey pricing, which gets at leisure by raising prices farther above costs on goods that have low (in absolute value) elasticities of demand. A higher mark up on goods that have less elastic demands is like a tax on leisure, because individuals want to spend their money on goods that have less elastic demands, and to buy them they have to work more and, thus, have less leisure time. The second-best policy gets at leisure indirectly by inviting more work and therefore less leisure.

The Ramsey rule—in its simple inverse elasticity form—is exactly like the profit-maximizing monopoly pricing rule except for the constant term, K. Monopolies are very efficient at raising money from consumers. In Ramsey pricing circumstances, raising money is socially desirable, to cover fixed costs and avoid a deficit. So Ramsey pricing uses monopoly methods but just enough to serve social welfare.

Avoiding Cross-Subsidy in the Multi-product Firm

Ramsey prices conceivably can contain cross subsidies. We can use average incremental cost to test for cross-subsidy, because if revenue from a good or service does not pay its average incremental cost it must be subsidized. In a two-good example, where the two goods are Q_1 and Q_2 and total cost is $C(Q_1, Q_2)$, the average incremental cost (AIC_1) of good Q_1 is

$$AIC_1 = (C(Q_1, Q_2) - C(0, Q_2))/Q_1.$$

BOX 11.5 Ramsey Pricing at the Lemonade Stand

One bright sunny afternoon the operator of the lemonade stand observes a difference between cars arriving between 4 and 5 PM and those arriving between 5 and 6 PM. The cars arriving after 5 PM tend to be fancier and more expensive. This prompts the operator to consider dividing the market and charging a higher price in the second hour. She conducts more pricing experiments, from which she estimates separate demands for the 4 to 5 PM period (P_1 and Q_1) and the 5 to 6 PM period (P_2 and Q_2):

$$P_1 = 2.50 - 0.0025 \, Q_1$$
$$P_2 = 6.50 - 0.01 \, Q_2.$$

We can also express these demands as $Q_1 = 1,000 - 400 \, P_1$ and $Q_2 = 650 - 100 \, P_2$. If we combine these demands, we can add the quantities as $Q = Q_1 + Q_2 = 1,000 - 400 \, P + 650 - 100 \, P = 1,650 - 500 \, P$, for $0 < p < 2.5$. Adding market quantities is ordinarily the proper way to combine separate demands. We can then convert the result into $P = 3.3 - 0.002 \, Q$, which is the same single-good demand that was estimated in Box 11.3. With the more detailed demands here, however, the welfare evaluations can change because—especially for Q_2—the estimated *consumer surplus* can change.

After experimenting in an attempt to find Ramsey prices, the operator settles on $P_1 = \$1.18$ and $P_2 = \$2.15$. These prices yield quantities of $Q_1 = 475$ and $Q_2 = 435$. At these prices the total contribution to fixed cost is \$652, which is very close to the sum of \$650 obtained from a single price of \$2.00 in Box 11.3. The question now is whether welfare loss is lower with these Ramsey prices than with the single price of \$2.00, which resulted in a dead-weight loss of \$250.

Pricing at marginal cost is shown in the table below to yield the greatest welfare, at \$1,312, but results in a deficit, and using taxes to cover that deficit may require payments from nonusers and, thereby, be unfair. Under Ramsey pricing the total surplus is lower, at \$1,228. When the operator prices above marginal cost, though, Ramsey pricing minimizes the consequent welfare loss. Setting the price at \$2.00 yields total surplus of \$1,062 (in round numbers). This is shown in the table as breakeven pricing. Pricing at \$2.00 to breakeven still causes a welfare loss of \$250 (\$1,312 − \$1,062), while Ramsey pricing causes a welfare loss of only \$84 (\$1,312 − \$1,228).

Price	Consumer Surplus	Contribution to Fixed Cost	Fixed Cost	Welfare CS+TR−TC
Marginal Cost Pricing				
$P_1 = \$1.00$	\$450			
$P_2 = \$1.00$	\$1,512			
Total	\$1,962	0	\$650	\$1,312
Ramsey Pricing				
$P_1 = \$1.18$	\$280	\$152		
$P_2 = \$2.15$	\$946	\$500		
Total	\$1,226	\$652	\$650	\$1,228
Breakeven Pricing				
$P_1 = \$2.00$	\$50			
$P_2 = \$2.00$	\$1,012			
Total	\$1,062	\$650	\$650	\$1,062

Average incremental cost is the per-unit increase in total cost that results from producing good Q_1 at all. Average incremental cost does not depend in any way on marginal cost.

If consumers of the good, Q_1, pay less than AIC_1 for it, the enterprise that produces both Q_1 and Q_2 must be losing money on Q_1. Assuming that the enterprise is breaking even, this means essentially that the other customers (those purchasing Q_2) are subsidizing good Q_1. Cross subsidies among products of a multi-product firm are undesirable because they represent inefficiencies. Good 1 is priced too low in that it causes two bad results. First, there is too much consumption of good 1, because customers are allowed to pay less than it costs. Second, consumers of good 2 pay too much, because they must pay the costs for the good they consume and also contribute to the costs of subsidized good 1. So they consume too little of the good 2. Average incremental cost is useful as a way to test for cross subsidy.

Because Ramsey prices are formed in the multi-product firm by marking up marginal costs inversely according to demand elasticities, they do not depend on incremental costs in any way. As a result it is possible, if marginal cost is much lower than average incremental cost, that the Ramsey price for some good (or goods) is lower than that good's average incremental cost, which can cause undesirable cross subsidy. To avoid this outcome, we need to compare Ramsey prices with average incremental costs to insure that the Ramsey prices are not lower. If, after such a comparison, we find that the Ramsey price for one (or more) good(s) to be lower than average incremental cost, the price of the good(s) should be raised at least to the level of average incremental cost(s). The Ramsey price for the fastest USPS offering, Express Mail, has been estimated to be below that service's average incremental cost, and price was set at least at that higher level to avoid subsidizing the Express Mail service.

11.3 │ NONUNIFORM PRICING

There is another class of prices that can help to alleviate the problems caused by economies of scale or economies of scope. These prices are not the same for every unit purchased, so they are called **nonuniform prices**. Two common forms are *two-part prices* and *block prices*. Two-part pricing often involves a fixed fee, which makes the first unit more expensive, as well as a price per unit, and it has commonly been used in pricing wire-line telephone service. Block pricing allows one price for a certain range of quantities, another price—usually lower—for the next range of quantities and so on in blocks of quantities, and it is common for electricity service.

Other forms of nonuniform pricing are also possible. While allowing consumers' marginal decisions to be based on low prices—prices close to marginal costs—these nonuniform pricing methods generally raise more money than marginal-cost prices would raise, because of the higher fees charged for units consumed earlier. Box 11.6 illustrates this point. Raising money, while also having marginal

---

BOX 11.6 Nonuniform Pricing at the Lemonade Stand

If all consumers of lemonade in each demand group in Box 11.5 are identical, we might expect that all would consume if we formed a lemonade club along the following lines. The consumers would pay a weekly fee and would then be able to buy lemonade at its marginal cost (of $1.00 per cup). Their demands are

$$P_1 = 2.50 - 0.0025\, Q_1 \text{ and}$$
$$P_2 = 6.50 - 0.01\, Q_2,$$

where Q_1 is demanded from 4 to 5 PM and Q_2 is demanded from 5 to 6 PM. At the marginal cost price of $1.00 per cup, suppose there are 230 customers, 120 buying 600 cups of Q_1 a week, and 110 buying 550 cups of Q_2 a week. A fixed fee of $2.85 per week, if paid by every one of the 230 customers, raises about $655, enough to cover the $650 in fixed cost plus the small added cost of maintaining a club membership list.

The club arrangement allows a fixed fee and a marginal price that amount to a two-part price, or a nonuniform price. It is nonuniform in that the effective price of the first unit, which includes the fixed fee and the unit price, is much more than successive units. If all consumers participate, consumer surplus is greater with this pricing, at $1,307, almost as much as the consumer surplus of $1,312 achieved by marginal-cost pricing. If all consumers do not participate then the success is not as great. But using a two-part price can ordinarily enable a welfare maximizing seller to achieve a higher level of consumer surplus.

---

prices near marginal costs, is desirable in industries that have decreasing average costs, and it can reduce the degree of reliance on Ramsey pricing. It does not *eliminate* the use of Ramsey pricing, because even the fixed fee in a two-part price rarely faces perfectly inelastic demand. Pricing according to Ramsey principles can reduce welfare loss, and Ramsey principles can apply even to the fixed fees in nonuniform prices.

Exchange and Other Problems with Nonuniform Prices

A nonuniform price for a single good or service might not persist. If there are many consumers, the possibility of exchange would allow them to trade until they agreed on a single uniform price. Nonuniform prices, can still be used where exchange is not possible, however, or at least where it is not easy, which is often the case with public services such as telephone or electricity.[8] Two consumers cannot exchange electricity easily, for instance, or phone service, so a degree of nonuniform pricing is feasible for those services. Wire-line telephone rates sometimes involve a fixed monthly fee plus a fee for usage, perhaps for long-distance calls. You must pay a fixed fee plus a unit price

---

[8] For careful analysis of this effect of transaction costs on the use of nonuniform prices, see McManus (2001).

to consume the first unit, and units after that cost only the unit price. The average price is nonuniform. Electricity rates for marginal units per time period often vary as total units consumed in the time period vary.

Difficulties still remain for nonuniform prices. How can the actions of many consumers be coordinated when the seller does not know the demand of each, particularly when the same price schedule must be offered to all consumers? Will some pay higher average prices than others because they prefer smaller quantities, even though the marginal cost of serving them is identical? Will all pay the same marginal price, but different fixed fees, depending on quantities? These questions arise when there are many consumers and they have different demands. If consumers' demands are similar, they will all choose virtually the same quantity, and, if resale by consumers is infeasible, an ideal solution to the decreasing cost-pricing problem is in principle achievable, because having consumers be very similar is like having only one consumer.

Two main tariff structures are used to produce reasonable nonuniform pricing solutions for the decreasing cost situation, the *two-part price* and the *block price*. Both can offer advantages over simple uniform prices.

The Two-Part Price

Even when a nonuniform price can improve welfare, there still may be problems in conveying its details to consumers so that they can choose soundly. Approximation may be desirable, to achieve some benefit of optimal pricing and yet not overburden consumers with highly complex price schedules. A crude approximation can be accomplished, for example, by a **two-part price,** which involves one price as a fixed fee that must be paid to consume even one unit, and a second price for each unit. Under a two-part price the supplier can set a price per marginal unit at marginal cost, $p = b$, and also charge a fixed fee, F, for consuming even one unit in a given time period. Proceeds from the fixed fee could go to cover what otherwise would be a deficit. If total fixed costs are B and n consumers each consume the same quantity, Q', for example, to cover costs the appropriate fixed fee would be $F = B/n$.[9]

The principles of Ramsey pricing can apply in setting two-part prices. Suppose there is a marginal cost of connecting an additional consumer, just as there is a marginal cost of delivering an additional unit of output, and there are additional fixed costs. The fixed fee can cover the cost of connecting the consumer and the unit price can cover the cost of delivering an additional unit. Then to cover fixed cost, both the price per unit and the fixed fee should be increased so the ratio of price minus marginal cost over price $((P - MC)/P)$ is inversely proportional to demand elasticity in each case, in keeping with Ramsey pricing principles.[10]

Because the fixed fee of our two-part price does not always reflect the cost of consuming a first unit, it can distort choices. If consumers differ in their demands, for

---

[9] Nobel laureate Ronald Coase (1946) effectively demonstrated this solution.
[10] See Schmalensee (1981) and Sherman and Visscher (1982a).

example, some who intend to consume smaller amounts might find the fixed fee so high they would decide not to consume at all, even though they might willingly pay more than the true marginal cost of their small consumption. The seller, however, lacks information about each consumer's demand. In such a case, offering a choice between tariffs might be beneficial. We examine this possibility by focusing on information.

Information and Two-Part Prices

How can a seller choose prices if the seller does not have information about consumers' demands? Suppose there is a fixed cost, B, and constant marginal unit cost, b, for any quantity of output; so total cost is $B + bQ$. If consumers are similar in their demands, a two-part price may serve ideally in a situation like this. If consumers differ considerably in their demands, however, some who intend to consume small quantities may find it better to forgo consumption of the good rather than pay the fixed fee, and the seller may not choose an optimal pricing scheme. Indeed, Figure 11.5 presents a two-part price example in which one consumer decides not to consume, making necessary an increase in the fixed fee for other customers.

The service in Figure 11.5 has a marginal cost of b per unit and total fixed cost B. Suppose, first, that every one of n consumers has the same demand at D_1 and all have zero income elasticity of demand (there is no income effect). To be eligible to buy at $p = b$, each consumer would also be required to pay a fixed fee. Each consumer would then be willing to pay a fixed fee up to the amount represented by consumer surplus, the large area abe in Figure 11.5. If there are n consumers, the fixed fee per consumer that covers all costs is B/n, and as long as the sum of all fixed fee payments, $n(B/n) = B$, is less than abe, the service can be provided without losing money. Indeed, if no consumer decides not to use the service because of the fixed fee this is an ideal solution. All consumers contribute to fixed costs and are able to consume at the marginal cost per unit.

Figure 11.5 *An Example in Which a Two-Part Price Causes Harm*

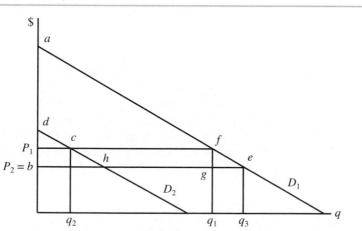

An equal sharing of fixed cost among consumers may cause a problem when consumers differ in their demands, however, and the seller does not know their demands. For then the fixed fee may drive away consumers who use small amounts of service. In Figure 11.5, suppose there are two consumers whose different demands for units of a service are shown as D_1 and D_2, again assuming zero income elasticity of demand (no income effect). Suppose the price, P_1, is equal to the average cost of producing the total quantity, $q_1 + q_2$. That is, suppose $P_1 = b + B/(q_1 + q_2)$. Consumer 1 consumes q_1 units at price P_1 while consumer 2 consumes q_2 units at that price.

Now suppose a fixed fee at the level of $F = B/2$ is introduced, a fee that is equal for both consumers, and paying it entitles customers to consume units at the lower price of $P_2 = b =$ marginal cost. This two-part price structure replaces the uniform price P_1, which is no longer available. In this case, a fixed fee equal to $B/2$ exceeds the consumer surplus for consumer 2 at marginal price b, the area dbh. Then consumer 2 decides not to purchase and is worse off than at the price of P_1, where consumer surplus of dP_1c was available. With consumer 2 out of the market, consumer 1 has to pay *all* of the capacity cost, or B, and so is also worse off than with the uniform price of P_1 when consumer 2 was participating. Thus the two-part tariff with equal fixed fees has made things worse than they were under the simple price-equals-average-cost-per-unit tariff.

What keeps the two-part price from being effective here is lack of information about consumer willingness to pay, preventing a two-part price from being tailored to the situation of each consumer. Such information is hidden from the seller. Even if asked, consumers have incentive to understate their willingness to pay, hoping to mislead the seller to obtain a lower fee. It is possible, however, to give consumers a choice through which they will essentially reveal their preferences. At the same time, they will face an appropriate rate tariff. This can be done in the situation of Figure 11.5 by offering a new two-part tariff while also leaving in place the old uniform price, P_1, so each consumer can choose either tariff. Then consumer 2 would consume at the uniform price of P_1, making some contribution to fixed cost, rather than leaving the market. Consumer 1 could pay the same contribution to fixed cost as before in Figure 11.5 (the area P_1fgP_2) while consuming the greater quantity, q_3, and consumer surplus *feg*. We call the principle involved **self-selection**. Consumers select themselves into the appropriate rate category, and welfare improves as a result.[11]

If everyone's demand were known, the unit price could reflect marginal cost per unit, and a different fixed fee could be set for every consumer. The monopoly seller could then attract consumers by making each consumer's fee always less than that consumer's surplus from consuming the good. As long as total consumer surplus exceeded fixed cost, the service could be provided, with positive benefit in economic welfare. This shows that the problem of pricing in this decreasing cost situation involves not only technology, the source of decreasing cost that can handicap the functioning of a competitive market, but also information. The seller does not know consumers' demands, except in the aggregate. Lacking information about individual

---

[11] See Willig (1978).

demands, the seller cannot find the optimal price structure for each individual. A desirable outcome can still be obtained, however, if consumers are given a chance to choose between rate structures. In doing so they essentially may reveal enough about their demands to allow a reasonably efficient outcome.

Block Prices

Let us return to the self-selection example in Figure 11.5, in which consumers were given a choice, for a certain time period, of either paying P_1 per unit *or* paying the fixed fee F and, thereafter, P_2 per unit. Figure 11.6 illustrates the outlays consumers have to make for different quantities under the two pricing structures. Figure 11.6a shows two outlay schedules, one at a simple per-unit price of P_1 and the other requiring a fixed payment F after which a price of P_2 per unit is required. Up to quantity q^* the simple P_1 price per unit allows the lowest outlay, and that is what consumer 1 would prefer. At quantities above q^* the two-part price involving F and P_2 allows a lower outlay. Thus, if they are given a choice, we should expect to find consumers along the solid portions of the two outlay schedules in Figure 11.6a, rather than the

Figure 11.6 *An Example of a Block Price*

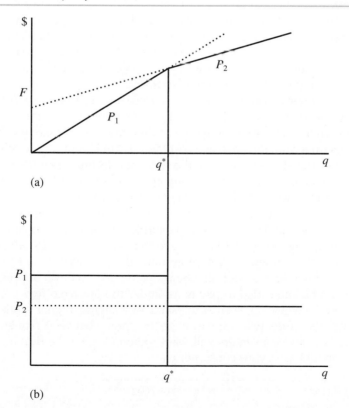

dashed portions. Prices in the solid-line portions dominate dashed-line portions of the outlay schedules. The marginal rates per unit, and the way they switch at q^*, are shown by the solid line in Figure 11.6b. The tariff shown in Figure 11.6 is called a **block price**; because a different price applies to different blocks of the quantity range. A block price is a nonuniform price, because the price per unit does not remain constant over all quantities consumed.

As we have seen, giving the consumer a choice among price structures can improve economic welfare compared with either the P_1, or the F plus P_2, rate structures taken alone. A block tariff can easily offer such a choice between rate structures. We already noticed for the two-part tariff in Figure 11.5 that P_1 could have an advantage over F plus P_2 if consumers differed substantially in the amount they would tend to consume and in the consumer surplus benefit they enjoyed. With a choice between rate structures, the consumer who wishes to consume more was shown to be better off by having access to marginal usage at marginal cost. That benefit could be shared by the two consumers through adjustment of F and P_1. The old price, P_1, might be set slightly lower, for example, with resulting lost revenue made up through a slight increase in F. Then both consumers could be better off.

To be sure that the benefits of block prices, or of a choice of price structures, can be achieved, a seller must meet two requirements. First, the seller must choose categories that consumers wish to select themselves into. We call this requirement the **incentive compatibility constraint**. In Figure 11.5, the consumer seeking less use of the service must prefer the uniform price, P_1, while the consumer who prefers the larger quantity can purchase under the rate structure of F plus P_2. If either consumer preferred the other arrangement, incentive compatibility would not be satisfied. Second, the parties must both be willing to participate in the seller's arrangement. We call this requirement the **participation constraint**.

Sellers can offer consumers a choice of price structures that meet the incentive compatibility constraint and the participation constraint. If consumers in Figure 11.5 are allowed such a choice, we have seen that the same revenue can be obtained from consumer 2 as under the P_1 = average cost tariff. From Figure 11.5 we also saw that a new fixed fee, F, equal to the value of the reduction in unit price $(P_1 - P_2)q_1$, or the area P_1fgP_2, could be charged to consumer 1 for the right to purchase at unit price $P_2 = b$, and this would yield the same revenue to the firm. Consumer 1 would be willing to consume q_3 units at the marginal price per unit of P_2, and would enjoy the added benefit represented by the consumer surplus triangle, fge. The consumer, therefore, would be willing to pay a fixed fee up to the larger area P_1feP_2, which means the firm could raise *more* revenue. Now how does this situation look to consumer 1? Consumer 1 is bound to be better off when consumer 2 is a buyer at price P_1. Because consumer 1 can be persuaded to pay more under the preferred two-part price, consumer 1 cannot be worse off, even at the same or a slightly higher profit level for the firm. The firm, therefore, will want to offer the choice between rate structures that improves welfare, and consumers will want to accept it; so the desirable offering is incentive compatible and wins consumer participation.[12]

---

[12] A general proof that this result is possible may be found in Willig (1978).

Figure 11.7 *The Choice between Two Blocks of a Three-Block Tariff*

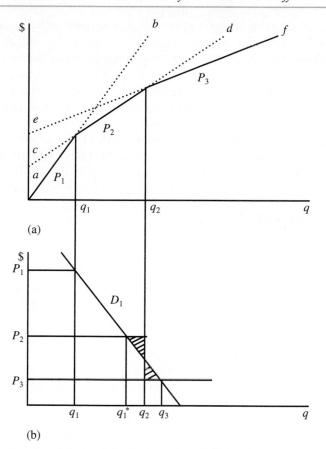

(a)

(b)

Figure 11.7a illustrates a rate structure involving three blocks. For quantities up to q_1, the total outlay for any quantity at price P_1 is represented by the line ab, which has slope of P_1. A lower slope, or lower marginal price, of P_2 is represented in the total outlay line cd for quantities above q_1. This line represents lower costs than line ab for quantities from q_1 to q_2. A still lower marginal price of P_3 is represented in the total outlay line ef for quantities above q_2. Figure 11.7b illustrates the marginal prices for each quantity range. There, the marginal price begins at P_1 for the block of consumption quantities up to q_1, then switches to P_2 for quantities up to q_2, then switches to P_3 for quantities greater than q_2. To maximize economic welfare, the lowest marginal price, P_3, must equal marginal cost, for otherwise an opportunity to benefit the consumer would go unexploited.

Having many blocks can complicate analysis at the market level, because buyers may choose quantities at different prices. A division between groups of consumers is created through self-selection at each price jump. Consider, for instance, the change in price from P_2 to P_3 in Figure 11.7. Consumers with demands that add to D_1 will demand $q_1{}^*$ units at price P_2. Consumers with demands of the sort represented by D_1 but who are willing to consume more than q_2 will switch into price block P_3. Consider consumers in the quantity range $q_1{}^*$ to q_3. Between paying P_2 at $q_1{}^*$ and paying P_3 at q_3, the consumer shown by D_1 is indifferent, because the striped areas are equal; the loss suffered on units from $q_1{}^*$ to q_2, where price exceeds the consumer's willingness to pay, is offset by the gain on units from q_2 to q_3, where consumer willingness to pay exceeds price. If other consumers have similarly sloped demands, no one will consume a quantity between $q_1{}^*$ and q_3. Demands within each price block are at the same marginal price and can reasonably be aggregated, so market-level analysis is still possible.

Interruptible Service Pricing

Thus far the two-part price has served primarily to raise funds from consumers so fixed costs can be covered. We did consider a two-part price above, however, where the fixed-fee portion of the price might reflect an installation or connection fee, in which case both parts of the two-part price would reflect costs. We now consider another case where both fixed and variable parts of the two-part price reflect costs. In this case, the fixed fee can represent a cost of capacity, and the variable, or per-unit, price can represent marginal cost.

Interruptible service pricing charges a fixed fee that varies with the assured rate of usage for which the customer wishes to pay. It is as if the customer pays to reserve a level of capacity that is to be kept available for that customer. The higher the fee paid, the more capacity the customer is assured. If you were considering such a contract in the case of electricity for your home, for example, you might pay to reserve a certain level of electricity below which you would not want to go. When capacity is scarce—as at peak times—that reserved level may be all you are allowed. Under an interruptible service contract, the supplier can cut back the electricity delivered, so it matches the assured level that was chosen and paid for by the customer through the appropriate fixed fee. That right of the supplier to cut back, or interrupt, the electricity chosen by the consumer is the crucial feature of interruptible service pricing.

When capacity is not scarce, the consumer may consume more electricity than indicated by the upper limit specified in the contract. When the demand on the distribution system is great, however, consumers can be cut back to the assured levels they purchased through their fixed fees. They may have only a rough idea how likely it is that they will be interrupted, but of course that probability will be lower as they choose a higher level of assured power. The interruptible-service-pricing scheme thus allows each consumer to choose an assured level of service, based on that consumer's own trade-off between price and assured supply. The contract also informs the supplier of how valuable reliability of service is to each consumer. Then the supplier can attempt to provide capacity to meet consumers' expressed preferences for reliable service.

11.4 | ACCESS PRICING

A new issue has arisen in recent years; How to price access to essential facilities, or bottleneck facilities, so that others besides the owners of the facilities may use them in providing services. A supplier of long-distance telephone service cannot reach a called party, for example, without access to the telephone network where the party is located. The pricing of such access takes on added importance when the party granting access provides the same service that is offered by the party to be allowed access, that is, when the parties compete. Suppose in this telephone case, for example, the local network also provides long-distance service. The grantor of access could then handicap its competitors by setting the access price high. On the other hand, if regulators take over and set the access price too low, the resource owner granting access is handicapped relative to its competitors.

To support competition in formerly regulated industries, the resources of one agent—say the operator of a local telephone network—are opened for use by another agent—say a long-distance service provider. Such access arrangements can foster competition among long-distance service providers, but they also raise the sensitive issue of how access to the first agent's resource is to be priced. After considering some examples of access we introduce the leading principles for determining access prices.

Examples of Access

Although telephone service is an area where access has systematically been introduced, access has also affected most other regulated industries. Tracks of one railroad have been made available to others for many years. Pipelines for natural gas can be an essential facility for the gas distributor who now has a form of access to the pipelines for transportation of natural gas. Transmission wires serve a similar purpose in the case of electricity. Mail delivery for mail transporters or for those who sort and code mail to make it easier for the Postal Service to handle can raise access pricing issues. Even a lemonade stand at a specially suitable location raises the question of access pricing, as Box 11.7 shows.

Often, access is arranged at only one level in the vertical stages from the origin to the completion of a service, as is the case when long-distance telephone service has access to local networks. Access is managed in two main ways. One policy settles for competition in one of the vertical stages, but prevents competition beyond that stage. Under terms of a 1982 court decision that opened the long-distance telephone service market, for example, local telephone networks were prevented from participating in other activities—such as long-distance service—on grounds that regulators would have difficulty ensuring fairness among competitors when some controlled both local and long-distance networks. While regulation might be simpler under such clear rules, the economic costs may also be considerable. If there are economies of scope in combining local and long-distance service, for example, those economies may not be realized when combining services is forbidden. If technology is changing rapidly, the initially best way of organizing may not continue to be the best way over time.

BOX 11.7 Access Pricing for Lemonade

In Box 11.3 we considered a lemonade stand facing a single demand,

$$P = 3.3 - 0.002\ Q.$$

The operator of the lemonade stand charged a price of $2.00, $1.00 greater than the marginal cost of $1.00, which led to sales of 650 cups a week and covered fixed cost of $650. That price of $2.00 also yielded consumer surplus of $422.50. What if another operator sought access to the little byway where the lemonade stand is located, the location being an essential facility, so the other operator could also sell lemonade?

Let the new operator be allowed access if he pays the existing operator $1.00 for every cup the new operator sells. If the new operator took a customer away from the existing operator, this access fee would cover the existing operator's fixed cost and, thus, enable her to continue to breakeven. This compensation makes her willing to grant access. Because the new operator probably cannot charge more than the existing price of $2.00, it must produce lemonade for $1.00 a cup ($2.00 price less $1.00 access fee) or less. That is, only an efficient new entrant can succeed. Incentive for the incumbent operator to grant access and attractiveness only to efficient entrants are desirable properties in an access fee.

The second way to manage access is to allow competition between the access provider and others. For instance, the Telecommunications Act of 1996 allows local telephone network operators to compete in long-distance markets, if they meet requirements for opening their local markets to competition. Here the most efficient organization can come into existence, but to foster it the access prices must be determined well. An error in setting the access price too high or too low unfairly benefits one party in the competition and harms another. In Figure 11.8, for example, the local network is a monopoly that also owns interexchange long-distance Network 1. Network 2 is a long-distance network that wishes to complete calls to customers in the local network, in competition with Network 1 and the local network. What access-price should Network 2 be charged? This question is treated in the next two subsections.

Figure 11.8 *Two Long-Distance Service Providers Connecting to a Local Network*

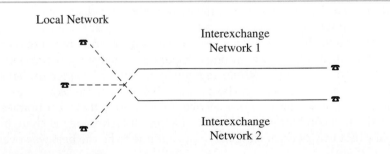

Requiring access to essential or bottleneck facilities is not new,[13] but requiring it on a broad scale and controlling its price are fairly new regulatory actions. The actions are justified on grounds that they foster competition where it did not exist before. Forcing access generally amounts to a significant redefinition of property rights, in that a monopoly owner of an essential facility—even a regulated owner—no longer controls use of the facility exclusively. The power to regulate price has been extended to a power to regulate a right of access and its price.

Two main ideas guide access pricing. First is *efficient component pricing (ECP)*, and second is the already familiar and more general idea of Ramsey pricing. We consider each in turn.

Efficient Component Pricing for Access

The **efficient component pricing rule (ECPR)** is a leading theoretical basis for determining access prices.[14] It calls for an access price to equal the incumbent provider's direct cost of arranging access, plus any opportunity cost of providing access. The inclusion of opportunity cost in the optimal access price allows the access provider to recover the profit it loses when a customer shifts to a competitor. That profit is the provider's opportunity cost of providing access to another supplier, and the ECPR compensates the provider for that loss. The good effect of this rule—allowing recovery of lost profit—is that it can motivate the provider to offer access, because granting access does not make the provider worse off. If a direct sale is lost by granting access, for example, in addition to its marginal costs of granting access, the ECPR allows the provider to include in its access charge its profit margin on its lost final sale.

Another good effect of the ECPR is that it motivates efficient entry and only efficient entry. That is, a potential supplier who can produce at the same or lower cost than the access provider in the *other* stages of producing the service wants access. Such a supplier makes the final service available at equal or lower cost and, thus, can only improve economic efficiency. It may be true that no other supplier wants to accept the offer of access, and the industry remains a monopoly, if the incumbent provider has lower cost, perhaps from being the first supplier and having superior technology. Requiring access could still be desirable, because it would put pressure on the incumbent monopoly to keep costs down and quality up, for if it slipped in either aspect of its service another supplier would be able to enter through the access offer.

To be concrete, let us introduce representations of cost for the telephone networks in Figure 11.8. Suppose the local network has total cost

$$TC_L = F + c_L Q,$$

where Q is the total number of calls, F is fixed cost, and c_L is the marginal cost of each call. Average cost in the local network is

$$AC_L = F/Q + c_L,$$

---

[13] See *United States v. Terminal Railroad Association of St. Louis*, 224 U.S. 383 (1912) and 236 U.S. 194 (1915).

[14] This idea was proposed by Robert Willig (1979). Important developments and applications have been made by William J. Baumol. See, for example, Baumol and Sidak (1994a).

which declines with Q, indicating that the local network experiences economies of scale. The total number of calls $Q = q_L + q_1 + q_2$, where q_L is the quantity of local calls, q_1 is the quantity of long-distance calls on the local monopoly's long-distance Network 1, and q_2 is the quantity of calls on independent Network 2. Assume no economies of scale on the long-distance networks, so costs there are

$$TC_1 = c_1\, q_1, \text{ and}$$
$$TC_2 = c_2\, q_2.$$

Prices to consumers are p_L for local calls, p_1 for long-distance calls on the local network monopolist's Network 1, and p_2 for long-distance calls on the competitor's Network 2. In addition, the long-distance networks must pay an access charge, a, to the local network for completing their calls.

Suppose that after paying the access fee of a, the competitive long-distance company has a competitive price,

$$p_2 = a + c_2.$$

Under the ECPR this value of a is the opportunity cost to the local network monopoly, which controls Network 1, plus the marginal cost of completing a call through the local network. Because p_1 must cover the entire cost of the call, including handling by the local network, the monopoly must charge enough to cover $c_L + c_1$, and its profit, so its opportunity cost is really $p_1 - (c_L + c_1)$. To follow the ECPR, the monopoly sets a equal to the marginal cost of completing the long-distance call through the local network, c_L, plus the opportunity cost, $p_1 - (c_L + c_1)$, so

$$a = c_L + p_1 - (c_L + c_1) = p_1 - c_1.$$

Then the price, p_2, of the competitive operator of Network 2 is

$$p_2 = a + c_2 = p_1 - c_1 + c_2.$$

Thus, $p_1 = p_2$ if $c_1 = c_2$. If Network 2 provides long-distance service more efficiently than Network 1, that is, if $c_2 < c_1$, Network 1 feels pressure to improve its efficiency.

If an unregulated monopoly chooses to allow access to an essential resource, it wants to recover the same monopoly profit it might have made by using the facility itself, and that is just what this ECPR access price allows. If the ECPR is imposed on a monopoly when the final product price is at a monopoly level, that high final product price makes the opportunity cost of granting access—and thus the access price—high. On the other hand, if the final product price is regulated at a "competitive" level, the ECPR calls for a competitive access price. Thus, the ECPR offers reasonable guidance for pricing access, but its ultimate reasonableness depends on the level of the final product price.

In the ECPR setting, either the original access provider or the entrant can have lower costs and, as a result, take over the entire market. There actually can be differentiated products or services, however, leading to less sharp and less extreme outcomes in which both (or more) firms survive. The ECPR also does not deal with the final service price but rather takes it as given. This is perfectly reasonable because its focus is on the access price alone, but it does not deal with the problem of pricing the final service in a regulated industry.

Ramsey Pricing for Access

With differentiated products or services, demand or supply elasticities is less than infinitely elastic, and the advantages of *Ramsey pricing* may be gained in access pricing.[15] A welfare maximizing problem for access can be posed and access prices can be derived to solve it, much like the Ramsey pricing problems considered in Section 2 above. Ramsey prices do not reflect the knife-edge conditions that are implicit in use of the ECPR, and they allow achievement of the greatest welfare when demands are not infinitely elastic.

The Ramsey problem was presented in Section 2 above by appending a constraint to the welfare maximizing problem, requiring that total revenue just equal total cost. If there are $j = 1, \ldots, n$ services to be provided, and they are all independent of one another (all cross elasticities are zero), the procedure followed in solving the constrained welfare problem yielded for the ith service the pricing rule:

$$(P_i - MC_i)/P_i = K/E_{ii}, i = 1, \ldots, n.$$

where K is a constant less than one and $E = - (\partial Q/\partial P)(P/Q)$ is the price elasticity of demand. It is perfectly logical to include access as one of the enterprise services in considering Ramsey prices. Ramsey prices for local service and two long-distance services would satisfy

$$(p_L - c_L)/p_L = K/E_L, \qquad \text{11.1}$$
$$(p_1 - c_L - c_1)/p_1 = K/E_1, \text{ and} \qquad \text{11.2}$$
$$(p_2 - c_L - c_2)/p_2 = K/E_2. \qquad \text{11.3}$$

Again, every ratio of price minus marginal cost over price is modified from the monopoly level by the same constant, K, to yield revenue merely sufficient to cover total cost. The term, K, is less than one, and it lowers the markups over marginal costs to a level that merely allows the firm to break even. Ramsey prices are like monopoly prices except that all elasticities are multiplied by the same constant to make them larger. Remember the advantage of Ramsey prices: They eliminate any deficit while minimizing the loss in welfare that results from setting prices above marginal costs.[16]

The access price for the competitive long-distance firm, $a = p_2 - c_2$, can be deduced by solving equation (11.3) for $p_2 - c_2$,

$$a = c_L + K\, p_2/E_L.$$

If the competitor and the monopoly face perfectly symmetric situations, with equal cost and identical demand elasticities, then $p_1 - c_L - c_1 = p_2 - c_L - c_2$, so $a = p_2 - c_2$ means that

$$a = p_1 - c_1,$$

which is exactly what the ECPR requires.

---

[15] See Laffont and Tirole (1996), Armstrong, Doyle, and Vickers (1996), and Armstrong and Vickers (1998) for treatments of access pricing using Ramsey principles.

[16] As noted in Section 11.2, because K is less than one and it multiplies the right-hand side of each Ramsey-pricing rule, it is as if a number greater than one was multiplied times all of the elasticities, or the E_is, in the denominators of the right-hand sides.

Elasticities for two services may differ, however, and then Ramsey prices could offer lower welfare losses than ECPR prices. If the competitive provider of long-distance service on Network 2 faces a more elastic demand (larger in absolute value) than the monopoly provider on Network 1, for instance, the optimal value of a is $a < p_1 - c_1$. This follows because Network 1, with its less elastic demand (lower in absolute value), should charge a higher price to consumers, so $p_1 > p_2$, and thereby make a greater contribution to fixed cost, F, of the local network. To implement such Ramsey prices across two separate firms is difficult, however, because the firm making a higher contribution to fixed cost may be handicapped in competition with the other firm. Although it may improve welfare, Ramsey pricing is hard to implement in a competitive setting.

It is also possible that the competitive Network 2 will attract some customers who would not have gone to Network 1. If so, this means that Network 1 does not face a full one-to-one loss in its customers for every call delivered by Network 2 because Network 1 would never have had some of the calls that come to Network 2. On such calls, Network 1 does not lose a customer. Then a should reflect just the fractional loss that Network 1 experiences for every Network 2 customer, rather than the full $a = p_1 - c_1$.[17] This adjustment would be needed to reflect opportunity cost properly under the ECPR, and it can be included as an effect in solving for Ramsey prices.

Ramsey prices can define ideal access prices, but it is difficult to find institutions that can implement them effectively. The simpler and more direct ECPR is easier to implement in practice, and for that reason it may have more widespread consideration.

SUMMARY

Applications with various representations of welfare show that socially optimal prices equal marginal costs. Peak-load pricing enable prices to equal marginal costs when demands are roughly predictable by time periods. Of course properly conceiving of marginal cost and estimating it can always be difficult, especially for short time periods. But when capacity is costly, the marginal cost of expanding it to serve customers at peak times can be very high. Then setting price high to match the high marginal cost at peak demand periods and low during off-peak periods can bring more efficient use of the capacity. More subtle adjustments are possible when a range of techniques are available. Techniques that have greater fixed cost may be utilized more to achieve low cost, while those with lower fixed cost may be used for just the peak periods because having them stand idle at off-peak times is less costly. Peak-load pricing is valuable because it achieves the efficiency that is possible from pricing at marginal cost.

Where economies of scale cause marginal cost to lie below average cost, marginal-cost prices cause losses. Although general tax revenues might be used to cover the resulting deficit for a public service, the result may be unfair, because some who pay

---

[17] For analysis of this displacement issue, and other important relations between the ECPR and Ramsey prices, see Armstrong, Doyle, and Vickers (1996).

taxes to cover that deficit never use the service. Welfare representations then are especially valuable in devising optimal departures of prices from marginal costs, perhaps in the form of Ramsey prices, to avoid a deficit. Ramsey prices are called second-best prices, because they achieve as great a level of social welfare as possible in the presence of realities that prevent the use of prices equal to marginal costs. The advantage of Ramsey prices is that they raise funds to cover fixed costs while causing the smallest possible welfare loss. This is true whether the object being priced is a final service or is access to an essential facility, and whether it is a price per unit or part of a nonuniform price.

Nonuniform prices can also be useful for raising more money from consumers to cover a deficit, and they can sometimes keep the marginal price close to marginal cost. In setting nonuniform prices a seller can be handicapped by not knowing the preferences of consumers. But allowing consumers to select from a set of rate structures, based perhaps on the quantity they wish to consume, was shown able to bring improvements, in part by conveying information about demands to the seller. Nonuniform prices may reflect costs, as when a two-part price has a fixed part that pays for an assured service level, calling on part of the supplier's limited supplier capacity, and a variable part that covers marginal cost. Then when capacity is scarce, the supplier can interrupt the consumer, to cut usage back to the agreed-upon upper limit according to the consumer's fixed payment.

Another important area of pricing arises when access is allowed to an essential facility, which is a way to introduce competition in otherwise monopoly circumstances. If the user and the grantor of access are competitors, the access price must be set just right. Otherwise, one side or the other has a competitive advantage. The efficient component pricing rule calls for the access price to cover the marginal cost to the facility owner for granting access plus the facility owner's opportunity cost in granting access. Such a rule has two virtues. It motivates the essential facility owner to grant access, and it also invites only efficient firms to take advantage of it.

Thus it is possible to develop optimal prices, sometimes using economic welfare as a goal, according to the representations of welfare already introduced. We now turn in Chapter 12 to consider institutions that might adopt some of these pricing rules. In the remainder of Part II we consider real-world industries in which the problem of inducing a monopoly firm to pursue the welfare goal, and so to adopt optimal pricing, is evident. That is why actual institutions are changing to accommodate new incentive arrangements.

QUESTIONS

1. The late Nobel laureate William Vickrey (1955) presented a striking marginal-cost pricing example involving a train that runs from A to B and returns each day. The question he raised in his example is whether the train should also go on to C and return, and the right answer to that question requires ideal pricing. If there were many trains each day (divisible service units), and only some

continued on to C, then ideal conditions could be satisfied on each part of the trip, and the problem would be easier. With only one train a day, however, we must reach an either-or decision about whether to serve C.

We'll call travel from A to B one leg of the train trip, and B to C another leg, with the CB and BA returns also called legs. Constant returns to scale prevail and costs are of three kinds: (1) 50 cents per seat per day for capital and similar charges on the equipment, independent of the distance operated; (2) $1.50 per seat for operating expenses for each leg of the trip; and (3) 50 cents per passenger for each leg of the trip for wear and tear on the equipment, cleaning, and service to passengers. We assume that equipment can be found to make the train up to any desired number of seats at strictly proportional costs. But, once determined, the train must be the same size in both directions. It is impractical to change the makeup of the train at B, so that if it is to run through to C, the entire train that traveled from A to B must run to C.

Demand each way for the AB leg is linear, ranging from 2,000 passengers at a price of $0.00 to a maximum price of $10.00 that the most eager passenger is willing to pay (the AB or BA demand equation is $P = 10.00 - 0.01Q$). Demand each way for the BC leg is one-fourth as great, ranging up to 250 passengers at a zero price, with the same maximum price of $10.00 (the BC or CB demand equation is $P = 10.00 - 0.04Q$).

a. Calculate the maximum sum of consumer surplus and profit that is obtainable through optimal prices and capacity for serving A to B and return. Show the optimal prices for the AB and the BA legs and show the optimal capacity of the train in seats.

b. Show the optimal prices for legs AB, BC, CB, and BA, and the capacity of the train in seats, for serving A to B to C and return, and calculate the consumer surplus. (Do not rush. This problem requires careful thought.)

c. Who gains the most from the solution you obtained in part b? Is your solution in part b sustainable?

d. Should train service be extended to C, on the basis of a comparison of your results in a and b? Might any other consideration be important here, other than maximizing welfare?

2. Consider the problem of a message service between two cities that faces demands for two periods of equal length (12 hours each) over the daily cycle, represented as

$$P_1 = 15 - 0.025 \, Q_1 \text{ and } P_2 = 10 - 0.025 \, Q_2,$$

where P_1 and P_2 are prices of messages in the two periods, and Q_1 and Q_2 are quantities per 12-hour period.

The service currently has capacity to produce 400 messages in each 12-hour period. Capacity to connect the two cities for a message costs $2 per day, but it can accommodate one message in each period. Operating cost is $1 per message. It is not possible to transmit more than the rated message capacity in the time guaranteed, so customers beyond that level must be turned away.

a. At the current capacity level of 400 messages per 12-hour period, which is *given*, what peak and off-peak prices maximize welfare?

b. What is the socially optimal capacity level?
c. What peak and off-peak prices maximize welfare at the socially optimal capacity level?
d. Is the capacity used as fully at the solution in c as at the solution in a? If it is, does that explain why the overall solution in c is more efficient? If it is not, how can the solution in c be preferable to that in a?
e. Suppose an unregulated monopoly operates the message service. What capacity and what peak and off-peak prices would the profit maximizing monopoly choose?

3. Suppose two products, good 1 and good 2, are produced at *zero* marginal cost. The demands for the two products are

$$P_1 = 7 - 0.02\,Q_1, \text{ and } P_2 = 5 - 0.01\,Q_2.$$

There are fixed costs of $900, so any prices must raise enough revenue to satisfy the constraint:

$$P_1\,Q_1 + P_2\,Q_2 = 900.$$

a. Determine Ramsey prices for the two goods. (*Hint:* The ratio of Q_1/Q_2 must be the same at the Ramsey solution as at marginal cost prices, because that is a property of Ramsey prices. You can use this relationship between the quantities and the budget constraint to solve the problem.)
b. Prices last period were $P_1 = \$2$ and $P_2 = \$4$. Do they meet the budget constraint? Calculate consumer surplus at these prices. Also calculate consumer surplus at the Ramsey prices you found in part a. Which set of prices offers the greater consumer surplus?

4. Suppose there are two identifiable groups, group 1 and group 2, that demand a service and their demands for the service are

$$P_1 = 22 - 0.01Q_1 \text{ and } P_2 = 12 - 0.01Q_2.$$

The service can be supplied according to the total cost function

$$TC = 8,000 + 2\,Q_1 + 2\,Q_2.$$

A single uniform price of $P_1 = P_2 = \$5.50$ covers operating costs plus fixed costs (actually this price raises $8,050 toward fixed costs of $8,000) and yields consumer surplus of $15,725.

a. Find prices for the two demand groups that are Ramsey prices. (*Hint:* The ratio of Q_1/Q_2 must be the same at the Ramsey solution as at marginal cost prices, because that is a property of Ramsey prices. You can use this relationship between the quantities, plus the budget constraint, to solve the problem. Along the way you have to solve a quadratic equation.)
b. Calculate total consumer surplus under the Ramsey prices found in part a and compare it with that under a single uniform price, which is $15,725. Explain any difference in consumer surpluses obtained under the uniform price of $P_1 = P_2 = \$5.50$ and under Ramsey prices.
c. Develop a multipart, self-selecting tariff for this situation but for simplicity assume each group is represented by one person (this prevents having to

divide the fixed fee by the number of consumers to get individual fees). (If F_1 and F_2 are entry fees, and P_1 and P_2 are marginal, per-unit, prices, you may set $F_2 = 0$ and have a simple one-part price for Q_2 if you wish. Then you must have $F_1 > 0$, and your overall rate structure must be incentive compatible so members of one group do not prefer prices intended for the other.)

d. Calculate total consumer surplus under the self-selecting tariff you developed in part c, and explain why it differs from that obtained under simple, uniform, Ramsey prices in part a.

5. A firm produces two goods, Q_1 and Q_2, with demands

$$P_1 = 50 - 0.0075 \, Q_1 \text{ and}$$
$$P_2 = 40 - 0.0040 \, Q_2.$$

Total cost is $TC = 19{,}200 + 20 \, Q_1 + 20 \, Q_2$. Because marginal costs are constant, pricing at marginal costs result in a loss of the fixed costs, 19,200. To eliminate this loss, prices have to be raised. There are many ways to do this so total costs are covered. Three sets of prices that cover costs are:

$$P_1 = 20 \quad \text{and } P_2 = 25.44,$$
$$P_1 = 26.25 \text{ and } P_2 = 20, \text{ and}$$
$$P_1 = 23 \quad \text{and } P_2 = 22.$$

One of these sets of prices constitute Ramsey prices.

a. Pick out which prices are Ramsey prices, and say why you think they are Ramsey prices.

b. Calculate the consumer surplus under each pair of prices. Because producer's surplus is the same in each case, Ramsey prices yield the greatest consumers surplus. Which pair of prices constitute Ramsey prices?

c. Consider the Ramsey pricing rule,

$$(P_1 - MC_1)/P_1 = K/(-E_1) \text{ and } (P_2 - MC_2)/P_2 = K/(-E_2),$$

or, on solving for K,

$$K = (-E_1)(P_1 - MC_1)/P_1 = (-E_2)(P_2 - MC_2)/P_2.$$

Find the value of K, the Ramsey price constant that reduces prices from the monopoly level, at the Ramsey prices you found in part b. (Doing this also checks whether the Ramsey prices are correct.)

6. Suppose demands and costs are the same as those in question 4. Assume that group 1 is one consumer who is comfortably self-supporting, while group 2 is a poor citizen for whom some "life-line" proposals of aid have been made. A workable rate proposal is to be developed that allows those in group 2 access to the service.

a. Consider one proposal that would give service free up to 1,200 units. Anyone wanting more than 1,200 units would have to pay an entry fee of $8,000 and then pay a marginal price of $2 per unit. Analyze this proposal to determine whether it succeeds and is incentive compatible.

   b. Consider another proposal that allows consumption of up to a maximum of 600 units at a price of $6 per unit, or a flat fee of $10,000 that entitles one to unlimited consumption at no additional cost per unit. Analyze this proposal to determine whether it succeeds and is incentive compatible.

   c. Suppose it is possible to distinguish group 1 from group 2 consumers. Then a tariff can be offered to each group alone, and it need not be incentive compatible for the consumers. As an example, let consumers in group 2 have the service free, and no subsidy is paid to the service provider. Then what is the best tariff to charge those in group 1, and why is it best?

   d. Is your solution in part c sustainable? Explain why or why not.

7. Consider a service that is offered to two markets that have the following demands:

$$P_1 = 2.50 - 0.0025 \, Q_1 \text{ and } P_2 = 6.50 - 0.01 \, Q_2.$$

Marginal cost for the service is $MC = \$1.00$, and there is a fixed cost of $650.

   a. Suppose the price is set at marginal cost, $MC = \$1.00$, in both markets. Find the consumers' surplus in each market and add the consumer surpluses for the two markets to find total consumer surplus. Then calculate total welfare as $W = CS + TR - TC$.

   b. Suppose a single price of $2.00 is set in both markets. What quantities are sold in each market, and what consumer surplus is obtained in each market? Find the total consumer surplus. Then calculate total welfare as $W = CS + TR - TC$.

   c. Find Ramsey prices and associated quantities for this service that allow the firm to break even. (*Hint*: Find the ratio of Q_1/Q_2 quantities when prices equal marginal costs. Because this ratio must also hold at Ramsey prices, you can use it to reduce the budget constraint to one variable in a quadratic equation, which you may solve for quantities and then Ramsey prices.)

   d. At the Ramsey prices obtained in part (c), find the consumer surplus in each market. Then add the consumer surpluses from the two markets and calculate total welfare as $W = CS + TR - TC$. (*Note*: This problem is treated in summary form in Box 11.5.)

APPENDIX 11.1 Socially Optimal Pricing

Let us now present a socially ideal price for a problem of maximizing a representation of consumer welfare. To represent welfare in these examples we use, first, consumer surplus and, second, a socially weighted sum of individual welfare indicated either by indirect or direct utility functions. Prices equal to marginal costs always maximize welfare as defined in these problems. We assume that marginal cost is constant and that total cost equals zero at $Q = 0$, so there is no excess profit or loss to consider at the solution. As a result, the net benefit to producers, or producers' surplus, is zero, allowing emphasis on consumer welfare measures. We call attention to the form of each problem and to the particular weighting of individual utilities that is implicit in the representations of welfare.

First we formulate the social problem as maximizing $W = CS + PS$ from areas below demand and above supply as identified in Chapter 2,

$$CS + PS = \int_{P_0}^{Q_d^{-1}(0)} Q(P)dP + \int_{Q_c(0)}^{P_0} S(P)dP.$$

Differentiating with respect to P and setting the result equal to zero, we obtain:

$$P = MC.$$

We could also use consumer surplus and add total revenue less total cost to represent producers' surplus in welfare:

$$CS + TR - TC = \int_P^{Q^{-1}(0)} Q(P)dP + PQ - C(Q).$$

Differentiating with respect to price, the necessary condition is

$$-q + q + P\, dQ/dP - MC\, dQ/dP = 0.$$

Solving for P we obtain

$$P = MC.$$

Alternatively, we might consider the social problem as maximizing total revenue plus consumer surplus less total cost:

$$CS + TR - TC = \int_0^Q P(Q)dQ - \int_0^Q MC(Q)dQ.$$

Differentiating with respect to quantity and solving for P, we again find

$$P = MC.$$

A similar procedure can be followed using a social welfare function. Let us use a socially weighted sum of individual utility functions, where each individual's utility depends on quantities of goods consumed. Our analysis is similar to one with the total revenue plus consumer surplus representation of welfare. This social problem would be to maximize

$$\Sigma_i \beta_i u_i - C(Q).$$

Here u_i is the ith person's utilty function and β_i is the social weight attached to that person. Social welfare is the sum of all the products of individuals' utilities times their social weights, less the total cost. Differentiating with respect to Q, and using the fact that $\partial u_i/\partial Q = \eta_i P$, yields

$$\Sigma \beta_i \eta_i P - MC = 0.$$

If we accept the current distribution of income, then each person's social weight is the reciprocal of that person's marginal utility of income. Total welfare is the same no matter who receives a benefit under this assumption. Suppose, for example, that $1 in benefit goes to person j. That person's gain in utility is η_j, the person's marginal utility of income. When weighted by person j's social weight, β_j, the product of the two $(\beta_j \eta_j)$, which is the social welfare gain, equals $1, no matter who person j is. It is clear from the above condition for maximizing welfare that, with

$$\beta_i = 1/\eta_i,$$

we again have

$$P = MC.$$

All of these optimal pricing problems show that price should equal marginal cost to maximize welfare. The welfare representation that is maximized with respect to prices is consumer surplus alone, without revenue (the area under the demand curve above price), so revenue must be added and cost subtracted to form producer's surplus. The welfare representation maximized with respect to quantities already includes total revenue plus consumer surplus (it is the area under the demand curve), and the social problem can be formed accordingly just by subtracting total cost. Consumer welfare can also be represented by a social welfare function, made up by the sum of individual utility functions multiplied by social weights for the individuals. In the latter case, when the social weights attached to individuals are explicitly set equal to the reciprocals of the consumers' marginal utilities of income, the solutions match those obtained with the consumer surplus representation. Thus, the consumer surplus representation implicitly requires also that the welfare weights of individuals (the β_is) equal the reciprocals of their marginal utilities of income $(1/\eta_i s)$.

These examples of socially optimal pricing have assumed that demand and cost functions are known perfectly and are unchanging. If demand fluctuates randomly, we can still obtain the same solutions, as long as marginal cost is constant and unaffected by level of output, and capacity does not limit output. When the level of output affects marginal cost, demand fluctuations that cause output to vary affects expected marginal cost, which complicates finding an optimal price. If price could be adjusted perfectly to every change in demand, and if new prices could immediately and costlessly be transmitted to consumers, who could then alter their consumption plans, a perfect solution would be possible. Such communication and consumer response, however, is either terribly costly or infeasible, and instead an attempt usually is made to maintain a single price that is optimal under the fluctuating circumstances.

Complications also arise when the level of marginal cost depends on the nature of demand fluctuations, because optimal price then depends on properties of demand. The complications are greater when capacity limits prevent some consumers from being served, because to evaluate welfare we must know who is served. We shall not explore the general problems of demand uncertainty here, but will examine specific cases of uncertain demand in chapters that follow.

APPENDIX 11.2 Long-Run Marginal-Cost Pricing

Demand is given by the function $Q = Q(P)$, where P is market price. We accept consumer plus producer surplus as our measure of welfare. Consumer surplus plus total revenue, or $CS + TR$, is the area under the demand curve up to the output produced, which can be represented mathematically as

$$CS + TR = \int_0^Q P(Q)dQ.$$

Total welfare, W, is represented by consumer surplus plus producer surplus, or $W = CS + TR - TC$, where total cost is $(b + B(Q))Q$ where the fixed cost, $B(Q)$ depends on Q. The social problem is therefore to maximize

$$W = CS + TR - TC = \int_0^Q P(Q)dQ - (b + B(Q))\,Q.$$

A necessary condition for a welfare maximizing solution to this problem can be obtained by differentiating W with respect to Q and setting the result equal to zero. Doing so yields the efficient pricing rule,

$$P = b + B(Q) + Q\,dB/dQ.$$

Since $b + B(Q) + Q\,dB/dQ$ is long-run marginal cost, the efficient price equals long-run marginal cost.

In this case average cost is $AC = b + B(Q)$, and it is decreasing with output Q. A price equal to marginal cost can cause a problem because, with $Q > 0$ and $dB/dQ < 0$, which goes with decreasing average cost, marginal cost lies below average cost. That means that a price equal to marginal cost is below average cost,[18] so charging the marginal cost price causes a loss for the firm. If the firm is privately owned, it cannot survive.

APPENDIX 11.3 Axiomatic Pricing

Another pricing principle bases prices on costs in a logically consistent way. Because these prices depend on certain logical principles, called *axioms*, we call them **axiomatic prices.** Cost-based axiomatic pricing has a different foundation from, say, Ramsey pricing. Axiomatic prices are based on costs in a consistent way, without

---

[18] Average cost minus marginal cost is $b + B(Q) - (b + B(Q) + Q\,dB/dQ) = -Q\,dB/dQ > 0$.

regard for demand influences. When entry is possible, as in a contestable market situation, costs determine firms actions and are crucial to market outcomes. Having costs drive pricing outcomes is then desirable, and that is where cost-based axiomatic pricing can be appropriate.

Imagine setting out desirable properties that prices should have, relative to costs, and then defining prices that satisfy those properties. Axiomatic prices are constructed in this way. Axiomatic prices are somewhat like average-cost prices but extended to multi-product circumstances. Most importantly, axiomatic prices have been shown to be sustainable. They rest on sound principles, rather than arbitrary rules that spread costs among products in *fully distributed–cost* pricing. Fully distributed costs also involve some procedure for imputing costs to products, and then setting prices at those cost levels, so all costs are distributed among outputs and revenues cover costs. But fully distributed costs do not follow carefully constructed principles. They follow ad hoc rules that are imposed arbitrarily, and they can lead to unwanted outcomes.[19] For example, such prices are not necessarily sustainable, so they do not support free entry in an industry. They are not necessarily efficient, so they cannot offer that advantage, either.

The desirable properties of axiomatic prices are specified in the form of requirements called axioms. As set out by Mirman, Samet, and Tauman (1983) the axioms begin with two simple principles. The first is *cost sharing*, the idea that costs are shared among products and services so that prices raise revenue to cover total costs. A second, *rescaling*, axiom requires simply that prices change correspondingly if scales of measurement of the goods or services are changed. Four remaining axioms deal with how prices are influenced by the cost function.

The first of these remaining four axioms imposes a *consistency* requirement on prices. If any subset of a firm's outputs together determine costs for the group, their prices should be the same. For example, if costs depend on the total of $Q_1 + Q_2$, then the price of Q_1 should equal the price of Q_2. Notice the orientation toward costs here, rather than toward demand elasticity as in the case of Ramsey prices. A *positivity* axiom requires that if one product has a higher marginal cost than another, it should also have a higher price.

Two other axioms concern the allocation of fixed costs, which are common to all outputs because they do not depend on output. An *additivity* axiom requires that if production can be separated into stages, with each stage having its own variable cost, then any fixed or common cost can also be assigned to the stages and added to variable cost by stage. Then the sums of variable costs plus assigned common cost, by stage, can be added together to obtain output cost. Another axiom makes the allocations of common costs for any pair of outputs *correlate* with the relative variable costs of those outputs. These latter two axioms allow fixed costs to be incorporated into axiomatic cost-sharing prices.

Contestable markets function effectively with few firms (perhaps one) and no barrier to entry. The lack of entry barriers presses existing suppliers to keep costs low and service quality high. If they do not do so, they lose to entrants who enter the market

---

[19] See Braeutigam (1980).

and replace them. Thus, social welfare can be higher when markets are contestable. This benefit arises only when prices are sustainable, however, meaning that only more efficient suppliers can enter. Sustainable prices can make legal entry barriers unnecessary, and efficiency incentives can be stronger without them. A great advantage of axiomatic prices is that they insure sustainable prices.[20]

Axiomatic prices are not necessarily the most efficient prices for maximizing welfare, an area where Ramsey prices excel. The main virtue of axiomatic prices is that they can prevent inefficient entry. This means they can avoid the need to impose legal barriers to entry, so they can open all the desirable incentives that accompany free entry. In addition to this advantage of eliminating the need for legal rules against entry, prices based on costs have been urged also as being less subject to political influences that can interfere with efficiency.[21]

Axiomatic prices have been difficult to apply. The conditions they require may not be met, and then they cannot deliver the benefit of sustainable prices. An application that implicitly assumed their conditions was the deregulation of the airline industry. Searching for places where they can be applied is desirable because they offer a means of using free entry as a motivating force for efficiency in place of governmental regulation.

---

[20] See Mirman, Samet, and Tauman (1983).
[21] See Von Weizsacker (1985).

12

Institutions of Industry Regulation

We know firms must be efficient to survive in competition. But when a government finds competition either to be unworkable or to produce undesirable outcomes, it may prevent it. In these circumstances, governments in the United States and in many other countries have often established monopolies to replace market competition and then imposed some form of regulation on the monopoly in an effort to sustain efficiency. How should this monopoly be regulated, or should some other form of organization be considered for the industry? This chapter considers governmental institutions that have replaced competition and other institutions that might modify competition as alternative forms of government regulation. These institutions are the flesh and blood of regulatory policy.

Once the competitive market is displaced, what institution will regulate the market? Many institutions have been created to provide goods or services under regulation, one usually providing service and another administering some form of regulation. Typically a monopoly replaces the competitive market, and a public institution regulates it. New means of regulating monopolies have come into use in recent years, in response partly to new knowledge about regulatory methods, and new institutions have been designed that offer a role for some form of competition.

We begin by describing traditional federal and state regulatory agencies and then turn to consider the enterprises that ordinarily supply services in regulated industries, primarily public enterprises and public utilities. Because it has been so widely used in the United States, the public utility is examined in detail. Principles involved in designing regulatory institutions are introduced, and their applications are described. Also discussed are alternative incentive devices, such as price-cap regulation, and new organizational arrangements coming into use, including those that foster competition through access for competitive providers.

12.1 | INDUSTRY REGULATORY AGENCIES

Regulatory agencies may exist at all governmental levels, and they take many forms. Local city and county agencies regulate activities from water supply to natural gas distribution to taxi cabs. State regulatory agencies often focus on public utilities and related institutions, but in some states they have broader powers. At the federal level there are many agencies with many goals, but we focus here on those federal agencies that oversee regulated industries.

Federal Regulatory Agencies

At the federal level, the major regulated industries and the agencies that regulate them are shown in Table 12.1. These agencies tend to be more specialized by industry than state regulatory agencies, and we examine them more carefully in the chapters to follow. For our purposes here one must understand the differences in jurisdictions of federal and state agencies.

The U.S. Postal Service is a national public enterprise and is regulated at the federal level. In telecommunications, local service tends to be regulated by states and long-distance service by federal regulators, although federal guidelines have covered local access pricing. Broadcast signals are federally regulated, while cable regulation is overseen by federal regulators with local participation. Transportation is regulated at all levels of government, but federal regulation is stronger in airlines and railroads, although states have participated in railroad regulation and local authorities participate in overseeing airports and regulating city buses, urban transit systems, and taxis.

TABLE 12.1   Major Federally Regulated Industries and Their Regulators

Industry	Federal Regulator(s)	Jurisdiction(s)
Postal service	Postal Rate Commission (PRC)	Federal
Telecommunications	Federal Communications Commission (FCC)	Federal (long distance) State (local service)
Broadcast and cable	Federal Communications Commission	Federal, local
Transportation	Department of Transportation (DOT) Federal Aviation Administration (FAA), Transportation Safety Administration Federal Transit Authority (FTA) Surface Transportation Board (STB)	Federal, state, and local
Energy	Department of Energy Federal Energy Regulatory Commission (FERC)	Federal and state
Electricity	Federal Energy Regulatory Commission Nuclear Regulatory Commission (NRC)	Federal and state

Energy is regulated at state and federal levels. New arrangements in electricity have states and regional authorities guiding retail operations and markets for generated electricity, but the Federal Energy Regulation Commission (FERC) influences transmission across state lines. Regulatory responsibilities are being shared in especially subtle ways in electricity and telecommunications, and in many other industries jurisdictional divisions are not as simple as they once were.

State Regulatory Commissions

All 50 states in the United States have regulatory commissions to regulate within state borders.[1] Some commissions regulate only public utilities, while others regulate insurance, transportation, or other activities. A common proceeding is a rate case, usually prompted by a utility's request to the commission for an increase in its rates. The commissions are quasijudicial in form, in that they render decisions after receiving evidence through hearings. Parties can appeal their decisions, and, if not satisfied, they have recourse to the regular court system.

Political influences on rate decisions have long been suspected, but efforts to explain rate decisions consistently on this basis have not been successful. The political explanations often see lower prices going to consumer groups that are more numerous and therefore can be expected to exercise more power at the polls. Commercial or industrial customers can also have political influence. Sometimes they have alternative sources of electricity, such as their own electricity generators, which enable them to bargain for lower rates. Politicians may use regulation to achieve specific income redistribution or other goals. The political arguments vary with the importance of politics in the regulatory process, as indicated at the state level, for example, by whether regulatory commissioners are appointed or elected by the public.

Regulatory commission performance must have some influence on outcomes, because major Wall Street advisory services spend time evaluating state regulatory commissions while analyzing the circumstances of individual public utilities. Where rate-of-return regulation is followed, for example, analysts systematically consider not only the generosity of the rates of return a commission allows but also many other factors such as how much time it takes to process rate cases, whether construction work in progress is counted as part of the firm's assets on which returns are allowed, whether automatic input-price adjustment clauses—which permit output price adjustments when input prices change—are allowed, and whether the basis for a decision is a recently completed "test" year or a hypothetical future period in which anticipated input price changes are taken into account.

The ratings given to commissions correlate well with bond ratings and stock values of the utilities they regulate, and the ratings are also explained empirically by political variables (for example, elected commissions tend to have less favorable ratings than appointed commissions) and competence measures (for example, higher

---

[1] Many regulatory commissions were formed at the start of the twentieth century. Anderson (1980, 1981) offers a history that emphasizes electric utilities' role, while Brock (1981) emphasizes regulation of telecommunications firms.

salaries tend to be earned at commissions with more favorable ratings).[2] Firms in less favorable regulatory climates are more apt to reduce capital expenditures by joint plant ownership (through cooperative power pools).[3] State regulatory commissions have scope, then, to create different environments for the firms they regulate, and firms respond to their regulatory environments.

12.2 REGULATED ENTERPRISES

We now turn from sketching the federal, state, and local regulatory institutions to considering the regulated institutions themselves, beginning with government enterprises and then examining public utilities. We call traditional privately owned regulated enterprises **public utilities**, but they are also coming to be known as "service providers." Two other main forms of public organization, **government departments** and **public enterprises**, also provide goods or services. Local governments, either by units of government or by public enterprises, provide about 15 percent of electricity, 5 percent of natural gas, and 40 percent of home trash collection in the United States. And recently local governments have moved into providing cable television service, especially in small communities, in competition with private cable television service providers.

Government departments take many different forms. Before becoming a public enterprise, for instance, the U.S. Postal Service was a large government department, called the Post Office Department. It was financed by federal government appropriations and its revenues went to the U.S. Treasury, so it was not a free-standing organization responsible for having its revenues cover its costs. Many cities that provide services, such as electricity, water, or natural gas, do so by using departments of government that already exist, such as the City Treasury and the Physical Plant Department. Although there may be a separate unit in government to manage the service, that unit may not handle all functions of the enterprise. The City Treasurer may handle financial matters, for example, while the department that takes care of Physical Plant—including streets and other government property—may build power lines, water pipes, or gas lines as the case may be. The sheer variety of organizational arrangements makes it difficult to describe how governments organize to provide services, and we focus here on the most common forms, starting with the public enterprise.[4]

The Public Enterprise

A public enterprise is an organization that is government owned, but is a coherent organization that takes in its own revenue to meet its costs. Although its history goes back to ancient times, the public enterprise came into much more widespread use after

---

[2] See Navarro (1980).

[3] See Gegax and Tschirhart (1984).

[4] It is possible that local governments provide services through government offices without forming a separate public enterprise because that gives them more control over provision of the service. In many states, if a city forms a separate public enterprise to provide a service, the regulatory agency of the state will claim regulatory authority over that enterprise, and, hence, over provision of the service.

World War II. Normally created by a legislative body, each public enterprise is a creature with its own distinctive features. This type of organization is more common in European countries than in the United States, where it is also quite widely used. For example, one of the largest public enterprises in the world is the U.S. Postal Service. Besides the U.S. Postal Service, the Corporation for Public Broadcasting, the Federal Deposit Insurance Corporation, the St. Lawrence Seaway Management Corporation, and the Tennessee Valley Authority are public enterprises at the federal level in the United States, and there are thousands of others at the state and local levels.[5] These enterprises are overseen in many different ways that are difficult to characterize, but generally some rule limits the profit or loss that each enterprise is allowed to earn.[6]

In Germany many railway, postal, and telephone services have been provided by special public enterprises that are like government departments, in that employees are civil servants, but with finances separated from the government budget. Local communities in Germany typically use public enterprises for electricity distribution. Many other forms of organization exist, including mixtures of public and private ownership, and changes are taking place. Federal legislation coordinates German electricity service through a national grid and imposes some broad requirements for pricing policy and data provision. It also exempts such enterprises from cartel (antitrust) law.

France has a renowned public enterprise providing electricity nationally, Electricite de France (EdF), which has led the world in applications of economics to problems of electricity pricing. It was created in 1946 out of many formerly private concerns, much damaged by war, that produced electricity, and it was extremely successful in developing an admirable national electricity network. Another well-known public enterprise is the Japanese National Railways, which has achieved the fastest train service in the world. Private firms provide electricity in Japan, and the Nippon Telegraph and Telephone Corporation (NTT) was sold to the public in 1986 and 1987 (at remarkably high prices, with price/earnings ratios above 200, for example). In the United Kingdom "privatization," or relying on private ownership, has proceeded beyond the aerospace, cable and wireless, automobile, and oil industries to gas, telecommunications, electricity, and water.[7] Movement in the direction of private ownership has also occurred in France, Italy, Spain, and Germany.

Virtually all countries have provided postal service either through a government department or a public enterprise. Sometimes the same enterprise provides postal and telecommunications services, which occurred in the United Kingdom until telecommunications service was separated from postal service and sold to private shareholders as British Telecom about 25 years ago. A public enterprise ordinarily is responsible for collecting its own revenue, out of which it pays for the expenses it decides to incur. In contrast, a government department usually has its expenditures

---

[5] See Walsh (1978).

[6] See Aharoni (1986).

[7] The British spelling, "privatisation," may be appropriate here because Britain started the conversion of nationalized industries to largely private ownership in the last two decades, and even in other languages the phenomenon is called "privatisation." For accounts, see Kay and Thompson (1986), Kay, Mayer, and Thompson (1986), Veljanovski (1987), Vickers and Yarrow (1985), and Waterson (1988). Most planned economies have also seen major change toward greater use of market processes, including Bulgaria, China, Czechoslovakia, Hungary, Poland, and Russia.

approved through a governmental budgeting process, and often the revenue from its services goes into the government's treasury. The public enterprise may need governmental approval for some of its expenditures, especially on major investments, and because it often has limited authority to borrow, its spending can be confined to the level of its revenue. Indeed, the common practice is to have a public enterprise break even by having its revenues equal its costs.

Box 12.1 indicates the high purpose that some have set for public enterprises. High purpose may have real meaning when one is considering the Royal Mint or the Scottish Development Agency in the United Kingdom, or the National Science Foundation in the United States, because these organizations clearly have goals beyond profit making. But when applied to enterprises in monopoly market positions, including even postal service, the idea may be more wishfully applied, with hope that the organizations are effective in place of competitive markets. Because pursuing welfare is difficult to motivate, however, how to bring about reliable public service in such circumstances is not self-evident.

Public enterprises usually face some degree of regulation, either by a ministry of government or by a regulatory commission, and sometimes by new oversight arrangements that are still developing. One advantage of organizing services through public enterprises is that, in principle, the government as owner can obtain by command the information needed for oversight. But the enterprise possesses the best information, and in practice ideal information seldom seems to be available to regulators. In addition, for better or worse, the enterprise can be managed to meet governmental objectives. For example, electricity price increases have been restrained during inflationary periods in France, and employment in the domestic coal industry appears to have been protected by public enterprise policies toward electricity in Germany and the United Kingdom. Incentives to keep costs low and to avoid discriminatory prices are not particularly strong in these organizations. Chapter 13 examines one very significant public enterprise, the U.S. Postal Service. We now turn to examine the most significant privately owned provider of public services in the United States, the public utility.

BOX 12.1 Public Enterprise and High Purpose

The broad goals that a public enterprise might pursue are represented in this statement by Lord Morrisson (1933), who provided part of the intellectual foundation for Labor Party nationalization of industries in Great Britain after World War II:

> The public corporation must be no mere capitalist business, the be-all and end-all of which is profits and dividends, even though it will, quite properly, be expected to pay its way. It must have a different atmosphere at its board table from that of a shareholders' meeting; its board and its officers must regard themselves as the high custodians of the public interest.

The public interest is a wholesome goal, but individuals may differ in interpreting it, and, even if they can agree, it may be hard to motivate an organization to pursue it.

The Public Utility

The public utility is a privately owned corporation serving public purposes. Its use is widespread in the United States because public services were usually provided by private firms early in the country's history, and they began to be regulated, as public utilities, little more than a century ago. In 1877 the states won the right to prescribe rates to be charged by private firms in certain circumstances, and that right led to the gradual establishment of state regulatory agencies in all states.[8] The guidelines for setting rates grew out of decisions handed down in often controversial court cases. Public utilities or other parties appealed the decisions of regulatory agencies through the regular court system, sometimes all the way to the Supreme Court. The resulting institution of regulation, therefore, is not neatly designed for a clear purpose but rather is a set of procedures and constraints that developed piecemeal through court decisions made largely out of actual experience.

Rate-of-return regulation is the name given the practice of determining a public utility's profit by setting an allowed return and multiplying it times the net value of the firm's assets. Such an allowed return reflects allowed interest payments to bondholders as well as profits to private owners of a public utility. The utility firm is allowed revenues sufficient to cover its operating costs plus the allowed return on assets that are employed in service to the public. To the extent the firm's costs influence allowed prices the result is **cost-plus regulation**, which just has costs determine prices. If TR represents total revenue, OC operating costs, A assets, D depreciation, and s the allowed rate of return, then allowed total revenue satisfies the equation,

$$TR = OC + s\,(A - D).$$

When a public utility feels that its prices need to be changed, it proposes changes to the agency that regulates it. A lengthy hearing may result. Often a recent "test period" is chosen as the basis for a factual history, and all questions are resolved using data from that period. Projections into a future period are sometimes used instead so that the result of lengthy deliberations will not be out of date once the rate case is completed.

In a rate case before it, the regulatory agency probes the accounting soundness of reported operating expenses and the appropriateness of included assets, and it puts much effort into determining the rate of return to be allowed on the assets. Historically, asset values have been enormous in many regulated industries. In the electricity industry, for example, the value of assets can amount to two or three times more than annual sales. As a result, the rate-of-return decision is a very important determinant of the firm's profit. The decision has such a crucial effect on stockholders that top officials of the public utility may devote much of their time to developing arguments for favorable returns and being present themselves at rate hearings.

---

[8] See the Supreme Court case of *Munn v. Illinois*, 94 U.S. 113 (1877).

If its allowed return exceeds its cost of capital, a rate-of-return regulated public utility may want to use more assets than is efficient. Besides serving a productive purpose, the assets in the rate-of-return-regulated monopoly justify profit.[9] More important, the firm's own costs are used to determine its revenues, so an inefficient firm may simply be allowed higher prices and, thus, more revenues to cover its higher costs. The incentive for efficiency or innovation is therefore weak. In addition, little attention is devoted to preventing inappropriate price discrimination by regulated firms, yet incentives and means for firms to use it are strong. Thus the rate-of-return regulation that has developed out of legal decisions has serious shortcomings. That is why governments have pursued alternative regulatory arrangements.

One arrangement that has come into use, primarily in telephone price regulation, is *price-cap regulation*. Instead of depending on the firm's costs, prices follow a price index less some amount for cost reduction that is deemed to be possible because of technological change in the industry. Because it does not rely in any direct way on the firm's own cost as an influence on prices, price-cap regulation preserves efficiency incentives in the firm. Having high costs leads to low profit, rather than to high prices, so the firm is motivated to keep costs low. Price-cap regulation can also elicit socially desirable pricing. With the passage of time, prices could turn out to be unreasonably above or below costs, however, because of changes in input prices that do not affect the price index. But regulators appear to have avoided that possible problem. Price-cap regulation thus offers better cost-control incentives in the firm than rate-of-return regulation does. On the other hand, it can permit greater short-term profit if the firm lowers cost by lowering quality, so it requires greater oversight of quality than does rate-of-return regulation.

Institutions of regulation often begin in circumstances in which some parties already have clear and well-defined interests. The possibility of change through government action causes other parties to defend their interests, and the contentious atmosphere that results shapes institutions. Clear interests of knowledgeable and influential parties receive more attention than smaller and more widely dispersed interests of many consumers. Seeking private advantage and finding compromise are apt to play a larger role in the outcome than the dictates of general economic welfare, which the institution presumably is to serve.

Competition provides remarkable guidance in a market economy, but some technologies do not allow it to function well. Then the same measure of economic well-being that competition maximizes—welfare representations—can be useful for designing alternative institutions and for determining socially optimal prices. Rate-of-return regulation was not designed, however, to maximize welfare, it grew out of court disputes—and compromises—and it is an imperfect institution. Price-cap regulation has come into use to overcome some of the incentive weaknesses of rate-of-return regulation. In addition, access to essential resources has been granted to foster a degree of competition where that might be possible. But rate-of-return regulation has been used longer, and more widely, than any other regulatory institution. So in the next section we examine rate-of-return regulation and its effects in some detail.

---

[9] Averch and Johnson (1962) were the first to formally set out this argument.

12.3 | RATE-OF-RETURN REGULATION

A longstanding institution of private monopoly regulation in the United States, rate-of-return regulation, is gradually being replaced by institutions that offer better incentives for efficiency. Rate-of-return regulation was not designed to achieve economic efficiency. It grew slowly out of a history of conflict, which the U.S. judicial system gradually resolved. More than a century ago the Supreme Court, in the case of *Munn v. Illinois*, affirmed the right of states to prescribe rates, but it did not make clear exactly how to prescribe rates.[10] In the nearly half-century between two ensuing Court cases, *Smyth v. Ames*[11] in 1898 and *Hope Natural Gas Company*[12] in 1944, the Court found a workable compromise. This history shows that once parties have had scope to entertain quite different positions, their disputes might result in a compromise that does not induce efficiency.

Although the *Hope Natural Gas Company* case settled legal issues, in the wake of this settlement economic issues became very complex. Rate-of-return regulation evolved before some economic principles that might have affected its design were fully known. These principles would have made untenable some of the positions that partisans in legal proceedings created (and that influenced the form of rate-of-return regulation). Its lack of a modern economic foundation is one reason the institution of rate-of-return regulation is now giving way to other arrangements.

Difficulties in determining the rate of return to allow on equity capital caused it to receive the most attention in rate cases, especially when heavy use of capital in regulated industries made it so important. This difficulty is the first of four weaknesses, which include claims that rate-of-return regulation (1) is inconsistent with financial theory and, therefore, impossible to apply faithfully, (2) biases the firm's choice among productive inputs in favor of the use of capital, (3) fails to control monopolistic reliance on price discrimination, and (4) does not encourage cost minimization or technological change. We briefly explore these problems here, beginning with the financial difficulties in application.

Finance under Rate-of-Return Regulation

For operational soundness, guidelines from the *Hope* decision require some basis for estimating a return to equity capital on the basis of current conditions. Yet the *Hope* framework complicates this task enormously and may even prevent it from being carried out. First, the *Hope* decision called for using current valuation principles for the rate of return allowed to equity and historical valuation principles for the return allowed to debt. This procedure does not match the valuation affecting unregulated firms, which are valued entirely on a current basis. So no true benchmark from observing unregulated firms reveals "comparable earnings" that can be applied to

---

[10] *Munn v. Illinois*, 94 U.S. 113 (1877).

[11] *Smyth v. Ames*, 169 U.S. 466 (1898).

[12] *FPC v. Hope Natural Gas Co.*, 320 U.S. 591 (1944).

regulated firms. Second, observing the returns earned by other regulated firms does not reveal true investor judgments reliably, because they can be affected by other regulators' actions.

The *Hope* guidelines are inconsistent with the financing of firms and their valuations. Remember that bonds tend to be relatively safe investments. They offer first priority to payments out of earnings of a firm—in specified interest payments—and first claim to assets, too, in the event the firm fails. We usually expect that making such an offer to bondholders raises the risk in common stock shares, for in allowing an assured payment of interest to bondholders the stockholders have to absorb all the fluctuations in earnings. The shareholders also have only residual claims to assets, after bondholders, if the firm fails. The regulated monopoly firm is not expected to fail, however, so these valuation processes are disrupted. Then valuations may not be determined as the *Hope* case specifies.

The absence of genuine competition in a regulated market derails the *Hope* guidelines, beginning with the lack of free entry. New entry determines overall returns in unregulated markets, because new entry responds to profitability in such markets. Because there is no entry in regulated industries, the capital market valuation mechanism cannot operate in the same way. Moreover, under *Hope* guidelines, only the return to the equity portion of capital in the rate-of-return regulated firm is to be based on current conditions, while the return to debt is based on the historical cost of debt. This is inconsistent with the Modigliani-Miller valuation process,[13] which determines firms' market values, so regulation according to *Hope* guidelines may interfere in a basic way with that process.[14]

That the *Hope* guidelines lack a sound basis for estimating the very rate of return they sanction is important beyond the obvious practical difficulty this causes. That practical difficulty gives regulators much discretion, when almost any decision they reach is feasible because the monopoly public utility they regulate usually is able to earn far more than they allow. In the worst cases, this discretion opens the way for corruption. Even in the best cases, it makes investors wonder not merely about inherent business risk, the risk of the business itself, but rather about what regulators decide, which allows the firm's return on equity capital to possess uncertainties that the regulatory process itself introduces.

Input Inefficiency

Although we can question the strength of its profit-seeking motivation, suppose for now that the monopoly firm whose rate of return on assets is limited according to *Hope* guidelines faithfully pursues profit for its shareholders. Suppose regulators can

---

[13] See Modigliani and Miller (1958); Chapter 4 discussed their valuation process. Jensen and Mechling (1976) and Sherman (1977) analyzed how policies can affect stockholders versus bondholders.

[14] Michael Keran (1976) found empirically that, with respect to dividend yields, equity shares in regulated firms behave much like bonds when the rate of inflation is high. This result probably follows from the reliance of most regulatory commissions on original (accounting) cost for valuing asset rate bases, which tends to make stockholder returns more like nominal bond returns. For more on the cost of capital in regulated firms, see Kolbe, Read, and Hall (1985). For effects of inflation, see Cross (1982) and Lebowitz, Lee, and Linhart (1976).

react immediately to all changes while controlling prices to maintain a particular allowed rate of return. Then, in choosing inputs to produce any particular level of output, the firm's profit incentives are distorted. If the regulated firm is allowed to earn a rate of return greater than the competitive cost of capital, but below the monopoly return, it wants to expand its capital beyond the monopoly level. This incentive by itself is desirable, because it leads to more output. But in hiring inputs other than capital, the regulated firm remains monopolistic. Indeed, the firm becomes schizophrenic in deciding capital use differently from the use of other inputs, and it succumbs to what is known as the Averch-Johnson effect: To produce any given output, it uses more capital relative to other inputs than is most efficient.[15]

The simplest way to view the incentive for capital use of the rate-of-return regulated firm is to realize that whereas an unregulated firm has one main aim, to maximize profit, the rate-of-return regulated firm has two. The rate-of-return regulated monopolist seeks not only to earn high profit but also to be allowed to keep it. Because the regulated monopolist's profit is limited to some fraction of its assets, the amount of profit it is allowed to earn can be increased as it employs more assets in its production process. Imposing rate-of-return regulation on the monopolist may therefore bring greater output as the monopolist expands its asset base from its original position, but such regulation also invites the use of more capital than is efficient when judged in relation to other inputs. A lower and lower allowed rate of return makes this input distortion more and more serious. Indeed, at the extreme where the equity rate of return almost satisfies the comparable earnings standard, there can be more inefficiency at the margin through distortion of input choice than social gain from a lower price.

One situation brings out especially well the potential distortion of incentives in the rate-of-return regulated firm. Suppose that as regulation is introduced, a single-product monopolist is forced away from its unregulated monopoly position. Soon the monopolist would have to enter an inelastic portion of its demand curve, because as price falls and output expands, quantity responds less to any given percentage change in price. The regulated firm would want to avoid an inelastic region of its demand curve, just as an unregulated monopolist would. For as the firm expands output where demand is inelastic, its total revenue *declines* while its total cost *increases*! Recall that when the own-price elasticity of demand is less than one in absolute value (that is, demand is inelastic), marginal revenue is *negative*. (When demand is inelastic, a cut in price of 5 percent brings an increase in quantity of less than 5 percent, so revenue, or price times quantity, declines.) Because marginal cost is always positive, a profit-maximizing firm trying to set marginal cost equal to marginal revenue wants to operate where marginal revenue is positive, not where it is negative.

The rate-of-return regulated monopoly has a simple way to avoid reducing its profit by expanding output; it merely wastes capital instead (if it can get away with it). Doing so lets it raise the amount of profit it is allowed to earn, as long as the rate of return it is allowed to earn on its assets exceeds its cost of capital. By needlessly

---

[15] For the classic analysis, see Averch and Johnson (1962). Sherman (1992) shows a more perverse possibility.

investing, the firm has more capital on which it is entitled to earn a return. And the inelastic demand allows the monopoly to raise more revenue when prices are higher. Regulatory commissions try to prevent such capital waste, of course, but the incentive to waste can come directly from rate-of-return regulation. It can even invite managers to deliberately pay high prices for assets, as Box 12.2 describes.

Regulatory commissions do not render immediate decisions. Indeed, rate cases can drag on for months. When no price change is possible for extensive intervals, efficiency incentives within a firm actually improve, because the firm's costs are not determining its prices. For example, a firm's use of excessive capital does not lead immediately to a greater profit allowance, and indeed with its prices fixed the only way the firm can act to improve profit immediately is to operate more efficiently. As a rate case approaches, however, the incentive to use more capital manifests itself again, as long as the allowed return exceeds the cost of capital, because a regulatory decision take costs and asset levels into account in setting prices.

Empirical tests based on years of normal operating conditions (after the great electrical equipment conspiracy in 1962 but before the 1970s oil embargo) have indicated a bias toward capital inputs.[16] These studies, all based on the electric utility industry, have tested a strong form of the Averch-Johnson hypothesis by focusing on new base-load electric plants to see whether any bias toward capital could be detected within them. A weaker hypothesis would allow for capital biases in the mixture of different kinds of plants, or even in the utilization of capacity, but the best studies have sought a bias only within a similar group of plants because more precise methods can be applied to such a sample. The finding of a bias in studies so narrowly confined is strong evidence that rate-of-return regulation reduces input efficiency.

BOX 12.2 The Great Electrical Equipment Conspiracy

Rate-of-return regulation has been shown to invite conspiracy between regulated firms and their suppliers to set high capital equipment prices. After a court convicted electrical equipment producers of price fixing in 1962, in what was called the "Great Electrical Equipment Conspiracy," economist Fred Westfield (1965) demonstrated convincingly "that it can be in the interest of a regulated private power generating company to pay a higher rather than a lower price for the plant and equipment it purchases." Producers could pass increased equipment costs through to the consumer in the form of higher prices, and at the same time they could increase the amount of profit they were allowed to earn by increasing their asset rate bases. Under rate-of-return regulation, the capital input side of the firm is essentially subject to cost-plus regulation; the higher the capital cost, the higher the prices and the greater the allowed profit.

---

[16] For a review of evidence and a well-constructed test that supports the Averch-Johnson hypothesis, see Jones (1983).

Output Inefficiency

When a monopoly produces only one product for which demand is everywhere elastic, and if the profit motive is still assumed, rate-of-return regulation can push the monopoly almost to an ideal price and output solution. The only problem comes from input inefficiency, the Averch-Johnson bias toward capital that can raise price by raising costs. However, when a regulated firm sells more than one product—and all public utilities sell more than one product—there is a question of whether it chooses efficient relative prices, that is, whether it chooses its mixture of *outputs* efficiently.

In choosing prices, the multi-product public utility that is regulated according to *Hope* guidelines will rely on demand elasticities, just as an unregulated monopoly would. Rate-of-return regulation does nothing to thwart this monopolistic behavior. Rate-of-return regulation introduces a capital bias through rate structures, too, causing the firm to favor with lower rates those products that contribute most to the capital rate base. Thus two factors influence the firm's mixture of output—demand elasticities in a monopolistic way plus a bias toward capital-intensive products—and these two factors distort the outputs of the firm away from an efficient combination.

We can see a special form of the pricing bias toward capital use in the failure of regulated firms to offer lower prices for services at off-peak times.[17] Sound economics calls for higher prices during peak demand periods, relative to off-peak periods, because only users at the peak demand press upon available capacity and call for its expansion, and so they should be the ones to pay for it. At off-peak times capacity is abundant, relative to demand, so consumers do not have to be turned away by a high price. Rate-of-return regulated firms lack incentive, however, to employ this sound pricing principle.

As long as allowed return exceeds the cost of capital, profit-seeking, rate-of-return regulated firms can prefer low prices for capital-intensive peak demands to justify more capital assets. They also charge high prices at off-peak times. Doing so helps them realize profit that the greater capital justifies.[18] This temptation is even stronger if, at an efficient outcome, demand would be inelastic. Then, having more capital to meet peaks can justify higher prices, especially at off-peak times, which yield more revenue. Moreover, long intervals between rate cases do not moderate this pricing tendency. Probably because the practice of rate-of-return regulation has been so widespread, the United States lags far behind other countries in the use of peak-load pricing. This perverse reluctance to lower off-peak prices is not something to be blamed on any unduly selfish utility president; it is directly motivated under rate-of-return regulation.

Cost Control and Technological Change

Even if rate-of-return regulation according to the *Hope* guidelines could somehow be employed perfectly and continuously, it still lacks incentive to control costs. Firms have to give up possible gains from improved efficiency, because prices fall as costs

---

[17] Wellisz (1963) provided an early demonstration of the peak and off-peak pricing problem caused by rate-of-return regulation. See also Eckel (1983).

[18] Demand elasticities can be in a relationship that can offset this tendency. See Bailey and White (1974).

fall. As long as prices depend on the firm's costs, the firm's incentive to improve is sapped. The *Hope* guidelines contain no great profit reward for efficiency, no incentive to elicit extra effort. Whether the firm would undertake research and development, for example, might depend on whether regulators count necessary resources in the cost and in the rate base, and how helpful to the firm the results might be. Some efficient exchanges are motivated among electricity producers, however, as Box 12.3 shows.

In part because of delays between price changes, rate-of-return regulation does not eliminate all efficiency incentive in regulated firms. Once the firm is bound to follow approved prices, it can benefit from lowering costs. This can motivate some cost control between rate cases, while the approved prices are in effect. Indeed, price-cap regulation was developed in part to exploit this incentive to lower costs that can arise when the firm's prices are fixed and, moreover, when costs do not influence prices. But the incentives that remain in firms regulated according to *Hope* guidelines do not serve the efficiency goal so faithfully, because such firms' costs do influence firms' prices.

Into this regulatory setting we want to introduce the possibility of technological change. The process of technological change is a complicated one, imperfectly understood even without rate-of-return regulation. We have assumed that technology is well known and is unchanging, but of course it changes, and firms using technology may devote resources in an effort to alter it. A monopoly may even have greater reason to use resources in this way, because by being alone in its market it can be assured of enjoying the benefits. A competitive firm must rely on patents to protect its

---

BOX 12.3 Exchanging Electricity

For more than 30 years a market for the exchange of electricity has operated in Florida through an institution called the Florida Coordinating Group Energy Broker. The Florida Coordinating Group (FCG) coordinates planning, construction, and utilization of generation and transmission facilities for 6 major private utilities, nearly 20 municipal utilities, and 10 rural electrical cooperatives in Florida. Every hour, the FCG Energy Broker arranges contracts after participants submit buy (bid) or sell (offer) quotes. The participants may enter up to three prices in each direction (buy or sell), for three sets of quantities, and the broker puts their bids (high to low) and offers (low to high) in rank order. The highest bid is matched with the lowest sell offer, then the next bid and offer, and so on, to maximize savings from electricity exchanges. The contract price is midway between the bid and offer prices; the difference between that contract price and the bid price is the gain to the buyer and the difference between the contract price and the offer price is the gain to the seller. Participants in this market maintain balance within their own networks, and they use power from the FCG Energy Broker to augment their own sources of power at lower cost.

Parties are motivated to deal in this exchange because the selling utility is allowed to keep its gain. This gain should ultimately benefit ratepayers, though, because it can postpone a rate case the firm would otherwise want to bring to request rate increases under rate-of-return regulation. The gain to the buying utility goes directly through to reduce the price paid by the final consumer.

rights, and it is more likely to waste resources in its effort to avoid having one of its competitors advance technology ahead of it. On the other hand, a monopoly can do very well without innovating and may even prefer to let existing equipment wear out before introducing new methods, whereas change can be forced on competitors.[19]

Consider the speed at which a rate-of-return regulated monopoly might innovate.[20] Suppose a regulator periodically sets prices under simple procedures, so the regulator bases price on cost. If the firm lowers its cost as much as it can in one period, it can experience a substantial profit gain, such as that represented by the striped area in Figure 12.1. In this example, the firm lowered cost from P_0 to P_5 by an innovation and enjoyed a profit gain for one period, but then the regulator lowered the price to the new cost level of P_5. The firm profits by innovating, and a considerable welfare gain goes to consumers as well. Now suppose the firm did not lower its cost to the maximum extent possible in one period but introduced the change gradually instead. Then costs would fall to a smaller extent in each period, and the regulator would institute slightly lower prices based on those costs, always allowing greater quantity to be sold than in the previous period.

As a result of such successive reductions, the firm can accumulate more profit. Figure 12.1 shows as a striped area the profit to be made by immediate innovation. If instead the firm can lower cost to P_1 while price is P_0, it profits by $(P_0 - P_1)Q_0$. The regulator then sets the price at P_1, but the firm then can lower cost to P_2 and profit by $(P_1 - P_2)Q_1$, and so forth. As a result of proceeding in this way, the firm can realize more of the area to the right of the striped area. This illustration assumes that

Figure 12.1 *The Advantage to the Public Utility of Slow Innovation*

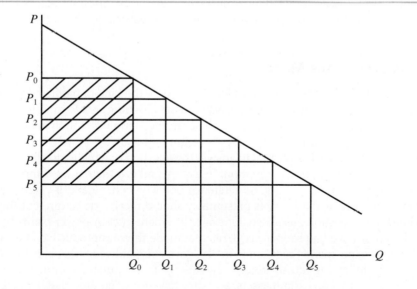

[19] For a discussion of technological change under regulation, see Berg and Tschirhart (1989).

[20] Sweeney (1981) examined the pace of introduction of an innovation and Figure 12.1 is based on his argument.

the periods are not very long, and that the discount rate for valuing future profits is low.

Requiring a long lag before price changes, as in price-cap regulation, can strengthen the incentive for innovation. Economists Bailey and Coleman (1971) observed that a lag, such as that central to Sweeney's (1981) model, is crucial to the incentive for innovation in a regulated firm. If regulators respond immediately to technological changes, price falls as the new technology is introduced and the firm realizes no benefit. Bailey showed that longer regulatory lag could enhance the incentive to reduce costs through innovation, although such a lag raised the benefit to firms of innovating by delaying the resultant benefit to consumers. A similar analysis applies to patent life, which also allows greater benefit to an innovator as the patent lasts longer.

12.4 │ DESIGNING A REGULATORY MECHANISM

Rate-of-return regulation grew out of a court decision that blended views of opposing parties. It was not carefully designed. Here we open the topic of institutional design, where we seek features of institutions that achieve a certain goal. A long line of theoretical developments has produced a substantial literature on the subject of designing regulatory mechanisms to achieve desired results. We begin by illustrating how rate-of-return regulation lacks any reference point for one of its most important decisions. We then go on to examine a way that induces firms to tell the truth about their costs or other information, which is an important problem of regulation. The remainder of the chapter considers a way to introduce a reference point to evaluate and motivate a regulated firm, price-cap regulation, and then treats how granting access to facilities can induce a form of competition into regulated industries.

Regulation versus Markets

Before turning to the design of institutions, let us note the kind of problem that currently can face a regulatory agency, How to value assets. Valuing assets to determine profit allowances under rate-of-return regulation has received more attention in rate cases (see Appendix 12.1) than a fundamentally more important question, which is whether to allow any return at all. It is difficult to answer the question of whether to allow any return in a regulated industry, because without free entry and exit there is no competitive market test for investment success, no reference point or benchmark. If putting assets in place was a mistake, those assets presumably should receive no return, but there is no good test. This question has arisen, for example, where nuclear power plants have been abandoned or have had serious accidents that made them unproductive. It exposes the weakness of extra-market regulation, the lack of a competitive market benchmark.

When following rate-of-return regulation, state regulatory commissions sometimes deny returns on certain assets, and they have long required that assets be "used and useful" for them to receive a return, so idle assets are not rewarded. They also imposed a **prudence test** on investment decisions, to see whether the investments were wise at the time they were made. Some commissions insist that assets be completed and productive before receiving any return, rather than receiving a return when they are only in a stage of construction. When utilities cancelled power plant construction projects, some state commissions did not allow shareholders any return of their investment costs. Some state commissions also have reduced in some way the rate base eligible to receive a return when they concluded that the utility had built excessive or unneeded capacity. State commissions thus attempted to mimic a competitive market, where excessive capacity in relation to demand—whatever the reason it was built—would not earn a normal return.

A transition from regulated to competitive circumstances can also be difficult. Competition has been introduced through deregulation or restructuring in some industries, for instance, and it is possible for such a change to impose losses on investors. Behind deregulation in the electric utility industry is the development of new, small-scale generating facilities that are more efficient than some large, aging plants belonging to regulated public utilities. As a consequence, costs can be lower, so deregulated electricity prices can be lower than utilities have been charging, and the utilities' aging plants are therefore worth less than they were when prices were regulated at higher levels. We call the lost asset values of the public utilities in such cases **stranded costs**. Utilities, which made investments with the understanding that their monopoly franchise positions would protect them, argue that they should be compensated for these losses in value. How to deal with such consequences is one of the problems that had to be negotiated in the movement toward restructuring the electric utility industry. We begin our discussion of designing regulatory mechanisms by examining how a regulator might reduce this problem by inducing truth telling in a regulated firm.

To Tell the Truth

Regulated firms often have a great advantage over their regulators: the firms know their costs while the regulators do not. One of the first lessons of mechanism design is that regulated firms can be induced to tell the truth. Truth telling is not achieved without cost, but it can be achieved. For an illustrative example, suppose that a regulated firm has either a low cost or a high cost of operation, and the firm knows whether cost is low or high but the regulator does not. To be specific, to the regulator the cost of producing output q is either Lq, if the firm has low cost, or Hq if the firm has high cost. Suppose also that the regulator is going to compensate the firm for its cost of producing q. Ultimately, the regulator knows the firm's cost of producing q, but a contract must be agreed upon in advance without such knowledge. The regulator asks the firm to report its cost in advance. The regulator can be fooled if the firm has low cost but reports high cost to obtain a larger payment. Can the firm be persuaded to reveal its true cost?

Consider an arrangement that compensates the firm partly through a fixed payment and partly through a weighted average of the firm's actual cost and the firm's reported cost. Let the payment to the firm be

$$F + [1 - \alpha]\, C_A + \alpha\, C_R,$$

where F is the fixed payment to the firm, α is a weight of either 0 or 1, and C_A and C_R are actual and reported costs respectively. The regulator can choose F and α after it receives the firm's report about its cost, C_R, but before it observes actual cost, C_A.

Now the regulator must consider how to respond to the firm's possible reports about its costs. Table 12.2 shows one way the regulator might choose F and α, based on the report by the firm about its cost. If the firm reports low cost, the regulator sets $F = 1$ and $\alpha = 1$. If the firm reports high cost, the regulator sets $F = 0$ and $\alpha = 0$. Thus, if we add subscripts to identify the regulator's choices of F and α in response to the firm's reported cost, the values are $F_L = 1$, $\alpha_L = 1$, $F_H = 0$, and $\alpha_H = 0$.

Now let us see how effective these choices of F and α will be. Just to keep cost differences large enough to be significant, we assume that $Lq + 1 < Hq$. Table 12.3 gives the reported cost and the actual cost, C_R and C_A, for three examples, one where the firm has high cost and reports high cost, a second where the firm has low cost and reports low cost, and a third where the firm has low cost but reports high cost. In the first two cases the firm tells the truth. In the third case, where the firm has low cost but reports high cost, the regulator faces the problem of overpaying the firm. But when the rules just set out in Table 12.2 determine F and α, so F and α depend on the firm's report of its cost, telling the truth can be rewarded. Let us see by substituting the values of C_A and C_R, together with the appropriate F and α values, to determine the firm's payment. As Table 12.3 shows, lying by the firm results in the lowest payment, Lq, which is less than $1 + Lq$ or Hq. Lying does not pay. This shows how a contract can be arranged to motivate the firm to tell the truth about its costs.[21]

TABLE 12.2   Firm Report and Regulator Choice

		Report of Firm	
		H	L
Choice of Regulator	F	0	1
	α	0	1

TABLE 12.3   Actual Cost, Reported Cost, and Payment to the Firm

C_A	C_R	F	α	Payment to Firm
Hq	Hq	F_H	α_H	$F_H + [1 - \alpha_H]\, Hq + \alpha_H Hq = F_H + Hq = Hq$
Lq	Lq	F_L	α_L	$F_L + [1 - \alpha_L]\, Lq + \alpha_L Lq = F_L + Lq = 1 + Lq$
Lq	Hq	F_H	α_H	$F_H + [1 - \alpha_H]\, Lq + \alpha_H Hq = F_H + Lq = Lq$

---

[21] We can also analyze the case in which the firm's actual cost is high and the firm reports low cost. One can easily see that the report of low cost is not then motivated. It is unprofitable to report low cost when costs are actually high.

Notice that when the low-cost firm tells the truth and reports low cost, it receives its low cost as payment plus a bonus fixed payment of $F_L = 1$, which may be regarded as a reward for telling the truth. The broader lesson here is that extra resources must be devoted to the task of teasing the truth out of the firm. Essentially, the firm owns a valuable bit of information—the level of its operating cost. It should not surprise us to learn that the firm has to be paid to reveal it. This simple example illustrates how incentives can induce truth telling quite easily. The same methods can also elicit truth telling in more complicated settings.[22]

Incentive Regulation

In the design of a regulatory mechanism, incentives have to be created to induce desirable behavior, and that is something that rate-of-return regulation ignored. An early form of incentive regulation in the local telephone industry involved **rate-case moratoria**, the postponement of rate-of-return rate cases, usually while granting some concession to a regulated firm. Keeping rates in effect without a rate-case motivated the regulated firm to control its costs, because cost increases could not bring rate increases during the moratoria. Regulators usually applied rate-case moratoria temporarily as a way to begin the transition to some form of regulation other than rate-of-return regulation.

A simple alternative to rate-of-return regulation is a sharing of improvement in earnings beyond a specified amount. Under rate-of-return regulation, a firm could not keep earnings above its allowed rate of return, and it would have to reduce prices to avoid higher returns. The effect was to give consumers the benefit of any extra gain in efficiency, while the firm gained nothing. **Earnings-sharing regulation** allowed the firm to share some fraction of an extra gain, which gives the firm greater incentive to produce efficiency gains. Some earnings sharing extended also to reductions in earnings below the specified range of allowed returns, so the firm would not have to bear the full consequences of, say, a reduction in demand.

A third form of incentive regulation is **price-cap regulation,** which sets prices for a firm independently of the firm's own cost and, thus, creates incentive for controlling costs because cost increases do not lead automatically to higher prices. Subject to a constraint on the sum of its revenue, the price-cap-regulated firm has some freedom to adjust its prices, and—surprisingly—incentive can be created within the firm to favor Ramsey prices. Over the last 15 years the use of price-cap regulation has become more widespread, especially in the local telephone industry.

Table 12.4 shows the gradual transition from rate-of-return regulation to price-cap regulation that occurred from 1985 to 2002 in the local telephone industry. All 50 states relied on rate-of-return regulation to regulate local telephones in 1985, and only 8 did in 2002. Rate-case moratoria came into effect in many states starting in 1986, but it began to decline in 1989. At about that time, earnings-sharing regulation began to grow, and its use peaked in 1993. Price-cap regulation started in 1990 in

---

[22] See, for example, Laffont and Tirole (1986, 2000).

TABLE 12.4   Number of States Employing Alternative Regulatory Means for Local Telephone

Year	Rate-of-Return Regulation	Rate-Case Moratoria	Earnings-Sharing Regulation	Price-Cap Regulation	Other
1985	50	0	0	0	0
1986	45	5	0	0	0
1987	36	10	3	0	1
1988	35	10	4	0	1
1989	31	10	8	0	1
1990	25	9	14	1	1
1991	21	8	19	1	1
1992	20	6	20	3	1
1993	19	5	22	3	1
1994	22	2	19	6	1
1995	20	3	17	9	1
1996	15	4	5	25	1
1997	13	4	4	28	1
1998	14	3	2	30	1
1999	12	1	1	35	1
2000	8	1	1	39	1
2001	7	1	1	40	1
2002	8	1	1	38	2

Source: C. Ai and D. E. M. Sappington, "The Impact of State Incentive Regulation on the U. S. Telecommunications Industry," *Journal of Regulatory Economics*, September, 2002, Vol. 22. p. 136, and D. E. M. Sappington, "The Effects of Incentive Regulation on Retail Telephone Service Qulaity in the United States," *Review of Network Economics*, December, 2003, Vol. 2, p. 357.

North Dakota. It was in use in half the states by 1996, and by 2002, 38 states used it to regulate local telephone service.

In a careful study of incentive regulation in local telephone service, which has been adopted across the states as shown in Table 12.4, economists Chunrong Ai and David Sappington (2002) and Sappington (2003) found benefits from its use although there were also some disadvantages. Compared with rate-of-return regulation, incentive regulation brought lower operating cost, lower prices for business customers, and more investment in modern facilities.[23] Price-cap regulation appears to be an effective form of incentive regulation.

---

[23] These results are mainly from Ai and Sappington (2002). Sappington is more equivocal about benefits (2003). On investment effects, see support from Greenstein, McMaster, and Spiller (1995). Crandall and Waverman (1995) found lower rates for both residential and business customers under price-cap regulation. Braeutigam, Magura, and Panzar (1997) also found lower rates under certain price-cap regimes.

12.5 | PRICE-CAP REGULATION

Price-cap regulation offers much better incentives—both for cost control and for socially desirable pricing—than rate-of-return regulation. Under price caps, a regulated firm's prices are fixed for a specified period of time, independent of the firm's costs. With prices fixed, the firm can profit only by keeping costs low. If it is allowed to retain its cost savings, the firm can be motivated to save costs. Regulators have to guard against reductions in quality, however, which offers another way for the firm to improve short-run profit. With quality controlled, the incentive for efficiency can be very effective.

Improving Cost Control

Under rate-of-return regulation, regulatory agencies evaluated price-change proposals in hearings that took months and sometimes years to resolve. Economists gave this delay in obtaining new prices the name **regulatory lag**. Professor William Baumol (1968) observed that regulatory lag could improve incentives within the firm, because prices were fixed and would not rise with costs, and he proposed its systematic use in regulation. Rates would be set for an agreed-upon period of time, perhaps three or five years, and the firm would have to live with whatever profit resulted during that interval.

Having a specified time period within which no price change can occur offers strong incentive for controlling cost, and that is what price-cap regulation is supposed to do. With prices fixed, the only way the firm can make profit is to keep its costs low. That yields profit because the firm can keep any savings it obtains by keeping its costs low. Once prices do not follow the firm's costs, the firm is motivated to control its costs precisely because higher costs do no longer lead to higher prices.

Setting rates without reference to costs can be difficult. One way to do it is to use **"yardstick" costs**, costs that are derived from other firms in similar conditions, as a guide to prices. Such a procedure may be feasible in some situations and not in others. Another way is to use a **price index**, reflecting costs for the industry in which the firm being regulated operates, and to set prices in keeping with that index. Setting price caps according to a price index not only improves cost control incentives, it can also create socially desirable pricing incentives in the firm.

Improving Pricing

Rate-of-return regulation leaves monopolistic pricing motives in the firm, and resulting prices can distort outputs from efficient levels. In contrast, rather than monopolistic tendencies, price caps can induce socially desirable pricing incentives and can even induce Ramsey pricing. Professors Ingo Vogelsang and Jorg Finsinger (1979) showed that if a multi-product firm was free to choose its prices but was constrained in a special way, its price choices would be socially desirable Ramsey prices. This finding is important because a major problem with regulation is controlling the firm's natural tendency to prefer monopolistic pricing.

To understand these pricing incentives, let's look briefly at the constraint on price adjustment that price-cap regulation requires. Suppose there is no change in price level from period to period. The firm is to take its new price for each product, multiply it times *last period's* quantity for that product, and add up the results to obtain the total revenue that procedure projects. The price-cap constraint is that this total projected revenue cannot exceed last period's total cost. Consider an example involving two goods. The firm is free to choose prices for the two goods, P_1 and P_2, this period. But the price choices must satisfy a constraint that revenue with the new prices at *last period's quantities* not exceed last period's costs,

$$P_1\overline{Q}_1 + P_2\overline{Q}_2 \leq C_1(\overline{Q}_1, \overline{Q}_2),$$

where $\overline{Q}_1$ and $\overline{Q}_2$ are last period's quantities of the two goods, and $C_1(\overline{Q}_1, \overline{Q}_2)$ is last period's total cost.

Intuitively, the advantage of imposing this constraint on the monopoly firm is that it breaks the connection the monopoly makes with demand when it calculates marginal revenue. Now there is no marginal revenue calculation; the firm chooses prices but must evaluate their effect using quantities that are *not affected* by those chosen prices. Ignoring marginal revenue turns the firm's motivation in another direction, where it seeks small incremental profit gains. With repeated application of this pricing rule, Professors Vogelsang and Finsinger (1979) showed that the new direction the firm pursues serves welfare by moving the firm toward choosing Ramsey prices.

A slightly different way to induce desirable pricing incentives is by limiting the firm so the new prices, when multiplied by last period's quantities and then summed up do not exceed last period's total *revenue*. Here last period's total revenue replaces last period's costs as a constraint on the firm's revenue this period. This form of the constraint leads to an interpretation in terms of a price index. Again consider an example involving two goods, where $\overline{P}_1$ and $\overline{P}_2$ are prices and $\overline{Q}_1$ and $\overline{Q}_2$ are quantities for the two goods in the initial period. The firm is free to choose P_1 and P_2 for the current period but must now meet the constraint,

$$P_1\overline{Q}_1 + P_2\overline{Q}_2 \leq \overline{P}_1\overline{Q}_1 + \overline{P}_2\overline{Q}_2. \qquad \textbf{12.1}$$

Thus, under the new prices, the projected revenue to be obtained based on old quantities must not exceed the old revenue. We may rearrange this inequality in the form,

$$(P_1\overline{Q}_1 + P_2\overline{Q}_2)/(\overline{P}_1\overline{Q}_1 + \overline{P}_2\overline{Q}_2) \leq 1. \qquad \textbf{12.2}$$

The term on the left-hand side of the inequality is the **Laspeyres price index**. In the Laspeyres price index, the initial period serves as the base period. The quantities from the base period are used to weigh the prices in the second period as well as in the base period, so any change comes only through prices, a property that we want in a price index. Under price-cap regulation the firm can change its prices however it wants, as long as the resulting price index, just for its services, does not exceed one, so it chooses prices that limit the rise in the price index.

These examples ignore the possibility that costs might rise, not because the firm is inefficient, but because input prices rise due, say, to a rise in the level of all prices.

It is desirable to allow prices to rise when input prices force costs to rise, because that is beyond the firm's control. For comparison, in a competitive industry all firms' costs rise when input prices increase, and so market price rises. To deal with this problem of price level change under price-cap regulation, the firm is usually allowed to adjust prices according to a price index. Then the right-hand side of equation 12.2 might contain the price index change from the previous year rather than 1. If the price level, as measured by the change in Consumer Price Index (CPI) from the previous year, rose 3 percent, for example, prices would be allowed to increase over the previous year by 1.03 rather than by 1.00. That is, if this year's price index divided by last year's price index is CPI_2/CPI_1, the constraint on prices would take the form:

$$(P_1\overline{Q}_1 + P_2\overline{Q}_2)/(\overline{P}_1\overline{Q}_1 + \overline{P}_2\overline{Q}_2) \leq CPI_2/CPI_1.$$

This price-cap formula often uses a general retail price index, such as the CPI in the United States, on the grounds that prices should be allowed to rise with the cost of living, out of fairness to the public utility. This arrangement also protects consumers from increases beyond changes in the cost of living. Input prices might also increase for some reason apart from the rate of inflation, however. Then it might be possible to use a more precise price index, focused on the particular industry being regulated.

Regulators usually make one further adjustment, to reflect gains from technological change. With productivity advance, costs should improve for the service provider. If productivity improves at 1 percent per year, for example, the right-hand side constraint on price increases in equation 12.2 should be reduced by 1 percent. If this percentage improvement in productivity is simply called X, the new price-cap constraint takes the form

$$(P_1\overline{Q}_1 + P_2\overline{Q}_2)/(\overline{P}_1\overline{Q}_1 + \overline{P}_2\overline{Q}_2) \leq CPI_2/CPI_1 - X.$$

Thus price increases are constrained by price caps to match a measure of inflation less an estimate for productivity gain. Within this price-cap constraint the firm is free to choose its prices, and resulting incentives control costs while inducing gradual adjustment to Ramsey prices.

Price-cap regulation has been used primarily in the telephone industry, first in England and then in the United States. Observers have judged it successful, and it would probably have seen more applications if alternative and more revolutionary regulatory devices had not been introduced. These other devices have transformed industries that rely on some form of access to essential facilities to induce a degree of competition as means of regulation. We now turn to these more revolutionary means of regulation.

12.6 | THE ROLE OF ACCESS IN TRANSFORMING REGULATED INDUSTRIES

Another recent development in regulated industries is the opening up of monopoly resources for use by others. Granting access for others to use a bottleneck resource, or an essential facility, is a blunt change in property rights. Owners of railroad tracks, telephone networks, electricity power transmission lines, natural gas pipelines, and other resources no longer possess the right of exclusive use of such properties.[24] Granting access often opens these resource owners to competition from the parties that receive access.

Access and Competition

Granting access to competitors raises very difficult pricing issues, because an error in pricing access can handicap either the grantor or the recipient of access. If the access price is high, the party that is being granted access is handicapped by it. If the access price is low, the incumbent who is the grantor of access is handicapped. Moreover, in the latter case, the grantor of access has no incentive to provide new and better facilities for use by the rival party that is to receive access. The ideal access price motivates the incumbent to offer access by making the granting of access sufficiently profitable, yet access is not to be priced so high that efficient entrants are discouraged from entering. Not all access involves competing enterprises, but much of it does. When competing parties are involved they participate very actively in whatever regulatory arena decides the access pricing issue. Pricing that fosters efficient decisions by potential suppliers is very desirable, and proper access pricing is intended to do that.

A related regulatory action is the requirement that a regulated firm purchase from an independent supplier. Electric utilities were required to purchase power from certain small qualifying generators, for example, under terms of the **Public Utility Regulatory Policy Act of 1978 (PURPA)**. In this case the transaction price was to be at or below the utility's avoided cost, although some contracts were made at higher prices. These arrangements later moved in the direction of competitive bidding by potential suppliers, which could yield greater efficiency.

Access and the Transformation of Industry Regulation

Access to transmission lines was made possible for independent suppliers of electricity by the **Energy Policy Act (EPA)** of 1992, which gave those independent generators a means of delivering their power to more than one buyer. Opening up transmission possibilities in this way allowed broader scope for competition in a serious restructuring of the electricity industry. Access to natural gas pipelines was also key to reorganizing that industry. Access to essential facilities is a long-standing feature of the railroad industry and is very important to the telephone industry, where access to local networks originally allowed competition among long-distance telephone service providers.

Access was also important to changes in electricity regulation. There, when independent generators were allowed to transmit power over transmission lines owned by others, competition in generating electricity was possible. A variety of new arrangements are now operating in different parts of the United States, as the

---

[24] The *Terminal Railroad* case opened a facility for use by others in 1912. See *United States v. Terminal Railroad Association of St. Louis*, 224 U.S. 383 (1912) and 236 U.S. 194 (1915).

industry is gradually being restructured and competition is playing a larger role. Access, then, is changing institutions of regulation by opening more opportunities to rely on competition as regulator.

SUMMARY

In some technological circumstances, a single monopoly firm can achieve lower costs than several competing firms. Conceptions of economic welfare can be useful to form pricing and other regulatory guidelines in such monopoly-firm conditions, but it is very difficult to induce welfare maximizing behavior in regulated firms. Government intervention to establish and regulate a monopoly is not without its own drawbacks. This chapter describes major institutions of industry regulation adopted in the United States and other countries and examines more generally the design of institutions and the incentives they elicit.

Rate-of-return regulation has developed over the last century through the gradual resolution of legally defined issues. The institution of rate-of-return regulation was not carefully designed for specific aims, however. Instead, it evolved as a compromise between vested interests arguing in courts. Unfortunately, rate-of-return regulation does not induce in regulated firms a strong motivation for cost efficiency or for welfare maximizing pricing. It can cause inefficient input choices as well as inefficient pricing. Its financial aspects are not in accord with economic and financial valuation processes, which leaves wide scope for discretion in the hands of regulators. Uncertainty about the use of such discretion is an added source of risk for investors. The discretion even has the potential for corruption. Jurisdictional boundaries between state and federal regulators complicate the scene and may even influence the way firms choose to organize.

State governments recognized serious weaknesses in rate-of-return regulation and began to consider alternative arrangements, some that grew out of academic research and some that were adopted in other countries. Several dynamic schemes, such as price-cap regulation, have been put into practice to improve incentives in the old organizations. Broader approaches have brought competitive forces to bear. Looking back, the simplest step was deregulation, merely removing regulation in industries like airlines where competition was able to function. Where deregulation was not so attractive, new incentive arrangements like price-cap regulation introduced better incentives, both for cost control and for pricing. In formerly monopoly circumstances, competition has been introduced in more complex ways, usually through the opening of an essential resource to use by others. Called access, this use of facilities by others has transformed industries. For instance, competition became possible in long-distance telephone service when long-distance companies could complete calls through access to local networks that belonged to other companies. Such initiatives are underway in many long-time regulated industries, and exciting prospects promise a greater role for competition that will revolutionize market regulation.

QUESTIONS

1. Explain the main features of the decision of the U.S. Supreme Court in *Federal Power Commission v. Hope Natural Gas Co.* Describe difficulties that a regulatory commission might have in following the guidelines of that decision.

2. How is responsibility for the regulatory task divided between state and federal government? Describe problems with this division of responsibility. Propose an alternative division of responsibilities that might reduce the problems.

3. Explain how rate-of-return regulation might induce a firm to make an inefficient choice of capital relative to other inputs.

4. Explain how rate-of-return regulation might induce a multi-service firm to choose prices for its services that are not ideal.

5. Table 12.3 shows payments to a firm for three different combinations of actual cost and reported cost. Work out a fourth case in which the firm actually has high cost (H) but reports low cost (L). Is this report of low cost by the firm warranted under the incentive scheme described in Table 12.2?

6. Compared with rate-of-return regulation, explain how price-cap regulation improves cost control incentives. Explain how price-cap regulation improves pricing incentives. Describe the main problem that might arise in a regime of price-cap regulation.

7. Suppose you produce two products, good 1 and good 2, at no cost. The demands for your two products are:

$$P_1 = 7 - 0.02Q_1, \text{ and } P_2 = 5 - 0.01Q_2.$$

Last period, your prices were $P_1 = 2$ and $P_2 = 4$, so quantities were $Q_1 = 250$ and $Q_2 = 100$. (Check these values in the demand curves.) Your total revenue was $900, so (with costs $2 per unit of each good) you made profit of $200 (($2 - 2$) $\times$ $250 + (4 - 2) \times 100 = 200$). You are subject to price-cap regulation, so in this period you may choose any prices you wish as long as those prices, when multiplied times last period's quantities and after the results are added up, do not exceed last period's total revenue. That is, your prices must satisfy the constraint:

$$P_1 \times 250 + P_2 \times 100 \leq 900.$$

a. Determine total consumer surplus under last period's prices and quantities (that is, last period's prices and quantities were $P_1 = 2$ and $P_2 = 4$, while $Q_1 = 250$ and $Q_2 = 100$).

b. Choose prices for this period that meet the price-cap constraint and improve your profit.

c. Calculate total consumer surplus under your new prices for this period.

d. Evaluate whether price-cap regulation has been effective in improving welfare.

8. Discuss similarities in the incentives that are induced by price-cap regulation and by the granting of access. Although they can seldom be employed in the same circumstances, evaluate whether they bring (1) similar incentives to control costs or (2) similar incentives to price efficiently.

APPENDIX **12.1** The Origins of Rate-of-Return Regulation

The question of what profit to allow the regulated firm, which was settled in the *Hope* case, goes back to the late nineteenth century, when the generally declining price level made that question all the more puzzling. Falling prices are hard for us to imagine today, because the price level essentially rose throughout the twentieth century and is still rising. Falling prices at that time, however, raised the issue of whether profit should be allowed on the amount investors originally invested in assets years earlier or on the lower current asset value that resulted after the price level fell. Basing profit on original investment value seemed fair, and the actual outlay had the added advantage of being precisely known. But using the current value appeared to follow more faithfully the competitive market, which reflects current conditions. So relying on it appeared more consistent with the market system on which the rest of the economy turned.

The price level finally began to rise after 1898. Utilities then seized on the Court's previous willingness to entertain current estimates of the value of property, because such values were growing larger and their use as an asset basis would benefit investors. Whether current values were appropriate and how to measure them—as physical replacement cost, the market value of stocks and bonds, or some other means—were still unclear, however.

Two Court decisions in 1923 (when the price level was twice as high as it had been in 1898) seemed to be consistent but gave two ways to impose rate of return as basis for determining the profit that utility owners would receive. In both *Southwestern Bell Telephone Co.*,[25] and *Bluefield Water Works and Improvement Co.*,[26] the Court endorsed the use of current reproduction cost as a basis for valuing assets. In an opinion in the *Southwestern Bell Telephone Co.* case (although he concurred in the decision), Justice Louis D. Brandeis called for the use of original cost, meaning accounting book value, as a basis for valuation. For valuing assets, reproduction cost or historical original cost were the main alternative valuation principles.

Justice Brandeis criticized the ambiguity of the *Smyth v. Ames* "fair-value" guideline in his opinion (joined by Justice Oliver Wendell Holmes, Jr.) in the *Southwestern Bell* case. He saw the investor contributing a sum of capital to the enterprise that was well defined. An explicit return on that capital also was demonstrably acceptable to the investors. These historical investment values and rates of return also would avoid the extreme variations in allowed profit that could follow if current estimates were used instead for the values of the firm's assets. The main drawback in this sound contractual view is that, as circumstances changed, the terms would no longer be current, so prices based on them would no longer be ideal signals to consumers of true current costs.[27] Historical measures, however, would be much easier to administer.

Although the *Bluefield* case was settled on quite a different basis from that urged by Brandeis in his *Southwestern Bell* opinion, it also sought consistency between valuing assets and allowing a rate of return. *Bluefield* valued assets at current

---

[25] *Southwestern Bell Tel. Co. V. Public Service Commission*, 262 U.S. 276 (1923).

[26] *Bluefield Waterworks and Improvement Co. V. Public Serv. Commission*, 262 U.S. 679 (1923).

[27] Sherman (1977) analyzes the Brandeis proposal.

reproduction cost and focused on comparable risk[28] as a basis for setting a current rate of return. Rather than merely listing possible factors to consider, as in *Smyth v. Ames*, the Court in *Bluefield* accepted a risk mechanism that presumably determined current returns in unregulated competitive markets and might, therefore, provide the logic needed for setting returns on current-valued assets in regulated markets.[29]

Using risk as basis for allowing profit to mirror the market process differed sharply from the Brandeis proposal, with its historical orientation. By tying rate of return consistently to rate-base valuation, however, each method offered coherence that had been missing before. Indeed, the two views are polar extreme ways of dealing with price-level change, the historical Brandeis proposal favoring consumers when the price level increases unexpectedly, since returns need not rise accordingly. Likewise, the current valuation proposal is better for investors when the price level increases more than anticipated.

---

[28] Comparative risk had been introduced in 1909 in *Willcox v. Consol. Gas Co.*, 212 U.S. 19 (1909), the first important case after *Smyth v. Ames*. A commission had found no constitutional basis for allowing a return greater than the rate of interest, but the Court said compensation for added risk bearing was appropriate beyond the rate of interest.

[29] Baumol and Malkiel (1967) showed the consequences of relaxing strong assumptions in the valuation process.

13

Postal Service

W e all send and receive mail. Yet beyond the corner mailbox that swallows our letters and the routine appearance in our mailboxes of incoming mail, just how the U.S. Postal Service operates remains for most of us something of a mystery. The U.S. Postal Service is certainly an enormous enterprise, spending more than $60 billion a year and employing more than 600,000 persons. Mail is a basic service, provided mainly by governments all over the world. How it is provided, how it is priced, and who, if anyone, receives favored treatment, are all important matters. Not only are the possible economic effects of mail service in the United States enormous, running into billions of dollars, but questions of public literacy and general knowledge as well as political community and rights of privacy also may be at stake.

The U.S. Postal Service today delivers more mail items than any other mail service in the world and at relatively low costs. But we can still raise questions about policies of the U.S. Postal Service, about the way it is regulated, and about its future in the electronic age. We begin in Section 13.1 by examining the budget-constrained public enterprise generally, because the U.S. Postal Service is that kind of an organization. Section 13.2 describes the creation of the U.S. Postal Service as a public enterprise and examines its behavior to see which goal it might have pursued. Section 13.3 derives pricing rules for the public enterprise under a budget maximizing goal rather than pricing to maximize welfare (Ramsey pricing) or to maximize profit (monopoly pricing). By observing prices in relation to costs, we may then be able to infer the U.S. Postal Service's goal. Section 13.4 and 13.5 consider Ramsey pricing and a form of access pricing for the U.S. Postal Service.

13.1 THE BUDGET-CONSTRAINED PUBLIC ENTERPRISE

The **budget-constrained public enterprise** is a government owned organization that produces public services in many countries. Being budget constrained means it is required to raise enough revenue from its services to cover its costs, or sometimes to achieve a target surplus or to incur a preannounced deficit. At the federal government level in the United States, examples of public enterprises besides the U.S. Postal Service are the Corporation for Public Broadcasting, the Tennessee Valley Authority (operating recreation areas as well as a huge hydroelectric dam), the Federal Deposit Insurance Corporation, and the St. Lawrence Seaway Management Corporation, among others. Mixed ownership arrangements that are partly pubic and partly private include Amtrak, Communications Satellite Corporation (COMSAT), Consolidated Rail Corporation (ConRail), and even the National Academy of Sciences. At state and local government levels public enterprises number in the thousands.[1] The magnitude of a public enterprise is often considerable, too, as spending of about $60 billion a year at the U.S. Postal Service suggests. Public enterprises provide electricity and telephone as well as postal services in many European countries. In other parts of the world, we can find government-owned enterprises in agriculture, health, manufacturing, and other areas. Given how widespread and powerful such public enterprises are, it is important to understand their behavior.

The Goal of the Public Enterprise

A large literature now combines knowledge from politics and economics to predict the consequences of providing goods or services through either public or private enterprise.[2] Direct implications of these theories are difficult to test, however, because they depend on unknowns such as the political importance and the costs of organizing affected interest groups. Moreover, the theories offer too many possible explanations for events. Sharper, or narrower, hypotheses are needed that can either be supported or disproved.[3]

Without competition, firms are not easily induced to pursue economic welfare. Under rate-of-return regulation, a privately owned firm presumably has a goal of maximizing profit while meeting constraints imposed by regulators that limit the firm's rate of return on its investment. Although private ownership creates a goal, public regulatory institutions have not manipulated the profit motivation so that it serves welfare ends perfectly. With public ownership, we have a different problem. Because profit in the private sense is no longer a goal under public ownership, we are not sure what sort of motivation takes its place.

---

[1] Examples might be public transportation, water, or other services. See Walsh (1978) for an estimate of how widely used public enterprises have been, and for a history of their origins in the United States. Canadian mixtures of government and private ownership are described in Boardman et al. (1983). Webb (1976) briefly reviews pricing principles for such enterprises, and Aharoni (1986) discusses their management.

[2] For historical references see Peltzman (1976) and the literature review by De Alessi (1974). More recent treatments often examine actions in other countries, such as Cassell (2002) examining the conversion of public enterprises to private form in Germany. Much work has treated the question of when private parties will seek government regulation. See especially Stigler (1971), Posner (1971), Borcherding (1981), and Peltzman (1976). General political forces in markets are examined in Wilson (2003).

[3] Some clearly political influences have been observed, such as the pricing under a state regulatory commission that benefits state residents relative to nonresidents (see Littlechild and Rousseau 1975) or that the rich benefit from telephone and postal pricing in Great Britain (see Waverman 1975). Much evidence is ambiguous or conflicting, however, as Posner (1974) has demonstrated.

What goal can we assume for the managers of a public enterprise? If the enterprise is subject to a budget constraint, its profit is limited to a specified amount, perhaps zero. Because profit (if any) is specified by the constraint, a profit goal has no meaning. For example, suppose that under a budget constraint an enterprise is supposed to raise enough revenue to cover its costs, or to break even, so profit will be zero. A monopoly can break even in many different ways.[4] Consumer welfare might be pursued as a goal, and Ramsey prices have been developed to meet that welfare goal. Yet we know consumer welfare is difficult to measure, and it is hard to give it operational form to motivate its pursuit within an organization. Instead, managers of public enterprises might indulge their own preferences, seeking a large organization, high salaries, or other personal goals, depending in part on the constraints imposed. The budget constraint itself is not very restrictive, especially if the management is free to propose prices for products or services.

We will see that several possible goals of the firm yield essentially the same pricing rule, and it is not a desirable rule. One goal that can yield some of the strongest consequences of managerial discretion is that of expenditure, or budget, maximization. Associated with "empire building," **budget maximization**, or **expenditure maximization**, has often been regarded as organizational goal for government agencies, where the goal is to make the budget as large as possible.[5] Budget maximizing is only a crude and unsubtle goal for government enterprises, but it yields sharp pricing implications.[6] **Revenue maximizing** was claimed as a goal for large private enterprises by economist William Baumol (1966), and under a budget constraint it leads to the same pricing rule as budget maximizing does.

The expenditure and revenue maximization goals lead to the same results as many other possible goals of managers, because either one of these goals fosters control over resources that could serve other goals. Expenditure maximization is the same as revenue maximization when a budget constraint is imposed because, when expenditures and revenues must be equal, maximizing one maximizes the other. Maximizing total output is another possible goal. These well-defined goals can yield clear implications for pricing in a multi-product enterprise.

Entry Protection and Pricing Discretion

The threat of new entry can force even a single firm in a market to price efficiently in serving consumers, but in many regulated markets entry is prevented. Whether entry is allowed into a market determines the discretion managers have in proposing prices. In a firm protected from entry it is easier for the managers to choose prices to serve whatever goals they want to pursue. Entry conditions in an industry thus affect the pricing practices that can be expected.

---

[4] Some other target may be set, but then the regulator must specify how to deal with a loss or what to do with a profit.

[5] Niskanen (1971, pp. 36–42) first articulated the budget-maximizing aim for bureaucracies, and in their study of regulated firms Crew and Kleindorfer (1979a) used it to represent managerial discretion.

[6] Lindsay (1976) has pointed out how blunt the goal is.

If the cost function for producing n services, $C(Q_1, \ldots, Q_n)$, has economies of scale and economies of scope and certain other properties that allow subsidy-free prices, adopting Ramsey prices may prevent entry even when entry is allowed.[7] That is, Ramsey prices can be sustainable. If those convenient properties for $C(Q_1, \ldots, Q_n)$ are lacking, however, so prices are not sustainable, a grant of monopoly protection may be needed to prevent socially inefficient entry into some or all of the public enterprises' markets.[8] Once law prevents entry in any market, demand elasticities seen by the incumbent firm are lower, because preventing entry effectively bans highly substitutable services. Then even a welfare-maximizing enterprise might be tempted to set a higher price in that no-entry market. As we will see, a budget-maximizing firm wants to set higher prices where demands are less elastic, because the enterprise makes full use of indicated demand elasticities rather than overstate them as called for by Ramsey pricing. Even though the resulting prices are not truly sustainable, they may persist because entry is barred.

To illustrate how entry conditions may effect pricing in a multi-product firm, suppose that of several markets the firm serves, entry is forbidden in one market that we call market 1. As a result, perceived demand elasticity for market 1 is lower, while entry is permitted in other markets. If the Ramsey pricing formula is then applied, the reduced demand elasticity in market 1 causes a rise in the Ramsey price, P_1, which should produce a greater contribution toward fixed costs from that market. Covering more of the fixed costs from this higher price in market 1 permits reductions of prices in other markets where entry is allowed, which makes entry into those markets more difficult. Thus, by affecting demand elasticities, the denial of entry in only one service may prevent genuine application of Ramsey pricing, even if the enterprise seeks to promote welfare, because the elasticities that can be observed are affected by the entry barrier that law imposes.[9]

The lower demand elasticities that result from barring new entry in one or a few markets can be more troublesome when goals other than welfare are being pursued. Section 13.3 shows how a budget-maximizing enterprise effectively understates its marginal costs and then acts like a profit maximizing firm with those understated marginal costs. Because marginal costs are understated, prices are lower than monopoly prices so the budget constraint can be satisfied. Demand elasticities have full influence on prices, though, so the prices are not Ramsey prices. Indeed, a price that is set close to its understated marginal cost may actually lie below *true* marginal cost, thereby resulting in cross-subsidization. Such cross-subsidization can follow if marginal costs and elasticities of demand across products differ substantially. Demand elasticities may differ more when statutory entry barriers reduce one or a few of the demand elasticities (in absolute value) while entry limitations do not protect other markets.

When entry to any of its markets is limited, the public enterprise also has more scope to pursue goals other than welfare. But it is not easy to distinguish which goal

---

[7] See Baumol et al. (1977).

[8] See Faulhaber (1975).

[9] See Sherman (1983).

the enterprise is pursuing by observing its prices. Revenue maximization and budget maximization are indistinguishable, as we have noted. If the enterprise maximizes output, its prices depend on weights it assigns its various services for its output goal. The output maximizing enterprise does not lead to a welfare maximizing result, either, but it does not try to avoid inelastic demand, which a revenue-or-expenditure-maximizing enterprise raises prices (and even costs) to avoid. We shall examine these pricing issues in more detail in Section 13.3, but first let us trace the origin of the U.S. Postal Service.

13.2 | CREATION OF THE UNITED STATES POSTAL SERVICE

Postal service in some form was provided early in the history of all countries. The U.S. Constitution gave Congress the power "to establish Post Offices," and a department of the federal government was accordingly created. This U.S. Post Office Department expanded dramatically in the early nineteenth century, easily raising revenues to cover the costs of its services. As the nation expanded, however, high delivery costs to the South and to the frontier West raised average postal costs nationally. Uniform national rates, when set to cover those higher average costs, attracted competitors within eastern cities, where private mail service could be provided to addresses in the same city at costs much lower than the national average.

To prevent competition from private express services, Congress passed the Postal Act of 1845, the so called **private express statutes** that literally forbid competition in letter mail by banning private express services. That legislation established what we refer to today as the **postal monopoly**. Without competition for mail service within cities, prices were high to cross-subsidize service in remote areas of the South and West. Unlike the public perception of most monopolies, therefore, the major postal service issues did not revolve around monopoly profits. Even today, the main concerns are rate relationships (are some users being subsidized and, if so, by whom?), costs, service quality, innovation, and competition from new forms of electronic communication.

When Congress passed the private express statutes in 1845, mail traveled the vast majority of miles outside cities by stagecoach and horseback. For five cents per ounce you could send a letter up to 300 miles, and to send a letter any farther you would pay 10 cents per ounce. The extraordinary expansion of railroads brought revolutionary economies to transportation, and with them came a reduction in postal costs and rates. In 1851 rates were reduced to three cents per ounce within 300 miles and five cents per ounce for up to 3,000 miles. And in 1855 the rate was set uniformly at three cents per ounce for distances up to 3,000 miles.[10] Postage stamps had been introduced by then, and specialized mail cars made their appearance in railroad trains. The United States was developing one of the largest and most efficient mail services in the world.

---

[10] An influential postal reform took place in England in 1841. It adopted a uniform rate (at one English penny for any distance, hence the term *penny post*), and it also introduced the postage stamp.

Postal developments in the twentieth century were not as promising. More and more communication went by telephone, which gradually eroded the power of the postal monopoly, and the 1960s were especially troubled times for the Post Office Department. Large financial deficits and serious service problems arose. Despite changing circumstances, the Post Office Department appeared unresponsive, and critics charged poor management and unfair cross-subsidization among the mail services. Reform came in 1970, when the **United States Postal Service (USPS)** was formed as an independent government enterprise rather than a department of the federal government as its predecessor had been.

The reorganization of postal service in the United States as a public enterprise led to improvements in operations and—after elimination of government subsidy— to increases in postal rates. As the twentieth century was coming to a close more mail moved to electronic form for routine business transactions like the payment of bills and, of course, for e-mail. The volume of First-Class Mail actually declined in 2000, and by 2002 the Postal Service had losses and debts totaling $11 billion. A commission was formed to recommend ways to reorient the Postal Service and to define its role for the twenty-first century, and modest reforms were introduced.[11]

The United States Postal Service

The United States Postal Service was created in 1970 by the **Postal Reorganization Act**, which converted the Post Office Department, a bureaucracy, into a public enterprise—the USPS—that delivers mail.[12] The USPS was to be operated with sound management methods, and postal services were to be made self-supporting. A **Postal Rate Commission (PRC)** was also created to enforce statutory requirements governing postal rates—in essence, to regulate postal rates. Under the Act, the initiative for proposing postal fees rests primarily with the Postal Service.

The Postal Reorganization Act placed new constraints on fees for postal services.[13] The most important constraint requires that fees cover costs for each service to avoid cross-subsidization. The PRC holds hearings on rate proposals from the USPS and recommends postal rates, which the **Board of Governors of the Postal Service** must approve. But the enterprise can break even in many different ways, so a break-even constraint is not very limiting. Indeed, while breaking even, the enterprise might maximize revenues, expenditures, or outputs. In this situation, with the letter-mail entry barrier, we should examine whether we can find any evidence for revenue- or expenditure-maximizing behavior by the way the USPS priced its services.

---

[11] See Christopher Marquis, "Commission Is Expected to Overhaul Postal Service," *New York Times*, December 11, 2002, p. A29.

[12] 84 Stat. 719 (August 12, 1970). The U.S. Postal Service was running a deficit that was to be reduced gradually until the USPS was able to break even. Ultimately, it was allowed 16 years to eliminate the deficit. There were also so-called phasing appropriations, which subsidized classes bearing especially sharp price increases under the Act, to ease the transition from old policies. The Act also was amended to allow greater one-time deficits by the Postal Reorganization Act Amendments of 1976, 90 Stat. 1303 (September 10, 1976).

[13] Guidelines for postal prices are contained in 39 U.S.C., § 3622(b), and a summary of them is contained in Appendix 13.2.

After its formation in 1970, critics repeatedly accused the USPS of understating its marginal costs to circumvent rules intended to prevent cross-subsidization among mail classes. The first postal rate case, decided by the newly created PRC, accepted as correct the Postal Service's imputations of costs to the various mail classes.[14] When the decision was appealed, however, the District of Columbia Court of Appeals described the Postal Service's cost estimates as inadequate.[15] Of the roughly 10 billion dollars of annual cost incurred by the Postal Service at that time, slightly less than half had been traced in any way to the classes of mail that might have caused it. The remainder was classified as fixed or institutional cost, unrelated to mail volume. With so much of total cost classified as fixed, the USPS inevitably claimed marginal costs were low. The Postal Service justified the resulting low marginal costs by claiming great economies of scale, an assertion that the court found unsubstantiated.[16]

Accounting methods that the Postal Service inherited from the Post Office Department were biased toward making economies of scale and economies of scope appear greater than they really were and marginal costs lower. First, the Postal Service for some time imputed only short-run costs to the classes of mail, as fixed or institutional costs, including long-run costs of capacity, were not attributed to any one mail class.[17] Second, as long as a particular cost was traceable to two or more classes of mail, the USPS did not attribute it to any class. For example, the bulk-mail system, which cost a billion dollars and is a set of sorting facilities devoted almost exclusively to Standard Mail parcels, was not attributed to that class by the Postal Service when it was first introduced but was classified instead as an institutional cost. Third, to be attributed to a class of mail, a cost had literally to vary in direct proportion to the volume of mail in that class. Such costs as mail sacks and stamps were not attributed to mail classes because they did not move perfectly proportionately to mail volumes, even though the movements were almost proportional, and a logical connection of the cost to the class of mail could easily be made.

Available empirical evidence, although incomplete because of limitations in data, failed to support the Postal Service's early claim that added mail volume required little increase in cost because of great scale economies in the postal network. With strong criticism from appeals courts, the PRC brought pressure on the Postal Service to trace its costs more fully to the classes of mail that cause them. In 1976 the PRC insisted that 60 percent of total cost be attributed to the classes of mail.[18] In 1977 the portion of total cost traced to mail classes went slightly above 70 percent.[19]

---

[14] See PRC Docket R71-1.

[15] Complaints about U.S. Postal Service pricing are set out in Chief Administrative Law Judge's Initial Decision, PRC Docket R74-1, May 28, 1975, Vol. 1, especially pp. 12–13. See also *Association of American Publishers, Inc. v. Governors, U.S. Postal Service*, 485 F. 2nd 768, D.C. Cir. 1973 and *National Association of Greeting Card Publishers v. U.S. Postal Service*, D.C. Cir., December 28, 1976.

[16] See *Association of American Publishers, Inc. v. Governors, U.S. Postal Service*, 485 F. 2nd 768, D.C. Cir. 1973, especially pp. 777–778.

[17] Stevenson (1973) charged the Postal Service with having excess capacity relative to demands, and he pointed out how the provision of excess capacity tend to make the observed marginal cost lower than the optimal level. The Chief Administrative Law judge found in Initial Decision on Postal Rate and Fee Increases, PRC Docket R74-1 (May 28, 1975) that many costs were classified as fixed, or institutional, costs even though they could have been traced to classes of mail; see vol. 1, pp. 8, 9 of Initial Decision. See also Miller and Sherman (1980).

[18] See PRC Docket R76-1.

[19] See PRC Docket R77-1.

The Postal Service practices that served to understate marginal costs generally affected all mail service costs as if by a percentage reduction, and such practices thus appear to be consistent with the pricing formula for expenditure, or total revenue, maximization. Distinguishing with subtlety among possible goals of the enterprise is not possible. Yet the evidence is consistent with pursuit of a set of goals different from welfare, and it suggests that the budget constraint alone is not sufficient to control the behavior of a public enterprise.

Today the Postal Service is using modern methods of cost estimation, and it has improved its cost estimates substantially. In a 1997 rate case, for instance, new costing methods represented economies of scale and economies of scope formally, and tests were carried out to ensure that prices exceeded incremental costs.[20] The Postal Service is a complex network industry, with challenging problems of cost estimation that are now receiving due attention. Cost information is an important basis for pricing decisions, including the use of Ramsey prices.

Any twenty-first century postal service faces increasing competition, and not just from facsimile machines, the telephone and its expanding wireless form, the Internet, or e-mail. Postal services also face competition from private parcel delivery services, such as United Parcel Service (UPS) and Federal Express (FedEx) in the United States. The letter monopoly is still strong, but many letters are being replaced by e-mail messages. Invoices comprise a much larger fraction of First Class Mail than letters, and the paying of invoices goes increasingly through Internet bill-pay services. The good news is that Internet e-commerce requires the delivery of goods that are purchased, so the demand for parcel delivery service is expanding. With the decline in letter writing and paying bills by mail, however, the mixture of postal services will change and the institution will also change.

Two other issues affect postal service pricing: universal service and international mail.

Universal Service

One important requirement is imposed by Congress on First Class Mail that restricts how it is priced. That requirement is **universal service**, which requires that First Class Mail service be offered to *every* destination in the nation for the *same* price. A single, uniform rate is charged for the first ounce of First Class Mail no matter where it is to be delivered.[21] This means that a person living in an apartment in New York pays the same price for mailing a letter to a friend in San Francisco as for mailing the same letter to a neighbor in the same apartment building in New York.

The reason originally given for universal service and for the uniform First Class Mail rate was that it would bind the nation together by allowing citizens to communicate regardless of where they lived. There was a greater range of costs for serving nearby versus distant letter destinations when the uniform rate was first chosen,

---

[20] In cases where originally proposed prices would not cover incremental costs, such as in the case of Express Mail service, the Postal Service raised prices to cover incremental costs.

[21] The rate is uniform also for successive ounces after the first ounce.

BOX 13.1 The Challenging Future for Postal Service

All over the world, postal services are facing intense competition from new technology, primarily the Internet, as communication by e-mail threatens to cut into letter mail, the most important source of postal revenue. In the United States, the USPS is offering Internet-based services in an effort to use the new methods and, thereby, limit the damage it will suffer, which is estimated at $10 to $15 billion in lost revenues over the next decade. A Postal Electronic Courier Service is now available from USPS, for example, that is like certified mail in informing a sender when a message is sent, when it is received, and when it is opened. The USPS also offers an eBillPay service, which allows customers to receive and pay bills on line. But the Computer and Communications Industry Association has objected to these USPS forays into e-commerce, arguing that the services often are already offered by private firms and are outside the scope of USPS purposes. They also argue that the USPS is not subject to the same tax, antitrust, and other law to which private firms must adhere, and so it has advantages in competition with private firms. This raises the question whether the USPS should be privatized and then allowed to compete in a range of services. Countries are moving in this direction. The Royal Mail in England has lost its 350-year-old monopoly on the delivery of letter mail, for instance, and faces competition from rivals such as Germany's Deutsche Post. Someday, postal service may be provided in the United States by a private organization, as is the case to a substantial degree in New Zealand, Holland, and Sweden.

---

because transportation was then a larger fraction of postal costs. Remember that private express services could then deliver letters within eastern U.S. cities at costs much lower than the required postage, which had to cover costs also for letters delivered to remote western locations by the famous pony express. That is why the private express statutes banned private services and created the postal monopoly in letter mail. Monopoly could preserve the ability of the Post Office Department to raise enough revenue to pay the high cost of serving remote areas. Today, transportation is a small part of the cost of handling an ordinary First Class letter. Distance can still be a factor influencing cost, however, because sorting is costly and a letter traveling a longer distance usually must be sorted more times.

Universal service is essentially a congressionally mandated cross subsidy, benefitting those who mail to remote locations where delivery is costly and imposing higher prices, relative to costs, on those who mail to areas where delivery is less costly. Requiring the same price for two services that differ in costs can have the same effect as charging two prices for a service that has a single known cost, the effect of cross-subsidy.

Besides the original aim to bind the nation together, universal service saves on transaction costs, because users of the mail do not have to bother with different prices depending on the destinations of their letters. Without universal service, you might have to check on the price of mailing to every city you might send mail and pay a different price, to the exact penny, for each destination. Instead, all costs are averaged together into a single uniform rate for First Class Mail. The resulting existence of cross-subsidy—from mail that is inexpensive to deliver, mainly within cities, to rural mail that is costly to deliver—makes it difficult to introduce competition in the delivery of letter mail and still preserve universal service. Competitors would seek out the postal services that were priced farthest above their costs, and as those services were lost to competitors, universal service could not be maintained.

Having prices vary by destination might allow the introduction of competition. Inefficient entrants could not enter markets where costs were low if prices in those markets were also low, and without universal service, prices can also be low where delivery costs are low. Proposals have been made to abandon universal service and introduce pricing distinctions within First Class Mail, say for letters to be delivered within the same city at a lower rate. As of 2007, the USPS has not adopted such pricing distinctions, and universal service remains.

International Mail

To round out this description of postal service we note the importance of international mail. Postal authority James Campbell (2001) has described today's global delivery services as a physical reflection of the Internet because it can reach so many places. A vast array of private express firms, parcel and freight companies, and major national post offices now make delivery of many materials possible all around the world, much like delivery of the same material within any one country. It was not always so. National postal monopolies controlled deliveries of parcels, mail, and much freight 30 years ago, and although private couriers of urgent documents existed, they were seen as a temporary appendage to an international system of national postal administrations. Generally, the sharing of responsibilities and agreements on pricing were necessary to make mail services across countries function effectively.

Formed in Switzerland in 1874, a Universal Postal Union sets rules primarily for exchange of mail among national postal administrations. Through vigorous reform efforts, led largely by private international couriers and private express firms, national postal administrations have gradually conformed their procedures to make possible the smoothly functioning international delivery of mail that exists today. Monopoly still exists for postal service within many countries, and this allows the use of Ramsey prices in an effort to maximize welfare.

13.3 | MAXIMIZING WELFARE OR EXPENDITURES

Prominent goals for a public enterprise like the U.S. Postal Service might be to maximize welfare, profit, or expenditures. Profit is not a sensible goal for a firm facing a budget constraint, because that constraint sets the profit (perhaps at zero) and leaves no profit-maximizing problem. It is still useful to use the prices implied by the profit goal as a point of reference, however. It is also useful to specify welfare-maximizing prices, even though welfare maximizing is not easy to induce. Our main interest lies in expenditure, or revenue, maximization, the goal that might be feasible and attractive for leaders of a public enterprise. Appendix 13.1 develops these three pricing rules more fully. We begin with welfare maximization.

Welfare Maximization

For a point of reference, consider a hypothetical budget-constrained public enterprise seeking to choose its outputs $Q_1, \ldots, Q_n$ to maximize welfare. We assume welfare is the sum of consumer surplus and producer surplus, represented for the multi-product firm by $W(Q_1, \ldots, Q_n)$.[22] For the n products, prices are $P_1, \ldots, P_n$ and total expenditures, or total costs, are represented by the cost function, $C(Q_1, \ldots, Q_n)$. With a budget constraint that makes revenues equal costs, welfare can be maximized if the enterprise follows the Ramsey pricing rule,

$$(P_i - MC_i)/P_i = K_W/-E_i,\qquad\qquad \textbf{13.1}$$

for the products $i = 1, \ldots, n$. Here $-E_i = -(\partial Q_i/\partial P_i)\, P_i/Q_i$ is own-price elasticity of demand for the ith service and K_W is a constant that is less than one. We assume cross-elasticities are zero. Appendix 13.1 shows that $0 < K_W < 1$. With $K_W < 1$, it is as if demand elasticities are *overstated* relative to the profit-maximizing case where K_W would equal 1. To solve for the welfare-maximizing prices, multiply all elasticities by a constant $1/K_W > 1$, making all elasticities larger. Then solving the problem as a profit maximizer with those larger elasticities yields prices that raise just enough revenue to cover all costs. Revenues raised by prices above marginal costs are like funds raised from taxes with the socially desirable purpose of covering fixed costs.

Expenditure Maximization

Now let's consider the budget-constrained public enterprise that does not maximize welfare but instead seeks to **maximize expenditure** while meeting the constraint that it break even. While meeting the constraint that revenues equal costs, the firm seeks the highest possible level of costs (or of revenues, which equal costs). Appendix 13.1 shows that under the same conditions as the welfare maximizing solution in equation 13.1, the enterprise with the budget maximizing goal implicitly follows the pricing rule,

$$(P_i - K_E MC_i)/P_i = 1/-E_i\qquad\qquad \textbf{13.2}$$

for $i = 1, \ldots, n$, with K_E a constant that is less than one. Thus, instead of overstating demand elasticities and then acting to maximize profit, as welfare maximizing in equation 13.1 requires, the pricing rule in equation 13.2 calls for the expenditure-maximizing, budget-constrained public enterprise to *understate marginal cost* for each

---

[22] Assume that income elasticity of demand is zero, so that consumer surplus can be well defined. The income elasticity of demand should be small for most public services that do not absorb a large fraction of private expenditures. See Willig (1976).

of its services. The enterprise thus reduces every marginal cost by the same fraction, $K_E < 1$, and then it acts to maximize profit using these modified, or understated, levels of marginal cost.[23] Solving this problem with understated costs as a profit maximizer yields just enough revenue so the firm can meet its budget constraint.

If the goal had been to maximize total revenue, rather than total expenditure, while the constraint remained the same, the resulting pricing rule would be the same as the one in equation 13.2. Intuitively, the budget constraint makes these two problems the same, because when it is effective the constraint forces revenue and expenditure to be equal. To maximize one is then to maximize the other. To pursue either goal, the enterprise would understate marginal costs rather than overstate demand elasticities for which welfare maximization calls.

Profit Maximization

We can also contrast the budget maximizing solution in equation (13.2) with the unconstrained firm that simply attempts to **maximize profit**, which yields the familiar monopoly pricing rule,

$$(P_i - MC_i)/P_i = 1/{-E_i}. \qquad \textbf{13.3}$$

Equation 13.1, the welfare-maximizing pricing rule therefore is like the profit-maximizing rule in equation 13.3, except the welfare-maximizing rule in equation 13.1 overstates demand elasticities. The budget or expenditure maximizing rule in equation 13.2 is similar to the profit-maximizing rule in equation 13.3 except the budget-maximizing firm understates marginal costs.

Comparison of Pricing Rules

Let us summarize and compare the pricing rules under different goals. The constrained welfare maximizing solution in equation 13.1 defines the Ramsey price, which, as noted, is similar to the monopolist's pricing rule shown in equation 13.3 except the welfare-maximizing Ramsey price solution systematically lowers all monopoly markups by a constant, K_W. It is as if the monopoly *overstates demand elasticity* for every i by a constant, $1/K_W$, which is greater than 1, and *then* maximizes profit. Moreover, the constant is just large enough to allow the enterprise to meet its budget constraint. The budget-constrained public enterprise that is trying to maximize expenditure also uses a modified monopoly pricing rule as shown in equation 13.2. Instead of overstating demand elasticity, however, it *understates marginal cost* for every i, multiplying by the same constant, K_E, which is less than one. Box 13.2 shows the effects of these pricing-rule differences in an example.

The expenditure-maximizing public enterprise, following the pricing rule in equation 13.2, does not act as if its elasticities are greater than they really are. Instead, it acts as if its marginal costs are lower than they are, somewhat as the USPS was found to do after it was formed in 1970. The expenditure-maximizing enterprise relies

---

[23] Sherman (1983) shows how this rule maximizes expenditure or revenue.

BOX 13.2 An Expenditure or Revenue Maximizing Example

Consider an enterprise serving two demands, $Q_1 = P_1^{-2}$ and $Q_2 = P_2^{-5}$, with constant marginal cost (equal to average cost) at \$1 per unit. Unconstrained profit maximizing prices, P_1^M and P_2^M, are $P_1^M = \$2$ and $P_2^M = \$1.25$. If a breakeven constraint is imposed, we know the welfare maximizing prices, P_1^W and P_2^W, are $P_1^W = \$1$ and $P_2^W = \$1$, because there is no fixed cost and so price can equal marginal cost. When similarly constrained to break even, however, a budget-maximizing firm chooses prices P_1^c and P_2^c so that $P_1^c = \$1.42$ and $P_2^c = 89¢$. At this solution, total revenue and, hence, total expenditure are larger at \$3.30, compared with \$2.00 at the constrained welfare optimum. The unconstrained profit maximizer can have much higher total revenue, at \$11.82, because it is not constrained to have revenue match costs.

The budget-or-revenue-maximizing solution obtained in this example involves cross-subsidization, because the service with more elastic demand, Q_2, at price $P_2^c = 89¢$, is priced below its marginal cost of \$1. Meanwhile, the service with less elastic demand, Q_1, is priced at $P_1^c = \$1.42$, to make a contribution above its \$1 marginal cost. Indeed, the constant, K_E from equation 13.2, is equal to 0.71 in this example, so it is as if marginal cost is seen as equaling only 71 percent of its true value, or \$0.71. Profit is then maximized on the basis of such artificially low marginal costs, which allows the enterprise to break even and also to raise more revenue. But it will not maximize welfare.

---

more on its monopoly power to raise revenue where demand is less elastic. To help see this intuitively, think of the case in which there are fixed costs, but marginal cost is zero for every good. A monopoly with marginal cost of zero for every good would set marginal revenue for every good equal to zero, which would maximize revenue from every good. So moving in the direction of reducing marginal cost tends to move the enterprise toward revenue maximization. We cannot expect the resulting prices to maximize welfare, however, and they can even lead to cross-subsidy.

It is also possible to examine a budget-constrained public enterprise that seeks to maximize output. Or suppose the budget-constrained public enterprise attempts to maximize a weighted sum of its outputs, where the weight given to output i is, say, w_i. The w_i's would allow more costly outputs to be weighted more heavily if that was desired. The main point is that such a budget-constrained, output-maximization problem leads to a nonoptimal pricing rule. Demand elasticities are not overstated as they are to maximize welfare. Instead, marginal costs are again understated but in a slightly different way. With output maximization subject to a budget constraint, a constant amount is *subtracted* from all marginal costs instead of a constant fraction being multiplied times all marginal costs. Again, once marginal costs are reduced in this way, the problem is solved like a monopolist's profit maximizing problem.

Our analysis has assumed the public enterprise operates on its cost function, but it can be motivated to operate inefficiently instead. The main difference between the behavior we can expect under an expenditure or revenue goal on the one hand,

and an output (or welfare) goal on the other, arises when demand is inelastic. Rather than operate where demand is inelastic, the revenue-or-expenditure-maximizing firm wants to depart from the efficient expenditure function, $C(Q_i, \ldots, Q_i)$, to raise costs. Raising costs can make expenditures higher and can justify higher prices, which, with inelastic demand, also yield higher revenue. To maximize output, on the other hand, or to maximize welfare, efficient operation is motivated, because that is needed either for more welfare or more output.

Public enterprises do not necessarily follow inefficient pricing rules; that is, they may not pursue the budget or revenue maximizing goals. Goals for public enterprises, are seldom perfectly clear, however, and the budget constraint is not very limiting. Because enterprises might pursue revenue, output, or expenditures (subject to the budget constraint), one should know the pricing rules such goals imply. The possibility of a wide range of pricing rules helps to show that the budget constraint is not very restrictive as an instrument of regulation.

13.4 RAMSEY PRICING IN THE UNITED STATES POSTAL SERVICE

If the Postal Service were to set prices for all mail service subclasses at their marginal costs, the outcome would be efficient, in that consumers could decide their usage of mail services based on the true marginal costs of those services. But a large deficit would result. Revenues would cover the variable costs but not the fixed costs. The resulting deficit can be avoided by pricing above marginal cost, although, of course, setting prices above marginal costs causes welfare losses. Welfare is lost when consumers no longer send some pieces of mail that are priced above marginal costs. The remarkable property of Ramsey prices is that they *minimize* the magnitude of these resulting welfare losses.

Alternatively, general tax revenues could be used to cover a postal deficit while prices were set at marginal costs. Such taxes, however, might fall partly on those who do not use the Postal Service at all, which is unfair. Requiring users of postal services to pay all their costs avoids that unfair possibility. Forbidding cross-subsidy also supports the fairness goal. It prevents one group from paying for another group's consumption. Pricing at marginal cost would not be perfectly efficient, either, because the Postal Service must still raise funds somehow to pay for the fixed cost, and even raising general tax revenues to cover fixed postal cost would impose some welfare loss. General tax revenues could be a more efficient source—they could be raised with less welfare loss—because the aggregate welfare loss from pricing above marginal cost can be lower when it is spread over more goods.

To restate the Ramsey pricing rule presented as equation 13.1 and in Chapter 11, if cross-elasticities of demand are zero, as is true for most subclasses of mail, we have

$$(P_i - MC_i)/P_i = K/-E_{ii}, \qquad \qquad \textbf{13.4}$$

where P_i is price for the ith service, MC_i is marginal cost, $-E_{ii}$ is own price elasticity of demand, and K is a constant between zero and one. Because the ratio, price minus marginal cost over price, is inversely related to demand elasticity, we call this pricing formula the inverse elasticity rule. The more general formula for the ith service is

$$\sum (P_j - MC_j)(-E_{ij}/P_j) = K,\qquad\qquad \textbf{13.5}$$

where E_{ij} is the cross-price elasticity, the effect of a change in P_j on Q_i. By including cross elasticity effects, this pricing formula allows a change in the price of service j to affect the volume of service i. The summation over all j ($j = 1, \ldots, n$) on the left side of equation 13.5 includes cross-elasticities times price-cost margins. If cross-elasticities are zero, so the price of one service does not affect volumes of other services, the only elasticity remaining is the case where $i = j$, which is the case of own-price elasticity, and then equation 13.5 will be equivalent to equation 13.4.

The USPS estimates costs and demand functions to calculate Ramsey prices. The most recent postal rate case to consider all postal prices, which is the scope needed for Ramsey pricing, came in 1997.[24] We compare proposed USPS prices with Ramsey prices using estimated long-run elasticities of demand.[25]

Costs, Demand Functions, and Welfare Measurement

By statute, the USPS is to cover all of its costs.[26] Estimating Ramsey prices that cover costs requires information on costs, demands, and demand elasticities. We take the costs of mail services from the record in the 1997 case.[27] The demand function used in USPS estimates of demand is logarithmic in form.[28] Initial postal rates and quantities in witness Bernstein's testimony[29] serve as an initial reference point to fix the functions numerically. We can then estimate from that starting point effects on volumes of any changes in prices.

Let us briefly examine the welfare loss from pricing above marginal cost. In Figure 13.1, the welfare maximizing price would equal marginal cost, at point A, where marginal consumers value the service at exactly what it costs. Figure 13.1 also shows the contribution toward fixed costs the USPS can obtain by raising the price of a service above its marginal cost. The rectangular area identified as "contribution" $((P - MC)\, V_P)$ represents both lost consumer surplus, in that consumers must pay $P - MC$ more for each of the V_P volume of units they consume, and the contribution the USPS obtains from the consumers that can be used to cover fixed costs. Because covering costs is a benefit, and the contribution for that purpose equals lost consumer surplus, these two amounts offset each other: the consumer loss equals the contribution benefit. The striped area ABC in Figure 13.1 is the dead-weight loss, which would

[24] Postal Service witness Peter Bernstein presented Postal Service prices in the 1997 postal rate case. See Testimony USPS-1 in Postal Rate Commission Docket R97-1.

[25] The USPS used short-run elasticities in its volume forecasts, which was consistent with the Postal Service plan that focused solely on the test year of 1998. We use the USPS long-run elasticities in Ramsey-price formulas to make longer-run comparisons.

[26] See 39 U.S.C., § 3622(b), which Appendix 13.2 summarizes.

[27] See PRC Docket R97-1, USPS-T-31, p. 55.

[28] See Witness Thress, USPS-T-7 and Witness Musgrave, USPS-T-8 in PRC Docket R97-1.

[29] See PRC Docket R97-1, USPS-T-31, p. 4 and p. 40.

Figure 13.1 *Welfare Loss from Price above Marginal Cost*

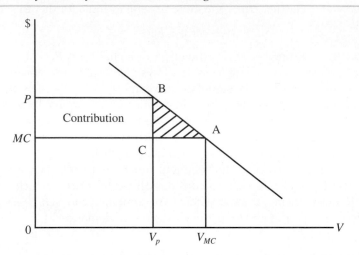

be consumer surplus if price equaled marginal cost. This striped area is lost when price is raised to P, because the units $V_{MC} - V_P$ simply are not consumed at the higher price P.

Although it would only cost MC to provide a unit of service, the USPS asks consumers in Figure 13.1 to pay P. The marginal consumer at B just values the service at the level of P, which exceeds what the service is worth to consumers who would have purchased at prices anywhere between A and B. So when the USPS sets the price at P, a range of possible consumption from A to B is lost. In this lost volume range, from V_P to V_{MC}, consumers value the service more than it actually costs (willingness to pay, or demand, exceeds marginal cost), but less than they are asked to pay. That is why the shaded area, ABC, represents the consumer surplus that is *lost* when the USPS sets the price at P to cover fixed costs and consumers no longer consume the volume $V_{MC} - V_P$.

We can estimate the welfare loss easily when demands are known and are linear and cross-elasticities are zero. Suppose demand is $V = a - bP$. When the USPS sets price above marginal cost, the triangular welfare loss (ABC) in Figure 13.1 is approximated by the price-minus-marginal-cost difference $(P - MC)$ times the quantity difference $(V_{MC} - V_P)$, times one half. This expression, $(P - MC)(V_{MC} - V_P) (1/2)$, comes from the rule for calculating the area of a triangle: one half the base of the triangle times its height. Substituting from the demand function, we can put this expression for welfare loss in the form:

$$(P - MC)(V_{MC} - V_P)(1/2) = (P - MC)(a - bMC - (a - bP))/2 = (P - MC)^2 (b/2). \quad \textbf{13.6}$$

Notice that the welfare loss in equation 13.6, $(P - MC)^2 (b/2)$, varies with the *square* of the difference between price and marginal cost. The squaring of these $P - MC$ differences means it would be better to have more smaller differences than a few large ones. That is why spreading the burden of covering the deficit over more goods can lower the total welfare loss, as relying on general taxation would do. But, as noted, to avoid the unfairness of having nonusers pay, prices are raised above marginal costs only on postal services.[30]

Still, because the welfare loss tends to rise with the *square* of that $P - MC$ difference, large differences between price and marginal cost are to be avoided if possible. The purpose of setting price above marginal cost is to make a contribution to fixed cost, so a greater contribution can justify a greater difference between price and marginal cost. Ramsey prices balance these two considerations. Indeed, they achieve this balance by making the marginal welfare loss per unit of marginal contribution *equal* across all services.

Other considerations might warrant departures from these Ramsey prices that keep welfare losses as small as possible. Departures from Ramsey prices, however, should take account of the consequences they have for welfare losses.

Estimated Ramsey Prices

Let us now compare USPS pricing proposals across six broad categories of mail with Ramsey prices for the same categories of mail services. The aim is to compare USPS rates with Ramsey prices for the same situation. Table 13.1 presents average revenue per piece of mail for the major mail classes as proposed by the USPS and as they might be with Ramsey prices at this aggregative level. The Ramsey prices represented here take into account the Revenue Foregone Reform Act, which favors certain

TABLE 13.1 Estimated Average Revenue and Contribution to Fixed Costs for 1998

Mail Class	Ramsey Average Revenue ($)	USPS Average Revenue ($)	Ramsey Contribution ($ millions)	USPS Contribution ($ millions)
First	0.352	0.38	16,365	19,372
Express	11.342	13.412	298	419
Periodicals	0.601	0.207	3,441	118
Standard A	0.146	0.172	4,431	5,321
Standard B	1.587	1.663	358	288
Special	2.563	1.556	923	298
Total	—	—	25,816	25,816

---

[30] By substituting the Ramsey price of $(P - MC)/P = K/(-E)$ into the welfare loss it is possible to express the welfare loss as $(-E)(P - MC)Pb/K_2$, which suggests that the welfare loss may be greater as the elasticity of demand is greater in absolute value, though the result also depends on $P - MC$.

preferred services such as periodicals so they have only one-half the markups of other classes. The Ramsey prices are adjusted also to comply with incremental cost tests that avoid cross-subsidy. Table 13.1 also reports levels of contribution to fixed costs that are obtained from each mail class, as $(P - MC)V_P$. These contributions come from the differences between price and marginal cost, multiplied times the volume for each mail class. The *total* contribution is the same under both sets of prices. This makes the comparison fair, in that welfare losses from both USPS prices and Ramsey prices will be the result of raising the *same contribution* to fixed cost.

Table 13.1 shows that, relative to Ramsey prices, the proposed USPS rates, as average revenues, raise little contribution to fixed costs from Periodicals mail (newspapers and magazines) or from Special Services (such as Certified Mail), and they raise less revenue than Ramsey prices from Standard B Mail. USPS rates draw a larger contribution than Ramsey prices from Standard A Mail, and they draw substantially greater contribution from First Class Mail, which includes Priority Mail, and from Express Mail.

Table 13.2 reports estimated welfare losses for the six broad mail categories, and it relates the loss in each category to its contribution-to-fixed-costs burden. Whenever a price is raised above marginal cost to contribute funds to support fixed costs, a welfare loss results, as described above in Figure 13.1. Consumption is reduced by the difference between volume at the marginal-cost price and volume at the higher price. The area below the demand curve and above the marginal cost curve over that lost volume range represents the welfare loss, which would have been consumer surplus but for the price increase. This is the dead-weight loss (ABC in Figure 13.1) from having the price greater than marginal cost. The question is, How much contribution to fixed cost is obtained relative to the welfare loss incurred? Ramsey prices minimize the overall loss by making that loss per contribution equal across all mail categories.

TABLE 13.2 Estimated Welfare Loss Relative to Contribution to Fixed Cost for 1998

Mail Class	Ramsey Welfare Loss ($ millions)	USPS Welfare Loss ($ millions)	Ramsey Advantage ($ millions)	Ramsey Loss per Contribution	USPS Loss per Contribution
First	1,176	1,982	808	0.072	0.101
Express	152	300	148	0.512	0.714
Periodicals	264	1	−263	0.077	0.007
Standard A	393	839	446	0.089	0.158
Standard B	25	18	−7	0.069	0.063
Special	83	19	−64	0.09	0.065
Total/ Average	2,094	3,159	1,065	0.081	0.122

Observe the "Ramsey Advantage" in column 4 (from the left) of Table 13.2, which results from subtracting the welfare loss due to Ramsey prices (column 2) from the welfare loss caused by USPS prices (column 3). Relative to Ramsey prices, the proposed USPS rates cause less welfare loss in Periodicals, in Special Services, and in Standard B Mail. As a consequence, the Ramsey advantage is negative for those services. At the same time, Postal Service prices impose greater welfare losses in First Class Mail, Standard A Mail, and Express Mail. The overall welfare loss is greater under the USPS's proposed rates than under Ramsey prices by more than $1 billion, as the bottom entry in column 4 of Table 13.2 shows. Thus, the low welfare losses from proposed USPS prices in Periodicals, Standard B Mail, and Special Services are more than offset by large welfare losses in First Class Mail, Express Mail, and Standard A Mail.

Table 13.2 also shows welfare loss per dollar of contribution by mail class for each set of rates in the table, and it gives some indication why USPS rates impose greater welfare loss than Ramsey prices. The average welfare loss per dollar of contribution is fairly constant across mail classes under Ramsey prices (at the margin they should be equal to minimize welfare loss, but they are affected by constraints on prices for preferred classes and to avoid cross-subsidy). The losses range from 0.069 to 0.090 over classes with modest constraints, and they go up to 0.512 for Express Mail, where rates substantially above pure Ramsey rates are needed to cover incremental cost.[31] The loss per contribution varies much more widely across mail classes under the USPS proposal, from a low of 0.007 to a high of 0.158 in classes with modest constraints and 0.714 in Express Mail, where the USPS rate is higher than the incremental cost test requires. The overall welfare loss is 12 cents per dollar of contribution under the proposed USPS rates, but only 8 cents per dollar of contribution under the constrained Ramsey prices.

Thus, to price above marginal costs so that fixed costs are covered, the USPS rates would impose greater welfare loss than Ramsey prices would. Whenever the ratio of welfare loss incurred per unit of contribution is much greater in some mail classes than others, as Table 13.2 shows the USPS rates to be, the overall welfare loss is greater. We can see the reason in equation 13.6, which shows how greater markups can impose more than proportionately greater welfare losses. The welfare loss goes up roughly with the square of the difference between price and marginal cost $(P - MC),^2$ as long as demand slopes are comparable. When larger numbers are squared they yield much larger products, and as a consequence the larger deviations from marginal cost tend to impose more welfare cost than smaller deviations would. (An example illustrates. Two equal numbers, with an average value of 2, are 2 and 2. Squaring both numbers and adding the result yields $4 + 4 = 8$. Two unequal numbers with an average value of 2 are 1 and 3. Squaring these two numbers and adding the result yields $1 + 9 = 10$, which is greater than 8.)

There can be explanations for the greater welfare losses in USPS rate proposals in this rate case. The USPS must serve goals beyond economic efficiency. Some of

---

[31] USPS later subcontracted Express Service to Federal Express, but it still needs to have prices cover incremental costs.

those other goals are represented here in Ramsey prices as well as in USPS proposals, however, through constraints on markups for preferred mail classes and the requirement to cover incremental costs.[32]

13.5 | UNBUNDLING POSTAL SERVICE FUNCTIONS

Besides pricing, an important question is, What services will the USPS offer? Many new services are being designed by USPS to take new electronic forms, but let us confine attention to mail-related choices. We might ask, for example, whether the USPS can separate some of the functions it performs so that mailers who can perform them more economically have an opportunity to do so. The USPS does allow mailers to perform such functions by unbundling service functions. These mailers need not always purchase complete packages; instead they can often purchase only the services they need. By allowing unbundling, the USPS not only improves overall efficiency, it also improves its own competitive position as more competing services are coming into existence.

Functions that come early in the processing of First Class Mail include collecting, sorting, and transporting the mail. Farther downstream is the delivery function. Some of these functions are unbundled, in that mailers can perform them rather than the Postal Service in exchange for a lower price for the remaining functions. For instance, companies or other organizations that are large mailers can presort their letter mail by delivery address Zip Code and receive a discount for doing so. These mailers place bar codes on their mail and the bar codes allow the postal service to sort the mail at lower cost. Farther downstream in the processing of mail come delivery costs, which may vary by location, and rates for parcel delivery vary by distance as well as weight. As a result, some mailers who operate their own trucking system may carry parcels part way to their destinations and then pay a lower delivery fee to the USPS for final delivery.

When universal service requires a uniform price for First Class Mail, regardless of delivery location, it is difficult to unbundle the downstream delivery service for that mail. If the delivery function for First Class Mail was unbundled, so entrants as well as the USPS could perform it at a uniform rate, entrants would be motivated to provide delivery service into low-cost delivery areas but not into high-cost delivery areas. Left only to perform delivery in the high-cost areas, the USPS would lose money as a result.

The unbundling of postal functions, whether they occur upstream or downstream in the flow of mail, are like access arrangements in their effects, because other agents perform the functions. This section considers upstream and downstream functions separately because of the special problems universal service raises for downstream unbundling.

---

[32] Indeed, such constraints affect 8 of the 21 subclasses of mail that are contained within the 6 broad mail categories examined here.

BOX 13.3 Parcels, Parcels, Everywhere

Along with the booming Internet purchases by consumers and companies, parcel delivery services are busy delivering them. The action is global. At its giant aircargo hub at the Cologne airport in Germany, UPS handled 225,000 packages in one evening late in 2005, and it now handles 14 million packages worldwide every day. Postal firms are sharing in this parcel delivery boom, which helps to offset the revenue lost to competing online e-mail and bill-pay services. According to comScore Networks, which tracks online consumer behavior, spending online grew 24 percent from 2004 to 2005 and more than that in fields like clothing, toys, home and garden products, and computer software. Some brick-and-mortar stores that have also developed an online presence, such as WalMart in the United States, allow consumers to purchase on line and pick up in a store, which restrains some of the delivery demand. But the delivery of online purchases, which is sometimes offered free by e-retailers to win business, will expand the demand for parcel delivery and bring added revenue to postal services.

See "Pass the Parcel," *The Economist,* February 9, 2006, p. 61.

Unbundled Upstream Mail Services

Let us begin with the unbundling of upstream mail services. The **worksharing discount** is a price reduction that invites large mailers to prepare their mail, usually by presorting or precoding (say by 9-digit destination Zip Code), so the USPS can handle it more efficiently. By carrying out some of the postal service tasks, the mailers, in return, receive the service for a lower price. Such a worksharing discount is comparable to an access charge that allows one supplier of a service to use the resources of another supplier, as when a long-distance telephone carrier uses a local telephone network or one railroad uses another railroad's tracks. But because the mailer uses this worksharing form of access essentially for its own consumption, the difficult issue of competition between the enterprise granting access and those who use it does not arise.

Worksharing can also be viewed as an unbundling of possible postal services. Only here, instead of purchasing an input, the mailer supplies one. That input is not an essential facility, but rather is a common input that the mailer may supply more efficiently than the postal administration. Some postal tasks, such as the sorting or barcoding of letters, can often be performed more efficiently by mailers, who can then save the Postal Service its cost of performing them. Worksharing discounts allow mailers to choose which services features they will do themselves and which they will leave for the Postal Service to do. Thus, worksharing is unbundling that allows tasks to be completed by the party best situated to carry them out.

The most significant example of worksharing at the USPS occurs in First Class letters, which account for about 45 percent of postal revenue. Of the roughly 95 billion pieces of First Class Mail that the USPS handles each year, about 40 billion, more than

40 percent, are workshared letters that are mailed in bulk. How to achieve optimal pricing of this significant volume of workshared mail is an important question. One answer lies in treating worksharing discounts as a problem of access pricing. It is possible to use the Efficient Component Pricing Rule (ECPR), which calls for the entity owning the resource to be compensated for its marginal cost plus its opportunity cost when granting access to others.[33] Allowing an access price consistent with this rule has the advantage that it can attract efficient firms to seek access and at the same time motivate the resource owner to allow access. The result can be ideal even when the enterprise offering the worksharing discount is a monopoly, although regulation of the final service price as well as the worksharing discount may then be in order.[34]

The ECPR idea assumes that volume shifts due to price changes will be abrupt. Suppose, for example, that all suppliers who workshare do it at a crucial access price, so they all workshare when the discount is at that level. On the other hand, when cross-elasticities are not infinitely elastic at the crucial access price, the elasticities should be taken into account in setting optimal prices. A ready-made means of doing that exists in Ramsey prices. Access can be seen as another service, and the USPS can follow Ramsey pricing principles to set prices that maximize welfare.[35]

The question remains, how should the postal worksharing activity be modeled to obtain Ramsey results? Whether identifying Ramsey prices or defining opportunity cost to apply the ECPR, knowing the relevant margin of adjustment is crucial. When the mailer can supply worksharing service at a cost lower than the offered discount, the mailer effectively faces a reduced price for mail service, which affects its marginal usage of the mail. On the other hand, when the mailer's marginal cost of worksharing rises to the level of the discount, the mailer stops worksharing. The discount then does not affect usage of mail service, because the effective postal price is unchanged. Instead, the mailer's marginal adjustment comes through the mailer's supply of worksharing. These two different marginal conditions imply two different forms for Ramsey prices.

Consider the demand for letters and the supply of worksharing as two different marginal adjustments. First, if the mailer can workshare all mail at a unit cost that is less than the discount, the effective price to that mailer is lower by that difference between the discount and the unit cost of worksharing. Account must then be taken of the possibility that the mailer will use the mail more. In this case, the marginal worksharing decision affects mail usage, so standard Ramsey prices apply to letter mail and to workshared mail as if they were two separate services. Then optimal profit margins depend on their respective demand elasticities.[36]

Second, if the mailer stops worksharing when its cost equals the discount, then the marginal decision is not about how much mail service to use, but rather it is about how much worksharing to supply. In this second case, the optimal profit margin for a

---

[33] An early form of efficient component pricing can be seen in Willig (1979). A full presentation can be found in Baumol and Sidak (1994a and 1994b).

[34] For analysis of ECPR when the final product price is unregulated, see Armstrong and Vickers (1998).

[35] The same is true for other multioutput pricing situations. See Armstrong, Doyle, and Vickers (1996), Laffont and Tirole (1996), and Sherman (2001a).

[36] The U.S. Postal Service described Ramsey prices close to this form in 1997, in the last postal-rate case that treated all mail classes at once so Ramsey prices could apply.

workshared letter depends on the supply elasticity of worksharing, because that is the marginal adjustment that is affected, and Ramsey principles can still be applied. The vast majority of worksharing mailers would probably have costs lower than the discount for worksharing, so applying Ramsey pricing to workshared mail as the mailer adjusts mail usage ordinarily works very well.

Unbundled Downstream Mail Services

Unbundling is possible for downstream services when they can be purchased in elemental parts. Because of the universal service requirement, First Class Mail has a uniform price regardless of the distance the mail travels. So for First Class Mail it is hard to unbundle, or separate, downstream services such as delivery from the overall Postal Service price. Parcels, on the other hand, have different mail prices, not only according to their weight but also according to the distance they must travel to their destinations. So a mailer who carries parcels for part of the distance to their destinations and deposits the parcels in the mail closer to their destination can save some of the cost for postal delivery. In this example, some of the transportation service is being unbundled. The outcome can be more efficient when the mailer has lower marginal cost than USPS for the portion of the delivery task that it performs. Other examples of possible unbundling include the use of insurance, certification of delivery, or return service, which are separate choices that are not bundled with letter mail service.

In First Class Mail, the only way to allow unbundling while also sustaining universal service would be to set different discounts for delivery into different delivery areas, so an entrant would receive a smaller reward for delivering into a low cost area. The compensation an entrant would receive for delivery should be great enough to cover whatever cost the Postal Service would have to incur to accomplish the same delivery task.[37]

A system of varying rewards for unbundled delivery would be difficult to administer, but it could permit unbundling of the delivery service. Departing from universal service would also be difficult to administer, because it would require different postage rates for mailing letters to different locations. Once in place, however, such a nonuniform pricing system might allow simple unbundling of the delivery function. And unbundling can bring competition with its incentives for efficiency.

SUMMARY

Postal service has been provided early in the history of all countries. Postal service began in the United States virtually when the country began, originally by a department of government called the Post Office Department. The U.S. Postal Service was created as a public enterprise in 1970, to be a quasi-independent organization that would collect its own revenue and apply that revenue to cover its costs. A public

---

[37] For descriptions of pricing principles to follow for unbundling in the presence of universal service, see Crew and Kleindorfer (2002) and Panzar (2002).

enterprise is a self-contained, or coherent, publicly owned enterprise that supplies goods or services. The form of organization is more common in some other countries, but it is also widely used in the United States. A public enterprise usually is required to cover some portion of its costs or to break even by just covering its costs, and in some cases it is expected to earn a profit. That budget constraint is the main instrument of control over a public enterprise.

To have some relation between revenues and costs, such as equality, is quite a different aim than, say, to maximize profit. It is not a very limiting constraint, because there are many ways to break even. Whereas profit maximization yields specific implications, control by budget constraints actually opens up a host of possible goals, such as revenue or expenditure maximization. By examining the pricing rules that such alternative goals imply, one can anticipate how an enterprise pursuing such goals might behave. In its early days, drawing perhaps on its history as a bureaucracy, the U.S. Postal Service seems to have functioned as if it pursued revenue or expenditure maximization. More recently the Postal Service has applied modern costing methods and has improved its pricing applications and may serve more closely general welfare aims.

When required to break even while pursuing maximum revenue or costs, the U.S. Postal Service would understate its marginal costs and then act like a profit maximizer. Evidence suggests this may have been the case when the Postal Service was first formed. Accounting methods that the Postal Service inherited from the Post Office Department were probably biased toward making economies of scale and economies of scope appear greater than they really were and, therefore, marginal costs lower. Understating marginal cost is consistent with pricing to maximize revenues or expenditures.

An examination of prices proposed by the Postal Service in 1997, the last year when the prices of all services were considered so Ramsey prices could be applied, shows the prices differed considerably from Ramsey prices and imposed hefty welfare losses. Welfare losses would be about $1 billion greater under the Postal Service proposal than under Ramsey prices, with First Class Mail (including Priority Mail), Express Mail, and Standard A Mail bearing greater burdens than Ramsey pricing would impose.

Some competitive force can be created for postal service, not so much by allowing others access to postal resources, but rather by allowing others to perform some of the work of the Postal Service, in exchange for a discount from ordinary rates. Postal service is then effectively unbundled, the service broken into parts so mailers can perform some of them at lower costs than the Postal Service. An example is the discount prices for companies and other organizations that are large mailers, who presort or prebarcode their mail to make it easier for the Postal Service to handle in what is called worksharing. Mailers of parcels, where rates vary with distance, may be able to save money by transporting parcels part way and then having access to the mail stream at a point closer to their destinations. The uniform rate for First Class Mail prevents such a saving for delivery service in that class of mail. But about 45 percent of First Class Mail involves worksharing, so the practice is important for the unbundling it allows.

QUESTIONS

1. Suppose the U.S. Postal Service offers only two mail services, First Class (at price P_1 and quantity Q_1) and Second Class (at price P_2 and quantity Q_2), with demands and costs as follows:

$$P_1 = 20 - 0.010 \, Q_1$$
$$P_2 = 15 - 0.005 \, Q_2$$
$$TC = 2{,}400 + 10 \, Q_1 + 10 \, Q_2.$$

   a. What prices maximize consumer surplus plus profit, subject to the constraint that total revenue must equal total cost? (*Hint*: The ratio of Q_1/Q_2 must be the same at the solution as at marginal cost prices, because that is a property of Ramsey prices. You can use this relationship between the quantities to simplify the problem.)
   b. Suppose that the Postal Service attempted to maximize revenue rather than welfare while subject to the same constraint that revenue equal cost. In what directions would the two prices in part a above be changed, if at all?
   c. Calculate the total consumer plus producer surplus at your solution in part a. Can you find any pair of prices for the two mail services that produce a larger total surplus while also covering all costs?
   d. If free entry is allowed into both mail services, are the solution prices in part a sustainable? Would you expect actual answers to the revenue maximizing prices for part b to be sustainable?

2. A uniform price has long been required for all First-Class letter mail, to invite citizens to correspond with each other and not be influenced by distance. The fact remains that delivery in dense urban areas costs less than delivery in sparsely populated rural areas. So having a uniform price makes entry into letter delivery tempting in urban areas where delivery costs tend to be low. To preserve uniform pricing, entry into letter mail services has been forbidden since 1845 by the Private Express Statutes. Discuss the advantages of uniform pricing, and explain the advantages that might be achieved if uniform pricing was abandoned.

3. Consider a postal service with two classes of mail, Q_1 and Q_2. The demands and total costs for the services are

$$P_1 = 25 - 0.025 \, Q_1$$
$$P_2 = 5 - 0.025 \, Q_2$$
$$TC = 2{,}500 + 2Q_1 + 2 \, Q_2.$$

   a. Find the prices and quantities a monopoly mail service would charge.
   b. Find Ramsey prices on the assumption that total revenue must equal total cost.
   c. Note the ratio of quantities at your solutions in a and b. There should be a pattern in these ratios. Can you explain it?

4. Compare the unbundling of elements that make up postal service, such as presorting of letters, with access to essential facilities. What is the main difference?

5. A public enterprise provides two mail services that have demands and costs of

$$P_1 = 15 - 0.025\, Q_1,$$
$$P_2 = 10 - 0.025\, Q_2,\text{ and}$$
$$TC = 1{,}250 + 5\, Q_1 + 5\, Q_2.$$

   a. Find Ramsey prices under the constraint that total revenue must equal total cost.
   b. Find prices charged by an unconstrained profit-maximizing monopolist.
   c. Compare the solutions in parts a and b. What is surprising about them? Give an explanation for what you find when you compare them.

6. Consider the privatization of the United States Postal Service. Describe the main problems you anticipate from such an action, and elaborate on its advantages and disadvantages.

APPENDIX 13.1 Expenditure versus Welfare Maximizing Prices

It is possible to analyze formally the problem of an enterprise seeking to maximize welfare or expenditure while subject to a budget constraint, and this Appendix provides a formal analysis. The profit maximizing problem is also examined for comparison.

For a point of reference, consider a hypothetical budget-constrained public enterprise seeking to choose its outputs $Q_1, \ldots, Q_n$ to maximize welfare, which we assume to be the sum of consumer surplus and producer surplus represented by $W(Q_1, \ldots, Q_n)$.[38] With prices $P_1, \ldots, P_n$, total expenditure or cost represented by the cost function, $C(Q_1, \ldots, Q_n)$, and the allowed budget deficit equal to D, the enterprise maximizes the Lagrangian function,

$$l(Q_1, \ldots, Q_n, \mu) = W(Q_1, \ldots, Q_n) + \mu[D + \Sigma_{i=1}^{n} P_i Q_i - C(Q_1, \ldots, Q_n)]. \quad \textbf{13.A1.1}$$

Maximizing with respect to the Q_i's yields the well-known Ramsey pricing rule,

$$P_i - (\partial C/\partial Q_i)/(P_i) = (P_i - MC_i)/P_i = (\mu/(1 + \mu)(1/E_i)) \quad \textbf{13.A1.2}$$
$$\text{or } (P_i - MC_i)/P_i = K_W/E_i,$$

for $1, \ldots, n$, where $E_i = -(\partial Q_i/\partial P_i)P_i/Q_i$ is own-price elasticity of demand for the ith service, $K_W = \mu/(1 + \mu)$, and cross-elasticities are assumed to be zero. We know from the form of the Lagrangian in (13.A1.1) that $\mu > 0$, so $0 < \mu/(1 + \mu) < 1$. Because the multiplier term, $K_W = \mu/(1+\mu)$, is less than one, at the welfare optimum the demand elasticities are *overstated* relative to the profit maximizing case. To solve for the welfare maximizing prices, it is thus possible to multiply all elasticities by some constant $1/K_W = (1+\mu)/\mu$. Because $1/K_W = (1+\mu)/\mu > 1$, this has the effect of making all elasticities larger (in absolute value). Once the elasticities are increased in this way, solving the resulting problem as a profit maximizer yields just enough revenue to cover all costs. Revenues raised above marginal costs are like funds raised from taxes, with the socially desirable purpose of covering fixed costs.

Now consider the budget-constrained public enterprise that does not maximize welfare but instead seeks to maximize expenditure while meeting the constraint that it break even. It faces the Lagrangian problem with expenditures rather than welfare as goal,

$$L(Q_1, \ldots, Q_n, \lambda) = C(Q_1, \ldots, Q_n) + \lambda [D + \Sigma P_i Q_i - C(Q_1, \ldots, Q_n)], \quad \textbf{13.A1.3}$$

where D is the deficit allowed to the firm. Still assuming that demands for the n services are independent of each other,[39] so cross-elasticities among the postal services are zero, necessary conditions are

$$\partial L/\partial Q_i = \partial C/\partial Q_i + \lambda [P_i + Q_i \partial P_i/\partial Q_i - \partial C/\partial Q_i] = 0, \quad \textbf{13.A1.4}$$

---

[38] Assume that income elasticity of demand is zero, so that consumer surplus can be well defined. The income elasticity of demand should be small for most public services that do not absorb a large fraction of private expenditures. See Willig (1976).

[39] Interdependencies among products or services complicate the analysis by bringing cross-elasticities into the solution and are not of major interest here. Indeed, we are interested to learn whether cross-subsidization might arise without nonzero cross-elasticities as a cause. See Mohring (1970) for an analysis of the effects of cross-elasticities in a welfare maximizing model and George (1973), Sherman and George (1979), and Scott (1986) for discussion of their importance in U.S. Postal Service pricing.

for $i = 1, \ldots, n$. When rearranged, these conditions yield the implicit pricing rule,

$$P_i - ((\lambda - 1)/\lambda)(MC_i)/P_i = 1/E_i,$$

$$\text{or } (P_i - K_E MC_i)/P_i = 1/E_i, \tag{13.A1.5}$$

for $1 = 1, \ldots, n$, and where $K_E = (\lambda - 1)/\lambda$ is a constant. The solution also calls for $\lambda \geq 0$. Indeed, with $\partial C/\partial Q_i = MC_i$ as marginal cost and $P_i + \partial P_i/\partial Q_i$ as marginal revenue, it is evident from equation (13.A1.4) that $\lambda = MC_i/(MC_i - MR_i)$. We can therefore expect $\lambda > 1$ as long as demand is elastic so $MR_i > 0$ and the firm operates beyond the monopoly output (which it should do to expand expenditures) so $MC_i > MR_i$.[40] It follows that $K_E = (\lambda - 1)/\lambda < 1$ because $\lambda > 1$. Thus the pricing rule in (13.A1.5) calls for the expenditure-maximizing, budget-constrained public enterprise to *understate* marginal cost for each of its services by the same fraction, $K_E = (\lambda - 1)/\lambda < 1$, and then to maximize profit using the modified, or understated, levels of marginal cost.[41]

If the goal (13.A1.3) had been to maximize total revenue rather than total expenditure, while the constraint remained the same, the resulting pricing rule would be essentially the same as the one in (13.A1.5). Intuitively, the budget constraint makes these two problems the same, because when it is effective it forces an exact correspondence between revenue and cost. To maximize one is then to maximize the other.

To aid in the interpretation of (13.A1.5), contrast it with the welfare-maximizing solution under the budget constraint (equation (13.A1.2)) and with the unconstrained firm that simply attempts to maximize profit. Maximizing profit, $P_i Q_i - C(Q_1, \ldots, Q_n)$, yields the familiar monopoly pricing rule,

$$(P_i - \partial E/\partial Q_i)/P_i = (P_i - MC_i)/P_i = 1/E_i. \tag{13.A1.6}$$

Thus, equation (13.A1.2) is the welfare-maximizing pricing rule that has the firm act as if its demand elasticities were larger and equation (13.A1.6) is the profit maximizing rule that does not alter elasticities. Both rules can be compared with the budget or expenditure maximizing rule in equation (13.A1.5) that has the firm act as if its marginal costs were lower. The welfare maximizing rule meets the budget constraint with minimal loss in welfare whereas the budget maximizing rule raises more revenue from consumers and can even lead to inefficient cross subsidy.

---

[40] Marginal cost must exceed marginal revenue at outputs beyond the profit maximum, from second-order conditions for that maximum. The budget-constrained expenditure-maximizing firm tries to avoid entering an inelastic region of demand, because marginal revenue would be lower there.

[41] This possibility was developed by Sherman (1983).

APPENDIX **13.2** Price-Setting Guidelines of the Postal Reorganization Act

The Postal Reorganization Act of 1970, as amended, set forth in section 3622(b) the following criteria to be considered in determining postal rate and fee levels:

1. The establishment and maintenance of a fair and equitable schedule;
2. The value of the mail service actually provided each class or type of mail service to both the sender and the recipient including, but not limited to, the collection, mode of transportation, and priority of delivery;
3. The requirement that each class of mail bear the direct and indirect postal costs attributed to that class plus the portion of all other costs of the Postal Service reasonably assignable to such class or type;
4. The effect of rate increases on the general public, business mail users, and enterprises in the private sector of the economy engaged in the delivery of mail matter other than letters;
5. The available alternative means of sending and receiving letters and other mail matter at reasonable costs;
6. The degree of preparation of mail for delivery into the postal system and its effect upon reducing costs to the Postal Service;
7. Simplicity of structure for the entire schedule and simple, identifiable relationships between the rates and fees charged the various classes of mail for the postal services;
8. The educational, cultural, scientific, and informational value to the recipient of mail matter; and
9. Such other factors the Commission may deem appropriate.

14

Communications Services

The modern telecommunications network is a marvelous achievement. In the United States alone it brings together more than 200 million telephones and other machines so that data and personal and business conversations can be passed among them. This network also allows the transmission of video signals, or the use of interactive TV. It is one way to connect to the Internet, and it is the closest thing we have to an information superhighway.

Yet the owners of this network face a revolutionary time. New ways of communicating, such as wireless phones and Internet telephony, are constantly being developed. Improvements in cost, speed, or capacity, are being made regularly even to old methods, just as digital subscriber line (DSL) technology allows broadband service through old telephone wires and cable networks are opening new forms of telephone service. Obtaining innovation and the efficiency benefits of competition in this high-investment, high-technology industry after its long history of government regulation is a continuing challenge.

Government regulates the telecommunications industry to provide compatibility, competitive access, and other desirable features for the network, as well as to influence prices. Resulting regulatory issues are often shaped by existing technology, and when that technology changes, regulatory practice does not always adapt easily. Moreover, network aspects of telecommunications technologies often require choice of one technical standard. Ideally, those who have perspective to make the collective decision also have genuine financial responsibility for results, but the same people seldom have both.

Special economic relationships arise in telephone networks, including network externalities, and this chapter discusses those relationships first. Next, we review the history of regulation in telecommunications, including the 1984 break up of the American Telephone and Telegraph Company (AT&T), then known as the Bell System, into eight different companies. Breaking up AT&T brought competition to long-distance services. To complete a reorganization of the industry, Congress passed the Telecommunications Act of 1996, the first major industry legislation since the Communications Act of 1934.

Among many other changes, the 1996 Act set out rules for competition among local telephone companies, opened the way for local companies to enter the long-distance market, and allowed telephone companies to offer cable service while cable companies could offer telephone service. In short, it transformed the telephone and cable industries. This legislation, together with challenges from new technologies and international competition, brought enormous change in the industry.

14.1 | THE ECONOMICS OF TELEPHONE NETWORKS

You would not want to be the only person connected to a telephone network. The network is more valuable when you can reach more people through it; it offers a **network externality**. Everyone joining the network benefits others. If separate networks are compatible, they can be interconnected, which allows each network to expand its network externality by reaching more people. Interconnection also raises a new pricing question, How much should Network 1 charge Network 2 so it can reach its customers through interconnection to Network 1? Separate owners of telephone networks determine not only a price to consumers for telephone service but also an access fee to admit other telephone companies to their networks. The network owners' incentives may not lead to ideal pricing outcomes. This section separately illustrates network externalities and interconnection effects in a simple one-service model to highlight how telephone networks function.

Externalities in a Telephone Network

Every new subscriber who joins a network increases the number of possible connections, and at any point the increase depends on the number of already existing subscribers. If there are n subscribers, the new subscriber can reach, and be reached by, every one of those n subscribers. Indeed, there is a formula from combinatorial mathematics that tells, for any number of subscribers, the number of connections that can exist between all possible *pairs* of subscribers. That formula is $P = n(n - 1)/2$, which is the possible combinations of n objects taken 2 at a time. This formula is appropriate because, in a telephone network, every pair of 2 subscribers can conceivably be connected for a conversation. Table 14.1 illustrates a network with a central switch, S, that shows how the number of connections (dashed lines) increases with the number of subscribers on the network.

Because connections to others is the main benefit of a telephone network, and connections depend on the total number of subscribers, we can expect demand to depend on the number of subscribers in the network. To represent such a demand relationship in simple form, consider what we call a type-1 individual. The type-1 individual makes an either-or choice about whether to connect to the telephone network, receiving utility (U_1) from the decision that we can express as

$$U_1 = \begin{cases} 0.1Q - p & \text{if connected to the network.} \\ 0 & \text{if not connected.} \end{cases}$$

TABLE 14.1 Possible Subscriber Connections in Networks

Network	Subscribers	Connections	Increase in Connections
	1	0	0
	2	1	1
	3	3	2
	4	6	3

The type-1 individual who is connected to the network receives utility (U_1), or satisfaction, (represented by $0.1Q$) from the number of *others*, Q, who are connected to the telephone system less the price, p, that is paid for connection. Because the individual's utility, U_1, depends on decisions by others, there is an external effect; utility depends on others' decisions to join the network. If not connected, the consumer receives no utility.

Consider now a type-2 individual, who may communicate more with other people and for that reason place even more importance on the number of others connected to the network. The type-2 individual's utility is

$$U_2 = \begin{cases} 0.2Q - p & \text{if connected to the network.} \\ 0 & \text{if not connected.} \end{cases}$$

Thus, the benefit that individuals obtain by connecting to the network increases as the total number of subscribers increases, and that network externality is greater for some individuals than it is for others. Assume that individuals are willing to be connected for a price less than or equal to the value they place on the network connection (for example, the type-2 individual pays as much as $0.2Q$ to be connected).

These representations of individual utility for telephone service yield demands for connections to the network. Once we have such demands, we can determine price responses by a monopoly provider of service. Consider, for example, a case in which there are no costs and there are four types of individuals who have utility for telephone service, much like 1 and 2 above but extending to a type-4 who receives utility of $0.4Q$ from connecting. Table 14.2 shows results for the four types of individuals,

TABLE 14.2 Demand, Profit, and Welfare with Network Externalities

n	i	U_i	Q	p	π	$W = \pi + 5 \Sigma_i U_i$ (for i of included groups)
5	4	$0.4Q - p$	5	2	10	$10 + 0 = 10$
5	3	$0.3Q - p$	10	3	30	$30 + 0 + 5[0.4(10)-3] = 35$
5	2	$0.2Q - p$	15	3	45	$45 + 0 + 5[0.4(15)-3] + 5[0.3(15)-3] = 67.5$
5	1	$0.1Q - p$	20	2	40	$40 + 0 + 5[0.4(20) - 2] + 5[0.3(20)-2] + 5[0.2(20)-2] = 100$

and it assumes that there are five members ($n = 5$) of each of the four types. Assume that costs are zero, and suppose a monopoly seller tries to maximize profit given the demands of these 20 individuals.

Headings in Table 14.2, starting at the left, show the number of each type, n (always 5), the index for each type, i, and then the utility for each member of each type, $U_i (i = 1, 2, 3, 4)$. Utility depends on the total number connected to the network, Q, and on p as well, and we assume that the individual decides to connect when utility equals or exceeds the price. Because the value of the network externality is highest for type-4 individuals, the first line in Table 14.2 considers their participation. That first line indicates that if service went only to type-4 individuals, Q would be 5, and utility for one individual, U_4, would be $0.4(5) = 2$. The monopoly, then, could charge a price of $p - 2$ and attract those five type-4 individuals, making a profit, π, of 10 ($2 \times 5 = 10$) and generating a net utility of 0 ($5 \Sigma_i U_i = 0$).

The monopoly would also want to consider attracting the type-3 individuals, to make $Q = 10$ thus increasing utility and how much all who purchase are willing to pay. In addition to raising the utility of type-4 individuals through the larger Q, type-3 individuals would gain utility of $0.3(10) = 3$ so the monopoly could charge them $p = 3$. This price would retain the type-4 individuals as customers, because with $Q = 10$ they would have utility of $0.4(10) = 4 > 3 = p$. Profit for the monopoly then goes from 10 to 30. Now if the monopoly can attract type-2 consumers, Q rises to 15. Notice that if $Q = 15$, utility of the type-2 consumers is $0.2(15) = 3$, so price can still be set at 3. That keeps type-3 and type-4 individuals willing to connect and thus maintains the output of 15. Profit increases again, to 45. Finally, consider what it takes to attract type-1 individuals so the quantity of subscribers reachs 20. At the quantity of 20, the utility of type-1 individuals is $0.1(20) = 2$, so price must be lowered to 2, and all other types continue to participate at that price. The monopoly profit, however, is only 40 with $p = 2$ and $Q = 20$, so we can expect the monopoly to choose $p = 3$ and serve only 15 subscribers to maximize its profit.

Individuals must act based on the number of individuals they *expect* will be connected to the telephone network. The number, Q, is actually an expectation an individual has when deciding whether to subscribe. We assume that individuals correctly estimate that number, so they have **perfect foresight**. Perfect foresight, which includes perfect knowledge of decisions by others, is a strong assumption. Yet if

Figure 14.1 *Illustration of Demand with Network Externalities*

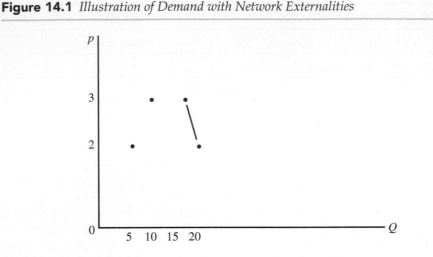

the telephone network has grown gradually over time, individuals have a good basis for forming expectations, and near perfect foresight is not unreasonable. This is not to say that a provider of telephone service will not try to influence that expectation, however, perhaps by claiming that its network is "Number One!"

Figure 14.1, which marks the four price-quantity points identified in Table 14.1, illustrates the responses of consumers to these pricing steps. Five type-4 consumers are willing to purchase at a price of 2, and 10 type-4 and type-3 consumers together are willing to purchase at a price of 3. Five more, type-2, consumers are willing to purchase at a price of 3, making $Q = 15$. Five type-1 consumers are attracted by a price of 2, making $Q = 20$. At any price, we can expect the largest quantity to prevail, so the effective demand is the downward sloping portion of demand indicated in Figure 14.1.

Table 14.2 shows that total profit is greatest when price is 3 and 15 subscribe, yet total welfare is greatest when price is 2 and all 20 consumers subscribe. Instead of maximizing welfare at $p = 2$, the monopoly charges $p = 3$ to maximize profit, and the result is inefficient. Can entry improve welfare? That is, at the monopoly solution, is it possible for a competing firm to enter and survive, particularly if the monopoly already has contracts with 15 consumers, making them unable to switch in the short run? If the competing entrant is compatible so its customers can call those on the monopoly's network, and vice versa, the answer is *yes*. With compatibility allowing 5 new consumers to join the monopoly's 15 customers, the entrant can set a price of 2 and bring utility of $0.1Q - p = 2 - 2 = 0$ to type-1 customers. Assume, as before, that even though they receive no extra surplus, type-1 customers will sign up. (The entrant, however, must win the five type-1 customers quickly; if the monopoly lowers price to attract them, the entrant fails.) Because the entrant's price is lower than the (former) monopoly's, it can expect in time to attract more consumers as the monopoly's contracts with its customers expire. Thus, in this example, entry can improve welfare.

Network externalities, then, can cause demand by all parties to increase with the number of individuals expected to participate in the telephone network. Yet we can expect an equilibrium to look very much like the equilibrium in any other market in that demand is ultimately downward sloping, even though consumers are willing to pay more as the number of subscribers grows. As in other market settings, a monopoly may prefer an equilibrium with a smaller output than is socially ideal. But the monopoly restriction of output lowers welfare more seriously when network externalities exist, because expanded output then enhances welfare more.

Interconnection of Telephone Networks

Network operators often want their networks designed to the same standard, because the resulting compatibility allows their interconnection, which expands network externalities. The case of entry in the Figure 14.1 and Table 14.2 example shows that a larger network may not want to interconnect with a smaller network. The smaller network, however, wants desperately to interconnect with the larger network so it can share the network externality of the larger network. When networks interconnect but are separately owned, they must reach agreement on terms for connecting each other's calls. For example, a long-distance carrier could interconnect with a local exchange carrier to complete its customers' calls to the final recipients of the calls. Agreement on access terms so calls can be completed on another network is the main new problem raised by the interconnection of separate networks.

 The problem of access payments between networks arises because each network collects a fee from the customer who originates a call, and the network may then have to compensate any other network that helps in completing the call. When only two parties are connecting—as when a long-distance company wants to complete a call through a local network—the bargaining may be quite simple. There is a complementary relationship that raises a double marginalization problem, however, in this case a vertical relationship between long-distance and local networks. Here double marginalization is more complicated than it was between manufacturer and retailer in Chapter 4, because it can now apply in two directions. We call it **double double marginalization**.

 Suppose each of two networks, called Foncall and Callfon, is a monopoly over its own local network. The two networks, illustrated in Figure 14.2, are symmetrical—they face similar demands—which simplifies some of the pricing issues that arise. Foncall (at the right in Figure 14.2) operates a local network and can transport long-distance calls to the local network operated by Callfon (at the left). Callfon

Figure 14.2 *Interconnection of Two Telephone Networks*

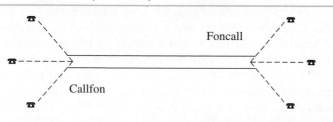

operates a local network and transports long-distance calls to Foncall. Each network now sets two prices: (1) a price, p, charged to individuals for connection to its network, and (2) a price, a, charged to the other network for completing that network's calls. Thus, each network collects fees from customers to whom it offers telephone service and from the other networks for completing their calls. Assume there are no costs other than these access charges networks pay each other. For simplicity, this section focuses on interconnection without treating the externality effect itself.

Double Double Marginalization

Suppose we know the demands for telephone service in two networks. Demand for calls originating in Foncall is given by $q_F = b - p_F$ and demand for calls originating in Callfon is given by $q_C = b - p_C$. Each network must pay the other for completing calls, but each also receives payment when it completes calls for the other network. The access charge for calls from Foncall to Callfon, which Callfon sets, is represented by a_C, while Foncall's access charge for calls from Callfon to Foncall is a_F. Assume that all who are connected to Foncall make calls to Callfon and vice versa, so Foncall pays $q_F a_C$ in access charges to Callfon and Callfon pays $q_C a_F$ to Foncall.

With all calls going from one network to the other when there is interconnection, we can represent the profit of Foncall, π_F, as

$$\pi_F = q_F(p_F - a_C) + q_C a_F, \tag{14.1a}$$

where q_F is the number connected to Foncall who call to Callfon, and q_C is the number who call from Callfon to Foncall. By the same reasoning, the profit of Callfon is

$$\pi_C = q_C(p_C - a_F) + q_F a_C. \tag{14.1b}$$

Notice that Callfon's decision in setting a_C determines marginal cost for Foncall, while Foncall's decision in setting a_F determines marginal cost for Callfon. By setting access fees for each other, the networks determine each others' costs.

Applying the same method as in Chapter 4, we find in Appendix 14.1 that by independently maximizing profit shown in equations 14.1a and 14.1b, Callfon and Foncall arrive at consumer prices of $p_F = (b + a_C)/2$ and $p_C = (b + a_F)/2$. Their profit maximizing access prices are $a_C = b/2$ and $a_F = b/2$, which imply that $p_F = p_C = 3b/4$. At that price, profit for the two firms is $\pi_F = \pi_C = b^2 3/16$. Suppose instead that the access fee is set at marginal cost ($a_C = a_F = 0$), as it was for the optimal manufacturer-retailer solution in Chapter 4. Then the price to consumers is lower at $p_F = p_C = b/2$, and profits are actually higher at $\pi_F = \pi_C = b^2/4$. Double double marginalization, therefore, can arise when networks independently maximize profit, and it leads to higher access prices, higher consumer prices, and lower profit than is possible with more efficient prices. Unlike the one-way relationship of manufacturer and retailer in Chapter 4, where a host of inducements was considered that would compensate one party for avoiding double marginalization, the symmetry of the networks' situations in this case can help them reach agreement. Here they share equally in the benefit of setting low access fees that avoid double double marginalization.

The Importance of Call Volumes

Networks may not be perfectly symmetrical, as Foncall and Callfon were. Specifically, if one of the networks is sending more calls than the other then they can have more of a one-way relationship, more like a manufacturer and a retailer, and their preferred access fees may differ. This possibility is considered in Appendix 14.1, which shows that the smaller network in that case sends fewer calls and receives more calls, so it wants a larger access fee for completing those calls.[1] Selling more service (for access) than it buys makes the smaller network resemble the manufacturer that wants to mark up its cost in the manufacturer-retailer case. Such a difference in motivation between telephone networks can complicate agreement on a common access fee.

Economists Michael Carter and Julian Wright (2003) have used this effect of asymmetry in call volumes to propose an access pricing rule for interconnection of telephone networks. Rather than have the parties bargain on an access fee or have a regulator impose an access fee, they propose to have the larger network choose the fee that both networks charge. They recommend this solution because the larger network can be expected to prefer a more efficient access fee. This rule can result in more efficient access charges because the larger network's preference for an access fee closer to marginal cost tends to rein in double double marginalization.

Remember that in these examples an individual who initiates a call is assumed to pay one network for all its service. If another network is needed to complete the call, then the first network, which is receiving the customer's payment, must negotiate an access charge with the second network. If the recipient of the call shared in paying its cost, a different pricing arrangement could result. Because the practice of having the initiator pay for calls is so widespread, it is assumed here that the initiator pays for the call.[2]

Incentives become even more complicated if instead of interconnecting merely to complete calls across networks of given sizes, each network competes for customers in an effort to enlarge its own network. The interconnection examples have so far assumed monopoly control of each network, where all calls from one network go to the other network. Suppose instead that the two networks compete for the same customers, and each network wants to increase its share of the single market. This incentive to have a larger market share can arise because all of one network's calls no longer go to the other network. Suppose, for example, that Callfon has three-fourths of the market. Then three-fourths of the calls from Foncall customers can be expected to go to customers of Callfon. As Callfon's share is larger, more calls from Foncall tend to go to Callfon, and if Callfon's access fee is above its marginal cost, Foncall must pay extra access charges to Callfon to complete all those calls. Foncall would prefer to complete those calls on its own network, which it can do by winning a larger market share.

So with competition for market share we can expect Foncall and Callfon to lower their prices to attract customers in an effort to enlarge their market shares.

---

[1] International access fees commonly follow this pattern, where the smaller country that has more calls arriving from larger countries imposes the larger access fee. See Wright (1999).

[2] For analysis of effects of having recipients contribute to the cost of calls, see DeGraba (2001).

Each network, however, also wants to raise its rival's costs by raising its own access fee. If both networks raise their access fees, prices to final customers could actually be higher even when there is competition for market share. We cannot predict perfectly how competition for market share will affect customer prices. To avoid double double marginalization, the ideal access fee should equal the marginal cost of access, but competition for market share motivates networks to raise access fees above marginal costs as each network tries to raise the other's cost. So competition between networks may not result in ideal prices either for access to other networks or for customers.

These examples of interconnection apply to a new age of telephony, in which many networks are available to provide local and long distance service. In the history of telephone service the problems that can arise from interconnection of networks were avoided by having only one long-distance network and simple arrangements with local networks. We now turn to consider this history of telephone regulation, to set the stage for the changes that have recently occurred.

14.2 | EARLY REGULATION OF THE U.S. TELEPHONE INDUSTRY

The telephone patent awarded in 1876 to Alexander Graham Bell is justly famous, and on it the Bell Telephone Company was founded. The company acquired the equipment manufacturer, Western Electric Company, in 1881, and thereafter produced its own equipment instead of buying from others. It licensed local telephone companies to use Bell technology, often in exchange for a portion of their ownership shares, which led to a holding company form of organization. In 1885 the Bell Company created a long-lines subsidiary for long-distance calls, named American Telephone and Telegraph Company (AT&T), to connect the local companies into what came to be known as the Bell System and was later called AT&T. Research by the company produced many more patents, including one that created a monopoly over long-distance service by the time the original Bell patent expired in 1893.

Early telephone service was nothing like what we enjoy today. Static interference could make it difficult to carry on a conversation, and service was provided only certain hours of the day, as from 8 AM to 6 PM. Initially every conversation required its own wire to connect parties, so in larger cities a maze of wires developed overhead. In New York City, the collapse of many poles and their nets of wires in the blizzard of 1888 caused such havoc that the city decided to place them underground. Other large cities followed this practice. Wires were gradually extended to more remote areas. Yet it was not until 1915 that a telephone call could be made across the United States.

Despite its inferiority, the early telephone service was very valuable. Conversation by telephone was much easier and cheaper than travel. Great profit came to the Bell System, which attracted a host of competitors into the business. This competition lowered prices and greatly expanded the number of people receiving telephone service.[3] The Bell System clearly wanted to capture for itself the advantages of network externalities, as it aimed to provide service from any one telephone to any other one in what it called **"end-to-end" service**. Indeed, it refused to connect independent companies to its long-distance network. When, in the period before World War I, the Bell System followed a policy of purchasing independent companies, it seemed to be embarking on a campaign to create a monopoly over telephone service in the United States.

The Beginnings of Regulation

The Interstate Commerce Commission (ICC), which was formed in 1887, was charged under the Mann-Elkins Act of 1910 with regulating AT&T. Later the **Communications Act** of 1934 created the **Federal Communications Commission (FCC)** to regulate radio and telephone common carriers. The FCC sought to make telephone service available to all as far as that was possible—a goal called **universal service**—and to do so at reasonable prices without unjust or unreasonable discrimination. AT&T's ownership of, and vertical integration with, the equipment supplier Western Electric quickly became a major issue for the new FCC.

When Bell bought Western Electric in 1881 and then insisted on owning all telephone instruments attached to its network, it essentially controlled the market for telephones. Such control was consistent with its end-to-end service aim, but there were complaints in the 1930s, especially from Congress, about high profit on unregulated Western Electric equipment sales to AT&T. The fact that paying high prices for Western Electric equipment would also lead to a high rate base for AT&T—and, thus, higher profits under rate-of-return regulation—was not lost on critics.

AT&T's large size was advantageous in facilitating national communications during World War II. After World War II ended, however, the Justice Department charged AT&T with conspiring to monopolize the telephone equipment market and to exclude others. In 1956 another consent decree, which was called the **final judgment,** resolved the antitrust issue for AT&T and its terms gave AT&T an apparent victory. The company was to license equipment patents, but because it controlled the market for telephone equipment, this was not a crucial issue. All of AT&T's activities were to be in regulated industries. Although it was not harmful to AT&T at the time, the 1956 consent decree restrained AT&T so it was not ready for the competitive threat that was to come.

After World War II, the FCC tended to support many AT&T arguments. For example, in the 1950s a small company called Hush-A-Phone sold a plastic device that would fit over the mouthpiece of a telephone to reduce the problem of background noise entering with the vocal sound. Even though the device had no electrical element, AT&T claimed it lowered signal strength and would lower service quality. The FCC supported AT&T in a 1954 decision barring the use of Hush-A-Phone. But Hush-A-Phone went to the Court of Appeals, which overturned the FCC decision on the ground that Hush-A-Phone was equivalent to cupping the mouthpiece in one's

---

[3] For descriptions of the development of the modern telephone network, see Compaine and Read (1999).

BOX 14.1 AT&T Accumulates Power

In 1913, after the U.S. Attorney General had filed a lawsuit over AT&T's acquisition of a small competing long-distance company, AT&T agreed to a **consent decree**, a statement of rules to be followed to which a defendant agrees to end a lawsuit. Under the decree, AT&T would no longer buy independent telephone companies or deny such companies connection to its long-distance network. AT&T also agreed to sell the Western Union Telegraph Company. Right after this consent decree came World War I, when the telephone system was placed under government control and supervised in 1918 and 1919 by the Postmaster General. He favored consolidation into a single national telephone system, and in 1921, Congress gave the ICC power to exempt AT&T from antitrust laws so it could acquire independent telephone companies. The part of the 1913 consent decree that limited horizontal integration was, thus, abandoned, and by 1930 the Bell System, by then widely known as AT&T, controlled four-fifths of the national market for telephone service.

See *U.S. v. AT&T*, No. 6082, U.S. Dist. Ct., Dist. Of Oregon, *Original Petition*, July 24, 1913, and letter from Nathan C. Kingsbury to James C. McReynolds, Dec. 19, 1913.

hand, and it could not harm the network. So Hush-A-Phone was used, especially in noisy environments. This opened a crack in the Bell System network and it was only the beginning. Regulatory procedures would also aggravate the Bell System.

The "Settlement" Conflict and the Regulatory Solution

Figure 14.3 illustrates a call network similar to the one in Figure 14.2. A call between stations (telephones) LA1 and LA2 (or NY1 and NY2) is local; it stays within one local exchange network, or loop. An interexchange call might go from LA1 to NY1, which involves both local and long-distance facilities.[4] Figure 14.3 also shows private line connections, which were like board-to-board transmissions but they connected stations directly. They could be used by private parties who set up their own communications channels and could be obtained by special arrangement from AT&T. The volume of messages between stations had to be large to justify construction of a dedicated private line, but banks, airlines, and television networks used them.

Whether the cost of processing the local part of a long-distance call should be counted in the cost of that long-distance call was an issue in the 1920s. Tracing local exchange costs of long distance calls is similar to determining access fees today, in that it influences how local and long-distance prices are established. In the 1920s, however, local service was offered to customers for a fixed monthly payment, with no

---

[4] Long-distance wireline transmissions occur by cable, microwave, or satellite means. Calls can go from a telephone (or "station") in one loop, or locality, to a distant telephone in another (Fig. 14.3). Alternatively, stations may be connected directly by private lines.

Figure 14.3 *Telephone Connections*

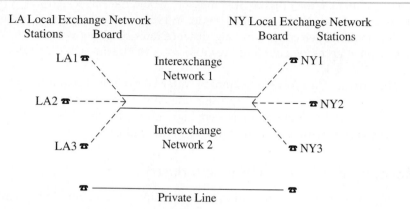

marginal charge per call, so a long-distance company expected the local part of a long-distance call to be free. Local exchanges argued that all cost, including the cost of handling a long-distance call within a local exchange, should be counted as cost of the long-distance call. After a complicated struggle through the court system, the Supreme Court ruled in 1931 that the telephones and the lines of a local exchange were indisputably used for long-distance calls, and regulators were, therefore, to include local exchange costs in what was called "station-to-station" accounting.[5]

The process of sorting local exchange costs between local and long-distance services for station-to station accounting was called "separations," because operating costs and capital stock had to be *separated* into local (usually intrastate) and long-distance (usually interstate) components. At the time, AT&T was regulated by the ICC, which also regulated railroads. The division of local exchange expenses between local and long distance traffic came to be based on a measure called "subscriber line use" (SLU), which counted the minutes used for local and long-distance calls and divided costs accordingly, much as railroad costs had been divided between passenger and freight service. There the fraction of a train that was used by each type of customer determined the division of train costs. A *Separations Manual* dictated the allocation of costs between local and long-distance service for decades.

There is no doubt that separations procedures allocated excessive amounts of cost to long-distance calls. Congressional pressure on the FCC worked to this end. Having low monthly rates for residential service was consistent with the goal of universal service,[6] and it was popular with the general voting public (and so with lawmakers). State regulatory commissions sought the same goal. Long-distance calls were paid for mainly by businesses, who tended not to organize around the issue of telephone rates and so were not very influential about it, whereas local calls and residential service affected citizens generally, and they were the nation's voters. By 1980, long-distance costs under

---

[5] *Smith v. Illinois Bell Tel. Co.*, 282 U.S. 133, 1930.

[6] Universal telephone service is so successful that fire alarms have been removed almost everywhere, the ubiquity of telephones making them unnecessary.

the separations procedures had climbed far above the level that the original SLU principle dictated. Indeed, the original SLU measure would have allocated 7 or 8 percent of total cost to interstate (long-distance) service in 1980, yet the separations procedure was allocating about 25 percent.[7] With long-distance rates so far above their true costs, any knowledgeable entrepreneur would want to enter the business if there were a way to do it.

The arrival of microwave technology after World War II made the possibility of constructing a separate low-cost, private-line connection more attractive, especially when long-distance telephone rates were high relative to costs. This possibility was to play a crucial role in revolutionizing the telephone industry.

A Revolution for the Telephone Industry

The reorganization of telecommunications that came to the United States in 1984 is a remarkable story.[8] This reorganization totally reshaped a large and complex industry, and it broke the largest private company in the world into eight main parts. It involved leading regulators, businesspeople, bureaucrats, politicians, and judges, who wrestled diligently over 25 years with the many problems, and their work culminated in a 1982 court decision that took effect in 1984. This vast change was driven by changes in technology—specifically microwave technology for long-distance calls—that drifted unceremoniously into a regulated world.

In late 1956, just after it agreed to the consent decree with AT&T, the FCC decided to consider the question whether to use certain radio frequencies above 890 megahertz for private microwave transmissions. The Bell System had for years offered special private-line services, connecting many calls between two points where no switchboard service from the Bell System was needed. Some of these private-line users wanted to transmit their own messages by the new microwave technology, which had only modest economies of scale, and they approached the FCC for permission to do so.

Opening this question of microwave transmission would invite more full and formal FCC hearings, because it would involve many parties besides AT&T, and it brought the prospect of competition from Motorola, a well-established and capable manufacturer of microwave equipment, against the AT&T subsidiary, Western Electric. In addition, a major potential user of private microwave facilities would be TV networks, carrying to the public a new medium that the FCC wished to encourage. The FCC had already allowed TV networks to build and operate private lines when the Bell System did not have capacity to transmit their messages. Finally, the prospect of possible competition for the Bell System from private lines was becoming more attractive. So when the FCC decided in 1959 to allow use of the above 890 megahertz range for private microwave operation, it was not a complete surprise.[9] The private microwave facility was only to be used by the organization building it, and the right to build it was to be granted only if a common carrier could not meet the user's demands at a reasonable price.

---

[7] See Temin (1987, p. 26).

[8] See Temin (1987).

[9] See *FCC Report and Order*, FCC Docket 11866, "Above 890 Mc.," July 29, 1959.

BOX 14.2 The TELPAK Controversy

AT&T complained about the FCC decision to allow private microwave operations, saying that it would invite "cream skimming," or selective construction of facilities in areas where regulated national average prices were high. Internally, the company created a task force to consider how to respond. The result was a new AT&T private-line service, called TELPAK, offered in 1961 at drastically reduced rates. The rates featured a fixed fee per mile regardless of use, the fee to vary depending on which of four capacity ranges a user chose. Choosing the smallest capacity AT&T offered would bring users a reduction in costs of roughly 50 percent, and the larger capacities involved even larger savings. Thus TELPAK represented a serious bid by AT&T to retain the private-line business against competition from microwave technology. But in the world of regulation, TELPAK turned out to give the word *controversy* a new meaning. The dispute over it was never entirely settled. Competing providers of private-line services objected that the TELPAK rates would not cover costs and were discriminatory. After a three-month suspension by the FCC, the TELPAK rates took effect, but whether they covered costs continued to be studied. After a blizzard of cost estimates were exchanged, the FCC ruled in 1964 that TELPAK rates were too low merely to be meeting competition, at least for the smaller two capacity choices, and it ended their use. The FCC continued to study costs for the other two, larger, capacity choices. It appeared that AT&T's response to possible competition had been too vigorous. That vigor probably raised concern about AT&T's power and how it might be used in the future.

See *FCC Tentative Decision,* FCC Docket 14-251, March 18, 1964 and *FCC Report and Order,* FCC Docket 11866, "Above 890 Mc.," July 29, 1959.

Interconnection to the Bell System Network

Interconnection to the Bell System network opened the way for competition in the telephone industry. Interconnection would ultimately bring questions of access pricing and double double marginalization, but it began as a simple extension to the Bell System through a device called Carterfone, which is described in Box 14.3. Carterfone extended the Bell System to two-way radio transmissions that seemed harmless to AT&T. Interconnection turned competitive when phone companies like MCI aimed squarely at completing calls on the Bell network. It is this competition through interconnection that would lead to the 1982 court decision, separating AT&T long-distance service from local service and breaking local service into seven regional telephone companies called Bell Operating Companies (BOCs).

Interconnection for competition actually began in 1963, when a small, fledgling enterprise called Microwave Communications, Inc., or MCI (MCI later merged with WorldCom, and after its bankruptcy the name reverted to MCI), asked the FCC to approve a private microwave connection linking St. Louis and Chicago. Too small to use the capacity itself, MCI planned to sell capacity to others. The FCC had foreclosed resale when it allowed private microwave systems in its *Above 890* decision, to preserve AT&T's monopoly over the sale of telephone services. Busy with AT&T

BOX 14.3 The Carterfone Connection

Carterfone was a clever radio, one that could be activated by the sound from a telephone handset so communication could be relayed to a mobile radio/telephone. It extended the Bell System network by allowing interconnection with radio telephones. Carterfone was electrical, but it made no electrical connection to the telephone network. It simply enabled a mobile radio/telephone to be connected to the AT&T network. Yet AT&T refused to allow its use. Indeed, AT&T attempted to discontinue service to any Carterfone customer. So Thomas Carter, the head of Carterfone, filed a private antitrust suit against AT&T on grounds that his company was being excluded unfairly from a market. The court referred the case to the FCC, saying that it fell under the Communications Act rather than the Sherman Act. The FCC approved the use of Carterfone.

For years, AT&T had claimed that the telephone network required extensive protection and only its own equipment could safely connect to it. In Carterfone, the FCC challenged this claim by requiring specific and concrete evidence as to what the harm would be. When it saw no evidence of genuine harm to the network, it allowed the device to be used. The Carterfone decision challenged AT&T's total control over the network, so AT&T again set to work to establish a policy in response. It developed interface equipment, called a "protective coupling arrangement," which customers could use to connect their equipment to the Bell System network. This was a more accommodating stance than AT&T had initially taken in the Carterfone case. AT&T imposed a charge for the arrangement, however, which was very unpopular.

---

pricing for these private lines, the Carterfone case, and its own inquiry into computers, the FCC was slow in getting to the MCI request. By the time it did, MCI was in the hands of the late William G. McGowan, an aggressive entrepreneur who would argue that long-distance competition was entirely feasible and the main question was how to implement it.[10] He proposed not only connecting customers' locations by private line but also connecting them to the switched network of AT&T.

McGowan claimed that MCI would provide a new service not available from AT&T, a service aimed at small users who could not qualify for AT&T's (Telecommunications Package, or TELPAK) rates. AT&T argued that MCI planned to offer a service that already existed but could do it at a lower fee than AT&T charged because MCI was not subject to the separations process or to averaging costs from a national network. For its part, the FCC could see approval of the MCI request as a possible experiment, on a small scale, to test the possibility of a form of competition in long-distance service. In a close four-to-three vote, the FCC approved the MCI request. So many requests were then made to build microwave systems that the FCC could not handle them on a case-by-case basis, so it approved a whole class of applications in what was called the Specialized Common Carrier decision. Despite its awareness that this decision essentially made

---

[10] See Kohaner (1986).

interconnection to the Bell System inevitable, the FCC may not have realized the threat it was creating to the Bell System. Continuing disputes about costs and separations procedures would limit the response AT&T could make to such new competition.

Notice that network externalities were enormous in the giant AT&T network but small within a separate MCI network, which is why MCI wanted access to the AT&T network and why AT&T wanted to block its access. Access to the AT&T network would give MCI the benefit of network externalities that it lacked, so being able to complete calls on the AT&T network was crucially important to MCI and to telephone competition as well.

In 1968, a presidential task force report had encouraged greater competition in the telecommunications industry,[11] so other influences were working against AT&T. Then problems developed with Bell System telephone service, especially in eastern cities. Expanding demand for service in the 1960s outran capacity. When several service breakdowns occurred in New York City, AT&T formed an emergency task force to repair the problems. Nevertheless, these events tarnished AT&T's image and put more pressure on the company's management to deal with its complicated and increasingly competitive environment.

14.3 | THE MODIFICATION OF FINAL JUDGMENT

The Department of Justice filed an antitrust complaint against AT&T in 1974, claiming monopolization or attempt to monopolize telecommunications markets, for example by excluding others from its network or by buying equipment only from Western Electric. As remedy, the DOJ proposed that Western Electric be divested, or sold off, and that some or all of the BOCs also be separated from AT&T and its Long Lines long-distance operations. With this lawsuit, combined with several private suits active at the time by competitors such as MCI, AT&T had it litigational hands full.

A solution was finally agreed to between AT&T and the Department of Justice, called the **Modification of Final Judgment (MFJ),** where Final Judgment stood for the 1956 Consent Decree that limited AT&T to regulated activities. The parties aimed at a short document that would supplant that Decree. Licensing and supply contracts between AT&T, the operating companies, and Western Electric were to be terminated. Seven regional BOCs were to be divested, and their ownership passed to AT&T shareholders. These operating companies, with AT&T's assistance, were to give all interexchange (long-distance) carriers equal access to their local exchange networks. This outline would vastly change AT&T and end the final-customer-to-final-customer, or "end-to-end," view of service the company had held for nearly all of its corporate life.

The Modification of Final Judgment left AT&T facing competition in long-distance service. AT&T was also allowed to compete in the unregulated computer industry, but after becoming established as a computer manufacturer it sold that business. Former BOCs were not to discriminate between AT&T and other long-distance

---

[11] President's Task Force on Communications Policy, *Final Report*, December 7, 1968.

carriers in arranging access to local exchange networks, or in a variety of other activities. They were to be monopoly providers, while AT&T—and its long distance service—would be competitive. This division of the industry into monopolistic and competitive parts was consistent with the idea that economies of scale were present in the local networks but not in long-distance service. Many difficult technical problems needed to be worked out for equal access to be achieved. Because of these circumstances, the court oversaw implementation of the Modification of Final Judgment.

For long-distance service, the FCC had all companies file rates with it, but it reviewed only AT&T's filings. Oversight of AT&T lasted until 1995 and probably restrained competition in long-distance rates because it limited the responses AT&T might make to competition. State commissions, which were less sympathetic than the FCC to competition, regulated local service and tended to favor residences with lower rates, especially rural residences, while setting higher rates for businesses, large cities, and long distance. Many of these rates did not reflect costs well, and some even involved cross-subsidy.

States gradually came to see the advantages of competition, however, and by 1991, 42 states were allowing some intrastate competition in long-distance service. Where competition could develop, as in paging services, cell phones, and private network services, state regulatory commissions allowed it. Intrastate long distance rates, however, and rates for calls within one area code, did not fall as sharply as unregulated long-distance calls, indicating that states were not allowing competition to play a full role.

Incentive Regulation

Various forms of incentive regulation came into use after the Bell System was broken up in 1984. States moved away from rate-of-return regulation as a means of regulating local telephone companies and toward incentive regulation, particularly price caps. Earnings share regulation allowed the firm to share with consumers in earnings gains above the allowed rate of return, and it grew in use in the latter 1980s. Under such arrangements, when the actual return exceeded the allowed return, perhaps half of the first 2 or 3 percent improvement in rate of return would be kept by the firm while the other half would go to customers in the form of lower prices. After 1996, price-cap regulation began to dominate. These methods of regulation led to lower operating costs and to lower prices, especially for business customers, who had been paying high prices in the pre-1982 world of regulation.[12] The station-to-station accounting of that period harmed businesses, which made most of the long-distance calls that were bearing disproportionately high costs.

Incentive regulation led to greater use of fiber-optic cable and modern switching technologies,[13] indicating that it made firms more willing to invest in new methods. Price-cap regulation of local telephone companies came to be used in half the states by 1996 and in 70 percent of the states by the end of the century. Having prices set without reference to the firm's own costs creates incentive for controlling cost, because higher

---

[12] See Ai and Sappington (2002), Braeutigam, Magura, and Panzar (1997), and Crandall and Waverman (1995).

[13] See Greenstein, McMaster, and Spiller (1995).

costs no longer lead automatically to higher prices as they did under rate-of-return regulation. Price-cap regulation also motivates desirable pricing by the firm.

Price-Cap Regulation

Price-cap regulation was introduced in England in the early 1980s, to regulate the national telephone monopoly, British Telecom, after it was separated from a national monopoly in telephone and postal service to be privatized. The aim of using price-cap regulation was to allow prices to rise with the cost of living, less a savings to be realized through productivity improvement. This way, consumers would benefit from productivity gains. The English called the price-cap formula RPI-X, where RPI is the retail price index in England and X is a required productivity improvement.

Calculating RPI-X is straightforward. Suppose a price exists in period 1, and we now ask what that price should be for period 2. If the retail price index in period 2 is 105 and in period 1 it was 100, then the price can rise 5 percent to 105. Then if productivity improvement of 2 percent is required by regulators, the price in period 2 can rise up to 3 percent over what it was in period 1: that is, RPI-X = $105 - 2 = 103$. This price-cap is a ceiling on the price increase that can occur in period 2 over the price in period 1.

With more than one service and, thus, more than one price, the *total revenue* for period 1—that is, the sum of the products of prices of all services times their quantities—can rise by 3 percent in period 2. Quantities for period 2 are not yet known when prices must go into effect, so let the firm use period-1 quantities to calculate hypothetical period-2 total revenue at the new period-2 prices. Under price caps, this hypothetical period-2 revenue is not to exceed 1.03 times total revenue in period 1. The firm is allowed to choose freely the prices for period 2, as long as it meets this constraint on hypothetical total revenue for period 2. When quantities from the base period (in this case, period 1) are used to calculate the resulting revenue in this way, the firm is motivated to choose socially desirable prices, in that they tend gradually with time to converge to Ramsey prices.[14]

Socially desirable pricing, which is so difficult to motivate in the regulated firm, can be induced through this procedure. The effect is not always perfect, in part because the firm may wish to take a long time to reach the ultimate ideal prices.[15] The procedure also may not operate exactly as expected, and then problems may develop in outcomes, although procedural modifications may preserve the desirable result.[16] Price-cap regulation removes any incentive to cross-subsidize, because firms earn less profit by doing so. Because prices are independent of the firm's own costs, the firm has no incentive to allow costs to rise. Indeed, the incentive is so strong to lower cost under price-cap regulation that regulators must focus more attention on service quality, to ensure that it isn't lowered as a means of lowering cost and thereby improving profit.

---

[14] See Vogelsang (1988) and Vogelsang and Finsinger (1979).
[15] See Sappington (1980).
[16] See Cox and Isaac (1987).

We can expect efficiency gains from the improved incentives under price-cap regulation, and having prices rise by less than some consumer price index allows these gains to be shared with consumers. Costs in one industry may not move as the consumer price index does, however. This would create risk for the firm because its prices, if tied to a consumer price index, could rise either more or less fast than its costs. Price-cap regulation focuses on price *changes*, and over time there is little basis for assessing whether costs and prices are where they should be. That is why regulatory agencies review features of price-cap regulation at intervals of several years. Despite improved incentives of regulatory arrangements, all was not well under the Modification of Final Judgment.

Problems with the Modification of Final Judgment

Under the Modification of Final Judgment, the BOCs could not compete in long-distance service among local access and transport areas (LATAs)—called inter-LATA service—while other companies could not offer the local exchange service the BOCs provided. BOCs might have been effective competitors in long-distance service, as long as they would not give themselves advantages in their own areas over other providers. The BOCs also could not manufacture telecommunications equipment, so they could not exploit advantages they might have in equipment manufacturing, based on their experience in using the equipment.

Biases in pricing persisted. Rural areas were favored with lower rates, and residences were favored over businesses in urban areas, so rates for businesses were high relative to costs. There was also a universal service obligation, aimed at making a minimal service level available at low cost throughout the nation so service would be widely (universally) enjoyed. This obligation was to be supported financially by established service providers, but not by fringe firms, and that put established service providers at a competitive disadvantage.

The obligation of Local Exchange Carriers (LECs) to connect others to their networks could also be turned against the LECs when they were required to price in a certain way and were prevented from responding to competition. For example, because regulated rates for business users in urban areas were set at high levels, some large businesses were motivated to set up their own connections between their main offices and interexchange, or long-distance, carriers. This action by a business was called **bypass**, because the company would be bypassing part of the LEC's network, and the LEC was not allowed to lower its rate to discourage the company from bypassing its network. Some enterprises, called **Competitive Access Providers (CAPs)**, built local networks in large cities, mainly in major office buildings and at switching locations for the interexchange carriers, and they sold bypass service to businesses. They usually installed fiber-optic networks that afforded high-quality transmission of calls, and they did not have to contribute to subsidies that would support universal service. Wireless cellular phones also grew rapidly in the 1990s and further disrupted the wire-line telephone industry.

Competition also loomed for LECs from cable television providers. Such providers were serving more than 80 percent of American homes and passing close by, and thus able to reach, 95 percent. With new technology, which requires some investment, these cable service providers would be able to carry telephone messages. Such service had been provided by cable operators in the United Kingdom and was growing in parts of the United States. Some cable companies also had financial interests in CAPs that bypass local networks to connect private users with long-distance services.

We can see many wrong turns by both regulators and regulated in this unusual history. Indeed, competition can be said to have developed in part because of faulty regulation, which resulted in high long-distance rates that tempted potential competitors. A crisis was evident in the 1970s and early 1980s when the FCC, the Department of Justice, and Congress were all working to find a way to bring competition from microwave technology into the industry. Radical change was accomplished when the Modification of Final Judgment was implemented in 1984, but still further change could be expected. A wireless network was growing, and a cable television network could reach the vast majority of American homes and could carry telephones calls, too. It was time for federal legislation to redefine the industry.

14.4 | THE TELECOMMUNICATIONS ACT OF 1996

In February, 1996, Congress passed legislation it had been unable to agree on for decades, the **Telecommunications Act** of 1996. The legislation was founded on the idea that competition could function broadly in the telecommunications industry, and it removed many barriers to entry that then existed. Whereas the 1982 Modification of Final Judgment had opened long-distance service to competition, the 1996 Act opened local service to competition. The law also allowed telephone service providers to offer video services and cable video providers to offer telephone services. Public utilities (mainly electric utilities, which have extensive wire connections) also might offer telecommunications services. Telecommunications service providers could enter equipment manufacturing and could also offer Internet connection services. Everyone, it seemed, could compete with everyone else.

But the law did not work out that way. It elicited more competition in courts than in markets and required two trips to the Supreme Court for decisions. Under the Act, the FCC was to devise pricing rules for sharing network facilities, but these rules were repeatedly turned aside in courts, most recently in 2004. Since then, the percentage of local markets served by new carriers—who lease parts of local exchange carriers' networks—has actually declined.

To the extent possible, the Act called for telephone numbers to be portable, in that they would move with subscribers from one telephone company to another. Access to directory assistance, operator call completion, white page directory listings, and 911 services were also required, along with access to telephone poles, ducts, conduits, and rights of way (for example, the right to run wires under streets) of the local exchange carrier. On opening its market to competition, an incumbent local exchange carrier would be allowed to enter long-distance service but had to enter through a

---

BOX 14.4 Cable and Telephone Competition

Here are some ways the Telecommunications Act encouraged competition between cable and telephone systems. A telephone local exchange carrier that was not affiliated with a cable company could offer video programming in the franchise area of the cable company, and at the same time, cable companies could not be prevented by their local franchising authorities from offering telephone service. A telephone company could own no more than 10 percent of any cable company that served the same area it served. When cable and telephone companies serve the same market, as long as it was not a smaller nonurban market, where there might be exceptions, no partnership or joint venture involving the cable and telephone companies was allowed for providing video or telephone service.

---

separate affiliate, and it had to grant access to all others on the same terms offered to that affiliate. Canada was less strict when it introduced competition to its telephone network, allowing a local exchange to enter long distance without a separate affiliate, and it seems to have achieved nondiscriminatory access successfully.

The law relied very much on the interconnection of networks and it encouraged new local exchange competition by empowering entrants to lease needed parts of the facilities of already existing local exchange networks. It spelled out how existing networks would be required to grant access to new operators. Implementation of these access requirements, however, repeatedly met resistance and legal challenges. Much of the competition that has developed recently has come from new technological developments in other modes of communications, which shows that a flexible regulatory arrangement is needed so new techniques can flourish.

Interconnection and Pricing Access

A host of access requirements were imposed on local carriers under the Telecommunications Act, essentially in exchange for the grant of rights to compete in long-distance markets. Local exchange carriers (LECs) had to share their network elements on an unbundled wholesale basis. That is, other phone companies could choose one service, such as switching, or several services, as they wished, at any feasible point in the local network. An LEC thus had to welcome a competitor to use its facilities to set up a competing service. This sharing of the incumbent carrier's facilities was to allow competitors to offer local telephone service, and sharing was to make elements of the network available on a nondiscriminatory basis at just and reasonable rates. LECs also had to permit resale of the services they provided. Indeed, any service a local exchange carrier provided its own customers was to be available also on a wholesale basis. Such unbundling was seen as crucial to competition at the local carrier level. Because of network economies, a new entrant would be severely limited in competing with a larger existing network but if it could lease elements from that network to get started, it might gradually build its own network of customers and become viable.

The Telecommunications Act called for the FCC to set guidelines for access pricing within six months of the law's passage. When the FCC revealed its pricing rules in August of 1996, however, the BOCs, GTE Corp., and other local service providers filed suit to block their application. The petitioners claimed that the FCC exceeded its authority in ordering states to use very specific pricing guidelines, in part because transactions occurred within states and thus were not interstate. They also claimed that the FCC guidelines overlooked significant elements of cost, particularly investments by the local exchange carriers.

This dispute over FCC pricing rules carried through several court cases and although it settled down 8 years after the passage of the Act, it was not quite settled. The FCC had called for access prices to be based not on efficient component pricing, nor on Ramsey pricing, but on what it called **Total Element Long Run Incremental Cost (TELRIC).**[17] TELRIC as a basis for price is like the long-run incremental cost for each service except it is "forward looking," in that it is based on the best available technology rather than the technology actually in use at the local exchange carrier. If TELRIC prices could be effectively implemented, their being based on such an external benchmark would offer desirable efficiency incentives, because the LECs could not raise rates simply by having high costs. By being set close to long-run marginal costs the rates also would tend to overcome double double marginalization. Because the rates resulting from the TELRIC rule would not be based on the *actual costs* of the local exchange carrier, however, the carriers objected that the basis for TELRIC rates was not sound. Efficient component pricing might have overcome this complaint by offering a profit allowance that would motivate incumbent carriers to offer access, but that would favor incumbent carriers rather than encourage new entry, and it might even foster double marginalization.

The FCC also allowed entering carriers to pick and choose among individual provisions of already existing interconnection agreements without accepting the terms and conditions of those agreements in their entirety. Essentially, the local

---

BOX 14.5 Energetic Communications

Operators of wired local networks, such as electric utilities, were invited to enter the telephone business under the Telecommunications Act of 1996, and some entry from such sources has occured. In September 1999, for example, the Public Utility Commission of Texas approved a request of Houston's Reliant Energy, the city's main electricity provider, to provide telephone service in the city. Such entry has not taken place on a large scale, however. Power lines are especially useful for Internet access, because Internet signals travel at higher frequencies than electricity and can coexist and not interfere with electricity transmission, and their use for this purpose is increasing.

See T. Serju-Harris, "Reliant Gets OK to Dial into Phones," *Houston Chronicle*, September 28, 1999, p. 1.

---

[17] For an argument that efficient component pricing should have been used to motivate incumbent cooperation, see Spulber and Yoo (2003).

exchange carriers had to unbundle these network elements one by one. The St. Louis appeals court found this rule to be unreasonable, and that the FCC had exceeded its authority. The FCC appealed this St. Louis decision to the Supreme Court, which, in January, 1999,[18] held that the FCC had the authority to specify rules for implementing the Telecommunications Act of 1996, but that its unbundling rules were not tied sufficiently to the goals of the Act. The Court did not consider the substance of the TELRIC rate-setting principles, because the case concerned whether the FCC had jurisdiction to set pricing rules, not the merits of those rules, and it sent the case back to the appeals court on remand, which meant the appeals court was directed to reconsider the case in light of the Supreme Court opinion.

After the appeals court decided the remanded case and allowed the FCC's TELRIC principles to be applied, its decision was again appealed to the Supreme Court, which in May 2002 confirmed the FCC's authority to impose the TELRIC pricing methodology, with qualifications.[19] For example, the Court dealt with the incumbent local exchange carriers' offer to competitors of unbundled network elements (UNEs), which are the signals, switches, loops, and other elements of the local network. The Act requires that they be made available to entrants but does not say who is responsible for combining them when less than the total set of them is leased. The Court ruled that the FCC could require incumbent LECs to combine leased UNEs for competitive LECs if they were unable to do it themselves.

The final blow came when the D.C. Circuit Court overturned the FCC access pricing guidelines in 2002.[20] The D.C. Circuit Court objected to the FCC's TELRIC rule because it was a national rule that did not consider the separate circumstances of each case, which could differ by number of competitors, economic conditions, or other relevant factors. The FCC then issued a 576-page opinion that provided guidance about which network elements had to be unbundled, but the opinion passed responsibility to the state regulatory commissions to determine which elements would be unbundled.[21] The FCC might have set further standards, perhaps different rules for different city sizes, for example, but its guidelines were not that concrete.[22] As it was, the D.C. court did not accept the FCC's response as sufficient to comply with the law.[23] Guidance on this important pricing issue is still being worked out.

In 2003, the FCC freed local exchange networks from having to share the broadband part of their networks with entrants.[24] Local networks were thought to be more willing to undertake the large investments that fiber installations required if they did not have to turn around and lease them to their competitors, and evidence indicated

---

[18] See *AT&T Corporation et al. v. Iowa Utilities Board et al.*, 525 U.S. 366, (1999). On page 397 of this opinion the Court said of the Act, "It is in many respects a model of ambiguity or indeed self contradiction. That is most unfortunate for a piece of legislation that profoundly affects a crucial segment of the economy worth tens of billions of dollars."

[19] See *Verizon et al. v. FCC et al.*, 535 U.S. 467 (2002). The *Review of Network Economics* published a symposium on the implications of this decision in September, 2002 (see www.rnejournal.com). See also Vogelsang (2003).

[20] See *United States Telecom Association v. FCC*, 290 F.3d 415 (D.C. Cir. 2002).

[21] See *Report and Order on Remand and Further Notice of Proposed Rule Making*, 18 F.C.C.R. 19.020 (2003).

[22] See Speta (2004).

[23] See *United States Telecom Association v. FCC* 359 F.3d 554 (D.C. Cir. 2004).

[24] See Saul Hansell, "High-Speed Service May Cost More," *New York Times*, February 21, 2003, p. C4.

that granting access had discouraged network investment by incumbent local carriers generally.[25] Thus, in not requiring sharing of broadband investments, the FCC intended to induce greater expansion of the broadband fiber network. Critics of this new national policy complained, however, that the policy would strengthen the local network monopolies of SBC, Verizon, Qwest, and Bell South, and make entry by new providers of local service much more difficult.

Another reason for the FCC to ease the requirement to share local broadband telephone networks is that it had classified cable service as an "information service" rather than a "communications service" like telephone. This classification meant that cable was not subject to the common carrier requirements of nondiscriminatory pricing, access to facilities, or contribution to the "universal service" fund. Although the FCC had the authority to do so, it had not required that cable service providers grant Internet service providers access to their networks, and the Supreme Court had endorsed its right to make that decision.[26] With cable companies able to refuse access to their networks, the FCC did not want to force local telecommunications companies to open the broadband part of their networks and, thus, be at a competitive disadvantage.

Historically, regulation within states was accomplished by states, while the federal government regulated interstate and international services. The FCC had claimed it was called upon to guide implementation of the Act, however, which its proposals would do by laying down federal principles to guide local rate setting by states.[27] There may be some advantage to having a national policy for a national network industry such as telecommunications, but doing so altered the simple jurisdictional boundary between states and the federal government that had existed for decades. Moreover, the new national policy was not entirely clear, which is why it has been debated in courts. Lengthy discussions are heard at policy levels in Washington, and vigorous lobbying continues. The FCC attempted more than once to forge a new policy, but it essentially preserved the existing compromise that has states regulating access fees according to FCC guidelines.[28]

Competitive Effects of the Telecommunications Act on Wireline Services

In the years after the Telecommunications Act of 1996 passed into law, the changes it was expected to cause came slowly. Court disputes delayed agreement on the pricing of access to elements of the local networks. Years passed before any local exchange carrier was deemed to have opened its network sufficiently that it could be allowed to enter the long-distance market. Cross-industry competition between telephone and cable providers of telephone service was slow to develop also. Some observers noted rising prices, especially in cable services where the price level rose at twice the rate of

---

[25] See Crandall (2005).

[26] See *National Cable and Telecommunications Assn. v. Brand X Internet Services* (04–277), 345 F.3d. 1120, reversed and remanded, June 27, 2005.

[27] For discussion of the issues involved in this case, see DeBow (1998).

[28] See Stephen Labaton, "F.C.C. Leaves Most Rules on Network Leasing In Place," *New York Times*, February 21, 2003, p. A1.

the consumer price index and wondered whether the law was a failure. Intrastate phone call rates rose almost as much, but rates on interstate phone calls rose only slightly more than the consumer price index from 1996 to 1999, and then they declined. Local service rates rose with the consumer price index until 2002 and then rose faster. On the whole, the prices of telephone services rose roughly with the consumer price index. But prices fell markedly from back in 1984, when the Modification of Final Judgment took effect, to 2001, when long-distance rates were only one-third as great. So consumers have not faced a telephone service pricing problem.

Local wire-line competition has not developed very successfully, however, in part because court disputes about access pricing have delayed the opening of local networks to competition. When it came, that competition was stymied by the 2002 D.C. Circuit Court decision and the FCC decision not to require access to broadband telecommunication services. Even the former BOCs that opened their networks to competition, so they would be allowed into the long-distance business, were not deluged by vigorous competitors. Less than 15 percent of local lines were operated by new local-exchange carriers in 2003.[29] One reason is that local service customers seem inclined to stay with their long-time providers of service, and it is hard for new suppliers to win them away. Another reason is that local residential rates were set so low by state regulatory commissions that entrants could not cut prices to win business and still earn profits.[30] Rural rates are often held at the same level as urban rates, even though the costs of providing service to widely dispersed rural telephones is greater. Urban residential rates are lower, relative to costs, than business rates. Both AT&T and WorldCom (now MCI) abandoned plans to enter local phone service, saying they could not make money reselling local residential phone service. WorldCom provided local service to businesses but mainly through its own networks.[31]

Telephone competition may still come from cable companies, who have to alter their networks from one-way distribution of video to two-way traffic with all its attendant switching requirements. Cox Communications, Inc., competes vigorously in parts of the country, combining local and long-distance telephone service with cable-TV and Internet service in one package for consumers. Comcast Corporation, the largest U.S. cable company, offers telephone service to all its cable subscribers and is offering telephone-TV-Internet packages. Partly in self-defense, Verizon is offering video service to homes and businesses over its fiber-optic lines.

In addition to competition from wireless services and cable and the Internet, wire-line telephone companies also face international competition. The World Trade Organization, after a year of negotiating, reached an agreement among countries in 1997 that allows telecommunications firms in any one country to enter foreign markets. As a result, the former monopoly telephone company in Germany has seen a 30 percent decline in phone service prices because of foreign competition, and many large telecommunications companies are entering markets in developing countries.

---

[29] See FCC reports at http://www.fcc.gov/Bureaus/Common_Carrier/Reports/FCC-State_Link/IAD/trend803.pdf.

[30] See Tom Fowler, "Telecom Issues Come Calling," *Houston Chronicle*, January 7, 2001, p. 1D.

[31] Only about 3 percent of local phone users can choose between local phone service providers. See Schiesel (2000).

Roughly 80 percent of the people in the world do not yet own a telephone, and half the people have never even used one, so the potential market being opened up is enormous. Existing telephone service providers in many such countries are inefficient, and this makes the competitive opportunity attractive to American and European firms.

Foreign ownership of domestic telephone companies has also expanded. The United States dropped its rule that allowed only 25 percent foreign ownership in a telecommunications company, and many other countries have dropped similar limitations. Canada still prevents foreigners from owning more than 46.7 percent of existing telecommunications facilities, and Japan sets the limit at 20 percent. But Japan allows a new firm with as much as 100 percent foreign ownership to *enter* its market. These terms from World Trade Organization negotiations require ratification in some countries, so all is not settled yet, but there clearly is a more open international market in telecommunications services, and there is wide acceptance of competitive organization for those services.

Thus, a revolution is visiting the telecommunications industry. It is not surprising that a U.S. law that was years in the making would take some time to have effect. Empirical studies across a range of countries indicate, however, that unbundling and sharing of local networks has not been very successful.[32] They do not seem crucial to local telephone competition, because changes in technology such as microwave and satellite transmission and the Internet and wireless telephones are bringing abundant competition. That is a major reason why financial consequences for existing carriers were not favorable.

Financial Effects of the Telecommunications Act

Within five years after the Act was passed, major providers of long-distance telephone service faced financial troubles. The Act spurred investment, as capital spending in the industry jumped from $40 billion in 1996 to $80 billion by 1999. Sales did not grow with capacity, however, and rates of return fell.[33] As a consequence, telecommunications stocks declined in value, upsetting investors. That is why AT&T reorganized into four separate companies in 2000, essentially repudiating its business plan of combining local, long-distance, and wireless services in one firm, which it had pursued for four years after the Act was passed. WorldCom changed its plans in a similar way. Then WorldCom fell into bankruptcy in a high-profile management scandal. Wireline service declined as wireless service expanded, and companies scrambled to reposition themselves.

One consequence of financial difficulty was a consolidation among both LECs and long-distance companies. As a result of mergers, the seven BOCs that were defined by the Modification of Final Judgment were quickly reduced to four. Two of

---

[32] See, for example, Hausman and Sidak (2005), who study Canada, New Zealand, Germany, the United Kingdom, and the United States.

[33] The rush to install network capacity came at a price that turned out to be excessive. See Gretchen Morgenson, "From WorldCom, an Amazing View of a Bloated Industry," *New York Times*, March 16, 2003, Sec. 3, p. 1.

the organizations formed from BOCs, Verizon and SBC Communications, Inc., were the first to meet the requirements for opening their systems to competition so they could compete in the long-distance market. Their competition is significant and has contributed to the decline in long-distance rates. Long-distance companies also consolidated. Financial pressure continues as wireless phone service, cable phone service, and Internet phone service using Voice-over-Internet-Protocol, or VoIP, have since added competition to local and long-distance wire-line networks.

The 1996 Act was followed in a few years by dramatic expansion of wireless services and substantial consolidation among the traditional wire-line companies. One of the original Bell operating companies, Bell Atlantic, and GTE Wireless and Vodaphone merged to form Verizon Wireless, while two other Bell companies, SBC and Bell South joined their wireless networks together to form Cingular. Then Bell Atlantic and GTE merged to form Verizon Communications. In 2004, a weakened AT&T stopped marketing its long-distance service to consumers and sold its wireless service to Cingular while WorldCom emerged from bankruptcy as MCI and Sprint acquired Nextel. In 2005 SBC bought AT&T, and the new firm adopted the AT&T name, while Verizon Communications acquired MCI. Then in 2006, in the largest merger of all, AT&T acquired Bell South, which brought the new company complete control of Cingular. The industry was moving back toward "one-stop" service, and preparing for battle against cable companies, which were moving into telephone service partly via VoIP. Wireline service was declining, and traditional companies wanted to participate in more promising service areas for the future. Wireless companies also wanted to have prominent name recognition among wireless users, to help their growth as networks. The mergers are hard to keep track of, but they leave us with fewer names to remember.

BOX 14.6 Telecommunications Deals

Independents*	Surviving Organizations
Nynex *Bell Atlantic* GTE Vodaphone	Verizon
AT&T *Pacific Telesis* *Southwestern Bell* *Bell South* *Ameritech* Cingular SNET	AT&T
US West Qwest	Qwest

* Former Bell Companies are in italics.

14.5 | NEW SOURCES OF COMPETITION

New developments continue to change the telephone industry. Wireless phones allow us to be more mobile while staying in touch with each other. They allow us to perform many other functions, such as communication by e-mail. The Internet is opening remarkable new avenues for voice communication as well as for e-commerce.

Wireless Services

Wireless phones can conserve the radio spectrum because they use low-power transmission within small areas.[34] The low power allows the same frequency to be used repeatedly in different areas that are not too close together and, thus won't interfere, so one frequency can afford many simultaneous uses. The wireless system currently requires access to the local loop for switching to wire-line phones. Wireless phones offer great advantages in remote areas, where wire connections must be long and usage rates are low. Quitague, Texas, an island community with a population of about 500, has a digital telephone network that is totally wireless.[35] An early wireless service in Mink, Louisiana, was recently replaced by a modern wireless service, and the community still has no wire.[36]

Wireless telephone service is booming, with many new competitors participating all around the country. Over a million wireless phones go into service each month, and some replace wire-line phones, which have declined slightly since 2001.[37] With technological improvements, wireless costs fell,[38] and prices, while unregulated, fell also. When the Omnibus Budget Reconciliation Act of 1993 required the FCC to auction electromagnetic spectrum for wireless communications, it called for at least two winners in any region and thereby served to instill competition. More than half of the U.S. population now owns a wireless phone, and this thriving wireless alternative puts growing pressure on regulators to sort out problems in other areas of voice communications.

In addition to their direct competition with wire-line phones, wireless telephones open up a variety of new applications. In some countries, for example, it is possible routinely to buy a soft drink from a vending machine and charge it to your bank account with a wireless phone. As another example, a patent has been awarded to inventors at Intel Corporation that allows a new form of bargain shopping.[39] A consumer with a scanner can scan a product bar code in a store and, using a wireless

---

[34] This concern with interference may not be lasting. New methods manage to send signals over available space by choosing among many channels rather than on dedicated channels. See "Launching Telecoms II," *The Economist Technology Quarterly*, March 15, 2003, p. 3.

[35] See Haynes (1993).

[36] See Ralph Blumenthal, "In the Age of the Wireless Phone, a Louisiana Town Awaits the Real Thing," *New York Times*, December 12, 2004, p. YT1.

[37] See Simon Romero, "Land-Line Rules in a Wireless World," *New York Times*, February 21, 2003, p. C1.

[38] Prices fell from the establishment of wireless phones in the early 1990s until 1998, when they rose slightly above 1997 prices. Prices have risen since then but a greater range of services has been offered for the higher prices in more recent years.

[39] See Sabra Chartrand, "Patents," *New York Times*, January 8, 2001, p. C6.

phone to which the scanner is connected, obtain—via the Internet—alternative prices from Internet sources, including shipping and handling speed and costs, and taxes if appropriate. This technology would make free riding by Internet sellers extremely easy, and it would raise more product-distribution issues for firms. In Japan you can point a specialized wireless phone at a restaurant or a historical monument and the phone provides information about it from the Internet.[40]

Wireless phones can even be used to solve the familiar problem of having keys locked inside a car. Telefonaktiebolaget LM Ericsson, the maker of wireless phones, has a patented system that offers access to an automobile's electrical system to unlock doors, turn off lights, or even turn off the engine (a useful feature in case the car is stolen). The car can also call its owner with a signal that the car's alarm has been activated.

Wireless technology might even solve the problem of "the last mile," the provision of broad-band service linking the Internet backbone to users' computers.[41] Capitalizing on the digital technology that came to wireless phones, a "wireless local loop" (WLL) technology may offer Internet connections 10 times faster than DSL telephone or cable service can provide. The technology conserves spectrum in a revolutionary way, as a software encoded chip constantly switches among channels to find gaps where information can be inserted. Such wireless technology solves the interference problem at the same time it makes the radio spectrum less serious as a constraint.

The Internet

The Internet became a commercial phenomenon in the early 1990s, and it now supports a flourishing e-commerce that reduces the need for telephone communications, especially for booking services such as air travel, so it indirectly competes with telephone

---

BOX 14.7 Joining Devices to the Internet without Wires

Sprint Nextel Corporation announced in 2006 that it planned a new network that blends wireless communication with broadband Internet access. The plan is based on a technology called Worldwide Interoperability for Microware Access (WiMax), which can connect to the Internet many devices that are not now connected, such as digital cameras, music players, or appliances. The network will compete not only against other wireless operators but also against telephone companies and cable companies that sell broadband. WiMax carries more data, at much less cost, than current technology. Because the technology is not yet deployed on a large scale and has to develop markets for the services it can provide, it is a substantial risk for Sprint Nextel to undertake. But the company plans to invest $3 billion to have the network running in 2008.

See "Up in the Air," *The Economist*, August 12, 2006, p. 52.

---

[40] See John Markoff and Martin Fackler, "With a Cellphone as My Guide," *New York Times*, June 28, 2006, p. B3.
[41] See "Launching Telecoms II," *The Economist Technology Review*, March 15, 2003, p. 3.

service, and cable and telephone service providers both battle for Internet service customers. The cable companies had been expecting little competition for this business until a consortium of Microsoft, Intel, and Compaq Computer Corporation, along with GTE, U.S. West, BellSouth, and SBC developed digital subscriber line (DSL) technology. Cable companies still have about two-thirds of the Internet service business.

Telephone communication directly through the Internet is also reaching a practical form. It presently requires broadband service, and early providers such as Vonage and Net2Phone are being joined by big telecommunications companies in offering it. They are soliciting customers aggressively at rates below either telephone or cable company rates.[42] The FCC is considering how to deal with such telephone service on the Internet, but it has tended so far not to treat it as a telephone service that is subject to regulation.[43] For local wire-line carriers already losing customers to wireless, and perhaps to cable telephone service competitors, a challenge from the Internet cannot be encouraging, but they have little choice except to join in adopting the technology.

Implications for Regulation

In restructuring the telecommunications industry, a major problem has arisen from the attempt to develop local competition, which the FCC micromanaged without great success. It labored under the Telecommunications Act prescriptions, though, that competition within a telephone technology, or intramodal competition, should be the main focus. Now that many other modes of communication are arising one should consider ways that regulation might focus on services and not be tied to technologies as it now is. The FCC is organized so it has a wire-line telephone bureau and a wireless telephone bureau, for example, when the two ways of communicating should be considered together. Indeed, wire-line is classified as a communications service while wireless is classified as an information service and is therefore not subject to regulation in the same way. Competition between technologies is increasingly important, and after many

---

BOX 14.8 The Example of Skype

Founded in Sweden and driven by Estonian software programmers who developed the file sharing program, Kazaa, Skype is a thriving Internet telephone service. It has just moved past reliance on voice communication between computers and can now connect to mobile phones. Before too long, it hopes to be available on a memory stick. Skype is unusual in having its customers talk with other Skype customers free of charge, and it profits when its customers call traditional phones for a small fee. In 2005 eBay, the auction and trading company, bought Skype for $2.5 billion and is optimistic about its future.

See "Communicating the Skype Way," *The Economist*, August 19, 2006, p. 56.

---

[42] See "Crossed Wires," *The Economist*, February 15, 2003, p. 60.
[43] See Stephen Labaton, "Thorny Issues Await F.C.C. on Internet Phones," *New York Times*, February 9, 2004, p. C1.

years in which regulators and politicians avoided it, improving competition between technologies, or intermodal competition, should be encouraged.

In addition to blending different technologies together, differences by geographic areas may also need some attention. Telephone companies complain that as they attempt to provide video service across the country they have to battle town by town because local authorities often want to protect their cable monopolies from competition. In Congress, the House of Representatives has supported legislation to give the FCC authority over the 30,000-odd local franchising authorities to eliminate this entry barrier.[44] The move by wire-line telephone companies into video service is part of the general convergence that is taking place, led by the very large firms that still remain from the telephone and cable industries that now aim to offer local, long-distance, wireless, video, and other services all from one organization.

The consolidation of technologies in large firms moves choices about which technology is good for which purpose within firms, and that may lead to better choices than might occur while the technologies are kept separate on regulatory grounds. For example, the United States regulated its transportation industries on a technological basis for years, with the Civil Aeronautics Board for airplanes and the Interstate Commerce Commission for trains, while Canada allowed firms to operate both technologies, as they deemed appropriate, and had efficient railroad-airline companies using both transportation modes. Regulation of more complex, multimodal, organizations may be harder. Yet if competition can be preserved among the firms, antitrust principles may be relied on more. It is a more general guide and more flexible than regulation by specialized agencies. A recasting of regulatory institutions to handle intermodal competition would help when technologies change so rapidly and might help the institutions function on what is now being called "Internet time."[45]

Many forms of competition are developing from wireless technologies, and that raises a host of policy questions about the electromagnetic spectrum. Except for the wireless telephone spectrum allocations that were made by auction, allocation of the spectrum to different uses is done by governmental authorities that retain government ownership. The FCC has made useful adjustments where it has authority to do so, by relocating services higher in the spectrum band where possible, creating flexible-use bands, and eliminating the need for licenses for low-power devices. But broader changes are needed. Without any market means to assess values, the spectrum does not always go to high-value uses, even though possible commercial uses are expanding. Valuable spectrum is reserved for many military, security, and other government agencies that do not need it, for example, and those agencies probably would not consider budgeting to pay the true value of the spectrum they occupy. Limiting available spectrum creates barriers to entry, especially for new services. Improved policies could increase the available spectrum, and new portions might be auctioned so they could go to the high-value uses that a market could help to identify.[46]

---

[44] See Stephen Labaton, "House Backs Telecom Bill Favoring Phone Companies," *New York Times*, June 8, 2006, p. B1.

[45] See Speta (2004).

[46] See Speta (2004).

SUMMARY

Telephone service is a perfect example of a network, where the service is more valuable as more people are connected to it. The resulting network externality favors a large operator that can offer network economies, which AT&T's Bell System did for years. The creation of separate networks can spur efficiency through competition, but separate networks also raise a host of interconnection issues. These problems of interconnection and competition have been tackled over the past two decades by government and industry representatives as the telecommunications industry has been restructured around the world.

Since the first scratchy conversation occurred over wires more than a century ago, telephone service has changed dramatically. Efforts by the Bell System to establish end-to-end service, connecting every telephone to every other telephone in the country, occasionally ran afoul of antitrust laws but came to dominate telephone service in the United States. Regulation of local service developed gradually at the state level. Congress created the Federal Communications Commission in 1934, and well past the middle of the twentieth century there was a single regulated provider of long-distance service and many monopoly providers of local services.

In 1956, AT&T signed a consent decree that limited its activities to common carrier telephone service. The decree allowed Western Electric to continue as a subsidiary but confined it to making telecommunications equipment and required that it license certain AT&T patents. Regulatory pricing decisions of the time raised the rates for long-distance calls well above their true costs while keeping local service prices low, especially for residences. Entry into highly priced long-distance service tempted operators of the new microwave technology, which lowered costs dramatically and lowered the efficient scale of operations. Soon, competitors were offering long-distance service and AT&T was the target of law suits for resisting various forms of competition. In 1982, an agreement settled a Department of Justice law suit against AT&T and called for the Bell System to be divided into seven regional telephone monopolies and one long-distance carrier, AT&T, which would compete with other long-distance providers. The regional companies provided connections for all long-distance companies on a nondiscriminatory basis.

Influenced by advances in technology and computer software, and from new ideas in economics, the Telecommunications Act of 1996 wrote entirely new rules for the telephone industry, allowing local service providers to become long-distance providers, and long-distance providers to become local service providers. Also under the Act, telephone companies can provide cable service, and cable television providers, or even electric utilities, can become telephone service providers. Local service competition that was proposed in the Act has not succeeded, in part because FCC implementation brought objections and court cases. Disputes over the pricing of access to admit local service competitors rose twice to the Supreme Court, which has supported an FCC role in guiding access pricing in local exchange networks, but questioned some features of its rules. Consumers benefitted from lower prices after the 1984 break up of AT&T and the 1996 Telecommunications Act, but investors have been disappointed by financial results.

When combined with competition from wireless telephone service, the Internet, and international competition, restructuring of the telephone industry has opened the way for a vastly different and more competitive telephone system that is still being created. As enterprises converge on offering the same full range of services, new approaches to regulation are in order. Regulation should not be separated into areas based on technology, as they have been, because when different technologies compete such areas don't have the scope to deal with problems that arise. If such broad competition can be sustained, greater reliance on more flexible antitrust law may be possible.

QUESTIONS

1. In response to terms of the Telecommunications Act of 1996, the FCC called for setting access prices according to its TELRIC method, which assumed that the incumbent service provider used the best available technology to provide whatever service was being priced. Thus, the price would not be based on the incumbent's *actual* technology.
   a. Discuss whether adherence to such a rule would create good incentives for the incumbent to be efficient.
   b. Discuss practical advantages or disadvantages of following this guideline.
2. Evaluate whether TELRIC rates, which the FCC proposed for access to local exchange networks, would be consistent with the Efficient Component Pricing Rule (ECPR). (The ECPR allows the incumbent network operator, in granting access, to recover its direct cost plus its opportunity cost through its access fee.)
3. Demand for calls in a local telephone exchange is $p = b - q$, where q is quantity of calls and p is price. The cost of completing calls on the network is c, and a monopoly operates the exchange.
   a. What is the monopoly quantity and price per call?
   b. Suppose access pricing is to be used to bring competition to the monopolized local exchange telephone network. The access price is to be determined by applying the ECPR. In words, what is that ECPR access price that the monopolist can charge a competitor for completing a call that the competitor brings to the network?
4. Consider two compatible telephone networks that may operate as one when they are interconnected. The networks are separately owned, however, and must agree on terms for connecting each other's calls. Assume the marginal cost of completing calls on either network is zero.
   Each of the two networks remains a monopoly in its own local network. Each network sets one price to customers for completing calls, a price of p_1 for Network 1 and p_2 for Network 2. The two networks negotiate a second price, a, which they charge each other for completing calls. All of the calls originating in one network terminate in the other.

Demand for calls originating in Network 1 is given by $q_1 = b - p_1$, and demand for calls originating in Network 2 is given by $q_2 = b - p_2$. One network must pay the other network an access charge, a, for completing one call, but it also receives that amount, a, when it completes one call for the other network. Then with interconnection, the profit of Network 1, π_1, and the profit of Network 2, π_2, is

$$\pi_1 = q_1(p_1 - a) + q_2 a, \text{ and } \pi_2 = q_2(p_2 - a) + q_1 a.$$

a. Suppose the networks negotiate an access price of $a = b/2$. Find the profit maximizing prices, p_1 and p_2, and the profits, π_1 and π_2.

b. Suppose the networks negotiate further and agree on an access price of $a = 0$. Find the profit maximizing prices, p_1 and p_2, and the profits, π_1 and π_2.

c. If you find the profit level is different in part a from what it is in part b, explain why there is a difference. If you find no difference in profit, explain why there is no difference.

d. If demands in the two networks differed (if they charged the same price, for example, suppose $q_1 > 5q_2$) would this complicate bargaining over the access price, a? If bargaining is just the same, explain why. If bargaining is different when quantities differ, explain why.

5. Consider the monopoly solution to the telephone network problem presented in Table 14.1 and Figure 14.1. Suppose an entrant is confined to serving only those customers who are excluded at the monopoly solution of $p = 3$ and $Q = 15$.

a. Show whether the entrant would be able to profit by entering the market for telephone service to serve only the five type-1 consumers in the market.

b. Now suppose interconnection to the incumbent monopoly network is allowed (customers of the entrant can call customers of the monopoly and vice-versa). Explain how interconnection of the telephone networks affects the profit outcome for both the incumbent monopoly and the entrant.

6. State regulators, who had great discretion in overseeing the local monopoly portion of telecommunications, were not eager to embrace competition when the possibility for it first arose. Do you think competition would be harder than outright regulation for state regulators to control, especially if there were distortions of prices away from costs? Could competition diminish the regulators' power?

7. The controversial TELPAK pricing for AT&T's private-line service represented new territory for the parties involved. Sketch the restraints that limited how AT&T, as a regulated monopoly, could respond to the competition it was being exposed to from microwave services. Specifically, how did the separations procedures affect the appearance of whose costs were lower?

8. In the 1920s, state regulatory commissions pushed to have local network costs of a long-distance call counted as part of the cost of a long-distance call, even though it was difficult to do. Apart from the pursuit of proper accounting for costs, why might they seek to have these local network costs included as long-distance costs?

9. A 1982 court decision broke AT&T into eight companies and opened long-distance competition. Explain how earlier regulatory decisions, such as the 1956 consent decree (the "final judgment") and the "separations" decision about local and long-distance costs set the stage for that outcome.

APPENDIX 14.1 Double Double Marginalization in a Telephone Network

Assume the demands for telephone service in two networks, Foncall and Callfon, are known. Demand for calls originating in Foncall is given by $q_F = b - p_F$ and demand for calls originating in Callfon is given by $q_C = b - p_C$. Each network pays the other for completing its calls but is also paid when it completes calls for the other network. The access charge for calls from Foncall to Callfon, which Callfon sets, is a_C, while Foncall sets an access charge for calls from Callfon of a_F. Assume for now that all who are connected to Foncall make calls to Callfon, so Foncall pays $q_F a_C$ in access charges to Callfon. All of those connected to Callfon also call to Foncall, so Callfon pays $q_C a_F$ to Foncall.

With all calls going from one network to the other when there is interconnection, we can represent the profit of Foncall, π_F, as

$$\pi_F = q_F(p_F - a_C) + q_C a_F, \qquad \text{14.A1.1a}$$

where q_F is the number connected to Foncall, who call to Callfon, and q_C is the number who call from Callfon to Foncall. By similar reasoning, the profit of Callfon is

$$\pi_C = q_C(p_C - a_F) + q_F a_C. \qquad \text{14.A1.1b}$$

Callfon's decision in setting a_C determines marginal cost for Foncall, while Foncall's decision in setting a_F determines marginal cost for Callfon. The vertical relationship examined in Chapter 4, where a manufacturer sets a price that became marginal cost to the retailer, had a similar pricing structure. When the manufacturer in Chapter 4 sets a monopoly price above its marginal cost to the retailer, who in turn marks up that price to a (socially nonoptimal) final product price, the result was called double marginalization. But here the relationship runs in both directions. Because we have networks in a reciprocal relationship, each imposes an access fee as a cost to the other, and resulting two-directional double markup is double double marginalization.

In choosing price p_F or output q_F to maximize profit, Foncall focuses on the first term in equation 14.A1.1a, because choice of price or quantity has no influence on the second term, $q_C a_F$. Essentially, it maximizes $\pi_F = q_F(p_F - a_C)$. By replacing p_F by $(b - q_F)$ from the demand function, we can express this relevant portion of profit in quantity rather than price terms as

$$\pi_F = (b - q_F)\, q_F - a_C q_F. \qquad \text{14.A1.2}$$

Expressing this problem in terms of quantity instead of price makes it perfectly analogous to the retailer's problem in the manufacturer-retailer vertical relationship considered in Chapter 5 except for the reciprocity element here with each network setting a price that is a cost for the other. Maximizing profit with respect to q_F in equation 14.A1.2 yields $q_F = (b - a_C)/2$. Following the same procedure for Callfon yields $q_C = (b - a_F)/2$. Substituting these quantities into demand functions yields prices

$$p_F = (b + a_C)/2 \text{ and } p_C = (b + a_F)/2. \qquad \text{14.A1.3}$$

Because it will be useful in a moment, we substitute Foncall and Callfon demands into profit function equation 14.A1.1 to obtain profits in terms of prices,

$$\pi_F = (b - p_F)(p_F - a_C) + q_C a_F, \text{ and} \qquad \textbf{14.A1.4a}$$
$$\pi_C = (b - p_C)(p_C - a_F) + q_F a_C. \qquad \textbf{14.A1.4b}$$

Then substituting prices from equation 14.A1.3 into the profit functions 14.A1.4 yields profits that depend on the access prices, a_F and a_C:

$$\pi_F = (b - a_C)^2/4 + (b - a_F)a_F, \text{ and} \qquad \textbf{14.A1.5a}$$
$$\pi_C = (b - a_F)^2/4 + (b - a_C)a_F. \qquad \textbf{14.A1.5b}$$

Now consider the choice of a_F and a_C. Callfon can infer the effect of its choice of a_C on Foncall's demand by substituting $p_F = (b + a_C)/2$ into Foncall's demand, $p_F = (b - q_F)$. This yields the demand Callfon experiences, $(b + a_C)/2 = (b - q_F)$, which reduces to $q_F = (b - a_C)/2$. Because Callfon receive $q_F a_C$ in access charges from Foncall, it sets a_C to maximize $q_F a_C$. By multiplying both sides of the demand just derived, $q_F = (b - a_C)/2$, by a_C, we see that $q_F a_C$ equals $a_C(b - a_C)/2$. Maximization of this latter term yields

$$\partial[a_C(b - a_C)/2]/\partial a_C = b/2 - a_C = 0, \text{ or}$$
$$a_C = b/2.$$

By the same analysis, Foncall finds

$$a_F = b/2.$$

The manufacturer in Chapter 5 followed exactly this procedure. It anticipated the retailer's behavior to infer its own demand and then, using that demand, it maximized profit.

Now consider the effects of the independently chosen, profit-maximizing access fee, $a_C = a_F = b/2$. Substituting this access fee into price equation 14.A1.3 yields

$$p_F = p_C = 3b/4. \qquad \textbf{14.A1.6}$$

Then, substituting $b/2$ as the access fee into profit equations 14.A1.5 yields

$$\pi_F = \pi_C = (b/2)^2/4 + (b/2)^2 = b^2\, 3/16. \qquad \textbf{14.A1.7}$$

Although each network may be drawn to a positive access price as it tries to profit from interconnection, this access price, $a_F = a_C = b/2$, is not the ideal solution, either for the networks or for society in general.

To see that a positive access price is not ideal, try an access price equal to marginal cost: $a = 0$. From equation 14.A1.3, this access price yields lower final consumer prices of

$$p_F = p_C = b/2, \qquad \textbf{14.A1.8}$$

and from equation 14.A1.5a with $a = 0$ the profits immediately increase to

$$\pi_F = \pi_C = b^2/4. \qquad \textbf{14.A1.9}$$

To repeat, with $a_1 = a_2 = 0$ rather than $a_1 = a_2 = b/2$, the profit $b^2/4$ in equation 14.A1.9 is greater than $b^2\, 3/16$ in equation 14.A1.7. Thus, in their own interests, the telephone networks should agree on an access charge of zero. In addition, the price to consumers is lower with $a_1 = a_2 = 0$ than with $a_1 = a_2 = b/2$, because the price of $b/2$ in equation 14.A1.8 is less than the price of $3b/4$ in equation 14.A1.6.

Networks Foncall and Callfon in the interconnection example were perfectly symmetrical. They faced the same demands and had the same call volumes, but if instead one of the networks is sending more calls than the other, they have more of a one-way relationship, like a manufacturer and a retailer. Incentives become even more complicated if instead of interconnecting merely to complete calls across networks of given sizes, each network competes for customers in an effort to enlarge its own network. We now consider effects of asymmetry in call volumes, and after that we will turn to competition for share of call volumes.

To understand this effect of differences in call volumes, suppose Foncall has greater demand than Callfon, such as $q_F = 5b - p_F$ compared with $q_C = b - p_C$. Then profit maximizing monopoly prices are

$$p_F = (5b + a_C)/2 \text{ and} \qquad \textbf{14.A1.10a}$$
$$p_C = (b + a_F)/2, \qquad \textbf{14.A1.10b}$$

and profits are

$$\pi_F = (5b - a_C)^2/4 + a_F(b - a_F)/2, \text{ and} \qquad \textbf{14.A1.11a}$$
$$\pi_C = (b - a_F)^2/4 + a_C(5b - a_C)/2. \qquad \textbf{14.A1.11b}$$

Now turn to the determination of access fees. Notice, first, that Foncall can easily pay the access fee of a_C which is set by Callfon because, in the first term of equation 14.A1.11a, its high demand intercept of $5b$ (in $q_F = 5b - p_F$) leaves plenty of room to pay. The demand intercept, $5b$, is much larger than the access fee, a_C, so the second term in equation 14.A1.11b can be larger as a_C is larger (up to $a_C = 5b/2$). This alone means that Callfon might want to set a high access fee or a high value of a_C. On the other hand, Foncall cannot set a_F as high, because Callfon has a smaller demand intercept and cannot pay as much, as indicated by the first term in equation 14.A1.11b. Foncall also cannot profit as much from a_F, as indicated by the second term in equation 14.A1.11a. Thus when networks differ in size, the smaller network is likely to send fewer calls and receive more calls, as Callfon does in this example, and it will want a larger access fee.[47] Selling more service (for access) than it buys makes it resemble the manufacturer that wants to mark up its cost in the manufacturer-retailer case. Such a difference in motivation between telephone networks can complicate agreement on a common access fee.

Instead of monopoly control of each network and all calls from one network going to the other, suppose the two networks compete for customers, so each network wants to increase its share of the single market. The incentive to have a larger market share arises when all of one network's calls no longer go automatically to the other network. The fraction of one network's customers making calls to customers of the other network are equal to that other network's share of the total telephone market. Each network would prefer to complete the calls on its own network, which it

---

[47] International access fees commonly follow this pattern, where the smaller country that has more calls arriving from larger countries imposes the larger access fee. See Wright (1999).

can do by winning a larger market share. So we can expect networks to lower their prices to attract customers in an effort to enlarge their market shares. Each network also wants to raise its rival's costs by raising its own access fee. If both networks raise their access fees, prices to final customers could actually be higher even when there is competition for market share. It is not possible to predict how competition for market share affects customer prices.

We know the ideal access fee should equal the marginal cost of access, but competition for market share motivates networks to raise access fees above marginal costs to raise competitor's costs. Even though competing networks may try to set lower prices to win customers to their networks, they may also raise access fees to raise their competitors's costs. Thus, competition between networks may not result in ideal prices either for access to other networks or for customers.

APPENDIX **14.2** Tariff Wars after Interconnection

For AT&T in the 1970s, aside from sagging morale and crucial organizational matters, an important question was how to respond to the specialized common carriers like MCI after they were allowed by the FCC to offer microwave private line services. For its own private-line service, AT&T finally settled on what was called a "Hi-Lo" tariff. Hi and Lo referred to high and low density routes, with rates for high-density routes roughly one-third as great as those for low-density routes. The Hi-Lo tariff abandoned national averaging, and it called for private-line rates merely to cover their costs. A year and a half passed before the new Hi-Lo tariff worked its way to FCC approval, and it became effective in 1974. The day after the tariff was effective MCI proposed a lower tariff and three months later it proposed a tariff for a metered-use service called "Execunet." Charges for MCI's Execunet service varied with usage, time, and distance, rather than with capacity alone, so it was essentially like AT&T's message toll service except it would serve only a limited number of cities. AT&T argued that this would be message toll service, which functioned in the AT&T network but was not authorized by the *Specialized Common Carrier* decision. MCI argued that preventing the Execunet service from being offered would be a violation of antitrust laws.

At this point, private-line service had been extended into switching services, so it was difficult to draw a line that would separate private-line from switched services. The FCC formed a distinction, however, and ruled that Execunet differed sufficiently from a private-line service that it should be rejected. MCI appealed the FCC decision against Execunet and in 1977 the D.C. Circuit Court of Appeals supported MCI. In a broad decision, the court did not dispute the finding that Execunet went beyond private-line service. It argued, however, that such a distinction was too narrow, and that the FCC had never properly considered whether competition in message toll service should be allowed. This question had to be considered by the FCC, the court said, and in the meantime MCI should be allowed to offer Execunet. This sweeping evaluation of developments reveals how each separate regulatory decision had moved the industry closer to outright competition in long-distance service, and how the full implications of each decision had not been seen.

AT&T's response to this decision was to propose interconnection charges, so that all long-distance carriers—itself included—would pay to support (because of separations procedures) the local exchange networks. All carriers agreed to a compromise arrangement for interconnection, and there the matter rested. Had the FCC then allowed systematic access to local exchange networks on a nondiscriminatory basis, it is possible that we would have had a smooth transition to competition in long-distance service. But we took a much more difficult route to telephone service competition.

15

Communication for News and Entertainment

Broadcast and cable services are important because "most Americans spend more time with radio and television than they do with any other activity, including working and sleeping, and most Americans get most of their news from television."[1] In retrospect, the rise of broadcast and cable to where they can claim so much of our attention is dramatic, even though it took a century. It was driven by advancing technology and guided by government regulation.

The federal government regulated broadcasting almost from its inception, primarily to keep radio broadcast signals from interfering with one another. Early radio was aimed not at general broadcasting, or at voice communications, but to replace wired telegraphy, a message communications code made up of dot-and-dash signals (Morse code). Radio broadcasting patents, shared through a patent pool by AT&T, General Electric Company (GE), Radio Corporation of America (RCA) (now part of GE), and Westinghouse Electric Corp., made general broadcasting possible. Congress considered placing radio broadcasting under government control as England had done but decided against it, although the government did control radio stations during World War I. A chaotic period followed the War in the 1920s, mainly over who could use certain frequencies, which the Federal Radio Commission finally settled after Congress created it to regulate radio broadcasting in 1927. Television reached commercial form as World War II began, and broadcasts began when the war ended.

An alternative means of reaching a broad audience is through cable connections. By traveling over wires, cable signals avoid interference. Unlike broadcast media, in principle a cable company can exclude from receiving the service those who do not pay for it, and this property allows cable providers to extract payments for services from consumers. Some theft of cable signals occurs, but it is small. Government regulation came to cable only after cable services began to broaden competition among over-the-air broadcasters, mainly TV stations, by extending their signals into each others' broadcast territories. The capacity for carrying signals without interference has been a growing advantage for cable.

---

[1] From Sterling and Kittross (2002, p. 5).

Cable TV has advantages over broadcast TV not only in better signal quality but also in the greater number of channels it can deliver. It has grown to where it is able to reach more than 95 percent of all households, and it is still growing rapidly. Cable-wired homes open the possibility of a range of additional services, such as two-way communication with movies on demand, banking, bill payment, Internet access, and even telephone service, especially as new technology allows more channels to use a cable connection.[2] Federal regulation of broadcast and cable is in the hands of the Federal Communications Commission (FCC).

Regulation of broadcast and cable services has been difficult at times, particularly when new technologies arose and existing arrangements had to be altered to accommodate them. This chapter first describes the need for compatibility, which allows separate networks to exploit network economies. To reveal biases in the timing and content of programs offered by competing broadcasters, the next section discusses public good aspects of broadcasting. The chapter then turns to explore cable service and such issues as the awarding of cable franchises and the bundling of cable channels. The last section considers remaining implications of having both broadcast and cable compete with each other and with satellite TV and podcasts, guided by the Telecommunications Act of 1996.

15.1 | NETWORK COMPATIBILITY IN BROADCASTING

The technology of communication includes famous inventions. First there was paper and then the printing press. The importance of communications technology soared with the discovery of electricity, when wires carrying electrical signals could travel almost any distance, in any weather, almost instantly, and convey meaning through the dots and dashes of Morse code. This technology was called **telegraphy**. After its adoption, telegraphy was called "a perpetual miracle, which no familiarity can render commonplace."[3] Indeed, telegraphy has been likened to the Internet for its impact on society.[4]

When Guglielmo Marconi developed radiotelegraphy in 1895, his aim was telegraphy without wires, which could be extremely valuable to ships at sea.[5] After the *Titanic* struck an iceberg on its maiden 1912 voyage, for example, a ship almost 60 miles away heard the *Titanic*'s radio call for help and was able to rescue about 700 passengers. Radio freed telegraphy from its dependence on wires not only over water but also over land. Morse code conveyed meaning through letters and words, but because it was broadcast through the airwaves in all directions, radio had the capacity to reach a large audience. Marconi's radio was useful only for carrying telegraphy, however, not for the voice or music that a large audience might enjoy. But the promise of Marconi's

---

[2] See "Launching Telecoms II," *The Economist Technology Quarterly*, March 15, 2003, p. 3.

[3] See Briggs and Maverick (1863, p. 13), quoted in Spar (2001, p. 61).

[4] See Standage (1998).

[5] See Spar (2001) for a revealing history of the development of what was called radiotelegraphy. See also Brian Carovillano, "100 Years Ago, Wireless Era Born," *Houston Chronicle*, January 18, 2003, p. 6A.

radio for such broader purposes attracted the interest of AT&T, Westinghouse, and especially GE, and their research led to the vacuum tube, which made radio the mass medium we know today.

Broadcasting over-the-air signals for general audio reception began in 1920 in Pittsburgh, Pennsylvania, when radio station KDKA went on the air for regular broadcasting.[6] How was early broadcasting financed? Makers of radios were the main promoters of this early service, and they provided financial support for early radio stations.[7] In time, general advertisers came to sponsor programs, which were delivered free over the air to radio receiving sets. After World War II, broadcast television was introduced and provided to viewers on the same advertiser-financed basis as radio had been. Cable television came soon after broadcast television. It extended signals mainly into remote areas that were hard to reach by over-the-air TV broadcasts, and, thus, it expanded the reach of such broadcasts. As it matured, however, cable television developed broad programming and came to compete with broadcast television.

A problem with early broadcasting involved the choice of frequency on which to broadcast. Some stations operated at such high power in territories so near to each other and on radio frequencies so close together that they interfered with each other.[8] Allowing stations to function so they were compatible with each other was difficult, in part because no clear coordinating body existed. We turn first to the problem of allocating the radio spectrum to alternative uses, because regulators' assignment of frequencies or channels has been a crucial coordinating function.

Allocating the Radio Frequency Spectrum

Many broadcasting stations were built in the years immediately after KDKA's broadcast in 1920, and their radio transmissions interfered with one another. The owners of most early radio stations were not primarily interested in broadcasting but had some related interest. In 1923, for example, about 40 percent of stations were owned by radio and electrical manufacturers and dealers.[9] The Radio Act of 1927 created a **Federal Radio Commission (FRC)**, which helped to control use of the radio spectrum by issuing licenses to legitimate broadcasters. This Commission became the Federal Communications Commission (FCC), with broader responsibilities, in 1934. The channels that the FRC and the FCC assigned to individual stations were meant to be used for "the public convenience and necessity" and were not to be owned by the assignees. The FCC continued to exercise control over broadcasting for the rest of the industry's history.

In addition to allocating the radio spectrum, the FCC reached decisions about the purposes of broadcasting, the ownership structure in the industry, amounts of

---

[6] There were earlier broadcasts, but KDKA—which started as an amateur station in 1916—is credited with being the first station established for regular broadcasting. See Sterling and Kittross (2002, pp. 44 and 66).

[7] Radio and electrical manufacturers and dealers owned about 40 percent of early stations, educational institutions and newspapers and other publications owned 25 percent. See Sterling and Kittross (2002, p. 70).

[8] See Sterling and Kittross (2002, pp. 141–145).

[9] See the U.S. Department of Commerce *Radio Survey Bulletin* (February 1, 1923), as cited in Sterling and Kittross (2002).

particular program types to be required, the prevention of specific forms of corruption, and other issues. The FCC never controlled prices or profits in the broadcasting industry, although it has exercised some control of pricing for cable service.

Radio stations in different parts of the country can be assigned the same frequencies as long as they are far enough apart and weak enough in their broadcast power to keep them from interfering with each other. For that reason, assignments to radio stations prescribe a maximum allowed power as well as a frequency. For television, the FCC defined 12 very high frequency (VHF) channels (channels 2–13) and 56 ultra high frequency (UHF) channels (channels 14–69). These channels can be assigned to more than 68 (12 plus 56) stations in different parts of the country in a manner that avoids interference. The quality of over-the-air UHF signals is lower than that of VHF signals, and largely for this reason not all possible UHF frequencies are used.[10] Table 15.1 illustrates the major spectrum allocations by purpose.

Spectrum Allocation through Lottery or Auction

Rather than assign channels to individual stations to be used for the public and not owned, the FCC might distribute the channels by lottery or by auction and convey them as property to the recipients. Nobel laureate Ronald Coase (1959) urged the auctioning of broadcast spectrum allocations roughly 50 years ago to avoid the discretion that is involved in governmental awards and to achieve greater efficiency. Frequencies for cellular telephones were distributed by lottery in 1993. Spectrum for personal communications services (PCS), the second-generation wireless telephone technology, was auctioned from 1994 to 1996.[11]

A **lottery** makes an award randomly among eligible applicants. The problem with a lottery for distributing spectrum rights is that frequencies or channels for

TABLE 15.1 Major Radio Frequency Spectrum Allocations

Frequency	Megahertz	Purpose
Very low	0.003 to 0.03	Sonar
Low	0.03 to 0.3	Loran, global positioning system (GPS)
Medium	0.3 to 3.0	AM radio; amateur
High	3.0 to 30	Short-wave; amateur
Very high	30 to 300	FM radio; VHF TV
Ultra high	300 to 3,000	UHF TV; citizen band (CB); radar, cellular
Super high	3,000 to 30,000	Satellite; microwave

---

[10] For analysis of the economic value of television stations and effects on such values that are traceable to UHF versus VHF quality differences, see Fournier (1981). See also Sterling and Kittross (2002, pp. 329–331) for criticism of spectrum allocations.

[11] See McMillan (1994) and Hazlett (1998).

broadcasting may not end up in the hands of the most efficient broadcasters. Nor may selection of broadcasters to fill a broad public goal, such as serving the public, necessarily succeed, because it is difficult for a regulator to judge in advance the best provider from among a set of applicants. Because a lottery conveys a property right to the recipient, that recipient would be motivated to find an efficient operator to whom it could sell the property to maximize its value.

An **auction** requires applicants to bid for a spectrum right, with the highest bidder winning. The advantage of an auction is that we can expect the most efficient provider of service or the broadcaster who can wring the most revenue out of a right to use the spectrum to make the highest bid and, thus, win the right to provide service. As with the lottery, once the spectrum right is privately possessed, its owner has an interest in placing it in the hands of whomever can make it most valuable. By avoiding discretionary assignment by government officials, an auction also can reduce political or even corrupt influences on spectrum allocations.

Either an auction or a lottery would ordinarily convey a property right to the broadcasting spectrum, which could complicate future change. If technological change calls for reassigning spectrum, for example, it may be difficult or costly to reassign spectrum rights that are privately *owned*. That is one reason why government has largely retained spectrum ownership. Another reason is that the public interest may be better served through government ownership than through private pursuit of profit. Without signals like prices indicating value, however, government is handicapped in trying to make efficient use of the broadcast spectrum. This problem grows more serious as more possibilities arise for spectrum use.

Regulation with Changing Technology

The broadcast and cable industries have not been easy to regulate, primarily because technological change has occurred often. Network aspects of the industry have called on regulators to set a standard to achieve *compatibility* that allows broadcast signals to be received by receivers. Regulators necessarily make such choices under conditions of uncertainty about the future. Choices were needed early in radio broadcasting, for instance, including the choice of a method of broadcasting and allocation of spectrum frequencies. FM broadcasting needed a single broadcasting method with appropriate frequencies. When television came along, a single broadcasting system again had to be chosen. There was a conflict with the FM radio frequency spectrum that had to be resolved before television broadcasting could begin. When color was developed in television broadcasting, that again called for setting a single standard.

Later choices became more difficult because many individuals had already invested in equipment to receive signals, and government regulators were naturally reluctant to make those investments obsolete. Several means of broadcasting television signals in color were developed, for example. What was wanted was a **downward compatible** technology, meaning it would allow old sets to receive new colored-television signals in black-and-white form, so the nation's stock of television sets did not have to be replaced. Examples illustrate how changes in technology complicate the government's regulatory problem.

Developments in Radio

From its beginnings as radio broadcasting, sending signals through the air was a high-technology service. The radio that thrilled its listeners in the 1920s used amplitude modulation (AM) to provide its information in the form of louder or softer signal emissions that were added to the carrier wave on a specific radio frequency. At the time that AM radio began broadcasting, laboratories were also working on frequency modulation (FM) versions of radio broadcasting, which conveyed information by varying the frequency of the signal. Although it would require wider frequency bands, when it was developed by Edwin Armstrong into a useable form, FM radio offered improved performance with less distortion.[12] The Radio Corporation of America (RCA), a large AM broadcaster and radio manufacturer, did not jump to introduce FM radio, though, even after it had supported its development, perhaps in part because the new FM radio medium could attract listeners away from RCA's already existing AM radio audience.

Although it was an improvement over AM radio, FM radio was not downward compatible. If you were an AM broadcaster, FM radio raised the **cannibalization** problem of taking business away from yourself. It is like an already established brick-and-mortar store hesitating to sell via the Internet for fear of losing its brick-and-mortar customers.[13] Brand new, Internet-only retailers are not so inhibited, and they may force the established store into selling via the Internet to avoid losing some of its physical-store customers to other Internet retailers. Similarly, FM broadcasting started very slowly through FM-only stations and came only gradually to complement AM broadcasting through AM/FM stations.

Another reason why RCA did not promote FM radio is that by 1935 it turned its research attention to television instead. Television was an exciting alternative medium, rather than an improvement on the AM system that might replace existing investments. World War II also prevented construction of new radio stations, so FM radio was dormant during the war years. FM radio had been chosen, however, to provide sound for television broadcasts. This led to the inclusion of FM radio receivers in some early television sets, in part because the FM radio spectrum was in television's very high frequency spectrum range. This tendency to include FM radios in television sets declined, however, and FM radio languished. In a reorganization of spectrum allocations that came after the war, the FCC set aside a range for FM radio. That did not help to expand its use, because the new range required added transmission-equipment investment from FM radio broadcasters.

In the mid-1950s, the development of the transistor cut the cost of combined AM/FM radio receivers, and once they were offered by radio manufacturers their popularity helped to save FM radio. The number of FM broadcasting stations had declined gradually after the war, while AM stations mushroomed, to the point where the capacity of the AM radio spectrum allocation was a major constraint on the number of AM stations. This limitation made AM broadcasters more willing to begin FM broadcasting.

---

[12] See Lessig (1956) and Hughes (1989) for biographies of Edwin Armstrong, who contributed also to the development of AM broadcasting.

[13] See Dinlersoz and Pereira (2005).

A new form of broadcasting from satellites in space was initiated by XM Satellite Radio Holdings, Inc., in 2002, and was followed a year later by Sirius Satellite Radio, Inc. These services collect monthly fees for providing more than 100 channels of music, news, talk, sports, and other programming. The satellite services are presently targeted primarily at automobiles, where they compete with Apple's iPod and other primarily musical entertainments. Indeed, XM offers a portable satellite radio called an Inno that stores individual songs heard on XM into playlists, much like an iPod, but it has been sued by the Recording Industry Association of America. Sirius offers a similar device, the S50, and it settled with the recording industry by making a payment to each recording company for every S50 that is sold. Satellite radio services also can feature performers like Howard Stern, who repeatedly ran afoul of FCC decency standards. They proposed to merge in 2007, which would keep them from driving up the price of talent through their competition and might allow compatibility, but would violate the terms of their FCC licenses.[14] These new forms of broadcasting add to the challenge that traditional broadcast radio faces from other extremely portable entertainment devices.

Radio and television broadcasting both face the prospect of a transition to digital technology. Digital radio, called HD radio, is the easier case, because it takes a form that is downward compatible. The FCC approved the new broadcasting technology in October 2002, and implementation began in 2003. Under this new technology, old radios are able to receive the new signals, which are substantially improved. Digital AM broadcasting sounds like FM broadcasting, and digital FM broadcasting almost reaches CD quality. Digital broadcasting also requires less radio spectrum than old AM and FM broadcasting, so digital stations broadcast more programming, sometimes without advertising. Radio stations see digital broadcasting as a way to respond to satellite radio and the popular MP3-player forms of downloaded music.[15]

Developments in Television

Although the FCC agreed on a system for broadcasting television in 1941, World War II delayed its appearance. When television came on the scene in the late 1940s it was organized for support by advertising, much as radio had been. Comedy, variety, and drama dominated early television shows. Radio stations adapted to the advent of television by moving away from dramatic productions, including serials that television could present better, toward music and news. Indeed, a fairly well-defined set of options—top 40, album-oriented rock, country, easy listening, news/talk, all news, and several others—can characterize the predominant programming of nearly all radio stations today, except for public broadcasting stations, which offer more public affairs programming.[16] Radio has become an especially cost-effective medium for local advertising.

Near the end of the twentieth century signal transmission quality improved in both radio and television. Early in the 1990s, high-definition television (HDTV)

---

[14] See Richard Siklos and Andrew Ross Sorkin, "A Proposed Merger Would End Satellite Radio's Costly Rivalry," *New York Times*, February 20, 2007, p. A1.

[15] See Eric Taub, "Move Over, HD-TV. Now There's HD Radio, Too.," *New York Times*, Jan. 23, 2006, p. C4.

[16] See Kehoe (1989).

looked very promising. Later, however, digital technology video (DTV) was acknowledged in the United States to be the best long-run route to higher-quality TV pictures. Further developments have improved the digital technology, and it is now called advanced TV (ATV). The Telecommunications Act of 1996 supported ATV by giving assurance to existing television stations that they would be awarded new spectrum to continue their broadcasting under any new technology.

The FCC approved a digital form of broadcasting for television, but in a form that is not compatible with existing receiving sets, and by 2011 the long-existing TV broadcasting standard that was first adopted in 1941 is to be replaced by the digital standard. Without downward compatibility, new receivers will be necessary to receive digital television, so the transition to digital TV will probably take longer than Congress has planned. Consumers have not rushed to purchase digital TV receivers because they are expensive, and with few receivers out there broadcasters have little incentive to broadcast digitally. But there is no doubt that digital television will be a significant development, and it should blossom when mass production techniques lower the cost of manufacturing receiving units.

Technology, then, has repeatedly forced change in this network industry called broadcasting. Because a network is involved, compatibility is essential for achieving network externalities, and compatibility has been orchestrated by the FCC. Examples of this coordinating function were evident even in the Marconi-led radiotelegraphy era, where uses of the radio frequency spectrum had to be decided and agreement on technology was often necessary for the network. Such examples of coordination are also clear now in broadcast radio and television.

A final network effect came in the development of the radio and television broadcasting networks themselves, organizations that were developed mainly for efficient production and distribution of programming for the broadcasting stations. In both radio and television there is a public-good element to the technology, in that once it is broadcast, a signal can be received by an additional receiver essentially at zero marginal cost. Broadcasting networks could combine many of these stations into

---

BOX 15.1 Digital Television by Cable

An agreement was reached at the end of 2002 among television manufacturers and cable operators that can simplify the cable delivery of digital television. The agreement would give digital television sets "plug-and-play" capability, so proprietary digital cable boxes, which would otherwise be part of the cable service, will no longer be needed. Instead, the function of the boxes would be built into the television sets in a uniform way. The agreement can simplify the implementation of digital cable service. The proposal also claims consumers have the right to record basic cable programming, something that may produce objections from movie studios. Involving 14 manufacturers and 7 cable companies (which reach 75 percent of cable subscribers), the proposal illustrates how negotiation can sometimes achieve compatibility in network circumstances.

See M. Musgrove, "Companies Reach Pact on Digital TV," *Washington Post*, December 20, 2002, p. E1.

organizational units that could negotiate efficiently with programming sources for content and with sponsors for advertising to help provide material to broadcast and advertising revenue to pay for it.

Broadcasting Networks

Soon after radio stations began broadcasting, national networks developed to provide programming to affiliated radio stations. Broadcast television also adopted this network pattern and relies on it to coordinate national advertising and programming even more than radio, where local advertising and local programming remain more important.[17] Two Boston and New York radio stations broadcast the same program simultaneously in 1923 and that established the feasibility of central programming for a network of radio stations. The National Broadcasting Company (NBC) network was formed in 1926, with radio manufacturers and broadcasters RCA, General Electric, and Westinghouse as its owners. The Columbia Broadcasting System (CBS) came soon afterward in 1928, and was put on a sound footing by a cigar company vice president, William S. Paley, who would go on to lead the network for 50 years. The American Broadcasting Company (ABC) dates from 1945 and the Fox network from the 1980s.

Producing a full day of television programs would be costly and difficult for a local station, and affiliation with a network helps to solve that problem through network scale economies. Television networks produce national and international news, sporting events, and other daytime and evening programming. They arrange for the broadcast of series programs, dramas, and movies that are produced by others. Larger stations sometimes deal directly with independent producers and broadcast their programs. Because economies are so great, however, networks provide most of the programming.[18] Stations affiliated with the network agree to broadcast a required amount of this network programming, which enables the network to count on an audience. For that reliable audience it can produce—or negotiate with independent producers to produce—extensive programming. Networks deliver the programming directly to local affiliated stations, using microwave relay, coaxial cable, and satellite communications. Networks also own some local stations directly, mainly in large cities.

The programming that networks provide attracts viewers, who become a target for advertisers. Broadcasting networks can assure predictable audiences through their arrangements with their affiliates, and they can, therefore, negotiate contracts with advertisers and their agencies to bring revenues to themselves and to the broadcast stations. This coordinating role of the broadcasting networks takes advantage of the inherent publicness of broadcasting by facilitating economical provision of programming and efficient development of advertising revenue. For both networks and stations, the advertising value of broadcasting has helped to foster a profitable business model.

---

[17] See Sterling and Kittross (2002, pp. 77 and 117) and Smith (1990).

[18] Networks have been prevented by the FCC since 1970 from participating fully in what is called the rerun syndication business. Independent producers develop TV programs, which they effectively lease to networks for the program's prime-time run, and they later sell the programs in syndication arrangements with local stations.

The broadcasting model that depends on advertising revenue can be challenged by easily programmed video recording devices, such as TiVo, that enable viewers to record shows and then skip the commercials when they watch them. TiVo works on cable broadcasts, too, but cable does not depend exclusively on advertising for revenue as broadcasting does. Although initially seen as an enemy of advertisers, TiVo is growing into an advertising tool, in part to foster its own success. TiVo can show that its 4.5 million subscribers spend roughly half their television watching time viewing previously recorded shows, and for those recorded shows they skip about 70 percent of the commercials. Again based on their records, TiVo can tell advertisers what kind of ads viewers are less likely to skip.[19] Broadcast network CBS entered into an agreement with TiVo for the Fall, 2006 TV season, in which TiVo would offer its subscribers previews of new CBS shows, another way TiVo is attempting to serve broadcasters.[20] Now TiVo offers a service called TiVo Product Watch, that allows viewers to download on demand particularly creative and informative commercials. TiVo is also developing ways to adapt Internet or Web video to broadcast on TV sets. TiVo can also improve the precision of Nielsen ratings, which used to estimate program viewers to determine broadcast advertising rates, but now tries to estimate commercials actually viewed.

New technology is encouraging new network forms, such as ITN Networks, Inc., which assembles customized national TV networks for advertisers using commercial time it buys from local broadcasters. ITN forms networks based on audience characteristics such as age and sex. If an advertiser wants to reach 25- to 54-year-old women to sell them a new bleach, for example, ITN can choose programs that reach that target group. These developments move broadcasting beyond a "one-size-fits-all" form into more exact advertiser matches, thus helping to preserve its business model. That business model has developed around the pubic-good character of broadcasting.

BOX 15.2 College Students and TV Advertising Rates

Without revenues from paying customers, television stations and networks rely on viewer surveys to learn how many viewers a program has and, thus, how much it can charge the advertisers who sponsor it. Until 2007, the largest TV-viewing survey firm, Nielsen Media Research, did not include college students in its surveys. This meant that not all viewers of programs that were popular with students, including (in 2007) "America's Next Top Model" and "Family Man," were counted. Nielsen changed its policy and began surveying students living away from home in 2007. The change is expected to benefit ESPN, the sports cable network, and stations like "Comedy Central," which both attract many 18-to-24-year-old viewers, because it can increase the advertising rates those networks will be able to charge.

See L. Story, "At Last, Television Ratings Go to College," *New York Times*, January 29, 2007, p. C1.

---

[19] See Saul Hansell, "TiVo is Watching When You Don't Watch, and It Tattles," *New York Times*, July 26, 2006, p. B1.

[20] See Stuart Elliot, "In a TiVo World, Television Turns Marketing Efforts to New Media," *New York Times*, September 5, 2006, p. C4.

15.2 | BROADCASTING AS A PUBLIC GOOD

It seems efficient to have advertisers pay for radio or television broadcasts—rather than those who receive signals—because there is no added cost of providing service for an additional receiver; marginal cost is essentially zero. A drawback arises in this organization of the broadcast service, however, because when they pay for programs, the advertisers choose them. As a result, programs produced by radio and TV broadcast systems do not reflect consumer preferences directly, they reflect instead the interests of the advertisers.[21] Advertisers prefer large audiences, so they support programs that appeal to many listeners or viewers, whereas payments by individuals might support more specialized programs for which only interested parties would be willing to pay.

As an alternative to commercial radio and television, commercial-free public radio and public television are provided with some government support, plus voluntary contributions from listeners and viewers and from businesses and universities. Government contributions are financed by payments that commercial stations make, essentially like taxes, from their revenues. Public stations accept responsibility to offer public affairs programming and cultural and educational offerings that might not be commercially viable. They exert some pressure on commercial stations for quality programming. The public-good property of the commercial broadcasting world and its pursuit of large audiences for advertisers still remains, however.

Broadcast service has the property of a public good in that once a program is broadcast anyone with a receiver can receive it, and consumption by one person in no way detracts from consumption by others.[22] All experience the same quantity and quality that is collectively provided, just as it is for a well-known public good, national defense. An organization that produces a public good usually lacks a simple for-profit business model because when a radio or television station sends out its public signal it has no direct way to collect revenues from listeners or viewers who receive it. The signal might be encoded, so only those who pay a fee can receive it, but any such encoding scheme is costly. Given this difficulty in collecting a fee from those who receive a broadcast, it is not surprising that broadcasting came to be financed by advertisers. Although broadcasters achieve short-run efficiency by avoiding a positive price per program, the selection of programs and their broadcast times are biased to produce the large audiences that advertisers seek.[23]

Program Selection and Broadcast Timing

As part of their business model, broadcasters attract audiences through their programs and then sell the attention of those audiences to advertisers. Those who pay—the advertisers—get to choose the programs, however, and the audience merely

---

[21] See Minasian (1964) and Spence and Owen (1977).

[22] See Samuelson (1954) for a classic description of the pure public good.

[23] The classic analysis of the drawback of advertising-supported television is by Minasian (1964). See also Spence and Owen (1977) for a model of programming choices and distortions when advertisers pay for programs.

BOX 15.3 The Lighthouse as a Public Good

One classic example of a public good is a lighthouse. A lighthouse can guide ships away from dangers and safely into harbors, but it can not easily reach out and make change for its paying customers. Nor can it deny its light from those who would not pay. By examining history, however, Nobel laureate Ronald Coase showed that early English lighthouse owners were able to collect fees from ships while they were in port, so lighthouses were not really perfect public goods. The broadcast signal constitutes a better example of a public good than the light of a lighthouse.

See R. H. Coase, "The Lighthouse in Economics," *Journal of Law and Economics,* 1974, Vol. 17, pp 357–381.

watches. It is true that audience choices are monitored and that they can influence the choice of programs to be offered, but the advertisers still make program choices based on their advertising goals. Some radio listeners or television watchers might prefer to pay for programs to influence more directly the offered programming. Some might even prefer to pay directly also to avoid the interruption of programs for commercials, but such desires are not met in the broadcast realm. We now turn to examine biases in program timing and in the selection of program content that come from these broadcasting choices.

Program Timing

Setting a time to broadcast a program is like locating a store, in that the time can match the convenience of some listeners or viewers. The Hotelling (1929) location model in Chapter 6 treated the physical locations of stores selling a homogeneous good to consumers who live on a long street. Suppose the Hotelling decision is about a broadcast time chosen from a time span by a television broadcaster, instead of a physical location chosen by a store. To focus on the main features of television broadcasting let us make some simplifying assumptions. First, assume that to make coordination easier for viewers, programs are broadcast on the hour every hour during the best viewing time, called prime time. Assume there is only one program to be broadcast, say a news program. Assume also that in their preferences for times, consumers are located uniformly across five program hours available during prime time. That is, a group of consumers prefers each of the five possible times across the prime-time broadcasting times, and the number of consumers in each group is the same. The satisfaction a consumer gains from watching a program is greater as the program is broadcast closer to that consumer's preferred time. Adjusting to a less preferred time is analogous to traveling in the Hotelling model to a more distant store; the farther a broadcast time is from a preferred time, the less satisfying the program.

Viewers' preferences for the single news program are focused at five evening program hours, labeled 6, 7, 8, 9, and 10 in Figure 15.1. It is as if one consumer is located at each of these five time preference points in Figure 15.1, or at least there is an equal number of consumers who prefer each program time. If more than one station broadcasts at the same time, we assume that the number who would prefer that

Figure 15.1 *Program Broadcast Times*

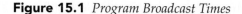
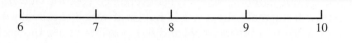

time is divided equally among the stations. We apply the same sort of tie-breaking assumption whenever two time slots are equally attractive. For example, if there is no broadcast at 7, then one broadcast at 6 and another at 8, each would win half of the viewers whose preferred time was 7. Two broadcasts at 7 would also split the viewers who prefer 7.

To attract viewers, a broadcaster wants to broadcast at a time they prefer. If there is only a single broadcaster locating along the time dimension in Figure 15.1, the best time to broadcast is 8, because that time is attractive to the most viewers. The broadcaster locates at 8 not to raise more revenue directly, because there is no price, but rather to ensure the largest audience, which in turn can bring the greatest advertising revenue. The monopoly broadcaster chooses the center of all preferred times, just as the monopoly store located at the center of Hotelling's street. At time 8, the program is available at the smallest inconvenience to the largest number of viewers. If only one program is broadcast, this central location in the time dimension is also socially ideal. It minimizes the inconvenience from nonpreferred broadcast times, which is the equivalent of total transportation cost along the Hotelling street.

To understand how broadcasters may locate in the time dimension, remember from Chapter 6 that for a consumer located at one end of the street, labeled 0, to reach the monopoly store at the center of the street cost 1/2, because the cost of traveling the whole street in that example was 1. Let inconvenience be represented in the same way here. Then if there are five consumers (we shall break them into fractions) each prefer one of the five possible times, the one who prefers the program at 6 but must see it at 8 has an inconvenience cost of 1/2, and the same cost of 1/2 applies to the consumer who prefers the program at 10. The inconvenience cost to the consumer who prefers the program at 8 is 0, while the inconvenience cost of a consumer preferring either 7 or 9 is 1/4. Thus, by aggregating total inconvenience cost on this basis, we can estimate inconvenience cost for the average consumer as $[2(1/2) + 2(1/4) + 0]/5 = 1.5/5 = 0.3$. You can experiment with other broadcast times to convince yourself that locating the program at any other time will result in a greater total inconvenience cost for the viewing audience and a greater average inconvenience cost per audience member.

Now consider a second broadcaster entering this market, after the first has taken the central programming time at 8. The second broadcaster also wants to broadcast at 8, the same time as the first broadcaster. Two broadcasters at 8 split the audience, which is the best outcome for the second broadcaster. Again, you can experiment with other times, but you will find you cannot attract a larger audience at any other time as long as the first broadcaster continues to broadcast at 8. Broadcasting at 8 is the Nash equilibrium strategy from Chapter 5, in that neither station can do any better as long as the other remains at time slot 8.

With two broadcasters, this Nash equilibrium solution to the problem of broadcasting times does not minimize overall inconvenience cost for viewers, just as two firms at the center of the main street would not be at socially optimal locations in the Hotelling model. With two broadcasters and five possible times, the socially optimal broadcast times are 7 and 9. Broadcasting at two different times, 7 and 9, meets two groups' preferences perfectly (inconvenience cost of 0) and are within 1/4 of the other three preferred times. Broadcasting at 7 and 9 results in average inconvenience time of $[1/4 + 1/4 + 1/4 + 0 + 0]/5 = 0.75/5 = 0.15$. All the viewers who prefer times 6, 8, and 10 incur an inconvenience cost of 1/4. Although one-half of the viewers who prefer 8 now go to 7, and the other half go to 9, they together incur an inconvenience cost of 1/4. Broadcasting at these two times, 7 and 9, is not a Nash equilibrium, however, because either broadcaster can increase its own audience by moving its broadcast time to 8. Thus, two broadcasters do not choose the socially optimal broadcast times.

With two broadcasters broadcasting at the Nash equilibrium time of 8, suppose a third broadcaster enters. The best result for society is to have the three stations broadcast at three different times. A third competing broadcaster is now looking for a larger audience. What broadcast time will this third broadcaster choose? Sharing the entire population by also broadcasting at 8 is a possibility. With a total population of 5, the third broadcaster can see that broadcasting at 8 brings $5/3 = 1\ 2/3$ viewers. The third broadcaster also thinks about broadcasting at a different time, say 9. Broadcasting at 9 would be privately better, because it would bring the viewers who prefer 9 and 10, or a total of 2, and leave only 3 viewers to be shared by the two broadcasters at 8.

The third broadcaster's choice of 9 does not produce an equilibrium, however. With the decline in viewers to 1.5 for each broadcaster at the 8 time slot, one of the broadcasters still at 8 shifts to 7, to attract an audience of 2 who prefer 6 and 7, leaving the remaining broadcaster at 8 with only one viewer. This outcome is unstable, because the broadcaster remaining at 8 can do better by moving to 7 or 9, where it is possible to split an audience of 2 1/2. The situation here is like the unstable outcome with three firms in the Hotelling model of Chapter 6, where the surrounded firm in the middle keeps moving to obtain customers. Economist Oz Shy provides a more formal analysis of this situation and points out that it is similar to television news in the United States, where the three main television networks, ABC, CBS, and NBC, do not usually broadcast news at the same time; two networks choose the same time, and the other network broadcasts at a later time.[24]

Thus, competition among broadcasters in their broadcast times may not result in a socially optimal outcome. We have ignored differences in the numbers of viewers who prefer the various times, and including that increases the range of possibilities. The main point is that the aim of maximizing audience does not usually bring the ideal selection of broadcast times. Free entry into broadcasting might bring broadcasts whenever they would be socially useful, but television programming is provided primarily by networks, which are limited in number, in part because entry to the

---

[24] See Shy (2001, p. 142). Shy also shows that with four broadcast times instead of five there are multiple Nash equilibria even with two broadcasters. Cancian, Bills, and Bergstrom (1995) treat one-way preferences, in which viewers prefer times at or later than particular times, and they show in that case that no equilibrium results.

industry as a network is difficult. The scale economies from operating a broadcast network are large, and they limit the number of networks that can exist. In the United States, there are only four main broadcast networks: ABC, CBS, Fox, and NBC.

Program Selection

In a classic treatment of program selection, which focused on advertising-supported radio broadcasting, economist Peter Steiner (1952) showed that a monopoly would choose a broader set of programs than an oligopoly of broadcasters. He assumed each competing broadcaster was trying to attract the largest possible audience (again because the audience is the source of advertising revenue). Whereas competing broadcasters pursue large audiences at the expense of other broadcasters, a monopoly is not exposed to the "business-stealing" efforts of competitors, and it seeks any profitable audience. Nobel laureate Michael Spence and economist Bruce Owen (1977) show a comparable bias in advertising-financed television programming. Having consumers pay for programs might avoid this bias in program offerings, but charging a price causes welfare loss when marginal cost is zero. It seems that either long-run program choices or short-run pricing is inefficient.

Now consider the program selection problem under broadcaster competition rather than monopoly.[25] To illustrate this problem of program selection, let us assume that all programs are broadcast at the same time, and suppose there are three types of program: (1) drama/adventure, (2) situation comedy, and (3) film. Assume the audiences for these three types of broadcast are A_1, A_2, and A_3. Let us also assume that the audiences differ in size so that

$$A_1 > A_2 > A_3,$$

because audiences for some programs actually are larger than for others.[26] Suppose three broadcasters, ABC, CBS, and NBC, operate three available television channels.

Notice immediately that if $A_1 > 3A_2$, all three broadcasters would want to broadcast drama/adventure shows and split the large A_1 audience. In that case, no other program selection can produce a larger audience for any broadcaster because the second largest audience, A_2 for situation comedy, is smaller than one-third of the drama/adventure audience, A_1. It is not ideal, however, to have only one type of program broadcast, for in that case two groups (A_2 and A_3) are not served at all. The socially ideal solution has all three program types broadcast, one on each channel, to meet the preferences of all three groups of viewers. A monopoly of three stations would probably offer all three programs.

Another imperfect set of programs is possible. If $A_1 < 3A_2$, while $A_1 > 2A_3$, then two broadcasters will want to show the drama/adventure program to the A_1 audience, while the third broadcasts a situation comedy to A_2. Again, this outcome is not ideal, because all three programs are not broadcast. All three programs will be broadcast through independent selections by the broadcasters if $A_1 < 2A_3$. But obtaining this

---

[25] Shy (2001, pp. 145–147) gives a simple treatment of the Steiner (1952) problem and Shy's treatment is drawn on here.

[26] As reported in Sterling and Kittross (2002), drama/adventure accounted for about 26 hours per week of prime-time TV in 1995 (when the last compilation of this kind was possible), situation comedy 24 hours, and film 14 hours. All other categories together accounted for 26 hours.

socially desirable outcome through broadcasters' choices requires a particular balance of preferences among programs, and ideal choices are not assured.

Thus, decisions about program content do not reliably serve social welfare when broadcasters attempt to maximize profit by maximizing audiences, which they are motivated to do when their revenue comes from advertisers. The programming bias from advertising support of television may be even more pronounced when advertisers seek particular segments of the viewing audience. For example, the 18-to-39 age group is large, has discretionary spending, and will be around for a while, so networks design programs to attract that age segment.

Ownership Restrictions

One issue raised by private ownership of TV stations is whether the owners offer independent views. Prior to the Telecommunications Act of 1996, to foster independent viewpoints the FCC restricted ownership by limiting how many national TV properties one person could own. One individual or company was to own no more than 12 TV stations, and even that was allowed only if they did not serve more than 25 percent of the national audience. One person or company could also own up to 12 AM and 12 FM radio stations. From each of these types, the individual or company could own only one station in any one location, however, again to foster more independent points of view. But competition from cable service brought more independent points of view, and the 1996 Act removed all of the ownership restrictions except for one that prevents an owner from serving more than 35 percent (formerly 25 percent) of the national audience. The FCC attempted to remove this limit but as the reach of one owner exceeded 35 percent, Congress froze the percentage at about 37 percent, where it now stands. Another limit comes on antitrust grounds, for the Department of Justice will block ownership of facilities on antitrust grounds when they generate more than half of the revenue in any one market, and this sets a limit on ownership concentration in each market.

To avoid local monopoly power over information, FCC rules had also prevented "cross-ownership." **Cross-ownership** is ownership across media, such as ownership of a TV station by a local newspaper publisher, or ownership of a cable company by a telephone company in the area where the telephone company provides service. Although television networks were not allowed to merge (except Fox, which was given more latitude to foster its growth), the 1996 Act allowed telephone companies or television networks (except Fox, which was not counted as a network for this purpose) to own cable systems. Many mergers ensued. Time Warner bought Turner Broadcasting System, Inc. Westinghouse Electric bought CBS plus the radio giant, Infinity Broadcasting Corporation. Rupert Murdoch's News Corporation added New World Communications to its Fox network. These mergers would not have been allowed before the 1996 Act.

Public Service and Avoiding Corruption in Broadcasting

Into the 1980s, the FCC was concerned about other aspects of advertising-financed TV broadcasting besides ownership arrangements. For instance, the FCC required that TV stations provide public service programming. The programming of commercial stations was to include at least 5 percent local material, 5 percent informational material, and 10 percent nonentertainment material, such as news, documentaries, and political and religious matters. The FCC reviewed a station's programming when its broadcasting right was up for renewal, to test compliance with these rules concerning programs by type. In the 1980s, however, the FCC greatly relaxed these rules, on grounds that competition—especially from cable systems—made it difficult for broadcast stations to comply with them.

The type of corruption the FCC remains alert for is the possibility that secret payments are made to win favors in having materials broadcast. A good example would be a payment to obtain the playing of a song that a recording company hoped to make popular, perhaps by bribing a disc jockey, a practice that has generally been given the name "payola" and was illustrated in the movie, "Dreamgirls." This practice has surfaced recently where large corporations have made bargains that involve the broadcasting of songs in exchange for in-kind services.[27] Another example of corruption was dramatized in the movie "Quiz Show," which told the true story of deception on a televised quiz show. The show provided answers to popular contestants to keep them on the show and thereby attract viewers. Unfair access to media in any way is a continuing concern for the FCC.

15.3 CABLE SERVICE

Television service is no longer dominated by broadcast media. Broadcasting faces vigorous competition not only from cable service but also from satellite television and from telephone networks, as well as from the many other ways to spend time that potential viewers and listeners now have. Cable service is the most prominent challenger to broadcast media, however, even though it began as an accessory to broadcast television. The regulation of cable system prices was largely a local matter for years. Communities would choose a cable provider, sometimes through an auction process, and retain some control over the rates to be charged. The cable service provider would then choose bundles of services to offer, leading to a range of offerings at different prices.

The basic cable system is a wired network, like a telephone network, except the typical cable network was designed to be hierarchical, to distribute signals in one direction without complicated switching. A "headend" and a "distribution system" constitute a cable system network. The headend receives signals from distant broadcast stations via microwave or satellite transmission and from local stations. The distribution system is a network that carries those signals to receivers used by the cable customers to display programming, perhaps by coaxial cable with up to 54 channels. More modern systems use two such cables to carry up to 108 signals, and more advanced systems can accommodate over 500 channels. The investment in a cable system's headend and distribution network can be substantial enough to make competing systems too costly

---

[27] See Lorne Manly, "How Payola Went Corporate," *New York Times*, July 31, 2005, Sec. 4, p. 1.

in many communities. That is, there are network economies of scale, and economies from greater density of consumers, so to achieve scale economies communities often award one cable system a monopoly franchise.

On Again, Off Again Government Regulation

Radio and television signals enter the home by cable as well as by over-the-air broadcast, and cable service started soon after TV broadcasting began in the late 1940s. Early cable systems extended the coverage of TV broadcast stations (and some radio stations, mainly FM Public Broadcasting System stations) by receiving signals and carrying them by wire into valleys and remote regions where over-the-air signals would not penetrate, such as hill-sheltered Mahoney City, PA, where cable service began in 1948. These cable systems were welcomed by broadcast stations because they enlarged audiences and thus raised advertising revenues. Indeed, in 1959 the FCC decided not to regulate such cable operations.

In the 1960s, cable systems were expanding into regular broadcast areas. They began to import more stations into given areas in part because microwave transmission allowed them to relay signals long distances at low cost. Although popular with viewers, these quality signals from other cities could reduce the audience for a local station. Rather than merely complementing local broadcast stations and extending their reach, the cable offerings now became competitors, and they were a potential challenge also to the major networks. To limit this development of cable, the FCC asserted regulatory power beginning in 1962 and restricted the number and type of signals that could be imported into any given area. It also required that cable systems originate programming and offer free channels for showing educational or government or public programming. The FCC gave a local station the right to prevent a cable service from carrying a show from an imported station if the local station was to air the show. This 1960s FCC regulation was clearly intended to prevent cable's growth from harming broadcasters.

In 1980, under the more conservative Reagan administration, the FCC retreated from this effort to restrain cable expansion. It relaxed the limit on imported signals and allowed cable systems to import programs that a local station was also broadcasting. Cable systems were greatly strengthened also when Congress passed the Cable Communications Policy Act of 1984, which prevented price regulation by local authorities and required good reasons not to renew cable franchises. Local authorities could still require that channels be assigned for educational, governmental, or public programming, but some other requirements, such as free services to the handicapped, were abandoned. The 1984 law came close to being a deregulation law for cable.

This near deregulation in 1984 led to a period of expansion in cable services, but it also led to higher rates. Congress did another about face and reregulated cable service in 1992, concluding that cable-service prices had risen too much after the 1984 legislation had prohibited most local regulation of cable rates. This return to federal regulation of cable service applied only to basic, or minimum, service, in areas where competition was weak, and it was to be carried out under FCC guidelines by local community governments.

New FCC rules to implement the 1992 law were slow to go into effect. The reason for this delay was that local communities were to apply to the FCC for authority to regulate. Near the end of 1993, only 5,000 out of 33,000 communities had applied, and the FCC wanted more communities ready to regulate before having the new law take effect. It froze average rates while waiting for applications, but rates for individual service options changed—both increasing and decreasing—during the freeze on average rates. The public complained about price increases for popular programming packages and for installation and the withdrawal of special discounts, such as for senior citizens. Yet some options, such as multiple outlets or remote controls, sometimes became less costly for consumers.

The announced purpose of the 1992 law was to make cable service prices no higher in the absence of competition than in places where competition functioned. An alternative to federal reregulation would have been an increase in competition, specifically from telephone companies, which might also open the way for new forms of cable service. The FCC long avoided this opening of competition between cable and telephone technologies, but the Telecommunications Act of 1996 finally allowed it. Yet it was a court decision that brought competition between cable and telephone providers into the realm of possibility.

Competition between Cable and Telephone Networks

Because most consumers have only one cable network provider available to them, so they have little choice, regulation might be in order, but should the FCC guide such regulation nationally? Instead, the FCC might have allowed competition from telephone companies, which was stimulated by court decisions and finally was allowed under the Telecommunications Act of 1996.

A court supported competition between telephone and cable in the 1990s. With the Chesapeake and Potomac (C&P) Telephone Company of Virginia, Bell Atlantic Corporation formed a new subsidiary, Bell Atlantic Video Services, for the purpose of providing cable service. On August 24, 1993, a District Court in Alexandria, VA, allowed local telephone companies to provide cable television service to homes.[28] Bell Atlantic Video Services was allowed to enter the territory of Jones Intercable, Inc., a cable company that had been serving Alexandria exclusively. Members of Congress and other observers raised immediate objections to the court decision. They feared that phone companies might provide unfair subsidies to new cable services or might buy cable companies and form even stronger monopoly positions. The Cable Communications Policy Act of 1984 had prevented telephone companies from providing cable service in the same area where they provided phone service. That law was overturned in the Alexandria decision, on grounds that it violated the telephone companies' first amendment rights.

The Alexandria, VA court decision opened the way for a redrawing of the cable and telephone service industries. The Telecommunications Act of 1996 accomplished

---

[28] See *Chesapeake and Potomac Telephone Company of Virginia v. U.S.*, 830 F. Supp. 909, 62 USLW 2152, 1993-2 Trade Cases P 70,339, 145 P.U.R. 4th 319 (E.D.Va., Aug. 24,1993) (NO. CIV. 92-1751-A).

that reordering, and in doing so it supplanted the Alexandria, VA court decision.[29] In 1993, the court decision had complicated life at the FCC, where it was known that Congress was treating this issue in the telecommunications legislation that it was considering. Even though the FCC was not entirely satisfied with the 1984 law, it was expected to enforce it. But it did not enforce the law while an appeal of the Alexandria decision was in process, which effectively was until the passage of the Telecommunications Act.

In the mid-1990s a host of proposed mergers resulted between telephone and cable companies, and the industry seemed on the brink of dramatic change that the FCC could not control. Before the 1996 Act, however, mergers could not combine potentially competing services. No telephone company absorbed a cable service company within its service area. For example, in a proposed $26 billion merger between Bell Atlantic and the nation's then largest cable company, Tele-Communications, Inc. (TCI), cable services within the Bell Atlantic telephone service area were specifically excluded from the merger and sold to other operators. This adjustment was part of the merger proposal because the merging companies did not think the Justice Department would permit a merger between potentially competing telephone and cable components.

Bidding for a Franchise

In the 1970s, many communities awarded monopoly franchises to cable systems. A form of auction was frequently used that, in principle, could achieve desirable results. The principle goes back to 1859[30] and in modern form[31] has been applied specifically to cable television.[32] Essentially, competitors who wish to provide the monopoly service offer prices they will charge for it, and the lowest price wins. The winner is franchised to provide the service as a monopoly for a specified period of time. This auction

---

BOX 15.4 The DVD as Competitor

Another form of competition that affects both broadcast and cable television is the rental and sale of movies as videos or digital video discs (DVDs), which can be seen on television sets through the use of VCRs and DVD players. With VCRs and DVD players in more than 85 percent of U.S. homes, providing movies has been a burgeoning business since the 1980s and is accomplished now through efficient Internet/mail services that distribute DVDs. Some joining of these sources of film entertainment has occurred. For example, Viacom owns both Blockbuster, a video rental company, and the CBS television network. DVDs now compete with videos and add to the usefulness of TV sets for entertainments beyond broadcast and cable.

---

[29] See *U.S. v. Chesapeake and Potomac Telephone Company of Virginia*, 516 U.S. 415, 116 S.Ct. 1036 (1993).
[30] See Sir Edwin Chadwick (1859).
[31] See Demsetz (1968).
[32] See Williamson (1976) and Prager (1990).

process can force the bidders to keep costs low and to provide desired services, and it can be repeated when the franchise expires.[33]

There are difficulties with such a system, however. Once a service provider becomes familiar with equipment and with the system operation, it probably has advantages over other bidders that may allow it to continue its monopoly position. It is also possible that the winning bidder is overambitious in its bidding and fails to achieve the costs on which its bid was predicated. When it asks for an adjustment in rates for that reason, a local authority may find it difficult to replace the existing provider, which might fail without relief from its contract, and so the authority is likely to grant an increase in the price charged to consumers. This pattern changed, however, as cable firms grew in size and came to serve more than one community. If a large cable provider should bid too low to make a profit in one community today, that community might not grant rate increases, because the large cable firm with revenues from other areas would probably not fail as a consequence of its low bid.

The Bundling of Cable Offerings

The provider of cable service can decide what services to offer and how to package them into different bundles for different fees. The cable service usually offers bundles of service instead of pricing every offering individually in what is called menu pricing. Bundling services can sometimes generate more revenue than selling single services alone through menu pricing.

Bundling of cable offerings is attractive to a cable operator in part because it often is already committed to certain programming and has already incurred its costs, so the aim is simply to bring in the greatest revenue from these available program offerings. The consumer valuations assumed in Table 15.2 illustrate how bundling may yield more revenue than menu pricing. With the aim of maximizing revenue from each of the three channels, HBO, ESPN, and the History Channel, what prices would be best for each channel? For either ESPN or the History Channel alone, a price of $8 is profit maximizing. This price attracts customer 3 to the History Channel and customers 1 and 2 to ESPN, thus raising $8 + $16 = $24.

TABLE 15.2 Consumer Valuations of Three Cable Channels

	Valuations ($) of Consumers		
Consumer	HBO	ESPN	History
1	8	8	2
2	6	8	2
3	3	2	8

[33] For analysis of this bidding process for a monopoly franchise, see Williamson (1976), Laffont and Tirole (1987), McAfee and McMillan (1987a), and Riordan and Sappington (1987).

A price of $6 attracts customers 1 and 2 to HBO and raise more revenue (at $12) than any other price. Total revenue from such separate, profit-maximizing, pricing by channel is $8 + $16 + $12 = $36.

Now consider bundling all of the channels together and selling them as a package. What would be the profit-maximizing price for the bundle that contains all three channels? Customer 3 would value the bundle the least and be willing to pay a total of $3 + $2 + $8 = $13. It would still be worthwhile to set the price at $13 to attract customer 3, because that wins all three customers and brings greater revenue, at $39, than the higher price of $16 for the bundle that attracts only two customers (1 and 2). Selling the bundle at $13 also raises more revenue, at $39, than selling individual channels, which would only raise $36, so in this case there is an advantage to bundling.

Do you think that mixed bundling, which involves selling channels alone and in bundles, might do even better? Try selling ESPN and the History Channel together as a bundle. At a price of $10, all three customers would buy, so this two-channel bundle would yield revenue of $30. The best price for HBO alone was shown above to be $6, a price that would attract customers 1 and 2 and yield revenue of $12. Thus, by selling ESPN and the History Channel as a bundle, and HBO separately, a total revenue of $30 + $12 = $42 is possible. Mixed bundling therefore yields more revenue in this example than bundling all three channels, and the cable operator can be expected to prefer it. This shows that the cable operator who has some monopoly control may package offerings into bundles that draw the most revenue from customers.

Broadcasters, who collect their revenue solely from advertisers, compete with cable operators who collect from viewers as well as advertisers. To attract advertisers, the broadcasters seek large audiences, but some cable offerings that include advertising have some of that same interest in large audiences and thus seek similar programs. At the same time, cable providers can supply more specialized programs to smaller audiences that are willing to pay for them, and this also may take some viewers away from the audience that is available to broadcasters.

The FCC completed a study that Congress required of menu, or à la carte, cable offerings in 2004, and found that such choice for consumers would be more expensive than bundles now available.[34] The study had many critics, however, in part because it focused on the extremes of either a forced á la carte choice *or* the current bundling, without treating seriously the advantage of adding an á la carte choice to existing bundling. In surveys, the vast majority of viewers favor an á la carte option, sometimes to limit what children are able to view, and sometimes because they only want to watch a few channels. We know that cable service providers can make more profit by using bundling. Network providers of programming, such as Time Warner and Disney, force cable and satellite companies to buy bundles of programs, and this affects what cable and satellites in turn offer. These network providers plus the National Cable and Telecommunications Association, a trade group of large cable providers, lobbied hard in support of bundling.

---

[34] See Frank Ahrens, "FCC Says A La Carte TV Would Cost More," *Washington Post*, November 20, 2004, p. E1.

Pay TV and Satellite TV

Like cable, pay TV, which requires a fee for specific services, both over-the-air and on cable, was also originally subject to restrictive FCC policies, again for the purpose of protecting free (advertising supported) television. Pay TV was considered extensively for over-the-air broadcasting through a system of encoding signals, which allowed fees to be charged, but the FCC resisted it.[35] In cable, the FCC prevented series programs from being carried on a pay-TV basis and limited the sporting events and even the movies that could be shown as pay TV. HBO went to court over FCC restrictions on its service, however, and the Court of Appeals for the District of Columbia struck down the FCC rules in 1977.[36] The FCC had argued that pay TV would draw programs from free television and deprive low-income viewers of entertainment, but the court held that the FCC had provided no evidence of a need for its restrictions. The court even questioned whether the FCC had jurisdiction to regulate pay TV. The FCC tried to appeal the decision, but the Supreme Court refused to hear the case.

A satellite launched in 1975 allowed cable systems to receive programming over long distances at even lower cost. This added to the competitive effectiveness of cable systems, and it spawned a new form of distribution for cable services that competes with cable. It also allowed delivery of television service by transmissions that are sent to satellites and then beamed back down directly to antennas at homes, thus allowing better reception than is possible with ordinary earth-bound, over-the-air broadcasting. A wireless-local-loop technology is no longer confined to line-of-sight paths and can travel as radio waves. It can offer much faster Internet service than telephone or cable alternatives and may provide competition for both. Technological change has also opened up more channels per cable connection, so more change can be expected in cable services.

Other Forms of Competition

Cable and telephone companies also compete vigorously for Internet access business. Cable companies had thought they had a great advantage in this market because cable modems offered generally greater band-width. But a consortium involving telephone companies GTE, U.S. West, Bell South, SBC Communications, and Ameritech, plus computer hardware and software companies Compaq, Intel, and Microsoft, developed DSL, a new way for telephone companies to serve this market. Through modem and software arrangements, DSL provides Internet access speeds 30 times faster than the telephone modems that were available in 1998. Nevertheless, from their strong beginnings cable systems still claim twice as many Internet connection customers as telephone systems.

Under the Telecommunications Act of 1996, cable systems were regarded as common carriers who were required to open their networks to access by others

---

[35] In the 1970s there was a continuing debate about having viewers pay for over-the-air television broadcasting. The debate was led by Zenith Corporation, which had developed a system of encoded signals that allowed exclusion of those who did not pay fees.

[36] *Home Box Office v. FTC*, 567 F. 2nd 9 (D.C. Cir., 1977).

without discrimination. The FCC, however, adopted a rule in 2002 making the Internet an "information service," a type of service largely unregulated, rather than a "telecommunications service," which the Act regulated. After a legal dispute over this rule and its implications, in June 2005 the Supreme Court accepted the FCC's right to interpret the law. This means that the FCC does not have to ensure that **Internet Service Providers (ISPs)** have access rights to cable systems. Soon after, in August 2005, the FCC also ruled that telephone companies did not have to grant broadband access at wholesale rates to the independent ISPs. Thus, telephone and cable companies are on similar footing in their dealings with ISPs, and by owning networks they have advantages over them. Telephone and cable systems, however, still face competition from each other.

Other forms of competition are developing between cable and telephone networks, even though the networks are configured differently. Telephone networks contain switches for two-way conversations, while cable networks were planned for one-way distribution of television programming and need changes to provide two-way telephone conversations. Cable wires have greater capacity, or band-width, than telephone lines, however, because they were designed to carry complex video signals that contain much information, whereas typical telephone lines are twisted copper wires that were intended to carry simple audio messages. The cable wires can carry telephone messages along with other content. With cleverness, the twisted copper wires can carry condensed signals for video and other content. Technology can thus make competition in telephone, video, Internet, and other services possible between these differing wire-line networks.

Cable companies can now compete more effectively with video stores in offering at-home movie entertainment through a video-on-demand cable service at reasonably low cost. This service allows viewers in their homes to order, from a substantial menu of films or TV series, one they want to watch. Viewers can then operate the film like a rented or owned video, including pausing and replaying. Time Warner Cable offers such video on demand, and as costs for the service fall, it is reaching more homes.[37] Not to be outdone, AT&T is introducing gradually through its network a package combining satellite service from Echostar Communications Corporation with videos and movies from the Internet.[38] The service is called Homezone and it includes the downloading of movies from Movielink. Downloading films over the Internet takes time, however, at roughly 30 minutes for sites such as CinemaNow or Movielink or the new Apple system, and all require a high-speed cable or DSL connection plus compression that harms slightly the appearance of the film. They also impose restrictions on how long the movie will last before being shown, whether DVDs can be burned, and other matters. A number of problems will probably slow the development of movie downloading, but it is likely to emerge in an effective form and have an effect much like music downloading, which changed the distribution of music.[39]

---

[37] See Seth Schiesel, "Video on Demand Is Finally Taking Hold," *New York Times*, November 25, 2002, p. C4.

[38] See Peter Grant, "AT&T Readies Service Uniting Internet and TV," *Wall Street Journal*, June 19, 2006, p. B1.

[39] See John R. Quain, "Films That Come Over the Internet Don't Come Easy," *New York Times*, August 31, 2006, p. C9.

15.4 CONVERGENCE OF BROADCAST, CABLE, AND TELEPHONE AND THE TELECOMMUNICATIONS ACT OF 1996

Technologies are being developed to meet consumer demand for information and entertainment, and, as demands are better known, the technologies tend to converge, all attempting to offer the same demanded services. Of course, the 1996 Telecommunications Act broadened the possibility for telephone and cable companies to compete with each other, and allowed public utilities such as electricity companies to offer cable or telephone service. The Act also restricted the FCC's regulation of cable prices. Market share and ownership or cross ownership limitations for broadcasting were relaxed and a variety of other features were introduced in the Act. Still, the Act is not adequate for the changes that have come since it was passed.

The Scope of Services Offered

The Telecommunications Act of 1996 affirmed developing trends in the cable and broadcast industries, yet its restrictions and requirements pale in comparison with the effects of new services that every day seems to bring. Technology has added a great variety of broadcast forms, including Web video, which allows distribution of TV programs to iPods. Together with TiVo devices to record programs and possibly skip commercials, these developments challenge the business model of broadcast TV stations and networks and may change in some degree their sources of revenue. Cable companies also face competition from satellite TV while trying to move to telephone and Internet service. Now radio stations often operate web sites where they present video fare, showing their announcers broadcasting, news clips, music videos, or other fare. Technologies are bending to serve the wishes of consumers, and the old broadcast-cable division is less important than developing the new services that each technology can fashion.

Retreating on Cable Rate Regulation

Parts of the 1984 law that suspended local cable rate regulation were essentially repealed in 1992, when the Act was passed that imposed rate reregulation on cable systems by local authorities under FCC supervision. Then the Telecommunications Act of 1996 overturned much of the 1992 Act. Indeed, under terms of the 1996 Act, FCC rules set out to control cable service rates that expired March 31, 1999, except for rates that apply to the basic level of service in exceptional cases. Small cable operators—those with less than $25 million in annual revenues—were given freedom from rate regulation immediately, as were larger cable systems that face effective competition from any local exchange carrier (LEC) that provides "comparable" video programming services. LECs may offer video services under the 1996 law, either by distributing programming or by creating an "open video system" to transport video programming as a common carrier. An open video system has up to two-thirds of its capacity available for unaffiliated programmers. The reduction in regulation allows more reliance on competition between technologies to discipline providers.

Under the 1996 Act, only franchising authorities are allowed to complain formally to the FCC about cable service rates. A franchising authority awards franchises, say for example to a local cable service provider. Only if it has received complaints from customers, and they are within 90 days of a price increase, can the franchising authority, in turn, file a complaint to the FCC.

Market Power in Broadcasting

Restrictions that had been intended to foster independent viewpoints and control market power were also relaxed under the 1996 Act. National restrictions on the number of television stations, or the number of AM and FM radio stations, that a single entity could own were eliminated. A limit on ownership, which allowed a single entity to reach no more than 25 percent of the national audience, was relaxed to allow one entity to reach 35 percent of the national audience and when the FCC allowed more than 35 percent, Congress froze the limit at 37 percent. The Department of Justice holds that a single owner of facilities cannot generate more than half the revenue in a market without violating antitrust law, and eventually that could become the effective limit on ownership concentration.

The Telecommunications Act of 1996 also eased cross-ownership restrictions between different types of media. A single entity can now own both a cable system and a network of broadcast stations. The FCC may grant waivers to permit cross ownership of radio and TV stations in any of the 50 largest markets in the country. TV stations may also affiliate with an entity that maintains two or more networks if the networks are not large. The Act also lengthened broadcast licenses to eight years, and it authorized new renewal procedures that presume the present holders of licenses are renewable so renewal is less uncertain.

Other Provisions of the Act

A variety of other provisions are contained in the 1996 Act. The FCC has authority to regulate direct-to-home satellite service and many features of advanced television (ATV). If the FCC issues additional licenses for ATV services, only existing television broadcast station licensees, or holders of permits to construct such stations, will initially be eligible. To receive such a license, after a period of dual broadcasting the recipient will have to give up its old license for reallocation to another party. The FCC may impose requirements to assure ATV quality, and it may specify hours of operation.

BOX 15.5 Clear Channel Radio

Founded in 1972, Clear Channel Radio is a private radio company that expanded mightily when ownership restrictions were removed by the Telecommunications Act in 1996. In 1996 it acquired 49 radio stations in 20 markets and made a large investment in New Zealand. It now operates 1,200 stations in 65 countries and is a large outdoor advertiser and a dominant organizer of concert tours.

The Act also sought to limit television violence and control "indecent" online communications. The new TV ratings system grew out of the V-chip requirement in the law, which makes manufacturers of TV sets equip them with chips that allow parents to prevent reception of certain types of programs. The V chips are not in wide use, and TV executives developed a "voluntary rating system" before government authorities did. The Act also forbids the use of telecommunications devices for transmitting " indecent materials," and it imposes similar prohibitions on computer use, particularly when aimed at children. Other provisions are concerned with access by disabled or handicapped citizens. As a result of the law, schools and libraries are connected to the Internet at greatly reduced rates, with costs to be borne by telephone companies or, effectively, by their customers.

SUMMARY

Radio was originally developed as a way to send messages without wires, as telegraphy, not as voice communications. This early wireless communication was narrowly focused, as from one ship to another at sea, and not intended for general broadcasting. After the vacuum tube was developed to allow audio broadcasting, radio manufacturers and others supported general broadcasting until advertisers came to support radio broadcasts to reach listeners and sell them goods. Commercial broadcast radio came in 1920. Television broadcasting started after World War II, and like radio it adopted financing by advertising. The FCC coordinates use of the radio spectrum and even decides which of contending technologies are implemented. Today, for example, new means of communicating and new uses of communication are available, but because network elements are so important, many centralized choices are necessary to implement the technologies.

Radio and television broadcasting have properties of public goods. Broadcasts are not sold directly to consumers, but audiences are sold instead to advertisers. Although advertiser-supported broadcasting avoids charging the marginal listener or viewer, which is desirable because the cost of reaching that marginal consumer is zero, the advertisers want large audiences, and they reach them through programs that might not be supported by fee-paying consumers. By offering programs free to listeners and viewers, broadcasters attract audiences, and advertisers in turn pay for the opportunity to appeal to those audiences. Competition among broadcasters in this public goods setting can lead to biases in the timing and in the content of programs. Advertisers seek large audiences, and they support programs that produce them, whereas individuals might willingly pay more to have programs that are more narrowly suited to their preferences.

Cable service, which initially expanded the reach of over-the-air television stations by relaying signals to remote locations, has grown to compete with over-the-air stations, offering more channels and higher quality reception. In principle, cable systems can charge customers for each program, but they also have extremely low marginal cost to serve an added customer. So for revenues they rely primarily on subscription fees, and many of their programs come from broadcast stations. Like broadcast stations, cable programs can also contain advertising.

The broadcast and cable industries are based on modern technologies and are currently moving through a revolutionary period. Technological advances have lowered the cost of delivering signals by cable and allowed transmission of signals having greater bandwidth, so dense information needed in video signals can be transmitted via cable. Technology has also made possible the transmission of video signals over telephone wires, so telephone service companies using DSL can provide cable service. By altering their one-way cable distribution systems, cable companies can provide telephone service. Competition thus extends to enterprises that are quite different in form. Telephone companies and cable service companies now enter each others' markets, a development that the FCC prevented for years. We can now expect competition to grow between the two methods of reaching viewers.

The FCC has gone back and forth in its regulation of cable. After deciding explicitly not to regulate cable operations in 1959, the FCC reversed itself and began to regulate cable in 1962, essentially to prevent cable from harming over-the-air broadcasters. Then in 1980 the FCC stopped restraining cable expansion and allowed cable systems to import programs that a local station was also broadcasting. Then Congress, with the Cable Communications Policy Act of 1984, prevented price regulation by local authorities and made it more difficult not to renew cable franchises. After this near deregulation of cable in 1984, cable expanded aggressively, and rates for cable service increased. Although services also increased along with rates, the rate increases motivated Congress to reregulate cable service in 1992, at least for basic cable service wherever competition was weak.

One of the important features of the revolution in broadcast and cable is a change in regulatory approach that allows more competition among service providers. Regulatory approaches have changed considerably from period to period. For example, the FCC shielded cable from regulation, imposed regulation, prevented regulation, and imposed regulation again. Present guidance is based largely on the Telecommunications Act of 1996, which changed many regulatory goals and restrictions. Cross ownership restrictions among communications media to preserve many points of view—ownership of both radio and television stations by one person, for instance—have been eased, on grounds that many views are now available from many sources. To support competition the 1996 Act sometimes requires the owner of a network to give others nondiscriminatory access to that network at reasonable prices. Current regulations also cover programming decency, particularly with regard to children, and access for disabled and handicapped individuals.

QUESTIONS

1. Suppose organizers of a new television station are considering their prospects. They have to devote $625,000 to construct the station, and they can operate it for virtually nothing. A reliable, high-quality demand study yielded the following information about demand:

Price ($)	TV Sets (thousands)	Total Revenue ($ thousands)	Average Cost ($) per TV Set
4	0	0	—
3	125	375	5.00
2	250	500	2.50
1	375	375	1.67
0	500	0	1.25

a. What is the best fee for the firm to offer under a pay-TV arrangement to achieve the most profit (or least loss)?

b. What is the consumer surplus at the fee you found in part a?

c. What fee generates the greatest consumer surplus, and what is that surplus?

d. Should this TV station be created? Will this TV station be created through the user-pays market if a price must be charged for its programs?

e. If advertising is allowed, can the TV station be supported on an advertiser-pays basis?

2. Suppose you are providing a cable service that distributes CNN, ESPN, and HBO to two customers (or two groups of customers of equal-size) whose utilities (or willingness to pay) for the three channels are described by the table below:

Customer	Valuations ($) of Consumers		
	CNN	ESPN	HBO
1	3	5	6
2	5	3	2

Your goal is to maximize profit. You need not serve every customer if it is not profitable to do so.

a. What prices would you charge if you sold each of the three channels separately?

b. What price would you charge if you bundled all three channels into one package?

c. You can bundle some channels together or price them separately, or do both, as you wish. What is the most profitable arrangement?

3. Suppose you are providing a cable service that distributes CNN, ESPN, and the History Channel to three customers (or three groups of customers of equal size) whose utilities (willingness to pay) for the three channels are described by the table on page 536.

| | Valuations ($) of Customers | | |
Customer	CNN	ESPN	History
1	8	10	9
2	6	9	7
3	2	8	5

Your goal is to maximize profit. You need not serve every customer if it is not profitable to do so.
   a. What prices would you charge if you sold each of the three channels separately?
   b. What price would you charge if you bundled all three channels into one package?
   c. You can bundle some channels together or price them separately, or do both, as you wish. What is the most profitable arrangement?

4. The FCC resisted competition between cable and wired telephone technologies for decades.
   a. Consider how the FCC might have introduced competition between these technologies in the 1970s. What steps could it have taken at what point in the history of the period, and what effects would you predict? Could the 1982 court decision that opened long-distance telephone service to competition have been avoided through your proposed actions?
   b. Consider how the FCC might have introduced competition between these technologies in 1990. What steps could it have taken, and what effects would you predict? Could the Telecommunications Act of 1996 have been avoided through your proposed actions?

5. Suppose the drama/adventure audience accounted for about 26 hours per week of prime-time TV, situation comedy 24 hours, and film 14 hours.[40] Suppose these hours of viewing represent the audience's true preferences.
   a. Would all of these three program types, drama/adventure, situation comedy, and film, be offered by three audience-maximizing television broadcasters?
   b. Explain why observations of the viewing audience may not reveal their true preferences, and say whether they might properly reveal preferences in this particular case.

6. Developments in all the forms of communication considered in this chapter affect newspapers. List some adjustments newspapers have made, or might make, to these developments. Do you think that newspapers, as we have known them, are threatened by these developments? Thomas Jefferson said " it is better to have newspapers without government than to have government without newspapers." Is the same statement appropriate today? Why or why not?

---

[40] These data were reported by Sterling and Kittross (2002, p. 858) for 1995, when the last compilation of this kind was possible.

16

Transportation

overed wagons dragged through rivers and over mountains in wild-west movies dramatize the effort individuals can put into moving themselves and their belongings from one place to another. Some travel affords pleasure, perhaps by glider or motorcycle or roller blades, but most transportation is instrumental. It allows us to be at point B rather than at point A. Over the last century how we move from A to B has changed dramatically.[1] Water transportation was once so important that it influenced the location of all major cities, but it has declined as the cost of transport over land has fallen sharply and air transport has made possible travel that could only be imagined a century ago. These changes, together with the growing cost of traffic congestion in cities, affect the shapes of cities and the locations of individuals, which determine in turn their need for transportation.

Modern transportation usually requires networks of highways, railroad tracks, airports, or waterways. Each network needs compatibility, such as railroad tracks of the same size, and may require some form of coordination, such as driving to the right side of public highways and observing rules about stop lights at intersections. For reasons that this chapter traces, in addition to compatibility and coordination, various commercial modes of transportation have been subject to governmental regulation, often as control over entry to the industry and over prices to be charged for services.

Efficient transportation is vital to economic activity and growth. Besides its importance to the economy, transportation requires public spaces for creating networks, and the difficulties of coordinating independent decisions within those networks led governments to regulate transportation industries. Indeed, transportation industries were the first to be regulated by the U.S. government, and the institutions created for this purpose were later applied to other industries. As these methods of regulation were

---

[1] For analysis of the decline in the transportation cost of goods and its effect on the form and function of cities see Glaeser and Kohlhase (2004).

questioned in recent decades, the transportation industries were also among the first to be deregulated.

The transportation industries are interdependent and are both substitutes and complements for one another. This chapter first considers ground transportation, including railroads, trucks, buses and urban transit, and automobiles. We then turn to air transportation, a twentieth century innovation. This chapter does not, however, examine water transportation, even though it is still significant. It takes quite different forms depending on natural circumstances of ports and rivers, and it involves a wide range of configurations (such as canals) that would complicate its treatment here. All of the regulated modes of transportation have seen some form of deregulation. In each of these cases we consider how regulation came about, the form that it took, why it changed or ended, and how the industry now functions.

16.1 | RAILROAD TRANSPORTATION

Railroads were especially important to the economic development of the United States.[2] They came to be regulated because competition among them did not seem to function well and because their price discrimination was seen as harming farmers and other large groups of shippers. Their regulation was subverted by substitute modes of transportation, however, such as trucks and buses, which were regulated to protect railroads. Automobiles were not regulated so easily, and their continuing unregulated presence challenged the other modes and their regulatory regimes.

Two centuries ago, without good roads and without a motor vehicle, movement of goods or people was by genuine horse power, which was slow, depending as it did on large and well-trained animals. Into this world came the "iron horse," the giant steam engine traveling on steel rails that was able to pull enormous loads from city to city. In its time, the railroad was a truly great innovation, the nineteenth century equivalent of today's broad band communications. While moving freight and passengers with punctuality and comfort, it changed commercial practices forever, fostered large new organizational forms, and even introduced new legal issues.[3] Supported in part by government grants of land for railway tracks, railroads also required immense private capital investments. Railroad leaders presided over extensive organizations and plotted complicated tactical battles. Excess capacity, price wars, monopoly positions, and price discrimination ensued. The federal government finally intervened to regulate the industry, and it created institutions for that purpose that would last almost without change well into the twentieth century.

---

[2] See Jenks (1944) and the less dramatic assessment by Fogel (1964).

[3] For example, early railroad engine sparks caused fires, and trains caused other new kinds of accidents. See Coase (1960) for illustrative legal cases.

The Early Period

Railroads drove the great nineteenth century economic expansion in America. Rail transportation of heavy freight fostered construction across America of all kinds—including railroad tracks—and solved the great problem of getting farm produce to large city markets in a timely fashion. Passenger service started in 1830 from Baltimore, first in cars resembling stage coaches. These cars quickly gave way to more comfortable forerunners of today's railroad cars, then called "exotic" cars that were lauded for their luxury features. Passengers considered it a sublimely comfortable way to travel. George Pullman introduced the upper-and-lower-berth sleeping car that bears his name in 1856, the same year rail service crossed the Mississippi River. With aid of the 1862 and 1864 Acts of Congress, railroads finally spanned the country in 1869. Changes of trains were needed for the trip, however, because rail network track widths were incompatible until railroads agreed on "standard gauge" tracks (4', 8 1/2" apart) in the 1880s. In addition to improving passenger travel, railroads made advancements between 1900 and 2000 that cut the shipping cost per ton-mile by roughly 90 percent.[4]

BOX 16.1 Railroad Wars and the Corporate Form of Organization

Railroads were the first businesses to adopt the corporate form of organization in the United States, and, after the Civil War, railway titans battled for their control. Daniel Drew, who was called the "Great Bear," ran the Erie Railroad in New York state. James Fisk and Jay Gould joined him in a struggle against the New York Central Railroad, headed by Commodore Vanderbilt and, later, by J. Pierpont Morgan. Vanderbilt bought Erie Railroad shares because that railroad was a competitor for the potential route to Chicago. He learned later that Drew was selling shares, while the Erie was borrowing money to purchase at vastly inflated prices certain properties Drew himself owned! Both sides used decisions by judges to help them in turn-by-turn legal ploys. Reports circulated of large sums of money being passed around the New York State legislature seeking favorable legislation.

Similar battles accompanied a race for control of railroads in the West. Collis Huntington in California and the Southwest and James J. Hill in the Northwest won substantial regional control, although skirmishing continued. Accounting tricks were as clever then as they are today, and their use to overstate earnings after excessive expansion led to a financial collapse of many western railroads in 1873.

Drew still held the Erie in the East, while Vanderbilt controlled the New York Central, and they faced as rivals the Pennsylvania and the Baltimore and Ohio railroads. J. P. Morgan worked for cooperation among railroads nationwide but encountered repeated difficulties, especially from the head of the Illinois Central Railroad, Edward H. Harriman. These early leaders played a sophisticated version of the present-day Monopoly board game. They were charged frequently with illegal acts, but they never went to jail.

---

[4] See Glaeser and Kohlhase (2004, p. 203).

Railroad Regulation

To avoid the seemingly debilitating effects of competition, in 1887 Congress created the **Interstate Commerce Commission (ICC)** (now the **Surface Transportation Board [STB]**) to regulate railroad power. The ICC was the first of our federal administrative agencies. These agencies are part legislative, part executive, and part judicial, because (1) they make rules that are almost like legislative statutes, particularly in form, (2) they decide disputes, and (3) they hold hearings and receive testimony that becomes the basis for rulings. These administrative agency rulings can be appealed through the federal judicial system. Whether the railroads actually favored the creation of this commission to avoid competition is still debated, because not all resisted it.

Railroads exercised monopoly control over some routes, and they routinely discriminated by charging different prices to different customers. Where it existed, competition revealed—and even contributed to—this disparity in rates. Competition might force modest prices on long hauls, which were often served by several railroads. The railroads followed different routes, however, and one railroad could have a monopoly in serving some, usually smaller, communities along its route. Users in these communities might pay very high short-haul rates, compared with rates for long-haul service. Because transportation was so important to farmers, who needed to move crops to markets, high railroad rates harmed the usually smaller communities that were served by only one railroad, putting them at an economic disadvantage in getting their products to markets relative to communities served by competing railroads.

Railroads were at the peak of their power in 1887, when the **Act to Regulate Commerce** created the ICC. The Act required the ICC to set rates that were "just and reasonable," and it outlawed "undue" discrimination among persons, companies, or communities. Discriminatory railroad pricing that caused some users to pay higher prices than others had offended the users of railroad services, and even the general public, and led to the Act to Regulate Commerce. The **Elkins Act** of 1903 strengthened the ICC mandate by specifically barring discrimination among different shippers, again so some would not have advantage over others. The **Hepburn Act** of 1906 enabled the ICC to set maximum rail rates. Then, in 1910, the **Mann-Elkins Act** specifically prevented long-haul versus short-haul railroad rate discrimination.

Finally, the **Esch-Cummins Transportation Act** of 1920 allowed the ICC to set minimum rates, which, along with the Hepburn Act allowing maximum rates, meant the ICC could control railroad prices. There were other restraints on competition in the Act, such as cooperative use of railroad terminals, but entry control and pricing were most important. High fixed costs in operating railroads encouraged a rough form of Ramsey pricing, predicated on monopoly regulatory power, which was discriminatory and called **"value-of-service" pricing**. The value of service was deemed to be high when shippers were willing to pay more for it, essentially when the demand for transportation was less elastic. Demand elasticity varied by commodity shipped, and it was usually low when the cost of transportation made up a small fraction of the commodity's final price so transportation cost was less important to the shipper. Under value-of-service pricing, the ICC set different rates for different commodities.

Because transportation is not ordinarily a source of pleasure, but rather is instrumental to some other benefit, the demand for it is called a **derived demand**. Demand is derived because transportation is not demanded for its own sake. Transportation moves a person from A to B or makes some good more useful by moving it to where it is wanted. For a valuable good, such as a wristwatch, transportation cost is a tiny portion of the final product price, so a shipper is not very sensitive to it. That is, the shipper's demand is not very elastic. Under value-of-service pricing, high prices were set on goods, such as watches, that had less elastic demands, so they could contribute more to the railroad's considerable fixed costs. This pricing, however, led to very high rates for some goods, which made them easy targets for any competitive alternative. Because railroads depended on value-of-service price discrimination, they suffered in the 1920s at the hands of the growing trucking industry, which was not regulated and could therefore easily beat the discriminating railroads' high prices. When it came in 1935, truck regulation helped the railroads, although trucks continued to attract some lighter and more valuable freight business while automobiles stole away passenger travel. The twentieth century was a time of railroad decline.

Railroad Deregulation and Its Effects

In the 1970s, many railroads were in serious financial difficulty, largely because ICC regulation prevented railroads from abandoning unprofitable routes. By then air travel and automobiles had drawn passengers from railroads, and railroad passenger service was notoriously unprofitable. In 1970, Congress passed the **Rail Passenger Service Act**, which created **Amtrak**, a partly private and partly public enterprise that now runs national passenger rail service. Amtrak absorbed facilities from railroads that were allowed to give up passenger service, and in exchange the railroads received common stock in the new enterprise.

BOX 16.2 Access to Railroad Tracks

Access has long been an issue in the railroad industry because, with their rail networks interconnected, railroads use each others' tracks to complete their routes. As early as 1912, railroad tracks and bridges were regarded as essential facilities, and railroads were required to share them with their competitors. The efficient component pricing rule (ECPR) for access was applied to railroad tracks early in the 1980s, and it continues to play a role in Surface Transportation Board hearings. As access to tracks became more routine after deregulation, some small new railroad companies negotiated rights to use the tracks of larger railroads, to gain network externality benefits and to offer competitive services. Railroads more equal in size have also negotiated flexible working arrangements for the use of each others' tracks.

See *United States v. Terminal Railroad Association of St. Louis*, 224 U.S. 383 (1912) and 236 U.S. 194 (1915).

With respect to freight traffic, in 1976 the **Railroad Revitalization and Reform Act** allowed railroads to abandon unprofitable routes. It also authorized procedural changes to expedite mergers, granted greater pricing freedom as long as a railroad did not have market dominance, and even awarded government subsidies. The Act was not very effective in improving the plight of railroads, however, so to strengthen the industry further Congress passed the **Staggers Rail Act** in 1980. The Staggers Act made route abandonments even easier, and it added more subsidies. It also permitted greater pricing flexibility, requiring merely that rates be no more than 60 percent above variable costs. The Staggers Act allowed railroads to abandon 30,000 miles of track, or about one-third of what had existed. Average rates actually went down after the Staggers Act was passed, yet the financial performance of railroads improved greatly. Today most rates are unregulated, although some commodities remain subject to maximum-rate guidelines.

Thus, after decades of railroad regulation had suffocated the industry, the iron horse was allowed to roam free once again in the 1970s and 1980s. Before all that happened, however, to preserve value-of-service pricing for railroads, government also regulated trucks and buses.

16.2 TRUCK TRANSPORTATION

Trucks account for roughly three-fourths of the expenditures on freight transportation in the United States today, although trucking involves only about one-fourth of total ton-miles (a ton-mile is one ton moved one mile). Trucks are more maneuverable than railroad trains, and they use a highway network that has a more extensive reach than the rail system. Trucks developed along with buses and automobiles after highways were expanded early in the twentieth century, and their greater flexibility made them effective competitors of the railroad. Trucks, however, have the disadvantage of not being able to carry the great weights that rail cars and railway tracks can bear.

Trucking Regulation

Trucking has been regulated in the United States since 1935, when the **Motor Carrier Act** of 1935 amended the **Interstate Commerce Act** of 1887 to extend ICC authority beyond railroads to trucks.[5] Railroads argued for such regulation, because trucking competition was harmful to them and had been since the 1920s. Because they were based on monopolistic value-of-service principles, the structure of railroad rates exposed them to competition. Unregulated trucks eagerly undercut the high value-of-service railroad rates for commodities such as watches. Losing this business to trucks left the railroads with less profitable items, such as coal, which is heavy and hard to handle, and whose shippers are very sensitive to price.

---

[5] For a description of the regulated trucking industry, see Strack (1987).

Trucking firms were quite willing to accept regulation, perhaps to avoid competition among themselves and to erect barriers to entry by others. Regulation of trucking certainly restricted entry. It also made rate structures similar to those used by railroads, differing by commodities according to value-of-service principles, which allowed comfortable profits. Trucking companies welcomed these essentially beneficial restrictions and controls in exchange for accepting a **common carrier** obligation, which required the trucking companies to supply service on announced terms to any customer who demanded it. The common carrier obligation effectively ruled out partial entry to the trucking market, because it prevented a trucking firm from refusing business to serve only part of the market. Entry meant receiving **operating authority**, a regulatory document that specified the services a carrier was permitted to offer. Operating authority was granted automatically to those carriers that already existed when regulation began.

A potential new entrant could not always acquire operating authority. Under the Motor Carrier Act, a firm had to be "fit, willing and able" to provide service in accord with the "public convenience and necessity." This language was eventually interpreted to allow entry only if existing firms could not provide the proposed service or would not be harmed by its introduction. Assurance on these points was very difficult to show in advance, so the ICC seldom approved an application if existing carriers objected. When entry was approved, it was usually to deliver only certain commodities in a limited region and possibly only along specific routes. Such patterns arose in part because the ICC received more applications than it could handle, so it asked parties to negotiate directly to work out solutions. To win approval in these circumstances, applicants accepted restrictions that would persuade existing carriers to tolerate them. As a result, entry occurred only where it caused little harm to incumbent firms.

The ICC also categorized regulated interstate carriers in ways that limited the services they could offer. First, they were either *common carriers*, carrying general freight, or *contract carriers*, carrying commodities that required specialized knowledge and techniques, such as automobiles. Common carriers handled some specialized freight, but their main cargo was general freight. Trucking companies carried freight either in *full truckload* quantities (weighing more than 5 tons) or in *less-than-truckload* quantities (less than 5 tons), with full truckload quantities receiving lower rates. Private "not-for-hire" trucks, such as those operated by a company for its own use, were not subject to ICC regulation. They also were not allowed to provide services to others. Farmers carrying unprocessed agricultural commodities were also exempted from regulation.

Rate Setting

In addition to deciding who might be in the trucking business, the ICC set "reasonable" trucking rates. The carriers themselves had a substantial influence on the rates, however, through **rate bureaus**, which the railroad and bus industries also used. Rate bureaus were groups of carriers that followed procedures approved by the ICC and were thus exempt from antitrust laws. Their use actually began before regulation came to trucking. They were not made fully legitimate until 1948, with passage of the **Reed-Bulwinkle Act**, which allowed agreements among carriers that specified their rate-making practices and procedures.

Ten large rate bureaus, each covering a part of the country, set rates for most of the general trucking freight traffic. They typically filed new rates twice a year. Rate bureaus held public meetings, where shippers could express views, to discuss and vote on rate changes. The meetings resulted in rates agreeable to the carriers, however, and the ICC would ultimately enforce those rates. Rates charged by a carrier had to conform to rates that were on file with the ICC. If viewed as a form of information exchange, or a list of announced sellers' rates, the rate bureau would be illegal under antitrust law because its rates were to be *effective in the future*. Rate bureaus sent rates to the ICC for approval, and, once approved, they also published the rates.

ICC regulation of trucks was widely criticized. Because the trucking industry lacked economies of scale, competition could function perfectly well, and its prevention only protected the railroads. Other problems existed because of the way trucking regulation worked. Operating authority, that is the right to operate trucks, was sometimes granted for traffic in only one direction between two cities, for example, which meant that a carrier could not fill a truck for its return home after making a delivery. The consequent empty one-way truck trips, called "empty back hauls," were inefficient.

Another complaint came from the purchase and sale of operating authority at sizeable values. Free entry would have eliminated these positive values for operating rights, and their existence indicated that ICC barriers to entry and high regulated prices were creating rents for those who held operating authority. Note how the existence of such positive values for operating authority also made deregulation difficult. Deregulation would bring entry, which would wipe out the values of operating rights. Those holding the operating rights had often purchased them for substantial amounts and would quite reasonably object to the losses that deregulation would force them to absorb.

Trucking Deregulation and Its Effects

On the heels of the Staggers Act for railroads, the **Motor Carrier Act** of 1980 brought reform to trucking regulation. Changes were already occurring under ICC auspices, but the legislation spelled out new policies. The Act facilitated entry and allowed individual carriers to set their own rates within certain ranges instead of relying on rate bureaus. Today, pricing, entry, and exit are fully deregulated at both state and federal levels, and competition effectively regulates the industry.[6] Empty back hauls, which caused trucks to return empty, are avoided. Antitrust immunity was withdrawn in phases from rate bureaus until they ceased to function.

The combination of ICC policy actions plus the 1980 Act brought a sharp increase in rate proposals from individual firms rather than from rate bureaus, as new companies entered the industry. The reforms lowered profits for trucking companies and almost eliminated the market value of operating authority, an indication that competitive

---

[6] See Winston (1998).

forces were affecting the industry. Trucks traveled empty for fewer miles, and this and other gains in flexibility reduced costs. For less-than-truck-load shipments, operating costs per vehicle mile are estimated to be 35 percent lower because of deregulation, and rates have fallen by the same percentage.[7] For truckload shipments, cost savings and rate reductions are estimated to be even greater, up to 75 percent, and transit times are also significantly better since deregulation.[8] Thus, deregulation of trucking, made possible by the deregulation of railroads, appears to be largely a success. We turn now to consider buses, which also use highways and have a history of regulation.

16.3 | BUS TRAVEL AND URBAN TRANSPORTATION

Buses carry passengers within cities, especially in large urban areas, and between cities. Federal policies have tended to shift transit service within cities into local government hands, but intercity bus travel remains private. The intercity bus industry serves about 15,000 cities, while airlines serve only about 600 and Amtrak serves about 500. Buses tend to serve smaller communities, but they carry more than half of all intercity passengers. We first consider this intercity bus travel and then devote the remainder of the Section to urban transit.

Intercity Buses

Passengers commonly travel between cities, especially small cities, by bus. Such intercity bus travel has been regulated at the federal level since passage of the Motor Carrier Act of 1935. The institution of the rate bureau operated to set rates in the bus industry as it had in trucking, but the bus industry had only one rate bureau, the National Bus Traffic Association. The rate bureau was immune from antitrust prosecution, but the ICC could overturn rates it deemed harmful to passengers or competitors. Still, the rate bureau essentially had the status and motives of a cartel. As observed in the trucking industry, positive values for operating rights in the bus industry suggested the effects of a cartel. It was almost 40 years before the ICC disallowed a rate bureau rate increase, which raised the question whether regulation of the industry was serving the public interest.

The Motor Carrier Act of 1935 preserved state authority to regulate entry, exit, and fares on routes within states. All states availed themselves of some form of this authority. Many states had regulated their bus transportation industries before 1935, and to save themselves that effort they tended to support federal regulation. Some states, however, saw drawbacks in bus regulation and thought competition would better regulate the industry. For example, Florida deregulated intrastate bus service in 1979, and Arizona, Indiana, Michigan and Wisconsin followed soon after.

---

[7] See Corsi (1996a).
[8] See Corsi (1996b).

The **Bus Regulatory Reform Act** of 1982 deregulated intercity bus travel at the federal level, soon after trucking deregulation. The Act made entry easier on interstate routes and reduced opportunities for fare collusion, much as similar steps had done for trucks. In addition, the ICC was allowed to preempt state regulatory agencies in intrastate cases, which gave greater scope to the new and more competitive ways of operating. The result is an industry that is free to respond to competitive forces.

It appears now that intercity buses should not have been regulated in 1935.[9] Economies of scale probably never existed in the bus industry. Regulation simply aided existing bus firms by protecting them from entry by others and by essentially allowing collusive price setting through the National Bus Traffic Association. Unionization also seems to have flourished in the industry after regulation began, because wages grew more rapidly in the bus industry than in other industries. With deregulation, the substantial market value of operating authority evaporated for buses, as it had for trucks, indicating again that government regulation had created benefits for firms in the industry and that deregulation had taken them away.

Early Urban Transit

The story of bus transportation within urban areas is quite different from that of trucks and intercity buses. Although the result was not intended, federal policy led to government operation of urban buses.[10] The technology of urban transit passed in the nineteenth century from horse drawn coaches to horse drawn rail cars to electricity powered street cars, and the street cars lasted into the twentieth century. Operators were licensed, mainly to control their behavior, and routes and schedules were usually published and followed.

During the electric streetcar era, the regulation of urban transit changed. The policy of simply awarding franchises to service suppliers developed into oversight by state or local public utility commissions. States created regulatory commissions in the aftermath of the 1877 *Munn vs Illinois* Supreme Court decision, which gave governments the power to regulate prices where the public interest was involved. States imposed service standards on streetcar companies and occasionally levied fees for licenses. Rates were more carefully regulated. Streetcars were an important means of urban transportation until automobiles and buses challenged them, starting in the 1930s.

Urban Transit with Automobiles and Buses

In 1914, passenger automobiles offered transportation service in Los Angeles, charging only 5 cents for a ride.[11] Called jitneys, these vehicles were soon accepting passengers in all major cities, typically along streetcar routes just before the scheduled

---

[9] See Johnson (1984).

[10] See Shipe (1992).

[11] See Eckert and Hilton (1972).

BOX 16.3 How Urban Ancestors Traveled

Fixed-route urban transportation systems date from 1827, when Abraham Brower offered service by four-wheel, horse-drawn, twelve-passenger coaches along Broadway in New York City. Called omnibuses, such vehicles provided service in many American cities and reached a popularity peak in the mid-nineteenth century. A railway opened on Fourth Avenue in New York in 1832, again powered by horses. The smoother ride and greater efficiency of rails caused such systems to grow, although at first more slowly than omnibuses. By the 1880s, however, they were the most common form of urban transportation. Regulation to this point was modest, usually taking the form of franchise awards through licensing, mainly to avoid disreputable operators.

In 1888, Frank Sprague built the first successful electric streetcar system, in Richmond, Virginia. The greater size, speed, and economy made possible by electric power spurred expansion of urban transit service, and in 1902 the national ridership reached 5 billion passenger rides. Economies of scale arose for the first time when electric streetcars were introduced, because such streetcars were major users of electric power that was produced under economies of scale. There was a tendency, then, toward consolidation into one transit company in a city, in an organization that also operated one power plant. Over-expansion weakened some companies and that became another reason for consolidation.

See Brian J. Cudahy, *Cash, Tokens and Transfers: A History of Urban Mass Transit in North America*, New York: Fordham University Press, 1990; John A. Miller, *Fares, Please!: From Horsecars to Streamliners*, New York: D. Appleton-Century, 1941; E. P. Schmidt, *Industrial Relations in Urban Transportation*, Minneapolis, MN: University of Minnesota Press, 1937; Richard T. Shipe, "Cost and Productivity in the U.S. Urban Bus Transit Sector, 1978–1989," Ph.D. Dissertation, University of Virginia, 1992.

arrival of the streetcars. Streetcars also charged 5 cents, but they traveled longer routes. While the uniform 5-cent price was low for long-distance travelers, that price was high for riders traveling short distances. Just as trucks sought to attract railroad shippers who were paying high value-of-service prices, these short-distance streetcar passengers were the target of the jitneys. Streetcar operators protested, claiming that jitneys were attracting the most profitable passengers without paying licenses or other fees, or complying with service regulations. The streetcar operators were even more successful in their complaints than the railroads had been against trucking. Instead of regulating the jitneys, Los Angeles banned them. By 1920 they were gone from almost every city in which they had operated.

The private automobile persisted as an alternative form of transportation, however, and it reduced streetcar ridership. Then, after World War I, motor buses became serious competitors to streetcars. Bus companies sprang up that were large enough to escape the devastating effects that government regulation had visited on the jitneys. Buses operated along regular streetcar routes again, and the streetcars sought to prevent this competition. Regulators responded by limiting entry of motor buses to these routes through terms in the operating certificates. Operating certificates were usually awarded to buses only in areas where streetcars did not operate, and even in those areas the number of competitors tended to be strictly limited. Streetcar operators then actively bought bus companies, which tended to be small, and consolidated them into community bus-and-streetcar monopolies.

Many smaller urban areas converted entirely to buses. Streetcar ridership had declined during the depression, when companies had trouble covering their sizeable fixed costs. Buses offered lower maintenance cost and lower capital cost, important advantages in hard economic times. In 1935 the diesel engine began to power buses with better reliability, fuel efficiency, and service life than gasoline engines. Motor-buses outnumbered streetcars before World War II and dominated urban mass transit after the war. Economist Ted Keeler (1971) showed that commuter railroads might have maintained services, and competitive costs, if they had invested more wisely and been able to change work rules, but they lost out to automobiles and buses for short trips and to airplanes for long trips.

Although transit ridership rose profoundly during World War II, it declined just as sharply afterwards. From an all time high of 23.3 billion yearly national passenger trips in 1946, ridership fell to 17.2 billion trips in 1950 and only 9.4 billion trips in 1960. Riders returned to the automobile as soon as wartime constraints were lifted while mass transit companies faced higher costs from wage increases plus a need to replace war-worn equipment. In addition, an increased peaking of transit service demands at morning and evening hours raised costs. This peaking could be traced in part to the **Fair Labor Standards Act** of 1938, which brought widespread use of the five-day work week and the eight-hour work day. Many potential riders moved to the suburbs, where automobiles were advantageous. Having purchased automobiles, owners had to pay only marginal cost to drive them back and forth to work.[12]

Suburbia

Suburban living was more affordable after the *amortized mortgage* came into use and helped to finance home ownership. Before the amortized mortgage, a family financing the purchase of a home would have their remaining loan principle come due after only five or seven years. They would then have to find another lender for the large remaining balance, called a "balloon balance," and in hard times that could be difficult. A great financial innovation of the 1930s, the **amortized mortgage** allowed equal payments to be spread over 20 years or more, so home owners no longer faced repeated negotiations for new mortgages every few years. Mortgage lending also expanded greatly after World War II because of the GI Bill, federal legislation that provided mortgage guarantees to returning war veterans.

Suburban living thus became possible for those who were reasonably well off and who had the travel flexibility made possible by automobile ownership. Suburbanites were aided also when Congress, in the Federal Highway Act of 1944, gave planning authority for urban highway funding to state rather than city officials. State planners took an area-wide perspective, and they focused on access to cities from surrounding areas instead of transportation within cities. Those who were poorer, or

---

[12] See Sherman (1967).

for reasons of age or health unable to drive, tended to remain in cities and depend on mass-transit systems, which were not aided by this Federal Highway Act.

Suburban living depended on the automobile, which, by taking passengers from urban transit and aggravating highway congestion, was antithetical to urban transit development. So the post–World War II growth of suburbia brought still harder times for urban transit. In many cities, transit ridership declined while highway congestion grew worse. Because transit service was important to the urban poor, city and state governments tried to keep transit rates low, but this policy also contributed to the financial problems of the transit companies. Congress passed the Transportation Act of 1958 to allow railroads to discontinue unprofitable commuter rail services. New York, New Jersey, and the city of Philadelphia responded with subsidies to keep commuter rail services going. Then, with the **Housing Act** of 1961 and the **Federal-Aid Highway Act** of 1962, came the promise of aid for urban mass transit. The first of these Acts offered demonstration projects to test new transit ideas, required mass-transit planning, and offered low interest loans to transit firms. The second Act required urban areas with populations above 50,000 to consider mass transit as an alternative to highways.

Federal Funding for Urban Transit

Really significant change in urban transit came with the **Urban Mass Transit Act of 1964**. State and local governments could apply for federal funds under this legislation, to cover up to two-thirds of the capital costs of mass transit projects. This money could buy buses, railways, and other assets. State and local governments were required to fund the share in these projects that the federal government did not fund, but local governments could not acquire private firms with these funds unless such a step could be shown to be essential to improving mass transit. Nor could they subsidize new private or public transit that would compete with, or otherwise cause injury to, existing private firms. Existing labor contracts and collective bargaining rights also had to be protected. Current employees were not to have their positions worsened because of federal funding, and employees of acquired mass-transit systems also were to be assured continued employment. Congress began the capital grant program with $375 million for 1965 to 1967 and added another $450 million for 1968 to 1970.

Federal capital funds allowed localities to replace old mass-transit vehicles and build new facilities. Bus activities benefitted first, but rail operations also received support after larger scale funding came in 1970 through the **Urban Mass Transit Act of 1970**, which committed the federal government to $10 billion in capital spending from 1971 to 1982 and added $3 billion more in the **Federal Highway Act** of 1973. Administration of such funds moved from the Department of Transportation in 1968, when the **Urban Mass Transit Administration (UMTA)** was created. UMTA was renamed the **Federal Transit Administration (FTA)** in 1991, and it now manages all federal transit programs.

This large infusion of federal funds actually had the effect of converting the mass transit industry from private to public ownership. Over 90 percent of national transit ridership was on public systems by 1973.[13] These conversions from private to public frequently occurred in emergencies, when a private firm was failing. Resulting consolidations often brought together urban and suburban services into regional transit authorities. In 1974, the federal government provided transit operating subsidies. About one-third of the subsidy funds were allocated by a formula involving population and its density. Reliance on a formula for subsidy awards was attractive because it reduced the possibility for political influence. The federal **Surface Transportation Act** of 1978 authorized $5.1 billion for operating support from 1979 to 1982, and $8.6 billion for capital grants. By 1981 this great increase in spending had arrested the decline in transit ridership. States also initiated subsidy programs that helped increase mass transit ridership.

In the 1980s, roughly two-thirds of subsidy funds came to be allocated by formula. A number of other changes occurred, but the federal role in urban transportation continued to be great. The **Intermodal Surface Transportation Act** of 1991 also substantially increased funding levels for federal transit programs. This Act allowed highway funds to be transferred by state and local governments to mass-transit capital projects, and it called for larger portions of each state's federal highway funds to go to urban areas.

Figure 16.1 shows urban transit ridership from 1870 to 2000. Stabilization of total ridership since 1970 is almost certainly due to substantial federal subsidies, which are shown in Figure 16.2. These subsidies are extremely important because fare revenue covers less than half of the total cost of transit operations.

Whether these great public subsidies solved transportation problems remains a question, in part because other steps have changed transportation needs. Observers have called attention to **edge cities**, for example, which are developments on the edges of cities that combine office parks with major retailing and housing.[14] By moving some urban activities to the edges of cities, where they depend on automobile travel, these developments reduce the need to travel to city centers and sometimes even make life difficult for the old central cities. Another phenomenon is the **edgeless city**, a sprawling form of office space outside the downtown that depends totally on the automobile.[15] These office buildings usually are not on transit lines, do not include mixed uses such as retailing and housing, and are not pedestrian friendly. Edge cities and edgeless cities are modern responses to the rise of suburbia and to traffic congestion in central cities.

The urban transit industry has undergone a gradual transition, from private to governmental ownership and operation. Declining demand for urban transit, a service that was deemed important to urban areas, brought federal funding to support it, and that funding ultimately went to governmental operators of urban transit. Federal subsidies to both capital and operating expenses kept fares low enough to retain riders. Costs of operating urban buses grew steadily, however, and in the 1990s questions were raised about their operating efficiency. The congested urban streets where

---

[13] See Shipe (1992).
[14] See Garreau (1991).
[15] See Lang (2003).

Figure 16.1 *U.S. Urban Mass Transit Ridership (Millions)*

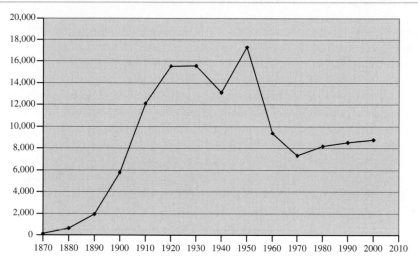

Source: B. J. Cudahy, *Cash, Tokens and Transfers: A History of Urban Mass Transit in North America*, New York: Fordham University Press, 1990; R. T. Shipe, "Cost and Productivity in the U.S. Urban Bus Transit Sector, 1978–1989," Ph.D. Dissertation, University of Virginia, 1992; and Federal Transit Administration National Transit Database at www.ntdprogram.com.

Figure 16.2 *U.S. Federal Transit Subsidy Appropriations (Millions $)*

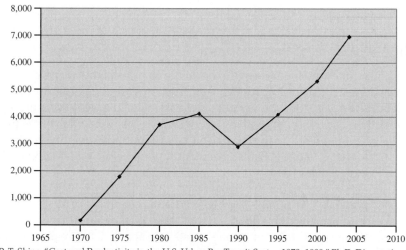

Source: R. T. Shipe, "Cost and Productivity in the U.S. Urban Bus Transit Sector, 1978–1989," Ph.D. Dissertation, University of Virginia, 1992; and Federal Transit Administration National Transit Database at www.ntdprogram.com.

buses—the most important mode of urban transit—operate contribute to the transit problem, and some activities are relocating out of central cities. These traffic congestion problems might be relieved, and the location of activities might be more soundly coordinated by the now feasible pricing of urban road use.

16.4 | PRICING THE ROAD NETWORK

All motor vehicles share the nation's highway network. Different parts of the network are broadly compatible in that highways have fairly standard widths and use the same traffic signals and consistent rules, such as driving on the right, to reduce the danger of accidents. The vehicles themselves are not uniform, and this affects the safety of highway travel. Highways ordinarily have been constructed with public funds, financed by taxes, and essentially given away free to drivers, with the consequence that highways become congested. As in other networks, excessive traffic congestion can develop when too many vehicles attempt to use a free highway network, and this congestion lowers speed and safety. Expanding a highway may not solve the problem of congestion, either, because vehicles still do not face the full social cost of their trips. The main way to ease this important problem is to price the use of scarce highway space, especially in crowded cities.

Without paying a price for highway use, private cars, buses, or trucks pay average private trip costs but do not bear the full marginal social costs of their road use. Substitute modes of travel, such as buses or commuter rail, have been subsidized, especially in urban areas, because they use less road space than automobiles and if they can attract commuters away from using cars, the subsidies can reduce congestion.[16] Allowing a price to be charged for the use of highways, however, is a more direct solution than offering subsidies to alternative modes of transportation, and by reducing congestion a price can improve highway efficiency.

The Highway Congestion Problem

Figure 16.3 illustrates the inefficiency that a failure to price highway use causes.[17] The vertical axis represents the full cost of an auto trip between two points, including fuel, oil, tire wear, and so on, plus the driver's (and passengers') time. In this example, we assume that time has the same value for everyone. On the horizontal axis is the number of vehicles attempting the trip in a given hour. Up to the quantity q_1, there is no congestion, and the AC curve is flat. The demand for trips, DD, is a function of the cost per trip. Given the cost and demand portrayed in Figure 16.3, consumers will demand more than q_1 trips. Curve AC shows the average cost of the trip, which is the total cost of all drivers divided by the number of drivers. The marginal cost of a trip, represented as MC, takes into account the added costs all drivers experience as a result of the marginal trip. Because MC takes everyone's costs into account, it is really the marginal *social* cost of a trip.

---

[16] For this argument, see Sherman (1971c, 1972).

[17] This is a classic problem that was first raised by A. C. Pigou (1920). For an early analysis, see Knight (1924). For a more modern analysis, see Mills (1981). For a history of the idea of road pricing and a current assessment of its standing among economists, see Lindsey (2006).

Figure 16.3 *Analysis of Road Congestion*

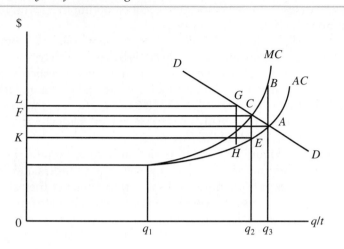

A problem arises because each individual decides whether to make an auto trip using the *average* cost rather than the *marginal* cost of the trip that is experienced by the community of drivers. An additional vehicle can join the traffic stream on the highway at any time, and thereafter it shares in the average costs and delays. Yet the marginal vehicle causes delays to all the other vehicles that the driver of the marginal vehicle *does not take into account* when joining the traffic stream. Marginal cost includes these marginal delays that an added vehicle imposes on others, while average cost does not. Because we decide to travel on the highway based on average cost, equilibrium occurs at point *A*, where demand meets average cost. There, the marginal benefit to consumers equals the private cost to them as individuals, which is the average cost for the trip. The efficient solution would occur at point *C*, where marginal benefit equals the marginal cost to society, including the cost of delays that each vehicle causes others.

Because the private cost to the consumer at point *A* is below the marginal cost to society, we have a loss in efficiency from too much consumption of road use. The triangular area *ABC* represents that loss, because every trip beyond the ideal quantity q_2 has a marginal cost to society that exceeds its marginal benefit (which the demand curve represents). Thus, the area *ABC* captures the amount by which the marginal costs exceed the marginal benefits. Resources devoted to the last $q_3 - q_2$ trips could be better used in other ways.

The optimal road use fee, or tax, should make private costs equal social costs at the ideal level of trips, q_2. Thus *CE* represents the ideal tax, because that amount, when added to average cost, presents to the decision maker a cost per trip just equal to marginal social cost. The difference between private cost, represented in curve *AC*, and social cost, represented in curve *MC*, is not constant; it depends on how many trips are being made. This makes it difficult to estimate the optimal level of tax without knowing also what output would be best. If we chose a tax greater than *CE*, such as *GH*, then consumers make too little use of the road, and some loss in consumers' surplus results. An aproximate solution may still be an improvement, however, over the one with no tax at *A* and with trips of q_3.

The area *FCEK* in Figure 16.3 represents the fees collected from the tax *CE*. The proceeds from these fees should ideally be distributed to all the people who were using the road at the no-tax level of q_3. Opposition to remedies such as this road-use tax can be strong, probably because individuals see the higher charge for road use as a new tax and cannot visualize receiving any of it as a benefit. If such proceeds could be paid, however, all parties potentially could gain under this tax-subsidy remedy for road congestion because it would improve road travel.

The example in Figure 16.3 is incomplete in two important respects. First, it assumes all vehicles are carrying the same number of passengers and all require the same road space. Buses require more road space than cars, but they also carry many more passengers so they cause less congestion per passenger mile traveled. To reduce congestion per passenger mile in the absence of road pricing, the price of mass transit might be subsidized, to make it lower relative to the inefficiently low private cost of automobile travel.[18] Increasing commuters per car from the current average of about 1.5 in the United States can also lower traffic congestion by reducing the number of cars on the road.

Congestion can be lowered if more passengers can be induced to travel in one car. That is the goal of **high occupancy vehicle (HOV)** lanes, which are commonly provided on commuter highways into large cities.[19] Smaller communities may use other means, such as traffic circles, to slow traffic and make it move more smoothly. But at rush hours in larger cities, HOV lanes are reserved exclusively for vehicles carrying at least two (HOV-2) or sometimes at least three (HOV-3), persons. Faster travel is possible in these HOV lanes, so commuters form car pools to take advantage of them. Many cities have informally come to establish points where individuals can wait to be picked up by single drivers who seek passengers so they can be eligible to travel in the HOV lanes. HOV lanes also have critics, who raise two main objections: (1) they are underused, and (2) they serve richer commuters (those who make this complaint call them "Lexus lanes"), but they remain an important tool for easing commuters' highway congestion.

The second shortcoming of the example in Figure 16.3 is that it assumes all travelers have the same value of time and, thus, the same dislike for congestion. Suppose values of time differ among travelers. At the one-price solution in Figure 16.3, all are forced to experience the same level of congestion even though they do not place the same value on any time savings from reduced congestion. Because those with the lowest time value are willing to tolerate a higher level of congestion, their actions may cause it to occur. Yet others would pay higher sums to avoid the congestion. Through bargaining, a small number of people who object most to congestion might pay others to stay off the road, but they have no opportunity to do so.

---

[18] See Sherman (1971c, 1972).

[19] See Peter T. Kilborn, "Slow Down, You Move Too Fast: Bulbs, Knobs, and Circles," *New York Times*, December 22, 2002, Section 1, p. 20.

It is difficult to design a general system to achieve a refined solution that can charge different fees to different vehicles for differing degrees of congestion. It would be ideal to have many separate highways, so each vehicle driver could choose a most preferred price and congestion combination. A rough approximation to that might be pursued through separate lanes for different drivers. Such a system is called "value pricing," and it is applied in what are called **high occupancy toll (HOT)** lanes, which are HOV lanes that allow access—for a fee—to vehicles with fewer than the required number of HOV-lane passengers in them.

Pricing road use can reduce road congestion, and modern technologies make it feasible. If distribution of proceeds from any road-use fee can be arranged in an equitable way, the tax or subsidy devices may even win endorsement by citizens. Without new technologies, crude rules may still be imposed, such as rules that prevent cars without special licenses from using city streets at certain times. Such rules allow less precise, and less efficient, adjustments than prices but can still offer improvement over the practice of giving highway use away free and inducing excessive congestion as a result. Higher fuel taxes may also be in order to help control air-pollution externalities from motor vehicles and to stimulate the development of more efficient motor vehicles.[20]

Road Pricing in Practice

More than 45 years ago, Sir Alan Walters estimated the magnitude of a tax that would restore efficient commuter road use in urban areas of the United States to be more than 2 cents per mile.[21] Adjusting for consumer price changes since then, a comparable figure today would be about 20 cents per mile, and if this charge was collected as a tax on gasoline today it would be more than $2.50 per gallon. Economists Ted Keeler and Kenneth Small (1977) estimated optimal peak-load road prices for rural, suburban, and urban roads. In today's dollars, their estimates would be about 7 to 25 cents per mile in rural areas, 7 to 32 cents per mile in suburban areas, and 21 cents to $1.25 per mile in urban areas. Thus, the fee that will reduce highway congestion to more efficient levels may be substantial;[22] but congestion imposes serious costs, too. Highway commuters in the United States spend the equivalent of 50 work days a year sitting in traffic, equivalent to about 20 percent of working time.[23]

Modern technology supports a market-like remedy for the external effect of highway congestion, although it requires that new property rights be defined and enforced. If persons cannot be charged for using a particular road when it is congested, then no property right to use the road can be enforced. Several means have been developed to monitor usage and to collect fees. An electronic device in each

---

[20] See "Gentlemen, Start Your Engines," *The Economist*, January 19, 2006.

[21] See Walters (1961).

[22] See Wayne Arnold, "Relief for Rush Hour: Pay as You Go," *New York Times*, August 9, 2001, p. D6.

[23] The Texas Transportation Institute has estimated the yearly cost of congestion in 68 urban areas to be $72 billion. Its congestion facts can be found at http://mobility.tamu.edu/ums/.

vehicle, which could respond to signals along the road, was proposed for this purpose in England as early as 1964. The device would record time on a road, much as an electricity meter records electricity consumption in a house.[24]

Many German and Scandinavian cities have banned motor vehicles from some urban areas, so space can be used for shopping or other purposes, and Paris and some Italian cities have followed.[25] Aiming more at congestion control, Singapore, Australia, and Norway have charged a fee essentially for a special license to operate a vehicle in a city area during certain hours of the day. A slightly more subtle program began in February, 2003, in London, the largest city so far to attempt congestion pricing.[26] Congestion was so bad in London that motor vehicle speeds had averaged about 9 miles per hour during the daytime hours. The London plan allows drivers to register their license plate numbers in advance and make payments for use of roads in a restricted eight-square-mile zone in central London. If they enter the restricted zone between 7:00 AM and 6:30 PM, photographs of their plates confirm their entry and a charge (of about $8) is deducted automatically from their accounts. Drivers can also pay by wireless phone. There are 700 video cameras to record license plates, which are then checked against payment records. Such cameras have been used for some time in Britain and elsewhere in Europe to document speeding offenses. The fee is to be charged every day the vehicle is in the zone, although it can enter any number of times in one day after paying a single fee.

The London usage fee is part of a comprehensive transit plan that seeks a 40 percent increase in London bus and subway capacity over the next 10 years. The aim is to shift people from cars to mass transit, so people can move more efficiently in the city with fewer motor vehicles on the streets. After one month under the plan, bus ridership was up 14 percent, traffic was reduced 20 percent, and average vehicle speed roughly doubled to 20 miles per hour.[27] The congestion fee so successfully reduced traffic in central London that it may raise only about $150 million per year to expand the transit infrastructure, instead of $200 million as originally estimated.

Singapore has made the most sophisticated application of road pricing, beginning with a license for central city travel 25 years ago, together with a day-pass system, which substantially reduced congestion. Singapore now uses a smart card, mounted in a transponder on the motor vehicle dashboard, which contains a paid balance. As the driver uses city-center roads during rush hours, that balance is automatically reduced.[28] The reductions extracted from the smart cards vary by traffic and time of day from about 30 cents to $3.50 per hour. Rush hour traffic has been reduced by 13 percent since the smart-card system was introduced in 1997 to replace a day-pass system. The city carefully monitors the effect of the smart-card program, and

---

[24] See Ministry of Transport (1964) and Walters (1968).

[25] See "Ken Livingstone's Gamble," *The Economist*, February 15, 2003, pp. 51–53. Rome also is introducing a sophisticated device to charge for road use in its congested central city.

[26] See "London Levies Toll on Traffic," *Houston Chronicle*, July 22, 2001, p. 1C; and Sarah Lyall, "Driving in London is Pound Foolish," *New York Times*, February 17, 2003, p. A1.

[27] See "Congestion Charge," *The Economist*, March 22, 2003, p. 51.

[28] See Wayne Arnold, "Relief for Rush Hour: Pay as You Go," *New York Times*, August 9, 2001, p. D6; and "Ken Livingstone's Gamble," *The Economist*, February 15, 2003, pp. 51–53.

every three months charges are adjusted up or down in an effort to improve traffic flow. The electronic system collects more than $40 million per year, a sum that is considerably less than was being raised before by the cruder day-pass system that it replaced. Despite this revenue reduction, Singapore authorities prefer the electronic system because it fosters more efficient use of the roads.

In the United States, our fondness for the "open road" brings widespread resistance to highway tolls. Nevertheless, more than 20 states have passed laws to allow usage tolls on roads.[29] Cities have experimented with road pricing because the problem of road congestion is so serious, and sympathy for paying a fee is growing. Houston reserves commuter HOV lanes for cars that carry three or more persons, for example, but the city also allows cars containing two persons to ride in this HOV lane if the two-person cars pay a $2 fee. This makes the HOV lane a HOT lane, and it offers drivers a trade-off between price and congestion. The fee is deducted automatically from a prepaid card by an overhead sensor on the highway. In addition to raising money, the system is credited with increasing car pooling by almost 14 percent since it was introduced in 1999.

A broader example of pricing road use is found on a northern commuter road into San Diego. Access to this road is free to car pools and is available to others for a fee. As in downtown Singapore, transponders are used to collect different fees for travel on the road, ranging from 50 cents to $4, depending on time of day and traffic conditions. The variable fee helps to control volume so traffic moves at an efficient speed. Travel times have improved, and proceeds from the fees support a commuter bus service. Denver, Los Angeles, and Minneapolis have similar toll systems on commuter roads, and Baltimore, Orlando, Salt Lake City, San Francisco, and Washington are studying them.[30]

A 2003 policy proposal to use HOT lanes more broadly in eight highly congested urban areas has drawn serious attention in the United States.[31] The eight urban areas are Miami, Atlanta, Dallas/Fort Worth, Houston, Seattle, Washington, D.C., San Francisco Bay area, and Greater Los Angeles. The proposal (1) examines legislative needs at federal and state levels to make such road pricing generally feasible, (2) reports on existing applications of road pricing, and (3) estimates costs and effects of new applications. HOT lanes use value pricing, the name given to imposing a price only for a higher quality of service. Such pricing can allow traffic congestion differences by lane in response to highway travelers' differing values of time. Prices would be adjusted in an effort to keep vehicles moving smoothly. The HOT lanes would be combined with bus rapid transit, which usually devotes lanes to bus traffic, but here the buses would share the HOT lanes with cars.

---

[29] See Timophty Egan, "Paying on the Highway to Get Out of First Gear," *New York Times*, April 28, 2005, p. A1.

[30] See Larry Copeland, "Solo in Car-Pool Lane? That's Hot," *USA Today*, May 9, 2005, p. 3A.

[31] See Robert W. Poole, Jr. and C. Kenneth Orski, "HOT Networks: A New Plan for Congestion Relief and Better Transit," Reason Public Policy Institute Policy Study No. 305, February, 2003 (available at http://www.rppi.org). For newspaper accounts see John Tierney, "Planners Say Tolls Will Ease Jams in 8 Cities," *New York Times*, February 25, 2003, p. A12; and Lucas Wall, "To Ease Congestion, Solo Drives Pay More," *Houston Chronicle*, Febarury 25, 2003, p. 13A. See also Robert W. Poole, Jr. and C. Kenneth Orski, "Building a Case for HOT Lanes: A New Approach to Reducing Urban Highway Congestion," Reason Public Policy Institute Policy Study No. 257, April, 1999 (available at http://www.rppi.org/257.html).

BOX 16.4 Driving in Seattle

A federally financed test of congestion pricing was conducted in Seattle, where the travels of 400 participating families were followed in detail as they faced sophisticated congestion tolls. These participating families receive monthly stipends of between $50 and $200, amounts chosen so that if no change in travel is made the families will spend their stipends in tolls. For economic reasons, however, they alter their road usage in response to the tolls, and thereby save money. Instead of only 400 families, 100 percent participation would improve the experiment, because that greater scale would produce changes in observable congestion levels. This small sample does not accomplish that, but it is still possible to observe individual responses to congestion tolls, which allows prediction of effects of road pricing in Seattle and in other cities.

See D. Leonhardt, "Toll-less in Seattle for Ages, But Ready to Move Forward," *New York Times,* November 12, 2002, p. A14.

Traffic congestion is a crippling problem in many of the world's cities.[32] Bangkok may be the worst city for traffic congestion, with speeds of 2 miles per hour during peak hours. Even on 10-lane access highways to Los Angeles, the increase in motor vehicles is expected to double commuting time in the next 10 years. As technological advances allow, road pricing will almost certainly be used to curb such congestion. Cities are using other strategies to improve traffic flow, including coordinating traffic signals better and metering ramp access to freeways, as well as expanding public transportation. Pricing, however, is also playing a role. Using satellites, the global positioning system (GPS) can record vehicle travel precisely and the European Commission is considering a plan to install GPS systems in commercial trucks to charge them for road use. When later extended to automobiles, such a system could further reduce wasteful traffic congestion.

16.5 | AIR TRANSPORTATION

The U.S. government regulation that came with the advent of commercial air travel in the 1930s was not aimed solely at protecting consumers but was intended in part to promote the magic of flying as a new mode of travel.[33] Regulatory control over entry and pricing limited the number of carriers serving each air travel route and prevented their competition in the realm of prices. Airlines could then compete only in nonprice ways, such as more frequent flights, which meant more convenient flights plus the

---

[32] See "Ken Livingstone's Gamble," *The Economist*, February 15, 2003, pp. 51–53.

[33] The thrill continues today. "General aviation" aircraft, or aircraft not operated by the military or by scheduled airlines, account for 90 percent of all aircraft in the United States. See Fallows (2002).

possibility of last-minute reservations, which produced a high quality of airline service. But flying more planes to accommodate passengers at the last minute was costly for the airlines, because it could only be done by flying many seats empty. When flights came to be operated by intrastate carriers within California and Texas in the 1970s, the flights were not subject to federal regulation, and they had low costs and low prices. This evidence suggested that costs could be lower without federal regulation. The airline industry was the first to be deregulated, before railroads, trucks, or buses. After deregulation, competition improved efficiency and brought lower prices. The industry remains volatile, however, with high fixed costs and traffic that fluctuates with the state of the economy, and with an oligopolistic market structure.

Airlines were changed dramatically on September 11, 2001, when terrorists hijacked four airplanes and then crashed two into the World Trade Center Twin Towers in New York City, one into the Defense Department Pentagon Building in Washington, D.C., and the fourth into a field in Pennsylvania after passengers battled with the terrorists on board for control of the airplane. Airports were shut down for a week because of these terrible events, and after airports reopened, because of safety concerns, air travel did not return to previous levels for years. To soften the financial effects, the federal government provided subsidies to the airlines. Passenger security, which had been the responsibility of airlines, was taken over by the federal government, and an uneasy period for air travel began.

Regulation by the Civil Aeronautics Board

Airplanes were developed early enough to play a significant role in World War I. After that war aviator Charles Lindbergh captured the imagination of the world by flying from New York to Paris for the world's first transatlantic flight. Less than 10 years after that, airplanes carried mail, and in the 1930s, passenger service began. Federal regulation came with the **Civil Aeronautics Act** of 1938, which created the *Civil Aeronautics Authority*, a regulatory agency specifically charged with promoting its fledgling industry. The Authority was renamed the **Civil Aeronautics Board (CAB)** soon afterwards, and regulation by the agency lasted more than 40 years. For roughly half of its life the CAB regulated safety as well as economic aspects of the industry, but in 1958 Congress created the **Federal Aviation Administration (FAA)** to regulate airline safety. The FAA still exists. Its rigorous inspections prevent financially troubled airlines from stinting on safety and are, thus, even more important when unregulated airlines compete with each other.

CAB economic regulation had two main features. First, the CAB controlled entry to routes, so the number of airlines serving any route was limited.[34] Entry through the regulatory process was difficult because, in addition to being "fit, willing and able," a new airline had to serve the "public convenience and necessity." As in the case of earlier ICC deliberations, especially in trucking, existing firms claimed they could meet demand adequately so no new provider was necessary. Opposition from existing

---

[34] For early criticism of CAB policy toward entry, see Keyes (1951).

carriers, who also could claim harm as a result of entry, usually prevented approval of the application for any new operating right. Indeed, there was no new entry to major airline routes for 40 years.

Second, the CAB established fares for each route. It used the average cost for all of the airlines serving a route as a basis for setting the fare on that route. A measure of rate-of-return on assets for all airlines was also considered as an influence in setting these rates, starting in 1960. Compared with using a monopolist's own costs in setting its prices, this procedure offers better incentives when there is more than one airline on the route. Whereas a rise in the monopolist's costs might go right through to higher prices, a rise in one airline's costs would have only a partial effect on average costs for all airlines serving the route. As a result, each airline could benefit from lowering its costs relative to others. Because the CAB controlled fares, there could be no competition in price, so any competition had to take nonprice forms. Moreover, the CAB set fares high.[35]

Suppose the same fare is set for all airlines serving a particular route, and the fare allows handsome profits. Each airline wants to attract such profitable customers. An airline cannot lower its fare, so it can attract customers only by nonprice competition, which includes advertising and such perks as tasty inflight meals. Even more costly, nonprice competition includes scheduling more flights in an effort to meet customers' most convenient travel times. Flying more planes raises costs because fewer seats on each plane are filled by passengers. The **load factor**, which is the percentage of seats filled on a plane, averaged less than 60 percent in the 1960s. To combat this inefficient utilization of aircraft, the CAB decided to set fares not on actual load factors, but on estimated costs based on a 65 percent load factor. This policy prevented airfares from rising still further, but it did not yield efficient results. Competitive airline markets within Texas and California had much lower fares per mile and load factors closer to 80 percent.[36]

The CAB also set rates higher on long-distance flights (more than 400 miles) and lower on shorter flights.[37] Such pricing was politically popular. Remember the cross-subsidization seen in telephone price regulation, where long-distance rates were higher relative to costs than local service rates? For similar reasons, politicians sought air service to small communities in their states, and they wanted it provided at low fares. Long-distance flights, on the other hand, more often served business travelers who were not as sensitive to price level nor so numerous as to be influential with Congress. These political preferences of elected officials worked their way into CAB decisions and resulted in a degree of cross-subsidization from long-distance to short-distance flights. Just as high long-distance telephone rates tempted entrants using microwave telephone technology to offer long-distance service, high fares on long-distance flights tempted successful transatlantic charter airplane operators to enter lucrative long-distance airline markets.

---

[35] See Bailey (2002). Before World War II airfares were set to match first-class railroad fares.

[36] See Keeler (1972). Assuming the cost of flying a given airplane from one airport to another is not affected by the number of passengers, which is close to the truth, increasing the load factor from 65 percent to 80 percent reduces average cost per passenger by 65/80 = 81 percent, which is a very significant savings.

[37] See Douglas and Miller (1974).

Airline Deregulation and Its Effects

In the early 1970s, the complaints of prospective airlines that had tried for years to enter long-distance, cross-country markets became especially loud. The inherent bias of CAB regulation toward high fares and thus high-cost service, and the tendency to favor shorter distances with lower rates, made the long-distance markets with their high fares *extremely* attractive to potential entrants. Commuter airlines were also flourishing, despite low regulated, short-distance fares. Some small airlines could set low fares by using newly developed airplanes that weighed just under 12,000 pounds and were very efficient. They escaped CAB regulation, because planes that weighed less than 12,000 pounds were not subject to CAB regulation.

During the Carter administration, under the leadership of economist Alfred Kahn as Chairman, the CAB moved to allow more entry into airline markets and to foster greater pricing flexibility for airlines. Instead of accepting slight harm to an existing airline as a reason for denying new entry, for example, the CAB came to require evidence that entry would *bankrupt* an existing airline. It permitted a band of price cutting, at first up to 5 percent below regulated fares. Congress also took an interest in airline-regulation reform, when Senator Edward Kennedy held hearings on the subject in 1975.

These CAB policy changes seemed to improve airline profits—which had suffered from significant fuel price increases in the 1970s. Such a favorable result, combined with evidence of low prices from unregulated intrastate experience and many analyses of the problems of high costs and prices under existing regulation, led Congress to pass the **Airline Deregulation Act** of 1978. This Act ended the CAB's control of entry and its control of airfares, and the CAB went out of existence in 1981. Once CAB regulation was abandoned, a wider variety of airline services came into existence, with "no-frills" airlines offering lower prices than "full-service" airlines. Economic deregulation does not appear to have affected safety, because the fatality rate, the fatalities relative to passenger-miles flown, has generally been on a downward trend since 1979, even though air travel increased dramatically after deregulation.[38] Congress pressured the FAA to release more information about airline safety.[39] One concern about deregulation was that it would reduce service to small communities, and to some degree it did. For some time after deregulation, average industry wages continued to rise, along with industry employment rates, but by September 11, 2001, salaries and employment at older airlines were both threatened.[40]

Although some aspects of service quality fell—when airplanes fly with more than 70 percent of their seats filled rather than 60 percent, it may be harder to find a seat—overall welfare was improved by deregulation.[41] Not all passenger miles are

---

[38] An exception is the increase in jet-airliner crashes around the world in 1996, which has no apparent explanation. There were 25 crashes of big jet airliners in 1996 compared with an average of 20.6 through the 1980s. See "Fasten Your Safety Belts," the *Economist*, January 11, 1997, pp. 55–57.

[39] Such information is available on the FAA Internet webpage, www.faa.gov.

[40] Some labor-management practices from the regulated world persisted into the deregulated world. See Roger Lowenstein, "Into Thin Air," *New York Times Magazine*, February 17, 2002, p. 40–45.

[41] See Morrison and Winston (1986, 1995, 2000).

flown at fares lower than they were under regulation, but evidence shows convincingly that fares are lower on average—by roughly 25 percent—than could be expected under regulation.[42] This is the case despite concerns about concentration in the industry.[43] Service quality also improved as schedules allowed round-trip, same-day travel between cities for the convenience of business travelers, and lower prices for leisure travelers.[44] Relative to the regulated world, economists Steven Morrison and Clifford Winston estimate gains, after considering changes in both price and quality, to be worth more than $20 billion per year.[45]

These benefits of deregulated airline service do not mean it is perfect. Flight delays increased 20 percent from 1999 to 2000.[46] These problems have been traced not to deregulation but to inefficient management of the air travel system, the airports and landing systems administered by governmental bureaucracies. Correcting the national traffic control system has been postponed since the events of September 11, 2001, in part because flights were cut back so capacity limits were less confining and because funds for such an effort were allocated instead to security and related activities.[47] Deregulated airline networks funneled more traffic into congested "hub" airports.[48] The FAA has admitted it makes inefficient use of the airways, with procedures that do not respond well to poor weather and that are not uniform across the country.[49] Perhaps deregulation will go farther, as it has in Canada, to include the air traffic control system. A serious proposal that has the backing of former airline regulators would form a government-owned corporation to operate the air traffic control system.[50] Such an organization might be able to coordinate the expansion of airports, which was widely called for in the United States before September 11, 2001.

Governments continue to own airports, and their management is not ideal. Airplanes use **landing slots**—time segments for take off and landing—which are limited, especially at rush hours. These slots were created to reduce congestion before deregulation, but the slots were not allocated efficiently and deregulation has not changed that very much. Many slots are still available exclusively for particular airlines at busy airports, although leasing of slots to other airlines has been allowed. Landing fees also are assessed, but they do almost nothing to control the scarcity of slots during rush hours at congested airports, and they barely cover costs of wear and tear of landings on runways. Market forces could improve the allocation of landing slots if the slots were auctioned to the highest bidder, so rights to land or take off

---

[42] See Morrison and Winston (2000). Fares declined in the 1990s. See Lee (2003).

[43] Fares under deregulation are higher in airline markets that have higher concentration, and that is inconsistent with contestable market theory. See Baker and Pratt (1989).

[44] See Bailey and Liu (1995).

[45] See Morrison and Winston (2000).

[46] A flight is delayed when it is held up 15 minutes or longer along its route. For a count of delays see the FAA web site, http://www.faa.gov/newsroom.htm.

[47] See Matthew L. Wald, "Effort to Cut Flight Delays Is Put Off," *New York Times*, January 7, 2002, p. A14. And see Morrison and Winston (2000).

[48] See Fallows (2002).

[49] See "A Jam at 32,000 Feet," *Economist*, February 5, 2000, p. 57.

[50] See Matthew L. Wald, "Experts Back Privatizing Flight Control," *New York Times*, February 23, 2001, p. A13. The proposal may be viewed at www.rppi.org.

would go to their most valuable use.[51] Market pricing of landing slots could bring a form of peak-load pricing, with higher auction prices when demand for slots is higher at peak times. Passing these landing fees through to passengers in the form of higher rush-hour airline fares would motivate passengers to shift to flights at less busy times, which could help to reduce congestion during rush hours and, thus, use limited airport capacity more efficiently.[52] Market prices for landing slots would also indicate when airports should be expanded, and the fees collected could be used for that purpose. Airlines have opposed market-based fees for landing slots, arguing instead for the expansion of airports at public (rather than airline) expense. It is perfectly reasonable, however, to have airlines, and then airline travelers through higher fares, pay for the airport capacity they use, and landing fees plus markets for landing slots can be a very effective instrument for achieving that result.[53]

BOX 16.5 Restraining Southwest Airlines

In 1979, shortly after airline deregulation began, today's Southwest Airlines was a discount upstart, operating out of Love Field near Dallas, Texas and attempting to expand and enter more markets. Such moves by Southwest threatened American Airlines and its home airport, the Dallas–Fort Worth International Airport. The airline and the airport were able to persuade Congress to restrict Southwest's flights in and out of Love Field to five states, Texas and its four neighboring states. Congress passed a law to achieve this effect, called the Wright Amendment after Jim Wright, who was Democratic majority leader in the House of Representatives from Texas. The legislation failed to stop Southwest because the airline went on to bring air service, and lower fares, all over the country, but the restriction still prevented some passengers from enjoying low fares. In December, 2005, Senator Christopher Bond of Missouri was able to get Congress to accept his amendment that exempted Missouri from the Wright Amendment's rule and Southwest now flies from Love Field to Kansas City and St. Louis. With the costs of the Wright Amendment becoming clearer each day, its repeal is expected. This barrier to airline competition will not go easily, however, because the arrangements being negotiated would now protect Southwest and American Airlines from competition and preserve traffic for the Dallas–Fort Worth airport. Now Southwest is not a small upstart that must suffer political barriers; it is a large player that can acquire them.

See D. Leonhardt, "Texas Skies May Finally Be Set Free," *New York Times*, March 22, 2006, p. C1; and S. Pearlstein, "Southwest Undercuts Competitors, and Competition," *New York Times*, July 28, 2006, p. D1.

---

[51] Complaints about allocation of slots persist despite the decline in air travel after September 11, 2001. See Matthew L. Wald, "Downturn in Air Travel Unclogs La Guardia's Runways," *New York Times*, January 25, 2003, p. A1.

[52] For criticism of present practices that limit entry, such as long-term leasing of landing slots and gates reserved for exclusive use by one airline, see FAA/OST Task Force Report, 1999, *Airport Business Practices and Their Impact on Airline Competition*, U.S. Department of Transportation. For criticism of slot allocations and other airport practices, see also Wendy Zellner and Lorraine Woellert, "Airport Hell," *Business Week*, September 4, 2000, pp. 38–40. For analysis of how fees might best be set, see Brueckner (2002b).

[53] For analysis of how congestion is internalized more effectively by an airline that has substantial market power, see Brueckner (2002a).

A competitive airline industry has to balance its capacity to supply airplanes against the passenger demand for its services.[54] Regulated airlines had limited experience with this problem, because the regulator provided stability through its monopoly power to limit entry and set fares. Airline capacity is costly—a wide-body jet costs $100 million—and after deregulation it took time for the airlines to learn ways to match capacity with reasonably good projections of demand. Airlines changed their ways of operating substantially after deregulation, and in responding to these changes new entrants brought different, low-cost ways of operating.

Changing Forms of Airline Competition after Deregulation

After deregulation, the major airlines developed networks called *hub-and-spoke* routing systems. A hub is an operating center for an airline. Rather than flying directly from every city to every other city in its route network, the airline schedules many flights as spokes into a hub, and from there they connect to other hubs, from which continuing flights fan out as spokes to smaller communities. By having its routes pass through the hub, which is a large airport, an airline typically achieves a saving in costs. It gathers passengers into hubs and then carries them on flights to hubs in other major cities using larger, more efficient, planes and achieving higher load factors. Flight frequency improved with the adoption of hub-and-spoke networks, and although travel times did not always improve, these hub-and-spoke designs formed more efficient networks for the airlines operating them.

An alternative to hub-and-spoke systems came later when low-cost carriers, led by Southwest Airlines, developed *point-to-point* networks. These networks pursued more direct flights of similar distances and could help to control costs by using the same type of aircraft on all flights. Figure 16.4 illustrates a hub-and-spoke network and a point-to-point network. Locations C and D are hubs in the hub-and-spoke network, and flights from A, B, E, F, and G go in and out of hubs. Many, though not all, points are connected by direct flights in the point-to-point network, yet some flights, as from A to C, do have to go through another airport (B). Using the same A through G cities helps to contrast the two types of network in Figure 16.4, but the airlines that create the networks may choose different cities. Southwest sometimes operates out of smaller airports, for example, and does not always reach the same locations as the hub-and-spoke networks.

The hub-and-spoke route design thus channels traffic from many places into fewer avenues. Although such hub-and-spoke networks may lengthen the total trip time for passengers, they also make more frequent flights possible, so passengers can fly at more convenient times.[55] The hub-and-spoke design, however, also raises fixed costs. A hub-and-spoke network usually needs more than one type of aircraft, small planes to carry passengers on spokes, and large planes to carry them from hub to hub.

---

[54] For description of this balancing of supply and demand see Virginia Postrel, "Economic Scene," *New York Times*, October 11, 2001, p. C2.

[55] See Brueckner (2003).

Figure 16.4 *Hub-and-Spoke and Point-to-Point Networks*

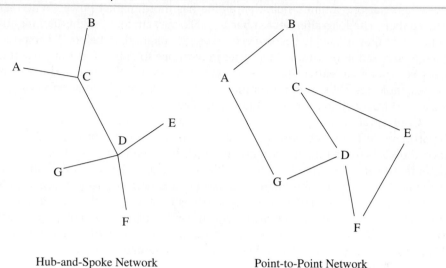

Hub-and-Spoke Network   Point-to-Point Network

Using more aircraft types requires higher maintenance and training expenses. Hub-and-spoke operations also tend to keep planes on the ground longer while passengers from more than one flight make their connections, so aircraft utilization is not as high. These higher fixed costs of hub-and-spoke networks can be overcome by a high volume of passengers, as such networks offer scale economies.

The scale economies of hub-and-spoke networks seemed to foster consolidation within the airline industry, as mergers caused the number of major carriers to decline.[56] Moreover, under the hub-and-spoke organization of routes, more passengers tended to remain on the same airline for their entire trip rather than switching airlines. For instance, connections with the same carrier increased from 25 percent to 45 percent in the six years between 1978, when deregulation began, and 1984.[57] Because the hub-and-spoke networks were intended to coordinate longer trips, it should not surprise us that they encouraged passengers to complete their trips on one airline. When they formed larger airline networks, however, these mergers raised fares more than they reduced costs.[58]

Although national measures of airline concentration are not very high, with top-4 concentration measures under 50 and HHI measures of concentration at about 1,000, concerns about market power might still arise about specific routes and airports.[59] Competition occurs among quite different hub-and-spoke systems, and because airlines have different hub locations, their locations serve as a basis for product

---

[56] See Borenstein (1989).
[57] See Doganis (1993, Ch. 10).
[58] See Brueckner, Dyer and Spiller (1992), and Kim and Singal (1993).
[59] These estimates are drawn from data presented in Table 1 of Lee (2003, p. 3).

differentiation. One airline tends to dominate at each hub, and as other airlines operate fewer flights at one airline's hub, that airline has more market power. When airlines reduced their schedules after September 11, 2001, they cut fewer flights at their hub airports, where they tended to become even more dominant than before.[60] The possibility of aggressive action by an existing carrier in response to entry at its hub airport might also give a potential entrant pause and keep entry from being free and unfettered as Box 16.6 indicates. Thus, high concentration can be more serious in its effects at a single hub airport than national concentration data might suggest.[61]

Concentration has been an issue in the deregulated airline industry. The Department of Transportation, which has been responsible for approving mergers since the CAB went out of existence in 1982, has been lenient in granting them, sometimes over Department of Justice objections. The Department of Transportation acts almost as if contestable market theory applies perfectly to the airline industry. Recall that contestable market theory assumes entry is so easy that concentration has no effect on market price. Even a single firm has to charge a minimum-cost price to avoid losing the contestable market to an entrant. Airline markets are not perfectly contestable, however, because airline fares under deregulation are higher on more concentrated routes.[62]

Soon after hub-and-spoke networks were formed, airlines encouraged customer loyalty through frequent-flyer programs, which reward accumulated miles on one airline with free trips. Having loyal customers, airlines followed pricing policies that involved some discrimination among customers, as well as having prices depend on how far in advance a flight reservation is made and on how close the flight is to being fully booked. Somewhat like complicated peak-load pricing plans, the pricing policy is set in computer software programs and dubbed **yield management**. This sophisticated pricing can offer a low price to a college student booking a month in advance and a high price to a business executive at the last-minute before her flight.

On the one hand, yield management helped the deregulated airlines use price to balance supply and demand, but on the other hand they discriminated in price among passengers. For example, airlines separated business travelers from

---

BOX 16.6 Airline Entry

American Airlines was sued by the Department of Transportation in 1999 for cutting prices to match those of new entrants at Dallas, Texas, and for adding to its capacity at the Dallas–Fort Worth International Airport. American operated a hub at Dallas and was charged with discouraging competitive entry. American Airlines won the case on the antitrust ground that it was merely matching the price of a competitor.

See J. R. Wilke and S. McCartney, "American Airlines Wins a Victory as Judge Dismisses Antitrust Case," *Wall Street Journal*, April 30, 2001, p.1

---

[60] See Laurence Zuckerman, "Airline Cutbacks With an Agenda," *New York Times*, November 20, 2001, p. C1.

[61] For evidence about lack of entry at hub airports, see Hendricks, Piccione, and Tan (1997).

[62] See Baker and Pratt (1989).

leisure travelers by whether they would stay over at their destinations on Saturday night, something business travelers usually prefer not to do, and travelers who revealed themselves to be business passengers by not staying Saturday night paid higher fares. Uncertainty about demand can also motivate airlines, who must set prices in advance, to set multiple prices, so some units (some airplane seats) are priced higher than others. Then, as lower-priced units are chosen first, the prices on other units effectively rise as a particular flight fills up.[63] Airlines introduced other special services at special prices to appeal to specific customer groups, with some fares five times as high as others. Many of these prices were not discriminatory because the services booked at different times were different, but discriminatory prices such as those against business travelers opened opportunities for competitors.[64] Low-cost operators of point-to-point networks tended to have simpler price schedules and to rely less on price discrimination.

On the whole, airline deregulation is still judged by most parties today to have been successful. For some years there was no decline in wages, employment, or airline safety, and fares on average moved lower. Travel time sometimes increased and sometimes fell. Taking into account both travel times and fares, however, overall welfare clearly improved. Deregulation led to a greater variety of services and more innovations, such as the hub-and-spoke network system and the point-to-point network into smaller airports. The industry has not been highly profitable on a consistent basis since deregulation, however, and the transition to a competitive industry is still bringing changes. The exposure of airplanes to deliberate acts of destruction also poses a serious problem for the future of the industry.

BOX 16.7 Airline Reservation Systems

The airline reservation scheme itself has been seen as an anticompetitive mechanism at times, because it could favor certain airlines by having their flights appear first on travel agents' computer screens when they search for flights. When computer reservation systems were first introduced, two systems dominated: American Airlines' Sabre System and United Airlines' Apollo System. The Department of Justice pressured both airlines to divest these scheduling businesses to avoid advantages they could otherwise have in operating them to improve their own sales. On being divested from airlines, both of these early scheduling systems moved to the Internet where they became Travelocity and Expedia. Five major airlines created an Internet site for fares, called Orbitz, and Northwest, Southwest, and America West developed their own sites. These systems now compete for Internet flight bookings, which are growing in popularity.

See S. Hansell, "As Big Airlines Struggle, Computer Booking System Prospers," *New York Times*, February 10, 2003, p. C1.

---

[63] For theoretical argument, see Sherman and Visscher (1982b) and Dana (1999a, 1999b). For supporting evidence, see Borenstein and Rose (1994).

[64] See Levine (1987, 2002) for analysis of airlines' yield-management pricing.

The Airline Industry after September 11, 2001

After airplanes were crashed by terrorists on September 11, 2001, into the World Trade Center in New York, the Pentagon in Washington, and a field in Pennsylvania, airline security became a paramount issue for air travel. Loosely operated by the airlines before those events, security at airports was taken over by the federal government in 2002 through the newly formed **Transportation Security Administration (TSA)**. The TSA employs thousands of agents to inspect passengers and their baggage and to otherwise try to reduce possible dangers to air travel from sabotage. Greater security tends to require more time of passengers, however, and is one reason some travelers began using cars, buses, or trains instead of flying.

The September 11, 2001, attacks and their aftermath brought serious financial problems for airlines, largely because of reduced demand for air travel, which strikes hardest at hub-and-spoke systems that have high fixed costs. The airlines suffered also from the Iraq war, which helped to increase fuel prices, and the SARS epidemic in 2003, which discouraged air travel. US Airways, Inc., and United Air Lines, Inc., were pushed into bankruptcy to protect them from creditors while they reorganized, and other large airlines including American, Delta, and Northwest followed soon after.[65] The federal government appropriated $10 billion to aid the industry through loan guarantees, but allocating that money among the needy airlines was not easy. In 2002 Congress formed the **Air Transportation Stabilization Board**, to decide who would receive the money. The Board had power to force mergers among airlines. It did not do so, but it indicated that the industry had changed, and that the old ways of operating would no longer support financial stability.[66]

Another step taken by the Department of Justice and the Department of Transportation in January, 2003, was to approve—with conditions—a **codesharing** alliance among three hub-and-spoke airlines—Continental Airlines, Inc., Delta Air Lines, Inc., and Northwest Airlines—to help them function as a single network.[67] Under code-sharing, participating airlines put their own identification codes on a route, and even though only one of them actually operates it, they all can sell it. Usually they also share each others' lounge facilities in airports and allow passengers to choose which frequent flyer program they want credited with miles. Code-sharing allows each participating airline to offer its passengers the advantages of a larger network than it alone can provide and, thus, extends the advantages of network externalities. In doing so, it also avoids the double marginalization problem that can arise in networks when two airlines provide complementary parts of a single trip.[68] If tickets

---

[65] See David Leonhardt, "UAL and Its Backers Scramble for Support and Financing," *New York Times*, December 6, 2002, p. C1; and Susan Carey, "UAL Strategy Chief Outlines Plans," *Wall Street Journal*, December 13, 2002, p. A2; and "Courts and Cuts," *The Economist*, January 19, 2006.

[66] See Michael E. Levine, "No Clear Way Forward for Airlines," *New York Times*, December 6, 2002, p. A33.

[67] Some conditions were attached to avoid anticompetitive behavior. See Edward Wong, "U.S. Approves Code Sharing By 3 Airlines, With Limits," *New York Times*, January 18, 2003, p. B1.

[68] Economist Jan Brueckner (2001) and Brueckner and Tom Whalen (2000) provide both rationale, including network externalities, and evidence for lower prices on international routes where airlines allied their services through codesharing arrangements. Park and Zhang (2000) provide similar empirical findings for North Atlantic routes.

were marked up separately, double marginalization might result, making prices for these complementary elements of the overall trip higher than even a single overall monopolist would choose.

Southwest Airlines Co. has grown to be one of the largest airlines in the United States, and it continued to be profitable after September 11, 2001. Southwest flies direct flights instead of using a hub-and-spoke network, and it flies often to smaller and less congested airports near large cities where it can land and take off in less time. By flying only Boeing 737s, Southwest also saves training and maintenance costs. Various estimates put its costs about 30 percent lower than those of major airlines. It offers simple pricing, which business and other travelers who were being discriminated against by major airlines may prefer because the simple prices lack the high fares aimed at business men and women that are part of yield management plans. Southwest's success in attracting passengers certainly puts pressure on major hub-and-spoke airlines, limiting the prices they can charge, the price discrimination and yield management practices they can use, and, hence, the profits they can earn. JetBlue Airways, which is the second largest low-cost airline, follows policies similar to Southwest's, as do other low-cost airlines such as Frontier Airlines, Inc., and Air-Tran Airways.[69] Growing travel by private jet aircraft, especially by corporations, also takes some business away from major airlines. Private jets can avoid delays caused by heavy security at major airports, and they can also save time by flying direct routes.

After September 11, 2001, the high fixed costs of maintaining hub-and-spoke networks with declining traffic handicapped large older airlines, relative to more flexible low-cost airlines such as Southwest that fly point-to-point routes. All the major airlines proposed scaled back, lower cost operations in an effort to compete and—especially when aided by court support while in bankruptcy—they renegotiated wage contracts with unions to lower their costs. One hub-and-spoke airline, America West Airlines, converted from a fare structure designed for yield management to a simpler structure like that of Southwest Airlines.[70] For instance, it dropped the effect on its fares of staying over Saturday night, and it cut last minute, "walk-up," fares by two-thirds. Competitors on America West's routes cut their fares in response, and now all have less opportunity to pursue yield management. America West then merged with troubled US Airways in 2005, moving the combined firm in the direction of a low-cost, point-to-point airline.[71]

Competition may help to answer the important question, Which airline organization can provide the best service at the lowest price? The threat of terrorist activities may alter the shape of the industry by reducing travel on commercial airlines. That favors more responsive and flexible airlines that can operate with lower costs

---

[69] One reason for United Airline's financial problems is that it faces low-cost competitors at or near many of the airports where its hubs are located. See Edward Wong, "United's Woes May Benefit Other Carriers," *New York Times*, December 12, 2002, p. C1.

[70] See Edward Wong, "Airline's New Diet Has Rivals Watching," *New York Times*, January 12, 2003, Sec. 3, p. 1.

[71] See Susan Carey and Melanie Trottman, "US Airways Talks To America West About a Merger," *Wall Street Journal*, April 20, 2005, p. A1.

and simpler price schedules relative to the large airlines that have hub-and-spoke commitments. As long as competition can be sustained, however, consumers will be able to decide which form of airline organization works best.

SUMMARY

Railroads, trucks, buses, and automobiles have all been regulated in important ways. Railroads were crucial to the early development of America, and their regulation in 1887 through the first federal regulatory agency, the Interstate Commerce Commission (ICC), established a pattern that would be repeated in other industries. Legislation allowed the ICC to control prices and entry and exit to the industry. The ICC employed value-of-service pricing to allow higher markups on commodities that had less elastic demands and to raise revenue so fixed costs could be covered. The ICC was drawn into very detailed pricing by commodity, however, and it also refused requests by railroads to abandon unprofitable routes, until the 1970s when railroads were financially weak. By 1980, deregulation allowed pricing flexibility and permission to abandon tracks, and that fostered a return to profitability for the industry.

As trucks developed they became competitors of railroads. Congress regulated trucks in 1935 largely to protect the railroads' value-of-service pricing, which could not survive unregulated competition from trucks that could charge lower prices for transporting the commodities on which the ICC had set high prices for railroads. Trucking companies did not resist regulation in part because they could expect to benefit from the entry protection it would afford. Interstate trucks were regulated federally, while trucks operating within a state were regulated by that state. Authority to operate over a particular route was commodified, or made tradable, and the substantial value of such authority suggests that regulation benefitted the trucking companies. Rate bureaus established rates in a process more like an illegal information exchange than like market competition, so rates were high while entry was controlled. Deregulation came in 1980 and seems to have improved the performance of the industry, which probably should not have been regulated in the first place.

Buses and urban transportation also have complex histories. For many passengers, intercity travel is available only by bus. Buses serve about 25 times as many locations as either railroads or airplanes, because they serve many small towns that railroads and airplanes do not reach. For many years, interstate buses were regulated federally and intrastate buses were regulated by states, but deregulation came to both federal and state levels by 1982, soon after truck deregulation in 1980. Urban transit followed a different path. After reaching a peak during World War II, urban transit passengers declined seriously. Because maintaining some form of transport within cities was important to their functioning, states and the federal government supported urban transit. They also regulated automobiles to conserve energy and to protect the environment, and communities have begun to control highway traffic congestion. Individual vehicles do not take account of the delays they cause others, and pricing road use offers a way to impose the costs of such delays on each driver. The evidence in many cities indicates that pricing road use, together with other steps, can greatly improve the efficiency of truck, bus, and auto travel on the road network.

Airline regulation began in 1938 with the purpose of promoting the airline industry, rather than to protect consumers alone or for some other, say natural monopoly, reason. Apart from safety regulation by the FAA, which still continues, the regulation of airlines involved control over entry to each route and over the setting of prices, or airline fares, by the Civil Aeronautics Board (CAB). It allowed firms serving a route to propose schedules, but all fares were regulated. Because regulated fares were set high, and airlines could not compete in price, they were drawn into nonprice competition, such as more frequent flights. Then planes were not very full, which raised costs. Inefficiencies of this regulation were implicated when, within the individual states of Texas and California where airlines were not subject to CAB regulation, the airlines had lower costs.

Airline deregulation was undertaken in 1978 and is estimated to have yielded savings worth $20 billion per year in current dollars. Air fares are lower on average, safety is no worse, and wages and employment did not initially suffer. The restructuring of routes into hub-and-spoke networks was an unanticipated innovation that the deregulated airlines frequently adopted. They raised revenue to cover the high fixed costs of hub-and-spoke systems partly by discriminating in price against business travelers. Low-cost airlines that flew point-to-point routes and used fewer airplane types undercut hub-and-spoke airlines, in part by not discriminating in price. Landing fees and other aspects of airport management are still protected from market forces, and their improvement might offer further gains.

The terrorist attacks of September 11, 2001, were especially harmful to the airline industry, which was shut down for a week. When air travel resumed, it was with more demanding security measures and fewer passengers, who had to plan on greater travel times. Congress allocated federal government funds to subsidize the industry in an effort to offset, at least partially, the losses it suffered. But major airlines operating hub-and-spoke networks still lost money because of the lower level of air travel demand, made worse by price competition from low-cost airlines that targeted discriminatory pricing systems. Reorganization is still sweeping through the airline industry, more than 25 years after it was deregulated.

QUESTIONS

1. Consider a railroad that runs freight trains between cities A and B, completing a round trip every day. The demand for freight traffic in tons is greater for the A to B trip (Q_{AB}) than it is for the B to A trip (Q_{BA}). The daily quantities of freight service demanded, in tons, for the two directions are given by demand functions

$$P_{AB} = 150 - Q_{AB}, \text{ and}$$

$$P_{BA} = 100 - Q_{BA},$$

where P_{AB} and P_{BA} are prices per ton in the A to B and B to A directions. The daily cost of train capacity to carry one ton is 200. That is, for an expenditure of 200, the railroad can carry one ton in *both* directions on one day. At that daily cost of 200 per ton of capacity, a train can be made up of any chosen size.

a. Is it more efficient to have the same price for freight in both directions, AB and BA, or should different prices be charged based on direction? Explain why your choice of pricing is more efficient than the alternative.

b. How large should the train be? That is, how many tons should the train be able to carry?

c. Find an optimal price, or optimal prices, per ton for AB traffic (P_{AB}) and for BA traffic (P_{BA}).

2. In many states, motor vehicles must periodically pass a safety inspection. Who gains by this regulation? Who loses? What advantage does this regulation offer over unregulated, decentralized decision making? Many states have compulsory automobile liability insurance. To what extent is the justification for this regulation similar to (and different from) the motor vehicle inspection regulation?

3. Assume that highway capacity theories are correct and that the average speed of a vehicle on a particular highway depends on the volume of traffic as follows:

$$\text{Average speed} = 50 \text{ mph} - 0.01 \times (\text{vehicles/hr}).$$

Consider a highway connecting two towns that are 45 miles apart.

a. Calculate the total time that 500 drivers experience at such a volume that 500 vehicles enter the road each hour (vehicles/hr = 500).

b. Calculate the total time that 501 drivers experience at a volume of 501 vehicles per hour.

c. The difference between your calculations in a and b represent the *marginal* trip time to all drivers—to society—of the 501st vehicle. What is the average trip time for each of the 501 vehicles, and how does it compare with the marginal trip time? If time is valued at $10 per hour by all drivers, what is the value of this difference between marginal and average trip time?

d. What would you need to know to determine an optimal congestion toll for this road?

4. Consider these rough cost approximations from Keeler (1971, pp. 159 and 161), adjusted to the current price level.

	Cost per Seat Mile
Bus (up to 200 miles), U.S. average	8.8 cents
Air	15 to 18 cents
Automobile (operating cost + user taxes)	26.5 cents
Railroad (with efficient work rules)	7.4 to 8.8 cents

Try to speculate about how these relative costs, and your own judgments about qualities of these modes, might explain the developments we have seen in passenger transportation in the last three decades.

5. Consider the *ABA* Airline, which flies from *A* to *B* once a month and from *B* to *A* once a month. The demands for trips in the two directions are symmetric, so consider only the *A* to *B* flight (the *B* to *A* flight is the same). The airplane that flies the route can carry 30 passengers, and once the flight is scheduled it must be flown (it will not be cancelled), so marginal costs per passenger are very low. Thirty days in advance of the flight, expected passenger demand can be represented by the demand function

$$Q = 31 - 0.01P.$$

Suppose the price per passenger is set at 100. Then the demand curve is true if one passenger signs up each day during the month in which reservations are accepted. Demand, however, may be higher or lower than this demand equation indicates. If an average of less than one passenger reserves a seat on the flight per day, the total demand is less than the demand indicates. If an average of more than one passenger reserves a seat on the flight per day, the total demand is more than the demand indicates.

a. After 10 days, 20 passengers have reserved seats on the plane. Would you recommend changing price? Why? If you changed price, would you raise or lower it? Why?

b. After 20 days, 10 passengers have reserved seats on the plane. Would you recommend changing price? Why? If you changed price, would you raise or lower it? Why?

c. Changing prices in response to changes in demand is one aspect of "yield management." Can yield management offer socially beneficial effects? Make an argument for or against this form of yield management by airlines.

d. Consider the practice of charging a lower round-trip fare to passengers who stay Saturday night at their destinations. Make an argument for or against this form of yield management by airlines.

6. Value-of-service pricing for railroads can be said to approximate Ramsey pricing. What were the advantages of this form of Ramsey pricing for railroads? What were the disadvantages of Ramsey pricing for railroads?

APPENDIX **16.1** Major Federal Railroad Legislation

1887 Act to Regulate Commerce—created the Interstate Commerce Commission (ICC)
1903 Elkins Act—barred discrimination among shippers
1906 Hepburn Act—allowed ICC to set maximum rail rates
1920 Mann-Elkins Act—barred discrimination between long and short hauls
      Transportation Act—permitted ICC to set minimum rates
1970 Rail Passenger Service Act—created AMTRAK passenger service
1976 Railroad Revitalization and Reform Act—allowed abandonment of routes, mergers, some pricing flexibility, some subsidy
1980 Staggers Act—eased route abandonment, added more subsidy

APPENDIX **16.2** Major Federal Truck, Bus, and Highway Legislation

1935 Motor Carrier Act—amended the Act to Regulate Commerce (1887) to have ICC regulate trucks and buses
1944 Federal Highway Act—granted state officials authority for urban highway funding
1948 Reed-Bulwinkle Act—allowed trucking rate bureaus without violating antitrust law
1958 Transportation Act—allowed commuter railroads to abandon unprofitable routes
1961 Housing Act—fostered mass transit planning and low interest loans
1962 Highway Act—allowed mass transit to be considered as alternative to highway spending
1964 Urban Mass Transit Act—supported up to two-thirds of capital cost of mass transit projects
1968 Urban Mass Transit Act—created Urban Mass Transit Administration (UMTA)
1970 Urban Mass Transit Act—committed federal government to spend $10 billion over 10 years on mass transit
1973 Federal Highway Act—allowed a portion of highway funds to go into mass transit projects
1978 Surface Transportation Act—added more federal funds for both operating and capital expenses of mass transit
1980 Motor Carrier Act—facilitated entry to trucking routes and allowed some rate flexibility
1982 Bus Regulatory Reform Act—allowed entry to interstate routes and gave ICC power over intrastate bus prices
1991 Urban Mass Transit Administration (UMTA) became Surface Transportation Board (STB)

APPENDIX 16.3 Major Federal Airline Legislation

1938 Civil Aeronautics Act—created Civil Aeronautics Authority (CAA), renamed as Civil Aeronautics Board

1958 Federal Aviation Administration Act—created Federal Aviation Administration (FAA) to regulate air safety separate from economic regulation by CAB

1978 Airline Deregulation Act—ended economic regulation of airlines by CAB

2002 Transportation Security Administration (TSA) created

2002 Air Transport Stabilization Board (ATSB) created

17

Energy

Energy is the power to do things. The power of a horse is a form of energy, and it even provides a unit of measurement: horsepower. Horses require open space, care, and training, however, so they are not as convenient to use as other forms of energy. Lightning is extremely high in energy but is very unpredictable, so it cannot be harnessed for constructive purposes. Effective sources of energy today are *coal, oil, natural gas,* and *nuclear energy*. Uses of energy sources change, as oil was first used for lighting, then heating, and then as fuel for electricity generation and myriad modes of transportation. Because all the current fuels cause externality problems, from air pollution to the danger of catastrophe in a nuclear explosion, and they are also exhaustible, changes in sources of energy can be expected in the coming decades.

Major oil companies are among the country's largest enterprises, and they provide fuel for all manner of motorized vehicle on land, at sea, or in the air. In addition to oil, the energy industry includes natural gas, which comes from the ground in an immediately useful gaseous state. Coal is an age-old source of energy, and it joins nuclear power, a modern marvel, to produce most electricity. The ever present light switch is a reminder that electricity is a most convenient form of energy.[1] Hydroelectric dams generate enormous amounts of power while also providing recreational opportunities. Dams offer a sustainable or renewable source of power. The sun, the earth, and the wind are other renewable sources of energy that are promising for the future as supplies of current nonrenewable sources decline.

Energy prices can profoundly affect the national economy. From World War II to 1975, sharp changes in the price of oil preceded five out of six U.S. recessions.[2] In the 1970s, the Organization of Petroleum Exporting Countries (OPEC) became an effective cartel for raising the international price of oil. Indeed, in 1973 the price was less than $3 per barrel; in 1981 it was more than 10 times that level. Because all sources of energy can substitute for each other to some degree, this jump in the price of oil increased the prices of all fuels.

---

[1] Electricity is the subject of Chapter 18.
[2] See Hamilton (1983).

Energy receives high-level government policy attention in most countries, including the United States, where the *Department of Energy* is a cabinet-level department that coordinates national policy.[3] The *Federal Energy Regulatory Commission* carries out regulatory functions in electricity, including hydroelectric projects, and in oil and natural gas.[4] Nuclear power is regulated separately by the *Nuclear Regulatory Commission*.[5] The Department of Energy is also concerned with long-term energy prospects, including renewable energy that eventually has to replace many existing fuels that come largely from fossil origins.

This chapter examines a range of regulatory issues in the energy industry. We turn first to explore coal and nuclear sources of energy that are so important in producing electricity. Then in Section 17.2 we discuss the special features of crude oil and consider a range of policies that attempted to interfere with and redirect market processes, sometimes improving but often reducing efficiency. Section 17.3 examines natural gas, and traces Federal Energy Regulatory Commission actions that restructured the industry to introduce more competition and improve efficiency. Finally, in Section 17.4, we consider renewable energy's promise for the future.

17.1 | COAL AND NUCLEAR POWER

The United States currently uses two fuels, coal and uranium, to generate most of its electricity. These fuels produce steam that runs the largest electricity generators, which provide what is called *base load* electricity all day, every day, at low cost. Other electricity generating units, usually using other fuels, are brought in to meet peak needs at higher cost, while coal and nuclear power produce electricity all the time. Coal is used for almost half of the electricity produced in the world, while nuclear power generates more than 15 percent. In the United States, coal fuels about half the electricity, while 20 percent comes from nuclear power.

Coal Power

An old and reliable source of energy, coal is our most lasting, with current supplies expected to last 150 years or more. Burning coal, however, produces carbon dioxide, an air pollutant that is linked to global warming, and the use of coal will have to be restrained unless ways can be found to capture, or sequester, the carbon dioxide to keep it from the air. Coal also poses dangers for the miners who extract it from the earth.

The production of coal has grown steadily, rising in the United States from half a billion short tons in 1950 to more than a billion short tons today.[6] Growth in

---

[3] Information about the Department of Energy is available at http://www.energy.gov.

[4] Information about the Federal Energy Regulatory Commission is at http://www.ferc.fed.gov.

[5] Information about the Nuclear Regulatory Commission is available at http://www.nrc.org.

[6] The short ton, or net ton, is an American measure of a ton, and it is 2,000 pounds. A long ton is a British ton, which is 2,240 pounds.

production over this period came from mines west of the Mississippi River, while the output of eastern mines remained quite stable. Whereas transportation together with steel making and industrial, commercial, and residential heating dominated in 1950, electricity generation is now by far the greatest user of coal.

Most coal is mined underground in dangerous and unhealthy conditions.[7] Partly as a result, some of the most bitter labor disputes have occurred in the coal industry. Some coal lies close to the surface of the earth and is obtained by *strip mining*, which is safer but disrupts the surface and calls for costly restoration after the coal is removed. Most of the growth in production of coal has come in surface mining, while production from underground mines has remained roughly constant. Coal is abundant and can be found in many countries.

The main advantage of coal is its low apparent cost per unit of energy, while the main disadvantage is its higher social cost due to externalities. Extracting coal endangers miners and presents restoration problems for landowners. Burning coal emits carbon dioxide, sulphur dioxide, and nitrous oxides into the air.[8] Carbon dioxide is a *greenhouse gas* that has been linked to *global warming*, which is the trend toward higher temperatures on the earth.[9] Global warming is a growing problem that may have very serious long-term consequences such as raising the levels of oceans and flooding major cities. Because carbon is the main culprit in the greenhouse effect, a tax has been suggested to reflect the negative externality from its use, whether as coal, oil, or any other fuel. Sulphur dioxide and nitrous oxides from coal form acids in the air, which fall to the earth as *acid rain* to harm vegetation and aquatic life in lakes and rivers.

To avoid the consequences of global warming, those who burn coal might capture and then *sequester* the emitted carbon dioxide. One way to sequester, or store, carbon dioxide is to pump it underground to emptied oil reservoirs. For years it has been pumped into oil and gas wells in late stages of production to force out the oil or gas, and the same pumping and monitoring methods can be applied for the sequestering purpose. The carbon dioxide might go a half mile to a mile into the ground, where it would be stored permanently. In one experiment a University of Texas team placed 1600 tons of carbon dioxide in an unused reservoir in Dayton, Texas, not far from the great Spindletop oil field, and other projects are also under way. Another approach is to compress carbon dioxide to make it dense and heavy, and sink it in the bottom of an ocean. When compressed, carbon dioxide becomes heavier than water, so if placed at the bottom of an ocean where pressure is very great, it would remain there. Methods like this will increase the cost of coal as an energy source, but may prevent an environmental effect that would otherwise limit its use.

---

[7] Mining safety is regulated separately by the Mining Safety and Health Administration. See Ian Urbina and Andrew W. Lehren, "U.S. Easing Fines for Mine Owners on Safety Flaws," *New York Times*, March 2, 2006, p. A1.

[8] Efforts are being proposed to lessen these problems. See Andrew C. Revkin, "U.S. Seeking Cleaner Model of Coal Plant," *New York Times*, February 28, 2003, p. A20; and Matthew L. Wald, "Skeptics Emerge on Technologies for Cleaner Coal," *New York Times*, February 21, 2007, p. C1.

[9] Global warming is examined in Chapter 21.

BOX 17.1 A Prize for Capturing Carbon Dioxide

A new incentive was created in 2007 to remove carbon dioxide from the air when Richard Branson, who operates Virgin Airways, offered a $25 million prize to anyone who could work out a way to remove a billion tons of carbon dioxide per year from the atmosphere. With roughly 6 billion tons being produced every year one billion tons would be a significant reduction and might even allow fossil fuels like coal to be used longer as a source of energy.

See J. Tierney, "A Cool $25 Million For a Climate Backup Plan," *New York Times,* February 13, 2007, p. D1.

Nuclear Power

Nuclear, or atomic, power began in 1957, when the first commercial plant produced electricity in Shippingport, Pennsylvania. Today, nuclear plants provide about 20 percent of electricity worldwide. Uranium, which is found in a rock-like ore, is used as a nuclear fuel because its atoms can be split apart relatively easily, and that fission process releases heat that can produce steam to generate electricity. One golf-ball sized piece of uranium can yield as much energy as the coal in 20 railroad cars. Indeed, in 1955 the submarine *Nautilus* traveled 62,000 miles on that much uranium. Uranium also causes very little air pollution when it is used to generate electricity. The major drawback of nuclear power is the radioactivity of used uranium fuel, which creates a disposal problem that can last for thousands of years. Concerns about safety and problems in disposing of the spent nuclear fuel restrain the expansion of nuclear power today.

The problems of nuclear power have grown more serious with time. So much heat is produced in splitting atoms that cooling towers and reservoirs are used to absorb the heat harmlessly. If the heat at the core of a nuclear reactor becomes too great, there is the danger of a *meltdown,* a break in the containment of radioactive material that allows it to spread over many miles to cause illness and death. In 1979 the Three Mile Island Nuclear Generating Station in Pennsylvania had a partial meltdown that was contained in time to avoid loss of life. A nuclear power plant at Chernobyl, in the former Soviet Union, had an explosion in a reactor in 1986, and it produced the worst nuclear accident to date. About 350,000 people were permanently relocated, and thousands died or became ill from radiation.

Even in the absence of a disaster, nuclear power causes a growing problem of toxic waste. Spent nuclear fuel rods, which introduce the fuel into reactors, must be handled so their remaining radioactivity is contained, and yet they continue to accumulate in reactors everywhere. There were 112 nuclear power plants operating in the United States in 1990, and a smaller number, 104, in 2001. Transporting wastes to a disposal center, if such a center is ever agreed upon, also presents risks.[10] And nuclear power plants themselves will be problems at the ends of their useful lives. Radioactivity

---

[10] For analysis of effects of these risks, see Riddel and Shaw (2002b).

BOX 17.2 Nuclear Waste on the Reservation

The Goshute Indian tribe in Skull Valley, Utah plans to use part of its barren 18,000 acre reservation for temporary storage of nuclear waste. A consortium of eight electric utilities is behind the plan, and it expects storage to last for 40 years, and longer if efforts to establish a long-term waste dump under Yucca Mountain in Utah do not succeed.

See A. Tanner, "Tribe Gambles on Nuclear Waste," *Houston Chronicle,* September 23, 2006, p. C1.

will prevent their use for other purposes, and they may have to be sealed up and remain unused for many more years.

After its dramatic use as a bomb at Hiroshima in World War II, atomic power became a subject of national policy with the Atomic Energy Act of 1954. Civilian use of nuclear materials was separated from military uses with the Energy Reorganization Act of 1974, which created the **Nuclear Regulatory Commission (NRC)**. In its regulation of the nuclear industry, the Commission is to protect the public health and safety, promote security, and protect the environment. Five members of the Commission serve five-year terms. The agency spends more than $600 million a year, but it collects fees for services such as licensing a nuclear reactor at a power plant, and they make up about 85 percent of its budget.[11]

The Price-Anderson Act

Early nuclear power plants found it difficult to insure against harm from meltdowns or other catastrophes because private insurers did not want to insure them. To ease this problem, and thinking that the private insurers were unwisely conservative, Congress passed the Price-Anderson Act in 1957 to indemnify operators of nuclear power plants against liability from damages. The aim was to support operators of nuclear reactors for 10 years while evidence could accumulate that would allow private insurers to take over the protection. The law authorized a fund to meet disaster claims to be financed by contributions from all nuclear power plants. As time has passed the private insurance industry has continued to avoid issuing extensive coverage for nuclear accidents, and the Price-Anderson Act may not offer adequate protection in the event of a major accident.

Despite the controversy that surrounds it, Congress has repeatedly revised and renewed the Price-Anderson Act. Indeed, the Energy Policy Act of 2005 renewed it until December 31, 2025. Although more nuclear power plants are not on the horizon, with renewal of the Act they need not hesitate for want of insurance protection. Currently nuclear reactor operators are required to have the maximum level of insurance available from private sources of $300 million. In the event of an accident, after that sum is exhausted further damages are to be paid by all other reactor operators under terms of the Act. Each reactor unit contributes nearly $100 million to a secondary

---

[11] Information about the Nuclear Regulatory Commission is available at http://www.nrc.org.

insurance pool, payable until complete in annual installments of $15 million per reactor. With slightly more than 100 reactors in operation, the private and public funds available for an accident total a little more than $10 billion.

Critics of the Price-Anderson Act emphasize that it sets an unrealistically low cap on the total damage that could result from a single nuclear accident. Evidence of possible harm, gathered after the Three Mile Island event, led to estimates of a more serious accident reaching almost $600 billion in today's dollars, or about 60 times as much as Price-Anderson would cover.[12] It has also been estimated that to privately provide the Price-Anderson level of insurance would cost reactor operators $3 billion annually, which is far more than they now pay into the reserve fund.[13]

Many other complaints can be made about the Price-Anderson Act. To the extent it provides a subsidy by protecting reactor operators, it can invite too much use of nuclear power relative to other sources of power. The law is also poorly designed as an insurance plan because it includes no risk adjustment. Old or poorly maintained plants—which may also be less well protected against terrorist attack—pay no more than new and well-maintained ones. The Act also ignores whether the reactor is built to contain or moderate a meltdown or is located near a large urban area where damage could be enormous. So in addition to motivating the construction of too many reactors, the Act may invite reactors to skimp on protections and locate too close to urban centers where the harm from an accident could be greatest.[14] Reactor operators can save on transmission costs by locating closer to their urban customers, but that means that a catastrophe would impose greater costs. Because it follows poor insurance practices by not adjusting for risks, the Price-Anderson Act makes the cost of such a catastrophe appear smaller than it is. In short, the Act invites the building of too many reactors that are located too close to cities.

Together, coal and nuclear power provide roughly three-fourths of our electric power, and although they are exhaustible they will last quite a while. They cause problems, however. Coal is seen as a major contributor to global warming, unless carbon dioxide can be sequestered, and nuclear power brings the threat of a catastrophic accident and the problem of storing used, but still radioactive, fuel. Thus, relying extensively on these two sources of energy has disadvantages, and unless problems can be solved alternative sources will be needed.

17.2 OIL

Oil passes through three main stages on its way to consumers: *production, refining,* and *distribution.* Before it can be produced it must be found, so we should add an *exploration* stage before production. Transportation is also necessary, and it brings risks of oil spills from tanker accidents that are a continuing problem for the industry. Crude

---

[12] See Fultz (1987).

[13] See Durbin and Rothwell (1990).

[14] For this argument, see Wood (1981).

oil is the output of production before refining yields products such as gasoline, and distribution carries those products to within easy reach of consumers. Major firms in the industry participate in all of these stages, and the dominant use of petroleum is for transportation. Supplies of oil are expected to last 40 years or so and will ultimately be exhausted. As oil approaches that point, it will grow scarce and its price will rise.

This section examines three illustrative policies that affected oil output and price in important ways, sometimes improving market performance and sometimes worsening it. The first policy, state output restrictions for oil wells, began early in the twentieth century and restricted domestic extraction of oil. Its purpose was to avoid too-rapid extraction of oil from wells, which reduces the amount recovered, and yet is motivated by the common pool problem when many owners share the same oil reservoir. The second policy restricted oil imports in the 1960s, when the world oil price was low, and had the effect of raising domestic oil prices and production. The third policy, controlling the price of crude oil, was imposed by Congress in 1973, after OPEC succeeded in limiting the supply and raising the international price of crude oil. By keeping market price low in the United States, these price controls encouraged oil use just when the OPEC cartel was limiting oil supply to increase its world price, and very serious shortages resulted.

Oil Output Restriction

When produced in a decentralized market economy, oil is subject to the common pool problem, where individual incentives do not lead to the best way to share a resource. Ownership of the oil usually follows the *rule of capture*, which essentially cedes the property right to whomever extracts the oil first. The rule of capture thus invites each of several well operators who tap into a single reservoir to pump oil out as fast as possible, before the others (who have the same incentive) pump out all of the oil. Such rapid extraction can lead to inefficiency and higher cost and may prevent recovery of some of the oil from the reservoir. In extreme cases, only one-third of the available oil can be withdrawn when the rate of extraction is too great. More wells are drilled into the reservoir than is desirable, because that can help in the race to withdraw oil from the common pool.

Prorationing

Initial regulatory efforts occurred in oil-producing states, especially Kansas, Oklahoma, and Texas, to limit crude oil production. A **prorationing** policy allowed a state to allocate its limited production on a pro-rata basis among wells in the state, so each well had a share of the state's total. Oklahoma adopted such a policy in 1909, and Texas followed for some areas in 1919.[15] Kansas adopted prorationing in 1931, and Texas passed statutes for that effect for new oil fields in East Texas in 1931 and 1932. To help control illegal production under these prorationing schemes, the federal

---

[15] Prorationing could also aid well operators when demand fell in the Depression as massive new reserves were discovered, particularly the great East Texas Spindletop oil field in October 1930. Prices fell dramatically from $1 per barrel in 1930 to $0.10 per barrel in May 1931. See Weaver (1994).

government passed the Connally "Hot Oil" Act in 1935, forbidding interstate transport of oil extracted outside the states' pro rata production allotments.

Prorationing operated in roughly the following way.[16] A state authority determined a maximum allowable rate of production for each well in the state. Generally, deeper wells tended to be allowed higher maximum allowable production rates. Then, each month, the state authority would forecast demand based on the current price. If this demand quantity equaled or exceeded the amount that could be produced by all wells operating at their allowable rates, the wells would be allowed to operate at those rates. If the forecast demand was lower, an amount first would be allowed for exempt wells, which could continue to operate at their maximum rates. Exempt wells were largely high-cost wells that produced at low rates, but they included many locally operated wells that regulators tended to favor for political reasons. This left an amount to be produced by nonexempt wells, and regulators assigned pro-rata quantities to them in proportion to their maximum allowable rates.

Spacing Wells

Pumping oil too rapidly from an existing well is not the only inefficient incentive that arises from the rule of capture in a common pool. More wells may be drilled also to extract oil rapidly. So states, and later the federal government, restricted the number of wells, by requiring a **minimal spacing between oil wells**. Limits on the acres needed to obtain a drilling permit had been set in Texas as early as 1919, but so many exceptions were granted that it had little effect. At the time of World War II the federal government required 40 acres of land per oil well, and this exceeded the requirements of some states. Because each owner of land who can reach the oil reservoir wants to drill as many wells as possible and extract the oil rapidly, to claim ownership of as much oil as possible, restricting the spacing of wells can help to restrain too-rapid extraction from the reservoir. Deeper wells were also granted higher maximum allowable production rates, and that might have created an inefficient bias toward deep wells.[17]

Unitization and Pooling

As long as the rule of capture defines property rights, land owners are motivated to drill more wells and operate them at high rates, thereby extracting oil as rapidly as possible but, in contrast, when only one owner owns access to an oil reservoir, that party is motivated to choose the optimal extraction rate for the reservoir. One owner weighs the gains and losses from alternative extraction plans and chooses the plan that offers the greatest present value for the resource. There is no common pool problem. So why not operate an oil reservoir as a single owner would, seeing it as a single resource to be operated, and shared, in the optimal way? **Unitization** and **pooling** are names given to such conservation plans, which would operate the reservoir as a single pool and have each operator share on a unit basis.[18] For example, each operator might share the oil in proportion to land acreage owned over the reservoir.

---

[16] See McDonald (1971).

[17] See Adelman (1964).

[18] See Weaver (1986).

Unitization, or pooling, has not always been adopted, however, largely because reaching agreement among several operators in the same oil field is difficult and sometimes impossible. Although we would expect governments to force agreement when waste was serious, they often failed to overcome well owners' reluctance to agree, and truly optimal oil extraction plans have seldom been pursued.

There is another reason why states might enter into efforts to restrict production: to raise incomes for owners of oil who live in the state. Limiting a state's output can be significant enough to a national market that it would affect the national oil price. If the government of an oil exporting state served as a cartel operator, the benefits would fall to state residents who operated oil wells while the costs of higher oil prices would fall mainly on residents of other states who buy oil. This argument might be less persuasive if wells were owned by nonresidents, but even then there might be advantages, such as higher tax revenue, in raising the value of the resource located within the state.

Assessment

Prorationing and spacing limits probably had the effect of easing the common pool problem in the domestic crude oil industry, although evidence is not conclusive. Creating an allocation to each well might also have motivated the drilling of too many wells, and granting larger allocations to deeper wells may have encouraged the drilling of deep wells. Well spacing requirements might have eased this problem for some periods, but many exceptions were granted that limited their effect. Also, many new drilling techniques allow drilling in all directions, not just straight down, so limiting the number of wells per unit of land over the reservoir is no longer an effective restraint. Unitization and pooling programs sometimes improved management of an oil field; but, they were difficult to achieve on a voluntary basis, and state regulators often shrank from imposing them on a compulsory basis, so they were not widely adopted until quite late in the twentieth century.

BOX 17.3 Problems of Pooling in Practice

In the 1930s, in the great East Texas oil field, 586 small independent operators owned 20 percent of the acreage but had produced 49 percent of the oil from the field. They were not about to agree to a sharing of output based on acreage. The Texas legislature, its courts, and the Texas Railroad Commission that regulated oil and gas, were all elected bodies, and they favored these independent operators over large corporations. After abundant evidence accumulated about waste from too rapid extraction in Texas oil and gas fields, the state passed a compulsory pooling law in 1961. But compulsory pooling would apply only to oil and gas fields discovered after March 8, 1961, so existing independent operators escaped its effects. Many other states drew rules, as in Texas, to favor local independent operators over large oil producers with mainly out-of-state owners.

See J. Weaver, "The Politics of Oil and Gas Jurisprudence: The Eighty-Six Percent Factor," *Washburn Law Journal,* Vol. 33, pp. 492–539, (especially pp. 500–501).

Oil Import Restrictions

In the 1950s, oil producers argued that growing dependence on foreign oil was creating a national security risk. The case was not entirely convincing, because it could just as easily—perhaps more easily—be argued that relying heavily on foreign oil would serve national security by preserving more domestic oil, which could be used in a national emergency. Indeed, in 1960 foreign supplies provided less than 20 percent of U.S. consumption, but they provide more than 50 percent now. It is true that conserving domestic oil might reduce the country's capacity to produce oil, which would have to be redeveloped in an emergency. It is likely, however, that a strong reason for limiting imports was to benefit producers by raising oil prices. Limiting imports is consistent with other policies that favored the oil industry up until the 1970s.

Restricting Oil Imports

Congress created the Mandatory Oil Import Program in 1959 to restrict crude oil imports to 9 percent of estimated demand for oil. In 1962 the quota was tied to domestic production rather than demand and targeted at 12.2 percent. So under the Program, after 1962, every oil refiner was given an import quota that limited the amount of crude oil it could import to 12.2 percent of its domestic production.

Figure 17.1 indicates how this program would work.[19] It shows $S(P)$ as the domestic supply of oil, which would determine the domestic price when it is below the world price, P_w, along the line segment ab. At that world price it would become worthwhile for a refiner to import crude oil, because it would be cheaper than domestically supplied oil. But only 12.2 percent could be imported, along the line segment bc. After that, domestic supply would again come into play because imports could not continue, although the allowed import of 12.2 percent could grow as domestic supply

Figure 17.1 *The Mandatory Oil Import Program*

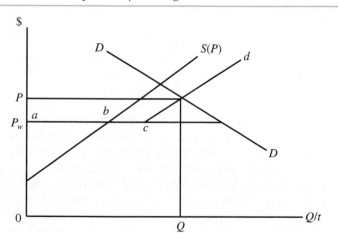

---

[19] See Burrows and Domencich (1970).

grew larger. The market would clear when demand met this total supply, which was domestic supply plus 12.2 percent imported crude oil, represented by line segment *cd*.

Assessment

Limiting imports raises the price of oil to domestic consumers, because the oil otherwise could be purchased at the lower world price of P_w. By 1970, this added cost to consumers was estimated at about $6 billion annually.[20] The import quotas were abolished in 1973, when the international price of oil rose dramatically and discouraged imports. The price rose after war came to the Middle East, the OPEC cartel grew stronger, and Arab countries imposed an embargo on shipments to the United States because of its participation on the side of Israel in the war.

Crude Oil Price Controls

During the 1970s, supply shocks following a 1968 war in the Middle East, and greater effectiveness of the OPEC cartel brought sharp increases in the international price of oil. Federal policy toward the oil industry then changed from generally supporting higher prices for oil to restraining increases in price. Just as import restrictions had raised the price of oil in the United States above the world level, crude oil price controls kept the price of oil below its market level. This made oil scarce and drew the government into allocating crude oil among refiners, who wanted more of it for its lower price. Although popular politically, keeping the price of oil low also strengthened the hand of the OPEC cartel, because it increased the amount of oil products demanded in the United States.

General and Industry Price Controls

President Nixon imposed general price controls to limit inflation in the early 1970s. After that program ended in 1973, the Emergency Petroleum Allocations Act (EPAA) continued to control oil prices. Through this Act, Congress imposed a price ceiling on domestically produced oil, a maximum price the producer could charge for the oil. In the Act, Congress also included a program of entitlements for distributing this low-price oil among refiners. The Cost of Living Council had managed general price controls, but as those general price controls eased, in 1974 the controls over oil prices that remained were shifted to the Federal Energy Administration. Then in 1975, Congress passed the Energy Policy Conservation Act (EPCA) with the aim of gradually decontrolling oil prices by 1981. Price controls ended in January of that year.

This episode of oil price control encouraged oil use through low consumer prices, while also making oil scarce by discouraging its production. More important, by discouraging exploration the controls probably raised the long-term cost of oil. Imports grew sharply during the period of the price controls. The price controls initially distinguished "old" from "new" oil, and price controls applied only to old oil. *Old oil* was oil produced from an existing well up to the rate of production for May 1972. Oil produced beyond that level, oil from small wells (less than 10 barrels per day), and oil from new

---

[20] See Bohi and Russell (1978).

fields constituted *new oil*, which was exempt from price controls. Moreover, for each barrel of new oil produced, a barrel of old oil was freed from price control.

This complex, multitiered pricing scheme was intended to retain incentives for oil exploration by leaving new and incremental oil production uncontrolled. The tiering became more complicated by 1975, however, when another old-oil tier was added and a distinction was made for oil produced after 1975. The rules became even more complicated with the addition of an overall average price as well as the tiered prices. By then it was clear to producers that new oil probably would soon come under price controls, so incentives to explore were seriously dampened.

Entitlements and Profits Taxes

The difference in price between old and new oil also grew markedly as the world price of oil went up sharply in the 1970s. As the world price increased, price-controlled oil became more attractive to refiners. The fraction of price-controlled oil in the total crude oil input was the basis for *entitlements*. One entitlement permitted the refiner to buy one barrel of price-controlled crude oil. If the price-controlled oil was 45 percent of total crude oil for a particular month, for example, then in that month any one refinery would receive entitlements equal to 45 percent of the crude input it used. If it processed 1,000,000 barrels, for example, it would receive entitlements worth 450,000 barrels. Entitlements were transferrable. Because they could be bought and sold, the refinery would surely want them, if only for the cash they represented.

The system of price controls with entitlements led to high profits for oil firms, and in 1980 Congress imposed a *Windfall Profits Tax* to capture some of that effect. It was really like an excise tax that applied to different tiers of crude oil, each tier being defined as of a certain date. In two tiers, it applied to the difference between the controlled price and the market price, and on that difference the tax was 60 percent for one tier and 70 percent tax for the other. On new oil, a tax of 50 percent was due on the difference between its sale price and the controlled price. The tax further dampened exploration incentives, which were already low because imported oil was so attractive, and it added another layer to the complexity of the program.

Assessment

Price controls reduced the supply of domestic oil by discouraging its production and encouraged consumption by keeping the price of crude oil low. Price controls were not well suited, then, to the oil-scarce 1970s. Moreover, a refinery could import a barrel of oil at the world price and in doing so become entitled to some fraction of a barrel of price-controlled domestic oil, the fraction being based on the fraction that price-controlled oil was of all crude oil input in the country. This effectively could make imports *more* attractive to a refinery, because a barrel of imported oil enabled it to buy domestic crude oil at a price that was below the world price.

The program also resulted in shortages of oil products such as gasoline. Limited quantities of gasoline were effectively rationed, allocated roughly to particular areas and gas stations based on past usage. With prices low relative to available supplies, gasoline was scarce and hard to find. As a consequence, it was difficult to plan a long auto trip in the middle 1970s for fear of finding gasoline unavailable. Cities and states adopted various nonprice rationing schemes. Some would allow cars with license plates ending in odd numbers to buy gasoline only on odd calendar days and those ending in even numbers to buy on even calendar days. Sometimes consumers could purchase no more than $5 worth of gasoline at one time, and yet long lines of cars would still wait to obtain it. The artificially low consumer prices were thus accompanied by serious inconveniences, which are added—but unmeasured—costs of the policies.

The Future

As recently as 1970, most of the world's oil was owned by large, privately held, and vertically integrated oil companies, such as British Petroleum, Chevron, ENI, Exxon, Mobil, Shell, Total, or Texaco. Today, however, the largest owners of oil are state monopolies such as Saudi Aramco, National Iranian Oil Co., Gazprom (Russia), Iraqi National Oil Council, Qatar Petroleum, Kuwait Petroleum, Petroleos de Venezuela, or Adnoc (United Arab Emirates).[21] Control over oil has moved to governments of the nations where the oil is located, and their participation in OPEC gives them market power over the price of oil. Monopoly state-owned companies also escape the common-pool problem. The change from commercial and market forces to political forces has made oil less reliable as an energy source for non-oil-producing countries. Oil production in the United States peaked in 1970, shortly after the oil import program favored domestic production over less costly foreign sources and just before the price-control program attempted to keep price low while OPEC was reducing world supply. The United States is now an oil importing country.

BOX 17.4 Trying for Oil Independence

In response to OPEC's embargo against the United States, for its intervention on behalf of Israel after Egypt attacked it in 1973, the United States tried to achieve independence from foreign sources of oil. One project was the Trans-Alaska Pipeline, which provided roughly 10 percent of the country's oil not long after it was completed in 1977. Another crisis came during the Carter administration in 1979, when revolution in Iran stopped its production of oil. Congress launched a Synthetic Fuels Corporation, an ambitious and costly effort to produce synthetic oil from shale that did not succeed because oil prices fell, making the effort uneconomical. Efforts since have largely granted tax subsidies to oil companies to increase production rather than develop alternative sources of energy, even though cries for energy independence are repeatedly heard.

See *America, Oil, and National Security*, National Environmental Trust, Ch. III, 2006, at http://www.net.org/proactive/newsroom/release.vtml?id=27555: and J. L. Weaver, "The Traditional Petroleum-Based Economy: An 'Eventful' Future," *Cumberland Law Review*, 2006, Vol. 36, pp. 1–75.

---

[21] See Weaver (2006).

Oil is plentiful enough to last 40 years or more at present consumption rates, but as production declines, the price will rise, and then oil may lose out to other fuels. Strong increases in demand for oil caused by economic growth in China and India, plus the Iraq War and other Mideast conflicts, contributed to a sharp rise in the price of oil in 2005 and 2006. Geopolitical uncertainties will probably keep the sources—and prices—of oil uncertain for the foreseeable future.

17.3 NATURAL GAS

Natural gas is often found where crude oil is found, and a significant fraction of the natural gas we use today comes from wells that also contain oil. Supplies of natural gas are expected to last 60 years or so, but supplies will decline and prices can be expected to rise. Natural gas needs no complicated refining, and its use does not cause as much pollution. It must be transported to final customers for use, however, and that transportation is complicated because natural gas requires a substantial volume to produce a unit of energy, even when it is compressed. Pipelines have proved to be the best way to transport natural gas in the United States, and today there is a large network of pipelines extending from sources, such as those in Texas, to other parts of the country. Pipelines raised many land-use and environmental questions, and when combined with the importance of the industry they invited government regulation. Until the 1970s, government policy often benefitted producers through policies that raised prices. But after high crude oil prices and shortages in the 1970s, important changes occurred in the regulation of natural gas. We begin by examining early regulation and price controls, and then consider how the industry was restructured.

Price Control

Congress applied price controls to natural gas as well as to crude oil. Natural gas is found, like crude oil, by drilling in the ground to strike a reservoir. The development of pipelines, accomplished mainly after World War II, allows transportation of natural gas for long distances. So the natural gas industry has production (from wells), transmission (by pipelines), and distribution functions. Natural gas is a clean burning and low-polluting fuel that competes effectively with other fuels and is used in some of the most modern and least polluting electricity generating facilities. Its advantages over other fuels led to great expansion in its use after 2000, and because supply was unable to increase rapidly enough its price has risen considerably.

Regulation

Federal regulation of natural gas began with the **Natural Gas Act** of 1938. Although the Act gave the Federal Power Commission (FPC) (now the Federal Energy Regulatory Commission) power to regulate transportation and sale of gas for resale (wholesale transactions) in interstate commerce, it did not appear to grant the agency control over producer prices, or so-called wellhead prices, where natural gas was produced in thousands of wells that constitute a competitive part of the industry. In 1954, however, the Supreme Court ruled in *Phillips Petroleum v. Wisconsin*[22] that the FPC also had the power to control wellhead prices of natural gas.

The FPC used rate-of-return regulation for the natural gas industry, allowing revenues to cover costs plus a reasonable return on investment. When the FPC set out to regulate wellhead prices, however, it was simply not able to process all the rate cases that developed, and there was an enormous backlog of cases by 1960. As a result, many prices stayed at the same levels for a long time. In setting wellhead prices, the FPC distinguished gas by vintage, old and new. As in the case for crude oil, the FPC hoped to retain exploration incentive by not regulating "new," recently discovered, gas, while limiting profit by regulating "old" gas. This policy encountered the same problem as in the case of crude oil: producers noticed that new gas would eventually become old gas subject to regulation, thus limiting the possible profit opportunity from exploration. From 1966 to 1978, proved or demonstrated gas reserves in the contiguous 48 states declined every year. Controlled prices led to shortages and to calls for change.

The Beginning of Restructuring

During the period of natural gas regulation, state or local authorities usually regulated the distribution function of carrying gas to final consumers, while the FPC regulated wellhead prices and pipelines, because they moved gas across state lines. Distribution had natural monopoly aspects, because it would be uneconomical to install competing distribution systems within a community. Pipelines also seemed to be natural monopolies because they required high fixed costs and had low operating costs, and often only one pipeline served to connect a particular consuming area with a source of natural gas.[23] Thus, unlike crude oil, the natural gas industry was regulated at every stage.

Pipelines and distribution companies had been subject to rate-of-return regulation, with exceptions including municipal distribution operations that were essentially controlled by their municipalities. Pipeline companies purchased gas from producers at regulated prices, transported it, and sold it to distributors, often under long-term contracts. The distributors liked long-term contracts, which assured availability of gas on which their customers depended for heating and other important uses. Pipelines also welcomed long-term arrangements to insure the use of their capacity and to facilitate planning. Pipelines also arranged long-term contracts with wells to assure their sources of supply. Under regulation, then, natural gas moved along an uncomplicated path from wellhead to final consumer, but regulatory procedures and the resulting prices seemed faulty as reserves dwindled. Interest in deregulation was mounting, especially when natural gas wells were so numerous that competition at this production level for the industry seemed perfectly feasible.

---

[22] See *Phillips Petroleum Co. v. State of Wisconsin et al.*, 347 U.S. 672, 74 S.Ct. 794.
[23] See Wellisz (1963).

The **Natural Gas Policy Act** of 1978 was intended to decontrol wellhead gas prices of natural gas gradually, starting with new gas (discovered after 1977). Power for such regulation moved to the **Federal Energy Regulatory Commission (FERC)** when it replaced the FPC in 1977. Old gas was still regulated and would be for some time. Apparent scarcity of natural gas was one reason for passage of the **Powerplant and Industrial Fuel Use Act (PIFUA)** of 1978, which prevented the use of oil or natural gas in new power plants built by electric utilities. But there was also growing awareness that price controls had exacerbated the problems for energy in the 1970s.

Restructuring of Natural Gas

A remarkable series of policy changes began in 1978 that would restructure the natural gas industry.[24] Shortly after the Natural Gas Policy Act of 1978 was passed to deregulate wellhead prices, a general scarcity of natural gas turned into a surprising surplus. Not believing that the abundant gas could last, pipeline companies entered into contracts with producers to insure their supplies, even at prices much higher than they had previously paid.

Being regulated by the FERC, the pipeline companies might reason that paying a high price for their input would enable them to have a high price approved for their delivered gas. Monopoly distribution companies could in turn pay that price by wringing more money from their retail customers. The pipeline companies even agreed to *take-or-pay clauses*, which obligated them to pay for some amounts of gas each month, whether they took the gas or not. They sometimes could protect themselves in turn through *minimum-bill contracts* with their customers, who would then be obliged to make payments of pipelines' fixed costs and even some variable costs, whether they took their gas or not.

The pipelines' expectations for continued scarcity of natural gas proved to be wrong. Release of natural gas producers from price control brought a sustained increase in supply, ending the scarcities of the price-controlled 1970s. Higher prices for gas persisted for some time, in part because of long-term contract arrangements, and the high prices had the effect of lowering demanded amounts. By 1981, industrial customers consumed about 25 percent less than they had 10 years earlier. And then in 1982, with calm in the Middle East and cracks in the OPEC cartel, world oil prices collapsed, opening up opportunities for natural gas customers who could switch to oil.

Competitive pressure, then, was mounting on the natural gas industry. In 1983, the FERC approved what were called *special marketing programs*, which allowed some large distributors to buy low-price gas directly from the producers at the wellhead. This essentially created a short-term, or "spot," market for natural gas, and it also created a situation in which pipelines were engaged merely to transport gas purchased by final users directly from producers. Large cities, which were likely to take advantage of special marketing programs, were sometimes served by competing pipelines, so there was also a possibility for competition in that transportation function.

---

[24] For a description of these changes, see Michaels (1993).

In these circumstances, the FERC moved to further encourage competition. It attacked the minimum bill contracts that required distributors to pay an amount to pipelines that would cover the pipeline's fixed cost and some variable cost, even if no gas was taken. The objection to these contracts was that they tied a distributor to a particular pipeline and made switching pipelines costly, thus inhibiting competition. In 1984, the FERC issued its Order 380, which eliminated variable cost as an element in minimum bill contracts with distributors and allowed pipelines to contract for help only in supporting fixed costs.

In 1985 the U.S. Court of Appeals for the District of Columbia found the special marketing programs, which allowed purchases of low-price gas directly from producers, to be discriminatory. The difficulty the court found with these programs was that only certain buyers, those large enough to bargain for low prices and arrange for the transportation of gas, were eligible to participate in them. Because the contracts were not really available to all buyers, the court held that they unlawfully discriminated among buyers.

The FERC liked the special marketing arrangements and the spot market they encouraged. The arrangements created a situation in which distributors could purchase directly from wells and pipelines merely transported the gas, without actually taking title to it. Whether pipelines would be transporters rather than owners of natural gas had been debated at the time the Natural Gas Act was passed in 1935. If pipelines only transported natural gas that their customers purchased at the wellhead from producers, the pipelines would not possess the degree of monopoly power they had as the owners of natural gas. A pipeline offering transportation service might have monopoly advantages that would call for regulation, but regulating transport service alone would be easier than regulating pipelines that owned natural gas and sold it to customers while also transporting it. In addition, the FERC could see some scope for competition in the transportation market. So the FERC set out to accomplish the same result as the special marketing programs but in other ways.

Open Access to Pipelines

The FERC's next step induced a restructuring of pipeline service. Through its Order 436 in 1985, the FERC offered pipelines an opportunity to choose to be open-access pipelines. Pipelines with **open-access** status would allow their customers to contract for natural gas with wellhead sources if they wished, and then have the pipeline transport the gas. The FERC offered two inducements. First, a pipeline that chose open-access status would be offered an *optional expedited certificate* for building new capacity. This certificate avoided much of the cost and delay, which could be years long, through the FERC construction approval proceedings. With the certificate, a project was essentially presumed to be in the public interest and could be quickly approved. Second, a pipeline that did not opt for open-access status could *not* transport gas; it could only resell gas to customers. Without open access it could then be at a disadvantage if some of its customers—perhaps a city distribution company that could be served by another, competing, pipeline—wished to have transportation service.

These FERC policies exerted pressure for pipelines to accept open access status. Pipelines supplied natural gas as monopolists at some of their delivery points but faced competition at others, especially at large cities. If a competitive pipeline that could serve one of those cities went to open access, it could probably win away the looming possible transport-only traffic from any pipeline that refused open-access status. If a pipeline opted for open access for such competitive reasons, the FERC required it also to offer access at delivery points where there was no competition! This spur to competition, plus the advantage of easy approval for pipeline expansion projects, successfully enticed pipelines into open-access status. By 1987 three-fourths of the gas that was being transported was not owned by the pipelines.

The use of FERC regulatory authority to force pipelines to offer transport service—by granting easy capacity construction approval—was challenged by some pipelines in court. The FERC's authority to require the open-access choice was upheld by the D.C. Court of Appeals in 1987, but the court also required the FERC to give more consideration to take-or-pay contracts. Specifically, the court wanted disputes over existing take-or-pay contracts to be resolved before producers could have access to pipelines for transportation. In response, the FERC issued Order 500 in 1987, requiring that gas transported by a pipeline for a producer would be credited as part of the pipeline's take-or-pay obligation to the producer. Although it involved modification of existing contracts, the court supported Order 500 in a 1989 decision.[25]

Ending Natural Gas Wellhead Price Control

While pipeline service was being reconstructed as a transportation service, authorities at the FERC were also evaluating wellhead price controls. In 1986, the FERC was distinguishing and setting maximum prices for 15 different vintages of natural gas, and it could see that some resulting prices did not cover replacement costs. As a consequence, the FERC decided that prices were neither just nor reasonable as regulated prices were supposed to be. So in that year the FERC issued Order 451, which collapsed the 15 vintages into one class and set a maximum price for it that was above the market level. This remarkable order effectively overturned the Natural Gas Policy Act's price controls, and it was challenged in court by Mobil Oil.

In 1989, the Fifth Circuit Court of Appeals decided Mobil's case against the FERC.[26] The court's line of argument was that the FERC was doing what only Congress could do. But in 1991 the Supreme Court unanimously reversed that decision, saying the FERC had not illegally deregulated because a price ceiling still existed, and that its concern for "just and reasonable" prices was sound.[27] The survival of Order 451, which ended complex price controls on natural gas at the wellhead, also eliminated efforts by strategically placed purchasers to seek advantage in obtaining low-price gas. Order 451 improved incentives by fostering market-based prices for

---

[25] See *American Gas Association, et al. v. Federal Energy Regulatory Commission*, 888 F.2d 136, 281 U.S.App.D.C. 123.

[26] See *Mobil Oil Exploration and Producing Southeast, Inc., et al. v. Federal Energy Regulatory Commission*, 885 F.2d 209.

[27] See *Mobil Oil Exploration and Producing Southeast Inc., et al. v. United Distribution Companies et al. Federal Energy Regulatory Commission*, 498 U.S. 211, 111 S.Ct. 615.

old as well as new gas. Despite thousands of sellers, price controls had prevented the gas-producing industry from functioning competitively. Acknowledging this, Congress passed the Natural Gas Wellhead Decontrol Act of 1989, which formally removed all price ceilings by January 1, 1993.

The Last Steps

Despite the radical changes brought about by these aggressive FERC actions, all was not well in the natural gas industry at the end of the 1980s. The rate structures for resale gas from pipelines continued as they were before, being high for usage and low for fixed fees that reserved capacity. This biased pricing structure invited distributors to reserve more capacity and create more peak usage than was efficient. Pipelines could not abandon sales arrangements to customers who preferred to purchase gas from them, so sales under this pricing arrangement continued. Some customers still bought gas that the pipelines had purchased to resell, even after open-access pipelines offered transportation-only service, because they did not want to manage delivery themselves.

With more competitive markets, the natural gas industry grew more complicated. Most pipeline companies formed affiliates, mainly for marketing gas they had purchased, so problems could arise if the pipeline offered more favorable terms to its affiliate than to transportation-only customers. There could be other problems when pipelines sold natural gas they owned themselves for resale to some customers while serving other customers only with transportation service. For instance, the pipelines had advantages over transportation-only customers when it came to allocating storage capacity they owned or deciding delivery points for customers. While the FERC did not require divestiture of affiliates, these affiliates were supposed to be kept separate in their operations, like independent firms.

To remedy these possible favoritism problems, the FERC issued Order 636 in April of 1992. Order 636 was 250 pages long, and it is known as the *final restructuring rule*. First, the Order required that bundled pipeline services be separated wherever possible, and it attempted to force fairness in treatment of gas between that owned by pipelines and that owned by customers. It gave transport customers specific rights to pipeline capacity and storage, not only on the pipeline delivering to them but also on upstream connecting pipelines where that was needed. Resales were to take place as near the wellhead as possible, so the customer would become a transport customer as soon as possible. The Order allowed market-based, or negotiated, rates for unbundled services and it permitted the pipelines to more easily abandon short-term obligations when they expired. The rights created for transport customers in Order 636 enabled them to duplicate all the services that a resale customer of the pipeline had and, thus, to be treated on the same footing.

Order 636 also restructured rates for transportation service. The capacity charge was to cover fixed costs, while the transport charge was to cover variable costs. Careful treatment of the pricing was intended to trace costs to those responsible for causing them more effectively than did traditional rate structures in the industry. Residences, which had uneven demands and did not pay the full costs of their peak demands under old rates, might face slightly higher overall rates after the changes, but some form of peak and off-peak pricing to the final customer would be encouraged under this rate structure. If the new rates raised fees to a customer class by more than 10 percent, however, the Order called for the pipeline to ease the impact of the change on that customer class by imposing it gradually over time.

Pipelines can resell gas at competitive market rates under Order 636, although they must comply with rules that govern sales to their affiliates. Pipelines can also sell their transportation capacity, and they are required to maintain electronic bulletin boards where shippers can post bids and offers for this capacity. In any transaction the original purchaser of the capacity must pay the pipeline, at regulated rates, and then collect from the actual user of the capacity.

The optional expedited certificate, which enabled transporting pipelines to expand their lines without delay, allowed pipelines to expand so they could connect to any large user seeking gas delivery. Allowing direct service to large industrial customers reduced the monopoly power that distribution companies had over such customers and cut much of the cross-subsidization of residences that high prices to industrial users had allowed. State and local regulators favored this cross-subsidization of residential customers, and they had some power to resist federal orders to achieve their local aims. Appellate circuit courts, however, ruled that bypassing a local distribution company with a pipeline direct to a customer is a transaction in interstate commerce, and they allowed it. These rulings brought competitive pressure to eliminate rate structures that were discriminatory in favoring residences at the expense of industrial customers, and it improved efficiency. State commissions have usually accepted the developing trends and moved to improve pricing practices, thereby avoiding cross subsidization.

A FERC task force on pipeline competition considered whether pipeline services could be sold at unregulated rates and whether sales should be allowed below regulated rates. Although it is true that few pipelines serve the same city, so their direct competition may appear weak, the fact that capacity rights are purchased and can be exchanged by many buyers and sellers opens up opportunities for competition. It is rather like a single highway that connects two cities supporting competition for space among many trucking companies that use the highway. With enough transport customers reserving capacity, their transactions may be sufficient to limit the price that the pipeline owner can charge, and, thus, competition could be effective at the pipeline transport service level. Transactions for capacity have taken place at rates below the regulated levels.

After these policy changes, some pipelines still had very large financial obligations, traceable to their ill-advised take-or-pay contracts. The FERC permitted pipelines to recover in their rates some of the costs of these old contracts, which in some cases were substantial. Order 636 almost certainly raised residential heating rates, because residences had previously been favored with uneconomically low rates. Evaluation of the Order shows that it caused firms to follow financial market incentives and to operate more efficiently.[28] On the whole, the prospect for a natural gas industry guided largely by competition is now realistic.

---

[28] See Finoff, Cramer, and Shaffer (2004).

Effects of Restructuring

This restructuring of the natural gas pipeline industry has led to improved efficiency and lower prices. Higher prices for the capacity part of pipeline tariffs have led to much more efficient use of pipeline capacity, especially at peak times.[29] Transmission and distribution costs for operations and maintenance are estimated to be 35 percent lower than before deregulation.[30] Service is judged to be more reliable. Natural gas prices are estimated to be 30 percent lower for residential consumers, and reductions are slightly better for industrial and commercial customers.[31] Also, the new policies that restructured the natural gas industry might have helped Canadian exporters into the U.S. market. Canadian exporters provided only about 4 percent of U.S. natural gas in the mid 1980s and they now provide more than 15 percent, a result consistent with our using the lowest price gas available. A summary of natural gas industry restructuring is presented in Table 17.1.

Instead of fairly simple transactions, along the direct line from wellhead producers to pipeline to distributor to final end user, natural gas transactions now occur through a maze of brokers, purchasing agents, and marketing companies. Gas follows the same path as before, but with more reliance on 30-day-spot contracts than on 20-year contracts and with more intermediaries to absorb the resulting uncertainties. Producers may sell to distributors, marketing companies may sell to distributors or end users, and pipelines can be involved in these transactions in complicated ways. With these new opportunities come a need for risk management strategies. Consider, for example, a northern city trying to obtain gas and gas transportation for a coming winter, without knowing just how cold the weather will be. It might engage a gas marketer, a new kind of firm that specializes in meeting such needs.

The presence of a variety of intermediaries gives rise to new markets for natural gas transactions, promoted by energy firms in the industry such as Enron.[32] Enron set out to be the e-Bay of energy trades and, being the largest, it became the market maker. For example, it agreed to supply energy needs for 20 plants in the United States

TABLE 17.1 Natural Gas Restructuring in the United States, 1978–1992

| Functions | Restructuring | |
	Before	After
Wellhead	Regulated prices	Competitive prices
Pipelines	Purchase for sale to distributors	Transport to order
Distributors	Purchase from pipelines	Purchase from wellhead and hire transportation

---

[29] See Henning, Tucker, and Liu (1995) and Herbert (1996).
[30] See Herbert (1996).
[31] See Costello and Duann (1996).
[32] For excellent descriptions of these new markets see Weaver (2004).

for 10 years.[33] Enron also introduced the "gas bank," an imaginary bank where producers could deposit promises of future gas for guaranteed payment and users could arrange promises of future delivery at guaranteed prices. The gas bank thus reduced risks for both sides, which is why producers would accept a lower price and demanders would pay more, with the result that Enron as broker intermediary could profit.

Institutions such as the gas bank inspired commodity exchanges to trade in natural gas futures. Through a futures contract, a producer can arrange the sale of future natural gas production at a known price today, thereby avoiding the risk of future price volatility. In 1990, the New York Mercantile Exchange (NYMEX) adopted standardized futures contracts for natural gas, so futures could easily be traded on its exchange, and this added another avenue for managing risk. Those who need gas, like that northern city planning for winter, can buy gas at a definite, known future price. All the while, speculators, who are willing to bear risk, also can take positions on future prices and help those who are accomplishing other functions avoid bearing risk.

Although restructuring of natural gas improved efficiency in the industry and lowered costs, it also gave rise to manipulation of prices in some newly formed markets. Such manipulation contributed to the electricity crisis that shook California in 2000.

The Future

With the lower pollution levels that its use allows, natural gas has a promising future. But much of the world's supply does not lie close to population centers. To be usable, this natural gas has to be converted to liquified natural gas (LNG) so it can be moved across oceans in tankers to regasification terminals in ports and then on to customers,

---

BOX 17.5 Treacherous Trading

Massive trading that developed in the deregulated natural gas environment turned out to be marred in important respects. Specifically in Western markets during the 2000–2001 California electricity crisis, the FERC found evidence of manipulation of gas markets by churning, or producing artificial sales, to affect market prices. Faulty and unverified reporting of transactions were used to manipulate price indices. The FERC found that EnronOnline manipulated actual prices of gas and electricity and profited on other contracts that were tied to those prices through actions that violated FERC and other rules. For example, merchant marketing affiliates of natural gas pipelines had advantages in obtaining capacity at crucial entry points to California, and they used the capacity to affect gas availability and its price. Procedural improvements, particularly in price reporting to form price indices, can help to avoid manipulations, but enforcement of existing FERC rules is also needed.

See R. A. Oppel, Jr., "Panel Finds Manipulation By Energy Companies," *New York Times*, March 27, 2003, p. A12; and T. Fowler and L. Goldberg, "Federal Report on Crisis Blasts Energy Companies," *Houston Chronicle*, March 27, 2003, p. A1.

---

[33] See Weaver (2004) and Fox (2003, pp. 165–170).

typically through pipelines. It is more difficult to protect tankers and long pipelines, so LNG offers less security than natural gas straight from wells, but LNG is a possible alternative source of energy when the price is right.

The added cost of converting natural gas to liquid form for transportation and then back to gas form for distribution and consumption would seem to limit its future. But energy prices are volatile. From a price of around $2.00 per thousand cubic feet (MCF) of gas in 1999, the price of natural gas surprisingly increased and reached $8.00 per MCF by 2003.[34] The future of LNG was thought in 1999 to be limited, unless the price of natural gas went above $4.00 per MCF, but now it has a bright future. Thus, although more expensive sources will have to be tapped, non-polluting natural gas will be available as a source of energy, but at higher prices than had been expected.

All fuel prices except coal increased sharply in 2005 and 2006, and these changes in prices affect the uses of fuels and the emergence of substitutes. As oil and gas decline in availability they can be expected to grow more expensive. As we have noted, LNG is more attractive as the price of natural gas rises. As the price of oil rises, a substitute can be obtained from shale. Although more plentiful, coal and nuclear energy have pollution and accident dangers, and like oil and gas they also ultimately are exhaustible. So at some point the hunt for new sources of energy will intensify, and as existing sources grow scarce, that hunt will focus on renewable sources of energy.

17.4 | RENEWABLE ENERGY

Current fuels that provide the bulk of our energy have two drawbacks. First, they pollute. For example, about half of all pollution in the United States today comes primarily from coal used in electricity generation, which also contributes to global warming. Second, current fuels are not renewable; we can ultimately expect to exhaust most of today's sources of fuel for electricity. Coal, uranium, oil, and natural gas are all found in the earth, and although they may be formed by natural processes, the processes operated over many years. Because we are using these resources faster than they can be formed, we call them nonrenewable sources of energy. This section examines some of the main sources of renewable energy, which come from the sun, wind, earth, and water, from organic materials such as trees, and from chemical energy. Renewable energy accounts for about 10 percent of all the energy the world uses today, and much of it is pollution free. Thus they offer a cleaner as well as a more lasting source of energy. Renewable energy often costs more than nonrenewable forms, but some sources of renewable energy, such as existing hydroelectric dams, are very economical, and others are economical in certain conditions.

---

[34] See Weaver (2006).

Solar Energy

We enjoy energy from the sun every day and could not live without it. *Passive solar heating* is as simple as a large window in a house, facing south, that receives daylight and the sun's warmth. More complex passive solar designs trap and route the heat more extensively through the house. An example would be a sun space, like a green house on the south side of a house, where the sun can heat air that is then circulated through the house. *Active solar heating* involves collectors containing air or water, usually on the roofs of buildings, that heat the air or water so it can be stored or pumped through the building to provide heat. Solar hot water systems have water run through tubes in solar collectors, again on the roofs of buildings, to heat water that is stored until used.

There are two main ways to produce electricity directly from the sun. One way is by concentrating the sun's power using mirrors, to obtain enough heat to operate a boiler which in turn can power a steam generator that produces electricity. Another way uses *photovoltaic solar cells* that convert sunlight into electricity. Small photovoltaic solar cells commonly power calculators and watches, and larger units can provide power for homes. Such sources are valuable in climates where sunshine is abundant, especially at remote locations that are expensive to reach with conventional electricity transmission lines.

Solar energy can be wisely used in small applications, such as the use of windows in building construction. It can be an economical renewable source of energy, in that it competes successfully with existing sources in certain conditions. Because it depends on rays from the sun reaching the earth, however, it is less reliable than existing sources and is promising mainly in areas that receive plentiful sunshine throughout the year.

Wind Energy

People have used windmills to pump water and grind grain for 3,000 years, and they have used sailing boats for even longer. Modern versions of wind turbines are usually about 100 feet high. That height reaches faster and less turbulent wind, which can spin turbine blades to rotate a shaft that can power an electricity generator. When built on a large scale, many turbines close together form a *wind plant*, also called a wind farm, that can produce a commercial quantity of electricity. A wind plant in Altamont Pass in California, for example, has 7,000 turbines that can produce more than a billion kilowatt-hours of electricity a year. Germany leads the world in capacity to produce wind energy, followed by the United States, Spain, Denmark, and India. Wind turbines, however, are only effective when the wind blows. Ideal areas for wind may not be close to population centers where electricity is consumed, so extensive transmission may be needed. Smaller stand-alone wind turbines can pump water or provide electricity for communications or for other specialized uses but are not large-scale sources of electricity.

BOX 17.6 Not in My Backyard

Coastal areas often provide desirable conditions for wind farms. That is why a wind farm of 130 turbines has been proposed for Nantucket Sound off the Massachusetts coast of the United States. Many environmentalists regard this location as one of the most promising in the country. Environmental lawyer Robert Kennedy, Jr., however, who supports the development of power from wind farms, has opposed this particular Nantucket Sound wind farm, almost certainly because it could mar the view from property he shares at Hyannis Port, Massachusetts. This same objection arises against other wind farms close to settled populations, and it can sometimes prevent their construction. The wind farms are often subsidized by federal tax breaks or state incentives. New York and California both require utilities to generate some of their power from renewable sources like wind farms. Thus, urged by government, utilities or private firms pursue promising sites, but they may encounter opposition from those who have to look at, or listen to, the wind farms and may oppose the government policies that promote them.

See J. Tierney, "Not in the Kennedys' Back Yard," *New York Times*, January 17, 2006 p. A25.

Wind energy is not highly expensive, and it competes successfully in some locations against existing generation methods. Spirited opposition to wind farms comes from those who do not like the threat they present to flying birds and bats or their noise, and they also complain about their relative inefficiency.[35] Ideal wind farm locations usually offer great views and are good for sailing or hiking or other activities enjoyed by many who resist interference for wind farming. But as concern for global warming grows, one consequence will probably be the expansion of wind farming, and many possible wind-farm locations are currently being evaluated.

Geothermal Energy

The earth itself can also be a source of energy. Extreme heat from the center of the earth raises underground water to very high temperatures. When that water is near the surface of the earth, say within two miles or so, it can be tapped and the steam it produces can be used to drive turbines to produce electricity. This is *geothermal energy*. It can be a low-cost source of energy where ideal conditions for it exist, but applications in less ideal circumstances grow more costly. Forty percent of El Salvador's electricity is produced from geothermal energy, and 85 percent of Iceland's houses are heated by geothermal energy. Around the world there are 250 geothermal power plants, including one that supplies electricity to San Francisco. Water as a source of geothermal energy can be returned to the ground, to be reheated, so a geothermal

---

[35] See Felicity Barringer, "Debate Over Wind Power Creates Environmental Rift," *New York Times*, June 6, 2006, p. B1.

plant is a sustainable resource that does not pollute the air. Sources are limited by natural circumstances, so geothermal energy will probably not be a large source of energy for much of the world.

We can use geothermal energy directly, by drilling a well into an underground reservoir of hot water and bringing the hot water to a heat exchanger to heat a building. Geothermal heat pumps are another source of heat. Merely from the difference between the almost constant temperature about ten feet below the surface of the earth and the temperature of the air above, heat-pump technology can produce heat in the winter and cooling in the summer.

Water Energy

The water of the world possesses enormous energy. Hydroelectric power is the most visible, commonly produced by a dam on a river that forms a reservoir to store water. When released from the reservoir, water can spin turbine blades to run generators to produce electricity. In ideal conditions water is a low-cost source of electricity. Many of the most promising locations for dams have already been developed, and they offer a significant supply of power.

Water can produce energy in other ways as well, but these other applications tend to be more expensive. Tidal movements of water in response to the moon's gravitational pull can be harnessed to turn turbines, much like river dams do. The tidal flow of water, unlike wind, is totally predictable. To harness tidal movements dams, called "barrages," are built across fairly narrow passages that the tidal waters pass through, and like river dams the water drives turbines to generate electricity. Especially in northern latitudes, tides are so great that the water level can rise and fall as much as 20 feet, and this great flow of moving water can generate power. Europe, where strong winds strengthen the tidal movements, is an especially promising region for tidal energy. A tidal power station built in 1966 in the Rance estuary in northern France is the largest in the world and is so far the only one in Europe. Only a limited number of locations allow tidal movements to be captured, but other technologies can produce power from movements in open oceans and may someday become economically feasible.

BOX 17.7 A Large United States Hydroelectric Power System

One large federal system operated by the Department of Energy contains 31 federal hydroelectric projects and is called the Bonneville Power Administration. The system provides about 45 percent of the power used in the Pacific Northwest. The Bonneville Power Administration also represents about three-fourths of the region's high-voltage transmission system. The power system raises enough revenue to break even on its operations, including the protection of fish and wildlife in the Columbia River Basin.

See http://www.bpa.gov.

Ocean temperature differences can also yield energy. Just as a heat pump takes advantage of the temperature difference between the earth and the air, similar technology can do the same with differences in temperature near the water's surface and at deeper levels. Such differences occur because the sun heats water near the surface while deeper water remains cold. This is a source of thermal energy. Oceans cover nearly three-fourths of the earth's surface, forming an enormous solar collector, and resulting temperature differences in water might become a substantial source of power.

Biomass Energy

Biomass energy comes from organic matter and provides 3 to 4 percent of energy in the United States. The most significant biomass energy source is *wood*, which has been used for thousands of years in fires to cook food and to generate warmth. Although burning biomass energy produces carbon dioxide, organic energy sources also remove carbon dioxide from the air as they grow. By removing about as much carbon dioxide as it produces, biomass energy can help to reduce greenhouse gas emissions.

Some biomass energy sources can be converted into liquid fuels. Leading ones for use in motor vehicles are *ethanol, methanol,* and *biodiesel*. Ethanol (a grain alcohol) is made by fermenting biomass materials such as starches or sugars available from cane sugar, corn, wheat, and other crops. Ethanol is used mainly as a fuel additive to save petroleum and reduce carbon emissions. Some vehicle engines are designed to use mixtures of gasoline with up to 85 percent ethanol. Methanol (a wood alcohol) can be made from many biomass resources, such as wood, but it is usually made from natural gas today because that is cheaper. Methanol is a single chemical, unlike gasoline which contains many chemicals and can vary considerably from one batch to another. Because it can be controlled and standardized to support fair auto races, methanol is the required fuel for the Indianapolis 500, which also shows that it can deliver abundant power. Biodiesel usually combines methanol with animal fat or vegetable oil so it can be added to diesel fuel to reduce emissions. It may also be developed into a renewable alternative diesel fuel.

Biomass can also play a role in generating electricity. Biomass materials may be added when coal is burned in boilers, for example, to reduce sulphur dioxide emissions. Gases are also produced in several ways from biomass materials and can fuel a gas turbine, which is like a jet engine, to generate electricity. When biomass decays it releases methane, which can fuel a boiler to produce electricity. Methane is especially effective in small *microturbines*, generators the size of a household refrigerator that produce modest amounts of electricity. Methane also can serve as fuel for a fuel cell. Many companies, especially in the wood and paper products industries, burn waste wood to produce steam and electricity for their own use.

Chemical Energy

Batteries that lead you to your car by flashlight on a dark night and then start your engine when you get to it run on chemical energy. Newer forms of this chemical energy, called *fuel cells*, are not only more powerful than ordinary batteries, but they do more than store energy. They continuously produce electricity and depend on common fuel sources, like hydrogen and oxygen, that are everywhere. The idea for the fuel cell is actually 150 years old, but it was developed for effective use when space travel began.[36] No power cord could be attached to space vehicles, and standard batteries were too heavy to carry. To provide needed power, the fuel cell used oxygen and hydrogen found in space. Fuel cells are not cheap, but they offer a great range of possibilities and some variations may produce power at costs only modestly above existing sources.

There are different kinds of fuel cells, but they usually trick a hydrogen atom in some way to separate its proton and electron elements to get electrons moving, which is electricity. Fuel cells are a form of *hydrogen energy*. Water is produced as a byproduct, but the water is pure and not a pollutant. Indeed, drinking water for the crew is a byproduct of hydrogen fuel cell operation in spacecraft. To power buses and automobiles by fuel cells would presently require compressed hydrogen as a fuel source. Hydrogen can also be obtained from methanol and ethanol, which can be easier than compressed hydrogen to handle in small applications, but they produce carbon dioxide waste. Small fuel cells, called microcells, promise applications for motor vehicle power, in part because they are expected to be competitive in price sooner.[37] Even though some electricity—with its associated pollution—would be needed to produce hydrogen, the total pollution would still be much lower than existing fuels. Also, the hydrogen this electricity would produce could be stored, rather than used on demand, so the electricity could be generated at off-peak times or by nonpolluting windmills or solar methods. Fuel cells thus promise a less-polluting source of power.

SUMMARY

The main sources of energy for electricity today are coal and nuclear power. Coal may last many years, but it causes environmental problems. Environmental regulation constrains the pollution that coal causes and mine safety regulation tries to protect the health and safety of miners who extract coal from the earth. One way to solve the problem of pollution is by sequestering, or saving and storing, the carbon dioxide that burning coal produces, and mine safety depends on a range of measures. If these problems cannot be solved economically, then fuels that do not pollute or endanger workers may replace coal. Nuclear power does not pollute the air but it raises concerns about safety, either from a catastrophic mistake or from an accident involving spent fuel, which can last thousands of years. The Nuclear Regulatory Commission focuses exclusively on these problems for the nuclear power industry.

---

[36] Its inventor was Sir William Grove, who noted that an electric current running through water separated hydrogen from oxygen, so he reversed the process to make electricity. Grove is described briefly at http://www.voltaic-power.com/Biographies/GroveBio.htm.

[37] See Barnaby J. Feder, "For Far Smaller Fuel Cells, a Far Shorter Wait," *New York Times*, March 16, 2003, Sec. 3, p. 1.

Oil and natural gas are less problematic sources of energy but their supplies are more limited than coal, so they will not last as long. Oil supplies are also concentrated in a few countries that do not enjoy stable governments and participate together in a cartel, the Organization of Petroleum Exporting Countries (OPEC). Natural gas is an especially clean-burning fuel. It also is concentrated in not-always friendly countries and much of it needs to be liquified so it can be transported in tankers long distances to reach markets.

In the United States, crude oil and natural gas have been subject to both federal and state regulation. Some state policies, such as prorationing, which limits extraction rates when many owners tap the same common pool, may increase efficiency by allowing more oil and gas to be drawn from the pool. Inefficiently rapid extraction is motivated when several land owners extract from a single reservoir of oil, and prorationing imposes quotas on wells in an effort to limit the rate of extraction. It offers benefits to well operators as a group, but individual operators may subvert it to seek their private interest to pump out oil before others do.

From 1959 to 1973, the federal Mandatory Oil Import Program raised domestic prices by limiting imports. It is difficult to defend the program because it limited citizens' access to lower-priced world oil, and in using domestic rather than foreign oil it also increased U.S. dependence on foreign countries for oil. Other federal price controls kept prices lower in the 1970s, but that was when OPEC made oil scarce and conservation was in order, so low prices were inappropriate from an efficiency standpoint. Fortunately, regulation has improved and these crude-oil import limits and price controls play little role today, but it is useful to understand mistakes that were made in the past.

In natural gas, the regulatory changes of the last 30 years are positive, despite manipulations that occurred in some newly formed markets. Starting at the end of the 1970s, natural gas prices at the wellhead were deregulated and in the 1980s pipelines were converted to transporters of natural gas rather than buyers and sellers of it. In place of traditional pipelines, which used to buy natural gas from many producers at controlled prices and resell it to distributors at regulated prices, we now have pipelines that essentially transport gas for distributors who use a new array of brokers, marketers, and traders to manage the delivery of gas so it meets their needs. Many producers now sell gas at competitive prices to distribution companies and other large users. Distribution to final customers remains the only portion of the industry that is regulated as before. As transporters, pipelines are regulated in new ways, with forms of competition increasingly important. This natural gas restructuring has had positive and significant effects.

Today's main energy sources are nonrenewable, in that they are being used faster than they can be replenished, and so at some point they will have to be replaced by less expensive substitutes. Substitutes for these nonrenewable energy sources include renewable power from the sun, the wind, and the earth, and water in rivers and oceans, organic matter such as wood, and chemical sources such as hydrogen fuel cells. Solar energy produces heating and lighting, and with photovoltaic cells it can be converted into electricity. Wind energy has powered windmills and sailing boats for thousands of years. Heat from within the earth yields geothermal energy. Water yields electricity from dams in rivers, from tidal movements, and even from the sun when it heats water. Biomass energy comes from wood and other organic material that can provide heat and light. Chemical energy is stored in batteries and can run fuel cells. These sources tend not to pollute, and because they will not run out, whatever energy they produce will grow in importance as other sources come to be exhausted.

QUESTIONS

1. Discuss the advantages and disadvantages of the Price-Anderson Act as a means of influencing insurance against the effects of nuclear reactor accidents.
2. What advantages and disadvantages would follow from repealing the Price-Anderson Act and relying on private insurers for protection from nuclear reactor accidents.
3. Regulation of natural gas pipelines converted the operators of pipelines into transporters of natural gas, rather than buyers and sellers of it. These transporting pipelines are required to maintain an electronic market where rights to use pipeline capacity (under contracts already arranged) are bought and sold. Discuss the effectiveness of this arrangement for competition into the transportation of natural gas, even where no other pipeline serves the same market. Explain advantages and disadvantages of the arrangement.
4. List the main environmental problems that are associated with the use of coal to produce electricity and sketch a way to moderate each one.
5. Explain in your own words the common-pool problem. Then evaluate with respect to oil whether (a) a prorationing policy and (b) limitations on the spacing of oil wells could help to overcome the common-pool problem. Do these policies offer a complete solution? Explain why or why not.
6. Evaluate whether the Mandatory Oil Import Program benefitted consumers. Explain how other groups might have been affected by the Program.
7. Deregulation has altered the production and transmission of natural gas. What steps taken by the Federal Power Commission were crucial in bringing about this deregulation?
8. Choose one form of renewable energy and summarize its advantages and disadvantages compared with the use of coal.

18

Electricity

The flick of a switch brings you power to enjoy lights, television, stereos, fans, air conditioners, radios, computers, can openers, juice extractors, coffee makers, or microwave ovens, to name only a few of many electrically powered pleasures. Instantaneous access to power is a great convenience, which is why we give up more than half the potential power when coal, natural gas, oil (all fossil fuels), or nuclear fuel is converted into electricity. Electric power is available just when you want it, and that extraordinary convenience makes the loss of energy worthwhile. Given our demand and the cost of electricity, it is no surprise that its sale in the United States amounts to more than $200 billion a year, more than is spent on new automobiles.

Electricity has special characteristics that place strong requirements on the markets that provide it. First and foremost, electricity cannot effectively be stored, and service to consumers ordinarily cannot be postponed. There is no busy signal for electric power. Second, demand for electricity is usually inelastic, in part because real-time pricing that allows consumers to respond has seldom been feasible. After being generated, electricity must pass through transmission networks to meet this real-time demand. Third, historically the industry required large investments for generation, transmission lines, substations, and related equipment, which led to economies of scale. A fourth characteristic of the industry is the pooling of demands into large aggregates, where the law of averages can help to smooth fluctuations that might arise in smaller areas.

Government regulation came to the electricity industry because of economies of scale, which seemed so great that monopoly organization could offer cost advantages. In the early part of the twentieth century, pioneers in the electricity industry formed large organizations that proved hard to regulate, so federal legislation in the 1930s simplified the organization of these electric utilities to support their regulation. From World War II until the 1970s, the electric utility industry was quite stable. In this generally expansionary period the electricity consumed per household rose substantially, yielding economies to the already installed networks of transmission and distribution systems.

Average costs for producing electricity actually fell slightly in the 1950s and did not rise markedly in the 1960s, so relations between utilities and their regulators were placid. In the 1970s, disruptions in the Middle East upset this calm, raising the price of fuels dramatically and once again drawing attention to regulation problems. Regulators considered many changes in the methods of regulating utilities in the 1980s, trying to improve efficiency incentives and to respond to fluctuating fuel prices. But deregulation and competition were not attempted.

Competition came to electricity in England and Wales in 1990 and is now being felt in parts of the United States electricity industry, where changes are being made in the form and extent of government regulation. Strictly speaking, the industry is not being deregulated, because government regulation continues to play an important role. It is being restructured, which involves the design of new markets in generation and retailing of electricity that probably would not emerge in such a network setting without conscious planning and design.

The first section of this chapter describes the generation, transmission, and distribution functions in the electricity industry and the special problems they cause for market regulation. In Section 18.2 we review the traditional organization of the industry, including the public utility organization and its functions, which are often separated in a restructured electricity industry. We also examine the major changes in federal regulation that have occurred. Section 18.3 examines markets for power as they have developed and functioned for years. Finally, in Section 18.4, we look at the role competition plays in restructured electricity markets.

18.1 | THE ELECTRICITY INDUSTRY

The electric power industry performs three main functions, the *generation* of electricity, the *transmission* of electricity at high voltages, and the *distribution* of electricity to final consumers at a voltage level they can use. Each of these functions itself is very complicated, and public utility organizations held them together for years. Restructuring of the industry has usually involved separation of these functions, with markets being expected to coordinate them.

Electricity is **generated** in giant turbines, which spin magnets inside coils of wires. This spinning of the magnetic field induces electrons to move in the coils of wires, and the moving electrons are electricity. The turbines are usually powered by steam, and they can require very large investments. Coal provides about half the heat source for making electricity in the United States, while nuclear power provides 20 percent and natural gas a little less. Petroleum provides about 3 percent, and less than 10 percent comes from hydroelectric dams and other sources. Only about 1 percent of electricity is produced in gas turbines or internal combustion engines, but recently developed natural gas turbines can be efficient even at a small scale, and their use is growing.

Transmission systems that move electricity from one place to another have limited capacities, and they can be damaged by sending too much electricity over them. When more electricity is needed through a line than its capacity allows, this congestion limits the movement of electricity. Transmission systems not only connect consumers to generators, they also connect the generators to one another. This means generators can exchange electricity when one has an unexpected outage, or one system might use another's excess capacity to help meet demand at a particular time of the day or season of the year.

When electricity is transmitted from one place to another, some is lost along the power lines. Even though the use of alternating current allows efficient movement and reduces such *line losses*, these losses still limit the distance over which it is feasible to transmit electricity. The voltage of electricity is usually raised, or "stepped up," for transmission across power lines to reduce such line losses. The laws of physics determine the flow of electricity, which courses over the transmission system without gates, unlike water that may be controlled by faucets. The flow of electricity is controlled by introducing and withdrawing it at the right places, to keep it flowing in the right direction.

Transmission systems carry electricity on to substations. From there it goes through **distribution systems** that carry electricity to final consumers. The voltage is lowered, or "stepped down," at substations so it can enter your home at 120 or 220 volts. Distribution systems accomplish this lowering of the voltage and delivery of electricity to final customers, which include residences, stores, restaurants, office buildings, and factories, although factories and other large users sometimes receive electricity at high voltages. Distribution systems also possess economies of scale, because once the distribution network exists, another customer can be added at small cost. In principle it is possible for competing retailer suppliers to win customers and then employ the distribution system to deliver power to them.

In both the transmission and distribution functions there is a substantial cost advantage for a single operator. It is feasible for one network to transmit power from several different generators, however, to support competition among the generators. A form of competition is also possible among retail suppliers, called marketing companies or **electricity service providers**, within the distribution function. These retailers can bill and otherwise deal with customers and arrange with a distribution system to deliver power they purchase for their retail customers.

This section describes the four functions of the electricity industry; generation, transmission, distribution, and retailing. We then discuss special features of electricity demand and supply that add to the complexity of electricity markets.

Electricity Generation

Let us begin with a word about units. The ability of electricity to do work is measured in watts, after James Watt, who invented the measurement. A kilowatt (KW) is 1,000 watts, and although electric power is not measured in horsepower a kilowatt equals about 1.34 horsepower (and one unit of *horsepower* is a force of 550 foot pounds per second). A megawatt (MW) is 1,000,000 watts. Your monthly bill charges you for use of electricity per unit of time. If you burn ten 100-watt light bulbs for one hour, for example, you use 1,000 watts for one hour, or one *kilowatt hour* of electricity, abbreviated one KWh. The average residence in the United States consumes almost 10,000 KWh of electricity in a typical year.

Historically, the great scale economies of electricity generation, relative to the sizes of markets that could be reached economically, invited monopoly organization for the industry. Traditional steam-powered electricity generating units were designed for 300 to 600 MWs of capacity to achieve the lowest possible average cost levels. Because transmission losses limit the distance that electricity can economically travel, this capacity could often serve an entire community's market but could travel no further. Today smaller scale generators, together with expanded demand for electricity that creates larger markets, have made scale economies less important than they once were. Combined-cycle gas-turbine plants, which are able to use more than half the energy in their fuel, can produce electricity at low cost when designed for only 100 megawatts of capacity. And new gas turbines, based on jet engine technology, can achieve competitive cost levels at a scale of only 20 megawatts. This decline in scale economies, together with greater populations of cities today and greater per capita use of electricity, allow more generators to serve market areas and, thus, make competition feasible.

With small generators it is also possible to achieve what is called **distributed generation**, which locates small generators close to those who consume power, thereby making transmission and distribution less important. While distributed generation reduces the need for transmission and distribution, it also forgoes the pooling advantage of large networks. If separate small users of electricity have volatile demands, they may be difficult to serve by distributed generation, because a generator is not easily turned on and off. When combined in a larger network, the demands may in part offset each other through the law of averages and result in a less volatile total demand.

Volatility of demand is a problem for electricity generation. Generators cannot be turned on and off quickly, so some must be available, held in reserve and ready to produce in case of unusually high demands. These generators are arrayed from low cost to high cost. Then as demand increases, and as constraints that affect how units can be started up and operated allow it, electricity companies try to bring generators on line in that low-cost to high-cost order. Using facilities in this **merit order**, or in order of cost from low to high, minimizes cost. Figure 18.1 represents the supply of and demand for electricity, where increasingly costly generating plants serve increasing demand (from *DD* to *D'D'*).

Having capacity is not sufficient in itself. As noted, a generator cannot be turned on in a few seconds to produce electricity. It takes time to get a generator going properly. An operator makes advance arrangements to have generation facilities "spinning," or *ready* to produce electricity if it is needed. Remember that if the amount of electricity demanded, or the *load*, is not met at all times, the entire electricity network can collapse. Wires that are overburdened can break down, and when wires carry too little power attached equipment can cease to function properly. Oversight is therefore needed to coordinate reserve capacity continuously, to know conditions at all points in an electricity network, and to insure that reserve capacity can always be brought on quickly to keep the network functioning.

A collapse of the electricity network from Ohio into the Northeastern United States and Canada occurred on August 14, 2003, affecting almost 50 million people,

Figure 18.1 *Supply and Demand for Electricity*

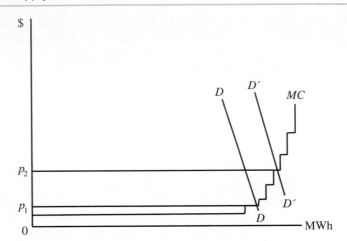

and it might have been caused in part by the greater burdens that restructuring has placed on the transmission system. An earlier failure, on November 9, 1965, when 30 million people went without power in the Northeastern United States, led to formation of the **North American Electric Reliability Council (NERC)**, a voluntary industry organization comprising 10 regional councils to which member utilities gave authority to intervene and coordinate the generation and transmission of electricity. Virtually all utilities in the nation belong to NERC today. The regional councils are charged with keeping electricity reliable in three synchronized electricity grids that cover Canada, the United States, and parts of Mexico.

Electricity Transmission

Because electricity is not always generated where it is consumed, utilities move it elsewhere for consumption through **transmission grids**. Suppose, for example, that a single transmission line connects the northern and southern parts of a state. Ideally, electricity is transmitted back and forth as needed to meet demands so that, except for small costs due to transmission losses, the price is the same in both north and south regions. If unit costs and, thus, prices differ in the two regions, improvement should be possible. Total cost can be reduced if generation in the high-cost region is reduced while generation in the low-cost region is increased and that low-cost electricity is transmitted to replace the high-cost electricity.

Figure 18.2 shows a transmission line connecting two areas, North and South. Both North and South can generate 1,000 MW of electricity, and each uses two technologies so that in each area 800 MW can be generated at $20 per MW, and 200 MW can be generated at $30 per MW. Suppose the demand for electricity, or the load, is 1,000 MW in North and 600 MW in South.

Ignoring transmission cost, what is the most efficient way to meet the combined loads of 1,600 MW in North and South with the capacities available? With transmission

---

BOX 18.1 Collapse of the U.S. Electricity Network

In a two-hour period beginning a little past noon on August 14, 2003, two electricity generators operated by the FirstEnergy Corporation in Cleveland, Ohio went out of service, and at about 2:00 a brush fire knocked out a transmission line and took away First Energy's reserve capacity to deal with further contingencies. Between 3:00 and 4:00 three transmission lines from eastern to northern Ohio went down, one from contact with a tree, and electricity from these lines moved to—and overloaded—other transmission lines and caused them to disconnect. Northern Ohio energy load was now served by so few lines that they disconnected, and heavy burdens in central Michigan caused a generator to trip and go down. As time passed the collapse spread through New York, Ontario, and much of New England. Examination of the event has shown that computer failures in the FirstEnergy system prevented managers from knowing of these failures and responding, and even the Midwest Independent System Operator, or regional network manager, was prevented from intervening for lack of information. Lack of communication of information thus prevented the continuous oversight that is needed to maintain a functioning electricity system or even to shut down portions to protect the remainder.

See U.S.-Canada Power Outage Task Force, *Final Report on the August 14, 2003 Blackout in the United States and Canada: Causes and Recommendations*, April, 2004, available at https://reports.energy.gov/BlackoutFinal-Web.pdf.

Figure 18.2 *A North-South Transmission System*

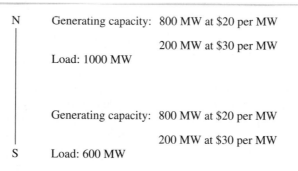

free, the low-cost generators in both North and South should run to produce 1,600 MW at only $20 per MW. Generating 800 MW in South meets the 600 MW load in South and allows 200 MW to be transmitted to North. When added to the 800 MW generated at $20/MW in North, the 200 MW transmitted from South meets North's 1,000 MW load. Thus, loads in both areas are met at a total cost of $32,000 (1,600 MW × $20/MW = $32,000).

Now what if the line from North to South serves other areas (such as Far North and Far South), and congestion from transmissions there limits the transmission capacity from South to North to 100 MW? Then South generates only 700 MW, at $20 per MW, consuming 600 MW and transmitting 100 MW to North. North can still generate 800 MW at $20 per MW and receive 100 MW from South, for a total of 900 MW costing $20 per MW, but it must produce an additional 100 MW at $30 per MW to meet its load of 1,000 MW. The marginal cost in North is now $30 per MW, while the marginal cost in South is $20 per MW. Total cost rises as a result to 1,500 MW × $20/MW + 100 MW × $30/MW = $33,000, or $1,000 more than the total cost would be with no congestion. Because congestion is preventing the transmission of lower cost electricity to North, the cost of the congestion is $10 per MW transmitted ($30/MW − $20/MW = $10/MW). This value of $10 per MW would be a reasonable fee to charge for transmitting from North to South, because it represents the opportunity cost of transmission that is being forgone.

Problems in managing the transmission grid and reckoning congestion costs may keep transmission regulated by means other than competition for some time to come. The present transmission network was developed by separate monopoly public utility organizations, each concerned with providing electricity in a well-defined area, usually within one state. Competition among generators requires a different kind of transmission grid that allows broader markets with fewer areas where one generator is dominant. Access to the transmission grid for other generators is important, too, so that any generator's electricity might be transmitted to the location where it is needed. Optimal pricing in transmission grids is complicated, involving peak-loads and interruptible service possibilities along with congestion and load management problems on the grid. Information available at each *node*, or each intersection of two transmission lines, conceivably can be used to price and otherwise manage the use of the transmission grids, as experiments along this line have suggested.

Electricity Distribution and Retailing

Even after electricity is transmitted so it is near the point of consumption it still has to be transported further, and readied, before the user can consume it. Distribution systems step down electricity to usable voltages and carry it to homes, office buildings, shopping centers, and factories through wires on poles or underground. Distribution companies also operate under economies of scale and are likely to remain regulated. They may, however, deliver electricity for independent retail suppliers or electricity service providers. These marketing companies arrange with consumers to provide electricity and metering and billing services. Such marketing companies could compete for customers. On the one hand they would purchase electricity from generators or from a wholesale market, and on the other hand they would employ a distribution system to deliver the electricity to final consumers.

In most parts of the United States, residences are still served by monopoly providers who meter usage and issue bills, while also generating, transmitting, and distributing the electricity. In other parts of the United States, competitive markets for generation have been created along with wholesale markets, and in some instances competition among retail suppliers is also occurring. Retailers are expected to search out pricing mechanisms to give consumers more opportunity to consume electricity when prices are lower, through more responsive peak and off-peak pricing. This responsive pricing in turn allows retailers to anticipate demands more accurately as they enter the wholesale market to purchase electricity. To design such markets for electricity, attention must be paid to special characteristics of the demand and supply of electricity.

Special Features of Electricity Demand and Supply

Let us briefly review the distinguishing features that complicate the sale of electricity in a competitive market. First, electricity moves through wires to the point where it is used, but congestion can limit that movement at peak times and electricity cannot be moved at off-peak times and stored until needed. Storage is possible for most goods that are exchanged in markets, so a supplier can use inventory to adjust for unexpected demand shifts, but storage of electricity is prohibitively costly, and that prevents the use of inventory as a buffer. With no storage, responses to shifts in demand must be immediate, and they must also come at the appropriate location.

There are three main categories of electricity user, commercial (stores and businesses), industrial (factories) and residential (homes), and their short-run demands for electricity tend to be inelastic. Residences are the most variable of users, with peak demands usually in morning and evening. We consumers want heat when it is cold; we want air conditioning when it is hot; we want light when it is dark. Yet in U.S. homes the price does not respond to short-run supply and demand conditions. Metering electricity by time of use is costly, and then users must be informed of current prices if they are to change their usage. Some other countries do better. In northern European countries, for example, time-of-use pricing is common, with higher prices in daytime than in nighttime. In response, homes use heat-storage devices at night when rates are low so heat can be released during the day when rates are high. Let us briefly explore the main pricing possibilities.

Time-of-Use Pricing Any regularity in periodic demand levels can make more efficient pricing easier. For example, suppose demand tends to be at a high level from 9 AM to 11 AM and from 4 PM to 6 PM and at a lower level at other times. A meter can distinguish demand by time of day and charge a different price accordingly. It is even easier to make distinctions by time of year. Prices that change by time or date with predicted average usage patterns are called **time-of-use prices**. The great advantage of such pricing is that consumers can be informed ahead of time of the price they can expect to pay by time of day, so where desirable they can arrange their activities to use electricity when capacity usually is less scarce and electricity is less costly (for example, they might do the laundry at night when rates are lowest).

BOX 18.2 Cooling the Empire State Building

Managers of the Empire State Building in New York City say they will save $200,000 in the summer season by switching between cooling methods depending on current prices. Under deregulated time-of-use pricing they can make ice at night when electricity is cheap and use the ice in their cooling system to help cool the building during the day when rates are high.

See E. McDowell, "Cooling the Empire State Building on the Cheap," *New York Times*, April 16, 2003, p. C7.

Real-Time Pricing Commercial users such as stores and office buildings tend to be more stable in their usage throughout the day than residences. Nevertheless, when their usage is large they might willingly respond to a market clearing price. Where they can be communicated to users, continuously adjusting **real-time prices** allow such responses. Large industrial users such as factories use a great deal of electricity, often receiving it at high voltage. They may not be able to change their usage if they are committed to activities that would be costly to interrupt. But, for example, simply raising their building temperatures a couple of degrees in summer to reduce air conditioning whenever the electricity price is high can yield significant savings.[1]

Interruptible-Service Pricing Factories are sometimes able to interrupt their electricity purchases, perhaps by using their own back-up generators. Then they might enter into what are called **interruptible-service contracts** that were described in Chapter 11. Such contracts permit the provider of electricity to interrupt the service at times of extremely high demands. Interruptible-service contracts seldom totally interrupt the use of electricity, they usually cut usage back to an agreed upon level the user selects by paying a fixed fee. The fee is higher for a higher minimum level, and the user can choose how drastic the interruption might be. Choosing a high level to be protected, even at times of unusually high demand, is costly; it is essentially what is called *firm service*, which is service that cannot be interrupted.

These three possibilities for market-type prices—time of use, real time, and interruptible service—are not widely used in the United States, and the resulting lack of any price adjustment is one reason electricity demand is inelastic. Figure 18.1 illustrated the inelastic demand for electricity as *DD*. The supply of electricity can also be inelastic in the short run, because older, less efficient facilities are brought into service to meet peak demand. This is also shown in Figure 18.1, where the marginal cost of electricity begins to rise steeply at large output levels. In an effort to augment supply, electricity might be borrowed from other areas, although congestion on the transmission lines may limit the amount that can reach the location where it is demanded. Indeed, limited transmission capacity can join limited generation capacity to make electricity supply inelastic, as Figure 18.1 shows.

When supply is inelastic, shifts in an inelastic demand function can produce very sharp swings in the market clearing price. Figure 18.1 illustrates this effect also. As demand moves from *DD* to *D'D'*, the market clearing price jumps from p_1 to p_2. For most electricity consumers, price is not effectively adjusted on a short-run basis, as from p_1 to p_2, but that is what real-time pricing would do. For routine or average fluctuations by time of day, time-of-use pricing helps to restrain peak demand, but real-time pricing might control extreme and unpredictable shifts. Some people may be unwilling or unable to change consumption in the short run if price could adjust and be communicated to them, but some would change, as industrial users do, and efficiency would improve. Interruptible-service contracts can also be valuable for cutting back peak demand and, thus, conserving supply when demand is unpredictably high.

---

[1] See Borenstein (2003).

18.2 | ORGANIZATION OF THE ELECTRICITY INDUSTRY

Complexities of managing electricity generation, transmission, and distribution fostered monopoly organization of the industry. A single supplier could achieve economies of scale and could also coordinate the complex delivery task of matching inelastic demand with potentially inelastic supply. In the United States, individual states typically granted one firm a monopoly franchise to generate, transmit, and distribute electricity in a defined area in exchange for public regulation of its affairs. This monopoly provider was usually a public utility, in a state that created a regulatory agency to oversee it. Through legislative initiatives beginning in the 1970s, Congress opened the way for a greater range of regulatory methods, including greater regulation of the industry by competition.

The Traditional Model

The traditional model for electricity industry organization is the public utility, a private corporation harnessed to serve the public interest by some form of regulation. Rigidities of this public-utility-with-regulator form of organization made change in the industry difficult.

The Public Utility Organization

In the United States, privately owned and unregulated firms originally produced electricity. Indeed, Thomas Edison began working to obtain city cooperation and Wall Street financing to produce and distribute electricity even before he perfected the light bulb, which of course would depend on electricity. Edison's Pearl Street Station in New York City began producing power in 1882. At the end of the nineteenth century, three-fourths of the nation's power companies, such as Edison and Westinghouse, were privately owned and unregulated, and competition among them was significant. The remaining one-fourth of the power companies were regulated mainly by municipal authorities who saw natural monopoly elements in the industry. In 1907, both New York and Wisconsin introduced state-level regulation of electricity companies, and other states gradually followed.

From the start of the twentieth century to World War I, private corporations built electric utility **holding company** empires, which owned other corporations and controlled their activities. By 1932 three holding companies, the Electric Bond and Share Company, the United Corporation, and the Insull Group, controlled almost half of the investor-owned utilities in the United States,[2] and the largest eight firms collected almost three-fourths of electricity sales. Concern about these powerful holding companies ran high, because their complicated capital structures and internal transactions fooled investors and seemed to subvert effective regulation.

Some electricity holding companies exacted high fees for paltry services to their subsidiaries; they arranged deals among the companies they held to raise asset values

---

[2] See Watkiss and Smith (1993).

fictitiously; they used intercompany borrowing for speculative purposes; and they included interest payments as costs in construction projects, which raised asset values, while they claimed the interest as earnings elsewhere. Outright violations of laws occurred in the sales of securities, such as paying dividends from capital surplus, or evading federal income taxes. The abuses resulted in excessive borrowing, which made the risk of insolvency high and resulted in manipulated security values. These abuses occurred without detection in the complex holding-company structure, which was made even less comprehensible by occasional reorganizations.[3]

After this holding-company form proved to be uncontrollable, the government stepped in to regulate the shape of the public utility. In 1935, Congress passed a proposal from President Franklin D. Roosevelt as the **Public Utility Act** of 1935. The law included two important parts. One part was the **Federal Power Act (FPA)**, which expanded the authority of the Federal Power Commission (FPC), known today as the Federal Energy Regulatory Commission (FERC). The FPC had been formed under the Federal Water Power Act of 1920 to regulate the sale of power from federal irrigation and water control projects. Its authority was expanded under the FPA to regulate the interstate sales, or essentially interutility sales, of electricity, where it would set "just and reasonable rates" for wholesale electricity.

The other part of the Public Utility Act was the **Public Utility Holding Company Act (PUHCA)** of 1935, which was passed to clear away the tangles of complex organizations and thereby allow more effective regulation. The PUHCA forced divestitures that simplified the organizational structure of public utilities. The Act greatly reduced the number of holding companies and made electric utilities take the form, primarily, of straightforward vertically integrated operating companies serving defined geographic areas.[4] More recently, as restructuring of the industry began to be considered, the PUHCA was repealed, but much of its influence on the organization of electric utilities remains.

Before any restructuring of the electricity industry in the United States, roughly 75 percent of consumers were served by privately owned and publicly regulated utilities, which were called *investor-owned utilities*. About 15 percent of customers were served by a large number of typically smaller, publicly owned systems, usually *municipal systems* operated by cities but also operated by districts or other public areas. The remaining 10 percent of customers were served by about 1000 *rural cooperatives* or other special agencies and a dozen federal power agencies. Although they have been the most important source of electricity, public utilities are not the only source. Municipalities sometimes own and manage electric utilities. Electric cooperatives were also formed after the Rural Electrification Act of 1936, which provided low interest loans to organizations that would extend electricity into rural areas. Cooperatives grew rapidly, and they still provide electricity in many rural areas today. Nonutility generators originally produced electricity for their own use. Recent policy changes extended their role by allowing them access to transmission services so they can sell

---

[3] See Sherman (1989).

[4] See Senate Report No. 621, 74th Congress, 1st Session 11 (1955).

electricity to utilities. These new independent generators are part of a restructuring that is changing the industry.

Suddenly in 1973 the Arab oil embargo tripled the price of oil, then raised it much more, and ushered in a decade of crisis. The Organization of Petroleum Exporting Countries (OPEC) was able to maintain high crude oil prices in the 1970s, which sharply increased fuel costs for utilities. Regulatory commissions approved only portions of the many rate increases requested by utilities, and processing the frequent requests overburdened the commissions. Many of them adopted procedures, called **automatic adjustment clauses**, which allowed changes in the price of fuel to automatically change—in a prescribed way—the final price for electricity. In effect, regulators treated the fuel-cost side of electricity generation on a "cost-plus" basis, meaning that cost determined price. While automatic adjustment clauses hastened the regulatory adjustment of price in response to input (primarily fuel) price changes, they also reduced the incentive for the utility to seek out lower-priced sources of fuel.[5]

Problems and Possibilities for Change

Electric utilities in different states developed in quite different ways over the years, in part because they faced different circumstances. They were all protected from competition, which explains why some states came to have costs twice as high as others.[6] In 1998 for example, when electricity cost averaged 6.7 cents per KWh in the United States, it was 11.9 cents per KWh in New Hampshire, 9 cents per KWh in California, and 4 cents per KWh in Washington or Idaho. Understandably, states with high-cost electricity had greater interest in restructuring the industry. Industrial activity depends heavily on electric power, so a state with high power costs may find it hard to attract new industry and may even see its industrial base decline. Attempting to lower the cost of electricity is one reason that 18 states and the District of Columbia introduced some form of competition by early 2003.[7] Although problems with restructuring in California slowed implementation in some of these states, many other states have programs under consideration to open electricity to some form of competition.

While consumers in high-cost states might seek possible benefits from restructuring, consumers in low-cost states may suffer if their states allow competition. Trade has such effects, for opening trade with a high-cost region can raise prices in a low-cost region.[8] Consider a low-cost state that is surrounded by high-cost states. With open markets, some low-cost electricity is transmitted to the high-cost states, and with less supply the formerly low-cost state may see higher prices. Open markets for electricity tends to make prices more equal. Owners of low-cost generators and their employees should benefit from this opportunity to sell in high-cost states. The owners may live in other states, however, and if electricity prices rise, the residents of

---

[5] See Scott (1979).

[6] Price differences among states are shown in Joskow (1997). For a description of the way the electricity industry has been organized historically and how it is being changed, see Kwoka (1997, 2005).

[7] The status of restructuring by state as of February, 2003, the last time the Department of Energy reported it, is available at http://www.eia.doe.gov/cneaf/electricity/chg_str/restructure.pdf.

[8] For analysis of this effect in electricity markets, see Barnett, Reutter, and Thompson (1998).

the formerly low-cost state may see little benefit from competition, and they may therefore resist it.

Capital has been very important to the techniques that produce electricity. Today, the investor-owned portion of the industry has about one trillion dollars in book value, or accounting value, of assets, and it is not unusual for the asset value of an integrated electric company's facilities to be so large that all sales must be added up for three years to match their value. If new technology and competition make some of these large investments uneconomical, the question arises, How are the resulting losses to be handled? Losses are not ordinarily expected in a regulated monopoly industry, yet when competition came to high-cost electricity generating markets, assets often fell in value. They had been valuable only as long as the monopoly producer was protected from entry. This loss in value is referred to as **stranded cost**, and legislators as well as regulators struggled with the question of what to do about such stranded costs when the industry is restructured. Should shareholders absorb the loss, even though they expected monopoly protection when they made their investments? Or should revenues be protected in some way so the investors can be compensated for the effects of a change in regulatory policy? Utilities have wanted help in recovering potential stranded costs before they would willingly agree to restructuring the industry, and they generally have received it.[9]

Moving from vertically integrated utilities to competitive markets is complicated also by the paths that existing transmission facilities follow. Built by integrated utilities to serve their local loads, these facilities were not built to foster competition across larger market areas. Indeed, the utilities would rather preserve some market power and avoid exposure to competition, so they might resist new transmission connections that would bring greater competition.

England and Wales restructured their electricity industries in 1990, and were followed promptly by Norway, Sweden, Argentina, Spain, Australia, and New Zealand.[10] Typically smaller than the United States, and often privatizing while restructuring, these countries were able to reorganize transmission to support competition according to clear plans. In the United States, however, many private parties already owned relevant assets and could insist on payments (such as stranded costs) that made the transition more difficult. Different states adopted different approaches, with only slight attention to the lessons from other countries.

Moreover, different restructuring arrangements were adopted at the state level with little central guidance from the FERC. This lack of an adequate blue print is especially troublesome in the transmission function, because transmission is so important to competition in generation, and because a national plan is ultimately needed. Change was first stimulated by the crisis from high oil prices in the 1970s and then expanded by states that wanted to reduce the high cost of their electricity in the 1990s. The stage was set for change by Congressional actions, beginning in 1978.

---

[9] In those few states where costs were low and utility assets gained (rather than lost) in value from competition, no symmetrical effort was made to take those gains away.

[10] The U.S. Energy Information Administration provides information on restructuring in Argentina, Australia, and the United Kingdom. See http://www.eia.doe.gov/emeu/pgem/electric/es.htm.

The Public Utility Regulatory Policy Act of 1978

With fuel prices high in the 1970s, the electric and gas power industries were suffering. In passing the **Public Utility Regulatory Policy Act** of 1978 **(PURPA)**, Congress sought to influence state public utility commissions in the way they regulated gas and electric utilities, to improve efficiency, to conserve energy—mainly to reduce dependence on petroleum exporting countries—and to insure equitable rates for consumers. In addition to high fuel prices, Congress was responding to concerns of environmentalists about electricity production and its effect on the environment.

Improving Efficiency

PURPA emphasized rate-making policies. Rates to each class of customer were to be based on the cost of serving that class. Moreover, rates were not to decline with customer usage, as declining-block rates do, unless the electric utility could show that average cost declined with aggregate consumption of electricity. Time-of-use rates and seasonal rates were also to be implemented if the efficiency gain from doing so was worthwhile. Interruptible rates were to be offered to industrial and commercial customers. Some businesses had emergency power sources of their own that they could fall back on when their power was interrupted, so they could accept interruptions in exchange for lower rates.[11]

PURPA also called for load management techniques to be offered to customers. Such techniques were expected to allow customers to moderate their peak needs, moving electricity consumption to other times of the day or year. For example, having a master meter in rental apartments, where all residents were served through a single electricity meter, was not to be allowed in new buildings. Master meters invited greater consumption through free riding, because they let consumers share in the total bill rather than pay for their own consumption as individual meters would require.

A related **Powerplant and Industrial Fuel Use Act (PIFUA)**, passed at the same time as PURPA, blocked most uses of oil or natural gas in new utility power plants, ostensibly to limit the use of these scarce fuels. The apparent scarcity of natural gas was fostered in part by price controls that had discouraged exploration, because once those controls were lifted the scarcity vanished. Independent or nonutility power producers were not restricted in their fuel use by this law, and they came to use natural gas extensively. In utilities, PIFUA stimulated the use of coal and nuclear power for generating electricity.

PURPA also limited automatic adjustment clauses, which adjusted electricity prices automatically for changes in input prices, primarily fuel prices. PURPA permitted automatic adjustment clauses but required periodic review to insure that they left the utility with incentives to be efficient. Other requirements involved information to be provided to customers about rates, and notification requirements and limitations

---

[11] More businesses produce their own power today. See Martha McNeil Hamilton, "Producing Their Own Power," *Washington Post*, August 22, 2003, p. A1,

that would apply in cases where electric service was being terminated. PURPA also imposed limitations on electric utility advertising, particularly advertising for promotional or political purposes.

The Purchase of Power by Electric Utilities

Not much noticed at the time, yet perhaps the most important part of PURPA, was its requirement that electric utilities purchase power from *cogenerators* and small independent power producers that used renewable sources of energy (for example, hydroelectric energy, solar energy, geothermal energy). Cogenerators produce heat as a by-product from a process that serves some other purpose, and rather than vent the heat into the air the cogenerators use it to make steam and then electricity. When combined with their other function, cogenerators often extract a relatively high fraction of energy from their fuels. The small producers using renewable sources of energy were called **qualifying facilities (QFs)**, and some states, such as California and New York, set high rates at which they could sell to public utilities. These high rates were not truly competitive, so their effects became part of stranded costs for utilities when competition was introduced. Encouragement of competition in some states led to the creation of small and specialized generators that were not qualifying facilities, called **independent power producers (IPPs)**. They might produce electricity by wind-energy machine or small hydroelectric facility, or they might operate a small, fossil-fuel, electricity generating plant.

Although it was limited, the purchase of power from separate producers showed that a market for power might be possible. Under PURPA a utility was to buy power from these new sources at a price up to its *avoided costs*, which are costs the utility would have incurred to produce the power itself. At peak times, when a public utility would be using its less efficient generating facilities, the avoided cost could be quite high. Some states auctioned opportunities to supply and obtained lower prices. The independent suppliers could sell only to utilities, for only utilities possessed the right to sell to final consumers. Exemption of small producers from terms of the PUHCA and greater access for such producers to use the national grid for transmission would come in 1992 legislation.[12]

The Energy Policy Act of 1992 (EPA)

The **Energy Policy Act** of 1992 **(EPA)** carried initiatives of PURPA to a level that was revolutionary.[13] It opened the possibility that the owner of a transmission grid would have to transmit electricity for any producer, which changed federal regulation of electricity because it fostered the development of a competitive market for wholesale

---

[12] The original plan of the Carter administration for PURPA was more ambitious. It would have mandated marginal cost pricing and exempted qualifying facilities from the Public Utility Holding Company Act (PUHCA). As passed, PURPA only made new rate-setting guidelines voluntary, but it still had influence on rate making. Without any PUHCA exemption, qualifying facilities still came into existence. With independent power producers (IPPs), they proved that some form of competition could be managed at the generation level.

[13] For a review of the Act, see Watkiss and Smith (1993, pp. 447–492).

electric power.[14] And the Act created a new class of electricity generator, called the **exempt wholesale generator (EWG)**. These EWGs (called "e-wogs") were exempt from organizational restrictions of the PUHCA and were free to use any technology, unlike the qualifying facilities under PURPA that could only use renewable energy sources and had to be small. A qualifying facility under PURPA or a cogenerator that produces electricity as a byproduct of another activity may become an EWG. EWGs are competitive producers of electricity.

In addition, public utilities were no longer required to buy from qualifying facilities at avoided cost. The qualifying facilities would be expected to win business through successful competition rather than by legislative favoritism. The 1992 Act also removed restrictions on owning foreign utilities, allowing American firms to became major investors in foreign electricity companies, especially in Australia and the United Kingdom.

Access to Transmission Lines

The 1992 Act amended the Federal Power Act to enable the FERC to require owners of power transmission lines to **wheel power**—that is, to transmit it for others. Generators of power and wholesale purchasers may thus carry out transactions to be executed over the transmission facilities of some intermediate utility. This access to transmission widened the potential market for wholesale generators. Eliminating PUHCA regulation for wholesale generators of power also freed them to compete without being subject to the many requirements that were then imposed on public utilities that held retail monopoly franchises.

Public utilities retained their monopoly positions for selling electricity at retail under the 1992 Act, primarily to avoid having independent power generators attract large industrial customers away from utilities. Given the scale economies in an integrated public utility system, loss of a large customer could raise average cost for the utility, which under rate-of-return regulation could bring price increases for remaining customers. Utilities also retained control over transmission but were required to provide transmission service to nonutility generators at reasonable fees. That is, they had to grant *access* to their transmission lines. In the generation function they faced alternative suppliers—independent power producers—who now had improved opportunities to sell their power output because utilities were required to transmit that power to eligible buyers.

Since its authority was expanded in 1935, the FERC has overseen the pricing of wholesale power transactions. But until the 1992 Act, it had no authority to require access to transmission lines and, thus, to make transmission service available to independent power producers. The 1992 law invited anyone generating electricity to apply to FERC for an order that would require a transmitting utility to wheel power for it.

---

[14] The right of access to a transmission service was established in an antitrust case, *Otter Tail Power, Inc. v. United States*, 410 U.S. 366, 93 S.Ct. 1022, 35 L.Ed.2d 359 (1973). It required a privately owned utility to transmit power for a municipal electric system when denial of the transmission service would have brought the municipal business to the privately owned utility.

The transmitting utility might even be asked to expand its capacity to be able to provide the wheeling service. The wheeling must be to a wholesale customer such as another utility, and not to an ultimate consumer, because the independent, nonutility generators cannot sell directly at retail. But FERC can decide to order provision of the wheeling service on fair terms.[15]

The 1992 EPA includes general directions specifying how FERC is to set rates for access to transmission systems. The rates are to enable the transmitting utility to recover "all the costs incurred in connection with the transmission services and necessary associated services," and "the costs of any enlargement of transmission facilities."[16] Rates also are to "promote the economically efficient transmission and generation of electricity," and "be just and reasonable, and not unduly discriminatory." These general guidelines leave FERC some latitude for devising pricing policies, and it has settled mainly on cost-based rules.

The Beginning of a Wholesale Electricity Market

How could independent EWGs be introduced into the complicated networks of electricity generation and distribution? Over the many years that integrated public utilities provided electricity, such utilities could maintain load in the face of demand fluctuations or even sudden loss of generation capacity within their complex systems. To do so required not only the generation of enough electricity to meet demand but also the provision of appropriate capacity in reserve, able to be brought on line immediately if needed to meet demand increases. Power to come on line as needed is called an *ancillary service*. Remember that electricity cannot be stored, is subject to inelastic short-run demand, and must be managed skillfully to avoid the collapse of a transmission and distribution network. The EPA introduced market transactions for electricity into this complex system and opened the possibility of genuine markets for power.

18.3 | MARKETS FOR POWER

In view of regulatory changes introduced by Congress in 1978 and 1992, the question arises whether markets for electricity can work. Evidence from other countries suggests the answer is "yes," but the transition is difficult when the electricity infrastructure is privately owned. This section first examines the role that competitive markets have long been allowed to play within the electricity industry in the United States, and it then introduces the new features that allow competition to expand. The new features involve new institutions that can function in and thereby contribute to a more competitive environment.

---

[15] Before ordering wheeling, FERC wanted other conditions satisfied. For example, the electricity generator must have requested wheeling service from the transmitting utility at least 60 days before applying to FERC, so parties try to work out arrangements on their own. An order to wheel was not to impair reliability of the electrical systems affected by the order.

[16] 16 U.S.C. § 824K (a).

Spot Markets and Contracting

Markets for power generation have existed for some time in many parts of the United States, and they take different forms. In Florida a spot market in power has been operating for over 30 years.[17] Six investor-owned utilities, nearly 20 municipal utilities, and more than 10 rural electrical cooperatives belong to an organization called the Florida Electric Power Coordinating Group, which operates the **FCG Energy Broker**. The **Florida Coordinating Group (FCG)** is intended to coordinate the planning, construction, and utilization of generation and transmission facilities in Florida. The FCG Energy Broker (hereafter, the Florida Broker) is a spot market that fosters hourly purchases and sales of electricity, which are motivated as long as incremental cost to a potential selling utility is lower than avoided cost to a potential buying utility.

The Florida Broker

The Florida Broker arranges contracts every hour. Utilities may submit both buy (bid) and sell (offer) quotes to the broker, entering up to three prices in each direction (buy or sell), for three sets of quantities. Usually a particular utility is only a buyer or a seller in any given period. The broker arrays in rank order the bids (high to low) and offers (low to high) and then matches highs and lows. The highest bid is matched with the lowest sell offer first, for example, then the next bid and offer, and so on, to maximize savings from electricity exchanges. Notice that participants in this market maintain balance within their own networks, using power from the Florida Broker to augment their sources of power.

Rules specify the cost calculations to be carried out as a basis for final-service pricing, and they provide for including transmission charges and profits on transactions. To trade, two utilities must have entered into preexisting bilateral contracts with each other. Trades are executed in the order starting with maximum unit savings (the highest bid and lowest offer) at a price halfway between the bid price and the offer price. The savings accruing to the buying utility go through to reduce the price paid for electricity by the final consumer. The selling utility is allowed to keep its gain, but under rate regulation this transaction should ultimately benefit ratepayers, because any gain to the utility can postpone a request to raise rates.

Contracting in Virginia

Virginia, in contrast, uses long-term contracts rather than a spot market. A number of independent producers sell power to a single dominant public utility buyer, Virginia Power.[18] The parties enter into long-term contracts, typically running under one set of terms for 15 years, renewable under another set of terms for 10 additional years, so a 25-year period is involved. The contracts include fixed payments to the independent producer, together with marginal payments per kilowatt hour actually produced.

---

[17] Linda Cohen (1982) describes this early electricity market.

[18] For a lucid description of this arrangement, see Easterbrook (1993).

The structure of the contracts in Virginia allows Virginia Power the right to dispatch the power. That is, Virginia Power can decide just when and how much power to take from any independent producer. The independent producers can earn some profit from the fixed payments in their contracts, apart from how much power they actually deliver, which makes them willing to accept these contract terms. Also, because the independent producers typically operate only one generating facility, they tend to have a single marginal cost. This makes possible the form of fixed-and-variable-cost contract under which it is simple and easy to operate. With control over when electricity is generated, Virginia Power can solve in a manageable way its problem of minimizing cost and maintaining load balance to meet demand fluctuations throughout its system.

Contracting versus the Spot Market

We might ask why the spot market flourishes in Florida, while Virginia uses long-term contracts with independent producers. In Florida a number of utilities and other producers, each with its own mix of electricity generating facilities and, therefore, its own pattern of fluctuating marginal costs can make the most of any situation in light of conditions faced every hour through a spot market. The supply and demand balancing requirement in the spot market helps to maintain load balance through the electric system in an efficient way. In Virginia, on the other hand, independent producers with simple cost conditions can sell to a single utility under negotiated long-term contracts, usually at single marginal cost rates plus fixed fees. With Virginia Power in position to dispatch power—from these suppliers or from its own facilities, whichever is cheaper—it can maintain balance throughout its electricity network. The long-term contracts also can foster needed financing for the independent producers, something unneeded by the Florida producers. Thus, the ways for organizing markets for power seem appropriate to the circumstances of each case.

Independent power producers and cogenerators, which PURPA and EPA encouraged to produce electricity for sale to utilities, are a growing source of electricity in the United States, and they have demonstrated that electricity generation can operate through a competitive market. More than 25 percent of power is produced by independent producers and cogenerators today, and more than half of new capacity in the past 10 years has been developed through this organizational form. In 1996, before industry restructuring began to separate generating facilities from some utility organizations, nonutility generators represented about 10 percent of total U.S. generating capacity.

Generating facilities have improved their efficiency in recent years. Some facilities, particularly those using natural gas, have quite mild effects on the environment. Alternative electricity sources, especially solar energy, are making even more dramatic progress and may provide power to many homes in the near future, at least in the southwestern United States, where sunshine is plentiful. Thus, generation facilities based on different technologies may compete in markets quite effectively. Transmission and distribution, however, appear to offer scale economics and monopoly advantages, so some form of regulation will probably continue in these two areas in the foreseeable future.

Increased Scope for Network Coordination

Expanded reliance on competitive markets for regulating electricity generation and distribution calls for new or modified institutions to help those markets function effectively. The essence of such new institutions is barely visible in the Virginia and Florida arrangements. Let's turn to consider some types of institutions that have been created to broaden the possibility for competition but contain potential problems that must be overcome.

A Poolco Spot Market

The **Poolco** is a name given to a coordinating system that relies on a centralized spot market for wholesale electricity transactions, somewhat like the Florida Energy Broker. The Poolco solicits offers from distributors to buy amounts of electricity they specify at proposed prices over an exact time period, say of 30 minutes in length, and it also solicits bids from generators as to prices and amounts they are willing to sell. The Poolco then finds the price at which bids and offers are equal and imposes it on the implied transactions. Normally all generators receive that price, and purchasers pay that price plus a surcharge to cover the cost of Poolco services.

Market power can be exercised in such a market, even without collusion, because owners of multiple generators can individually be tempted to behave strategically. Suppose you own six generating plants that you can offer in such a market, and you expect demand to be high. You might either (1) use **physical withholding**, by keeping some of your capacity, say one plant, idle to heighten scarcity, or (2) use **economic withholding**, typified by **"hockey-stick" offers**, which offer low prices for power from most of your plants (along the hockey stick handle) but jump to a very high price for, say, one plant (as a hockey stick bends sharply to the section where it meets the hockey puck). Although you face a possible loss in not having one plant operate under either of these strategies, the strategies might also raise the spot price if your last plant is needed to meet demand. Physical withholding can reduce supply and raise price to yield higher profit from all your other plants, and the high price you offer for power from one plant under economic withholding may be accepted, yielding high profit at all of your plants.[19]

Notice that **long-term contracts**, or **forward contracts**, can moderate this urge to make strategic offers. Long-term contracts may apply for a year or more and forward contracts apply for a future date and, thus, can be regarded as long-term contracts. If long-term contracts have essentially tied up the output of three of your six plants, for example, sacrificing one plant to win higher prices in the spot market would benefit only two other plants rather than five others. The odds of success must now be considerably higher for you to try strategic offers, and your eagerness to use them falls accordingly.

As a Poolco becomes larger it can take responsibility for system balance across a broader area than separate utilities were coordinating. Here the Poolco differs from

---

[19] For experimental markets that demonstrate such a result, see Holt, Langan, and Villamil (1986) and Rassenti, Smith, and Wilson (2000).

the Florida Broker, where separate producers balanced their own separate systems, because the Poolco undertakes to balance supplies and demands across the system. To be able to balance, the Poolco could operate markets in what are called **ancillary services**, most importantly reserve capacity to be available when needed. This market would array bids and offers under various readiness conditions, with fixed as well as variable, or per unit, payments to compensate generators for being ready to produce even if no production turns out to be needed. So in addition to a current market for exchange of electricity, there can be a reserve market in ancillary services, to insure adequate capacity is always ready to meet the possible electricity demand. The reserves can also be used for **congestion management** of the transmission system, by providing power to areas where fully used lines prevent it from being transmitted. Such arrangements would be part of the Poolco's management of **real-time balancing**, or keeping supply in line with demand at each location all the time.

A Poolco would probably be subject to some form of regulation. The surcharge to purchasers for maintaining reserve capacity, for instance, is one element that might be subject to regulation. Separate, possibly long-term, contracts might also exist among participants in a Poolco system for a portion of the transactions. Parties would notify the Poolco about the contracts so it could take them into account in coordinating overall demand and supply. The Poolco would still be in position to act monopolistically, so it would be subjected to some form of oversight to prevent exploitation of its position.

The Independent System Operator and Transcos

When the tasks of a Poolco increase, and market participants have less ability to coordinate their own systems, a market coordinator may be created. In a contracting system such as the arrangements between Virginia Power and its nonutility suppliers, for example, a single coordinator maintained balance over the entire system. As demands rose or fell unexpectedly, adjustments could be made to supplies by Virginia Power to avoid a system failure. A coordinating entity created for this purpose is usually called an **independent system operator (ISO)**. Such an ISO coordinating function is provided in many parts of the United States by a **regional transmission organization (RTO)**, a voluntary arrangement that oversees power supplies in each of the 10 regional councils in the NERC.

In response to unanticipated ups and downs in the demand for electricity, an ISO would have authority to start up or shut down generators, and it would arrange for emergency sources in advance to have electricity available as needed to maintain the system. This ISO agent would probably be subject to some form of regulation, to insure that the power it was given was exercised solely to maintain a balance between electricity demand and supply. It probably would not be allowed to own any generation capacity, to avoid conflicts of interest.

Suppose a grid company owned and operated a transmission grid that connected generating companies with purchasers of electricity. As long as it did not own a generating company, such a grid company could serve as the ISO for the grid. The grids in many countries are operated by independent **transmission companies**, called **Transcos**, rather than electricity-producing companies. The regulation of such

Transcos, while concerned with pricing for transmission services, also seeks nondiscriminatory access to the transmission services for all generators that want to transmit electricity. Such access is crucially important to competition in generation, to prevent some generators from having an advantage over others, either in the convenience of transmission service or in the rates paid for it.

A Transco owns a transmission grid, but ownership is not necessary to carry out ISO functions. It might be possible to have ISOs as large as one of the three synchronized electricity grids in North America. As noted, a form of ISO operates as an RTO in each of the 10 regional councils in the NERC. Alternatively, ISOs might be created in each state in the United States, especially if this form of competition develops separately in each state. But questions about incentives in ISOs remain, because it is not clear that they can provide totally efficient, unbiased, and ownerless oversight.

The purpose of an ISO is to insure balance in the system by coordinating supply and demand in three main ways: (1) grid congestion management, (2) ancillary services, and (3) real-time balancing. The ISO can manage grid congestion through control of transmission by calling on generators to increase or decrease generation on each side of congested lines. The ISO can also pay generators for ancillary services, so they are in position to respond at once to provide needed power or to maintain spinning or nonspinning reserves to be available in a few minutes by operating but not producing. Finally, the ISO can achieve real-time balancing by overseeing electricity provision, which means calling on available generators to maintain the system at all points and at all times in the most cost efficient way.

In 1996, the FERC issued two orders for transmission systems as part of a framework to support the functioning of competition in the U.S. market for electricity. First, the FERC required the owner of a transmission line to offer nondiscriminatory access to any company wishing to send electricity to any wholesale buyer, such as a local distribution system or a power marketer.[20] A specific tariff must be published for all transmission services, and the tariff is to include, for instance, interruptible service as well as ordinary service (firm service) that is not to be interrupted but is more costly. The Order also required that if the transmission line operator is an integrated firm with generating capability, it must make services available to other generators on a separate, or unbundled, basis. Then any user can choose just the services it wishes to use, and units of the integrated firm have to pay the same fees to the transmission company that other users pay. Second, FERC required any party that operated transmission facilities in interstate commerce to participate in an "open-access, same-time information system," to provide information electronically about available capacity, prices, and other necessary information for a market in power to operate.[21].

Fair access to transmission service for electricity generators brings efficiency by opening opportunity for the best provider, just as access on equal footing was sought for long-distance providers to local telephone networks in telephone restructuring.

---

[20] Order 888, "Promoting Wholesale Competition through Open Access Non-Discriminatory Transmission Services by Public Utilities; Recovery of Stranded Costs by Public Utilities and Transmitting Utilities," issued April 24, 1996, 75 FERC §61,080.

[21] Order 889, "Open Access Same-Time Information Systems," issued April 24, 1996, 75 FERC §61,078.

Without such access, a transmission company that is part of a vertically integrated utility could maintain a monopoly for its generating facilities by denying transmission access to other generators, or it could make connection more difficult or more costly for others. Avoiding such outcomes is one reason some states require divestiture of transmission and distribution facilities from electricity generation plants as part of industry restructuring plans.

Competition Among Generators

Consider two geographic areas that had been served by two public utilities, each having a monopoly in one of the areas over both generation and transmission. If new transmission facilities connect the two areas, that creates a new, broader, market where the once-monopoly generators now form a duopoly. For generators of about equal size, it turns out that not very much of this interconnecting transmission capacity is needed to bring about the duopoly result, because not much electricity needs to flow from one area to the other to bring about a single market.[22] The mere threat of transmission between areas can induce duopoly rather than monopoly behavior, because each of the two generators is better off expanding output than trying to maintain its monopoly output while having the other enter its market.

Each generator would prefer to maintain its market power without interconnection, because interconnection supports competition. Where transmission is limited, and congestion occurs, price is higher in what are called "load pockets," spots where the load is high and transmission facilities cannot import electricity to serve the load. Local generators then have to run less efficient facilities, and they may even have market power. Congestion of transmission facilities leads to congestion charges for transmission out of low-cost areas, and the resulting fluctuation in transmission costs is an added source of uncertainty.

Sophisticated transmission rights can allocate scarce transmission capacity to suppliers and consumers without forcing them to bear all the risks of fluctuations in transmission prices.[23] These rights come in two forms, **physical transmission rights**, which entitle the holders to transmit electricity, and **financial transmission rights**, which focus on price and can yield rents if the charge for congestion goes up. These rights are broadly similar in allowing suppliers and consumers to use markets for these rights to hedge the risks associated with congestion charges for transmission.

Retail Electricity Service Providers

How can competition function at the retail level for electricity? Suppose a distribution company exists to deliver electricity to users. A promising framework allows for the development of marketing companies for electricity, which would purchase electricity from generators and distribute it to customers, ordinarily by purchasing delivery service from the distribution company. Such an electricity service provider (ESP) might not own either generating, transmitting, or distributing facilities. The ESP would specialize in identifying consumers' needs and finding ways to serve them. In particular,

---

[22] For analysis of this point, see Borenstein, Bushnell, and Stoff (2000).
[23] For explanation of these devices, see Joskow and Tirole (2000).

ESPs might develop time-of-use or other efficient rate structures that would convey true costs of electricity to users. ESPs would ensure that bills were properly rendered and collected.[24]

Traditional distribution companies, as public utilities, essentially sold two bundled services, electricity and delivery. With restructuring, the ESPs would take over selling the electricity, while the former distribution company would provide delivery service, including stepping down the voltage and carrying the electricity to the final users. These distribution or delivery companies would probably be regulated in the prices they could charge for their delivery services. To the extent ESPs would make no great investments, their activities might be quite competitive—somewhat like telephone service resellers—so regulation of them may be unnecessary. But door-to-door ESP sales efforts after restructuring in England were found to mislead consumers and some problems with sellers' claims have surfaced in the United States as well.

18.4 COMPETITION IN A RESTRUCTURED ELECTRICITY INDUSTRY

Competition can be introduced to electricity in many different ways, and state practices illustrate this variety. Most states have imposed retail price caps of some form. Pennsylvania, for example, froze rates to customers at existing levels, while California and Massachusetts required reductions.[25] Usually states separate the generation, transmission, and distribution functions to avoid favoritism, say in access to a transmission system and a schematic illustration of restructuring is shown in Appendix 18.2. Such plans typically require separation or unbundling of generation from transmission activities, and they sometimes require formal divestiture so the functions are split into separate, independent organizations. States sometimes imposed rules to handicap incumbents, not only requiring separate organizations for transmission and distribution and for marketing electricity but also limiting incumbents' prices and market shares. This section examines specific restructuring plans. But first we explore stranded costs and the long-standing relationship between public utilities and their regulators.

Stranded Costs and the Regulatory Compact

One practical economic issue that has complicated the transition to competitive markets for electricity in the United States is the *regulatory compact*, an implicit agreement between utilities and their regulators that owes utilities a return *of* their principle and a return *on* that principle. Remember that electric utilities had to make large, long-lasting investments, which their owners might not have made if regulatory rules

---

[24] The example of retail competition for New Hampshire is reported at the web site www.powerischoice.com/pages/Update.html.
[25] See descriptions in Kleit (2006).

could easily be changed in ways that would harm them. On the other hand, if regulators have allowed returns high enough to compensate utility owners for the risk that competition would arise to lower their asset values, it might be argued that no further compensation is warranted. As a practical matter, because moving to greater reliance on competition needed the cooperation of utilities, almost every restructuring has offset in some way the harm to those utilities. Some states limit the price reduction under competition by essentially imposing a tax, sometimes called a transition fee, and the proceeds are used to compensate existing utilities for the losses they suffer when competition ends their monopoly positions.[26] California and Texas provide examples of major industry restructuring.

Restructuring in California

As the 1990s began, electricity rates in California were more than 30 percent higher than the average for the country, and these higher costs handicapped California businesses relative to those in other parts of the country. After Congress passed the EPA in 1992, the California Public Utilities Commission set out to explore alternative ways to regulate the industry to improve its performance. The effort was influenced in part by reforms already in place in telecommunications and the natural gas industry in the United States and by electricity restructuring in Chile, Argentina, England, and Wales.

In April, 1994, the **California Public Utility Commission (CPUC)** proposed a competitive electricity generation industry, which would replace existing regulation of electric utilities. In addition, under the original proposal, consumers would be able to buy electricity from any source by the year 2002. This would make California the first state to embrace retail competition in electricity.

Managing Competition

To manage its markets, California mixed the ISO and Poolco models. The CPUC proposed to allocate market functions to two organizations in 1995, a spot market for day-ahead power and an ISO to ensure system balance. The state legislature passed the plan, which went into effect April 1, 1998.[27] Besides using these two market organizations, California created oversight boards for each of them that included representatives of all interested parties, almost ensuring there would be conflicting views at the highest levels.

California, therefore, created a market for electricity, called the **California Power Exchange, or CALPX**, as a day-ahead market that might be compared to the Florida Energy Broker. An important difference is that CALPX arranged *all* transactions instead of just extra ones, say to cover an integrated company's peak needs, which was the case in Florida. Generators belonging to former utilities that still had transmission or distribution facilities had to sell power in the CALPX while the distribution company also bought it there. This requirement ensured a large volume of trades in the spot market to support its establishment and effective function.

---

[26] New Hampshire is the only state so far granting less than full recovery of stranded costs. For an explanation of stranded costs and ways they were recovered, see Brennan, Palmer, and Martinez (2003).

[27] For description of the California plan see Joskow (2000, 2001) and Kleit and Considine (2006).

The **California Independent System Operator (CAISO)** was to be responsible for maintaining system balance, and it operated hour-ahead and real-time markets. This ISO coordinating function is similar to that provided by Virginia Power under its arrangements with independent power producers, but it is more complex. While Virginia Power had to provide reserves beyond the amounts planned to meet projected loads, it also controlled all generators in the system. In California, many independent generators made agreements to produce, while many users were agreeing to take electricity, and the transmission and distribution network was more extensive, in part because on average California drew 25 percent of its electricity from neighboring states.

Long-term forward contracts were discouraged for the first four years of the market's operation because full cost recovery for them was not guaranteed by the CPUC. Economist Frank Wolak argues that the utilities, who were divesting generating capacity and would now be buying electricity, did not expect to need the benefit that long-term contracts promised for hedging against price increases. He also points out that when generating capacity was divested it might have been pressed into long-term supply contracts with formerly affiliated distribution companies in what are called "vesting contracts."[28] Such procedures had been followed in restructuring elsewhere with good effects. Not having long-term contracts could make entry easier, because no customer would be tied up by contract. But it aggravated the temptation to make strategic offers in wholesale markets, a temptation that long-term contracts could moderate. By tying up capacity, long-term contracts dampen the incentive to withhold a unit or bid it at a high price, because the gain across fewer uncommitted units is then smaller.

California's generation capacity had been expanded very little in the 1990s, due to a combination of slow economic growth in the early part of the decade, strict environmental requirements that complicated new construction, and even uncertainty about industry restructuring itself. When it came, the restructuring plan asked California utilities to sell off much of their conventional generating plants to separate the generation of electricity from its transmission and its distribution. Much of the capacity was purchased by five power companies, AES, Duke, Dynegy, Mirant, and Reliant, with each acquiring roughly equal amounts. California utilities also owned extensive hydroelectric facilities, but environmental issues complicated their sale.[29] Not all of California participated in the deregulation of electricity. Officials in Los Angeles, for instance, where electricity is provided through the city's Department of Water and Power, decided in 1997 not to join in the restructuring program, and ended up selling power to other parts of the state.

Frozen Retail Rates

To win public support for electricity restructuring and to solve the stranded cost problem, retail rates were fixed at a level 10 percent lower than before. The 10 percent retail price reduction was subsidized in a complicated way by bonds issued by utilities

---

[28] See Wolak (2003b).

[29] For a history of electricity restructuring in California, see Blumstein, Friedman, and Green (2002).

but guaranteed by the state. Expected wholesale prices for electricity and transmission and distribution costs would allow these retail rates to cover ordinary costs and yield enough money to cover the utilities' stranded costs. The difference between the fixed retail rate and the ordinary cost was called the **Competitive Transition Charge (CTC)**. This CTC would be collected until stranded costs had been covered or until April 1, 2002, whichever came first. As long as wholesale prices are low enough, the CTC gives utilities revenues to cover their stranded costs, but if wholesale prices were to rise markedly the utilities could suffer dearly. After the CTC had served its purpose or expired, retail prices would be based on the average spot price in the CALPX plus transmission and distribution costs.[30] For up to four years, however, while retail prices for electricity would be fixed, wholesale prices could follow the dictates of supply and demand in the CALPX. Although not expected at the time, increases in the wholesale price could force enormous losses on the former utilities that became distribution companies, when they had to buy wholesale electricity at high market rates and distribute it at low fixed rates.

The state of California spent $80 million to inform consumers about the retail competition that was part of the restructuring plan. New retail suppliers could not escape paying the CTC, however, and this limited their opportunity to undercut incumbents' prices. Without a price advantage, new entry was difficult. Later, when wholesale prices rose and distribution companies were losing money, new entry to serve the retail market was out of the question.

The CALPX ran smoothly when it opened in April, 1998. From the beginning the CAISO faced problems, however, largely in markets for ancillary services where, according to FERC rules, generators had to make offers on the basis of their costs. When generators could obtain higher rates in the CALPX market they did not want to make offers based on their costs in the ancillary services market run by CAISO. So even though it could force generation, it was hard for CAISO to obtain reserve power when generators preferred to sell in the CALPX. FERC made some changes in rules to remove rigidities and to impose price ceilings and finally allowed generators to make offers on bases other than cost.

California's monthly wholesale prices per MWh averaged less than $30 in 1999, as shown in Table 18.1. At the end of 1999, San Diego Gas and Electric (SDG&E) was able to announce that its stranded costs had been repaid so it could abandon the fixed retail rate for electricity. Less than a year later, in September, 2000, Southern California Edison (SCE) and Pacific Gas and Electric (PG&E) also declared their stranded costs recovered. But they were not allowed to abandon fixed retail rates, and the legislature reimposed fixed retail rates on SDG&E as well. These actions protected consumers from price jumps in the summer of 2000, when electricity was suddenly scarce and expensive, but they hurt the power distribution companies.

As Table 18.1 shows, the wholesale price averaged $132.40 per MWh in June of 2000; from June through September it averaged $137.00. In June, San Francisco suffered rolling blackouts, as power was cut for short times in successive neighborhoods

---

[30] Littlechild (2003) describes problems with having retail price depend on market price at the wholesale level, in large part from volatility in such markets.

Table 18.1   Average Wholesale Electricity Prices in California ($/MWh)

Month	1999	2000	2001
January	21.6	31.8	272.0
February	19.6	18.8	304.4
March	24.0	29.3	249.0
April	24.7	27.4	265.9
May	24.7	50.4	239.5
June	25.8	132.4	159.8
July	31.5	115.3	137.8
August	34.7	175.2	120.1
September	35.2	119.6	126.8
October	49.0	103.2	69.4
November	38.3	179.4	74.8
December	30.2	**385.6**	69.6
Average	29.9	114.0	174.1

Source: Joskow (2001) for 1999–2000 and CAISO and California Department of Water Resources data reported by CPUC for 2001 (at http://www.cpuc.ca.gov/static/industry/electric/electric+markets/historical+information/average+ energy+costs+2000+thru+2001.xls), as reported in C. Blumstein, L. S. Friedman, and R. J. Green, "The History of Electricity Restructuring in California," University of California Energy Institute Working Paper, CSEM WP103, August, 2002, Berkeley, CA, p. 20. They note that 2001 data are not strictly comparable to earlier years because they include some longer-term contract prices, while earlier years are based only on day-ahead prices.
Note: The highest average wholesale price for the three-year period is **385.6**, which occurred in December, 2000.

to keep the power system going. The FERC proposed rule changes in the California system, to cap prices and to allow utilities to buy electricity from any source rather than be confined, as they had been, to purchasing from the CALPX.[31] FERC also proposed that the unwieldy boards of the CAISO and the CALPX be reconstituted to be less representative—and, therefore, less political—than they initially were.

The Crisis and Its Causes

The California electricity markets began to collapse at the end of 2000. Surprisingly, the average wholesale price hit its maximum of $385.6 per MWh in the usually off-peak month of December, 2000. Even though demand was well below the summer peak, rotating blackouts were needed to constrain demand and protect the network

---

[31] See Banerjee (2000, p. 1).

on seven days during the winter and spring of 2001.[32] With wholesale rates so high, even increasing retail rates by 7 to 15 percent, as regulators did in January 2001, could not prevent enormous losses at SCE and especially at PG&E, which was driven to bankruptcy. The CALPX had to suspend operations in January 2001 and declared bankruptcy itself in March. The CAISO became insolvent but was able to survive. The California Department of Water Resources took over purchasing electricity for the state to keep the electricity network functioning.

The failure of electricity markets in California does not mean electricity markets cannot work, because they do work in other parts of the country and in other parts of the world. But operating markets in electricity is difficult. Although exact causes are hard to identify, several forces contributed to California's problems. As noted, generating capacity expanded very little in the 1990s, so the capacity of California generators was not abundant. The problem is not just in the level of generating capacity, which existed in amounts that could have avoided blackouts, but whether electricity from that capacity was available when and where it was needed. The period from 1999 to 2001 brought less than usual rainfall in the Pacific Northwest, which reduced the exports of electricity from hydroelectric sources in that region that usually would flow to California, especially in the summer months. Summers were also unusually warm, so use of air conditioning—which accounts for 30 percent of summer electricity demand in California—was high.

The price of fuel, particularly the natural gas price that is a large element of marginal cost when it is used in electricity generation, also contributed to a rising cost of producing electricity that began in January, 2000. The price of natural gas doubled by June and tripled by September, and in December it was almost 10 times higher than it had been in January.[33] These increases were so great they alone drove the marginal cost of producing electricity at some generators so high that, with fixed retail electricity rates, large losses were inevitable. Costs could even go above the price caps that had been put in place, so some generators would then lose money selling electricity, and they were better off shutting down.

Environmental policy had an influence, too. Emissions of nitrous oxide from stationary sources, such as power plants, were controlled in Southern California by a so-called cap-and-trade system, which allows trading of permits that are needed to emit pollution. With trading, a market price is established for the permits. Power plants must have enough of these permits, or rights to pollute, to match their emissions, and the permits are gradually being reduced over time to improve air quality. Between April and September of 2000 the price of these permits rose almost tenfold. Economist Paul Joskow estimated this increase in permit prices alone could raise the marginal cost of electricity in a gas-fired steam unit by $30 to

---

[32] See Blumstein, Friedman, and Green (2002, p. 22).

[33] For effects of these natural gas price increases, see Blumstein, Friedman, and Green (2002, p. 23). In March 26, 2003, the FERC reported evidence that market prices had been manipulated; inappropriate withholding of capacities had elevated prices. See Richard A. Oppel, Jr., "Panel Finds Manipulation By Energy Companies," *New York Times*, March 27, 2003 p. A12; and Tom Fowler and Laura Goldberg, "Federal Report on Crisis Blasts Energy Companies," *Houston Chronicle*, March 27, 2003.

$40 per MWh and in a peaking turbine by $100 to $120 per MWh.[34] When combined with wholesale price caps, these increases could again make some generating units decide not to produce.

The interrelatedness of markets plays a role in these effects. One factor contributing to the increase in permit prices for nitrous oxide emissions was probably the reduction in imported electricity from the Pacific Northwest when dry conditions reduced hydroelectricity generation there. To make up for that loss of imported power, power plants in California had to produce more electricity with less efficient, more polluting, plants, which increased the demand for permits and raised their price.

Market power and strategic bidding of generators was also a problem. Generators exaggerated the scarcity of their capacity by withholding some capacity from the market or offering some of their capacity at high prices. Inelastic demand, which exists in part because many consumers cannot respond to short-run prices, makes this strategy more promising because a higher price does not affect quantity demanded very much. Expenditures on wholesale electricity were four and one-half times greater in the summer of 2000 than they were in the summer of 1999, a remarkable increase. Economists Borenstein, Bushnell, and Wolak trace almost 60 percent of the increase in price to the exercise of market power.[35] Wolak also showed how market power developed in the CAISO real-time market in 2000, as California demand increased relative to 1998 and 1999.[36] When large producers strategically withhold some of their generating capacity, the result is not only a higher price but also generation inefficiency, because the withheld capacity is often more efficient than the capacity that replaces it to produce power.[37]

By its design, the California electricity market was not adequate to deal with this collection of unexpected causes of scarcity and high wholesale prices. Requiring all transactions to go through the CALPX prevented the cushioning hedge that long-term forward contracts might have provided against short-lived high prices. Forward contracts might also have reduced market power by reducing the capacity output still to be priced, thereby making efforts to influence the spot price less profitable. Other market rules, including some pricing rules, compounded the problem by causing transactions to leave the CALPX and spill over into the ancillary services market, where prices could be higher but supplies had to be arranged at the last minute.[38] Great increases in natural gas prices, made worse by market manipulation, added to the cost of electricity. High prices in the wholesale market wreaked havoc on distributors, who were required to serve customers at fixed retail prices that would not cover their costs.

---

[34] See Joskow (2001).

[35] See Borenstein, Bushnell, and Wolak (2002) and Joskow and Kahn (2002).

[36] See Wolak (2003a, 2003b).

[37] See Wolak and Patrick (1997) and Wolfram (1998).

[38] For analysis of these rules and their effects, see Wolak, Nordhaus, and Shapiro (2000), available at http://www.ucei.berkeley.edu/ucei/restructuring.html. See also Wolak (2003a, 2003b).

Restructuring in Texas

Texas produces and consumes more electricity than any other state. Electricity costs and rates are lower in Texas than the national average so, unlike California, Texas did not restructure to overcome a competitive disadvantage from high electricity costs. More important to Texas was the fact that some areas of the state had higher costs than others, suggesting that efficiency improvements would be possible. Electric power also had great significance for Texas, where roughly 9 percent of all electricity in the United States is purchased.

Texas became the last state to regulate electricity when it created the **Public Utility Commission of Texas (PUCT)** in 1975 with passage of the Public Utility Regulatory Act (PURA). Texas contains entirely the **Electric Reliability Council of Texas (ERCOT)**, one of the 10 Electric Reliability Councils that make up the North American Reliability Council (NERC). Extreme eastern and western parts of the state belong to other Reliability Councils, but ERCOT oversees reliability for about 85 percent of the electricity in Texas. Moreover, the United States is also divided into three major interconnected systems, and one of these systems coincides with ERCOT. This scope made ERCOT an ideal candidate to serve as ISO for a restructured electricity industry in Texas, thus avoiding the need for building from scratch a new institution that would lack experience in its task.

In the 1980s the PUCT was affected by legislation narrowing its responsibilities to electricity and local telephone and broadening its powers to approve new generating plants and encourage the use of alternative fuels. In the 1990s, however, the emphasis shifted to actions that would restructure the electricity industry. Amendments to the PURA in 1995 exempted from rate regulation both ESPs, who sell at retail but do not generate or transmit electricity, and exempt wholesale generators (EWGs). The EWGs can sell only wholesale power, although they are allowed to affiliate with utilities who in turn can sell power at any level. The 1995 legislation also required the PUCT to develop an integrated resource planning process.

Another feature of the 1995 Texas legislation, aimed more at restructuring, called on the PUCT to create a nondiscriminatory wholesale transmission service and to introduce flexible pricing for wholesale and retail sales. In response to this legislation, ERCOT reorganized and began operating as a nonprofit ISO in 1996. As part of the 1995 law, utilities that owned or operated transmission grids were required to provide access to their networks at announced terms and conditions. These terms and conditions were to be comparable to those they charged themselves for the same services. Utilities could charge less than their approved rates, although not less than their marginal costs.

In 1999 Texas passed broad restructuring legislation. First, it required functional unbundling of public utilities, so generation, transmission, and distribution activities were to be separated within the utilities. This is expected to result eventually in formal division of utilities so each becomes three separate companies: (1) a Power Generation Company (PGC), (2) a Transmission and/or Distribution Service Provider (TDSP), and (3) a Retail Electricity Provider (REP). Moreover, no PGC is to own more than 20 percent of installed capacity in the ERCOT region. The TDSPs continue to be regulated.

Retail competition would be set up in the area formerly "belonging" to each utility, with a price benchmark established. In the service area of the TDSP affiliated with the utility, the REP affiliated with that utility had to provide a "price to beat," which was to be 6 percent lower than the price charged by the utility on January 1, 1999. Except for adjustments to be allowed for fuel cost (up to two times a year), this price would hold until 36 months after retail competition started, or until 40 percent of customers in the TDSP service area had switched to a different retail provider. Thus, retail competition was set up to favor entrants by not allowing the incumbent to cut price, but only for three years or until entrants have a significant share of the market. Competitors are expected to offer different forms of tariffs from which consumers can make choices.[39]

The Texas restructuring took effect without major difficulty and has operated successfully. Retail service from new nonutility providers is small but growing and even comes from environmentally clean sources like wind power. No sweeping changes were made to the industry, as there was no exchange where trades were required and no forced divestiture of functional units. The overseeing agency serving as independent system operator was ERCOT, an organization that had played a similar role since it was formed in 1970. The transition to greater competition was thus less radical and less disruptive than California's, and that may account for its success.

Restructuring the Electricity Industry in Other States

The unhappy ending for California's restructuring caused some other states to delay their programs. Nevertheless, Arizona, Connecticut, Delaware, Illinois, Maine, Maryland, Massachusetts, Michigan, New Hampshire, New Jersey, New York, Ohio, Oregon, Pennsylvania, Rhode Island, Texas, and Virginia restructured their electricity industries within the last 10 years. Many, though not all, of these states had relatively high electricity prices. In January, 1997, Massachusetts regulators approved a plan of the New England Electric System to sell its generating plants, which are located in six states and include hydroelectric facilities. These separate generating companies are now competing with one another for customers. Electricity rates were initially cut by 10 percent and consumers could choose from whom to purchase electricity.

A major eastern U.S. wholesale market, called PJM, involves Pennsylvania, New Jersey, and Maryland and stretches as far west as Illinois. It also affects parts of nearby states in which generators compete. Like Texas and the Midwest, these states broadened existing exchange institutions, instead of creating new institutions as California had done. PJM relied on a regional power exchange like Florida's. The Pennsylvania government gave high priority to informing consumers about retail choices through advertising, with the result that more than 10 percent of the consumers chose new providers shortly after they had the opportunity. Those new providers, in turn, built new capacity in or near Pennsylvania. The state claims consumers saved almost $3 billion in

---

[39] As Littlechild (2003) shows, however, presenting complex rates to consumers and explaining attendant risks in an understandable way is difficult.

three years because of lower electricity bills under agreements that prevented price increases while competition was developing in the generation of electricity.[40]

Restructuring of electricity has not always gone smoothly. In normal times, a megawatt hour of electricity could cost between $25 and $125. In the Midwest during the summer of 1998, for example, the wholesale price of electricity in Chicago briefly reached $2,000 per megawatt hour because of supply scarcity, or a load pocket, in a small area. The wholesale price again went almost that high in the summer of 1999, and the price in load pockets in some other parts of the Midwest went even higher. The fall of many active energy traders, and the Enron bankruptcy, also dampened enthusiasm for electricity markets. But Enron was a stimulating developer of markets for electricity and many of those markets survive and are now growing.[41]

The years 2006 and 2007 brought increases in fuel prices plus huge increases in the cost of power-plant construction, and when frozen electricity rates expired in many states the rates rose substantially.[42] Rate caps have expired in Connecticut, Delaware, Illinois, Maryland, Massachusetts, and Texas, and are soon expiring in Ohio, Pennsylvania, Rhode Island, and Virginia. Despite the great price swings in some restructured regions, we are unlikely to see the return of the public utility and its narrowly administrative regulatory commission after the utility has been replaced. Twenty-five states have enacted electrical restructuring legislation or issued regulatory orders to that effect and a host of other states have regulatory orders or legislation pending, but many delayed any action after the California experience and are still waiting to see how restructuring works. But only seven states have taken no action so far on electricity restructuring. New institutions, which continue to change and develop, control the pricing and allocation of electricity in many regions, and they do it every hour of every day.

In airlines, the design and location of facilities changed after deregulation, and although it may occur more slowly in electricity, change is similarly taking place after restructuring. Competition will probably spark innovations in metering, and its strong incentives should bring other changes, particularly in the organization of transmission systems, which are crucial to the success of restructuring. FERC is facilitating the transition, although it also is feeling its way and was painfully ineffective in the California crisis. Restructuring of the industry is occurring by degrees, especially in high-cost states, and lessons from state-by-state experiments can benefit all. The big question that is yet to be answered is whether decentralized decisions can produce better results in this volatile industry than central coordination can. So far, the development of a competitive market for electricity generation is quite an achievement, and time will tell whether it will improve efficiency while reducing the role of external regulation.[43]

---

[40] See Kleit and Considine (2006) for a comparison of restructuring in Pennsylvania and California.

[41] See Neela Banerjee, "Who Will Needle Regulators Now That Enron's Muzzled?" *New York Times*, January 20, 2002, p. BU1; and Alexei Barrionuevo, "Energy Trading, Post-Enron," *New York Times*, January 15, 2006, p. C1.

[42] See Alexei Barrionuevo, "Soaring Utilty Prices Bring Calls to Re-examine Regulation," *New York Times*, February 17, 2007, p. B1.

[43] For examples of work by economists that tries to understand possible strategic behavior in these new markets, see Newbery (1998) and Fernando, Kleindorfer, and Wu (2000). For empirical studies of possibly strategic behavior, see Wolfram (1998, 1999) and Borenstein, Bushnell, and Wolak (2002).

SUMMARY

Although electricity began as an unregulated, privately financed business, its producers were subject to regulation as public utilities for almost all of the last century. The industry was greatly affected by the Public Utility Holding Company Act of 1935, which—although now repealed—essentially barred the complex holding company form of organization in the industry. In related 1935 legislation, the Federal Power Commission, which became the Federal Energy Regulatory Commission, gained authority to regulate interutility sales of electricity. Electric utilities remained vertically integrated across the functions of electricity generation, transmission, and distribution, and until the 1970s they grew faster than the growing United States economy.

The Middle-East oil crisis of the 1970s raised the price of fuel dramatically, and electric utilities suffered in two ways. Either regulators were slow to allow the higher fuel prices to affect the price of the electricity output, so profit fell, or they did raise the electricity price and consumer responses cut needed output so that capacity utilization fell and profit suffered. The Public Utility Regulatory Policy Act of 1978 attempted to improve efficiency in the industry through pricing that reflected costs and attention to other issues. It also encouraged generation by small units using renewable energy sources. This legislation, together with technological changes that enabled smaller units to produce electricity at low cost, brought new, nonutility, generators into the industry as suppliers of electricity to the well-established utilities.

In 1992 Congress passed the Energy Policy Act, which broadened opportunities for nonutility generators and set the stage for competition at the generation level. It removed the requirement that these nonutility generators had to use renewable energy sources, and it required the owners of electricity grids to transmit electricity between nonutility generators and their utility customers at reasonable terms. Additions to industry generating capacity now come mainly from nonutility generators, and many state regulators are concerned with ways to allow them to engage in competition with each other and with traditional utilities.

With competition for customers at either the wholesale or retail level, however, problems might develop on the electricity grid in the interactions between electricity generators and final customers. For one thing, electricity flows in an electric power system according to rules of nature, and because electricity cannot be held to a preset path, congestion is hard to manage in the transmission grid. Because electricity cannot be stored, an electric power system has to balance constantly the amount supplied to match the amount demanded. This task is complicated by the inelastic demand for electricity, which results in part because price has not been able to respond to short-run conditions to influence consumption.

To deal with these special features of electricity, while allowing competition, two structural arrangements have been proposed, one based on a system of contracting that can be guided by an independent system operator and the other on short-term market clearing, through a spot market. States that restructured their electricity industries have used both of these institutions. Apart from serious problems with electricity markets in California, due to complex and unusual causes, markets that allow competition in the generation of electricity appear to be working reasonably well, although price promises to be more volatile than it used to be.

Retail competition is not flourishing like wholesale competition, but with time, new strategies may develop to help entrants. Thus far, retail competitors have found it hard to undercut the rates of incumbent providers in many states. Unchanging rates for residences limit efficiency by preventing customers from knowing about scarcity through price changes to which they can respond. Low-cost metering that can adjust prices could have important effects on the efficiency of the entire system, and it might alter the retailing landscape.

Electricity restructuring came at a bad time in California. Generating capacity was scarce relative to demand, because few new power plants had been built in the 1990s. Then, while a booming economy in the late 1990s stimulated electricity demand, dry weather reduced hydroelectric generation in the Northwest that usually served California in summer, and summers were unusually warm, which increased the demand for air conditioning. As the electricity markets functioned, generators were motivated to withhold units, to drive up wholesale prices. Sharp increases in fuel prices, especially for natural gas, and in the price of Southern California pollution permits, also raised wholesale prices and, when combined with legislatively fixed retail prices, brought financial disaster to electricity distributors. The institutions guiding wholesale markets failed, and other institutions took over guidance of California markets.

Competition functions in a variety of forms in 18 states, including Texas which is the largest electricity market in the United States. Fuel prices and construction costs for new power plants are both rising, however, just as the frozen retail prices that accompanied restructurings in many states are expiring. In these circumstances the effects of restructuring are still being judged.

QUESTIONS

1. Suppose that demand for electricity is constant every day for 12 hours at one level and for the other 12 hours at another level. A rate-of-return regulated public utility offers electricity services in the two 12-hour time periods, or two markets, an off-peak market Q_1 and a peak market Q_2. Annual demands in the two markets are

$$P_1 = 10 - 0.025Q_1, \text{ and}$$

$$P_2 = 15 - 0.025Q_2.$$

The cost of producing Q_1 is $5 per unit. Peak service Q_2 requires capital, while off-peak service Q_1 does not. To produce a unit of Q_2 requires $100 in capital that lasts forever and that can be adjusted perfectly to meet demand. Suppose that the allowed rate of return is 7 percent and the cost of capital is 5 percent. Then a unit of Q_2 costs $5 (5 percent of $100 each year), but (because the allowed rate of return is 7 percent) the regulator thinks it costs $7. Assume the regulator is not concerned with profit obtained from either Q_1 or Q_2 separately but only looks at total actual profit and total allowed profit.

a. Find socially optimal prices on the assumption that total revenue must equal total cost and the cost of capital is 7 percent (rather than 5 percent). An approximation is fine. Find the quantities of Q_1 and Q_2 at optimal prices.

b. Find prices for the profit-maximizing public utility subject to the rate-of-return constraint.

c. Explain the difference between answers in a and b.

d. Is your answer in b sustainable?

2. Consider the following electricity generation capacities and demand loads in two communities, North (N) and South (S), that are connected by a transmission grid:

N| Generating capacity: 700 MW at $20 per MW

                                      300 MW at $30 per MW

   Load: 1500 MW   200 MW at $50 per MW

   Load: 500 MW

                                        700 MW at $20 per MW

S| Generating capacity: 300 MW at $30 per MW

a. Assuming that transmission is costless and there is no congestion, describe an efficient solution for the two communities, North and South. Calculate the total cost of electricity for both communities under your solution.

b. Now suppose that congestion limits the use of the line between North and South so only 300 MW can be transmitted in either direction. Describe an efficient solution for the two communities in this situation. Calculate the total cost of electricity for both communities under your solution.

c. For your answer in part a, what would be a reasonable access fee for transmitting electricity from South to North?

d. For your answer in part b, what would be a reasonable access fee for transmitting electricity from South to North?

3. In the following questions, assume that each pricing arrangement is set so it yields the same profit.

a. What is the difference between time-of-use pricing and real-time pricing? What advantages and disadvantages does each have for consumers, relative to a single price that is the same at all times? What makes time-of-use pricing effective?

b. What is the main advantage of interruptible service pricing?

4. Restructuring of the electricity industry came in part from federal legislation and in part from conditions in certain states. What pieces of legislation played a role,

and what role did each piece of legislation play? Would the level of costs play a role in the state's decision to restructure? Why?

5. Nuclear power projects have sometimes been unpopular with neighboring citizens. Under rate-of-return regulation, do you think consumers might be motivated to oppose the *completion* of such construction when capacity was not greatly needed?

6. Consider a wholesale electricity market supplied by 10 generating companies that are roughly equal in size. Each generating company operates six generators. Demand in the market is inelastic in the short run and shifts considerably at different times during the day.

   a. Explain whether one generating company, on suspecting an outward or increasing shift in demand, might withhold one of its generators from the market or set a high price for one generator's output. To what extent can the company benefit from such an action?

   b. The top-4 concentration ratio in this market is not exceptionally high, at about 40, yet withholding of the sort that part a considers might occur to raise market price. Is this a typical example of market power? The FERC used to evaluate whether to allow wholesale electricity pricing by market forces by considering concentration ratios of sellers in the market. Can you criticize this practice?

   c. Now suppose that each of the generating companies has long-term contracts to provide electricity that ties up the output of three of its six generators for the foreseeable future. Might this change cause you to modify your answer to part a? Explain why or why not.

APPENDIX 18.1 Transmission Grid Illustration of Congestion Cost

The services that a transmission system might offer are actually more complicated than a diagram of one line connecting a generator to a customer may suggest. First, transmission lines are interconnected in complex ways, so electricity can flow in many directions and electricity to balance the system may be obtained from many locations. Electricity, however, does not necessarily flow over the routes to the locations desired. Consider the analogy of water in pipes. With no valves to control it, as more pipes are opened up the water flows through them whether that is desired or not. With electricity, valves that might control water flows are not economically available, so electricity flows where it can most easily go. As a result, where two transmission systems are interconnected, one system may help to carry another's electricity even though it is the other system that earns revenue for the service.

To illustrate the transmission task, consider the example represented in Figure 18.A1.1, where a transmission grid connects three areas, North, South, and East.[44] North and South generate electricity and consume it, while East consumes but does not generate any electricity. Indeed, North generates 1,000 MW but consumes only 300 MW, South generates 1,000 MW and consumes 700 MW, and East, which generates none, consumes 500 MW. Generation is more costly in North, at $40 per MW, while the cost is just $20 per MW in South. There is one other constraint: because of characteristics of the grid, when power flows from South the flow to East *will always be twice what it is to North.*

Figure 18.A1.2 illustrates an efficient solution for generating and transmitting power. South, the low-cost producer, generates its maximum output of 1,000 MW, consumes 700 MW, and transmits the remainder on the grid, which travels in the two-to-one ratio so that 200 MW go to East and 100 MW go to North. North receives these 100 MW from South and produces 500 MW, so it has 600 MW available. It consumes

Figure 18.A1.1 *Transmission Grid for North, South, and East*

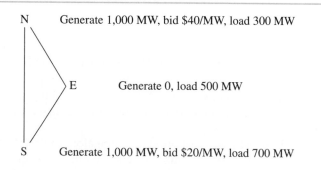

N   Generate 1,000 MW, bid $40/MW, load 300 MW

E   Generate 0, load 500 MW

S   Generate 1,000 MW, bid $20/MW, load 700 MW

---

[44] This example is drawn from "ERCOT, The Texas Connection," University of Houston Institute for Energy Law and Enterprise, February 22, 2001, pp. 40, 41.

Figure 18.A1.2 *Transmissions on the North, South, and East Electricity Grid*

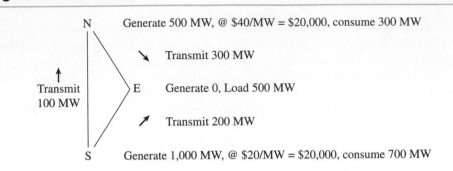

Figure 18.A1.3 *Transmissions with Congestion for the North, South, and East Grid*

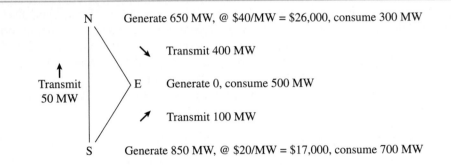

300 and transmits 300 to East. Thus, East receives a total of 500 MW, which is the amount it wishes to consume. This solution meets all constraints and produces the needed 1,500 MW at the lowest possible cost of $40,000.

Now suppose the line connecting South to East can safely handle only 100 MW. Because the line would ideally handle 200 MW, there is 100 MW of congestion on the line. Figure 18.A1.3 shows the best solution with this amount of congestion. Now South can send only 100 MW to East because of the congestion. Given the two-to-one ratio of amounts it can send to East and North, South can send only 50 MW (one-half of the amount to East) to North. This means that South can send only 150 MW, so it should produce only 150 MW above its own consumption of 700 MW, for a total of 850 MW. North now receives 50 MW from South and produces 650 MW, so it has 700 available. It consumes 300 and sends 400 to East. Again, this solution meets all load requirements.

Under the revised plan that responds to congestion, the total cost is higher, at $43,000 rather than $40,000, because more electricity must now be generated in the high-cost area of North. The cost of the line congestion between South and East is, thus, $3,000. If no other solution can be found to this problem (perhaps by arranging for other generators to come on line) the cost of transmitting from South to East is set at $30 per MW ($3,000 in added cost caused by congestion on the line divided by 100 MW transmitted). The cost of congestion is, thus, inferred from its consequences in higher-cost generation, and that cost is imposed on those using the line, so only those who have a need for transmission worth that much use the line.

APPENDIX 18.2 Illustration of Restructured Electricity Industry

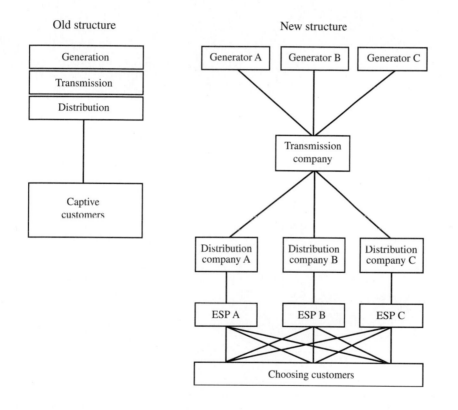

PART 3
SOCIAL REGULATION

Even when markets can function without monopoly, they may still be imperfect. Chapters 19 and 20 describe imperfections that can arise and discuss alternative means of remedying them. Chapter 21 shows how externalities prevent markets from being efficient when costs are borne by innocent victims who are not in on the decisions. For instance, decentralized decisions are not efficient if business firms disregard important costs, as when a power plant in the Midwestern United States sends sulphur dioxide into the air to form sulphuric acid, which prevailing winds can carry as far as Canada and New England to fall into lakes and kill aquatic life. A wide range of policies aim at controlling these costs borne by others. For instance, markets have been created where those who pollute must purchase "rights to pollute," and the value of that right can reflect the costs that pollution imposes on others.

Imperfect information can also prevent markets from operating efficiently. Workers and employers may be uninformed about risks and dangers in the workplace, for example. Chapter 22 explores ways government regulation helps to prevent discrimination in the workplace, reduce dangers of occupational health and safety, and support the provision of retirement pensions and other worker benefits. In a multicultural workplace, some workers face discrimination that competition and regulation can help to prevent. Courts sometimes grant redress to harmed individuals, and state workmen's compensation laws provide low-cost insurance against physical injuries suffered at work. Consumers are also exposed to injury when information about products and services is imperfect. Chapter 23 examines protections afforded consumers, especially for purity and effectiveness of foods, drugs, cosmetics, and medical devices. Motor vehicle safety is supported by highway requirements and motor vehicle design features that are intended to avoid crashes and limit harms when they occur. Courts also play a role in protecting consumers from injury.

A competitive market economy has one inescapable side effect: some firms fail. Governmental regulation is intended to moderate the possible effects of firm failure. Chapter 24 shows that although owners are expected to bear the burden of firm failure, it can bring workers and retirees unexpected and devastating losses. To clarify their meaning, pensions are defined by government authorities for uniformity, and some federal pension insurance protects employees and retirees when their employer fails. Government agencies also oversee corporate governance to minimize conflicts of interest and to insure proper reporting, all intended in part to guard against the unexpected collapse of business firms. Social regulation thus tries to overcome economic conditions that interfere with the effectiveness of competitive markets in serving citizens.

19

Social Regulation of Markets

I n 1894, William T. Love started to dig a canal to link the Niagara River in upstate New York to Lake Ontario, and he hoped to locate an ideal community around what he named Love Canal. Although a trench was dug, the canal was never completed, and in the 1920s the trench became a dump site. In 1947 the Hooker Chemicals and Plastic Corporation owned the original 15-acre site and used the trench to dispose of chemical waste. Just 6 years later, in 1953, Hooker covered the canal with dirt and sold the site to the City of Niagara Falls Board of Education for $1. The Hooker Company wrote into the deed a disclaimer for any future damage its discarded chemicals might cause. After a school was built on the property, and land surrounding the school was sold for the construction of about 100 homes, damage came. And it turned out to be devastating. After a heavy rain in 1978 many chemicals rose to the surface, where they turned trees and gardens black and burned children's hands and faces. After miscarriages and birth defects were suffered by residents, studies found more than 80 dangerous chemical compounds in the area, 11 of them suspected carcinogens. The school was closed, and residents, even in the surrounding area, were evacuated. President Carter called it "one of the grimmest discoveries of the modern era."

Love Canal takes us beyond regulating competition or regulating industries to a third form of market regulation. Called social regulation, this third form focuses on broad goals, cutting across industries to protect employee and consumer health and safety and to pursue environmental, financial, or other concerns. As early as 1906, concern for health and safety motivated formation of the *Food and Drug Administration* to protect food and drug purity. A burst of social regulation dates from the 1960s, however, when highway and workplace deaths increased markedly, dangers of consumer products became apparent, catastrophes from nuclear power plants could be imagined, and harmful side effects of pesticides such as dichlorodiphenyl-trichloroethane (DDT) became known. Congress responded by creating laws and agencies having social regulatory purposes to control unwanted consequences of what might be called modern life.

The *Environmental Protection Agency*, the *Consumer Product Safety Commission*, the *Occupational Safety and Health Administration*, the *Equal Employment Opportunity*

Commission, the *National Highway Traffic Safety Administration*, and the *Nuclear Regulatory Commission* were all created in the 1960s and 1970s. In terms of their total cost, these social regulatory agencies now exceed all other forms of regulation. When first introduced, regulation in these new forms was not always effective, especially in light of the aims Congress set for them. Nor was it welcomed initially, because it intruded into decisions of businesses and individual consumers. For example, "fasten your seatbelt," or "wear your motorcycle helmet," were not welcome admonitions before evidence that supported their value was available. As time has passed, social regulation has come to be more accepted, in part because it gradually took more effective forms that can achieve desirable goals while imposing lower costs.

The concerns that motivate social regulation, such as protection of the environment, of consumers, of worker health and safety, or of retirement pensions in the event of firm failure, are properly labeled as social concerns. The causes that lead to social regulation, however, can usually be traced to problems in the functioning of markets. If decentralized decisions are taken without considering all consequences for society, or if socially beneficial effort is not motivated, or if parties to transactions are not well informed, or if firm failure inflicts great harm that falls unfairly among workers, consumers, and others, then outcomes under an otherwise well-functioning competitive market system may fall far short of what ideally could be possible. Finding the causes of these market failures is crucial to the diagnosis of social problems that can arise in a market economy.

Here in Part III we examine possible failures of markets as the result of imperfect information and externality, including firm failure. These problems are not limited to one industry, so industry regulation is not a solution, and they are not avoided by supporting competition through antitrust policy. Treatment of these problems of social regulation calls for subtle diagnosis, and Chapter 20 considers tools for solving them. Succeeding chapters examine problems and their remedies in areas of environmental protection, worker protection, consumer protection, and firm failure as it affects banking, insurance, and employee pensions. We begin by considering the market problems that social regulation is intended to correct: externalities, imperfect information, fairness, and side effects of firm failure.

19.1 | EXTERNALITIES

Even though competitive markets can drive prices down to the level of costs faced by firms, they still may not serve society efficiently when *externalities* exist. When there are externalities, such as highway congestion, decentralized decisions are not based on marginal social costs, so they do not produce ideal outcomes. A chemical company may not consider the costs it imposes on residents. Competition functions to drive prices to the level of the costs that are considered, but all costs are not considered. So the result cannot be ideal.

When disposing of smokestack waste in the air, a factory manager does not take all social costs into account largely because property rights to the air cannot easily be defined. In principle, where property rights can be defined parties can negotiate to solve such externality problems, although necessary agreements can involve many parties and be very costly, perhaps so costly they are not even feasible. Taxes, subsidies, and new forms of tradeable property rights can all have a role in solving externality problems by correcting the costs or benefits that decision makers act on. It is especially difficult, however, to convey to decision makers the costs and benefits of their decisions when property rights are not well defined.

Unclear Property Rights

Property held in common and not individually owned, such as the air we breath and the water in lakes and rivers, may be used—even exploited—by everyone. No user faces a price or a cost for using these collectively owned resources, yet the use by one may detract from effective use by others. That is why property held in common may be overused. It is the classic common pool problem. Air, land, and water were plentiful for many centuries, relative to the demands placed on them by the world's population.[1] In many parts of the world today this is no longer true. For instance, land was once so plentiful that it was not owned privately, even in places where private property was well accepted. As land became scarce, people abandoned common use to foster better control and more efficient use. Similarly, for many years the use of air and water by one person did not detract from use by others, but with population growth and industrialization, the nature and amount of emissions into the air and water grew so serious that rules were created to control them.

Property rights to air or to lakes and rivers are much harder to define than property rights to land. No one owns a river, which explains why factories as well as fishermen may try to use it. When a factory uses a river to dispose of waste, that use may interfere with the fishermen who use the river to catch fish. Without clear property rights, the responsibilities of parties cannot be specified, and decentralized coordination of activities is difficult. Unclear property rights also handicap negotiation. How can a contract be drawn if ownership is not clear?

In principle, a merger between fishermen and factories might control pollution by "internalizing" the externality, that is, forming an organization that would motivate factories to consider the costs borne by fisherman. But such mergers seldom appeal to the disputing parties. New firms or additional fishermen might not be drawn into the merged enterprise. The merged firm would still not take into account effects that others might suffer, such as those who want to swim in the river. With others, such as the swimmers, merger is not even feasible.

Externalities are likely, therefore, to follow when property rights are unclear. When land, water, or air is communally owned, the private costs or benefits seen by individuals in using them can differ from the true social consequences of their actions, so decentralized decisions fail to produce an optimal allocation of resources. There are three main solutions. First, a *command system* may set allowed levels of an activity to force improvement. For example, in an effort to impose minimal standards

---

[1] For wasteful use of plentiful land in early Australia, see Blainey (1975).

of house maintenance, some communities require that lawns be mowed before they reach a certain height. Second, taxes or subsidies may be used in an effort to correct private costs so they reflect social costs. A tax on pollution discharged from a smoke-stack is an example. Third, rights to engage in the activity that causes the externality may themselves be defined and then traded so a newly created market that puts a price on the externality can efficiently restrain it.

Sometimes it is possible to establish clear property rights. For many years it was assumed that when externalities existed in production, an optimal allocation of resources was impossible without some sort of imposed remedy, such as a tax, a subsidy, or a restriction. An important argument by Nobel laureate Ronald H. Coase (1960) qualified this presumption, and showed that a solution could follow simply by establishing clear private property rights. We turn to Coase's ideas first, before returning to situations in which the definition of property rights is more difficult or impossible.

The Coase Theorem

Professor Ronald Coase showed how defining property rights could solve externality problems. In an example involving a rancher and a farmer, in which unfenced cattle could create an externality by destroying crops, Professor Coase (1960) showed that defining property rights motivated the rancher and the farmer to negotiate a solution. Whether the farmer had the right to be free from damage caused by cattle or the

---

BOX 19.1 Honey Bees and Pollination

As honey bees collect nectar to produce honey, they transfer pollen from one plant to another, which fertilizes the plants and enables them to bear fruit. This is a positive externality that results from the bee's own goal of producing honey, and it is crucial to the production of fruits, vegetables, and nuts that we enjoy every day. Bees pollinate apples, almonds, oranges, blueberries, peaches, cotton, and about 90 other crops. This bee pollination has been organized commercially so it no longer depends on a side effect of bees' efforts, and to this extent the beneficial externality has been internalized. Bee keepers now profit not only from the honey and wax their bees produce, but also from moving their bee hives to apple orchards and to other clients to facilitate the pollination process. For some so far unexplained reason, many bee colonies around the U.S. did not return to their hives when released to pollinate in 2006 and 2007, and commercial bee hives in 24 states have lost large fractions of their bees. Some losses come in any year, but these losses are so extraordinary they are being called "colony collapse disorder." Until this mystery is solved, the fall in honey production will be trivial compared with the loss of crops that depend on pollination by honey bees. These crops provide an estimated one-third of our diet, and arguably the healthiest part, too.

See S. N. S. Cheung, "The Fable of the Bees: An Economic Investigation," *Journal of Law and Economics*, 1973, Vol. 16, pp. 11–34; A. Barrionuevo, "Honeybees, Gone with the Wind, Leave Crops and Keepers in Peril," *New York Times*, February 27, 2007, p. A1; and May R. Berenbaum, "Losing Their Buzz," *New York Times*, March 2, 2007, p. A21.

rancher was entitled to let his cattle roam free, once the property rights were clarified Professor Coase deduced that the two parties could reach the same efficient solution! This does not mean that the two parties themselves would not care how rights were assigned. To the contrary, each would benefit more when its rights were stronger. The final outcome of their negotiations, however, would involve *exactly the same output* under either arrangement, barring large income effects. In this instance, the parties are few enough to make negotiation and other transaction costs low. Although he recognized their importance generally, Coase assumed transaction costs to be zero in his example. Property rights can be defined easily in this case, too. Figure 19.1 illustrates the logic of Coase's argument.

The vertical axis of Figure 19.1 shows the profit of the cattle rancher, which curve P traces as a function of the number of cattle raised, or herd size. The lower part of Figure 19.1 shows crop loss damage to the farmer (for a given crop size) as a function of the number of cattle the rancher raises. If the rancher has the legal right to raise cattle without liability for damage to neighboring crops, he chooses to raise q_1 head of cattle, for that number maximizes his profit. This outcome is not a socially optimal one, however. In setting private marginal cost equal to the price for which cattle can be sold, that is, in maximizing profit, the rancher has omitted—or failed to consider—the costs the farmer bears. The rancher causes these costs, but creates a negative externality when the farmer is forced to pay for them. Thus price does not equal social marginal social cost at herd size q_1, because price is less than the marginal cost to the rancher plus the marginal cost to the farmer.

Notice, however, that because the damage increases with herd size, the farmer is motivated to pay the rancher to reduce the herd size. Indeed, the farmer in Figure 19.1 is willing to pay an amount up to AB to persuade the rancher to reduce his herd size from q_1 to q_2, because that is the loss the farmer suffers due to the larger herd.

Figure 19.1 *The Coase Case: An Optimal Solution Independent of Property Rights*

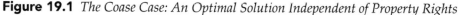

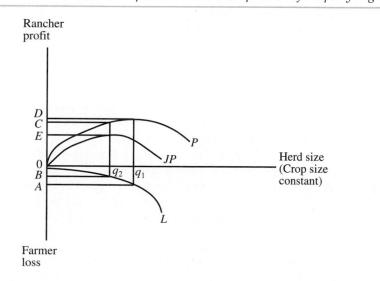

Meanwhile, the rancher makes the reduction in herd size for a payment greater than CD, the profit lost by reducing the herd size to q_2. Because $AB > CD$, a mutually beneficial agreement should be possible. The best agreement would permit the farmer and rancher to maximize their combined profit from cattle-raising decisions, with the rancher raising q_2 head of cattle. The curve JP represents the joint profit from the cattle-raising output decision, which is the rancher's profit less the farmer's loss, and it is maximized at E, where output is q_2. Reducing output any further reduces the rancher's profit by more than it reduces the farmer's loss, so negotiation does not go there. We assume that there is no problem in determining the amount of damages the farmer suffers, although such determination might actually be difficult.

The herd size q_2 reflects all social costs, and so it is the efficient herd size. Notice that this efficient outcome could also have been achieved, and more directly, if the rancher did not have a legal right to raise cattle without being liable for damage they cause. If instead the rancher was liable for all damages caused to the farmer, then the rancher would effectively incur the losses resulting from crop damage as the herd expanded. Then, in an attempt to maximize profit, the rancher would be led directly to output q_2. As another alternative, the two parties might consider fencing their boundary lines, but this option would require the invention of barbed wire.

Bargaining Problems and Transaction Costs

Even though negotiation is possible, it is not always easy to reach an agreement, as we have presumed the farmer and rancher would do. Aside from the problem of property rights being unclear, even when they are clear and well defined an agreement can still be difficult to reach and enforce.

Consider an example of competitive landlords who are deciding whether to invest to improve their properties. Professors Otto Davis and Andrew Whinston (1961) demonstrated how two property owners may be led to allow their properties to deteriorate, thus contributing to urban blight. Table 19.1 presents the situation. If both owners invest, they earn 7 percent returns on their investments. In this example, investment by both owners yields efficient resource allocation. But if one invests and

---

BOX 19.2 The Role of Barbed Wire

Expansion of agriculture to the Great Plains of the United States was stymied in the 1870s because fencing could not protect farmers' crops from damage by roaming cattle. When ranchers' herds damaged farmers' crops, the resulting conflicts created the plot lines for many Western movies. Neither smooth wire fences nor thorny hedges stopped cattle from harming crops until inventors combined their properties into barbed wire. By protecting agriculture, barbed wire had a great impact on the development of the West and was so important that one could be hanged for cutting a barbed wire fence.

See H. D. and F. T. McCallum, *The Wire That Fenced the West*, University of Oklahoma Press, Norman, OK, 1965.

TABLE 19.1 A Prisoner's Dilemma in the Investment to Maintain Urban Property

		Other Owner's Return	
		Invest	Do Not Invest
		7%	10%
One Owner's Return	Invest	7%	3%
		3%	4%
	Do Not Invest	10%	4%

the other does not, the investor earns a lower return. The noninvestor hurts the neighborhood. Despite the commitment of funds by the investor, the area in which the investor's apartment is located will be less attractive because of deterioration of the other owner's property. Yet the noninvestor even benefits from an enhanced environment because of the first owner's investment. The investor earns only a 3 percent return with its increased investment while the noninvestor's return is increased to 10 percent because of neighborhood improvement. If neither owner invests, each earns a return of 4 percent because the neighborhood declines further. This frustrating structure of payoffs is an example of a prisoner's dilemma, one in which private motives can take parties away from the socially ideal outcome.

The two property owners represented in Table 19.1 face **reciprocal externalities**, in that each party affects the other. The reciprocal effects may help the two neighbors to understand their dilemma and rise above it. If the owners act independently, however, they will not invest, thereby inviting deterioration of their properties and the neighborhood where they are located. Here, even though property rights are well enough defined that an agreement might be negotiated, motivation remains for each party to defect from the agreement unless some clear legal responsibility for harm can be invoked to avoid it.

Building and occupancy codes, or zoning laws, are rules aimed at coordinating behavior when negotiation would be costly and difficult.[2] Building and occupancy codes in cities may help to reduce the force of the dilemma described by requiring both of the two owners to invest. There is little evidence, however, that building and occupancy codes are strong enough to solve the dilemma, and the costs of enforcing such codes are considerable. Typically, more than two owners would be involved, making negotiation more difficult.

Another problem in reaching socially optimal solutions by bargaining when externalities exist can be traced to flexibility in the status quo, whenever the status quo might influence legal rights. For example, if a glue factory is polluting a stream, and the seriousness of the pollution affects the ultimate bargained outcome, then the

---

[2] For examination of zoning laws and their effects, see Davis and Whinston (1961) and Siegan (1970).

polluter may prefer to begin at a very high level of pollution to make any concession appear greater. The polluter is in somewhat the position of a monopolist who can estimate the effect of an initial status quo point on the ultimate outcome, at least when the bargaining is to occur in a dynamic context.[3]

There is a further incentive problem when long-run adjustment is considered. We considered only the immediate short-run problem of the farmer and rancher, yet the outcomes of the bargaining described might affect decisions to create farms and ranches in the first place. If ranchers have the right to run their herds regardless of harm to farmers, for example, there may be more entry into ranching than into farming, and meat could appear less costly relative to vegetables than it really is.

Thus, ill-defined property rights and problems of gathering reliable information about the effects of actions can so increase transaction costs that the external effects of certain actions, while significant, might be ignored. Incentives to reach a socially optimal solution remain, but the transaction costs of reaching it stand in the way. When only a few, say two, parties are involved the transaction costs are lower so negotiation is more promising. Even then, hard bargaining by either party over how to divide gains might prevent their reaching any agreement.

Tax-Subsidy or Property-Right Solutions

When many persons make decentralized decisions based on private costs or benefits that do not reflect all social costs or benefits, then their combined decisions produce an inefficient allocation of resources. This inefficiency problem can be more serious than the two-person problem suggests. With many persons involved, there may be diverse reactions to external effects, and at the same time the costs of negotiations among these persons are much higher simply because they are many. In addition, the economy-wide income distribution effects that follow from alternative property rights rules can lead to alternative solutions—even alternative efficient solutions—rather than the unique one the farmer and rancher could reach in the example above.[4]

With externalities present, the problem is not that a polluting firm, say, is necessarily "bad." The signals it acts on in making its decentralized decisions are wrong, in the sense that they do not reflect all social costs or benefits. You may do the same sort of thing as the polluting firm when you drive downtown at the rush hour. You pay for your own fuel, tire wear, other maintenance costs, and your time, but you do not account for the costs you impose on others in delays you cause them, the elevated accident risk you present to them, or the polluting exhaust from your vehicle's engine. In the two problems of air pollution and traffic congestion, we are failing to coordinate our economic affairs efficiently.

As noted, an early remedy for externalities was to have government impose taxes or subsidies to eliminate this divergence between private costs and social costs.[5] Professor Coase showed, however, that such action might be unnecessary. Where

---

[3] See, for example, Kamien, Swartz, and Dolbear (1966).

[4] Dolbear (1967) shows graphically for the two-person problem broader and more complex general equilibrium effects.

[5] The classical analysis of the externality problem, with an early suggested cure through taxes, is by A. C. Pigou (1920).

Figure 19.2 *Pollution Cost Is the Difference between Private Cost and Social Cost*

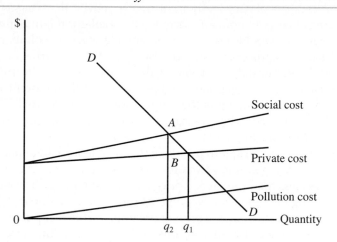

parties can negotiate a solution, a tax or subsidy distorts their assessments and might get in the way of an efficient outcome. On the other hand, where transaction costs are so high that they rule out negotiation, and an alternative scheme is needed, a tax or subsidy may offer a relatively efficient solution. Figure 19.2 shows how an externality, such as a pollution cost, can be added to private cost to determine the cost of the activity to society, the social cost.

Any solution to the externality problem requires some measurement of the externality effect, such as the pollution cost in Figure 19.2. Without any treatment of pollution cost, the firms follow their private costs and the market settles into equilibrium at q_1. A tax essentially sets a price for the external diseconomy, a price that reflects its social cost so those who face the tax determine the socially optimal amount of the activity. A tax equal to the pollution cost, AB, can yield the social optimum of q_2 in Figure 19.2. When the tax of AB is assessed on decision-making producers, their costs rise to include the pollution costs, and the market can then yield a socially optimal quantity. As a remedy for externality, a tax offers desirable incentives because it properly motivates the decentralized decision makers. Those who can avoid pollution at a cost that is less than the tax will do so, while those that would have to incur higher costs to avoid polluting will pay the tax instead.

Externality taxes may be difficult to apply, because their purposes and premises can be very demanding. We know from Chapter 16 the difficulties that arise in trying to apply a gasoline tax to control highway congestion, for instance, because congestion occurs at different times of the day and a gasoline tax makes no distinction by time. Air pollution occurs at different places, and a general tax may not be appropriate at different locations. Traffic congestion and air pollution are both external diseconomies, in that they impose excessive costs on victims. Analogous problems can also arise for external economies that bring benefits to third parties, where subsidies may be appropriate to induce socially desirable action.

An alternative means of correcting the costs used in decentralized decisions can come from the creation of a property right in the activity that causes the external effect. In the area of air pollution, for example, the regulator might define a "right to pollute." The regulator would also set an acceptable level of pollution and would accordingly create an appropriate number of *pollution rights* to achieve only that acceptable level. Next, those rights would be distributed, perhaps by outright sale, or possibly by allocation to existing polluters in proportion to their current, or *status-quo*, levels of pollution. Finally, trading of these rights would be permitted. The amount of pollution that is determined to be acceptable thus leads to a price for discharging pollution (a price for the right to pollute).

A market price for the right to pollute, which would arise in a market for pollution rights, creates desirable incentives for decentralized firms. If a firm is able to reduce pollution at less than the market price for pollution rights, it will do it, and sell the rights, pocketing the difference as profit. At the same time, those that find pollution reduction more costly than the price of pollution rights will purchase rights and use them. Private and social costs can thus be brought into line and decentralized choices can again produce efficient outcomes. Pollution is costly when rights to emit it must be purchased, so such rights motivate firms to reduce it. The market for pollution rights can determine the value of a unit of pollution reduction.

If they anticipate the award of pollution rights in proportion to previous levels of pollution, parties might strategically increase pollution before the rights are awarded to improve their bargaining positions. Approximately ideal taxes or subsidies, occasionally readjusted, also can accomplish a great deal. Thus, either tax-subsidy devices or property rights can serve to confront decision makers with all the social costs and benefits of their actions. Taxes require regulators to estimate social costs per unit in the price-setting dimension, whereas the granting of rights to pollute requires regulators to estimate the appropriate level of activity in the quantity-setting dimension. Over time, adjustments in either dimension can approach a social optimum.

Effects on Income Distribution

To remedy equitably the misallocation that an external effect causes, we often need more than a tax that makes each decision maker face all the costs of actions taken. The proceeds of that tax payment also have to be distributed so no great inequity results from the tax. Fair distribution of tax proceeds can be a very difficult task, and yet without attention to it, sound economic remedies for externalities may be politically infeasible. Approximations are possible. The costs of air pollution, for instance, might be deemed to be borne by everyone, and so the proceeds of a pollution tax might be used for community purposes in an effort to compensate everyone. Or, because sufferers of bronchitis, emphysema, and lung cancer appear to bear more of the effects of air pollution, the tax might finance expenditures to benefit them.[6]

In the case of road use, drivers bear many of the effects of road congestion themselves, and the proceeds of any congestion tax could be passed through to them,

---

[6] Lave and Seskin (1970) describe consequences of air pollution for human health.

too. The market effect we hope to achieve in the road case is to have those most willing to pay for the use of the road be the ones who use it and have those least willing to pay be the ones who refrain from using it. We can't easily arrange to have the right group bribe the other to stay off the road. We might hope to accomplish roughly the same result, however, by charging just the road users a tax and then dividing the proceeds of that tax among users of roads at peak traffic times and those who become nonusers, possibly by subsidizing mass transit for the latter. The net effect will be as if the final users had paid the others to become nonusers. Making the payment to the affected party is usually an equity matter, whereas the tax that alters marginal behavior is a matter of efficiency. Without attention to the equity issue, however, voters may not accept a proposal to accomplish the efficiency goal alone.[7]

Having a right to act, such as a right to pollute, also has implications for income distribution, but they are narrower and more transparent. Pollution taxes raise costs for firms and revenue for government. Again, if a government sells pollution rights to firms, the government gains revenue and the firms—which previously had polluted without cost—suffer losses. Distributing pollution rights instead of selling them to firms would harm the firms less and might help to win their acceptance. Rights to pollute would be allocated in a market after that, so some firms would be rewarded for reducing pollution while others would have to pay to pollute. Citizens, who suffer less pollution, would gain.

Thus, externalities lead to nonoptimal outcomes because in their presence private, decentralized decision makers do not consider all the consequences of their decisions. Similar problems for efficiency can follow when decision makers are imperfectly informed, because their decisions will not reflect social costs properly. Major problems from externalities occur as forms of environmental pollution, which are examined in Chapter 21.

19.2 | IMPERFECT INFORMATION

In a risky world, information can be a valuable commodity. It can reduce risk and uncertainty. It can guide a consumer to a lower price or a better product and protect one from dangers. When information is lacking, markets may not work well. Price may be high or product quality may be low, all because of the ways that competitive markets work. On the other hand, imperfect information may help the inventor of a new idea, because others do not immediately know about the idea. How information may affect markets, then, is an important issue. Many information problems arise in employment situations examined in Chapter 22 and in consumer choices considered in Chapter 23.

As noted in Chapter 3, *imperfect information* affects the functioning of competitive markets in many possible ways. One-sided, or asymmetric, information would seem to give the informed party an advantage over the uninformed party in transacting. Yet

---

[7] For illustration of the conflict that can arise, see Sherman and Willett (1969).

when less informed parties recognize their information disadvantage they can compensate for it by expecting the worst, as when buyers who cannot judge quality simply expect it to be low. With the buyer making such pessimistic assumptions about quality, the seller of a higher quality item will find it hard to obtain fair value, and the market will not function effectively. The market may even cease to exist, because parties cannot agree on the value of the item to be exchanged. Consequences of imperfect information can affect workers in the workplace as well as consumers in product markets.

The Market with Imperfectly Informed Consumers

Let us begin by representing the effect of imperfect information in a retail market. Consider a model with consumers who know product quality but are uninformed about prices. The consumers have to travel to a store to purchase one unit of a good but do not know its price until they arrive. Moving from one store to another also involves a cost, which we estimate to be c. Then store A could set a price, P_A, that was above the average of all store prices by less than that travel cost, or less than $P_B + c$ as shown in Figure 19.3, and still retain the customers who are already at its store A. Even if the consumer thought a price of P_B was possible at store B he might realize that once he went to store B he would effectively have to pay $P_B + c$ because it costs c to reach store B.

Other possibilities arise in this situation where it costs a positive amount, c, to visit a store. For instance, suppose some, but not all, of the consumers in the market are informed about prices. They might be local residents in a town that also has uninformed tourists. The informed consumers go to stores offering lower prices, which motivates the stores to set prices low to win their business. What if only a small fraction of the consumers is informed? Some stores may still set low prices to attract the informed consumers, but other stores may find it worthwhile to set higher prices. For the uninformed consumers are in somewhat the same position as the consumers in the earlier example where there was no information, so they tolerate a higher price rather than incur the cost of c to visit another store. For tourists, the cost to visit

Figure 19.3 *Costs of Imperfect Information*

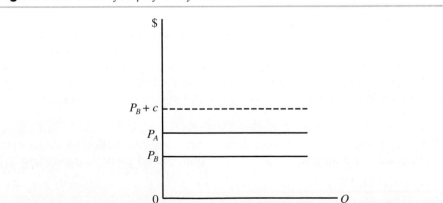

another store, c, may be higher because they do not know the area well. If the fraction of informed consumers is high enough, there is an equilibrium at the low competitive price. On the other hand, if the fraction is low and a large fraction of consumers is uninformed, there could be an equilibrium with two prices, one low for locals and one high for tourists.

Stores might also find ways to discriminate among consumers, perhaps by loyalty programs that reward repeat customers such as "buy-five-get-one-free," or by offering bargains on large sizes that tourists would not want to purchase. When a significant number of consumers is uninformed, markets may not perform well.

Consumers may lack information about product quality as well as about price. And some players in a market may know more about the quality of an item than others do, as for example when a seller of a used car knows more about its quality than the buyer does. This is a case of *asymmetric information*.

Asymmetric Information

Where one party to a transaction has more or better information than the other, we say there is **asymmetric information**. For example, a case in which buyers can have more information than sellers is that of insurance. You know more about your own health condition than a health insurance company. If the insurance company can learn nothing about possible customers' health conditions, it will have to set rates based on an average for everyone. The healthiest will find such rates unattractive and may decide against buying insurance, while the least healthy happily buy the insurance. As healthy individuals leave the market, the average level of health of remaining customers declines. Because this process selects the least attractive prospects, the effect is called **adverse selection**. Poorer risks are more costly to insure, so the rate charged for the insurance must increase. This process can continue until only the least healthy are interested in insurance. If their number is too low to support insurance, the market can disappear. Because of asymmetric information, competition can fail and the market will not exist. To avoid this asymmetry in information, insurance companies incur costs in seeking more information, such as requiring a physical examination before granting health insurance coverage.

A second problem can arise when one party not only has information, such as their health condition or their risk of causing an automobile accident, but also has discretion that can influence those risks. For example, once you have insurance against an automobile accident, you may drive more carelessly and be more likely to have an accident. That is, the fact of insurance changes incentives and may change behavior. This problem is called the **moral hazard** problem, although it is not as much a moral issue as it is a possible rational response to contractual protection.

Remedies

When buyer and seller are equally well informed markets may perform better, because the process of adverse selection is not so strong. The force of the asymmetric information problem can be weakened by requiring the better-informed party to disclose information. In the sale of real estate, for example, most states now require the seller to disclose certain types of problems with the property, such as a leaking roof or an air conditioner that does not function. It is also illegal in most states for a seller to tamper with a motor vehicle's odometer and thus deceive a buyer about the miles the vehicle has traveled. States also require extensive disclosure in the sale of new securities. Sellers in markets do not always resist these requirements either, because to the extent it improves the functioning of the market disclosure can benefit them, especially when they are sellers of higher-quality items. In the case of health insurance, large groups of customers such as all employees of a company may be served by a health insurance company. The insurance company can then expect an average incidence of health problems, because the whole group is insured. Because members of the group are determined primarily by their employment decisions, there is no problem of healthy clients leaving the program while unhealthy clients join.

Another way to limit the consequences of imperfect information is to set **standards** that products are required to meet. Standards may define acceptable processes, such as the pasteurization of milk, or standards of quality, such as the weight that a ladder is supposed to hold. Water quality standards might have solved the problem of impure water sold in the early days of New York City, for example.[8] Consumer organizations, industry organizations, or governments may set standards. In 1972 Congress created a federal institution to advance consumer protection, called the **Consumer Product Safety Commission (CPSC)**, and it has established safety standards for products such as lawn mowers, glass shower doors, and play pens. Standard setters also usually certify products that meet their standards, thereby giving assurance to consumers about quality.

Standard setting is not without problems, however. The standards need to be changed as technology changes, and this can be difficult when some varieties of a product use one technology and other varieties use another. Plumbing and building codes often called for copper pipe, for example, and were slow to change when lower cost, but effective, plastic pipe became available. Product standards usually take a blunt form, also, so products either meet them or do not meet them. This situation invites producers to provide whatever quality the standard requires, but no more. Even if the standards include several grades rather than one acceptable one, the incentive will be to qualify barely for each grade. If producers in a market are able to control the standard, they might set it too high, to limit the number of competitors, with the result of denying some consumers options they would like to choose. Or they might set it too low, to save cost, lower price, and expand their market.

Licensing serves in professions somewhat as standard setting does in manufacturing, and it has some of the same problems. Other means of certification accomplish the same end, such as degree requirements for teachers, lawyers, and doctors, but these professionals also must pass licensing examinations. Economists and students of other disciplines draw authority simply from being awarded a Ph.D. Because licensing procedures and even degree requirements are typically controlled

---

[8] For a history of impure water in early New York City, see Koeppel (2000).

by the members of the profession involved, often with government support, they may serve themselves by limiting entry excessively while controlling quality. Yet at the same time, many professions have been criticized for not disciplining members who do not serve their clients effectively.

Producers of high-quality products may attempt to establish **reputations** for their high quality. Such a reputation can reduce inefficiency and be a sound source of information, because it can be developed more easily by the producer of a genuinely high-quality product. It helps to operate in a stable market where many customers return repeatedly, so their judgments about quality can influence further purchases. Reputations can be difficult to establish in markets where there is little repeat business, such as in tourist destinations, because buyers cannot develop experience with sellers, but sources of information such as travel guides may effectively certify the better providers of service. Many sources provide information about college and university quality, and Box 19.3 illustrates one of them.

In addition to standard setting and licensing, companies may use contractual devices for building consumer confidence. We call such a device a **warranty**. The warranty promises a certain level of performance and offers corrective measures if that level is not met. Warranties tend to reflect the qualities of the products they are tied to. Only the maker of a reliable product can offer an especially strong warranty, for example, because if the product fails frequently, the maker is swamped with demands for repair that are costly to provide. This reality and the rights they advance to consumers give warranties their credibility.

BOX 19.3 Rating College and University Teaching

Many factors influence reputations and ratings of colleges and universities, but among them teaching itself may not be the most important. In reviewing books about colleges, political scientist Andrew Hacker presented results from a survey conducted by the *Princeton Review* of 110,000 undergraduates at 357 colleges. The following table lists the institutions ranked highest and lowest in the survey by their students when showing agreement with the statement, "Professors bring material to life."

Highest Scores		Lowest Scores	
Reed	99	UCLA	61
Carlton	99	Texas	65
Wabash	99	Michigan	68
Middlebury	98	Harvard	69
Kenyon	98	Penn	69

The high-scoring institutions are small, not nationally prominent, and without graduate programs, while the low-scoring institutions are large, nationally known, research universities. Such results suggest that for the student pursuing excellent teaching, the overall national rankings of universities might not be the best source of information.

See A. Hacker, "The Truth About the Colleges," *New York Review of Books*, Vol. 52, Number 17, November 3, 2005.

19.3 | FAIRNESS FOR WORKERS

Although the Internet may help workers find information about jobs at relatively low cost, the information is limited, and labor markets traditionally have poor information. The information that exists may also be asymmetric, because it is usually easier for a hiring firm to obtain information about job candidates than it is for the candidates to gather information about jobs. Law has influenced the employment relationship in important ways historically, and it continues to influence the fairness that employees experience in labor markets.

Employment "At Will"

Workers and employers have considerable scope to define their relationship. Employment can be so important to the worker that, with the passage of time, the worker has won a range of protections. Going back to the nineteenth century, common law in the United States regarded the employment relationship as an **"at-will" relationship**, in which employers could hire or dismiss workers "at will," meaning the employer did not have to give a reason. Employers could refuse to hire racial minorities or women, for example, and they could give opportunities for advancement to whomever they wished. Employee unions similarly could deny membership to whomever they wished.

By the middle of the twentieth century, the common law started to limit this employment-at-will principle. In 1959, for instance, a California court found that an employee who was discharged for refusing to commit perjury had been wrongfully discharged, meaning that the discharge was unlawful.[9] Many states passed laws to protect employees from retaliation by employers when the employees simply exercised their legal rights. States extended this idea specifically to prevent retaliation against **whistleblowers**, who provide information about potential violations of law, although states differ in the nature and extent of these protections.

Some courts have prohibited dismissal of an employee when dismissal would deny the employee an accrued benefit, such as a pension right for example, on the ground that it violates the principle of good faith and fair dealing on which all contracts depend. Abusive treatment of an employee may also be found to be a tort, or noncontractual offense, not only for physical abuse such as assault and battery but also for invading a private work space, humiliating an employee, or behaving in other ways that can be seen as causing emotional harm to the employee.[10] Contracts are sometimes drawn to moderate the reign of employment-at-will, and terms in company employment manuals that offer employee protections have been interpreted to be terms of a contract.

Fairness Legislation

Legislation to promote fairness goes beyond employers' hiring and firing decisions. Early in the twentieth century, for example, states began developing workers' compensation

---

[9] See *Petermann v. International Brotherhood of Teamsters*, 174 Cal. App. 2d 184, 344 P.2d 25 (Cal. App. 2 Dist., 1959).
[10] See Player (1999).

laws to provide reliable compensation for injuries suffered at work. Private workers also have the right to organize collectively to protest wages or hours or other conditions of employment under the **National Labor Relations Act** of 1935, which extended the right granted earlier to workers in the railroad industry through the **Railway Labor Act** of 1926. As long as they behave lawfully (not trespassing, for example), workers can act in concert over treatment of minority workers or over discrimination generally. An elaborate set of laws and rules exists to guide the organization of collective action through labor unions.

Principles of fairness thus came to the workplace, but they were quite limited, and they depended on collective agreement for action. Fairness at work, however, came to be viewed as an important right in a country such as the United States composed of people of different ages, physical conditions, and races and ethnic backgrounds, and Congress adopted legislation in the 1960s to provide it. Three important federal laws are intended to prevent discrimination in the workplace: (1) **The Civil Rights Act** of 1964, (2) The **Age Discrimination in Employment Act** of 1967, and (3) The **Americans with Disabilities Act** of 1990.

Title VII of the Civil Rights Act of 1964 prohibits discrimination in any aspect of the employment relationship because of race, sex, color, religion, or national origin, and it applies to employers, labor unions, and employment agencies. Title VII also created the **Equal Employment Opportunity Commission (EEOC)**, a five-person

---

BOX 19.4 Statistical Discrimination

Discrimination may arise when members of one recognizable group are thought by employers to be less productive on average than members of another group. All members of the group that is thought to be less productive may then be discriminated against if the employer relies on group membership when making hiring decisions. Suppose, for example, that an employer has four candidates for a job, two Red people (1 and 2) and two Green people (3 and 4), and Green people are known to be more productive. The employer knows the average productivities, as shown in the row "Average" in the table below, but does not know the individual productivities. Individual productivities may be determined but only through added effort, which is costly to the employer. The employer might not take the trouble to determine individual productivities and instead choose one of the Green candidates, even though, by making an effort, the more productive Red candidate (1) could be identified. The Red candidate, 1, with a productivity of 20, which is 10 percent better than the best Green candidate, would not be hired. This is an example of statistical discrimination.

Candidates	Candidate Productivities	
	Red	Green
1,3	20	18
2,4	12	16
Average	16	17

See Nobel laureate E. S. Phelps, "The Statistical Theory of Racism and Sexism," *American Economic Review*, September, 1972, Vol. 62, pp. 659–661.

commission appointed by the President, which receives discrimination complaints in offices throughout the country and attempts to resolve them. The prohibition against discrimination was extended to age soon afterward, in the Age Discrimination in Employment Act of 1967, to prohibit discrimination against those 40 and older who are otherwise qualified for the work. Some exemptions apply to firefighters or police, and employees that face demanding stress, such as FBI agents or airline pilots, who may be refused work because of age. The Americans with Disabilities Act prohibits discrimination against individuals with mental or physical disabilities who are otherwise qualified for jobs. A host of other laws provide related protections and rights for employees.

Claims of discrimination against employers have been difficult to win in court, and this has led to other kinds of lawsuits, such as suits brought against employers for retaliation against a complaining employee. Court cases have helped to foster a realm of case law that defines offenses and specifies remedies, which makes fairness protection more concrete. Besides passing legislation pursuing fairness in employment, Congress has also enacted legislation to further the health and safety of workers.

Health and Safety

Accidents increased by more than 25 percent in the United States in the 1960s, as the work force expanded rapidly, motor vehicles traveled faster, and new technologies came into use in many fields. Congress passed the **Occupational Safety and Health Act** in 1970 to "assure so far as possible every working man and woman in the nation safe and healthful working conditions." The Act created the **Occupational Safety and Health Administration (OSHA)** to set and enforce safety and health standards. OSHA quickly imposed mandatory workplace standards that became controversial because they were detailed and were not tied closely to effective performance. As time has passed, the agency has shifted to more flexible and workable standards that companies have accepted more willingly. These standards focus heavily on safety. Health has been more difficult to protect, because the effects of materials that are harmful to health are not as easily traced. Still, a central agency has advantages in identifying health hazards and in exercising responsibility to moderate their effects.

19.4 CONSEQUENCES OF FIRM FAILURE

Firm failure is common. Restaurants or other small businesses go out of existence regularly, and even large firms such as Enron or WorldCom occasionally fail. Although losing a convenient or desirable source of goods or services may be disappointing, consumers do not usually suffer greatly when a firm fails. Employees or retirees of a firm that fails, however, can lose their pension benefits or retirement savings, and this harm to employees can be very serious. In some industries, such as banking or insurance, customers also can suffer greatly from a failure. Regulation aims primarily at fostering trust in these industries, but protecting consumers is another reason they are regulated. Chapter 24 describes problems caused by firm failure along with accounting and corporate governance issues that are intended to prevent company fraud from causing it.

Banks and Insurance Companies

Consumers ordinarily are not well positioned to evaluate the banks in which they deposit their money. It is even harder to evaluate insurance companies before turning savings over to them. Yet consumers depend financially on the continued survival of these institutions. Regulation aims at protecting consumers by insuring that banking and insurance companies follow sound practices to reduce the chance of failure. In the Great Depression of the 1930s many banks failed, and the experience led to regulatory actions in an effort to prevent that from happening again. The insurance industry is less thoroughly regulated, and the regulation that does exist occurs primarily at the state level. Further insurance is also arranged to protect consumers if, despite these safeguards, an individual bank or insurance company should actually fail. In banking, such insurance was augmented from general tax revenues in the 1980s to compensate depositors and to avert a more serious crisis among **thrift institutions**, or thrifts, such as savings and loan companies or credit unions.

Thrifts usually specialized in one form of investment: real estate mortgages. Designed to finance houses, mortgages are long-term loans, often lasting 20 or 30 years, and thrift institutions financed them with short-term borrowing, usually in the form of savings deposits. Great risks result from this set of activities. If short-term rates rise above long term rates, the fixed income from mortgage payments is less than the high-interest payments needed to attract short-term deposits to finance the mortgages. So the mortgage lender loses money. Despite repeated crises in the thrift industry, Congress did not recognize its flaws until an especially serious crisis in the 1980s, and implementing remedies for them then was not easy.

Broadening activities of banks may help them to survive hard financial times, on the same theory that urges investors to diversify their portfolios. Results over a wide range of activities are less apt to be extreme, because many good and bad outcomes can offset each other when they are averaged. Laws confining banks to operate in one state have also been relaxed, so one bank is not confined to economic ups and downs of one area. That allows greater regional diversity in banks' investments, and the pooling effect reduces risk for the individual bank. Laws have also removed many restrictions on the activities of thrift institutions, allowing them a wider range of investment opportunities and, thus, a more diversified asset base.

Insurance companies are regulated at the state level. Like thrifts, they can have difficulty diversifying. For instance, some companies that have insured substantial property in Florida have stopped issuing policies there, because so many properties can be damaged by a single hurricane that they find their risks are too concentrated. The insurance industry also has a problem with fraud, and preventing it can require extensive and costly oversight. Asymmetric information in insurance markets complicates their operation. Potential clients may know more about their conditions—their health or driving habits for examples—than insurers, who are then handicapped. Clients have difficulty evaluating the financial condition of their insurance company because the clients have less information. A similar problem can arise in an employee's effort to evaluate the financial soundness of her employer's promised pension.

Pensions

Another possible consequence of firm failure is that retirees lose the pension benefits that provide their retirement incomes when they are no longer in position to work. Employees as well as retirees of a firm that fails may also lose health insurance benefits, even though the employees served the employer loyally for years. If the employer fails, they may find that money for their promised pensions or health insurance is not available.

Retirement pension plans are among the most valuable benefits employees receive. The regulation of federal pension plans is guided by the **Employee Retirement Income Security Act (ERISA)** of 1974. Pensions are of three main types. **Defined-benefit plans** promise specific *benefits* to the retiree upon retirement, while **defined-contribution plans** involve employee and/or employer *contributions*, invested as the employee directs to form a retirement fund. The third type, **cash-balance plans**, are managed by the firm, which invests money for each worker and accumulates it at a modest rate of return. Defined-contribution plans are called 401k plans, and like other plans they defer income tax payments on funds invested. Firms' incentives are not strong to set aside funds to meet future defined-benefit pension obligations, but some federal insurance protection is available if they fail. Defined-contribution pension plans allow employees to make tax-free contributions to a retirement account and to direct how the contributions are invested. The employee, therefore, has responsibility for funding and managing a defined-contribution pension plan, while the employer either invests with the purpose of providing all the benefits for a defined-benefit or cash-balance plan or expects to pay some part of them out of company profits.

If employees who have defined-contribution plans concentrate their investments in their employer's stock, something that company stock-purchase plans often invite, they can suffer greatly if the firm fails. Employers that make contributions to defined-contribution plans in the form of stock often require that it be held for some length of time. The bankruptcy of the Enron Corporation in 2001 devastated many employees who, before the bankruptcy, had more than half their retirement funds in Enron stock, in part because Enron's contributions to the plans were to be held until age 50. Employees who have defined-benefit pension plans depend on their employers for pension fund management. Employers sometimes fail to fund pensions adequately, however, and in hard times they may not meet their pension obligations.

Accounting and Corporate Governance

For markets to function well, information about firms' financial conditions must be known to investors, so they can allocate resources soundly among the available firms. Corporations are supposed to use sound accounting principles to reveal their financial conditions to investors and others. Regulators require audits of public corporations and oversee accounting principles, but the auditing process remains imperfect in part because of conflicts of interest. Audit firms are paid by the firms they audit, which makes them hesitate to be any more strict than they have to be. In passing the Sarbanes-Oxley Act of 2002, after fraud led to high-profile bankruptcies at Enron and WorldCom, Congress took some steps against conflicts of interest and increased the accountability of senior executives for financial reporting of the firms they lead.

Two protections are intended to prevent corporations from issuing faulty financial reports: (1) audits of the corporations that attest that their accounting reports reflect their financial condition, and (2) having accountants follow strong, generally accepted accounting principles (GAAP) in carrying out the audit. As a result of the Sarbanes-Oxley Act, a **Public Company Oversight Board** oversees this process of corporate accounting in the future. A competitive market economy needs high accounting standards and procedures, so that financially strong and honest firms are not confused with weak firms that issue false and misleading reports about their condition.

Some conflicts of interest arise from the incentives that are offered to top managers. Stock options, for example, are rights to buy stock, usually at the price on the day they are issued. They are given to managers to motivate them to raise the value of stock, because raising the stock value makes the options more valuable. In some cases, however, the options may have created too much incentive, as managers bent accounting rules and took other deceptive actions to raise stock values. There were also scandals in the award of options, as the options were illegally backdated to make them more valuable.

BOX 19.5 Backdating Stock Options

It is possible to make stock options more assuredly valuable to their top management recipients by choosing dates for the granting of them *after the fact*. That is, the option awards may be dated on a day in the past when the stock had a low value, as if they had been granted that day, so a gain from that low value can be assured. Doing so is misleading, and, if done secretly, it is illegal because it passes more earnings to the option recipients, usually top executives, than had been approved by formal and open procedures. It may also violate tax laws. Suspicions about backdating began with academic studies finding that, had the options been awarded randomly, the chances that the actual option gains would have occurred were very low. This meant it was very unlikely that options had actually been awarded on the dates as claimed.

See "Walking the Plank," *The Economist*, October 21–27, 2006, pp. 73–74; and Stephanie Saul, "Study Finds Backdating of Options Widespread," *New York Times*, July 17, 2006, p. C1.

SUMMARY

Competitive markets let individuals express their own preferences through their market decisions, and such expression can yield an efficient allocation of resources if judgments can be based on genuine social costs and benefits. Externalities interfere with this ideal result, however, by making the private cost or benefit to individual decision makers differ from the cost faced by the whole society. In the presence of externalities, decentralized choices do not yield an ideal solution because privately perceived costs and benefits are misleading—they do not reflect all costs or benefits.

When one neighbor creates external economies for another, or when one producer (say, a rancher) imposes external diseconomies on another (say, a farmer), clear property rights may motivate the parties to negotiate until they reach a socially desirable solution. Although their bargaining might break down, in principle they can reach an optimal solution no matter which way property rights are defined, whether the rancher is entitled to run cattle anywhere with impunity or the rancher is liable for damage caused by his cattle. If property rights are not well defined, that limits the grounds for bargaining. The Environmental Protection Agency is concerned at the federal level with limiting pollution externalities, and it works with state agencies to do so.

Imperfect information also can interfere with the effectiveness of markets in achieving efficient outcomes. Consumers who are not well informed are handicapped in market transactions. The same is true of workers who select employment without knowing what dangers various jobs involve. The Occupational Safety and Health Administration at the federal level and comparable units at the state level seek safe workplaces for American workers. The Consumer Product Safety Commission and many consumer protection agencies at the state level try to make products safe to protect consumers.

There are other remedies for imperfect information in markets. Standards may be set, and products can be certified as meeting the standard. This assurance of minimal quality can protect consumers from unsafe or inadequate products. Licensing accomplishes a similar effect in the professions. Sellers can also establish reputations for quality, especially in stable markets where transactions can be repeated with the same parties, so that reputations can be established. Warranties give consumers added protection, by offering concrete remedies if problems arise. The consumer, however, still has to pursue the issuer of the warranty when there is a problem. Business firms may fail, and the warranties of a failing firm may not be honored.

When a firm fails in a market, it can cause problems beyond the shareholders, who knowingly place their funds at risk, and reach consumers, employees, and even retirees, whose decisions do not cause the failure and who are not in good position to predict when such failure might happen. The cost of the firm's failure that spills over to others besides the owners of the firm is an externality. Employees may face staggering losses if their employer fails, including not only their jobs but also the pensions they had been promised and which, if retirees, they may already depend on for their incomes. If the worker has a defined benefit pension plan, which has specific pension benefits, those benefits may not be paid by a failing firm. If the worker has a defined contribution plan, benefits depend on the worker's own investment decisions. If the failed employer's stock made up a large fraction of a worker's retirement funds, the worker's pension benefits suffer.

Consumers are not usually much affected by the failure of a firm, because they can switch to another firm; however, if the firm that fails is a bank—or an insurance company—customers may lose their savings and suffer dearly. One reason the government regulates banking and insurance companies is to avoid their failure and the consequent harm customers suffer. The regulation of banking institutions is influenced by a desire to avoid failures, and the institutions are held to operating practices that reduce that possibility. Congress also created Federal Deposit Insurance to protect bank depositors from loss of their savings in the event of bank failure. Insurance companies are subject to state regulation for the same purpose of avoiding failure, and many states provide some form of insurance in the event an insurance company fails.

QUESTIONS

1. Consider the farmer-rancher problem analyzed in Figure 19.1.
   a. What profit does the rancher earn under each of the two liability-for harm rules: (1) the rancher pays for harm to the farmer, and (2) the farmer must bear the cost of harm to his crop?
   b. Suppose that an effective barbed-wire fence can be built at a total cost of F, which is less than the amount CD, and that the rancher's output and revenue possibilities are as shown for any herd size. How is the solution to be changed for such a fence?
   c. In principle, would a merger of farmer and rancher solve the externality problem? What might prevent a merger from serving as an effective remedy?
2. Consider two health insurance companies. One company, Ace, sells to individuals. The other company, Bee, sells insurance services to companies under which it provides coverage for all the companies' employees. What problem does company Ace have that company Bee avoids? How, if at all, might company Ace avoid this problem? In light of this problem faced by individual insurer Ace, can you see why some nations provide health insurance for all their citizens? Discuss any similarity between the health insurance problem and the case of automobile insurance, where most states require all drivers to carry liability insurance to protect against the harm they might cause from accidents.
3. The city of London has introduced fees for traveling by motor vehicle on city streets during daylight hours, and efficiency gains are already being experienced. What uses for the funds raised from such fees would you recommend to make the program successful by not having it cause serious shifts in the distribution of income?

4. In areas of both occupational health and safety and consumer product safety, regulation is concerned with protecting individuals from harm. Compare and contrast the methods of regulation you might propose for use in these two areas. Evaluate whether differences in methods you would propose are appropriate, given differences you see in the two types of regulatory tasks.

5. Three major types of employer-sponsored pension plans exist: defined-benefit, defined-contribution, and cash-balance plans. All of them can raise problems for workers or retirees if the employers that sponsor them fail. Consider two alternative ways to organize pensions that might avoid these different problems. Any organization may be considered. Be sure to work through your plans, to anticipate problems that might arise if they were put into effect. Then see if you can find ways to moderate the seriousness of any problems. Do you think you have an alternative that is more attractive than the present plans? Say why or why not.

6. Is it possible to interpret fairness legislation, such as the Civil Rights Act of 1964, as legislation to remedy an externality? To start an answer, ask whether the cost is borne by those against whom a decider discriminated—rather than by the decider—and does the legislation aim to avoid such external cost?

7. Externality problems are described here as arising among decentralized decision makers in a market economy. In a centrally controlled, nonmarket, economy, externalities have been serious problems. Explain why a centralized economy could have externality problems.

20

Pursuing Social Regulation

Should firms that pollute air or water or land be required to pay the costs that result? Should a worker be compensated who loses her hearing because of noise levels at the machine she tends? Should a seller of coffee have to pay damages to customers who are burned because the coffee is so hot, or should an automobile manufacturer whose gas tank placement causes harmful fires in vehicle crashes be responsible for damages? You may find such questions easy to answer, but others may disagree with you, and even if agreement is found, identifying these problems in advance and developing enforceable solutions for them is not easy. Identifying and solving these problems are the means of social regulation.

Social regulation pursues many goals, but this chapter emphasizes the pursuit of a narrow set of goals that reflect efficiency concerns, in part because we stress social problems that can be traced to failures of markets to deliver efficiency. We seek remedies for these market failures, remedies that enable markets to serve social goals. Such market failures are due to three main problems: (1) externality, (2) imperfect information, and (3) firm failure. Remedies do not always simply return the market machinery to its functioning form, however, and new forms of intervention in markets, and new forms of analysis, may be appropriate.

Initial social regulation relied on "command and control" methods by which regulators demanded compliance with outright orders. More decentralized forms were later pursued, and by creating incentives to improve decentralized decisions they are more consistent with market organization of the economy. They can function when a clear set of rules exists, and an enforcement body can force compliance. Tax or subsidy schemes can sometimes serve in this way to correct faulty market price signals. Tradeable rights, such as rights to pollute, can also motivate efficient action by decentralized agents.

Command and control regulation usually imposes the same solution on all who are subject to the regulation, whereas decentralized means of regulation allow different adjustments by different agents. Yet both methods seek to elicit the socially optimal level of an activity, which *benefit-cost analysis* can help to determine. It arrays the benefits that follow from successive actions and sets them against the costs those actions require. If actions are chosen well, meaning that activities promising greatest net benefits are chosen first, moving down the list of possible activities should bring declining benefits and increasing costs. This means we can find a point at which marginal benefits equal marginal costs, and that is the optimal stopping point because that is where total benefit are as large as possible.

To calculate benefits and costs for social regulation, we must sometimes consider the values of factors that are not traded in markets. A change in the risk of death, for example, is inherently difficult to value. Yet if the use of a faulty drug can increase the chance of death, a value must be placed on that risk. So we examine how the value of a life, or of other nonmarket notions, might be estimated. Assigning a value to a human life can guide the allocation of limited life-saving resources more efficiently, and it is desirable for that practical reason, however unappealing the estimation itself may appear.

We first consider in Section 20.1 benefit-cost analysis, which offers a means of pursing economic efficiency as a goal for social choices. Then in Section 20.2 we consider the difficult task of placing values on nonmarket objects for such analysis. Such values are implicit in social regulation decisions, and if everyone can agree upon the values, the decisions can be better made. Next, in Section 20.3, we take up the command-and-control means that have been used for social regulation. Two means of social regulation that can work on a more decentralized basis are then explored in Section 20.4: tax-subsidy policies and the trading of newly created property rights. These regulatory instruments have advantages over command-and-control methods, because they preserve the incentives and information-conveying features of a market system. Finally, Section 20.5 considers improving information as a means of regulation.

20.1 | BENEFIT-COST ANALYSIS

Imagine air pollution being controlled by banning the release of all pollutants into the air. Although it could achieve a substantial benefit, that policy could also be extremely costly, as it would effectively ban many goods that are produced with air pollution as a side effect. Banning pollution altogether is too severe, but then just how should another rule be chosen that allows only a certain amount of pollution? Benefit-cost analysis helps in that decision by offering a way to maximize social benefit.

Maximizing Social Benefit

Benefit-cost analysis arrays marginal benefits and marginal costs in an attempt to maximize the total benefit from a policy choice. Figure 20.1 shows marginal benefits and marginal costs from a regulatory activity, such as imposing increasingly more demanding—and more costly—noise-level standards in the workplace. As the regulatory activity expands, say to place lower and lower decibel limits on acceptable noise, the severity of the injuries being avoided declines. That is, as the standard becomes more demanding, milder harms are avoided, so marginally less added benefit is realized. This means that

Figure 20.1 *Marginal Benefit and Marginal Cost Functions*

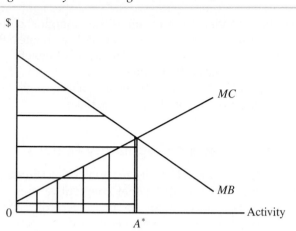

marginal benefit declines. We can expect such an outcome because the most beneficial actions—in relation to cost—should be chosen first. On the other hand, the costs tend to rise with successive actions because it is more and more difficult to accomplish lower and lower sound levels. The result is a benefit function and a cost function like those illustrated in Figure 20.1.

Maximum total net benefit—that is, total benefit minus total cost—occurs where marginal benefit and marginal cost are equal, at level of activity A^* in Figure 20.1. The marginal benefit curve can sometimes be interpreted from an estimated demand curve, with willingness to pay along the demand curve being equivalent to marginal benefit. The area under the marginal benefit curve, up to any point along the horizontal axis, is the total benefit at that point, or the consumer surplus. The consumer surplus up to level of activity A^* is indicated by horizontal lines. The area under the marginal cost curve is total cost, and for the level of activity A^* it is indicated by vertical lines. Total benefit minus total cost is maximized at the point on the horizontal axis where marginal benefit and marginal cost are equal, because that makes total benefit (horizontal lines) minus total cost (vertical lines) as large as possible. To choose a smaller level of activity below A^* would fail to bring some marginal benefits that exceed their marginal costs, and to choose a larger level beyond A^* would impose marginal costs that are greater than marginal benefits.

Sometimes regulators must choose separate programs, such as automobile safety standards like shatter-proof glass, hydraulic brakes, seatbelts, and other separate items. Now some of these programs, such as brakes and seatbelts, may be aimed at saving the same lives, and if so their interaction with each other needs to be taken into account. The same sort of interaction can arise with costs when the cost of one activity affects the cost of another. Also, when projects are separate and discrete like this, the ordering may not be as smooth as Figure 20.1 suggests. It would not be possible to list the auto safety standards in decreasing order of marginal benefit *and also* to choose the lowest cost projects first, because the orders of costs and benefits may not be consistent. That is, the safety standard offering the greatest marginal benefit may not also have the lowest marginal cost. The projects might then be ordered by their net benefits—their marginal benefits minus their marginal costs.

When uncertainty surrounds the benefit and cost estimates, the net benefit in relation to total cost might be considered as an expected benefit per dollar of cost. Here the level of cost can indicate how much money is at risk. Incurring very high cost means accepting more risk, and without a similarly high expected marginal benefit, a high cost project may be too risky to undertake.

Income-Distribution Effects of Regulatory Actions

There is a major difference between benefit-cost analysis to choose worthwhile projects and the kind of welfare maximizing that competitive markets perform. Both frameworks seek maximum efficiency. Projects chosen according to the rules of benefit-cost analysis, however, may benefit some members of the population and impose costs on others or on all members. The choices are not like exchanges in ideal markets where all parties participate only if they benefit from transactions. When a benefit-cost analysis favors construction of a new airport at taxpayer expense, for example, air travelers may benefit more than other taxpayers. Choices made by applying benefit-cost analysis alter the community's income distribution unless, through some sort of averaging across projects, the benefits and costs are spread over the population. Then, over time, net benefits of chosen projects may be shared in an equitable way among members of the community, and the efficiency advantage of the rule allows greater total benefit than would otherwise be possible from the same resources.

Recall the Pareto Rule, which in these social choices could take the form: *Any action that benefits some person(s) and harms none is an improvement.* This appealing statement expresses a value judgment, but a very weak one because so many people would agree to it. The rule, however, does not determine which action is best in many social choice situations. Such choices typically have only one level of output, such as the number and type of automobile safety standards to be implemented, and we all have to consume at least the particular level of safety that allows. In such cases it is hard to move away from an existing *status quo* point because a change usually harms someone and, thus, does not meet the Pareto Rule. The Pareto Rule essentially requires unanimous agreement, for if anyone is harmed by an action, that action cannot satisfy the Pareto Rule.

A way around this problem is to compensate those who are harmed, to satisfy the Pareto Rule. In principle, the total benefit for the gainers from a soundly chosen project should be adequate to compensate the losers. If this were not true, the project's costs would exceed its benefits, and it would be unsound. Arranging for compensation in a realistic setting, however, would be almost impossible. Effects of regulatory actions are difficult to identify with specific individuals, and if we attempted to do that we would probably have disagreement among members of the community about what the benefits are. Moreover, it would be very hard to develop ways to arrange the compensation payments, even if we could agree on them.

In 1939 economist Nicholas Kaldor suggested evaluating proposals as if compensation would be paid and then adopting those that would pass, *even though compensation would not actually be paid*. The criterion became known as the **Kaldor Rule**: *Any action that leads those who gain to evaluate their gain at a greater value than the losers place on their loss is an improvement*. The Kaldor Rule uses the valuations of those affected to assess benefits and losses, which it uses in turn to evaluate the project. But no compensation is paid. The Kaldor Rule would use information that yields a reasonable judgment about whether a project is efficient, but it ignores effects on income distribution of actually implementing the project. Thus, it does not necessarily meet the crucial requirement of the Pareto Rule, that anyone must always be made better off. The Kaldor Rule could be fair only if projects benefitted some persons some times and other persons other times, so that—on average—all would benefit.

Relying on benefit-cost analysis for deciding regulatory actions is similar to using the Kaldor Rule. It takes individuals' assessments of their benefits, estimated perhaps as a demand function and represented as consumer surplus, and compares that with estimated cost. If the outcome offers positive benefits, the action is taken. There is no compensation, however, in that those who benefit pay nothing while those who bear costs—perhaps by paying taxes and not benefitting from the action—are not compensated. Taking the action can improve efficiency, but it can also have unwanted effects on income distribution. The rich may benefit from applications because they are in a position to place a high value on wanted projects, and if their projects are repeatedly chosen without compensating losers the result, from an income distribution standpoint, might seem perverse. That is why government policy makers should attend to income distribution effects of decisions reached through benefit-cost analysis, so that certain people do not benefit while others lose repeatedly.

This distributional issue is less important in the realm of regulatory policy than in some other areas, such as where to build roads or airports. One reason is that the beneficiaries of regulatory policies are often broad groups that include almost everyone, such as "consumers." Some goals, like protecting those who save and insure from the failure of a firm serving them, may offer large benefits—especially in the fairness realm where the benefit-cost criterion tends to be inherently weak.

One advantage of benefit-cost analysis is that it fosters consistent decisions across units of government. This emphasis on efficiency is valuable, and it can help to offset the political motives that might result in less efficient projects that would favor particular groups. Benefit-cost analysis can serve to restrain agencies by requiring explicit economic justification for actions, and that process of analysis also leads to more transparency for the resulting decisions. It does not insure perfect outcomes, however, in part because social regulation involves consequences that can be difficult to value in a quantitative way. So we must take extra care in considering these difficult valuation problems.

20.2 | VALUING NONMARKET OBJECTS

Many aspects of welfare are not bought and sold in markets, and they do not have agreed-upon monetary values. Estimating the values of such nonmarket objects can, therefore, be difficult. One of the most difficult valuations is that of *life*, which is relevant because many regulations aim to save lives or reduce the risk of death. These regulations implicitly value life because they commit resources to save lives, and they thus contain a dollars-per-life measure. But valuing life is a terrifying task. If you could pay a sum of money to avoid *certain* death, for example, you would probably be willing to offer all your wealth with no upper limit. Yet we all take risks, which suggests we place some finite value on life.

Although it may be very difficult to provide a totally persuasive single value for life, having such a value can support consistent life-saving efforts. Consistent decisions—that is, using the same resource commitment to save a life across different activities—helps to save more lives from any given amount of resources. With diminishing returns to life-saving effort, whether it is limiting arsenic in the environment or installing air bags in automobiles, life-saving efforts should be carried to the same level in each area. If instead more resources per life saved are devoted to limiting arsenic than to installing air bags, some of the resources being used to limit arsenic should be shifted to installing devices like air bags, where they can save more lives. We begin by examining how a value of life can improve the efficiency of life-saving efforts and then turn to the problem of estimating the value of a life to guide the extent of the total life-saving effort. We finally consider valuing other nonmarket effects.

The Advantage of Placing a Value on Life

Regulation can serve many good purposes, and protecting lives is certainly one of them. To pursue such a purpose, however, requires comparisons for deciding how to use resources in the most effective way, and some of those comparisons are seemingly impossible. How can lives be compared with expenditures, and who can decide how much to spend to save a life? The key to understanding the setting for this truly formidable question is to realize that we actually make such terrifying choices, whether we admit it or not. For instance, suppose a dangerous section of a road is straightened to make it safer. Comparing the cost of the road improvement with the reduction in loss of life, or with the lives saved, implicitly sets a value on life. In building roads, such assessments are inescapable. Whether any "correct" answer to the question is possible is less important than the fact that it is better to make such judgments consistently, because the same effort across different areas yields the greatest benefit from the resources applied.

Remember that if activities are undertaken in a desirable order, with the most beneficial actions first, there will be a form of diminishing returns, because later chosen efforts will be less productive. In that situation, suppose the Occupational Safety and Health Administration (OSHA) was devoting twice as many resources as the Consumer Product Safety Commission (CPSC) toward saving a life. Then it would be better to reduce the effort of the OSHA, which is experiencing lower marginal returns and expand the effort of the CPSC. Expending the same effort per marginal life saved at both agencies is efficient and allows more to be done with limited resources—in this case, more lives saved. Box 20.1 shows the benefit from using a consistent value of life, quite apart from the ease or difficulty with which it can be done.

BOX 20.1 The Usefulness of a Value for Life

To illustrate the advantage of having a general value of life to use in guiding policy, suppose agency A spends $100,000,000 at the margin to save a life, and agency B spends $100,000 at the margin to save a life. Suppose also that the benefit functions have the usual properties, so benefits decline and marginal costs rise as effort expands. Then agency A is devoting too many resources to life saving, and agency B is devoting too little. Agency A should transfer funds for life saving to agency B, because agency B can save more lives with the resources that Agency A is currently devoting to this purpose.

Notice that having a single value of life in this example, say a value between $100,000,000 and $100,000, would call for a transfer of funds from agency A to agency B. Suppose the value of life is taken to be $5,000,000. Agency A is spending too much, at $100,000,000 per life saved, because the marginal benefit from that spending is only $5,000,000. Agency A should cut back its effort so that agency B, which is spending too little at $100,000 per life saved, can expand its effort. Agency A is well beyond the ideal intersection point of marginal benefits and marginal costs, while agency B is short of that optimal point.

Working to a common value of life can improve the allocation of resources, even if the common value that is used is in some sense wrong. Having a truly sound assessment of the value of a life is desirable for deciding how much resources to allocate to the life-saving purpose in general, but for allocation among agencies, a single approximation can be very useful even if it is not perfectly correct (as it may never be). To obtain the most benefit from whatever resources two agencies have, they should make the same marginal effort, and benefit-cost analysis with a single value of life can induce that result.

In raising the question of the value of a life, we want to consider life in a general way, rather than any specific life, say the life of a specific person in a concrete, life-or-death choice. Fictional treatments have used such choices in dramatic ways, but they do not lead to a general value of life that might be used to guide regulatory policy.[1] What we need is an average value for a typical citizen that can guide the allocation of life-saving efforts in society. Such a value is called the **value of a statistical life**.

The Value of a Statistical Life

How can we assign a value to a life? We describe three methods here, one based on individuals' estimates through an indirect route, another based on procedures that have been used in court cases involving compensation for loss of life, and finally a statistical value of a life that is deduced empirically from decisions individuals make,

---

[1] See, for example, *The Prisoner*, by novelist Graham Greene (1986), which examines the sale of a life in a prisoner-of-war setting.

first in choosing among jobs that carry different risks of death, and second in the choice of highway speed limits. None of the methods can provide a true value of life, and indeed life cannot be valued in monetary terms. Public decisions, however, about highway improvements, automobile standards, air quality levels, medical procedures, or other similar matters affect the risk of death, so those decisions determine an implicit value of life. It is sensible to estimate an explicit value in part to achieve consistency and, thus, greater efficiency in life saving efforts across agencies. Knowing the value of a statistical life can also serve to guide the decision of how large the total life-saving effort should be.

Individuals' Judgments

As in other questions of valuation, it is desirable to have estimates based on individuals' judgments. Asking individuals to place a value on their lives is not very promising, however, because it is such a difficult question, and it borders on the life-or-death choice we want to avoid. (Each of us would probably choose a very high figure and be troubled by budgetary limitations.) An easier question, partly because it is smaller, is to ask how much an individual would pay to reduce the risk of death.[2] This method can escape the limitation of a budget constraint, because if the change in the risk of death is small, only a modest payment for risk reduction may be appropriate. That allows the estimate to reflect individuals' valuations rather than their budget constraints alone. If estimates could be obtained from a sizeable sample of individuals who represent the population, their average value can provide a general value for a statistical life. Such individual estimates might come from answers to the following question: *Suppose there is one chance in 10,000 that you will die this year because of risks on your job. How much would you pay to avoid that risk?* (Think about this, and choose an amount you would pay before proceeding further.)

If your answer to this question is, say $500, meaning that you would actually pay $500 to eliminate this 1 chance of death in 10,000 in the next year, that number offers a basis for estimating the value you attach to life. If you take the probability of death and multiply it times the value of life, the resulting expected value is the expected loss from being in the job for the next year. That is the sum you might pay to avoid the risk of death. That is, the amount you are willing to pay (WTP) should equal the probability of death (P) times the value you attach to life (X), or

$$WTP = PX, \text{ or } X = WTP/P.$$

To infer your value of life if your answer was $500, we can calculate

$$X = WTP/P = \$500/(1/10,000) = \$5,000,000,$$

or five million dollars. If you chose an amount for WTP different from $500, use your amount in this same way to calculate the implied value you attached to life.

This method for estimating values of lives has the advantage of asking for a payment. Because the payment equals only a fraction of the value of life, however, the method reduces the problem of the budget constraint, which might otherwise keep a

---

[2] See Schelling (1968).

person from offering a large sum. On the other hand, the exercise is hypothetical and, therefore, less effective than actual transactions in risk reduction could be. Also, we have a tendency to be biased in probability judgments. We overestimate the probability of unlikely events.[3] Here, this problem may be moderated by specifying the risk explicitly, although there may still be a lingering bias in our judgments. Values of life found in this way do tend to be lower than values found by other means. Still, there is a great advantage in eliciting judgments from individuals for these values rather than constructing them arbitrarily by other means. Hypothetical choices offer a feasible way to do that. Some averaging of a large sample of estimates is still needed to find the value of a statistical life.

Law-Suit Estimates

Courts frequently estimate the value of a life, to propose damages when a life is lost, say through a defendant's negligence. Most of these estimates rely on what is called a *human-capital* approach, which uses evidence about one's earnings to place a monetary value on one's life.[4] Although objection might reasonably be made to a method that relies on estimating such a market value, the method is feasible, because earnings prospects often can be calculated from market evidence such as rate of pay. This approach lacks information in the case of a person who does not work in the market, however, such as a housewife or a child, though estimates are offered for such situations based on other market data. Future lifetime earnings are usually estimated as of a current date, in present-value form. The deceased individual's consumption is often estimated and subtracted from lifetime earnings to give a net present value measure of the individual's contribution to society.

While its concreteness may make this human-capital method of valuing life useful in settling disputes, it is not a good basis for choosing the amount of resources to be devoted to reducing the general risk of death in social regulation.[5] It tends to yield low values for elderly citizens, who have little workforce time remaining, and it tends to yield high values for children. Although it represents one's contribution to gross domestic product (GDP), it does not focus on how much we value a reduction in the risk of death. We all might want more resources devoted to reducing the risk of death by a small fraction than the amount that would be indicated by our net contributions to GDP.

Imputed Values

A statistical value of life has also been imputed to individuals through empirical analysis of employment or other choices the individuals actually made. Because workers prefer a low risk of death on the job, that risk, together with a host of other factors having to do with the individual and the job, should influence wage payments. If everything else about jobs and workers are the same, the payments workers receive tend to be greater in jobs having greater risk of death. To identify this effect, one must

---

[3] See Fischhoff, et al. (1981).

[4] See Mishan (1971).

[5] For a survey and critique of these measures, see Viscusi (2000).

control for the many other influences that the job and the individual can have on earnings and then to isolate a separate effect for the risk of death. Such studies include personal characteristics such as age and education, for instance, as well as job characteristics that describe working conditions, such as working at an air-conditioned desk or lifting 70-pound packages in a hot warehouse.

We can represent the types of regression equations for such studies as follows:

$$Y = \Sigma_{i=1}^{n} \alpha_i I_i + \Sigma_{j=1}^{m} \beta_j J_j + \lambda R$$

where Y represents annual earnings from the job, I_i represents individual characteristics, J_j represents job characteristics, and R represents the annual risk of death in the job. The coefficients, α, β, and λ, are to be estimated from observations on individual workers, so—for the population studied—they indicate how each characteristic affects annual earnings. The workers in the sample accept this or a riskier job, so the value estimated is an upper limit of dollars per unit of risk. The coefficient λ indicates this marginal effect on annual earnings of a marginal change in the risk of death on the job. Thus, λ is the coefficient of interest. Its estimation is better when other coefficients are able to account for, and thus hold constant, other influences on earnings. Indeed, if important influences are omitted from the analysis their effects may be erroneously absorbed into λ and thereby throw off the estimate of the imputed value of a life.[6]

The change in annual earnings a worker wants for bearing greater risk of death is something like the willingness to pay for a reduction in the risk of death. In that comparison, R represents the risk of death, so λ represents the value of a life. A number of studies have estimated the value of a statistical life by this method, and results of an early and influential one are considered in Chapter 22. Estimates from different studies vary, due to differences in the sample of workers studied, the risk of death data, and the individual and job data. The estimates of the value of life obtained in this way tend to fall between \$2,000,000 and \$7,000,000.[7]

The value of a statistical life has also been imputed to decisions about highway speed limits. After war in the Middle East in 1968, together with strengthening of the OPEC cartel in the 1970s, oil became scarce. In 1974, as part of an effort to conserve the use of oil, the United States adopted a national highway speed limit of 55 miles per hour (mph), a lower speed limit than was in effect in any of the 50 states at the time. To enforce its national speed limit, the federal government required compliance measures in the states. Then, if compliance was low in a state, federal highway funds for that state would be cut. Many states were not pleased with this arrangement, and finally in 1987 the federal government allowed states to adopt a 65 mph speed limit on rural interstate highways if they wished, and in 1995 the national 55 mph speed limit was repealed. There was some resistance to increasing the speed limit, out of fear that doing so might reverse an effect it turned out to have: Highway fatalities fell 15 percent after it was passed in 1974.

---

[6] For criticism of studies on this ground, see Black and Kniesner (2003).

[7] For a review of value-of-life studies, see Viscusi (1992, 1993) and Blomquist (1994).

Higher speed limits have two main effects. They save drivers' (and passengers') time and they increase highway fatalities, so comparing effects under different speed limits can yield an estimate of dollars (time value) per life (fatalities). Economists Orley Ashenfelter and Michael Greenstone (2004) made such a comparison between the 40 states that increased their speed limit to 65 mph and states that remained at 55 mph. They studied states before the change (1982–1986) and after the change (1988–1993), to form a basis for comparing across the states after the change. Although state officials rather than individuals made these decisions, they would do so on behalf of their citizens, an ideal target group to use in deciding social policy.

Ashenfelter and Greenstone found actual speeds rose 2.5 mph, or 4 percent, with the higher 65 mph speed limit, while fatality rates rose by about 35 percent. Using the value of time saved traveling because of the gain in speed, based on average wage rates, and comparing it with increased fatalities at the higher speed limit, they estimated the value of a statistical life at about $2.0 million (in 2006 dollars). Many possible effects were controlled in the natural experiment that this contrast in state speed limits allowed. There was a substantial difference in estimates by state, however, suggesting that the value of a statistical life is not estimated without considerable possible error.

Other Nonmarket Effects

Any effect that does not pass through a market is difficult to value because it has no price. One way to estimate values is to collect individuals' judgments through well-designed surveys. A second way is to infer values from market data. In the same way that the risk of death is used to imputed value of life from earnings data or speed limit

---

BOX 20.2 The Costs of Saving Lives

Policies of social regulation often save lives, but the costs incurred vary widely. Economist John Morrall reported estimates of lives saved and average costs per life saved for many programs, such as standards for automobile steering columns or for the control of arsenic in the workplace. Morrall found the steering column standard imposed a cost of $100,000 per life saved, making it a very attractive program. Seat belts in automobiles are also effective, costing an estimated $300,000 per life saved. But Morrall found the program of arsenic protection cost $92,500,000 per life saved, placing it among the highest cost programs. Because these programs are often discrete and independent, they cannot always be substituted for one another. Some programs, however, impose costs far beyond others, and well above most estimates of the value of a life, so it is reasonable to question whether they should continue in effect as they are. Note once again how an accepted amount for the value of a life could help in the effort to save lives. Such a value would justify adoption of productive programs and would discourage unproductive ones, thereby leading to more effective use of all resources available for the life-saving effort.

See J. F. Morrall, "A Review of the Record," *Regulation*, Nov./Dec., 1986, pp. 25–34.

choices, a variety of other effects can be estimated. When measures of air pollution are used along with many influences to estimate house prices, for instance, the influence of air pollution on house prices can be assessed. We consider each of these two methods in turn.

Surveys

One of the main devices used to determine values for nonmarket effects, such as smog or odors in the air, is the **survey**. A survey puts questions to a sample of individuals to estimate their views. Opportunities for quantitative empirical estimates of nonmarket effects are rare, and surveys provide at least some information about valuations. How accurate they are will depend on how realistic the questions are and how carefully the subjects answer them.

In designing sound surveys, direct estimates of specific effects are rarely solicited, just as individuals are not usually asked directly how much they value their lives in value-of-life estimates. Instead of asking a worker for the value of a particular injury, for example, the worker would be asked how large a payment would be warranted to secure a specific reduction in the risk of that injury. This method is called the **contingent valuation** method, because it presents questions that are contingent, or that depend on, a certain choice being available in a market-like setting where payments actually could be made. The researcher follows a variety of procedures, sometimes with open-ended questions, sometimes with multiple-choice questions, and sometimes with auction-type procedures where amounts are successively raised or lowered until the respondent will go no further. But in all cases the purpose is the same: to obtain an estimate of the value of some effect that is hard to estimate otherwise. Box 20.3 shows the results of a simple survey from a very specialized audience.

Hedonic Indexes

One can sometimes estimate a value for nonmarket effects because they influence the value of other objects. One method constructs what is called a hedonic index because it traces how a set of features affects the pleasure, and hence the value, of an object. For instance, economists Brookshire, Thayer, Schulze, and d'Arge (1982), used variables such as the age of a house, its lot size, and neighborhood school quality to explain house-sale prices, and they also included measures of air pollution. Their purpose was to observe the effect of air pollution on house values. The equation they estimate is comparable to the labor market equation that yielded a value of life from

---

BOX 20.3 Valuing True Love, or Being President

A survey by *Worth* magazine asked a sample of Americans earning at least $250,000 per year how much they would pay to find "true love," and how much they would pay to be President of the United States. Their answers indicated that the average amount they were willing to pay for "true love" was $487,000. To be president, the average amount was $55,000.

See "Harper's Index" in *Harper's Magazine*, June, 1998.

risk of death effects on earnings after controlling for other influences on earnings. Estimating this pollution equation has the same requirement that all influences be included, so the estimated effect of air pollution does not erroneously include effects of factors that were omitted.

In their study of factors affecting house-sale prices, Brookshire, Thayer, Schulze, and d'Arge found that air pollution levels had a negative effect on house prices. They also conducted surveys, to compare them with these results, asking individuals to estimate how much they would be willing to pay their utility company in exchange for lower levels of air pollution. Results from the survey did not exactly match those estimated by the equation. Survey results, with their subjective assessments of hypothetical situations, did not produce valuations that were as high. That they might not yield accurate estimates is a typical concern about surveys.

Hedonic valuations, which trace how measured influences affect value, apply to specific circumstances, and they often do not generalize, at least in quantitative terms, to other situations. For example, a landfill was found by estimation of a hedonic index to affect nearby property values in a small Virginia community.[8] The magnitude of this effect would probably not be the same in another community with another landfill, however, where the houses as well as other aspects of the neighborhood might be different. A separate study may be necessary in each situation. The method is useful, however, and it affords an empirical basis for estimating nonmarket effects.

<table>
<tr><td>**20.3**</td><td>**COMMAND-AND-CONTROL MEANS OF SOCIAL REGULATION**</td></tr>
</table>

Once social goals for an activity can be specified, the question is: How can they be achieved? Social regulation usually involves some interference with the market process, either to change the prices firms act upon, or to change firms' decisions in some more direct way. Direct orders, as rules or regulations, are **command-and-control** methods, in that they take the form of a command that must be obeyed. Limits on the noise that equipment can emit in the workplace is an example of such a rule. The rules or standards that such methods establish must be enforced to be effective, and the necessary monitoring and enforcement efforts may be substantial.

Command-and-Control Methods

Command-and-control systems set out commands and then monitor and enforce them to control the outcomes.[9] For controlling some forms of pollution to achieve an acceptable level of air quality, for example, the **Environmental Protection Agency (EPA)** essentially prescribes the types of technology firms can use. The EPA enforces this prescription by requiring any producer of effluent, such as smoke from a smokestack at a

---

[8] See DiCalogero (1997).

[9] For description of an entire economy organized on a command-and-control basis, see Gregory and Stuart (1998).

specific location, to have a permit that allows it to produce at all. OSHA has imposed many requirements with respect to noise and other dangers in the workplace, at times by requiring certain attachments or modifications to machinery. CPSC has established standards for glass shower doors, lawnmowers, and a vast array of other consumer products. These requirements all take the command form, and they usually involve some type of standard.

Standards specify requirements to be met, such as maximum sound decibels for workplace machines, or how resistant glass shower doors must be to shattering, and they can be desirable in principle. They may help to internalize an externality by limiting the methods to be used. For example, when information is imperfect so buyers cannot judge products well, competitive pressure might tempt sellers to produce cheaper—and less effective or more dangerous—products. Standards offer one means of moderating such a "race to the bottom" that can grow out of imperfectly competitive circumstances. They also impose the same burden at each point where they apply, thus requiring equal efforts by all parties. Especially when uncertainties are great, so any step is problematic, standards can be an effective means of reliably achieving some level of quality.[10]

Standards, however, have disadvantages, too. First, their concrete specification gives them sharp edges, in that product manufacturers may just barely meet them, and then the standards determine the level of product quality or worker protection for the market. Manufacturers also must meet the standards without deviation, even when an innovative deviation might actually offer an improvement. Second, changing a standard may be difficult, precisely because a standard is so specific. Parties subject to standards commit to the forms they take, perhaps by purchasing equipment or installing procedures. So a change in the standard can impose serious costs on those who are committed to its old form, and for that reason alone a change can face resistance. Third, because change is difficult, the standards tend not to change. Standards can, thus, become out of date, and they can delay introduction of improved products, workplaces, pollution abatement methods, or other benefits. As an example, the sealed-beam headlamp was once the standard headlamp for automobiles in the United States, and it took a long time to change that standard so that halogen lamps could be used. These characteristics of standards make setting them difficult. Not only do the standards take rigid and lasting form, but centralized information to establish them is seldom as rich and plentiful as the information available on a decentralized basis across many markets.

Monitoring and enforcing standards can also be costly, especially when taking account of the responses of the regulated parties. A regulatory organization must conduct some form of monitoring of compliance with its rules and standards, which becomes another cost of regulation. Enforcement also must be established at an appropriate level for the task. Another cost of this regulation is the cost borne by businesses and others in understanding and complying with the rules and standards.

To have effect, the government must usually establish separate regulatory agencies, each with specific goals. The goals of any one agency are usually narrower than

---

[10] For a description of advantages of command-and-control regulation, see Cole and Grossman (1999).

the broad national interest. For example, three federal government units focus on the automobile industry, one concerned about fuel economy, another with highway safety, and the third with air pollution from motor vehicles. Because safer cars may be heavier and, therefore, less fuel efficient and more polluting, we can see how conflicts arise. Thus, the structure of government can make it difficult to set rules or standards, even without considering the many other contending political and economic interests that may also be at work.

Rule-Making Procedures

Establishing rules at the federal level has special procedural complications. Rules are usually numerous when they take the command-and-control form. In proposing a rule, an agency is supposed to stay within the range of activities that Congress legislated for it. When an agency finds that a matter within its area of responsibility is in need of regulatory attention, it must announce its intention to examine the matter and propose a program for it. The **Office of Management and Budget (OMB)** then reviews the agency's proposed program. Such a review prevents interference with other agencies' responsibilities and can block undesirable or unwanted programs. If the OMB does not object to the program, the agency must prepare a **Regulatory Impact Analysis (RIA)** for its proposed regulation, usually including estimates of expected benefits and costs, plus a description of possible alternative means of achieving the same ends.

The RIA goes to the OMB for a formal review, which must be completed within 60 days. Although it seldom happens, the OMB may reject the proposed regulation. More often, if it finds a problem it negotiates with the agency to make changes in the regulation. Usually it approves the proposed regulation, which allows the agency to issue a **Notice of Proposed Rulemaking** to explain the proposal, including a statement of justification for the new regulation. This Notice of Proposed Rulemaking is published in the *Federal Register*, which covers all government matters and notifies the public of pending proposals and adopted rules. This appearance in the *Federal Register* informs the public. The public then has a specific period, usually 30 to 90 days, in which to respond. Not surprisingly, most reactions come from affected business, environment, employee, or other interests and their lobbyists. The regulatory agency finally completes the proposed regulation and passes it, along with a revised RIA, to the OMB, which has 30 days in which to review it finally, before the agency can publish it in the *Federal Register* as an adopted regulation. Box 20.4 traces this approval process.

Regulation at the federal level requires many decisions to set up the various rules and standards that effect command-and-control regulation. Progressing through this process to approval can be a time-consuming task involving many parties, especially when the rule is to serve in all circumstances. Yet the circumstances differ in different parts of the country. Monitoring and enforcement efforts may then require coordination with local authorities.

Social regulation often relies on command-and-control methods because, except for the case of environmental externalities, it is difficult to use taxes, subsidies,

BOX 20.4 The Creation of a Federal Rule

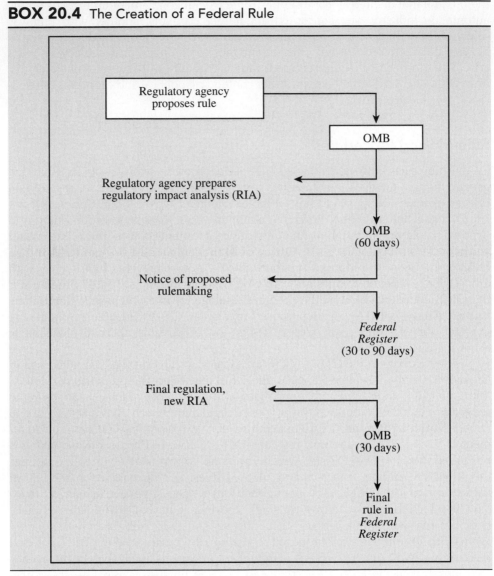

OMB = Office of Management and Budget.

or property rights to control or influence business firms' actions. It might be possible to impose a tax on employers for workplace injuries, and workers' compensation laws have some of the effects of such an instrument. We have many rules and regulations for the workplace, for products, and for institutional procedures, and for most of them tax or subsidy policies are not presently workable.

The rules and standards that grow out of command-and-control regulation usually must take a single form. That is, only one rule, or one standard, is set for all to follow, whether in New York, Louisiana, or Oregon. Essentially, the rule or standard involves a collective choice. But sometimes several equally effective rules can be put forward to allow the firm a choice, based on its circumstances, and such flexibility can reduce the cost to firms of compliance.

20.4 TAX-SUBSIDY AND PROPERTY-RIGHT MEANS OF SOCIAL REGULATION

A less blunt instrument of social regulation than command-and-control is a tax or a subsidy, which can correct the private incentives of firms. A tax is ideally chosen to represent the difference between the private cost that a firm sees when it acts—the cost an electric utility sees in producing electricity, for example—and the social cost of its action, which for an electric utility would include the cost others bear from the air pollution that it causes. Air pollution is an *external diseconomy*, in that it has negative effects on others, and a tax is then appropriate because it raises the polluter's cost to include costs others now bear. On the other hand, pollution abatement conveys *external economies*, because it brings external benefits to others, and so its production may be subsidized. Another approach to solving externality problems is to create a property right, such as a right to pollute. Although the distribution of such rights can be problematic, active trading in them creates prices for the rights to pollute that a polluter must own, and which can lead in turn to desirable efficiency incentives. Tax or subsidy schemes are examined first.

Tax-Subsidy Solutions

A tax can force the firm that produces external diseconomies to face the added social cost it causes and consequently reduce its production, while a subsidy can lower private cost and induce a firm to expand production of a good that brings external economies. We begin by illustrating taxes or subsidies and then note problems in implementing them.

Taxes or Subsidies Can Correct Prices

Taxes or subsidies can be important in controlling external effects, especially in a market economy that relies on decentralized decisions. The main advantage of taxes or subsidies is that they function amid decentralized decision making in a market to eliminate the difference between private and social cost, so private decisions in markets reflect social costs. In attempting to choose an ideal tax, regulators seek to place a value on an external effect, when there is no market available to do so.

A unique optimal tax or subsidy rate may be hard to determine and difficult to implement. Estimating the external cost or benefit may be difficult, and then implementing an appropriate tax or subsidy so it takes effect at the right time or place can also be difficult. But given time to make marginal adjustments, the tax or subsidy can often be workable. Where it is workable, a tax or subsidy can serve better than blunt rules or standards, or outright prohibition of particular acts. When taxes and subsidies can adjust prices so they reflect true social costs, they avoid the rigidities and enforcement problems of standards, and they enable us to choose an efficient solution through our decentralized responses to them in a market economy.

A form of taxation is part of workers' compensation laws, which provide compensation for workplace injury. Courts were slow to compensate workers for injury, because they tended to find that workers had accepted the risk of injury when they accepted employment. The courts required convincing evidence of an employer's negligence before they would grant relief to a harmed worker. Going to court was costly and might not succeed, with the result that workers seldom sought court relief. To protect workers in this situation, many states passed workers' compensation laws beginning in 1902. All states had them by 1950.

A major change in workplace safety came after states adopted workers' compensation laws, because they raised the costs to employers of operating unsafe workplaces. Workers' compensation laws call for paying compensation to injured workers, even where the employer was not negligent. The compensation to workers is financed by fees, like taxes, charged to employers in proportion to the injury claims lodged against them. As a result, the employers are motivated to lower risks in their workplaces to lower the workers' compensation claims against them. Workers' compensation laws thus use a tax-like instrument to force employers to bear costs for unsafe conditions in their workplaces.

Problems with Taxes or Subsidies

It is not always easy to make private cost equal social cost by adding a single tax to prices. For instance, suppose we attempt to impose a tax for using streets to reduce traffic congestion. Even if a companion reduction can be found for other taxes, to keep total tax payments about the same, some persons may want a higher road tax than others. The reason such disagreement may arise is that some persons would prefer less congestion than others, perhaps because they place a higher value on the time they could save. Yet we all must agree on one road tax and one level of congestion, a level we all must bear. Each person cannot buy a personal level of traffic congestion. It might be possible to have two alternative roads, perhaps charging an added toll on one to offer a choice of two congestion levels, but even this would be imperfect in that it would not suit all users ideally. It certainly is not possible to have a personal level of air pollution.

For air pollution it can be very difficult to track down the source and impose a tax that makes final product price equal marginal social cost. First, the source might be in the Midwest, and effects may occur in New England or even in Canada. Consequences across state boundaries, and especially across national boundaries, make governmental remedies harder to form because of jurisdictional problems. Second, the effects are hard to trace to their sources. Many polluters may contribute, and the effect of their effluent depends on complex processes and even on the combination of other substances that are in the air. Although problems with water pollution are not exactly the same, they are similar, and applying tax-subsidy solutions to water pollution problems also can be difficult.

Finding an optimal tax may even be harder in the case of air or water pollution than in the case of highway congestion. Reducing highway congestion can save us time, and by evaluating such savings we can define an optimal tax for road use, even though it must be a compromise over all our various preferences. The marginal amount of air pollution might impose even more wide ranging marginal costs on different persons. It also seems harder to quantify bleary eyes, nausea, and illness than road travel delays. More generally, in the case of air pollution the technological cause-and-effect relationships are less well defined than those for highway use. Approximations can improve matters, though, and crude taxes and subsidies can still offer remarkable improvements in the effectiveness of resource use.

In addition to finding a unique optimal tax, other problems can complicate implementation. To continue with the automobile congestion example, we can trace the private cost of an automobile trip to a complex mix of inputs. No one of these inputs alone typically could bear the tax without affecting resource allocation in unintended ways. If we place the tax on fuel only, for instance, we would cause people to use the streets less, as intended, but they also would make inefficient substitutions, using less fuel by their choice of speeds, and vehicle design might even be affected. For controlling air pollution, on the other hand, which we can trace directly to fuel use, a tax on fuel alone may be a most effective instrument. It can induce the choice of lower speeds and the design of more fuel-efficient vehicles.[11]

If highway traffic congestion is the problem to be solved, taxing all inputs would be desirable. It is difficult to imagine a tax scheme that would affect all inputs equally, however. For one thing, the costs of levying and collecting taxes is much higher for some inputs than for others, and this circumstance alone could make proportional taxation of all inputs inappropriate. Moreover, congestion is a problem only at certain times during the day. Because the travel inputs need not be purchased right at the time they are used, taxes on them cannot achieve any desired timing in their effects. Any tax must be in effect at all hours of the day, even in the middle of the night when congestion may not exist. If the tax is appropriate in a city, where congestion is a problem, and not in nearby communities, drivers may buy gasoline outside the city and avoid the congestion tax. In the case of motor vehicle air pollution, on the other hand, one input such as gasoline may be the cause. If the offending input can be taxed directly, that can be an ideal solution.

One other subtle problem arises if the optimal tax level responds very much to total quantity, either of air pollution or of traffic congestion. For if it does, then designing an optimal tax may require knowledge of the ideal quantity ahead of time. It often is feasible to administer only a constant per-unit tax, where the tax rate is independent of quantity. If the difference between private and social marginal costs does not change very much with quantity, then consumers can pick an approximately optimal quantity (for which marginal social benefits equal marginal social costs) as they respond to a constant tax. If the optimal tax changes very much as quantity changes, however, then the choice of the constant tax per unit is difficult. It is only correct if the final equilibrium quantity consumers choose is the one that was anticipated. But then,

---

[11] For analysis of this possibility of targeting an offending and taxable input, see Plott (1966).

decentralized decisions are not serving their purpose if the outcome must be predicted correctly in advance. Nevertheless, a roughly approximate tax, adjusted over time, may still lead to more efficient use of resources than no tax at all.

The advantage of taxes or subsidies is that they correct an error in perceived costs that the externality causes. Tradeable rights can do the same thing, but they allow the regulator to set the quantity of pollution rather than its price.

Creating and Trading Property Rights

Creating rights that are needed to engage in an activity, such as polluting the air, can—perhaps paradoxically—help to control the activity. When such rights exist they can be traded, and trading can yield a market price for the activity.

Rights to Pollute

When firms must purchase rights to pollute, if the price is "right," their total private cost can be set equal to social cost, and the externality can be neutralized. A patent right is another example of a created right. It has been valuable to society to create this patent right to an idea, because the value of that right motivates the creation of new ideas. The right to pollute is different, but it also is an invented right that can improve market functioning.

A right-to-pollute solution for pollution control is similar to a tax, but it relies even more on markets. Government defines a **right to pollute**, which is a specified amount of a pollutant that can be emitted into the air. In the case of sulphur dioxide, for example, the defined unit is called an *allowance*, and a firm must submit an allowance for every ton of sulphur dioxide pollution it emits. Government also creates a system to measure the amount of pollution actually emitted so it can collect the right number of allowances from any polluter. Government is then able to specify the total amount of pollution it allows and issue a corresponding number of allowances—total rights to pollute—to achieve that target. Thus, within the limits of the available measurement and enforcement systems, the level of pollution can be specified.

A market can then be created where the rights to pollute, or allowances, can be traded. Owners of the pollution rights would want to maximize the value of those rights once a market price for a given supply of them was established. Those who could reduce pollution most efficiently—that is, for less than the value of a right to pollute—would reduce pollution and sell to others their rights to pollute. On the other hand, those who face higher pollution abatement costs would buy the pollution rights and use them. At a market equilibrium, the price of pollution rights would reflect the marginal cost of controlling pollution to the level that the available pollution rights allow.

The Allowed Level of Pollution

The use of pollution rights enables regulators to set an allowable amount of pollution and to distribute rights for that amount. Choosing the total level of pollution still requires an assessment of the marginal harm the pollution causes. That level may not be socially ideal if it does not reflect the benefits consumers realize from the marginal reduction in pollution. There could be too much pollution, if citizens valued marginally cleaner air by more than it would cost to produce. Or there could even be too little pollution if more was being spent to contain it than citizens really wanted. The marginal benefit of pollution abatement should be set equal to its marginal cost under pollution rights trading, just as it should be under tax-and-subsidy schemes.

The effectiveness of pollution-rights trading can depend on how localized the effects of pollutants are. Rights to emit the pollutant sulphur dioxide have worked well, for example, because those who produce it are spread out geographically and the pollution moves broadly in the air, so using a national market does not result in troublesome concentrations of the pollutant. Using a national market for mercury, on the other hand, could be problematic, because dangerous concentrations would be likely in particular geographic locations. Then a national price for pollution rights in mercury probably could not reflect the different social costs that would arise at different locations. Either localized taxes, or smaller localized pollution rights markets, would then be in order.

Both pollution-rights trading and pollution taxes can strike fully at the heart of the efficiency problem because both induce firms to make the effort that is best in their particular situations. The tax-subsidy arrangement imposes on all firms the same charge—as a tax—for units of pollution, regardless of their abilities to reduce pollution. As a result, firms that can reduce pollution at low cost can be motivated to do so to reduce their tax payments, while others that find the tax cheaper will pay it instead. Having an optimal outcome requires that the pollution tax reflect the marginal social cost of pollution, which should equal the marginal social benefit from reducing it. The regulator essentially must set a *price* for pollution reduction. The firms, in response, determine the amount of pollution at that price.

The pollution trading solution also motivates greater effort from those who can reduce pollution at lower cost, but pollution trading does so in an equilibrium that delivers a specified *quantity* of pollution. That is, instead of having to set a tax properly at the marginal social cost of pollution, the regulator now must choose the right level of pollution rights to distribute. Trade in those rights determines the marginal social cost of pollution abatement at that level of pollution.

The pollution-rights solution can present different implications for income distribution than the pollution tax, and that is one of its advantages. A pollution tax produces governmental income in the form of tax revenues collected from polluting firms. Pollution rights may also be sold to firms, and that again produces revenue for the government at the cost of firms. But pollution rights can be distributed free to firms in proportion to benchmark levels of their pollution effluents, and from there the firms buy or sell rights so they gain or lose based on their efficiency at reducing pollution. When they have to pay taxes to pollute, or buy rights to pollute, firms will object, saying it would be unfair to make them pay the government for pollution from plants that complied with all laws when they were constructed. Giving pollution rights away free to firms instead, based on past levels of pollution or past outputs, can avoid a transfer of income from firms to the government and, thus, can reduce conflict with the firms about introducing the policy. We now turn to examine the income-distribution effects of alternative policies in more detail.

Income-Distribution Consequences

In a very simple framework it is possible to consider a variety of efficient solutions that differ in their income distribution effects. To do so requires us to assume that income effects do not alter demands and that changes in output cause no changes in input prices. We shall compare different policies using Figure 20.2.[12] Pollution increases more than proportionately as output quantity increases, as was the case in Figure 19.2. Here, output has a constant private marginal cost (PMC) at the level of P', while pollution has an added cost—borne by others—that makes social marginal cost (SMC) rise with output along the line SMC. The marginal benefit of production is reflected by the demand curve and is labeled in the figure as marginal benefit. A private market equilibrium occurs at output Q' and price P', where marginal benefit is equal to PMC. The sum of consumer surplus ($A + B + C + D$) plus private producer surplus ($G + H - G - H = 0$) is maximized there at output Q', but a social cost ($C + D + E + F$) is incurred that is an externality, and this externality is ignored in private decisions.

In this framework we begin with the private market solution at Q' and P', and introduce alternative policies to correct for the externality. We first illustrate the Coase solution in this framework and then proceed to consider command-and-control, tax-subsidy, and pollution-right forms of environmental policy.

Figure 20.2 *Effects of Alternative Policy Solutions*

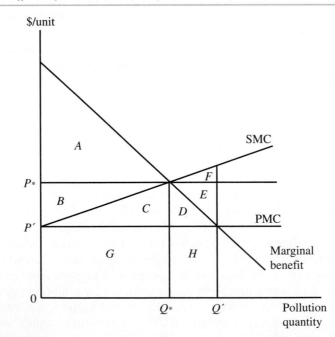

---

[12] This framework was developed by Don Fullerton (2001).

Coase

Recall that in the Coase situation, defining property rights brings incentives for an efficient solution. In Coase's analysis, property rights are well defined, although the definition can go one of two ways. Either the victims who suffer from the external effect—in this case, pollution—have the right to be free of it, or the party who is responsible for the pollution has the right to emit it. The parties in Coase's case have low transaction costs, which allows them to negotiate a solution.

Suppose the polluters have the right to pollute and they face competition from one another. Then the polluters face only private cost PMC and produce as much as demand allows at cost and price of P' until output is Q' at the private market solution. The victims of pollution suffer harm represented by areas C, D, E, and F. The area under the social marginal cost curve and above private marginal cost at output Q', or $C + D + E + F$, is the sum of social marginal pollution costs up to that output, so it represents the total pollution cost at output Q'. Even though the polluters have the right to pollute, the victims can bribe the polluters to reduce output and, thus, pollution. It will be hard to persuade the polluter to produce less than Q^*, because at any lower output consumer willingness to pay is higher and some competitor could sell more even at a higher price. The victims, however, would be better off by $D + E + F$ if output is reduced from Q' to Q^*. In view of this potential gain, the victims would be willing to offer the polluters a side-payment, S, in the amount $S \le D + E + F$. At the output, Q^*, the polluters can clear the market with a price of P^* and gain profit of $B + C$, plus the side-payment, S. The polluters may need a device, such as payment into a fund of an amount $P^* - P'$ per unit, which they later divide among themselves, to enforce the equilibrium without competitive undercutting. With that rise in price, however, consumers would lose consumer surplus of $B + C + D$. Thus, after negotiation between victims and polluters, victims gain $D + E + F - S$, polluters gain $B + C + S$, and consumers lose $B + C + D$. The net result is $D + E + F - S + B + C + S - B - C - D = E + F$, a net gain for society.

If victims have the right to avoid pollution damage, polluters have to compensate for the harm their production causes. Essentially, then, they have to include SMC as their private cost, so they could reach output Q^* and price P^* directly. This solution maximizes consumer plus producer surplus, but it is not certain to be selected. Victims have the right to be free of all harm, so they can prevent production altogether. Polluters not only have to compensate victims for harm at output Q^*, they have to get the victims to agree to that much pollution. Victims could ask not only for their harm, C, but also for part of B, which would otherwise be polluters' profit. To win their agreement, polluters would, therefore, be willing to offer victims a side-payment, S, between C and $B + C$, or $C \le S \le B + C$. Thus, under either definition of property rights, an efficient solution might be negotiated, although the property rights that are assigned have a significant effect on income distribution consequences.

Command and Control

Using command-and-control methods, regulators could set the output and pollution level. If they chose the optimal level, output would be set at Q^*. At that output, polluters effectively would set price at P^* to clear the market. As a consequence, compared with the unregulated solution at Q' and P', consumers lose $B + C + D$ in consumer surplus, polluters gain $B + C$, and victims gain $D + E + F$. Thus, there is a net gain of $B + C - (B + C + D) + D + E + F = E + F$.[13]

Tax and Subsidy

A tax is a classic solution to the externality problem.[14] A regulator can assess the difference between social marginal cost and private marginal cost at the ideal solution to be $t = P^* - P'$ and impose that tax per unit of output on the polluters. Faced with this tax, the polluters would now face costs equal to P^*, and the market would clear at price P^* and quantity Q^*, the welfare-maximizing equilibrium. At the P^*, Q^* solution, government would receive tax revenue of $B + C$, consumers would lose consumer surplus of $B + C + D$, and victims would experience reduced harm of $D + E + F$. Thus, the net effect of the tax policy would be a gain of $B + C - (B + C + D) + D + E + F = E + F$.

It might be difficult for the regulator to select the ideal tax of $t = P^* - P'$ when the market had settled at the private equilibrium of Q' and P'. At that solution, the regulator might estimate the difference between social marginal cost and private marginal cost as SMC − PMC at output Q' as a basis for the tax, an amount that is greater than the ideal tax, $t = P^* - P'$. Once imposed, this larger tax would lead the market to an equilibrium at an output below Q^*, where the regulator could see that the outcome was not ideal and could then lower the tax. It would thus be possible through adjustments for the regulator to converge to the ideal tax.

As an alternative to the tax on pollution, the regulator might provide a subsidy for pollution abatement. That is, the polluter would be paid to reduce pollution. At the private market equilibrium, suppose the regulator offered a subsidy of $s = P^* - P'$ to the polluter for each unit of pollution it abated or prevented. If you were polluting at level Q' and would receive $s = P^* - P'$ for reducing your output you would gladly reduce your output. You would continue to reduce output until it was at Q^*. Any further reduction would raise price above costs and thereby bring undercutting by competitors, so it could not last. The polluters gain in profit plus abatement subsidy the amount $B + C + D + E$, the government loses $D + E$ in abatement subsidy payments, consumers lose consumer surplus of $B + C + D$, and victims gain $D + E + F$. The net effect is thus a gain of $B + C + D + E - (D + E) - (B + C + D) + D + E + F = E + F$. Selecting the correct subsidy would be difficult but, as with the tax, it might be approached by marginal changes until the ideal was reached. Because the subsidy is intended to induce a *change* from an existing equilibrium, it could invite strategic behavior. Polluters might raise their outputs before the subsidy goes into effect to receive larger subsidy payments for reducing output to the ideal level.

---

[13] Regulators might try to avoid the rise in price to P^* by setting price at P' and quantity at Q^*. This policy, however, would remove the market clearing function that price serves. See Question 7.

[14] See Pigou (1920).

Pollution Rights

A property right to pollute might also be defined and used to control pollution. Under this policy the regulator would create tradeable pollution rights in the quantity Q^*. Once the polluters have to buy these rights, they will pay $B + C$ for them, which is a gain to the seller of rights (the government). Price will rise accordingly to P^*, where consumers will lose $B + C + D$ and victims will gain $D + E + F$. Thus the net gain is $B + C - (B + C + D) + D + E + F = E + F$. The question remains, who gains $B + C$ from the sale of the pollution rights?

First, the government might sell the rights at auction. Then the government would receive the proceeds of $B + C$. Often in these situations, however, the polluters have been polluting for years. They object through political institutions. They argue that they invested under old rules and should not have to suffer from a change of the rules that imposes such a cost on them. Governments often concede in these situations, and instead of auctioning pollution rights they give them away, perhaps in proportion to firms' past levels of pollution or past outputs. The efficiency incentive still arises, because the permits are tradeable and they become valuable as rights to pollute. When they are given to polluters, the polluters receive the value of the permits, $B + C$, rather than the government. Permits, therefore, allow the government to win the agreement of polluters more easily than with a tax and at less cost than with a subsidy.

Effects of these alternative policies on income distribution are summarized in Table 20.1. When means of reducing pollution are introduced, analyzing such effects

TABLE 20.1 Income Distribution Effects of Alternative Policies

Policy	Gains Experienced by Each Group				
	Polluters	Victims	Consumers	Government	Net Effect
Coase					
Victim rights	$B+C-S$	$D+E+F+S$	$-(B+C+D)$	0	$E+F$
Polluter rights	$B+C+S$	$D+E+F-S$	$-(B+C+D)$	0	$E+F$
Command and control					
Quantity restriction	$B+C$	$D+E+F$	$-(B+C+D)$	0	$E+F$
Tax and subsidy					
Tax	0	$D+E+F$	$-(B+C+D)$	$B+C$	$E+F$
Subsidy	$B+C+D+E$	$D+E+F$	$-(B+C+D)$	$-(D+E)$	$E+F$
Pollution rights					
Government sale	0	$D+E+F$	$-(B+C+D)$	$B+C$	$E+F$
Government gift	$B+C$	$D+E+F$	$-(B+C+D)$	0	$E+F$

Source: D. Fullerton, "A Framework to Compare Environmental Policies," *Southern Economic Journal*, 2001, Vol. 68, pp. 224–248.

on parties can determine which type of policy is politically feasible. Polluters may have enough political influence to prevent the imposition of policies that harm them, and that is one reason why tracing effects on income distribution is useful.

20.5 | INFORMATION AS REGULATION

The distribution of information can be a form of regulation, and it is relied on heavily in protecting workers, consumers, and investors. We begin with an example from pollution control.

Information and Pollution Control

A variety of social regulations focus on information to achieve desired ends. An example is a new device for regulating toxic wastes: the **Toxic Release Inventory (TRI)**. This instrument requires all facilities that exceed certain minimum size and emission thresholds to report annual releases of specific toxic substances through standard reporting procedures. Merely by requiring that firms announce these events publicly, after they occur, has had some success in discouraging accidental release of toxic substances.[15]

Congress created the TRI after the 1985 tragedy in Bhopal, India, involving the accidental release of a toxic chemical (methyl isocyanate) from a subsidiary of Union Carbide Corporation. The release resulted in more than a thousand deaths and in injury to hundreds of thousands. In light of this tragedy some states passed laws imposing information requirements on facilities, not just to warn about them but more on the principle that the public had a right to know about any potentially harmful toxic release. At the time, the action by Congress to create TRI seemed merely to be taking some sort of action, without expecting it to have any genuine effect.

Toxic releases are seldom an important aspect of a company's environmental externalities. Nevertheless, they can serve as an indicator, so companies may try to cast themselves in a favorable light by improving the indicator. The rankings of a university's sports teams in the United States may not properly reflect the university's quality either, but the rankings provide an indicator. Such rankings bring public awareness and positive media attention, which affect the image of the university. Perhaps reporting toxic releases is seen as offering similar indications of a company's achievement, although of a negative rather than a positive kind, and because it receives attention companies seek to improve it.

Since 1987, when the first reports were required under TRI, reported toxic releases have declined 57 percent.[16] TRI effectively introduced a form of benchmarking

---

[15] For examination of the TRI program, see Karkkainen (2001).

[16] See EPA, *Toxics Release Inventory*, 2004 Public Data Release (2006), or www.epa.gov/tri.

and performance monitoring, because companies pay attention to the releases of competitors and want to compare favorably in their effectiveness at combating accidental releases. The information requirements of TRI have helped move companies to be more careful about releasing toxics into the air.

Protecting Workers and Consumers

OSHA requires the labeling of chemicals and the training of workers in their handling. Providing information to workers in this way helps them to know about and avoid the inherent dangers of chemicals. Similar to the TRI program, chemical labeling also reflects overall attention to health by the employer. Informing workers of such hazards is desirable because it was a way to attack health dangers, which tend to have long-term effects that are more challenging for OSHA to pursue than safety. The wide range of safety requirements that OSHA has created also conveys information to workers about safety.

To avoid consumer harm, which can bring costly court punishment, manufacturers try to anticipate the uses that might be made of their products and provide information to consumers about possible dangers. For example, automobile manufacturers affix warning stickers inside vehicles, cautioning about the dangers of air bags. Instruction manuals that accompany appliances also contain frequent mention of possible dangers in their use. Manufacturers are motivated to provide such information in part to show that they have tried to inform consumers, so they bear less responsibility for consumer harms in court.

The FDA requires that food items be labeled for the benefit of consumers. Since May, 1994, for example, U.S. manufactured foods have had to present basic "nutrition facts" on labels for their products so consumers can take health effects into account in an informed way while choosing among available foods. Manufacturers must report the amount of fat, saturated fat, cholesterol, sodium, protein, and other elements that are contained, and what fraction of daily normal consumption of each category that amount represents. Producers of meat and poultry products, which are regulated by the U.S. Department of Agriculture, also have to comply with the law.

Besides providing information to help consumers make sound nutritional judgments, food labels prevent sellers from making misleading claims. The FDA defines terms like *low fat* and *fat free* so they have consistent meanings. Similar limits are specified for meanings of other terms such as *light* or *lite*, *low calorie*, *sugar-free*, or *cholesterol-free*. Serving sizes are also defined in a uniform way. Even a "fresh" chicken has to meet standards that insure consistency, and the FDA requires that makers of grains and breads called "enriched" must include folic acid.

The FDA also requires cautions on drug labels. Makers of unpasteurized fresh fruit and vegetable juices must label them as such and warn that the products may contain harmful bacteria. Tylenol is required to warn against the consumption of alcohol while using the headache remedy. Labels can reveal ingredients that cause allergic reactions, such as certain nuts, where the information is important because the reactions can be fatal.

Protecting Investors

Accounting information is supposed to reveal the income, expenses, and asset status of a firm. Such information not only aids in the sound management of the firm but also informs interested parties such as investors about the firm's condition and, thus, fosters efficient allocation of capital in the economy. Timely and reliable information helps investors judge whether to buy or sell a company's stock. To prevent surprises and to support investor judgments for sound resource allocation, corporations are required by government to issue financial reports that follow generally accepted accounting practices.

Congress passed the Sarbanes-Oxley Act in 2002 to improve corporate governance and securities regulation, and the law sought to improve information available to investors and others. Among other things, the law aimed to reduce conflicts of interest that could mar the auditing process in accounting. For example, the law prohibits an accounting firm from offering a wide range of consulting services to a publicly traded company it audits. As an auditor that is not providing consulting services it has no temptation to be lenient to protect its sales of consulting services. Under the Act, auditors also have to change periodically. The Act broadens the definition of fraud by corporate leaders and strengthens penalties for such crimes. The Act creates a new accounting regulatory board, called the Public Company Oversight Board and overseen by the Securities and Exchange Commission, to strengthen the uniformity of accounting practices and foster better comparisons across firms.

Under the Act, a corporation has to disclose publicly, as quickly as possible, any "material" change in its financial condition. Chief executives and chief financial officers of corporations have to personally certify the accuracy of the financial statements they issue.[17] For "knowingly or willfully" providing materially misleading information in such statements, they can go to jail for up to 20 years.

SUMMARY

Social regulation focuses on areas where markets fail to serve social goals effectively. Environmental pollution is an example. If individual firms discharge effluents into the air that impose costs on others, they face less than the true social costs of their actions. The environment is harmed by such an external effect, products appear to be less costly than they really are, and the economy does not perform efficiently. Prominent regulatory solutions include command-and-control methods, in which firms are told exactly how to avoid polluting, tax (or in other settings subsidy) schemes, and creation of rights to pollute, which the firm must obtain to pollute. By informing participants, information requirements can also lead to more efficient outcomes in markets.

---

[17] Based on a large sample of firms, including firms that certified and some that failed to certify after an SEC demand just before the Sarbanes-Oxley Act became effective, Bhattacharya, Groznik, and Haslem (2002) found that the certification requirement had no effect. That is, investors had already discounted for the reporting soundness, or the transparency of earnings, in firms with weaknesses before the certification requirement called attention to it.

There is still the problem of determining the proper level, or extent, of regulation. In many areas of social regulation, a decision about how much to regulate can be made along one continuous dimension. Setting a limit on the amount of ozone in the air is an example. The marginal benefit from further regulation falls as the target increases along that one dimension, and the marginal cost rises. The socially optimal level of regulatory activity is then where marginal benefit equals marginal cost, because that is where total benefit is maximized. That is the essence of benefit-cost analysis. Benefits and costs may fall on different parties, however, and attention to income effects may be needed, beyond the role income distribution plays in the welfare representation that defines benefit.

Government has pursued social regulation by several means, but command-and-control methods have been especially important. These methods call for the setting of standards or the imposition of rules, and they are able to go directly to the result desired. They are heavy-handed methods that may not yield ideal solutions, however, and they leave little scope for innovation or even effort on the part of the complying party. They also tend to be rigid and unchanging, possibly lasting past the time when they should change as technological improvement allows. They are also costly for regulators to monitor and enforce, and compliance with them tends to be more costly for the regulated parties than alternative methods.

Valuing benefits and costs for social regulation can be very challenging. For example, many regulations involve risk of death, and the value of saving a life is conceptually elusive. A perfectly accurate value is not essential (or even possible), however. With or without any explicit value of a life, decisions are regularly made—such as whether to improve a dangerous section of a highway—that implicitly value life. That value of life may as well be considered carefully, to help decide how far to carry regulatory activities that affect risks of death. Activities that involve risk of death occur in many different areas of regulation, and efforts to save lives can be consistent if regulators use a single value of life. If far more resources are used for the purpose of lowering the risk of death in one area than others, for example, more lives can be saved by taking some resources from that one area and applying them in others. A single value of life helps guide that kind of allocation.

There are several ways of estimating the value of life. It is callous to ask individuals what their lives are worth directly, and the question is surely hard to answer. But it is possible to ask what individuals would pay to reduce their risk of death by a small fraction. It is also possible to infer valuations of life from decisions we make in the risks we accept in different activities, including employments. To the extent these efforts succeed, they help us determine how great our regulatory efforts should be in areas that affect the risk of death. The same argument applies to other nonmonetary factors, such as the values we place on clean air or water. For those estimates, surveys have frequently been used and values have also been inferred from market decisions.

In some areas it is possible to use taxes or subsidies in pursuing the goals of social regulation by making private cost closer to social cost. Where they can be applied, such means are attractive because they improve decentralized decisions to overcome externalities, for example. There are difficulties, however, which setting taxes can illustrate. First, a tax level can be difficult to choose, because it is to represent the difference between private and social cost, and that may be hard to estimate. It can also be awkward to choose which items to tax when, for practical reasons, all cannot be taxed, and the items are to a degree substitutable. Taxing any one or even some may cause unwanted distortions in choices. The tax may be needed only at certain times during the day, too—as in the case of traffic congestion—yet imposing it *only* then is costly or impossible. Or the tax may be needed only in certain geographical areas, when the means of implementing the tax must apply everywhere.

Rights may be created, such as pollution rights, which also use markets as taxes or subsidies do. Whereas a tax is based on the added, social, external cost of an activity, and it acts like a price to which market quantities adjust, pollution rights are defined for a chosen total quantity of allowable pollution. Rights are created to match that quantity and distributed to firms, and their trading in the pollution rights determines a price for that chosen level of pollution. As in the case of a pollution tax, pollution rights motivate efficient decisions. Firms able to reduce pollution more efficiently will do so while others will purchase and use pollution rights.

Means by which social goals are pursued are important. Exhortation by politicians, newspaper editors (and writers of letters to them), well-intentioned action groups, and authors of books, together with great progress by scientists and engineers, cannot halt environmental pollution or make products and workplaces safe if our decentralized actions in markets are not also properly coordinated. With prices that do not reflect marginal social costs of our actions, it is difficult for us to choose efficient outcomes. The problem is as simple, and as complicated, as that.

QUESTIONS

1. A law protecting endangered predators (for example, eagles or timber wolves) stipulates a fine of $500 or one year in jail or both for, say, killing a bald eagle without a permit. In the early 1970s, there was a rash of killings of both bald eagles and golden eagles in Wyoming (by poisoning and by shooting from helicopters), because they were a nuisance to ranchers. Bounties of up to $25 per dead eagle were reported in Congressional testimony. The general reaction of government officials was to propose an increase in the fine, to $10,000 and one year in jail, or both, and the confiscation of any equipment (such as helicopters) used in the killing of eagles.
   a. Why, when the existing penalty for killing eagles was $500 or one year in jail, or both, would anyone kill an eagle for $25?
   b. Will the proposed increase in penalty to $10,000 or one year in jail, or both, be an effective method of deterring the killing of eagles?
   c. Is it an equitable method of doing so?
   d. Can you think of other ways (besides higher fines) that might be more desirable for protecting endangered predators?
2. Many states require that automobiles be inspected at least once per year to examine brakes, tires, and other elements that are related to the vehicle's safety

on the road. Newly manufactured automobiles also must contain air bags and seat belts. Describe a form of evaluation that can determine whether such policies are warranted.

3. Discuss possible effects on income distribution of relying on benefit-cost analysis for social decisions. Specify conditions that help to make the use of benefit-cost analysis reasonably fair, and describe how these conditions might be satisfied.

4. The National Academy of Science has called for a new federal agency to regulate the delivery of medical care in the United States. The academy makes this recommendation after completing a thorough study of medical errors, which it estimates to cause the deaths of 44,000 to 98,000 people a year, which is more than die from highway accidents. More than 7,000 are estimated to die from "medication errors," which includes prescribing or dispensing the wrong drugs, and this is more than the 6,000 who die from workplace injuries. The Academy points out that information on faulty procedures and mistakes is not available and, indeed, is essentially concealed. Twenty states have some type of reporting requirement, but some of these reporting requirements are not true requirements because they are voluntary. The Academy wants uniform reporting of mistakes to be required, first by hospitals, then by doctors, clinics, outpatient surgery centers, nursing homes, and others who care for patients. From such information, the Academy believes many causes of errors can be identified and remedied. Consider how such a new federal agency might function. Sketch a proposal for such an agency, indicating what its purpose will be, what enforcement power it should have, and what main problems it will have to overcome to be successful.

5. Consider a command-and-control policy that specifies equipment to be used to reduce air pollution from industrial smokestacks. Compare the effects of such a policy with a tax on measured levels of pollution. Which policy is more flexible in the scope it allows firms for compliance? Say which policy will lower pollution by a specified amount at less cost, and explain why.

6. Suppose you may choose between two routes in your commute by automobile to work each day. Over a year, the risk of death on route A is 0.0001 while the risk of death on route B is 0.0002. Because route B takes 30 hours of commuting time a year, compared with 80 hours a year on route A, assume you choose route B. You value commuting time at $10 per hour. Use this information to infer the value you place on your life.

7. Consider the command-and-control solution for externality that is presented in Income-Distribution Consequences in Section 20.4, where regulators choose output Q^*. Suppose that, in an attempt to avoid the rise in price to P^*, the regulators also set price at P' at the same time that they set quantity at Q^*. Will this policy succeed in preserving all consumer surplus while also reducing the externality cost?

8. The cost of a pollution tax on polluters is shown in Table 20.1 to be 0. The tax, however, raises price and, thus, reduces industry output, so polluters still object to it because they lose money in a transition to lower output. Is there any way that permits, representing rights to pollute, can overcome this objection by an industry and win their agreement? If not, explain why not, and, if yes, explain how the pollution-rights system would function.

21

Environmental Protection

Humans escaped the confining grip of Earth's gravity by a flight to the Moon in July of 1969 and were able for the first time to look down (or up) at the Earth. They could see a thin layer of blue vapor that filters out damaging rays from the sun and saves us from the extreme temperatures of outer space.[1] That blue layer holds air within the space close to Earth, where oxygen for animals and carbon dioxide for plants are exchanged. The movement of this air draws water from the Earth, purifies it, and returns it as rain or snow every day.

Our atmosphere has been explored only in recent centuries, first by mountain climbers, then by balloonists, and later by airplanes and space ships. Before the nineteenth century, mountain climbers had shown that air grows thinner and lighter farther from the Earth's surface. With the greater reach of balloon exploration, it was a surprise to discover that temperature fell consistently with altitude only up to about 8 miles, or 40,000 feet. That level is called the *tropopause*, and it marks the top of the *troposphere*. After that altitude is reached, the temperature levels off (at −60 degrees Celsius) and then begins to *rise* slowly with altitude.[2] This *"temperature inversion"* at 40,000 feet keeps the cooler, and thus heavier, air from rising any further. As a consequence, 85 percent of the atmosphere is held in the troposphere. This means that whatever we spread into the atmosphere is not dissipated into space; it remains in the troposphere to affect our weather and our health.

Temperature inversions also occur closer to Earth. They result when the Earth cools at night, which cools the air close to the ground and keeps it there by making it heavier, at least until the sun warms it again the next day. Such inversions occur on more than half the nights in the United States, and they make air pollution more serious. Discarding pollutants into the air can then harm others (an externality) because the pollutants do not rise and move away from the ground. Inversions can even last for several days, and that is the condition behind the most serious problems of smog in cities like Los Angeles. A striking episode from lasting temperature inversion

---

[1] For description of this layer, on which this account draws, see Young (1990, p. 72).

[2] It later falls again, to a minimum at −130 degrees celsius at an altitude of about 50 miles, or 260,000 feet. Then it again rises before continuing its fall with movement farther into space.

occurred in Denora, Pennsylvania in 1948. It caused 40 percent of the city's population to become ill, and 20 people died.

Water pollution can result from acid rain falling on the surface of lakes and rivers or from a range of impurities in ground water. Some water pollutants, such as lead, mercury, or DDT are not degraded by water. Toxic chemicals, such as benzene, vinyl chloride, and DDT, can cause cancer, neurological damage, and sterility, and they present the most ominous danger to ground water. Other pollutants, such as sewage, degrade in water but in doing so may use up oxygen and thus threaten aquatic life. Land pollution comes from acid rain and toxic substances and includes scrapped appliances and automobiles. Highway construction, strip mining, and poor agricultural or forestry practices reduce the uses that land can offer.

We first discuss in Section 21.1 the main problems pollution causes in air, water, and land. We then turn in Section 21.2 to explore the initial command-and-control regulatory actions taken to combat air pollution. Section 21.3 considers the pollution-rights-trading solutions that came later. Water pollution is a wide-ranging problem that is limited primarily by command-and-control means, similar to those originally used against air pollution, and we examine it, along with land pollution, in Section 21.4.

21.1 | AIR, WATER, AND LAND POLLUTION

Not being owned, air and water can be used by all of us, and some uses have external effects in the forms of air and water pollution. Air pollution takes a range of forms, from effects on ozone, which influences how our environment functions, to chemicals that can make rain harmfully acidic, to the rising global temperature of the Earth, which can change the Earth's water level and have other effects. Many problems of water pollution involve not only drinking water but lakes and streams, estuaries, wetlands, and watersheds that affect recreation, natural beauty, and aquatic life. Pollution of land has resulted primarily from disposing of waste materials, including toxic substances, in the land. This section first discusses the three broad forms of air pollution.

Three Main Air Pollution Problems

We are all confined to breathing the air in the troposphere, and that makes air pollution especially serious. It is fair to say that our growing population and our advancing technologies have upset the balance in the troposphere and left us with three main problems of air and water pollution: (1) a depleted level of protective *ozone* in the stratosphere, (2) chemicals forming acids in the air and falling to Earth as *acid rain*, and (3) a rising average temperature on Earth, called *global warming*. We consider ozone first.

The Ozone Problem

Ozone is a three-atom molecule of oxygen, formed after the sun breaks oxygen into single oxygen atoms in the upper atmosphere. These separate atoms react with ordinary oxygen molecules to form ozone. The sun also has the effect of breaking down ozone molecules and converting them back into ordinary oxygen molecules. So ozone is forming and breaking down all the time. In one of the world's great marvels, photosynthesis created the beginning of life on Earth by producing additional oxygen, and that oxygen led in turn to ozone, which fostered more life on earth by taming the sun's rays.

Ozone lies in a layer in the *stratosphere*, above the tropopause, where the atmosphere is less dense. If brought down to sea level and compacted by atmospheric pressure there, this ozone layer would be only about an eighth of an inch thick. Yet this thin layer protects life on earth, for without it we would be exposed to harmful ultraviolet radiation. The temperature inversion at the tropopause is actually caused by ozone in the stratosphere. Stratospheric ozone absorbs ultraviolet radiation from the sun and converts it into energy and heat to make the higher altitude it occupies actually warmer. This causes the temperature inversion that holds cooler air in the troposphere, where its movements cause what we call weather. A change in the ozone layer, therefore, could change our weather.

The Halley Research Station at Halley Bay, Antarctica started to monitor ozone at that location in the 1960s. Since 1977, a hole in the ozone layer has been observed each year from late September into November. This ozone hole is surprising because there is little life in Antarctica that might explain this effect. NASA observations have confirmed the ozone hole, which appears to become larger as time passes. Thin ozone in Antarctica now occurs over an area about the size of the United States.

A most likely cause of this reduction in stratospheric ozone is widespread use of **chlorofluorocarbons (CFCs)**, which were developed in the early twentieth century as nontoxic and nonflammable refrigerants in air conditioning systems. One manufacturer, DuPont, gave CFCs the trade name, freon, and it came to be used as a propellant in bug sprays, paint sprays, hair conditioners, and other spray products. When CFCs, which are normally inert, rise to high altitudes, they meet ultraviolet radiation and break down. One product of the breakdown is a chlorine atom, which acts as a catalyst to cause an oxygen atom and an ozone molecule to form two molecules of ordinary oxygen. Each reaction removes a molecule of ozone, and the chlorine atom catalyst can go on and cause the same process to occur again. The chlorine atom can remain active in this way for one or two centuries, so even though the use of CFCs is now being phased out under an international agreement called the **Montreal Protocol**, it will still take a long time to stop their harmful effect on ozone.[3]

Because ozone is forming while it is also being destroyed, we can view it as a renewable resource. In the upper reaches of the ozone layer, where ultraviolet radiation is most strong, the lifetime of an ozone molecule may only be a few minutes, but it can last months at lower levels. Forming and vanishing at the same time, it swirls in the atmosphere and is constantly changing in concentration. It is even affected, for example, by sun spots, which occur when the spectrum of solar radiation is most favorable for creating ozone, and by El Niño, the periodic warming of the South Pacific Ocean surface that affects wind movements over the earth. Because ultraviolet

---

[3] Chemical reactions in Antarctica may help to explain the loss of ozone there. See Kenneth Chang, "The Melting (Freezing) of Antarctica," *New York Times*, April 2, 2002, p. D1.

radiation itself fluctuates, it is difficult to tell from observations of it how much protection ozone is providing.

Acid Rain

Rain that contains acid is called **acid rain**, and it results from a complex process that is part of the weather cycle in the troposphere. The burning of fossil fuels spews sulfur dioxide and nitrogen oxides into the atmosphere. (The worst fossil fuel on this score is high-sulfur coal.) When water that has evaporated from the surface of the earth makes its way back as rain or snow, it meets these chemicals in the air, and one result of that meeting can be an acidic rain.

Ozone also plays a role in the formation of acid rain, even though ozone is quite scarce in the lower atmosphere. It can help transform nitrogen dioxide into nitric acid and sulfur dioxide into sulfuric acid. In addition, carbon dioxide, which is always present in the atmosphere, combines with water to form carbonic acid. Although this is a milder acid, it can erode silicate rocks, limestone and marble. Nitric acid and sulfuric acid are far more harmful to these stones.

Acid rain can be measured over time from ice cores and other sources, and the concentrations were increasing into the 1990s. Moreover, measures showed the greatest concentrations to be in densely populated regions, particularly near coal-burning plants.[4] Effluent from Midwestern United States manufacturing and power plants was carried by prevailing winds to Eastern regions, including the Adirondack Mountains and Canada. The distances over which effluents travel is greater when the offending smokestacks are higher, which is how they are often built to avoid complaints from residents who are nearby or to meet local air quality standards. The introduction in 1995 of pollution rights trading for the major causes of acid rain, such as sulphur dioxide and nitrous oxides, has brought an important reduction of the ingredients that form acid rain.

BOX 21.1 Acid Rain

Acid rain has destroyed aquatic life in hundreds of lakes in the Adirondack Mountains and in Ontario, Canada. Lakes that are naturally alkaline, perhaps from native limestone, can neutralize the acid and protect water life, but even these lakes suffer from extended exposure to acid rain. Lakes with sandy soil or igneous rocks, such as granite or quartz, offer no alkaline protection, and suffer immediately from deposits of acid rain. Besides its harm to aquatic life, acid rain reacts with metals in the soil to release metal ions that can be toxic to humans. Aluminum, lead, cadmium, manganese, nickel, mercury, and zinc are found in soil, and lead from drinking water pipes can also cause a problem. Acid rain upsets the balance of nature also by destroying algae in water, which is important to water life, and insects that play a role in maintaining the algae.

See L. B. Young, *Sowing the Wind*, New York: Prentice Hall, 1990.

---

[4] See Young (1990, n.1, p. 24).

Global Warming

Global warming is a more controversial environmental subject than acid rain, in part because long trends in global temperatures can run in different directions and so, on seeing a trend, it is difficult to infer cause and thus to predict future effects. Reliable temperature data began to be maintained in about 1850, at least for the northern hemisphere, and from this time until about 1940 the Earth's temperature tended to rise. As a result, glaciers retreated, growing seasons lengthened in northern regions, and seaports in such regions were open a greater part of the year. In the late 1940s, average temperatures turned colder, especially in northern regions where fluctuations in temperature tend to be greater, and in the 1970s scientists warned that a new ice age was coming.

Theories to explain global temperature change have been accepted by scientists for a long time. Several trace gases that are a small but important part of the atmosphere, such as carbon dioxide and methane, do not absorb energy flowing from the sun to the Earth as short-wave radiation, but they block it from traveling away from the Earth at long wavelengths. Indeed, they reradiate it back to Earth. The result is labeled a **greenhouse effect** because it acts like a greenhouse window, allowing energy to flow in freely but not out freely. The trace gases are called greenhouse gases, and they lead to global warming. Other air pollutants, however, can bring cooling. For instance, little particles in the atmosphere called particulate matter interfere with the sun's radiation reaching Earth and may have contributed to the Earth's cooling in the middle of the twentieth century. Although volcanic eruptions are a source of particulate matter, the largest share of it comes from industrial activity. Industrial activity can thus cause both warming and cooling of the Earth.

Temperatures began to rise after the 1970s, and the 1980s and 1990s represented the warmest decades of the twentieth century. Fears of global warming revived. Industrialization probably was not responsible for the warming trend from 1850 to 1940, because burning fossil fuels was not advanced enough to increase carbon dioxide and induce the greenhouse effect. From the 1950s to the 1980s, however, the concentration of carbon dioxide in the atmosphere increased by more than 10 percent. Because carbon dioxide can remain in the atmosphere a long time, continuation of such a trend is a serious cause for concern about future climate.

There is some evidence that growing seasons are getting longer, based on images from National Oceanic and Atmospheric Administration satellites that record plant photosynthesis.[5] The longer growing season is coming to the arctic and high northern latitudes, roughly north of a line through Boston, Massachusetts, in the United States and Bordeaux, in France. In this region over the last 10 years the spring thaw has moved earlier by about eight days, although there is very little effect over the same period in lower latitudes. This change adds to other evidence indicating a warming trend, even though more carbon may be taken up by vegetation over the longer growing season, which can help to moderate the trend.

---

[5] See Ranga Myneni, et al. (1997).

Signs of global warming are especially troublesome because they can increase in magnitude as they develop.[6] Scientists do not expect the favorable effects of warming that occurred until the 1940s to continue, and further warming can bring considerable harm as glaciers melt and ocean waters rise. Ice is definitely melting on land and that can raise the sea level, causing problems not only for low-lying countries such as Bangladesh but also for parts of Florida in the United States and for large coastal cities such as New York, London, or Hong Kong. As ice on land melts, the land reflects less heat than the ice did, and so the land absorbs more heat. If the ocean warms it will be able to absorb less carbon dioxide, while if the land warms it will release more carbon dioxide, which can only increase global warming. The melting of ice brings less salinity and can change the flow of the Gulf Stream, which currently moderates the climate of Europe and Scandinavia. Warming oceans can also make our weather more volatile and less hospitable, with greater variance in rainfall, more storms, and a gradual rise in hurricane intensity.[7]

An international organization called the Intergovernmental Panel on Climate Change (IPCC), sponsored by the United Nations and the World Meteorological Organization, has worked since 1988 to trace whether human activity has influenced the Earth's temperature. The organization's four reports have grown steadily stronger in supporting the connection between human activity and warming and most recently found the connection "very likely."[8] The most recent IPCC report estimates that without immediate aggressive measures to curb fossil fuel emissions global temperatures may rise up to 5 degrees C in the next century, with oceans rising one to two feet as a result. Other estimates put the possible rise in ocean levels quite a bit higher, so this is an externality that can have very serious consequences.

Irreversible Effects

An extra consideration is illustrated by greenhouse gasses; they can have **irreversible effects**. Effects are irreversible once the elements that cause them are already in the atmosphere and may continue to cause changes that are impossible to reverse. Some of the causes of global warming are long-lasting pollutants, such as carbon dioxide, which will have further effects for years even if we stop now the activities that produce them. Some of its consequences are melted glaciers that are difficult to replace. It may not be possible to restore some of the harms to vegetation and animal life that global warming can cause. In a case of irreversible harm, it is reasonable to control *possible* causes, even if we are not certain of their effects, because if they *are* the causes they will bring irreversible harm to the Earth's environment.

To put this threat of irreversible effects in economic terms, the British government analyzed the costs that global warming could inflict if no international action

---

[6] See "The Heat is On," *The Economist*, September 9–15, 2006, p. 4 of Special Report on Climate Change.

[7] See Andrew C. Revkin, "But Where Is It Going?," *New York Times*, Sept. 13, 2004.

[8] The most recent report, Fourth Assessment Report of the Intergovernmental Panel on Climate Change, is available at www.usgcrp.gov/usgcrp/links/ipcc.htm#4wg1. A further installment will examine consequences of expected global warming. See also Bill McKibbon, "Warning on Warming," *New York Review of Books*, March 15, 2007, pp. 44–45.

was taken to limit it.[9] The U.K.'s Government Economic Service issued a report in October 2006 estimating harm after 2050 that would equal the scale of damage from World War II, costing the world economy 5 to 20 percent of the world's gross domestic product.[10] Actions to limit global warming were estimated to cost much less, in the range of 1 percent of the 2050 world gross domestic product, if taken now to prevent the greatest harms. Needless to say, these consequences are hard to predict. The study did not analyze effects of the time-value of money, to find the difference between present value and future value. It treated the discount rate as zero, which makes future values appear larger than they would look with discounting. As a result, future benefits and costs appear larger than they should or as a positive discount rate would reveal them to be. The consequences are instructive nonetheless, as they dramatize the "act-now-or-act-later" choice.

Figure 21.1 illustrates the conclusion of the British Government Economic Service report. The vertical axis represents percentages of 2050 world GDP, and the horizontal axis represents time in years. If we begin now, the cost of moderating global warming is 1 percent of 2050 GDP. These are costs of altering energy sources or modifying methods of producing electricity and following conservation, reforestation, and other policies. As time passes these costs grow larger, though they can be estimated only over a wide range. In 2030, for instance, the costs would fall between 3 percent and 10 percent of 2050 world GDP, whereas in 2050 the costs would fall between 5 percent and 20 percent of 2050 GDP. They grow largely because the goal is to be reached in the latter half of the twenty-first century and having more time to do it makes it less costly.

Figure 21.1 *Costs of Global Warming Reduction, Based on the Year Started*

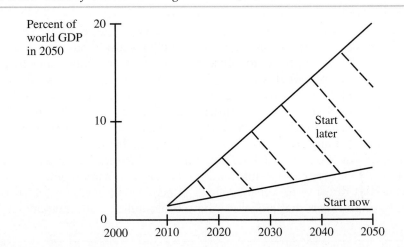

[9] See Andrew C. Revkin, "British Government Report Calls for Broad Effort on Climate Issues," *New York Times*, p. A15; Juliet Eilperin, "Warming Called Threat to Global Economy," *Washington Post*, October 31, 2006, p. A18; and Kevin Sullivan, "In Britain, All Parties Want to Color the Flag Green," *Washington Post*, October 30, 2006, p. A18.
[10] The Stern Report on the Economics of Climate Change is available at www.sternreview.org.uk.

Limiting global warming is extremely difficult, however. Not only do effluents that contain carbon dioxide last for years, but on average a large new electricity generating plant is being built somewhere in the world every week, many of them in China and India, and they will last 30 or 40 years. Expanding forests through reforestation can help to absorb carbon dioxide, but both reforestation and deforestation are occurring in the world.[11] New methods might capture carbon dioxide emissions from electricity generation before they reach the atmosphere and store them, either in the ground or at the bottom of an ocean. Power sources other than coal-fired generation might be developed also, but research on these matters has actually fallen in the last 30 years and will have to be increased substantially to produce solutions.[12]

The Problem Substances for Air

A range of substances contribute to air and water pollution. Table 21.1 shows trends in levels of concentration of some of the air pollutants as indicators of the quality of ambient, or surrounding, air. CFCs, which escape from refrigerants and solvents to harm the ozone layer, are not included in Table 21.1. In 1970, the concentration of CFCs in the atmosphere was about 1.6 parts per billion, rising to 2.5 in 1980 and then to 3.2 in 1990. Such a sharp increase, together with the growing ozone hole in Antarctica that CFCs would worsen, brought international attention and cooperation leading to the agreement reached in Montreal, Canada in 1988 called the Montreal Protocol. This agreement is phasing out the use of CFCs around the world.

Total suspended particulate matter in the air is often visible as soot or dust or smoke but is also formed in the atmosphere from sulfur dioxide and nitrous oxides. Particulate matter up to 10 micrometers in diameter, labeled **PM(10)**, is usually visible in the air. Fine particulate matter is 2.5 micrometers in diameter or less, labeled **PM(2.5)**, and is usually formed in the atmosphere, and fuel combustion in stationary

TABLE 21.1 Estimates of Ambient Air Quality in the United States

Year	PM(10)* ($\mu g/m^3$)	SO_2 (ppm [avg.])	NO_2 (ppm [avg.])	O_3 (ppm [1 hr.])	CO ($\mu g/m^3$)	Pb ($\mu g/m^3$)
1980	—	0.010	0.024	0.090	8.3	0.60
1990	30	0.008	0.022	0.087	6.0	0.08
2000	24	0.006	0.017	0.080	3.7	0.02

Source: EPA Latest Findings on National Air Quality: 2000 Status and Trends, available at www.epa.gov/otaq.
ppm = parts per million by volume; mg/m^3 = milligrams per cubic meter of air; $\mu g/m^3$ = micrograms per cubic meter of air.
*Smaller particulate matter (2.5 micrometers in diameter or smaller, labeled PM(2.5)) has not been monitored as long as PM(10), and its concentrations are observed regionally. The method of estimating smaller particulate matter changed in 1998, making comparisons difficult.

---

[11] Reforestation tends to rise with prosperity and is growing in India and Asia. Some biologically diverse forests, however, are being logged or burned, and tropical rain forests are declining.
[12] See Andrew C. Revkin, "Budgets Falling in Race to Fight Global Warming," *New York Times,* October 30, 2006, p. A1.

sources is a major source. Respiratory ailments plus poor visibility are consequences of particulate matter, but PM can also help to block harmful ultraviolet radiation. **Sulfur dioxide**, or **SO₂**, comes primarily from the combustion of fossil fuels, such as coal and oil, billowing into the air from smokestacks at stationary sources such as factories and electric power plants. In addition to its role in causing acid rain, SO_2 has also been associated with respiratory disease. **Nitrogen dioxide**, or **NO₂**, causes smog and can contribute to acid rain. It comes primarily from electric power plants and motor vehicles. Nitrogen dioxide belongs to a family of **nitrous oxides**, or **NOₓ**. All members of the family have similar effects, and they contribute to ground-level ozone.

Ground-level ozone (O₃) is formed in the presence of heat and sunlight from nitrous oxides and a variety of **volatile organic compounds (VOCs)**, which come from power plants, motor vehicles, chemical plants, refineries, factories, and other sources. Hospital admissions for respiratory problems, especially among children and the elderly, have been linked to high concentrations of ground-level ozone. Ozone also reduces growth and survival of plants and trees, and it can lower agricultural yields. **Carbon monoxide**, or **CO**, comes primarily from motor vehicle exhausts. It aggravates lung diseases, such as asthma or emphysema, and contributes to acid rain. **Lead (Pb)** can be inhaled or ingested in food. By accumulating in blood, bone, and soft tissues, it can harm the kidneys, liver, nervous system, or other organs. Reducing the content of lead additives in gasoline has reduced lead emissions dramatically, and it has cut back the amount of lead in the air.

Carbon dioxide and other trace gases such as methane contribute to global warming through their greenhouse effects.[13] Some argue that gases like methane be included in the Montreal Protocol. These gases would be easier to control that way than carbon dioxide, which plays a central part in worldwide plant-animal exchanges and results from burning fossil fuels.

There are more serious air pollutants that do not depend on complex chemical reactions but are dangerous in themselves. Currently 188 such substances are recognized, such as benzene, and they are called **hazardous air pollutants**. They come from many sources, and a small amount of them can do serious damage, so controlling them is both challenging and important.

Water and Land Pollution

Water pollution results from acid rain, but many other forms also occur in ground water and in the surface water of lakes and rivers. Some forms of water pollution can be changed by water, or is *degradable*, through a process that alters the waters ecology, while others are *nondegradable*. **Nondegradable pollutants**, such as cadmium, lead, mercury, polychlorinated biphenyls (PCBs), and DDT, are unchanged by water. They can be directly poisonous, and some of these water pollutants, such as DDT, can accumulate in animals high in nature's food chain and affect their reproduction.[14] Toxic chemicals pres-

---

[13] See Dickinson and Cicerone (1986).

[14] Rachel Carson's book, *Silent Spring* (1962), revealed the unseen—until then—side effects of DDT, and it moved citizens to support government efforts to protect the environment.

ent the most ominous danger to ground water. They include benzidine, PCBs, vinyl chloride, and DDT, which can cause cancer, neurological damage, and sterility. In the late 1970s, Love Canal in Niagara Falls, New York, which had been a dumping site for Hooker Chemicals and Plastics Corporation from 1947 to 1953, became a site for homes and a school. Residents complained of abnormal numbers of birth defects and cancers, and damage suits from Love Canal amounted to more than $3 billion.

In contrast to nondegradable pollutants, **degradable pollutants** are modified by water through chemical and biological processes. Even that cleansing process can be problematic, however. A side effect of the degradation that bacteria can accomplish in water is that it uses oxygen, which water life needs for survival. Degradable pollutants are measured, or graded, according to the oxygen needed to degrade them, which is called **biochemical oxygen demand (BOD)**. Animal wastes deposited in the Pagan River in Virginia from nearby meat processing plants, for example, had high BOD. Because of the amount of oxygen their degradation required, these animal wastes upset the local balance of nature and threatened some sensitive and immobile species, such as oysters. Indeed, the commercial taking of oysters in this area has almost vanished as a livelihood.

Pollution can also affect the value and usefulness of land. Acid rain harms land as well as water, for example, and disposal of toxic substances in land has caused illness and even death, as, for example, at Love Canal. Solid wastes, including scrapped appliances and automobiles, are lodged all around the country in what are called **landfills**, or disposal sites, which can adversely affect the land and its possible uses. Highway construction, strip-mining, and poor agricultural or forestry practices also can reduce the uses that land can offer. Ground-level ozone also affects agricultural yields from the land, because it can harm all forms of plants, trees, and vegetation.

Property rights to land are clearer than they are to air or water, because land is defined in units that can be owned and exchanged. So the externality problem might seem to be less serious. But air and water pollution, which are clear externalities, can affect the land. Rights to use land can be altered in unexpected ways to open possibilities for new external effects. For instance, a century ago some land owners sold coal-mining rights under their land, which would allow the digging of a mine by then existing methods. Today, giant mining machines bore subterranean caverns 40 stories

---

BOX 21.2 Oil on Alaska's Tundra

Very early one March morning in 2006, a British Petroleum (BP) oil worker discovered oil over roughly 2 acres of tundra near Alaska's Prudhoe Bay, caused by a small leak in an old pipe. It turned out that the pipe had been leaking five days without being discovered, releasing over 200,000 gallons of crude oil to form the largest oil spill ever on the North Slope of Alaska. Working in temperatures as low as 40 degrees below zero, cleanup crews hoped to save 90 percent of the oil. But the leak raised questions about the diligence of oil companies to protect the environment, just as Congress was considering expanded drilling for Alaskan oil.

See N. Thornburgh, "A Crude Warning," *Time Magazine*, March 20, 2006, p. 47.

below the surface of the Earth, and they disrupt the surface, causing damage to structures that the old methods would not have inflicted.[15] The sale and transfer of rights that did not anticipate these new technologies, and their effects can create legal difficulties today.

Thus, air, water, and land pollution are interrelated. Indeed, the **Environmental Protection Agency (EPA)** was created in part because separate agencies were thought unable to see and respond to these complex interrelationships.[16] Data collection alone has been a valuable product of environmental protection efforts, because it makes possible analysis of the effects that pollutants can have. Measurements indicate that efforts to harness pollutants have been worthwhile, although market methods now coming into use can elicit reductions at much lower cost. We next explore steps taken to protect the air, to be followed by those to protect water and land, but interconnections frequently arise.

21.2 | COMMAND-AND-CONTROL MEANS OF PROTECTING THE AIR

Largely because no one owns them, air and water are common properties, often regarded as free and available for all to use. Our use, however, can harm the air or water, as when we use them to dispose of a wide range of substances, like smoke from our chimneys or wastes from our factories. Like many other governments, that of the United States has taken action to prevent disposal into the air and water those substances that are toxic or otherwise dangerous and to control the disposal of less troublesome but still unwanted substances.

Congress passed the **Clean Air Act** in 1970 and added important **Clean Air Act Amendments** in 1977 and 1990. The Act established the EPA to control pollution by working with states in areas of air, water, toxic substances, noise, radiation, and solid waste. The general approach was to specify air quality standards as goals and to specify emission standards at the state level to meet them. Thus, although there would be national goals, their implementation could vary with the different conditions in different parts of the country.

Setting standards is a command-and-control approach that imposes rules rather than adjusting the perceived, or private, costs faced by polluters. Congress chose command-and-control methods in part because it wanted to control pollution quickly, and issuing orders was a direct way to do that. Alternatives such as effluent taxes or rights to pollute would require measures of effluent at each location, a task too extensive and time consuming for an impatient Congress. But as time has passed regulatory devices that rely on markets have come into use, and they have great efficiency advantages. This section explores both approaches, beginning with the standards approach and its command-and-control procedures.

---

[15] See Francis X. Clines, "A House is Braced for Underground Tunneling," *New York Times*, March 25, 2001, p. A14.

[16] A memo to President Nixon presenting this argument for a new agency can be seen at www.epa.gov/history/org. origins/ash.htm.

Beginning Air Pollution Regulation

The Clean Air Act's air quality standards took the form of upper limits to be set for crucial pollutants that circulated in the atmosphere. A set of other, less ubiquitous but more hazardous, pollutants were also identified and controlled more tightly. We begin with the path-breaking legislation that initiated serious federal environmental policy.

The Clean Air Act of 1970

Besides creating the EPA, the Clean Air Act required the establishment of **National Ambient Air Quality Standards (NAAQS)** to protect public health and public welfare. Once standards were available, the Act called for each state to develop a **State Implementation Plan (SIP)** for meeting those standards. The SIP would include **emission standards** as controls on sources of air pollution, and the standards had to be approved by the EPA. Under a framework that has air quality standards set on a national basis and emission standards set by states, the strictness of the emissions limitations can vary around the country depending on how polluted the air is.

The Act also imposed **New Source Performance Standards (NSPS)** on newly constructed sources of pollution, like new power plants. New plants were required to meet stringent pollution standards, while older plants were "grandfathered," or allowed to remain at their existing, often much higher, pollution levels. It was impossible politically to force owners of the old plants to meet standards that did not exist when the plants were built. When older plants retired the new-source emission standards would prevail. The new-source emission standards, however, were so strict that new plants were very costly to build so older plants were kept in service and became a serious pollution problem.

National Ambient Air Quality Standards for Criteria Pollutants

National ambient standards were defined for what are called **criteria air pollutants**: particulate matter, sulfur dioxide, nitrogen dioxide, carbon monoxide, ozone, and lead. These six criteria air pollutants are not dreadfully noxious substances, but they are common in the air and they can be harmful in many ways. In setting ambient standards for these criteria pollutants, Congress assumed that they cause a problem only when they reach a certain "threshold" level. The idea of an **air quality threshold** has been criticized because even low levels of pollution can be harmful, but the standards for criteria pollutants rest on it.

The ambient air quality standards are measured either as parts per million (ppm) by volume or as an amount by weight in a cubic meter of air (either milligrams per cubic meter, mg/m^3, or micrograms per cubic meter, $\mu g/m^3$). The standards also contain a time element, a period over which average levels are calculated, which can be annually, quarterly, over 24 hours, 8 hours, 3 hours, or 1 hour.[17] Sometimes the

---

[17] The EPA proposed the 8-hour standard for ozone, in addition to the 1-hour standard, in July, 1997, on grounds that health was affected by 8-hour concentrations. At the same time, a new standard for small particulates, those below 2.5 micrometers in diameter, was introduced (PM(2.5) in Table 21.2). Corporations and some states opposed the new standards in court, and the standards were not effective until supporting court decisions came in 2002. See Neely Tucker and Michael Grunwald, "U.S. Court Upholds Pollution Standards," *Washington Post*, March 27, 2002, p. A1.

standards are set for two time periods, such as an average over a year and an average over 24-hours, thus allowing a higher average level of the pollutant for a short time period and a lower average level over a longer time period.

The allowable limits or standards for the appropriate time periods are of two kinds, called primary and secondary, to serve two purposes. **Primary standards** are intended to protect public health, including especially those in greatest need, such as asthmatics, children, and the elderly. **Secondary standards** are intended to protect public welfare, including good visibility and protection of crops, vegetation, and buildings. Different primary and secondary standards were set only for sulphur dioxide, and in the case of carbon monoxide no secondary standard exists. The air quality standards for criteria pollutants are summarized in Appendix 21.1.

In October, 1997, the EPA proposed two new elements for the national ambient air quality standards aimed at smog and related respiratory problems. Industry representatives opposed the standards, which an appeals court decision finally made effective in 2002 after a lengthy court battle.[18] The first of the two new elements involves smaller particulates (called "fine" particles because they are only 2.5 micrometers in diameter). A number of studies linked them to more serious respiratory problems than larger particulates.[19] As Table 21.2 shows, compared with the 10-micrometer particles, those 2.5 micrometers in diameter have a more demanding annual-average standard of only 15 $\mu g/m^3$ rather than 50 $\mu g/m^3$, and a more demanding 24-hour average of 65 $\mu g/m^3$ rather than 150 $\mu g/m^3$. The second new standard involves ground-level ozone. As Table 21.2 indicates, it is now held to an 8-hour standard of 0.08 ppm, as well as the older 1-hour standard of 0.12 ppm. Motor vehicles as well as factories and power plants contribute both to the particulates in the atmosphere and to ground-level ozone.

Hazardous Air Pollutants

The EPA identifies more noxious substances than the six criteria pollutants as hazardous air pollutants; they are called **toxic air pollutants**, or "air toxics." These pollutants are deemed too dangerous for the threshold criterion to be used. They can cause cancer, for example, or birth defects. The EPA sets emission standards directly for 188 hazardous air pollutants, and the standards are to protect public health with "an ample margin of safety." These hazardous air pollutants include, for example, benzene, which is in gasoline, and methylene chloride, a solvent and paint stripper. A complete accounting of emissions for all 188 toxic pollutants is not available, but many measures exist. For example, measures of benzene emissions from 87 urban monitoring sites—where emissions tend to be greatest—indicate a decline of 40 percent from 1994 to 1999 (from 3.1 to 1.9 micrograms per cubic meter of air). But these air toxics are numerous, they can arise from many sources, and small amounts can be very

---

[18] See *American Trucking Associations, Inc., et al. v. Environmental Protection Agency,* 283 F3rd 355, March 26, 2002. See also Neely Tucker and Michael Grunwald, "U.S. Court Upholds Pollution Standards," *Washington Post,* March 27, 2002, p. A1.

[19] For illustrations of effects see Andrew C. Revkin, "E.P.A. Finds Some Soot Is Bad, Other Soot Is Worse," *New York Times,* September 11, 2001, p. D1.

TABLE 21.2 National Ambient Air Quality Standards for Fine Particulates and Ozone

Pollutant	Time Period	Primary Standard	Secondary Standard
Particulate Matter			
PM(10)	Annual average	50 μg/m^3	50 μg/m^3
	24-hr. average	150 μg/m^3	150 μg/m^3
PM(2.5)	Annual average	15 μg/m^3	15 μg/m^3
	24-hr. average	65 μg/m^3	65 μg/m^3
Ozone			
O$_3$	1-hr. average	0.12 ppm (235 μg/m^3)	0.12 ppm (235 μg/m^3)
	8-hr. average	0.08 ppm (157 μg/m^3)	0.08 ppm (157 μg/m^3)

Source: National Ambient Air Quality Standards, Environmental Protection Agency, http://www.epa.gov/airs/criteria.html. ppm = parts per million by volume; mg/m^3 = milligrams per cubic meter of air; μg/m^3 = micrograms per cubic meter of air.

harmful, so adequately controlling them is more difficult than controlling the criteria pollutants.

An important device in the control of toxic air pollutants is called the Toxics Release Inventory (TRI). The TRI program requires facilities that meet certain size and emission thresholds to report in a routine and standardized way their annual releases of toxic air pollutants. The report of releases brings firms unwanted public attention, which in turn motivates them to reduce the emissions.[20] At the time it was legislated, the TRI was seen as a possibly foolish effort by Congress to do something visible after a tragic toxic release in Bhopal, India killed thousands of people. Yet by bringing attention to polluters, the law is credited with reducing releases of toxic pollutants, and the general idea of using publicity in such ways is winning support.

The Clean Air Act Amendments of 1977

It was obvious by 1975 that many states would not meet ambient air quality standards by the deadlines set in the Clean Air Act. Political problems developed as the command-and-control policies began to have effect. Congress added amendments to the Act in 1977 to extend deadlines and to deal with three major political problems.

One problem stemmed from the different standard for new versus old plants. High emission levels from grandfathered old plants made attainment of the air quality standards difficult. Harsh emission limits for new plants essentially made the old plants more valuable, and owners of these dirty old plants kept them in service longer. The second problem was that some areas, particularly western states that had access to low-sulphur coal, were meeting the ambient air quality standards easily, and

---

[20] For description of the TRI program and its effects, see Karkkainen (2001).

environmentalists wanted to prevent having them deteriorate to the levels of the standards. The third problem arose because producers of high-sulphur coal wanted scrubber technology mandated to clean the polluting sulphur from the coal as it went up smokestacks, even though that was more costly than using low-sulphur coal. If effluent was cleaned in the smokestack, the sulphur content in the coal would not matter much and high-sulphur coal could still have a market. This set of differences hints at how regions of the country could hold different views about command-and-control rules for air pollution.

The political problems were interrelated. Old power plants were concentrated in states like Ohio, Indiana, Illinois, and Missouri. Some states produced coal that was high in sulphur content (Kentucky, Pennsylvania, West Virginia), and some produced coal that was low in sulphur content (Colorado, Montana, Wyoming). Some states imported coal (North Carolina), and some exported coal (Kentucky, Pennsylvania, West Virginia). Some states imported power (Idaho), and some exported power (Washington, Wyoming). Some states were growing rapidly and needed energy (California, Louisiana, Texas), and some were declining in industrial activity (Ohio, Illinois, Indiana). These and other differences in position made political negotiation difficult, and yet agreement was needed to impose command-and-control rules.

The Clean Air Act Amendments of 1977 benefitted the producers of high-sulphur coal by mandating **scrubber technology** in electricity generation to remove pollutants from effluent as it went up a smokestack. Without this provision, eastern and midwestern producers of high-sulphur coal would have suffered, because low-sulphur coal would be the low-cost way to meet the emissions standard for sulfur dioxide, and demand for high-sulphur coal would fall. But the areas that produced high-sulphur coal had enough votes in Congress to make the use of scrubber technology mandatory.[21]

To overcome environmentalists' concern about air quality deteriorating in areas where it exceeded the ambient air quality standards, the 1977 Amendments placed limits on allowable deterioration. The 1977 Amendments labeled areas where standards are met **attainment areas,** and they divided them into three classes:

I—Areas where essentially no deterioration is permitted, such as national parks,

II—Areas where moderate deterioration is permitted (vast majority of country), and

III—Areas where deterioration to the threshold level is allowed.

The Amendments designated areas where national ambient standards are *not* attained as **nonattainment areas**. In such areas, guidelines for states called for more stringent emission standards for new sources and even urged "reasonably available control measures" for old sources. This policy discouraged expansion in nonattainment areas, because building new plants called for reducing pollution at other locations so the degree of nonattainment would not grow worse. Old plants were kept in service, and no solution was found to the problem they caused.

---

[21] See Ackerman and Hassler (1981) and Crandall (1984).

Setting and Implementing Emission Standards for Air

After ambient air quality standards were agreed upon came the crucial step of imposing Emission Standards for Air on specific sources of pollution. Because the problems of dealing with stationary and mobile sources differ, a distinction is made between (1) **stationary sources**, such as electricity generating plants, and (2) **mobile sources**, such as automobiles. For stationary sources, the Clean Air Act Amendments of 1977 distinguished between attainment areas, where quality standards were met, and nonattainment areas, which faced stricter emission standards. Stationary sources are granted permits by the states, while mobile sources are controlled by the EPA.

Stationary Sources of Air Pollution

State environmental protection agencies are responsible for setting and enforcing emission standards for stationary sources of air pollution. The state agencies issue **permits** to sources, such as electricity generating plants, and they dictate methods to contain pollution within the allowed emission standards. In setting emission standards for stationary sources, states follow guidelines from the 1977 Amendments, which distinguish whether the ambient air quality standards are being attained in the area. They also consider whether the source is old or newly built. Table 21.3 summarizes these guidelines.

In attainment areas, there is no requirement to make changes to old sources unless the source is modified so much it becomes a new source. Whether an old source is changed into a new source is a contentious issue that led to constant wrangling between companies and the EPA. New sources must use the best control technology available to achieve the maximum reduction, but cost can be considered, and that puts some limit on the scope of the antipollution effort. The EPA retains authority to set NSPS for certain new sources, such as coal-burning electricity generating plants. These standards are demanding, and they compare to state guidelines for new sources in nonattainment areas.

In nonattainment areas, the state authorities usually choose a percentage-reduction target to reach attainment, and they pursue it by the policies they follow for specific categories of sources. These policies can also be complicated by changes in federal requirements. In 1997, for example, the EPA proposed large new reductions in

TABLE 21.3 Guidelines for State Emission Standards

	Old Sources	New Sources
Attainment areas	No alternative required	Use "best available control technology for maximum degree of pollution reduction achievable, taking into account cost"
Nonattainment areas	Use "reasonably available control measures"	Use technology with "lowest achievable emission rate" plus an offset from old sources, considering cost

nitrogen oxide emissions in 22 eastern and midwestern states, effectively making more areas into nonattainment areas. It came partly in response to international pressure to reduce pollution and partly from complaints in affected areas. The goal of the proposal is to reduce emissions from power plants and factories where prevailing winds can bring emissions to other states and regions. That is the reason the largest reductions—roughly in the 40 percent range—would be required of Ohio, Indiana, Missouri, Kentucky, West Virginia, and Illinois. The EPA urged the states to focus on electric utilities, which produce the most ozone-and-acid-rain-causing nitrogen oxides, and to accomplish the reductions through a market trading system.

California officials agreed in 2006 to cut carbon dioxide emissions 25 percent by 2020, with strict controls taking effect in 2012.[22] Global warming is a concern in California, where a long coastline is vulnerable to a rise in sea level and where drinking water comes from the Sierra-Nevada snow pack, which may decline as much as 30 percent in the next century if no action is taken. Any one state faces difficulties in imposing strict limits by itself, because it might send producers to more lenient states, but California is attempting action in the absence of greater federal effort and a handful of other states are taking similar, but smaller, steps.

Enforcement Stationary sources need federal permits to operate, and the EPA and state and local agencies share responsibility for "permitting" these emission sources. The permit allows operation with certain technology that can meet specified emission limits. State and local authorities, who inspect sources and test smokestacks, carry out most monitoring. The EPA inspects a small portion of major sources annually. Remedies for stationary sources that violate standards begin with the **notice of violation**, which the EPA issues as a warning, and extend to civil and criminal penalties that may be imposed.

Mobile Sources of Air Pollution

Mobile sources of air pollution, primarily motor vehicles, account for about 40 percent of oil consumption and nearly one-third of all air pollution in the United States. Mobile sources are regulated federally, and their manufacturers must satisfy EPA

BOX 21.3 A Merger Solution for Externality

An unusual way to satisfy pollution requirements was avoided in one case by adoption of a strategy that is similar to the merger solution, which internalizes the external effect by changing ownership. In the spring of 2002, American Electric Power bought the small Midwestern town of Chesire, Ohio. The company destroyed most of the buildings in the town, and made the town part of the power plant, thereby avoiding obligations to residents and others who had sold and moved from the town.

See A. Goodheart, "Something in the Air," *The New York Times Magazine,* February 8, 2004, pp. 38–47.

---

[22] See Felicity Barringer, "Officials Reach California Deal to Cut Emissions," *New York Times,* August 31, 2006, p. A1; and Jad Mouawad and Jeremy Peters, "California Plan to Cut Gases Splits Industry," *New York Times,* September 1, 2006, p. C1.

standards that vary by type of vehicle and by model year. The motor vehicle emission standards are expressed in grams of pollutant allowed per mile. As of 2006, for example, during the first 5 years or 50,000 miles of a passenger car's life, the limit is 3.4 grams per mile of carbon monoxide and 1.0 gram per mile of nitrogen oxides.[23] Because California imposed emission standards on vehicles before the federal government did, it still sets separate regulations, which are slightly more demanding than federal requirements. Table 21.4 presents estimates of major air pollution emissions from mobile sources and shows a marked decline since 1970.

Light trucks, including minivans and sport utility vehicles (SUVs), have faced easier emission standards than automobiles for years. When they weigh more than 3,750 pounds, but less than 5,750 pounds, the standards have allowed such vehicles to release pollutants in amounts roughly 30 percent higher than passenger cars. This easier standard allows greater size and power in vehicles that qualify as light trucks, and it favors U.S. manufacturers who tend to be large producers of light trucks.

In 1975, Congress also imposed gasoline mileage standards on motor vehicles, requiring each automobile manufacturer's entire fleet of produced cars to satisfy **Corporate Average Fuel Economy (CAFE)** standards. The CAFE standards set a miles-per-gallon for a manufacturer's entire fleet of produced vehicles, and companies that fail to meet the CAFE standards must pay fines or penalties. Fines of $5 per tenth-of-a-mile per-gallon, per-vehicle produced, are charged by the **National Highway Traffic Safety Administration (NHTSA)** on amounts by which the CAFE standards are not met. The design of the CAFE standards makes payments in the

TABLE 21.4 **Estimates of Air Pollutant Emissions from Mobile Sources in the United States (Millions of Metric Tons per Year)**

Year	PM(10)	SO_2	NO_x	CO	Lead
1970	12.2	31.2	26.9	197.3	0.221
1975	7.0	28.0	26.4	184.0	0.160
1980	6.2	25.9	27.1	177.8	0.074
1985	3.6	23.3	25.8	169.6	0.022
1990	3.2	23.1	25.2	143.6	0.005
1995	3.1	18.6	24.7	120.0	0.004
2000	2.3	16.3	22.3	102.4	0.003
2005	2.0	15.0	19.0	89.0	0.003

Source: Environmental Protection Agency, www.epa.gov/airtrends.

---

[23] See www.epa.gov/otaq.

BOX 21.4 The CAFE Standards

Passenger cars are currently required to achieve 27.5 miles per gallon on average, while light trucks, including minivans and SUVs, have been held to a roughly 22 percent lower standard of only 21.6 miles per gallon. That mileage standard for light trucks will rise gradually to 24 miles per gallon in 2011, when more categories of vehicles—up to six—will be introduced, based in part on how far apart the vehicle's wheels are. Mileage standards will also extend to larger vehicles, up to 10,000 pounds. The standards will apply separately to each category of vehicle, and fleet wide averages will no longer be applied. Certifying that vehicles meet these standards is done under ideal conditions. In actual performance, the EPA estimates that miles per gallon are 10 to 15 percent lower than the certified level.

See M. L. Wald, "U.S. Raises Standards in Mileage," *New York Times*, March 30, 2006, p. B1.

United States come largely from foreign producers.[24] The standard for a motor vehicle manufacturer is a weighted average of the mixture of vehicles in the fleet it produces.

The CAFE standards have not been successful. When the CAFE mileage standards distinguished between automobiles and light trucks, they invited manufacturers to produce more of the least demanding, or least fuel efficient, type of vehicle, the light truck. Auto companies expanded the form of light trucks into minivans and SUVs, which were popular with consumers who would not have purchased trucks, so vehicles that were less fuel efficient were produced in greater numbers.[25] Primarily as a consequence of this increasing number of light trucks, the average fuel economy of all new vehicles in 2002 was the lowest it had been since 1981.[26]

In addition to using fuel, motor vehicles also cause excessive highway traffic congestion and vehicle crashes, both of which are external costs of highway travel. By raising the private cost of vehicle use and fuel consumption, a fuel tax would reduce the externality more efficiently than the CAFE program. Indeed, making CAFE standards more restrictive than their present levels could worsen the efficiency of highway travel, for although such standards force better mileage, it is estimated that improved mileage under the restrictive CAFE standards encourages more driving and, thus, raises externality costs.[27] To reduce the externality costs to an efficient level would require a fuel tax of about $1.75 per gallon or perhaps a tax of $1.50 a gallon together with a modest CAFE program.[28]

---

[24] In 2005, BMW ($12 million), Daimler-Chrysler ($8.5 million), Volkswagen ($3.5 million), Porsche ($3.2 million) and Ferrari-Maserati ($1.5 million) paid the largest fines. See Jeff Plungis, "MPG Violations Cost Carmakers," *Detroit News*, January 6, 2006, p. 1.

[25] See Danny Hakim, "The Station Wagon Is Back, But Not as a Car," *New York Times*, March 19, 2002, p. A1.

[26] See Danny Hakim, "Fuel Economy Hit 22-Year Low," *New York Times*, May 3, 2003, p. B1.

[27] For analysis of this possibility following from the tighter standard for light trucks (from 20.7 to 22.2 MPG) effective in 2007, see Lutter and Kravitz (2003). They put the marginal externality costs at 10.4 cents per mile. More general analysis of such effects of the CAFE standards is provided in Kleit (2003), who finds that the CAFE standards impose pollution, congestion, and crash costs totaling about 70 to 78 cents for every gallon of gas saved.

[28] These estimates are drawn from Gerard and Lave (2003).

Gasoline and automobile companies have successfully resisted higher fuel taxes more effectively in the United States, where taxes averaged $0.40 per gallon in 2006, than in other countries like the United Kingdom, where at the same time taxes were 10 times as great, at more than $4 per gallon (Germany, France, and Italy have tax levels not far below the United Kingdom).[29] Without a high tax on fuel to reflect at least the negative externalities it produces, using fuel in motor vehicles is cheap. This can motivate consumers to buy larger and less fuel efficient vehicles. Even when market prices for fuel rise, motor vehicle purchasers do not choose vehicles as small as they would choose under a $4 per gallon fuel tax. By distinguishing between cars and light trucks, the CAFE standards also distort the mix of vehicles from an efficient one.

Enforcement For mobile sources, such as automobiles, manufacturers are subject to **certification** requirements. A prototype of each automobile model is tested by the EPA, and only if it meets emission requirements for its year and type (and thus is certified) can it be sold to the public. Later monitoring includes assembly-line testing in automobile factories and testing of cars on the road by states (the emission standards are to be satisfied by a vehicle for its first 5 years or 50,000 miles). For vehicles that fail to meet emission standards there are several remedies. The most mild is a notice of violation, which is like a warning. A vehicle model may be recalled for correction of a problem, and civil penalties such as fines may be imposed for repeated failure. In extreme cases, criminal penalties are possible. Fines are the main penalties imposed for failure to meet gasoline mileage standards. Notice that it is

---

BOX 21.5 "Chicken-and-Egg" Problems for the Fuel-Cell Car

If and when a fuel cell can economically power a motor vehicle with no air pollution, it will need to have fuel conveniently available. Developing a nationwide network of 10,000 or more pumps that can deliver the needed hydrogen to fuel-cell vehicles is an ambitious task. To get such development started, in the early 1990s California required that, by 2003, 10 percent of cars sold there be emission free. It modified the requirement in 2001 to lower targets and allow a wider range of vehicles to qualify including hybrids that are not entirely emission free (called low-emission vehicles or LEVs). California abandoned the zero-emissions requirement entirely in 2003 after auto companies and even the Bush administration sued to prevent its adoption. Nevertheless, some other states, including New York, Massachusetts, and New Jersey, have adopted or are considering similar laws. Movement toward a serious reduction in air pollution from motor vehicles may thus be induced more by state government actions than by the federal government, despite the problems individual states face when imposing restrictions by themselves.

See A. Appelbaum, "Ulterior Motors," *The New York Times Magazine*, December 10, 2000, p. 64.

---

[29] See Daniel Gross, "Raise the Gasoline Tax? Funny, It Doesn't Sound Republican," *New York Times*, October 8, 2006, Sec. 3, p. 3.

manufacturers rather than the consumers who face the brunt of this mileage regulation, although many states test privately owned vehicles to insure that emission limits are not exceeded.

International Agreements to Combat Global Warming

Because pollution, especially air pollution, is a global problem, it has become the focus of international efforts. Early international efforts used command-and-control methods. An example is the Montreal Protocol, which scheduled the end of the use of CFCs by the many signatory nations. Substitutes, which are sometimes more expensive, will replace CFCs, and scientists expect that by 2050 the concentration will be so low that the hole in the ozone layer over Antarctica will no longer occur.

A major international agreement on intentions was reached in South America in 1992 that focused on world pollution. An ensuing conference was held in 1997 in Kyoto, Japan, with the aim of taking action to restrain global warming. Although negotiations had been actively conducted for two years before this meeting, reaching agreement—primarily on emission of greenhouse gasses like carbon dioxide—was difficult.

A compromise was finally reached in July of 2001 by 178 nations, but in milder form than originally intended and without the United States, where the Bush administration did not support it.[30] Almost all nations except the United States ratified the agreement, and it became effective in February, 2005. The agreement frees developing countries from pollution reduction goals and provides funds to help them acquire technologies to deal with effluents. It calls on the 38 participating industrialized countries to cut emissions of greenhouse gases, principally carbon dioxide, to a level that is 5.2 percent below 1990 levels by 2012, or delinquent countries will face harsher emissions goals. Although expressed primarily in the form of goals, this substantial cooperative international effort is regarded as a success, despite the lack of participation by the United States.[31]

An important element of this Kyoto plan is the possibility of international trading in pollution, or emission, rights. Participating nations included the outline of an international pollution-rights trading system as part of their agreement. The European Union operates an Emissions Trading Scheme (EU ETS) that is similar to the U.S. system, but it differs in a number of details, in part because the European Union is an organization of separate countries. Where it can function, pollution-rights trading has been found efficient as a way to reduce polluting emissions, as the program to reduce acid rain in the United States shows.

---

[30] See Andrew C. Revkin, "178 Nations Reach a Climate Accord; U.S. Only Looks On," *New York Times*, July 24, 2001, p. A1.

[31] There are some nonfederal efforts in the United States. California and Oregon are attempting to reduce carbon emissions in the spirit of the Kyoto agreement, as is the city of Boulder, Colorado, which has imposed a "carbon tax" on electricity to reduce pollution. See Katie Kelley, "City Approves 'Carbon Tax' in Effort to Reduce Gas Emissions," *New York Times*, November 18, 2006, p. C1.

21.3 POLLUTION-RIGHT MEANS OF PROTECTING THE AIR

When provisions of the Clean Air Act were implemented, efforts to comply with them were costly. Command-and-control methods focus on average effects. The Act ordered the same technologies to be used everywhere, even though some firms could reduce pollution more easily or more efficiently than others. If rights to emit pollutants are defined, a market value for those rights can be determined, and once such a price is attached to the right to pollute that can create incentives to reduce pollution. Then firms that can reduce pollution most efficiently are motivated to do it because the alternative is to buy costly pollution rights. Pollution taxes could induce the same incentives, but they would differ in their income distribution effects. That is where pollution trading offered special advantages.

Trading Pollution Rights to Combat Acid Rain

Considerable improvement in air quality had been achieved by 1985. In that year, however, power plants that did not meet the 1971 NSPSs were generating 83 percent of power-plant sulphur dioxide emissions.[32] By 1985 it was obvious that old generating plants were being kept in service longer, and fewer new plants were being built because of the strict NSPSs. This bias against new plants from the NSPSs was so evident it was even labeled the "**new-source bias**," and it embodied the persistent political problem of reigning in pollution from grandfathered old plants. In any case, in the 1980s electricity generation using coal was a dominant contributor to sulphur dioxide emissions, which in turn was a major cause of acid rain.

Early Forms

We first note rudimentary forms of exchange that foreshadowed genuine pollution-rights trading. The EPA introduced a practice called **netting** in 1974 to allow a firm creating a new emissions source within a plant to reduce emissions from another source to prevent *net* emissions from increasing significantly. Because the exchange among emission sources is within the firm, netting was also called **internal trading**. In nonattainment areas, a practice similar to netting has been followed since 1977. To create a new source in a nonattainment area, a larger reduction in emissions, called an **offset**, must be obtained from already existing sources. This policy of netting allows the construction of new sources that would otherwise be banned in nonattainment areas. If an offset is negotiated with another firm, that would involve **external trading**.

In 1979, the EPA introduced **bubbles** to apply to existing sources rather than new sources. A firm could sum the emission limits for individual sources of pollutants in a plant to determine an aggregate limit for a large "bubble" area surrounding that plant. The firm could then adjust the different sources to meet the aggregate emissions level in the most efficient way. This policy allows a firm to meet the *aggregate*

---

[32] See Ellerman, et al. (2000).

emission limit by using its knowledge of pollution control methods to minimize its cost. In conjunction with the bubble policy, the EPA allowed **banking**, so firms could save credits for their emissions reductions to be used in future emissions trading. The EPA left development of rules and administration of banking programs to the states, subject to EPA guidelines.

Since they were introduced, bubbles and offsets are estimated to have saved compliance costs without any decline in air quality.[33] Netting, which is the most commonly used market-like device, is estimated to have worsened air quality slightly but to have generated substantial savings in compliance costs. Banking has provided little cost savings but has afforded a very slight improvement in air quality.

Through the 1980s, acid rain was a growing problem, causing especially serious harm to lakes and streams in New England and eastern Canada, where the government objected formally to pollutants crossing the border. Changes in political leadership in the United States toward the end of the 1980s also brought more attention to environmental policy. So efforts intensified to solve the very great political problem of reaching agreement on how to reduce industrial emissions. Because it was the dominant source of sulphur dioxide emissions in the United States, efforts to control acid rain focused on the electric power industry.

The Clean Air Act Amendments of 1990

The 1990 Amendments to the Clean Air Act included an attack on acid rain through pollution-rights trading. All electricity generating plants together produced about 70 percent of U.S. sulphur dioxide emissions in 1985, and of that amount over 95 percent came from the use of coal. So coal-burning electricity generators were a special target for attention, and the new-source bias was a large part of the problem. A market-based plan for reducing these emissions emerged from several sources.[34] Although EPA staff and others had opposed market-based methods, no other means of restricting old plants was feasible politically.

The market-based plan that emerged for sulphur dioxide emissions is called a **"cap-and-trade"** plan, because it puts a limit, or a cap, on total emissions, allocates among plants these rights to emit effluent, and then lets the plants trade the pollution rights among themselves. Controls of a more traditional kind on nitrous oxides were included in the effort against acid rain, but eventually rights to emit nitrous oxides came to be traded.

Now note how the cap-and-trade market institution can overcome the enormous political problem of old dirty plants that NSPSs caused. Instead of merely exempting old plants, a cap-and-trade program can extend large pollution allowances to them. This gives their owners incentive to reduce pollution to save their pollution allowances, so they can sell them. Thus, for the first time under the Clean Air Act, the owners of old plants could now decide to reduce emissions in response to market incentives.[35]

---

[33] See Hahn and Hester (1987).

[34] See Ellerman, et al. (2000, Ch. 2).

[35] Political influences resulted in a program of bonus allowances for installing scrubber technology to help producers of high-sulphur coal; nevertheless, the cap-and-trade program was a revolutionary use of market forces to reduce pollution efficiently.

The Clean Air Act Amendments of 1990 first required all electricity generating units to install **continuous-emission-monitoring equipment**, which reliably assessed the emissions of plants and thereby determine the pollution rights they would have to submit. Rights to release emissions were called **allowances**, and they were introduced in two phases. Phase I involved the largest and "dirtiest" electricity generating plants. It began in 1995 for sulfur dioxide and lasted until 1999. Phase II extended the use of allowances to all electricity generating plants for 2000 to 2009. Slightly simpler allocation rules take effect for 2010 and beyond. Generating units have 30 days after the end of each calendar year to deliver to the EPA enough allowances to cover their emissions for the previous year. Pollution allowances can be banked, for use in later years, but not borrowed from the future for current use. Phase I focused on the 263 most polluting units in 110 generating plants in the country. The goal of Phase I was to bring early relief by attacking the "dirtiest" plants and, at the same time, to establish the market for trading allowances.

Marketable rights to pollute allow the establishment of an enforceable goal for emissions. Once a level of emissions is chosen, enough allowances can be distributed to permit only that level of emissions. If the allowable level of emissions is not very restrictive, the price of allowances is low; if the level is strict, the price of allowances is high. The higher the price of allowances, the more firms are willing to spend to reduce emissions. Ideally this value of allowances can be brought into line with the social cost of the emissions. Once a level of emissions is chosen, some means of distributing, or allocating, the allowances is needed.

We have seen that giving more allowances to old plants offered the great advantage of motivating emission reductions in the most polluting plants, while also being politically acceptable. In principle, the government might have sold the allowances, which would impose large dollar costs on all electricity generators[36] and would have punished the old plants especially. Forcing them to buy many allowances was probably as unacceptable politically as requiring retrofitting to reduce pollution at old facilities or of imposing taxes on pollution. The allowances might also have been distributed in equal amounts per unit of output of the plants, which would have immediately forced on older plants the purchase of many allowances because they had higher than average pollution rates per unit of output.

The EPA actually distributed pollution allowances free to plants in accordance with base-line heat input, or fuel use, levels, roughly from averages for the 1985 to 1987 period. Plants that burned more fuel produced more pollution and, thus, started off with more allowances. This allocation is fair in the sense that it does not burden old plants with newly imposed rules. In time the trading of pollution rights invites all plants to consider the social value of reducing emissions, which is revealed through the market price of emissions, so a gradual movement to efficient emission control can be expected. Although old plants now faced controls they had previously escaped, their high pollution levels were accepted as benchmarks. Here was the great political advantage of a market-based solution. It allowed pollution controls to be

---

[36] See Van Dyke (1991) for support of this position.

imposed without greatly disadvantaging the older, "dirtier" plants that had been built under old rules, and yet at the same time it motivated those plants to restrain their pollution.

Effects of Trading Pollution Allowances

Before examining effects of trading pollution allowances, we need to understand the indirect role of railroad deregulation in reducing sulfur dioxide emissions, to keep that effect separate from the effect of the cap-and-trade program.[37]

The Effect of Railroad Deregulation

Low-sulphur coal is produced in Montana and Wyoming—an area called the Powder River Basin (PRB)—at lower cost than that of producing high-sulphur coal in the Midwest. But because transportation of coal was expensive and could be a large fraction of its final cost if the coal traveled far, this low-cost, low-sulphur coal was burned close to the Powder River Basin, where pollution levels were low.

The Staggers Act, which brought railroad deregulation, removed restrictions that had prevented competition on railroad routes out of the PRB, where Burlington Northern effectively had held a monopoly. From 1979 to 1993, competition from the Union Pacific Railroad cut in half the railroad rates for coal going out of the PRB. This lower transportation cost extended substantially the range over which it was economical to move low-sulphur coal, and it went as far as the Midwest where it helped to lower sulfur dioxide emissions. The PRB Abatement row of Table 21.5 shows the effect that Powder-River-Basin coal had and allows that to be kept separate from effects of tradeable emission allowances.[38]

TABLE 21.5 Sulfur Dioxide Emissions from Phase I Generating Units
(in Thousands of Short Tons Each Year)

	1991	1992	1993	1994	1995	1996	1997
Actual Emissions	9,585	9,206	8,615	8,415	5,383	5,681	5,628
PRB Abatement	1,231	1,436	1,641	1,846	2,051	2,256	2,462
Phase I Abatement	0	50	398	537	4,153	3,791	3,955
Combined Total	10,816	10,892	10,644	10,798	11,587	11,728	12,045

Source: A. D. Ellerman, P. L. Joskow, R. Schmalensee, J-P. Montero, and E. M. Bailey, *Markets for Clean Air: The U.S. Acid Rain Program*, Cambridge: Cambridge University Press, 2000.

[37] For analysis of this effect of railroad deregulation on delivered low-sulphur coal prices, see Ellerman et al. (2000, pp. 80–105).

[38] Ellerman et al. (2000) carried out separate estimation of the effect on Powder River Basin coal use from railroad deregulation.

The Trading of Allowances

Phase I in the cap-and-trade program of trading allowances to emit sulfur dioxide worked smoothly, and as Table 21.5 shows it led to a substantial reduction in sulfur dioxide emissions. At the end of each year, every unit subject to allowance requirements surrendered allowances to cover its emissions on time. Indeed, in the aggregate there was over-compliance, as emissions were lower than allowed by the allowances issued. Some allowances were being banked for use in future years, probably because Phase II requirements would be stricter so allowances in that period were expected to be more expensive. Table 21.6 shows the sulfur dioxide emissions for various types of coal used in electricity generation.

As Table 21.6 shows, in 1995 when Phase I began, total sulfur dioxide emissions from all coal used in making electricity was 11,603 thousand short tons, about 2,700 thousand short tons lower than the 14,313 thousand level of 1994. The total level of emissions was not very much higher in 1999. Much of this reduction in sulfur dioxide emissions starting in 1995 came from the large, high-emission units that were required to submit allowances in Phase I, as shown in Table 21.5. Actual emissions from units included in Phase I had emissions of 8,415 in 1994, and that level dropped to 5,383 in 1995, roughly 3,000 thousand short tons lower. Thus, the considerable reduction in emissions in 1995 can be traced to implementation of Phase I of the allowances trading program. Table 21.7 shows evidence of sulfur dioxide emissions

TABLE 21.6 Sulfur Dioxide Emissions from Electricity Generation (in Thousands of Short Tons Each Year)

Coal Type	1993	1994	1995	1996	1997	1998	1999
Bituminous	12,212	11,841	8,609	8,998	9,517	9,357	8,806
Subbituminous	1,796	1,988	2,345	2,632	2,490	2,486	2,427
Anthracite and lignite	519	484	649	576	608	627	623
Total	14,527	14,313	11,603	12,206	12,615	12,470	11,856

Source: Technological Transfer Network, Environmental Protection Agency, www.epa.gov/ttn/chief/trends/trends99/tier3_yrsemis.pdf.

TABLE 21.7 Sulfur Dioxide Emissions under Acid Rain Program (in Millions of Short Tons Each Year)

Phase	1985	1990	1995	1996	1997	1998	1999	2000	2001	2002	2003	2004	2005
I	6.8	7.0	6.6	7.1	7.5	7.8	7.6	—	—	—	—	—	—
II	9.3	8.7	5.3	5.4	5.5	5.3	4.9	—	—	—	—	—	—
Total	16.1	15.7	11.9	12.5	13.0	13.1	12.5	11.2	10.6	10.2	10.6	10.3	10.2

Source: Annual Report of the Environmental Protection Agency for 2006, Section II, Goal 1, available at www.epa.gov.

since the first phases ended, and emissions in 2004 are lower than those in 1995 when Phase I began. With respect to the achievement of this program, environmentalists and economists who studied it, Denny Ellerman, Paul Joskow, Richard Schmalensee, Juan-Pablo Montero, and Elizabeth Bailey say, ". . . it has been more successful in reducing emissions than any other regulatory program initiated during the long history of the Clean Air Act."[39]

Trading of allowances to pollute under the program was extensive.[40] Some plants emitted sulfur dioxide per unit of electricity at *three times* the rate of the average of all units. Other units had very low emissions, because of their pollution-abatement, which enabled them to sell allowances to those needing them. The advantage in this divergent outcome is efficient emissions reduction. Units able to reduce emissions at the lowest cost do so, and they benefit by selling allowances for more than it cost them to lower emissions, while those for whom emission reductions are expensive find it is less costly to buy the allowances. Emission levels may thus differ markedly, but overall emissions are reduced in a low-cost way.

Two private businesses, Cantor-Fitzgerald Environmental Brokerage and Emission Exchange Corporation, created markets in sulfur dioxide emission allowances. Continuous trading was possible, somewhat the way stocks can be traded on the New York Stock Exchange. The two market makers published indexes indicating the values at which the allowances were trading. The EPA also held back a fraction of the allowances (less than 3 percent) and distributed them through a public auction in March of each year. Because it took place at one time, the EPA auction provided public information about the value of allowances.

The price of a sulfur dioxide allowance averaged about $125 during Phase I and gradually rose when Phase II began in 2000, passing $200 at the end of 2003. These were fairly low values, caused in part by the greater use of low-sulph ur coal as an alternative way to reduce emissions that was made possible, as noted above, by railroad deregulation. Innovations also lowered the cost of scrubber technology, which is another way to reduce sulfur dioxide emissions. In late 2005, however, the price of allowances rose to around $1,500, because of uncertainty about an EPA plan to require further emission reductions in many eastern states.[41] That plan was made definite, and in 2006 the price of an allowance fell back to the $600 range, which is more appropriate for the lower emission levels that are now required. There is a forward market in allowances, so trades can be exercised on future dates. Such information about future prices of allowances helps firms in their decisions now about emission control in future periods.

Compared with command-and-control methods, which mandate technologies that all units are to use, regardless of the suitability to the unit, the trading of

---

[39] See Ellerman et al. (2000, p. 141).

[40] See Ellerman et al. (2000, p. 142). Prices for emissions can be viewed at www.epa.gov/airmarket/trading/index.html.

[41] See the Acid Rain Program 2005 Progress Report at www.epa.gov/airmarkets/arp.

allowances induces less costly emission reduction. As allowances grow scarce, and thus costly, operating a "dirty" unit may no longer be feasible.

The Future of Trading Allowances

Northeastern states of Maine, New Hampshire, Vermont, Massachusetts, Connecticut, Rhode Island, New York, New Jersey, Maryland, and Delaware, and the District of Columbia reached an agreement in 1994 to limit summer-time emissions of nitrous oxides to reduce ground-level ozone, which exceeded ambient air quality standards throughout much of the region (of these states, only Maine and Vermont met the NAAQS for ozone). The plan calls for setting emission levels by state and allocating allowances to emit among sources in each state. These emission allowances can then be traded, as they are in the acid rain cap-and-trade program for sulfur dioxide.

When the air quality standard for ground-level ozone was made more restrictive in 2002, after five years of legal battles, many eastern states in the United States were unable to comply immediately. The EPA set out unified procedures for cap-and-trade systems that states could use in their efforts to reduce ozone during summer time in the northeastern United States. By 2004, 21 states and the District of Columbia operated cap-and-trade programs in nitrous oxide and substantial reductions were made. There are a variety of ways to reduce nitrous oxide emissions, and many other programs were in use for that purpose. Cap-and-trade programs made significant reductions, however, and they used efficiency incentives in doing it.[42] From these efforts nitrous oxide emissions were reduced from 6.7 million tons in 1990 to 3.6 million tons in 2005.

The continuous emission monitoring, which was part of the cap-and-trade program from the Clean Air Act Amendments of 1990, makes market trading workable for nitrous oxide, carbon dioxide, and sulfur dioxide, because they are all monitored under the continuous emissions monitoring program. A "Clear Skies" program would expand the cap-and-trade plan more broadly to these other monitored pollutants and perhaps to include others. Expanding the trading of emission allowances could bring the same kind of efficiency gains that were seen in sulfur dioxide and nitrous oxide emission trading. It should also end the contentious and troublesome battles over NSPSs that prevented control of emissions since the standards were first applied.[43]

The EU ETS is much like the U.S. system, although the allocation of allowances is more complicated because individual countries choose what industries to include and, within E.U. guidelines, what targets to set. The EU ETS does not allow the banking of allowances, and there is currently some uncertainty about targets beyond 2012, but it is a promising pollution-rights trading institution that is expected to flourish in similar forms around the world.[44]

---

[42] Evaluation of these programs may be found at www.epa.gov/airmarket/trading/index.html.

[43] General information about cap-and-trade programs is available at www.epa.gov/airmarkets/cap-trade-resource.html.

[44] See Joseph Kruger, "Companies and Regulators in Emission Trading Programs," Resources for the Future, February, 2005; and Lars Zellerberg, Kristina Nilsson, Markus Ahman, Anna-Sofia Kumlin, and Lena Birgersdotter, "Analysis of National Allocation Plans for the European Union Emission Trading System," IVL Swedish Environmental Research Institute, Ltd., 2006.

21.4 | PROTECTING WATER AND LAND

Water covers about three-fourths of the earth's surface. The remainder is land, and both water and land need protection. A dramatic example of harm to them came in 1989 when an oil tanker, the *Exxon Valdez*, ran aground on Bligh Reef in the Bay of Alaska, releasing 11 million gallons of oil that covered 1,100 square miles and went 470 miles southwest from Bligh Reef. The oil spill caused extensive damage to 9,000 miles of shoreline and harmed such a wide range of water life that some species have not recovered roughly 20 years later. More routine challenges to pure water and aquatic ecosystems arise everywhere. Because polluted air, perhaps containing acid rain, can harm water and land, remedies for such air pollution serve also to moderate water and land pollution. We begin by examining water regulation in the first two subsections and then turn to land in the third subsection.

Water Pollution Regulation

The Water Pollution Control Act Amendments of 1972, commonly known as the **Clean Water Act,** was to eliminate the discharge of pollutants into navigable waters by 1985.[45] Through the command-and-control means chosen to achieve this aim, sewage treatment facilities and industries were to adopt by 1977 what was defined as the **Best Practicable Control Technology (BPCT),** technology that would bring improvements at reasonable cost. Then by 1983 the industries were to achieve **Best Available Control Technology (BACT),** to clean water virtually without regard to cost. The goal was to have "fishable and swimmable waters" throughout the nation.

Congress passed the Clean Water Act due in part to dramatic examples of unsafe water, as when the Cuyahoga River in Cleveland, Ohio, caught fire in 1969 because of a waste slick on its surface. Emotions of the day help to account for the ambitious aims in the Act, which turned out to be unrealistic. In 1977, when only about 80 percent of industrial sources and 60 percent of municipal sewage plants were in compliance, Congress postponed the BPCT standards to 1979 and moderated the BACT standards. It held toxic pollutants, such as arsenic, lead, and mercury, to the same standard as before, but it eased standards for conventional pollutants such as human waste. These rules applied only to **point sources,** like factories or sewage treatment plants, which can be observed, yet much water pollution arises from **nonpoint sources** that are difficult to observe. Nonpoint sources include runoff from city streets and fertilizer use on farms. Control of the point sources that were the targets of this legislation, even if achieved, could not alone ensure fishable and swimmable waters.

EPA policies to limit water pollution take many different forms. Among other things, the EPA sets standards for drinking water and pursues their attainment, oversees the management of waste water, and protects watersheds, wetlands, coastal

---

[45] See 33 U.S.C. § 1251 *et seq.*

areas, and estuaries. The EPA often prescribes technologies that must be used, and it defines forbidden actions. Besides distinguishing between point sources of pollution and nonpoint sources, it categorizes pollutants as either degradable or nondegradable, depending on whether they can be neutralized in water. Neutralizing degradable pollutants usually consumes oxygen, however, and reduced oxygen levels can upset an ecosystem. Major nondegradable water pollutants are cadmium, lead, phosphorous, mercury, PCBs and DDT, and water purification processes cannot reliably remove all of them.

Emission levels have been established for point sources all over the country under the **National Pollutant Discharge Elimination System (NPDES)**. For identifiable pollutants, the system usually specifies the average amount that can be contained per unit of product over a 30-day period, with a maximum also in any 24-hour period. Every public or private point source that discharges wastes into waters of the United States must obtain a permit to do so. The permits place requirements on their holders to submit reports on compliance and sometimes to upgrade their control technology. State agencies and the EPA monitor point sources, with the EPA focusing on "major" sources that are either high in volume or dangerous in content. Notices of violation are used as warnings, as in the case of air pollution, and the EPA's "administrative orders" for correction can be enforced by fines.

Dealing with pollution that originates from nonpoint sources reveals how complex water pollution can be and why it is only partly understood. Phosphorous, for example, is commonly used in fertilizers at nonpoint sources, such as farms that cover large areas, and rain often washes it into lakes or rivers. When overabundant, phosphorous along with nitrogen stimulates excessive production of organic matter (for example, algae, or seaweed). When excessive, the organic matter reduces the sunlight for submerged forms of vegetation, thereby reducing the oxygen they can produce. The organic matter may decompose, but that also raises **biochemical oxygen demand (BOD)**, which consumes oxygen in the water and can disturb the ecosystem. To minimize damaging phosphorous run-off into lakes and streams, the EPA defines best-practice methods for farming and other activities and tries to win their implementation.

BOX 21.6 Too Much Fishing

No one owns fish in the ocean, and so we all may try to catch them. Fisheries and ecology experts predict that if the current fishing pace continues unabated, the species currently fished will vanish by 2050. The Sea is a complex ecosystem, in part because of the way different species depend on other species, and as fished species decline that will induce other changes in the system. One effect is a loss in the diversity of species, which lowers stability and even water quality. At this point the problem is reversible. Effective international arrangements for limiting the taking of fish do not exist, however, and will be needed to save the bounty of the sea.

See C. Dean, "Study Sees 'Global Collapse' of Fish Species," *New York Times*, November 3, 2006, p. A1; and B. Worm, et al., "Impacts of Biodiversity Loss of Ocean Ecosystem Services," *Science*, November 3, 2006, pp. 787–790.

Preserving the habitat for shellfish in large estuaries is important to our food chain as well as to recreational fishing and swimming activities. Shellfish provide a staggering amount of protein for the meal table each year, and states, together with the EPA, determine where they can be safely harvested. Some water life, such as oysters in the Chesapeake Bay, are immobile and unable to move from areas where oxygen is depleted, so they may not survive, while more mobile creatures may not suffer as much.[46]

For protection of drinking water, the EPA defines standards, somewhat like the ambient air quality standards for air, to impose limits on impurities to protect public health. They are called **National Primary Drinking Water Regulations (NPDWRs)**. These regulations apply to a large number of contaminants, categorized as microorganisms (a total of 7, including viruses), disinfectants and their byproducts (7, including chlorine), inorganic chemicals (16, including arsenic and lead), organic chemicals (53, including benzene), and radionuclides (4, including uranium).[47] Secondary standards also exist for many contaminants that cause cosmetic effects (tooth discoloration) or aesthetic effects (taste, odor, color). The EPA does not enforce these secondary standards, but states may choose to enforce them.

More than 200,000 public drinking water systems serve over 240 million people in the United States. About 20 percent of the population is served by systems that violate some purity regulation in the course of a year. When that happens, the system must remove the contaminants and notify the public. The goal is to have less than 5 percent of the population face this possible risk of drinking water contamination.[48]

BOX 21.7 Bottled Water

Vendors in Roman times sold bottled water, and although it has grown into an $8 billion business today, the industry's water can be imperfect and is occasionally recalled. In 1989, for instance, the leading importer of bottled water in the United States, Perrier from France, withdrew 70 million bottles from the market after North Carolina regulators discovered its water was contaminated with benzene. The regulators tested 88 brands of bottled water, and besides benzene in Perrier they found freon, kerosene, trichlorethylene, and other impurities in some of the other brands. In 2006 Natural Spring Water and Price Chopper Desert Spring Water recalled their water, saying it may be contaminated with coliform bacteria and algae. Bottled water is sometimes drawn from the same aquifers as public tap water, but the public water is required to meet more stringent tests.

See G. Bolduc, "Pressure Increases on State's Groundwater Sources," *Morning Sentinel*, Kennebec, Maine, March 24, 2006; and "The Bottle Boom," at www.second-opinions.co.uk/ bottle.html.

---

[46] For descriptions of the scale and methods of fishing by Chesapeake Bay "watermen," see Warner (1977) or Chowning (1990).

[47] These standards can be seen at www.epa.gov/safewater/mcl.html.

[48] See Douglas Jehl, "A New Frontier in Water Wars Emerges in East," *New York Times*, March 3, 2003, p. A1.

A Broader Problem for Water

Pollution may not be the biggest nor even the gravest problem for water; supply is a broader problem. Deep aquifers made of porous rock and sand contain underground water that can be pumped to the surface, but they are being drained at an unsustainable rate.[49] About 70 percent of the water humans use goes for irrigation, and aided by the development of efficient pumps, irrigation draws water from aquifers all around the world. Generally, no one owns an aquifer, making it a perfect example of a common pool that all may use. The great Ogalalla Aquifer that stretches across the Great Plains of the United States is being drawn down, and aquifers like it in China, India, Pakistan, and elsewhere have falling water levels. So even if water can be kept pure, it will grow scarce without conservation. The lack of a market price for water in most places discourages its conservation.

The year 2004 marked the fifth straight year of drought in the western United States, when Arizona experienced, according to tree-ring evidence, its driest year in the last 1,400.[50] And drought conditions continue across 60 percent of U.S. land area. Tree-ring analysis in Arizona shows that there have been two droughts lasting almost 20 years, so it is hard to tell whether this dry spell is simply due to the vagaries of weather or is due in part to global warming. If global warming is at work, it may also reduce snowpacks in the Cascade and Sierra mountain ranges, which are the source of much of California's water. Western development and California lifestyles may be at stake. Whatever the causes of a dwindling water supply, countries around the world need to take steps to store rain water more effectively to offset scarcity and to conserve existing supplies.

Thus, water for drinking and other uses is increasingly scarce and prices are seldom used to guide its allocation. In the western United States, allocation of water from important sources, like the Colorado River, has been the subject of detailed agreements for years, and disputes have been settled by the Supreme Court. In 2000, for example, the Court supported the pursuit of claims to Colorado River water by five tribal reservations with historic interests. The Court also referees disputes between Kansas and Nebraska about whether they are following a 1943 agreement on the use of Colorado water. Recently, similar water-use issues have opened in the East. For instance, an agreement between Alabama, Georgia, and Florida to share the Apalachicola-Chattahoochee-Flint basin is encountering implementation problems as parties disagree. In Virginia and Maryland, rulings from 1632 by King Charles I are still in effect. King Charles gave the whole Potomac River to Maryland, rather than follow the usual practice and divide it in the middle with neighboring Virginia which, along with West Virginia, draws water from the river. Rather than using the edge of the river it clearly owns, Virginia wants to draw water from farther into the river, where the water is purer. These disputes will almost certainly become more frequent as water becomes more scarce.

---

[49] See Brown (2006).
[50] See editorial, "The Arid West," *New York Times*, May 10, 2004, p. A24.

BOX 21.8 A Drop to Drink

Failure to understand limits to the supply of water, together with legal principles formed without that understanding, such as the rule of capture, have prevented reliance on markets and led to inefficient uses of water in the United States and many other parts of the world. In extreme cases, groundwater pumping—which accounts for 25 percent of the water used—has destroyed springs and rivers and caused land to collapse. Cotton, alfalfa, and rice are grown by pumping scarce groundwater in arid western regions of the United States, while plentiful rain in eastern regions could easily grow those crops and leave western water for better uses. Better uses are not the golf courses and artificial lakes that have been developed in water-scarce western regions, but drinking water and sensible irrigation needed for living. Existing water rights are often based on historic land ownership and the rule of capture, which can be a barrier to better water use. These rights will not soon change, because they belong to politically powerful landowners. The water rights usually cannot be traded, for example, yet tradeable rights could shift water to more valuable uses as owners of the rights sought out their greatest value. Even taxes for using groundwater and higher fees for consuming water are in order. Reliance on these market mechanisms could help to bring efficient water use, allowing more benefit from whatever water is available and better conservation to expand its availability.

See R. J. Glennon, *Water Follies: Groundwater Pumping and the Fate of America's Fresh Water,* Washington, D.C.: Island Press, (2002) and B. McKibben, "Our Thirsty Future," *New York Review of Books,* September, 2003, Vol. 50, pp. 58–60.

Land Pollution Regulation

Land pollution misuses the soil by dumping industrial waste, following poor agricultural practices, exploiting minerals, or disposing of other harmful materials. To protect the land, a host of EPA and other regulations guide the uses of landfills, strip-mining, and other activities that can harm the land. Metals, glass, plastic, and paper can be recycled to reduce the damage they may cause in landfills. Those who strip-mine are required to reclaim uses of the land once they complete their mining. More serious problems can also arise, and they require broader rehabilitation of damaged land.

Superfund and Brownsfields

On the heels of environmental disasters of the 1970s, including Love Canal, Congress passed the Comprehensive Environmental Response, Compensation, and Liability Act in 1980, also known as the **Superfund Act**. Under the law, the EPA was to develop capabilities for containing and treating hazardous waste on land. It can take years of work and great expense to remove contamination from a hazardous site, and the task of reclaiming many sites is a major one for the EPA.

State agencies, EPA regional offices, and observant citizens bring possible hazardous sites to the EPA's attention, and the EPA has an information system to keep track of them. It evaluates sites and adds those in need of treatment to the **National Priorities List (NPL)**. The EPA also judges which sites are most serious or solvable, and it undertakes clean up efforts. As time has passed, easier cases that could be cleaned up in a shorter time have been treated, and now a larger fraction of cases require longer-term projects. In the year 2000, there were 1,509 NPL sites, and construction to remedy contamination had been completed at roughly half of them.

The financing for Superfund projects has come largely from firms that were guilty of causing the damage. A tax on chemical and oil firms poured revenues into the Superfund for years. In addition, firms responsible for contamination have voluntarily financed cleanups at roughly 70 percent of Superfund sites. When firms that were responsible for damage resist requests for payment, the Superfund law can sometimes force compliance, even where the guilty party is no longer in business, by attaching its assets or placing a claim on them. If the firm still refuses to contribute to any restoration, the EPA can pursue it in court. In 1995, Congress did not renew the Superfund tax, and since then federal allocations to the fund have come from general tax revenues.[51] The Superfund itself has declined from about $3.5 billion in 1996 to less than $0.5 billion in 2002, and this decline in resources affects how aggressively authorities can pursue projects.

The EPA undertakes another category of cleanup, called **brownsfields**, to restore sites after manufacturing plants or military bases that occupied them close or relocate. Brownsfields sites are usually not as dangerous as Superfund sites, but without some genuine reclamation efforts their economic redevelopment will be hindered. The EPA has provided funds to evaluate sites for many communities as pilot projects, and it has launched a small number of corrective actions at sights more contaminated than is normal for sites in the brownsfields program.

SUMMARY

Common ownership of air and water cause common-pool problems, in which each party may have a different use for the resource. If one party seeks to dispose of wastes while another wants to see handsome views or enjoy fresh air or drinking water, the first party imposes an external effect on the second. As a result, air may be polluted and water may not be efficiently conserved. In the presence of such externalities, decentralized choices that depend on private costs and benefits do not yield an ideal solution because those private costs and benefits do not reflect all social costs and benefits. When natural purification processes are not adequate to maintain high-quality air and water, governmental regulation may be needed to help them do so.

The atmosphere has a temperature inversion about eight miles above the earth's surface, which prevents most air from rising further and keeps effluents that are discharged at the surface from moving out into the cosmos. This means we must live with whatever we put in the air, just as we must live with what we deposit in lakes and rivers. Sulfur dioxide, caused by the combustion of fossil fuels, is one element that is

---

[51] See Tom Zeller, "The Future of the Superfund: More Taxing, Less Simple," *New York Times*, March 24, 2002, p. WK16.

discharged into the air, and it can make rain take on a harmful acididty, causing damage to rocks, water, and aquatic life in lakes and rivers. Carbon monoxide comes mainly from motor vehicle exhausts; it aggravates lung diseases and contributes to acid rain. Carbon dioxide comes from our own breathing and from burning fossil fuels, and in the air it absorbs radiation and redirects it back to earth, contributing to global warming. Fuel combustion in stationary sources also worsens soot and dust in the air. Such particulate matter, suspended in the air, causes respiratory ailments as well as poor visibility. On the other hand, particulates also can help to block harmful ultraviolet radiation. Nitrous oxides and hydrocarbons come from power plants and automobiles. They both cause smog, and nitrogen dioxide also contributes to acid rain. When combined with heat and sunlight, nitrous oxides can help to form ozone at ground level, where it causes respiratory problems and reduces agricultural yields.

Mainly since 1970, when Congress passed the Clean Air Act and formed the Environmental Protection Agency (EPA), policies have been developed to moderate these environmental problems. The EPA established National Ambient Air Quality Standards for air and set similar standards for water quality. Then states prescribed emission standards to meet these quality standards. The EPA sets emission standards for mobile air pollution sources, such as automobiles, through manufacturer certification requirements, while the states set standards for stationary air pollution sources, such as factories, refineries, or power plants, for the EPA to approve. Emission standards for stationary sources are set at levels intended to achieve the national quality standards, and they are enforced through a system of permits for all stationary sources of pollution. Having states set emission standards allows them to vary across the country depending on regional air qualities. The EPA also sets water quality standards and pursues their achievement by setting emission standards and granting permits to sources of the emissions.

Politically, it was impossible to force old plants to meet new command-and-control standards when they were introduced. So the EPA treated old sources leniently and "grandfathered" them at their old levels of pollution while imposing strict standards on new sources. This distinction between old and new sources caused a bias against building new sources, called the "new-source bias," because air pollution standards for them were so strict. Old sources were simply kept in service longer, and air pollution worsened as old "dirty" sources had their useful lives extended.

Markets to control emissions of air pollution came with the Amendments to the Clean Air Act of 1990, which mounted an attack on acid rain through tradeable rights to emit sulfur dioxide at coal-fired power plants, the dominant source of such emissions. The program required Continuous Emission Monitoring at power plants, and it introduced phases of emission trading, beginning with power plants that produced the most pollution. Rights to pollute, called allowances, were initially distributed free to sources based on their historical pollution levels, so old plants received more allowances and, thus, were not penalized for their high pollution levels. Once the old plants had tradeable pollution rights, they were motivated to reduce pollution, to save their pollution allowances because the allowances became valuable. The program brought a reduction in sulfur dioxide emissions of about 35 percent and did it with great efficiency by eliciting emission reductions from firms that could do it at the lowest cost.

Mobile sources of pollution, primarily motor vehicles, which account for roughly one-third of air pollution in the United States, are controlled federally by the EPA. Emission standards are set by type of vehicle and enforced at the manufacturer level. Corporate Average Fuel Economy (CAFE) standards are also imposed across all of a corporation's vehicles. The CAFE standards are less efficient than fuel taxes, because they do not directly affect the price of fuel so fuel prices remain low and as a result vehicles are driven more.

International cooperation in controlling pollution is also growing, mainly because some problems, such as the ozone hole and global warming, depend on worldwide activity. Cooperation is often needed among people living in separate political boundaries, as when effluents from midwestern U.S. factories and power plants caused acid rain to fall in New England and in Canada. So solutions to environmental problems call for new institutions and may involve new forms of political cooperation.

Water pollution also results from acid rain, but many other forms of water pollution occur in ground water and in the surface water of lakes and rivers. Nondegradable pollutants are unchanged by water and can even be directly poisonous. Toxic chemicals present the most ominous danger to ground water and even to land. Degradable pollutants are modified by water through chemical and biological processes, allowing domestic sewage, or organic wastes from food preparers, to be cleaned and absorbed. Even that cleansing process can be problematic, however, because it uses oxygen, which water life needs for survival.

Property rights to land are clearer than they are to air or water, because land is defined in units that can be owned and exchanged. But air and water pollution, which are clear externalities, can affect the land. Acid rain can harm land as well as water, and solid wastes, including scrapped appliances and automobiles in landfills, can adversely affect the surrounding land and its possible uses for many years. Highway construction, strip-mining, and poor agricultural or forestry practices also can reduce the uses of nearby land. Remedies for serious harms to land have been pursued federally through the Superfund Program, although its funding has recently been reduced. Another federal program rehabilitates less seriously damaged land, called brownsfields, so they can be economically useful.

QUESTIONS

1. The Coase theorem indicates that the same result can be achieved, regardless of which way property rights are defined. However, one way of defining property rights may make transaction costs lower. Can the Clean Air Act be interpreted as a redefinition of property rights, aimed at making a socially desired outcome easier to reach?

2. In a nonattainment area, where air quality standards are not being met, the EPA requires firms to use "reasonably available control measures" for old sources of

pollution and, for new sources, technology with "lowest achievable emission rate," plus offsets from old sources. Suppose, instead, that rights to pollute were issued in numbers that would achieve the same average local-area level of pollution and that those rights would be tradeable. Explain whether the tradable-rights system would allow more flexibility to firms that produce and compete in a national market. Why or why not?

3. Suppose a new technology is discovered along the Wet River that allows production of a high-quality color TV set at a constant cost of only $60 per unit. And suppose the current annual demand for this TV set can be represented by

$$P = 170 - 5Q,$$

where Q is the number of TV sets in thousands, and P is the price per set in dollars.

a. Find the competitive price and quantity for these TV sets.

b. Production of these TV sets also produces effluent that pollutes the Wet River, at the location where the TV sets are built. Suppose damage, C, from this water pollution increases with TV set production at an increasing rate and is reliably estimated by the equation, $C = 0.25Q^2$. This means the marginal damage cost (MDC) is $0.5Q$. Without any correction for this pollution, what is the marginal social cost of a TV set at the competitive equilibrium? (*Note*: MDC $= 0.5Q$ because $dC/dQ = d(0.25Q^2)/dQ = 0.5Q$.) (*Hint*: The marginal social cost at any output Q is now $60 plus MDC, or $60 + 0.5Q$.)

c. Find the socially optimal number of TV sets, taking into account this harm to the river from production of the TV sets that is described in part (b).

d. Estimate a tax per TV set that could bring about the socially optimal result. What would be the effective price per TV set at that optimal solution?

e. Suppose a technology is developed that neutralizes the harmful effect of the effluent that is discharged into the Wet River. Using this technology, it costs $12 to remove the effluent caused by the production of one TV set. Will this technology ever be used?

f. Regulators might (1) ban unneutralized effluent into the Wet River, (2) impose a tax per TV set, or (3) impose a tax per TV set on the unneutralized effluent volume that is generated by production of one TV set. Given that the conditions described in part (e) exist, and given a strong possibility of demand growth, which is the worst of these three policies and why is it the worst? Which is the best of the three policies and why is it the best?

4. When Congress passed the Clean Air Act, the harms from pollution and the benefits of its reduction were not reliably known. Because the amount of pollution and thus its harms would differ at different locations, each location would require detailed study to determine an optimal effluent tax for that location. Would the same problem arise for a system of tradable pollution rights? Compare the requirements of these two means of influencing polluters, effluent taxes or tradeable pollution rights, and indicate the efficiency advantages of each pollution control system.

5. CAFE standards impose an average requirement that all vehicles of particular types produced by a firm must meet a miles-per-gallon standard. Specifically, suppose automobiles that are produced are to meet an average 27.5 mpg, while light trucks can average 20.7 mpg, and fines are imposed for noncompliance. Compare this CAFE policy with a tax on fuel, evaluating possible effects on (1) vehicle design, (2) corporation size and shape (the product line produced), and (3) the control of air pollution.

6. A "cap-and-trade" system is currently used to control sulfur dioxide emissions at U.S. electric power generating plants. Explain (a) how this system came into use, (b) how the system functions, and (c) how effective it has been.

APPENDIX 21.1 National Ambient Air Quality Standards

Pollutant	Time Period	Primary Standard	Secondary Standard
Particulate matter, PM(10)	Annual average	50 μg/m^3	50 μg/m^3
	24-hr. average	150 μg/m^3	150 μg/m^3
Particulate matter, PM(2.5)	Annual average	15 μg/m^3	15 μg/m^3
	24-hr. average	65 μg/m^3	65 μg/m^3
Sulphur dioxide, SO$_2$	Annual average	0.03 ppm (80 μg/m^3)	
	24-hr. average	0.14 ppm (365 μg/m^3)	
	3-hr. average		0.050 ppm (1,300 μg/m^3)
Nitrogen dioxide, NO$_2$	Annual average	0.053 ppm (100 μg/m^3)	0.053 ppm (100 μg/m^3)
Carbon Monoxide, CO	1-hr. average	35 ppm (40 mg/m^3)	(No secondary standard)
	8-hr. average	9 ppm (10 mg/m^3)	
Ozone, O$_3$	1-hr. average	0.12 ppm (235 μg/m^3)	0.12 ppm (235 μg/m^3)
	8-hr. average	0.08 ppm (157 μg/m^3)	0.08 ppm (157 μg/m^3)
Lead, Pb	Quarterly average	1.5 μg/m^3	1.5 μg/m^3

Source: National Ambient Air Quality Standards, U.S. Environmental Protection Agency, http://www.epa.gov/airs/criteria.html. ppm = parts per million by volume; mg/m^3 = milligrams per cubic meter of air; μg/m^3 = micrograms per cubic meter of air.

22

Worker Protection

A dults spend much of their lives at work, where they form important relationships with their coworkers and identify with the work they do. Workers in the United States also find their social safety net on the job, rather than from the government, as workers depend on their employers for health care, pensions, and other important benefits when they are ill, disabled, or retired. The employer-employee relationship was historically intended to be long-term, with workers remaining loyal to their employers in part to receive retirement benefits that were more generous after a full career of service. The decline in this life-long relationship with an employer is not the only change that U.S. workers feel today.

In the last 30 years the workplace has been quietly transformed. Greater competition in product markets, partly from the deregulation of formerly regulated industries and partly from more vigorous international competition, places greater productivity demands on workers. Changes in shareholdings and in the vigor of shareholder representations also increase pressure on managements to deliver financial performance, which in turn increases the demand for worker productivity, while the power of labor unions to protect workers has declined. The pace of technological change quickened in the computer age, led by remarkable advances in communication that alter the nature of work. Such technological changes open new opportunities for some workers while forcing difficult job transitions on others. The workforce itself has also changed in the last 30 years, from one comprising mainly males working to support wives and children to a diverse workforce that often claims two or more workers from a family.

New issues abound in this new age. First, employment is so important to individuals' financial and other forms of security that fair opportunity to obtain it is important to the decency of our society. Law and court decisions have attempted to insure a degree of fairness in hiring and firing decisions and freedom from abuse at work. Second, the workplace can be physically dangerous, and attempts have been made to protect workers from these dangers insofar as that is possible. Finally, after a life of hard work and saving, employees should be able to enjoy a secure retirement. Legislation to support that goal guides the form and scope of workers' pension plans.

We begin in Section 22.1 by examining how well markets protect workers in the areas of employment discrimination, health and safety, and pensions, and then we consider legislation in these three areas. Section 22.2 treats the Civil Rights Act of 1964, which is one of the most significant pieces of U.S. federal legislation in the twentieth century. It inspired additional legislation that focused on avoiding discrimination in employment. Section 22.3 considers statutory worker protection, which began with Maryland's Workers' Compensation law in 1902 and by 1949 all states had such laws. The federal governmental effort to regulate health and safety came soon after, in 1970, with the Occupational Safety and Health Act (OSHA). Section 22.4 examines 1974 federal legislation to guide pension plans, the Employee Retirement Income Security Act (ERISA).

22.1 | PROTECTION IN MARKETS

How can markets, with assistance from the legal system (1) protect against employment discrimination, (2) provide for occupational health and safety, and (3) protect employees' pensions? Competitive firms seek efficiency in matching workers to jobs, but discrimination may interfere with the matches. Markets will require higher wage payments from employers whose jobs are riskier, thus creating an incentive for employers to make jobs safer. Courts help to define employer liability, which motivates employers to prevent accidents and provides limited protection for retirement pensions.

Employment Discrimination

In the late nineteenth century in the United States a practice called *employment at will* came to dominate the employment relationship. **Employment at will** allowed either the employer or the employee to terminate their relationship at any time, for good reason, bad reason, or no reason at all.[1] In earlier centuries, going back to England, employment was based on long-term practices that amounted to social policy, for example to make agricultural employment for a year rather than for one harvest only. U.S. courts welcomed and supported the idea of employment at will, however, and they even barred legislative attempts by states to regulate working conditions because such laws would rein in the right of employers to engage in at-will employment contracts.[2] Under employment at will, employers controlled completely the employment relationship, from hiring through pay and promotion to retirement or termination.

With exceptions that effectively began in the 1930s to protect union supporters, and were broadened in the 1960s when resistance to discrimination resulted in the Civil Rights Act and the Age Discrimination in Employment Act, employment at will still serves as the default principle for the employment relationship. For some

---

[1] See Feinman (1976).

[2] See, for example, *Adair v. United States*, 208 U.S. 161 (1908).

time Congress resisted legislation to bar discrimination on grounds that (1) it would be expensive and (2) markets could bring it about anyway. But discrimination was evident and persistent in labor markets. The unfairness of discrimination in employment opportunities was extremely costly to those who bore the effect of reduced employment opportunities. It was also inefficient, because it prevented the most productive assignments of workers to jobs. Eventually, Congress passed laws against discrimination.

Competition in Labor Markets

Many employers argued that competition could root out discrimination, so passing laws to prevent it was unnecessary. As profit seeking employers sought more productive workers, the argument went, those employers would not focus on race, sex, or other extraneous factors instead of productivity. For if they did, competitive pressures could push them under. Studies in the 1960s showed that market competition could improve efficiency over a regime that practiced racial discrimination,[3] and provided some evidence that there was less discrimination in markets with more competition relative to monopoly.[4]

It was also possible, however, to explain how discrimination could arise in competitive markets. Nobel laureate Gary Becker argued that an employer with some preference among potential employees might discriminate, to select workers congenial to the employer's taste. Such a "taste for discrimination" could apply if the employer was willing to accept lower profit to indulge the taste.[5] That is, the employer would hire workers to satisfy the employer's preferences, even at the cost of efficiency. An employer with some monopoly power would find it easier to sacrifice profit for such a purpose, so the argument could help to explain why competition might result in less discrimination.

Some lawyers and economists have tried to defend discrimination.[6] One argument is that freedom of contract between workers and employers is a powerful and desirable freedom that makes productivity the dominant factor in hiring decisions. The homogenous work force that discrimination produced would be easier to manage, because by sharing similar backgrounds and characteristics the employees could function more efficiently. As an example, gains have been found when workers speak a common language.[7] Despite such arguments, the importance of fairness in employment opportunity and the ultimate promise of efficiency dominated such considerations and Congress passed national laws that banned discrimination even in private sector employment. The antidiscrimination laws are narrowly focused, however, to prevent discrimination according to specific characteristics, such as race, sex, national origin, religion, age, or disability, or particular conduct such as whistle-blowing or certain union-related activities. Discrimination can be shown to occur,

---

[3] See Hutt (1964). He showed how South Africa's apartheid system prevented assignment of workers to jobs where they would be most productive.

[4] See Alchian and Kessel (1962).

[5] See Becker (1971).

[6] See Epstein (1992).

[7] See Lang (1986).

even when the employer has no desire to discriminate, through a possibility called statistical discrimination.

Statistical Discrimination

A worker who is a member of an identifiable group can suffer from a kind of statistical discrimination that is based on expected productivity for members of that group.[8] The key statistic is the average productivity of the group. To illustrate, suppose that average productivity for those without high school diplomas is low, and suppose an employer can save time by simply using identity in that group as an indicator of productivity. Then all members of the group lacking a high school diploma will be regarded as low in productivity, and they will be handicapped when seeking employment. This result can follow even when some who lack a high school diploma are high in productivity, but the employer has to spend considerable time and effort to find that out in the case of each individual applicant. With management time and effort scarce, true productivity might not be discovered in time for a favorable employment decision. Statistical discrimination saves employer search cost but may result in lower productivity, and it can occur even in a competitive market.

The possibility of statistical discrimination arises when an employer economizes on effort in reaching an employment decision by using a rough statistic, such as the average productivity of the group to which an applicant belongs. It is like an insurance company charging all male drivers who are age 25 and younger higher rates because, *on average*, the drivers in that group have more accidents. The practice is similar also to stereotyping, which arises when we are lazy and think in terms of types, to economize on the effort of perceiving and processing information.[9] The mind uses convenient categories, including perhaps race, age, or sex, giving them a set of unquestioned (but possibly false) characteristics. Either practice can appear useful on average, and although it can lead to the hiring of a less efficient worker it can seem to save costs for an employer. Beyond the employer's calculations, the discriminatory consequences are just as serious for the excluded worker as they would be if the employer acted deliberately out of bias.

Discrimination Based on Conduct

Imperfect information can thus prevent the selection of workers on the basis of their productivity alone and thereby contribute to bias in employment. An employer may discriminate deliberately against workers who engage in activities that may not be in the employer's interest. An employer may try to punish workers for serving on a jury, for instance, or for refusing to lie for the firm. Courts have allowed workers to sue employers for damages in limited circumstances to prevent such punishments. Employers might also fire workers for union activity, to which they have a right, or for informing authorities against illegal management practices, when informing about them can be socially valuable. To avoid employer actions against employees who are benefitting society, courts protect a worker who is

---

[8] See Nobel laureate Edwin Phelps (1972).
[9] For description and evaluation of stereotyping, see Krieger (1995).

wrongfully discharged, although such protection is not reliable without clear rules that statutes provide. Congress passed laws to protect workers against retaliatory action, and without these laws, markets would offer only slight protection against such employer action.

With widespread adherence to the employment-at-will rule, markets may not prevent discrimination in employment. The unfairness to those who suffer from discrimination, however, plus the inappropriateness of the advantages that are enjoyed by those who benefit from it, were deemed to be so serious that courts slightly weakened the at-will rule, and Congress passed laws that limit its application. In addition to avoiding discrimination at work, employees are also concerned about their safety and their health, and Congress responded with laws to protect occupational safety and health.

Occupational Safety and Health

Some jobs are dangerous, and although risks of some kind arise in almost every line of work, risks vary considerably by occupation. When the Labor Department reported the first national census of job-related deaths in 1993, it noted that, although men represented 55 percent of the workforce, they accounted for 93 percent of job-related fatalities. Women accounted for 7 percent of job-related deaths, but 40 percent of their deaths are due to murder, whereas 15 percent of deaths among men are by murder. Another census published in that year by the National Institute for Occupational Health and Safety found similar patterns.[10] Falls, electrocutions, being struck by falling objects, exposure to harmful substances, and fires or explosions are other major causes of death on the job.

One reason that preventing job-related fatalities is difficult is that they arise in part from the dangers that are present even in the nonwork realms of society. For instance, the greatest number of job-related fatalities can be traced to highway vehicle accidents (including those involving tractor trailers, delivery vans, and cars driven by sales representatives). Machine-related accidents are second highest among the causes of job-related fatalities, and sound workplace policies could reduce this loss of life. Next in importance as cause of death at work are homicides, which result from violence in the workplace that is difficult to prevent through regulatory policies.

Market Wage Premium for Job Risk

Markets motivate employers to prevent accidents because workers normally prefer less risk to their health and safety. When risks on the job are known, workers who bear greater risks want a **wage premium,** a higher wage to compensate for bearing added risk. Economists have estimated how job risk can explain wages through

---

[10] See "Fatal Injuries to Workers in the United States, 1980–1989: A Decade of Surveillance," U.S. Department of Health and Human Services, Center for Disease Control and Prevention, National Institute for Occupational Safety and Health, August, 1993.

statistical regressions, by using observations that include characteristics of workers and properties of jobs plus a measure of job risk. Using many factors to explain the wage paid in each job enables researchers to isolate the effect that job risk has on the wage.[11] It is difficult to control for all influences on wages to identify a market risk premium for bearing risk, but a number of studies have attempted to do so.

Table 22.1 shows that more dangerous occupations tend to have greater wage premiums for bearing added risk. In its own financial interest, then, an employer is willing to spend money to improve workplace safety to reduce the compensation that it must pay to workers for the risks they bear. The workers must be informed about risks, however, before the wage premiums can reflect sound judgments about them. In addition, workers can choose their preferred amount of risk only if they have a range of work opportunities from which to choose. The supplies of workers who have different willingness to bear risk also determine what kind of risk premium might be observed. When ideal information and opportunity conditions are met, the market can function well and workers can allocate themselves rationally across different jobs. Then those more willing to bear risk find the premium paid for doing so attractive, so they gravitate to the riskier jobs, while those who most dislike risk find the risk premiums inadequate and settle into lower risk jobs.

It is desirable, on the whole, that workers are able to consider health and safety risks when choosing among available jobs. The individual knows his or her views about facing risk, at least better than someone else, so the individual can make the best choice. Providing risk information to workers, who can use it in market decisions about where to work, can thereby foster an allocation of risk bearing that is better than other ways of assigning workers to jobs, because the market allocation can reflect individual preferences. For the market to work, however, workers need information about risks and they have to have opportunities from which to choose. Estimating risks, especially for new workers, can be difficult.

TABLE 22.1 Wage Premiums for Risk

Occupation	Occupational Deaths per 100,000 Workers per Year	Estimated Wage Premium per Year (2006 dollars)
Police Officer	78	820
Sailor	163	1,717
Bartender	176	1,850
Taxi Driver	182	1,911
Lumberjack	256	2,695

Source: R. Thaler and S. Rosen, "The Value of Saving a Life: Evidence from the Labor Market," in Nestor E. Terleckyi, ed., *Household Production and Consumption,* New York: N.B.E.R., 1976, pp. 265–298.

---

[11] For a description and review of this kind of study, with emphasis on estimating the value of life, see Viscusi (1992, 1993). See also Ashenfelter (2006).

The Problem of Estimating Job Risks

In some occupations, such as mining, risks are quite well known and are separately regulated.[12] In most cases, however, the risks to safety in a workplace are difficult for workers to judge.[13] Health risks are even more difficult to judge, in part because effects of exposure in the workplace to certain substances, such as asbestos, may take years and even decades to develop. Moreover, only a small fraction of those workers exposed may develop a health problem. The problem may be serious and costly, making it important to control even if only a small fraction of workers suffer it, but a low probability that a worker will be affected makes tracing the cause more difficult.

Safety risks may be judged better with experience, and that leads to one reason why workers quit their jobs. Partly because of a substantial risk premium, for example, high pay may attract an uninformed worker to a job. After being exposed to the risks of the new job, however, and thus becoming informed about them, the new worker may identify the compensating differential being paid for bearing these risks and judge it to be inadequate. He or she can then quit. This result is fairly common, because new and inexperienced workers often begin in risky jobs, which contributes to the higher accident rates of younger and less experienced workers.

Thus, although substantial, the allocation of risks through markets may not be ideal. Workers may not be fully informed, and even with good employer intentions it is sometimes hard to make them so. Plentiful employment opportunities are also important, so workers are able to use their knowledge of safety or health risks in choosing a job. Some workers may have less choice of their employments and may be pressed into bearing more risk than they would like, simply to earn enough to meet their needs. Life in a mining town may offer mainly mining work with the risks it brings. So job-risk information and job opportunities, as well as risk preferences, may affect the allocation of risks.

Workers' Compensation Laws

The possibility that workers can obtain compensation in the courts gives employers an incentive to avoid accidents. The incentive may seem to come after the fact or after the harm is done. Knowing that redress is available to employees, however, motivates an employer to avoid dangers that might lead to suits against it before they happen. Indeed, law often affects our behavior through this anticipation of consequences. The legal process is also important in defining responsibilities. For example, judicial decisions clearly establish forms of negligence and rules for identifying it, and they provide valuable guidance for specifying the kind of error that can lead to liability for harm.

Courts, however, were slow to protect worker health and safety. Nineteenth-century courts, assuming that workers earned higher wages by bearing greater workplace risks, often denied compensation for workplace injuries on grounds that workers had accepted the risks when they accepted the employment. Courts also demanded

---

[12] Mining safety is regulated by the separate Mine Safety and Health Administration. For a description of recent relaxation in mine safety regulation, see Ian Urbina and Andrew W. Lehren, "U.S. Easing Fines for Mine Owners on Safety Flaws," *New York Times*, March 2, 2006, p. A1.

[13] See Viscusi and O'Conner (1984) regarding worker judgments of risks in the chemical industry.

convincing evidence that an employer's negligence caused harm. Nevertheless, a negligent employer could be sued under common law and found liable for compensation to the worker. Going to court is costly, however, and even after doing so, a worker may not succeed in establishing negligence on the part of the employer. After some significant awards were won, states began to pass *workers' compensation laws*. Table 22.2 shows how coverage and benefits (in constant 2000 dollars) grew from 1970 to 2000.

Workers' compensation laws called for compensating injured workers even where the employer is not negligent, and they brought a major change in workplace safety. The laws are not very effective in some states because of weak enforcement and small awards as compensation. The existence of workers' compensation also makes it much more difficult, if not impossible, for an injured worker to sue successfully, because the laws usually bar lawsuits for workplace injuries or death in return for unchallenged compensation. Workers' compensation laws still tend, overall, to raise the cost to firms for unsafe working conditions, and they offer a direct avenue for workers to obtain compensation when injured. As in the area of product liability that protects consumers, they also place responsibility on the party best positioned to control safety—in this case, the employer.

Employers have incentive to reduce injuries under workers' compensation laws, whether the laws cover compensation expenses through private or state-run insurance programs. Private insurance plans are used in most states, and they charge higher fees to employers who have more accident claims. In states where employers' payments go into state workers' compensation funds, those payments vary according to the compensation claims the employers actually experience, much as private insurance plans do. Employer self-insurance has been growing and now accounts for more than 20 percent of payments, and here, too, incentives for reducing harms to workers are strong. This means that on economic grounds, the employers are motivated to lower workplace dangers to lower workers' compensation claims against them and, thereby, to lower payments either to insurance companies, state workers' compensation funds, or company funds. Evidence shows that in states where workers' compensation benefits are more generous, fewer fatal injuries occur.[14]

TABLE 22.2 Workers' Compensation Coverage and Payments

	1970	2000
Workers Covered (millions)	59	124
Labor Force (millions)	83	135
Percent of Labor Force Covered	71	92
Benefits Paid (billions of 2000 dollars)	13.3	41.7

Source: U.S. Bureau of the Census at www.census.gov and workers compensation information at www.allcountries.org/uscensus/621_workers_compensation_payments.html.

---

[14] See Ruser (1993).

Workers' compensation laws started with the early twentieth-century Progressive Era of reform and grew throughout the century, and they improved the well-being of workers. Indeed, evidence suggests that after passage of workers' compensation laws, workers set aside less savings to protect against consequences of injury at work.[15] Before workers' compensation laws, few workers won negligence law suits against their employers, and even though the awards to those winners might have been sizeable, the average prospect was not great. Workers' compensation laws enabled a greater fraction of injured workers to be compensated, and on average the amount of compensation also increased. These were valuable improvements in a working environment that was growing more dangerous with more complicated manufacturing processes.

It should be obvious that better information about health and safety risks can aid workers in making their employment decisions. Furthermore, the risk premiums that result in labor markets can inform employers about the value of reducing risks. Information about practices that lower risks also can aid employers by enabling them to achieve safer workplaces. Employers are financially motivated to use available knowledge in this way because it can save them from liability in court cases, from greater payments to workers' compensation funds, and from paying higher wages to workers in the form of risk premiums.

Although laws, courts, and markets all provide desirable economic incentives for employers to control the risks faced by their employees, these incentives alone are not adequate. At almost every step, the main problem is imperfect information, which keeps incentives from reflecting effects fully. Lack of information can even make it difficult for workers to assess the soundness of retirement pensions when they are managed by others on their behalf, and this can undermine their security in retirement.

Retirement Security

Employees are concerned about their retirement years as well as their working years, and that is why pension benefits are valuable to them. Offering a more generous pension may allow an employer to attract more productive workers and that appeal to workers, together with tax advantages, motivates employers to offer pensions. Protections to preserve those pensions may still be necessary, however. There have been cases where employees have been fired just before they become eligible for pension benefits, for example. Also, firms may fail, and not provide the pensions they owe their workers. Firms compete in demanding product markets and to survive they may take actions that reduce promised pensions and are not fair to workers.

Tax laws influence pension programs. It is socially desirable to have individuals plan for retirement, and tax laws invite such planning by postponing taxes to make some forms of saving for retirement attractive. In the United States, pension plans include specific tax provisions that reward certain kinds of retirement savings with reduced tax obligations. Thus, the federal government indirectly influences the types of pension plans that exist.

---

[15] For an excellent analysis of workers' compensation laws and their origins, see Fishback and Kantor (2000).

Employers sponsor three main types of pension plans. First, some pension plans are defined in terms of the benefits retirees receive. For such a **defined-benefit** plan, the employer either invests with the purpose of providing the defined benefits for retirees or expects to pay some part of the benefits out of company profits. Second, an employer might sponsor a variation on the defined-benefit plan called a **cash-balance** plan, in which the employer invests in and maintains funds for individual employees, usually at a modest promised return. Cash-balance plans accumulate funds that are paid out either as a lump sum upon retirement, when they can be rolled into a retirement plan, or taken along by the worker who transfers to another employer. Finally, an employer might sponsor a **defined-contribution** pension plan, in which the employee is responsible for managing as well as contributing the funds.

Defined-benefit pension plans depend on the financial health of the firm offering them, and if the firm fails retiree income and health care may fail as well. Defined-contribution plans and cash-balance plans depend less on the health of the firm, in that the retirement fund is owned by the employee and exists even if the employer fails. Federal insurance helps to protect retirees of firms that participate in defined-benefit or cash-balance plans, but that insurance benefit almost always is less than the employee had been promised.

Laws can prevent some objectionable actions by employers in labor markets and protect workers who are entitled to retirement benefits from being exploited. We turn now to consider legislation in the first of three main areas of worker protection, the effort to limit discrimination in employment to foster a fair and equitable society.

22.2 | EMPLOYMENT DISCRIMINATION LAWS

Employment discrimination may occur (1) in the hiring decision, (2) in opportunities during a career, such as in promotions, or (3) in the termination of employment. As noted, in the late nineteenth century, when *laissez-faire* was the watch word of commerce, employers could hire and fire at will. Indeed, employment at will was articulated as a principle to guide courts in employment disputes. The at-will principle allowed an employer to fire an employee who practiced a religion the employer disliked, and the employer could also discriminate in hiring on race, sex, or other grounds. Such employer discretion has gradually been limited in two ways. First, members of protected groups according to race, color, sex, national origin, religion, or age cannot be discriminated against because of membership in those groups. Second, public employees and union members can be fired only for "just cause," meaning the employer must explain inadequacies of job performance as cause for firing. Thus, it is fair to say the public sees that a free and fair society requires limitations on the freedom of employers to hire and fire as they please.

Limiting Employment At Will

Federal statutes banning discrimination go back to the Civil Rights Acts of 1870 and 1871. However, these laws did not explicitly apply to employment, and courts did not enforce them vigorously until the 1970s. Effective protection against discrimination started in the 1930s to prevent retaliation against workers who exercised newly won rights to engage in union activity. Then 30 years passed before the **Equal Pay Act** of 1963[16] required that men and women be paid the same wage for the same work. This act was a forerunner of broader antidiscrimination laws, which followed soon after.

Attention focused broadly on discrimination in the Civil Rights Act of 1964,[17] which prohibited discrimination on the basis of sex, race, color, religion, or national origin and created the Equal Employment Opportunity Commission (EEOC), which has the authority to enforce laws against discrimination. The EEOC is not funded adequately to handle all cases brought to it, so it tries to bring cases it thinks will be influential. All other cases are brought in courts as private claims. Discrimination against anyone of age 40 or over was prohibited by the Age Discrimination in Employment Act of 1967.[18] Then in 1990 Congress passed the Americans with Disabilities Act[19] to bar discrimination against persons with disabilities and in some situations to require reasonable efforts to accommodate persons with disabilities. Various amendments in 1972, 1978, and 1991 extended coverage to federal and state government employees, overruled Supreme Court decisions that had been hostile to some provisions, and clarified other matters.

Discrimination against Protected Classes

Laws beginning in the 1960s protected employees from discrimination or different treatment at work owing to the employee's membership in certain recognizable classes or groups. Race, color, sex, national origin, or religion can define groups, as can age, particularly age 40 or older. In the simplest terms, this means for example that whites cannot be favored over blacks, males cannot be favored over females, and younger workers cannot be favored over those who are age 40 or older.

When employees, or potential employees, suffer discrimination because of their group membership, they are responsible for making a charge and proving their case.[20] That is, the remedy relies on courts rather than a central agency. Somewhat as triple damages induce remedies by stimulating private suits in antitrust law, the victim of discrimination initiates discrimination cases and pursues them. The EEOC may aid a victim but is able to handle very few cases, so the victim typically uses protection of the law to seek compensation for harm through the courts.

Discrimination laws are part of a patchwork of legislation that guides employment law generally in the United States. In addition to laws and court decisions, executive orders have banned discrimination, not only in federal employment but also in employment by contractors to the federal government. Many states and cities have passed their own statutes with coverage that goes beyond federal coverage. For example, some, but not all, cities protect against discrimination based on sexual orientation.

---

[16] See 29 U.S.C.A. § 216(d).

[17] See 42 U.S.C.A. §§ 2000.

[18] See 29 U.S.C.A. §§ 621–634.

[19] See 42 U.S.C.A. §§ 12,101–12,213.

[20] For description of this dependence on private causes of action for enforcement see Moohr (1999).

BOX 22.1 National Origin Bias

In March, 2006, the Equal Employment Opportunity Commission announced settlement by consent decree of a case against the Melrose Hotel in New York City for discrimination on the basis of national origin. The hotel and its management company agreed to pay $800,000 to the workers and to take substantial steps to prevent discriminatory conduct in the future. The hotel and the management company had been charged with creating a hostile work environment, requiring Hispanic workers to speak English even while on breaks, firing Hispanic workers, and retaliating against employees who complained of discrimination. Besides compensating workers, the settlement required the hotel to change some practices, amend and reissue their nondiscrimination policy, train employees and managers in equal employment law, and provide periodic reports to the Equal Employment Opportunity Commission.

See www.eeoc.gov/press/3-16-06a.html; and *EEOC v. Berwind Props. Group, Ltd.*, Consent Decree, CV-04-7514 (S.D.N.Y., March 16, 2006).

Retaliation for Conduct

Union activity was the first kind of worker conduct that Congress protected. As labor unions developed in the United States, a host of disputes arose that were difficult for courts to settle in a broad way. For example, an employer seeking to resist a union might refuse to recognize it, while at the same time forming its own union, so it could seem to recognize organized labor but through an organization it was able to control. Or the employer might fire workers for engaging in union activity. In 1935 Congress set out the **National Labor Relations Act (NLRA)**, also called the **Wagner Act**, to provide a method of establishing employee representatives for collective bargaining and to prevent employer interference with employees' rights to engage in collective activity. The result is a contractual system based on private bargaining.

A whistleblower is an employee who informs the outside world about dangerous or illegal behavior inside a firm. Such an employee can provide a social benefit, yet his or her manager may want to fire a whistleblower. To avoid retaliation against whistleblowers in the civil service of the federal government, Congress passed the **Whistleblower Protection Act** of 1989. Congress also passed the Sarbanes-Oxley Act of 2002, which among other reforms protects whistleblowers who report wrongful conduct by private firms, either internally or to external investigators. This Act even makes retaliation against such whistleblowing behavior a crime.[21] Without these laws, markets operating under the employment-at-will principle could offer only slight protection, and although courts might protect a worker who is wrongfully discharged, they have not been able to offer reliable protection. In any case, under discrimination laws generally, the victim is responsible for pursuing a claim of discrimination and proving that it occurred.

---

[21] See Moohr (2003).

BOX 22.2 Whistleblowing

Sherron Watkins, who is famous for writing to her boss, Enron CEO Ken Lay, about questionable accounting practices at Enron, is not a typical whistleblower. First, she did not notify internal or external auditors about the problems she saw at Enron, she informed her boss, and the public only learned of her concern after Enron had collapsed. Second, she has triumphed as a witness against Enron top management and is now widely praised. True whistleblowers inform the outside world about problems with management decisions, and management is often able to punish them for it or malign them as "crazy." Indeed, in the Enron case Mr. Lay's lawyer described whistleblower Margaret Ceconi, who had gone to the Securities and Exchange Commission five months before Enron collapsed, as a "nutcake." Despite laws intended to protect whistleblowers, the persistence of employment at will often allows firms to fire them. Increasingly strong legislation is being passed as cases come to light, however, so protections may grow stronger.

See "Tales from the Back Office," *The Economist*, March 25, 2006, pp. 67–68.

Proving Discrimination

The first form of discrimination by class involves intentional **disparate treatment**, essentially different treatment. The question here is whether a person is treated less favorably because of race or sex or membership in some other protected class. Sometimes direct proof comes in an employer's conduct or policy that contains a "smoking gun" showing discriminatory intent. Suppose a prison follows a policy of employing males to guard male prisoners. A potential female employee might charge that the policy discriminates against females. The employer can then try to rebut the claim, by offering a defensible reason for the policy, like arguing that male guards are more effective in dealing with male prisoners. The employee can then try to claim the employer's reason is only a pretext for discrimination, and a court decides whether discrimination occurred. In a case alluded to here involving prison guards, the Supreme Court found that employing guards of the same sex as their prisoners was legitimate and not discriminatory, because the employer proved that maleness was a bonafide occupational qualification for the job of guarding males.[22] That is, the employee had to be male to perform the job.

Far more commonly, employees must establish proof of discrimination by circumstantial evidence, using facts to infer a discriminatory purpose because no explicit policy proclaims it. The employee, or more generally the plaintiff, must show a prima facie case that discrimination occurred, which then requires the employer to respond with a nondiscriminatory reason for its action. The employee then tries to show the action was discriminatory. In cases concerning promotion or firing, the worker's record can provide evidence bearing on the case, but in charges of discriminatory hiring such evidence usually is not readily available, so discrimination is harder to prove.

---

[22] See *Dothard v. Rawlinson*, 433 U.S. 321 (1977).

An employment practice might be shown to have a **disparate impact**, specifically a harmful effect, if the practice handicaps members of a protected class. The issue in such a case is not whether the employer intended to discriminate, but rather it is whether a disparate impact that is not justified by business necessity resulted. For example, an employer's requirement that job applicants have a high school diploma might not seem to discriminate because the requirement applies to all employees. But in a labor market where African Americans were much less likely to have diplomas, the Supreme Court found the requirement caused a disparate impact on blacks that was not justified by business necessity. That is, the diploma was not shown to be essential for the work so requiring it was not allowed.[23] Any hiring requirement that is not related to the work and that has a disparate impact on a protected class of workers may be unlawful.

An employer may defend limited types of discrimination when the decision is based on an affirmative action program that is intended to remedy past discrimination. **Affirmative action** began in federal government contracting, to require contractors not only to avoid discriminating but to favor those who had suffered discrimination in the past. Specifying who had suffered injustice, and so deserved advantages, has not been easy, but affirmative action has made employment opportunity more equal. An affirmative action program is required to be effective in breaking past patterns of discrimination and cannot run roughshod over rights of other employees in the process. An affirmative action program also has to be temporary.

Discrimination based on an employee's conduct is approached more straightforwardly than discrimination involving protected classes. Questions are asked about the retaliation for an employee's conduct, such as whether the conduct was harmful to the employer firm or to a manager in the firm. Was the conduct desirable from the standpoint of society—such as whistleblowing? Such questions are not necessarily easy to answer, but the answers to them can decide cases. Discrimination against a member of a protected class are usually more difficult to prove.

Special Problems

Special problems develop in several of the protected classes that are unique to that class. For instance, pregnancy raises special problems of gender discrimination. Congress passed the Pregnancy Discrimination Act of 1978 to make decisions based on pregnancy a form of sex discrimination. Under the Act, a woman who is pregnant is to be granted the same sort of leave granted to others. For example, if a firm would grant a worker leave to have back surgery, it should also grant leave so a pregnant woman can have her baby. If, however, the employer never grants leaves for any purpose, it can legally refuse a request for pregnancy leave.

Sexual harassment is also a problem of sex discrimination, and it takes two possible forms. First, harassment results when a supervisor puts the choice to a subordinate: sex or your job? This is called quid pro quo harassment because of the trade it proposes, and when the employee submits, or suffers some loss in job rights for not submitting,

---

[23] See *Griggs v. Duke Power Company*, 401 U.S. 424, 91 S.Ct. 849, 28 L.Ed.2d 244 (5th Cir. 1993).

quid pro quo harassment has occurred. A second form of sexual harassment can occur through a hostile environment, when a workplace is "permeated with discriminatory intimidation, ridicule, and insult."[24] The frequency and severity of insult are considered in judging whether an objective, reasonable person would agree that a hostile environment exists. Hostile environment claims can apply to all protected classes.

Members of a religion are protected from discriminatory conduct like other protected classes. Religious beliefs are also to be accommodated in the workplace if doing so is not very costly to the employer. Accommodation is different from disparate impact or disparate treatment, where religion should be ignored, and it requires some adjustment by employers to meet the employee's genuine religious beliefs. Religious discrimination is also allowed, however. For example, when a religious school hires teachers for a religious curriculum, it may require the teachers to hold a particular religious belief.

Discriminatory employment decisions against persons over 40 are generally unlawful, but age can be used in decisions in which it affects an employee's ability to perform the needed work. That is, in employments where age is deemed to affect performance, age discrimination is allowed. For example, retirement is enforced at a specified age—usually earlier than a normal retirement age—for airline pilots, FBI agents, and police or firefighters. Pension plans may also use age to determine eligibility for benefits for voluntary retirement.

22.3 | OCCUPATIONAL SAFETY AND HEALTH LAWS

In the 1960s, the accident rate increased in the United States by more than 25 percent. Fast and powerful vehicles on the highways, complex production equipment, and a youthful workforce all played a role. Congress passed the Occupational Safety and Health Act in 1970 in an atmosphere of crisis, to "assure so far as possible every working man and woman in the nation safe and healthful working conditions." The Occupational Safety and Health Administration (OSHA) was created by the Act to set and enforce safety and health standards, and it was located in the Department of Labor. The Act also created an **Occupational Safety and Health Review Commission**, an independent commission that reviews OSHA decisions. There is also a **National Institute for Occupational Safety and Health**, part of the Health and Human Services Department, that carries out research on occupational safety and health and recommends standards to OSHA.

OSHA Standards

The Occupational Safety and Health Act of 1970[25] authorized OSHA to set standards to insure worker safety and health, but it neither indicated fully what the nature of the standards would be nor how severe or demanding they would be. If standards were to

---

[24] See *Harris v. Forklift Systems, Inc.*, 510 U.S. 17 (1993).
[25] See 29 U.S.C.A. §§ 651–678.

BOX 22.3 Danger at Work

Job-related deaths have held steady, first above and then a little below 6,000 per year almost since the Bureau of Labor Statistics began conducting a census of fatalities at work in all 50 states in 1992. The number includes accidents, homicides, and suicides on the job but not deaths from natural causes, which are larger. For comparison, there are approximately 2,500,000 fatalities in the United States in a year. On average, the occupational fatality rate has been about 4.5 per 100,000 workers since 1996, but the highest rates (all above 25 per 100,000) were among commercial fishermen, loggers, airplane pilots, metalworkers, taxi drivers, construction laborers, roofers, electrical workers, truck drivers, and farm workers.

See U.S. Department of Labor Bureau of Labor Statistics, Census of Fatal Occupational Injuries at http://www.bls.gov/iif/oshcfoi1.htm.

---

require protective additions to factory equipment, for example, how extensive should those required additions be? This question concerns the balance between costs and benefits, a balance that was not struck in the Act. A related question concerns enforcement, for without enforcement the realized standards could fall short of the prescribed standards. On the other hand, vigorous enforcement with high fines might wring full compliance from affected firms. The fledgling OSHA had to strike these balances itself.

Fast Action

One goal of Congress was clear: action to protect the workplace was to be taken quickly. To bring fast action, Congress urged the adoption of existing standards as requirements. Because consensus standards already had been established by the American National Standards Institute, the National Fire Protection Association, and other groups this set of guidelines seemed a reasonable place to begin. The consensus standards had been worked out with industry representatives and were intended as guidelines for safe and sound practices.

The form of various consensus standards was technological, or design-based, in that they prescribed the width of ladders or the height from the floor to mount fire extinguishers. An alternative, performance approach would specify the purpose to be achieved, such as the weight-bearing strength of a ladder or the accessibility of a fire extinguisher. To move rapidly, OSHA used the design-based consensus standards as the basis for over 4,000 industry standards it quickly promulgated. Originally intended only as guidelines, these consensus standards were not well suited for mandatory implementation. The design form of the standards thus led OSHA to enforce seemingly trivial requirements and involved OSHA in enforcement disputes that seemed remote from safety or health. As a consequence, implementing OSHA standards was costly, and the new OSHA became a subject of ridicule and derision.

Aside from the public relations damage it caused, early OSHA standard setting also took a design and technological form that would continue to be a problem. Standards that specified design details led to a regulation effort that seemed doomed to focus on trivial, yet rigid, details rather than on the important purpose of protecting health and safety. The most troublesome of these details were combed out of OSHA standards in 1978, but this reform effort was modest and the design form of the standards remained.

Lack of Benefit-Cost Analysis

OSHA's general approach in setting standards was to extend them to the point where the costs would rise steeply with any increase in stringency. OSHA asked questions about whether the standard would be feasible and affordable, where affordable meant it could be paid without putting the affected firm out of business. The Occupational Safety and Health Act did not call for benefit-cost analysis to be used, and it was not applied. That is, OSHA authorities did not analyze marginal benefits and marginal costs as part of an effort to equate them to maximize efficiency. Marginal cost exceeds marginal benefit if risk is reduced too far, or marginal benefit exceeds marginal cost if risk is not reduced enough. The OSHA policy was seen by critics as carrying efforts to reduce risk beyond an efficient level, and because OSHA did not compare marginal benefits with marginal costs, it was unable to satisfy its critics.

OSHA decisions could be appealed in the court system, but court decisions in appeals did not support a benefit-cost approach, either. The issue was central in the *American Textile Manufacturers Institute v. Donovan* case in 1981, the so-called "cotton dust" case.[26] Cotton dust causes byssinosis, or "brown lung" disease, a breathing disorder that in some cases can be fatal. OSHA set a standard for cotton dust of 0.2 milligrams per cubic meter of air. The textile industry argued that standard would cost $2 billion to implement and urged a weighing of benefits relative to costs in choosing a standard. OSHA had made a benefit-cost analysis in this instance, but its estimates of benefits and costs differed markedly from the industry's. The Supreme Court concluded that benefits did not have to be weighed relative to costs, largely because Congress did not specify that in the Act and probably did not intend to, because it included benefit-cost guidelines in some other legislation where it intended to have the benefit-cost analysis applied. Instead, the occupational safety and health legislation spoke of feasibility, which is a question of achievability rather than a weighing of benefits relative to costs.

Another characteristic of OSHA standards is that they concern safety more than health. Safety standards are easier to set and implement than health standards. Given the greater difficulty workers have in assessing health risks, however, standards in the health area would seem to be more valuable. Dangers to health also can be far more difficult to determine and would more likely be found through the wide-ranging and systematic studies that an agency like OSHA might perform. OSHA probably should have given more attention to protecting health, where it could have a genuine comparative advantage.

Revised Forms of OSHA Actions

As OSHA gained experience it learned that rigid rules of the command-and-control type were meeting objections that reduced their effectiveness. So it tried to make rules more flexible, and it tried to make greater use of information. To set more persuasive

---

[26] *American Textile Institute, Inc. v. R. J. Donovan, Secretary of Labor,* 69, L. Ed. 2nd, 185 (1981).

standards, it introduced benefit-cost analysis. It also tried to make use of ergonomic knowledge in designing standards.

Flexible Standards

Aware that its rigid, rule-setting approach was meeting resistance, and that such resistance was not unjustified, OSHA attempted to revise the way its rules would work. Greater flexibility of OSHA standards came with a grain-elevator dust standard in 1984. Rather than specify a single form of standard for dealing with grain-elevator dust, OSHA allowed operators of grain elevators to clean up the dust in several ways: (1) to sweep it up once per shift, (2) to sweep it when it was an eighth of an inch in thickness, or (3) to use pneumatic (blower) equipment to remove it. This flexibility signifies more of a performance approach to standards, allowing several ways to achieve a desired result and placing focus on the result. A main advantage of flexibility is that it would allow grain elevator operators to accomplish the goal in a lowest cost way, which could differ for different operators.

Improving Information

Another important OSHA step, which started during the Carter administration, required the labeling of chemicals. Regulation in this informational form, which, in addition to labels, calls for training of workers in the handling of chemicals, can strengthen the functioning of the market. It can do so because it provides information workers can use to judge risks and, in turn, evaluate the compensating wage differentials they were receiving for bearing those risks. Furthermore, focusing on specific dangers reflects overall attention to health by the employer, somewhat as the Toxics Release Inventory (TRI) program called attention to environmental protection. Informing workers of hazards was a desirable activity also because it was a way to attack health dangers, which had received less attention from OSHA than had safety.

Benefit-Cost Analysis

OSHA also attempted, after President Reagan's Executive Order 12291 in 1981 called for it generally, to compare benefits with costs in choosing standards. With time, the logic behind allocating resources to achieve the most beneficial result has won supporters. One area in which this might alter OSHA tendencies is in the choice between mandating machine modifications or requiring personal protections. For example, to lessen the risk of damage to workers' hearing, a machine may be modified or workers may wear ear covers. The latter is often far less costly, but OSHA tended to prescribe engineering modification of equipment. Such a solution is more popular with workers, and might also be more reliably implemented because it does not depend on worker behavior. When the cost is far higher than personal protective steps, however, the wisdom of modifying machines can be questioned, because the same funds used in another way could probably improve health and safety more.

Ergonomic Regulation

In the late 1980s and early 1990s, one of OSHA's major efforts involved the development of policies based on ergonomic knowledge—knowledge about jobs and tools that fit the physical and psychological limits of individuals—that would be aimed at reducing injuries caused by repetitive motions and related features of work. Ergonomic injuries grew over the last 20 years in many jobs, such as assembly line work, meat-packing, and computer programming. Hundreds of thousands of workers are afflicted. From 1987 to 1993, the number of cases per 10,000 workers went from 10 to 38, perhaps in part because it was more readily diagnosed but also because it truly was occurring more frequently. Roughly 40 percent of the workforce now works at computer keyboards, where this type of problem is serious. To address these problems, rule-writing efforts to specify new regulations began at OSHA in 1990.

The National Association of Manufacturers and other opponents objected to the new rules because they feared that the rules would force large cost increases. They claimed the OSHA proposal to be based on imprecise science and to impose high costs on firms while offering uncertain benefits. In response, OSHA sharply reduced the scope of the proposal. Rather than applying to the nation's entire workforce of nearly 100 million, as originally planned, new rules would apply to 21 million workers in high-risk jobs where they repeat the same motion, lift heavy objects, or perform other physically stressful tasks. After Congress aimed budget cuts at the program, OSHA finally abandoned it altogether.

OSHA attempted to revive this program of ergonomic regulation in the workplace late in the 1990s by offering information to employers on ergonomic research and warning of ergonomic hazards. OSHA provided technical assistance to automobile manufacturers, meat-packers, and nursing home owners. It sponsored conferences for employers on the subject. The agency also announced it would use its authority to cite employers for ergonomic hazards in the workplace. Such hazards could include speeding up assembly lines, repetitive and heavy lifting, or intensive work at keyboards. OSHA developed and issued a standard and rules in 2000. Partly in response to feverish appeals from businesses large and small, Congress passed a joint resolution disapproving the rules, which essentially nullified them. Thus, the question of ergonomic regulation is unsettled. It reveals the possible advantages of constructive action, such as providing information to affected parties in an effort to win their support. It also shows how political winds can influence the policies of regulatory agencies.

BOX 22.4 The Advantage of a Standard for Enforcement

In 2000, OSHA cited Pepperidge Farm, Inc., for lifting and repetitive motion injuries at its Downingtown, Pennsylvania plant. The Occupational Safety and Health Review Commission (which considers workplace health and safety disputes) reviewed the citation. It supported OSHA's general authority to issue citations for these recognized hazards, but the Review Commission did not find Pepperidge Farm liable for consequences. It said OSHA could not prove that its recommendations would remedy the problem. Had a standard been in effect, OSHA could have shown that the standard was not being met, and that would have strengthened OSHA's case. Without a standard, OSHA is handicapped in enforcing its recommended practices.

See A. B. Crenshaw, "Fax Attack Helped Kill Ergonomics Regulations," *Washington Post*, March 12, 2001, p. E3.

Enforcement

OSHA, in cooperation with state agencies, inspects workplaces and issues citations for noncompliance with its standards. It imposes fines for these citations, which vary with the seriousness or the willfulness of the violation. Firms can reduce fines by up to 30 percent if they make serious efforts to meet the standards. Most OSHA inspections are systematically programmed to take inspectors to sites that are more likely to have violations based on statistical sampling principles. Through these methods the agency has gradually come to focus more inspection effort on high-risk industries, such as construction and metal fabricating.[27] Indeed, in 2004 almost 60 percent of OSHA inspections were in the construction industry and more than 20 percent were in manufacturing.[28]

Other categories of inspections are prompted by accidents, worker complaints or other referrals, or previous violations. A serious accident involving death or other catastrophe leads to an OSHA inspection. Employee complaints can also spur an OSHA inspection if the circumstances appear dangerous, and referrals come from other government agencies. Previous citations for willful, serious, or repeated violations can bring follow-up inspections. So too will a court restraining order involving anything that is perceived to be an imminent danger.

Despite a 2000-person army of OSHA inspectors, any typical workplace has a very small chance of being inspected,[29] and fines have been modest, although recently they have increased.[30] Moreover, follow-up inspections to see whether violations have been corrected occur only about 5 percent of the time, although OSHA now gives special attention to repeat offenders.[31] Harm to a firm's reputation, which is important in attracting workers, might be more important than a fine, so most firms prefer to comply. In industries with greater hazards, the chances of inspection are now greater, and the fines can be substantial. Together, those factors raise the incentive to comply. Perhaps because OSHA initially gave more than proportional attention to small firms, and those firms complained, Congress insisted in 1978 that for firms with fewer than 10 nonserious violations, no penalty should be imposed. Although OSHA has moved to inspect large firms more, it is still criticized for giving too much enforcement attention to smaller firms, even though larger firms are more likely to provide training and to have safety and health policies in place.[32]

The combination of rare inspections and modest fines that have characterized much of OSHA's enforcement leads to the conclusion that enforcement is weak. Even if standards are always sound and valuable, weak enforcement does not force their

---

[27] For a description of how OSHA targets its inspections, see Wokutch (1990). Siskind (1993) reports numbers of inspections. For OSHA enforements strategies, see U.S. Department of Labor, OSHA Enforement, at www.osha.gov/dep/enforcement/enforcement_results_06.html.

[28] See inspections at www.osha.gov.

[29] See Lofgren (1989).

[30] For example, after investigating a BP refinery explosion in March, 2005 at Texas City, Texas, that killed 15 workers and injured 180, OSHA fined BP $21 million.

[31] See Weil (1996).

[32] See Smith (1979).

implementation. As long as any employer might calculate that it can save money by skimping on safety, the aims of OSHA programs are at risk.[33]

State Enforcement of OSHA Regulation

The Occupational Safety and Health Act contained a provision that allowed states rather than OSHA to enforce OSHA standards, and 24 states and 2 territories have elected to do so in some form.[34] State enforcement has the advantage of local knowledge, and having a large number of states involved increases the chance for an innovative improvement. A state's interest in competitive success, with both workers and employers, may also elicit a more cooperative attitude between regulators and regulated firms. The possibility that states would compete to lower costs and attract firms through lenient enforcement of standards in a "race to the bottom" is a potential drawback. Workers and citizens may oppose such an outcome, however, so efficiency might win out. OSHA monitors state programs and provides up to 50 percent of a state's cost.

It is possible to contrast the 21 states that have full enforcement responsibility with the remaining states where federal authorities enforce OSHA rules. By comparing fatality rates under such state enforcement versus federal enforcement over the 1981 to 1995 period, economist John Bradbury (2006) found that where states enforced OSHA rules there were roughly 25 to 35 percent fewer deaths. He controlled for many characteristics across states, including the composition of employment by industries and income per worker. The states that enforced OSHA standards had slightly higher death rates overall, but they had relatively more workers in dangerous industries. They also had considerably higher workers compensation payments per worker. After taking into account the effects of these differences, the states enforcing OSHA standards were left with lower death rates. While further study of the matter is warranted, it appears that decentralized enforcement of occupational safety by states may offer advantages over federal enforcement.

Effects of OSHA Regulation

No observation is possible of a world with OSHA and a world without OSHA to allow an ideal basis for comparison. Conditions before and after OSHA was created can be observed, but that comparison cannot yield a simple answer either. There is a long trend in many of the measures of occupational safety or health that we might use to estimate effects. Such measures show steady improvement, so we cannot draw conclusions by looking at measures before and after OSHA came into existence. To make matters worse, data gathered by the U.S. Bureau of Labor Statistics changed just when OSHA was created, so a full comparison is impossible.

---

[33] A three-part *New York Times* series highlighted such an employer. See David Barstow and Lowell Bergman, "At a Texas Foundry, an Indifference to Life," *New York Times*, January 8, 2003, p. A1; "Family's Profits, Wrung from Blood and Sweat," *New York Times*, January 9, 2003, p. A1; and "Deaths on the Job, Slaps on the Wrist," *New York Times*, January 10, p. A1.

[34] Twenty-one states with their own complete enforcement programs are Alaska, Arizona, California, Hawaii, Indiana, Iowa, Kentucky, Maryland, Michigan, Minnesota, Nevada, New Mexico, North Carolina, Oregon, South Carolina, Tennessee, Utah, Vermont, Virginia, Washington, and Wyoming. Connecticut, New York, and New Jersey enforce OSHA standards at state government agencies, and Puerto Rico and the Virgin Islands are the territories that operate their own OSHA programs.

Early studies of the effect of OSHA actions, such as the number of inspections on measures of safety or the rate of lost workdays due to accidents found no effect. But in more recent periods, and with larger samples, studies have revealed positive effects on safety from OSHA efforts. Companies' compliance with OSHA standards has been quite good.[35] Inspections do improve compliance, and repeat inspections are especially effective. The compliance rate, or the fraction of standards met, roughly tripled in the second inspection after a first.[36] Given the low penalties, good compliance might be surprising, but it can be rationalized. Harm to a firm's reputation might follow from publicity about citations, although that can be avoided if inspections are rare. Firms might be expecting greater fines, and they also may learn about the benefits of complying with standards from a first inspection. Organizational behavior might play a role, too, as responsible workers and managers in firms respond to problems in constructive ways, without private cost-benefit calculations. For instance, the presence of a union appears to improve compliance.[37]

Even when there is greater compliance with OSHA standards, there is a question whether safety and health improve. Evidence does show that enforcement reduces injuries, but the role compliance plays is not clear.[38] The effect might come directly through improved compliance with standards, but that connection is not totally convincing.[39] And if compliance does not reliably reduce injury and health, that could explain why some studies have not found strong improvement from OSHA effort.[40] We just noted that OSHA programs administered by states had fewer workplace fatalities, which seems to show that regulatory federalism can offer advantages.

One lesson from examining OSHA's attempts to improve occupational safety and health is that the competitive market process, together with courts and workers' compensation laws, accomplish a great deal. An OSHA policy aimed at strengthening that market process, by improving information that workers have about the workplace and that employers have about risks, also appears to be fruitful.

22.4 | RETIREMENT SECURITY LAWS

One of the most valuable employee benefits is a retirement pension that provides income after the employee stops working. Basic retirement protection comes to workers through federal Social Security payments, but private pensions are more significant as sources of retirement income.[41] Such private pensions and employee health insurance can be at risk when firms fail. As we noted in Section 22.1, pension plans

---

[35] See Bartel and Thomas (1985) and Gray and Jones (1991a, 1991b).

[36] See Weil (1996).

[37] See Bacow (1980).

[38] See Cooke and Gautschi (1981) and Scholz and Gray (1990).

[39] See Weil (1996) for limited support for the connection of compliance to safety and health.

[40] See, for example, Viscusi (1986), who found accident rates might be slightly lower because of OSHA effort.

[41] For evaluation of Social Security, see Diamond (2004).

are of three main types.[42] If they promise specific *benefits* to the employee upon retirement, they are defined-benefit plans. If they involve employee and/or employer *contributions*, often invested as the employee directs to form a retirement fund, they are defined-contribution plans. For example, tax advantaged 401k plans, which defer income tax payments on funds a worker invests, are defined-contribution plans. The assets in these plans are owned by the employees. Pension payments from defined-contribution plans therefore depend less on the survival of the firm and more on the success of the investments made. A third type of plan is the cash-balance plan, which accrues funds for the employee at a regular rate through the employee's career, rather than rising markedly at the end as traditional defined-benefit plans do.

Pension payments are explicitly specified in defined-benefit plans. The retirement benefit is usually low in early years and grows larger after more years with the employer, because it is based on years with the employer and on the most recent hourly or salaried wage. Such high end-of-career benefits are designed to invite life-long employment. The plans, however, are not always adequately funded. The employer that sponsors a defined-benefit plan either invests with the purpose of providing all the defined benefits or expects to pay some part of them out of company profits. The employer that sponsors a cash-balance plan invests funds on behalf of the employee, usually at a modest promised return so the fund grows uniformly over the worker's career. The worker owns that fund and can take it when leaving the firm. The employer that sponsors a defined-contribution plan may contribute but leaves to the employee the responsibility for managing the pension plan and for most of its funding.[43] All of these pension plans qualify for lower taxes, and since such plans began to be developed over 30 years ago, defined-contribution plans and cash-balance plans have grown more important, while defined-benefit plans have declined.[44] Indeed, employees now contribute as much to retirement savings as employers do on their behalf.[45]

Federal pension plan regulation is complicated and is guided primarily by the **Employee Retirement Income Security Act (ERISA)** of 1974.[46] The ERISA was formulated in response to serious pension failures, such as the withdrawal of pension benefits by the Studebaker Corporation, a failing automobile company, in 1963. It is a complex law with four titles, or parts, one of which is in the nation's tax code. Only a few important features can be examined here, to illustrate pension financing and show where economic problems may exist. The ERISA regulates defined-benefit, cash-balance, and defined-contribution pension plans, all of which are examined in this section.

---

[42] For analysis of the role of pensions in the employment contract relationship, see Ippolito (1985).

[43] Self-managed defined contribution plans tend to perform less well than professionally managed plans, presumably because individuals are not skilled at managing them. See Ed Dravo, "The 4 Percent Solution," *Slate*, April 30, 2004, at http://slate.msn.com/id/2099695/.

[44] See Friedberg and Owyang (2002).

[45] See Edward Wyatt, "Pension Change Puts the Burden on the Worker," *New York Times*, April 5, 2002, p. A1.

[46] See 29 U.S.C.A. §§ 1011–1145 (1988).

Defined-Benefit Pension Plans

Defined-benefit pension plans cover about 40 million workers and are the earliest form of large-scale pension plans in the United States. They promise specific pension payments for an employee's retirement years. These payments are usually in proportion to the years worked by the employee and to the final rate of wage or salary earned. There was a time when such pensions were not "vested," or were not the property of the employee, and they could be forfeited by an employee who quit or was fired.[47] Such pensions encouraged longer employee tenure because an employee could not leave without sacrificing pension benefits. Changes in the ERISA law in 1986 required that defined-benefit plans be vested, usually within five years of initial employment,[48] so after some point employees now have a right to the funds invested on their behalf.

Investments in defined-benefit plans must comply with stricter federal guidelines than those for defined-contribution plans. An obvious reason for this is that employers manage defined-benefit plans, while defined-contribution plans allow employees great control over the investment of their accumulated retirement funds.[49] To avoid having the employer bias the portfolio in its defined-benefit plan toward its own stock, such stock is limited to no more than 10 percent of the portfolio. There is presently no such limit for investments in defined-contribution plans.

Broadly, employers need not pay taxes on the funds they set aside for the purpose of providing defined pension benefits to their employees. Because of this tax saving, offering a pension can attract employees to the firm at lower cost than an equivalent amount of salary or wages. Employees would otherwise have to take after-tax salaries and wages for that pension purpose, which would be more costly to them.

There are essentially two ways to value defined-benefit pensions. One value takes into account all that is needed to fund the promised pension. The other value is a bare minimum, to be provided if the employee stopped working tomorrow. This lower amount is the legal obligation of the firm, but the firm can set aside tax-free funds in excess of this legal obligation. Consider these two different ways to value a defined-benefit pension, say for a 40-year-old employee named Mary who has worked 15 years with a company. First, consider that professionals, called actuaries, calculate the life expectancy for an average person at any age.[50] Using such information, it is possible to estimate the value of the full retirement payments that Mary will receive if she stays with the company 25 more years, until she retires at age 65, and then lives as long as actuarial tables predict (almost 20 more years). Performing this calculation now for Mary, and for all other employees, determines a total pension obligation for the firm. In principle, this obligation can be represented in its present-value form, as long as a

---

[47] For a rich description of effects of these earlier plans, in which funds did not belong to employees, see Glendon and Lev (1979).

[48] As an alternative, vesting may be accomplished gradually over as many as seven years. See Conison (1998).

[49] For comparison of defined-benefit and defined-contribution plans, see Ippolito (1985).

[50] See *65+ in the United States: 2005*, U.S. Census Bureau Economics and Statistics Administration, publication P23–209, for a description of life after age 65.

discount rate can be agreed upon. This present value of the pension obligation is called the **ongoing pension liability**, and the firm can shield from taxes enough money to generate it.

A second value of the pension, which we can also represent in present-value form, assumes that Mary does not work another day. The funds accumulated to date to provide her current retirement benefit would then constitute the value of her pension, without considering her further work. Because defined-benefit plans offer lower retirement payments in early years, this might be a modest sum. In part because it represents what exists today, this sum is called the firm's **termination pension liability**. The termination pension liability is the *legal* liability of the employer, to which the employee is entitled if the employer terminates its pension plan. The ongoing pension liability normally exceeds the legal obligation of the firm, the termination pension liability, in part because the pension amount depends on years of service and final wage payments, so it usually increases substantially in the last years of a worker's career. That final obligation is reflected in the ongoing pension liability but not in the termination liability.

Now suppose a firm that has funded its ongoing pension liability desperately needs funds. The firm can terminate its pension plan, provide the termination pension liability for its employees, and take for its own purposes the difference between the on-going pension liability and the termination pension liability. The firm will have to pay corporate taxes on this amount, because that tax will not have been paid. This action is common enough that it has a name: **reversion**.

Company takeovers, when outsiders acquired enough stock to control a company, were common in the 1980s. After a few out of the many that occurred, pension funds in the acquired firm were reduced through the process of reversion. That is, in the wake of the takeover, the newly formed organization terminated a well-funded pension plan and claimed the reversion assets as its own. Although this happened in only a few takeovers, it caused such outrage that Congress taxed reversions in 1986, and in 1990 it raised the reversion-tax rate to 50 percent.[51] This Congressional action overlooked the possibility that employers would respond by contributing less to defined-benefit pension plans. There now is convincing evidence that after this change, employers stopped funding beyond the minimum legal obligation (not all firms provide even that amount). There has been some effort to reduce the high tax on reversion.[52]

If firms that offer defined-benefit pensions fail without having them adequately funded, insurance for retirees may be available through the federal Pension Benefit Guaranty Corporation (PBGC). Employers decide whether to participate in this insurance, however, so retirees are not covered at every employer, and any pension the PBGC provides will almost certainly be less generous than that originally promised to employees. A rough illustration of employer liabilities under a defined-benefit plan is

---

[51] With a reversion tax rate of 50 percent, plus a corporate tax rate of, say 34 percent, a corporation might obtain only 16 percent of the reversion amount. See Ippolito (2001).

[52] See Ippolito (2001) for evidence about the effect of a high tax on reversions. On efforts to change the tax, see Mary Williams Walsh, "New Tug of War over Excess Pension Cash," *New York Times*, March 3, 2005, p. B1.

Figure 22.1 *Defined-Benefit Pension Plan Prospects over a 40-Year Career*

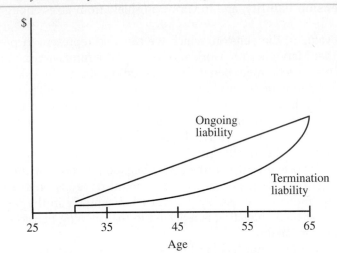

contained in Figure 22.1. The employee pictured begins work at age 25 and is vested, or has a claim on assets if they are there, at age 30. Pension benefits rise gradually over the career but more steeply near retirement, while the need to save funds to provide the pension—the ongoing liability—rises at a constant rate over the worker's career.

Cash-Balance Pension Plans

The difference between ongoing liability and termination liability of defined-benefit plans emphasizes how pension benefits affect workers of different ages differently. The termination valuation reflects the way the value of a pension rises for older employees late in their careers, because the benefits to which they are entitled increase dramatically as they approach retirement. An alternative, cash-balance, pension plan promises a steady conservative rate of return, which approximates the ongoing liability of a defined-benefit plan.[53] Compared to ordinary defined-benefit plans, the steady accumulation of assets in cash-balance plans tends to offer higher values for younger employees and lower values for older employees. Figure 22.2 shows the steady asset build up in cash-balance pension plans, and those assets are formally owned by the employee. Nevertheless, like defined-benefit plans, cash-balance plans are also protected by PBGC insurance.

Some companies have terminated their older defined-benefit pension plans and replaced them with cash-balance plans.[54] They say this helps them recruit younger workers, and that cash-balance plans are better for workers who expect to

---

[53] For a description of cash-balance plans see Sandra Block, "As More Companies Adopt Cash-Balance Plans, What You Need to Know," *USA Today*, August 8, 2006, p. 3B.

[54] See Richard A. Oppel, Jr., "Companies Cash In On New Pension Plan," *New York Times*, August 20, 1999, p. C1.

Figure 22.2 *Cash-Balance Pension Plan Prospects over a 40-Year Career*

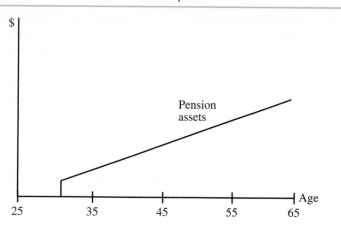

change employers rather than stay with one employer all their working lives. A change from a defined-benefit to a cash-balance plan breaks an implicit promise made to older workers who no longer have the pension program they anticipated when they were hired.[55] Cash-balance plans invest funds on behalf of the employee at some promised rate of return, which may be variable according, for example, to some government bond rate. When there is ambiguity about that rate, some companies have skimped on funding their cash-balance plans.[56]

Cash-balance pension plans are a response to changes in recent years. The tax deductibility of pension funding once caused firms to accumulate sizeable reserves to meet their defined-benefit pension obligations. That was when employees were more closely tied to their employers, in part because pensions were not movable to a new employer and because benefits were larger when an employee worked for only one employer until retirement. A pension would be lost if an employee quit.[57] Because legislation adopted in 1986 required it, employees have become the owners of their pensions after a waiting period. With such vesting, pensions became portable across employers and less effective for retaining workers. Cash-balance pension plans allow employers to attract younger workers by accruing pension benefits for them steadily over the workers' careers, without asking them to wait for a big increase at the end. That is why firms have moved away from defined-benefit plans toward cash-balance plans and defined-contribution plans.

---

[55] The IBM corporation replaced its defined-benefit plan with a cash-balance plan in 1999 and withstood legal challenges brought on age discrimination grounds. See Stephanie Armour, "Court Rules IBM Pension Change Didn't Discriminate," *USA Today*, August 8, 2006, p. 1B.

[56] See Steven Greenhouse, "Wrong Payouts are Uncovered in Pension Plan," *New York Times*, May 8, 2002, p. A22.

[57] See Glendon and Lev (1979).

Defined-Contribution Pension Plans

Defined-contribution plans were stimulated by federal legislation in 1978 that created tax advantages for retirement plans to encourage workers to save more for retirement. Most plans that qualify for the tax advantage are administered by corporations for their employees and are designated as 401k plans. On average, however, the employer now contributes less than the employee to defined-contribution plans. Although the government places limits on the amount of their annual contributions, employees have the advantage that contributions into the plans are deducted from their taxable income. Not only are income taxes on these contributions deferred, but taxes on income earned on the contributions are also deferred. Taxes are paid later, however, as the funds are withdrawn in the form of income for retirement years.

Defined-contribution plans are regulated for compliance with tax law but not for investment soundness. Investments are overseen by the employee directly, so such regulation seems unnecessary. On average, the employees' portfolios perform less well, however, than professionally managed portfolios.[58] Defined-contribution retirement portfolios tend to be heavily weighted in employers' stock, for example, rather than being diversified. In many plans, employer contributions to the pensions are made in company stock, and some plans require that their contribution remain in the form of company stock, at least for some time period. In the case of Enron, for example, the employee was not to sell the company's contributed stock until age 50, and almost 60 percent of the value of the average retirement portfolio was in Enron stock when the company went bankrupt. Company stock may be over weighted in retirement portfolios because it is offered to employees at attractive terms when they make their acquisition choices. Figure 22.3 shows a range of possible values for pension assets, depending on investment success, and indicates that retirement need not occur at age 65.

Figure 22.3 *Defined-Contribution Pension Plan Prospects over a 40-Year Career*

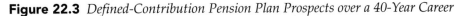

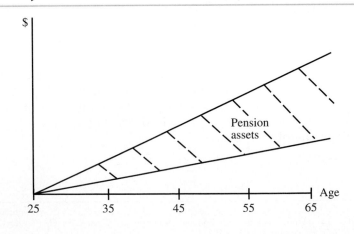

---

[58] See Ed Dravo, "The 4 Percent Solution," *Slate*, April 30, 2004, at http://slate.msn.com/id/2099695/.

Since their inception in 1978, defined-contribution plans have grown handsomely. Indeed, from 1984 to 2000, so many companies adopted them that assets in defined-contribution 401k plans grew at 20 percent a year. They sometimes exist in the same firms along with defined-benefit plans,[59] but usually an individual employee has one plan or the other. In 1995, the total assets in defined-contribution plans passed those of defined-benefit plans, and they now exceed $2 trillion. Companies were glad to pass to employees the responsibility for providing retirement income, and employees like the greater control they have of defined-contribution plans. Companies also saw employee stock ownership as a way to motivate employees to work harder, because they would benefit from company success. Unlike the original defined-benefit plans, defined-contribution plans are immediately portable. An employee owns the defined-contribution retirement funds from the start and can take the funds along when changing employers.

The timing of employee retirement decisions can vary more under defined-contribution plans, as Figure 22.3 suggests. Whereas defined-contribution plans are quite straightforward investment plans, defined-benefit plans were designed to induce specific retirement behavior. For example, defined-benefit plans often rise considerably in value when an employee reaches age 60 or 62 or 65, and they improve little after that. Employees must often stay with the firm until they reach the required age to be entitled to the full defined-benefit pension, and their lack of eligibility for improved benefits after they pass that "trigger" age tends to induce retirement at that age. Defined-contribution plans do not focus benefits at a specific age in this way, so workers under them may work until they feel ready to retire. As a result, workers who have defined-contribution plans tend to retire later than workers who have defined-benefit plans. Eighty percent of defined-benefit plan workers are retired by age 65, but only 60 percent of defined-contribution plan workers are.[60] Freedom from mandatory retirement at colleges and universities also has delayed the retirement of faculty and may result in faculties that are slightly older on average.[61]

SUMMARY

Although competition in markets can harness forces against discrimination in employment, competition can be imperfect, and the effects of discrimination are very harmful to those who suffer them. Efforts to improve employment fairness in the workplace started with laws to protect employees in the 1930s. The National Labor Relations Act of 1935 (also called the Wagner Act) protected workers who were union supporters from retaliation by their employers. Other forms of conduct, such as

---

[59] About 17 percent of companies offer both types of retirement plan. See Edward Wyatt, "Pension Change Puts the Burden On the Worker," *New York Times*, April 5, 2002, p. A1.

[60] See Friedberg and Webb (2000).

[61] See Ashenfelter and Card (2002).

whistleblowing to reveal bad behavior within a firm, are also protected. The Equal Pay Act, the Civil Rights Act, and the Age Discrimination in Employment Act, came in the 1960s. They protected certain classes of workers, particularly workers age 40 or older and women, and they barred discrimination based on race, color, religion, or national origin. In 1990 the Americans with Disabilities Act extended protection from discrimination to qualified individuals who had disabilities, in some circumstances requiring that employers accommodate the disability.

In addition to pursuing fairness in workplaces, Congress has sought to combat the physical dangers that workplaces inherently possess. Workers can gain compensation in markets for being exposed to such dangers, in the form of wage premiums. Injured workers may be compensated for harm under state workers' compensation laws, or, in exceptional circumstances, they may sue employers directly. Employers, in turn, are motivated to offer safer work places, either to persuade employees to accept lower wages because risks are lower or to be entitled to lower contributions to state workers' compensation funds because injuries are fewer. For this market process to work well, information has to be readily available in markets, a range of job opportunities has to exist for workers, and awards for injuries under workers' compensation programs need to be significant.

Federal efforts to improve workplace safety came in the Occupational Safety and Health Act of 1970. The Act specified standards for the workplace and the main agency created under the Act, the Occupational Safety and Health Administration (OSHA), set out to enforce them. These standards were hurriedly imposed, they stressed safety over health when information about health risks might have been more valuable, and they focused on design more than performance. The OSHA has since introduced more flexible standards that are focused more on performance and has moved also to provide information to help workers and firms understand dangers. It has targeted its inspections better on industries with high risks of accident. Under the 1970 Act, states can choose to enforce the standards, and the 21 states that do this have fewer workplace fatalities than the OSHA regulated states after other effects are controlled. In any case, the enforcement task is enormous, even in light of the substantial resources available to the OSHA. Thus, although the OSHA may have brought improvements to the workplaces of America, its effects on health and safety are not dramatic. Markets and courts, and state workers' compensation laws, will continue to play a major role in promoting health and safety in the workplace.

Congress has also moved to protect retirement security for workers through federal regulation of private pension plans. Such regulation is guided primarily by the Employee Retirement Income Security Act (ERISA) of 1974, which now supports three main types of plans. A defined-benefit plan offers a specific formula to determine the employee's pension, which usually remains low for some years and then rises considerably as the employee approaches retirement. A cash-balance pension plan accrues pension benefits more steadily over a career, and gives ownership of the funds to the employee. A federal insurance program exists for these defined-benefit and cash-balance plans, but the insurance is not generous and employers are not required to participate in it. If a firm fails, employees and retirees who have a cash-balance plan own its funds, and thus have some protection, but when they have a defined-benefit plan that is not adequately funded, they may lose significant pension benefits. In the future, accounting rules will pay more attention to firms' pension liabilities, so unfunded obligations to their employees will be revealed as a prominent financial liability of the firms.

A third type of pension plan is the defined-contribution pension plan, which sets aside funds the employee owns and manages. In this case the pension ultimately depends on how well the employee's investments perform. A major problem arises when employees keep a large fraction of their funds in their employer's stock, because if the employer fails the retirement funds may lose much of their value. Recent bankruptcies have revealed the importance of having employers properly fund their defined-benefit and cash-balance pension plans, and of having employees diversify their investments in defined-contribution retirement plans.

QUESTIONS

1. Suppose there are two classes of worker, green and red. An employer has four candidates, two green and two red, for a single job. Although the employer does not know the productivities of the individual workers, the employer knows that on average the productivities tend to be higher for red workers. The information not available to the employer is that the first and second green workers have productivities of 4 and 10, while the first and second red workers have productivities of 7 and 9. By expending more effort, the employer can determine this information about the productivity of each candidate. Could statistical discrimination apply in this case? Explain why it could or could not.

2. Discuss the "employment at will" doctrine. Note advantages the doctrine offers to workers and to employers. Which side of the employment arrangement can suffer most from it, the employee or the employer? How can product market conditions affect this balance between the employee and the employer?

3. Consider the data on wage premia and deaths per 100,000 workers by job in Table 22.1. Taking the wage premium for a police officer as the amount the officer is willing to pay (WTP) to make the risk of death zero, use the formula $WTP = PX$ (where P is the probability of death and X is the value of life) to estimate the value of life for a police officer. Do the same thing for a lumberjack and compare the resulting values of life. Does the value attached to saving a life increase or decrease as the risk is greater? Explain why or why not.

4. Having markets allocate workers to jobs based on risks can be useful, in that workers more tolerant of risk can bear greater risks and be compensated for doing so. Evaluate this advantage of the market by considering how market organization and available information can affect its robustness and its reliability.

5. Employees have relied on employer promises for years. Distinguish among the three types of pension plans, defined-benefit pension plans, cash-balance pension plans, and defined-contribution pension plans, in how much each

requires the employee to trust the employer. Explain whether the plan that requires the greatest trust in the employer comes with any offsetting benefit.

6. List weaknesses in the accounting for defined-benefit pension plans. Discuss reasons why accounting properly for defined-benefit pension obligations is important, both for investors and for employees.

7. Explain the difference between the "ongoing pension liability" and the "termination pension liability" of defined-benefit pension plans. Why are there these two bases of value, and what problem does the existence of two bases cause?

23

Consumer Protection

The printed warning on a Superman costume reads, "Cape does not enable user to fly." This simple statement neither surprises nor informs the typical customer. The costume maker is simply trying to avoid liability in case a cape wearer leaps from a tall building. Protections for consumers have grown enormously in the last century, and manufacturers now try to limit their liability wherever possible. Swimmers in early swimming pools bore all risk of injury, for example, but the pool operator today has to protect swimmers. Indeed, diving boards have almost disappeared from motel and hotel swimming pools because owner liability is costly, in the form of either a lawsuit from an injured diver or of insurance payments to protect against such a lawsuit. As another example, the production of small airplanes virtually ceased in the United States until federal legislation in 1994 limited the liability of small airplane manufacturers to only the first 18 years of an airplane's use. Before this legislation, manufacturers' liability for airplane accidents—especially accidents involving old airplanes—was so great that manufacturers could not afford to produce airplanes. Caveat emptor, or let the buyer beware, no longer rules in markets for dangerous consumer products.

Uncertain and unreliable product quality can greatly reduce the effectiveness of a competitive market when information is costly for consumers to obtain. If the product or service involved is one that is important to society, information problems under competitive market organization may not be tolerated, and even monopoly might be imposed in its place. Before New York City built remarkable underground tunnels in 1927 that could bring water from reservoirs in the Catskill Mountains, for example, it relied on competitive markets for drinking water. Anyone who owned a pond and a long hose seemed to be in the water business then, and there were serious problems with contamination.[1] Quality standards, enforced by inspection, might have controlled the situation without resort to monopoly control by the city, because regulation in the form of quality standards can allow a competitive market to avoid dangerously low levels of quality.

---

[1] See Koeppel (2000).

A regulator must still determine quality standards and enforce them. Once in place, standards can support competition among firms that all have to comply with them. When a monopoly seeks to evade standards, consumers may be harmed more than under competition, because they have no competing supplier to turn to. Competing firms meeting safety, quality, or reliability standards, as in the airline, drug, lawn mower, and other industries, can then perform better than monopoly. Each competing firm must meet at least minimal standards, but it also faces pressure to perform better than others because consumers have a choice and turn to other suppliers if they perform better. The disadvantage is that firms might barely comply with the standard, so the standard determines product quality, and its rigidity may even prevent useful change.

Initial federal efforts to improve consumer safety, while relying on markets, focused on foods and drugs with the formation in 1906 of the Food and Drug Administration (FDA). The FDA relied heavily on quality and purity standards, but because drugs and medical devices can have such harmful effects the agency also has power to approve them *before* they can be marketed. Starting in the 1960s, consumer safety regulation exercised greater control over product designs, including safety features for automobiles, glass shower doors, baby cribs, rotary lawnmowers, and other potentially dangerous products. More recently, governments have taken steps to influence individual behavior more directly. Many U.S. states require the actual use of seat belts installed in cars, for instance, or they impose tight drunk-driving definitions and enforcement efforts, or mandate lower highway speed limits (although the initial purpose of lower speed limits in the 1970s was to conserve fuel) and higher minimum drinking ages. Thus recent regulatory steps have gone beyond product design, to change the way we actually use products that might cause harm.

Throughout these recent decades, liability awards have grown dramatically, both in number and in the amounts awarded. Insurance to protect against such claims consequently became far more expensive than it had been before. Indeed, it was this rise in insurance costs to prohibitive levels that caused motel and hotel diving boards and newly manufactured small airplanes to become rare objects. But more generally manufacturers have had to examine their products in an effort to prevent them from causing injury, because a victim can sue for large amounts of money if harm needlessly occurs.

Over the past 50 years, court decisions have gradually shifted in the direction of protecting consumers, and legislation also has afforded greater protections, often by creating agencies focused on particular problems. The development of class-action lawsuits, in which a whole class of consumers achieve economies by filing one suit against a producer, supported this trend. In addition, state and federal governments created agencies to protect consumers. Most states have consumer protection legislation in force, and state governments also file class action suits on behalf of their citizens.

Section 23.1 examines the role courts play in protecting consumers from harm in the use of products or services they purchase, an area known generally as *product liability*. Then in Section 23.2 we consider efforts to protect consumers at the state government level. We then turn to consumer protection activities of major federal regulatory agencies, the Food and Drug Administration in Section 23.3, the National Highway Traffic Safety Administration in Section 23.4, the Consumer Product Safety Commission in Section 23.5, the Federal Trade Commission in Section 23.6, and the Securities and Exchange Commission in Section 23.7.

23.1 | THE COURTS AND PRODUCT LIABILITY

Courts deal with claims of actual loss, and the liability of a manufacturer for a product that causes loss is called **product liability**. Treating these liability claims after the losses have occurred does not mean court decisions have no preventive effect because parties can anticipate the penalties imposed for causing harm based on past court decisions. When the potential liability is great, firms try to avoid such penalties through preventive actions. Nevertheless, at any given time, courts may not have ruled on risky products that have yet to cause harm, and firms may be unaware of their risks.

In principle, government regulation can anticipate such problems before they occur. That would mean regulators could alter product designs or practices to prevent injuries before they happened, which would seem to make regulation more reliable than courts for ensuring consumer safety. Regulators, however, simply cannot anticipate all, or even many, potential problems before they occur. Anticipating problems before they occur is at least as difficult for regulators as it is for firms. For this reason, the age-old role of courts in affording remedies and thus in creating incentives to protect consumers is in no danger of being made redundant by regulatory agencies.

Tort Law

If you are injured by a product today, you may sue its manufacturer, and you may even have a reasonable chance of winning. There was a time when the buyer of a product from an intermediary—the buyer of a car from a car dealer, for example—had no standing to sue the manufacturer, even if the product's design or negligent manufacture had caused harm to the buyer. Early in the twentieth century one could sue for harm only if it arose out of a failure to satisfy some contractual obligation. The injured party in this car example probably did not have an explicit contract with the car's manufacturer, because the faulty product was purchased from an independent (franchised) intermediary, a car dealer.

A **tort** is a civil wrong, and it was first applied as a product liability matter in the *McPherson v. Buick* case of 1916,[2] which involved injury to an automobile passenger when a defective wheel fell off a car. Benjamin Cardozo, who served as chief judge of the New York Court of Appeals from 1914 to 1932 and had a great influence on the development of U.S. tort law, decided this case in favor of the injured plaintiff.

---

[2] See *McPherson v. Buick*, 111 N.E. 1050 (N.Y. 1916).

He noted that there was precedent for finding manufacturers liable to consumers in the absence of direct contracts when the product was "imminently dangerous"—a finding that had been applied to poisons—and he judged automobiles to fall in that general category.[3]

The *McPherson* case established the need for a manufacturer to anticipate how its product would be used, even by someone with whom it had no direct transaction. Later cases broadened this responsibility of the manufacturer, making it necessary to anticipate even unintended uses to which its product might be put. As a result, manufacturers warn consumers of uses for which the product is not suited or is incapable of performing in an effort to prevent inappropriate use and, thus, to protect themselves against tort suits. That is why we see such warnings as "Cape does not enable user to fly."

Tort liability tends to place responsibility for injuries from products in the hands of those with the most information and control over product dangers, the manufacturers. Tort liability also invites consumers to be responsible in their uses of products. For if a driver uses a car while intoxicated, or a handyman uses a chain saw carelessly, any claim for injury against the manufacturer will be less strong. The consumer will have contributed to his or her injury and this will result in the reduction or elimination of any award that the consumer might otherwise have obtained. Large awards in product liability cases thus raise the stakes for consumers as well as for manufacturers to behave responsibly.

Manufacturers of products may be held to "implied warranties" for their products, based on claims they made about them. Indeed, a manufacturer may now prefer to issue an explicit **warranty**, spelling out assurances as to how the product will perform and what will be done to remedy problems, so that liability can be more precisely asserted and even limited. Warranties also offer a way for a producer of a high-quality product to persuade a consumer as to that quality, by making a commitment to perform as specified. Developing a reputation for quality alone may enable a seller to persuade consumers that a product is high in quality, but a warranty is more concrete because it guarantees the consumer a specified level of performance. A generous warranty for a product's performance is only economical if the product performs so the manufacturer is not swamped by costly warranty claims.

Torts and Punitive Damages

When the manufacturer of a product is negligent in its production, and a consumer is harmed as a result, the manufacturer is guilty of a tort. The plaintiff in a tort action today is not only able to pursue **compensatory damages**, which are to cover costs of the harm that was suffered, and damages for their pain and suffering. The plaintiff can also seek **punitive damages**, which are intended to punish the defendant for its transgression. The unusual feature of punitive damages is that they can depend on the wealth of the defendant. That is why cases involving punitive damages routinely involve investigations of the wealth of the defendant. In law, this is the only situation in which the defendant's wealth is a consideration in determining the level of punishment.

---

[3] See G. Edward White (1980, p. 120).

Consideration of the defendant's wealth in assessing a punishment actually is consistent with diminishing marginal utility of wealth in individuals. For example, consider a rich person and a poor person who are alike (have the same utility function) and are to be punished for the same wrongful behavior. A greater sacrifice in wealth must be asked of the richer person to inflict the same absolute reduction in utility as would be imposed on the poorer person by a smaller financial sacrifice. If the same loss in utility is desired for the two persons, different monetary punishments—punishments in relation to wealth—would seem to be necessary.

Defendants in product liability cases are often large, wealthy corporations, and the Supreme Court has limited the punitive damages they must suffer. Under the principle that punishment should depend on wealth, the wealth of corporations opens them to enormous punitive damage assessments. For example, a woman who was seriously burned by a cup of McDonald's coffee received a punitive judgment of nearly $3 million against this large and wealthy corporation that had been warned repeatedly about the danger of high coffee temperatures in more than 700 previous cases.[4] But after BMW was required to make a $2 million punitive damages payment (in addition to $4,000 in compensatory damages) to the purchaser of a new car who received a repainted car that was actually not new, the award was adjusted.[5] The Supreme Court even suggested that a 4-to-1 ratio of punitive to compensatory damages might be high enough. In 2003, the Supreme Court overturned a punitive damage award against State Farm Insurance of $145 million and compensatory damages of $1 million, because it considered the 145-to-1 ratio to be too high.[6] So wealth may be considered, but courts can limit the punitive damages that are based on wealth.

Congress has also made efforts to put an upper limit on product liability damage awards, often under the label of "reform." The word *reform* is used by those who think damage awards are too high and need to be limited. There is considerable debate about the need for reform, because the average award is less than $100,000. One proposal that has been introduced in Congress would limit the amount of any total damage award to either $250,000 or to twice the level of compensatory damages awarded, whichever is greater. Opponents of such national legislation point out that it would not deter corporations from negligent manufacture of products. Consumer advocates in particular oppose any limit on grounds that large damage awards are precisely what is needed so manufacturers of products will make sure they are safe to use, and trial lawyers oppose a maximum that would limit possible gains from law suits. A national limit could also intrude on state responsibilities.

There can be little question that large damage awards in tort suits have made manufacturers more conscious of safety in the use of their products and more concerned about avoiding tort suits. For example, some observers feel that improved highway safety since the 1960s is due not only to safety standards imposed by the

---

[4] The case was settled for a smaller, but unknown, sum. See Anthony Ramirez, "For McDonald's, British Justice Is a Different Cup of Tea," *New York Times*, April 7, 2002, p. WK7.

[5] See *BMW of North America, Inc., v. Gore*, 517 U.S. 559, 116 S.Ct. 1589 (1996).

[6] See *State Farm Mutual Automobile Insur. Co. v. Campbell*, 538 U.S. 408(2003); and Linda Greenhouse, "Supreme Court Sets Limit on Size of Damage Awards," *New York Times*, April 8, 2003, p. A16.

National Highway Traffic Safety Administration (NHTSA), but at least as much to increased punitive damages against vehicle manufacturers that began to be awarded at about the same time the NHTSA was created.

Labeling

In an effort to avoid costly punishment for consumer harm, manufacturers try to anticipate the uses that might be made of their products and warn consumers about possible dangers. For example, automobile manufacturers distributed warning stickers to be affixed inside vehicles to caution about the dangers of air bags, even though they were not required to do so. Instruction manuals that accompany appliances contain frequent mention of possible dangers in the use of such products. In addition to the benefit in avoiding dangers these warnings may bring, they also may be used in law suits as part of a manufacturer's effort to show that consumers could have been informed of dangers.

Labeling will not always protect a manufacturer from liability, especially when labels are unclear or offered only in fine print. Labels also may be less effective for products that are inherently dangerous, such as firearms or skis, that require training for skilled and proper use. Thoughtful and well-designed labels, however, can be useful in educating consumers about proper and improper use of many products, and manufacturers provide them to limit the liability for injury that they might otherwise incur.

23.2 | STATE LAWS

The 50 states enact sometimes different and sometimes similar consumer protection laws. National companies complain that they must satisfy 50 different laws, and they occasionally lobby for national legislation to bring uniformity to the rules they are to follow. But they also seek federal legislation to avoid especially strict requirements that any one state may impose. Yet regional differences, due to climate, altitude, taste, or other characteristics, may make different standards of consumer protection appropriate in the different states.

Motorcycle helmet laws provide an example of differences across states. Twenty-five states and the District of Columbia require all motorcycle riders to wear helmets, while another 22 require only minors to wear them. Only Illinois, Colorado, and Iowa presently have no helmet law. The federal government has pressured states into adopting helmet laws by making more federal highway funds available to states that have them. There is evidence suggesting that helmet laws reduce head injuries and fatalities from motorcycle accidents. For example, five of the six states that adopted mandatory helmet laws since 1989 saw reductions in fatalities from motorcycle accidents, ranging from 15 percent in Washington to 33 percent in Oregon. The sixth state, Maryland, had no decline in fatalities, although motorcycle fatalities made up a slightly smaller fraction of all highway fatalities after the law was in effect.

States' attorneys general may pursue class-action law suits under state consumer-protection laws. In the 1990s many states sued five leading tobacco companies, charging that the companies withheld knowledge about the adverse health consequences of smoking, with the result that the states incurred billions of dollars annually in added health care costs. Tobacco companies reached agreements with Texas (involving $14 billion) and Minnesota ($6 billion) in 1999, and later that year a Master Settlement Agreement was reached with 46 states that involved payments totaling $206 billion over 25 years. Because Congress passed federal legislation in 2005 requiring class-action plaintiffs to bring their suits only in federal courts, class-action suits are expected to be less effective for such cases in the future.

Conflicts are possible between state and federal laws, or at least the laws may differ, and which law rules is not always clear. A plaintiff or a defendant may prefer either federal or state law, and in such a case each side maneuvers to obtain a jurisdictional ruling in its preferred direction. We may never eliminate this problem, which results from our federal form of governmental organization. Federal regulatory institutions can dominate state institutions, however, where interstate commerce is significant. We now turn to examine the first federal agency created to protect consumers, the Food and Drug Administration.

23.3 | THE FOOD AND DRUG ADMINISTRATION

Early in 1906, a novel appeared by Upton Sinclair called *The Jungle*.[7] It became an international success in only 6 weeks and was soon translated into 17 languages. The book described Chicago's turn-of-the-century slaughterhouses, where immigrant workers suffered safety and health hazards and lived lives exposed to disease and deprivation. The filth in the slaughterhouses also affected consumers of the products. Vivid descriptions of conditions so moved the public that the book is credited with inspiring passage of the **Pure Food and Drug Act** in 1906. This Act created the Food and Drug Administration (FDA), a federal agency that protects against impure or adulterated foods or drugs. Sinclair, who sought to promote socialism with his book, said, "I aimed at the public's heart, and by accident I hit it in the stomach."[8]

Scope of the FDA

The FDA represents President Theodore Roosevelt's insistence that rules of commerce be fair to all parties.[9] He asserted that government had a responsibility to intervene when commerce was functioning in a way that harmed consumers, and the Pure Food and Drug Act was the vehicle to guide such intervention. Science grew enormously in the twentieth century, bringing giant pharmaceutical and food industries that chafed under FDA guidance but benefitted from the public confidence it fostered. After sulfanilamide, an early antibiotic, was combined with a toxic sweetener and caused 107 deaths in 1937, Congress introduced testing for safety *before marketing* in the **Food, Drug, and Cosmetic Act** of 1938.

---

[7] See Sinclair (1988).

[8] As quoted at pg. xiii of James R. Barrett's "Introduction" to *The Jungle*; see Sinclair (1988).

[9] For description of the establishment of the FDA, plus a history of its regulatory role for a century, see Hilts (2002).

In 1961 a world-wide thalidomide disaster was limited in the United States by the FDA's refusal to approve it without evidence of safety, a reluctance that confined its harm to those taking pills its manufacturer had distributed free on a test basis to doctors. The tragedy ultimately served to strengthen the FDA's power to protect consumers. In 1962 Congress passed the Kefauver-Harris Amendment to give the FDA authority to require proof that drugs and, in 1976 medical devices, are **efficacious**, that is, that they do what they are claimed to do. The amendment also required informed consent by patients participating in drug trials and the reporting of any adverse effects to the FDA.

For food, cosmetics, drugs, and medical devices, there can be health and safety dangers that consumers are ill equipped to judge, and scientific information can help to guide their decisions. Even if many sellers are careful and responsible, one illicit purveyor could fool consumers and cause great harm. Matters of safety, purity, and cleanliness in production are of primary concern to the FDA, and public health is also a broad concern. As noted, for drugs and medical devices, efficacy—actual effectiveness—is a requirement. Clinical trials are needed to satisfy this requirement, and they delay the introduction of drugs and medical devices, but the requirement ensures that consumers do not waste time and money using products that are not effective in their purpose.

The FDA therefore pursues safety of food, cosmetics, drugs, and medical devices in slightly different ways. For foods and cosmetics, the aim is to eliminate all risk, with few exceptions. For instance, the Delaney Amendment to the Food, Drug, and Cosmetic Act banned additives found to cause cancer in humans or animals. For drugs and medical devices, on the other hand, a trade off is faced between risk and benefit, because substantial benefit may be possible where risk cannot be avoided. The FDA is willing to accept greater risks for drugs when other remedies seem unable to prevent death.[10] All foods, cosmetics, and drugs are to be pure, in that composition

---

BOX 23.1 Ranchers as Neighbors

A deadly outbreak of *E. coli* bacteria in California in 2006 killed 3 people and made 200 others seriously ill in 26 states and Canada. The FDA's Center for Food Safety and Applied Nutrition, and the Centers for Disease Control (both part of the Department of Health and Human Services) worked with the state of California to find the cause of the outbreak. The source of the *E. coli* was traced to one of four suspected produce ranches in Salinas Valley, California, where the strain was found in cattle feces, but how it might have reached the food supply is still unclear. This is a more serious possible externality from ranching than the Coase problem of ranchers' cattle causing problems for farmers (Chapter 19), in that it involved loss of life and its effects were felt far beyond the immediate neighborhood of the source.

See L. Sanders, "Source of Deadly *E. Coli* Is Found at California Ranch," *New York Times*, October 13, 2006, p. A18; and C. Larkin and M. B. Marios, "One Source Not Found for *E. Coli* in Spinach," *New York Times*, March 24, 2007, p. D6.

---

[10] See Andrew Pollack, "Drug's Approval Hints at Flexibility in F.D.A. Process," *New York Times*, May 6, 2003, p. C1.

and potency are to be within specified tolerances. Producers must also avoid contamination by all reasonable means. The FDA can prescribe good practices to achieve production cleanliness, and if it finds a production process is unclean, it can label the product adulterated and prevent its sale.

As an example of the enforcement of these aims, the FDA closed down drug firm Warner-Lambert for a period in 1993. The FDA claimed no "critical health risk," but a variety of complaints against the company had accumulated without effective remedy. There had been 14 recalls of products in less than a year. The company had not been reporting the quality control test results required by the FDA, had used lab workers who were not properly trained, and had followed procedures not approved by the FDA. The FDA took legal action, and the shut down resulted from a consent decree entered in U.S. District Court in New Jersey. Under the decree, Warner-Lambert could sell existing supplies of products, and it could manufacture under FDA supervision products that had no close substitutes. Warner-Lambert estimated it lost $150 million in revenue as a result.

Food and Drug Labeling

An example of FDA policy is the mandatory labeling of food items. Since May of 1994, the FDA has required U.S. manufactured foods to present basic "nutrition facts" on their products to enable consumers to make informed choices among available offerings. The facts to be reported include the amount of fat, saturated fat, cholesterol, sodium, protein, and other elements that the product contains, as well as what fraction of daily nutritional requirements of each category that amount represents. Meat and poultry products, which the U.S. Department of Agriculture regulates, also have to comply with the law.

The labels are supposed to provide information consumers can use to make sound nutritional judgments in selecting foods. They are also intended to prevent sellers of these products from making misleading claims about them (such as "low fat!"). "Low fat" is defined to mean 3 or fewer grams of fat per serving, and "fat free"

BOX 23.2 Bad Apples

In 1998 Odwalla, a producer of fresh fruit drinks, pleaded guilty in a Chicago court to selling apple juice tainted with *E. coli* bacteria or other impurities that in 1996 had made 70 people sick in California, Colorado, Washington, and Canada. This group included 14 children who were very seriously ill and one 16-month-old girl who died. In addition to the criminal penalty of $1.5 million that resulted from the settlement of that suit, the company paid over $12 million to settle a dozen civil suits. After the incident, the company began pasteurizing (raising the temperature to 140 degrees for 30 minutes to kill germs) its apple juice and it overhauled its production process to insure the safety of its products. Criminal penalties are rare in food safety cases, in part because it is difficult to trace widespread food poisoning to its source. The case of the Odwalla fresh fruit drink company provides an example of FDA enforcement through court cases involving the FDA, states, and private parties.

means less than 1/2 gram of fat per serving. The FDA specified similar limits for meanings of other terms such as "light" or "lite," "low calorie," "sugar-free," or "cholesterol-free." The FDA also defined serving sizes in a uniform way. The FDA imposes standards that foods must meet if they bear certain labels. For example, makers of grains and breads called "enriched" must include folic acid, which has been found valuable in reducing birth defects. The **Nutrition Labeling and Education Act** of 1990 extended labeling requirements to dietary supplements.

Labels also can serve to define products and, thus, to influence activities in markets, sometimes in questionable ways. For example, Agriculture Department regulations allow poultry that has been frozen at temperatures as low as 1 degree Fahrenheit (and warmed no higher than 40 degrees) to be labeled as "fresh." Fresh poultry bring a premium price of 40 cents per pound or more, so poultry producers who do not freeze their birds are angry about having birds they regard as frozen bear the same "fresh" label they are entitled to use.

Although not as systematic as food labeling, the FDA also requires drug-label cautions. After the tainted Odwalla apple juice case, for example, the FDA required makers of unpasteurized fresh fruit and vegetable juices to label them as such and to warn that they may contain harmful bacteria. In an unusual 1994 case, a jury in Alexandria, Virginia awarded $8.8 million to a man who lost his liver after consuming moderate amounts of alcohol—in the form of wine—while also taking Tylenol. Even before the judgment was affirmed by an appeals court, the FDA announced that warning labels would be required to warn against mixing the Tylenol ingredient, acetaminophen, with alcohol. Liver damage also developed in individuals who took acetaminophen without alcohol, however, and in 2002 an FDA advisory panel recommended an explicit warning about liver damage from Tylenol alone.[11]

Product Liability and the FDA

Should the opportunity to sue for harm under product liability be relied upon in the case of medical devices? Congress moved away from relying on courts when it passed the **Medical Device Amendments** of 1976 **(MDA)**, which required FDA approval of the riskiest class of medical devices, such as pacemakers, before they could be marketed. The law came after injuries suffered from the Dalkon Shield intrauterine device, and it was intended to insure the safety of inherently risky medical devices. Devices already on the market at the time Congress adopted the Amendments did not have to be approved by the FDA, however, nor did devices made since then but considered "substantially equivalent" to a pre-1976 device.

One question that arose since the passage of the MDA is whether the Amendments preempt state-level, personal-injury laws. A case involving a pacemaker that is substantially equivalent to a pre-1976 product and therefore never explicitly subjected to FDA approval, was kept from state court decision on grounds that federal law preempts state law. Appeals from such rulings reached the Supreme Court in the

---

[11] See "Pain Killer," *The Economist*, October 4, 2002, p. 59–60.

1996 case of *Medtronics v. Lohr*, and the Court decided that state law is not preempted and can still be controlling.[12]

Tobacco

In the 1990s, the FDA sought to control tobacco as a drug after concluding that tobacco companies adjusted the amount of nicotine in their products. More specifically, the FDA accused the companies of developing super-high-nicotine tobacco, which could be combined with the use of ammonia compounds to fine tune nicotine levels in cigarettes. Armed with this information, FDA Commissioner David A. Kessler argued in 1996 that if tobacco companies intend to sell their products as drug delivery systems, they should come under the authority of the FDA for regulation. In 2000, the Supreme Court ruled that the FDA lacked authority to regulate tobacco unless Congress passed legislation granting it such authority, which Congress did not do.

The FDA also pursued an effort to reduce smoking of cigarettes or chewing of smokeless tobacco by the young. FDA rules, effective in 1997, made selling cigarettes to anyone under 18 years of age a federal violation and made retailers require picture identification from any tobacco purchaser under the age of 27. Rules also banned outdoor cigarette advertising, including window signs as well as billboards within 1,000 feet of a school or playground, and they banned vending machines or self-service displays anywhere those under 18 are allowed. Additional limitations prohibited redemption of coupons for cigarettes or smokeless tobacco through the mail, banned free samples of these products, and denied companies the right to offer T-shirts, caps, or other articles bearing tobacco brand names.

This effort to reduce smoking and chewing was predicated on the FDA's position that the use of cigarettes or smokeless tobacco is a means of administering nicotine. Except for buyer identification requirements, these FDA rules were successfully challenged in federal courts and are not in effect now. Bills were introduced in Congress as recently as 2006, however, to restrict in these same ways the sale of tobacco to minors. The bills also require more disclosure of ingredients in tobacco products and larger health warning labels on them. With tobacco classified as the leading preventable cause of death in the United States, it is likely that one of these years Congress will call for stronger regulation of it by the FDA.

23.4 | THE NATIONAL HIGHWAY TRAFFIC SAFETY ADMINISTRATION

In 1966, for the first time, traffic fatalities in the United States exceeded 50,000. Traffic fatalities had grown with the dramatic increase in motor vehicle travel in the first half of the twentieth century, but because fatalities did not grow as fast as miles traveled the fatality rate per 100 million vehicle miles declined, and highway travel seemed to

---

[12] See *Medtronic, Inc. v. Lohr*, 518 U.S. 470, 116 S.Ct. 2240 (1996).

be getting safer. Then, quite suddenly, from 1961 to 1965, as vehicle miles still increased, the fatality rate per 100 million vehicle miles jumped 6 percent, from 5.2 to 5.5, a rise in fatalities that dramatized concern about highway safety. A popular book written in 1965 by Ralph Nader, *Unsafe at Any Speed*, catalogued design problems of the General Motors rear-engine car, the Corvair, and it contributed, along with the rising traffic fatalities, to passage of the **National Traffic and Motor Vehicle Safety Act** of 1966.

Motor Vehicle Safety Standards

The National Traffic and Motor Vehicle Safety Act of 1966 established the National Highway Safety Bureau, which became the **National Highway Traffic Safety Administration (NHTSA)**. The Act granted the Secretary of Transportation authority to establish appropriate Federal Motor Vehicle Safety Standards, and it called for initial standards to be issued within five months. The Secretary delegated this authority to the NHTSA. Another law, the **Highway Safety Act** of 1966, was intended to give federal guidance to states about driver education, traffic law enforcement, highway construction, and other highway safety programs. These steps and many others—including great increases in court-awarded damages against automobile manufacturers—probably helped to lower the motor vehicle fatalities per 100 million miles in the United States from 5.5 in 1965 to 1.5 for the past five years (compare with 1.2 for England). Highway fatalities over the last 10 years in the United States are reported in Appendix 23.1.

In 1964, Congress instructed the General Services Administration (GSA) to set safety standards for cars purchased by the federal government. By 1966, automobile manufacturers had largely met the GSA standards on all cars built in the United States. Because of the short time allowed for setting standards, NHTSA essentially adopted these GSA standards for the nation, and this meant that manufacturers could immediately be in compliance with the initial standards. For example, more than 30 states required seatbelts on cars by the 1966 model year, and because seatbelts were required by the GSA standards, the seat-belt requirement was extended to every state. The current safety standards are of two types: (1) crash-avoidance standards, which concern brakes, tires, windshields, lights, and transmission controls, and (2) crash-worthiness standards for occupants, such as seat belts, head restraints, energy-absorbing steering columns, padded instrument panels, energy absorbing bumpers, fuel system integrity, and the resistance of interior materials to fire.[13]

Regulatory standards do not stand on their own in motivating manufacturers to produce safe cars. First, consumers prefer greater safety, especially as their income levels rise and they can afford it, and manufacturers want to offer features consumers want. An unsafe car can also harm a manufacturer's reputation, as the Corvair did for General Motors in the 1960s. Product liability claims from tort suits can be very costly. In 1993, for instance, an Atlanta jury ordered General Motors to pay $105.2 million to

---

[13] Detailed standards are available at http://www.nhtsa.gov.

parents of a teenager who died in a 1989 crash when side-mounted gas tanks on a GM pickup truck burst into flames. Of the total award, $4.2 million was for compensatory damages, and $101 million was for punitive damages. With manufacturers bearing responsibility for liability claims of this magnitude, government standards will not be the only influence on vehicle safety design.

The NHTSA enforces vehicle standards by examining automobile designs before models go into production. Manufacturers must certify that vehicles are produced to meet the safety standards. One of the other main enforcement mechanisms of NHTSA is the vehicle recall. A vehicle recall results from an order to a manufacturer, requiring that owners of a vehicle be notified of a problem that has been found with that vehicle. Owners are also asked to bring their vehicles in to a dealer, where corrective work will be carried out at no expense to them.

The Effects of Automobile Safety Standards

Auto manufacturers did not, then, strongly resist the NHTSA standards, although the manufacturers did oppose a bumper standard that is intended to prevent significant vehicle damage at low speeds and is very costly to meet. We can summarize here the results of some studies of specific standards. Instrument panel padding has only limited effect, for instance, especially in preventing serious injuries.[14] Head restraints are generally thought to reduce neck injuries from accidents, and one study found head restraints reduced injuries 14 percent.[15] Energy-absorbing steering columns can reduce the chances of death or serious injury to drivers, partly because they are effective in front-end collisions, which cause a large portion of vehicle-accident fatalities.[16] Windshield and other glass standards probably have beneficial effects. Gates and Goldmuntz found high-penetration-resistant windshield glass reduces serious and fatal injuries by 0.4 to 2.7 percent.[17]

Seat belts are seen by analysts as one of the most effective motor-vehicle safety devices.[18] A number of studies find they offer reductions in fatalities of 30 percent or more, and their cost is not excessive. Side door strength reduces injuries and fatalities from side-door-impact in single-vehicle crashes by 25 percent, and from multiple-vehicle crashes by 8 percent.[19] Dual braking systems reduce accident rates by about 1 percent.[20] The overall effect on safety of all of these standards appears to be significant.

---

[14] See Howard Gates and Lawrence Goldmuntz (1978, pg. 30), and Lester B. Lave and W. E. Weber (1970, pp. 265–275).

[15] See General Accounting Office, *Effectiveness, Benefits, and Costs of Federal Safety Standards for Protection of Passenger Car Occupants*, National Highway Traffic Safety Administration, Department of Transportation, CED-76-121, 1976, p. 42.

[16] See Gates and Goldmuntz (1978, p. 27) for an estimate that serious and fatal injuries are reduced 8 to 10 percent.

[17] See Gates and Goldmuntz (1978, p. 25).

[18] See, for example, Lester B. Lave and W. E. Weber (1970, pp. 265–275).

[19] See Department of Transportation, NHTSA, *An Evaluation of Side Structure Improvements in Response to Federal Motor Vehicle Standard 214*, DOT HS-806-314, 1982, p. xxiii.

[20] See Department of Transportation, NHTSA, *A Preliminary Evaluation of Two Braking Improvements for Passenger Cars: Dual Master Cylinders and Front Disk Brakes*, DOT HS-806-359, 1983, p. 43.

BOX 23.3 Extreme Recall

An extreme form of recall occurred in 1994, when Nissan North America announced it would *buy back* 30,000 C-22 Nissan minivans. The vehicles had been involved in 160 fires, and although Nissan had recalled the vehicles four times, the company had not succeeded in fixing the problem. Fortunately, there had been no serious injury or fatality from the fires, but they had caused harm, and the vehicles seemed to present a constant and continuing danger. State attorneys general were investigating the problem, and class action suits had been filed. NHTSA demanded action by Nissan and agreed to their offer to buy back the vehicles and crush them. Critics objected to this buy-back solution, however. Some consumers who had lost their vehicles in fires, for example, had nothing left that could be repurchased, so their losses were uncompensated. And the $5,000 to $7,000 that was offered might not entice all owners to give up the vehicle, so some of these vehicles could be expected to remain on the road. Nevertheless, attempting to take a problem vehicle off the road is a very strong result of regulatory action.

Studies of traffic fatalities over long time periods have been carried out while controlling as many influences as possible, to estimate the role these safety standards may have had in reducing fatalities. Factors influencing fatalities per year, for instance, included income, average speed, a measure of the fraction of all drivers who are between the ages of 15 and 25, alcohol consumption per person, the costs of medical and accident repairs, the average weight of cars on the road, the share of vehicle miles accounted for by trucks, the share of miles driven on limited access highways, the total number of miles driven, and the weighted average age of cars on the road. When all of these variables explain fatalities, it is possible also to add a variable to represent whether the federal safety standards were in force. This might take the simple form of a variable that is zero in years before the standards, and one in years when the standards have been in effect.

The safety standards tend to have a significant and favorable effect in reducing fatalities in these studies.[21] Significant influences that tended to increase the total deaths were vehicle miles driven, the fraction of miles by truck, and average income. Vehicle weight reduced deaths, which indicates that heavier vehicles were relatively safer. The same variables were used to explain another dependent variable, pedestrian and bicyclist deaths. For these deaths, quite remarkably, the safety standards appear to make things worse. One explanation for this result is from Professor Sam Peltzman of the University of Chicago, who pointed out early that, when assured of more protection from their vehicles, drivers might partly offset that benefit by driving more aggressively.[22] Here the result shows up as an increase in deaths of pedestrians and bicyclists, who are outside the vehicles. Variables that were not significant

---

[21] See Crandall, Gruenspecht, Keeler, and Lave (1986, p. 63).

[22] See Peltzman (1975, pp. 677–725).

in explaining total deaths but become significant factors in increasing deaths of pedestrian and cyclists are the fraction of young drivers (ages 15 to 25) and the level of alcohol consumption.

Other factors that are difficult to incorporate in these studies may also have contributed to the reduction in fatalities after federal safety standards were implemented. The rise in tort liability came at about the same time, for instance, first in suits against General Motors involving the Corvair. The placement of the gasoline tank in the Ford Pinto resulted in a number of much publicized tort suits in the 1970s. This was a period when product liability awards rose markedly. From the period 1960 to 1964 until the period 1975 to 1979, for instance, product liability awards in Cook County, Illinois—after adjustment for inflation—rose nearly 900 percent.[23] Manufacturers would surely be aware of these trends, which give them financial incentive to make vehicles safer to reduce the chance of tort suits with their costly adverse judgments.

Safety standards and vehicle designs alone will not solve all highway safety problems. More recent effort has focused on driver behavior. A safety standard may require seat belts in vehicles, for example, while a law requiring their use focuses on behavior. Although about 80 percent of drivers and passengers fasten seat belts in the United States, fewer than half the states have what are called primary seat-belt laws, which require that seat belts be used and which authorize police to stop vehicles carrying people without seat belts fastened. Other seat-belt laws authorize penalties for not using seat belts only after a vehicle is stopped for violating some other law, such as speeding. Australia and Canada have primary seat-belt laws and achieve about 90 percent compliance. NHTSA estimates that increasing the use of seat belts to 90 percent in the United States would save about 4,000 lives a year.[24]

Roughly two-thirds of accidents involving fatalities are caused by overly aggressive driving, and states are attempting to reduce that. If the day is divided into 3-hour time segments, the segment from midnight to 3 AM sees more single-vehicle crashes than any other 3-hour time segment, and three-fourths of those midnight-to-3-AM crashes are alcohol related. Indeed, alcohol is involved in about 40 percent of all motor vehicle crashes. States have responded by reducing the alcohol level that defines drunk driving from 0.10 percent to 0.08 percent, and some states—like Colorado—set the drunk driving level at 0.02 percent for drivers under 21. Many states have vigorous campaigns against drunk driving and some are considering for first drunk-driving offenders the mandatory installation of ignition interlock systems, which prevent a vehicle from operating if alcohol is detected.[25]

Teenage drivers are four times as likely as older drivers to have accidents, and 16-year-olds are three times as likely to die in a crash than the average of all drivers. Some states are introducing "graduated" licensing procedures that require a year of probationary driving, sometimes to be accompanied by a licensed driver, sometimes without carrying any passenger below a specified age, sometimes without using cell

---

[23] See Peterson and Priest (1982, p. 31).

[24] See Danny Hakim, "Once World Leader in Traffic Safety, U.S. Drops to No. 9," *New York Times*, Nov. 27, 2003, p. B1.

[25] See Matthew L. Wald, "A New Strategy to Discourage Driving Drunk," *New York Times*, November 20, 2006, p. B1.

phones, and sometimes allowing driving only during certain hours. Illegal drivers—those who do not have effective driver's licenses—are another group much more likely to have accidents. California impounded the vehicles of illegal drivers when they were caught, and found that impounding vehicles reduced the accident rates of illegal drivers.[26]

Child Safety Seats and Air Bags

Seat belts restrain drivers and passengers from being thrown in motor vehicle crashes, but they provide only limited protection. Safety seats for children and air bags for adults help to cushion the impact of a crash. A major problem with child safety seats has been a lack of uniformity and compatibility in their designs. With many different child seats on the market, to be held in place mainly by seat belts, and with auto makers using about 30 different seat-belt systems, it is not surprising that child seats were often installed incorrectly. Seat-belt systems did not hold many child seats well, largely because they are not intended for that purpose. Safety officials claimed that safety seats were only half as effective as they could be, because they were improperly installed so often. In 1998, NHTSA proposed separate child-seat arrangements be included in new cars, for holding child seats in place, and a simpler arrangement was adopted in 1999.[27] OSHA now evaluates child safety seats and grades them for their effectiveness. In 2007, 101 different child seats were graded, with 81 percent receiving "A" grades.[28]

Another area of NHTSA activity has involved air bags for automobiles. NHSTA first called for air bags to be installed in new automobiles in 1970, but various forms of resistance from automobile manufacturers kept the air-bag requirement from being implemented. Finally, in 1993, NHTSA amended the air-bag standard and required that air bags be installed in all new passenger cars for driver and front passenger by September 1, 1997. Although air bags had been installed in some automobiles as much as 10 years earlier, results of their effectiveness are only now becoming evident. The NHTSA has estimated that air bags have saved more than 2,000 lives in the past 10 years. When combined with seat belts, they make frontal collisions less dangerous than they used to be.

Auto companies are now also offering side air bags, which protect front-seat occupants—especially near the neck and head—from side-impact collisions. Such collisions pose an increasing problem, and they account now for roughly one-fourth of the deaths from motor vehicle collisions. Light trucks, including sport utility vehicles (SUVs), play an increasing role in such collisions and make them more dangerous, in part because such vehicles are higher and rise above automobile frames to

[26] See "An Evaluation of the Specific Deterrent Effect of Vehicle Impoundment for Suspended, Revoked and Unlicensed Drivers in California," California Department of Motor Vehicles, Research and Development, Sacramento, CA, November, 1997.

[27] See Matthew L. Wald, "U.S. Plans New Rule to Install Child Safety Seats in New Cars," *New York Times*, November 7, 1998, p. A11.

[28] The child-safety-seat ratings are available at www.nhtsa.dot.gov/CPS/CSSRating/Index.cfm.

BOX 23.4 The Air-Bag Standard

Although they were never strictly imposed, initial NHTSA rules for air bags called for them to protect 172-pound males in 30-mile-an-hour, head-on crashes, whether they were wearing seat belts or not. To protect occupants in such crashes the air bags must deploy at speeds in the 200 m.p.h. range. To protect smaller drivers and passengers, critics called for milder speeds of air- bag deployment (less than 200 m.p.h.) and for optional deactivation of the air bags. The final amended standards for air bags do not contain the initial requirements, even though they probably guided development of the initial air bag technology. As evidence has accumulated, planning for 30-mile-an-hour crashes has been criticized, because not only are crashes rare at speeds that great, but to protect against them requires the enormous 200 m.p.h. burst from the air bag, which is what makes it so dangerous. Moreover, harm from air bags often results when they erupt in minor accidents, sometimes involving speeds of less than 10 m.p.h., sometimes when a car simply strikes a pothole, and—rarely—for no apparent reason at all. In all such cases, slower deployment of air bags would be adequate to protect occupants.

For review of the air-bag standard see P. J. Norton, "What Happens When Air Bags Kill: Automobile Manufacturer Liability for Injuries Caused by Air Bags," *Case Western Reserve Law Review,* 48: 569–599.

strike the automobiles' occupants. There is also some evidence that drivers of cars equipped with air bags are more aggressive.[29] This is consistent with the evidence that safer cars generally lead to more aggressive driving.[30]

Air bags have been found harmful to children and small adults, particularly women, seated in the front seats of cars. They may have caused roughly 100 deaths over the last 10 years, with almost two-thirds of the deaths being children and the vast majority of remaining adults being women. Deploying within hundredths of a second at speeds of up to 200 miles per hour, the air bags can harm small riders. Indeed, children under 12 years of age, or under 65 pounds, are not to be in the front seats of cars equipped with air bags, mainly for that reason. The Insurance Institute for Highway Safety found that of 73 persons killed by air bags in low-speed crashes in the 1990s, 53 were children between the ages of 1 and 11.[31] Of these 53 children who died, only 10 were wearing seat belts and 6 of these had only the lap part of the lap-and-shoulder belt fastened. Even adults are at greater risk from air-bag injury when they do not have seat belts fastened. An accident usually involves braking, which throws passengers forward, closer to the air bag when it deploys, and that is where injury from the erupting bag is more likely.

Air bags can also go off inadvertently. The driver might hit road debris, or a curb, or a pothole, and set off an air bag. Some motorists were simply driving and saw no cause that would explain the deployment of the air bag. The first lawsuit over an air

---

[29] See Peterson, Hoffer, and Millner (1995).

[30] The original idea of such "offsetting behavior" is from Professor Sam Peltzman (1975).

[31] See Benjamin Weiser, "Automaker Ordered to Pay $750,000 to Estate of Bronx Boy Killed by Air Bag," *New York Times,* December, 5, 1998.

bag causing a child's death was decided in a federal court in New York in December, 1998, and it resulted in a jury award of $750,000 to the estate of a 5-year old boy, Michael Liz Crespo. In this case the boy's father was driving a 1995 Dodge Caravan down a steeply inclined driveway in Puerto Rico at 9 miles an hour when he struck another slow moving car and the front seat passenger air bag inflated.[32] Because the boy was in the front seat and not wearing a seat belt, the initial award of $1,500,000 was cut in half. Then the jury award was later set aside, so no award was made, because the defendant, Chrysler Corporation, had warned of the dangers of the air bag, and its air bag design adhered scrupulously to every regulation and even met additional requirements recommended by safety experts.[33]

In March of 1997, the NHTSA announced that automobile manufacturers could "de-power" the air bags so they would open with less force. The NHTSA allowed up to a 35 percent reduction in force, effective in the 1998 model year. And consumers who meet certain conditions—such as traveling frequently with more children than their back seat holds—can now have air bags deactivated altogether. In the future air bags are expected to sense the size and position of driver or passenger and adjust their action accordingly to avoid harm to small passengers.

Compatibility of Vehicle Size and Shape

Motor vehicles come in many sizes and shapes. This raises a question about the designs of highways and of the vehicles that use them and about the compatibility of the vehicles that share the highway network. Trucks are shaped differently from cars to carry more cargo. Large semitrailers carry loads that verge on exceeding the weight limits that states impose to protect their highways. Pickup trucks also carry more than cars and can travel over less smooth surfaces. Such trucks are also designed so they can climb over obstacles more readily, a design feature that may even cause problems when trucks encounter highway guardrails. Indeed, after October 1, 1998, two main types of guardrails were no longer used on federally financed highways, because in accidents they could cause full-size pickup trucks to roll over.[34]

There is an obvious externality in motor vehicle travel on the highway. My safety can depend on choices you make, and your safety can depend on my choices. These choices involve how fast and how carefully we operate our vehicles and which vehicles we choose to drive. To the extent larger vehicles afford more protection, there may be a prisoner's dilemma influence on choices by safety conscious consumers: choosing a larger vehicle offers more protection as long as others choose small ones. If all choose large vehicles, that advantage may be neutralized, for crashes between large vehicles of the light truck type may be more harmful than those between small, well-designed cars. The cooperative solution would have us all drive small cars. In November 1998,

---

[32] See Weiser, fn. 31.

[33] See 75 F.Supp.2d 225, 1999.

[34] The Texas Transportation Institute at College Station, Texas crashed two-wheel-drive pickups repeatedly into the types of guardrails to be banned—at an angle of 25 degrees and at speeds of about 60 miles per hour—and found the trucks usually rolled over. Other guardrails can be installed on new highways that are less likely to cause the trucks to roll over.

however, for the first time, light trucks outnumbered automobiles in sales,[35] and in 2005, SUVs accounted for about 40 percent of all registered vehicles.[36]

Faced with this clear vehicle compatibility issue, the NHTSA focused on the effects of the relative sizes of the vehicles involved in crashes. Evidence has accumulated that when midsized automobiles crash with light trucks—including SUVs, pickup trucks, and minivans—the driver of the automobile is three times as likely as the driver of the light truck to die from the accident. Based on a review of fatal crashes from 1991 through 1994, the NHTSA found that several features of SUVs, pickup trucks, and vans could account for this disparity in their capacity to harm others.

First, trucks, vans, and SUVs are heavier than cars. They also are higher off the ground, which allows them to override the side structure protection of a car and reach its occupants directly. Trucks and SUVs usually have "stiffer" frames, built along two steel rails that run the lengths of the vehicles. Automobiles tend to use a lattice structure of lighter steel and aluminum parts that collapses gradually to absorb some of the impact in a crash. By not collapsing in this way, stiff frames absorb less of the force of a crash, and they transfer more of the sudden force of the crash to the vehicle occupants.

Under threats from the NHTSA that it would adopt light-truck design standards to make them more compatible with automobiles, 15 automakers from four nations agreed in 2003 to adopt standards for light trucks. To meet the new standard for light-trucks, their front and rear bumpers would be lowered, or else have hollow impact-absorbing bars placed below them, so they would match bumpers or structural parts of automobiles in crashes. Although the standard is not mandatory until 2009, light trucks began to be made with this new bumper arrangements in 2003. The Insurance Institute for Highway Safety studied results of accidents involving 2001 to 2003 vehicles to compare effects of vehicles that met the new standard versus those that did not.[37] In side impact collisions, the new standards caused the number of deaths to fall by almost half because the new bumpers on light trucks made them less likely to rise above the door sills of automobiles and enter passenger compartments. The new designs also reduced by 20 percent the chance that an SUV would kill the driver of an automobile in a front-end collision. Thus, making highway vehicles compatible so their protections can be effective promises to improve highway safety enormously.

In addition to being heavy, SUVs and trucks have a high center of gravity, and as a result they tend to roll over more readily than cars do.[38] Fatal rollovers are three times as common for SUVs as for passenger cars. This is an important difference, because while rollovers account for only 3 percent of crashes, they cause 32 percent of crash deaths.[39] After more than 15 years of indecision about how to test rollover risk, the NHTSA now uses "real world," or actual crash tests, the type of test they use for other aspects of crash protection. Congress passed the Transportation Recall Enhancement, Accountability, and Documentation Act (called TREAD) after deaths

---

[35] See Keith Bradsher, "Light Trucks Exceed Cars In U.S. Sales," *New York Times*, December 4, 1998, A23.

[36] See "Auto Crashes," Insurance Information Institute, 110 William St., New York, N.Y., April, 2006.

[37] See Jeremy W. Peters, "Gains Seen In Redesign of S.U.V.'s," *New York Times*, February 3, 2006, p. C1.

[38] For criticism of SUV design, see Bradsher (2002).

[39] See Fara Warner, "Rollover Safety Moves to Center Stage," *New York Times*, March 16, 2003, Sec. 8, p. 11.

from blowouts of Firestone tires on Ford Explorers in 2000, and that Act mandated "real-world" rollover tests.

Manufacturers are giving more attention to rollover risk, and they are attempting to improve designs to reduce the hazard.[40] The building of SUVs was motivated in large part by easier light truck mileage standards that were established for them under the Corporate Average Fuel Economy (CAFE) program. The SUVs were initially designed hurriedly, combining car features with truck frames to allow greater hauling capacity and more rugged use than cars permitted, and they were not particularly safe. More recent designs are less top heavy and they contain electronic stability controls that reduce the tendency to roll over.[41] Vehicles that were built on older designs, however, will remain on roads for many years to come.[42]

Tires can also be an important element in highway safety. Tires are sometimes barely adequate for the weights imposed, and when tires are imperfect, the vehicles may be treacherous to drive, particularly at high speeds. Almost 150 deaths were claimed to be the result of failures of an identified set of Firestone tires in 2000.[43]

Benefit-Cost Analysis of the Total Highway Safety Program

It is very difficult to trace the effects that regulations have had on measures of highway safety because many complex interrelationships affect outcomes. The safety-standards program, however, has had a significant and favorable effect, and studies make possible a quantitative estimate of the lives saved. Fatalities are not the only consequence of motor vehicle accidents. But researchers have noted the incidence of other injuries and found them related to observed fatalities in a way that allows the total loss from traffic accidents to be estimated as 1.5 times the value of the loss of life. Using such estimates, and bringing vehicle miles, fatalities, and price levels up to date, the benefit from our highway safety standards can be estimated to be 24,200 to 43,500 lives saved in 2004.[44] Using a conservative value of life between $1,000,000 and $3,000,000 in 2006 dollars, the values of these savings in lives would range from a low value of $24.2 billion ($1,000,000 per life times 24,200 lives saved) to $130.5 billion ($3,000,000 per life times 43,500 lives saved).

Costs have also been estimated per car for all the NHTSA safety regulations.[45] In 2006 dollars, these estimates ranged from $1,340 to $1,960 per car. Assuming that 17 million cars would be produced in a year, the total cost would range from $22.7 billion to $33.4 billion in 2006 dollars. (If the costly bumper standard had not been included, the range would be from $15.9 billion to $22.4 billion.) Although the costs of this program would exceed benefits by about 50 percent if we compare pessimistically high costs with

---

[40] See Keith Bradsher, "Documents on Design of Explorer Reveal a Series of Compromises," *New York Times*, December 7, 2000, p. A1.

[41] See Ken Thomas, "More SUVs Pass Safety Test," *Washington Post*, June 23, 2005, p. D3.

[42] See Danny Hakim, "Used SUVs Come Loaded, With Safety Concerns," *New York Times*, June 26, 2005, Sec. 4, p. 3.

[43] See David Stout, "29 More U.S. Deaths Linked to Firestone Tires," *New York Times*, December 7, 2000, p. C7.

[44] See Crandall, Gruenspecht, Keeler, and Lave, (1986, p. 77).

[45] See Crandall, Gruenspecht, Keeler, and Lave, (1986, Ch. 3).

pessimistically few lives saved, together with a low value per life, that is the worst case possibility. Benefits more likely exceed costs, because any movement from pessimistic values—more than the minimum lives saved, a greater value for life, or values in the lower part of the range of estimated costs—will make benefits exceed costs. Standards can probably be met at lower costs now than when cost estimates were originally made. These rough estimates indicate that the highway traffic safety program has been a beneficial one for consumers overall. This comparison of overall benefit with overall cost does not examine marginal benefits or costs of separate programs, so it cannot tell us whether the effort is the right size.

23.5 | THE CONSUMER PRODUCT SAFETY COMMISSION

Many other consumer products, besides foods, drugs, or motor vehicles can cause harm. The Consumer Product Safety Commission (CPSC) was created in 1972 and it administers laws that are intended to protect consumers from such other products. Before the CPSC was formed, Congress had passed special legislation to deal with each of several specific problems as they arose, such as problems with refrigerator doors, poisons, hazardous substances, and flammable fabrics. Refrigerators were a very dangerous product before the development of magnetic latches, because early door latches locked automatically when the door was slammed closed. That meant that children playing in discarded refrigerators could be trapped alive inside. Congress called for magnetic latches, so anyone caught inside could push the door open. Magnetic latches are now almost the only kind in use, and discarded refrigerators are much less dangerous than they once were.

Poisons are subject to labeling requirements and their availability is restricted. Medications, such as aspirin and prescription drugs, must be available in containers with "child-proof" caps, which Congress mandated in the 1960s. Protections in such form may not be as effective as anticipated, however, if we think a child cannot open the bottle of sleeping pills and so do not place it beyond the reach of children. If the bottle cap is not really child proof, children can be harmed.[46] Congress banned flammable fabrics as clothing and as part of many household products. Hazardous substances also are restricted in their use. The most problematic category is that of toxic substances, which are regulated primarily by the Environmental Protection Agency (EPA). For instance, the EPA enforces rules about disposing of automobile batteries because of the acid they contain.

As the twentieth century wore on, business firms developed more marvelous, and more dangerous, products. By the 1970s, quite a range of dangerous consumer products existed, from rotary lawn mowers to shattering glass shower doors, and Congress realized it could not legislate protections separately for every one of them. Instead, in 1972 Congress created the CPSC that could recognize product dangers and remedy them, mainly by recalling unsafe products and suggesting better designs.

---

[46] See Viscusi (1984, pp. 325–331).

The CPSC administers all the consumer product legislation Congress has passed in an effort to protect the public from unreasonable risks of injury from consumer products. It takes steps to assist consumers in evaluating the comparative safety of products. It also tries to develop uniform standards, to avoid conflicting state and local standards, and it promotes research into causes and prevention of deaths and injuries consumer products may cause.

Consumer Products

The focus of the CPSC is on consumer products, and one of its primary activities is to gather information about problems with products and negotiate improvements with manufacturers. An important source of information is customer complaints, which come more from lower priced, lower quality products.[47] To illustrate the form and scale of CPSC activities, consider that in December, 1994, the CPSC announced the recall of 2,000,000 beanbag chairs, 186,000 mountain bike seat posts, 46,000 Christmas books, 30,000 Christmas lights, 42,000 tea sets, 14,000 baby toys, 1,000 toy trucks, and 500 music makers. In December, 2004, the CPSC announced the recall of 265,000 battery packs for portable DVD players, 13,000 Christmas tree toppers, 2,800 childrens' bicycles, 104,000 baby cribs, 22,000 notebook computer batteries, 6,600 gas ranges, 41,000 childrens' books, 144,000 plastic siren whistles, and 202,000 oil-filled radiator heaters. Most of these recalls were carried out voluntarily by manufacturers, and full refunds were available for most of the products on returning them to the place where they had been purchased.

Small parts that can cause a child to choke often lie behind a recalled product. One book had plastic jewels decorating a page, for example, that a small child could peel off and swallow. A 19-month-old Missouri boy had unzipped a bean bag chair, crawled into the pellets inside, and drowned in the plastic foam. Another child had almost suffocated after her brother had put her inside the chair and zipped up the opening. For these chairs, the CPSC called for an alternative to the zipper opening. The seat posts on mountain bikes had broken and caused some injuries, as had 21,000 other bikes because of problems with the front forks breaking. Recalled batteries could overheat and cause fires. Mattress supports in baby cribs could come loose and cause part of the mattress to fall creating a suffocation hazard. The CPSC gathers information on such problems with consumer products and helps manufacturers to organize recalls and make their products less dangerous.

Fires

More than 4,000 die each year in home fires in the United States, making fires one of the leading causes of death in the home and giving the United States one of the highest fire death and injury rates in the world. A special CPSC program focuses on preventing fires through study of products that cause them: heating devices, upholstered furniture, bedding, cigarette lighters, matches, and clothes. Fires related to

---

[47] For an analysis of consumer complaints, see Sharon Oster (1990, pp. 603–609).

BOX 23.5 Cigarettes and Fires

Congress has considered assigning responsibility for the fire safety aspects of cigarettes to the CPSC but has not yet done so. The CPSC did participate in a congressionally sponsored study of fires caused by cigarettes. Smoke detectors remain the most important protective device. Studies have shown that some cigarettes are significantly less likely than others to start fires. The National Institute of Standards and Technology found that the best-selling brands were about equally likely to start fires if lighted and placed on cotton upholstery fabric. But five brands were found less likely to start fires: More White Light 120s, More 120s, Virginia Slims Superslims 100s, Capri Light 100s, and Eve Light 120s. All five of these brands are marketed to women.

---

smoking have declined as smoking has declined over the last two decades, but such fires still account for thousands of injuries (3 to 4 thousand injuries annually) and deaths (1,200 to 1,500 deaths annually).

23.6 THE FEDERAL TRADE COMMISSION ON UNFAIR AND MISLEADING CLAIMS

Unscrupulous sellers can take advantage of imperfectly informed consumers if they persuade them to buy through claims that are false. A specific responsibility of the Federal Trade Commission (FTC) is to protect consumers from false and misleading claims, and the agency investigates claims in an effort to weed out false ones. Some early FTC actions in this realm seemed frivolous and harmed its credibility. For example, an ice-cream manufacturer substituted mashed potatoes for its ice cream in television ads after the heat from television lamps melted the ice cream, and the FTC sought to prevent broadcast of the ads on the ground that the ice cream was not shown. In this case, many observers sympathized with the ice-cream maker.

The FTC's more recent efforts have aimed at more constructive targets. In 1994, Haagen-Dazs agreed to stop advertising its ice cream products as "low fat" and "98 percent fat free" after the FTC charged that the company made misleading claims to consumers. The FDA defines low-fat products as having three grams of fat or less per serving, and the FTC found some of Haagen-Dazs ice creams had as many as 12 grams of fat per serving. Seven of Haagen-Dazs' nine frozen yogurt flavors were also found not to be low in fat. The FTC charged that three of its eight flavors of yogurt bar had as many as 230 calories per serving rather than 100, as claimed. Although Haagen-Dazs provided some qualifications to their ads in small type, the FTC would not accept that as a defense. FTC spokesperson Christian S. White said, "If the advertisement taken as a whole is deceptive, the fact that there is a tiny disclaimer isn't sufficient to cure it." Haagen-Dazs was one of the first ice-cream companies to reveal contents on its packages, and, since its tussle with the FTC, it has lowered the fat content of its products.

The FDA helps the FTC in this consumer information effort by defining terms such as ".low fat" or "reduced calorie." It also tries to make sure that the nutritional information on labels is correct. Labels can be especially important for revealing ingredients that cause allergic reactions, because some of these reactions can be fatal. In cooperation with regulators in Minnesota and Wisconsin, the FDA examined practices of 85 companies and found that 25 percent failed to list ingredients that could be harmful to some allergic individuals.[48]

The FTC engages in other consumer protection efforts, especially where national companies are involved and separate state efforts would be more costly or less effective. For instance, in 1994 the FTC charged Bally's, the nation's largest health club chain, with overbilling and harassing, or ruining credit ratings, of customers nationwide. Bally's agreed to pay a civil penalty of $120,000 and to restore credit ratings of those it damaged, without admitting or denying wrongdoing.

23.7 | CONSUMER PROTECTION FOR SECURITIES TRADING

Many consumers are also investors who purchase stocks, bonds, and other securities. The Securities and Exchange Commission (SEC) is concerned about the functioning of capital markets in the United States, and it has an active office of consumer affairs that attempts to improve the lot of consumers as investors. A hallowed principle of regulation at the SEC has rested on the disclosure of information, on grounds that investors can make their own choices if they are fully informed. Aware that investors can also be inundated with information, the office of consumer affairs at the SEC tries to make information that is presented to investors focus on important matters and be presented in understandable ways. In keeping with SEC rules, reputable accounting firms certify the soundness of reports by all corporations that issue securities to the public. Generally Accepted Accounting Principles (GAAP) are applied by accounting firms, although such firms have discretion in judging what is "material" or important.[49] When an accounting firm makes a poor judgment, the results can be very harmful to investors.[50]

The GAAP themselves are also important. In the United States, these accounting standards are set by a private organization that is financed by industry, called the **Financial Accounting Standards Board (FASB).** The SEC requires that corporations follow these FASB standards. As a result of the Sarbanes-Oxley Act of 2002,[51] a Public Company Oversight Board now oversees this process of corporate accounting.

The SEC receives about 800 letters and 300 telephone calls per day, and investor complaints trigger roughly 20 percent of the agency's enforcement cases. The SEC is trying to make it easier for consumer-investors to reach them with complaints (a consumer information line is 1-800-SEC-0330). Mutual funds now hold roughly

---

[48] See "F.D.A. Finds Faulty Listings of Possible Food Allergens," *New York Times*, April 3, 2001, p. C1.

[49] For criticism of the enforcement of accounting standards see Benston, Bromwich, Litan, and Wagenhofer (2003).

[50] For examples involving the accounting firm, Arthur Andersen, see Floyd Norris, "From Sunbeam to Enron, Andersen's Reputation Suffers," *New York Times*, November 23, 2001, p. C1.

[51] See 116 Stat 745.

$2.5 trillion in assets, more money than is on deposit in commercial banks. With consumers investing through mutual funds more than ever before, attention to the amount and quality of information available to them seems appropriate.

The stock exchanges themselves are also changing, moving gradually from member-owned operations, trading stocks in one large room, to shareholder-owned operations, trading stocks electronically. The National Association of Securities Dealers, parent to the NASDAQ, or "over-the-counter," stock exchange, purchased a large electronic market, Instinet, LLC, in 2005 and merged with the American Stock exchange and the Philadelphia stock exchange.[52] It began trading options in 2007, about when the Chicago Board Options Exchange planned to begin trading stocks.[53] Nasdaq also discussed an alliance with the German stock market and went heavily into debt to purchase a 25.1 percent interest in the London Stock Exchange. Then in 2006 it proposed to buy the rest of the shares of London Stock Exchange, although its offer was turned down. In 2005, the New York Stock Exchange merged with Archipelago, which was one of the largest electronic trading operators, to form the NYSE Group.[54] The NYSE Group broadened electronic trading and allowed faster execution of trades, and it also shifted the exchange from being a nonprofit organization to a profit-seeking, shareholder-owned enterprise.[55] Then in 2006 it merged with Euronext, the operator of European stock exchanges in Paris, Amsterdam, Brussels, and Lisbon, which have largely converted to electronic transactions.[56]

BOX 23.6 Stock Markets Wheel and Deal

Stock markets have struggled to acquire prominent international positions, partly to gain large network advantages so they can offer good large-market prices. Nasdaq's 25 percent stake in the London Stock Exchange does not give it control of that exchange but does allow it to veto any deal the London Exchange might want to make with another exchange. The German Exchange, the Deutsche Borse AG, had failed earlier in an effort to acquire the London Stock Exchange. Nasdaq is now able to prohibit such a merger. The NYSE Group bid vigorously and successfully against the German Exchange for Euronext, the operator of largely electronic European stock exchanges in Paris, Amsterdam, Brussels and Lisbon, and it pursues an alliance with the Tokyo Stock Exchange. In principle, a combined trading organization could allow greater scope for forming a single market price and could make global diversification easier for investors, so many exchanges would like to win a global position.

See A. MacDonald and A. Lucchetti, "NYSE Group and Euronext Agree to Merger," *Wall Street Journal*, June 2, 2006, p. C1; and Kazuhiro Shimamura and Margot Patrick, "Discussions Among Global Stock Exchanges Run Hot and Cold," *Wall Street Journal*, January 24, 2007, p. C3.

---

[52] See Jenny Anderson, "Big Board vs. Nasdaq: Let Round 2 Begin," *New York Times*, April 22, 2005.

[53] See Jenny Anderson, "Nasdaq is Planning to Start an Options Exchange," *New York Times*, September 7, 2006, p. C3.

[54] See Jenny Anderson, "Big Board to Acquire Leading Electronic Trading System," *New York Times*, April 21, 2005.

[55] See Aaron Luchetti, "The NYSE: Faster (and Lonlier)," *Wall Street Journal*, January 24, 2007, p. C1.

[56] See Alistair MacDonald and Aaron Lucchetti, "NYSE Group and Euronext Agree to Merger," *Wall Street Journal*, June 2, 2006, p. C1.

Stock exchanges know there are advantages when a greater range of securities can be priced in a single market, thereby saving traders from having to compare prices across markets. This advantage in reducing search costs may be offset, however, by delays that can arise as markets become very large and must process many transactions, because that might slow down the execution of trades. Traders want speedy transactions to have their trades occur before prices change. Electronic technology has improved the speed of transactions and may thus allow larger stock markets. As part of the globalization trend, international trading of stocks connects traders in different time zones, and capital markets seek broader network externalities as they take advantage of this technological change and the globalization trend.

While the globalization and consolidation of exchanges makes them larger and helps them to support economic globalization, they also alter the tasks for regulators.[57] In the short term, regulation will continue as it is presently, but the integration of global exchange operations will require new definitions of regulators' tasks and greater international cooperation.

SUMMARY

More protection is available now than in the past for consumers of a wide variety of products. One cause is a change in the interpretations of courts, which now recognize the advantages manufacturers have in greater information about products and their dangers and which are imposing greater responsibilities on manufacturers to share this information with consumers. Legislation has also created administrative agencies to protect consumers. The change in law may also be a response to products in the modern age being inherently more dangerous than was once possible and more complex and harder to understand.

Class-action law suits, organized by specialist law firms and by state attorneys general, have benefitted consumers by allowing them to band together and seek remedies in cases that one consumer might be unable to pursue alone. Courts also now interpret torts more broadly to protect consumers, and they impose large punitive damages to punish firms that mislead or impose great risks on consumers. Companies have responded with improved product designs and with careful labeling to warn of dangers. Most states now have consumer protection agencies. At the federal level, the FDA, the NHTSA, and the CPSC are major agencies promoting consumer product safety. The FTC and the SEC also conduct significant consumer protection programs.

Formed in 1906, the FDA is the first federal agency established to protect consumers, primarily to assure the purity of food and drug products, and for food and cosmetics to avoid virtually all risks. For drugs and medical devices a trade-off between risks and benefits is allowed because benefits are sometimes possible only with risks when no other option is available. After disasters occurred in the 1900s, the

---

[57] See Bernard Wysocki, Jr. and Aaron Lucchetti, "Global Exchanges Pose a Quandry for Securities Cops," *Wall Street Journal*, June 5, 2006, p. A1.

agency was given power to approve drugs and medical devices before they could be marketed and to certify that the drugs and devices were efficacious in that they actually would do what they were supposed to do.

Highways became increasingly unsafe in the early 1960s and Congress responded by forming the NHTSA. NHTSA adopted standards, to be incorporated into motor vehicle designs, that are intended to avoid crashes and to make crashes less harmful when they do occur. Important additions to the standards include air bags and a uniform way to install child safety seats. NHTSA has also tried to moderate the incompatibility of motor vehicles when they are of different sizes and shapes and yet are sharing the same highway networks.

The CPSC attempts to reduce harm from about 15,000 other products consumers use, mainly by observing problems with products and negotiating remedies with manufacturers more cheaply than individuals could do. A common remedy is to recall products that pose problems and see to their repair, and the CPSC oversees procedures to accomplish this purpose. The FTC focuses on information, to guard against unfair and misleading claims that may deceive or trick consumers. The SEC protects investors in a number of ways, but primarily it seeks soundness and transparency of financial reports by publicly held corporations.

The policies of these various agencies differ, depending on the nature of the problems they face. They often impose product standards and in some cases advance approvals, and they require labeling or other means of providing information about dangers. Product and process approvals are used by the FDA and by the NHTSA. For consumer products generally, it is difficult to anticipate behavioral responses to requirements that might be imposed, and so the CPSC depends more on gathering information about safety problems as they arise and then negotiating solutions with manufacturers. Centralized action at the federal level often takes away evidence of alternative policies, because no other domestic action can be observed, but it also collects information more broadly and is able to carry out large scale analyses of problems. Study of policies in other countries can also yield evidence about alternative policies.

QUESTIONS

1. In areas of both occupational health and safety and consumer product safety, regulation is concerned with protecting individuals from harm. Compare and contrast the methods of regulation used in these two areas. In your answer, evaluate whether the differences you observe are appropriate, given the differences you see in the two types of regulatory tasks.

2. Much consumer protection regulation depends on the specification and enforcement of standards for product design. Discuss the advantages of pursuing protection through design standards, including the conditions in which standards may be most useful. Discuss the disadvantages of relying on product standards to protect consumers and the conditions that may make them less effective.

3. Describe whether occupational health and safety regulation focuses more on safety or on health. Discuss why the emphasis you describe may occur.

4. Motor vehicle seat belts, air bags, and child safety seats all require resources that may go unused. The same is true of almost all safety standards, in that a collapsible steering wheel, for example, may never protect a driver of a particular motor vehicle because that vehicle may not be involved in a crash that would require it to function. Sketch broadly how to evaluate such a standard. Specifically, what data are needed to evaluate the standard along benefit-cost lines?

5. Quality discrimination, to achieve price discrimination through self-selection, was described effectively by Jacques Dupuit in 1849 when he noted that a Paris railroad degraded its lower quality service to wooden benches and open roof cars to "hit the poor, not because it wants to hurt them, but to frighten the rich." Is such a choice of quality offerings by the railroad a subject for consumer protection action? Explain why or why not.

6. The NHTSA sets standards for motor vehicle design to make the vehicles safer. Compatibility of vehicle designs for travel on the highway network has received attention only recently, yet preliminary evidence from (voluntary until 2009) new, more compatible, bumpers promises substantial life-saving benefit. Give reasons for this delay in improving motor vehicle compatibility and for why the improvement is coming now.

7. Other agencies of the U.S. federal government are concerned with the fuel economy of motor vehicles and with the air pollution they cause. Note any conflicts that might arise between these agencies and the NHTSA.

8. Before electronic trading was as widespread as it now is, the Securities and Exchange Commission proposed a plan to overhaul securities markets by modifying the so-called *trade-through* rule. This rule required that trades be executed on the exchange where investors could be given the best price available. Yet at any one time, the apparently best price actually may not be achieved if the exchange where it exists is slow in executing a transaction so it actually occurs at another, perhaps less attractive, price. If there is a chance that the best price will not be achieved, it is possible the investor will not want to transact under this trade-through rule. That is why smaller exchanges (Nasdaq or Fidelity, which execute transactions quickly) criticized the trade-through rule, saying that in awarding trades it favors the largest exchange (the NYSE, which was slow in executing transactions) when that exchange may not actually deliver the best price. Explain how this issue of low price versus transaction speed can affect the sizes of stock exchanges. Does viewing the exchange as a network help to understand this conflict? How would you expect the adoption of electronic trading to affect the trade-off between market size and transaction speed?

APPENDIX 23.1 Fatal Highway Crashes in the United States, 1996–2005

	1996	1997	1998	1999	2000	2001	2002	2003	2004	2005
Fatal crashes	37,494	37,324	37,107	37,140	37,526	37,862	38,491	38,477	38,444	39,189
Deaths										
Vehicle occupant	35,695	35,725	35,382	35,875	36,348	36,440	37,375	37,341	37,304	37,594
Vehicle nonoccupant	6,368	6,288	6,119	5,842	5,597	5,756	5,630	5,543	5,532	5,849
Total deaths	42,065	42,013	41,501	41,717	41,945	42,196	43,005	42,884	42,836	43,443
Deaths per 100,000,000 vehicle miles	1.69	1.64	1.58	1.55	1.53	1.51	1.51	1.48	1.45	1.47
Deaths per 100,000 population	15.86	15.69	15.36	15.30	14.86	14.80	14.93	14.74	14.59	14.66

Source: The Fatality Analysis Reporting System (FARS) of the National Highway Traffic Safety Administration (NHTSA), at http://www-fars.nhtsa.dot.gov/.

24

Protecting against Effects of Firm Failure

Business firms fail every day. Although painful for owners and lenders, such failure can be economically useful because the less efficient firms tend to fail. In some cases, however, consumers, employees, and especially retirees, can suffer when a firm fails, and they can suffer dearly. Think, for example, what could happen to a depositor in a bank if there was no deposit insurance. She might lose all her savings if her bank failed, or she might lose her retirement fund and her bequest to heirs if the life insurance company that collected her premiums for a lifetime should fail. Beyond banks or insurance companies, the failure of a business firm can destroy retirement funds in its employee pension plans. The great harm that firm failure can cause innocent parties is an important reason for regulation to moderate its effects.

In addition to preventing harm to individuals as a result of firm failure, regulation of financial institutions helps the economy function effectively. The *Federal Reserve System* is responsible for guiding the economy by wisely exercising its control over banking policy, and for these efforts to be effective widespread confidence in the monetary and banking system is required. Putting to rest worries about the capacity of the system to maintain credit helps to support the economy by making cash available and avoiding financial panic that could undermine the entire system. It protects depositors, who are not in good position to evaluate their bank's financial condition. Nor are policy holders of an insurance company in good position to evaluate the condition of the company or to protect themselves from a failure, so governmental protections may also serve a useful purpose in aiding customers in the insurance market.

The failure of a business firm can extend harm beyond owners to employees and can cost employees more than their jobs. Because the failed firm may be worthless, the firm may stop severance payments that it owes employees, eliminate health insurance, and refuse to make pension payments to them. In bankruptcy proceedings, employees' claims for wages have priority; however, the firm pays obligations to the employee only after it pays secured creditors, such as bond holders, and taxes. Employee health insurance is not well protected and may be lost. Bankruptcy procedures afford some protection for vested pension rights, and if that fails, a federal insurance program may provide retirement payments for some pension plans.

This chapter describes the problems of firm failure and the major regulatory institutions that prevent or cushion its effects in banking, insurance, and employee pensions. Section 24.1 examines banks, where the emphasis is on preventing failure or easing its effects. We explore the consequences of poorly conceived regulation, which led in the 1980s to deregulation of a portion of the banking industry. We turn in Section 24.2 to the insurance industry, which is also regulated in part to avoid, or moderate, the effects of firm failure. This regulation comes mainly at the state level. Section 24.3 discusses the forms of employee pension plans, along with the protections they have in the event of firm failure. We also cover the twenty-first century's increase in bankruptcies and describe subsequent reforms in corporate governance.

24.1 BANKING INDUSTRY REGULATION

Banking supported the lively development of the United States economy, and we begin with a brief history of the industry's features. One weakness of the system was a specialized "thrift" segment, which dealt mainly in residential mortgages and thus lacked diversification that could reduce risk. We describe reforms that were undertaken to remedy this weakness.

A Brief History of the Banking Industry

The nineteenth century was a time of great economic development in the United States, and financial institutions were an important source of capital for business firms. Lasting federal regulation of banks started in the 1860s, with the National Currency Act in 1863 and the National Bank Act in 1864. Aimed at unifying the banking system, these laws created national commercial banks, to be chartered and regulated by a new federal government Office of the Comptroller of the Currency. States had already chartered state banks, and with bank charters now available from either the state or the federal government, a form of regulatory competition was created. Regulators at both levels had to limit the severity of their restraints, once banks had a choice between state and federal regulation, because the banks could move to the less restraining jurisdiction.

Features of the United States Banking System

Stringent national bank requirements limited interaction between banks across state lines. A requirement that national banks possess a great deal of capital kept their numbers small, which tended to limit their competition. State banks were more leniently regulated and did interact across states lines. They developed continuing **correspondent banking** relationships, bank-to-bank arrangements through which small rural banks could gain access to the resources of financial centers in large cities.

The generally easier capitalization requirements that states allowed also fostered banking competition. Competition helped to lower interest rates, and correspondent relationships together with competition helped to move capital among different parts of the country.[1] Resources went to industries and regions where they could be most productive, and regional interest rates became more alike.

A great weakness of the banking system became apparent at the beginning of the twentieth century. Many independent banks existed that had no connection to other banks. Their loans tended to be concentrated in local activities, within their own geographic areas. So their financial risks were not diversified. When these undiversified banks had many claims to meet, they also had no lender of last resort they could turn to, such as a central bank. Congress passed the Federal Reserve Act in 1913 to create the **Federal Reserve System**, which could pool bank resources into reserves, again to avoid panics and to give stability to the national banking system. The system included a central bank, today called the **Fed**, which could pursue monetary policy and lend as necessary to other banks. The Act required national banks to join the Federal Reserve System and to keep deposits at the Fed. Although state chartered banks were allowed to join the Federal Reserve System, they tended to prefer the lower reserve requirements and weaker regulation that existed at the state level.

The Act allowed national banks to operate only at one location. Banks within some states, called "unit banking" states, were subject to the same restriction. In contrast, California allowed a bank to operate branches throughout the state. A few other states allowed some branching but imposed geographic limits within the state. Such differences between state and federal branching rules have gradually been reduced as time has passed. In 1927, the **McFadden-Pepper Act** allowed national banks to operate branches within the cities in which they were located, if the state where they operated allowed it. And the **Banking Act** of 1933 extended to national banks the same branching privileges as were open to state-chartered banks in their states. Although such branching restrictions have been eased since the 1930s,[2] it was not until the 1990s that Congress permitted interstate banking.

Correspondent bank relationships were useful through the twentieth century because of the tendency in the United States to limit branch banking and to prevent interstate banking. Such policies reduced the opportunity for diversification of loan risk and probably weakened the banking system as a consequence. At least there is evidence that states allowing branch banking had fewer bank failures, and in countries that encourage branching such policies also seems to moderate the incidence of bank failure.[3] But by limiting branching, by confining banks to operate in one state, and by only rarely granting charters to operate new banks, Congress limited competition. At the time, this limitation was thought to strengthen banks.

The Great Depression, however, sent the banking system into crisis. Congress's resulting Banking Act of 1933 had three major effects. First, it prevented banks from paying interest on demand deposits in checking accounts. Members of Congress

---

[1] For analysis of the banking system and its effects in the postbellum period, see James (1978).
[2] See Golembe and Holland (1983).
[3] See Calomiris (1991).

BOX 24.1 The "Bank Holiday" and the Great Depression

The Great Depression threatened the banking system in the United States. Whereas an average of about 600 banks had failed per year in the 1920s, the average rose to more than 2200 per year in the years 1930 through 1933. For comparison, in the last 10 years, the average is about 160 bank failures per year. Soon after he took office in 1933, President Franklin D. Roosevelt declared a "bank holiday" and closed the banks. He wanted to stop customers from withdrawing balances in panic and thereby destroying the banking system. Although most banks reopened after about one week with confidence in the system restored, the experience convinced Congress that new banking legislation was needed.

---

believed that bidding among banks in the interest rates they offered, to attract potential depositors' funds, had weakened banks. Under the Act, the Federal Reserve set out rules (known as Regulation Q) to contain such competition, mainly by price control in the form of a maximum interest rate banks could pay on savings deposits and by allowing no interest to be paid on checking deposits. Second, the Act separated commercial banking from investment banking. Congress saw the investment banking activity of underwriting new securities as a source of great risk and forbid it for commercial banks by a portion of the Act that has come to be called the **Glass-Steagall Act**, after its major drafters.[4] (Whether pre-Banking-Act banks made riskier commercial loans to firms to win their investment banking business is still debated.) Third, the Banking Act of 1933 created the **Federal Deposit Insurance Corporation (FDIC)** to provide federal insurance for deposits, initially up to $2,500 and today up to $100,000. The insurance was financed by an annual charge on the domestic deposits of any bank covered by the insurance. Although there are serious criticisms of the way it operates, the FDIC has generally been regarded as a valuable institution that has reduced bank failures to minimal levels. State deposit insurance had existed for a century before the FDIC was created, but state provisions differed and they lacked the great pooling advantage of a national system.

Bank failure illustrates perfectly how customers can suffer when a firm fails; in the banking case they lose their deposits. **Deposit insurance** can reduce this suffering of customers when banks fail, and the assurance it gives depositors can also help to prevent bank panics. Many other early features of bank regulation could also be seen as protecting against firm failure and panics. For example, states set reserve requirements and equity capital requirements for the banks they chartered, and they intended such requirements to ensure financial soundness. States imposed many other financial requirements, and they curtailed banking competition. The process of chartering itself was expected to limit the number of banks and, in turn, the vigor of their competition.

---

[4] For a contrary view of the effect of combining commercial and investment banking, see Benston (1990).

The banking sector contains more than standard commercial banks. Savings and loan associations, mutual savings banks, and credit unions all perform bank functions and are called **thrift institutions**. Thrift institutions emphasize mortgage lending, and they spearheaded the popularity of the amortized mortgage, which began in the 1930s and allowed monthly payments over long periods so individuals could finance homes. The Great Depression caused difficulties for savings and loan associations (S&Ls) as well as for banks. Congress moved to establish the **Federal Home Loan Bank Board** in 1932, which provided a structure for S&Ls somewhat like the Federal Reserve System for commercial banks. The **Home Owners' Loan Act** in 1933 created federal charters for S&Ls. In 1934, the **National Housing Act** brought into existence the **Federal Savings and Loan Insurance Corporation** (abbreviated **FSLIC** and pronounced Fizz-Lick) to offer deposit insurance for S&L depositors. Federal charters were also made available to credit unions, another bank-like institution, through the **Federal Credit Union Act** in 1934. Thus, by the mid-1930s, Congress had created comparable protection for all forms of deposit banking institutions.

A Weakness in the Thrift Business

Thrift institutions, primarily S&Ls and mutual savings banks, began by investing mainly in long-term mortgage loans at fixed interest rates. They financed these loans through short-term liabilities—such as savings deposits—that could be withdrawn on short notice. Investing in long-term mortgages and financing them with short-term deposits constitutes a pattern, called **borrowing short and lending long**, that is inherently dangerous. While income from long-term loans is quite stable, the cost of financing the loans can fluctuate with current short-term interest rates. Low current rates produce handsome profits. High current rates can produce punishing losses.

The risks of borrowing short and lending long were revealed clearly in the 1960s, when short-term interest rates rose, in part from heavy borrowing to finance U.S. involvement in the Vietnam war. Through 1964, 1965, and 1966, interest rates continued to rise. Thrift institutions were being squeezed in these years as short-term interest rates went up, because that made the cost of borrowing rise while income from long-term mortgage loans remained pretty much the same. Selling mortgages to reduce exposure was not a solution because high current interest rates made all long-term, income-producing assets, including mortgages, less valuable. So the thrifts would also lose money if they tried to sell their mortgages.

This weakness in the structure of thrifts increased their chances of failure, but treatments for this problem focused mainly on symptoms. In an effort to protect the thrifts from high current interest rates, Congress passed the **Interest Rate Control Act** of 1966. The Act gave the Bank Board power to set interest rate ceilings, thereby limiting what thrifts would pay on deposits somewhat like (but slightly higher than) the ceilings set for commercial banks by the Federal Reserve under Regulation Q. But because deposits were still needed to finance the mortgage loans, competition continued in nonprice forms. Thrift institutions tried to get around price ceilings by offering consumers toasters or other prizes for opening accounts (the value of such prizes even came to be regulated). Another form of nonprice competition was improved service, such as longer opening hours and more convenient locations. These nonprice forms of competition were less costly to thrifts than open interest rate competition would have been.

Thus, by the 1970s commercial banks and thrift institutions came to share comparable regulatory controls, including demanding requirements for entry into the business, location and product-line limits (thrifts were narrowly confined to mortgage lending), financial and performance standards, and insurance to protect depositors. The design of these regulatory arrangements was not ideal, however, because of the flaw in the borrowing-short-and-lending-long structure of the thrifts. Some of the arrangements, such as interest rate control, merely contained the down-side risk of thrifts borrowing short and lending long. Flaws in the regulatory arrangements would be revealed—at considerable cost to the nation—when pressures built up against the interest rate limits, and Congress attempted partial deregulation of thrifts as a cure.

Deregulation of the Thrifts

New financial institutions challenged regulatory control over banks and thrifts when interest rates rose in the 1970s. The new institutions were called **money market mutual funds**. They would place investor's deposits in Treasury bills, bank certificates of deposit (CDs), and high-quality, short-term corporate bonds that were exempt from interest rate controls. Not being banks, the money market mutual funds were exempted from Regulation Q that limited interest rates, so they could offer returns beyond regulatory limits. They also allowed investors to write checks, although only for fairly large sums ($400 or $500). Another break from the past came in the 1970s when state chartered mutual savings banks introduced interest-bearing checking accounts. Based on the name given to the checks they could issue, the accounts were called **negotiable order of withdrawal**, or **NOW**, accounts. You can probably predict the effects that money market mutual funds and NOW accounts would have on banks and thrifts.

Banks and thrifts lost deposits to the new institutions. Supply scarcities in oil and food and wage inflation from earlier years account in part for the high peacetime inflation of the 1970s, and both factors contributed to a marked rise in market interest rates. In 1978 the three-month U.S. treasury bill rate went above 9 percent. Because of interest rate ceilings, thrifts were limited to paying 5.25 percent, and banks to 5 percent, which is why funds shifted from accounts in banks and thrifts over to higher yielding money market funds and NOW accounts. Once this alternative money market investment was created, regulatory limits on interest rates could not save the banks and thrifts from interest-rate competition. Investment in money market funds tripled in 1978. Market interest rates were to go well above 9 percent over the next three years, while the total investment in money market funds went up almost 20 times, to nearly $200 billion.

By the late 1970s the thrift industry, now facing high short-term rates to finance long-term mortgage loans that had been committed at lower rates, was in deep trouble. By now, Congress recognized the problem of borrowing short and lending long.

Congress was bringing deregulation to airlines and would soon deregulate railroads and trucking, so the idea of ending restrictions on thrifts arose quite naturally. Deregulation of thrifts could broaden their activities to save them from solely borrowing short and lending long on mortgages.

First in the deregulation of the thrifts came the **Depository Institutions Deregulation and Monetary Control Act**, signed by President Carter in 1980. The Act allowed banks and thrifts to offer interest bearing checking accounts, or NOW accounts. The Act also extended deposit insurance protection to all types of accounts, including those at thrifts. With interest rates remaining high, however, the new legislation alone was seen as inadequate. In 1982 Congress passed the **Garn–St. Germain Depository Institutions Act**. Together, the 1980 and 1982 legislation phased out Regulation Q (by 1986) and encouraged the use of adjustable-rate mortgages for both state chartered and federally chartered thrifts. The Act also permitted federally chartered thrifts to expand their lending into credit cards, consumer loans, commercial loans, commercial real estate loans, and in certain limited circumstances equity investments, with some limitations on the fraction of assets that could go to any one of these loan categories. States followed with similar, sometimes even more lenient, permissions in lending opportunities for the state chartered thrifts, to avoid losing them to federal charters.

While each of these steps could be defended as a sensible improvement on previous regulatory policy, when combined with the deposit insurance provisions and the weakened condition of the thrifts, they were a recipe for disaster.[5] Although the thrifts faced a profit-and-loss risk in mortgage investing, due to possible changes in short-term interest rates, there was little risk of default. Moving into loans for

---

BOX 24.2 Adjustable-Rate Mortgages as a Solution

Congress had supported thrift mortgage lenders repeatedly, but it had denied them the use of adjustable-rate mortgages. Adjustable-rate mortgages, which allow the interest rate on long-term mortgage loans to change based on current conditions, would have solved the problem of borrowing short and lending long. But federal regulation prevented adjustable-rate mortgages from being used, mainly because Congress opposed them. Congressional leaders apparently feared that thrifts would arbitrarily raise rates if the rates were adjustable. In 1979, when the Bank Board proposed rules that would permit federally chartered thrifts to offer adjustable-rate mortgages, Congress did not prevent it. But it was too late. Adjustable-rate mortgages might ease a future problem, but they could not solve the present problem because it resulted from all the conventional mortgages that were already in existence.

See N. Strunck and F. Case, *Where Deregulation Went Wrong: A Look at the Causes Behind Savings and Loan Failures in the 1980s*, Chicago, IL: U.S. League of Savings Institutions, 1988.

---

[5] See White (1991).

commercial ventures, including commercial real estate investment, was inherently more risky, and it required knowledge that neither thrift managements nor their regulators had developed. Yet besides opening up such investment opportunities for thrifts, the legislation also made more funds available to them. By phasing out the Regulation-Q type of interest rate limit, and extending insurance protection to thrift depositors, the legislation enabled thrifts to attract deposits. The legislation not only opened up new and unfamiliar investment opportunities for thrifts, but it also fostered the financial wherewithal to pursue them.

The opportunity for thrifts to attract deposits completed the recipe for disaster. With their depositors insured for up to $100,000 by the federal government, the thrifts were tempted to attract deposits and make risky new investments. If the investments worked out well, the gains could be enormous; if they worked out badly insurance would protect the providers of funds, so consequences would be cushioned for them. Moreover, risky investment possibilities were especially attractive to many thrifts because the high short-term interest rates from 1978 to 1982 left them essentially bankrupt. For some of these thrifts, risky investments that might succeed offered the only possibility for survival.

In view of the choices that new legislation created in thrift institutions, it is fortunate that more of them did not pursue risky investments. But some failed, and indeed a few engaged in illegal and fraudulent activities. Even without such activities, a thrift moving into new lending fields without experience could make poor decisions. Many investments that these risk-taking thrift institutions financed turned out to be unwise. When completed, the projects were simply not worth as much as they had cost. Even if foreclosure was pursued for such a project, there would be a loss, because its value would be less than the amount of the loan foreclosed.

Many thrift institutions failed because they financed poor investments. The loss of deposits had to be made good by the FDIC and FSLIC organizations. There were so many failures in the 1980s that the deposit insurance reserves were soon exhausted, and despite increases in insurance rates on deposits, general tax revenues had to be tapped to make good on the federal deposit insurance obligations.

The Thrift Industry Crisis and Its Consequences

By 1984 and 1985, problems were becoming more visible for thrift institutions. Thrifts were growing at alarming rates, and some were failing. Specialized brokers had come into existence as intermediaries to gather deposits for them. The Federal Home Loan Bank Board expanded its field force and imposed stricter rules, but insolvencies mounted. The FSLIC funds were not adequate to meet all claims for deposit insurance, and Congress took up the question of appropriating additional funds. Congress did not urgently pursue the debate, however, and it was August of 1987 before it granted borrowing authority through a new agency. A maximum of nearly $11 billion (but only $3.75 billion in any one year) could be borrowed, but much greater obligations already existed. And before the banking crisis was over, estimates of its cost ranged from $150 billion to $200 billion.

More Remedies

In 1989 Congress passed the **Financial Institutions Reform Recovery and Enforcement Act (FIRREA)**. This Act authorized $50 billion in additional borrowing and substantially reorganized the regulatory institutions. It altered some accounting rules that applied to S&Ls to make them more demanding. The Act replaced both the Federal Home Loan Bank Board and FSLIC by new institutions. It created an **Office of Thrift Supervision** to charter and regulate thrift institutions and a **Federal Housing Finance Board** to oversee lending by the Federal Home Loan Bank, which is owned by thrifts. For deposit insurance, the Act merged the FSLIC into the FDIC, although their funds were kept separate. The FDIC protected commercial banks and some savings banks, while FSLIC had protected depositors in savings and loans. The Act created a new **Savings Association Insurance Fund (SAIF)** to protect S&Ls depositors by managing FSLIC's insurance funds. The Act created one more agency, the **Resolution Trust Corporation (RTC)** to deal with insolvent thrifts, a task that had fallen previously to FSLIC.

These reorganizational steps may have been sensible. But carrying out the reorganization was an added complication in an already very difficult time for these regulatory agencies. The most necessary and important part of the 1989 Act was probably the additional borrowing authorization, which enabled the new RTC to pay off the depositors of closed thrifts. The RTC attempted to sell assets of failed thrifts to provide at least part of the funds needed to meet deposit obligations. In an effort to minimize the needed outlays, the RTC tried to find buyers of failing thrifts or parts of them. Buyers that could absorb the troubled thrifts might enable them to survive, and this would keep the RTC from having to make good the deposits of failed thrifts. The RTC sometimes paid buyers to take over thrifts, where the thrift balance sheets were negative. There is potential for costly errors in an activity of this sort, especially if bureaucratic delays affect timing and funds are sometimes inadequate when

---

BOX 24.3 An Extra Cost of FIRREA

The FIRREA's adjustment of accounting rules proved costly. Tougher rules in the 1989 FIRREA Act made S&Ls look less sound, for example by preventing them from including "good will" as an asset on their balance sheets. The purchasers of some S&Ls under earlier, pre-FIRREA, rules charged the government with undermining their financial soundness when it changed these accounting rules. In 1996, the Supreme Court held that by toughening accounting rules, the 1989 Act breached contracts that had been reached between investors—who were rescuers of failing S&Ls—and regulators. And in April, 1999, a federal judge in the United States Court of Claims originally awarded the Glendale Federal Bank of California $909 million, an estimate of its loss because the bank almost went bankrupt after FIRREA changed the accounting rules in 1989. The award was later reduced to about $380 million. There were many similar cases, and a variety of awards resulted.

See *Glendale Federal Bank v. United States*, 43 Fed.Cl. 390 (1999); and *Glendale Federal Bank, FSB v. United States*, 239 F.3rd 1374 (2001) and 54 Fed.Cl. 8 (2002). See also S. Labaton, "West Coast S&L Wins $909 million from Government," *New York Times*, April 10, 1999, p. B1.

immediate payment would be the lowest cost option. Yet, on the whole, reasonably sensible disposition of troubled thrifts seems to have been accomplished.

For professional negligence, the RTC pursued lawyers, accountants, and others who worked in responsible positions for the failed thrifts. They recovered roughly $400 million, and all cases from the crisis are now closed. In connection with the failure of the Lincoln Savings and Loan Association, for example, $14 million was recovered from its accounting firm, Arthur Anderson and Company, and $51 million was recovered from its law firm, Jones, Day, Reavis and Pogue, a Cleveland-based law firm that is the nation's second largest. Neither firm admitted wrong doing in settling the claims.

One problem with regulation that banks currently point to is that it comes from many different agencies. The Comptroller of the Currency is responsible for overseeing all federally chartered banks. Some banks have branches that are S&Ls, and so are subject to the Office of Thrift Supervision. The FDIC is concerned with depositors and borrowers and their protection. Banks also are subject to regulations of the SEC, the Commodities Future Trading Commission, Securities Investor Protection Corporation, and the FTC. And then there is the Federal Reserve Board. Each of these agencies has a specialty, but the effect is that banks face a maze of regulatory forces.

Deposit Insurance

At the start of the thrift crisis of the 1980s, all deposit institutions in a given category, banks or thrifts, paid the same insurance rate on their deposits, regardless of the risk exposure they represented.[6] An institution had no incentive to improve and to maintain a sound loan portfolio, because doing so would not entitle it to a lower insurance rate. Risk-adjusted insurance rates are common in the insurance industry, largely because a firm that offered insurance without attending to risk would go broke. That is exactly what happened to Federally provided deposit insurance.

In the case of savings and loan institutions, the existence of deposit insurance that made no adjustment for risk was an unwitting catastrophe in the making.[7] Remember that the thrift institutions were beset with enormous financial problems, caused by the unfortunate imbalances that could arise in the business of borrowing short and lending long. They essentially were invited to gamble to survive, because high-risk investments, if they succeeded, could save them. This encouragement to gamble was magnified by deposit insurance that paid no attention to the riskiness of their investments. Because insurance fees did not increase with the riskiness of investments made, there was little reason not to make risky investments. Even if the investments failed, depositors would not suffer; they would be compensated by FSLIC.

In 1989, commercial banks paid a deposit insurance fee of 0.0833 percent of their deposits, while thrifts paid a higher fee, at 0.2083 percent of their deposits. Starting in 1989, these deposit insurance rates gradually increased for commercial banks

---

[6] For analysis of risk adjusted insurance, see Lereah (1985).

[7] For analysis of the role of deposit insurance, see Kane (1989).

and declined for thrifts until, in 1998, the rates matched at 0.15 percent. This plan was not adequate, however, to meet all obligations it was intended to meet. The funds raised by the fees did not quite pay requirements of bonds floated in 1987 to clean up the S&L problems. Commercial banks did not want to contribute more to pay for a problem they did not create. Surviving S&Ls did not feel responsible either for effects caused by those that did *not* survive. So Congress contributed funds to meet obligations and strengthen the banking industry, even after it had already spent $140 billion, or more than 80 percent of the clean up costs.

Had the fees for deposit insurance been tied to the riskiness of a thrift institutions' investments, "going for broke" by making risky investments might have been restrained. The FDIC now makes crude risk adjustments that affect the fees charged for deposit insurance. Having to pay a greater cost for deposit insurance because of riskier investments can make such investments less attractive. It is possible, however, that under the great strain of open interest-rate competition that affected the thrift industry, even adjustments for risk in deposit insurance would not have prevented many failures. It is difficult to evaluate investment risk, except crudely, and adjustments for risk would take time to implement. Some attention to thrift policies, however, would have been stimulated by a program that adjusted deposit insurance rates based on investment risk. This failure to condition deposit insurance fees to the risks of how depositors' funds were used certainly contributed to the thrift industry problems of the 1980s.

Conglomeration in Financial Services

At the end of the twentieth century, Congress ended limitations on bank activities that it imposed in the Great Depression. In October 1999, Congress repealed the Glass-Steagall Act, part of the Banking Act of 1933,[8] which had required commercial banks to be separate from investment banks that sell new stock securities. The fear in the 1930s was that the greater risks of investment banking would make commercial banking less safe, and separating them prevent shocks in the stock market from damaging the commercial banking system. Separating them also prevented a commercial banking arm from unfairly favoring clients of the investment banking arm. Besides being separated, commercial banks were allowed to derive no more than 10 percent of their income from securities markets. The **Bank Holding Company Act** of 1956, which had restricted bank participation in the insurance business, was also modified. Together, the 1933 and 1956 laws had confined firms to only one of the three distinct activities, commercial banking, investment banking, or insurance, but these limitations were dissolved in 1999.

From the time the Banking Act of 1933 was passed until the end of the twentieth century, commercial banks in the United States declined in importance, while pension funds and investment companies grew. Commercial banks controlled more

---

[8] See Stephen Labaton, "Accord Reached on Lifting of Depression-Era Barriers Among Financial Institutions," *New York Times*, October 23, 1999, p. A1.

than 50 percent of major financial assets in 1929 and little more than 22 percent in 1999.[9] In contrast, European commercial banks have long participated in securities and insurance markets, and they flourished under globalization. In Germany, for instance, bankers not only hold important positions as directors of private companies, they may also help to negotiate mergers involving firms in which they hold ownership positions. Commercial banks that participate in investment banking and insurance are called "universal banks" in Europe, where they are seen as offering convenience to consumers and financial strength through diversification of risks. With competition now taking place on a global scale, countries that severely constrain banking activities might handicap banks and limit their success.

After 1999 commercial banks, investment banks, and insurance companies in the United States can operate in what was formerly each others' areas. Bringing large and able new competitors into each of the three fields is expected to increase competition. Regulation of possible banking and insurance conglomerates that take advantage of the new freedom will be shared by the Treasury, the Federal Reserve, the SEC, other federal agencies, and various state insurance regulators. Despite the possibility of greater competition, the opportunities offered by the new law may produce larger and more secure firms, which will have lower probabilities of failure. No groundswell of banking and insurance mergers followed the new law, perhaps because, for other reasons, banking shares were depressed after passage of the law.[10] The primary example is Citigroup Global Markets, Inc., a $72 billion merger involving Citibank, Travelers Insurance, and Salomon Smith Barney investment bank accomplished just as the repeal was being considered. J. P. Morgan Chase & Co. combines investment and commercial banking.

The 1999 law allows the commercial banking arm of a combined banking firm to favor clients of the investment banking arm, making loans available more easily, as may have happened at Enron. Indeed, Citigroup and J. P. Morgan Chase have been accused of structuring debt and cash flow for Enron in misleading ways and of proposing similar arrangements to other firms.[11] Motives to meet client needs in this undesirable way may be stronger in a firm that seeks both investment banking and commercial banking business. Thus, allowing these banking activities to be combined in the same firm has to offer important advantages to offset this undesirable possibility that risky loans may be subsidized.

Consumer privacy can also be affected by these multiservice banking and insurance enterprises. For instance, insurance information about a medically ill consumer may be used to deny that consumer a home mortgage. The law does not prevent the use of such information within companies, although it does require the customer's permission before information can be sold to others outside a given company.

---

[9] See Saunders and Walter (1999).

[10] See Riva D. Atlas, "Few Banks or Insurers Capitalize on Their New Freedom to Merge," *New York Times*, December 18, 2000, p. C1.

[11] See Jathon Sapsford and Paul Beckett, "Citigroup, J. P. Morgan Marketed Enron-Type Deals to Other Firms," *Wall Street Journal*, July 23, 2002, p. A1; and Richard A. Oppel, Jr., "Citigroup and Chase Defend Their Enron Roles," *New York Times*, July 24, 2002, p. C1.

These features of bank organization show how Congress has controlled and adjusted them, often with the aim, at least in part, of preventing bank failure. Preventing insurance companies from failing is also important, but that activity is carried out primarily at the state level.

24.2 | INSURANCE INDUSTRY REGULATION

Insurance is a protective response to risks, a way to pool them together as in a large portfolio so the unlucky bad outcome can be compensated for because the many other outcomes are not bad. It is the opposite of gambling, for instead of many losers rewarding the gambling winner, many nonlosers compensate the insured loser. Historically in the United States individual states regulated the insurance industry that developed.

The Insurance Industry

A party seeking insurance often knows more about the risks to be covered than the insurance company does. Such asymmetric information complicates the operation of the insurance industry because choices by informed parties can harm uninformed parties. To open the topic and illustrate some essential problems in insurance markets, we briefly describe one of the world's great insurers, Lloyd's of London.

Lloyd's of London

One of the best-known insurance companies in the world, Lloyd's of London, has been almost unregulated through much of its more-than-300-year history.[12] Britains's Parliament has passed acts setting rules for Lloyd's, but the rules mainly captured existing practices, and essentially Lloyd's has been exempted from regulation in the United Kingdom and, at least in some respects, in much of the rest of the world. This privileged position was justified in part by some of Lloyd's procedures, which grew from operations in seventeenth century coffee houses (Edward Lloyd founded a London coffee house in 1687) where insurers were financially able to shoulder insurance risks.

Lloyd's development was assisted by the United Kingdom's Bubble Act of 1720, which outlawed the joint stock company, a corporate form of organization, and made full liability common. Stock holders in the joint stock company had limited liability; they could lose the amounts they had invested, but nothing more. In contrast, merchants fully insured risks through Lloyd's, and they sometimes underwrote risks of friends and associates by joining in proposals that came through the coffee houses. These risk bearers were well informed about the situations (mainly maritime undertakings in the early days of Lloyd's) and were known well enough that the amount of risk their wealth might cover also could be known. They functioned then, and

---

[12] For description of Lloyd's and its history, see Finsinger, Hammond, and Tapp (1985).

through the twentieth century, under complete liability, so clients expected their insurance obligations to be met.

At Lloyd's, the individuals who bear insurance risks, called "Names," organized into groups, called syndicates, which would compete with each other for writing specific policies. The late actor, Christopher Reeves, was insured for $20 million during the filming of the "Superman" movies, for example, and Bruce Springsteen insured his voice with Lloyd's for more than $5 million. Claims against Lloyd's from the sinking of the *Titanic* in 1912 exceeded $1 million (about $20 million in today's dollars). For years the Names were quite well known to each other. They managed their affairs closely and settled disputes among themselves, without resorting to the courts. Lloyd's functioned like a market in which parties were well informed and contracts were complete.

In the 1970s Lloyd's grew substantially, and with the Names numbering in the thousands, fair play and integrity among them seemed to decline. Disputes involving them and the syndicates spilled into the court system and received substantial publicity. Lloyd's delegated greater authority to outside underwriting agents, some of which were corporations. This reduced the cohesive participation of the Names, who became more like passive investors. Brokers, who controlled large numbers of underwriting syndicates, grew more concentrated, and this put the Names at a disadvantage by giving them fewer and more costly sets of insurance policies as options. Problems led finally to The Lloyd's Act of 1982, British legislation that established a new constitution for Lloyd's and resulted in substantial reorganization to avoid concentrations of power and conflicts of interest.

Reorganization as a result of the Lloyd's Act of 1982 may not have been adequate, however, for the once great insurance company fell on hard times. Partly because of bad luck (such as plane crashes and hurricanes) at the end of the 1980s and the beginning of the 1990s, Lloyd's lost billions of dollars, and many Names were financially ruined. Charges in lawsuits are plentiful and more than bad luck may be involved.[13] After terrorist attacks in 2001, insurance claims against Lloyd's reached roughly $2.7 billion, more than any other insurer, although many of these obligations were shared with other insurers. In response, Lloyd's announced sweeping changes, including new accounting practices to make its activities more transparent.[14] It would also phase out its more than 2,000 Names, and replace them with corporate investors, who already provided most of the company's capital. These steps would make Lloyd's more like other large insurers in the world.[15]

Asymmetric Information

The special information problems that can afflict insurance companies may have reached Lloyd's of London. Differences in information between buyers and sellers, called asymmetry of information, is a well-known cause of market inefficiency.

---

[13] See "Shipshape?" *The Economist*, February 22, 2001.

[14] See Joseph B. Treaster, "Lloyd's of London Weighs a New Path to Profitability," *New York Times*, January 18, 2002, p. C2.

[15] See Joseph B. Treaster, "Lloyd's Plans to Alter How It Finances Its Insurance," *New York Times*, July 19, 2002, p. C8.

It arises when a party on one side of a transaction, say the seller of a used car, has more information about the item than a possible buyer. Asymmetric information can exist in financial markets when a firm's managers know more about the firm than do investors. It is especially likely in the case of insurance, where a possible client may know more about her own health than the company that is offering her life insurance.

As Lloyd's of London grew, and Names and those who dealt with them could not be as well informed as before, the company may have fallen prey to these informational problems. On the one hand, the insurance company is apt to know much more about its own financial soundness than the customer does. On the other hand, the customer can know more about the risk that is to be insured. Indeed, two particular problems result from this form of asymmetric information. First, there is adverse selection, the possibility that customers who are the poorest risks are precisely the ones who seek insurance.[16] Second, there is moral hazard, which is the possibility that, once insured, a customer is less careful because insurance protection makes the consequences of careless action less harmful.[17]

Insurance companies can guard against the informational advantages of their customers. To protect against moral hazard, for instance, the company can offer less than full insurance, perhaps 80 percent coverage rather than 100 percent. This leaves the policy holder to bear significant harmful consequences from an unwanted outcome (such as a house fire), and as a result that policy holder still has incentive to be careful. Moral hazard takes other forms, however. For example, when involved in a motor vehicle accident, a person may feign a whiplash neck injury or other hard-to-confirm injury to collect damages, perhaps as pain and suffering awards.[18] Insurers attempt to distinguish these claims from legitimate ones but cannot always, and false claims add to the cost of insurance protection.

To protect against adverse selection, an insurer can do two things. First, it can gather enough information about customers to place them in risk classes, with fees to match the risks. More expensive auto insurance for customers under the age of 25 is an example, arising from the higher accident rate among drivers in that age group. More generally, "experience rating" can be used to categorize drivers, based on their driving records, and leads to higher prices for drivers with poorer records. In the case of health insurance, a physical examination could serve this purpose. Without any examination the company might offer a policy for people of average health but attract mainly customers with serious health problems. By giving examinations it is possible for the insurance company to adjust rates according to health condition and thereby avoid having less healthy customers choose policies designed for customers of average health. Failure to adjust the rate charged according to the riskiness of deposit insurance coverage for banks, as discussed in Section 24.1, is another example of this problem of adverse selection.

---

[16] For a classic description of this consequence of asymmetric information and adverse selection, see Akerlof (1970).

[17] No-fault automobile insurance reduces administrative costs by eliminating the right to sue for personal injuries while the injured's own insurance company compensates them instead. When free of the danger of a law suit, however, there is some evidence that drivers are less vigilant, as they are more likely to have accidents. See Cummins, Phillips, and Weiss (2001).

[18] For evidence of such moral hazard problems, see Cummins and Tennyson (1996).

Second, to avoid adverse selection the insurer can attempt to choose its customers rather than have customers choose it. For example, when they cover *all* employees of a firm, health insurers effectively choose their clients, because employees do not choose them. As another example, credit card companies attempt to approach customers with certain characteristics (such as college graduates) rather than respond only to requests from potential customers. After all, the person who intends to default is more likely to approach the company. By choosing customers itself, the company is better able to avoid such customers and can do it without exerting great investigative effort.

Automobile Insurance

Auto insurance illustrates particularly well the problem of asymmetric information, where drivers know more than insurance companies about their driving habits. One way the insurers of automobile drivers try to overcome this problem of asymmetric information is by using age as a signal of experience and of the ability to avoid accidents. Drivers below the age of 25 generally have to pay higher rates for insurance, because as a group they are more likely on average to have accidents. Drivers who are over age 25 and have bad driving records also pay higher rates. For those under 25, having better grades in school can bring discounts from the high rates, because students with good grades are less likely to have accidents.

One regulatory question that has arisen prominently in the automobile insurance industry is whether to organize insurance on a "no-fault" basis.[19] As its name suggests, no-fault insurance does not assess blame. After an accident, the motorists involved each make claims against their own insurance companies. The respective insurers simply pay medical bills, car repairs, and other losses. The advantage is that the insured do not pursue high claims as often, and lawyers are not brought in to fix blame in court and to pursue large damage awards. As a result, a higher portion of premiums can go directly to loss payments, and less to legal and administrative costs, than under ordinary tort liability.[20] A recent study by the Joint Economic Committee of Congress estimated that the average family's auto insurance premium of approximately $771 could be reduced by $221 under an effective no-fault insurance system. The Committee found no-fault insurance to be especially promising for reducing insurance costs in urban areas.

A second feature of no-fault insurance is that it usually bars tort claims. Except for very serious losses, law suits are not allowed in no-fault insurance plans. Barring lawsuits helps to overcome the moral hazard problem of accident "victims" falsely pursuing pain and suffering awards in court. Yet lawsuits are not totally wasteful. The threat of harsh penalties in law suits may force drivers to exercise great care. Without the care induced by threat of law suits, accidents may rise. Indeed, there is evidence, at least for crash fatalities, that states with no-fault insurance have 7 to 13 percent higher fatality rates than states with tort liability.[21]

---

[19] See Cummins and Tennyson (1992) for description of how no-fault insurance may lower costs.

[20] See Grabowski, Viscusi, and Evans (1989).

[21] See Cummins, Phillips, and Weiss (2001).

A number of states have adopted no-fault insurance but have not achieved expected benefits.[22] For one thing, injured parties have not wanted to renounce their right to sue, although states have acted to limit law suits. New York and Michigan, for example, permit suits only after dismemberment, permanent disfigurement, loss of some bodily function, or other severe injuries. Some states set monetary limits, so there is a right to sue only for losses above a specified amount. Having such a limit apparently has led to inflated claims, as insured parties attempted to qualify by suing for awards that were large enough to exceed the limit.

Interest in no-fault auto insurance has increased recently because accident claims have been rising at 4.4 percent annually, even though accidents have been declining slightly and their severity has been constant. Congress is considering legislation that would allow consumers to choose whether they wanted to retain the full right to sue or be sued, or choose a version of no-fault insurance that would allow recovery of economic damages only. If their damages exceeded the limit of their own policy, they would be permitted to sue the other party.

Another problem for automobile insurance is the presence on the highway of uninsured drivers. Although more than half the states make motor vehicle insurance mandatory, these states require only minimal amounts of insurance and their enforcement is weak, which allows uninsured drivers on the roads.[23] Uninsured drivers are seldom able to cover the costs they cause. As a result, when they fail to collect for damages from the uninsured, the insurance companies end up compensating their clients who suffered damages, and this brings higher rates to those who pay for insurance. As insurance rates rise, more drivers may attempt to drive with no insurance. This process can continue until accidents involving uninsured motorists push insurance rates quite high. Rates for automobile insurance protection vary markedly across American cities, and the varying proportions of uninsured drivers is an important reason. For example, early 1990s insurance rates in Philadelphia were more than twice as high as in Seattle; in Philadelphia 27.5 percent of liability claims involved uninsured motorists while in Seattle only 8 percent did.[24]

The example of automobile insurance illustrates how a market can fail, and various policies have been adopted in efforts to avoid such failure. Notice, first, that competition is part of the problem. Some of the uninsured motorists are drivers with poor records, whom insurance companies do not want to insure because such clients put one company at a disadvantage relative to its competitors. In their efforts to avoid such unprofitable clients, the companies can provoke a market failure. A monopoly over an insurance market could offer lower prices for "good" drivers and engender a more efficient equilibrium. The monopoly would be motivated to overcome these failures to insure, which competition can cause, although the monopoly might be inefficient in other ways. Instead of adopting monopoly market organization, states have adopted "assigned-risk" insurance plans as a way to increase coverage for drivers

[22] At least 13 states have no-fault automobile insurance programs and 12 more states have features of no-fault insurance but do not limit the right to make tort claims. See Cummins, Phillips, and Weiss (2001).

[23] The states without mandatory insurance impose financial responsibility requirements, but these also are not enforced reliably.

[24] See Smith and Wright (1992).

who have poor records. These plans assign the drivers with poor records to insurance companies on a "fair-share" basis, usually in proportion to the company's share of the state's insurance business. Under rates that are subsidized, but still high, insurance is thereby made available, and the number of uninsured drivers is reduced.

Under no-fault insurance, drivers are paid damages by their own insurance companies, so no-fault insurance can avoid the cost of unsuccessful lawsuits against uninsured motorists. The problem such drivers cause would still remain, but if rates were lower, the adverse selection problem that pushes better drivers away from insurance could be moderated. Stiffer enforcement of mandatory insurance laws also might help, but that is costly, and it tends to strike at the poorest members of a community.

Insurance Regulation Issues

The failure of an insurance company can devastate its clients, and largely to avoid such an outcome, regulation attempts to avoid insurance company failure. When failure does occur, all states offer some form of back up insurance to fill in for the failed insurance. These state reinsurance arrangements, however, vary in their provisions, which raises the question whether insurance should be regulated at the state or federal level.

When Insurance Companies Fail

The late 1980s and the beginning of the 1990s were bad times for many insurance companies besides Lloyd's of London. In 1991, 26 U.S. life and health insurers became financially impaired or insolvent. The accounting book value of their assets exceeded $40 billion, making it by far the largest failure year ever in life and health insurance. The failing insurers had often made high-risk investments, in junk bonds for example, which plunged in value in 1990, or in commercial real estate, which also lost value. The loss in asset value made them unable to meet their financial obligations. When news of these financial difficulties reached them, many policyholders sought to cash in their policies, which aggravated the weak financial conditions of insurance firms and probably accelerated takeover of the firms by regulators. But withdrawal of funds may also have served to limit the ability of such a firm to make more risky investments in a desperate survival effort to earn high returns.

Customers have difficulty overcoming the informational disadvantage they face in judging the financial soundness of an insurance company, and to protect customers against firm failure is a major reason why insurance companies are regulated. In the United States this regulation is accomplished primarily at the state level, through state insurance commissioners. All states maintain insurance guarantee funds to protect residents from the failure of property liability, life, and health insurance companies (the District of Columbia protects for property liability but not life and health insurance), mainly by assessing surviving companies up to 1 or 2 percent of their premiums.

State insurance guarantee funds do not always provide adequate protection when an insurance company fails. Richard Montejo, Jr. was injured playing baseball in

Texas when he was 9 years old, and when he did not receive timely hospital care for his head injury he developed cerebral palsy. A lawsuit against his hospital finally resulted in a $600,000 award, but on the day the funds were to be released, the hospital's insurer, Insurance Company of America, was declared insolvent and placed under state supervision. The Texas Department of Insurance provides payments when insurance companies fail, but its maximum of $100,000 would not satisfy Richard's claim, and some outstanding claims were substantially larger than Richard's. The funds to make this reduced award come from the Texas Property and Casualty Guaranty Association, which is financed by assessments on insurance companies and is intended to moderate the impact of insurance company failure. All states and the District of Columbia have such insurance guarantee associations, but they differ considerably in the protection they provide. Some observers have called for a federal fund to protect consumers of failed insurers, much as the FDIC protects depositors of failed banks.

State or Federal Insurance Regulation?

Congress has expressed concern over the cost of insurance-company insolvencies and the effectiveness of widely varying state regulation, which sometimes has insurance commissioners appointed and sometimes elected. Yet thus far Congress has prevented federal regulation of the industry. Congress has focused more on property-liability insurers and has raised the possibility of federal regulation to overcome problems with inconsistent state regulation. Congress also considered a bill that would modify the **McCaren-Ferguson Act** of 1945 to almost repeal the antitrust exemption enjoyed by insurance companies, which allows them to cooperate in several areas such as developing similar policy forms and means of estimating prospective losses on policies. Some consumer activists argue that the Act also shields the industry from price-fixing charges.

BOX 24.4 Insurance Regulation Failure

Consumers may have lifetime savings with their insurance companies, and with so much money at stake, fraud is a serious potential problem for the industry. One of the biggest insurance frauds in history was revealed in 1999 when CEO Martin R. Frankel fled to Europe after taking hundreds of millions of dollars from Franklin American Corporation, a company that promised high returns to insurance companies that invested with it. It is now clear that regulators in states where the company operated should have uncovered Franklin American's deceptive practices. Indeed, Tennessee's Commerce and Insurance Department noted irregularities as early as 1993 but failed to act on them, and five especially strict states that employ over half the country's insurance regulators—California, Connecticut, Florida, New York, and Texas—also appear to have been fooled.

See J. Kain, "Insurance Fraud Shows Gaping Holes in States' Regulatory Net," *New York Times*, July 6, 1999, p. C1.

Congress is concerned about possible fraud, rising rates for auto and medical insurance, failure of life insurers, and efforts by some home insurers to withdraw from Florida and other areas that are exposed to risks of hurricanes. Some reinsurers, who pool risks for insurance companies, are often kept from helping to spread these risks because they are foreign companies that face greater entry barriers in most states.[25] Congress has also noted with suspicion that insurance fees escalated substantially along the eastern United States coast after the crash of planes into the World Trade Center in New York on September 11, 2001. There is concern that property insurers deny insurance coverage to homeowners and businesses in minority neighborhoods. One type of legislation that Congress has proposed would require insurers to report data on the cost and quality of their policies by metropolitan area; legislation would also require race and gender information of policyholders by census tract, so Congress could follow insurance trends and notice if biases developed among customers. Some large companies propose a choice of state or federal chartering, somewhat as bank regulation allows. Congress, however, has not passed any such legislation.

Federal regulation could help to overcome two problems. First, the state that regulates an insurance company may contain only a fraction of its policyholders, so the state regulator may be more concerned about the company and not be as strongly motivated to protect consumers as it would if all consumers of the insurance were residents of its state. Federal regulators might focus on consumers more reliably. Second, foreign insurance companies are subject to higher requirements, such as a need to maintain more collateral, than U.S. companies when they operate in the states. These requirements go back to a time when some foreign countries did not regulate well, but they now interfere with an increasingly global insurance market that federal regulation might better coordinate. On the other hand, federal regulation of, say, banks and savings and loan associations, has not been perfect, so it is not clear that regulation of insurance at the federal level—which typically is more remote from the circumstances and could preempt stronger state regulations—would be better.[26]

The **National Association of Insurance Commissioners** has taken a number of actions to improve regulation by states. For instance, it has developed model insurance regulation bills that improve management in many ways and increase required reporting about loss reserves and other matters, and it urges state legislatures to pass them. It now has an accreditation process and is instituting risk-based capital value standards for property-liability and life and health insurers. In the crucial step of judging when an insurer is insolvent and moving to control the effects, state regulators can have important advantages because they know local conditions better than federal authorities normally would. So regulation of insurance may continue to operate at the state level, at least for the near future.

On the whole, observers judge the insurance industry to be quite strong. The life and health insurance industry holds about one-third of all corporate bonds and nearly one-third of all commercial mortgages, so it is an important player in capital

---

[25] See "American Exceptionalism," *The Economist*, August 12, 2006, p. 62.

[26] For evaluation of insurance regulation in the United Kingdom and Germany, see Finsinger, Hammond, and Tapp (1985).

markets. But fractured regulation across many states may discourage foreign competitors and prevent some benefits of global risk spreading. The very size and significance of the industry makes its effective functioning important. Sound regulation that efficiently spreads risks and reduces the possibility of insurance-firm failure will be important in achieving that end.

24.3 │ FIRM FAILURE IN THE TWENTY-FIRST CENTURY

The first few years of the twenty-first century saw a remarkable increase in bankruptcies, especially of large firms. Indeed, three-fourths of the bankruptcies that occurred between 1980 and 2003 occurred after the year 2000. There was a shake-out among dot-com start-ups, problems in the new world of energy trading, and overinvestment by telecommunications firms. And there was outright fraud. The most famous bankruptcies were Enron in 2001 and WorldCom in 2002.[27] Officers of Adelphia Cable were arrested in handcuffs for allegedly looting that company,[28] and the leader of Tyco International received enormous compensation, borrowed further from the firm and still appeared to avoid taxes in questionable ways.[29] Strong corporate executive motivation, often from widespread use of stock options, invited aggressive efforts to raise share values. Accounting rules were bent, and protections against corporate misbehavior were inadequate, in part because they had been weakened by Congress, and not strengthened when needed, in the 1990s.

The Role of Financial Information

Accounting information is supposed to reveal the income, expenses, and asset status of a firm, to facilitate its sound management and to inform interested parties of its condition. This information can give early warning of financial problems, which can help to prevent firm failure because it can force remedial actions and avoid the crash that may follow if risky practices go unnoticed and are extended too far. Investors, in particular, need prompt and reliable information to judge whether to buy or sell a company's stock. To prevent surprises, and to support investor judgments for sound resource allocation, the federal government requires publicly held corporations to issue financial reports that follow Generally Accepted Accounting Principles (GAAP). The purpose of accounting reports is to make a firm's financial condition transparent to investors and to others.[30]

---

[27] See Simon Romero and Riva D. Atlas, "WorldCom Files for Bankruptcy; Largest U.S. Case," *New York Times*, July 22, 2002, p. A1.

[28] See Andrew Ross Sorkin, "Founder of Adelphia and 2 Sons Arrested," *New York Times*, July 25, 2002, p. C1.

[29] See David Leonhardt, "A Prime Example of Anything-Goes Executive Pay," *New York Times*, June 4, 2002, p. C1.

[30] For illustrative problems in the Enron case, see Gretchen Morgenstern, "Enron Letter Suggests $1.3 Billion More Down the Drain," *New York Times*, January 17, 2002, p. C1; and for another example from WorldCom see Simon Romero and Alex Berenson, "WorldCom Says It Hid Expenses, Inflating Cash Flow $3.8 Billion," *New York Times*, June 26, 2002, p. A1.

Some Problems with Financial Information

Firm failure is especially painful to employees who lose their jobs and their retirement funds at the same time, and the effect is worse when it comes without warning. Committed as they are to a single employer, when that employer fails, the employees must hunt for new positions. Some might begin hunting earlier if prospects for the company are reliably reported. They might also reduce their commitment to the employer's stock in their pension plans. So employees also have an interest in sound accounting reports from their employers. Experience from the beginning of the twenty-first century showed weaknesses in the financial information that corporations issued, and we now know that faulty reports were often followed by shocking bankruptcies.

Management incentives can tempt individual business firms to "push the envelope" of accounting practice. Institutional investors such as mutual funds press managements to improve their performance. In part because issuing stock options did not have to be reported as an ordinary corporate expense, their use was also widespread through the 1990s. Using them allowed top managers to profit enormously from increases in share values. Feverish pursuit of share price increases therefore should not surprise us. In the 1990s, however, firms that distributed a greater fraction of options to their top five executives actually had poorer performances than those that distributed a smaller fraction to their leaders.[31]

There are two main protections against faulty accounting reports. First, by conducting audits, reputable accounting firms certify (or not) the soundness of reports issued by firms. Accountants apply GAAP rules with reasonable consistency across a great range of firms with usually satisfactory results. The accounting firms have some discretion in applying GAAPs, however, especially in judging what is "material," or important, and what is not.[32] Here an accounting firm may make poor judgments, and in some cases, the results can be disastrous.

The second source of protection from faulty reports are the GAAPs themselves, the rules that accountants follow and the ways they are defined and enforced. In the United States, accounting standards are set by the Financial Accounting Standards Board (FASB), a private organization that is financed by the industry. The FASB follows advice from leading accounting authorities. Although it is difficult to avoid all ambiguity, the FASB attempts to pursue standards that will make accounting reports reflect reality. Standards set by the FASB are followed by practicing accountants in part because the SEC requires that public corporations follow them. As a result of the Sarbanes-Oxley Act of 2002, a **Public Company Oversight Board** will oversee this process of corporate accounting in the future.

Having clear and demanding accounting standards is important to a competitive market economy. Without such standards, firms with the most misleading reports might flourish, at least for a time, and the most honest firms could be handicapped in attracting investment funds or employees. Resources then would not reliably flow

---

[31] See Bernstein, Blasi, and Kruse (2003), and Gretchen Morgenson, "When Options Rise to Top, Guess Who Pays," *New York Times*, November 10, 2002, Sec. 3, p. 1.

[32] For criticism of the enforcement of accounting standards see Benston, Bromwich, Litan, and Wagenhofer (2003).

BOX 24.5 An Accountant's Reputation

The Arthur Andersen accounting firm had been called the "conscience of the industry," partly because in the 1950s it had urged greater independence for accountants, and in the 1980s it was the only large firm to argue for improved pension accounting. But Andersen came under scrutiny in 2001 after the Securities and Exchange Commission filed fraud complaints against a partner of the firm and against the firm itself in cases involving the Sunbeam Corporation and Waste Management. Then Enron repudiated financial statements that Andersen had certified, and Andersen never recovered. In each of these instances, Andersen had identified accounting problems but had judged that the effects were immaterial and often had allowed the accounting practices that were involved. Making such trade-offs between client wishes and accounting purity is treacherous, because when the judgments depart too much from accounting purity the accounting firm can lose its reputation and then its customers.

See F. Norris, "From Sunbeam to Enron, Andersen's Reputation Suffers," *New York Times*, November 23, 2001, p. C1.

---

where they could be used best, so output would not be as valuable as it could be. Opportunities for fraud and deception would be greater, and their occurrence would diminish trust in markets and reduce market effectiveness. The adoption of functional accounting standards is not always left to the judgment of the FASB, however, despite its auspicious competence to formulate them.

Problems in Overseeing Accounting

Many existing corporations (including accounting firms) are large Congressional lobbyists and contributors to Congressional election campaigns, so interference by Congress with the development of FASB standards or related matters may not be surprising.[33] For example, in the early 1990s the FASB attempted to put into effect a rule requiring that stock options be reported as an expense by a firm, like any other form of employee compensation. Members of Congress moved to prevent the change. By various means, such as considering an amendment to the Securities Exchange Act of 1934 to require SEC approval of *every* FASB proposal, Congress forced the FASB to withdraw the proposal. Moreover, Congress made lawsuits against corporate managements harder to bring and to win. Congress also resisted changes that would have clarified accounting for mergers and acquisitions. It is difficult to justify this regulatory intervention by Congress into the rules of accounting and business practice, especially to make them weaker.

Accounting firms also face natural conflicts of interest. As auditors, they are paid by the very clients they audit. As a result, they may be tempted to be lenient to the

---

[33] For examples that reveal how Congress weakened accounting rules and limited enforcement in the 1990s, see Michael H. Granof and Stephen A. Zeff, "Unaccountable in Washington," *New York Times*, January 23, 2002, p. A23, Don Van Natta Jr., "Bipartisan Outrage but Few Mea Culpas in Capital," *New York Times*, January 25, 2002, p. C1, and Stephen Labaton, "Now Who, Exactly, Got Us into This?" *New York Times*, February 3, 2002, Sec. 3, p. 1.

clients who pay their bills. To make this temptation worse, they have also served as consultants to those same client firms in often lucrative arrangements. In the Enron example, the accounting firm Arthur Andersen received from Enron about $25 million in annual revenues in auditing fees and another $27 million in consulting fees. A firm might be more reluctant to disapprove a client's accounting practices and lose the client, especially when that could also mean the loss of significant consulting income. To remedy this conflict, the SEC proposed in the 1990s that accounting firms be separated from consulting firms, but vigorous resistance from Congress prevented adoption of the proposal.

Conflicts of interest also arise in investment banking firms, where analysts evaluate stocks to give investment advice. Investment banks want to attract lucrative investment banking business, especially to handle the sale of new stock issues. To further this aim, their analysts may resist criticizing existing or potential clients, and the result can be faulty advice for investors. Charges about self-serving advice flourished after the dot-com investment bubble burst in the late 1990s, and they even arose as part of the Enron wreckage.[34] The SEC adopted some rules in 2002 to restrain misleading practices, but legislation may impose more thorough remedies.[35]

A conflict of interest may also arise for insiders, those who function within a corporation. First, suppose a senior executive who holds shares in the firm sees the fortunes of the firm about to rise or fall. Current law makes it a felony for the executive to buy or sell stock shares on such **insider information**. Such a law is based on the idea that those with access to inside information about the firm should not be able to profit from it. The main enforcement mechanism to prevent insider trading on privileged information is the public reporting of trades by those in the firm. These required reports come about a month after the trade occurs, however, and proposals call for much faster reporting, perhaps within a few days, which modern communication makes possible.[36] If stock options are awarded just before good news is released by the company, that can then amount to an institutional form of insider trading, to the extent that it is like buying on favorable information. Such opportunistic timing of awards seems more prevalent when directors also receive the options, and it may lead to rules that call for periodic award of options without discretion by the firm as to the timing of the awards.[37]

A second insider problem arises when top executives can make millions of dollars from increases in share price, which make their stock options valuable, and so they may pursue misleading accounting practices to inflate reported cash flow or conceal debt in an effort to make the share price move higher. This problem is aggravated by the failure to account for stock options as an expense at the time they are granted, which makes them attractive for compensating executives and others because this form of compensation does not immediately reduce firm profit. While it is difficult to

---

[34] See John C. Coffee Jr., "Guarding the Gatekeepers," *New York Times*, May 13, 2002, p. A19.

[35] See Stephen Labaton, "S.E.C. Adopts New Rules for Analysts," *New York Times*, May 9, 2002, p. C1.

[36] See Floyd Norris, "S.E.C. Seeks Tighter Curbs On Insiders," *New York Times*, April 12, 2002, p. C1.

[37] See Gretchen Morgenson, "Are Options Seducing Directors, Too?" *New York Times*, December 12, 2004, Sec. 3, p. 1.

value options, because they depend on future movements in share prices, several reasonable means have been proposed, including FASB and SEC proposals in the early 1990s.[38] Some companies are now treating stock options as an expense when they are granted, and some business leaders are urging that all companies do so.[39] Another proposal, aimed at restraining the short-term incentives that stock options can induce, would have executives retain any stock options they are awarded until the time comes for them to leave the company that awarded them.

Although stock options are usually justified by firms as management motivation devices, to induce managers to pursue the goals of shareholders, they have been misused to pass large rewards to managers who did not cause rising share values. A number of cases were investigated in 2006, based largely on suspicious option awards made in the 1990s.[40] Some option awards were backdated, so recipients could benefit from selling shares that appeared to have been awarded earlier at low prices. Backdating essentially is lying about the option award and unjustly rewarding the option recipients. The Sarbanes-Oxley Act curtailed this practice, by requiring that

---

BOX 24.6 Accounting for Stock Options

Stock options grant rights, usually extending over several years, to buy stock shares at a specified price per share once the stock reaches a specified price (the "strike" price) that is usually at or above the current price when the options were awarded. The holder of the option gains the difference between that specified price and the higher market value that is received when the option is exercised. Stock options are usually awarded as incentive for employees, to motivate them to improve the stock price, because the employees can gain only if share price rises so they can exercise the options. If the firm merely issues new shares when the options are exercised there is no outright expense, but the firm's profit will be divided among more shares, so the earnings per share will be reduced. Although this "dilution" of earnings may reduce the value of shares, shareholders have to look carefully through footnotes in the firm's accounting reports to see this potential effect. If the firm buys shares to satisfy its need when the options are exercised, that will of course require the expenditure of real money, which will affect cash flows in the firm. So handling options is a thorny accounting problem, but fuller reporting of their issuance and better information about them would clearly be an improvement. The issue is increasingly important because the use of options grew from a value of about $10 billion in 1994 to over $100 billion in 2000.

See H. R. Varian, "In Accounting for Options, Knowing about Diluted Earnings Is a Powerful Tool," *New York Times,* May 9, 2002, p. C2.

---

[38] For further analysis, see David Leonhardt, "Options Calculus: Who Gets It Right?" *New York Times*, March 30, 2003, Sec. 3, p. 1.

[39] See, for example, Warren E. Buffett, "Who Really Cooks the Books," *New York Times*, July 24, 2002, p. A21.

[40] See "Nuclear Options," *The Economist*, June 3, 2006, pp. 56–57.

option awards be reported within two days rather than at the end of the year as under previous reporting requirements that left room for cheating on option award dates. The timing of option awards can still come just before a rise in stock price is expected and, thus, serve as a payment to managers rather than as a reward for effects of their management actions. Strategic dating might be minimized by making option awards on preset dates each year, although even then stock prices might be manipulated by saving good news until just after option award dates.

There are still other ways for highly motivated corporate leaders to issue misleadingly high-profit reports in their own private interest. One muddy area, for instance, is in the reporting of returns for defined-benefit pension funds. The pension fund returns can be reported as part of profit on an estimated basis that allows considerable discretion. Concealing pension performance information when it is convenient to do so has also been possible.[41] An optimistic estimate of pension earnings result in higher current profit but may be followed by a disappointing profit adjustment at a later date that is hard to uncover. Profit on long-term contracts is sometimes booked in the year the contracts are signed, even though the actual profit occurs later. Such rules create ambiguities in accounting practice, and they have often contributed to the misleading profit reports that preceded giant bankruptcies in recent years.

Rating Corporate Bonds

In addition to possible problems with the reports that corporations issue, there may be weaknesses in a separate set of independent agencies that evaluate the soundness of the corporations' debt instruments, primarily their bonds. By rating the quality of these corporate securities, bond-rating agencies can influence the cost of financing for corporations. In 1975, the SEC decided that bond-rating agencies needed to be certified, and it introduced a certification procedure. The avowed aim was to insure that no untrustworthy agency gave misleading ratings. The three bond-rating agencies that existed at the time, Fitch, Inc., Moody's Corporation, and Standard and Poor's Equity Research, were certified, and four new entrants since 1975 have been absorbed into the original three agencies. In February, 2003, after a two-year evaluation process, the SEC approved a Canadian firm, Dominion Bond Rating Service, as a fourth authority to rate bonds, and it may approve others.[42]

Three rating agencies operated as oligopolists for nearly 30 years. Having only three agencies evaluating all corporate bonds probably limited the effectiveness of the bond-rating process.[43] Until the 1970s, income for the rating agencies came from

---

[41] See Gretchen Morgenson, "It's Time to Move Pension Reporting Out of the Dark," *New York Times*, November 10, 2002, Sec. 3, p. 1.

[42] One applicant, Egan-Jones Ratings, has been trying to win approval since 1998 and may yet succeed. See Leslie Wayne, "Credit Raters Get Scrutiny And Possibly A Competitor," *New York Times*, April 23, 2002, p. C1. Egan-Jones does not take payments from firms whose credit it rates. Instead it sells its rating service to investors. It was one of very few advisory firms to detect financial problems at Enron and Worldcom before they collapsed.

[43] See Lawrence White, "Credit and Credibility," *New York Times*, February 24, 2002, p. 13. For a detailed analysis of the bond rating industry, see White (2001).

publication of their ratings to bond investors, but when copying machines threatened to take away that source of revenue, the companies began collecting fees directly from the issuers of bonds, the parties whose bonds they rate. Indeed, the bond rating companies are exempt from SEC corporate disclosure rules, so they can receive sensitive information from clients without having to pass it along to other investment analysts.

When substantially protected from entry by SEC certification, the three rating agencies did not face effective competition. Ratings by *all* agencies are valued, so a client corporation doesn't really choose among them, which means there is no strong price competition. As for the quality of analysis, the rating agencies simply publish their ratings by placing bonds in rating categories and do not have to justify them. This makes it easy for the three agencies to lean toward favorable ratings and thereby avoid irritating their fee-paying clients. Suppose instead that the rating agencies had to justify their ratings in public, so their justifications could reveal the efforts they had made and the soundness of their analysis. Public justification could foster competition to make the judgments more compelling. Most importantly, however, it would allow fuller evaluation of the bond evaluators. Then, SEC barriers to entry into the ratings agency business could more easily be eliminated.

The past bond-rating performance is not impressive.[44] For instance, the rating agencies did not detect weakness in Enron's debt ahead of other observers, despite being privy to more information because rating agencies receive more information from clients who pay for their ratings, as nearly all clients do.[45] The ratings need not be soundly based to have effects on bond interest rates. The rating agency simply issues a rating, which like a signal can influence bond interest rates. Such influence could be due in part to regulations that constrain the investment portfolios of banks, which must achieve a target average bond rating. If a rating agency downgrades a bond, some banks may have to sell it, and that will affect the interest rate of the bond, whether the market finds the rating itself informative or not.

Information about the financial conditions of firms is crucially important to the functioning of markets. It is an area where important improvements seem to be possible, but improvement is neither simple nor easy. Evaluating evaluators is always difficult, in part because self-serving opportunities and incentives get in the way. Eliminating entry barriers for bond evaluators holds promise because it would allow their evaluation in the market place.

Protecting Employee Pensions

Even with well-applied accounting rules and reliable bond ratings, a firm's poor performance can lead to its failure. If a firm fails, can pension benefits of employees be lost? Yes, they can. Such a loss can devastate affected employees. Employees with defined-contribution pension plans may have portfolios that are particularly risky if

---

[44] See Partnoy (1999).

[45] See White (2001). See also Richard A. Oppel Jr., "Credit Raters Face Inquiry over Enron," *New York Times*, March 20, 2002, p. C1.

they concentrate their investments in their employer's stock. Before the Enron Corporation went bankrupt in 2001, for example, almost 60 percent of the average employee's portfolio of retirement funds was in Enron stock, which in a few months fell from a high of about $90 per share to less than $1 per share. Even firms that do not fail may cut back so drastically that workers are affected as if they had failed, because both jobs and pensions are lost. Lucent Technologies cut 30,000 jobs in 2001, for instance. Many employees held a large fraction of Lucent stock in their defined-contribution pension plans, and the value of the stock fell more than 90 percent from 1999 to 2001.[46]

Where the employer's stock is an investment option for the employee in a defined-contribution plan, almost a third of the average retirement portfolio tended to be in such stock in 2001. Where the employer influences pension investments by *contributing* stock, more than half of the average retirement portfolio was in the employer's stock.[47] Employees in many companies, including Procter and Gamble, Sherwin-Williams, Abbott Laboratories, Pfizer, Coca-Cola, Anheuser-Busch, and General Electric, had far more of their employers' stocks in their defined-contribution pension plans than did Enron employees.[48] Stimulated by the fall of the Enron Corporation, which wiped out defined-contribution pension benefits for employees who were heavily invested in Enron stock, many proposals were made with the aim of lowering employee risk. They included calls for employee education about the benefits of diversification, rules to prevent requirements that funds remain for long periods in the employer's stock, and limits on the fraction to be invested in the employer's stock.

Employees who have defined-benefit pension plans also lack protection against their employer's failure, although general rules for these plans limit investment in the employer's stock to 10 percent of the pension portfolio value. Employees have to depend on their employers for sound management of their pension plans, for they do not participate themselves in managing the funds collected in their plans, and they have only limited information about them.[49] As a result, employees are not usually in a very good position to evaluate the financial condition of their defined-benefit plan or to determine the status of pension assets. Lack of information can be a problem when employers fail to fund pensions adequately and employees do not know it. If their industry declines, as the steel industry did in the 1990s, for example, employers may not be able to meet their defined-benefit pension obligations and employees suffer. Even when employees know that the financial condition of their employer is weak they may be helpless to act, except by leaving the employer and attempting to take their inadequately funded pensions with them.

---

[46] See Danny Hakim, "Former Workers at Lucent See Nest Eggs Vanish, Too," *New York Times*, August 29, 2001, p. C2.

[47] See Richard A. Oppel, "The Danger in a One-Basket Nest Egg Prompts a Call to Limit Stock," *New York Times*, December 19, 2001, p. C1; and Daniel Altman, "Experts Say Diversify, but Many Plans Rely Heavily on Company Stock," *New York Times*, January 20, 2002, p. A26.

[48] See Steven Greenhouse, "Response to 401(k) Proposals Follows Party Lines," *New York Times*, February 2, 2002, p. C1.

[49] See Gretchen Morgenson, "It's Time to Move Pension Reporting Out of the Dark," *New York Times*, November 10, 2002, Sec. 3, p. 1.

The FASB issued new rules in early 2006 that require fuller reporting of a corporation's pension obligations. Until then, one had to search footnotes in a corporation's annual report to learn the financial obligations that its pensions represented, and even then tracing true obligations could be difficult. As a result, investors were handicapped in assessing the true financial condition of the firm, and employees had difficulty determining the soundness of their pensions. Under the new FASB rules, corporations have to include their pension obligations in standard reports as liabilities. Following the new rules will reduce substantially the equity value of many corporations, but financial statements will reflect more transparently their financial conditions.[50]

Pension insurance can also help. To avoid the loss of defined-benefit pensions due to firm failure, Congress created the **Pension Benefit Guaranty Corporation (PBGC)** in 1974. The PBGC was to be a self-sustaining insurance fund, collecting small annual premiums from participating defined-benefit pension plans to cover the losses of pension plans unable to meet their obligations. Plans might fail to meet obligations either because the company sponsoring them falls on hard times without having the plan fully funded, or because the plan is poorly managed. In the 1990s, reduced pension funding by firms dampened the prospects for this PBGC insurance as a protection for employees. By 2003, many of the 32,000 participating defined-benefit plans were not adequately funded, meaning that their pension funds alone would not meet their expected future obligations. On average, they could almost meet their termination pension liabilities, or what they would owe if everything stopped today, but they could not meet their on-going pension liabilities, which include obligations in the future. The companies sponsoring these plans would expect to cover their obligations out of profits when necessary, and perhaps to increase their commitments to the plans until they are adequately funded.

Estimates of "underfunding" for defined-benefit pension plans vary with financial conditions, which affect the value of pension fund assets, as well as the interest rates that are used to forecast how those assets will grow to meet pension obligations in the future. Congress eased the funding requirements for defined-benefit pension plans in April, 2004, and it added special concessions for airline and steel companies.[51] Under existing practices and with a depressed economy, estimates of underfunding in 2003 ran as high as about $300 billion.[52] Roughly $80 billion of this was concentrated in the airline, automobile, auto parts, and tire industries, with obligations to airline pension plans exceeding $25 billion. More than half of all claims from the PBGC through 2001 went to steelworkers, and pension claims in the year 2002 exceeded claims for all previous years (back to 1974) *combined*. Reserves of the PBGC appear inadequate to meet all the claims it may receive. Although with rising interest rates the condition of the PBGC has improved, it is still precarious.

---

[50] See Albert B. Crenshaw, "Pension Rule May Wipe Out Equity," *Washington Post*, April 13, 2006, p. D1.

[51] See Mary Williams Walsh, "Negotiators Reach Accord on Pension Bill," *New York Times*, April 2, 2004, p. A1.

[52] See statement of Steven A. Kandarian, Executive Director Pension Benefit Guaranty Corporation, Before the Subcommittee on Select Revenue Measures, Committee on Ways and Means, United States House of Representatives, April 30, 2003. See also Mary Williams Walsh, "Discord Over Efforts at Valuing Pensions," *New York Times*, May 1, 2003, p. C1. For effects of bankruptcy on pensions, see Micheline Maynard and Mary Williams Walsh, "Judge Rules US Airways Can End Pilots' Pension," *New York Times*, March 3, 2003, p. C2.

Premiums charged to pension plans by the PBGC were increased to strengthen reserves. This is not a genuine solution, however, because pension plans have a choice whether to participate in the PBGC program and there is no effective risk adjustment in the fees they pay. This means that as premiums rise, adverse selection can operate. Because the premiums rise for all pension plans, regardless of how strong they are, the well-funded pension plans may find the added protection of PBGC too costly. If they stop participating, that will leave a greater fraction of the remaining plans at PBGC underfunded. Such a transition is already underway, because 97,000 defined-benefit plans have been terminated since 1986, and the overwhelming majority of those plans were able to meet their obligations to their workers.[53]

An asymmetric information problem lies behind this possibility of adverse selection among firms offering defined-benefit plans. Clients of the insurance protection provided by PBGC know more about their condition than the insurer, PBGC, and the most risky clients have the greatest interest in having the insurance protection. Poorly funded pension plans are motivated to accept PBGC insurance protection largely because—as in the case of early bank deposit insurance—rates do not vary with their risks of failure. On the other hand, the well-funded pension plans that have smaller risk of failure may find the undifferentiated fee for insurance protection too high and decide not to incur it.

Companies with underfunded pensions also have a perverse incentive that can motivate behavior reminiscent of the S&Ls discussed in Section 24.1. Recall how S&Ls in weak financial condition were motivated to make risky loans. The loans could either work out well and save the company or not work out well, in which case the depositors could at least collect deposit insurance. Here, in the case of pensions, employers may offer attractive pension packages, knowing that if they attract productive workers and succeed in their businesses, all will be well. Even if they should fail, the workers will be able to turn to the PBGC for retirement benefits, although the PBGC benefits are usually substantially lower than employers had promised.

The PBGC itself has urged Congress to take steps that would alter this situation. For example, Congress requires firms to make contributions to cover unfunded commitments; however, it allows the firms such a long period of time in which to do it that they can add more new unfunded obligations by the time they cover the old ones. The PBGC has proposed that, as long as old benefits are not provided for, new benefits not be guaranteed. The PBGC also proposed a requirement that annual contributions at least equal annual pay outs, so reserves in pension plans could not be depleted. The PBGC also requested that it be given higher standing in bankruptcy proceedings, to improve its chances of recovering funds, a proposal that seems reasonable because wages have higher standing. Congress adopted none of these proposed improvements in pension protection for workers.

---

[53] See statement of Steven A. Kandarian, Executive Director Pension Benefit Guaranty Corporation, Before the Subcommittee on Select Revenue Measures, Committee on Ways and Means, United States House of Representatives, April 30, 2003.

Accounting and Corporate Governance

In 2002 Congress passed the Sarbanes-Oxley Act to reform accounting and other aspects of business law.[54] Reforms in the Act are aimed at accounting practices, fraud, corporate governance, and securities regulation. For accounting, the law is intended to reduce the conflicts of interest that can mar the auditing process. As noted, the largest U.S. accounting firms[55] earned substantial amounts of money by selling consulting services to the very firms they audited, which can cause a conflict to the extent that lenient accounting might win more consulting profit. The Act now prohibits accounting firms from offering a wide range of consulting services to publicly traded companies that they audit. Auditors will also have to change every five years, although one firm may be able to retain a client by changing the partner of the firm who is leading its audit. It may, therefore, still be possible for an accounting firm to win business by lenient auditing, without fear that it will be noticed by a separate, entirely independent, auditing firm. The board of directors of corporations, with shareholder approval, still chooses the auditor.

Another feature of the Act includes a new accounting regulatory board, called the Public Company Oversight Board, with investigative and enforcement powers, to be overseen by the SEC. The Act broadens the definition of fraud by corporate leaders in dealing with their shareholders, and it strengthens the penalties for such crimes. Language in the Act requires firms to disclose publicly, as quickly as possible, any "material" change in their financial condition. The Act also gives analysts at investment banking and brokerage firms new protections, forbidding their employers from retaliating if their recommendations differ from the employer's interests and making it easier for them to win retaliation cases against their employers if retaliation occurs. Investors also will have more time in which to bring lawsuits against corporations for securities fraud.

The Act prohibits corporations from making loans to their insider executives unless such loans are also available to outsiders. Executives cannot dodge liability for securities violations by declaring bankruptcy, either. When issuing financial statements, chief executives and chief financial officers of corporations will be required to certify them. A study based on a large sample of firms, including some that certified and some that failed to certify just before the Sarbanes-Oxley Act became effective, found that the certification requirement had no effect.[56] That is, investors had already discounted for the reporting soundness, or the transparency of earnings, in firms with weaknesses before the certification requirement called attention to it. Under the certification procedure, however, if leaders "knowingly or willfully" provide materially misleading information in statements, they can go to jail for up to 20 years.

---

[54] See 116 Stat 745. The Sarbanes-Oxley Act of 2002 was passed July 30, 2002.

[55] First called the "big-eight" when the number of giant accounting firms in the United States was eight, that number dwindled to five by 2002: Andersen, Deloitte Touche Tohmatsu, Ernst & Young, KPMG, and Price Waterhouse Coopers. After a series of challenged audits, Andersen was found guilty of obstruction of justice in the Enron case and was unable to survive as a major accounting firm, leaving only a "final four" large accounting firms.

[56] See Bhattacharya, Groznik, and Haslem (2002).

The Sarbanes-Oxley Act does not deal with the problem of accounting for stock options. Perhaps the Public Company Oversight Board will implement a solution to that problem, based on FASB recommendations. A proposal by the New York Stock Exchange to have shareholders approve all stock option plans could have very significant effects, because such a requirement would almost certainly reduce the use of stock options.[57] Because stock options seem to invite short-run efforts to raise share values and may even tempt top executives to fraudulently manipulate earnings, curbing their use might improve corporate governance.

SUMMARY

Firm failure is common in a competitive market economy. But it can have consequences that are harmful, especially in the banking or insurance industries where consumers may suffer enormously if a firm collapses with their savings. Much regulation in those two industries aims at preventing large-scale harm from the failure of firms.

Banking has changed a great deal since the National Currency Act of 1863 and the National Bank Act of 1864. The Federal Reserve System was created in 1913, and federal insurance to protect deposits of failing banks began with the Banking Act of 1933. Congress developed similar protections for thrift institutions in the 1930s. But thrift institutions had to borrow at short-term rates to support their long-term mortgage investments. Because short-term rates fluctuate more than long-term rates, the borrowing rate could exceed the rate determining income and thus cause losses. This inherent weakness led to repeated crises for thrift institutions, and Congress responded by placing ceilings on short-term interest rates they and banks would have to pay. In the 1970s, however, the development of alternative financial institutions such as money market mutual funds and interest bearing checking, or NOW, accounts, resulted in high interest rates being offered for deposits. The resulting open competition for deposits caused serious problems for both the regulated banks and the thrifts, and led to forms of deregulation in the 1980s. Neither thrifts nor their regulators were knowledgeable about the new opportunities deregulation opened for them. Many thrift institutions failed, and deposit insurance funds alone were not adequate to meet demands placed on them.

Reforms resulting from the thrift industry debacle of the 1980s gradually made thrift institutions more like banks, and the reforms relaxed some of the regulations to which banks had been subject. The reforms also reorganized regulatory institutions, especially for the troubled thrift industry. They reconstituted the form of deposit insurance, making thrifts comparable with commercial banks and adjusting the fees

---

[57] See Jonathan D. Glater and David Leonhardt, "Both Sides Say Bill Addressing Business Fraud is a First Step," *New York Times*, July 25, 2002, p. C1.

for deposit insurance protection so they reflected the risks involved. Legislation passed by Congress in 1999 overturned the regulatory restrictions that had confined commercial banks, investment banks, and insurance companies each to their separate lines of business for much of the twentieth century. Now all of these financial services may be offered by one conglomerate. This freedom to choose organizational boundaries may produce at least some firms that offer all of the services, leading to more competition and to the development of larger firms that may be less likely to fail. Approval of interstate commercial banking in the 1990s was another step that reduced regulatory barriers and, together with more liberal branch-banking rules, may also reduce the probability of bank failure.

The insurance industry, like banking, has gone through a difficult period recently, and the problems are visible in exaggerated form at Lloyd's of London. The buyer of insurance may know more about risks than the seller—an example of asymmetric information—which can cause problems for the seller. Adverse selection occurs when high-risk potential buyers, who are poorer insurance risks, choose insurance, while low-risk potential buyers do not buy insurance. A second possible problem is moral hazard—the idea that, once insured, a client may behave in a riskier way. All of these problems surfaced at Lloyd's.

More generally, a host of problems face regulators trying to avoid the problems of insurance firm failure. There is the question of what level—state or federal—is best for regulation, which now rests primarily at the state level. No general federal insurance is available to protect insurance funds, as there is for bank deposits, and such a program may be desirable. But sound design for such an institution is difficult to achieve, as we can see from bank deposit and pension insurance examples, so more work is needed.

Pension plans that are provided by employers have been especially hard to design so they do not collapse when the employer fails, bringing disaster to employees who depend on them. There are two main types of pension plans, defined-benefit plans that specify exactly the retirement benefits to be paid, and defined-contribution plans that allow employees to decide (up to a limit) the amounts they invest for retirement but leave actual retirement benefits to depend on the performance of their investments. A third type of plan, called a cash-balance plan, offers immediate employee ownership of funds but has them accrue steadily at a specified rate under management by the employer. There is some regulation of the types of investing that is allowed in defined-benefit plans, and they are insured by the federal Pension Benefit Guaranty Corporation. The main problems for defined-benefit plans arise from the failure of employers to fund them adequately, and although the Pension Benefit Guaranty Corporation offers valuable insurance protection, it is not adequate to protect all such plans. Strengthened accounting standards now make accounting for defined-benefit pensions more transparent. Defined-contribution plans presently have no similar insurance protection, and because employees often invest substantially in the stock of their employers, firm failure can be doubly harmful to them. Regulation of defined-contribution plans restricts the contribution levels so that they are tax deductible.

Accounting practices can help to avoid firm failure by alerting investors to risks of a firm and thereby prompting corrective action. Assurance that accounting reports reflect the true state of a corporation's finances depends on careful and honest auditing. With that, there have been two main problems. First is the question whether an accounting firm objectively follows Generally Accepted Accounting Practices in auditing the books of a client who pays it, and for whom it once might have performed lucrative consulting services. Second, the GAAPs themselves must be sound. They are set by an independent accounting industry organization but in the 1990s Members of Congress interfered to weaken accounting rules on behalf corporations. Congress also clouded merger accounting and made shareholder lawsuits against management harder to bring.

The Sarbanes-Oxley Act of 2002 repaired some of these accounting flaws and improved other practices. It created the Public Company Oversight Board to investigate and enforce sound accounting practices under the guidance of the Securities and Exchange Commission. It made document destruction easier to find in obstruction of justice cases, and penalties for it were increased. The Act prohibited auditors from providing a range of consulting services to firms they audit, and required a change in the auditor in charge at least every five years. The Act gives security analysts new protections that should make them more independent in the recommendations they provide to investors. Under the Act, securities fraud charges are easier to bring, and maximum sentences for fraud are greater. The law requires rapid disclosure of material information, and sanctions the corporate executive who misleads or wrongfully benefits. Fortunately, even without these reforms, sound procedures greatly outweighed the inappropriate actions that some firms take, and accounting generally reveals reasonably well the financial conditions of the vast majority of corporations.

QUESTIONS

1. Describe what is meant by "borrowing short and lending long." Would the same type of problem that accompanied "borrowing short and lending long" ensue for a banking institution that was "borrowing long and lending short?" Explain your answer.

2. What problems may follow if bank deposit insurance is offered on the same terms to all banks, regardless of the riskiness of their financial conditions? What problems may arise if automobile insurance is offered on the same terms to all potential customers, regardless of their driving records and chances of having a motor vehicle crash? Can a similar problem arise in connection with insurance to protect defined-benefit pension plans against the consequences of firm failure?

3. Can you make an argument that, to be diversified, an employee's defined-contribution plan should contain *none* of her employer's stock?

4. Congress considered the following proposals to reduce the risk to employees of a collapse in their defined-contribution pension plans when their employers fail: (1) employee education about the benefits of diversification, (2) rules to prevent having funds frozen for long periods in employer's stock, and (3) limits on the

fraction (for example, 20 percent) to be invested in the employer's stock. Evaluate each of these proposals for their effects, if any, on (1) employee loyalty and work incentives, and (2) the protection they might afford employees from harm if their employers fail.

5. There is a trend away from defined-benefit pension plans toward cash-balance and defined-contribution pension plans. Explain this trend and offer a prediction as to where it will lead.

6. Evaluate each of the major provisions of the Sarbanes-Oxley Act for its effect on the soundness of the financial information that will be available from corporations. Can you see possible undesirable side effects of any of the provisions?

7. One element of the government's protection against effects of firm failure is the Pension Guarantee Benefit Corporation, a federal insurer of defined-benefit pension plans that can cushion the blow to retirees when firms fail. Describe the strengths and weaknesses of this institution. Is there any way that such an insurance plan could also cover defined-contribution pension plans?

GLOSSARY

absolute cost advantage An advantage in cost that an incumbent firm has over an entrant because of experience in learning a production technique, scale economies, or other reason.

acid rain Precipitation formed in the atmosphere that contains acid.

Act to Regulate Commerce U.S. legislation of 1887 that created the Interstate Commerce Commission and required it to set rates that were "just and reasonable" and outlawed "undue" discrimination among persons, companies, or communities.

administered pricing The setting of prices by large enterprises that does not seem to reflect fully the effect of supply and demand because the prices do not change very much.

administrative law A body of law that governs decisions of government agencies and is relevant to regulatory agency proceedings.

adverse selection A possible consequence of imperfect information in markets, as when the quality of products is unknown and higher prices cannot be obtained for high-quality products, so only low-quality products are offered for sale.

advertising-to-sales ratio The ratio of advertising expenditure to sales.

affirmative action A temporary effort to remedy past discrimination by allowing employers to take into account such characteristics as race and gender.

Age Discrimination in Employment Act U.S. legislation of 1967 that prohibits discrimination against those 40 and older who are otherwise qualified for the work.

agency costs Actual and intangible costs of motivating and monitoring agents.

agent The party who is obligated to act on behalf of the employer, or the principal.

aggregate concentration A crude measure of economic power in a whole economy, measured, for example, as the percentage of an economy's total sales, employment, value added, or other measure of activity that originates in the largest 50, or perhaps the largest 200, firms.

air quality threshold The basis for setting ambient air-quality standards for criteria pollutants is a certain threshold level, an approach that has been criticized because even low levels of pollution can be harmful.

Airline Deregulation Act U.S. legislation of 1978 that ended the Civil Aeronautics Board's control of entry and airfares in the airline industry and disbanded the CAB in 1981.

Air Transportation Stabilization Board U.S. federal agency created in 2002 because of events of 9/11/01 to administer $10 billion to aid the airline industry through loan guarantees.

allowances Rights to release emissions under the U.S. sulphur dioxide (SO_2) cap-and-trade pollution rights trading program.

American Inventors Protection Act A law that requires public access to patents 18 months after the application date of a patent, whether or not the patent office has made a decision about the application.

Americans with Disabilities Act U.S. legislation of 1990 that prohibits employment discrimination against individuals with mental or physical disabilities who are otherwise qualified for jobs.

amortized mortgage A long-term loan, as for house construction, to be repaid through regular specified payments over a long time period, such as 30 years.

Amtrak A partly private and partly public U.S. enterprise that now runs national passenger rail service.

ancillary services A range of services, such as available reserve generating capacity, that support a wholesale electricity market.

Antitrust Improvements Act U.S. legislation of 1976 that requires firms planning a large merger to notify the Federal Trade Commission and the Department of Justice in advance of the merger and allows state attorneys general to bring suits on behalf of state citizens.

applied research Scientific effort that is designed to achieve a specific outcome.

asset specificity A term that recognizes the specialization of assets for narrow purposes.

asymmetric information A condition in which one party to a transaction is better informed, perhaps about product quality, than the other.

attainment areas Areas defined by the 1977 Amendments to the Clean Air Act to be attaining emission standards, as part of a plan to control allowable deterioration in air quality by category of attainment.

attempting to monopolize Attempting to gain a monopoly position, which was declared to be illegal by the Sherman Act.

"at-will" relationship A judicially created employment rule by which employers can hire or dismiss workers "at will"; in particular, the employer does not have to give a reason.

auction A procedure that makes an award to a winning bidder.

automatic adjustment clause Electricity industry procedure that allows changes in the price of fuel to automatically change the final price for electricity.

average cost Total cost divided by output quantity.

average fixed cost Total fixed cost divided by output quantity.

average incremental cost Incremental cost of a product divided by the output of the product.

average variable cost Total variable cost divided by output quantity.

avoidable costs Costs that reflect less commitment than sunk costs because they can be terminated in a fairly short time.

B2B transactions Internet transactions between firms, including wholesale trade and company purchases of parts, components, and capital equipment.

Bank Holding Company Act U.S. legislation of 1956 that restricted bank participation in the insurance business.

Banking Act U.S. legislation of 1933 that prevented banks from paying interest on demand deposits in checking accounts, separated commercial banking from investment banking, and created the FDIC to insure bank deposits.

banking pollution An early U.S. air pollution control practice allowing firms to save credits for their emissions reductions to be used in future emissions trading.

barometric price leadership A form of price leadership in which one firm initiates changes in price and others follow, not because the leader has power but because it is responding to conditions in the industry.

basic research Scientific effort that is not designed for, but may lead to or be used in, specific applications.

Best Available Control Technology (BAT) Practice adopted in 1983 of the Environmental Protection Agency specifying technology for industries and sewage treatment facilities to clean water virtually without regard to cost.

Best Practicable Control Technology (BPT) Practice adopted in 1977 of the Environmental Protection Agency specifying technology for industries and sewage treatment facilities that would bring improvements at reasonable cost.

best-response function Gives one firm's best output choice as a function of the other firm's (or other firms') output(s).

biochemical oxygen demand (BOD) The oxygen needed to degrade a pollutant in the water.

block price A nonuniform price such that a different price applies to different portions, or blocks, of the quantity range.

Board of Governors of the Postal Service The governing body of the United States Postal Service.

bond covenant Promise made to bondholders, such as a limit on the fraction of debt in the firm's capital structure, that serves to protect the collateral of the bonds.

bondholder A provider of capital to the corporation who is owed the value of the bond and is usually paid a fixed interest rate on the capital the bond provides.

book value The accounting value of assets based on the actual historical cost of each asset minus some estimate of loss in value due to depreciation.

borrowing short and lending long A pattern of financing long-term loans with short-term deposits that is inherently dangerous because the cost of financing the loans fluctuates with short-term interest rates.

bounded rationality An expression that conveys our human limitations in considering every possibility in any situation.

brownsfields Polluted land sites (though not as dangerous as Superfund sites) that the Environmental Protection Agency undertakes to cleanup, such as sites manufacturing plants or military bases have vacated, that need reclamation efforts to preserve their prospects for economic redevelopment.

bubble An early U.S. air pollution control practice applied to existing sources that allowed a firm to sum the emission limits for individual sources of pollutants in its plant into a large "bubble" area within which the firm could adjust the different sources to meet its aggregate emissions level in the most efficient way.

budget-constrained public enterprise A government-owned organization, used to produce public services in many countries, that is required to raise enough revenue from its services to cover its costs, or sometimes to achieve a target surplus or to incur a preannounced deficit.

budget maximization A possible goal for a budget-constrained public enterprise.

bundled Two or more goods are bundled when they are offered for sale together.

business-stealing effect A consequence of one firm taking business from another or others.

Bus Regulatory Reform Act U.S. legislation of 1982 that deregulated intercity bus travel at the federal level by making entry easier on interstate routes and reducing opportunities for fare collusion.

bypass A private telephone connection to carry calls between a business (usually a large one) and an interexchange, or long-distance, carrier, so the business does not use the local exchange network.

California Independent System Operator (CAISO) Coordinator, as an Independent System Operator, responsible for maintaining system balance in the California electricity markets.

California Power Exchange (CALPX) The California wholesale market for electricity, comparable in form to the Florida Energy Broker but arranging all transactions rather than marginal trades.

California Public Utility Commission (CPUC) The California regulatory commission that proposed a competitive electricity generation industry to replace then existing regulation of electric utilities.

cannibalization An expansion by a firm into a service that actually competes with and takes business away from another of the firm's services.

"cap-and-trade" A program that puts a limit, or a cap, on total emissions, allocates among plants rights to emit effluent, and then lets the plants trade the pollution rights among themselves.

capital gains Appreciation in the value of capital assets.

capital structure The mixture of shareholder equity, bond debt, and other financial sources for a corporation.

capture theory A theory that sees an industry "capturing" its regulators because they often come from the industry being regulated and share its values.

carbon dioxide An air pollutant that contributes to global warming through the greenhouse effect.

carbon monoxide (CO) An air pollutant that comes primarily from motor vehicle exhausts.

cartel Organization of firms in a market that enables them to control price and quantity.

cash-balance plan A pension plan managed by the employer, which invests money for each worker and accumulates it at a modest rate of return.

Celler-Kefauver Act U.S. legislation of 1950 that defined mergers more fully than the Clayton Act and permitted enforcement against mergers.

certification For automobile air pollution control, the Environmental Protection Agency tests a prototype of each automobile model and imposes emission requirements that certify the vehicle for its year and type before it can be sold to the public.

chicken game A game situation that has one player's payoff depends on the other's action in a dangerous way, as when two entrepreneurs each promote a conference center in a town that is large enough to support only one.

chlorofluorocarbons (CFCs) Nontoxic and nonflammable refrigerant (named freon by Du Pont), now banned, that is a likely cause of damage to the protective ozone layer.

Civil Aeronautics Act U.S. legislation of 1938 that created a regulatory agency, known since 1940 as the Civil Aeronautics Board, to promote and develop the airline industry, to award routes, and set fares.

Civil Aeronautics Board (CAB) A U.S. federal agency created in 1938 that regulated economic aspects of the airline industry for more than 40 years before it was eliminated in 1981.

civil law Laws implicated in settling private disputes in areas such as property, contracts, and torts.

Civil Rights Act U.S. legislation of 1964 that, among other provisions, prohibits discrimination in any aspect of employment of protected groups and applies to employers, labor unions, and employment agencies.

class of customer A way sellers may divide markets—one seller selling wireless phones to individual consumers while another sells to professional or business users, for example—to reduce their competition.

Clayton Act Antitrust legislation of 1914 that is more specific than the Sherman Act in making particular business practices unlawful.

Clean Air Act U.S. legislation of 1970 that established the Environmental Protection Agency (EPA) to control pollution by working with states in areas of air, water, toxic substances, noise, radiation, and solid waste.

Clean Air Act Amendments Amendments to the U.S. Clean Air Act passed in 1977 and 1990.

Clean Water Act Water Pollution Act of 1972 that called for the elimination of the discharge of all pollutants into navigable waters by 1985.

codesharing An alliance among airlines to help them function as a single network.

collusion Agreement among existing sellers that restrains trade.

command-and-control A method of regulation that issues commands that must be obeyed.

commitment A strategic action that makes a threat credible, as when an existing firm actually expands its capacity to threaten a potential entrant with increased output upon its entry.

common carrier A governmentally endorsed service provider who is to serve all who want service at announced rates.

common knowledge Widely held knowledge, in a game, for example, where all players know the rules of the game and all know that they all know the rules.

common law A form of law developed by courts that relies on past judicial decisions and on judicial interpretations of legislation.

common-pool problem Arises when multiple owners of a resource all try to use it.

Communications Act U.S. legislation of 1934 that created the Federal Communications Commission to regulate telecommunications services in the United States.

compatibility Separate operations use the same standard, such as the same railroad track widths, so the operators can use one another's systems.

compensatory damages An award to cover damages suffered, possibly including damages for pain and suffering, when the manufacturer of a product is negligent and a consumer is harmed as a result.

competitive access provider (CAP) Unregulated provider of local network services, usually at major office buildings in large cities, to reach switching locations for interexchange carriers so businesses can bypass a local exchange.

Competitive Transition Charge (CTC) The difference between the fixed retail electricity rate and expected cost in California's electricity restructuring plan, which was intended to compensate electricity producers for their stranded costs.

complements Two products are complements if, when the price of one rises, the quantity demanded of the other falls.

concentration measures Ways to characterize the number of firms in a market and their different sizes.

concentration ratio A measure of the percent of an industry's sales, assets, employment, or value added that is in the hands of a small number of firms in an industry.

congestion management Management of an electricity transmission system to provide power to areas where fully used lines otherwise prevent it from being transmitted.

conglomerate A multiproduct business firm that produces seemingly unrelated products.

conglomerate merger A merger between firms in unrelated businesses.

conjecture An assumption, according to Augustin Cournot, that a firm makes about the quantities that other firms will offer for sale.

consent decree A judicial order in the United States based on an agreement between the government and a defendant.

Consumer Goods Pricing Act U.S. legislation of 1975 that repealed the Miller-Tydings Resale Price Maintenance Act and the McGuire-Keogh Fair Trade Enabling Act, to remove federal antitrust exemption for resale price maintenance agreements.

Consumer Product Safety Commission (CPSC) A U.S. federal agency created in 1972 to administer laws intended to protect consumers from dangerous products.

consumer's surplus The difference between what a consumer is willing to pay for all the units of a good consumed and the price actually paid.

contestable market When an industry has no sunk costs, no great investment needs, and no other barrier, entry is very easy so even a small rise in price will induce entry.

contingent valuation A method for evaluating public projects that presents to subjects contingent survey questions that depend on a choice available in a market-like setting where payments actually could be made.

continuous-emission-monitoring equipment Equipment for monitoring emissions of plants to determine the pollution rights they have to submit.

contract carriers Specialized transporters of commodities that require specialized knowledge and techniques, such as carriers of automobiles.

coordination game A situation in which players have to coordinate their actions, as when two players have to arrive at a meeting place at the same time for the meeting to succeed.

copyright A statutory scheme that protects certain rights of creators of original works.

corporate acquisitions and mergers The joining of two or more firms into one, a process regulated by the Department of Justice and the Federal Trade Commission.

Corporate Average Fuel Economy (CAFE) Federal U.S. standards for fuel economy as a miles-per-gallon target for a weighted average of the auto manufacturer's entire fleet of produced vehicles.

corporate governance The rules through which corporations and their managers are governed.

corporation A form of business organization that is owned by holders of ownership shares who select a board of directors to pursue the organization's interests.

correspondent banking A relationship between large and small banks through which small rural banks could gain access to the resources of financial centers in large cities.

cost-plus regulation The practice of regulating a firm's allowed prices based on its costs.

credible A requirement for a firm's threat to be believed is that carrying it out does not go against firm's own interest, for if it does the threat may not be credible and may be ignored.

criminal law A set of rules all citizens must obey under threat of punishment by fine or incarceration by states or the federal government.

criteria air pollutants Substances that are common in the air but can be harmful and are measured to give an indication of air quality: particulate matter, sulphur dioxide, nitrogen dioxide, carbon monoxide, ozone, and lead.

cross-ownership An arrangement in which one owner operates in different media, for example, as the same owner of a TV station and a newspaper in the same city.

cross-subsidy One product in a multi-product firm benefits from a cross-subsidy if the price of that product is below cost, while the resulting loss is covered by prices of other products that are above their costs.

dead weight loss The surplus that is lost when a market is not in equilibrium, usually because price is higher than marginal cost.

defendant Party against whom a plaintiff files a complaint because of a claimed injury.

defined-benefit plan A pension plan provided by the employer that promises specific benefits to the retiree upon retirement.

defined-contribution plan A pension plan that involves employee and/or employer contributions, invested as the employee directs to form a retirement fund for the employee.

degradable pollutants Pollutants that are modified by water through chemical and biological processes, though the processes use oxygen that water life needs for survival.

demand curve A representation of consumer demand for a good or service.

democratic capitalism Capitalism that is restrained by democratic political institutions.

Department of Justice (DOJ) A cabinet office of the U.S. government whose antitrust division initiates both civil and criminal antitrust actions.

deposit insurance Insurance for bank deposits that can reduce the suffering of customers when banks fail.

Depository Institutions Deregulation and Monetary Control Act U.S. legislation of 1980 that allowed banks and thrifts to offer interest bearing checking accounts, or NOW accounts, and extended deposit insurance protection to accounts at thrifts.

derived demand Demand for a good or service is derived when the good or service is not demanded for its own sake, as is the case for transportation that moves a person from A to B or makes some good more useful by moving it to where it is wanted.

development The effort that goes into moving a new application into a profitable product, and arranging ways to present it to the public.

differentiated products A characterization of products when consumers believe the products of different sellers in the same market are not the same, and the consumers differ in their preferences for the different products.

discount rate The interest rate you could earn in alternative uses of your funds, and which can be used to calculate the present value of an income stream.

discovery procedures Rules that allow parties in legal disputes to obtain information about the dispute from each other.

disparate impact A practice, such as a requirement that job applicants have a high school diploma, may have a disparate impact if the requirement is not needed for job performance yet handicaps members of a protected class.

disparate treatment An unlawful employment practice in which race, sex, national origin, color, religion, or disability played a motivating role in an employment decision.

distributed generation An electricity industry policy that locates small generators close to consumers of power, thereby making transmission and distribution less important.

distribution systems Electricity industry networks that deliver electricity to final consumers.

diverse technology A case in which two or more available techniques have different operating and capacity costs.

dominant-firm price leadership A form of price leadership in which all price-setting power resides in the market's dominant firm.

Dorfman-Steiner condition A condition for optimal pricing and advertising by a monopoly that has the ratio of advertising elasticity to price elasticity (in absolute value) equal to the advertising-to-sales-ratio.

double double marginalization A name given to double marginalization when it is present in two directions, and the reciprocity may foster agreement on a solution to double marginalization.

double marginalization A problem that arises when each of two firms possess a degree of monopoly power and one sells to the other who in turn resells to others, because each firm independently marks up its costs and as a result the final price is above what a monopolist would charge.

downstream In the path from raw material to final consumer, the firm closer to the final consumer is called the downstream firm.

downward compatible A property of changing technology that allows old units to receive new signals; for example, colored-television signals could be received by old television sets in black-and-white form so the nation's stock of sets did not have to be replaced.

Drug Price Competition and Patent Term Restoration Act U.S. legislation of 1984 that extends patent protection for proposed branded drugs by the amount of time required for Food and Drug Administration review, subject to some other limiting constraints, and, when this extended period of patent protection expires, makes approval easier for generic producers of the drug.

duopoly A market with only two firms.

earnings-share regulation A simple alternative to rate-of-return regulation that sets a range of allowed returns and allows a sharing in the improvement in earnings above the range and in reductions in earnings below the range.

economic profit An amount of net revenue earned beyond the normal amount to be expected.

economic withholding Strategic behavior by the owner of multiple generators in an electricity market, who can be tempted to offer low prices for power from most of the generators but jump to a very high price for one generator with the aim of raising the spot price if that generator is needed to meet demand.

economies of scale A pattern that exists when a fall in long-run average cost occurs as output increases.

economies of scope A cost pattern when producing more than one good in a single firm is more economical than producing the goods in separate firms.

edge cities Developments that ring the suburban outskirts of cities and include office parks, retailing, and housing.

edge-less cities Cities that do not have developments at their edges, but instead have a sprawling form of office space outside the downtown area.

effective price Consumer price that includes all costs of the product, including the cost of transportation by the consumer to obtain the product.

efficacious A requirement that a drug or medical device performs as the seller claims it will.

efficient components pricing rule (ECPR) A rule for pricing access to essential facilities that sets the price high enough to motivate resource owners to offer access but just high enough that only efficient providers can enter.

elasticity of advertising The percentage change in quantity divided by the percentage change in advertising ($(\delta q/\delta a)a/q$, where a is advertising and q is quantity).

electricity service provider Electricity industry retailer who bills customers and otherwise deals with them and arranges with a distribution system to deliver power.

Electric Reliability Council of Texas (ERCOT) One of the 10 Electric Reliability Councils that make up the North American Reliability Council (NERC) that is located entirely within the state of Texas.

Elkins Act U.S. legislation of 1903 that specifically barred transportation price discrimination among different shippers of goods so some shippers would not have a price advantage over others.

emission standards Standards that are approved by the Environmental Protection Agency as controls on sources of air pollution.

Employee Retirement Income Security Act (ERISA) U.S. legislation of 1974 that regulates employee pension plans.

employment at will A feature of the employment relationship that allows either the employer or the employee to terminate their relationship at any time for any reason.

endogenous Outcome determined by forces operating within a model that represents an economic process, such as price as determined in a market by supply and demand.

"end-to-end" service The Bell System's historical aim to provide telephone service from any one telephone to any other one.

Energy Policy Act (EPA) U.S. legislation of 1992 that required the owner of a transmission grid to transmit electricity for any producer of it.

Energy Policy Conservation Act (EPCA) U.S. federal legislation of 1975 to decontrol regulation of natural gas prices by 1981.

entry Occurs when a firm enters a market as a new supplier.

Environmental Protection Agency (EPA) A U.S. federal agency created by the Clean Air Act of 1970 to control pollution by working with states in areas of air, water, toxic substances, noise, radiation, and solid waste.

Equal Employment Opportunity Commission (EEOC) A U.S. federal commission that receives discrimination complaints in offices throughout the country, issues guidelines, and attempts to resolve cases.

equilibrium Occurs when neither suppliers nor demanders are motivated to raise or lower price or change output or consumption. In a market it is where supply and demand curves intersect.

equity The ownership interest in a firm after accounting for the corporation's debt obligations.

Esch-Cummins Transportation Act U.S. legislation of 1920 that sought consolidation of railroads and charged the Interstate Commerce Commission with granting stockholders a fair return and setting fair rates for freight and passenger traffic.

essential facility A resource that is owned by one organization but is essential to the provision of a service by other organizations.

establishments Independent physical production locations, such as factories.

exclusion A practice that excludes some sellers from a market.

exclusive dealing To deal only with one party, as when a retailer agrees with a manufacturer not to carry competing brands.

exclusive territories A product distribution strategy that separates sellers of a single brand of product through control of seller locations to reduce their intrabrand competition.

exempt wholesale generator (EWG) Electricity generators (called "e-wogs") that were created by the Energy Policy Act of 1992, exempt from organizational restrictions of the Public Utility Holding Company Act and free to use any technology.

exit Occurs when a firm stops being a supplier and leaves a market.

exogenous Factor determined independent of a model that represents an economic process, such as the weather in a model of an agricultural market.

expenditure maximization A possible goal for a budget-constrained public enterprise.

experience goods Goods whose quality consumers cannot easily judge without using them.

externality A consequence of a decision that is borne at least in part by those who did not participate in the decision.

external trading An early U.S. air pollution control practice that allowed a pollution reduction to be negotiated with another firm.

Fair Labor Standards Act U.S. legislation of 1938 that established the minimum wage and a 40-hour work week and authorized overtime pay.

FCG Energy Broker The operator of a spot market in electricity in Florida called the Florida Coordinating Group.

federal administrative agencies Agencies created by the U.S. government, such as the Federal Communications Commission, to create and enforce specific regulations and develop the expertise necessary to do so.

Federal Aid Highway Act U.S. legislation of 1962 that mandated highway planning in urban areas, including consideration of mass transit.

Federal Aviation Administration (FAA) A U.S. federal agency created in 1958 to regulate airline safety.

Federal Communications Commission (FCC) A federal agency created in 1934 to replace the Federal Radio Commission and regulate radio and telephone common carriers.

Federal Credit Union Act U.S. legislation of 1934 that allowed the federal government to charter credit unions.

Federal Deposit Insurance Corporation (FDIC) A U.S. federal agency that provides federal insurance for bank deposits, today up to $100,000.

Federal Energy Regulatory Commission (FERC) A U.S. federal energy regulatory agency that replaced the Federal Power Commission in 1977.

Federal Highway Act U.S. legislation of 1973 that added $3 billion more in capital spending for transit than the Urban Mass Transit Act had provided.

Federal Power Act (FPA) U.S. legislation of 1935 that expanded the authority of the Federal Power Commission (FPC), now the Federal Energy Regulatory Commission (FERC).

Federal Radio Commission (FRC) A U.S. regulatory commission created in 1927 to control use of the radio spectrum by issuing licenses to legitimate broadcasters.

Federal Reserve System The U.S. central bank, created by the Federal Reserve Act in 1913, which could pool bank resources, serve as a lender of last resort, and give stability to the national banking system.

Federal Savings and Loan Insurance Corporation (FSLIC) A U.S. federal agency that offers deposit insurance for Savings and Loan (S&L) and other thrift depositors.

Federal Trade Commission (FTC) A federal agency created by the FTC Act of 1914 to ban unfair methods of competition and unfair and deceptive acts or practices.

Federal Trade Commission Act U.S. legislation of 1914 that created the Federal Trade Commission (FTC) to ban unfair methods of competition and unfair and deceptive acts or practices.

Federal Transit Administration (FTA) U.S. transit regulatory agency created in 1991 to replace UMTA and that now manages all federal transit programs.

final judgment Used here to denote a 1956 consent decree that resolved an antitrust issue for AT&T when it agreed to license equipment patents and confine its activities to regulated industries.

Financial Accounting Standards Board (FASB) A U.S. panel that sets accounting standards and maintains a body of generally accepted accounting practices that accountants are to follow throughout the country.

financial transmission rights Sophisticated transmission rights that focus on price and can allocate scarce transmission capacity to suppliers and consumers without forcing them to bear all the risks of fluctuations in transmission prices.

first degree price discrimination Price discrimination between customers that sets a different price for each customer and is so precise it takes almost all consumer's surplus from every consumer.

fixed cost Costs that cannot be adjusted in a short-run time period.

fixed inputs Inputs that cannot be adjusted in a short-run time period.

Florida Coordinating Group (FCG) An organization of electricity producers in Florida that coordinates planning, construction, and utilization of generation and transmission facilities in the state.

focal point A basis for common understanding when parties seek it in an uncertain situation.

follower In the Stackelberg theory, a firm that responds passively by accepting the output of a leader and responding in a predictable way, which allows the leader an advantage.

Food and Drug Administration (FDA) A U.S. federal agency formed in 1906 to protect consumers from impure or adulterated foods or drugs.

Food, Drug, and Cosmetic Act U.S. legislation of 1938 that requires tests for drug safety before a drug may be marketed.

forward contracts Forward contracts in electricity markets apply for a future date, and, like long-term contracts, they can discourage strategic offers by tying up the capacity that could benefit from strategic offers.

free-rider Shirking behavior that is motivated by a situation where responsibility is shared, as when shareholders do not oversee management but leave the task for the board of directors.

full entry A government policy that requires an entrant to serve all who wish to consume at whatever price the entrant announces.

full price Consumer price that includes all costs of the product, including the cost of transportation by the consumer to obtain the product.

full truckload Trucking shipment quantities weighing more than 5 tons.

functional organization A form of business organization in which divisions of the organization carry out its functions, such as sales, finance, or manufacturing.

game theory A theory that emphasizes strategy and is intended to capture the essence of strategic interactions to reveal the most effective strategies.

Garn-St. Germain Depository Institutions Act U.S. legislation of 1982 that phased out bank interest rate controls, encouraged the use of adjustable-rate mortgages, and permitted federally chartered thrifts to expand their lending into credit cards, consumer loans, commercial loans, commercial real estate loans, and, in certain limited circumstances, equity investments.

Generally Accepted Accounting Practices (GAAP) Practices that accountants are to follow in the United States. See Financial Accounting Standards Board (FASB).

generate To create electricity through inducing the movement of electrons by spinning magnets inside coils of wire.

geographical extension merger A merger that brings together two (or more) firms in the same product line, such as two grocery store chains, but in different sections of the country, so no relevant market concentration measure is affected.

geographic division A way sellers may divide markets—one seller in the East and one in the West, for example—to reduce their competition.

Glass-Steagall Act A part of the Banking Act of 1933 that separated commercial banking from investment banking.

global warming A tendency for the temperature of the earth to rise, which scientists trace to air pollution emitted by human activity.

going-private A transaction in which the management of a firm, perhaps with others, buys a controlling interest in the firm.

golden parachutes High severance payments granted to management in the event of a takeover, which serve to discourage takeovers and to reward managers in the event that a takeover occurs.

government department A government organization that can be used for providing government services, usually at the municipal level.

greenhouse effect An effect of trace gases in the atmosphere such as carbon dioxide and methane that do not absorb energy flowing from the sun to the earth but block it from traveling away from the earth, thus acting like a greenhouse window that warms the earth.

greenmail A strategy to discourage takeovers that involves buying shares from a would be raider at a premium to deflect the takeover effort.

ground-level-ozone (O_3) is formed in the presence of heat and sunlight from nitrous oxides and a variety of volatile organic compounds (VOCs), which come from power plants, motor vehicles, chemical plants, refineries, factories, and other sources.

Hart-Scott-Rodino Antitrust Improvements Act See Antitrust Improvements Act.

hazardous air pollutants Very serious air pollutants that are dangerous in themselves, such as benzene, and 188 of them are separately regulated by the Environmental Protection Agency.

Hepburn Act U.S. legislation of 1906 that enabled the ICC to set maximum rail rates.

Herfindahl-Hirschman Index (HHI) A measure of industry concentration used in the United States that involves calculating firms' market shares (usually measured by value added or value of shipments or employment of each firm), squaring it, and summing those squares.

hidden conspiracy A conspiracy in which participants keep secret their agreement to fix prices or allocate markets.

high occupancy toll (HOT) Highway lanes that are high occupancy vehicle (HOV) lanes but allow access—for a fee—to vehicles with fewer than the required number of HOV-lane passengers.

high-occupancy vehicle (HOV) Highway lanes, usually carrying commuters into and out of cities, that are reserved during rush hours for vehicles carrying two (HOV-2) or three (HOV-3) people.

high-powered incentive A strong incentive, felt by a residual claimant of profit who seeks high sales and low costs because the difference between them is profit.

Highway Act U.S. legislation of 1962 that required urban areas with populations above 50,000 to consider mass transit as an alternative to highways.

Highway Safety Act U.S. legislation of 1966 that was intended to provide advice to states about driver education, traffic law enforcement, highway construction, and other highway safety programs.

"hockey-stick" offers A strategic offer in an electricity market involving low prices for power from most generators (along the hockey stick handle) but jumps to a very high price for, say, one generator (as a hockey stick bends sharply to the section where it meets the hockey puck).

holding company An organization that owns other companies and controls their activities.

Home Owners' Loan Act U.S. legislation of 1933 that created federal charters for Savings and Loan Associations (S&Ls).

homogeneous products Goods that are the same.

horizontally differentiated products Goods that are similar in quality but offer different characteristics and can substitute for one another.

horizontal restraint of trade A trade restraint among firms in the same industry that can have some of the same effects as a monopoly.

Housing Act U.S. legislation of 1961 that offered low interest loans to public transit firms, offered demonstration projects to test new transit ideas, and required mass-transit planning.

imperfect information A state in which actors are not fully informed, as when a

consumer at one store does not know the price at others or a buyer does not know the quality of a product.

incentive compatibility constraint A particular price structure, called a self-selection tariff, allows consumers to choose a price category, and to be effective the price categories must have this constraint that consumers wish to select the categories that are intended for them.

incremental cost The increase in a firm's total cost when a particular product is produced by the firm compared with total cost when the firm does not produce that product.

incremental cost test A test of whether a multiproduct firm has a cross-subsidy among its products; the firm fails the incremental cost test for cross-subsidy if revenues for any subset of goods are not great enough to cover the incremental costs of that subset.

independent power producers (IPPs) Small electricity generators using wind-energy or small hydroelectric facility or small fossil fuel electricity generating plant.

independent system operator (ISO) A party to oversee an electricity market so adjustments can be made to supplies as demands rise or fall unexpectedly to avoid a system failure.

industrial revolution A development of the eighteenth and nineteenth centuries that brought unprecedented economic growth and change.

industry concentration A measure of influence by few firms in an industry, measured, for example, as the percentage of sales, employment, or other activity that occurs in the largest 3, 4, 8, or 20 firms in an industry.

information exchanges Arrangements among competitors that allow them to share information, such as the prices they charge, that may or may not violate antitrust laws.

injunction An injunction forbids certain future antitrust action without imposing a penalty for the action having been carried on in the past.

insider information Information available to an insider working within a firm, which is not available to the general public, that may not be used by the insider as a basis for buying or selling stock.

intellectual property A certain right to original or functional ideas, such as copyrighted or patented material.

interbrand competition Competition between brands, as when each retailer sells one brand exclusively and the separate brands compete.

Interest Rate Control Act U.S. legislation of 1966 intended to protect thrifts from high current interest rates by giving the Bank Board power to set interest rate ceilings.

interlocking directorates The same directors control several firms in the same industry, a practice that is outlawed by the Clayton Act when the firms are beyond certain sizes.

Intermodel Surface Transportation Act U.S. legislation of 1991 that substantially increased funding levels for federal transit programs and allowed highway funds to be transferred by state and local governments to mass transit capital projects.

internal trading A U.S. air pollution control practice applied in areas that do not attain air quality standards; similar to netting, it has been followed since 1977.

International Accounting Standards Board (IASB) An international panel that sets standards for accounting practices that are followed by many countries to make their accounting practices sound and consistent.

Internet service providers (ISPs) Independent firms that provide access to the Internet.

interruptible-service contracts Electricity customer contracts that permit the provider of electricity to interrupt the customer's service at times of extremely high demands.

interruptible service pricing A two-part price structure in which the fixed fee varies with the assured rate of usage, so the customer effectively pays to reserve a level of assured capacity.

Interstate Commerce Act U.S. legislation of 1887 that created the Interstate Commerce Commission to regulate railroads rates to be "just and reasonable" and to ban price discrimination.

Interstate Commerce Commission (ICC) The first U.S. federal administrative agency, created in 1887 by the Act to Regulate Commerce, to regulate railroads (the ICC is now the Surface Transportation Board (STB)).

intrabrand competition Competition within one brand, as when many retailers compete in selling the same brand of product.

inverse elasticity pricing rule A pricing rule that raises revenue by pricing above marginal cost, perhaps to cover fixed cost, but minimizes the welfare loss from doing so.

irreversible effects Effects of pollutants that are irreversible because once the elements that cause them are in the atmosphere they may continue to cause changes that are impossible to reverse.

joint ventures Joint ventures are usually contractual arrangements among separate firms for specific purposes, sometimes for limited periods of time.

junk bonds Indebtedness used to finance a management buyout or a going-private transaction that carries unusually high risk and pays unusually high interest rates.

Kaldor Rule A criterion for social decisions that approves an action when those who gain evaluate their gains at a greater value than the losers place on their losses.

kinked demand A pessimistic view a firm may have that if it lowers price all firms will join it but if it raises price no one will join it, so there is a kink in the effective demand curve that discourages the firm from changing its price.

land fills Disposal sites for solid wastes, including scrapped appliances and automobiles, which can adversely affect the land and its possible uses.

landing slot An airline industry term for the time segments that are assigned for take off and landing.

Lanham Trademark Act U.S. legislation of 1984 that specifies how firms can register trademarks with the federal government as service marks or with states that have adopted similar statutes.

Laspeyres price index A particular form of price index in which quantities from the early, or base, period are used to weight prices in that period and also in the second period.

Lead (Pb) A metal element that, as a pollutant, can be inhaled or ingested.

leader In the Stackelberg theory, a firm that leads by deciding its output before another, or follower, firm does, while also anticipating the behavior of the follower.

learning by doing As learning occurs within firms, methods improve with cumulative output, and as a result costs are lowered.

less-than-truckload Trucking quantities weighing less than 5 tons.

leverage Ratio of debt to all capital in a firm's capital structure, or debt divided by the sum of debt plus equity.

leveraged buyout (LBO) A name used when the funds to carry out a management buyout or a going-private transaction are raised by issuing debt.

liberalization The allowance of limited entry in a formerly regulated industry that opens opportunity for competition.

licensing An arrangement that allows a patent holder to allow others to use the patent for a fee; a proof of qualification in some professions.

limit price An upper limit on the price that existing firms in a market can charge without attracting new entry.

load duration curve A diagram that shows how demand for generated electricity, the electrical load, is distributed over the hours of the day or any other periodic cycle.

load factor An airline industry term for the average percentage of seats filled on planes.

lobby An effort by private parties to persuade legislators and regulators to support their positions.

long-run average cost Average cost over a long time period, a period long enough that all inputs can be adjusted.

long-run equilibrium A state in which no firm and no consumer wishes to make any change in its position even over a long time period.

long-run firm supply curve A representation that shows the output of a single firm in the long run for every possible price in the market.

long-run marginal cost Marginal cost over a period of time long enough that all inputs can be adjusted.

long-run market supply curve A representation that shows the output of all firms in the long run, existing firms and entrants, for every possible price in the market.

long-term contracts Legally enforceable agreements in electricity markets may apply for a year or more and can discourage strategic offers by tying up capacity that would benefit from strategic offers.

lottery A procedure that makes an award randomly among eligible applicants.

Magnuson-Moss FTC Improvements Act U.S. legislation of 1975 that expanded the powers of the Federal Trade Commission by adding remedies, granting rule making authority, and broadening its scope from anything "in" interstate commerce to anything "in or affecting" interstate commerce.

major innovation An innovation so dramatic that, based on the reduction in cost it allows, the new monopoly price in the market lies below the old competitive price.

management buyout (MBO) A transaction in which the management of a firm buys a controlling interest in the firm, usually by issuing debt. See junk bonds.

managerial control An ownership condition in which owners—usually shareholders—are not in full control of their hired managers.

Mann-Elkins Act U.S. legislation of 1920 that specifically prevented long-haul versus short-haul railroad rate discrimination.

marginal cost The increase in total cost of producing one more unit of output.

marginal product For a particular input, the increase in output from adding one more unit of that input in production.

marginal revenue The increase in total revenue a firm receives from selling one more unit, taking into account the reduction in price that is needed to sell one more unit.

market demand curve A representation of demand from all consumers for a good or service that shows quantity demanded at every price.

market for corporate control Control of a corporation may be purchased in this type of market by buying enough shares to obtain a large stake in the firm and win board representation to install new management.

market foreclose Prevents entry to markets through vertical integration, either by "squeezing" one level in the vertical chain by influencing prices on both input and output sides of it, or by forcing entry as an integrated firm, which can require much greater investment.

market structure The organization of a market judged largely by the number of firms it contains such as monopoly, oligopoly, or competition, and by how difficult is entry into the market.

markup Price-setting procedure that adds a percentage of cost to the level of cost to determine price.

maximize expenditure The possible goal of a public enterprise that cannot maximize profit because its profit is not to exceed its revenue.

maximize profit The goal that may be forced on a private business firm by product-market competition and may be pursued also by a monopoly.

McCaren-Ferguson Act U.S. legislation of 1945 that exempted insurance companies from antitrust laws so they could cooperate in several areas, such as developing similar policy forms and means of estimating prospective losses on policies.

Medical Device Amendments (MDA) U.S. legislation of 1976 that required the Food and Drug Adminstration to approve the riskiest medical devices, such as pacemakers, before they could be marketed.

merger The joining of two or more firms into one.

merger waves The waves, or clusters, of mergers that seem to be stimulated when new technologies, high stock values, changes in government regulation, or new ways of organizing occur.

merit order The order in which electricity generating units are used, roughly in order of cost from low to high.

Miller-Tydings Act U.S. legislation of 1937 that exempted manufacturers and retailers from prosecution under Section 1 of the Sherman Act for resale price maintenance when the retailers adhered to minimum prices, wherever state laws allowed them to do so.

minimal spacing between oil wells State or federal requirements for the number of acres of land needed for each oil well, which restricts the number of wells drawing oil from a reservoir.

minimum efficient size (M.E.S.) A meas ure for an industry that indicates how large a firm has to be in a particular industry to have costs low enough to succeed.

minor innovation An innovation that lowers cost, but not by so much that the monopoly price after innovation will be below the original level of average cost.

mobile sources Sources of air pollution, such as automobiles, that are mobile and whose pollution is controlled by the EPA.

Modification of Final Judgment (MFJ) Used here to indicate the 1982 modification to a 1956 consent decree (called the final judgment, which had limited AT&T to regulated activities) that broke AT&T into seven Regional Bell Operating Companies and a long-distance company.

money market mutual funds New institutions in the 1970s that placed investor's deposits in Treasury bills, bank certificates of deposit (CDs), and high-quality, short-term corporate bonds that were exempt from interest rate controls and paid high interest rates.

monopolistic competition A market structure in which sellers offer differentiated products and have some monopolistic advantage over some customers, and where entry by substitute products limits the profit that can be earned.

monopolize To reach or attempt to reach a dominant position in a market, and thus to have power to control the market price, a position that was made unlawful by the Sherman Antitrust Act.

Montreal Protocol An international agreement that banned the use of chlorofluorocarbons.

moral hazard A temptation that arises under a contract, as when a driver is insured and then drives more carelessly.

Motor Carrier Act of 1935 U.S. legislation that amended the Interstate Commerce Act of 1887 to extend ICC authority beyond railroads to trucks.

Motor Carrier Act of 1980 U.S. legislation that brought reform to trucking regulation by facilitating entry and allowing individual carriers to set their own rates within certain ranges instead of relying on rate bureaus.

multidivisional organization A form of business organization in which divisions operate as separate firms, in that they deal with their own products and are responsible for earning profit.

multi-market contact Occurs when conglomerate firms face each other in more than one market, which opens strategic possibilities because their competition—or cooperation—can extend across markets.

multinational enterprise A business firm that operates in more than one nation and can move operations from one nation to another.

Nash equilibrium An equilibrium in which each player takes the action that is best for that player against the actions taken by others, whose actions in turn are best for them.

National Ambient Air Quality Standards (NAAQS) Air quality standards required by the Clean Air Act to protect public health and public welfare.

National Association of Insurance Commissioners A national organization of state insurance commissioners that, among other things, has attempted to improve insurance regulation, for example by proposing model insurance regulation laws.

National Cooperative Research Act U.S. legislation of 1984 that invited firms conducting joint venture research to register with the government and thus avoid treble damages or punitive damages in case of antitrust suits involving the research.

National Highway Traffic Safety Administration (NHTSA) A U.S. federal agency created in 1966 and authorized to establish appropriate federal motor vehicle safety standards.

National Industrial Recovery Act U.S. legislation of 1933 that created the National Recovery Administration and gave regulatory powers to the executive branch in an effort to pull the economy out of the great depression.

National Institute for Occupational Safety and Health Part of the Health and Human Services Department that carries out research on occupational safety and health and recommends standards.

National Labor Relations Act U.S. legislation of 1935 that gave private workers the right to organize collectively and negotiate wages or hours or other conditions of employment.

National Pollutant Discharge Elimination System (NPDES) A system for establishing water pollution emission levels for point sources all over the United States for identifiable pollutants.

National Primary Drinking Water Regulations (NPDWRs) Standards defined by the Environmental Protection Agency for protection of drinking water, somewhat like the ambient air quality standards for air, to impose limits on impurities to protect public health.

National Priorities List (NPL) A U.S. list of possibly hazardous sites that the Environmental Protection Agency maintains as it judges which sites are most serious or solvable, where it undertakes clean up efforts.

National Traffic and Motor Vehicle Safety Act U.S. legislation of 1966 that created the National Highway Traffic Safety Administration (NHTSA) to regulate motor vehicle and highway safety.

Natural Gas Act U.S. legislation of 1938 that gave the Federal Power Commission power to regulate transportation and sale of natural gas for resale (wholesale transactions) in interstate commerce.

Natural Gas Policy Act U.S. legislation of 1978 intended gradually to decontrol wellhead prices of natural gas.

natural monopoly An industry that can achieve lowest cost when organized as a monopoly.

negotiable order of withdrawal (NOW) Interest bearing checking accounts introduced by state-chartered mutual savings banks in the 1970s.

netting A U.S. air pollution control practice introduced in 1974 to allow a firm creating a new emissions source within a plant to reduce emissions from another source, to prevent net emissions from increasing significantly.

network A means of connecting separate units or participants and make them more effective, either by lowering costs or raising benefits.

network economies Reduced average cost or more valuable consumption that can be achieved as a network becomes larger.

network externality A condition in which those in a network benefit as more join the network.

New Source Performance Standards (NSPS) Stringent emission standards imposed on newly constructed sources of pollution, like new power plants.

nitrogen dioxide (NO_2) An air pollutant that causes smog and contributes to acid rain and that comes primarily from electric power plants and motor vehicles.

nitrous oxides (NO_x) A family of air pollutants that have similar sources and effects.

nonattainment areas Geographic areas designated under the 1977 Amendments to the Clean Air Act because ambient air quality standards are not attained; nonattainment calls for states to impose more stringent emission standards for new sources and "reasonably available control measures" for old sources.

nondegradable pollutants Pollutants such as cadmium, lead, mercury, PCBs (polychlorinated biphenyls) and DDT that are unchanged by water.

nonpoint sources Sources of pollution, like runoff from city streets and fertilizer used on farms, that are difficult to observe and control.

nonuniform price A category of prices in which prices are not the same for every unit purchased, such as two-part prices and block prices.

North American Electric Reliability Council (NERC) A voluntary electricity industry organization comprising 10 regional councils to which member utilities gave authority to intervene and coordinate the generation and transmission of electricity to achieve reliability.

North American Industry Classification System (NAICS) A U.S. industry classification system to support industry data collection that is consistent with systems used by Canada and Mexico.

Notice of Proposed Rulemaking A notice, published in the Federal Register to explain a proposed new regulation, including a statement of justification and inviting public comment.

notice of violation A notice issued by the Environmental Protection Agency as a warning for air pollution violations that may be extended to civil and criminal penalties.

Nuclear Regulatory Commission (NRC) A U.S. regulatory agency created by the Energy Reorganization Act of 1974 to regulate the civilian nuclear industry and protect the public health and safety, promote security, and protect the environment.

Nutrition Labeling and Education Act U.S. legislation of 1990 that extended labeling requirements to dietary supplements.

Occupational Safety and Health Act U.S. legislation of 1970 that was intended to assure as far as possible every working person safe and healthful working conditions; it created also the Occupational Safety and Health Administration.

Occupational Safety and Health Administration (OSHA) A U.S. federal agency, created by the Occupational Safety and Health Act of 1970, that sets and enforces workplace safety and health standards.

Occupational Safety and Health Review Commission An independent commission that reviews Occupational Safety and Health Administration decisions.

Office of Management and Budget (OMB) A U.S. federal agency that reviews agencies' proposed programs to avoid interference with other agencies' responsibilities and can block undesirable or unwanted programs.

offset An early U.S. air pollution control practice, applied to nonattainment areas, that required existing sources of pollution to make a larger reduction in emissions, called an offset, before a new source could be created.

oligopoly A market with just a few firms.

ongoing pension liability The present value of a firm's future defined-benefit pension obligation assuming employees continue working to retirement.

open access Status of natural gas pipelines that transport gas for customers, who purchase gas directly from wells.

operating authority A document that allowed entry into a regulated trucking route and specified the services a carrier was permitted to offer.

opportunistic behavior Occurs if one party to a contract takes advantage of the other when circumstances allow it.

Pareto optimality An economic welfare achievement when no action remains that could improve one person's situation, as that person sees it, without harming any one else.

partial entry A government policy that allows a supplier to serve only a part of a market that it wishes to serve.

participation constraint A requirement of an effective self-selection tariff that parties be willing to participate in the seller's arrangement.

patent The right of exclusive use granted for a limited time period to the inventor of a new and nonobvious technique.

peak-load pricing The practice of setting higher prices when demand is high and capacity is scarce because cost is then higher.

perfect competition An idealized representation of a market or an economy that shows benefits competition is ideally able to achieve.

perfect foresight A strong assumption that individuals correctly estimate a future quantity and know about decisions by others.

per se illegal Mere participation in a practice is illegal so it is not necessary to show unreasonable consequences.

physical transmission rights Sophisticated transmission rights that allow holders to transmit electricity and allocate scarce transmission capacity to suppliers and consumers without forcing them to bear all the risks of fluctuations in transmission capacity.

physical withholding Strategic behavior by the owner of multiple generators in an electricity market to keep some capacity idle to reduce supply with the aim of raising market price.

piece rate A basis for employee pay in which pay depends on the number of units, or pieces, the employee produces.

plaintiff The party who initiates a legal action by filing a complaint against another party, usually to obtain money damages.

plea bargain An agreement under which a criminal defendant agrees to forego trial and plead guilty to a charge in return for some certainty in sentencing.

point sources Sources of pollution, like factories or sewage treatment plants, that are at specific locations and can be readily observed and controlled.

poison-pill A strategy to discourage takeovers that makes shares of stock available at low prices to original shareholders but not to the new, takeover, shareholders, thus diluting the value and the voting power of the latter's shares.

Poolco The name given to an electricity coordinating system that relies on a centralized spot market for wholesale electricity transactions.

pooling Oil industry conservation plan that operates a reservoir as a single pool and each operator shares the oil on a pro-rata basis.

postal monopoly A monopoly over letter-mail services, created in the United States by private express statutes in 1845.

Postal Rate Commission (PRC) An organization created under the Postal Reorganization Act of 1970 to regulate postal rates.

Postal Reorganization Act U.S. legislation of 1970 that created the U.S. Postal Service to replace the Post Office Department as provider of mail services.

Powerplant and Industrial Fuel Use Act (PIFUA) U.S. legislation of 1978 that prevented the use of oil or natural gas in new power plants built by electric utilities.

predatory pricing Pricing to harm a competitor, as for example charging very low prices in one market to harm a competitor there.

present value Amount of money that a stream of future payments is worth right now, calculated by using a discount rate that converts future to present payments.

price-cap regulation A form of regulation that determines prices on a basis other than the firm's costs and offers desirable efficiency incentives for both cost control and pricing.

price discrimination Offering different prices to different consumers even though marginal costs of serving them are the same.

price index A measure of the change in price level from one period of time to another, usually obtained by using the same weights on prices in the periods being compared.

pricing policy Formula for setting price—usually based on cost and determined by high-level managers in a firm—that subordinate managers within the firm can implement.

primary line Injury from price discrimination in vertical markets that can drive direct competitors of the discriminating firm out of business.

primary standards Ambient air quality standards that are intended to protect public health, including especially those most vulnerable such as asthmatics, children, and the elderly.

principal The party who sets goals and seeks their pursuit from employed agents.

principal-agent A relationship in which one party, the principal, attempts to motivate another, the agent, to do as the principal wishes.

principal-agent problem The problem of the principal to monitor and motivate an agent when doing so also forces the agent to bear risk.

prisoner's dilemma A game situation with both cooperative and competitive motives in which two players can cooperate at a high price but then each wants privately to undercut the price, so the equilibrium might come at a lower, less profitable, price.

private express statutes U.S. legislation in 1845 that prevented competition in letter mail by banning private express services that would compete in providing postal service.

process innovations Innovations that affect production processes, usually to lower costs.

producer's surplus The difference between the marginal cost of all units produced and the price that can be charged for them, less any fixed cost.

product extension merger A merger between producers of different products that share the same manufacturing process or marketing methods, so the merger does not affect concentration in any one product market.

product innovations New products that can serve new uses.

product liability The legal responsibility of a manufacturer for injury and losses caused by its product.

property right A set of rights that flow from ownership of personal, real, or intellectual property.

prorationing A policy in the oil industry that allows a state to allocate its oil production on a pro-rata basis among wells in the state.

prudence test A regulatory standard to evaluate the soundness of investment decisions made by public utilities, based on the soundness of the investment at the time it was made.

public choice A field of study concerned specifically with how collective choices are made and the incentives that might prevent them from being well made.

Public Company Oversight Board A U.S. government board created by the Sarbanes-Oxley Act of 2002 to oversee the accounting profession, to evaluate the effect of generally accepted accounting practices and to ensure that accounting firms accurately reveal information about the financial health of corporations.

public enterprise A publicly owned and operated enterprise usually providing goods or services in which the general public has great interest.

public interest A theory of regulation that urged governmental regulatory intervention when ideal outcomes were not achieved by the market.

public utility A privately owned and publicly regulated producer of goods or services in which the general public has great interest.

Public Utility Act U.S. legislation of 1935 to remedy abuses by complicated public utility organizations through two parts, the Federal Power Act (FPA) and the Public Utility Holding Company Act (PUHCA).

Public Utility Commission of Texas (PUCT) Texas regulatory commission created in 1975 with passage of the Public Utility Regulatory Act (PURA) in Texas.

Public Utility Holding Company Act (PUHCA) U.S. legislation of 1935 that forced divestitures and simplified the organizational structure of public utilities, thereby allowing more effective regulation.

Public Utility Regulatory Policy Act (PURPA) U.S. legislation of 1978 to influence state public utility commissions to improve efficiency, conserve energy, and ensure equitable rates for consumers.

punitive damages An award of damages that may be pursued by a plaintiff and that is intended to punish the defendant for its transgression.

Pure Food and Drug Act U.S. legislation of 1906 that created the Food and Drug Administration.

qualifying facilities (QFs) Small U.S. electricity generators using renewable sources of energy that were allowed to sell power to public utilities.

quantity-forcing A practice that sets a quota, or minimum quantity, one party must accept in a time period, as when a retailer agrees to accept a specified quantity of units to sell in a time period.

Rail Passenger Service Act U.S. legislation of 1970 that created the rail passenger service, Amtrak.

Railroad Revitalization and Reform Act U.S. legislation of 1976 that began railroad deregulation by allowing railroads more freedom, including abandoning some unprofitable routes.

Railway Labor Act U.S. legislation of 1926 that granted workers the right to organize collectively in the railroad industry.

Ramsey pricing A price-setting principle that uses monopoly power to raise price above marginal cost and thereby cover fixed cost and break even, or meet some other public goal, and to do that with the least possible loss in welfare.

rate bureaus Railroad and bus industry rate-setting institutions that were made up of groups of carriers that followed procedures approved by the Interstate Commerce Commission and were thus exempt from antitrust laws.

rate-case moratoria The postponement of public utility rate-of-return rate cases, usually while granting some concession to the utility.

rate of return on investment Revenue of a firm, minus its costs, divided by the value of the firm's assets.

rate-of-return regulation A form of regulation that sets a firm's profit as a reasonable rate of return on the value of assets the firm uses in providing a public service and bases prices the firm is allowed to charge on that allowed profit together with the firm's other costs.

real-time balancing An electricity industry requirement to keep supply in line with demand at each location all the time.

real-time prices Electricity prices that adjust continuously to market-clearing levels.

reciprocal externalities Externalities involving two parties when each party's decisions affect the other.

Reed-Bullwinkle Act U.S. legislation of 1948 that allowed railroads to fix rates, thus exempting them from antitrust laws, as long as their procedures were public.

refusing to deal Refusal of a buyer or seller to deal with another party when the refusal serves the purpose of creating or maintaining a monopoly.

regional transmission organization (RTO) A voluntary organization in electricity markets of the United States that oversees power supplies in each of the 10 regional councils in the North American Electricity Reliability Council (NERC).

Regulatory Impact Analysis (RIA) A require ment for approval of a proposed federal regulation, usually including estimates of expected benefits and costs and a description of possible alternative means of achieving the same ends.

regulatory lag A period over which no change is made in a regulated firm's prices, so in that period the firm has an incentive to control costs.

rent seeking The effort made to acquire a monopoly position, perhaps one that is to be awarded by government, when the effort to win the monopoly may absorb expected monopoly profit.

reputation Public understanding about a product's quality or durability.

resale price maintenance Occurs when an upstream firm (e.g., manufacturer) controls the final price at which a downstream firm (e.g., retailer) can sell its product.

research joint ventures An arrangement that allows two (or more) firms in the same industry to join together for a research project and have some exemption from antitrust laws.

residual claimant Individual who is entitled to profit from the remainder between sales and costs.

residual demand The demand one firm sees after subtracting another firm's (or others') output from the total market demand.

restraint of trade A practice that negatively affects commerce in some way, as when sellers collude to keep price high.

restructuring Changing the structure of a regulated industry but not deregulating, because government regulation continues to play a role in the industry.

revenue maximization A possible goal for a large private enterprise or for a budget-constrained public enterprise, in which case it leads to the same pricing rule as budget maximizing does.

revolving door A name given to the practice of choosing government regulators from the industry to be regulated and then allowing them to return to jobs in that industry.

reward Possible method of motivating innovation, used to determine longitude for ships at sea or to fly an airplane across the Atlantic ocean.

right to pollute A right to emit a defined unit of pollution that may be traded in markets and must be submitted to authorities for each unit of pollution actually emitted.

risk averse Characteristic of a person who dislikes the possibility of losing and whose disutility from a loss exceeds the utility from a gain of the same amount.

risk loving Characteristic of a person who prefers the chance of a gain and whose utility from a gain exceeds the disutility from a loss of the same amount.

risk neutral Characteristic of a person who is indifferent to chances of loss or gain, in that the utility from a gain is the same as the disutility from a loss of the same amount.

rivalrous behavior Occurs when the players in a game focus on the differences between their payoffs, each wanting to do better than the other.

Robinson-Patman Act U.S. legislation of 1936 amending Clayton Act provisions against price discrimination to limit differences in prices charged to small retailers and chain stores.

Roman law An early form of Western law that relies more on legislation than on judicial bodies to produce clear rules that regulate society; the basis for civil law in Western Europe.

rule of capture A rule that grants ownership to whomever captures property, for example, as oil in a reservoir is owned by whomever extracts it first from the reservoir.

rule of reason Basis for court decisions that does not depend on strict rules but instead probes the consequences of a firm's behavior in the circumstances of each case.

salary Employee pay that is not based on actual time worked.

Sarbanes-Oxley Act U.S. legislation of 2002 that created new regulatory and criminal offenses and increased sentences for many corporate misdeeds.

satisficing A process in which a decision maker in a large organization works in turn on different goals so that as one prescribed goal is met, rather than pursue it further the decider turns to another goal.

scrubber technology A technology for air pollution abatement in electricity generation to remove pollutants from effluent as it passes through a smokestack.

search goods Goods for which consumers are able to judge quality by inspection.

secondary line A scope of injury to competition from price discrimination that arises among possible buyers from the discriminating firm and is the main target of the Robinson-Patman Act.

secondary standards The levels of ambient air quality standards that are intended to protect public welfare, including good visibility and protection of crops, vegetation, and buildings.

second degree price discrimination Price discrimination that allows customers to choose between alternative rate structures, as is sometimes possible for electricity or phone service, but designed by the seller so that different amounts of profit can be taken from different customers.

Securities and Exchange Commission (SEC) The U.S. federal agency that oversees corporation financing, securities trading, and other capital market practices, created by the Securities Exchange Act of 1934.

self-selection Property of a price structure that allows consumers to select themselves into an appropriate rate category.

sequential-choice game A game situation in which players choose actions in sequence, first one and then another.

service mark A representation of trade name or trademark that, after being registered with the U.S. federal government, allows its holder to bring an infringement claim against use of the mark by another.

share-cropping An age-old solution to the principal-agent incentive problem that compensates an agent partly by granting a fixed payment and partly by granting a share in the agent's crop harvest.

shareholder Corporation owner, also called stockholder, who holds shares of stock issued by the corporation as an instrument of ownership.

Sherman Act The initial 1890 U.S. antitrust law, which barred restraint of trade and monopolizing or attempting to monopolize a market.

shifting peak A case in which peak and off-peak prices are introduced, but the quantity of service demanded at what was expected to be the off-peak period actually exceeds the quantity demanded at what was to be the peak, so revised pricing is needed.

short run A time period in which a firm must make adjustments, but which is too short to allow all inputs to be adequately adjusted.

short-run average cost Total cost divided by output in a short period of time.

short-run firm supply curve A representation that shows the output of a single firm in the short run for every possible price in the market.

short-run marginal cost The increase in total cost when a firm produces one more unit in a short period of time.

short-run market supply curve A representation that shows the output of all firms in the short run for every possible price in the market.

simultaneous-choice game A game situation in which players choose actions at the same time, or at least without knowledge of others' actions.

size distribution of firms A pattern of sizes and numbers of firms for an industry, from few firms that have quite large market shares to a more competitive industry representing little difference in the sizes of firms.

social choice A field of study concerned specifically with how collective choices are made.

speculation Activity that markets accommodate by allowing trading, for example, in the future possible values of a good to reconcile differing interests.

Staggers Rail Act U.S. legislation of 1980 that made route abandonments even easier than had 1976 legislation, added more railroad subsidies, and permitted greater railroad pricing flexibility.

stand-alone test A test of whether a multiproduct firm has a cross subsidy among its products; when a subset of customers pays more than the costs of serving them the firm fails the test, because customers would be better off serving themselves and going their own way (they "stand alone").

standard A framework—usually technological such as VHF TV—that can be duplicated by many operators to achieve compatibility. Also a minimal level of quality, as in drinking water or automobile brake systems, that may be required by regulators.

stare decisis A rule of law that requires courts to adhere to the rules of law that were developed in previous cases.

State Implementation Plan (SIP) A state plan in the United States for meeting the National Ambient Air Quality Standards.

stationary sources Sources of air pollution that are stationary, such as electricity generating plants, and that are granted permits by the states.

status quo market shares Historic or "normal" market shares that firms may respect and preserve to prevent drastic price cutting.

Statute of Monopolies Legislation in England in 1624 to void monopolies, although its effective use against monopolies came many years later.

stock options Allows holders to purchase stock, usually at the price of shares when the options were issued.

stranded costs Changes (usually losses) in asset values of regulated firms that resulted from the transition to competitive markets.

subsidy-free prices If an incumbent firm in a market breaks even, then to be free of subsidy its prices must yield revenues for any subset of products that do not exceed the costs of serving that subset.

substitutes A relation between two goods such that a rise in the price of one good causes the quantity consumed of the second good to rise.

sulfur dioxide (SO_2) An air pollutant that causes acid rain and comes primarily from the combustion of fossil fuels, such as coal and oil.

sunk costs Costs that represent a long-term commitment because they cannot be recovered for a long time.

Superfund Act The Comprehensive Environmental Response, Compensation, and Liability Act of 1980 that required the EPA to develop capabilities for containing and treating hazardous waste on land.

super majority A requirement to gain control of a corporation that a new owner must obtain more than a simple majority of shareholder votes, which makes it more difficult for a takeover effort to win shareholder approval.

supply curve A representation of the quantity of a good or service that firms in a market will supply at every possible price.

Surface Transportation Act U.S. legislation of 1978 that authorized $5.1 billion for transit operating support from 1979 to 1982 and $8.6 billion for capital grants.

Surface Transportation Board (STB) U.S. transportation regulatory agency created in 1995 to replace the Interstate Commerce Commission, to resolve disputes over railroad rates and services and to review railroad mergers.

sustainable price Price an incumbent firm can set that allows the firm to break even and at the same time prevent entry by an efficient potential entrant.

switching cost A cost of switching from one source to another, as when a buyer switches from one seller to another.

tacit collusion Collusion among firms that is achieved without sending any message except the message implicit in pricing and other actions.

Telecommunications Act U.S. legislation of 1996 that allowed competition in the telecommunications industry and removed many entry barriers that then existed.

telegraphy Coded signals originally carried over wires and later by radio waves that conveyed meaning through the dots and dashes of Morse code.

termination pension liability The present value of a defined-benefit pension obligation if the worker stopped working today.

tertiary line A rare scope of injury from price discrimination that involves harm to competitors of a favored buyers' customers.

third degree price discrimination Price discrimination between customers, as for example charging autos and trucks different tolls for crossing a bridge.

threat A strategic act used by one firm to convince another or others to cooperate or else it will take some harmful action.

thrift institution Historically, a savings institution such as a credit union or a savings and loan company that specialized in mortgages but now operates much like an ordinary commercial bank.

time-of-use prices Prices that change by time period or date so consumers can be informed ahead of time of systematic changes in prices.

top-4-firm concentration ratio (C4) A measure of industry concentration used in the United States that is the percentage of activity (usually value added or value of shipments or employment) accounted for by the largest four firms in the industry.

tort A civil wrong for which the injured party may recover damages because the injury usually was deliberate or due to negligence.

total cost function A relationship between cost and output that yields total cost for any product output or combination of outputs that is specified.

Total Element Long Run Incremental Cost (TELRIC) Telecommunications pricing the Federal Communications Commission implemented under the Telecommunications Act of 1996 that is like long-run-incremental-cost pricing for each service except it is "forward looking" in that cost is based on the best available technology rather than the technology actually used by the local exchange carrier.

total requirements contract A contract in which a buyer agrees to accept all that it might need of a certain line of product from a single seller over a specified time period.

total suspended particulate matter Air pollutant often visible as soot, dust, or smoke and formed in the atmosphere from sulfur dioxide and nitrous oxides; particulate matter up to 10 micrometers in diameter is labeled **PM(10)** and up to 2.5 micrometers in diameter is labeled **PM(2.5)**.

toxic air pollutants "Air toxics" are deemed too dangerous for use of the threshold criterion; 188 hazardous air pollutants that are separately regulated by the EPA to protect public health with "an ample margin of safety."

Toxic Release Inventory (TRI) Regulatory instrument that requires any facility exceeding a certain minimum emission threshold to report annual releases of specific toxic substances through standard reporting procedures.

trade associations Groups of firms in the same trade or business that may serve as information exchanges or perform other industry functions such as setting standards.

trademark Mark that identifies the producer of a particular product.

trade secret Scientific or technical information, including business-related information, that is secret and has value; misappropriation of such information is grounds for civil and sometimes criminal action. A secret of a firm in a line of business that the firm can protect from theft as long as it takes measures to protect it, such as telling employees of its status as a secret; then one who steals it can be responsible for the loss its holder suffers.

transaction costs Costs of participating in an exchange of goods or services in a market.

Transco Independent electricity transmission companies that exist in many countries.

transmission companies Organizations that do not produce electricity but operate electricity grids; also called Transcos.

transmission grid Electricity industry network that moves electricity from a generation point to other locations for consumption.

transmission systems Electricity industry networks that move electricity from places where it is generated to places where it can be consumed.

Transportation Act U.S. legislation of 1920 that allowed the Interstate Commerce Commission to set minimum rates and, in combination with the Hepburn Act of 1906 allowing maximum rates, gave the ICC power to control railroad prices.

Transportation Security Administration (TSA) U.S. federal agency formed in 2002 to inspect air passengers and their baggage and to otherwise reduce possible dangers to air travel.

treble damages The basis for compensating victims and punishing violators of the Sherman Act, three times the loss suffered.

trust Organization of the late nineteenth century that exchanged its own certificates for shares of separate firms in its industry and, thus constituted, could coordinate actions of firms in the industry; "trust busters" sought and obtained legislation banning such organizations

two-part price or **two-part tariff** A price structure having two parts, one that is a fixed fee that must be paid to purchase any units and the other that is a price per unit.

tying A practice under which one or more goods are made available for sale (such as a camera) only on the condition that another good (such as film) or goods also be purchased.

unfair acts and practices Acts and practices that are unfair to competitors and may harm consumers and that were made illegal by the Federal Trade Commission Act.

unfair methods of competition See unfair acts and practices.

uniform price A price that is the same for every unit sold.

United States Postal Service (USPS) A public enterprise created in 1970 to replace the Post Office Department as provider of mail service in the United States.

unitization Oil industry policy that employed a conservation plan that would operate a reservoir as a single pool and have each operator share on a pro-rata basis.

universal service The aim of making a service available to all, as far as that is possible, at reasonable prices without unjust or unreasonable discrimination.

upstream In the path from raw material to final consumer, the firm closer to the raw material is called the upstream firm.

Urban Mass Transit Act of 1964 U.S. legislation that invited state and local governments to apply for federal funds to cover up to two-thirds of the capital costs of mass transit projects.

Urban Mass Transit Act of 1970 U.S. legislation that committed the federal government to $10 billion in capital spending for transit from 1971 to 1982.

Urban Mass Transit Administration (UMTA) U.S. federal regulatory agency for urban transit created in 1968.

value added A measure of the magnitude of a firm's contribution to economic activity as the difference between value of shipments, or sales, and value of purchases, or inputs.

"value-of-service" pricing Railroad pricing imposed by the Interstate Commerce Commission that deemed the value of delivering a commodity to be high when shippers were willing to pay more for it, essentially when the demand for the commodity's transportation was less elastic.

value of statistical life The value of a life that is estimated from individuals' decisions, as when they trade off the risk of fatal injury at work against the higher wages paid for bearing that risk.

variable cost Cost that varies with output in a short-run time period.

variable inputs Inputs that can be adjusted even in a short time period.

vertically differentiated products Goods that differ in their quality, some being higher in quality and some lower.

vertical restraints Limitations on a downstream firm's pricing actions imposed by an upstream firm not through vertical integration but through contract terms, including two-part pricing arrangements, franchising, profit sharing, and resale price maintenance.

volatile organic compounds (VOCs) Air pollutants from power plants, motor vehicles, chemical plants, refineries, factories, and other sources.

wage premium An addition to an employee's wage to compensate for bearing dangerous or otherwise distasteful working conditions.

warranty A guarantee to a customer that promises a certain level of performance from a good or service and offers corrective measures if that level is not met.

welfare economics Deals with representations of economic welfare and analyzes means for its achievement.

Wheeler-Lea Act U.S. legislation of 1938 that amended the Federal Trade Commission Act to stress "deceptive acts or practices."

wheeling power Transmitting power for others over an electricity grid.

whistleblower Employee who informs the outside world about dangerous or illegal behavior within an organization such as a business firm or government agency.

Whistleblower Protection Act U.S. legislation of 1989 to prevent retaliation against whistleblowers in the federal civil service.

white knight A more congenial partner sought by a firm that is the subject of a takeover attempt by a raider.

"yardstick" costs A regulatory standard used as a basis for prices that depends on the costs of other firms in similar conditions and avoids using the firm's own costs.

yield management An airline industry term for sophisticated pricing that is intended to raise the most revenue possible for each airplane flight.

REFERENCES

Abrams, Roger I. 1998. *Legal Bases*, Philadelphia: Temple University Press.

Acemoglu, Daron, Simon Johnson, and James A. Robinson. 2001. "Reversal of Fortune: Geography and Institutions in the Making of the Modern World Income Distribution," MIT, Economics Department Working Paper, August 9.

Ackerman, Bruce, and William T. Hassler. 1981. *Clean Coal, Dirty Air*, New Haven, Conn.: Yale University Press.

Adams, William J., and Janet Yellen. 1976. "Commodity Bundling and the Burden of Monopoly," *Quarterly Journal of Economics*, 90: 475–498.

Adelman, Morris A. 1982. "OPEC as a Cartel," in James M. Griffin and David J. Teece, eds., *OPEC Behavior and World Oil Prices*, London: George Allen and Unwin.

Adelman, Morris A. 1964. "Efficiency of Resource Use in Crude Petroleum," *Southern Economic Journal*, 31: 101–122, October.

Agarwal, Anup, and Michael Gort. 2001. "First-Mover Advantage and the Speed of Competitive Entry, 1887–1986," *Journal of Law and Economics*, April, 44: 161–177.

Aharoni, Y. 1986. *The Evolution and Management of State-Owned Enterprises*. Cambridge, Mass.: Ballinger.

Ai, Chunrong, and David E. M. Sappington. 2002. "The Impact of State Incentive Regulation on the U.S. Telecommunications Industry," *Journal of Regulatory Economics*, September, 22: 107–132.

Akerlof, George A. 1970. "The Market for Lemons: Quality Uncertainty and the Market Mechanism," *Quarterly Journal of Economics*, 84: 488–500.

Alchian, Armen A., and Reuben A. Kessel. 1962. "Competition, Monopoly, and the Pursuit of Pecuniary Gain," in *Aspects of Labor Economics*, Princeton, N.J.: Princeton University Press.

Alexander, Donald L., and Robert M. Feinberg. 2004. "Entry in Local Telecommunications Markets," *Review of Industrial Organization*, September, 25: 107–127.

Allais, Maurice. 1968. "Vilfredo Pareto," *International Encyclopedia of the Social Sciences*, Vol. 11. New York: Crowell-Collier and Macmillan, pp. 399–411.

Anderson, D. D. 1981. *Regulatory Politics and Electric Utilities*, Boston.: Auburn House.

Anderson, D. D. 1980. "State Regulation of Electric Utilities," in James Q. Wilson, ed., *The Politics of Regulation*, New York: Basic Books.

Andrade, Gregor, Mark Mitchell, and Eric Stafford. 2001. "New Evidence and Perspectives on Mergers," *Journal of Economic Literature*, Spring, 15: 103–120.

Aoki, Rieko, and Yossi Spiegel. 1998. "Disclosure of Patent Applications, R & D, and Welfare," Tel Aviv University Working Paper No. 30–98.

Areeda, Phillip E. 1986. *Antitrust Law*, Vols. 6, 7, Boston: Little, Brown.

Areeda, Phillip E. 1967. *Antitrust Analysis*, Boston: Little, Brown.

Areeda, Phillip E., and Donald F. Turner. 1978. *Antitrust Law*, Vols. 1–5. Boston: Little, Brown.

Areeda, Phillip E., and Donald F. Turner. 1975. "Predatory Pricing and Related Practices under Section 2 of the Sherman Act," *Harvard Law Review*, 88: 697–733.

Armstrong, Mark. 2001. "Access Pricing, Bypass, and Universal Service," *American Economic Review*, May, 91: 297–301.

Armstrong, Mark, and John Vickers. 1998. "Access Pricing with Deregulation: A Note," *Journal of Industrial Economics*, 46: 115–121.

Armstrong, Mark, Chris Doyle, and John Vickers. 1996. "The Access Pricing Problem: A Synthesis," *Journal of Industrial Economics*, 44: 131–150.

Arrow, Kenneth J. 1963. *Social Choice and Individual Values*, 2nd ed., New York: John Wiley and Sons.

Arrow, Kenneth J. 1962. "Economic Welfare and the Allocation of Resources for Invention," in *The Rate and Direction of Economic Activity*, Princeton, N.J.: Princeton University Press for the National Bureau of Economic Research.

Arrow, Kenneth J., and R. C. Lind. 1970. "Uncertainty and the Evaluation of Public Investment Decisions," *American Economic Review*, 60: 364–378.

Association of American Railroads. 1996. *Analysis of Class I Railroads, 1980–1995*, Washington, D.C.: Association of American Railroads.

Ashenfelter, Orley. 2006. "Measuring the Value of a Statistical Life: Problems and Prospects," *Economic Journal*, March, 116: C10–C23.

Ashenfelter, Orley, and David Card. 2002. "Did the Elimination of Mandatory Retirement Affect Faculty Retirement?" *American Economic Review*, September, 92: 957–980.

Ashenfelter, Orley, and Michael Greenstone. 2004. "Using Mandated Speed Limits to Measure the Value of a Statistical Life," *Journal of Political Economy*, 112: S226–S267.

Auletta, Ken. 2001. "Leviathan: How Much Bigger Can AOL Time Warner Get?" *The New Yorker*, October 29, pp. 50–61.

Austin, John. 1875. *Lectures on Jurisprudence, or the Philosophy of Positive Law*, Robert Campbell, ed., New York: J. Cockcroft.

Autor, David H., and David Scarborough. 2004. "Screening for Hourly Wages Jobs: Is There a Trade-Off between Efficiency and Equality?" Working Paper, MIT Department of Economics, February.

Averch, Harvey, and Leland L. Johnson. 1962. "Behavior of the Firm under Regulatory Constraint," *American Economic Review*, 52: 1053–1069.

Bacow, Lawrence. 1980. *Bargaining for Job Safety and Health*, Cambridge, MA: MIT Press.

Bagnoli, M., Stephen Salant, and J. Swierzbinski. 1989. "Durable Goods Monopoly with Discrete Demand," *Journal of Political Economy*, 97: 1459–1478.

Bailey, Elizabeth E. 2002. "Aviation Policy: Past and Present," *Southern Economic Journal*, July, 69: 12–20.

Bailey, Elizabeth E., and Doug Liu. 1995. "Airline Consolidation and Consumer Welfare," *Eastern Economic Journal*, 21: 463–476.

Bailey, Elizabeth, and Lawrence J. White. 1974. "Reversals in Peak and Off-Peak Prices," *Bell Journal of Economics*, 5: 75–92.

Bailey, Elizabeth, and Roger D. Coleman. 1971. "The Effect of Lagged Regulation in an Averch-Johnson Model," *Bell Journal of Economics*, 2: 278–292.

Baily, Martin N., and Robert Z. Lawrence. 2001. "Do We Have a New Economy?" *American Economic Review*, May, 91: 308–312.

Bain, Joe S. 1956. *Barriers to New Competition*, Cambridge, Mass.: Harvard University Press.

Baird, Douglas G., Robert H. Gertner, and Randal C. Picker. 1994. *Game Theory and the Law*, Cambridge, Mass.: Harvard University Press.

Baker, Samuel H., and J. B. Pratt. 1989. "Experience as a Barrier to Contestability in Airline Markets," *Review of Economics and Statistics*, May, 71: 352–360.

Bakos, Yannis. 2001. "The Emerging Landscape for Retail E-Commerce," *Economic Perspectives*, Winter, 15: 69–80.

Bakos, Yannis, and Erik Brynjolfsson. 2000. "Aggregation and Disaggregation of Information Goods: Implications for Bundling, Site Licensing, and Micropayment Systems," in Brian Kahin and Hal Varian, eds., *Internet Publishing and Beyond: The Economics of Digital Information and Intellectual Property*, Cambridge, Mass.: MIT Press.

Banerjee, Ajeyo, and W. Ward Eckard. 1998. "Are Mega-Mergers Anti-Competitive?: Evidence from the First Great Merger Wave," *RAND Journal of Economics*, 29: 803–827.

Banerjee, Neela. 2000. "U.S. Proposes Changes in Electricity Marketing in California," *New York Times*, November 2, p. C1.

Barber, Brad M., and Terrence Odean. 2001. "The Internet and the Investor," *Economic Perspectives*, Winter, 15: 41–54.

Barnett, Andy, Keith Reutter, and Henry Thompson. 1998. "Electricity Substitution and Deregulation: Some Local Industrial Evidence," *Energy Economics*, 34: 411–419.

Bartel, A. P., and L. G. Thomas. 1985. "Direct and Indirect Effects of Regulation: A New Look at OSHA's Impact," *Journal of Law and Economics*, 28: 1–25.

Barton, David M., and Roger Sherman. 1984. "The Price and Profit Effects of Horizontal Merger: A Case Study," *Journal of Industrial Economics*, December, 33: 165–177.

Barzel, Yoram. 1968. "Optimal Timing of Innovations," *Review of Economics and Statistics*, 50: 348–355.

Baumol, William J. 1968. "Reasonable Rules for Rate Regulation: Plausible Policies for an Imperfect World," in Almarin Phillips and Oliver E. Williamson, eds., *Prices: Issues in Theory, Practice, and Public Policy*, Philadelphia: University of Pennsylvania Press.

Baumol, William J. 1966. *Business Behavior, Value and Growth*, rev. ed., New York: Harcourt Brace and World.

Baumol, William J., and Burton G. Malkiel. 1967. "The Firm's Optimal Debt Equity Combination and the Cost of Capital," *Quarterly Journal of Economics*, November, 81: 547–578.

Baumol, William J., and Gregory J. Sidak. 1994a. "The Pricing of Inputs Sold to Competitors," *Yale Journal on Regulation*, 14: 145–163.

Baumol, William J., and Gregory J. Sidak. 1994b. *Toward Competition in Local Telephony*, Cambridge, Mass.: MIT Press.

Baumol, William J., and Robert D. Willig. 1981. "Fixed Costs, Sunk Costs, Entry Barriers, and Sustainability of Monopoly," *Quarterly Journal of Economics*, 95: 405–431.

Baumol, William J., John C. Panzar, and Robert D. Willig. 1982. *Contestable Markets and the Theory of Industry Structure*, New York: Harcourt Brace Jovanovich.

Baumol, William J., Elizabeth Bailey, and Robert D. Willig. 1977. "Weak Invisible Hand Theorems on the Sustainability of Multiproduct Natural Monopoly," *American Economic Review*, 67: 350–365.

Baye, Michael, Keith Crocker, and Jiandong Ju. 1996. "Divisionalization, Franchising, and Divestiture Incentives in Oligopoly," *American Economic Review*, March, 86: 223–236.

Baylis, Kathy, and Jeffrey M. Perloff. 2002. "Price Dispersion on the Internet," *Review of Industrial Organization*, November, 21: 305–324.

Beaver, William H., Catherine Shakespeare, and Mark T. Soliman. 2006. "Differential Properties in the Ratings of Certified vs. Non-Certified Bond Rating Agencies," *Journal of Accounting and Economics*, December, 42: 303–334.

Bebchuk, Lucian Arye, and Assaf Hamdani. 2002. "Vigorous Race or Leisurely Walk: Reconsidering the Competition over Corporate Charters," *Yale Law Journal*, December, 112: 553–615.

Becker, Gary. 1971. *The Economics of Discrimination*, 2nd ed., Chicago: University of Chicago Press.

Becker, Gary, and K. Murphy. 1993. "A Simple Theory of Advertising as a Good or Bad," *Quarterly Journal of Economics*, August, 108: 941–964.

Benham, L. 1972. "The Effects of Advertising on the Price of Eyeglasses," *Journal of Law and Economics*, October, 15: 337–352.

Bennathan, Esra, and Alan A. Walters. 1969. "Revenue Pooling and Cartels," *Oxford Economic Papers*, July, 21: 1961–1976.

Benston, George J. 1990. *The Separation of Commercial and Investment Banking*, New York: Oxford University Press.

Benston, George J., Michael Bromwich, Robert E. Litan, and Alfred Wagenhofer. 2003. *Following the Money: The Enron Failure and the State of Corporate Disclosure*, Washington, D.C.: AEI-Brookings Joint Center.

Bentham, Jeremy. 1945. *The Limits of Jurisprudence Defined* (written in 1782 and first printed from the author's manuscript with an introduction by Charles Warren Everett), New York: Columbia University Press.

Bentham, Jeremy. 1879. *An Introduction to the Principles of Morals and Legislation*, Oxford, England: The Clarendon Press.

Berg, Sanford V., and John Tschirhart. 1989. *Natural Monopoly Regulation: Principles and Practice*, New York: Cambridge University Press.

Berle, Adolph A., and Gardiner C. Means. 1968 (1932). *The Modern Corporation and Private Property*, rev. ed., New York: Harcourt, Brace and World.

Berndt, Ernst R. 2002. "Pharmaceuticals in U.S. Health Care: Determinations of Quantity and Price," *Journal of Economic Perspectives*, Fall, 16: 45–66.

Berne, Robert, and Richard Schramm. 1986. *The Financial Analysis of Governments*, Englewood Cliffs, N.J.: Prentice Hall.

Bertrand, J. 1883. "Review of Cournot's Researches into the Mathematical Principles of the Theory of Wealth," *Journal des Savants*, September, 499–508.

Besanko, David, Julia D'Souza, and S. Ramu Thiagarajan. 2001. "The Effect of

Wholesale Market Deregulation on Shareholder Wealth in the Electric Power Industry," *Journal of Law and Economics*, April, 44: 65–88.

Besen, Stanley, Paul Milgrom, Bridger Mitchell, and Padmanabhan Srinagesh. 2001. "Advances in Routing Technologies and Internet Peering Arrangements," *American Economic Review*, May, 91: 292–296.

Bhattacharya, Utpal, Peter Groznik, and Bruce Haslem. 2007. "Is CEO Certification of Earnings Numbers Value-Relevant," *Journal of Empirical Finance* (forthcoming).

Biglaiser, Gary, and Michael Riordan. 2000. "Dynamics of Price Regulation," *RAND Journal of Economics*, Winter, 31: 744–767.

Bittlingmayer, George. 1985. "Did Antitrust Policy Cause the Great Merger Wave?" *Journal of Law and Economics*, 28: 77–118.

Bittlingmayer, George. 1982. "Decreasing Average Cost and Competition: A New Look at the Addyston Pipe Case," *Journal of Law and Economics*, 25: 201–230.

Black, Bernard. 2000. "The First International Merger Wave (and the Fifth and Last U.S. Wave)," *University of Miami Law Review*, 54: 799–818.

Black, Dan A., and Thomas J. Kniesner. 2003. "On the Measurement of Job Risk in Hedonic Wage Models," *Journal of Risk and Uncertainty*, December, 27: 205–220.

Blainey, Geoffrey. 1975. *Triumph of the Nomads: A History of Ancient Australians*, Melbourne: Sun Books.

Blainey, Geoffrey. 1966. *The Tyranny of Distance: How Distance Shaped Australia's History*, Melbourne: Sun Books.

Blasi, Joseph R., Douglas Kruse, and Aaron Bernstein. 2003. *In the Company of Owners: The Truth about Stock Options and Why Every Employee Should Have Them*, New York: Basic Books.

Blass, Asher A., and Dennis W. Carlton. 2001. "The Choice of Organizational Form in Gasoline Retailing and the Cost of Laws That Limit That Choice," *Journal of Law and Economics*, October, 44: 511–524.

Blomquist, Glenn C. 1994. "Self Protection and Averting Behavior, Values of Statistical Lives, and Benefit Cost Analysis of Environmental Policy," *Review of Economics of the Household*, 2: 89–110.

Blumstein, Carl, L. S. Friedman, and R. J. Green. 2002. "The History of Electricity Restructuring in California," *Journal of Industry, Competition, and Trade*, June 2: 9–28.

Boardman, Anthony E., Catherine Eckel, M. Linde, and A. R. Vining. 1983. "An Overview of Mixed Enterprises in Canada," *Business Quarterly*, 48: 101–106.

Bohi, Douglas R., and Milton Russell. 1978. *Limiting Oil Imports*, Baltimore: Johns Hopkins University Press.

Boiteux, Marcel. 1960. "Peak-Load Pricing," *Journal of Business*, 33: 157–179.

Boiteux, Marcel. 1956. "Sur la Gestion des Monopoles Publics astrients a l'Equilibre Budgetaire," *Econometrica*, 24: 22–40.

Bolton, Patrick, Joseph F. Brodley, and Michael Riordan. 2000. "Predatory Pricing: Strategic Theory and Legal Policy," *Georgetown Law Journal*, 88: 2259–2297.

Bolton, Patrick, Joseph F. Brodley, and Michael Riordan. 2001. "Predatory Pricing: Response to Critique and Further Elaboration," *Georgetown Law Journal*, 88: 2495–2528.

Borenstein, Severin. 2006. "Time-Varying Retail Electricity Prices: Theory and Practice," in James M. Griffin and Steven Puller, eds., *Electricity Deregulation: Where to From Here?*, Chicago: University of Chicago Press.

Borenstein, Severin. 2002. "The Trouble With Electricity Markets: Understanding California's Restructuring Disaster," *Journal of Economic Perspectives*, Winter, 16: 191–211.

Borenstein, Severin. 1999. "Rapid Price Communication and Coordination: The Airline Tariff Publishing Case," in John E. Kwoka and Lawrence J. White, eds., *The Antitrust Revolution: Economics, Competition, and Policy*, 3rd ed., New York: Oxford University Press.

Borenstein, Severin. 1992. "The Evolution of U.S. Airline Competition," *Journal of Economic Perspectives*, 6: 45–73.

Borenstein, Severin. 1990. "Airline Mergers, Airport Dominance, and Market Power," *American Economic Review*, May, 80: 400–404.

Borenstein, Severin. 1989. "The Evolution of U.S. Airline Competition," *Journal of Economic Perspectives*, 6: 45–73.

Borenstein, Severin, and Nancy L. Rose. 1994. "Competition and Price Dispersion in the U.S. Airline Industry," *Journal of Political Economy*, August, 102: 653–683.

Borenstein, Severin, and Garth Saloner. 2001. "Economics and Electronic Commerce," *Journal of Economic Perspectives*, Winter, 15: 3–12.

Borenstein, Severin, and Andrea Shepard. 1996. "Dynamic Pricing in Retail Gasoline Markets," *RAND Journal of Economics*, Autumn, 27: 429–451.

Borenstein, Severin, James Bushnell, and Steven Stoff. 2000. "The Competitive Effects of Transmission Capacity in a Deregulated Electricity," *RAND Journal of Economics*, Summer, 31: 294–325.

Borenstein, Severin, James B. Bushnell, and Frank A. Wolak. 2002. "Measuring Market Inefficiencies in California's Restructured Wholesale Electricity Market," *American Economic Review*, December, 92: 1376–1405.

Bork, Robert H. 1966. "Legislative Intent and the Policy of the Sherman Act." *Journal of Law and Economics*, October, 9: 7–48.

Bosselman, Fred, Joel Eisen, Jim Rossi, David Spence, and Jacqueline Weaver. 2006. *Energy, Economics, and the Environment*, 2nd ed., Eagen, MN: Foundation Press.

Bowman, Ward S., Jr. 1973. *Patent and Antitrust Law*, Chicago: University of Chicago Press.

Bradbury, John Charles. 2006. "Regulatory Federalism and Workplace Safety: Evidence from OSHA Enforcement, 1981–1995," *Journal of Regulatory Economics*, March, 29: 211–224.

Bradley, Michael, Anand Desai, and E. Han Kim. 1988. "Synergistic Gains from Corporate Acquisitions and Their Division between the Stockholders of Target and Acquiring Firms," *Journal of Financial Economics*, 21: 3–31.

Bradsher, Keith. 2002. *High and Mighty: SUVs— The World's Most Dangerous Vehicles and How They Got That Way*, New York: Public Affairs.

Braeutigam, Ronald R. 1980. "An Analysis of Fully Distributed Cost Pricing in Regulated Industries, *Bell Journal of Economics*, 11: 182–196.

Braeutigam, Ronald R., Matthew Magura, and John C. Panzar. 1997. "The Effects of Incentive Regulation on U.S. Telephone Rates," Northwestern University, Working Paper.

Brealey, Richard A. 1969. *An Introduction to Risk and Return from Common Stocks*, Cambridge, Mass.: MIT Press.

Brennan, Timothy J., Karen L. Palmer, and Salvador A. Martinez. 2003. *Alternating Currents: Electricity Markets and Public Policy*, Washington, D.C.: Resources for the Future.

Bresnahan, Timothy F., and Shane Greenstein. 1999. "Technological Competition and the Structure of the Computer Industry," *Journal of Industrial Economics*, March, 47: 1–40.

Bresnahan, Timothy F., and Peter C. Reiss. 1991. "Entry and Competition in Concentrated Markets," *Journal of Political Economy*, October, 99: 977–1009.

Bresnahan, Timothy F., Erik Brynjolfsson, and Lorin M. Hitt. 2002. "Information Technology, Workplace Organization, and the Demand for Skilled Labor: Firm-Level Evidence," *Quarterly Journal of Economics*, February, 97: 339–376.

Bresnahan, Timothy F., Scott Stern, and Manuel Trajtenberg. 1997. "Market Segmentation and the Sources of Rents from Innovation: Personal Computers in the Late 1980s," *RAND Journal of Economics*, Special Issue, 28: S17–S44.

Briggs, Charles F., and Augustus Maverick. 1863. *The Story of the Telegraph*, New York: Rudd and Carleton.

Brock, G. W. 1981. *The Telecommunications Industry*, Cambridge, Mass.: Harvard University Press.

Brock, James. 2000. "Industry Update: Airlines," *Review of Industrial Organization*, 16: 41–51.

Brodley, J. 1990. "Antitrust Law and Innovation Cooperation," *Journal of Economic Perspectives*, 4: 97–112.

Brodley, Joseph F., and Ching-to Albert Ma. 1993. "Contract Penalties, Monopolizing Strategies, and Antitrust Policy," *Stanford Law Review*, 45: 1161–1232.

Brookshire, David, Mark Thayer, William D. Schulze, and Ralph C. d'Arge. 1982. "Valuing Public Goods: A Comparison Survey of Hedonic Approaches," *American Economic Review*, 72: 165–177.

Brown, Lester R. 2006. *Plan B 2.0. Rescuing a Planet under Stress and a Civilization in Trouble*, New York: W. W. Norton.

Brown, Jeffrey R., and Austan Goolsbee. 2002. "Does the Internet Make Markets More Competitive? Evidence from the Life Insurance Industry," *Journal of Political Economy*, 110: 481–507.

Brozen, Yale. 1971. "Bain's Concentration and Rates of Return Revisited," *Journal of Law and Economics*, 14: 351–369.

Brueckner, Jan K. 2004. "Network Structure and Airline Scheduling," *Journal of Industrial Economics*, June, 52: 291–312.

Brueckner, Jan K. 2003. "International Airfares in the Age of Alliances: The Effect of Code-sharing and Antitrust Immunity," *Review of Economics and Statistics*, February, 85: 105–118.

Brueckner, Jan K. 2002a. "Airport Congestion When Carriers Have Market Power," *American Economic Review*, December, 92: 1357–1375.

Brueckner, Jan K. 2002b. "Internalization of Airport Congestion: A Network Analysis," University of Illinois, Economics Department Working Paper, October 21.

Brueckner, Jan K. 2001. "The Economics of International Codesharing: An Analysis of Airline Alliances," *International Journal of Industrial Organization*, 19: 1475–1498.

Brueckner, Jan K., and Tom Whalen. 2000. "The Price Effects of International Airline Alliances," *Journal of Law and Economics*, 43: 503–545.

Brueckner, Jan K., and Yimin Zhang. 2000. "Scheduling Decisions in an Airline Network: A Hub-and-Spoke System's Effect on Flight Frequency, Fares, and Welfare," *Journal of Transport Economics and Policy*, 35: 195–222.

Brueckner, Jan K., Nicola J. Dyer, and Pablo T. Spiller. 1992. "Fare Determination in Airline Hub-and-Spoke Networks," *RAND Journal of Economics*, 23: 309–333.

Bryce, Robert. 2002. *Pipe Dreams: Greed, Ego, and the Death of Enron*, New York: Public Affairs.

Brynjolfsson, Erik, and Lorin M. Hitt. 2000. "Beyond Computation: Information Technology, Organizational Transformation and Business Performance," *Journal of Economic Perspectives*, Fall, 14: 23–48.

Brynjolfsson, Erik, and Brian Kahin, eds. 2000. *Understanding the Digital Economy*. Cambridge, Mass.: MIT Press.

Brynjolfsson, Erik, Yu (Jeffrey) Hu, and Michael D. Smith. 2003. "Consumer Surplus in the Digital Economy: Estimating the Value of Increased Product Variety at Online Booksellers," *Management Science*, November, 49: 1580–1596.

Buchanan, James M. 1968. "A Public Choice Approach to Public Utility Pricing," *Public Choice*, 2: 1–17.

Buchanan, James M. 1962. "Politics, Policy, and the Pigovian Margins," *Economica*, 29: 17–28.

Buchanan, James M., and Gordon Tullock. 1965. *The Calculus of Consent*, Ann Arbor, Mich.: University of Michigan Press.

Burnett, William B. 1994. "Predation by a Nondominant Firm: The Liggett Case (1993)," in John E. Kwoka and Lawrence J. White, eds., *The Antitrust Revolution: The Role of Economics*, New York: Harper Collins.

Burrows, James C., and Thomas A. Domencich. 1970. *An Analysis of the United States Oil Import Quota*, Lexington, Mass.: D.C. Heath.

Bush, Darren, and Carrie Mayne. 2004. "In (Reluctant) Defense of Enron: Why Bad Regulation Is to Blame For California's Power Woes (Or Why Antitrust Law Fails to Protect Against Market Power When the Market Rules Encourage Its Use)," *Oregon Law Review*, 83: 207–285.

Bush, Darren, and Salvatore Massa. 2004. "Rethinking the Potential Competition Doctrine," *Wisconsin Law Review*, 2004: 1035–1160.

Bushnell, James, and Celeste Saravia. 2002. "An Empirical Assessment of the Competitiveness of the New England Electricity Market," Center for the Study of Electricity Markets Working Paper No. 101, available at http://ucie.berkeley.edu/PDF/csemwp101.pdf.

Bushnell, James, Erin T. Mansur, and Celeste Saravia. 2004. "Market Structure and Competition: A Cross-Market Analysis of U.S. Electricity Deregulation," University of California, Energy Institute Working Paper No. 126, March.

Cabral, Luis M. B., and Jose Mata. 2003. "On the Evolution of the Firm Size Distribution,"

American Economic Review, September, 93: 1075–1090.

Cairns, Robert D. 1994. "Asymmetry of Information and Contestability Theory," *Review of Industrial Organization,* 9: 99–107.

Call, G. D., and Theodore E. Keeler. 1985. "Airline Deregulation Fares and Market Behavior: Some Empirical Evidence," in Andrew F. Daugherty, ed., *Analytical Studies in Transport Economics,* New York: Cambridge University Press, pp. 222–247.

Calomiris, Charles W. 1991. "Regulation, Industrial Structure, and Instability in U.S. Banking: An Historical Perspective," University of Pennsylvania, Department of Economics Working Paper, December.

Cameron, Lisa, and Peter Cramton. (1999). "The Role of the ISO in U.S. Electricity Markets: A Review of Restructuring in California and PJM," *Electricity Journal,* April, pp. 71–81.

Campbell, James I., Jr. 2001. *The Rise of Global Delivery Services,* Washington, D.C.: J. Campbell Press.

Cancian, M., A. Bills, and T. Bergstrom. 1995. "Hotelling Location Problems with Directional Constraints: An Application to Television News Scheduling," *Journal of Industrial Economics,* 43: 121–124.

Caritat, M. J. A. N. (The Marquis de Condorcet). See Condorcet.

Carlton, Dennis W. 1991. "The Theory of Allocation and its Implications for Marketing and Industrial Structure," *Journal of Law and Economics,* 34: 231–246.

Carlton, Dennis W., and Judith A Chevalier. 2001. "Free Riding and Sales Strategies for the Internet," *Journal of Industrial Economics,* December, 49: 441–461.

Carroll, Glenn R., and Michael T. Hannan. 2000. *The Demography of Corporations and Industries,* Princeton, N.J.: Princeton University Press.

Carson, Rachel. *Silent Spring,* Boston: Houghton Mifflin, 1962.

Carter, Michael, and Julian Wright. 2003. "Asymmetric Network Interconnection," *Review of Industrial Organization,* February, 22: 27–46.

Casadesus-Masanell, Ramon, and Daniel Spulber. 2000. "The Fable of Fisher Body,"

Journal of Law and Economics, April, 43: 67–104.

Cassell, Mark. 2002. *How Governments Privatize: The Politics of Divestment in the United States and Germany,* Washington, D.C.: Georgetown University Press.

Cave, Martin E., Sumit K. Majumdar, and Ingo Vogelsang, eds. 2002. *Handbook of Telecommunications Economics,* Cambridge, Mass.: North Holland Elsevier

Caves, Richard E., and D. P. Green. 1996. "Brands' Quality Levels, Prices, and Advertising Outlays: Empirical Evidence on Signals and Information Costs," *International Journal of Industrial Organization,* 14: 29–52.

Caves, Richard E., Michael D, Whinston, and Mark A. Hurwitz. 1991. "Patent Expiration, Entry and Competition in the U.S. Pharmaceutical Industry," *Brookings Papers on Economic Activity,* 1–48.

Chadwick, Sir Edwin. 1859. "Results of Different Principles of Legislation and Administration in Europe: of Competition for the Field, as Compared with the Competition within the Field of Service," *Journal of the Royal Statistical Society,* 22: 381–420.

Chamberlin, Edward H. 1933. *The Theory of Monopolistic Competition,* Cambridge, Mass.: Harvard University Press.

Chandler, Alfred D. 2001. *Inventing the Electronic Century,* New York: Free Press.

Chandler, Alfred D., Jr. 1977. *The Invisible Hand: The Managerial Revolution in American Business,* Cambridge, Mass.: Belknap Press.

Chandler, Alfred D., Jr. 1962. *Strategy and Structure: Chapters in the History of the Industrial Enterprise,* Cambridge, Mass.: MIT Press.

Chay, Kenneth Y., and Michael Greenstone. 2005. "Does Air Quality Matter? Evidence from the Housing Market," *Journal of Political Economy,* April, 113: 376–424.

Chenery, Hollis B. 1949. "The Engineering Production Function." *Quarterly Journal of Economics,* May 63: 507–531.

Cheung, Steven N. S. 1970. "The Structure of a Contract and the Theory of a Non-Exclusive Resource," *Journal of Law and Economics,* 13: 49–70.

Chow, Gregory C. 1957. *Demand for Automobiles in the United States*, Amsterdam: North-Holland.

Chowning, Larry S. 1990. *Harvesting the Chesapeake*, Centreville, Md.: Tidewater Press.

Cirace, John. 1978. "CBS v. ASCAP: An Economic Analysis of a Political Problem," *Fordham Law Review*, 47: 277–306.

Clark, Victor S. 1928. *History of Manufactures in the United States, 1860–1914*. Washington, D.C.: Carnegie Institution.

Clay, Karen, Ramayya Krishnan, and Eric Wolff. 2001. "Prices and Price Dispersion on the Web: Evidence from the Online Book Industry," *Journal of Industrial Economics*, December, 49: 521–539.

Coase, Ronald H. 2000. "The Acquisition of Fisher Body by General Motors," *Journal of Law and Economics*, April, 43: 15–31.

Coase, Ronald H. 1974. "The Lighthouse in Economics," *Journal of Law and Economics*, 17: 357–381.

Coase, Ronald H. 1972. "Durability and Monopoly," *Journal of Law and Economics*, 15: 143–149.

Coase, Ronald H. 1960. "The Problem of Social Cost," *Journal of Law and Economics*, October, 3: 1–44.

Coase, Ronald H. 1959. "The Federal Communications Commission," *Journal of Law and Economics*, 2: 1–40.

Coase, Ronald H. 1946. "The Marginal Cost Controversy," *Economica*, 13: 169–180.

Coase, Ronald H. 1937. "The Nature of the Firm," *Economica*, N.S., October, 4: 386–405.

Coate, Malcolm B., and Shawn W. Ulrick. 2005. "Transparency at the Federal Trade Commission: The Horizontal Review Process, 1996–2003," Bureau of Economics, Federal Trade Commission, February.

Coffee, John C., Jr. 2003. "What Caused Enron? A Capsule Social and Economic History of the 1990s," Columbia University Law School, Center for Law and Economics Studies Working Paper No. 214, January 20.

Cohen, Julie E. 1998. "Lochner in Cyberspace: The New Economic Orthodoxy of 'Rights Management,'" *Michigan Law Review*, 97: 462–563.

Cohen, Linda. 1982. "A Spot Market for Electricity: Preliminary Analysis of the Florida Energy Broker," RAND Corporation, RAND Note N-1817-DOE.

Cohn, E., S. L. Rhine, and M. C. Santos. 1989. "Institutions of Higher Education as Multi-Product Firms: Economies of Scale and Scope." *Review of Economics and Statistics*, May, 71: 284–290.

Cole, Daniel H., and Peter Z. Grossman. 1999. "When Is Command and Control Efficient? Institutions, Technology, and the Comparative Efficiency of Alternative Regulatory Regimes for Environmental Protection," *Wisconsin Law Review*, 71: 887–938.

Comanor, William S. 1967. "Market Structure, Product Differentiation, and Industrial Research," *Quarterly Journal of Economics*, November, 81: 639–657.

Compaine, Benjamin M., and William H. Read, eds. 1999. *The Information Resources Policy Handbook*, Cambridge, Mass.: MIT Press.

Condorcet, Marie Jean Antoine Nicholas Caritat. 1785. *Essai sur l'Application de l'Analyse aux Probabilites des Decisions Rendues a la Pluralite des Voix*, Paris: Imprimateur Royale.

Conison, Jay. 1998. *Employee Benefits in a Nutshell*, 2nd ed., St. Paul, MN: West Group.

Connor, John M. 2001. "Our Customers Are Our Enemies: The Lysine Cartel of 1992–1995," *Review of Industrial Organization*, 18: 5–21.

Cooke, W. N., and F. Gautschi. 1981. "OSHA, Plant Safety Programs, and Injury Reduction," *Industrial Relations*, 20: 245–257.

Coockenboo, L. 1955. *Crude Oil Pipelines*, Harvard University Press.

Corsi, Thomas M. 1996a. "Current and Alternative Federal Size and Weight Policies: Less-Than-Truckload Motor Carriers," University of Maryland, College of Business and Management Working Paper.

Corsi, Thomas M. 1996b. "Current and Alternative Federal Size and Weight Policies: Truckload Motor Carriers," University of Maryland, College of Business and Management Working Paper.

Costello, Kenneth W., and Daniel J. Duann. 1996. "Turning up the Heat in the Natural Gas Industry," *Regulation*, 1: 52–59.

Cournot, Augustin A. 1963 (orig. 1838). *Researches into the Mathematical Principles of the Theory of Wealth*, translated by

Nathaniel T. Bacon, 1927. Homewood, Ill.: Richard D. Irwin.

Coursey, Don, R. Mark Isaac, Margaret Luke, and Vernon L. Smith. 1984. "Market Contestability in the Presence of Sunk (Entry) Costs," *Rand Journal of Economics*, Spring, 15: 69–84.

Cox, James C., and R. Mark Isaac. 1987. "Mechanisms for Incentive Regulation: Theory and Experiment," *RAND Journal of Economics*, 18: 348–359.

Crandall, Robert W. 2005. *Competition and Chaos: The U.S. Telecommunications Sector Since 1996*, Washington, D.C.: Brookings Institution Press.

Crandall, Robert W. 2001. "The Failure of Structural Remedies in Sherman Act Monopolization Cases," *Oregon Law Review*, Spring, 80: 109–198.

Crandall, Robert W. 1984. "An Acid Test for Congress," *Regulation*, September–December, 8: 21–28.

Crandall, Robert W., and Jerry Ellig. 1997. "Economic Deregulation and Customer Choice: Lessons from the Electricity Industry," George Mason University, Center for Market Processes Working Paper.

Crandall, Robert W., and Jerry A. Hausman. 2000. "Competition in U.S. Telecommunications Servioces: Effects of the 1996 Legislation," in Sam Peltzman and Clifford Winston, eds., *Deregulation of Network Industries: What's Next?* Washington, D.C.: AEI-Brookings.

Crandall, Robert W., and Leonard Waverman. 1995. *Talk is Cheap: The Promise of Regulatory Reform in North American Telecommunications*, Washington, D.C.: The Brookings Institution.

Crandall, Robert W., Howard K. Gruenspecht, Theodore E. Keeler, and Lester B. Lave, 1986. *Regulating the Automobile*, Washington, D.C.: The Brookings Institution, p. 63.

Crawford, Gregory S. 2000. "The Impact of the 1992 Cable Act on Household Demand and Welfare," *RAND Journal of Economics*, Autumn, 31: 422–449.

Crew, Michael A. ed. 1992. *Economic Innovations in Public Utility Regulation*, Dordrecht: Kluwer.

Crew, Michael A. 1968. "Peak Load Pricing and Optimal Capacity: Comment," *American Economic Review*, 53: 168–170.

Crew, Michael A., and Paul R. Kleindorfer, eds. 2002. *Postal and Delivery Services: Delivering on Competition*, Norwell, MA: Kluwer.

Crew, Michael A., and Paul Kleindorfer. 2002. "Balancing Access and the Universal Service Obligation," in Michael A. Crew and Paul R. Kleindorfer, eds., *Postal and Delivery Services: Delivering on Competition*, Norwell, MA: Kluwer.

Crew, Michael A., and Paul R. Kleindorfer. 2000. *Current Directions in Postal Reform*, Boston, MA: Kluwer.

Crew, Michael A., and Paul Kleindorfer. 1992. *The Economics of Postal Service*, Norwell, MA: Kluwer.

Crew, Michael A., and Paul Kleindorfer. 1986. *The Economics of Public Utility Regulation*, Cambridge, Mass.: MIT Press.

Crocker, Keith J., and Scott E. Masten. 1996. "Regulation and Administered Contracts Revisited: Lessons from Transactions-Cost Economics for Public Utility Regulation," *Journal of Regulatory Economics*, 9: 5–39.

Cross, John G. 1970. "Incentive Pricing and Utility Regulation," *Quarterly Journal of Economics*, 84: 236–253.

Cross, Steven M. 1982. *Economic Decisions under Inflation: The Impact of Accounting Measurement Errors*, Greenwich, Conn.: JAI Press.

Cudahy, Brian J. 1990. *Cash, Tokens and Transfers: A History of Urban Mass Transit in North America*, New York: Fordham University Press.

Cummins, J. David, and Sharon Tennyson. 1996. "Moral Hazard in Insurance," *Journal of Risk and Uncertainty*, 12: 29–50.

Cummins, J. David, and Sharon Tennyson. 1992. "Controlling Automobile Insurance Costs," *Journal of Economic Perspectives*, 6: 95–115.

Cummins, J. David, Richard D. Phillips, and Mary A. Weiss. 2001. "The Incentive Effects of No-Fault Automobile Insurance," *Journal of Law and Economics*, October, 44: 427–464.

Cyert, Richard M., and James G. March. 1963. *A Behavioral Theory of the Firm*, Englewood Cliffs, N.J.: Prentice-Hall.

Dales J. H. 1968. *Pollution, Property, and Prices: An Essay in Policy-Making and Economics*, Toronto: University of Toronto Press.

Dana, James D. 1998. "Advance Purchase Discounts and Price Discrimination in

Competitive Markets," *Journal of Political Economy*, 106: 395–422.

Dana, James D., Jr. 1999a. "Using Yield Management to Shift Demand When the Peak Time Is Unknown," *RAND Journal of Economics*, 30: 456–474.

Dana, James D., Jr. 1999b. "Equilibrium Price Dispersion under Demand Uncertainty: The Roles of Costly Capacity and Market Structure," *RAND Journal of Economics*, Winter, 30: 632–660.

d'Aspremont, Claude, Jean Jaskold Gabszewicz and J.-F. Thisse. 1979. "On Hotelling's Stability in Competition," *Econometrica*, 47: 1145–1151.

Dasgupta, Partha, and Joseph Stiglitz. 1980. "Industrial Structure and the Nature of Innovative Activity," *Economic Journal*, January, 90: 266–293.

Davis, Douglas D., and Charles A. Holt. 1994. "Market Power and Mergers in Markets with Posted Prices," *RAND Journal of Economics*, 25: 467–487.

Davis, Joseph A. 1986. "Acid Rain to Get Attention as Reagan Changes Course," *Congressional Quarterly*, March 22, 44: 675–676.

Davis, Joseph S. 1917. *Essays in the Earlier History of American Corporations*, Cambridge, Mass.: Harvard University Press.

Davis, Otto A., and Andrew B. Whinston. 1965. "Welfare Economics and the Theory of Second Best," *Review of Economic Studies*, January, 32: 1–14.

Davis, Otto A., and Andrew B, Whinston. 1964. "The Economics of Complex Systems: The Case of Municipal Zoning," *Kyklos*, September, 17: 419–440.

Davis, Otto A., and Andrew B. Whinston. 1961. "Economics of Urban Renewal," *Journal of Law and Contemporary Problems*, Winter, 24: 105–117.

Dean, Robert C., Jr. 1999. "Patent Law's Impact on Invention and Innovation," *Texas Review of Law and Politics*, Fall, 4: 95–102.

Deane, Phyllis. 1965. *The First Industrial Revolution*, Cambridge, England: Cambridge University Press.

DeBow, Michael E. 1998. "Congress, Federal Courts, and Administrative Agencies: How Much Authority Did Congress Give the Federal Communications Commission to Hasten Telecommunications Deregulation?"

PREVIEW of United States Supreme Court Cases, American Bar Association, 49–54.

Deck, Cary A., and Bart J. Wilson. 2000. "Interactions of Automated Pricing Algorithms: An Experimental Investigation," *Proceedings of the 2nd ACM Conference on Electronic Commerce 2000*, Minneapolis, Minn.: ACM Press, pp. 77–85.

DeGraba, Patrick. 2001. "Efficient Interconnection for Competing Networks When Customers Share the Value of a Call," October, Charles River Associates, Boston, Working Paper.

Demsetz, Harold. 1968. "Why Regulate Utilities," *Journal of Law and Economics*, 11: 55–65.

Demsetz, Harold. 1967. "Toward a Theory of Property Rights," *American Economic Review*, May, 57: 347–352.

Deneckere, R., H.P. Marvel, and J. Peck. 1997. "Demand Uncertainty and Price Maintenance: Markdowns as Destructive Competition," *American Economic Review*, September, 87: 619–641.

Denison, Edward F. 1985. *Trends in American Economic Growth 1929–1982*, Washington, D.C.: Brookings Institution.

Denison, Edward F. 1967. *Why Growth Rates Differ*, Washington, D.C.: Brookings Institution.

Denison, Edward F. 1962a. "How to Raise the High-Employment Growth Rate by One Percentage Point," *American Economic Review*, May, 52: 74–75.

Denison, Edward F. 1962b. *The Sources of Growth in the United States and the Alternatives Before Us*, New York: Committee for Economic Development.

Department of Transportation, NHTSA. 1983. A Preliminary Evaluation of Two Braking Improvements for Passenger Cars: Dual Master Cylinders and Front Disk Brakes, DOT HS-806–359, p. 43.

Department of Transportation, NHTSA. 1982. An Evaluation of Side Structure Improvements in Response to Federal Motor Vehicle Standard 214, DOT HS-806–314, p. xxiii.

Destler, Chester McArthur. 1967. *Roger Sherman and the Independent Oil Men*, Ithaca, N.Y.: Cornell University Press.

Dharan, Bala, and Nancy Rapoport. 2003. *Enron: Corporate Fiascos and Legal Implications*, New York: Anderson.

Diamond, Peter. 2004. "Social Security," *American Economic Review*, March 94: 1–24.

Dias, R. W. M. 1964. *Jurisprudence*, London: Butterworth.

DiCalogero, Sarah. 1997. "The Ivy Land Fill," Senior Thesis, University of Virginia, School of Engineering.

Dickinson, Robert E., and Ralph J. Cicerone. 1986. "Future Global Warming from Atmospheric Trace Gases," *Nature*, January 9, 319: 109–115.

Dinlersoz, Emin M., and Ruben Hernandez-Murillo. 2005. "The Diffusion of Electronic Business in the United States," *The Federal Reserve Bank of St. Louis Review*, Jan./Feb., 87: 11–34.

Dinlersoz, Emin M., and Pedro Pereira. 2005. "Patterns of Diffusion of Electronic Commerce in Retail Industries: Theory and Evidence," *CESifo Economic Studies*, 51: 261–294.

Dinlersoz, Emin M., and Pedro Pereira. 2007. "On the Diffusion of Commerce," *International Journal of Industrial Organization*, 25: 541–574.

Djankov, Simeon, Rafael LaPorta, Florencio Lopez-de-Silanes, and Andrei Shleifer. 2002. "The Regulation of Entry," *Quarterly Journal of Economics*, February, 117: 1–37; and available at http://www.nber.org/papers/w7892.

Doganis, Rigas. 1993. *Flying Off Course: The Economics of International Airlines*, 2nd ed., London: Routledge

Dolbear, F. Trenery. 1967. "On the Theory of Optimum Externality," *American Economic Review*, March, 57: 90–103.

Dolbear, F. Trenery, et al. 1968. "Collusion in Oligopoly: An Experiment on the Effect of Numbers and Information," *Quarterly Journal of Economics*, May, 82: 240–259.

Dolbear, F. Trenery, et al. 1965. "Factors Affecting Cooperation in the Prisoner's Dilemma," *Behavioral Science*, June, 10: 26–38.

Donohue, John J. 2003. *Foundations of Employment Discrimination Law*, New York: Foundation Press.

Donaldson, G. 1994. *Corporate Restructuring*, Boston: Harvard Business School Press.

Dorfman, Robert, and Peter O. Steiner. 1954. "Optimal Advertising and Optimal Quality," *American Economic Review*, December, 44: 826–836.

Doriot, Georges F. 1963. *The Management of Racial Integration in Business*, New York: McGraw Hill.

Douglas, George W., and James C. Miller, III. 1974. *Economic Regulation of Domestic Air Transport: Theory and Policy*, Washington, D.C.: The Brookings Institution.

Duetsch, Larry L. ed. 1998. *Industry Studies*, New York: M. E. Sharpe.

Dupuit, Jules. 1844. "On the Measure of the Utility of Public Works," reprinted in K. Arrow and T. Scitovsky, eds. 1969. *AEA Readings in Welfare Economics*, Homewood, IL: Richard D. Irwin.

Durbin, J. A., and G. S. Rothwell. 1990. "Subsidies to Nuclear Power Through Price Anderson Liability Limits," *Contemporary Policy Issues*, 7: 73–79.

Easterbrook, Gregg. 1993. "The Future of Electric Power," *Atlantic Monthly*, July.

Eaton, B.C., and N. Schmitt. 1994. "Flexible Manufacturing and Market Structure." *American Economic Review*, September, 84: 875–888.

Eckbo, Espen B. 1983. "Horizontal Mergers, Collusion, and Stockholder Wealth," *Journal of Financial Economics*, 11: 241–274.

Eckel, Catherine C. 1983. "Customer Class Pricing by Electric Utilities." Ph.D. dissertation, University of Virginia.

Eckel, Catherine C., and Theo Vermaelen. 1986. "Internal Regulation: The Effects of Government Ownership on the Value of the Firm," *Journal of Law and Economics*, 29: 381–403.

Eckert, Ross D., and George W. Hilton. 1972. "The Jitneys," *Journal of Law and Economics*, 15: 293–325.

Economides, Nicolas. 2001. "United States v. Microsoft: A failure of antitrust in the New Economy," *UWLA Law Review*, April, 32: 3–44.

Economist, "Fasten Your Safety Belts," January 11, 1997, pp. 55–57.

Edgeworth, Francis Y. 1925. *Papers Relating to Political Economy*, Vol. 1, London: Macmillan.

Edlin, Aaron S., and Joseph E. Stiglitz. 1995. "Discouraging Rivals: Managerial Rent-Seeking and Economic Efficiencies,"

American Economic Review, December, 85: 1301–1312.

Ehrlich, Isaac, and Richard A. Posner. 1974. "An Economic Analysis of Legal Rule Making," *Journal of Legal Studies*, 3: 257–286.

Eichenwald, Kurt. 2000. *The Informant: A True Story*, New York: Random House.

Eisenach, Jeffrey A., and Thomas M. Lenard. 1999. *Competition, Innovation, and the Microsoft Monopoly: Antitrust in the Digital Marketplace*, Boston: Kluwer Academic Press.

Ellerman, A. Denny, Paul L. Joskow, Richard Schmalensee, Juan-Pablo Montero, and Elizabeth M. Bailey. 2000. *Markets for Clean Air: The U.S. Acid Rain Program*, Cambridge, England: Cambridge University Press.

Ellig, Jerry, and Joseph P. Kalt. 1996. *New Horizons in Natural Gas Deregulation*, Westport, Conn.: Praeger.

Elzinga, Kenneth G. 1977. "The Goals of Antitrust: Other than Competition and Efficiency, What Else Counts?" *University of Pennsylvania Law Review*, June, 125: 1191–1213.

Elzinga, Kenneth G. 1969. "The Antimerger Law: Pyrrhic Victories?" *Journal of Law and Economics*, April, 12: 43–78.

Elzinga, Kenneth G., and William Breit. 1976. *The Antitrust Penalties*, New Haven, Conn.: Yale University Press.

Elzinga, Kenneth G., and David E. Mills. 2001a. "Independent Service Organizations and Economic Efficiency," *Economic Inquiry*, 39: 549–560.

Elzinga, Kenneth G., and David E. Mills. 2001b. "Predatory Pricing and Strategic Theory," *Georgetown Law Journal*, August, 89: 2475–2494.

Elzinga, Kenneth G., and David E. Mills. 1994. "Trumping the Areeda-Turner Test: The Recoupment Standard in Brooke Group," *Antitrust Law Journal*, 62: 559–584.

Elzinga, Kenneth G., and David E. Mills. 1989. "Testing for Predation: Is Recoupment Feasible?" *Antitrust Bulletin*, Winter, 34: 869–893.

Epstein, Richard A. 1992. *The Case Against Employment Discrimination Law*, Cambridge, Mass.: Harvard University Press.

ERISA Industry Committee. 1996. A White Paper on Emerging Pension Issues, Washington, D.C: ERISA Industry Committee, July.

Evans, David S., and Michael Salinger. 2005. "Why Do Firms Bundle and Tie? Evidence from Competitive Markets and Implications for Tying Law," *Yale Journal on Regulation*, Winter, 22: 37–89.

Evans, William N., and Joannis N. Kessides. 1994. "Living by the 'Golden Rule': MultiMarket Contact in the U.S. Airline Industry," *Quarterly Journal of Economics*, 109: 341–366.

Evans, William N., and Ioannnis N. Kessides. 1993. "Localized Market Power in the U.S. Airline Industry," *Review of Economics and Statistics*, February, 75: 66–75.

Fallows, James. 2002. *Free Flight*, New York: Perseus Books Group.

Lynch-Fannon, Irene. 2003. *Working Within Two Kinds of Capitalism: A Consideration of the Role of Employees as Stakeholders within the EU and US Corporation*, Oxford: Hart Publications.

Faulhaber, Gerald R. 1975. "Cross Subsidization: Pricing in Public Enterprises," *American Economic Review*, 65: 966–977.

Feinberg, Robert. 1985. "'Sales at Risk': A Test of the Mutual Forbearance Theory of Conglomerate Behavior," *Journal of Business*, April, 58: 225–241.

Feinberg, Robert, and Donald Alexander. 2004. "Entry in Local Telecommunications Markets," *Review of Industrial Organization*, September, 25: 107–127.

Feinberg, Robert, and Roger Sherman. 1988. "Mutual Forbearance Under Experimental Conditions," *Southern Economic Journal*, April, 54: 985–993.

Feinman, Jay M. 1976. "The Development of the Employment At Will Rule," *American Journal on Legal History*, 20: 118–200.

Feldman, Alan M. 1980. *Welfare Economics and Social Choice Theory*, Boston, Mass.: Martinus Nijhoff.

Fellner, William. 1960. *Competition Among the Few*, New York: Augustus M. Kelly.

Feltovich, Nick. 2000. "Mergers, Welfare, and Concentration: Results from a Model of Stackelberg-Cournot Oligopoly," Working Paper, University of Houston.

Fernando, Chitru S., Paul Kleindorfer, and D-J Wu. 2001. "Strategic Gaming in Electric Power Markets," *European Journal of Operational Research*, 130: 156–168.

Finoff, David, Curtis Cramer, and Sherrill Shaffer. 2004. "The Financial and Operational Impacts of FERC Order 636 on the Interstate Natural Gas Pipeline Industry," *Journal of Regulatory Economics*, May, 25: 243–270.

Finsinger, Jorg, Elizabeth Hammond, and Julian Tapp. 1985. *Insurance: Competition or Regulation*, London: Institute for Fiscal Studies.

Fischhoff, B., S. Lichtenstein, P. Slovic, S. L. Derby, and R. L. Keeney. 1981. *Acceptable Risk*, Cambridge: Cambridge University Press.

Fishback, Price V., and Shawn Everett Kantor. 2000. *A Prelude to the Welfare State: The Origins of Workers' Compensation*. Boston: National Bureau of Economic Research.

Florida, Richard. 2002. *The Rise of the Creative Class*, New York: Basic Books.

Fogel, Robert W. 1964. *Railroads and American Economic Growth: Essays in Economic History*, Baltimore: Johns Hopkins Press.

Folsom, Ralph H. 1990. *State Antitrust Law and Practice*, Englewood Cliffs, N.J.: Prentice-Hall.

Fouraker, Lawrence E. and Sidney Siegel. 1963. *Bargaining Behavior*, New York: McGraw-Hill.

Fournier, Gary M. 1981. "The Determinants of Economic Rents in Television Broadcasting," Ph.D. dissertation, University of Virginia.

Fox, Loren. 2003. *Enron: The Rise and Fall*, New York: Wiley.

Frankena, Mark W., and Paul A. Pautler. 1984. "An Economic Analysis of Taxicab Regulation," Bureau of Economics, Federal Trade Commission, May.

Fraumeni, Barbara M. 2001. "E-Commerce: Measurement and Measurement Issues," *American Economic Review*, May, 91: 318–322.

Freeland, Robert. 2000. "Creating Holdup through Vertical Integration: Fisher Body Revisited," *Journal of Law and Economics*, April, 43: 33–66.

Friedberg, Leora, and Michael T. Owyang. 2002. "Not Your Father's Pension Plan: The Rise of 401k and Other Defined-Contribution Plans," Federal Reserve Bank of St. Louis *Review*, January/February, 84: 23–34.

Friedberg, Leora, and Anthony Webb. 2000. "Retirement and the Evolution of Pension Structure," Working Paper No. 2000–30, University of California at San Diego, January.

Friedlaender, Ann F., Clifford W. Winston, and Kung Wang. 1983. "Costs, Technology, and Productivity in the U.S. Automobile Industry." *Bell Journal of Economics*, Spring, 14: 1–20.

Friedman, Lawrence M. 1985. *A History of American Law*, 2nd ed., New York: Simon and Schuster.

Fuller, John G. 1962. *The Gentlemen Conspirators: The Story of the Price Fixers in the Electrical Industry*, New York: Grove Press.

Fullerton, Don. 2001. "A Framework to Compare Environmental Policies," *Southern Economic Journal*, 68: 224–248.

Fultz, Keith O. 1987. "A Perspective on Liability Protection for Nuclear Plant Accidents," United States General Accounting Office, Government Printing Office, GAO/RCED 87–124, June.

Galbraith, John, Kenneth. 1952. *American Capitalism: The Concept of Countervailing Power*, Boston: Houghton Mifflin.

Gallini, Nancy T. 2002. "The Economics of Patents: Lessons from Recent U.S. Patent Reform," *Journal of Economic Perspectives*, Spring, 16: 131–154.

Gallini, Nancy T. 1992. "Patent Policy and Costly Imitation," *RAND Journal of Economics*, 23: 52–63.

Gallini, Nancy T., and Suzanne Scotchmer. 2001. "Intellectual Property: When Is it the Best Incentive System?" in Adam Jaffe, Josh Lerner, and Scott Stern, eds., 2001. *Innovation Policy and the Economy*, Vol. 2, Ch. 2, Cambridge, Mass.: MIT Press.

Garcia-Murillo, Martha, and Lee W. McKnight. 2005. "Internet Telephony: Effects on the Universal Service Program in the United States," *Review of Network Economics*, September, 4: 205–219.

Garicano, Luis, and Steven N. Kaplan. 2001. "The Effect of Business-to-Business

E-Commerce on Transaction Costs," *Journal of Industrial Economics*, December, 49: 463–485.

Garreau, Joel. 1991. *Edge City: Life on the New Frontier*, New York: Doubleday.

Garrett, Martin A., Jr., and Zhenhui Xu. 2003. "The Efficiency of Sharecropping: Evidence from the Postbellum South," *Southern Economic Journal*, January, 69: 578–595.

Gates, Howard, and Lawrence Goldmuntz. 1978. *Automotive Safety*, Washington, D.C.: Economics and Science Planning.

Geddes, Rick. 2003. *Saving the Mail: How to Solve the Problems of the U.S. Postal Service*, Washington, D.C.: AEI Press.

Geertz, Clifford. 1978. "The Bazaar Economy: Information and Search in Peasant Marketing," *American Economic Review*, 68: 28–32.

Gegax, Douglas, and John Tschirhart. 1984. "An Analysis of Interfirm Cooperation: Theory and Evidence from Electric Power Pools," *Southern Economic Journal*, 50: 1077–1097.

Geller, Howard, and Sophie Attali. 2005. "The Experience with Energy Efficiency Policies and Programmes in IEA Countries," International Energy Association, Paris, France, Working Paper, August.

Gellhorn, Ernest, and William E. Kovacic. 1994. *Antitrust Law and Economics in a Nutshell*, St. Paul, MN: West.

General Accounting Office, 1976. *Effectiveness, Benefits, and Costs of Federal Safety Standards for Protection of Passenger Car Occupants*, National Highway Traffic Safety Administration, United States Department of Transportation, CED-76–121, p. 42.

George, Anthony. 1973. "Second-Best Pricing and the U.S. Postal Service," Ph.D. Dissertation, University of Virginia.

Geradin, Damien. 2002. *The Liberalization of Postal Services in the European Union*, The Hague: Kluwer.

Gerard, David, and Lester B. Lave. 2003. "The Economics of CAFÉ Reconsidered: A Response to CAFÉ Critics and a Case for Fuel Economy Standards," *Regulatory Analysis*, October, 21: 3–10.

Gerber, David. 1988. "Rethinking the Monopolist's Duty to Deal: A Legal and Economic Critique of the Doctrine of Essential Facilities," *Virginia Law Review*, 14: 1069–1113.

Gertner, Robert H., and Robert S. Stillman. 2001. "Vertical Integration and Internet Strategies in the Apparel Industry," *Journal of Industrial Economics*, December, 49: 417–440.

Gilbert, Richard J. 2000. "Exclusive Dealing, Preferential Dealing, and Dynamic Efficiency," *Review of Industrial Organization*, March, 16: 167–184.

Gilbert, Richard J., and Edward P. Kahn. 1996. *International Comparisons of Electricity Regulation*, Cambridge, England: Cambridge University Press.

Gilbert, Richard J., and David Newberry. 1982. "Pre-emptive Patenting and the Persistence of Monopoly," *American Economic Review*, June, 72: 514–526.

Ginsburg, Douglas H. 1991. "Vertical Restraints: De Facto Legality Under the Rule of Reason," *Antitrust Law Journal*, 60: 67–83.

Glaeser, Edward, and Janet E. Kohlhase. 2004. "Cities, Regions, and the Decline of Transport Costs," *Papers in Regional Science*, 83: 197–228.

Glaeser, Edward, and Andrei Shleifer. 2003. "The Rise of the Regulatory State," *Journal of Economic Literature*, June, 41: 401–425.

Glendon, Mary Ann, and Edward R. Lev. 1979. "Changes in the Bonding of the Employment Relationship: An Essay on the New Property," *Boston College Law Review*, 20: 457–491.

Goetz, Charles J., and Fred S. McChesney. 1998. *Antitrust Law*, Charlottesville, Va.: Lexus Law.

Golbe, Devra L., and Lawrence J. White. 1988. "A Time Series Analysis of Mergers and Acquisitions in the U.S. Economy," in Alan J. Auerbach, ed., *Corporate Takeovers: Causes and Consequences*, Chicago: University of Chicago Press.

Golembe, C. H., and D. S. Holland. 1983. *Federal Regulation of Banking, 1983–84*, Washington, D.C.: Golembe Associates.

Goolsbee, Austan. 2001a. "The Implications of Electronic Commerce for Fiscal Policy (and Vice Versa)," *Journal of Economic Perspectives*, Winter, 15: 13–23.

Goolsbee, Austan. 2001b. "Competition in the Computer Industry," *Journal of Industrial Economics*, December, 49: 487–499.

Goolsbee, Austan. 2000. "The Impact of Taxes on Internet Commerce," *Quarterly Journal of Economics*, 115: 561–576.

Gompers, Paul, and Josh Lerner. 2001. "The Venture Capital Revolution," *Journal of Economic Perspectives*, Spring, 15: 145–168.

Gompers, Paul, and Andrew Metrick. 2001. "Institutional Investors and Equity Prices," *Quarterly Journal of Economics*, February, 116: 229–259.

Gompers, Paul, Joy Ishii, and Andrew Metrick. 2003. "Corporate Governance and Equity Prices," *Quarterly Journal of Economics*, February, 118: 107–155.

Gort, Michael, and Steven Klepper. 1882. "Time Paths in the Diffusion of Product Innovations," *Economic Journal*, September, 92: 630–653.

Grabowski, Henry, W. Kip Viscusi, and William Evans. 1989. "Price and Availability Trade-offs of Automobile Insurance Regulation," *Journal of Risk and Insurance*, 56: 275–299.

Gray, W. B., and C. A. Jones. 1991a. "Are OSHA Inspections Effective? A Longitudinal Study in the Manufacturing Sector," *Review of Economics and Statistics*, 73: 504–508.

Gray, W. B., and C. A. Jones. 1991b. "Longitudinal Patterns of Compliance with Occupational Safety and Health Administration Health and Safety Regulations in the Manufacturing Sector," *Journal of Human Resources*, 36: 623–653.

Green, Mark J. ed. 1973. *The Monopoly Makers*, New York: Grossman.

Green, Richard. 2006. "Restructuring the Electricity Industry in England and Wales," in Griffin and Puller, eds., *Electricity Deregulation: Where to From Here?* Chicago: University of Chicago Press.

Green, Richard J., and David M. Newbery. 1992. "Competition in the British Electricity Spot Market," *Journal of Political Economy*, October, 100: 929–953.

Greene, Graham. 1986. *The Tenth Man*, New York: Simon and Schuster.

Greenstein, Shane. 2000. "The Evolving Structure of Commercial Internet Markets," in Eric Brynjolfsson and Brian Kahin, eds., *Understanding the Digital Economy*, pp. 295–324, Cambridge, Mass.: MIT Press.

Greenstein, Shane, and James B. Wade. 1998. "The Product Life Cycle in the Commercial Mainframe Computer Market, 1968–1983" *RAND Journal of Economics*, 29: 772–789.

Greenstein, Shane, Susan McMaster, and Pablo T. Spiller. 1995. "The Effect of Incentive Regulation on Infrastructure Modernization: Local Exchange Companies' Deployment of Digital Technology," *Journal of Economics and Management Strategy*, 4: 187–236.

Gregory, Paul, and Robert Stuart. 1998. *Russian and Soviet Economic Structure and Performance*, Reading, Mass.: Addison Wesley.

Griffin, James M. 1985. "OPEC Behavior: A Test of Alternative Hypotheses," *American Economic Review*, 75: 954–963.

Griffin, James M., and Steven Puller, eds. 2006. *Electricity Deregulation: Where to From Here?* Chicago: University of Chicago Press.

Griffin, James M., and David J. Teece, eds. 1982. *OPEC Behavior and World Oil Prices*, London: George Allen and Unwin.

Griffin, James M., and Weiwen Xiong. 1997. "The Incentive to Cheat: An Empirical Analysis of OPEC," *Journal of Law and Economics*, 40: 289–316.

Griliches, Zvi. 1958. "Research Costs and Social Returns: Hybrid Corn and Related Innovations," *Journal of Political Economy*, October, 66: 419–431.

Grimm, Curtis, and Clifford Winston. 2000. "Competition in the Deregulated Railroad Industry: Sources, Effects, and Policy Issues," in Sam Peltzman and Clifford Winston, eds. 2000. *Deregulation of Network Industries: What's Next?* Washington, D.C.: AEI-Brookings

Grossman, Gene M., and Elhanan Helpman. 2001. *Special Interest Politics*, Cambridge, Mass.: MIT Press.

Grossman, Sanford J., and Joseph E. Stiglitz. 1980. "On the Impossibility of Informationally Efficient Markets," *American Economic Review*, 70: 393–408.

Hackl, Jo Watson, and Rosa Anna Testani. 1988. "Note: Second Generation State Takeover Statutes and Shareholder Wealth: An Empirical Study," *Yale Law Journal*, 97: 1193–1231.

Hahn, Robert, and Gordon L. Hester. 1987. "The Market for Bids: EPA Experience with

Emissions Trading," *Regulation*, 11(4): 48–53.

Hall, Sir Robert, and Charles J. Hitch. 1939. "Pricing Theory and Business Behavior." *Oxford Economic Papers*, May, 2: 12–45.

Hall, Brian J., and Jeffrey B. Liebman. 2000. "The Taxation of Executive Compensation," Working Paper, National Bureau of Economic Research, Boston,

Hall, Brian J., and Jeffrey B. Liebman. 1998. "Are CEOs Really Paid Like Bureaucrats?," *Quarterly Journal of Economics*, 112: 653–691.

Hall, Bronwyn H., and Rosemary Ham Ziedonis. 2001. "The Patent Paradox Revisited: An Empirical Study of Patenting in the U.S. Semiconductor Industry, 1979–1995," *RAND Journal of Economics*, 32: 101–128.

Ham, Mikel Rex. 1998. "Rental Car Service Tenure and Downstream Vertical Integration in the Automobile Industry," Ph.D. Dissertation, University of Virginia.

Hamilton, James D. 1983. "Oil and the Macroeconomy Since World War II," *Journal of Political Economy*, April, 91: 228–248.

Hannan, Timothy H., and J. Nellie Liang. 1993. "Inferring Market Power from Time-Series Data: The Case of the Banking Firm," *International Review of Industrial Organization*, June, 11: 205–218.

Harris, Milton, and Arthur Raviv. 1981. "Monopoly Pricing Schemes with Demand Uncertainty," *American Economic Review*, 71: 347–365.

Harrison, G. W., and M. McKee. 1985. "Monopoly Behavior, Decentralized Regulation, and Contestable Markets, An Experimental Evaluation," *RAND Journal of Economics*, 16: 51–69.

Hart, Oliver. 2001. "Financial Contracting," *Journal of Economic Literature*, December, 39: 1079–1100.

Hartman, Raymond S. 2001. "Price-Performance Competition and the Merger Guidelines," *Review of Industrial Organization*, February, 18: 53–75.

Hastings, Justine S. 2004. "Vertical Relationships and Competition in Retail Gasoline Markets: Empirical Evidence from Contract Changes in Southern California," *American Economic Review*, March, 94: 317–328.

Hausman, Jerry A., and Gregory K. Leonard. 2002. "The Competitive Effects of New Product Introduction: a Case Study," *Journal of Industrial Economics*, September, 50: 237–263.

Hausman, Jerry A., and J. Gregory Sidak. 2005. "Did Mandatory Unbundling Achieve Its Purpose? Empirical Evidence from Five Countries," *Journal of Competition Law and Economics*, 1: 173–245.

Hausman, Jerry A., and J. Gregory Sidak. 2002. "Do Long-Distance Carriers Price Discriminate Against the Poor and the Less-Educated?" Working Paper, American Enterprise Institute, Washington, D.C.

Hausman, Jerry A., J. Gregory Sidak, and Hal J. Singer. 2001. "Cable Modems and DSL: Broadband Internet Access for Residential Customers," *American Economic Review*, May, 91: 302–307.

Hausman, Jerry A., Timothy Tardiff, and Alexander Belinfante. 1993. "The Effects of the Breakup of AT&T on Telephone Penetration in the United States, *American Economic Review*, May, 83: 178–184.

Hausman, W. J., and J. L. Neufeld. 1984. "Time-of-Day Pricing in the U.S. Electric Power Industry at the Turn of the Century," *RAND Journal of Economics*, 15: 116–126.

Hawley, Ellis W. 1966. *The New Deal and the Problem of Monopoly*, Princeton, N.J.: Princeton University Press.

Hay, George A. 2000. "The Meaning of 'Agreement' under the Sherman Act: Thoughts from the 'Facilitating Practices' Experience," *Review of Industrial Organization*, March, 16: 113–129.

Hayes, Kathy J., and Leola Ross. 1996. "Measuring Changes in Multiproduct Market Structure: An Application to Airlines," *Review of Industrial Organization*, 11: 493–509.

Haynes, Peter. 1993. "Survey: Telecommunications," *The Economist*, October 23: p. 7.

Hazlett, T. 1998. "Assigning Property Rights to Radio Spectrum Users: Why Did the FCC License Auctions Take 67 Years?" *Journal of Law and Economics*, 41: 529–575.

Heilbroner, Robert L. 1977. *The Economic Transformation of America*, New York: Harcourt Brace Jovanovich.

Heilbroner, Robert L. 1962. *The Making of Economic Society*, Englewood Cliffs, N. J.: Prentice-Hall.

Hendricks, Ken, Michelle Piccione, and Guofu Tan. 1997. "Entry and Exit into Hub-Spoke Networks," *RAND Journal of Economics*, 28: 291–303.

Henning, Bruce, Lee Tucker, and Cindy Liu. 1995. "Productivity Improvements in the Natural Gas Distribution and Transmission Industry," *Gas Energy Review*, February, 23: 17–20.

Herbert, John H. 1996. *The Emergence of Natural Gas Market Centers*. August. Washington, D.C.: Energy Information Administration, U.S. Department of Energy.

Heron, Randall A., and Erik Lie. 2007. "Does Backdating Explain the Stock Price Pattern Around Executive Stock Option Grants?" *Journal of Financial Economics*, 83: 271–295.

Higgins, Richard S. 1997. "Diagonal Merger," *Review of Industrial Organization*, August, 12: 609–623.

Hill, J. E. Christopher. 1961. *The Century of Revolution 1603–1714*, Edinburgh: Thomas Nelson and Sons.

Hilts, Philip J. 2002. *Protecting America's Health: The FDA, Business, and One Hundred Years of Regulation*, New York: Adolph A. Knopf.

Hirshleifer, Jack. 1971. "The Private and Social Value of Information and the Reward to Inventive Activity," *American Economic Review*, September, 61: 561–574.

Hofstadter, Richard. 1955. *The Age of Reform*, New York: Alfred A. Knopf.

Holliday, Andrew, Jackson. 1995. "The Definition and Measurement of Antitrust Enforcement," Ph.D. dissertation, University of Virginia.

Holmes, Thomas J. 2001. "Bar Codes Lead to Frequent Deliveries and Superstores," University of Minnesota Working Paper, July.

Holstrom, Bengt, and Steven N. Kaplan. 2001. "Corporate Governance and Merger Activity in the United States: Making Sense of the 1980s and 1990s," *Journal of Economic Perspectives*, Spring, 15: 121–144.

Holt, Charles A. 2007. *Markets, Games, and Strategic Behavior*, Boston: Addison-Wesley.

Holt, Charles A., L. Langan, and A. Villamil. 1986. "Market Power in Double Oral Auctions," *Economic Inquiry*, January, 24: 107–123.

Holt, Charles, and Roger Sherman. 1999. "The Market for Lemons," *Journal of Economic Perspectives*, Winter, 13: 205–214.

Holt, Charles, and Roger Sherman. 1990. "Advertising and Product Quality in Posted-Offer Experiments," *Economic Inquiry*, 28: 39–56.

Hood, Christopher, Henry Rothstein, and Robert Baldwin. 2001. *The Government of Risk: Understanding Risk Regulation Regimes*, Oxford, England: Oxford University Press.

Horowitz, Morton J. 1977. *The Transformation of American Law*, Cambridge, Mass.: Harvard University Press.

Hotelling, Harold. 1929. "Stability in Competition," *Economic Journal*, 39: 41–57.

Houthakker, Hedrik H. 1951. "Electricity Tariffs in Theory and Practice," *Economic Journal*, 61: 1–25.

Howard, Michael. 1976. *War in European History*, London: Oxford University Press.

Hughes, Thomas P. 1989. *American Genius: A Century of Invention and Technological Enthusiasm, 1870–1970*, New York: Viking.

Huneke, William F. 1983. *The Heavy Hand: Government and the Union Pacific, 1862–1898*, New York: Garland.

Hutt, William H. 1964. *The Economics of the Colour Bar*, London: Andre Deutsch.

Ippolito, Richard A. 2001. "Reversion Taxes, Contingent Benefits, and the Decline in Pension Funding," *Journal of Law and Economics*, April, 44: 199–232.

Ippolito, Richard A. 1998. *Pension Plans and Employee Performance*, Chicago: University of Chicago Press.

Ippolito, Richard A. 1985. "The Labor Contract and True Economic Pension Liabilities," *American Economic Review*, 75: 1031–1043.

Jaffe, Adam B. 2000. "The U.S. Patent System in Transition: Policy Innovation and the Innovation Process," *Research Policy*, 29: 531–537.

Jaffe, Adam, Josh Lerner, and Scott Stern, eds. 2001. *Innovation Policy and the Economy*, Vol. 2. Cambridge, Mass.: MIT Press.

James, John A. 1978. *Money and Capital Markets in Postbellum America*, Princeton, N.J.: Princeton University Press.

Jenks, L. H. 1944. "Railroads as an Economic Force in American Development," *Journal of Economic History*, IV, May, 1: 1–20.

Jensen, Michael C. 1993. "The Modern Industrial Revolution," *Journal of Finance*, 48: 831–880.

Jensen, Michael C. 1988. "Takeovers: Their Causes and Consequences," *Journal of Economic Perspectives*, 2: 21–48.

Jensen, Michael C., and W. H. Mechling. 1976. "Theory of the Firm: Managerial Behavior, Agency Costs, and Ownership Structure," *Journal of Financial Economics*, 3: 305–360.

Jewkes, John, David Sawers, and Richard Stillerman. 1959. *The Sources of Invention*, New York: St. Martin.

Jin, Ginger Zhe, and Phillip Leslie. 2003. "The Effect of Information on Product Quality: Evidence from Restaurant Hygiene Grade Cards," *Quarterly Journal of Economics*, May, 118: 409–451.

Johnson, Bruce K. 1984. "Regulation of the Intercity Bus Industry: A Comparison of the Public Interest Theory and the Economic Theory of Regulation," Ph.D. dissertation, University of Virginia.

Johnson, Simon, John McMillan, and Christopher Woodruff. 2002. "Property Rights and Finance," *American Economic Review*, December, 92: 1335–1356.

Johnston, John. 1960. *Statistical Cost Analysis*, New York: McGraw-Hill.

Jones, Fred. 1983. *Input Biases under Rate-of-Return Regulation*, New York: Garland Press.

Jones, Leroy P. 1985. "Public Enterprise in Less-Developed Countries," *The Economic Journal*, December, 95: 1133–1134.

Jordan, W. A. 1972. "Producer Protection, Prior Market Structure and the Effects of Government Regulation," *Journal of Law and Economics*, 15: 151–176.

Josephson, Matthew. 1934. *The Robber Barons*, New York: Harcourt, Brace and World.

Joskow, Paul L. 2006. "The Difficult Transition to Competitive Electricity Markets in the U.S.," in James M. Griffin and Steven Puller, eds., *Electricity Deregulation: Where to From Here*, Chicago: University of Chicago Press.

Joskow, Paul. 2001. "California's Energy Crisis," *Oxford Review of Economic Policy*, Autumn, 17: 365–388.

Joskow, Paul. 2000. "Deregulation and Regulatory Reform in the U.S. Electric Power Sector," in Sam Peltzman and Clifford Winston, eds. *Deregulation of Network Industries: What's Next?* Washington, D.C.: AEI-Brookings.

Joskow, Paul L. 1997. "Restructuring, Competition and Regulatory Reform in the U.S. Electricity Sector," *Journal of Economic Perspectives*, Summer, 11: 119–138.

Joskow, Paul L. 1987. "Contract Duration and Relation-Specific Investments: Empirical Evidence from Coal Markets," *American Economic Review*, 77: 168–185.

Joskow, Paul L. 1974. "Inflation and Environmental Concern: Structural Changes in the Process of Public Utility Regulation," *Journal of Law and Economics*, 17: 291–327.

Joskow, Paul L. 1973. "Pricing Decisions of Regulated Firms: A Behavioral Approach," *Bell Journal of Economics*, 4: 118–140.

Joskow, Paul L. 1972. "The Determinants of the Allowed Rate of Return in a Formal Regulatory Hearing," *Bell Journal of Economics*, 3: 632–644.

Joskow, Paul L., and Edward Kahn. 2002. "A Quantitative Analysis of Pricing Behavior in California's Wholesale Electricity Market During Summer 2000," *Energy Journal*, 23: 1–35.

Joskow, Paul L., and Jean Tirole. 2000. "Transmission Rights and Market Power on Electric Power Networks," *RAND Journal of Economics*, Autumn, 31: 450–487.

Joskow, Paul L., and Alvin K. Klevorick. 1979. "A Framework for Analyzing Predatory Pricing Policy," *Yale Law Journal*, 89: 213–270.

Jovanovic, Boyan. 1982a. "Selection and the Evolution of Industry," *Econometrica*, 50: 649–670.

Jovanovic, Boyan. 1982b. "Truthful Disclosure of Information," *Bell Journal of Economics*, Spring, 13: 36–44.

Jovanovic, Boyan, and Serguey Braguinsky. 2004. "Bidder Discounts and Target Premia in Takeovers," *American Economic Review*, March, 94: 46–56.

Jovanovic, Boyan, and Glenn M. McDonald. 1994a. "The Life Cycle of a Competitive Industry," *Journal of Political Economy*, April, 102: 322–347.

Jovanovic, Boyan, and Glenn M. McDonald. 1994b. "Competitive Diffusion," *Journal of Political Economy*, February, 102: 29–52.

Jovanovic, Boyan, and Yaw Nyarko. 1996. "Learning by Doing and the Choice of Technology," *Econometrica*, November, 64: 1299–1310.

Kahn, Alfred E. 1970. "The Future of Local Telephone Service: Technology and Public Policy," University of Pennsylvania, Wharton School Discussion Paper.

Kahn, Alfred E. 1959. "Pricing Objectives in Large Companies: Comment." *American Economic Review*, September, 49: 674–680.

Kahn, Alfred E., Peter C. Cramton, Robert H. Porter, and Richard D. Tabors. 2001. "Uniform Pricing or Pay-as-Bid Pricing: A Dilemma for California and Beyond," *Electricity Journal*, July, 14: 70–79.

Kaldor, Nicholas. 1939. "Welfare Propositions of Economics and Interpersonal Comparisons of Utility," *Economic Journal*, September, 49: 1–27.

Kamien, Morton I. 1992. "Patent Licensing," in Robert J. Aumann and S. Hart eds., *Handbook of Game Theory*, Amsterdam, The Netherlands: North Holland/Elsevier.

Kamien, Morton I., and Nancy Schwartz. 1982. *Market Structure and Innovation*, Cambridge, England: Cambridge University Press.

Kamien, Morton I., Nancy L. Schwartz, and F. Trenery Dolbear, Jr. 1966. "Asymmetry between Bribes and Charges," *Water Resources Research*, 2: 147–157.

Kane, Edward J. 1989. *The S and L Insurance Mess: How Did It Happen?* Washington, D.C.: Urban Institute Press.

Kaplan, A. D. H., Joel B. Dirlam, and Robert F. Lanzillotti. 1958. *Pricing in Big Business*, Washington, D.C.: Brookings Institution.

Karkkainen, Bradley C. 2001. "Information as Environmental Regulation: TRI and Performance Benchmarking, Precursor to a New Paradigm?" *Georgetown Law Journal*, 89: 257–370.

Katz, Michael L. 2002. "Recent Antitrust Enforcement Actions by the U.S. Department of Justice: A Selective Survey of Economic Issues," *Review of Industrial Organization*, December, 21: 373–397.

Kay, John A., and D. J. Thompson. 1986. "Privatization: A Policy in Search of a Rationale," *Economic Journal*, 96: 18–32.

Kay, John A., C. Mayer, and D. J. Thompson. 1986. *Privatisation and Regulation—The UK Experience*, Oxford: Clarendon.

Kearney, Joseph D., and Thomas W. Merrill. 1998. "The Great Transformation of Regulated Industries Law," *Columbia Law Review*, October, 98: 1323–1409.

Keeler, Theodore E. 1994. "Highway Safety, Economic Behavior, and Driving Environment," *American Economic Review*, June, 84: 684–693.

Keeler, Theodore E. 1972. "Airline Regulation and Market Performance," *Bell Journal of Economics*, Autumn 3: 399–424.

Keeler, Theodore E. 1971. "The Economics of Passenger Trains," *Journal of Business*, 44: 148–174.

Keeler, Theodore E., and Kenneth A. Small, "Optimal Peak-Load Pricing, Investment, and Service Levels on Urban Expressways. 1977. "*Journal of Political Economy*, 85: 1–25.

Kehoe, Michael. 1989. "The Choice of Format and Advertising Time in Radio Broadcasting," Ph.D. dissertation, University of Virginia.

Keran, M. W. 1976. "Inflation, Regulation and Utility Stock Prices," *Bell Journal of Economics*, 7: 268–274.

Keyes, Lucille S. *Federal Control of Entry into Transportation*, Cambridge, Mass.: Harvard University Press, 1951.

Kim, Han E., and Vijay Singal. 1993. "Mergers and Market Power: Evidence from the Airline Industry," *American Economic Review*, 83: 549–569.

King, Ross. 2000. *Brunelleschi's Dome*, London: Chatto and Windus.

King, Willford I. 1939. "Can Production of Automobiles Be Stabilized by Making Their Prices Flexible?" *Journal of the American Statistical Society*, December, 34: 641–651.

Kirzner, Israel. 1973. *Competition and Entrepreneurship*, Chicago,: University of Chicago Press.

Kitch, Edmund W. 1980. "The Law and Economics of Rights in Valuable Information," *Journal of Legal Studies*, 9: 683–723.

Klein, Benjamin. 2000. "Fisher-General Motors and the Nature of the Firm," *Journal of Law and Economics*, April, 43: 105–141.

Klein, Benjamin, Robert G. Crawford, and Armen A. Alchian. 1978. "Vertical Integration, Appropriable Rents, and the Competitive Contracting Process," *Journal of Law and Economics*, 21: 297–326.

Kleit, Andrew N. ed. 2006. *Electric Choices: Deregulation and the Future of Electric Power,* Oakland, Calif.: The Independent Institute.

Kleit, Andrew N. 2001. "Creating a Public Good to Fight Monopolization: The Formation of Broadcast Music, Inc.," *Review of Industrial Organization,* September, 19: 243–256.

Kleit, Andrew N., and Timothy Considine. 2006. "Restructuring in California and Pennsylvania," in Andrew N. Kleit ed. *Electric Choices: Deregulation and the Future of Electric Power,* Oakland, Calif.: The Independent Institute.

Knight, Frank H. 1924. "Some Fallacies in the Interpretation of Social Cost," *Quarterly Journal of Economics,* August, 38: 291–293.

Koeppel, Gerard T. 2000. *Water for Gotham: A History,* Princeton, N.J.: Princeton University Press.

Kohaner, Larry. 1986. *On the Line,* New York: Warner Books.

Kohlhase, Janet E. 1991. "The Impact of Toxic Waste Sites on Housing Values," *Journal of Urban Economics,* 30: 1–26.

Kolbe, A. L., J. A. Read, and G. R. Hall. 1985. *The Cost of Capital: Estimating the Rate of Return for Public Utilities,* Cambridge, Mass.: MIT Press.

Kolko, Gabriel. 1965. *Railroads and Regulation, 1877–1916,* Princeton, N.J.: Princeton University Press.

Kolko, Gabriel. 1963. *The Triumph of Conservatism, 1900–1916,* New York: The Free Press.

Kovacic, William E. 1993. "The Identification and Proof of Horizontal Agreements under the Antitrust Laws," *Antitrust Bulletin,* 38: 31–55.

Kovacic, William E. 1992. "The Antitrust Law and Economics of Essential Facilities in Public Utility Regulation," in Michael A. Crew ed. *Economic Innovations in Public Utility Regulation,* Dordrecht: Kluwer.

Kovacic, William E., and Carl Shapiro. 2000. "Antitrust Policy: A Century of Economic and Legal Thinking," *Journal of Economic Perspectives,* Winter, 14: 43–60.

Kremer, Michael. 1998. "Patent Buyouts: A Mechanism for Encouraging Innovation," *Quarterly Journal of Economics,* November, 113: 1137–1167.

Kreps, David M., and Jose Scheinkman. 1983. "Quantity Precommitment and Bertrand Competition Yield Cournot Outcomes, *Bell Journal of Economics,* Autumn, 2: 326–337.

Krieger, Linda Hamilton. 1995. "Content of Our Categories: A Cognitive Bias Approach to Discrimination and Equal Employment Opportunity," *Stanford Law Review,* 47: 1161–1248.

Krotoszynski, Ronald J., Jr. 2002. "Expropriatory Intent: Defining the Proper Boundaries of Substantive Due Process and the Takings Clause," *North Carolina Law Review,* March, 80: 713–772.

Krueger, Alan B., and Alexandre Mas. 2004. "Strikes, Scabs, and Tread Separations: Labor Strife and the Production of Defective Bridgestone/Firestone Tires," *Journal of Political Economy,* April, 112: 253–289.

Kwerel, Evan, Jonathan Levy, Robert Pepper, David Sappington, Donald Stockdale, and John Williams. 2002. "Economic Issues at the Federal Communications Commission," *Review of Industrial Organization,* December, 21: 337–356.

Kwoka, John E., Jr. 2005. "Electric Power Distribution Economies of Scale, Mergers, and Restructuring," *Applied Economics,* 32: 2373–2386.

Kwoka, John E., Jr. 2001. "Automobiles: The Old Economy Collides with the New," *Review of Industrial Organization,* August, 19: 55–69.

Kwoka, John E., Jr. 1998. "Automobiles: Overtaking an Oligopoly," in Larry L. Duetsch ed. *Industry Studies,* New York: M. E. Sharpe.

Kwoka, John E., Jr. 1997. "Transforming Power: Lessons from British Electricity Restructuring," *Regulation,* Summer, 20: 42–49.

Kwoka, John E., Jr., and David J. Ravenscraft. 1986. "Cooperation v. Rivalry: Price-Cost Margins by Line of Business," *Economica,* 53: 351–363.

Kwoka, John E., Jr., and Lawrence J. White, eds., 1999. *The Antitrust Revolution: Economics, Competition, and Policy,* 3rd ed., New York: Oxford University Press.

Kwoka, John E., Jr., and Lawrence J. White, eds. 1994. *The Antitrust Revolution: The Role of Economics,* New York: Harper Collins.

Laffont, Jean-Jacques, and David Martimort. 2002. *The Theory of Incentives,* Princeton, N.J.: Princeton University Press.

Laffont, Jean-Jacques, and Jean Tirole. 2000. *Competition in Telecommunications*, Cambridge, Mass.: MIT Press.

Laffont, Jean-Jacques, and Jean Tirole. 1998a. "Network Competition: I. Overview and Nondiscriminatory Pricing," *RAND Journal of Economics*, 29: 1–37.

Laffont, Jean-Jacques, and Jean Tirole. 1998b. "Network Competition: II. Price Discrimination," *RAND Journal of Economics*, 29: 38–56.

Laffont, Jean-Jacques, and Jean Tirole. 1996. "Creating Competition through Interconnection: Theory and Practice," *Journal of Regulatory Economics*, 10: 227–256.

Laffont, Jean-Jacques, and Jean Tirole. 1987. "Auctioning Incentive Contracts," *Journal of Political Economy*, 95: 921–937.

Laffont, Jean-Jacques, and Jean Tirole. 1986. "Using Cost Observations to Regulate Firms," *Journal of Political Economy*, 94: 614–641.

Laffont, Jean-Jacques, Scott Marcus, Patrick Rey, and J. Tirole. 2001. "Internet Peering," *American Economic Review*, May, 91: 287–291.

Lafontaine, Francine. 1993. "Contractual Arrangements as Signaling Devices: Evidence from Franchising," *Journal of Law, Economics, and Organization*, October, 9: 256–289.

Landes, William M., and Richard A. Posner. 1989. "An Economic Analysis of Copyright Law," *Journal of Legal Studies*, 28: 325–363.

Landes, William M., and Richard A. Posner. 1987. "Trademark Law: An Economic Perspective," *Journal of Law and Economics*, 30: 265–309.

Lang, Kevin. 1986. "A Language Theory of Discrimination," *Quarterly Journal of Economics*, 101: 363–382.

Lang, Robert E. 2003. *Edgeless Cities: Exploring the Elusive Metropolis*, Washington, D.C.: Brookings Institution Press.

Langlois, Richard N., and Nicolai J. Foss. 1999. "Capabilities and Governance: The Rebirth of Production in the Theory of Economic Organization," *Kyklos*, 52: 201–218, Fasc. 2.

Lanjouw, Jean, and Josh Lerner. 2001. "Tilting the Table? The Use of Preliminary Injunctions," *Journal of Law and Economics*, 44: 573–603.

Lanzillotti, Robert F. 1958. "Pricing Objectives in Large Companies." *American Economic Review*, December, 48: 921–940.

Lasok, D., and J. W. Bridge. 1973. *An Introduction to the Law and Institutions of the European Communities*, London: Butterworth.

Lave, Lester B., and Eugene P. Seskin. 1970. "Air Pollution and Human Health," August 21, *Science*, 19: 723–733.

Lave, Lester B., and W. E. Weber, 1970. "A Benefit-Cost Analysis of Auto Safety Features," *Applied Economics*, October, 4: 265–275.

Lebowitz, J. L., C. O. Lee, and P. B. Linhart. 1976. "Some Effects of Inflation on a Firm with Original Cost Depreciation," *Bell Journal of Economics*, 7: 463–477.

Lee, Darin. 2003. "An Assessment of Some Recent Criticisms of the U.S. Airline Industry," *Review of Network Economics*, March, 2: 1–9.

Lee, Francis E., and Bruce I. Oppenheimer. 1999. *Sizing Up the Senate*, Chicago: University of Chicago Press.

Lenard, Thomas M. 1999. Statement at FTC Workshop on Market Power and Consumer Protection Issues Involved with Encouraging Competition in the Electric Utility Industry, September 13, Federal Trade Commission, Washington, D.C.

Lereah, David A. 1985. *Insurance Markets: Information Problems and Regulation*, New York: Praeger.

Lerner, Josh. 1995. "Patenting in the Shadow of Competitors," *Journal of Law and Economics*, 38: 463–495.

Lerner, Josh. 1994. "The Importance of Patent Scope: An Empirical Analysis," *RAND Journal of Economics*, 25: 319–333.

Lerner, Josh, and Jean Tirole. 2002. "Some Simple Economics of Open Source," *Journal of Industrial Economics*, June, 50: 197–234.

Lessig, Lawrence. 2001. *The Future of Ideas: The Fate of the Commons in a Connected World*, New York: Random House.

Lessig, Lawrence. 1999. *Code: And Other Laws of Cyberspace*, New York: Basic Books.

Lessig, Lawrence. 1956. *Man of High Fidelity: Edwin Howard Armstrong*, Philadelphia: Lippincott.

Letwin, William. 1965. *Law and Economic Policy in America*, New York: Random House.

Lev, Baruch, and Doron Nissim. 2002. "Taxable Income As an Indicator of Earnings Quality," N.Y.U. Stern School, Working Paper, November, 2002.

Levenstein, Margaret C., and Valerie Y. Suslow. 2006. "What Determines Cartel Success?" *Journal of Economic Literature*, March, 54: 43–95.

Levin, Richard C., Alvin K. Klevorick, Richard R. Nelson, and Sidney G. Winter. 1987. "Appropriating the Returns from Industrial Research and Development," *Brookings Papers on Economic Activity*, 3: 783–820.

Levine, Michael E. 2002. "Price Discrimination Without Market Power," *Yale Journal on Regulation*, Winter, 19: 1–36.

Levine, Michael E. 1987. "Airline Competition in Deregulated Markets: Theory, Firm Strategy, and Public Policy," *Yale Journal on Regulation*, Spring, 4: 393–494.

Levitan, R., and Martin Shubik. 1972. "Price Duopoly and Capacity Constraints," *International Economic Review*, 13: 111–122.

Lewis, Michael. 2006. *The Blind Side: Evolution of a Game*. New York: W. W. Norton.

Lieber, James B. 2000. *Rats in the Grain: The Dirty Tricks and Trials of Archer Daniels Midland*, New York: Four Walls Eight Windows.

Liebermen, Marvin B. 1987. "Patents, Learning by Doing, and Market Structure in the Chemical Processing Industries," *International Journal of Industrial Organization*, 5: 257–276.

Lindsay, Cotton M. 1976. "A Theory of Government Enterprise," *Journal of Political Economy*, October, 84: 1061–1078.

Lindsey, Robin. 2006. "Do Economists Reach a Conclusion on Road Pricing? The Intellectual History of an Idea," *Econ Journal Watch*, May, 3: 292–379.

Lipsey, Richard, and Kelvin Lancaster. 1956. "The General Theory of Second Best," *Review of Economic Studies*, January, 24:11–32.

Lipsky, Abbott B., Jr., and J. Gregory Sidak. 1999. "Essential Facilities," *Stanford Law Review*, May, 51: 1187–1248.

Litan, Robert E., and Alice M. Rivlin. 2001. "Projecting the Economic Impact of the Internet," *American Economic Review*, May, 91: 313–317.

Littlechild, Stephen C. 2003. "Reflections on Incentive Regulation," *Review of Network Economics*, 2: 289–315.

Littlechild, Stephen C., and J. J. Rousseau. 1975. "Pricing Policy of a U.S. Telephone Company," *Journal of Public Economics*, 4: 35–46.

Locay, Luis, and Alvaro Rodriguez. 1992. "Price Discrimination in Competitive Markets," *Journal of Political Economy*, October, 100: 954–965.

Lofgren, D. J., 1989. *Dangerous Premises: An Insiders Perspective of OSHA Enforcement*, Ithaca, NY: ILR Press.

Long, William F., and David J. Ravenscraft. 1984. "The Misuse of Accounting Rates of Return: Comment," *American Economic Review*, June, 74: 494–500.

Long, William F., Richard Schramm and Robert D. Tollison. 1973. "The Economic Determinants of Antitrust Activity," *Journal of Law and Economics*, 16: 351–364.

Longstaff, Patricia Hirl. 1999. "Regulating Communications in the 21st Century: New Common Ground," in Benjamin M. Compaine and William H. Read, eds. *The Information Resources Policy Handbook*, Cambridge, Mass.: MIT Press.

Luce, R. Duncan, and Howard Raiffa. 1957. *Games and Decisions: Introduction and Critical Survey*, New York: John Wiley & Sons.

Lucking-Reiley, David, and Daniel F. Spulber. 2001. "Business-to-Business Electronic Commerce," *Economic Perspectives*, Winter, 15: 55–68.

Lynch, J. G., Jr., and D. Ariely. 1998. "Interactive Home Shopping: Effects of Search Cost for Price and Quality Information on Consumer Price Sensitivity, Satisfaction with Merchandise, and Retention," INFORMS College of Marketing Mini-Conference on Marketing Science and the Internet, Cambridge, Mass., March 6–8.

Machlup, Fritz. 1968. "Patent," *International Encyclopedia of the Social Sciences*, vol. 11. New York: Crowell Crown and Macmillan, pp. 461–472.

Magat, Wesley A. 1976. "Regulation and the Rate and Direction of Induced Technological Change," *Bell Journal of Economics*, 7: 478–496.

Maine, Henry S. 1920. *Ancient Law*, London: John Murray.

Maloney, M. T., R. E. McCormick, and Robert D. Tollison. 1984. "Economic Regulation, Competitive Governments, and Specialized Resources," *Journal of Law and Economics*, 27: 329–338.

Mann, Michael. 1966. "Seller Concentration, Barriers to Entry, and the Rates of Return in Thirty Industries, 1950–1960" *Review of Economic Statistics*, 48: 290–307.

Mansfield, Edwin. 1968. *Industrial Research and Technological Innovation: An Econometric Analysis*, New York: W. W. Norton.

Mansfield, Edwin. 1964. "Industrial Research Expenditures: Determinants, Prospects, and Relation to Size of Firm and Inventive Output," *Journal of Political Economy*, August, 72: 319–340.

Mansfield, Edwin. 1963. "Size of Firm, Market Structure, and Innovation" *Journal of Political Economy*, December, 71: 556–576.

Mansfield, Edwin. 1961. "Technical Change and the Rate of Imitation," *Econometrica*, October, 29: 741–766.

Marais, Laurentius, Katherine Schipper, and Abbie Smith. 1989. "Wealth Effects of Going Private on Senior Securities," *Journal of Financial Economics*, 23: 155–191.

March, James G., and Herbert A. Simon. 1958. *Organizations*, New York: John Wiley.

Mariotti, Renato. 2000. "Rethinking Software Tying," *Yale Journal on Regulation*, Summer, 17: 367–406.

Markham, Jesse W. 1957. "The duPont–General Motors Decision," *Virginia Law Review*, 43: 881–888.

Markham, Jesse W. 1951. "The Nature and Significance of Price Leadership," *American Economic Review*, December, 41: 891–905.

Marshall, Alfred. 1920. *Principles of Economics*, London: Macmillan.

Martin, Albro. 1974. "The Troubled Subject of Railroad Regulation in the Gilded Age—A Reappraisal." *The Journal of American History*, September, 61: 339–371.

Martin, Stephen, Hans-Theo Normann, and Christopher M. Snyder. 2001. "Vertical Foreclosure in Experimental Markets," *RAND Journal of Economics*, Autumn, 32: 466–496.

Marx, Karl H. 1928 (1867). *Capital*, trans. by Eden and Cedar Paul. London: George Allen and Unwin.

Mason, Edward S. 1968. "Corporation," in *International Encyclopedia of the Social Sciences*, Vol. 3. New York: Crowell Collier and Macmillan.

Masten, Scott E., and Edward Snyder. 1993. "United States v. United Shoe Machinery Corporation: On the Merits," *Journal of Law and Economics*, 36: 33–70.

Mazon, Cristina, and Pedro Pereira. 2002. "Some Trade-offs of Electronic Commerce," Working Paper, Universidad Carlos III de Madrid, Spain.

May, James. 1990. "The Role of States in the First Century of the Sherman Act and the Larger Picture of Antitrust History," *Antitrust Law Journal*, 93: 59–107.

McAfee, R. Preston, and John McMillan. 1987a. "Auctions and Bidding," *Journal of Economic Literature*, 25: 699–738.

McAfee, R. Preston, and John McMillan. 1987b. "Competition for Agency Contracts," *RAND Journal of Economics*, Summer, 18: 296–307.

McAfee, R. Preston, Hugo M. Mialon, and Michael A. Williams. 2004. "What Is a Barrier to Entry?" *American Economic Review*, May, 94: 461–465.

McChesney, Fred S., and William F. Shugart II. 1995. *The Causes and Consequences of Antitrust*, Chicago: University of Chicago Press.

McCormick, Robert E., William F. Shugart, II, and Robert D. Tollison. 1984. "The Disinterest in Deregulation," *American Economic Review*, 74: 1075–1079.

McDonald, John. 1950. *Strategy in Poker, Business and War*. New York: W. W. Norton.

McDonald, Stephen L. 1971. *Petroleum Conservation in the United States: An Economic Analysis*, Baltimore,: Johns Hopkins University Press.

McEachern, William A. 1975. *Managerial Control and Performance*, Lexington, Mass.: D.C. Heath.

McKean, Roland N., and John H. Moore. 1972. "Uncertainty and the Evaluation of Public Investment Decisions: Comment," *American Economic Review*, 62: 165–167.

McKibben, Bill. 2003. "Our Thirsty Future," *New York Review of Books*, September, 50: 58–60.

McManis, Charles R. 1992. *Unfair Trade Practices in a Nutshell*, 3rd ed. St. Paul, MN: West Publishing.

McManus, Brian. 2001. "Two-Part Pricing with Costly Arbitrage," *Southern Economic Journal*, October, 68: 369–386.

McMillan, John. 2002. *Reinventing the Bazaar: A Natural History of Markets*, New York: W. W. Norton.

McMillan, John. 1994. "Selling Spectrum Rights," *Journal of Economic Perspectives*, 8: 145–162.

Merges, Robert P. 1997. "The End of Friction? Property Rights and Contract in the 'Newtonian' World of On-line Commerce." *Berkeley Technology Law Journal*, 12: 115–136.

Merges, Robert P., and Richard R. Nelson. 1990. "On the Complex Economics of Patent Scope," *Columbia Law Review*, 90: 839–916.

Merrill, Thomas W. 2002. "Introduction: The Demsetz Thesis and the Evolution of Property Rights," *Journal of Legal Studies*, June, 31: S331–S338.

Michaels, Robert J. 1993. "The New Age of Natural Gas," *Regulation*, 17: 68–79, Winter.

Miller, Arthur Selwyn. 1976. *The Supreme Court and American Capitalism*, New York: W. W. Norton.

Miller, John A. 1941. *Fares, Please!: From Horsecars to Streamliners*, New York: D. Appleton–Century.

Miller, James C., III. 1999. *Monopoly Capital*, Hoover Institution Press.

Miller, James C., III, and Roger Sherman. 1980. "Has the Postal Reorganization Act Been Fair to Mailers?" in Roger Sherman, ed., *Perspectives on Postal Service Issues*, Washington, D.C.: American Enterprise Institute.

Miller, Merton, and Franco Modigliani. 1958. "The Cost of Capital," *American Economic Review*, 48: 261–297.

Mills, David E. 1986. "Flexibility and Firm Diversity with Demand Fluctuations," *International Journal of Industrial Organization*, 4: 203–215.

Mills, David E. 1984. "Demand Fluctuation and Endogenous Firm Flexibility," *Journal of Industrial Economics*, 33: 55–71.

Mills, David E. 1981. "Ownership Arrangements and Congestion-Prone Facilities, *American Economic Review*, 71: 493–502.

Mills David E., and Lawrence Schumann. 1985. "Industry Structure with Fluctuating Demand," *American Economic Review*, 75: 758–767.

Minasian, Jora. 1964. "Television Pricing and the Theory of Public Goods," *Journal of Law and Economics*, 7: 71–80.

Ministry of Transport. 1964. *Road Pricing: The Economic and Technical Possibilities*, London: H.M.S.O.

Mirman, Leonard J., Dov Samet, and Yair Tauman. 1983. "An Axiomatic Approach to the Allocation of Fixed Cost through Prices," *Bell Journal of Economics*, 14: 139–151.

Mishan, Ezra J. 1971. "Evaluation of Life and Limb: A Theoretical Approach," *Journal of Political Economy*, 79: 706–738.

Mitchell, Bridger M., and Ingo Vogelsang. 1991. *Telecommunications Pricing: Theory and Practice*, New York: Cambridge University Press.

Mitchell, Lawrence E. 2002. *Corporate Irresponsibility: America's Newest Export*, New Haven, Conn.: Yale University Press.

Mitchell, Matthew F., and Andrzej Skrzypacz. 2002. "Industry Dynamics with Network Externalities," University of Iowa, Working Paper, November 11.

Mitchell, M., and H. Mulherin. 1996. "The Impact of Industry Shocks on Takeover and Restructuring Activity," *Journal of Financial Economics*, 41: 193–229.

Modigliani, Franco, and Merton Miller. 1958. "The Cost of Capital, Corporation Finance, and the Theory of Investment," *American Economic Review*, 48: 281–297.

Mohring, Herbert. 1970. "The Peak-Load Problem with Increasing Returns and Pricing Constraints," *American Economic Review*, 60: 693–705.

Moohr, Geraldine Szott. 2003. "An Enron Lesson: The Modest Role of Criminal Law in Preventing Corporate Crime," *Florida Law Review*, September, 55: 937–975.

Moohr, Geraldine Szott. 2002. "The Problematic Role of Criminal Law in Regulating Use of Information: The Economic Espionage Act," *North Carolina Law Review*, 80: 853–921.

Moohr, Geraldine Szott. 1999. "Arbitration and the Goals of Employment Discrimination Law," *Washington and Lee Law Review*, Spring, 56: 395–460.

Moohr, Geraldine Szott. 1998. "Don't Make a Federal Case of Everything," *Legal Times*, March 2.

Moohr, Geraldine Szott. 1997. "The Federal Interest in Criminal Law," *Syracuse Law Review*, 47: 1127–1184.

Moore, Barrington., Jr. 1966. *Social Origins of Dictatorship and Democracy*, Boston: Beacon Press.

Moore, Thomas G. 1986. "U.S. Airline Deregulation: Its Effects on Passengers, Capital, and Labor," *Journal of Law and Economics*, April, 29: 1–28.

Morck, Randall, Andrei Shleifer, and Robert Vishny. 1990. "Do Managerial Objectives Drive Bad Acquisitions?" *Journal of Finance*, March, 45: 31–48.

Morison, Samuel Eliot, Henry Steele Commager, and William E. Leuchtenburg. 1969. *The Growth of the American Republic*, London: Oxford University Press.

Morrison, Lord Herbert. 1933. *Socialization and Transport*, London: Constable.

Morrison, Steven A., and Clifford Winston. 2000. "The Remaining Role for Government Policy in the Deregulated Airline Industry," in Sam Peltzman and Clifford Winston, eds. *Deregulation of Network Industries: What's Next?* Washington, D.C.: AEI-Brookings.

Morrison, Steven A., and Clifford Winston. 1995. *The Evolution of the Airline Industry*, Washington, D.C.: The Brookings Institution.

Morrison, Steven A., and Clifford Winston. 1986. *The Economic Effects of Airline Deregulation*, Washington, D.C.: Brookings.

Morton, Fiona Scott, and Joel Podolny. 2002. "Love or Money? The Effects of Owner Motivation on the California Wine Industry," *Journal of Industrial Economics*, December, 50: 431–456.

Morton, Fiona Scott, Florian Zettelmeyer, and Jorge Silva-Risso. 2001. "Internet Car Retailing," *Journal of Industrial Economics*, December, 49: 501–539.

Moss, David A. 2002. *When All Else Fails*, Cambridge, Mass: Harvard University Press.

Mossin, Jan. 1969. "Security Pricing and Investment Criteria in Competitive Markets," *American Economic Review*, 59: 753–763.

Mueller, Dennis C. 2001. "Delusions Regarding the Proper Role of Markets and Antitrust Policy," *Review of Industrial Organization*, August, 19: 27–36.

Mueller, Dennis C. 1997. "Merger Policy in the United States: A Reconsideration," *Review of Industrial Organization*, 12: 655–685.

Mueller, Dennis C. 1996. "Lessons from the United States Antitrust History," *International Journal of Industrial Organization*, 14: 415–445.

Mueller, Dennis C. 1990. *The Dynamics of Company Profits*, Cambridge, England: Cambridge University Press.

Mueller, Dennis C. 1989. *Public Choice II*, Cambridge, England: Cambridge University Press.

Mueller, Dennis C. 1986. *Profits in the Long Run*, Cambridge, England: Cambridge University Press.

Mueller, Dennis C. 1980. *Public Choice*, New York: Cambridge University Press.

Murdock, Kevin. 2002. "Intrinsic Motivation and Optimal Incentive Contracts," *RAND Journal of Economics*, Winter, 33: 650–671.

Mussa, Michael, and Sherwin Rosen. 1978. "Monopoly and Product Quality," *Journal of Economic Theory*, 18: 301–317.

Myneni, Ranga, Charles D. Keeling, Compton J. Tucker, G. Asrar, and R. R. Nemani. 1997. "Increased Plant Growth in the Northern High Latitudes from 1981 to 1991," *Nature*, April, 386: 698–701.

Nasar, Sylvia. 1998. *A Beautiful Mind*, New York: Simon and Schuster.

Nash, John F., Jr. 1950. "The Bargaining Problem," *Econometrica*, 18: 155–162.

Navarro, P. 1981. "Electric Utility Regulation and National Energy Policy," *Regulation*, 5: 20–27.

Navarro, P. 1980. "Public Utility Commission Regulation: Performance, Determinants, and Energy Policy Impacts," Harvard University, Energy and Environmental Policy Center Discussion Paper E-80-05.

Neal, Phil C., Chairman. 1968. "The White House Task Force Report on Antitrust Policy," July 5, Washington, D.C.: Bureau of National Affairs.

Neale, A. D. 1970. *The Antitrust Laws of the U.S.A.*, 2nd ed. Cambridge, England: Cambridge University Press.

Nelson, Philip. 1974. "Advertising as Information," *Journal of Political Economy*, August, 82: 729–754.

Nelson, Philip. 1970. "Information and Consumer Behavior," *Journal of Political Economy*, May, 78: 311–329.

Nelson, Richard R. 1959. "The Simple Economics of Basic Scientific Research," *Journal of Political Economy*, June, 67: 297–306.

Neumann, John von, and Oskar Morgenstern. 1944. *Theory of Games and Economic Behavior*, Princeton, N.J.: Princeton University Press.

Neumark, David, and Steven A. Sharpe. 1992. "Market Structure and the Nature of Price Rigidity: Evidence from the Market for Consumer Deposits," *Quarterly Journal of Economics*, May, 107: 657–680.

Newbery, David M. "Competition, Contracts, and Entry in the Electricity Spot Market," *RAND Journal of Economics*, 29: 726–749.

Niskanen, William A. 1971. *Bureacracy and Representative Government*, Chicago: Aldine-Atherton.

North, Douglass C., and Robert Paul Thomas. 1973. *The Rise of the Western World*. Cambridge, England: Cambridge University Press.

Norton, Patrick J. 1998. "What Happens when Air Bags Kill: Automobile Manufacturers' Liability for Injuries Caused by Air Bags," *Case Western Reserve Law Review*, 48: 569–599.

Nussbaum, Helga. 1986. "International Cartels and Multinational Enterprises," in Alice Teichova, Maurice Levy-Leboyer, and Helga Nusbaum, eds. *Multinational Enterprises in Historical Perspective*, New York: Cambridge University Press. pp. 131–145.

O'Donoghue, Ted, Suzanne Scotchmer, and Jacques-Francois Thisse. 1998. "Patent Breadth, Patent Life, and the Pace of Technological Progress," *Journal of Economics and Management Strategy*, 7: 1–32.

Oerlemans, Leon A. G., and Marius T. H. Meeus. 2001. "R&D Cooperation in a Transaction Cost Perspective," *Review of Industrial Organization*, February, 18: 77–90.

Oi, Walter Y. 1971. "A Disneyland Dilemma: Two-Part Tariffs and a Mickey Mouse Monopoly," *Quarterly Journal of Economics*, 85: 77–96.

Okuguchi, Koji. 1975. "The Implications of Regulation for Induced Technological Change," *Bell Journal of Economics*, 6: 703–705.

O'Rourke, Maureen A. 1995. "Copyright: Protection after the ProCD Case: A Market Based Approach," *Berkeley Technology Law Journal*, 12: 53–91.

Orbach, Barak Y. 2004. "The Duropolist Puzzle: Monopoly Power in Durable-Goods Markets," *Yale Journal on Regulation*, Winter, 21: 67–119.

Ordover, Janusz A., and Robert D. Willig. 1981. "An Economic Definition of Predation: Pricing and Product Innovation," *Yale Law Journal*, 91: 8–53.

Oster, Sharon. 1990. "The Determinants of Consumer Complaints," *Review of Economics and Statistics*, Vol. 62, pp. 603–609.

Owen, Bruce M., and R. Braeutigam. 1978. *The Regulation Game: Strategic Use of the Administrative Process*, Cambridge, Mass.: Ballinger.

Panzar, John C. 2002. "Reconciling Competition, Downstream Access, and Universal Service in Postal Markets," in Michael A. Crew and Paul R. Kleindorfer, eds. *Postal and Delivery Services: Delivering on Competition*, Norwell, MA: Kluwer.

Panzar, John C., and Robert D. Willig. 1981. "Economies of Scope," *American Economic Review*, May, 71: 268–272.

Panzar, John C., and Robert D. Willig. 1977. "Free Entry and the Sustainability of Natural Monopoly," *Bell Journal of Economics*, Spring, 8: 1–22.

Park, Jong-Hun, and Anming Zhang. 2000. "An Empirical Analysis of Global Airline Alliances: Cases in the North Atlantic Markets," *Review of Industrial Organization*, 16: 367–384.

Partnoy, Frank. 1999. "The Siskel and Ebert of Financial Markets: Two Thumbs Down for the Credit Rating Agencies," *Washington University Law Quarterly*, 77: 619–712.

Patterson, Mark R. 2001. "On the Impossibility of Informational Intermediaries," Fordham University School of Law, Working Paper, August 5.

Paulter, Paul A. 2001. "Evidence on Mergers and Acquisitions," Working Paper No. 243. Washington, D.C.: Bureau of Economics, Federal Trade Commission.

Peitz, Martin, and Gerhard Illing, eds. 2005. *The Industrial Organization of Digital Goods and Electronic Markets*. Cambridge, Mass.: MIT Press.

Peltzman, Sam. 1976. "Toward a More General Theory of Regulation," *Journal of Law and Economics*, April, 19: 211–240.

Peltzman, Sam. 1975. "The Effects of Automobile Safety Regulation," *Journal of Political Economy*, 83: 677–725.

Peltzman, Sam. 1971. "Pricing in Public Enterprise: Electric Utilities in the United States," *Journal of Law and Economics*, 14: 109–147.

Peltzman Sam, and Clifford Winston, eds. 2000. *Deregulation of Network Industries: What's Next?* Washington, D.C.: AEI-Brookings.

Peoples, J., A. Hekmat, and A. Moini. 1993. "Corporate Mergers and Union Wage Premiums," *Journal of Economics and Finance*, 17: 65–75.

Perry, T. 2000. "Incentive Compensation for Outside Directors and CEO Turnover," Arizona State University, Working Paper.

Peteraf, Margaret A. 1995. "Sunk Costs, Contestability and Airline Monopoly Power," *Review of Industrial Organization*, 10: 289–306.

Peterman, John L. 1975. "The Brown Shoe Case," *Journal of Law and Economics*, 18: 81–146.

Peterson, Mark A., and George L. Priest, 1982. *The Civil Jury: Trends in Trials and Verdicts, Cook County, Illinois, 1960–1979*, R2881-ICJ. Santa Monica, Calif.: RAND Corporation, p. 31.

Peterson, Steven, George Hoffer, and Edward Millner. 1995. "Are Air-Bag-Equipped Cars More Aggressive? A Test of the Offsetting Behavior Hypothesis," *Journal of Law and Economics*, 38: 251–264.

Petrin, Amil. 2002. "Quantifying the Benefits of New Products: The Case of the Minivan," *Journal of Political Economy*, August, 110: 705–729.

Phelps, Edmund S. 1972. "The Statistical Theory of Racism and Sexism," *American Economic Review*, September, 62: 659–661.

Phillips, Almarin. 1959. "A Critique of United States Experience with Price-Fixing Agreements and the Per Se Rule," *Journal of Industrial Economics*, October, 8: 13–32.

Phlips Louis, and J. Thisse. 1982. "Spatial Competition and the Theory of Differentiated Products: An Introduction," *Journal of Industrial Economics*, 31: 1–11.

Pickering, J. F. 1966. *Resale Price Maintenance in Practice*, New York: August M. Kelley.

Pigou, Arthur C. 1920. *The Economics of Welfare*, London: Macmillan.

Player, Mack A. 1999. *Federal Law of Employment Discrimination in a Nutshell*, 4th ed. Eagan, Minn.: West Group.

Plott, Charles R. 1966. "Externalities and Corrective Taxes," *Economica*, February, N.S.33: 84–87.

Plott, Charles R., and Michael E. Levine. 1978. "A Model of Agenda Influence on Committee Decisions," *American Economic Review*, 78: 146–170.

Polanyi, Michael. 1944. "Patent Reform," *Review of Economic Studies* 11: 61–76.

Posner, Richard A. 2001. *Antitrust Law: An Economic Perspective*, 2nd ed., Chicago: University of Chicago Press.

Posner, Richard A. 1975. "The Social Cost of Monopoly and Regulation," *Journal of Political Economy*, 83: 807–827.

Posner, Richard A. 1971. "Taxation by Regulation," *Bell Journal of Economics*, 2: 22–50.

Posner, Richard A. 1970. "A Statistical Study of Antitrust Enforcement," *Journal of Law and Economics*, October, 13: 365–419.

Posner, Richard A. 1969. "Natural Monopoly and Its Regulation," *Stanford Law Review*, February, 2: 548–643.

Poterba, James, and Andrew Samwick. 1995. "Stock Ownership Patterns, Stock Market Fluctuations, and Consumption," *Brookings Papers on Economic Activity*, 2: 295–357.

Pound, Roscoe. 1959. *Jurisprudence*, Vols. I–V. St. Paul, Minn.: West Publishing.

Prager, Robin A. 1990. "Firm Behavior in Franchise Monopoly Markets," *RAND Journal of Economics*, Summer, 21: 211–225.

Prendergast, Canice. 2002. "The Tenuous Trade-off between Risk and Incentives," *Journal of Political Economy*, October, 110: 1071–1102.

Prendergast, Canice. 2000. "What Trade-off of Risk and Incentives?" *American Economic Review*, May, 90: 421–425.

Prendergast, Canice. 1999. "The Provision of Incentives in Firms," *Journal of Economic Literature*, March, 37: 7–63.

Prescott, Edward, and Michael Visscher. 1977. "Sequential Location among Firms with Foresight," *Bell Journal of Economics*, 8: 378–393.

Pryor, Frederic L. 2002. *The Future of U.S. Capitalism*, New York: Cambridge University Press.

Pulley, Lawrence B., and Y. M. Braunstein. 1992. "A Composite Cost Function for Multiproduct Firms with an Application to Economies of Scope in Banking," *Review of Economics and Statistics*, May, 74: 221–230.

Ramsey, Frank. 1927. "A Contribution to the Theory of Taxation," *Economic Journal*, 37: 47–61.

Rapoport, Anatol, and Albert M. Chammah. 1965. *Prisoner's Dilemma*, Ann Arbor, Mich.: University of Michigan Press.

Rapoport, Nancy, and Bala G. Dharan, eds. 2004. *Enron: Corporate Fiascos and Their Implications*, New York: Foundation Press.

Rassenti, Stephen J., Vernon L. Smith, and Bart Wilson. 2000. "Market Power in Electricity Networks," George Mason University, Working Paper.

Ratner, James. 1988. "Should there Be an Essential Facilities Doctrine?" *U.C. Davis Law Review*, 21: 327–382.

Ravenscraft, David J., 1993. "Structure-Profit Relationship at the Line of Business and Industry Level," *Review of Economics and Statistics*, February, 65: 22–31.

Ravenscraft, David J., and F. Michael Scherer. 1987a. "Life After Takeover." *Journal of Industrial Economics*, December, 36: 147–156.

Ravenscraft, David J., and F. Michael Scherer. 1987b. "Mergers and Managerial Performance," in John C. Coffee, Jr., Louis Lowenstein, and Susan Rose-Ackerman, eds., *Takeovers and Contests for Corporate Control*, Oxford, England: Oxford University Press.

Ravenscraft, David J., and F. Michael Scherer. 1987c. *Mergers, Sell-Offs, and Economic Efficiency*, Washington, D.C.: The Brookings Institution.

Read, William H., and Ronald Alan Weiner. 1999. "FCC Reform: Does Governing Require a New Standard?" in Benjamin M. Compaine and William H. Read, eds. *The Information Resources Policy Handbook*, Cambridge, Mass.: MIT Press.

Reinganum, J. 1983. "Uncertain Innovation and the Persistence of Monopoly," *American Economic Review*, June, 73: 741–748.

Reinganum, Jennifer. 1989. "The Timing of Innovation: Research, Development, and Diffusion," in Richard Schmalensee and Robert D. Willig, eds., *The Handbook of Industrial Organization*, Amsterdam: North Holland, pp. 849–908.

Rey, Patrick, and Joseph Stiglitz. 1995. "The Role of Exclusive Territories in Producer Competition," *RAND Journal of Economics*, Fall, 26: 431–451.

Ribstein, Larry E. 2002. "Market vs. Regulatory Responses to Corporate Fraud: A Critique of the Sarbanes-Oxley Act of 2002," Paper Prepared for Conference at Tilburg University, September 5–6, 2002.

Riddel, M., and W. D. Shaw. 2006. "A Theoretically Consistent Empirical Non-Expected Utility Model of Ambiguity: Nuclear Waste Mortality Risk and Yucca Mountain," *Journal of Risk and Uncertainty*, 32: 131–150.

Riordan, Michael H. 1998. "Anticompetitive Vertical Integration by a Dominant Firm," *American Economic Review*, December, 88: 1232–1248.

Riordan, Michael H., and David E. M. Sappington. 1987. "Awarding Monopoly Franchises," *American Economic Review*, December, 67: 375–387.

Riordan, Michael H., and Steven C. Salop. 1995. "Evaluating Vertical Mergers: A Post-Chicago Approach," *Antitrust Law Journal*, Winter, 63: 513–568.

Robertson, Ross M. 1955. *History of the American Economy*, New York: Harcourt, Brace.

Robinson, E. Austin G. 1958. *The Structure of Competitive Industry*, Chicago: University of Chicago Press.

Robinson, Joan. 1933. *Economics of Imperfect Competition*. London: Macmillan.

Romano, Roberta. 1992. "A Guide to Takeovers: Theory, Evidence, and Regulation," *Yale Journal on Regulation*, Winter, 9: 119–180.

Romeo, Charles, Russell Pittman, and Norman Familabt. 2003. "Do Newspaper JOAs Charge Monopoly Advertising Rates?" *Review of Industrial Organization*, March, 22: 121–138.

Rose, Nancy L., and Andrea Shepard. 1997. "Firm Diversification and CEO Compensation: Management Ability or Executive Enrichment?" *RAND Journal of Economics*, Autumn, 28: 489–514.

Rosenfeld, Richard N. 2004. "What Democracy? The Case for Abolishing the United States Senate," *Harper's Magazine*, May, pp. 35–44.

Ross, Marc, and Tom Wenzel. 2002. "An Analysis of Traffic Deaths by Vehicle Type and Model," Berkeley National Laboratory Report No. T021, Prepared for U.S. Department of Energy under LBL Contract No. DE-AC03-76SF00098, Report No. LBNL-49675.

Ruderman, Henry, Mark D. Levine, and James McMahon, "The Behavior of the Market for Energy Efficiency in Residential Appliances including Heating and Cooling Equipment," *The Energy Journal*, 8: 101–124.

Ruffin, Roy. 2007. "The Structure of Vertical Markets," University of Houston, Working Paper.

Ruffin, Roy. 1971. "Cournot Oligopoly and Competitive Behavior," *Review of Economic Studies*, 38: 493–502.

Ruser, John W. 1993. "Workers' Compensation and the Distribution of Occupational Injuries," *Journal of Human Resources*, Summer, 28: 593–617.

Rutledge, Gary L., and Mary L. Leonard. 1993. "Pollution Abatement and Control Expenditures, 1987–91," *Survey of Current Business*, May, 73: 22–44.

Salant, Stephen, S. Switzer, and Robert Reynolds. 1983. "Losses from Horizontal Merger: The Effects of an Exogenous Change in Industry Structure on Cournot-Nash Equilibrium," *Quarterly Journal of Economics*, 98: 185–213.

Salop, Steven C. 2000. "The Kodak Case, the First Principles Approach and Antitrust at the Millennium," *Antitrust Law Journal*, 68: 187–202.

Salop, Steven C. 1979. "Monopolistic Competition with Outside Goods," *Bell Journal of Economics*, 10: 141–156.

Salop, Steven C. 1976. "Information and Monopolistic Competition," *American Economic Review*, 66: 1011–1032.

Samuelson, Paul A. 1954. "The Pure Theory of Public Expenditure," *Review of Economics and Statistics*, 36: 386–389.

Samwick, Andrew A., and Jonathan Skinner. 2004. "How Will 401(k) Pension Plans Affect Retirement Income?," *American Economic Review*, March, 94: 329–343.

Sappington, David E. M. 2003. "The Effects of Incentive Regulation on Retail Telephone Service Quality in the United States," *Review of Network Economics*, December, 2: 355–375.

Sappington, David E. M. 2002. "Price Regulation," Chapter 7 in Martin E. Cave, Sumit K. Majumdar, and Ingo Vogelsavig, eds., *Handbook of Telecommunications Economics*, Vol. 1, Amsterdam, The Netherlands: North Holland Elsevier.

Sappington, David E. M. 1980. "Strategic Firm Behavior under a Dynamic Regulatory Adjustment Process," *Bell Journal of Economics*, 11: 360–372.

Sappington, David E. M., and Dennis L. Weisman. 1996. *Designing Incentive Regulation for the Telecommunications Industry*, Cambridge, Mass.: MIT Press.

Saunders, Anthony, and Ingo Walter. 1999. *Universal Banking: Financial System Design Reconsidered*, Washington, D.C.: Federal Reserve Board of Governors.

Schankerman, Mark. 1998. "How Valuable is Patent Protection? Estimates by Technology Field," *RAND Journal of Economics*, 29: 77–107.

Scheffman, David T., and Mary T. Coleman. 2002. "Current Economic Issues at the FTC," *Review of Industrial Organization*, December, 21: 357–371.

Schelling, Thomas C. 1963. *The Strategy of Conflict*, New York: Oxford University Press.

Schelling, Thomas C. 1968. "The Life You Save May Be Your Own," in Samuel B. Chase, ed., *Problems in Public Expenditure Analysis*, Washington, D.C.: Brookings Institution.

Scherer, F. Michael. 1967. "Market Structure and the Employment of Scientists and Engineers," *American Economic Review*, June, 57: 524–531.

Scherer, F. Michael, Alan Beckenstein, Erich Kaufer, R. Dennis Murphy, and Francine Bougeon-Maassen. 1975. *The Economics of Multi-Plant Operation*, Cambridge, Mass.: Harvard University Press.

Schiesel, Seth. 2000. "AT&T Takes Full Control of Home Cable Venture," *New York Times*, March 30, p. C1.

Schmalensee, Richard. 1992. "Sunk Costs and Market Structure: A Review Article,"

Journal of Industrial Economics, June, 40: 125–134.

Schmalensee, Richard. 1981. "Monopolistic Two-Part Price Arrangements," *Bell Journal of Economics*, 12: 445–466.

Schmidt, E. P. 1937. *Industrial Relations in Urban Transportation*, Minneapolis: University of Minnesota Press.

Scholz, John T., and Wayne R. Gray. 1990. "OSHA Enforcement and Workplace Injuries: A Behavioral Approach to Risk Assessment," *Journal of Risk and Uncertainty*, 3: 283–305.

Schramm, Richard, and Roger Sherman. 1977. "A Rationale for Administered Pricing," *Southern Economic Journal*, July, 44: 125–135.

Schramm, Richard, and Roger Sherman. 1976. "Advertising to Manage Profit Risk," *Journal of Industrial Economics*, June, 44: 295–311.

Schramm, Richard, and Roger Sherman. 1974. "Profit Risk Management and the Theory of the Firm," *Southern Economic Journal*, January, 40: 353–363.

Schumann, Laurence. 1993. "Patterns of Abnormal Returns and the Competitive Effects of Horizontal Mergers," *Review of Industrial Organization*, 8: 679–696.

Schumann, Laurence, Robert P. Rogers, and James D. Reitzes, 1992. *Case Studies of the Price Effects of Horizontal Mergers*, Washington, D.C.: Bureau of Economics, Federal Trade Commission.

Schumpeter, Joseph A. 1942. *Capitalism, Socialism, and Democracy*, New York: Harper.

Scitovsky, Tibor. 1950. "Ignorance as a Source of Oligopoly Power," *American Economic Review*, 40: 48–53.

Scotchmer, Suzanne. 1996. "Protecting Early Innovators: Should Second-Generation Products be Patentable?" *RAND Journal of Economics*, 27: 322–331.

Scotchmer, Suzanne. 1991. "Standing on the Shoulders of Giants: Cumulative Research and the Patent Law," *Journal of Economic Perspectives*, Winter, 5: 29–41.

Scott, Frank A., Jr. 1986. "Assessing USA Postal Ratemaking: An Application of Ramsey Prices," *Journal of Industrial Economics*, 34: 279–290.

Scott, Frank A., Jr. 1979. "An Economic Analysis of Fuel Adjustment Clauses," Ph.D. Dissertation, University of Virginia.

Seager, Henry R., and Charles A. Gulick, Jr. 1929. *Trust and Corporation Problems*, New York: Harper and Brothers.

Selten, Reinhard. 1978. "The Chain Store Paradox," *Theory and Decision*, 9: 127–159.

Selten, Reinhard. 1975. "Reexamination of the Perfectness Concept for Equilibrium Points in Extensive Games," *International Journal of Game Theory*, 4: 25–55.

Selwyn, Arthur Miller. 1976. *The Modern Corporate State*, Westport, Conn.: Greenwood Press.

Shaked, Avner, and John Sutton. 1982. "Relaxing Price Competition Through Product Differentiation," *Review of Economic Studies*, 49: 3–13.

Shapiro, Carl, and Robert D. Willig. 1990. "On the Antitrust Treatment of Production Joint Ventures," *Journal of Economic Perspectives*, 4: 113–130.

Sharpe, William F. 1965. "Risk Aversion in the Stock Market: Some Empirical Evidence," *Journal of Finance*, 20: 416–422.

Shavell, Steven, and Tanguy van Ypersele. 2001. "Rewards versus Intellectual Property Rights," *Journal of Law and Economics*, 44: 525–547.

Shepard, Andrea. 1991. "Price Discrimination and Retail Configuration," *Journal of Political Economy*, February, 99: 30–53.

Shepherd, William G. 1972. "The Elements of Market Structure," *Review of Economics and Statistics*, February, 54: 25–37.

Sherman, Roger. 2004. "Designer Markets: The Art of Restructuring," paper given at Encore Conference, University of Amsterdam, available at www.encore.nl/documents/paper_sherman_001.pdf.

Sherman, Roger. 2003. "Restructuring Industries: The Carrot and the Stick," *Review of Network Economics*, 2: 376–403.

Sherman, Roger. 2001a. "Optimal Worksharing Discounts," *Journal of Regulatory Economics*, 19: 81–92.

Sherman, Roger. 2001b. "The Future of Market Regulation," *Southern Economic Journal*, 67: 782–800.

Sherman, Roger. 1992. "Capital Waste in the Rate-of-Return Regulated Firm," *Journal of Regulatory Economics*, 4: 197–204.

Sherman, Roger. 1989a. *The Regulation of Monopoly*. Cambridge, England: Cambridge University Press.

Sherman, Roger. 1989b. "Efficiency Aspects of Diversification by Public Utilities," in Michael A. Crew, ed., *Deregulation and Diversification of Utilities*, Norwell, Mass.: Kluwer.

Sherman, Roger. 1983a. "Is Public Utility Regulation Beyond *Hope*," in Albert L. Danielson and David R. Kamerschen, *Current Issues in Public Utility Economics: Essays in Honor of J.C. Bonbright*, Lexington, Mass.: D.C. Heath, 1983.

Sherman, Roger. 1983b. "Pricing Behavior of the Budget Constrained Public Enterprise," *Journal of Economic Behavior and Organization*, 4: 381–393.

Sherman, Roger. 1980. "Hope against *Hope*," in Michael A. Crew, ed., *Issues in Public Utility Economics and Regulation*, Lexington, Mass.: D.C. Heath.

Sherman, Roger. 1977a. "Ex Ante Rates of Return for Regulated Utilities," *Land Economics*, 53: 172–184.

Sherman, Roger. 1977b. "Financial Aspects of Rate-of Return Regulation," *Southern Economic Journal*, October, 44: 321–332.

Sherman, Roger. 1974. *The Economics of Industry*, Boston: Little, Brown.

Sherman, Roger. 1972a. *Oligopoly: An Empirical Approach*, Lexington, Mass.: D.C. Heath.

Sherman, Roger. 1972b. "Subsidies to Relieve Urban Transit Congestion," *Journal of Transport Economics and Policy*, 6: 1–10.

Sherman, Roger. 1971a. "An Experiment on the Persistence of Price Collusion," *Southern Economic Journal*, April, 37: 489–495.

Sherman, Roger. 1971b. "Entry Barriers and the Growth of Firms," *Southern Economic Journal*, October, 38: 238–247.

Sherman, Roger. 1971c. "Congestion Interdependence and Urban Transit Fares," *Econometrica*, 39: 565–576.

Sherman, Roger. 1970. "The Design of Public Utility Organizations," *Land Economics*, February, 46: 51–58.

Sherman, Roger. 1969. "Risk Attitude and Cost Variability in a Capacity Choice Experiment," *Review of Economic Studies*, October, 36: 453–466.

Sherman, Roger. 1967. "A Private Ownership Bias in Transit Choice," *American Economic Review*, 57: 1211–1217.

Sherman, Roger, and Anthony George. 1979. "Second-Best Pricing for the U.S. Postal Service," *Southern Economic Journal*, 45: 685–695.

Sherman, Roger, and Thomas D. Willett. 1969. "Regional Development, Externalities, and Tax-Subsidy Combinations," *National Tax Journal*, June, 22: 291–293.

Sherman, Roger, and Michael Visscher. 1982a. "Rate-of-Return Regulation and Two-Part Tariffs," *Quarterly Journal of Economics*, 97: 27–42.

Sherman, Roger, and Michael Visscher. 1982b. "Nonprice Rationing with Monopoly Price Structure When Demand is Stochastic," *Bell Journal of Economics*, 13; 254–262.

Sherman, Roger, and Michael Visscher. 1978. "Second-Best Pricing with Stochastic Demand," *American Economic Review*, 68: 41–53.

Shiller, Robert J. 2003. *The New Financial Order*, Princeton, N.J.: Princeton University Press.

Shipe, Richard T. 1992. "Cost and Productivity in the U.S. Urban Bus Transit Sector, 1978–1989," Ph.D. Dissertation, University of Virginia.

Shleifer, Andrei. 2000. *Imperfect Markets—An Introduction to Behavioral Finance*, Oxford: Oxford University Press.

Shleifer, Andrei. 1985. "A Theory of Yardstick Competition," *RAND Journal of Economics*, 16: 319–327.

Shleifer, Andrei, and Lawrence Summers. 1988. "Breach of Trust in Hostile Takeovers," in Alan J. Auerbach, ed., *Corporate Takeovers: Causes and Consequences*, Boston: NBER.

Shy, Oz. 2001. *The Economics of Network Industries*, Cambridge, England: Cambridge University Press.

Shy, Oz. 1995. *Industrial Organization*, Cambridge, Mass.: MIT Press.

Sidak, J. Gregory. 1983. "Debunking Predatory Innovation," *Columbia Law Review*, 83: 1121–1141.

Sidak, J. Gregory, and Daniel F. Spulber. 1997. *Deregulatory Takings and the Regulatory*

Contract, New York: Cambridge University Press.

Siegan, Bernard H. 1970. "Non-zoning in Houston," *Journal of Law and Economics*, April, 13: 71–148.

Simon, Herbert A. 1979. "Rational Decision Making in Business Organizations." *American Economic Review*, September, 69: 493–513.

Simon, Herbert A., and Charles P. Bonini. 1958. "The Size Distribution of Business Firms," *American Economic Review*, September, 48: 607–617.

Sinclair, Upton. 1988. *The Jungle*, with "Introduction" by James R. Barrett, Urbana, Ill.: University of Illinois Press.

Singer, Charles, E. J. Holmyard, and A. R. Hall, eds. 1954. *A History of Technology, Vol. 1, From Early Times to Fall of Ancient Empires*, New York: Oxford University Press, chapter 9.

Singer, Joseph W. 2002. *Property Law: Rules, Policies, and Practices*, 3rd ed., Boston: Little, Brown.

Singer, Joseph W. 2001. *Introduction to Property*. Boston: Little, Brown.

Sirower, Mark L., and Stephen F. O'Byrne. 1998. "The Measurement of Post-Acquisition Performance: Toward a Value-Based Benchmarking Methodology," *Journal of Applied Corporate Finance*, Summer, 11: 107–121.

Siskind, F. B. 1993. *Twenty Years of OSHA Federal Enforcement Data*, Washington, D.C.: U.S. Government Printing Office.

Small, Kenneth A. 2003. "Road Pricing and Public Transport," University of California Energy Institute, Energy Policy and Economics Working Paper 010, UC Berkeley (www.ucei.org).

Smith, Adam. 1937 (1776). *The Wealth of Nations*, New York: The Modern Library.

Smith, Eric, and Randall Wright. 1992. "Why is Automobile Insurance in Philadelphia So Damn Expensive?" *American Economic Review*, September, 82: 756–772.

Smith, Michael D. 2001. "The Law of One Price? The Impact of IT-Enabled Markets on Consumer Search and Retailer Pricing," H. John Heinz III School of Public Policy and Management, Carnegie Mellon University, Working Paper.

Smith, Michael D., and Erik Brynjolfsson. 2001. "Consumer Decision-Making at an Internet Shopbot: Brand Still Matters," *Journal of Industrial Economics*, December, 49:541–558.

Smith, Richard A. 1961. "The Incredible Electrical Conspiracy," *Fortune*, April and May, 63: 135–140.

Smith, Robert S. 1979. "The Impact of OSHA Inspections on Manufacturing Injury Rates," *Journal of Human Resources*, 14: 145–170.

Smith, Sally Bedell. 1990. *In All His Glory: The Life of William S. Paley—The Legendary Tycoon and His Brilliant Circle*, New York: Simon and Schuster.

Smith, V. Kerry. 1974. "The Implications of Regulation for Induced Technological Change," *Bell Journal of Economics*, 5: 623–632.

Smithies, Arthur. 1941. "Optimum Location in Spatial Competition," *Journal of Political Economy*, 49: 423–439.

Sobel, Dava. 1996. *Longitude: The True Story of a Lone Genius Who Solved the Greatest Scientific Problem of His Time*, Harmondsworth, England: Penguin Books.

Solow, Robert M. 1957. "Technical Change and the Aggregate Production Function," *Review of Economics and Statistics*, August, 39: 312–320.

Soma, John T., and Kenin B. Davis. 2000. "Network Effects in Technology Markets: Applying the Lessons of Intel and Microsoft to Future Clashes Between Antitrust and Intellectual Property," *Journal of Intellectual Property Law*, Fall, 8: 1–36.

Spar, Debora L. 2001. *Ruling the Waves: Cycles of Discovery, Chaos, and Wealth from the Compass to the Internet*, New York: Harcourt.

Spence, Michael. 1975. "Monopoly, Quality, and Regulation," *Bell Journal of Economics*, 6: 417–429.

Spence Michael, and Bruce Owen. 1977. "Television Programming, Monopolistic Competition, and Welfare," *Quarterly Journal of Economics*, 91: 103–126.

Speta, James B. 2004. "Deregulating Telecommunications in Internet Time," *Washington and Lee Law Review*, 61: 1–91.

Spiller, Pablo T., and Carlo G. Cardilli. 1997. "The Frontier of Telecommunications Deregulation: Small Countries Leading the Pack," *Journal of Economic Perspectives*, Autumn, 11: 127–138.

Spulber, Daniel F., and Christopher S. Yoo. 2003. "Access to Networks: Economic and Constitutional Connections," *Cornell Law Review*, 88: 885–912.

Sraffa, Piero. 1926. "The Laws of Returns under Competitive Conditions," *Economic Journal*, 36: 535–550.

Stackelberg, Heinrich von. 1934. *Marketform and Gleichgewicht*, Berlin: Wien and Berlin.

Standage, Tom. 1998. *The Victorian Internet*, New York: Walker and Company.

Stango, Victor. 2002. "Pricing and Consumer Switching Costs: Evidence from the Credit Card Market," *Journal of Industrial Economics*, December, 50: 475–492.

Starmer, Chris. 2000. "Developments in non-Expected Utility Theory: The Hunt for a Descriptive Theory of Choice Under Risk," *Journal of Economic Literature*, 38: 332–382.

Steiner, Robert L. 1985. "The Nature of Vertical Restraints," *Antitrust Bulletin*, Spring, 143–197.

Steiner, Peter O. 1957. "Peak Loads and Efficient Pricing," *Quarterly Journal of Economics*, 66: 194–223.

Steiner, Peter O. 1952. "Program Patterns and Preferences, and the Workability of Competition in Radio Broadcasting," *Quarterly Journal of Economics*, 71: 585–610.

Sterling, Christopher H., and John M. Kitross. 2002. *Stay Tuned: A History of American Broadcasting*, Belmont, Calif.: Wadsworth.

Stevenson, Rodney E. 1973. "Postal Pricing Problems and Production Functions," Ph.D. Dissertation, University of Michigan.

Stewart, James B. 1991. *Den of Thieves*, New York: Simon and Schuster.

Stigler, George J. 1971. "The Theory of Economic Regulation," *Bell Journal of Economics*, 2: 3–21.

Stigler, Chair, George J. 1969. The Report of the President's Task Force on Productivity and Competition, *Congressional Record—Senate*, June 16, pp. 56473–56480.

Stigler, George J. 1964. "A Theory of Oligopoly," *Journal of Political Economy*, October, 72: 44–61.

Stigler, George J. 1950. "Monopoly and Oligopoly by Merger," *American Economic Review*, 40: 23–34.

Stigler, George J. 1947. "The Kinky Oligopoly Demand Curve and Rigid Prices," *Journal of Political Economy*, October, 55: 432–449.

Stigler, George J. 1939. "Production and Distribution in the Short Run," *Journal of Political Economy*, 47: 305–327.

Stigler, George J., and C. Friedland. 1962. "What Can Regulators Regulate?: The Case of Electricity," *Journal of Law and Economics*, 5: 1–16.

Stiglitz, Joseph E. 2002a. *Globalization and Its Discontents*, New York: W.W. Norton.

Stiglitz, Joseph E. 2002b. "Information and the Change in the Paradigm in Economics," *American Economic Review*, June, 92: 460–501.

Stiglitz, Joseph E. 2000. "The Contributions of the Economics of Information to Twentieth Century Economics," *Quarterly Journal of Economics*, November, 115: 1441–1478.

Stiglitz, Joseph E. 1989. "Imperfect Information in the Product Market," in Richard Schmalensee and Robert Willig, eds., *The Handbook of Industrial Organization*, New York: Elsevier Science Publishers.

Stiglitz, Joseph E. 1972. "On the Optimality of the Stock Market Allocation of Investment," *Quarterly Journal of Economics*, February, 86: 25–60.

Stiglitz, Joseph E. 1969. "A Re-Examination of the Modigliani-Miller Theorem," *American Economic Review*, 59: 784–793.

Strack, Walter. 1987. "Productivity, Technological Change, and Regulatory Reform in the Interstate Trucking Industry: General Freight carriers from 1974 to 1982," Ph.D. Dissertation, University of Virginia.

Strunck, N., and F. Case. 1988. *Where Deregulation Went Wrong: A Look at the Causes Behind Savings and Loan Failures in the 1980's*, Chicago: U.S. League of Savings Institutions.

Sunstein, Cass R. 1990. *After the Rights Revolution: Reconceiving the Regulatory State*, Cambridge, Mass.: Harvard University Press.

Suslow, Valerie Y. 2005. "Empirical Evidence from Inter-war International Cartels," *Industrial and Corporate Change*, 14: 705–744.

Sutton, John. 1991. *Sunk Costs and Market Structure*, Cambridge, Mass.: MIT Press.

Swan, Peter L. 1977. "Product Durability under Monopoly and Competition: Comment," *Econometrica*, 45: 229–235.

Swan, Peter L. 1970. "Durability of Consumption Goods," *American Economic Review*, 60: 884–894.

Sweeney, G. 1981. "Adoption of Cost-Saving Innovations by a Regulated Firm," *American Economic Review*, 71: 437–447.

Sweezy, Paul M. 1939. "Demand under Conditions of Oligopoly," *Journal of Political Economy*, August, 47: 568–573.

Szymanski, Stefan. 2003. "The Economic Design of Sporting Contests," *Journal of Economic Literature*, December, 41: 1137–1187.

Taylor, Charles T., and Aubrey Silberston. 1973. *The Economic Impact of the Patent System*, Cambridge, England: Cambridge University Press.

Teece, David J. 1980. "Economies of Scope and the Scope of the Enterprise," *Journal of Economic Behavior and Organization*, 1: 223–247.

Teichova, Alice, Maurice Levy-Leboyer, and Helga Nusbaum, eds. 1986. *Multinational Enterprises in Historical Perspective*, New York: Cambridge University Press.

Temin, Peter. 1987. *The Fall of the Bell System*, New York: Cambridge University Press.

Thorelli, Hans B. 1955. *The Federal Antitrust Policy*, Baltimore: Johns Hopkins University Press.

Tierney, John. 2004. "The Autonomist Manifesto (Or, How I Learned to Stop Worrying and Love the Road)," *New York Times Magazine*, September 26, pp. 58–65.

Tirole, Jean. 1988. *The Theory of Industrial Organization*, Cambridge, Mass.: MIT Press.

Toynbee, Arnold. 1969 (1884). *Toynbee's Industrial Revolution*, New York: Augustus M. Kelley.

Trebing, Harry M. 1985. "The Impact of Diversification in Economic Regulation," *Journal of Economic Issues*, 19: 463–474.

Tullock, Gordon. 1967. "The Welfare Costs of Tariffs, Monopolies, and Theft," *Western Economics Journal*, June, 6: 224–232.

Turvey, Ralph. 1968. *Optimal Pricing and Investment in Electricity Supply*, London: Allen and Unwin.

Usher, Abott P. 1954. *A History of Mechanical Inventions*, Cambridge, Mass.: Harvard University Press.

Van Dyke, Brennan. 1991. "Emissions Trading to Reduce Acid Deposition," *Yale Law Journal*, 100: 2707–2726.

Varian, Hal R. 2000. "Versioning Information Goods," in Brian Kahin and Hal R. Varian, eds., *Internet Publishing and Beyond*, Cambridge, Mass.: MIT Press.

Veljanovski, C. 1987. *Selling the State*, London: Weidenfeld and Nicolson.

Vickers J., and G. Yarrow. 1985. *Privatisation and the Natural Monopolies*, London: Public Policy Centre.

Vickrey, William S. 1963. "Pricing in Urban and Suburban Transport," *American Economic Review*, May, 53: 452–465.

Vickrey, William S. 1961. "Counterspeculation, Auctions, and Sealed Tenders," *Journal of Finance*, March, 16: 8–37.

Vickrey, William S. 1955. "Some Implications of Marginal-Cost Pricing for Public Utilities," *American Economic Review*, 45: 605–620.

Vickrey, William S. 1948. "Some Objections to Marginal-Cost Pricing," *Journal of Political Economy*, 56: 218–238.

Viscusi, W. Kip. 2000. "The Value of Life in Legal Contexts: Survey and Critique," *American Law and Economics Review*, 2: 195–222.

Viscusi, W. Kip. 1993. "The Value of Risks to Life and Health," *Journal of Economic Literature*, December, 31: 1912–1946.

Viscusi, W. Kip. 1992. *Fatal Tradeoffs*, New York: Oxford University Press.

Viscusi, W. Kip. 1986. "The Impact of Occupational Safety and Health Regulation," *RAND Journal of Economics*, 17: 567–580.

Viscusi, W. Kip. 1984. "The Lulling Effect: The Impact of Child-Resistant Packaging on Aspirin and Analgesic Ingestions," *American Economic Review*, May, 74: 325–331.

Viscusi, W. Kip, and Charles O'Conner. 1984. "Adaptive Responses to Chemical Labeling: Are Workers Baysian Decision Makers?" *American Economic Review*, December, 74: 942–956.

Vogelsang, Ingo. 2003. "Price Regulation of Access to Telecommunications Networks," *Journal of Economic Perspectives*, September, 41: 830–862.

Vogelsang, Ingo. 1988. "Price-Cap Regulation of Telecommunications Services: A Long-Run Approach," Rand Note N-2704-MF, February. The RAND Corporation, Santa Monica, Calif.

Vogelsang, Ingo, and Benjamin M. Compaine. 2000. *The Internet Upheaval: Raising Questions, Seeking Answers in Communications Policy*, Cambridge, Mass.: MIT Press.

Vogelsang, Ingo, and Jorg Finsinger. 1979. "A Regulatory Adjustment Process for Optimal Pricing by Multiproduct Monopoly Firms," *Bell Journal of Economics*, August, 10: 157–171.

Waddams Price, Catherine. 2004. "Spoilt for Choice? The Costs and Benefits of Opening UK Residential Energy Markets," University of California Energy Institute, Berkeley, Calif., CSEM WP 123, February.

Walsh, A.H. 1978. *The Public's Business*, Cambridge, Mass.: MIT Press.

Walters, Sir Alan. 1968. *The Economics of Road User Charges*, Baltimore: Johns Hopkins University Press.

Walters, Sir Alan. 1961. "The Theory and Measurement of Private and Social Cost of Highway Congestion," *Econometrica*, October, 29: 7–99.

Walton, Clarence C., and Frederick W. Cleveland. 1964. *Corporations on Trial: The Electrical Cases*. Belmont, Calif.: Wadsworth.

Warga, Arthur, and Ivo Welch. 1993. "Bondholder Losses in Leveraged Buyouts," *Review of Financial Studies*, 6: 37–71.

Warner, William W. 1977. *Beautiful Swimmers*, New York: Penguin Books.

Warsh, David. 2006. *Knowledge and the Wealth of Nations*, New York: W.W. Norton.

Waterson, Michael. 1988. *Regulation of the Firm and Natural Monopoly*, Oxford: Basil Blackwell.

Watkiss, Jeffrey D., and Douglas W. Smith. 1993. "The Energy Policy Act of 1992—A Watershed for Competition in the Wholesale Power Market," *Yale Journal on Regulation*, Summer, 10: 447–492.

Waverman, Leonard. 1975. "Peak-Load Pricing under Regulatory Constraint: A Proof of Inefficiency," *Journal of Political Economy*, 83: 645–654.

Weaver, Jaqueline Lang. 2006. "The Traditional Petroleum-Based Economy: An 'Eventful' Future," *Cumberland Law Review*, 36: 1–75.

Weaver, Jaqueline Lang. 2004. "Can Energy Markets Be Trusted? The Effect of the Rise and Fall of Enron on Energy Markets," in Nancy Rapoport and Bala G. Dharan, eds. *Enron: Corporate Fiascos and Their Implications*, New York: Foundation Press.

Weaver, Jaqueline Lang. 1994. "The Politics of Oil and Gas Jurisprudence: The Eighty-Six Percent Factor," *Washburn Law Journal*, 33: 492–539.

Weaver, Jaqueline Lang. 1986. *Unitization of Oil and Gas Fields in Texas: A Study of Legislation*, Baltimore: Johns Hopkins University Press.

Webb, Michael G. 1976. *Pricing Policies for Public Enterprises*, London: Macmillan.

Weil, David. 1996. "If OSHA Is So Bad, Why Is Compliance so Good," *RAND Journal of Economics*, Autumn, 27: 618–640.

Weiler, Paul C. 2000. *Leveling the Playing Field: How the Law Can Make Sports Better for Fans*, Cambridge, Mass.: Harvard University Press.

Weiler, Paul C. 1990. *Governing the Workplace: The Future of Labor and Employment Law*, Cambridge, Mass.: Harvard University Press.

Weiss, Leonard W. 1989. *Concentration and Prices*, Cambridge, Mass.: MIT Press.

Weiss, Leonard W. 1971. "Quantitative Studies of Industrial Organization," in Michael D. Intriigator, ed. *Frontiers of Quantitative Economics*, Amsterdam: North Holland.

Weizsacker, Christian C. von. 1985. "Free Entry into Telecommunications?" *Information Economics and Policy*, 1: 231–242.

Weizsacker, Christian C. von. 1980. *Barriers to Entry: A Theoretical Treatment*, New York: Springer-Verlag.

Wellisz, Stanislaw H. 1963. "Regulation of Natural Gas Pipeline Companies: An Economic Analysis," *Journal of Political Economy*, February, 55: 30–43.

Wenders, John T. 1976. "Peak Load Pricing in the Electric Utility Industry," *Bell Journal of Economics*, 7: 232–241.

Werden, Gregory J. 2000. "Market Delineation under Merger Guidelines: Monopoly Cases and Alternative Approaches," *Review of Industrial Organization*, March, 16: 211–218.

Westfield, Fred. 1965. "Regulation and Conspiracy," *American Economic Review*, 55: 424–443.

White, G. Edward. 1980. *Tort Law in America: An Intellectual History*, New York: Oxford University Press, p. 120.

White, Lawrence J. 2002. "Trends in Aggregate Concentration in the United States," *Journal of Economic Perspectives*, Fall, 16: 137–160.

White, Lawrence J. 2001a. "The Credit Rating Industry: An Industrial Organization Analysis," paper given at Southern Economics Association Meetings, Tampa, Florida, November 18.

White, Lawrence J. 2001b. "Lysine and Price Fixing: How Long? How Severe?" *Review of Industrial Organization*, February, 18: 23–31.

White, Lawrence J. 1991. *The S&L Debacle*, New York: Oxford University Press.

White, Michelle J. 2004. "The 'Arms Race' on American Roads: The Effect of Sport Utility Vehicles and Pickup Trucks on Traffic Safety," *Journal of Law and Economics*, October, 47: 333–355.

Williams, J. D. 1954. *The Compleat Strategist*, New York: McGraw-Hill.

Williamson, Oliver E. 2002. "The Theory of the Firm as Governance Structure: From Choice to Contract," *Journal of Economic Perspectives*, Summer, 16: 171–195.

Williamson, Oliver E. 2000. "The New Institutional Economics: Taking Stock, Looking Ahead," *Journal of Economic Literature*, September, 38: 595–613.

Williamson, Oliver E. 1987. *Antitrust Economics*, Cambridge, Mass.: Basil Blackwell.

Williamson, Oliver E. 1985. *The Economic Institutions of Capitalism: Firms, Markets, and Relational Contracting*, New York: The Free Press.

Williamson, Oliver E. 1981. "The Modern Corporation: Origins, Evolution, Attributes," *Journal of Economic Literature*, December, 19: 1537–1568.

Williamson, Oliver E. 1976. "Franchise Bidding for Natural Monopolies In General and with Respect to CATV," *Bell Journal of Economics*, 7: 73–104.

Williamson, Oliver E. 1975. *Markets and Hierarchies: Analysis and Antitrust Implications*, New York: Free Press.

Williamson, Oliver E. 1970. *Corporate Control and Business Behavior*, Englewood Cliffs, N.J.: Prentice-Hall.

Williamson, Oliver E. 1968. "Economies as an Antitrust Defense: The Welfare Tradeoffs," *American Economic Review*, March, 58: 18–36.

Williamson, Oliver E. 1966. "Peal-Load Pricing and Optimal Capacity under Indivisibility Constraints," *American Economic Review*, 56: 810–827.

Williamson, Oliver E. 1965. "Innovation and Market Structure," *Journal of Political Economy*, February, 73: 67–73.

Willig, Robert D. 1979. "Customer Equity and Local Measured Service," in Joseph A. Baude, et al., eds., *Perspectives in Local Measured Service*, Kansas City, Mo.: Rocky Mountain Telephone Company.

Willig, Robert D. 1978. "Pareto-Superior Nonlinear Outlay Schedules," *Bell Journal of Economics*, 9: 56–69.

Willig, Robert D. 1976. "Consumer Surplus Without Apology," *American Economic Review*, 66: 589–597.

Wilson, Graham K. 2003. *Business and Politics*, New York: Chatham House Publishing.

Winerman, Marc. 2003. "The Origins of the FTC: Concentration, Cooperation, Control, and Competition," *Antitrust Law Journal*, 71: 1–97.

Winston, Clifford. 1998. "U.S. Industry Adjustment to Economic Deregulation," *Journal of Economic Perspectives*, Summer, 12: 89–110.

Winston, Clifford, and Steven A. Morrison. "Another Look at Airport Congestion Pricing," *American Economic Review*, (forthcoming).

Winston, Clifford, Thomas M. Corsi, Curtis M. Grimm, and Carol A. Evans. 1990. *The Economic Effects of Surface Freight Deregulation*, Washington, D.C.: Brookings.

Wiseman, Alan. 2000. *The Internet Economy: Access, Taxes, and Market Structure*, Washington, D.C.: Brookings Institution Press.

Wokutch, Richard E. 1990. *Cooperation and Conflict in Occupational Safety and Health: A Multination Study of the Automotive Industry*. New York, Praeger.

Wolak, Frank A. 2003a. "Measuring Unilateral Market Power in Wholesale Electricity Markets: The California Market 1998–2000," *American Economic Review*, May, 93: 425–430.

Wolak, Frank A. 2003b. "Lessons from the California Electricity Crisis," in James M. Griffin and Steven Puller, eds. *Electricity Deregulation: Where to From Here?* Chicago: University of Chicago Press.

Wolak, Frank A. 1998. "Price-Cap Regulation in Newly Privatized Industries," *Oxford Energy Forum*, 12–14, available at http://www.stanford.edu/~wolak/.

Wolak, Frank A., Robert Nordhaus, and Carl Shapiro. 2000. "An Analysis of the June 2000 Price Spikes in California ISO's Energy and Ancillary Services Markets," University of California at Berkeley, Energy Institute Working Paper, September 21.

Wolak, Frank A., and Robert H. Patrick. 1997. "The Impact of Market Rules and Market Structure on the Price Determination Process in the England and Wales Electricity Market," University of California, Energy Institute, April, POWER Working Paper PWP-047.

Wolfram, Catherine D. 1999. "Measuring Duopoly Power in the British Electricity Spot Market," *American Economic Review*, September, 89: 805–826.

Wolfram, Catherine D. 1998. "Strategic Bidding in a Multiunit Auction: An Empirical Analysis of Bids to Supply Electricity in England and Wales," *RAND Journal of Economics*, 29: 703–725.

Wood, William C. 1993. "Costs and Benefits of Per Se Rules in Antitrust Enforcement," *Antitrust Bulletin*, Winter, 38: 887–902.

Wood, William C. 1981. *Nuclear Liability, Nuclear Safety and Economic Efficiency*, Greenwich, Conn.: JAI Press.

Worm, Boris, Edward B. Barbier, Nicole Beaumont, J. Emmett Duffy, Carl Folke, Benjamin S. Halpern, Jeremy B. C. Jackson, Heike K. Lotze, Florenza Micheli, Stephen R. Palumbi, Enric Sala, Kimberley A. Selkoe, John Stachowicz, and Reg Watson. 2006. "Impacts of Biodiversity Loss on Ocean Ecosystem Services," *Science*, November 3, 314: 787–790.

Wright, Julian. 1999. "International Telecommunications, Settlement Rates, and the FCC," *Journal of Regulatory Economics*, 15: 267–291.

Young, Louise B. 1990. *Sowing the Wind*. New York: Prentice Hall, p. 72.

Zimmer, Michael J., Charles A. Sullivan, Richard F. Richards, and Deborah A. Calloway. 2000. *Cases and Materials on Employment Discrimination*, 5th ed. New York: Aspen Publishers.

Zimmerman, Martin B. 1988. "Regulatory Treatment of Abandoned Property: Incentive Effects and Policy Issues," *Journal of Law and Economics*, 31: April, 127–144.

INDEX